Cooking Essentials

for The New Professional Chef™

Cooking Essentials

for The New Professional Chef™

THE FOOD AND BEVERAGE INSTITUTE

Mary Deirdre Donovan

Editor

JOHN WILEY & SONS, INC.

New York   Chichester   Weinheim   Brisbane   Singapore   Toronto

The Culinary Institute of America Staff:

Project Director: Tim Ryan

Editor: Mary Deirdre Donovan

Assistant Editor: Terry Finlayson

Editorial Assistant: Jessica Bard

Graphics Coordinator: Henry Woods

Photographers: Elizabeth C. Johnson, Lorna Smith

Consultants: Richard Czack, Fritz Sonnenschmidt, Fred Mayo, Tim Rodgers, Markus Färbinger, Jonathan Zearfoss, Cathy Powers, Uwe Hestnar, John Kowalski, Bob Briggs

Line Illustrations: TCA Graphics, Inc., Tom Cardamone, Ann Cardamone

Cover photography: © Louis Wallach

This book is printed on acid-free paper. ♾

Copyright © 1997 by The Culinary Institute of America. All rights reserved

Published by John Wiley & Sons, Inc.

Published simultaneously in Canada.

This publication is designed to provide accurate and authoritative information in regard to the subject matter covered. It is sold with the understanding that the publisher is not engaged in rendering professional services. If professional advice or other expert assistance is required, the services of a competent professional person should be sought.

Library of Congress Cataloging-in-Publication Data:

Cooking essentials for the new professional chef.   The Food & Beverage Institute / Mary Deirdre Donovan, editor.
    p.   cm.
  At head of title: The Culinary Institute of America.
  Includes bibliographical references and index.
  ISBN 0-471-28717-2 (hard cover)
  1. Quantity cookery. I. Donovan, Mary Deirdre, 1955–
TX820.C673   1996
641.5'7—dc20
                                         96-21066

Printed in the United States of America

3   4   5   6   7   8   9   10

Contents

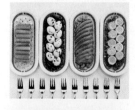

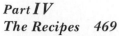

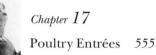

Recipe Contents

Preface

People often find cooking mysterious. They assume that all gifted chefs have a bag full of special tricks and closely guarded recipes that enable them to prepare the dishes that seem so amazing to the uninitiated. Really, though, it is the chef's reliance on basic cooking principles and fundamental preparation techniques that provides the canvas for the artwork.

Creativity takes on a substance only when it is paired with the primary lessons of cooking. Mastery of these lessons eliminates the mystery and makes it easier to differentiate the merely trendy from the valid and valuable innovations.

It is not enough to know how to prepare a particular dish, or to produce a complicated recipe. As professionals, we all need to move our orientation away from memorizing a particular combination of ingredients to reach a prescribed, predetermined finished dish. It is even more important to delve behind the "formulas" so that we can grasp the basics of cooking such as roasting, poaching, grilling, baking, and charcuterie.

As students of cooking, we must all continue to gain confidence through experience, so that we can answer the questions How much? How long? When? When we learn where the benchmarks of quality are found, we can begin to answer these questions. It is important that the true flavors of foods—earthy, comfortable, honest, identifiable—be allowed to speak for themselves. At the same time, the intriguing interplay of contrasting colors textures, shapes, and cooking techniques on the plate can provide depth, excitement, and interest.

What we have tried to accomplish in this book is to provide professionals and students with a text that can function as a reference point. By reading and learning the lessons set down in this book, a student can begin a lifelong process of education by first learning the fundamentals of identifying and working with a variety of foods, then actually cooking the food. The next part of the process is to examine closely what is contained in the book and hold its lessons up against the experiences that you have had in the kitchen. Learning is the most effective when you are engaged in critically evaluating, investigating, and challenging the written word through practical application. If we have accomplished our purpose in developing this text, you will be inspired to go beyond the lessons explained here.

This book's aim is to act as an inspiration to always learn more, for there is always more to learn. The youngest apprentice and the experienced master chef alike are only truly at their best when they continue to search for the greatest perfection of technique, the most ideal harmonies of flavors and foods. It is simplicity, in cooking as in all arts, that demands the greatest artistry and offers the greatest rewards.

The motivation for this new book was our desire to incorporate into it as many contemporary cooking concepts as possible, while remaining true to the principles that govern all good cooking. Increased interest in nutritional cooking, working profitably with a dwindling supply of high-quality fish and shellfish, the excitement of learning about cuisines from our own and other countries—all of these elements have combined to change the way we view a culinary education. In addition, we know that issues regarding management of resources, time, and people are perhaps the greatest single challenge facing chefs and restaurant owners today.

By reorganizing the book, we have brought the important lessons more clearly into focus. The book is arranged in a progressive, logical sequence, separated into four parts. We begin with a brief his-

SPECIAL PEDAGOGICAL FEATURES

There are a number of special features in *Cooking Essentials for the New Professional Chef* intended to act as an aid to both students and instructors.

Chapter objectives list the major topics covered within each chapter. The **summary** recaps the lessons that should be mastered.

Self-study questions and **activities** act as a means to further enhance the content provided in the chapter, by bringing students and instructors back to the text as well as by asking that the lessons of the chapter be applied in a problem-solving situation.

Key terms and concepts offer a quick recap of the language that a chef should be able to use fluently.

"Footnotes" define terms that might be unfamiliar when they first appear in the text.

Another feature found throughout the text chapters are sidebars, which offer information about **techniques, chef's tips,** or **historical or anecdotal information.**

torical overview of the chef's role in society. Then we move on to an in-depth discussion of the specific areas of concern for the professional, including food safety and sanitation, nutrition, and the ability to purchase and fabricate foods and to use equipment efficiently and safely.

In the third part of the book, Cooking in the Professional Kitchen, the emphasis is on providing a clear picture of the basic cooking techniques using both words and pictures. Cooking is not always a perfectly precise art, but a good grasp of the basics gives the chef or student the ability not only to apply the technique, but also to learn the standards of quality. Once the lessons step out of the book and into the kitchen, you can begin to develop a sense of how cooking works. The arrangement of cooking techniques moves in a progression, beginning with Mise en Place, on into soups and sauces, then the basic cooking methods, pantry cooking and garde manger, and concluding with baking and pastry.

The surest way to "de-mystify" cooking is to understand that it is not recipes or an arsenal of secret ingredients that make the chef. Rather, it is the chef's knowledge and expertise in three key areas: selecting ingredients with an eye to quality and seasonality; handling foods and equipment carefully to get the best results with the least waste; and applying fundamental cooking techniques with due respect for the food and the intended effect of the finished dish. These are the supports that hold the recipe up.

The recipes themselves, found in the fourth part of the book, are grouped according to the way that professionals will use them. Five separate chapters include entrée recipes.

New recipes can be found for marinades, relishes, grains, and legumes throughout the book. These recipes have been developed, reviewed, and prepared by our chef instructors and students. Yields have been regulated and standardized. Additional information, or "trucs," have also been incorporated, so that you can find the following information: ways to make nutritional modifications, variations, substitutions, historical and anecdotal information, and serving suggestions.

The recipes given here have been written with metric equivalents; it should be noted the conversions have usually been rounded to the nearest even measurement. Whenever teaspoon and tablespoons offer the most accurate measurement, we have left them the same for both U.S. and metric measures.

Photographs throughout the book were prepared using equipment that allows us to show the technique clearly. This has meant that in some cases we have prepared a much smaller batch, in a smaller pan, than you might select.

Ours is a dynamic profession, one that provides some of the greatest challenges and some of the greatest rewards. There is always another level of perfection to achieve and another skill to master. It is our hope that this book will function both as a springboard into further growth and as a reference point to give ballast to the lessons still to be learned.

—*The Editors*

Acknowledgments

Cooking Essentials for the New Professional Chef marks a brand new level of cooking textbook. We are proud to be able to offer a volume designed to meet the specific needs of students and instructors in cooking schools of all types. This project was crafted to meet the same high standards as the sixth edition of *The New Professional Chef*. We wish to thank and acknowledge the following people for their vision and dedication:

Tim Ryan
Mary Donovan
Terry Finlayson

Jessica Bard
Richard Czack
Fritz Sonnenschmidt
Henry Woods

The heart of this book is the detailed explanation of cooking methods, in words and in images, as well as the amazingly diverse collection of recipes, running the gamut from simple broths to multilayered dishes composed of sauces, stuffings, garnishes, and side dishes. Other areas of the kitchen are no less important: the bakeshop, pantry, and charcuterie. In addition, there are many subjects that a chef must master, including management, food safety issues, nutrition, purchasing, and the selection of equipment. For their dedication to excellence in several areas (reading and critiquing the text, testing and reviewing recipes, and being the hands you see in the photographs throughout the book), the following individuals are to be congratulated and thanked:

Mark Ainsworth
Wayne Almquist
Gunther Behrendt
Pat Bottliglieri
Ed Bradley
Liz Briggs

Robert Briggs
John Canner
Shuliang Cheng
Corky Clark
Amy Coleman
Richard J. Coppedge, Jr.

Phil Delaplane
Bob DelGrosso
Ron DeSantis
Dieter Doppelfeld
Joseba Encabo
George Engel
Mark Erickson
Markus Färbinger
Dieter Faulkner
Anton Flory
Craig Goldstein
Peter Greweling
Uwe Hestnar
George Higgins
Julia Hill
Morey Kanner
Tom Kief
Jean-Luc Kieffer
Anthony Ligouri
Frank Lopez
Jim Maraldo
Noble Masi
Fred Mayo

Joseph McKenna
Peter Michael
Al Natale
John Nihoff
John O'Haire
Claudio Papini
Norman Peduzzi
Bill Phillips
Cathy Powers
Paul Prosperi
Frank Rinaudo
Tim Rodgers
Eric Saucy
Walter Schreyer
Kathy Shepard
Rudy Smith
Jay Stein
David St. John-Grubb
Claude Swartvagher
Dan Turgeon
Marianne Turow
Rich Vergili
Mark Westfield

The images in this book were created in the new photography studio under the direction of Henry Woods. Many thanks to the photographers: John Grubell, Liz Johnson, and Lorna Smith.

For additional photographs we wish also to thank Will Faller and The Oldways Preservation & Exchange Trust. And a special acknowledgment to Louis Wallch for the image on the book's cover.

The foods you see in the photographs were selected from among those in our school's storeroom; Brad Matthews and Todd Perkins went beyond the call of duty.

We particularly wish to recognize all of the students and graduates of The Culinary Institute of America, to whom this book is dedicated. They use these recipes, each and every day. It is in the crucible of the classroom that this book came into being. We thank all the students who have helped to make this book what it is, but especially wish to mention: Julia Vega, Jewel Bishop, Tim Champness, and Thomas Schroeder.

Van Nostrand Reinhold, our partners in this grand effort, showed great dedication, patience, and an extraordinary degree of flexibility in bringing this book home:

Marianne Russell   Stephen McNabb
Renee Guilmette   Mike Suh
Marie Terry   Louise Kurtz
Melissa A. Rosati

And Van Nostrand Reinhold's support staff: Karen Abrams, Paul Aljian, Elizabeth Curione, Jill Elias, Rose Grant, Dionicia Hernandez, Mia McCroskey, Laura Morelli, Joe Ruddick, Karen Verde.

We would like to thank the following corporations and groups for the equipment, china, and foods used in the testing and photography portions of this book:

F. Dick   J.B. Peel
Villeroy and Boch   Susan Shaffer,
AllClad   creator of ExecuChef
Cuisinart

This book has had an enormous impact on many lives. It is with great joy that we extend our heartfelt thanks to our families.

Cooking Essentials

for The New Professional Chef™

CHAPTER OBJECTIVES

- Discuss some of the key historical events and figures that shaped the modern foodservice industry

- Trace the history and evolution of restaurants

- Explain the influence of society and its structure, science and technology, and nutrition on the development of the food service industry

- Identify some of the first American chefs who began to define our national cuisine

- Understand how science and technology have affected the modern foodservice industry

- Identify some of the most significant currents and trends in today's foodservice industry

---

A Historical Perspective

Humans tend to seek out and prefer the familiar, reassuring foods of their native countries. Brillat-Savarin (see "Major Historical Figures") knew this well when he said, "Tell me what you eat and I will tell you who you are." The foods that grow in a particular region, the cooking methods typically used, the seasonings, and the style of eating are all part of a community's shared behavior.

There is an equally strong tendency in humans to explore new regions, to learn about other societies, and to acquire as our own whatever we come across that fits into our ideas of what is "right." Travel has a broadening influence, not only on the kinds of foods that are deemed suitable, but also on the ways in which familiar and unfamiliar foods are prepared. Although some peoples have tended to stay in one area for generations, others have roamed from one end of a continent to the other, ventured out onto the high seas, and discovered new lands.

The quest to conquer other lands has been another potent spur to the growth and evolution of cooking. The Greeks and Romans were, perhaps, the most effective at bringing about changes that completely altered the eating habits of most Western hemisphere inhabitants. The delicacies and choicest goods of each conquered country became their "property." Leavened breads, sweet wines, forcemeats, sauces, and "composed dishes" all became part of the Greek repertoire after they gained control of Egypt, Persia, Babylon, and India.

This exchange was never completely one-sided. When the Romans marched through what would one day become Europe, they brought along their own way of seasoning dishes, as well as recipes for pickles, cheeses, and special cakes and breads. Several of these influences can still be seen today; examples include the sweet-sour sauces of modern Italy and the sauerkraut or sauerbraten of modern Germany.

Another example of culinary influence through conquest is that of the Moors over the Spaniards. The use in Spain and Portugal of typically Moorish ingredients, such as sweet syrups, pastries, and almonds, is evidence today of their centuries-long dominion.

As the world moved into the Dark Ages, travel began to diminish, although crusaders in the eleventh to the thirteenth centuries still were making journeys to the Holy Land, and the devout continued to make pilgrimages to various shrines and holy places. Most of the books that discussed food and cookery and the formulas for rich exotic dishes were safeguarded in monastaries' libraries, while outside their walls the people continued to prepare the rough, simple dishes that had sustained them for generations.

Exploration of new worlds was slow, and it took many decades before any real influence on the established European cuisines was felt. Eventually European explorers traveled to the Americas and the West Indies. They returned with such "new world" foods as chocolate, chilies, beans, corn, tomatoes, and potatoes.

Many of these items were at first regarded as poisonous. Potatoes, a member of the deadly night-

---

forcemeats: an emulsion of lean meat and fat used to make sausages, pâtés, and terrines.

sauerbraten: beef, marinated in red wine and braised; a classic German dish.

I

Introduction to the Profession

*As far as cuisine is concerned, one must
read everything, see everything, try
everything, observe everything, in order to
retain, in the end, just a little bit!*

—FERNAND POINT

*Humans are distinct from other species in that we, for the most part, prefer to make
eating a social act. We have created elaborate systems of manners, rituals, and taboos
to govern how we eat, what, where, and with whom. The role of the chef in such a
complex system is a fascinating story. This overview of the history of cooking, dining,
and hospitality as a whole will touch on many aspects of human endeavor—
communal living, social structure, war and conquest, and much more. In particular,
we will concentrate on the way that a special institution—the restaurant—has come
into being. All of this is, of course, a way of understanding the background and
significance of a very special career path—that of being a professional chef.*

shade family, met with especially strong resistance. A famous French agronomist, Antoine-August Parmentier (1737–1813), finally broke through the deep-seated fear of potatoes with a campaign begun in 1774. By the time the French Revolution began in 1789, they were as familiar on the French table as bread. Other new foods that seemed more familiar, or at least bore a surface resemblance to foods already available in Europe, such as the turkey, were taken up immediately and enthusiastically.

With the end of the Dark Ages came a resurgence of travel by the wealthy. At first, this was a time-consuming and hazardous undertaking. However, new modes of travel, such as improved ships able to make long sea journeys, made it possible for the noble classes to move with greater freedom. They carried their own approach to foods and cookery with them, but also were influenced by the foods they found. The number of French chefs in Russia in the eighteenth and nineteenth centuries is a testimony to the way in which cuisines tended to travel from one part of the world to another. Thomas Jefferson's repeated trips to Europe introduced macaroni, ice cream, and a host of new fruits and vegetables to the United States.

Immigrants traveling from one country to another, whether to escape religious persecution or in pursuit of a better life, brought with them their traditional dishes and ways of cooking. Each new group's special drinks, breads, cakes, and other foods eventually were intermingled with the foods brought by previous arrivals and with indigenous foods.

The soldiers from the United States who fought in the World Wars returned to this country with a newly acquired taste for the traditional foods of France, Italy, Germany, and Japan. As the twentieth century wore on, the middle class was able to afford foreign travel for pleasure. Today, travel influences the type of cuisines featured in contemporary restaurants. Foods from the Caribbean, the Middle East, and previously lesser-known French and Italian regions have become more familiar as the world continues to "shrink." Chefs and patrons alike are discovering the pleasures of foods from countries as diverse as Portugal, Thailand, and New Zealand. Just as travel has made it easier for the guest to get to the food, it is also a far simpler, faster, and cheaper matter to get food from all over the world to the chef's kitchen.

Royalty and the Rise of the Middle Class

European royal families often intermarried for reasons of state and to form political alliances. With the union of these families came a blending of the customs of different countries. This mingling resulted not only in the exchange of cooking styles and special dishes, but also of social etiquette as well. For example, Caterina de Medici, a sixteenth-century Italian princess who came to France as the result of a royal alliance, brought her chefs and many Italian products from Florence. The number of "Florentine" dishes in the classic French repertoire attests to their influence.

Once the monarchies and the feudal system began to decline, a change occurred in the social structure. The chefs who had once worked in royal households took positions in the wealthy homes of a newly rich and "nonnoble" class. The result was an expansion of the cuisine of the nobility, first to the upper class, and eventually to the large and growing middle class.

The gradual dissolution of strict class lines, and the ability of people to move from the lower class to the middle or upper classes allowed the cookery of the upper class or nobility, known as **haute cuisine,** to blend with the cooking of hearth and home, **cuisine bourgeoisie.** This exchange between domestic cooks and classically trained chefs in all countries produced a number of innovations and refinements. The effect was to spur growth and change, and to prevent classic cooking from becoming dull and stale.

Restaurant History

The first restaurant (as we know restaurants today) opened in Paris in 1765. Monsieur Boulanger, a tavern-keeper, served a dish of sheep's feet in a white sauce. He called this dish a restorative or *restaurant,* which is where we get the word **restaurant** today. Once the ice was broken, other restaurants followed in fairly rapid succession.

Florentine: typically a dish containing spinach.

The French Revolution (1789–99) had a particularly significant effect on restaurant proliferation, because many chefs who previously had worked for the monarchy or nobility fled the country to escape the guillotine. Although some sought employment with the nobility in other countries, others began to open their own establishments.

Restaurants became increasingly refined operations. Although they were at first frequented only by men, this would change as customs in society and in the foodservice industry as a whole changed. Today, the variety of dining establishments reflects the interests, lifestyles, and needs of a modern society: brasseries, bistros, "white tablecloth" or fine dining, ethnic restaurants, fast food spots, take-out companies, hotel dining rooms, banquet halls, and the list goes on.

The Evolution of Restaurant Cuisines

From the time of M. Boulanger to the present day, there has been a virtual explosion in the kitchen. New or rediscovered cooking styles have changed the landscape of restaurants throughout the world. Each new style of cuisine has swept onto the scene with enormous force.

Grande Cuisine

The *grande cuisine,* a careful code established by Antonin Carême (1784-1833) detailed numerous dishes and their sauces in *La Cuisine Classique* and other volumes. This style came to restaurants much more slowly than it did to nobility's kitchens. The menus of most hotels and restaurants offered a simple *table d'hôte,* which provided little if any choice. The *grande cuisine* offered a *carte* (or list) of suggestions available from the kitchen. The *à la carte* restaurant had begun to make inroads on the traditional "men's club" atmosphere of most restaurants and cafes.

When the Savoy Hotel opened in London in 1898 under the direction of Cesar Ritz and Auguste Escoffier, *grande cuisine* was still the exception. These two gentlemen waged a successful campaign to assure that their *à la carte* offerings were of the finest, that their service was the best, and that it was all delivered to the guest on the finest china and crystal. As a result, ladies and gentlemen of good standing finally could be found in the dining rooms of restaurants in England, France, and elsewhere.

Classic Cuisine

Carême played an important role in establishing French cuisine by writing it down in an organized manner. He had a great influence on another major figure in the history of Western cuisine, Georges Auguste Escoffier (1847-1935). Escoffier was the individual most responsible for continuing to refine and simplify the French repertoire of classic dishes. His work was built on that of Carême.

In addition to his many great culinary contributions, Escoffier also devised the **brigade system,** which turned the chaos of a typical kitchen into a smooth operation. We model our kitchen structure on this system even today. Escoffier's writings are furthermore considered classics and ought to be part of every chef's library, particularly his masterwork, *Le Guide Culinaire,* published in 1903.

Nouvelle Cuisine

The next major shift in French cuisine occurred gradually. Fernand Point (1897-1955), another extremely influential chef, took Escoffier's message of simplification even further, and laid the ground work for the next upheaval in restaurant cooking styles.

Several chefs are credited with "inventing" **nouvelle cuisine,** including such luminaries and Paul Bocuse, Alain Chapel, Françoise Bise, and Jean and Pierre Troisgros. They were all influenced by Fernand Point. The end result was a whole new approach to the selection of ingredients for a dish, cooking and saucing styles, and plate presentation.

Nouvelle cuisine became popular during the early 70s. It was seen as a long-needed break from the elaborate, costly, and time-consuming dishes served by restaurants of the grand or classic style. Smaller portions, more artful presentation, and the combination of new ingredients became the hallmarks of this cooking style. The considerable inter-

ACTIVITIES

- Make a list of the restaurants that you admire in your community and visit at least one of them. Ask to talk with the chef and have a tour of the kitchen during a slow period in the day.

- Find several recent articles in food magazines that identify a new, "hot" style of cuisine that is receiving attention in major cities around the country. Try to name the chefs practicing this new cooking style, where they work, and what their influences were.

- Locate at least three sites on the World Wide Web dedicated to professional cooks, chefs, and restaurant owners. What do they offer? What don't they offer?

KEYWORDS

à la carte	carte	*haute cuisine*	pasteurization
American cuisine	*cuisine bourgeoisie*	hybridization	restaurant
animal husbandry	freeze-drying	irradiation	table d'hôte
brigade system	*grande cuisine*	*nouvelle cuisine*	vacuum packing

areas and the ability to use foods once considered "out of season." High-quality produce is now available year-round, and special items once usable only in the area where they were produced are now available worldwide. This has had a negative impact, too. We have become increasingly less aware of what foods are native to a given region, when and for how long they are in season, and how they taste when they ripen on the vine instead of in transit.

Nutrition

Nutrition has become so much a part of everyday life that we can easily forget just how young a science it actually is. The study of how foods help the body grow, rejuvenate, fight diseases, and prevent the onset of certain conditions is constantly uncovering clues as to how we can eat "smarter." The chef's role is challenging in this regard.

The first task is to learn the rudiments of nutrition. In Chapter 3 you will learn the basic components of foods as they relate to nutrition. You will also see the dietary recommendations currently suggested. This type of information is important for your overall menu plan, production techniques, and recipe development.

Your guests have as much access to this information as you do. Remember that much of the data released by the popular press is seen as contradictory. People remain perplexed by such topics as cholesterol in the diet versus cholesterol in the blood. They find it difficult to separate the hard facts about alcohol as a beverage from the reports about the French Paradox. They are no longer certain if it is butter that is evil, margarine that must be avoided, or coconut and palm kernel oils that are responsible for cardiovascular disease, or if they should immediately start pouring extra-virgin olive oil over everything they eat.

It is no easier for a professional chef to glean the most pertinent and accurate facts and put them to practical use. Reading current books and magazines is a starting point. Work with professional nutritionists or use some of the excellent software available. There are courses available to you through various continuing education programs that can help you to apply new techniques to creating a whole new menu or individual menu items.

Family Structure Changes

The extended family—grandparents, parents, children, and assorted aunts, uncles, and cousins all living together—is now a rarity. The traditional "nuclear" family—working father, mother at home, two children in school—also is getting harder to find. It is far more likely that both the father and mother are working, or that the family has only a single parent.

"Baby boomers" who waited until much later in life to start their families, are often unwilling to give up their careers. For any family in which the major caregivers are also the major wage earners, finding ways to minimize demands on time is essential. More and more often, meals are either eaten in a restaurant or they are takeout foods.

The double-income family and increasing numbers of single professional people have brought about significant growth in the foodservice industry. These people have more disposable income but less time to cook at home, so they tend to eat out more often. This circumstance also has spurred the growth of "carryout cuisine" or "takeout," which is offered by gourmet shops, delicatessans, and supermarkets, as well as by restaurants filling orders for home consumption.

Single professionals and the growing numbers of retired persons have shifted the demographics of this country dramatically. Though the requirements of these two groups may not be identical, they are both looking to the foodservice industry to meet their special needs, whether it be gourmet shops or "early bird" specials.

---

pasteurization: the exposure of perishable food products to heat and/or gamma ray radiation to partially sterilize them and increase their shelf life.

freeze drying: a process for drying heat-sensitive foods by freezing them and then placing them in a vacuum packaging.

vacuum packing: eliminating as much air as possible from packaging to preserve freshness.

irradiation: exposing food to radiation to preserve freshness, a technique especially common for dried spices.

French Paradox: apparent inconsistency between levels of fat in French diet and incidence of fat-related disease.

cardiovascular disease: the general term used to describe diseases of the heart and blood vessels, such as stroke and heart attack.

Media and the Information Superhighway

There are many ways to get information. Print media, including books, magazines, periodicals, and newsletters, crowd the shelves of the local newsstand and bookstore. Special-interest publications are among the most-often used resources for any professional. Videos, videoconferencing, and multimedia forums, such as CD-ROM, on-line services, and interactive software are moving rapidly onto center stage as sources for information, inspiration, and networking.

Information overload is a very real concern. It has become a more difficult task to sort out what is truly reliable. Fads grow (and die) quickly. In fact, it is becoming increasingly difficult to distinguish a passing fad from a newly emerging trend. "Stars" and "hot spots" come and go rapidly as well. The pressure of being the latest, hottest, and best can be overwhelming. It is no longer uncommon to hear a talented chef bemoan the fact that he or she is away from the kitchen too much, is being pulled in too many directions, and feels burned out. Media attention can be a mixed blessing.

Accurate and timely reporting has and will always be a valued commodity. Journalists have assumed a larger importance in the food world as well as in the total news and media picture.

Summary

The social act of dining is one of the ways that humans are distinct from other species. We eat, not just to nourish our bodies, but also to strengthen our ties as a group. Foods are prepared before they are eaten. They are grown, hunted, or gathered; cut, cleaned, and trimmed; cooked and presented to the assembled group. This collection of activities has become a central focus of daily life and one of the unifying factors of all human society and culture. Chefs have played a critical role in the spread of these civilizing behaviors. Understanding how this profession first began, how it has changed, and what its potential can be is the first step on a lifelong path toward becoming a professional chef.

SELF-STUDY QUESTIONS

1. How has travel, exploration, and conquest changed the nature of cooking and cuisine?

2. Briefly describe the evolution of cuisine from the *grande cuisine* to contemporary cuisine. Name significant contributors to each style.

3. What role did M. Boulanger play in the development of restaurants?

4. Describe briefly the following historical figures: Brillat-Savarin, la Varenne, Escoffier.

5. What are the possible effects on this industry of changes to the traditional family structure?

6. Why is Caterina de Medici considered an important figure in the evolution of French cuisine and culture?

7. Describe two popular farming practices and two food technologies of the twentieth century.

MAJOR HISTORICAL FIGURES

The following list of additional influential figures in culinary history is by no means complete. Further reading about notable figures throughout the history of cooking is recommended. Refer to the Recommended Readings at the end of this book for other sources.

Caterina de Medici (1519–1589), an Italian princess from the famous Florentine family, married the Duc d'Orleans, later Henri II of France. She introduced a more refined style of dining, including the use of the fork and the napkin. Her Florentine chefs influenced French chefs as well, most particularly in the use of spinach.

Anne of Austria (1601–1666), wife of Louis XIII, was a member of the Spanish Hapsburg family. Her retinue included Spanish chefs who introduced sauce Espagnol and the use of roux as a thickener for sauces.

Pierre François de la Varenne (1615–1678) was the author of the first cookbook to summarize the cooking practices of the French nobility. His *Le Vrai Cuisinier François* was published in 1651.

Jean-Anthelme Brillat-Savarin (1755–1826) was a French politician and gourmet and a renowned writer. His work, *Le Physiologie de Gout (The Physiology of Taste)*, is highly regarded to this day.

Marie-Antoine Carême (1784-1833) became known as the founder of the *grande cuisine* and was responsible for systematizing culinary techniques. He had a profound influence on the later writing of Escoffier, and was known as the "chef of kings, king of chefs."

Charles Ranhofer (1836–1899) was the first internationally renowned chef of an American restaurant, Delmonico's, and the author of *The Epicurean*.

Georges Auguste Escoffier (1847-1935) was a renowned chef and teacher. He was the author of *Le Guide Culinaire*, a major work codifying classic cuisines that is still widely used by professional chefs. His other significant contributions include simplifying the classic menu in accordance with the principles advocated by Carême, and initiating the brigade system. Escoffier's influence on the food-service industry cannot be overemphasized.

Georges Auguste Escoffier

Fernand Point (1897-1955) was the chef/owner of La Pyramide restaurante in Vienne, France. He went even further than Escoffier in bringing about a change in cooking styles and laid the foundations for *nouvelle cuisine*.

---

action and sharing of ideas between these chefs and others have led to contemporary cuisine's growth and development.

American Cuisine

As the seventies wore on, there was a growing sense that **American cuisine** had a legitimate place among world cuisines. Larry Forgione (The River Cafe), Jeremiah Tower (Stars), Alice Waters (Chez Panisse), and Dean Fearing (Mansion on Turtle Creek) were among those in the front lines of this new cooking style. And, for the first time, chefs trained in the United States were achieving worldwide recognition.

Into the Future

If you read magazines or watch television, you are already aware that the types of cuisine popular today are more numerous, and faster-changing, than they ever were before. Italian, Southwestern and Tex-Mex, Mediterranean, and Latin American cuisines are growing in importance all the time. Cuisines from the Pacific Rim are also increasingly popular, including Thai, Vietnamese, Japanese, and Korean.

Today's Currents and Trends

Keeping track of the latest "hot" chef in the restaurant world has become a nearly impossible task. Media attention on new restaurants, "rising star" chefs, and the latest dining trends has continued to grow in importance. As we enter the twenty-first century, the face of this industry is changing just as surely as other industries are changing.

Throughout the world, individual chefs are raising the standards of this profession. They are well-trained and highly motivated. Today, the profession has attained a level of respect that was not always forthcoming in this nation. The interaction and exchange between cultures, the more widespread availability of special foods, and an increasingly sophisticated clientele have been the driving forces behind the growth, diversity, and excitement found in the restaurant world today.

Chefs are not the only people to attain status and high regard in the foodservice industry. Writers, critics, and reviewers have made a mark on the evolution of the field. While there is a great tradition of food writing from time immemorial, today's food writers have become versed in such specialized areas as nutrition, history and culture, ecology as it relates to the foodservice industry, and health issues. Teachers, photographers, and food stylists help to shape what appears on menus and plates throughout the country.

The list of names of those who have had a measurable impact on the public's perception of all manner of food-related issues is long and grows longer each day.

The restaurant business as a whole is subject to the same changes that affect our entire culture. Today's family is not what is was 20 or 30 years ago. There are whole new ways to go to work, study, and be entertained now. The future is bristling both with possibilities and uncertainties.

Science and Technology

From the time that humans first learned to control fire, advances in science and technology have had a direct relationship on food production and preparation. Many of these changes have been heralded as great advances, while others have been met with resistance.

Advances in farm technology have increased yields and improved quality and overall availability of many foods. One of the less desirable changes is an increased reliance on single-crop farming on a more "industrial" scale. This style of farming encourages a strong reliance on chemical fertilizers, pesticides, and other man-made substances in order to enhance crop yields. Some of this has been done at the expense of soil quality. It certainly has changed the face of farming across the world, as small family farms are less and less part of the overall picture.

Hybridization of crops has increased the variety of foodstuffs that are grown. This means that unless a crop has been preserved in a seed bank, an entire strain could be lost. We are only now beginning to understand the consequences of allowing cultivated and wild species to become extinct.

Animal husbandry, the ability to breed desirable characteristics in and undesirable ones out, allows us to raise animals that provide better yield and flavor, as well as less fat. It has also led to ever-increasing problems with diseases that need to be treated with antibiotics. These drugs and others, such as growth hormones used to stimulate milk production in cattle, are being looked at with some alarm.

Equipment and tools have undergone an evolution, from the rudimentary cutting tools and cooking vessels that first allowed foods to be boiled in liquids to the gas and electric stoves, microwave ovens, and computerized equipment of today. The advent of refrigeration also has allowed foods to be held longer and shipped farther, without significant loss of quality.

Scientific developments have allowed us to improve on techniques for food storage, increasing both the shelf life and wholesomeness of foods and reducing the incidence of food spoilage, contamination, and poisoning. Examples of these technical advances include **pasteurization**, **freeze-drying**, **vacuum packing**, and **irradiation**.

Improved methods of transportation make possible the availability of food from other geographic

---

hybridization: the process of creating a new plant strain by combining two or more other strains.

seed bank: a place where seeds from heirloom or unusual plant varieties are preserved.

II

The Foodservice Professional

*The cook, considered and employed until
then as a slave at the lowest cost, became
extremely expensive. What had been only a
job became an art.*

—TITUS LIVY, CIRCA A.D. 15, WRITING OF A ROMAN
INCURSION IN SYRIA

There are many pieces in the makeup of a professional chef. Just like any other craftsman, you must begin with a thorough knowledge of how to work as a professional, including a code of behavior, knowledge of the tools of the trade, and the raw materials you will use in applying your craft.

The first chapter in this part of the book discusses what it means to be a chef. Education, (whether in a professional cooking school or as an apprentice), networking, and a brief survey of the current status of society and how that impacts the definition of "chef" are topics of great significance to the working chef.

Next, you must be able to work in a safe manner. This means not only handling foods carefully to avoid transmitting a foodborne disease to a guest, but also developing proper technique in order to prevent the numerous accidents that seem to be part and parcel of a job that puts you in nearly constant contact with hot, sharp, and heavy objects.

Nutrition has become a topic of great significance to this profession. Chefs and patrons alike are wondering how they can eat better to ensure greater energy. Weight control, health concerns, and an upsurge of interest in vegetarianism have influenced the types of foods featured on menus and the ways in which they are being prepared. As a chef, you need to have the rudiments of nutrition well in hand.

Chapter 4 introduces the large and small equipment that you will work with on a daily basis. Some items, such as knives and sieves, haven't changed design or function in centuries. Others (microwave ovens, convection steamers, and induction cooktops) represent the con-tinued march of technology. Many kitchens have reverted to equipment patterned on old-style items, such as wood-fired grills and ovens, to provide foods with a special appeal.

The basic ingredients you will use to create the items offered on your menu are illustrated and explained in Chapter 5. The quality of the foods you purchase will determine the quality of the finished dish.

Working efficiently, carefully, and creatively with the foods, staff, and equipment at your disposal in the kitchen is one of the greatest challenges you will face as a professional.

1

The Professional Chef

*It's a lot of hard work to become a good
chef...It's a long road and it's not always
gratifying*

—DANIEL BOULUE, RESTAURANT DANIEL

*The term "chef," although frequently used to describe anyone who cooks, is considered a
mark of respect by those within the profession. The title is one that can only be earned
through diligent practice and dedication. Those chefs who have made (or will make)
the most lasting impression on this industry know that their success depends on their
ability to fulfill many different roles. A true chef is, among other things, a lifelong
student, a teacher, a craftsperson, a leader, and a manager. An open and inquiring
mind; an appreciation of, and dedication to, quality and excellence; and a sense of
responsibility to self and the community are among the professional chef's
cardinal virtues.*

Today's chefs are often looked upon as a new breed—respected, even admired, for their skill and artistry. Some chefs have received so much press that their names are household words. Books, magazines, entire sections of the newspaper, even a television network are devoted to food and cooking, commanding an impressive share of the consumer's disposable income. The elevation of the chef to a legitimate profession has helped to attract bright and talented people to the industry.

It has been estimated that at the turn of the century, there will be one million more foodservice industry jobs available than there will be trained people to fill them. This industry's evolution has been one of steady growth, increased diversification, and expanding opportunities. The interaction of new trends in foods and dining, combined with the traditions and customs of other eras and other social groups, creates new styles of cooking, new dishes, and new types of eating establishments. The increasing communication between chefs and professionals in other areas (production, farming, and computers, for example) has stimulated growth and opened up new potentials.

At the same time, it has increased the number of businesses offering a vast array of services and goods. Competition between restaurants for clients is growing each day. Learning more than just how to sauté and make a good sauce is more important than ever before.

CHAPTER OBJECTIVES

- Define the important personal attributes of a professional chef
- Explain the importance of a good basic education as well as continuing education to the professional chef
- Name the positions in a classic brigade system for the kitchen and dining room
- Name several possible career options in the foodservice industry
- Explain how to network and why networking is important to a strong career in the foodservice industry
- Define the chef's role as an executive, administrator, and manager
- Explain the significance of marketing to a restaurant's success

---

Becoming a Craftsman

There is something fascinating about watching a chef who wields a knife with the dexterity of Jacques Pépin or Martin Yan. They can reduce an onion to a pile of exquisitely even dice within seconds. Acquiring the skills that enable you to handle a knife with authority, to flip an omelet with finesse, or to poach a piece of salmon in a court bouillon that appears to barely quiver is all part of a chef's education.

Getting an Education

There are many chefs today who learned the basics of their craft by attending an accredited school. Under the tutelage of experienced chefs, they begin a journey that starts with simple skills, such as dicing onions and peeling carrots, and progresses through the intricacies of preparing French pastries and such elaborate composed dishes as *Veal à l'Orloff.* Formal training in a school supplies a solid grounding in basic and advanced culinary techniques. It is also a good laboratory where you can become "fluent" in the language of the trade. There is no substitute for experience, however. It is only with a great deal of hands-on practice that class-learned theory can be fully assimilated.

Veal a l'Orloff: a classic French preparation of veal loin, soubise sauce, truffles, béchamel sauce, and Parmesan cheese before being finished in an oven.

FIGURE 1-1 Chefs Selecting Produce for the *Bocuse d'Or* Competition

FIGURE 1-2 Research in the Library

Others may begin their training as an apprentice *(stagiare)*, either in a special apprenticeship program or a self-directed course of study, advancing from kitchen to kitchen, learning at the side of chefs who are involved in the day-to-day business of running a professional kitchen.

For most individuals, training is an ongoing matter. Whether you learn your trade in school, through an apprenticeship program, or on the job, the responsibility for acquiring that training is yours. It is never fully complete at any point. Instead, it is achieved in a variety of guises, all of which are important to your education at various stages throughout your career.

Continuing Education

Once initial training has been completed, continuing education is equally important, because the foodservice industry is constantly evolving. Attending classes, workshops, and seminars helps keep practicing cooks and chefs in step with new methods and new styles of cooking, or it may serve to hone skills in specialized areas.

The more you keep abreast of changes and new developments in the restaurant industry, the more clear the need for continuing education becomes. As a case in point, consider the enormous impact the following areas have had over the last several years:

- *Nutrition*
  Chefs no longer can afford to ignore nutrition. It is as much a part of the dining experience of many individuals as whether or not a restaurant has a wine list or serves a wonderful hot soufflé. The ability to make nutritional adaptations to dishes, to identify to your waitstaff or guests those items that are good choices for individuals with concerns about eating a low-fat or low cholesterol diet, or to simply enhance the overall nutritional value of any meal, is a critical asset to today's professional chef.

  There are many excellent books available that address nutrition. But you may find that enrolling in a class, or even meeting with a registered dietitian or nutritionist is valuable.

- *Food safety issues*
  One of the areas of great concern to customers and people who work in this industry is that of food safety. Regulations and standards are under constant review. Changes to existing standards occur quickly, often in almost immediate response to a specific foodborne illness outbreak. The glove law, requiring food handlers to wear gloves whenever handling a food that will not be cooked again before it is served to the guest, is a case in point. The recommended safe handling procedures for eggs, beef, chicken, and other po-

tentially hazardous foods are also under scrutiny and revision.

- **Organic foods**

Organic farming has become an increasingly important issue for virtually all sectors of our society. Farmers, restaurateurs, and consumers are all looking at **organic foods** more carefully than ever before. The concept behind organic farming is simple: Farmers use organic matter to enrich the soil, control pests, and enhance the yield they can generate.

At this time, farmers who use organic methods are at a slight disadvantage in relation to large-scale "industrial" farms. First, there are relatively few farms producing organic foods, so the supply does not yet meet the demand. Second, the cost of organic farming is still greater than it would be to grow foods using chemicals. There may be several reasons to account for this, but the net result is that until there are more farms using organic farming methods, costs will remain slightly higher for organic meats, poultry, wines, fruits, vegetables, and herbs.

How do you know if foods labeled as organic are actually any different than nonorganic products? There are several organizations on the national and state level that monitor organic farming. Regulations may vary from organization to organization, but in essence, the farmer must have used no chemicals on the fields for a specified number of years before any foods grown there can be labeled organic. So, if you are purchasing foods that are supposedly organic but you want to be sure, ask the farmer or purveyor who has done the inspection of the farm.

The other big question regarding organic foods is: Are they better for you? The jury is still out. Some reports seem to indicate that any nutritional edge that they have is wishful thinking. Others swing to the other end of the scale, claiming greatly improved nutritional levels. While there is no clearcut answer to this question, you will certainly find that there is a particular clientele who will prefer organic foods, and will actively seek them out on the menus of restaurants they frequent.

- **Environmental concerns**

Probably the main purpose of moving toward organic farming has to do with its impact on the en-

FIGURE 1-3   Wear Food-Handling Gloves to Keep Foods Safe.

vironment. The farmer works to improve the quality of the soil by introducing organic matter, such as compost. Enriching the soil is seen as the best way to ensure a good harvest.

Other environmental concerns for this industry include concerns about solid waste disposal. Composting, recycling, and overall reduction in the materials used in each phase of your operation are all ways to contribute to the solution. In some communities, you may be able to find farmers willing to take your compost, for example.

Each community has its own standards about recycling. It is important that you know what can be recycled and how it should be prepared for recycling. Appropriate containers should be set up in any kitchen to encourage the practice.

Conservation of water, electricity, and oil is another way that chefs can contribute to the health of our environment. Ths also results in a reduction in operating costs. As you review your daily operation, think long and hard about how you can cut down on your energy and water consumption. This means reviewing when certain tasks are done; for example, if you can cluster a number of roasting tasks into a specific time slot, you won't need to have the stoves turned on when they aren't actually in use. If you like additional information or assistance in finding ways to conserve resources, contact your local utility company.

- *Vegetarianism*

  Many more individuals than ever before have adopted a vegetarian diet. To capture this share of the market, you need to learn what types of vegetarians there are. Then you need to develop a set of menu options to reach these people. Even those who are not strict vegetarians may look for meatless options on menus. As interest in traditional diets from cultures around the world continues to be a strong influence, it is relatively easy to incorporate appetizers, entrées, and soups into menus so that you can that meet the needs of all types of vegetarians. For more information, read about vegetarians in Chapter 3.

The list of concerns that you and your guests bring to your restaurant will depend upon what type of service you offer and the general makeup of your audience. Evaluate your market, and then take the appropriate steps to keep on top of the latest information in the areas they are most concerned about. Magazines, newsletters, electronic bulletin boards, government publications, and books are all excellent sources. Whenever possible, you should try to attend seminars, workshops, and lectures. To find out more in any given area, consider joining professional organizations in order to network with other professionals in the field.

A Chef's Professional and Personal Attributes

Every member of a profession is responsible for upholding the profession's image, whether he or she is a teacher, lawyer, doctor, or chef. As our profession continues to become accessible to individuals who might formerly have been denied a spot in the professional kitchen, a consistent **code of conduct** is even more important.

A Commitment to Service

The foodservice industry is predicated on service. Therefore, you, as a future chef, should never lose sight of what that word implies. Good service includes (but is not limited to) providing good food, properly and safely cooked, appropriately seasoned, and attractively presented in a pleasant environment—in short, your job is making the customer happy. The degree to which an operation maintains a standard of excellence in these areas is the degree to which it will succeed. The customer must always come first.

A Sense of Responsibility

When you are truly responsible, it means that you have considered what effect your actions will have not just on yourself, but on those directly around you and beyond, out into the community. As we learn more about how things work in the world at large, it becomes abundantly clear that "community" means far more than a few surrounding blocks. As long as you are able to see and accept the fact that what you do does make a difference, even to people you may never meet, you are acting as a responsible member of the world community.

When employees and guests feel that their needs are given due consideration, the entire operation will benefit. Employees self-esteem will increase and their attitudes toward the establishment will improve. Making each staff member a part of the team will help to increase their productivity and reduce pilferage and absenteeism. Guests will enjoy their dining experience, certain that they are getting good value for their money. They will come back and they will tell friends and colleagues about your restaurant.

Foods, equipment, staff, and the facility are all valuable assets that must be treated with care and respect. This will become the norm when you make it clear by your own actions that this is the only acceptable way to behave. Waste, recklessness, disregard for others, and misuse and abuse of any commodity are clearly unprofessional and unacceptable. Abusive language, harassment, ethnic slurs, and profanity do not have a place in the professional kitchen. No operation, in any business, can afford to act as if there were people, assets, or time to waste.

Judgment

Although it is not easy to learn, a sense of what is right—whether you are seasoning a dish, developing new menu items, making out a weekly schedule, or disciplining an employee—is a litmus test for evaluating professional behavior. This sense of what is appropriate is acquired throughout a lifetime of experience. Good judgment is never completely mastered; rather, it is a goal toward which one should continually strive.

Looking the Part

A chef's uniform is an outward symbol of the profession. Looking like a professional will help you to act like one. The uniform's history is intriguing, reflecting both a practical, utilitarian side as well as some of the "romance" associated with being a chef.

The traditional uniform consists of the ***toque blanche*** (tall white hat), double-breasted white jacket, neckerchief, black and white houndstooth checked pants (or solid black pants in Europe), an apron, side towel, and hard leather shoes.

The most recognizable part of the uniform is the *toque blanche.* There are many explanations for the shape of the hat. Some believe, for example, that the chimney-like white hat may have originated in the fifth century at the time the Byzantine Empire was under siege by the barbarians. Men from all walks of life (including philosophers, and artists, as well as chefs to royalty) fled to Greek Orthodox monasteries for protection. They adopted the same dress as the priests so that they would not be recognized. After the threat of persecution lessened, the chefs began wearing white hats to differentiate themselves from the ordained priests.

The pleats on a chef's hat also have a story. Legend has it that the hundred pleats represent the one hundred different ways a chef can prepare eggs. For more information about the chef's uniform, refer to Chapter 2.

Career Paths for Professionals in Foodservice

A typical career in this industry usually begins as a **prep cook,** cleaning and cutting vegetables, watching over stocks and soups, preparing such basic preparations as mirepoix, roux, and clarified butter. Once you are ready to assume greater responsibilities, you may move into the **pantry,** preparing salads and cold appetizers.

Or you may move into one of the positions "on the line." To understand the organization of the kitchen and its hierarchy, read the description of

FIGURE 1-4   The Proper Chef's Uniform.

FIGURE 1-4   The Proper Chef's Uniform.

the brigade below. The brigade system was instituted by Escoffier to streamline and simplify work in hotel kitchens. Under this system, each position has a station and defined responsibilities. The French names for these positions are still used, even in restaurants that are not themselves "French." It is just as likely, however, that an English equivalent term will be used.

The Kitchen Brigade System

The **brigade system** was instituted by Escoffier to streamline and simplify work in hotel kitchens. It

---

mirepoix: a combination of chopped aromatic vegetables used to flavor stocks, soups, braises, and stews.

roux: a cooked mixture of fat and flour, used to thicken liquids.

clarified butter: butter from which the milk solids and water have been removed, leaving pure butterfat.

THE DINING ROOM BRIGADE SYSTEM

The other "traditional" type of foodservice industry positions are classified under the term "front of the house." The traditional line of authority in a dining room is as follows:

- The *maître d'hôtel,* known in American service as the dining room manager, host, or hostess, is the person who holds the most responsibility for the front-of-the-house operation. The maître d'hôtel trains all service personnel, oversees wine selection, works with the chef to determine the menu, and organizes seating throughout service.

- The wine steward *(chef de vin,* or *sommelier)* is responsible for all aspects of restaurant wine service, including purchasing wines, preparing a wine list, assisting guests in wine selection, and serving wine properly. If there is no wine steward, these responsibilities are generally assumed by the maître d'hôtel.

- The head waiter *(chef de salle)* is generally in charge of the service for an entire dining room. Very often this position is combined with the positions of either the captain or the maître d'hôtel.

- The captain *(chef d'étage)* deals most directly with the guests once they are seated. The captain explains the menu, answers any questions, and takes the order. Any tableside food preparation is generally done by the captain. If there is no captain, these responsibilities fall to the front waiter.

- The front waiter *(chef de rang)* assures that the table is properly set for each course, that the food is properly delivered to the table, and that the needs of the guests are promptly and courteously met.

- The back waiter or busboy *(demi-chef de rang* or *commis de rang)* is normally the first position assigned to new dining room workers. This person clears plates between courses, fills water glasses and bread baskets, replaces ashtrays, and assists the front waiter and/or captain as needed.

served to eliminate the chaos and duplication of effort that could result when workers did not have clearcut responsibilities. Under this system, each position has a station and defined tasks, as outlined below.

- The *chef* (chief) is responsible for all kitchen operations, including ordering, supervision of all stations, and development of menu items. He or she may be known also as *"chef de cuisine"* or executive chef.

- The *sous* ("under") *chef* is second in command, answers to the chef, may be responsible for scheduling, filling in for the chef, and assisting the station chefs (or line cooks) as necessary. Small operations may not have a sous chef.

- Station chefs *(chefs de partie)* are considered "line cooks" and include the following:

  - The sauté station *(saucier)* is responsible for all sautéed items and their sauces. This position is often considered the most demanding, responsible, and glamorous on the line.

  - The fish station *(poissonier)* is responsible for fish items, often including fish butchering and their sauces; this position is sometimes combined with the saucier position.

  - The roast station *(rôtisseur)* is responsible for all roasted foods and related *jus* or other sauces.

  - The grill station *(grillardin)* is responsible for all grilled foods; this position may be combined with rôtisseur.

  - The fry station *(friturier)* is responsible for all fried foods; this position may also be combined with rôtisseur.

  - The vegetable station *(entremetier)* is responsible for hot appetizers, and frequently has responsibility for soups and vegetables, starches, and pastas. (In a full, traditional brigade system, soups are prepared by the soup station or *potager,* vegetables by the *legumier.)* This station may also be responsible for egg dishes.

---

jus: a sauce based on meat's natural juices.

FIGURE 1-5   Fine Dining Restaurant Organization.

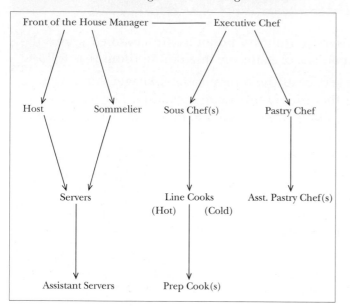

FIGURE 1-6   Hotel Organization

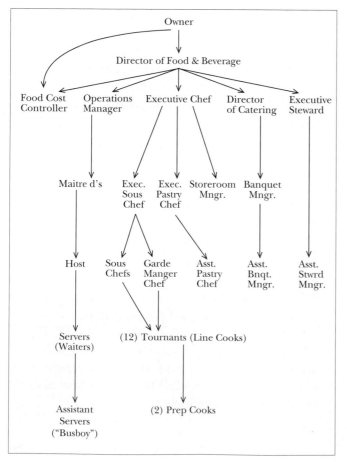

- The roundsman *(tournant)* is also known as the swing cook. This individual works as needed throughout the kitchen.

- The pantry chef *(garde manger)* is responsible for cold-food preparations, including salads, cold appetizers, and pâtés. This is considered a separate category of kitchen work.

- The butcher *(boucher)* is responsible for butchering meats, poultry, and (occasionally) fish. The butcher may also be responsible for breading meat and fish items, and is often considered part of garde manger.

- The pastry chef *(pâtissier)* is responsible for baked items, pastries, and desserts. The pastry chef frequently supervises a separate kitchen area or a separate shop in larger operations. This position may be further broken down into the following areas of specialization: *confiseur* (prepares candies, petits fours), *boulanger* (prepares nonsweetened doughs as for breads and rolls), *glacier* (prepares frozen and cold desserts), and *decorateur* (prepares show pieces and special cakes).

- There are other brigade positions: The expediter or announcer *(aboyeur)* accepts orders from the dining room and relays them to the various station chefs. This individual is the last person to see the plate before it leaves the kitchen. In some operations, this may be either the sous chef or kitchen steward. The *communard* cooks for the staff; the *commis,* or assistant, works under a chef de partie to learn the station and its responsibilities.

Types of Restaurants and Other Foodservice Establishments

Chefs are needed not just in hotel dining rooms and traditional restaurants but in a variety of settings—public and private, consumer-oriented, and institutional. An increased emphasis on nutrition, sophistication, and financial and quality control means that all settings, from the "white-tablecloth" restaurant to the fast-food outlet, can offer you interesting challenges.

---

pâté: a forcemeat loaf, typically served cold.

petits fours: small cakes, pastries, or cookies.

- *Hotels* often have a number of different dining facilities, including fine dining restaurants, room service, coffee shops, and banquet rooms. The kitchen staffs are large, and there will often be separate butchering, catering, and pastry kitchens on the premises.

- *Full-service restaurants* such as *bistros*, *"white table-cloth,"* or *family-style restaurants* feature a full menu, and the patrons are served by trained waitstaff.

- *Private clubs* generally provide some sort of foodservice to their members. It may be as simple as a small grill featuring sandwiches, or it may be a complete dining room and banquet hall. The difference is that the guests are paying members and the food costs generally are figured differently than they would be for a public restaurant.

- *Executive dining rooms* are operated by many corporations. The degree of simplicity or elegance demanded in a particular corporation will determine what types of food are prepared, how they are prepared, and what style of service is appropriate.

- *Institutional catering* (schools, hospitals, employee cafeterias, colleges, airlines, correctional institutions) often requires a cycle menu. In a cafeteria, the guests serve themselves, choosing from the offered foods. The range of menu selections depends a great deal on the institution's needs, available monies, and the preferences of those operating the cafeteria.

- *Caterers* provide a particular service specifically tailored to meet the wishes of a special client for a special event, whether it be a wedding, a cocktail reception, or a gallery opening. Caterers may provide either on-site services (the client comes to the caterer), off-site services (caterer comes to the client), or both.

- *"Carryout"* foodservices are growing in importance as more couples, single professionals, and families try to enjoy meals at home without having to spend time preparing them. These shops prepare entrées, salads, side dishes, and desserts.

Alternative Careers in Foodservice

As long as the foodservice industry continues to grow, a continual need will exist for well-trained personnel to fill the traditional careers of chef, sous chef, saucier, and other "back-of-the-house" positions. Of great importance as well, are other opportunities available to a well-trained and motivated *cuisinier*. A growing number of less-traditional opportunities exist, many of which do not involve the actual production or service of foods.

- *Consultants and design specialists* will work with restaurant owners, often before the restaurant is open, to assist in developing a menu, designing the overall layout and ambiance of the dining room, and establishing work patterns for the kitchen. Joe Baum, restaurant consultant, made an indelible mark on the design of restaurant interiors, setting new standards in such renowned establishments as The Four Seasons in New York. Barbara Lazaroff has made an equally strong impact through her design work at Spago and Chinois on Main in Los Angeles.

- Well-informed *salespeople* help chefs determine how to best meet their needs for food and equipment, introduce them to new products, and demonstrate how to properly use the new equipment that is essential to the well-run, modern kitchen.

- The number of cooking schools in this country has swelled from one to nearly 300 over the course of the last five decades. *Teachers* with solid experience in addition to teaching skills are what set the good schools apart. Chefs who turn to classroom instruction bring with them the experience that gives students a more thorough understanding of what restaurant cooking is like. Culinary historians, writers, and table service instructors are all playing an increasing role as the education of a chef becomes more fully rounded.

- For those who read about food as voraciously as some people devour mystery novels, good food writing is a cherished commodity. There are several different types of *food writers*: cookbook authors, historians, reviewers, critics, and journalists. Individual writers have, over time, played crucial roles in setting the tone for this profession. M.F.K. Fisher, Elizabeth David, James Beard, Jane Brody, Craig Claiborne, Bryan Miller, Paula Wolfert, and Florence Fabricant have all had an impact, directly or indirectly, on the restaurant industry.

- *Food photography and styling* has become a significant factor in the promotion of new products, as well as in magazines and books. This has become an increasingly specialized field. As food continues to have a starring role in television programs, videos, and movies, this area will remain an important avenue for professional growth.

- *Research and development kitchens* employ a great many chefs. These may be run by food manufacturers who are developing new products or food lines. Advisory boards, such as the American Dairy Association or the California Prune Board, may also operate research, development, and testing facilities. Magazines for both the industry and consumers also maintain test and development kitchens. *Eating Well* and *Saveur,* for example, have a great deal of prestige and pride invested in their test kitchens.

The Chef as Executive, Administrator, and Manager

As you continue your career, you will move from positions where your technical prowess is your greatest contribution into those where your skills as an executive, administrator, and manager are more clearly in demand. This does not mean that your ability to grill, sauté, or roast foods to the exact point of doneness is less important than it was before. It does mean however, that you will be called upon to learn and to assume tasks and responsibilities that are more managerial, marking a shift in the evolution of your career.

Becoming a Good Executive

What do executives do? They are the individuals who develop a mission or a plan for a company or organization. They are also the individuals responsible for developing a system that allows that plan to come to fruition. As an executive, then, you will be called upon to shoulder a large portion of re-

sponsibility for the success or failure of your restaurant.

Executives cannot operate in a vacuum, however. Nor do they emerge full-blown one day out of the blue. Even before you wear a jacket embroidered with "Executive Chef," you will have begun to exercise your abilities as an executive.

Becoming a Good Administrator

Once a restaurauteur has laid down an overall goal and game plan, the next task is to establish systems to implement and track those plans. Now your role becomes that of an administrator. Some administrative duties may not sound at all glamorous—preparing schedules, tracking deliveries, computing costs, and so forth—but a sound restaurant business cannot be run without them. If a restaurant is small, the "executive" and "administrator" will be the same person. That same person also might be the one who dons a uniform and works the line.

The best administrators are those who can create a feeling throughout the entire staff that they have a stake in getting things done correctly. When you give people the opportunity to help make decisions, and provide them with the tools needed to perform as well as they can, you will see that it is easier to achieve the goals you have established on an executive level.

There are tools that you can and should learn to use. Computers, accounting systems, and careful

FIGURE 1-7   Using a Computer as a Management Tool

record-keeping all play a role. Many organizations, from large chains and hotels down to the smallest one-person catering company are relying more and more on software systems that enable them to track purchases, losses, sales, profits, food cost, recipes, and customer comments. If you (or the professionals that you employ to do this for you) are not already using a system capable of incorporating all of this information and more, you cannot be as effective as you need to be.

Becoming a Good Manager

Management issues have received a good deal of attention in this industry, as well as in others. All businesses must operate more effectively and efficiently, with fewer resources. Managing a restaurant, or any other business, is a job that requires the ability to manage four areas effectively:

1. Physical assets
2. Time
3. Information
4. People (human resources)

The greater your skills in managing any of these areas, the greater your potential for success will be. Many management systems today stress the use of quality as a yardstick. Every aspect of your operation needs to be seen as a way to improve the quality of service you provide your customers. As we look at what you might be expected to do in order to manage resources, information, people, and time effectively, the fundamental question you need to ask, over and over, is this:

How does a change (or lack of change) affect the quality of service or goods that I am offering my customer?

Unless you are different, better, faster, or unique in some way, there is every chance that, as competition continues to increase, you may not survive, let alone prosper.

Managing Physical Assets

The primary purpose of being in business is to make money. If you squander your assets, then you cannot make a profit. The increasingly complex problems of budgeting, taxes, wages, and many other business considerations make it a good idea to hire professionals trained specifically to handle these areas. In order to be sure that these professionals are able to do what a specific operation requires, you need to be aware of how a business operates—and you must be realistic about what can be expected.

When we talk about managing physical assets, we are considering how anything that you must purchase or pay for affects your ability to do business well. This includes, but is certainly not limited to, the items listed below:

- Food and beverage
- Operating costs such as utilities, waste removal, taxes, and insurance
- Rent, mortgage, or lease payments
- Tables, chairs, linens, china, flatware, glassware
- Computers, cash registers
- Pots, pans, and other large and small kitchen equipment
- Cleaning supplies and/or services, ware washing machines

The first step to bringing the expenses associated with your physical assets under control is to know what your expenses actually are. Then, you can begin the process of making the adjustments and instituting the control systems that will keep your organization operating at maximum efficiency.

Each restaurant has different needs, and only you, along with your management team, can decide how best to purchase, lease, or rent various commodities that you need. For instance, you may find that buying linens and washing them on the premises represents a slight increase over the cost of renting. Still, you might decide not to rent, since owning your own linens allows you to have a specific quality, style, or color not available through the companies in your area. Or, you might compromise on linens and opt to apply the money saved by using a linen service toward purchasing better quality flatware. There are no hard and fast

MANAGING TIME

It seems that, no matter how hard you work or how much planning you do, the days aren't long enough. Learning new skills to become as efficient and competitive as possible ought to be an on-going part of your education. The more time you can save using any of the following strategies, the greater your potential for profit can be. The top five time wasters, in most operations, can be categorized as:

- no clear priorities for tasks

- poor, inadequate, or nonexistent training standards for staff

- poor communication

- poor organization

- missing or inadequate tools to accomplish tasks

To combat these time wasters, use the following strategies:

Invest Time in Reviewing Daily Operations   Consider the way you, your coworkers, and staff spend the day. Does everyone have a basic understanding of which tasks are most important? Do they know when to begin a particular task in order to bring it to completion on time?

It can be an eye-opening experience to take a hard look at where the work day goes. Once you see that you and your staff need to walk too far to gather basic items, or that the dishwasher is sitting idle for the first two hours of the shift, you can take steps to rectify this.

You can try to reorganize storage space (see below for more about organization). You may decide to train the dishwasher to do some prep work or you can rewrite the schedule so the shift begins two hours later. Until you are objective about what needs to be done, and in what order, you can't begin the process of saving time.

Invest Time in Training Others   Assigning work to others is one area where managers often tend to waste time, both theirs and their staffs. If you expect someone to do a job properly, take enough time to explain the task carefully. Let the person who will be receiving orders know what you expect: where items should be stored, how to handle and process invoice slips, and where packing boxes go for recycling, for example. Walk yourself and your staff through the jobs that must be done, and make sure that everyone understands how to do the work, where the tools they need can be found, how far their responsibility extends, and what to do in case a question or emergency crops up. Give them the yardsticks they need to evaluate the job and determine if they have done what was requested, in the appropriate fashion, and on time. If

rules, just principles that you will apply to your own situation.

One of the biggest expenses for any restaurant will always be food and beverage costs. You or your purchasing agent will have to work hard to develop and sustain a good purchasing system. The principles outlined in "Purchasing" offer a way to analyze and improve what you are already doing or to act as a guide in establishing a new system. You should constantly re-evaluate your purchasing practices to accommodate changes in your operation and in the marketplace.

Controlling Food Cost   The food and drink that are ultimately served to the guest are the raw materials of our industry. It is impossible to overemphasize how important it is for you to be aware of what your own food cost and to take steps to maximize the use of these raw materials. You must make a great effort to squeeze the most out of every product that passes

you don't invest this time up front, you may find yourself squandering precious time following your workers around, picking up the slack, and handling work that shouldn't be taking up your day.

Learn to Communicate Clearly Whether you are training a new employee, introducing a new menu item, or ordering a piece of equipment, clear communication is important. Be specific, use the most concise language you can, and be as brief as possible, without leaving out necessary information.

If some tasks are handled by a number of different people, be sure to write that task out, from the first step to the last. Encourage people to ask you questions if they don't seem to understand you. You may find that your terminology isn't the same as theirs, or that a phrase you find succinct someone else finds baffling.

Spoken, written, and nonverbal communication is fundamental to all you do throughout the day. If you need help learning communication skills, consider taking a workshop or seminar to strengthen any weak areas.

Take Steps to Create an Orderly Work Environment If you have to dig through five shelves to find the lid to the storage container you just put the stock in, you haven't been using your time wisely. Planning work areas carefully, thinking about all the tools, ingredients, and equipment you need for preparation and throughout service, and grouping like activities together are all techniques that can help you better organize your work.

Schedules are another effective and time-honored means of achieving organization. If this is Thursday, you must plan your meat order so that it be phoned in on Friday. If this is January, you know that you need to get your fryolater serviced and the fire extinguishers inspected.

Purchase, Replace, and Maintain All Necessary Tools A well-equipped kitchen will have enough of all the tools necessary to prepare every item on the menu. If you are missing something as basic as a sicve, your cream soups won't have the right consistency. If you put pizza on the menu and don't have enough oven space, will pizza orders start to crowd out other baked and roasted items on your menu? If you have a menu with several sautéed appetizers, entrees, and side dishes, are you and your line cooks cooling your heels while the pot washer scrambles to get you restocked with sauté pans? If you can't purchase new equipment, then think about restructuring your menu to even out the workload. If you can't remove a menu item, then invest in the tools you need to prevent a slow-up during service.

Poor placement of large and small tools is a great time waster. Use adequate, easy-to-access storage space for common items like whips, spoons, ladles, and tongs. Electrical outlets for small equipment such as food processors ought to be within reach of everyone who works in your kitchen. While you may be forced to work within the limits of your existing equipment and floor plan, be on the lookout for products or techniques that can turn a bad arrangement into one that works smoothly and evenly.

through the door, all the while keeping quality standards intact.

Controlling spoilage and waste is one of the first lines of defense. Many of the materials you work with are perishable. Having adequate space to store foods properly is imperative. Refrigerators, walk-ins, reach-ins, freezers, and dry storage should be carefully maintained and monitored. Insist that foods be labeled, dated, and used in sequence (first in, first out).

Whenever foods are cut, trimmed, and cleaned, there is a possibility that you can lose money through carelessness or mishandling. The cost of the food when it is received is referred to as the **as purchased/AP** cost. Once it is properly processed, prior to cooking, you can determine its **edible portion/EP** cost. When all of the trim has been removed, the food is measured again and the resulting EP weight is divided by the AP cost in order to determine how

(Continued on page 28)

PURCHASING

Purchasing has a direct impact on cost control. An adequate store of supplies is needed so that the restaurant can operate efficiently. This includes not only food but nonfood items, such as cleaning supplies, small tools, and equipment. Having too little of any given item is a clear sign of poor planning. On the other hand, it is wasteful to have more supplies than can be used in a reasonable amount of time, or to own unnecessary equipment and tools. An excess of anything is simply tying up money, space, and time.

When you apply the nine steps outlined here, foods, supplies, and equipment can be purchased wisely and efficiently.

1. Develop a list of your needs.

All food and equipment purchased for the kitchen should have a direct relation to the menu. Review your menu carefully. Create master lists for foods, small and large equipment needs, and any special service items.

2. Develop quality and purchasing specifications.

This is a precise description of the product, including trade or common names, type of container, brand names or federal grades, container size, and the unit (pound, case, bunch, can, and so on) on which the item's price is quoted. Any other pertinent specifications, such as whether meats should be aged, should also be included. These specifications should take the form of a written communication between you and the purveyor.

You may wish to make use of local farmer's markets to get some or all of your food. If so, use the same standards you would in purchasing food from a purveyor. There are often bargains to be had, especially if you can time your trip to coincide with the opening of the market. An alternate strategy might be to wait until the market is about to close. Restaurants can often make use of the very large tomatoes or other "odd"-sized produce that the home cook is less likely to want.

3. Select purveyors.

It is best to have a minimum of two purveyors for any item purchased. Well-chosen purveyors can provide an operation with products of consistent quality. They will also work with an operation to help set up delivery schedules. To find a good purveyor, check with the Better Business Bureau and with other restaurant owners. There are many ways you can determine if your purveyor is giving you the best possible service:

- The price quoted by the salesperson should be the same as the price paid upon receipt of the goods
- Foods should be of the quality and quantity requested
- Delivery trucks should be clean, and refrigerated if necessary
- Invoices should be clearly written
- Returns of unacceptable products should be handled quickly
- Foods should arrive in appropriate containers

4. Organize a delivery schedule.

A consistent and reliable delivery schedule is one way that you even out the workload. If you cannot be certain when a delivery will arrive, it may force you into unwise purchasing patterns. You may find it necessary to overpurchase some items in order to be prepared in case a delivery is delayed. Or, you may be in the position of removing a dish from the menu in the middle of service if the fish that normally arrives at 4 o'-clock on Thursday afternoon is not on hand until 10 o'clock in the evening.

5. Develop a parstock.

Parstock refers to a basic inventory that should be consistently on hand. Being overstocked can be as bad as having too little stock. If there is too much stock, valuable space and money are tied up. If there is not enough, it may be impossible to produce a given menu item. It is one thing to run out of a "special" but it is bad business to have to apologize that a regular menu item is unavailable.

6. Take purchase inventory.

This is a physical count of what is available. You and your staff should take a quick physical inventory of the food items, linens, and equipment for each station at the end of every shift. A more detailed and accurate count should be taken weekly, monthly, quarterly, and yearly. The amount you have on hand should then be "brought to par" by ordering enough of an item to replace the depleted stores.

7. Forecast contingency needs.

Keeping full and complete business records can help predict what times of the year, month, or week may be busier than others. If your restaurant is located in a tourist area, there may be a predictably busy season. Other factors to consider are parties, banquets, and special events, such as festivals in the area. Additional stock may then be ordered to cover especially high-volume times. If your restaurant is a new operation, you can learn some of this information by talking with other owners or chefs in the area.

8. Take market quotes.

Many factors can affect what you pay for food and beverage items. A strike, a flood or hurricane, poor growing conditions, a drought, or an unexpected shortage of certain goods due to seasonal swings can send the cost of certain goods soaring. When you find, for instance, that broccoli or red pepper are no longer within your operating budget, you may need to make adjustments.

9. Maintain a purchase log.

Keeping good records of all orders, invoices, and price lists helps to make ordering, receiving, and storing procedures efficient. An up-to-date purchase log eliminates costly guesswork when you must decide what foods and beverages to purchase from which vendors. You may be required by local ordinance, state, or federal law to produce certificates or receipts for specific foods, such as shellfish.

much the food that you serve your guests is actually costing.

To cut down on trim loss, be sure that your kitchen staff is trained properly. If you can use the ends of the red pepper to make a coulis, then let the person who does the advance preparation of peppers know how to process every bit of the pepper, including where to store the usable trim so that it can be retrieved and used in a timely fashion.

Keeping food costs in line is your responsibility. You can only be effective at this job if you are constantly aware of what food and beverage costs are, and how to maximize each dollar you spend. You should know what yield you can expect from particular foods, from fish to foie gras. Then, you will be able to tell quickly if you are experiencing undue loss, and where that loss is occurring.

Recipes as Tools   We often think of recipes as performing one function—telling someone the steps in preparing a dish. That is one of the primary purposes of a recipe of course. For a restaurant, recipes have an equally important role in helping to control costs, ensure consistency, and maintain quality standards.

Standard recipes need to be carefully written so that everyone can prepare a dish correctly from start to finish. They should be revised whenever modifications are made. The measurements need to be very accurate, so that there is as little loss as possible during production. Check the yields and measurements periodically to be sure that you are getting what you expect from a recipe. Check, too, that both you and any other line cooks involved in food preparation haven't strayed too far from the recipe.

In many establishments, proper procedures for maintaining wholesomeness and safety are also identified, along with methods for monitoring proper food handling. Recipes written in a HACCP model (see Chapter 2 for more information) clearly identify "critical control points" and correct cooking, holding, and service temperatures. Careful handling at all phases of production is important, not only to ensure that your customers don't suffer from foodborne illness at your hands. But it also increases the life of foods that might otherwise

foie gras: the fattened liver of a goose.

become part of the "loss" column when the books are done at the end of the day.

Portion Control   Equally important to controlling loss is establishing the appropriate portion size of all the items you serve your guests. This includes large and small items alike.

Once **standard portion sizes** for foods have been established, it is important that this information be passed along to anyone who plates the food. So, if soups are handled by the waitstaff, your salads are prepared and plated in one part of the kitchen, and desserts in another, all of these stations need to be informed about what is considered an acceptable portion.

This important point needs to be constantly monitored and reinforced. It has a bearing on more than just the bottom line. It also can have a very direct influence on how customers perceive the dining experience. If a steak or ice cream sundae is consistently the same in both quality and quantity, that speaks loudly about the care and concern that is promoted in all aspects of the operation.

Menu Pricing   Once you have calculated the true food cost and determined the correct serving or portion size for a menu item, your next task is establishing a **menu price.** A variety of methods may be used. You will need to assess the market, the cost of food you want to serve, and the type of establishment you will be operating.

All three of these factors will play an important part in deciding final menu prices. For instance, some restaurants will keep their menu prices relatively low and rely upon volume to make a profit. Others will use a higher markup, making their menu prices relatively higher, but requiring a lower sales volume to make a profit.

There are several different methods used for menu pricing. Remember that no matter which method you actually use, the price charged for a menu item will have to cover not only the cost of food and the labor of those preparing and serving the food, but also any and all additional operating expenses, such as rent, utilities, and advertising.

1. **Factor method.** The factor method reflects the idea that the cost of the food sold should fall

within a range that is equal to a specified percentage of the sales in dollars.

To use this method, you must first determine the raw cost of food using your standardized recipes. Then, you need to decide what an acceptable food-cost percentage is for your operation. If you select, for example, a food-cost percentage of 25 percent of the total sales, you can calculate your factor as follows:

Divide the desired percentage, 25 percent, into 100. The resulting number, 4, is the "factor" you would use to multiply the food cost in order to arrive at the selling price.

So, if the raw food cost for a serving prepared according to a standardized recipe is $2.50, you multiply by 4 to arrive at a menu price of $10.

There are some advantages to this method, such as its relative simplicity. But, there are also some serious disadvantages as well. Your calculated profit may not match your actual profit, since many operating costs won't be deducted from the profit until the end of the month, when costs other than food, can be calculated.

2. **Prime cost.** This pricing method is more complex than the factor method and, if done exactly as specified according to its definition, might be an extremely complex and time-consuming process. Most managers that use this particular strategy will modify the method slightly. They make a few initial assumptions, based on a good understanding of the total operating costs for their restaurant. Percentages of the prime cost are assigned to cover raw-food, direct-labor, and operating costs.

Once these percentages are established as standards, you need only use raw-food cost and cost of labor for food preparation to determine a menu price.

3. **Actual cost.** If you have accurate records on hand, this method can be used to determine menu prices as follows: First, you need to determine as accurately as possible the actual cost of the raw ingredients, using your standardized recipes. You would also use payroll records or other sources to determine the actual cost of labor involved in food preparation. Finally, you

will determine the cost of all of the other fixed and variable expenses involved in operating the restaurant. All of these costs are assigned a percentage of the actual sales. Use the percentages to determine what the dollars-and-cents value for these items ought to be, so that you will have actual figures to work with.

Then you determine your menu price by adding together actual food cost, actual labor cost, other variable costs, other fixed costs, and an amount for your profit. The sum is the menu price.

Menu pricing is a complex process and there are a number of books that can assist in determining which method is appropriate to an operation and how to use the chosen method. Such books include *The Restaurant Operator's Manual* by Allen Z. Reich (1990, Van Nostrand Reinhold), *Foodservice Organizations* by Marion C. Spears (1994, Macmillan), and *The Business Chef* by Tom Miner (1989, Van Nostrand Reinhold). Also refer to the resources listed in the Recommended Readings.

Cost of Errors   One area that many chefs tend to overlook is the cost of errors. This can have a great impact on your profit. Say, for example, that a steak is overcooked and returned by the guest. Not only are you losing the cost of the food that must be discarded, you are also losing the time spent in preparing the food, including any advance work

FIGURE 1-8   A Management Training Session

done during the day as well as the time lost by the chef and waiter during service. If you "comp" a dessert or after-dinner drink, you are also losing that food and labor cost. You may also be losing return business, and cutting into potential new customers who won't come on the basis of a negative review.

In a similar vein, overportioning should be considered an error. If you are giving away an extra ounce or two of salmon on each plate, at the end of the month, the loss will tally up to quite an impressive figure. Inaccurate or inconsistent portioning will have the same effect, compounded by the fact that repeat customers will notice the swings in portion sizes, and may decide to take their business elsewhere.

If this happens only once in a great while, the damage to your overall business is not going to be too substantial. If it happens consistently, however, the actual cost can be staggering.

Managing Information

It often seems that there is so much information available that you can never keep current in all the important areas of your work. And, at our current rate of growth in the sheer volume of information being generated each day, you are probably right. The ability to tap into the information resources you need, as well as the ability to use information gathering tools, has never been more important.

Restaurants, menus, and dining room design have all been dramatically impacted by such societal trends as an increased interest in health and nutrition and Mediterranean or other ethnic diets. There are also a number of influences that may not seem, at first glance, to have much to do with restaurants and food. Yet, the prevailing tastes in politics, art, fashion, movies, and music also have no small effect.

Gathering all of the information you need to successfully operate your business is a full-time task. You need to learn ways to manage both gathering and processing tasks so that information becomes a useful tool, rather than a staggering burden.

Computers as Kitchen Tools Unlike other labor-saving devices, such as food processors, one of the most useful tools to show up in the kitchen in recent years has no direct interaction with the food itself. The computer, however, is almost as essential today as a stove to allow a chef to operate successfully. Chefs are using them for everything from tracking inventory to submitting purchase orders to purveyors. Given a computer's many advantages to a foodservice operation, computer literacy is now a vital part of every chef's education.

Selecting the appropriate computer system and software is extremely important. You should spend some time doing research and testing out a variety of systems to find one that is most suited to your needs. Systems are available that can act as a database for recipes, create menus for special events, track salaries, or be a watchdog to help avoid loss through spoilage, pilferage, or inaccuracy in writing checks.

Computers are one of the best ways to gather, store, process, and retrieve all sorts of information about virtually every phase of your operation. One of the most basic computer functions is to assist in maintaining accurate business records: bookkeeping, inventory, costing, reservations, customer lists, staff schedules, and budget information.

Interactive software, CD-ROM, the Internet, and other computer applications are being used throughout the country, permitting chefs wider and easier access to information of all sorts. Networking and information gathering are the two other important areas in which computers can provide an invaluable service. Updates to FDA regulations regarding safe food-handling practices, information about product availability on a local, national, and worldwide scale, and answers to questions are available to you 24 hours a day through on-line services, forums, bulletin boards, and databases.

The Media Newspapers, magazines, newsletters, journals, and books about food have become a major part of the newsstands and bookstores throughout the world. Even those publications that are not directly aimed at the professional audience may offer some special insight, recipe, tip, or news item that you can turn to your use. For more information, review the Recommended Readings list at the end of this book.

Professional Organization There are professional organizations in this industry that you will want to

LEGAL RESPONSIBILITIES FOR MANAGERS

Everyone has the right to work in an environment that is free from physical hazards. This means that if you own a restaurant one day, you must provide a work space that is well lit, properly ventilated, and free from obvious dangers, such as improperly maintained equipment. Employees must have access to potable water and bathroom facilities. Beyond these bare minimum requirements, you may offer a locker room, a laundry facility that provides clean uniforms, aprons, and side towels, or other such amenities.

Workers compensation, unemployment, and disability insurance are also your responsibility. You are required to make all legal deductions from an employee's paycheck and to report all earnings properly to state and federal agencies. Liability insurance (to cover any harm to your facility, employees, or guests) must be kept up to date and at adequate levels.

Your workers may require additional forms of assistance, which you may be able to offer as part of an employee benefits package. Life insurance, medical and dental insurance, assistance with such things as dependent care, family leave, adult literacy training, and enrollment in and support for those enrolled in substance abuse programs are all items of which you need to be aware. You may have a legal responsibility in some cases. The responsibility may be ethical but not legal in others.

This industry is notorious for its problems with illegal aliens. You need to be familiar with the regulations that could affect you or those you employ.

join. An affiliation with a national or international group, such as the American Culinary Federation (AFC) or National Restaurant Association (NRA), or with more special-interest and locally-run groups (National Association of Catering Executives (NACE) or Culinary Historians of New York, for example) is one way to reap the benefits that only such a group can offer. Not only do they have various memberships services, they are also one of the best sources of job opportunities, pending legislation that might affect you, and other types of "insider" information. There is a list of food associations at the back of this book.

Networking with Other Chefs   Creating a **professional network** is a task that should be taken seriously. Working with other professionals to share information and knowledge is an important avenue of growth—both professional and personal. Networks can be formal or informal. The way to begin is simply to introduce yourself to others in your field. Have business cards with you when you go out to restaurants or to trade shows.

When you make a good contact, follow up with a phone call or a note. Keep the names and cards that you acquire organized in some sort of filing system. An established network makes it much easier for you to find a job once you've completed school.

It also makes any travel that you may begin to do more pleasurable and effective, since you will already know colleagues in other cities and countries before you arrive. The communication that you develop with your peers will keep your own work fresh and contemporary.

Managing Human Resources

Restaurant operations rely directly on the work and dedication of a number of people, from executives and administrators to line cooks to waitstaff and maintenance and cleaning staff. No matter how large or small your staff may be, the ability to engage all your workers in a team effort is one of the major factors in determining whether you will succeed or not.

Your goal should be creating an environment in which everyone feels that they have a distinct and measurable contribution to make within the organization. Knowing how they can work within the team and how their efforts will be part of the bottom line makes it much easier to understand and accept organizational policies that might otherwise seem to have little to do with an individual's needs or wants.

The first task for a good manager is to establish clear criteria, otherwise known as a job description. Having created that description, it is a far easier task to recruit employees and get them oriented and trained.

Training is another key component. If you want someone to do a job well, you have to first show them exactly what the quality standards are that you expect to see. You need to continually reinforce those standards with clear, objective evaluation of an employee's work through feedback, constructive criticism and, when necessary, additional training or disciplinary measures.

The classic brigade systems, used in both the kitchen and dining room have clearly defined jobs. These systems provide a good place to begin the work of writing job descriptions.

Marketing

There may have been a time when restaurants were not actively concerned with courting and cultivating a market. In today's climate, however, a restaurant chef who is ignorant of the problems of **marketing** is willfully ignoring an area that can make or break a business.

When you develop your organization's mission statement, you need to make it clear who you think is likely to come to your restaurant. To a large extent, your answer may lie in geographic location. If you are in a busy downtown area where business and government offices are located, then you are talking about one subset of the city's population. If you are in a resort location, it is another group altogether. Your mission and your market need to line up. If they don't, you need to go back to the drawing board.

Just as menu development is not a single-stage operation, a marketing plan is also something that should be part of the review and analysis of virtually every day's business. It should be looked at carefully, so that elements that are working well get reinforced, and those that are less successful are modified. It is an ongoing challenge—one that you need to stay fully aware of, even if it is not your primary charge.

The way in which a foodservice establishment presents itself to its customers has a definite influence on whether or not the business will succeed.

Defining the Customer Base

If you haven't opened your doors yet, then you should at least know who you would like to come through the door. If you are in business already, then it is clear who is coming to your restaurant. But, there may be other, wider markets you think you could tap. How do you find out what will appeal to your intended market? Having gotten that far, how do you determine what will sway someone to choose you over the other restaurants within reach of your potential guest?

There are numerous marketing strategies and, as with virtually every area we have touched on throughout this chapter, it is a good idea to arm yourself with additional information. Beyond the broad definitions and overviews we can offer here, you will be ahead of the game if you keep up with current journals, publications, books, and on-line services that can keep you and your business out in front.

Today's clientele is a more sophisticated and widely traveled group than ever before. These consumers' "food savvy" has had a direct impact on the types of food served in restaurants, as well as what is offered now in supermarkets and specialty shops. Small farms and bakeries producing specialty produce, cheeses, and breads are becoming more widely known and appreciated. The continuing demand for such foods will provide a great avenue for growth. It is already opening doors for those who wish to participate in less "mainstream" operations, as entrepreneurs supplying restaurants and retail outlets.

The public's growing interest in grains, legumes, fish, vegetables, and fruits, along with a desire to decrease overconsumption of animal fat, protein, and sodium, have helped popularize nutritional cooking. This has spurred fundamental changes in the preparation and presentation of traditional foods. Favorite dishes from both the classical and peasant traditions are being reevaluated to reduce or eliminate fats, sodium, and cholesterol.

Going out for dinner has become a form of entertainment and the restaurant has become a destination, not just a place to have a quick meal before moving on to another activity. Rather than spending an evening at the theater followed by supper, or a night of dancing preceded by a light dinner, lingering over dinner at a restaurant has become "the evening."

The Menu as a Marketing Tool

A menu is a powerful tool. It can be a marketing and merchandising vehicle. It can establish and reinforce the total restaurant concept, from the style of china and flatware selected to the training needs for the service staff. It can assist the chef in reducing waste and increasing profits.

The way a menu is developed or adapted is a reflection of how well the total concept has been designed. Sometimes, the two evolve hand in hand. In other scenarios, the concept comes first and the menu comes later. In still others, the menu may be the guiding principle that gives a particular stamp to the way the restaurant concept evolves.

You may engage in **menu development,** redesign, or overhaul at any time. It is fairly certain that, whenever you turn your attention to the menu, you will need to address a number of issues. The following list of questions is not meant to be exhaustive. Each operation has special needs, and as you look over this list, you will see that this is just the jumping-off point.

- Do you have a particular cuisine or cuisines in mind? Or, do you have a different set of standards to guide you in making selections? What are they?

- What meal period is the menu geared toward?

- Is your menu seasonally driven, cycle driven, or set?

- Do you expect to have, or do you already have, signature dishes?

- Do you have both the staff and the equipment necessary to properly serve your guests from the menu you have established?

- How large is your menu, and how does that translate into stations and staff in the kitchen, equipment needs, service needs?

- How is your menu pricing structured? Is it an *á la carte* (all items priced individually), *prix fixe* (one single price for a meal, that is all inclusive), *table d'hôte* (a single price for an entrée that includes a set number of accompanying dishes, which may or may not allow the guest some choice), or a combination of pricing strategies?

- Do you have a wine list? Does it complement your menu, both in terms of wine and food pairings as well as in pricing? Can your waitstaff use it to promote wines with foods, especially with special menu items?

- What are your portion sizes? Can you assure that they are consistently adhered to?

- Can your menu incorporate some profit-engineering techniques such as cross-utilization of foods, promotion and merchandising efforts, use of in-season items to take advantage of their low cost?

- Is your menu varied enough that regular customers will have enough selections to keep them from being bored? At the same time, are your signature dishes available consistently so that the regular customer doesn't feel cheated when his or her favorite dish is not on the menu?

- Will you have supplemental or special menus: grazing menus, light fare menus, pub menus?

- Do you have a set of menus established for special events, banquets, or catered events (Mother's Day brunch, Thanksgiving, New Year's Eve, weddings, for instance)?

- Is the descriptive language on the menu appropriate to your concept? For instance, a family-style restaurant might not be the best place to use unfamiliar Italian or French names for dishes, while a bistro could more easily incorporate a foreign language.

- Do you have a system that allows you to analyze your sales?

- How easy is it for you to cost out and price a new item?

After you have developed or refined your menu, you can clearly see that it is far more than a simple list of dishes offered to the customer. It sets the tone and style for your restaurant in a way no other single element of your business can, and it impacts directly and indirectly on virtually everything you do, from ordering linen to choosing a computer system to selecting new kitchen equipment.

This brief look at menus is meant only as an introduction to the topic and its potential value to the chef. For further information on menu development and use, refer to the resources noted in the Recommended Readings list, found at the end of the book.

Restaurant Design and Ambiance

First and foremost, a foodservice establishment should be appealing to the eye and the nose. This means keeping all visible areas clean, well lit, and well maintained. Lighting should be appropriate and adequate to allow the menu to be read easily. It should be flattering to the food and to the guest, in order to promote a pleasant feeling. Chairs should be comfortable. Tables should be sturdy and appropriately appointed with flatware and china that are suitable to both the food and to the atmosphere of the restaurant. Music may be good for some styles of operations, but it should be at a level that makes it easy to hear without intruding on the meal or conversation.

Other areas in the restaurant where customers are welcomed, including bathrooms, bars, or "open kitchens," need to be given the same degree of thought and care as the dining room and the tabletop.

Service

In an industry based on service, the type and quality of service offered to the guest is of ultimate importance. You should realize, however, that the definition of quality service can and does change from one establishment to another. In a fast-food restaurant, courtesy is important but speed is paramount. In a white-tablecloth restaurant, other skills are more valuable: the ability to help a guest select an appropriate wine, to "intuit" how to pace the meal to avoid rushing the guest, and to provide as much or as little interaction as the customer appears to want.

Proper training for service staff at all levels is the only way to be sure that the caliber of service provided is appropriate to the menu offered, the prices charged, the style of the dining room, and the clientele you hope to serve. Schedule sessions to bring the kitchen and dining room staff together. Airing concerns about communication and finding solutions before tempers flare on a busy Saturday night is good for everyone.

Summary

As a chef, you will deal with a great many people every day: salespeople, waitstaff, kitchen staff, customers. In order to be successful in these dealings, you must constantly work at upholding the standards of the profession.

It is not always easy to define what makes someone a true professional. It is actually much simpler to describe it in terms of what it is not. Anyone can recognize behavior that is below the industry's acceptable standards.

Education, work experience, more education, more experience, and still more education are the cornerstones of true professionalism. Learning through daily contact with other professionals what professionalism means, and how it shows itself to coworkers and guests, will do much to elevate the chef's image both within the profession and to our guests. Carrying professionalism into all areas is your responsibility.

Becoming a chef is a task that requires a great deal from any individual. In order to be the best at this job you can, you should have a good understanding of many different aspects of the foodservice industry.

Gaining knowledge in the following areas is a good starting point:

- The paths by which one becomes a professional chef

- The personal attributes a chef needs in order to be successful

- The ways in which you can develop a career, including both traditional and alternative paths

- The importance of being able to assume the duties of executive, administrator, and manager

SELF-STUDY QUESTIONS

1. How can one begin to develop a sense of judgment?

2. Name three possible paths to getting an education in the foodservice industry as a chef.

3. What are the "line cook" positions? Name at least four and describe their duties.

4. Name at least three important uses for computers.

5. What issues in farming and food processing have a direct impact on food safety concerns?

6. What is meant by the term "organic," and why is it of concern to the chef?

7. What are physical assets? Name several examples.

8. What is meant by parstock? Why is it important?

9. Define the terms as "purchased/AP" and "edible portion/EP." Explain how they relate to menu pricing and food cost control.

10. Name the nine steps in purchasing foods.

11. Name two methods that can be used to arrive at a menu cost.

12. What are some of the key elements the chef should analyze when working to develop a marketing plan.

13. What is the most basic component in providing excellent service to your guest?

ACTIVITIES

- Make a monthly schedule, and break the tasks down into weekly segments. Prepare a weekly schedule, and track how many items on your schedule you are unable to accomplish over the month. Review your schedule and try to determine where you could have been more efficient.

- Try to find a better way to organize your own work space. Try to eliminate wasted steps and motions, excess prep, and unnecessary distractions.

KEYWORDS

actual cost	factor method	pantry	sous chef
as purchased/AP	food cost	prep cook	standard portion sizes
code of conduct	marketing	prime cost	standardized recipes
brigade system	menu development	professional network	*toque blanche*
cost of errors	menu price	purchasing	
edible portion/EP	organic foods	quality service	

2

Food and Kitchen Safety

*There's a simple rule of thumb: I look at
the ceiling, I look at the floor, I look at
your apron, your shoes. And I've made up
my mind.*

—GRAY KUNZ, CHEF DE CUISINE, LESPINASSE

*There is a belief that in the good old days all foods were pure, unadulterated, and
wholesome. With each newly reported food poisoning outbreak, fears about food safety
escalate. This is of enormous concern to the entire foodservice industry. Over three-
quarters of all foodborne diseases reported to the Centers for Disease Control in Atlanta
can be traced to improper food handling in restaurants. This number overshadows all
other sources of foodborne disease. Around 20 percent of foodborne diseases are due to
improper cooking and handling of foods in the home, and of the other cases, less than
5 percent of the total can be attributed to food processing and handling plants.*

Improved methods of food processing and handling procedures, as well as enhanced inspection practices have helped to reduce the total number of officially reported outbreaks of foodborne illnesses. At the same time, it should be noted that the new processing technologies (aseptic packaging, vacuum-packed foods, and foods prepared by a cook/chill process) may have created a number of new problem areas.

Chefs working together with health officials have developed their own standards, aimed at improving the quality and safety of the foods prepared and served to the public. Additional information to help chefs set and meet high standards for health, sanitation, and safety in the kitchen can be found in Appendix 2.

This chapter will look at three important facets of maintaining a working environment that helps promote food and worker safety in a commercial kitchen: food safety, running a clean kitchen and dining room to reduce the risk of foodborne illnesses and worker safety. All three areas are so firmly intertwined that, as you will see, keeping standards high in one area will automatically upgrade the others.

CHAPTER OBJECTIVES

- List the three ways in which foods can become contaminated and name some of the strategies for avoiding contamination in the kitchen

- Name different types of foodborne illnesses, their sources, and symptoms

- Explain what is meant by potentially hazardous foods

- Define danger zone and name several critical temperatures in safe food-handling practices

- Understand the connection between personal hygiene and the prevention of foodborne illness

- Learn to apply the correct procedures for cooling and reheating foods

- Explain HACCP

- Name several key points for keeping the kitchen safe and sanitary

---

Safe Foods

A brief survey of food journalism from ancient times to your favorite current food magazine will quickly assure you that the problem of adulterated or otherwise "unclean" foods is as enduring as recorded history. As T. Braun writes in "Ancient Mediterranean Food" (*The Mediterranean Diets in Health and Disease*): "It is not a modern failing to adulterate food with chemicals. What is modern is adequate consumer protection." A big part of that adequate consumer protection is a news-reporting system that transmits stories of food poisoning outbreaks accurately, rapidly, and widely.

Yesterday's worries about alar on apples has become today's concern about genetically engi-neered foods and irradiation. Stories in magazines, newspapers, and on television stress the fact that more and more foods are likely to be contaminated with *E. coli* **bacteria,** the same bacteria responsible for the 1993 deaths of three toddlers in the Northwest, all of whom had eaten contaminated ground beef.

Still other stories detail parasites or viruses found in fish harvested from polluted waters. Herbicides and pesticides banned from use in the United States are found in high concentrations in

---

alar: a growth regulator which was sprayed on apple trees to control the ripening of fruit. Residual levels of alar on supermarket apples were found to be harmful when consumed, so it is no longer used in the American market.

the produce we import from countries that do not have the same standards.

There is enough information given to frighten and even anger consumers, but often not enough to really understand the issues or the ways in which they can be addressed. It is your responsibility, then, to learn what you can about these questions, and to take the appropriate action. That is the only way you can make sure that guests will feel confident dining on food you've prepared. As anyone involved with the disastrous Jack-in-the-Box incident can tell you, recovery from an official outbreak of foodborne poisoning that originated in your restaurant is painfully slow, if it comes at all.

A Safe Food Supply

One of the major concerns today regarding foods is that they have become tainted with life-threatening substances. Current agricultural practices do tend to rely heavily on fertilizers, feeds, pesticides, and herbicides made from a variety of chemicals, antibiotics, and hormone supplements. The argument is made that, without the aid of these technological advances, our world food supply would fall dramatically short of current needs. Since alternatives to the current growing methods are not yet widely practiced, organically grown foods or those with minimal amounts of chemicals remain hard to find and expensive.

Once foods are ready to be harvested or butchered, the potential for contamination is certainly not lessened. Food-processing plants are inspected by agents of the Food and Drug Administration. The foods themselves may undergo testing to determine wholesomeness—meats, dairy products, and all processed/prepared foods are supposed to be tested regularly.

Whether or not these tests are adequate is a subject of debate. The sheer volume of food produced in this country and imported into the country is overwhelming. Logic would indicate that there is a limit to the number of trained inspectors available, as well as to the quantity of food they can physically inspect. In addition, inspection standards first established near the turn of the century were not designed to cope with modern issues. Revisions to food safety codes have begun to address these issues. Updated codes from federal, state, and local agencies are being issued in response to current needs.

We are still unsure what, if any, long-term effects there might be with regard to such techniques as irradiation and biologically or genetically engineered foods. Other foods do not yet have established safety standards or inspection procedures. However, most food processors are using Hazard Analysis Critical Control Point (HACCP) systems to identify when foods are most at risk, and what can be done to eliminate food hazards throughout the processing operation.

While there is a sense of urgency about maintaining safe foods and offering adequate protection to the consumer, the process of making changes or establishing new systems is slow. It remains to be seen how consumers will react to a tomato that has had a gene spliced into it to promote longer vine ripening combined with sufficient firmness to withstand the rigors of shipping.

It is clear, then, that simply trying to buy foods from reputable purveyors is not always going to be enough. You may even begin to wonder if it is possible to find foods that are "safe." As a chef, you need to make a choice about food purchasing practices based on an understanding of the quality of the food purchased, the reliability of the purveyors used, and the degree of commitment to sustainable and organic agriculture the business can afford.

FIGURE 2-1 A Flat of Eggs Can Harbor Salmonella

FIGURE 2-2   Stuffings are Thoroughly Chilled Before Adding to Meats

Types of Foodborne Diseases

Nearly everyone has had a brush with a **foodborne disease**. The culprit might be a **pathogen** such as a bacteria, a virus, a yeast or mold, or a parasite. The symptoms vary, but typically include that unholy quartet: vomiting or nausea, diarrhea, fever, and cramps. Not a pretty picture, and certainly not something you would like to be responsible for inflicting on one of your most valuable commodities: the guest.

Each pathogen will produce a particular set of symptoms, with the actual onset of the disease occurring anywhere from within an hour or two up to several days after eating **contaminated foods.** You could even be unfairly blamed for someone else's poor kitchen safety. It may also mean that a guest who contracted the illness at your restaurant will not necessarily be able to identify the ultimate culprit. They may even write it off to a "bug" that they picked up from some other source.

Foodborne illnesses fall into two categories:

1. **Food intoxication** is true food poisoning. It occurs when a person consumes food with toxin-containing microbes. The production of these toxins is a natural part of the pathogen's life cycle. Once in the human body, the toxins act like a poison. Food intoxication typically occurs within 1 to 12 hours and is associated with specific kinds of bacteria, such as staphylococcus and botulism, both of which are discussed in greater detail in the section that follows.

2. **Food infection** occurs when we consume food that contains a great number of microbes, which attack the gastro-intestinal track. In this case, bacteria are actually living and reproducing inside the human body and illness generally takes from 12 to 48 hours to strike. Salmonella is an example.

Staphylococcus is the number one cause of foodborne illness. The organisms are commonly found in the nasal passages, cuts, and throats of infectious humans and they can easily be passed on to moist food such as meat, poultry and pastry filling.

Some of the more common diseases include the following:

Salmonellosis is a bacteria found in the intestinal tracks of animals and in insects. Common food carriers include undercooked poultry, eggs, mayonnaise, milk, soft cheese, even unrefrigerated sliced fruits such as melons. Laboratory studies have shown that chickens and eggs may harbor salmonella on their skin or shells. Even "free-range" and "organically grown" birds appear to have as good a chance of being contaminated as those raised in large factory-style operations. Scrupulous attention to **personal hygiene,** the religious use of sanitizing solutions to swab work surfaces and cutting equipment, and proper cooking are the best ways to combat this common foodborne disease.

Trichinosis is the disease brought on by eating infected pork products. Proper cooking to an internal temperature of at least 155°F(68°C), according to the latest United States Food and Drug Administration (USFDA or more commonly called FDA) standards, is the only way to be sure that any existing parasites have been killed.

Botulism is another foodborne disease that is well fixed in the public mind. Typically caused by consuming improperly canned or jarred foods, it is of great concern to the foodservice industry. Discard

FIGURE 2-3   Potentially Hazardous Foods—Poultry, Eggs, Custard, Rice, Potatoes, and Melon

any bulging or otherwise "mysterious" cans or jars. Avoid storing foods in their original jars or cans. There are also advisories against leaving oils infused with garlic and shallots at room temperature for long periods of time.

Toxic poisoning from eating mushrooms is an issue of concern as well. Learn to identify the wild mushrooms that you typically use, and purchase them from reputable purveyors. No matter what, don't accept a basket of mushrooms that were harvested by an amateur forager. While some mushrooms only cause minor discomfort, others can kill the unlucky guest who has one bite too many.

There are other diseases that are contracted by eating infected foods. For a more complete list, along with a description of their likely sources, symptoms, and appropriate preventative measures, refer to the table in Appendix 2.

The majority of foodborne illnesses can be traced to biological sources, particularly specific bacteria. As we look at the types of foodborne illnesses, remember that this danger can usually be eliminated by making sure that bacteria are not introduced to foods through careless handling or cross-contamination. In addition, foods such as eggs in the shell or raw chicken, which may arrive at your establishment carrying a particular bacteria, should be properly handled so that bacteria is not able to become so well established that it can cause

illness. This is accomplished primarily through temperature control and strict adherence to safe food-handling guidelines.

Reducing the Risk of Foodborne Illness

A professional chef needs to have a thorough understanding of how to operate a kitchen safely. Certification programs are available throughout the country, and it is strongly recommended that at least one member of the kitchen staff have certification.

The FDA has prepared a Food Code that is intended to act as a model for the prevention of foodborne disease. Local and state health departments may have other regulations and requirements intended to meet the particular needs of a given location. Be sure to check with local health authorities about any permits, inspections, or certifications that might be necessary.

A certificate, by itself, is no guarantee that a commercial kitchen is preparing foods that are safe and wholesome. The real issue is consistent, day-to-day application of the standards and guidelines for keeping foods as safe and clean as possible. A good knowledge of how foods can become the carriers of disease offers the chef a battle plan for preventing such outbreaks.

Foods may become contaminated at many points: while they are being grown or raised, in processing or packaging plants, or during shipping. As such, contaminants can take on different forms. The three primary forms of contamination are: (1) chemical, (2) physical, and (3) biological.

Chemical Contamination in the Kitchen

Chemical contaminants can cause serious illness if consumed in sufficient quantities. The onset of symptoms may take from minutes to hours. There are a variety of chemicals that have been known to make their way into food, and they come from four primary sources:

1. Residuals from food supply growers such as insecticides, herbicides, antibiotics, steroids, and hormones.

2. Toxic cleaning compounds and disinfectants, such as ammonia, chlorine, and silver polish.

PREVENTING CHEMICAL CONTAMINATION

It takes some care and proper work habits to prevent chemicals from getting into the foods you cook and serve. Here are some prevention strategies:

• Try to learn more about the methods used to raise the foodstuffs you buy. Whenever possible, buy from farmers and processors you are sure don't use chemical contaminants

• Store all kitchen cleaners in a separate area, away from any food storage.

• Use storage containers made only from approved materials, such as **food-grade plastics,** glass, and stainless steel.

• If you use copper cookware or serving pieces, be sure the lining is intact

• Lobby to investment in new plumbing if your establishment has old lead pipes.

• Do not use earthenware or ceramics, unless you are certain they were properly and safely produced, without lead or other toxic metals

3. Toxic metals from cooking vessels and utensils, including corroded or unlined copper cookware, galvanized (zinc-coated) or chipped enamel cookware, and cadmium-coated ice cube trays.

4. Water from old lead pipes.

Physical Contamination in the Kitchen

Physical contaminants include any of the wide array of items that might be accidentally left in foods. Sometimes this occurs during harvesting or butchering. It is equally likely to occur in the kitchen. Bits of plastic wrap, dirt, hairs, bandages, fingernails, glass or wood splinters, even whole insects are all examples. While these contaminants can cause disease (if nothing more, revulsion could cause someone to feel nauseated), the most obvious danger is causing injury. If someone unwittingly eats a bit of shell or a shard of crockery, the gastrointestinal tract could be lacerated, or worse. Swallowing a bit of broken glass or biting down on a piece of metal might cause a wound, a lost filling, or a broken tooth.

The government has established standards known as **GRAS,** "Generally Recognized As Safe." These guidelines, while they might elicit some unhappy reactions from consumers, are a concession to the way in which foods are handled. A certain level of physical contamination is consider reasonable and accepted. The restaurant's staff should be aware, however, that even if the government consid-

ers several parts per million of rodent hair to be an acceptable quantity of contamination, the guest who finds just one eyelash floating on the soup will be hard to appease.

Biological Contamination

The majority of foodborne illnesses are caused by **biological contamination.** Sometimes molds are responsible. A classic example is ergot, which attacks rye and can cause hallucinations and convulsions. Viruses, such as hepatitis, can also be transmitted through foods. Parasites, such as the one responsible for trichinosis, are also found in foods. However, far more foodborne illnesses are caused by a wide range of bacteria.

Throughout the next section, we will look at the types of foods likely to carry a foodborne disease, the way in which they can become contaminated, and steps that can be taken to prevent contamination from taking hold. Many of the same procedures that help to keep bacterial contamination at bay are those required to inactivate viruses and parasites as well.

Potentially Hazardous Foods

The first line of defense is knowledge about why it is that some foods are likely to be culprits in a case of food poisoning and others are not.

When we think about the types of illnesses a customer might contract in a restaurant, terms like sal-

---

PREVENTING PHYSICAL CONTAMINATION

- • Be sure all bandages are secure and, if necessary, wear a finger cap or glove.
- • Keep fingernails trimmed and clean.
- • Remove all jewelry that might fall into food (earrings, necklaces, rings, etc.).
- • If a glass breaks in your work area, discard any food that might have bits of glass in it. (When in doubt, throw it out.)
- Constantly be aware of what you are doing, as well as what is going on around you.

---

monella, trichinosis, botulism, and hepatitis come to mind. Some foods are more likely to act as good carriers for these types of disease. These foods are referred to as **potentially hazardous foods.**

All foods are teeming with a variety of microorganisms. Some are harmless to humans, others are beneficial, and some, known as pathogens, can cause humans to become ill when they are found in sufficient quantity in foods, or are ingested by someone whose natural defenses are unable to combat them even in much smaller quantities. Unless pathogens find an environment that will encourage them to grow and reproduce, however, they cannot make anyone sick.

The Three Requirements of Pathogens

Pathogens thrive when three basic living conditions are readily available: (1) protein, (2) water, and (3) appropriate **pH**. A large percentage of foods typically contain these three elements in ratios favorable to the rapid growth of pathogens. The greater the abundance of protein and water and the more favorable the pH, the higher the likelihood that foods will become contaminated. In addition, some bacteria do best with a good supply of oxygen, others when oxygen is absent. Some can get along either way. The handling procedures noted in sections on cooling, reheating, and thawing help to prevent any single condition from becoming so predominant that it will favor the pathogen's growth and reproduction.

Protein

Most foods contain some protein. Meats, fish, poultry, and eggs are among the foods with the greatest percentage of protein, making them, and prepared foods containing them, highly susceptible to the pathogens that cause food poisoning and intoxication. But grains, potatoes, and legumes also contain protein in significant quantities. They become vulnerable once cooked, especially rice and potatoes. Vegetables contain very small amounts of protein, and fruits contain very little protein at all, if any.

Water

Foods that are moist enough to be soft and easy to chew are also moist enough to support the growth of many types of pathogens. There are some foods that are naturally "dry" and have a lesser chance of becoming infected: certain root vegetables have a relatively low moisture content. Other foods, once processed, lose much of their moisture: very hard cheeses such as Romano or Parmesan cheeses; dried, salted, or preserved foods such as olives and hams; nuts and seeds; and uncooked grains, cereals, and meals. These are the foods that we treat as "nonperishables," a recognition of the fact that they can be stored at room temperature without fear of immediate loss of quality or wholesomeness.

Moderate pH

The pH of most foods falls within a range considered "moderate," a state that makes foods attractive for the growth and reproduction of many different types of microorganisms. A substance

---

pH: the symbol used to express the acidity or alkalinity of a substance.

FIGURE 2-4   The pH Scale

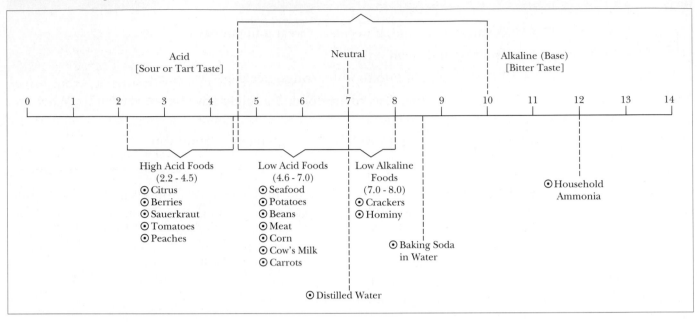

that is extremely **acid** (e.g., lemon juice) will be closer to a value of 0. Those that are extremely **alkaline** (e.g., baking soda) will measure closer to 14.

Most foods tend to fall within a range of about 4 to 10. Foods more acidic or more alkaline than that will generally no longer be susceptible to microorganisms. Vinegar, lemon or lime juice, and other very tart and sour-tasting foods are acid; baking soda, alum, and cream of tartar are bitter-tasting and cause the mouth to pucker; these items are alkaline. We use this general principle to preserve foods when we pickle, salt, or brine them in order to change their pH level to above 10 or below 4, increasing the shelf life of the food.

The Danger Zone

There are two other variables that can affect the levels of pathogens: time and temperature. The disease-causing microorganisms found in food need to be present in significant quantities in order to make someone ill. Once pathogens have established themselves in a food source, they will either thrive or be destroyed, depending upon how time and temperature are manipulated while foods are in the so called **danger zone.**

Temperature

There are pathogens that can live at all temperature ranges. For most of those capable of causing foodborne illness, however, the most "friendly" environment provides temperatures within a range of 40 to 140°F (4 to 60°C). Most pathogens are destroyed at temperatures above 140°F. Storage at temperatures below 40°F will also destroy some pathogens; in others the cycle of growth and reproduction will only be slowed or interrupted.

Time

When conditions are favorable, pathogens can grow and reproduce at an astonishing rate. There are four distinct stages of bacterial growth.

1. **Lag phase,** during which newly introduced bacteria become adjusted to their environment.
2. **Accelerated growth phase,** in which the bacteria reproduce rapidly. Bacteria reproduce asexually; as each bacterium grows, it will split into two bacteria of equal size. Under ideal circumstances, each bacterium can reproduce every 20 minutes. One bacterium could produce 72 million bacteria in just 12 hours.
3. **Stationary phase,** a plateau during which the

rate of growth and reproduction is matched by the rate of death. At this point, there is no increase in the number of bacteria.

4. **Decline phase,** when the essential elements for life are exhausted. The death rate exceeds the growth rate.

Controlling the time during which foods remain in the danger zone is critical to the prevention of contamination through foodborne illness. The techniques outlined below are intended to shorten the total amount of time that foods spend in the danger zone.

Handling Foods Safely

From the time that foods arrive at your restaurant until they are placed in front of the guest, it is important that they be carefully handled during storage, cooking, cooling, and reheating.

Storing Foods

As soon as a shipment of food is delivered and has been properly checked in, it should be placed in storage. Three types of storage are used in most establishments: refrigerated units, freezers, and dry storage. A storage principle that effectively rotates stock of both perishable and nonperishable items helps to prevent foods from spoiling or rotting. This system is known as "First In, First Out," or **FIFO.** It means that any food or preparation that is newly delivered or freshly prepared goes to the back of the shelf so that older products get used first.

Refrigeration and freezing units should be regularly maintained and equipped with thermometers to make sure that the temperatures remain within a safe range. Although cold temperatures do not kill pathogens, they can drastically slow down reproduction. In general, refrigerators should be kept between 36 and 40°F (2 and 4°C), but food quality is better maintained if certain foods can be stored at specific temperatures:

Meat and poultry—32 to 36°F (0 to 2°C)

Fish and shellfish—30 to 34°F (−1 to 1°C)

Eggs—38 to 40°F (3 to 4°C)

Dairy products—36 to 40°F (2 to 4°C)

Produce—40 to 45°F (4 to 7°C)

Using separate refrigerators for each of the above categories is ideal, but if necessary, a single unit can be divided into sections. The front of the box will be the warmest area, the back the coldest.

Reach-in or walk-in refrigerators should be wiped out and put in order at the end of every shift. Before being put in the refrigerator, food should be properly cooled, stored in clean containers, wrapped, and labeled clearly with the contents and date. Store raw products below and away from cooked foods to prevent **cross-contamination** by dripping. Make sure the fan is not blocked and that the doors close properly.

Freezers should be at 32°F (0°C) or below. They also should be cleaned and put in order regularly. Foods need to be very clearly labeled and a system for checking and rotating frozen goods should be maintained. Freezer burn, primarily caused by inadequate wrapping, makes foods unfit for any use.

Dry storage is used for foods such as canned goods, spices, condiments, cereals, and staples such as flour and sugar, as well as for some fruits and vegetables that do not require refrigeration and have low perishability. Keep this area clean and be sure that there is proper ventilation. Moisture, direct light, and heat are likely to reduce shelf life for many foods.

Foods should not be stored directly on the floor or near the walls. Provide adequate shelving to prevent crowding and permit air circulation. All containers (including boxes and cans) should be labeled with a date. Use a separate area for cleaning supplies.

Cooling Foods Safely

To cool liquids such as stocks, soups, and sauces:

1. Transfer to a clean container

    Stainless steel or other metal containers are most effective at dispersing heat. Glass is next best, and plastic is least appropriate for cooling. Be sure

---

cross-contamination: the transference of disease-causing organisms from one source to another through physical contact.

FIGURE 2-5   Cooling a Hot Liquid Properly

FIGURE 2-6   Cooling Custard Over an Ice Bath

that the containers you use for cooling and storing foods are properly cleaned and sanitized.

2. Place the container in a cold water bath.

Special cooling tables may be available in some larger kitchens, but failing that, a setup such as that shown in Figures 2-5 and 2-6 should be used. An overflow pipe is ideal, allowing a constant stream of cold water to run into the sink. Or, add more ice and/or drain out the water as it warms and replace it with cold water.

3. Stir the liquid as it cools.

This prevents **anaerobic bacteria** from gaining a foothold and speeds the overall cooling process by equalizing the temperature.

4. Label, date, and store properly

Once the entire batch has been cooled to a temperature of 40°F(4°C) it may be covered and labeled with the name of the contents and the date. Should you prefer, the liquid can be transferred

to plastic containers for storage purposes so you do not tie up valuable cookware in storage.

The larger the quantity of liquid, the more time it will take to cool completely. If possible, split large batches into two or more smaller batches.

To cool very small batches of items such as custard sauce, lemon curd, or leftover stew, place the container in a large bowl or tub filled with equal quantities of ice and cold water as shown in Figure 2-6. Remember to stir the contents of the container as it cools.

The greater the surface area that is exposed to the cold water bath (through a bain-marie or other container), the more quickly the liquid will cool.

To cool semi-solid or solid foods, a different approach may be required. For example, a stuffing mixture added to a chicken or used to fill a pork chop should be well chilled before it is introduced to the bird or chop. Sautéed onions, carrots, celery, and peppers should be removed from the pan, spread in a thin layer on a clean baking sheet and placed in a refrigerator to cool quickly before combining the stuffing with other ingredients.

This same principle is used to cool cooked pasta, rice, or other items that cannot easily be stirred as

---

anaerobic bacteria: requires the absence of oxygen in order to survive and reproduce.

they cool, or would be damaged by being piled up in a large pot or bain-marie.

Large cuts of meat or other solid foods should be cut into slices or chunks whenever possible. The idea is to reduce the diameter of the food, enabling it to cool within a safe time period (less than two hours). Place the sliced or chunked food into clean containers, and cool, uncovered, until the item is thoroughly chilled. Then, cover, label, and date properly.

Reheating Foods

Prepared foods should be kept chilled at 40°F (4°C) or less until you are ready to reheat them. At that point, they should be heated as quickly as possible to a safe service temperature—165°F (72°C). Use an instant-reading thermometer to check the food's temperature after it has been stirred.

Liquid or semi-liquid foods should be placed in clean pots and reheated over direct heat. Simply placing soups and sauces into steam table inserts is not a good method. The food will take far too long to come up to a safe serving temperature, if it ever does.

Individual portions, or small batches, can be reheated successfully in a microwave. Use the highest

FIGURE 2-7   Fried Eggs Prepared Sunny Side Up May Be Potential Carriers of Foodborne Illness

power setting you can without harming the food. If the microwave does not have a turntable, turn the food manually at regular intervals as it reheats. Stir soups and stews as they reheat so the food becomes evenly hot.

Solid foods, such as roasted items, are more difficult to reheat, especially meats that need to be at a particular doneness. Reheating them in an oven or convection oven is usually the best method.

To cut back on the amount of food you must discard at the end of service, reheat batches that are only large enough to last through a meal period, or part of a meal period. This approach may seem a little more time-consuming if you have been accustomed to filling a pot with more soup than you think you need so you only have to heat it once. However, the overall savings and increased quality of your food will more than repay any nuisance you may experience (See "Batch Cooking" in Chapter 3).

Holding Cooked Foods at Service Temperature

Keeping foods such as sauces, soups, stews, grains, and potatoes hot during a meal period is an important concern. Not only do you want foods to be at the best possible temperature to assure your guests enjoyment, you also want them to stay safe and wholesome. Check to be sure that heat lamps, steam tables, or other holding devices are maintained properly. This includes a thorough cleaning at the end of each meal period.

Use an instant-reading thermometer to be sure that foods that have been first properly heated or cooked are staying above 140°F (60°C). This needs to be done consistently throughout service. Any foods that are not at a safe temperature should be immediately brought back to within the desired range. If you cannot be certain how long they have been in the danger zone, the best decision would be to get rid of the food item and start over, reheating or preparing a fresh batch.

Thawing Foods

There are a number of foods purchased in a frozen state purchased by restaurants, including vegetables, fruits, meats, processed foods, prepared items, and more. Handling these foods properly as they

IDENTIFYING CRITICAL CONTROL POINTS

Here's a recipe with safety strategies highlighted in **boldface** at each critical control point (CCP). You should make every effort to extend these practices into your own cooking.

New England-Style Clam Chowder

Yield: 1 gallon (3.75 liters)

Chowder clams, washed	90 each	90 each
Water	2 quarts	2 liters
Potatoes, 1/4-inch dice	20 ounces	.5 kilograms
Salt pork, minced to a paste	8 ounces	225 grams
Onions, minced	1 pound	450 grams
Flour	5 ounces	145 grams
Milk	40 ounces	1 kilogram
Heavy cream	8 ounces	225 grams

1. Steam clams in water in a covered pot until the shells open. (Discard any clams that did not open; this is an indication that the clam was already dead.)

2. Strain broth through a very fine filter or cheesecloth. **Reserve and hold broth at 140°F (60°C) or higher.**

3. Pick, chop, and reserve the clams. **Hold at 140°F (60°C) or higher.**

4. **Cook potatoes in clam broth to 145°F (62.8°C) or higher for 15 seconds.** Separate potatoes and broth. **Hold both broth and potatoes at 145°F (62.8°C) or higher.**

5. Render (melt) fat in the soup pot; add onions and sweat (cook gently) until translucent.

---

thaw is of great importance in order to retain the quality of the food, as well as to avoid possible contamination.

The best way to thaw a frozen item is to move it from the freezer to a refrigerator. It should be left in its wrapping, placed in a shallow container, and allowed to thaw, taking as much time as necessary. The reality, however, is that many times you will need to speed up the process in order to meet the demands of service. When this is the case, there are two alternatives that can be employed, depending upon the nature of the item being thawed and the amount of time available to thaw it.

1. Place the well-wrapped item in a container and set it in a sink. Turn the cold water on and allow it to flow over the food constantly, until it is thawed. Very large items will still take a long time to thaw, but it is crucial to keep the temperature of the item below 40°F (4°C) as much as possible, both to avoid creating an environment that would favor the growth of pathogens and to prevent the loss of quality often associated with improperly thawed foods.

2. Place the food in a microwave, using the defrost setting or lower power. This is most effective for foods that are small, thin, and relatively uniform in composition. It is not the best way to thaw meats, since the uneven thawing could destroy the tissue of the meat, causing a significant loss of flavor and moisture in the meat once it is cooked. Foods defrosted in the microwave should be cooked immediately after they are thawed.

It is never a good idea to simply remove an item from the freezer and place it on a counter or anywhere else at room temperature in order to thaw it

6. Add flour; cook to make a blond roux (lightly cooked mixture of flour and fat, used as a thickening agent).

7. Add reserved broth gradually and stir it completely, working out any lumps that might form.

8. Simmer for 40 minutes until **145°F (62.8°C) or higher is reached for 15 seconds.** Skim surface as necessary.

9. Scald milk and cream and add to the soup.

10. Add seasoning.

11. **Finish cooking to a product temperature of 145°F (62.8°C) or higher for 15 seconds.**

12. **Hold chowder at 140°F (60°C) or above for service.** Do not mix new product with old.

13. Cool in shallow pans with a product depth not to exceed two inches. **Product temperature must reach 40°F (4.4°C) or lower within 4 hours.**

14. **Store at a product temperature of 40°F (4.4°C) or lower in refrigerator unit.** Cover.

15. **Reheat chowder to a product temperature of 165°F (73.9°C) or higher for at least 15 seconds within 2 hours.**

Sanitation Instructions: Measure all temperatures with a calibrated food thermometer. Wash hands before handling food, after handling raw foods, and after any interruption that may contaminate hands. Wash, rinse, and sanitize all equipment and utensils before and after use. Return all ingredients to refrigerated storage if preparation is interrupted.

more quickly. It is also rarely advisable to cook foods from a frozen state, unless directions from the manufacturer specifically state that it is acceptable to do so (for instance, some prepared items, such as frozen pastries or pizza dough, can be prepared directly from a frozen state).

Hazard Analysis Critical Control Point (HACCP)

The **HACCP** system has been adopted both by food processors and restaurants, as well as by the FDA in its latest code (1993). At this time, there are no particular mandates that HACCP inspection forms must be used by all foodservice establishments. However, instituting such a plan may prove advantageous on a variety of levels.

If you decide to begin instituting HACCP procedures in your restaurant, you should know that an initial investment of time and human resources is required. It is becoming obvious, however, that this system can ultimately save money and time, and improve the quality of service you are able to provide your customers.

Computer systems help make many of the parts of a HACCP system easier to institute: flowcharts, standards and measures to control hazards, and tracking how and when control measures are used by you and your staff.

The heart of HACCP is contained in the following seven principles:

1. Assessment of hazards and risks.

2. Determining the **critical control points (CCPs).**

3. Establishing critical limits (CLs).

4. Establishing procedures for monitoring CCPs.

5. Establishing corrective action plans.

6. Establishing a system for maintaining records.

7. Developing a system to verify and record actions.

The way in which an individual operation may apply these principles will vary. Not only is it permissible to make the system fit your establishment's style, it is imperative. Chain restaurants receive and process foods differently than à la carte restaurants.

In order to make full use of a HACCP system, you need to clearly identify where foods are most likely to be in danger of contamination, and when and where you can do something to eliminate the risk or reverse the danger.

Foods can become contaminated at many points as they travel from their point of origin to your guests. Examples of these critical control points include any of the following situations:

- Raw foods come in contact with pathogens through exposure to contaminated cutting boards, an employee's hands, or through cross-contamination. For instance, a knife is used to cut a chicken, and then used to cut cabbage for cole slaw without cleaning and sanitizing the knife between tasks.

- Egg yolks or hamburgers are not cooked to a safe temperature, thus allowing pathogens that might have been killed at proper temperatures to survive and establish themselves in the food.

- Foods, especially those considered potentially hazardous, are allowed to remain at a temperature within the danger zone for more than three hours.

- Foods are not cooled to below 40°F (4°C) before storing.

- Foods are stored in containers that are not properly cleaned.

As you look over the path that foods travel, from the time you receive them until they are served, you will be able to establish acceptable procedures for handling them safely. This may include a set of standards for receiving, storing, and reheating that out-lines acceptable temperatures, containers, procedures for thawing, cooling and reheating, and other food-handling issues addressed in this chapter.

Maintaining High Standards of Cleanliness

Customers today want to be sure their meals are prepared in a clean kitchen, free of grease, rats, cockroaches, and flies. They want the people who handle their food to be clean and to take enough pride and care in their work to do things the right way. The glasses, silverware, plates, and linens that are on the table are also under careful customer scrutiny. The image of a fussy diner automatically wiping down his knife and fork, and sending back glasses that are spotty may get a few laughs on a situation comedy. It is not so funny if it is your restaurant, however.

Should word spread that your staff in the kitchen and dining room are well groomed and careful, your bathrooms are spotless, and your napery faultless, you are ahead of the game. On the contrary, charges of hair in the soup, flies in the sauce, and fingerprints all over the plate can spell failure, no matter how brilliant the menu. Somehow, this kind of informal review spreads more rapidly and means more to the potential guest than any three- or four-star critique in a newspaper or guidebook might.

Keeping the kitchen and dining room clean is important on many other levels as well. It is clear that it plays a key role in keeping foods safe. It also helps prevent many of the common accidents that can occur in the workplace, as well as the transmission of diseases that might happen from person-to-person contact.

An additional benefit of keeping standards of cleanliness high is that it sends a clear message to others. If you take pride in the restaurant and all that goes on there, people will sense that you want everyone to have a safe, pleasant experience, whether they have come to dine or to work.

The Role of the Uniform

There is a standard of dress for professionals working in a kitchen that has come to be accepted by both the professional and the public. The white jacket, tall hat, apron, side towel, are all part of the image. Pants (typically a houndstooth check in this country, solid black in European countries), hard shoes, and a neckerchief are all considered important elements as well. More than simply completing the look of the chef, these parts of the typical uniform have important roles to play in keeping workers safe as they work in what is a potentially dangerous (some might say hostile) environment.

The Hat

Escoffier wore a black beret, and Gordon Sinclair wears a baseball cap. Most chefs in this country and throughout the world, however, have adopted a tall, chimney-like hat. The idea is to help contain the chef's hair, preventing it from falling into the food. There may be some absorption of sweat from overheated brows as well.

The Jacket and Pants

A sparkling clean jacket does more than give the chef a crisp professional look. The fact that the jacket is double breasted means that there are two layers of cloth to protect the chest area from steam burns, splashes, and spills. Interestingly, the jacket is one item of apparel that knows no gender, since it can be buttoned on either side. In fact, you can easily rebutton your jacket to cover up any stains, should you need to appear in all your glory in the dining room for an interview with the press.

Sleeves on chef's jackets are long and should be worn long, so that as much of the arm as possible is covered to protect against burns and scalding splashes. The same is true of pants. Shorts, while they may seem like a good idea for such a hot environment, are inappropriate, offering no protection from hot stoves, accidental encounters with steam kettles, and splashes from sloshing pots of stock or pasta water.

The jacket and pants should be clean at the start of each shift, and kept as white as possible by proper laundering. If you do not have a linen/laundry service, be sure that you use the correct technique for washing your uniform. (See "A Germ Free Uniform" below.)

Apron and Side Towels

The apron is worn to protect the jacket and pants from excessive staining. It should be clean at the start of the shift and, if necessary, should be changed during the course of a working shift.

Most chefs use side towels to protect their hands when working with hot pans, dishes, or other equipment. They are not meant to be used as wiping cloths. If you do use a side towel to clean up a spill or wipe off a cutting board, replace it with a clean one.

Side towels used to lift hot items must be dry in order to provide protection. Once they become even slightly wet, they can no longer insulate your hands; the heat passes through the wet cloth

---

A GERM-FREE UNIFORM

As unlikely as it may seem, jackets, pants, side towels, and aprons can harbor bacteria, molds, parasites, and even viruses. It is not so difficult to see the ease with which these pathogens could be transmitted from your uniform to foods. Properly laundering can sanitize your uniform to make it safe and clean.

Uniforms, aprons, and side towels can be kept bright white and stain-free with proper laundering. Some restaurants, particularly in hotels, have a linen/laundry service for chefs' attire, but if you are washing your own "whites," be sure you use the correct method for cleaning them: hot water, a good detergent, and a sanitizer, such as Borax or chlorine bleach to remove bacteria and grime. Adding a half cup of coarse dishwasher detergent helps to brighten and whiten.

quickly. If, like most people, you react by dropping the pan or pot, it is likely that you will wind up with even more burns from the hot food that splashes on your legs and feet.

Shoes

While athletic shoes are very comfortable, they are not ideal for working in a kitchen. If a knife or other sharp object should fall from a work surface onto your feet, most athletic shoes could offer very little resistance, and you could wind up with a puncture wound. Hard leather shoes with slip-resistant soles are recommended, both because of the protection they offer from knives and because of the support they can give to your feet.

A job that involves standing for several hours in a row, without moving around a great deal (chefs typically spend most of their day standing in a single spot at their work station or on the line) puts a premium on good-quality, supportive, protective foot gear. There are several brands available, and it is worth the time and trouble to try on several different types of shoes to determine which are most suitable for you.

Neglecting your feet is a bad business, one that will pay you back with foot trouble, back pain, and discomfort throughout your life. If you develop trouble with your feet, seek professional help, consider orthotics, and carefully heed advice about what shoes and other devices are best for your particular needs.

Neckerchief

Some chefs feel that, without a neckerchief the uniform has an unfinished look. Others find it bulky or fussy, and prefer to go without, except possibly for a press photo. If the neckerchief is worn, it should be impeccably clean, and replaced as necessary throughout a shift to keep the neck cool and clean. Neckerchiefs do absorb perspiration.

Pest Control

Rodents, flies, and other pests are a real problem. Take the necessary steps to prevent them from gaining a foothold in the kitchen. Keep screens on all doors and windows that might allow them entrance. By covering garbage cans and dumpsters, getting rid of trash promptly, and closing up any holes around the foundation of the building, infestation will be kept to a minimum. Cleaning the kitchen, storing foods carefully, and checking incoming deliveries is also part of a first line of defense. When necessary, you may need to rely on insecticides, traps, or other pest-control measures. If you use these defenses, be sure that you or the service hired handles all such items with extreme care to avoid contaminating the food, air, and water in the restaurant.

Cleaning and Sanitizing

Cleaning something means that you have removed all visible traces of soil, food particles, or grease. **Sanitizing** something means that moist heat or chemical agents have been used to destroy disease-causing pathogens.

Cleaning is not enough for some things, such as pots, pans, cutting boards, knives, plates, glassware, and silverware. Sanitizing food-contact surfaces is an extremely important part of preventing food-borne illnesses.

At your work station, you should have a cloth in a double-strength sanitizing solution on hand to wipe down your knives, steel, and cutting board between each use. This is not done in place of careful cleaning; it is done to assure that you won't inadvertently transmit pathogens through cross-contamination. Iodine, chlorine, or quaternary ammonium compounds are all common sanitizing agents. Be sure to learn how to use these compounds properly and safely.

Ware Washing

Ware washing must be handled properly as well. Both three-compartment sinks and ware-washing machines can be used to properly clean and sanitize utensils, pans, and service ware.

Hand-washing of dishes is performed as follows:

1. Fill the first sink with water and an approved detergent. The water should be at least 120°F(49°C). Wash the dishes well. Remember

FIGURE 2-8 Proper Setup for a Three-Compartment Sink.

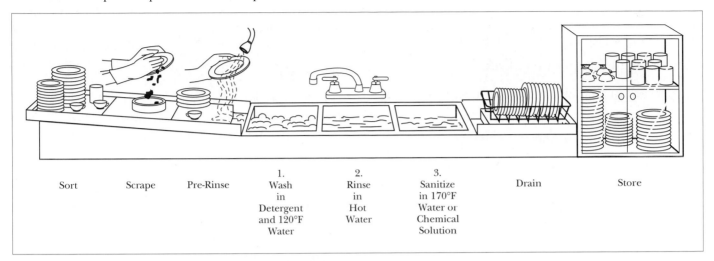

| Sort | Scrape | Pre-Rinse | 1. Wash in Detergent and 120°F Water | 2. Rinse in Hot Water | 3. Sanitize in 170°F Water or Chemical Solution | Drain | Store |

to drain and replace the water and detergent as necessary, so that all grease and food particles are being completely removed.

2. The second sink should hold water at about 130°F(54°C). This is used to rinse the dishes, removing any traces of detergent.

3. The third sink is used to sanitize dishes. This can be accomplished by filling the sink with water that is 170°F(77°C). Dishes are submerged in this water for at least 30 seconds, then transferred to a clean area where they can drain and air dry. Or, you may use a chemical sanitizer. Dilute it properly and follow the manufacturer's instructions. Generally a water temperature of 75°F(24°C) and a one-minute submersion is adequate.

Allow pots, pans, and all tableware to air-dry completely before storing them.

If you have an automatic ware-washing machine, be sure to check that the water reaches the correct temperature for each stage of washing and sanitizing. Keep the equipment properly serviced and use only approved cleaning and sanitizing compounds.

If your water is "hard," it will contain high levels of iron, calcium, or magnesium. These minerals can interfere with detergents and sanitizers. If necessary, use water-softening additives or install a water-softening system.

Safety Issues

Making your restaurant safe for everyone who walks through the door means many things. Foods need to be kept safe and wholesome, of course. Making the surrounding environment as hazard free as possible also means keeping equipment functioning and having established procedures in case of fires or choking incidents. It means having safe drinking water, adequate ventilation, and keeping the workplace free from such obvious hazards as asbestos, lead in the water or paint, and unnecessary distractions and noises.

Kitchens and dining rooms are filled with potential dangers. Sharp knives, hot coffee, broken glassware, frayed electrical wires, wet floors, and heavy crates or pots and pans seen as part of day-to-day life in a restaurant. Train new employees and remind everyone that working safely means working "smart." Several guidelines for handling knives and large equipment can be found in Chapter 4. In addition, make sure that everyone is aware that keeping the kitchen and dining room safe is part of their official job description. You should:

• Wipe up spills immediately. Throwing a handful of salt or cornmeal over the spill isn't enough. Take the time to clean away all traces of grease or oil.

• Warn coworkers when you are coming up behind them with something hot or sharp.

- Alert the pot washer when pots, pans, and handles are especially hot.

- Respect knives and handle them carefully.

- Know what to do in case of fires.

- Learn about first aid, including how to deal with cuts and burns.

- Pick up anything on the floor that might trip the unwary.

- Get help before lifting anything heavy, and use your legs, not your back.

- Learn how to administer the Heimlich maneuver, CPR, and mouth-to-mouth resuscitation.

Occupational Safety and Health (OSHA)

The Occupational Safety and Health Administration (**OSHA**) is a federal act instituted during the Nixon presidency in 1970. This federal organization falls within the Health and Human Services branch of the federal government. Its goal is helping employers and workers to establish and maintain a safe, healthy work environment. Among its regulations is the mandate that all places of employment must have an adequate and easily accessible first-aid kit on the premises.

In addition, if an organization has more than ten employees, records must be kept of all accidents and injuries to employees requiring medical treatment. Any requests for improvements to the safety of the workplace, including repair or maintenance of the physical plant and equipment necessary to perform one's job, must be attended to by the organization.

As money for many health and human service organizations has dwindled, OSHA's ability to make on-site inspections has also been reduced. It now concentrates its efforts on providing services where the danger of risk to the worker's safety is greatest.

Heimlich maneuver: an emergency procedure to aid a person choking on food.

CPR: cardio-pulmonary resuscitation. An emergency procedure to aid a person whose heart has stopped beating.

mouth-to-mouth resuscitation: an emergency procedure to aid a person who has stopped breathing.

This does not mean that small businesses can operate with impunity. Employees can call OSHA offices and report violations.

Fire Safety

It only takes a few seconds for a simple flare-up on the grill or in a pan to turn into a full-scale fire. Grease fires, electrical fires, even a waste container full of paper going up when a match is carelessly tossed into it are all easy to imagine happening in any busy kitchen. Burns and blisters are almost certainties for people who work over open flames, serve hot coffee, or deep-fry potatoes. Just because they are common injuries and accidents does not mean that they should be thought of as "part of the territory." A comprehensive **fire safety plan** to reduce burns and open fires should be in place and a standard part of all employee training.

The first step to take in avoiding fires is to make sure that the entire staff for both the kitchen and dining room are fully aware of the potential dangers of fire everywhere in a restaurant. If you see someone handling a situation improperly, get the situation under control, and then take the time to explain what your concern is, and how to avoid the situation in the future.

Next, be sure that all equipment is up to code. Frayed or exposed wires and faulty plugs can all too easily be the cause of a fire. Overburdened outlets are another common culprit. Any equipment that has a heating element or coil must also be maintained carefully, both to be sure that workers are not likely to be burned as well as to prevent fires.

Another key element in any good fire safety program is thorough training. Everyone should know what to do in case of a fire. Having fire drills often is a good idea. Instruct your kitchen staff in the correct way to handle a grill fire and grease fire.

There should also be fire extinguishers in easily accessible areas. Check the extinguisher to see what type of fire it is meant to control, and make sure you understand when and how to operate each type.

Proper maintenance of extinguishers and timely inspections by your local fire department are vital. Fire control systems such as an Ansel system need to be serviced and monitored so that, if you need

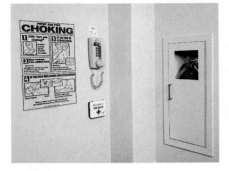

FIGURE 2-9
Safety Measures: Posted Emergency Numbers, Fire Extinguisher, and the Heimlich Poster

them, they will perform correctly. Above all make sure you never try to put out a grease, chemical, or electrical fire by throwing water on the flames.

Everyone should know where the fire department number is posted and who is responsible for calling the department in case of need. The exits from all areas of the building should be easy to find, clear of any obstructions, and fully operational. Your guests will have to rely on you and other staff to get them safely through any crisis that requires them to quickly exit the building. Identify one spot outside the building at a safe distance where everyone should assemble when they've exited safely. Then, you will know immediately who may still be inside the building and might need to be rescued by firefighters.

The main rule for fires is to be prepared for all possibilities. You cannot assume it won't happen to you.

Americans with Disabilities Act (ADA)

This act is intended to make public places accessible and safe for those with a variety of disabilities. Any new construction or remodeling done to a restaurant must meet **ADA** standards. This includes being sure that telephones are located so that they can be reached by a person in a wheelchair, and providing toilets with handrails. Most contractors will have the necessary information, but if you are unsure, contact a local agency.

A Special Note about Smokers

Many restaurants today have already opted to ban smoking completely. Those that have not yet done so may find that public pressure or even legislative mandates will force their hands in the future. While this may improve the air quality within the restaurant itself and provide a more pleasant dining experience for nonsmoking guests, there is one thing that should be kept in mind: Simply banning smoking from the dining room and the bar may not ban smoking from the entire premises. Common sense will tell you that smokers will very likely smoke cigarettes up to the moment they walk in the door, and light up as soon as they step back outside. One carelessly flung match, or a single smoldering cigarette butt can spell ruin.

Place sand-filled buckets or urns near the areas you expect or prefer to have smokers take their cigarette breaks. If you do allow smoking in your restaurant, make sure that bartenders, bus people, and waitstaff have a safe way to dispose of the contents of ashtrays.

Drugs and Alcohol in the Workplace

One final topic that is of great importance in the workplace is the right of all workers to be free from the hazards imposed by a coworker who comes to work under the influence of drugs or alcohol. The abuse of any substance that can alter or impair one's ability to perform his or her job is a serious concern. Reaction times are slowed. The ability to concentrate and to comprehend instructions is reduced. Inhibitions are often lowered and judgment is generally impaired.

People's lives may be at stake: A poorly judged effort when emptying the hot oil from the fryolater could result in permanent disability. A playful attempt at passing a knife could literally put out an eye. Forgetting to take the time to properly store and reheat foods could lead to an outbreak of foodborne illness that could kill someone. The responsibilities of a professional working in any kitchen are too great to allow someone suffering from a substance abuse problem to diminish the respect and trust you have built with your customers and staff.

Summary

Professionals dare not take foolish chances with the public's health, their own reputations, or the tremendous investment of resources involved in any foodservice operation. It is in caring about the details of maintaining a clean and safe establishment that you provide the most tangible evidence that a restaurant and its patrons are in the hands of a dedicated and responsible professional.

You should be comfortable with a wide range of information, skills, and safe work habits, especially the following:

- The importance of sanitation and safety in the kitchen
- The serious consequences of foodborne illness
- The many ways in which foods can become contaminated
- The role of sanitary work habits and personal hygiene
- Keeping the restaurant safe and free from hazards

SELF-STUDY QUESTIONS

1. Define food safety and explain why it is important in a professional kitchen.
2. Name three sources of contamination for foods.
3. Name the three characteristics of potentially hazardous foods.
4. Name four types of biological contaminants.
5. Name five improper food handling procedures that tend to promote the growth and reproduction of pathogens.
6. Name several practices that promote a safe working environment.
7. What is the danger zone?
8. List the steps involved in safely cooling the following types of foods:
   - large batches of hot liquids
   - semi-solid foods
   - solid foods
9. What is the difference between food infection and food intoxication?
10. What is the best procedure for thawing foods? What are two alternatives?
11. What is HACCP? What are the seven key points in the HACCP system?
12. What is the correct setup for ware washing by hand?
13. How can pest infestation be controlled in the kitchen?
14. What should you know and do in case of fire?

ACTIVITIES

- Choose one of your favorite recipes, examine it thoroughly, and identify critical control points along with proper handling/preparation procedures, as recommended by HACCP.

- Inspect one of the kitchens at your school or at work and look for any potential violations of safe, sanitary working habits. Write a report to review with your instructor or your boss.

- Contact the local board of health and ask them how and where you can receive a certificate in sanitation.

KEYWORDS

accelerated growth phase
acid
ADA (Americans with Disabilities Act)
alkaline
anaerobic bacteria
bacteria
biological contamination
botulism
chemical contaminants
contaminated foods
CPR
critical control points (CCP)

cross-contamination
danger zone
decline phase
FIFO (first in, first out)
fire safety
foodborne disease (or illness)
food infection
food intoxication or poisoning
food-grade plastics
GRAS (Generally Recognized as Safe)

HACCP (Hazardous Analysis Critical Control Point)
Heimlich maneuver
lag phase
mouth-to-mouth resuscitation
OSHA (Occupational Safety and Health Administration)
pathogen
personal hygiene
pH
physical contaminants

potentially hazardous foods
salmonellosis
sanitizing
staphylococcus
stationary phase
toxic poisoning
toxins
trichinosis

3

Nutrition and Healthy Cooking

*Too much in this country, we think of food
as poison, or how it relates negatively to
our health and diet. What about the
pleasures of the table? Have we forgotten?*
—ANN ROSENZWEIG, CHEF/CO-OWNER, ARCADIA

*Nutrition is the study of the way humans make use of the foods they eat in order to
fulfill the body's needs for growth, repair, and maintenance. Our knowledge of
nutrition has increased tremendously over the past several years. Restaurant patrons
are increasingly asking for menu options that are lower in fats and cholesterol, or
with sauces served on the side. When you stop to think about the changes in the way
people select food, both to prepare at home and when they dine out, it is clear that
things are quite different now from even a few short years ago.*

*Healthy cooking refers to the ways that a chef or restaurant owner can meet
guests' needs for dishes that fit some specific nutritional guidelines. The level of
sophistication that a typical restaurant consumer has in the field of nutrition makes
it more important than ever that you continue to learn more about dietary guidelines
and recommendations. You need to not only be able to respond to your guests'
requests, but also be sure that you have not crossed the line on your menu from
informative copy into an area that might be looked upon as making health claims.*

Unless you are creating an entire menu devoted to nutritional cooking, however, it is not necessary to exclude such items as foie gras and Camembert from your selections. The responsibility for making selections from your menu, and throughout the entire day, belongs to the individual. You should not be seen as a dictator of what people can or ought to eat.

The dietary guidelines and recommendations from the United States Department of Agriculture (USDA), the World Health Organization (WHO), the American Heart Association (AHA), and the American Diabetes Association (ADA) have undergone some dramatic changes over the last two decades. This has resulted in a whole new clientele interested in different foods, different menu options, and a broader sense of what "eating healthy" means.

For the chef, this might translate into some simple modifications—using olive oil to replace butter on the table, including whole grain breads in the bread basket, offering skim milk and nonfat yogurt. It also offers opportunities to give a whole new look to appetizers, soups, and entrées.

Grains that were not familiar a few years ago are now finding greater acceptance. Vegetables, dried beans, and fruits are taking a more dominant spot on the plate. A greater variety of foods are being combined on individual plates. This means that not only are dishes more interesting in terms of colors, textures, flavors, and aromas, they are also a better source of a wider range of nutrients.

News stories about the USDA Food Guide Pyramid, the Mediterranean diet, the role of antioxidants and phytochemicals in maintaining health and preventing disease, the role of olive oil and other monounsaturated fats in the diet, and the French Paradox have made their mark on our collective consciousness. Sometimes that mark is clearly a question mark.

The personal health and diet concerns your guests have today may not be the same ones they will have tomorrow. It is likely, however, that one of the greatest motivators for selecting a menu item that fits particular nutrition guidelines is a concern with weight loss.

We will look at some of the current issues in nutrition that your guests may hope to find reflected on your menu: The lessons of traditional diets from around the world, an upswing in the number of individuals who consider themselves vegetarians, the USDA Food Guide Pyramid and other dietary guidelines, the impact of continuing studies in the relationship of food choices and the prevention or reversal of certain diseases.

CHAPTER OBJECTIVES

- Explain what is meant by dietary goals and recommendations

- Describe the USDA's Food Guide Pyramid, as well as the Mediterranean and Vegetarian Pyramids

- Define and properly use the basic language of nutrition

- Discuss the different types of diets and special nutritional concerns for vegetarians

- List the major dietary vitamins and minerals

- Name the seven guidelines for nutritional cooking

- Explain how to put these guidelines into practice through recipe development, "healthy" plate compositions, and purchasing for nutrition

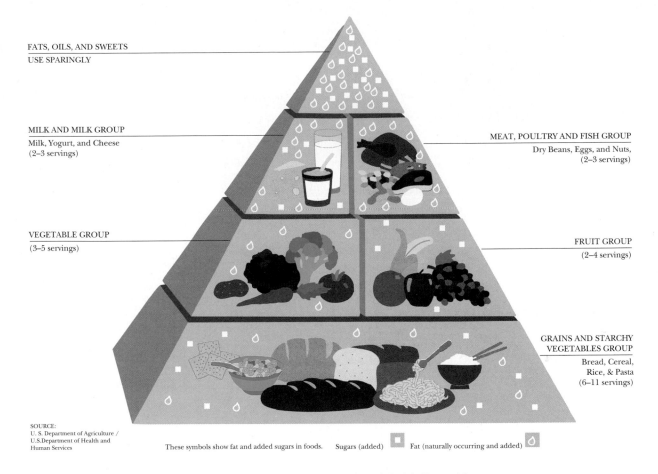

FATS, OILS, AND SWEETS
USE SPARINGLY

MILK AND MILK GROUP
Milk, Yogurt, and Cheese
(2–3 servings)

MEAT, POULTRY AND FISH GROUP
Dry Beans, Eggs, and Nuts,
(2–3 servings)

VEGETABLE GROUP
(3–5 servings)

FRUIT GROUP
(2–4 servings)

GRAINS AND STARCHY
VEGETABLES GROUP
Bread, Cereal,
Rice, & Pasta
(6–11 servings)

SOURCE:
U. S. Department of Agriculture /
U.S.Department of Health and
Human Services

These symbols show fat and added sugars in foods.   Sugars (added) ▪   Fat (naturally occurring and added) ⬦

FIGURE 3-1   The USDA Food Guide Pyramid

Dietary Goals and Recommendations

The **USDA Food Guide Pyramid** (see Figure 3–1) is a set of dietary recommendations that translates the suggested number of servings of various sorts of foods into a graphic image. The broad base of the pyramid includes pasta, rice, cereals, breads, and other foods made from grains. The majority of the foods eaten throughout the day should come from this group. Fruits and vegetables make up the next layer. Dairy products such as milk, yogurt, and cheeses are included on the same tier as meats, poultry, fish, eggs, beans, and nuts. The top of the pyramid, to be consumed sparingly, includes fats, oils, and sweets.

The **Mediterranean Food Pyramid** (see Figure 3-2) gives a strikingly similar message. There are some differences to be noted. Olive oil is considered important enough in the diet to deserve its own tier. Red meats occupy the top tier of the pyramid; it is suggested that they be consumed only a

few times per month. Poultry and fish can be eaten a few times per week. Wine in moderation can be seen near the top of the pyramid, and is an optional component of the diet. Regular physical exercise is also made part of this traditional healthy diet.

The **Vegetarian Pyramid** (see Figure 3-3) gives the option of replacing dairy products with milk substitutes, such as soy or nut milks and cheese, and suggests that they be fortified with calcium and vitamins B_{12} and D. If a vegan diet is followed, the meats, poultry, and fish suggested for those following a nonvegetarian diet can be replaced with dry beans, nuts, seeds, tofu, and nut butters. The top tier of the pyramid includes some foods that vegans must consume daily to maintain optimal levels of specific nutrients: vegetable oil, blackstrap molasses, and brewer's yeast.

The USDA's Department of Health and Human Services has targeted the end of this century to turn around some of the less desirable dietary habits found in this highly industrialized Western

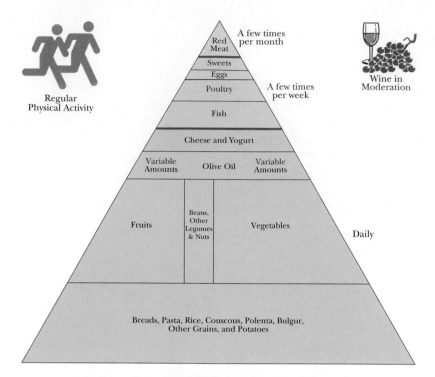

FIGURE 3-2   The Mediterranean Food Pyramid

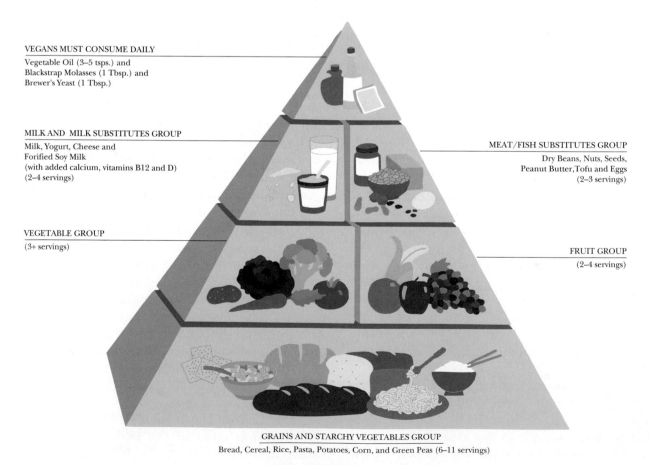

VEGANS MUST CONSUME DAILY

Vegetable Oil (3–5 tsps.) and
Blackstrap Molasses (1 Tbsp.) and
Brewer's Yeast (1 Tbsp.)

MILK AND MILK SUBSTITUTES GROUP

Milk, Yogurt, Cheese and
Forified Soy Milk
(with added calcium, vitamins B12 and D)
(2–4 servings)

MEAT/FISH SUBSTITUTES GROUP

Dry Beans, Nuts, Seeds,
Peanut Butter,Tofu and Eggs
(2–3 servings)

VEGETABLE GROUP

(3+ servings)

FRUIT GROUP

(2–4 servings)

GRAINS AND STARCHY VEGETABLES GROUP

Bread, Cereal, Rice, Pasta, Potatoes, Corn, and Green Peas (6–11 servings)

FIGURE 3-3   The Vegetarian Pyramid

culture. This program, known as Healthy People 2000, is aimed at making it easier for people to understand what constitutes a healthful diet, and to make informed choices about what they eat.

This will continue to have enormous impact on what all restaurants, from fast-food restaurants to chain restaurants to upscale restaurants, are offering to their guests. As more Americans start to adopt the USDA Food Guide Pyramid (see Figure 3-1), a broader range of grains, legumes, vegetables, and fruits is being featured in virtually every course of the menu. Couscous, bulgur, barley, quinoa, kasha and other grains are no longer seen as unusual. Cooking greens (including collards, turnip greens, and escarole), squashes, sweet potatoes, and broccoli rabe are featured not only as side dishes, but also as the main element on the plate.

There are many different sets of dietary recommendations, including those shown here (USDA, Vegetarian, and Mediterranean). The American Heart Association, and the American Cancer Society, as well as other organizations whose aim is to help those with specific health concerns to eat well and live better through controlling their diets, also have standards and recommendations that they offer to their members.

When you look at these recommendations as a group, one thing is clear. Every set of these goals recommends the following:

- Maintaining a healthy body weight through a combination of a healthful diet and exercise
- Thinking of a balanced diet as something to be achieved over the course of a day or week, rather than in each dish, recipe, or meal

couscous: very small, round pieces of semolina pasta; used typically in North African dishes of the same name.

bulgur: cracked wheat that has been hulled and parboiled; slightly nutty in flavor.

quinoa: the seed of a plant, indigenous to South America, which has been used as a staple grain since the time of the Incas.

kasha: grains of buckwheat that have been hulled, crushed, and cooked; used heavily in Russian cooking.

broccoli rabe: *a.k.a. broccoli raab* or *rapini*. A vegetable that is related to broccoli and known for its assertive, bitter-flavored stalks, leaves, and florets; popularly used in Mediterranean cuisine.

FIGURE 3-4   Regular and "Tasting" Portions of Wine

- Reducing total calories
- Keeping total fat intake at or below about 30% of the day's total calories
- Replacing saturated fats with monounsaturated fats
- Drinking sufficient water throughout the day
- Eating more fruits, vegetables, and starchy foods, as well as selecting a good variety of these foods to assure adequate levels of vitamins, minerals, and fiber
- Reducing portion sizes and the frequency with which meats, poultry, fish, eggs, and whole milk cheeses are included in the diet
- Reducing the amount of refined sugars consumed
- Avoiding highly processed or refined foods
- Keeping sodium consumption below approximately 3000 milligrams per day
- Reducing the amount of dietary cholesterol in the diet
- Keeping alcohol consumption at moderate levels (for instance, one to two glasses of wine a day for men, one per day for women)

Some dietary programs recommend completely eliminating meat from the diet or keeping total fat intake below 20, 15, or even 10 percent of the day's total calories. These programs may be important for individuals with specific dietary needs—for instance, heart disease patients, diabetics, or those with severe hypertension. If you are preparing menus to meet these needs, be sure to get assistance either from medical professionals and nutritionists, or from books, software, and journals that specialize in these areas.

The Lessons of Traditional Diets

Traditional Mediterranean cultures, as well as those of the Pacific Rim and South America, have relied for centuries upon a combination of foods and eating habits that appear to result in a more healthful, disease-free life. There are many lessons that we can learn from these traditional food habits.

Snack foods, small meals, and street foods play an important role. Unlike our fat- and sugar-laden junk foods, the traditional choices in the Mediterranean, Asian, and South American countries are predominantly those based on grains, pastas and noodles, breads, fruits, and vegetables. Grazing has many benefits. It is often easier to control your appetite, since you never really become ravenous waiting for dinner to arrive. Blood sugar levels remain even throughout the day and it is more likely that you will eat a wider variety of foods.

Cooking oils tend to be monounsaturated and are derived from nuts, olives, and vegetables. Saturated fats, such as those found in butter, lard, and cheeses, play a far less significant role. When they are used, they play the part of a condiment or seasoning. Meats, fish, and poultry are viewed similarly as flavoring ingredients, not the main event.

In those cultures where alcohol is part of the diet, wine often is the basic alcoholic beverage (see Figure 3-4). It is consumed moderately, with food, and in a social setting.*

Which brings us to what may well be the most elusive but important component of these traditional cultures: Coming together at the table to dine is an important part of the day. It is becoming harder and harder for Americans to carve out time each day to devote to relaxing at the table, enjoying a meal and each other's company.

Vegetarianism

Many people today prefer to reduce or completely eliminate animal foods from their diets. Nearly 12.5 million people refer to themselves as **vegetarians**, a number that has nearly doubled over the last ten years.

The reasons for becoming a vegetarian can range from a concern with health to ethical, environmental, or moral concerns. From a health standpoint, diets that cut out meats are likely to have lower levels of fats, especially saturated fats. They may also, depending upon the type of vegetarian diet adopted, greatly reduce or even eliminate a dietary source of cholesterol.

Just as there may be many reasons for becoming a vegetarian, there is more than one type of vegetarian. The following list provides some definitions and standards for a range of vegetarian options:

Vegans: This diet is based purely on vegetable foods, and excludes all forms of animal-based foods, including eggs, honey, fish, dairy foods, poultry, and red meat. There are some special concerns vegans need to be aware of so that they can balance their nutritional needs adequately.

Fruitarian: Similar to a vegan diet, eating predominantly fruits, nuts, and seeds.

Ovo-vegetarians: This diet adds eggs but no animal flesh or dairy to the vegan's diet.

Lacto/ovo-vegetarian: This indicates an individual who eats dairy products (milk, yogurt, cheese) in addition to eggs. All animal flesh is excluded.

Pesco-vegetarian: Fish is included, but no other type of animal flesh.

Semi-vegetarian: All foods, excluding only beef, veal, pork, lamb, and game, are eaten. Fish and chicken are occasionally part of a meal.

One phenomenon today's chef needs to keep in mind is the growing number of individuals who consider themselves **situational vegetarians,** or **alternivores.** An alternivore is any person who might,

---

*Not all dietary recommendations condone or suggest that alcohol is important or beneficial. This is an optional part of any diet.

given an attractive choice, opt to order a vegetarian or a meatless meal.

Many restaurant operators have found that introducing such selections on a menu has numerous benefits. It offers guests an agreeable new choice, and may increase their inclination to return. These offerings may have a reduced food cost, and provide a real chance to make a better margin of profit on that menu item. They are a viable way to introduce new flavors, ingredients, or preparations to an audience that is already disposed to be more adventurous in their food choices.

Dietary Supplements and "Nutraceuticals"

Dietary supplements are looked upon by many as an alternative to medical care. When antioxidants, lecithin, or beta-carotene hit the headlines or the nightly news, people are anxious to learn if taking a pill is likely to cure or reverse a medical condition.

In addition to vitamin and mineral supplements, we are beginning to see the possibility of engineering foods to increase levels of certain nutrients. This might mean that a "super food" could be developed that your doctor would prescribe as part of the treatment for cancer, hypertension, or heart disease.

The FDA has become increasingly concerned about the blurring of lines between foods and medicines. Making health claims about a food is no longer an acceptable practice. What this means in terms of the menu is that you should stay away from any claim, whether it is obvious or implied, that eating a single food or menu item will guarantee health, provide a cure for, or prevent a disease. You can still tell your clients that a dish is low in fats, calories, cholesterol, and sodium, however.

The Language of Nutrition

Nutrition is the study of the way humans make use of the foods they eat in order to fulfill the body's needs for growth, repair, and maintenance. **Nutrients** are not foods all by themselves. They are, in-

---

lecithin: a kind of lipid (or fat) produced in the liver, which is a vital component of cell membranes and acts importantly as an emulsifier to hold fat in solution in the blood.

stead, the elements found in foods. We do not eat pure nutrients, we eat the foods that offer them in good supply. You should still be seeing a beautiful, ripe, juicy, and delicious piece of fruit when you look at an apple—not a carbohydrate-/fiber-/vitamin-/mineral-/water-delivery system!

A well-nourished body requires adequate supplies of all of the nutrients known to be important in maintaining health. While it is likely that there are some essential nutrients not yet identified, we do know that eating a wide variety of foods should provide enough of those we have identified as essential—protein, carbohydrates, fats, vitamins, and minerals—as well as those that we know less about.

The following discussion of the various nutrients our bodies use in the day-to-day processes of maintainance, growth, and repair is meant as a brief introduction. These are the terms that are frequently used to discuss food and its preparation with nutrition as a basic concern, along with flavor, texture, color, and overall appeal.

Calories

A **calorie** is a unit of measure used to indicate the energy value of a particular food or beverage. Counting calories is a time-honored method of weight control. It is a simple formula: When the energy you consume equals the energy you expend, your weight remains the same. If you take in more calories than you use up through your metabolism, daily activities, and exercise, you will gain weight. If you take in fewer calories than you body needs, you will lose weight. (See "Determining Daily Calorie Needs," page 66)

Of course, it is not all that simple to lose or gain weight, as the number of weight loss books and programs available attests. It appears that the calories from certain foods, especially fats and oils, are handled differently by the body. An individual's metabolism has a big part to play as well. If your metabolism has slowed because of repeated sessions of dieting, or if it has been boosted by a program of physical activity, your ability to gain or lose weight is similarly confounded or enhanced.

We need to maintain a concern about the amount of calories we put on a plate, since overconsumption of calories, in combination with a lack of exercise, is the major cause of overweight—one of this country's leading health problems. Americans, on average, are still well over their ideal weights. This health hazard can become manifest in a number of secondary diseases. High blood pressure, eating disorders, heart disease, stroke, certain types of cancer, and diabetes have all been linked to overweight and obesity. Arthritis is aggravated by carrying around extra pounds. Sleeping problems,

back problems, foot problems, and a variety of emotional disorders have all been shown to have a direct correlation to overweight and obesity.

Empty Calories

All nutrients provide calories. Carbohydrates and proteins contain four calories in each gram. Fats contain more than double the number of calo-

---

DETERMINING DAILY CALORIE NEEDS

Examples:

John is 6'1", 210 pounds
  with a large build.
He is moderately active.
  He wants to lose
8 pounds

Mary is 5'6", 125 pounds
  with a medium build.
She works out strenuously
  every day.
She wants to gain 5 pounds.

1. Determine Desirable Body Weight (DBW)

Build	Men	Women
Medium	Allow 106 lb. for first 5 feet, plus 6 lb. for each additional inch.	Allow 100 lb. for first 5 feet, plus 5 lb. for each additional inch
Small	Subtract 10%	Subtract 10%
Large	Add 10%	Add 10%

2. Determine Daily Caloric Needs *(BC + AC = Total Daily Calories)*

Basal Calories (BC)	Activity Calories (AC)
DBW **x** 10 (men)	DBW **x** 3 (Sedentary)
DBW **x** 9 (women)	DBW **x** 5 (Moderate)
	DBW **x** 10 (Strenuous)

3. Adjust Calories to Gain, Lose, or Maintain Weight

- Add zero (0) calories to maintain weight
- Subtract calories to lose weight (the suggested amount is 1 to 2 lbs. per week)
- Add calories to gain weight (the suggested amount is 1/2 lb. per week)

Key: One pound of body fat is equal to approximately 3500 calories

- To lose 1 lb. per week, subtract 500 calories per day
- To gain 1/2 lb. per week, add 250 calories per day.

1. DBW=202 lbs.

2. (BC=2020 + AC=1010) = 3030 cal/day

3. Reduce daily caloric intake to 2530 cal. for 8 weeks to lose 8 lbs.

1. DBW=130 lbs.

2. (BC=1170 + AC=1300) = 2470 cal/day

3. Increase daily caloric intake to 2720 cal. for 10 weeks to gain 5 lbs.

ries with nine per gram. Alcohol has seven calories per gram.

Foods that have been significantly refined sometimes offer nothing beyond **empty calories.** Processing and refining often strips away those elements from the food that your body needs, including vitamins, minerals, and fiber. Alcohol also offers no nutritive elements for your body.

Carbohydrates

When the USDA Food Guide Pyramid was released, the broad base of the pyramid showed clearly that a healthful diet should be selected primarily from foods that provide good-quality **carbohydrates.** Carbohydrates are your body's preferred source of energy.

Carbohydrate-rich foods include a wider selection of items than you might at first imagine. Figure 3-5 illustrates just how broad the possibilities are. These foods contribute to a healthful diet by providing an energy source that is released in an even, gradual manner. When your body breaks down the starches in these foods into **glucose,** it actually expends some energy. Your body's organs and muscles can use protein and fats to provide energy, but these nutrients must first be altered into a form that your body is able to use. This taxes the body, and also generates toxins that must be cleared out of your system

Complex Carbohydrates

When **complex carbohydrates** are made part of the meal in the form of whole grains, cereals and meals, starchy vegetables, and dried legumes, they provide additional elements your body requires, including fiber, proteins, vitamins, and minerals.

Many whole foods are refined or processed in some way. In some instances, this can be beneficial. Cracking grains makes it easier to both cook and eat them. However, some foods can be refined to the point that they offer little more than starch, without the nutritional benefits you can derive from the unprocessed version. Steel-cut oats, cooked into a rich porridge, are a better value than cookies made with quick-cooking instant oats. This is true not only because the cookies have added fats and refined sugar, but also because the process of refining the oats has removed much of the vitamins, minerals, and fiber of the unrefined oats.

Simple Carbohydrates

Often referred to as simple sugars, **simple carbohydrates** are found in great concentration in fruits, as well as in vegetables and milk. The naturally occurring sugar found in fruit is referred to as **fructose.** Milk contains **lactose,** and grapes contain a simple sugar known as **maltose.**

When you eat whole fresh fruits, you get the added benefit of a whole host of additional nutrients, including vitamins, minerals, fiber, and water.

Refined Sugars

Clever food-label writers realize that the term fructose or "fruit sugar" will often give the consumer a false sense that they are getting something "healthful" when in fact, the type of fructose they are using is no better than any other type of **refined sugar.**

Honey, maple syrup, molasses, white and brown sugar, corn syrups, and other sweeteners are all refined, and offer very little beyond a few traces of minerals and calories. These calories provide nothing beyond empty calories to distinguish them from other sugars.

Refined sugars do play an important part in many recipes, however. They moisten, preserve, and flavor foods. But they can also boost the calorie level of foods without offering any other benefit. Too many calories in your diet will result ultimately in weight gain.

Fiber

Your body cannot digest **fiber;** it is not really a source of nutrition. Still, it has an important role in regulating the body properly. In some studies, soluble fiber has been shown to aid in reducing the overall levels of cholesterol in the blood. Insoluble fiber helps to move foods through the gut quickly, preventing various gastrointestinal upsets such as constipation, diarrhea, and diverticulitis.

---

glucose: *a.k.a. blood sugar,* the body's most important source of energy.

FIGURE 3-5 Foods Rich in Carbohydrates

(1) Complex carbohydrates are found in foods made from whole grains and cereals.

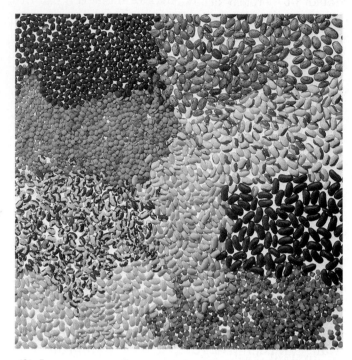

(2) Legumes are another source of complex carbohydrates.

(3) Fruits and vegetables provide both simple and complex carbohydrates.

Meeting Carbohydrate and Fiber Requirements

Most dietary guidelines recommend that at least 50 percent of your day's total calories come from carbohydrates, with as few of those calories as possible derived from refined sugars found in sweeteners, jams, jellies, and confections.

Fiber is another important part of a healthful diet. Most Americans do not include enough fiber-rich foods in their diets at the correct level.

The suggested number of servings of carbohydrate-rich foods ranges from eight to twelve, depending upon how many calories a person needs each day.

Proteins

Most Americans remember learning in grade school that **protein** was one of the most important of all nutrients. It is certainly one of the essential nutrients, but Americans and most Western people rarely suffer from a protein deficiency. Instead, our diets tend to be skewed heavily toward protein, especially in the form of meats. Over consumption of

FIGURE 3-6 Protein-Rich Lean Foods

meat has the effect of increasing the quantity of dietary fats in our diets, resulting in an unbalanced diet that shortcuts carbohydrates, includes more than adequate quantities of protein, and has us consuming far more saturated fat than is necessary or beneficial.

Shifting toward leaner cuts of meat, and away from those with high levels of saturated fats (and cholesterol), and using more poultry, fish, and foods such as dried beans and tofu are good ways to offer high-quality foods that provide good sources of protein without overdoing fats in the diet (see Figure 3-6).

Essential Amino Acids

Proteins are composed of smaller groups of compounds known as amino acids. There are 20 amino acids, and our bodies are capable of creating over half of them. The remaining amino acids are referred to as the **essential amino acids.** This means that in order to produce proteins, we need to find a dietary source for that particular amino acid. De-

pending on age and other physical conditions, there may be eight or nine essential amino acids.

Plant-based Proteins

Animal foods, including meat, milk, cheese, and eggs, provide **complete proteins.** This means that a single food can supply all of the essential amino acids. Plant-based foods are also a good source of protein, even though some plants may have low levels of particular amino acids.

This was once considered an issue of some concern for vegetarians. If they were eating foods low in the amino acid tryptophan, for instance, they were cautioned to be sure to eat a food that was a good source of that amino acid at the same meal.

It is no longer thought to be critical to get all of the essential amino acids combined in a single meal, as long as you do get them over the course of the day. Most well-balanced vegetarian meals rely on time-honored food combinations, such as rice and beans, that provide all of the essential amino acids.

Meeting Protein Requirements in a Typical Diet

Getting an adequate supply of protein in our diets is not a mysterious process. The recommended amount of protein for most adults of average size ranges from 56 to 65 grams each day. In general, a single 6-ounce portion of meat, coupled with a few servings of low- or nonfat dairy foods throughout the day will meet an individual's needs quite well.

What this means to the chef is that the "standard" portion of 6 to 8 ounces of meat, fish, or chicken is really fine. The trick is in making it appear bountiful, attractive, and filling to patrons who are accustomed to thick center-cut chops, platter-size steaks, chicken halves, and whole pan-ready fish. Certainly you will not be in the position of dictating whether or not an individual can or ought to have more meat at another meal. But even if this were the only meal that person ate all day, a larger portion offers no nutritional advantage.

Fats and Oils

Fats and **oils** are essential, but over-consumed, elements in any healthful diet. For most chefs, they are a critical staple in the restaurant larder. Fats do more than supply some important nutrients. They also make foods feel and taste rich and satisfying. They signal the stomach that enough food has been eaten, giving people the feeling of satiety that encourages them to stop eating before they overeat.

High concentrations of fats are found in some foods, notably meats, poultry, fish, cheeses, eggs, and nuts. Different foods contain different types of fat, which fall into three categories: monounsaturated, polyunsaturated, and saturated. Each appears to have a different effect on the body (see Figure 3-7).

Monounsaturated Fats

When findings about the Mediterranean diet were released, it seemed clear that the use of olive oil in those diets played a role in a generally lower incidence of cardiovascular disease.

Monounsaturated fats have a tendency to lower the levels of certain types of cholesterol in the blood and raise others. The net result of this is that diets that rely upon monounsaturated fats, rather than saturated fats, are likely to encourage low levels of serum cholesterol. This means that the chances of developing **atherosclerosis** are reduced.

Nuts and olives, as well as oils made from those foods, contain primarily monounsaturated oils.

Polyunsaturated Fats

Oils made from corn, safflower, and rapeseed (canola), and other vegetable sources are referred to as **polyunsaturated fats.** While these oils are still preferred over saturated fats in a healthful diet, they do not appear to have precisely the same benefits as monounsaturated fats.

Vegetable oils are frequently used to prepare shortening and margarine. This process, known as hydrogenation, changes the overall structure of the fat. Instead of pouring at room temperature, these hydrogenated oils become "plastic," or solid, at room temperature.

Saturated Fats

Saturated fats are found typically in animal foods including butter, marbling in meats, lard,

chicken skin, bacon, sausages, and eggs. The so-called **tropical oils** are also saturated fats: coconut and palm oils, for example.

Saturated fats have been linked to increased levels of serum cholesterol and an increased risk of developing cardiovascular diseases.

Cholesterol

This is a type of fatty acid found in animal foods. There is a distinction between **dietary cholesterol** and **serum cholesterol.** Dietary cholesterol is that which is found in the foods themselves. Serum cholesterol is found in your bloodstream.

When you have a blood test done to determine your cholesterol levels, the doctor will review specific components found in the blood, known as lipoproteins. **Low-density lipoproteins (LDL)** are associated with an increased risk of developing arteriosclerosis. **High-density lipoproteins (HDL)** appear to reduce the risk, since HDL actually removes LDL from your blood.

Certain individuals are more sensitive to dietary cholesterol than others. Learning how to reduce the amount of foods containing cholesterol in your diet is critical if you are one of those individuals. But it may not always be enough. Your body produces cholesterol on its own, whether or not you eat foods containing it. (Consult your doctor if necessary.)

Plant-based foods, even those high in fats and oils, do not contain cholesterol. This means that peanut butter, almonds, olives, beans, and sesame seeds are all "cholesterol free." They always have been.

Maintaining Proper Levels of Fat and Cholesterol in the Diet

A significant dietary problem facing most Westerners, and Americans in particular, is that we consume far more fat, both the fats that occur in foods

---

atherosclerosis: a disease, primarily affecting the larger arteries, in which they become thickened and clogged with deposits of fat, cholesterol, and other debris.

cardio-vascular diseases: the general term used to describe diseases of the heart and blood vessels, such as stroke and heart attack.

arteriosclerosis: a general medical term that refers to the hardening and obstruction of arteries in the body.

FIGURE 3-7   Fats and Oils

(1) Corn oil, sesame seeds and sesame seed oil, and walnut oil are all sources of polyunsaturated fats.

(2) Olive oil, avocados, most nuts, and nut oils are monounsaturated.

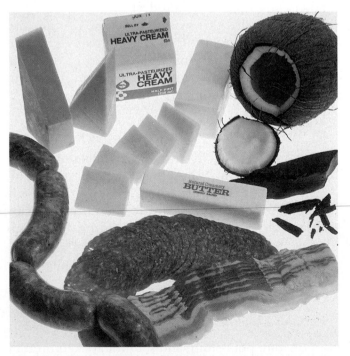

(3) Saturated fats are found in meats, butter, cheese, cream, and coconuts.

(4) Foods high in cholesterol include egg yolks and organ meats such as liver, sweetbreads, and kidneys.

naturally and those that are added to foods during cooking or other processing, than we actually require. There is a great correlation between increased fat intake and the increased risk of developing certain diseases.

The stance taken by most nutritionists and expounded in various eating plans and pyramids is that current levels of fat intake should be reduced to at or below 30 percent of the day's total calories.

Vitamins and Minerals

Vitamins and minerals are crucial to your health. Even though they do not provide you with energy per se, they are important to various functions in the body (see Figure 3-8). A deficiency of a particular vitamin or mineral can cause disease. Many folk cures are based on the fact that a specific food could replenish the missing nutrient. Around the turn of the century, chemists were able to isolate these compounds. They were given letter names, and later on, more specific names. Deficiency diseases were also linked to them. The **United States Recommended Daily Allowance (USRDA)** recommendations for vitamins and minerals were established based on the levels required to prevent those diseases. (see Table 3.1)

Water-Soluble Vitamins

Vitamin C (ascorbic acid) and the B vitamins can be dissolved in water. This means that you need to replenish stores of these vitamins daily, since they are readily lost from the body in waste fluids. They are also sensitive to prolonged exposure to heat, air, and light. Cooking foods to retain maximum levels of the **water-soluble vitamins** is a challenge for the chef.

Since the body can excrete water-soluble vitamins with ease, you normally need not worry about building up toxic levels of these vitamins. It is possible to take too much of these vitamins, however.

Beta-Carotene

This vitamin is found in red and orange vegetables, leafy greens, and members of the cabbage family. **Beta-carotene** is a precursor for vitamin A, and has been shown to have a variety of health benefits.

FIGURE 3-8   Vegetables are Good Sources of Vitamins and Minerals

Antioxidants

The **antioxidants** include vitamins C and E. These compounds help to prevent other substances, such as the membranes of red blood cells and vitamin A, from being destroyed. They do this by bonding with the oxygen that would otherwise destroy white and red blood cells, as well as cell membranes in the lungs. This means that the mechanisms required to keep the immune system strong and functioning are preserved.

Fat-Soluble Vitamins

Vitamins A, D, E, and K are **fat-soluble vitamins.** This means that they are stored in fat, which is far less simple to remove from the body than water. Megadoses of those vitamins can easily cause toxic levels to build up, leading to serious disease, even death.

Unlike water-soluble vitamins, these vitamins are relatively stable during cooking.

Major Minerals

Calcium, potassium, and sodium are required by your body in significant quantities. They are essential to maintaining a proper balance of fluids in your body, as well as the proper **acid/base balance.** Calcium is associated with bone strength and density.

FIGURE 3-9 Sodium and Salt

(1) Salt, a common sources of sodium, may need to be controlled if an individual has hypertension.

(2) Use other flavorings to reduce or replace some salt in recipes.

Potassium has been linked to maintaining the heart's rhythm, while sodium has a great deal to do with blood pressure (hypertension). These minerals need to be part of your daily diet.

Trace Minerals

Other minerals known to be important to maintaining health are required in very small amounts. Iron, zinc, manganese, and fluoride are all **trace minerals.**

Dietary Requirements for Vitamins and Minerals

Today, as we continue to learn more about the role of vitamins and minerals in maintaining health, questions about the value of supplementation are cropping up. Many people are attempting to use vitamin and mineral supplements to bolster their immune systems, fight diseases, and prevent the development of everything from osteoporosis to cancer. Self-medicating can have serious consequences if an individual takes megadoses, especially of the fat-soluble vitamins and some minerals.

For most people, supplementation is unnecessary if a varied diet rich in whole grains, fruits, and vegetables is followed. For those who do not get a good dietary source of some vitamins or minerals, supplementation may be suggested.

Water: "The Forgotten Nutrient"

Like vitamins and minerals, water is a noncaloric essential nutrient, which means that you need it to keep your body running properly, but it does not provide you with energy or with building materials for growth or repair of tissues. Our bodies are mainly water. Drinking the recommended eight glasses of water per day keeps joints properly cushioned, and increases the body's ability to get the necessary nutrients to the spot where you need them, and to clean out toxins from your system.

The Seven Guidelines for Nutritional Cooking

Bringing nutrition out of the textbook and into the kitchen requires far less in terms of actual change than many people fear. If you are already doing

	TABLE 3-1	VITAMINS AND MINERALS		
Vitamin *RDA for Adults* *Ages 25–50*	*Sources*	*Function*	*Deficiency/* *Excessiveness*	*Stability*
Thiamine (B₁) **RDA: Men 1.4 mg** **Women 1.0 mg**	pork, liver, legumes, fresh green vegetables	carbohydrate metabolism; maintaining healthy nerves, normal appetite	def.: beri-beri	destroyed by heat and water
Riboflavin (B₂) **RDA: Men 1.7 mg** **Women 1.5 mg**	milk, liver, lean meats, eggs, leafy vegetables	breakdown of fatty acids for energy, release of energy from food	def.: rare, except in alcohol abusers	destroyed by U.V. rays and fluorescent lights, stable in heat and acid
Niacin **Men 18 mg** **Women 14 mg**	liver, lean meats, wheat germ, leafy green vegetables	carbohydrate metabolism	def.: pellagra excess: liver damage skin rashes. peptic ulcer	
Vitamin B₆ **Pyridoxine** **RDA: 2 to 2.2 mg**	meat, liver, whole grain cereals, vegetables	aids in synthesis of nonessential amino acids, fat, and carbohydrate metabolism	def.: convulsions, anemia, depression, nausea	stable to heat, light, oxidation
Vitamin B₁₂ **RDA: 3 μg**	liver, meats, milk, eggs (only animal foods)	growth, blood formation, amino acid synthesis	def.: pernicious anemia	stable during normal cooking
Folacin **(most common** **vitamin deficiency)** **RDA: 400 μg**	green leafy vegetables, liver, milk, eggs	blood formation, amino acid metabolism	def.: megaloblastic anemia, diarrhea	unstable to heat and oxidation
Ascorbic Acid **(vitamin C)** **RDA: 60 mg**	citrus fruits, strawberries, cantaloupe, broccoli, cabbage	production and maintenance of collagen (base for all connective tissue), healing, resistance	def.: scurvy (smoking cigarettes seems to interfere with use of vitamin C)	unstable; destroyed by oxygen, water
Vitamin A **(retinol)** **RDA: 1000 R.E.**	liver, carrots, sweet potatoes, green leafy vegetables, egg yolk, milk fat	building of body cells, healthy tooth structure, normal vision in dim light	def.: night blindness excess: joint pain, nausea, rashes	fairly stable in light and heat, easily destroyed by air and ultraviolet light
Vitamin D **RDA: unknown**	animal fat, fortified milk. sunlight	bone development (promotes the absorption of calcium and phosphorus)	def.: rickets excess: hypercalcemia	stable to heat, aging, and storage
Vitamin E **(tocopherols)** **RDA: 10 I.U.**	leafy vegetables, egg yolk, legumes, vegetable oils, peanuts	protects cell structure, (rare)	def.: blood disorder	destroyed by rancidity
Vitamin K **RDA: unknown**	cabbage, leafy vegetables, liver, vegetable oils	essential for clotting of blood	def.: lack of prothrombin (important in blood clotting) excess: jaundice	destroyed by strong acids, alkalis, and oxidizing agents

your best to select foods that are fresh, fully flavored, ripe, and wholesome, you are well on the way. Cook these foods as quickly as possible in as little water as possible to maximize nutrient retention. Serve a variety of foods, including as many whole grains, unprocessed fruits and vegetables, and legumes as possible.

The guidelines below for introducing healthful cooking practices into any kitchen capitalize on this approach to selecting, preparing, and serving

TABLE 3-1   VITAMINS AND MINERALS (*continued*)

Mineral RDA for Adults Ages 25–50	Sources	Function	Deficiency/ Excessiveness	Stability
Calcium **RDA: 800 mg**	milk, dairy products, canned salmon w/ bones	bone and tooth formation, coagulation of blood, regulates muscle contraction	def.: osteoporosis	stable
Phosphorus **RDA: 800 mg**	milk, poultry, fish, meats, cheese, nuts, cereals, legumes	energy exchange, buffer system	def.: unknown	stable
Sodium **500 mg***	common salt, some canned foods, salt-cured meats, pickles	regulates electrolyte and water balance (extracellular fluid)	excess: linked to hypertension	stable
Potassium **2000 mg***	meats, cereals, vegetables, legumes, fruits	regulates electrolyte and water balance (intracellular fluid), muscle contractions		stable
Iron **RDA: Men 10 mg** **Women 18 mg**	liver, meat, whole or enriched grains, green vegetables	essential for hemoglobin production, constituent of tissue cells, transporting oxygen	def.: anemia	stable
Iodine **RDA: 150 µg**	iodized salt, seafoods	necessary for the formation of thyroxine (a hormone of the thyroid gland)	def.: goiter	stable

Other minerals: Magnesium, chloride, sulfur, zinc, copper, manganese, chromium, fluorine, molybdenum, selenium, cobalt

*There is no RDA for sodium or potassium. These numbers are minimum estimated requirements.

FIGURE 3-10   Water: The Forgotten Nutrient

foods. You will undoubtedly begin to see a change for the better in all aspects of your foodservice establishment as healthful practices become the norm.

1. Cook all foods with care to preserve their nutritional value, flavor, texture, and appeal.

Match the cooking method you select to the food you are preparing. Whenever possible, opt for methods that do not introduce additional fats and oils. Grilling, roasting, and steaming are good examples.

Whenever possible, cook foods close to the time that they are to be served. This will minimize nutrient loss and ensure that the food is at its best when you serve it to your guests. For those foods or in those situations where it is not reasonable to do an à la carte preparation, use **batch cooking** (see "Batch Cooking", page 76).

2. Shift the emphasis on plates toward grains, legumes, vegetables, and fruits as the **"center of the plate"** (see "Center of the Plate" on facing page).

3. Serve appropriate portions of foods; know what a **standard serving** for all foods is (see Table 3.2).

4. Select foods that help to achieve the nutritional goals and guidelines your guests are striving to meet.

   In general, the closer a food is to its natural state, the higher its nutritional value. Locally picked fruits and vegetables, for example, do not travel as far or as long to get to the market. This means that they will retain more of their nutrients. Whole grains, with the germ and bran intact, are a better source of a wider variety of nutrients than polished, refined, or quick-cooking varieties.

   There are still instances when processed foods may be necessary, but you can exert some control over what effect these foods have on the overall value of the foods you prepare for your guests. Be sure to read the label on any processed, packaged, canned, or frozen food. Make comparisons to be sure that you are getting the most flavor, the best quality, and the least unwanted additives possible.

5. Opt for monounsaturated cooking fats and oils whenever possible and reduce the use of saturated fats.

   The average American consumes nearly 37 percent of a day's calories in the form of fats. This is well above the current recommendations from any of a number of sources. Limiting the use of foods that contain too much fat and cholesterol need not be the punishment many fear. Chefs know a great deal about how to get the full flavor value from foods without falling back on classic "disguises."

6. Use calorie-dense foods (eggs, cream, butter, cheeses, and refined sugars) moderately.

BATCH COOKING

Batch cooking means preparing or reheating small quantities of a single food item, rather than preparing enough to last through an entire service, or for a few days of service. This technique helps to retain nutrients present in the foods that may be either reduced or even destroyed during extended exposure to heat.

In many institutional foodservice operations, as well as à la carte restaurants, vegetables are often prepared in the morning, placed in steamer inserts, cooked and then held until lunch is served. By the time the vegetable is served to the customer, it may be suffering from dehydration, discoloration, and a significant compromise of flavor and nutrient integrity. Instead, vegetables can be cleaned, trimmed, and peeled in the morning, and then, as lunch draws closer, a continuous supply may be steamed in batches of reasonable size and taken directly to the serving line. They will be fresher tasting, more appealing, and more nutritious.

The same principle holds true for any foods that are typically prepared in large batches, such as soups. If the soup was prepared correctly, promptly cooled, and stored, it will be wholesome and safe to eat. However, each time the soup is reheated, it will lose some of its nutritive value. Constantly reheating and cooling soup will eventually flatten its flavor, affect its appearance and texture, and reduce its vitamin and mineral content. Reheating only small batches and supplying the service line with enough to get through approximately two hours of service is far preferable.

Ultimately, the quantity of food that is prepared in each batch should be determined by evaluating (1) how much food is actually served during a typical meal period, and (2) the time at which a dining room is at its busiest. Learning how to respond to these concerns will allow you to prepare ample amounts of fresh and nutritious food in any foodservice establishment.

CENTER OF THE PLATE

The term "center of the plate" refers to the main component of an entrée. This component has traditionally been meat, fish, or poultry. Today however, many nutritionists are asking chefs to look at traditional "side" dishes, such as rice pilaf, noodles, potatoes, vegetable or dried bean stews, and other vegetable- or grain-based dishes, as the most important part of the plate.

Whenever the main attraction on the plate becomes a carbohydrate-rich food, such as a grain, vegetable, or fruit, the chef is left with two options: (1) meat or fish can be used as the garnish or flavoring ingredient, or (2) the entire entrée selection can be left meatless, as long as the plate contains nutritional variety.

For example, consider a stir-fry entrée that consists primarily of vegetables, but includes about 2 ounces of slivered poultry or pork. This is far less than the standard 6- to 8-ounce portion of meat. But since the purpose of the meat is to add flavor and texture, it is sufficient in this quantity to accomplish the goal and still satisfy. Serving the stir-fry with rice, and perhaps a second vegetable dish, makes excellent sense from a nutritional and culinary point of view.

To illustrate further, consider the classic Italian dish of polenta topped with stewed mushrooms and tomatoes. Adding a selection of additional steamed or braised vegetables would further give the plate color and variety. This is a filling, satisfying, and wholesome meal, even without any meat, fish, or poultry.

In both examples, you can see how traditional "side dishes" may become the "center of the plate" and the meat, if any is used, takes a healthy back seat as the "side of the plate."

This recommendation often presents a great challenge to anyone who is accustomed to relying on rich foods as the major carriers of flavor on a plate. Cutting calories nearly always includes cutting fats. Cream, cheese, butter, and oils add more calories, gram for gram, than other foods. When you do add them to a dish, use them sparingly.

7. Learn a variety of seasoning and flavoring techniques to help reduce reliance on salt.

With the possible exception of cholesterol, there is probably no single topic relating to nutrition that causes such confusion and alarm as controlling salt and sodium. The current recommendations for sodium vary but are relatively generous. There is no guarantee that a lifetime of moderate salt consumption will keep an individual free of **hypertension.** However, it is fairly certain that, once hypertension has been diagnosed, controlling the amount of salt and sodium consumed will have a benefit. Nor is there anything to indicate that keeping one's sodium consumption at or under the recommended levels is harmful.

Salt is relied upon as a seasoning and flavor enhancer in many dishes. Learning to add the minimum quantity needed to get the taste benefit may be enough. If your palate is less likely to detect salt in foods before a significant quantity is added, you may need to take the time to measure at first, until your own palate adjusts. Remember, there are many other ways to add flavor to foods that will not add salt. Wines, vinegar, citrus juices, fresh herbs, and low-sodium soy sauces can all be used (see Figures 3-9[2] and 3-11).

If you add an ingredient to a dish—such as capers, olives, or hard grating cheeses—that is high in sodium, you should make even further reduction in the amount of salt you add. Processed, canned, or frozen foods also may be high in salt or sodium. Read the labels carefully and opt for reduced sodium versions.

Putting Nutrition Guidelines into Practice

These are the ways that a chef can make solid, practical use of the suggestions to modify a typical "American" diet in favor of one that relies more on whole grains, meals, cereals, fresh fruits and vegetables, leaner meats, fish, poultry, and a more judicious use of ingredients that are typically high in fats, sodium, and cholesterol.

TABLE 3-2   Standard Portion Sizes

The following list provides basic standards for portion sizes according to the 1992 USDA Food Guide Pyramid. These should be modified in professional kitchens, as suitable for appetizer or entrée portions, as well as to match the restaurant's philosophy and style with regard to appropriate portions for particular foods.

Food Product	Portion Size
Breads	1 slice (about 1 ounce)
Cooked grains	$1/2$ cup
Cooked pasta	1 cup
Ready-to-eat cereals	1 ounce (varies by type)
Cooked vegetables	$1/2$ cup
Raw vegetables	$1/2$ cup
Salad greens	1 cup
Fruit or melon	1 piece, or 1/4 melon
Juice	$3/4$ cup
Canned fruit	$1/2$ cup
Dried fruit	$1/4$ cup
Milk	1 cup
Yogurt	1 cup
Cheese	$1 1/2$ to 2 ounces
Cooked lean meat, poultry, or seafood	4 to 6 ounces
Cooked beans	$1/2$ cup
Eggs	1 each
Peanut butter	2 tablespoons

Developing Menu Items and Recipes

Recipe development and modification is one of the chef's main tools for introducing nutrition into the menu. If you want to begin slowly, you can make some simple adaptations of existing recipes. You might grill a piece of chicken rather than sautéing it. Or you might replace a fattier cut of meat with a leaner one. For some operations, it will be helpful to use nutrition software to evaluate where existing recipes fall with respect to suggested guidelines.

Current interest in dishes from cuisines around the Mediterranean, the Southwest, and the Pacific Rim offer new flavors, textures, and ingredients to feature on menus. Books, magazines,

FIGURE 3-11   Flavor is the Key

(1) A selection of seasonings used in Asian cooking: gingerroot, tamarind, wasabi powder, lemongrass, and mustard.

(2) Herbs, spices, and seeds used to flavor foods.

RECIPE MAKEOVER

 Imagine you have a wonderful recipe for lasagna that you would like to make healthier. How can you accomplish this without sacrificing the flavor, texture, and aroma of the original recipe? The following four steps will show you.

1. **First examine all of the ingredients and see if there are any low-fat or low-calorie substitutions possible.**

Instead of	Use	To cut back on
whole-milk ricotta	part-skim ricotta	calories, fat, sodium, and cholesterol
whole-milk mozzarella	part-skim mozzarella	calories, fat, sodium, and cholesterol
whole eggs	egg whites	calories, fat, sodium, and cholesterol
Parmesan cheese	reduced-fat Parmesan	calories, fat, sodium, and cholesterol

2. **Then think if there are any ingredients that could be substituted for other, more nutritious items.**

Instead of	Use	To cut back on
ground beef	spinach	calories, fat, sodium, and cholesterol, while also adding vitamins, minerals, and carbohydrates to the dish
meat sauce	reduced-sodium tomato sauce, flavored with herbs	calories, fat, sodium, and cholesterol

3. **Next consider cutting back the quantities of other ingredients, for even greater reductions in fat, calories, sodium, and cholesterol. Mind that you don't want to cut back so far that the dish doesn't have the good taste and texture you'd expect in lasagna. However, with repeated testing you will discover the point at which too much has been taken out.**

Instead of	Use	To cut back on
4 ounces olive oil	1 ounce	calories and fat
3 pounds grated mozzarella	1 1/2 pounds	calories, fat, sodium, and cholesterol
2 tablespoons salt	2 teaspoons	sodium

4. **Finally, think about any ways you might be able to change the cooking methods used in the original recipe to cut back on added fats.**

Instead of	Try	To cut back on
frying the onions for the sauce in oil	dry-sautéing them in a cast iron skillet	calories and fat
sautéing the spinach	steaming it	calories and fat

TABLE 3-3   THE MEANING OF NUTRITIONAL CLAIMS

Nutritional Claim	Related Nutrient(s)	Definition of Claim
Free	fat, calories, sodium, cholesterol	no, or only "physiologically inconsequential" amounts
Low, Little, Free, Low Source of	fat, saturated fat, cholesterol, sodium, calories	may be eaten frequently without exceeding dietary guidelines
Low Fat	fat	3 grams or less per serving
Low Saturated Fat	saturated fat	1 gram or less per serving, not more than 15% of calories from saturated fat
Low Sodium	sodium	140 milligrams or less of salt per serving
Very Low Sodium	sodium	35 milligrams or less of salt per serving
Low Cholesterol	cholesterol	20 milligrams or less per serving
Low Calorie	calories	40 or fewer calories per serving.
Reduced, Less, Fewer	fat, sodium, calories	nutritionally altered to contain 25% fewer of the nutrient or calories than FDA standard reference
Light or Lite	fat, sodium	nutritionally altered product contains 50% less fat or sodium than FDA standard reference
High	fiber, vitamins, minerals, protein	contains 20% or more of a desirable nutrient's daily value
More	protein, vitamins,	contains 10% more of the daily value than the reference product
Good Source	calcium, fiber, vitamins minerals, protein	10 to 19% of daily value per serving
Lean	fat, saturated fat, cholesterol	meat, poultry, fish items containing less than 10 grams of fat, 4 grams of saturated fat, 95 milligrams of cholesterol per 100-gram serving.
Extra Lean	fat, saturated fat, cholesterol	meat, poultry, fish items containing less than 5 grams of fat, 2 grams of saturated fat, 95 milligrams of cholesterol per 100-gram serving.

and newspapers can offer inspiration and recipes to help.

Portion control is an important point. Even if you remove the skin from chicken breasts, trim all of the visible fat from steaks, and omit the heavy cream sauces from fish entrées, you can still exceed optimal amounts of fat, sodium, cholesterol, and calories if your entrée is too large. If you are worried about customer acceptance of small portions of meats, fish, and poultry, make changes slowly. Be sure that as the size of the steak becomes more in line with current recommendations, you are keeping the plate full and appetizing by serving generous and varied portions of grains, vegetables, and legumes.

Identifying Healthful Cooking Techniques

Grilling, roasting, steaming, poaching, and baking are all excellent ways to prepare foods without adding fats during the cooking process. When possible, opt to use these techniques instead of pan-frying, broiling in butter, or deep-frying.

Sauces made from vegetables and herbs, salsas, and chutneys are popular alternatives to heavier toppings and side dishes.

Purchasing for Nutrition

Identify those foods that naturally fit this style of cooking. They have been noted throughout this discussion. When an ingredient you might typically use in a recipe falls into the category of foods too high in fat, total calories, or sodium, consider using substitutes. Remember that no one expects to sacrifice flavor when they attempt to make their diets more healthful, so be sure to sample different brands of products to get the best quality.

Sometimes you may find that there is no really good substitute, in which case it is better to simply reduce the ingredient, or change the quantity in which it is used in a menu item. Instead of blending a large amount of heavy cream into a soup, for instance, try floating a rosette or dollop on top of the soup. It will still add richness and flavor, without as many calories.

Whether you are using a modified version of an ingredient or replacing an ingredient with something entirely different, there is one question you can ask to judge the success of the substitution or alternative: Does the finished dish look, feel, and taste as good as the original? (see "Recipe Makeover," on page 79).

Reading Labels for Nutritional Information

Food labeling can be an effective way for food manufacturers and processors to provide a wide range of information about the products. There have been many instances in the past, however, when the language on the label has been used more to promote a product than to provide accurate information. In response to this concern, the Food and Drug Administration has developed a set of labeling requirements, which now apply to most processed food products (see Table 3.3). This information can act as a guide for making more healthful choices among various brands.

Summary

Nutrition is more important in professional kitchens than ever before. Guests are looking for and demanding more interesting healthy alternatives. Throughout this chapter, we have looked at several ways to incorporate healthy cooking techniques into the kitchen. Some of the key points include:

- Dietary goals and recommendations have changed dramatically, with the most recent USDA Food Guide Pyramid being released in 1992, showing the importance of a diet based on grains, pastas, cereals, fruits, and grains

- The elements of nutrition, including a brief description of the essential caloric and non-caloric nutrients, and information about meeting basic requirements for those nutriens.

- Seven guidelines for nutritional cooking, and information about how to put these guidelines into practice, including recipe makeovers, creating attractive plates, and purchasing for nutrition.

SELF-STUDY QUESTIONS

1. Define nutrition and healthy cooking. Explain why these concepts are so important in professional kitchens.

2. According to the USDA's Food Guide Pyramid, what types of foods should be consumed most? What foods should be consumed least?

3. Name several grains, besides rice, that might be featured in a contemporary healthy entrée.

4. How important do you think it is for today's chef to be able to cook healthful vegetarian items? Please explain.

5. Which of the following percentages is the suggest percentage for daily fat calories?

   30%　　　　38%　　　　　　40%

6. What makes a protein "complete"?

7. Fats in foods may be described as saturated, monounsaturated, or polyunsaturated. Which of these three is most associated with health problems such as cardiovascular disease? Name several food items that contain high concentrations of this particular fat.

8. Are all foods that are high in saturated fats also high in cholesterol? Please explain.

9. Vitamins may be separated into two categories. Please name them and explain the difference between the two.

10. Name three minerals, including one trace mineral, and provide food sources for them.

11. What are the seven guidelines for nutritional cooking?

12. What would the standard portion sizes be for each item in a dish containing cinnamon couscous with grilled vegetables and seared salmon?

ACTIVITIES

- Calculate your daily calorie needs, and then determine the maximum suggested number of calories that can come from fats.

- Read several food labels, and determine which foods make the best choice for a nutritional menu item. Indicate if the product was nutritionally modified from its original form (e.g., reduced sodium, low calorie, light, etc.)

- Find a current article about fat substitutes or other food substitutes (salt replacement, artificial sweeteners, non-dairy toppings or creamers). What are the potential benefits or disadvantages for the chef using these ingredients.

KEYWORDS

acid/base balance
alternivore
antioxidants
atherosclerosis
beta-carotene
batch cooking
calorie
carbohydrates
center of the plate
complete proteins
complex carbohydrates
dietary cholesterol
dietary supplements
empty calories

essential amino acids
fat soluble vitamins
fats
fiber
fructose
fruitarian
glucose
high-density
  lipoproteins (HDL)
hypertension
lactose
lacto/ovo-vegetarian
low-density
  lipoproteins (LDL)

maltose
Mediterranean Food
  Pyramid
monounsaturated fats
nutrients
nutrition
oils
ovo-vegetarian
pesco-vegetarian
polyunsaturated fats
protein
refined sugar
saturated fats
semi-vegetarian

serum cholesterol
simple carbohydrates
situational vegetarian
standard serving
trace minerals
tropical oils
USDA Food Guide
  Pyramid
USRDA
vegan
vegetarian
Vegetarian Pyramid
water-soluble vitamins

4

Equipment Identification

Who you are is completely reflected in your knives—are they sharp, are they clean, and are they put away in the proper manner?

—*Gray Kunz, Chef De Cuisine Lespinasse*

Using the right tool for the job is one of the hallmarks of a professional. Equally important is the ability to handle and care for all tools, whether it is a cutting board, a knife, a mandoline, or a stockpot. Tools, large and small, are what make it possible for a chef to do the job well. This does not mean that you cannot perform well without the newest, most advanced, or most expensive piece of equipment. Many of the pieces described in this chapter are simple items—including pots, pans, and other utensils whose design and construction have not changed in decades, even centuries.

Assembling a personal collection of knives is one of the first steps in becoming a professional. Just as an artist gathers together the tools necessary for painting, sculpting, or drawing, you will need to begin a lifetime of selecting the knives that fit your hand the best. They will become as important to you as your own fingers—quite literally an extension of your own hands.

In addition to knives, well-equipped kitchens need a variety of other items: bowls, pots, pans, stoves, refrigerators, storage and service pieces, mixers, blenders, food processors, slicers, and smokers. Learning to handle all types of equipment with care and respect is a crucial part of your training. As technology continues to refine old tools and introduce new ones, you will need to learn constantly about innovations. Trade shows, journals, and your own network of contacts will expose you to various tricks and tools, from a food-grade piece of PVC pipe used as a mold, to a new time-saving kitchen tool, to a software program that tracks sales, inventory, prep lists, staffing, and payroll.

CHAPTER OBJECTIVES

- Understand the rules for knife care, use, and storage

- Identify the different parts of a knife

- Understand the differences in knife construction and quality

- Describe a variety of sharpening and honing tools and their function

- Name a variety of hand tools and their uses

- Identify some of the most frequently used pieces of small equipment

- Learn the basic rules for working safely with large and small equipment

- Identify pots and pans, their composition, purpose, and appropriate care

- Identify the equipment used in several categories of work, including:

  - slicing, grinding, and grating
  - mixing and puréeing
  - cooking: stovetops, ovens, grills, fryers, steamers, kettles
  - refrigeration and freezing

Knives

The importance of knives to a professional chef or cook cannot be overstated. The only piece of equipment more basic to cooking is the human hand. All knives should be treated with great respect and care. The following rules concerning knife care, use, and storage should be automatic behavior for professionals:

1. Handle knives with respect.

Professionals have their own collection of knives, which they care for, maintain, and use daily. You should never use someone else's personal knife without first obtaining permission. Handle it with the same care that you would your own, and be sure to return it promptly.

Many people will engrave their name on the blade of the knife, so that they can identify which knives belong to them. If you work in a large kitchen, this is generally a good idea.

2. Keep knives sharp.

Learn the proper techniques for both sharpening and honing knives. (See Figures 4-1 and 4-2.) A sharp knife not only performs better but is safer to use because less pressure is required to cut through the food. When too much pressure is exerted, there is a good possibility the knife will slip and cause injury to the user.

Various tools are used to sharpen knives. A steel should be within reach at all times. Use a stone periodically to sharpen knives, or use a sharpening machine. Severely dulled or dam-

FIGURE 4-1   Sharpening a Knife on a Stone

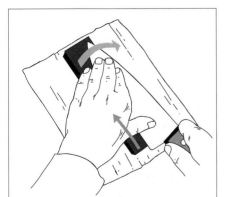

(1) Place the stone on a towel to prevent slipping. Hold the knife at a 20-degree angle and push it over the stone's surface, using your guiding hand to keep even pressure on the blade.

(2) Continue to push the knife over the surface, so that the entire length of the blade is sharpened.

(3) Pull the knife off the stone smoothly, making sure that the total length of the blade has been sharpened, from the tip to the heel.

(4) Turn the knife over and repeat the process on the second side. Notice that the position of the guiding hand changes.

aged blades may need to be reground in order to restore the edge. This is usually done on sharpening wheels by professionals who specialize in the maintenance of knives.

3. Keep knives clean.

Thoroughly clean knives immediately after using them. Work carefully, and pay attention to what you are doing, so that you do not cut yourself as you wipe down the blade. Sanitize the entire knife, including the handle, bolster, and blade as necessary, so that the tool does not become a site for cross-contamination. Keeping knives clean helps to prolong their lives.

Never drop a knife into a full pot sink. The knife might be dented or nicked by heavy pots; also, someone who reaches into the sink could be seriously injured by grabbing the blade. Do not clean knives in a dishwasher, because the handles are likely to warp and split.

4. Use safe handling procedures for knives.

When you are passing a knife to another person, lay it down on a work surface so that the handle is extended to the person who will pick it up. Whenever you must carry a knife from one area of the kitchen to another, hold the knife down at your side with the blade pointed down and let people know you are passing by with a sharp knife. Ideally, you should sheathe or wrap the knife before walking anywhere with it, or transport it in a carrier.

When you lay a knife down on a work surface, be sure that no part of it extends over the cutting board or worktable. That will avoid harm to both the knife and people walking by who could brush against it or knock it onto the floor.

Knives are intended for specific cutting tasks. They are not built for opening bottles and cans, prying lids loose, or other such tasks. Using them inappropriately can at best nick or mar the blade. At worst, the blade could break, and pieces may fly off into the surrounding area.

5. Use an appropriate cutting surface.

Cutting directly on metal, glass, or marble surfaces will dull and eventually damage the blade of a knife. Wooden or composition cutting

FIGURE 4-2   Honing a Knife with a Steel

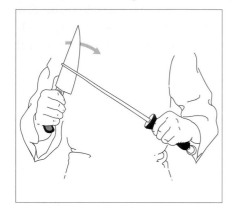

(1) Hold the steel away from the body in one hand and hold the knife in the other. Start with the knife nearly vertical, with the blade resting on the inner side of the steel at a 20-degree angle.

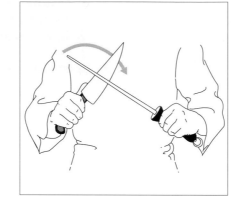

(2) Pass the blade along the entire length of the steel, bending at the wrist as the blade moves. Keep the pressure even and light.

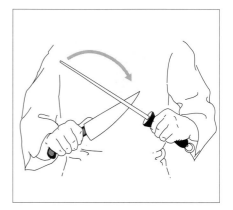

(3) Keep the blade in contact with the steel for the last few inches for proper honing.

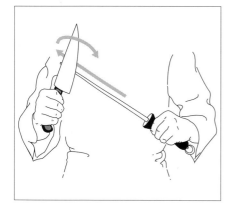

(4) Return the blade to a nearly vertical position, this time on the outer side of the steel, to hone the other side of the blade.

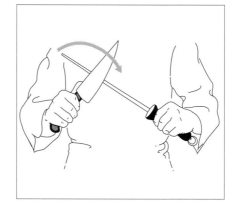

(5) Use the thumb to maintain even, light pressure.

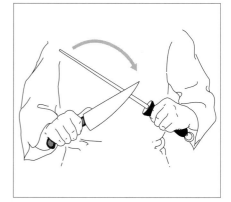

(6) Finish the second pass, making sure the entire length of the blade, including the tip, is properly honed.

boards should always be used to prevent dulling the knife edge.

6. Keep knives properly stored.

   There are a number of safe, practical ways to store knives. They may be kept in knife kits or rolls for one's personal collection, and in slots, racks, and magnetized holders in the kitchen. Storage systems should be kept just as clean as the knives. Cloth rolls should be washed and sanitized periodically. Proper storage will prevent damage to the blade or harm to an unwary individual. Knives should be carefully dried after cleaning, then stored in sheaths to help retain their edge.

The Parts of a Knife

Selecting a knife of good quality that fits the hand and is suitable for the intended tasks depends on a basic knowledge of the various parts of the knife (see Figure 4-3).

Blades

The most frequently used material for good-quality **blades** is **high-carbon stainless steel.** Other materials, such as stainless steel and carbon steel, are also available.

For many years, **carbon steel** was used to make most knife blades. Although carbon steel blades

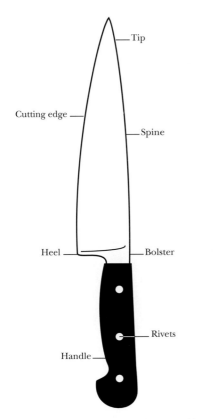

FIGURE 4-3   Parts of the Knife

out of a single sheet of metal and has been ground so that it tapers smoothly from the spine to the cutting edge, with no apparent beveling. Frequently used knives should be made with taper-ground blades.

Hollow-ground blades are made by combining two sheets of metal; the edges are then beveled or fluted. Although hollow-ground blades often have very sharp edges, the blade itself lacks the balance and longevity of a taper-ground blade. This type of blade is often found on knives, such as slicers, which are used less frequently in the kitchen.

Tangs

The **tang** is a continuation of the blade and extends into the knife's handle. Knives used for heavy work, such as chef's knives or cleavers, should have a **full tang;** that is, the tang is as long as the entire handle. A **partial tang** does not run the length of the handle. Although blades with partial tangs are not as durable as those with full tangs, they are acceptable for less-used knives. **Rat-tail tangs** are also used. These are much thinner than the spine of the blade and are encased in the handle (not visible at the top or bottom edges); these tangs tend not to hold up with heavy or prolonged use.

Handles

One of the best materials for knife handles is rosewood, because it is extremely hard and has no grain, which helps to prevent splitting and cracking. Impregnating wood with plastic protects the handle from damage caused by continued exposure to water and detergents. Some state codes require that plastic handles be used in butcher shops because they are considered more sanitary than wood. Care must be taken to thoroughly remove grease, however, because it adheres more persistently to plastic than it does to wood.

Whatever kind of handle you choose, it should fit your hand comfortably. Manufacturers typically produce handles that fit a variety of hands. Spend some time holding the knives you're interested in before you purchase them. A comfortable fit will improve the ease and speed with which you work. A poor fit can result in hand fatigue, or cramping. People with very small or very large hands should

take a better edge than either regular or high-carbon stainless steel, they tend to lose their sharpness quickly. Also, carbon steel blades will discolor when placed in constant contact with high-acid foods, such as tomatoes or fruits.

Carbon steel blades must be treated carefully to avoid discoloration, rusting, and pitting; they should be washed and thoroughly dried between uses and before storage. The metal is brittle and can break easily under stress.

Stainless steel is much stronger than carbon steel and will not discolor or rust. It is very difficult to get a good edge on a stainless steel blade, although once an edge is established, it tends to last longer than that on a carbon steel blade.

High-carbon stainless steel is a relatively recent development that combines the advantages of carbon and stainless steel. The higher percentage of carbon allows the blade to take and keep a keener edge, while the stainless steel content prevents the blade from discoloring or rusting quickly.

The most desirable type of blade is **taper-ground.** This means that the blade has been forged

be sure that they are not straining their grip to hold the handle. Some knives are especially constructed to meet the needs of left-handed chefs.

Rivets

Metal fasteners called **rivets** are used to secure the tang to the handle. The rivets should be completely smooth and lie flush with the surface of the handle to prevent irritation to the hand. Good construction will also avoid pockets in the wood and under rivets where microorganisms can gather.

Bolsters

In some knives there is a collar or shank, also known as a **bolster.** This feature is found at the point where the blade meets the handle and it is a sign of a well-made knife, one that will hold up for a long time. Some knives may have a collar that looks like a bolster but is actually a separate piece attached to the handle. These knives tend to come apart easily and should be avoided.

Types of Knives

The knives that a chef will accumulate over the course of a career will undoubtedly include a number of special knives. There are, for example, several special knives and cutting tools found exclusively in bakeshops; still others are required for butchering meats and fabricating fish. This list is intended as a guide to the knives that may be found in nearly any well-outfitted knife kit but it is by no means comprehensive. See Figures 4-4 and 4-5 for illustrations.

Chef's Knife, or French Knife This all-purpose knife is used for a variety of chopping, slicing, and mincing chores. The blade is normally 8 to 14 inches long.

Utility Knife This smaller, lighter chef's knife is used for light cutting chores. The blade is generally 5 to 7 inches long.

Paring Knife This short knife, used primarily for paring and trimming vegetables and fruits, has a 2- to 4-inch blade.

FIGURE 4-4   Knives

(from left to right) Chef's knives of various sizes, paring knife, clam knife, oyster knife.

FIGURE 4-5   Knives

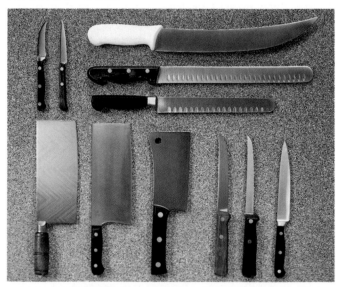

(clockwise from top left) Tourné knives, scimitar, slicers (two sizes), utility knife, boning knife, filleting knife, meat cleavers, Asian cleaver.

Boning Knife A boning knife is used to separate raw meat from the bone. The blade, which is thinner and shorter than the blade of a chef's knife, is about 6 inches long, and is usually rigid.

Filleting Knife Used for filleting fish, this knife is similar in shape and size to a boning knife, but it has a flexible blade.

Slicer This knife is used for slicing cooked meat. It has a long blade with a round or pointed tip. The blade may be flexible or rigid and may be taper-ground or have a fluted edge that consists of hollow-ground ovals.

Cleaver Used for chopping, the cleaver is often heavy enough to cut through bones. It has a rectangular blade and varies in size according to its use.

Tourné Knife This small knife, similar to a paring knife, has a curved blade to make cutting the curved surfaces of tournéed vegetables easier. It is also called a bird beak knife.

Sharpening and Honing Tools

The key to the proper and efficient use of any knife is making sure that it is sharp. A knife with a sharp blade always works better and more safely because it cuts easily without requiring the chef to exert pressure, which may cause the knife to slip and an injury to result. Knife blades are given an edge on a sharpening stone and maintained between sharpenings by honing with a steel (see Figure 4-6 for a variety of sharpening and honing tools).

Sharpening Stones

Sharpening stones are essential to the proper maintenance of knives and are used to sharpen the blade by passing its edge over the stone at the correct angle. The **grit**—the degree of coarseness or fineness of the stone's surface—scrapes the blade's edge, creating a sharp cutting surface. When sharpening a knife, always begin by using the coarsest surface of the stone and then move on to the finer surfaces. A stone with a fine grade should be used for boning knives and other tools in which an especially sharp edge is required. Most stones may be used either dry or moistened with water or mineral oil. Once oil has been used on a stone's surface, however, oiling the stone should be continued. Three basic types of stones are commonly available in the standard size of $8 \times 2 \times {}^{15}/_{16}$ inches:

FIGURE 4-6   Sharpening and Honing Tools

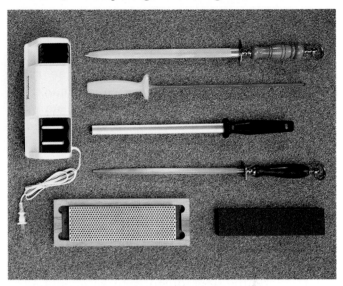

(from top left) Electric knife sharpener, variety of steels, carborundum stone, diamond-impregnated stone in case.

- **Carborundum stones** have a fine side and a medium side.

- **Arkansas stones** are available in several grades of fineness and some consist of three stones of varying degrees of fineness mounted on a wheel.

- **Diamond-impregnated stones** are expensive, although some chefs prefer them because they feel these stones give a sharper edge.

Before using a stone, the chef should be sure that it is properly stabilized. Place carborundum or diamond stones on a dampened cloth to brace them. Make sure you have enough room to work. A triple-faced stone is mounted on a rotating framework that can be locked into position so that it will not move. The blade should be held at a 20-degree angle to the stone's surface and the entire length of the blade should be drawn across the stone. This process is repeated on both sides of the blade. (See Figure 4-2 for an illustration of sharpening a knife on a stone.)

Grinding wheels, electric sharpeners, leather strops (such as those used to sharpen barbers' blades), and other grinding tools may be necessary to replace or restore the edge of a badly dulled knife.

Steels

A **steel** should be used both immediately after sharpening the blade with a stone and also between sharpenings to keep the edge in alignment. The length of the steel's working surface can range from 3 inches for a pocket version to over 14 inches. Although traditionally made from hard steel, other materials, such as glass, ceramic, and diamond-impregnated surfaces, are also used in steel construction today.

Steels come with coarse, medium, or fine grains. Some are magnetic, which helps the blade retain proper alignment and also collects metal shavings which might otherwise fall into food. A guard or hilt between the steel and the handle protects the user, and a ring on the bottom of the handle can be used to hang the steel for storage.

When using a steel, the knife is held almost vertically, with the blade at a 20-degree angle as it rests against the steel. The blade should be drawn along the entire length of the steel. (See Figure 4-2 for an illustration of honing a knife on a steel.)

Hand Tools

Every well-equipped professional knife kit includes a number of small tools in addition to knives (see Figure 4-7). It should be noted that in addition to the hand tools listed here, there are many others used in the professional kitchen for various specific functions. Tools designed to scale fish, open clams and oysters, or even cut eggs can be found in some knife kits.

Rotary or **Swivel-Bladed Peeler** This tool is used to peel the skin from various vegetables and fruits. The swivel action accommodates the contours of various products. Because the blade is sharpened on both sides, it will peel in both an upward and downward motion. Using it correctly will greatly increase the speed with which you can "prep" vegetables.

Parisienne Scoop (Melon Baller) This tool is specifically designed for scooping out balls or ovals (depending upon the shape of the scoop) of vegetables and fruits.

Kitchen Fork The fork is used to test the doneness of braised meats and vegetables, for lifting finished items to the carving board or plate, and to steady the item being carved. A kitchen fork should never be used to turn foods as they are sautéed, grilled, or broiled. This is because when the tines pierce the food, the juices escape and the resulting finished product will be dry.

Palette Knife (Metal Spatula) This is a flexible, round-tipped tool used in the kitchen and bakeshop for turning pancakes or grilled foods, spreading fillings and glazes, and for a variety of other functions. A palette knife with a serrated edge is useful for preparing and slicing sandwiches.

Whips Whips are used to beat, blend, and whip foods. Balloon whips are sphere-shaped and have thin wires to incorporate air for making foams. Sauce whips are narrower and frequently have thicker wires. The chef should have a number of whips in various sizes.

Offset Spatula This spatula is used to turn or lift foods on grills, broilers, and griddles. It has a wide, chisel-edged blade set in a short handle.

Pastry Bag This plastic, canvas, or nylon bag is used to pipe out puréed foods, whipped cream, and various toppings. Pastry bags have uses in both the kitchen and the bakeshop.

Other kitchen hand tools include (but are not limited to) items such as cherry pitters; strawberry hullers; tomato knives (also known as tomato witches); rubber scrapers; ladles of various sizes; skimmers for skimming the surface of stocks, soups, etc.; "spiders" for lifting foods out of liquids or fats; spoons of various sorts, wooden and metal serving spoons, tasting spoons, and slotted or solid spoons; scoops of various sizes; hardwood rolling pins; and plastic or wooden cutting boards.

Small Equipment

The tools outlined in this section are available in any well-equipped kitchen. For the sake of clarity, they have been categorized here according to their general function.

Measuring Equipment

Measurements are determined in many different ways in a professional kitchen, depending upon the ingredient to be measured and the measuring system (weight in U.S. or metric, volume, or a combination) employed by a specific recipe. For this reason it is important to have equipment for liquid and dry volume measures for both U.S. and metric, as well as a variety of scales for accurate measurement by weight. Thermometers should display both Fahrenheit and Centigrade temperatures.

Graduated Measuring Pitchers and Cups   These are used for measuring liquids and are generally available in pint, quart, and gallon sizes. Cup sets include $^1/_4$-, $^1/_3$-, $^1/_2$-, and 1-cup measures

Scales   These are used to weigh ingredients for preparation and portion control. Ounce/gram and pound/kilo scales both should be available. Scales may be spring-type, balance beam, or electronic.

Thermometers   An instant-reading thermometer is used to measure the internal temperature of food. The stem, inserted in the food, gives an instant reading. Candy and deep-fat thermometers are also helpful.

Measuring Spoons   Measuring spoons typically come in the following sizes: tablespoon, teaspoon, ½ teaspoon, and ¼ teaspoon. Some sets also have ½ tablespoon and ⅛ teaspoon measures.

Bowls for Mixing

Most kitchens are equipped with a variety of bowls, usually a nonreactive material, such as stainless steel. Copper bowls are often included in the kitchen's stock of mixing bowls too, since they are considered best for whipping egg whites.

Bowls should be reserved for mixing, rather than using them for storage containers, unless there is no other option.

Storage Containers

Foods in the kitchen are stored in several stages: as raw products, partially prepared items, as cooked

FIGURE 4-7   Small Tools

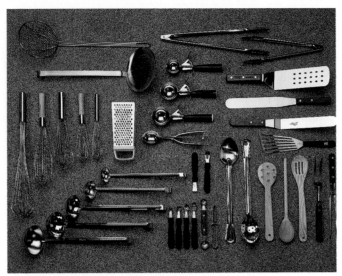

(from top left) spider, skimmer, tongs, offset spatula, flexible spatulas, fish spatula (peltex), kitchen forks, wooden spoon (slotted and solid), pasta fork/spoon, slotted and solid kitchen spoons, swivel-bladed peeler, zester, channel knife, parisienne scoops/melon ballers, ladels, whips, box grater, and in center, scoops.

items that are to be held for the next day's service, or as frozen items for longer periods of storage. It is crucial to have an adequate supply of containers to hold foods safely in the refrigerator or freezer. In addition to plastic or stainless steel containers (which may or may not have fitted lids), you will also require butcher's paper, plastic wrap, foil, and freezer wrap. You should additionally have tools for securing and marking stored foods, including tape and waterproof markers.

Sieves, Strainers, and Chinois

Sieves and strainers (see Figure 4-8) are used to sift, aerate, and help to remove any large impurities from dry ingredients. They are also used to strain or purée cooked or raw foods.

Food Mill   This is a type of strainer used to purée soft foods. A flat, curving blade is rotated over a disk by a hand-operated crank. Most professional models have interchangeable disks with holes of varying fineness. An exception is the Foley food mill, which has a mesh disk that is fixed in place.

FIGURE 4-8   Sieves, Strainers, and Chinois

(from top left) salad spinner, cheesecloth, pasta machine, colander, ricer, food mill with interchangeable disks, parchment, cone sieve/chinois (regular and fine), and food-handlers gloves, in center.

Note: Many mixing machines may be used like a food mill with the addition of attachments that allow them to strain and purée foods.

Drum Sieve (Tamis)   This sieve consists of a tinned-steel, nylon, or stainless-steel screen stretched in an aluminum or wood frame. A drum sieve is used for sifting or puréeing. A *champignon* (mushroom-shaped pusher) or a rigid plastic scraper is used to push the food through the screen.

Chinois   This conical sieve is used for straining and/or puréeing food. The openings in the cone can be of varying sizes, from very large to a fine mesh. A fine chinois (also known as a bouillon strainer) is a valuable piece of equipment and should be treated with great respect. It should be cleaned immediately after each use and stored properly; never drop it into a pot sink where it could be crushed or torn.

Colander   This stainless-steel sieve, with or without a base, is used for straining foods. Colanders are available in a variety of sizes.

Ricer   This is a device in which cooked food, often potatoes, is placed in a hopper, which is pierced

with holes. A plate on the end of a lever pushes the food through the hopper walls. Garlic presses and french-fry cutters operate on the same principle.

Cheesecloth   This light, fine mesh gauze is frequently used in place of a fine chinois and is essential for straining some sauces. It is also used for making sachets. Before use, cheesecloth should be rinsed thoroughly in hot water and then cold water to remove any loose fibers. Cheesecloth also clings better to the sides of bowls, chinois, and so forth when it is wet.

Pots, Pans, and Molds

Various materials and combinations of materials are used in the construction of pots, pans, and molds. Because form and function are closely related, it is important to choose the proper equipment for the task at hand.

Pots made of **copper** transfer heat rapidly and evenly. Direct contact with copper will affect the color and consistency of many foods, however, so copper pots are generally lined. (An exception is the copper pan used to cook jams, jellies, chocolates, and other high-sugar items, often known as a preserving pan.) Great care must be taken not to scratch the lining, which is usually a soft metal, such as tin. Copper also tends to discolor quickly, and it requires significant time and labor for proper upkeep.

Cast iron has the capacity to hold and transmit heat effectively and evenly. The metal is somewhat brittle however, and must be treated carefully to prevent pitting, scarring, and rusting. Cast iron is sometimes coated with enamel during manufacture to simplify care and make it last longer.

Stainless steel is only a moderately good conductor of heat, but is often preferred because it has other advantages, including easy maintenance. Other metals, such as aluminum or copper, are often sandwiched within layers of stainless steel to improve heat conduction. Stainless steel will not react with foods; this means, for example, that white sauces will retain a pure white or ivory color.

Blue-steel, black-steel, pressed-steel, or **rolled-steel pans** are all prone to discoloration but trans-

---

sachet: a small bundle of aromatic ingredients, encased in cheesecloth, used to flavor stocks and sauces.

PROPER CARE AND CLEANING OF COPPER PANS

There is a technique that chefs have used through the years for cleaning and shining copper cookware. It is still favored by many because it is fast, inexpensive, and efficient:

1. Mix equal parts of flour and salt, then add enough distilled white vinegar to form a paste. The vinegar will react with the copper to erase any discoloration caused by oxidation and heat. Any other acid, such as lemon juice, would work equally as well; however, white vinegar is typically the most economical choice. The salt acts as a scouring agent and the flour provides the binder.

2. Coat copper surfaces completely with this paste, then vigorously massage clean with a cloth.

Clean the tin-lined cooking surfaces as you would other pots and pans, with a gentle scouring pad and cleaning detergent.

Note: Delicate copper serving dishes and utensils should be cleaned with a commercial cream or polish without abrasives, to avoid scratching.

---

mit heat very rapidly. These pans are generally thin and are often preferred for sautéing foods because of their quick response to changes in temperature.

Aluminum is also an excellent conductor of heat, however it is a soft metal that wears down quickly. When a metal spoon or whip is used to stir a white or light-colored sauce, soup, or stock in an aluminum pot, it could take on a gray color. Anodized, or treated, aluminum tends not to react with foods, and it is one of the most popular metals for pots used in contemporary kitchens. The surfaces of treated aluminum pans tend to be easier to clean and care for than most other metals, with the exception of stainless steel.

Nonstick coatings on pans have some use in professional kitchens, especially for those that offer foods that are cooked with less fats and oils. These surfaces are not as sturdy as metal or enamel linings, so care must be taken to avoid scratching during cooking and cleaning. New methods of adding nonstick coatings as well as new materials used to create these coatings have produced more-durable nonstick pans, suitable in many cooking situations.

The following guidelines should be observed when choosing a pan or mold:

- *Choose a size appropriate to the food being cooked.*

The chef should be familiar with the capacity of various pots, pans, and molds. If too many pieces of meat are crowded into a sauteuse, for instance, the food will not brown properly. If the sauteuse is too large, however, the drippings could scorch. If a small fish is poached in a large pot, the sauce will not have the proper flavor intensity. It is also easier to overcook the fish in a pot that is too large. If the pot is too small, there may not be enough cuisson available for the sauce.

- *Choose material appropriate to the cooking technique.*

Experience has shown, and science has verified, that certain cooking techniques are more successful when used with certain materials. For instance, sautéed foods require pans that transmit heat quickly and are sensitive to temperature changes. Braises, on the other hand, require long, fairly gentle cooking, and it is more important that the particular pot transmit heat evenly and hold heat well than respond rapidly to changes in heat.

- *Use proper handling, cleaning, and storing techniques.*

Avoid subjecting pots to heat extremes (for example, placing a smoking-hot pot into a sinkful of water) because some materials are prone to warping. Other materials may chip or even crack if allowed to sit over heat when they are empty or if they are handled roughly. Casseroles or molds made of enameled cast iron or steel are especially vulnerable. In order to protect the **seasoning** of rolled steel pans, do not clean the surface with detergents or abrasives such as steel wool or cleansing powders.

- *Be sure to dry pans before storing.*

Air drying is best to prevent the pitting and rusting of some surfaces, as well as to keep them clean and sanitary. Proper and organized stor-

SEASONING PANS

Chefs who use pans made of cast iron or rolled steel, which are porous metals, will often season their pans to seal the pores and preserve the cooking surface before use. To do this, pour enough cooking oil into the pan to evenly coat the bottom. Place the pan over high heat, on a stovetop, or in a very hot oven. Heat the oil until it begins to shimmer and smoke. Remove the pan from the heat. Rub the oil into the pan with a dense bundle of paper towels, taking care not to burn yourself. This procedure should be repeated every so often to renew the seal.

To clean a seasoned pan, use a bundle of paper towels to scour salt over the surface of the pan until all food particles have been removed. This procedure effectively cleans the pan without stripping the metal base.

---

age prevents dents, chips, and breakage, and expedites the work load because staff can more readily find what they need.

Pots and Pans for Stove Top Cooking

Pots and pans are not only available in a variety of materials but they are also produced in a number of different sizes.(See Figure 4-9.) Different manufacturers however, may use different styles of handles, loops, or lids. All must be able to withstand direct heat from a flame. A poorly produced pot will have weak spots that will eventually warp.

Stockpot (Marmite) This large pot is made of medium-gauge metal. It is taller than it is wide and it has straight sides. Some stockpots have a spigot at the base so that the liquid can be drained off without lifting the heavy pot. Anodized aluminum and stainless steel are the preferred materials.

Saucepot This pot is similar in shape to a stockpot, although not as large. It has straight sides and two loop handles for lifting.

Saucepan This pan has straight or slightly flared sides (a pan with flared sides may be known as a *fait-tout*) and it has a single long handle.

Rondeau This is a wide, fairly shallow pot with two loop handles. When made from cast iron, these pots are frequently known as **griswolds,** and they may have a single short handle rather than the two loop handles. A brazier is similar to a rondeau but it may be square instead of round.

Sauteuse This shallow skillet with sloping sides and a single long handle is often referred to as a sauté pan.

Sautoir This shallow skillet has straight sides and a single long handle. It is also often referred to as a sauté pan.

Omelet Pan/Crêpe Pan This shallow skillet has very short, slightly sloping sides, and is most often made of rolled or "blue" steel.

Bain-Marie (Double-Boiler) These are nesting pots with single long handles. The bottom pot is filled with water that is heated to gently cook or warm the food in the upper pot. The term also refers to the stainless-steel containers used to hold food in a steam table.

Griddle This is a heavy round or rectangular surface for griddling. A griddle is flat with no sides or handles and may be built directly into the stove. There may be a groove or indentation around the edge to allow grease to drain away.

Fish Poacher This is a long, narrow pot with straight sides It may include a perforated rack for holding the fish.

Steamer This consists of a set of stacked pots. The upper pot has a perforated bottom and is placed over a larger pot, which is filled with boiling or simmering water. The perforations allow the steam to

---

seasoned pan: a pan that has had its cooking surface conditioned before use.

FIGURE 4-9 Pot Rack

(top row) stock pot, steamer insert, colander; (second row) various sauteuse, saucepans, and small sauce/stock pot; (third row) in foreground, various sizes of sauteuse; stainless steel, bimetals/copper, anodized aluminum; in background; lids, couscousière, fish poacher, small copper roasting pan/baking dish; hanging: paella pan; (fourth row) foreground, crêpe pan; background, nested sauce pots with loops handles, copper saucepan with handle, sauce pot with loop handles, and copper roasting pan, rondeau and nested sauce pots; hanging, wok; (bottom row) marmite/stockpot, half-size sheet pans, chinois, perforated insert for hotel pan and hotel pan, roasting pan (with various lids) on full-size sheet pans.

rise from the pot below to cook the food above. Tiered steamers are also available.

Specialty Pots and Pans: Woks, couscousières, paella pans, and **grill pans** (the latter is essentially a skillet with ridges that can simulate grilling) are among the stove-top pots and pans used to prepare special, usually ethnic, dishes.

Pots and Pans for Oven Cooking

Pans used in ovens are produced from the same basic materials as those used to make stove-top pots and pans. Glazed and unglazed earthenware, glass, and ceramics are also used. The heat of the oven, less intense than that of a burner, prevents these more delicate materials from cracking and shattering because of extreme temperature. It is important to remember to avoid submerging these materials into water immediately after removing them from the oven.

Roasting Pan This rectangular pan with medium-high sides is used for roasting or baking and comes in various sizes.

Sheet Pan This shallow, rectangular pan is used for baking and may be full or half size.

Hotel Pan This is a rectangular pan, used occasionally for preparing foods, but more often as a container to hold foods that are already cooked in steamtables, hot boxes, or for use in electric or gas steamers. It is also frequently used to marinate meats or for food storage under refrigeration. It may be shallow, deep, divided, or half-size. **Chafing dishes** usually are of standard sizes, so that most hotel pans will fit them properly.

Pâté Mold A deep rectangular metal mold, the pâté mold usually has hinged sides to facilitate re-

moval of the pâté. Special shapes (oval, triangular, and others) may be available.

Terrine Mold The terrine mold may be rectangular or oval, with a lid. Traditionally an earthenware mold, it may also be made of enameled cast iron.

Gratin Dish A shallow oval baking dish, this may be ceramic, enameled cast iron, or enameled steel.

Soufflé Dish This is a round, straight-edged ceramic dish which is available in various sizes.

Timbale Mold This small metal or ceramic mold is used for individual portions of various molded, cooked vegetables, usually made with a custard base.

Specialty Molds These include dariole, savarin, ring, and other molds that are used to achieve varying shapes.

Large Equipment

Safety precautions must be observed and proper maintenance and cleaning must be consistently applied in order to keep equipment functioning properly and to prevent injury or accident. Observe the following guidelines when working with large equipment:

1. Obtain proper instruction in the machine's safe operation. Do not be afraid to ask for extra help.
2. First turn off and then unplug electrical equipment before assembling or breaking down the equipment.
3. Use all safety features: Be sure that lids are secure, hand guards are used, and the machine is stable.
4. Clean and sanitize the equipment thoroughly after each use.
5. Be sure that all pieces of equipment are properly reassembled and left unplugged after each use.
6. Report any problems or malfunctions promptly and alert coworkers.

Grinding, Slicing, and Puréeing Equipment

Grinders, slicers, and cutting equipment (see Figures 4-10 and 4-11) all have the potential to be ex-

---

couscousière: a pot specially designed to cook the classic North African dish, couscous. It has two compartments. The couscous grains are cooked in the top, while chunks of meat, vegetables and other items are cooked in the bottom.

paella pan: a wide shallow pan with two handles used to prepare the classic Spanish, saffron-flavored rice dish, paella.

chafing dishes: a metal dish with a heating unit, used to keep foods hot for buffet or tableside service.

FIGURE 4-10 Blenders

(clockwise from top left) bar blender with stainless jar, glass jar, and immersion (burr/stick) blender.

tremely dangerous. The importance of observing all the necessary safety precautions cannot be overemphasized. These tools are essential for a number of different operations however, and all chefs should be able to use them with confidence.

Meat Grinder This is a freestanding machine or an attachment for a standing mixer. A meat grinder should have **dies** of varying sizes and in general will have a **feed tray** and a **pusher.** All food contact areas should be kept scrupulously clean. To make sure all the food has been pushed through the **worm,** feed a twisted coil of plastic wrap through the feed tube.

Vertical Chopping Machine (VCM) This machine operates on the same principle as a blender. A

---

dies: punctured metal discs that fit into a grinder.

worm: the spiral shaped piece of a grinder which pushes the food forward, through the die.

motor at the base is permanently attached to a bowl with integral blades. As a safety precaution, the hinged lid must be locked in place before the unit will operate. The VCM is used to grind, whip, emulsify, blend, or crush foods.

Food Chopper (Buffalo Chopper) The food is placed in a rotating bowl that passes under a hood, where blades chop the food. Some units have hoppers or feed tubes and interchangeable disks for slicing and grating. Food choppers are available in floor and tabletop models and are generally made of aluminum with a stainless-steel bowl.

Food Processor This is a processing machine that houses the motor separately from the bowl, blades, and lid. Food processors can grind, purée, blend, emulsify, crush, knead, and, with special disks, slice, julienne, and shred foods.

Food/Meat Slicer This machine is used to slice foods in even thicknesses. A carrier moves the food back and forth against a circular blade, which is generally carbon steel. There may be separate motors to operate the carrier and the blade. To avoid injury, all the safety features incorporated in a food slicer, especially the **hand guard,** should be used.

Mandoline This slicing device is made of nickel-plated stainless steel with blades of high-carbon steel. Levers adjust the blades to achieve the cut and thickness desired. As with food slicers, be sure

FIGURE 4-11 Mandoline with Guard

to use the guard—the carriage device that holds the food—to prevent injury. The mandoline can be used to make such cuts as slices, juliennes, gaufrettes, and batonnet.

Kettles and Steamers

Kettles and steamers enable a chef to prepare large amounts of food efficiently, since the heat is applied over a much larger area than is possible when a single burner is used. Cooking times for dishes prepared in steamers and large kettles are often shorter than for those prepared on a range top.

Steam-Jacketed Kettle This freestanding or table-top kettle circulates steam through the walls, providing even heat. Units vary; they may tilt, may be insulated, and may have spigots or lids. Available in a range of sizes, these kettles are excellent for producing stocks, soups, and sauces. They are generally made of stainless steel and sometimes have a specially treated nonstick surface. Gas or electric models are available.

Tilting Kettle This large, relatively shallow free-standing unit is used for braising and stewing. Most tilting kettles have lids, allowing for steaming as well. They are usually made of stainless steel and are available in gas or electric models.

Pressure Steamer Water is heated under pressure in a sealed compartment, allowing it to reach higher than boiling temperature (212°F/100°C at sea level). The cooking time is controlled by automatic timers, which open the exhaust valves at the end. The doors cannot be opened until the pressure has been released.

Convection Steamer The steam is generated in a boiler and then piped to the cooking chamber, where it is vented over the food. Pressure does not

build up in the unit; it is continuously exhausted, which means the door may be opened at any time without danger of scalding or burning.

Stoves, Ranges, and Ovens

It is difficult to imagine a kitchen without a stove. The stove top is known as the **range;** the oven is usually below the range. There are a number of different variations on this standard arrangement, however, just as there a number of different range tops and ovens available today.

Ranges

Gas or electric ranges are available in many sizes with various combinations of open burners, flat-tops (not to be confused with griddle units), and ring-tops. Open burners and ring tops supply direct heat, which is easy to change and control. Small units known as **candy stoves** or **stockpot ranges** have rings of gas jets that allow for excellent heat control. Flat-tops provide indirect heat, which is more even and less intense than direct heat. Foods that require long, slow cooking, such as stocks, are more effectively cooked on a flat-top.

Open Burner This is an individual grate-style burner that allows for easy adjustment of heat.

Flat-Top This consists of a thick plate of cast-iron or steel set over the heat source. Flat-tops give relatively even and consistent heat but do not allow for quick adjustments of temperature.

Ring-Top This is a flat-top with concentric rings or plates that can be removed to widen or close the opening, supplying more or less direct heat.

Induction Burner This is a relatively new technology based on the transference of an electric current into a magnetic vibration. It is the vibration that heats the pan as it sits on top of the burner. The food is cooked via heat transferred from the pan while the burner itself stays cool. All pans used on this type of burner must be made of steel or iron; copper and aluminum cookware will not respond to it.

---

julienne: a knife cut that produces thin strips measuring 1/16-inch square by 1 to 2 inches long.

gaufrette: a lattice shape cut made on a mandoline, usually associated with potatoes, which are then deep fried until light brown and crispy.

batonnet: a knife cut, slightly thicker than a julienne, but similar in shape, measuring 1/4-inch square by 2 to 2 1/2 inches long.

Ovens

Ovens cook foods by surrounding them with hot air, a gentler and more even source of heat than the direct heat of a burner. Many types of roasted and baked food are prepared in ovens. Delicate foods such as custards are also cooked in an oven usually in a hot water bath (bain-marie). Different ovens are available to suit a variety of needs, and both the establishment's menu and its available space should be evaluated before determining what type and size oven to install.

Convection Oven Hot air is forced through fans to circulate around the food, cooking it evenly and quickly. Some convection ovens have the capacity to introduce steam. They are available in gas or electric models, in a range of sizes, with stainless steel interiors and exteriors, and glass doors. Special features may include infrared and a convection-microwave combination.

Conventional/Deck Ovens The heat source is located on the bottom, underneath the deck, or floor, of the oven. Heat is conducted through the deck into the cavity. Conventional ovens can be located below a range top or as individual shelves arranged one above another. The latter are known as deck ovens, and the food is placed directly on the deck, instead of on a wire rack. Deck ovens normally consist of two to four decks, though single-deck models are also available. Some deck ovens have a ceramic or firebrick base. Deck ovens usually are gas or electric, although charcoal and wood-burning units are also options. The basic deck oven is most often used only for roasting, but several variations are available for other purposes.

Additional styles of ovens include pizza ovens, rotary ovens for spit roasting, conveyor ovens, and rotating deck ovens.

Slow Cookers/Combi Stoves These stoves have been used extensively in Europe and are becoming more common in this country. The stove cooks at low temperatures, and may also steam foods. It can be used for both cooking foods and holding them at the correct service temperature, making them desirable in a number of different instances (catering, banquets, large scale operations, and so forth.) Some versions of these stoves are capable of smoking foods as well.

Smokers

A true **smoker** will treat foods with smoke (after they have been properly brined and cured, if necessary) and can be operated at either cool smoking or hot smoking temperatures. Racks or hooks are generally installed, allowing foods to hang so that the smoke circulates evenly around the item.

Small home-style smokers can be ideal in some operations when only a small volume of specialty items, such as smoked trout or cheese, is being prepared.

Griddles and Grills

Two other oven/range features, the griddle and the grill, are part of the traditional commercial foodservice setup.

Griddle Similar to a flat-top range top, a griddle has a heat source located beneath a thick plate of metal, generally cast-iron or steel. The food is

---

TANDOORI OVEN

The tandoori oven is used in classic Indian food preparations. It is shaped with a round top and a deep pit, traditionally made from clay and elephant hair. Brick and clay adaptations are available in the United States. The tandoori oven heats up to between 500° and 1500°F (260° to 815°C). The heat source is a fire built of wood, charcoal, or a combination of the two in the bottom of the oven. The ovens are used primarily to cook small, skewered items very quickly; however, when the temperature is adjusted to the lower range, tandoori ovens can also be used to roast large items, such as a whole leg of lamb. Ovens are available in a range of sizes, which are measured by the amount of bread, called "naan," they can hold—30 naan, 40 naan, and so forth.

cooked directly on this surface. A griddle may be gas or electric.

Grills, Broilers, and Salamander In a grill, the heat source is located below the rack; in a broiler or salamander, the heat source is above. Some units have adjustable racks, which allow the food to be raised or lowered to control cooking speed. Most units are gas, although electric units with ceramic "rocks" create a bed of coals, producing the effect of a charcoal grill. Salamanders are small broilers, used primarily to finish or glaze foods.

Refrigeration Equipment

Maintaining adequate refrigeration storage is crucial to any foodservice operation; therefore, the menu and the available refrigeration storage must be evaluated and coordinated. All units should be maintained properly, which means regular and thorough cleaning, including the insulating strips. Such precautions will help reduce spoilage and thus reduce food costs. Positioning the units so that unnecessary steps are eliminated will save time and labor. Both of these factors will save money for the operation.

Walk-In

This is the largest style of refrigeration unit and usually has shelves that are arranged around the walls. It is possible to zone a **walk-in** to maintain appropriate temperature and humidity levels for storing various foods. Some walk-ins are large enough to accommodate rolling carts for additional storage. The carts can then be rolled to the appropriate area of the kitchen when needed. Some units have pass-through or reach-in doors to facilitate access to frequently required items.

Walk-ins may be situated in the kitchen or outside the facility. If space allows, walk-ins located outside the kitchen can prove advantageous, because deliveries may be made at any time without disrupting service.

Reach-In

A **reach-in** may be a single unit or part of a bank of units, available in many sizes. Units with pass-through doors are especially helpful for the pantry area, where salads, desserts, and other cold items can be retrieved by the waitstaff as needed.

On-Site Refrigeration

These are refrigerated drawers or undercounter reach-ins, which allow foods on the line to be held at the proper temperature during service. **On site refrigeration** eliminates unnecessary trafficking of food during peak periods, which can create a hazard.

Portable Refrigeration

Portable refrigerators are basically refrigerated carts that can be placed as needed in the kitchen.

Display Refrigeration

These are display cases that are generally used in the dining room for desserts, salads, or salad bars.

Ice Cream Freezer

A small, freestanding **ice cream freezer** can be kept at the appropriate temperature for ice cream. There are separate lids allowing you to easily reach the appropriate container without letting out too much cold air.

Summary

Knives, hand tools, cookware, and other kitchen equipment, lagre and small, are essential to the work you will do in any professional kitchen, as well as in your own home. The ability to properly select, care for, and maintain kitchen equipment is an indispensable skill. Careful consideration will be required when choosing the equipment you will encounter throughout your career. This knowledge includes the following:

• Explaining the basic construction of knives, including the blade and handle, and how that affects the knife's quality

• Cleaning and storing knives and hand tools

• Identifying and properly using a number of specialty knives and hand tools

- Sharpening a knife using a sharpening stone and honing a knife using a steel

- Understanding the importance of a sharp blade for safety and work efficiency

- Understanding the basic use and proper operation of a variety of small kitchen equipment and cookware including, measuring equipment, mixing bowls, sieves, strainers, and chinois, pots, pans, and molds

- Understanding how to properly care for cookware including cleaning, drying, and storing

- Being able to describe the basic use and operation of large kitchen equipment including, stove, ranges, and ovens and refrigeration equipment

- Understanding the basic rules for working safely with large and small equipment

SELF-STUDY QUESTIONS

1. Why is the chef's knife so important, and why is it a good idea to buy the best knife you can find?

2. Name the three materials commonly used to make knife blades.

3. Explain the difference between taper ground and hollow ground blades.

4. Name the three types of tangs and explain the differences.

5. How should you care for a knife?

6. Describe the procedure for sharpening and honing a knife.

7. Name three types of materials used to construct a steel.

8. What pieces of equipment are used to perform the following tasks?

   - Cutting up a chicken
   - Peeling carrots
   - Making whipped egg whites or heavy cream
   - Puréeing strawberries

9. Name four food items measured by volume and four food items measured by weight.

10. What pieces of cookware are used to strain sauces?

11. Name three types of material used to make pots and pans. Give advantages and disadvantages of each. Describe any special instructions for proper care.

12. Give two reasons why a fish should be cooked in the right size pot.

13. What are the benefits and disadvantages of copper cookware?

14. Give two reasons why proper and organized storage of cookware is important.

15. What are the relative benefits of deck ovens, convection ovens, and slow cookers?

ACTIVITIES

- Go to three different kitchen supply stores or well-equipped department stores and compare four brands of chef's knives. They are often locked up in glass display cases, so ask a salesperson assist you. Hold each one and write brief observations of how the knife feels in your hand—the balance, weight, etc.—and the price. State which knife you prefer and why?

- Use a mandoline to cut a carrot into julienne and rondelles (rounds). Use a food processor with appropriate attachments to make the same cuts. Compare the results.

- Review the following recipes and make a list of all the tools, pots, pans, large and small equipment you might need:

  - Italian Meat Balls (page 550)
  - Paella (page 605)
  - Garlic Cheese Grits (page 643)

KEYWORDS

aluminum
Arkansas stone
bain marie
  (double boiler)
black steel
blade
blue steel
bolster
boning knife
broiler
candy stove/stock pot
  range
carbon steel
carborundum stone
cast iron
chafing dish
cheesecloth
chef's or French knife
chinois
cleaver
colander
convection oven
convection steamer
conventional oven
copper
couscoussière
deck oven
diamond-impregnated
  stone
die
drum sieve (tamis)

feed tray
filleting knife
fish poacher
flat-top range
food chopper
  (Buffalo chopper)
food mill
food processor
food/meat slicer
full tang
graduated measuring
  pitchers and cups
gratin dish
griddle
grill pan
grill
griswold
grit
hand guard
high-carbon stainless
  steel
hollow-ground
hotel pan
ice cream freezer
induction burner
kitchen fork
mandoline
measuring spoons
meat grinder
nonstick coating
offset spatula

omelet pan/crêpe
  pan
on-site refrigeration
open-burner range
paella pan
palette knife
paring knife
parisienne scoop
  (melon baller)
partial tang
pastry bag and tips
pâté mold
portable refrigeration
pressed steel
pressure steamer
pusher
range
rat-tail tang
reach-in refrigeration
ricer
ring-top range
rivets
roasting pan
rolled steel
rondeau
rotary peeler
salamander
saucepan
saucepot
sauteuse
sautoir

scales
seasoning
sharpening stone
sheet pan
slicer
slow cooker/
  combi stove
smoker
soufflé dish
stainless steel
steam-jacketed kettle
steamer
steel
stockpot (marmite)
tang
taper-ground
terrine mold
thermometer
tilting kettle
  (Swiss kettle)
timbale mold
tourné knife
utility knife
vertical chopping
  machine (VCM)
walk-in refrigeration
whips/whisks
wok
worm

5

The Raw Ingredients

Personally, I like to use as few things as possible and buy the finest ingredients I can get. It's sort of like insurance—buy the best and do the least with it.

—MARCEL DESAULIER, CHEF/COOK BOOK AUTHOR,
THE TRELLIS RESTAURANT

The successful operation of any foodservice establishment demands careful attention to many areas. One of the most critical is the selection and purchase of the foods. This chapter offers a look at the factors that should be taken into account when deciding which foods to buy.

There is a great deal more to purchasing foods than could be covered here. You will find a number of other books listed in the Recommended Readings list—found at the end of this book—that can provide more information.

Whether the purchasing is handled directly by the chef or by a separate purchasing agent, it is the chef's

responsibility to assure that all foods received and accepted are of excellent quality. They must be handled properly from the time they enter the back door, to the time they go out on a plate. You will find a good deal of information in Chapters 1 through 4 to help you make the most of one of the most precious commodities in a restaurant—the raw ingredients.

CHAPTER OBJECTIVES

- Describe the availability, quality indicators, common uses, and cooking applications for a wide variety of foods, including:

  - beef, veal, lamb, pork, and game
  - domestic poultry and game birds
  - fish and shellfish
  - fresh fruits, vegetables, and herbs
  - dairy, cheese, and eggs
  - grains, meals, flours, and dried pastas
  - dried legumes, nuts, and seeds
  - oils, shortenings, vinegars, and condiments
  - extracts, flavorings, wines, cordials, and liqueurs
  - dried herbs and spices
  - sugars, sweeteners, syrups, and chocolate
  - coffees and teas
  - leaveners and thickeners
  - frozen and convenience goods

- Name the factors taken into account when purchasing ingredients.

- Describe proper storage techniques for a variety of ingredients.

Meat Identification and Purchasing

For most restaurants, the purchase, preparation, and service of meats is one of the most expensive, as well as one of the most potentially profitable, areas of the business. In order to get the most value out of the meats purchased, it is important to understand how to select the right cut for a particular menu item.

Meat Basics

The meat, poultry, and game cuts that a restaurant should buy will depend upon the nature of the particular operation. A restaurant featuring predominantly *à la minute* preparations—especially those with a preponderance of grilled or sautéed items—will need to purchase extremely tender (and more expensive)

cuts. A restaurant that uses a variety of techniques may be able to use some less tender cut, for example, the veal shank in a braise such as osso buco.

Meats can be purchased in a number of forms, and at varying degrees of readiness to cook. The chef should consider several factors when deciding what type of meat to buy. Storage capacity, equipment required to prepare a menu item, the kitchen staff's capability to butcher, or fabricate, larger cuts, and the volume of meat required must all be taken into consideration. Once this information is evaluated, you can determine whether it is more economical to purchase large pieces, such as whole legs of veal, or prefabricated meats, such as veal already cut into a top round, or perhaps even precut *scaloppine*, which have been trimmed and cut into portions (known as "pc").

---

osso buco: braised veal shank.

FIGURE 5-1   Meats in Cryovac

FIGURE 5-2   Inspection Stamp

Storage

Meats, poultry, and game should be loosely wrapped and stored under refrigeration. When possible, they should be held in a separate unit, or at least in a separate part of the cooler. They should always be placed on trays to prevent them from dripping onto other foods or onto the floor.

The chef should separate different kinds of meats; for example, poultry should not come in contact with beef, or pork products in contact with any other meats. This will avoid cross-contamination.

Meats packed in **Cryovac**® (shown in Figure 5-1) can be stored directly in the Cryovac®, as long as it has not been punctured or ripped. Once unwrapped, meats should be rewrapped in air-permeable paper, such as butcher's paper, because airtight containers promote bacterial growth that could result in spoilage or contamination.

Meat stored at the proper temperature and under optimal conditions can be held for several days without a noticeable quality loss, although there may be some loss of volume and weight due to moisture loss. Variety meats, poultry, and un-cured pork products all have short shelf lives and should be cooked as soon as possible after they are received.

Inspection and Grading

Government inspection of all meats is mandatory. Inspections are required at various times—on the farm or ranch and at the slaughterhouse (**ante-mortem**), and, again, after butchering (**post-mortem**). This is done to assure that the animal is free from disease, and that the meat is wholesome and fit for human consumption. Inspection is a service paid for by tax dollars. (See Figure 5-2.)

Most states have relinquished the responsibility for inspecting meats to federal inspectors. Those states that still administer their own inspections of meat must at least meet, if not exceed, federal standards.

Quality grading, however, is not mandatory. The United States Department of Agriculture (**USDA**) has developed the specific standards used to assign grades to meats. The organization also trains graders. The costs involved in grading meats are absorbed by the individual meatpacker, not the taxpayer, since it is voluntary. The packer may, however, choose not to hire a USDA grader and may assign his or her own grader instead.

Depending upon the particular animal, the grader will consider the overall carcass shape, the ratio of fat to lean meat, ratio of meat to bones, color, and **marbling** of lean flesh. The grade placed on a particular carcass is then applied to all the cuts from that animal. (See Figure 5-3.) The eight USDA beef grades are Prime, Choice, Select, Standard, Commercial, Utility, Cutter, Canner. Only a small percentage of meats produced will receive the "Prime" grade. Choice and Select are more often

scallopine: a thin slice of meat.

marbling: thin strips of intramuscular fat; its presence or absence is a factor in determining a meat's quality grade.

FIGURE 5-3 USDA Grade Shield

FIGURE 5-4 USDA Yield Grade

FIGURE 5-5 Kosher Stamp

Market Forms of Meat

The obvious step after slaughtering, inspection, and grading the animal is to cut the carcass into manageable pieces. These divisions break the animal into what are referred to as **sides, quarters,** and **saddles.** Sides are prepared by making a cut down the length of the backbone. Quarters are made by cutting sides into two pieces, dividing them between specifically determined vertebrae. Saddles are made by cutting the animal across the belly, again at a specified point or vertebrae. The exact standards for individual animal types govern where the carcass is to be divided.

The next step is cutting the animal into what are referred to as **primal cuts.** There are also uniform standards for beef, veal, pork, and lamb primals. These large cuts are then further broken down into

available. Grades lower than Select are generally used for processed meat products. They are of no practical importance to the restaurant (or retail) industry.

Some meats may also receive **yield grades** (see Figure 5-4). This grade is of the greatest significance to wholesalers. It indicates the amount of salable meat in relation to the total weight of the carcass. Butchers refer to this as **"cutability."** In other words, it is a measure of the yield of edible meat from each pound of the carcass.

Table 5-1 indicates the range of quality and yield grade designations possible for beef, veal, pork, and lamb.

Kosher Meats

Kosher meats are specially slaughtered, bled, and fabricated in order to comply with religious dietary laws. In this country, only beef and veal forequarters, poultry, and some game are customarily used for kosher preparations. The stamp for kosher meats is shown in Figure 5-5. Kosher meats are butchered from animals that have been slaughtered by a scholet. The animal must be killed with a single stroke of a knife, and then fully bled. All the veins and arteries must be removed from the meat. This process would essentially mutilate the flesh of loins and legs of beef and veal; therefore, they are generally not sold as kosher meat.

TABLE 5-1			
Beef	*Veal*	*Pork*	*Lamb*
Quality grades			
Prime*	Prime*	U.S. No. 1	Prime*
Choice*	Choice*	U.S. No. 2	Choice*
Select	Good	U.S. No. 3	Good
Standard	Standard	U.S. No. 4	Utility
Commercial	Utility	U.S. Utility	Cull
Utility	Cull		
Cutter			
Canner			
Yield Grades			
1	None		1
2			2
3			3
4			4
5			5

*These grades are used widely in foodservice and retail operations. Others are used for commercial operations, processing, and canning.

scholet: a kosher slaughterer who butchers animals in accordance with kosher dietary lavs.

FIGURE 5-6 Carcass Division

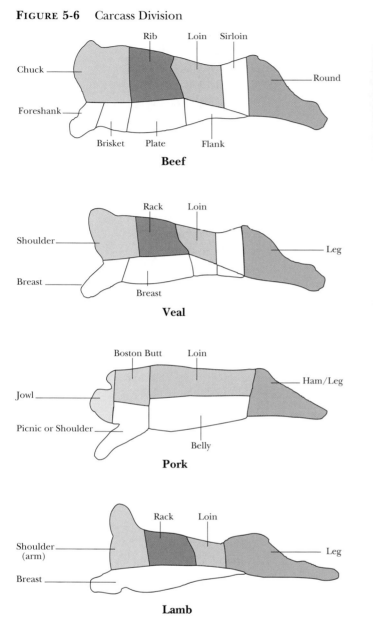

Beef

Veal

Pork

Lamb

FIGURE 5-7 Hanging Meat

While it is still possible to purchase **hanging meat,** as shown in Figure 5-7, most operations will buy what is referred to as **boxed meats.** This indicates that the meat has been fabricated to a specific point (primal, subprimal, or retail cut), then packed in Cryovac®, boxed, and shipped for sale to purveyors, butchers, chain retail outlets, and so forth.

Beef

The beef industry is of great importance to the United States. We devote nearly 600 million acres to pasture land to raising livestock. We produce more beef (and veal) than any other nation or group in the world. We also consume more on a per-capita basis than any other country in the world, with the exception of Argentina.

Special types of beef, including the Japanese "Kobe," French "Limousine," and, in this country, "Brae," "Certified Angus," "natural," "organic," and "aged" beef, are each reputed to have specific benefits. Special meats do cost more, but they also command a higher price on menus. Whenever they are used, it should be indicated on the menu, so the value is communicated clearly to the customer.

subprimals. These cuts are generally trimmed and packed. There may be even more fabrication (butchering) done in order to prepare steaks, chops, roasts, stew, or ground meat. These cuts are referred to as **retail cuts.**

As the illustrations of the cuts of beef, pork, veal, and lamb shown in Figure 5-6 indicate, the divisions follow a similar pattern, whichever animal is being butchered, with only minor variations by type.

The amount of butchering done in packing plants has increased over the past several years.

(continued on page 112)

TABLE 5-2 BEEF CHART

NAMP Item Number	Product/Cut	Weight Range (Pounds)	Suggested Cooking Method
103	Rib	28–38	roast, sauté, pan-fry, broil, grill
104	Rib, oven-prepared, regular	22–30	roast, sauté, pan-fry, broil
107	Rib, oven-prepared	19–26	roast, sauté, pan-fry, broil
107A	Rib, oven-prepared, blade bone in	19–26	roast, sauté, pan-fry, broil
109	Rib, roast ready	16–22	roast
109A	Rib, roast ready, special, tied	16–22	roast
109B	Rib, blade meat	over 3	stew, braise
109C	Rib, roast ready, cover off	15–21	roast
109D	Rib, roast ready, cover off, short cut	14–20	roast
110	Rib, roast ready, boneless, tied	13–19	roast
112	Rib, ribeye roll	6–10	roast, sauté, pan-fry, broil
112A	Rib, ribeye roll, lip-on	7–11	roast, sauté, pan-fry, broil
113	Chuck, square-cut	79–106	roast, braise, simmer
114	Chuck, shoulder clod	15–21	roast, braise, simmer
114A	Chuck, shoulder clod, roast	15–21	roast
114B	Chuck, shoulder clod, roast, tied	15–21	roast, braise
115	Chuck, square-cut, boneless	65–88	roast, braise
116B	Chuck, chuck roll, tied	15–21	roast, braise
117	Foreshank	8–12	braise, simmer
118	Brisket	14–20	braise
120	Brisket, boneless, deckle-off	8–12	braise
121	Plate, short plate	27–35	braise, cook in liquid
121C	Plate, skirt steak (diaphragm), outer	2–up	sauté, braise, grill, broil
121D	Plate, skirt steak, inner	3–up	sauté, braise, grill, broil
121E	Plate, skirt steak, skinned, outer	2–up	sauté, braise, grill, broil
123	Short ribs	3–5	braise
123A	Short plate, short ribs, trimmed	amount as specified	braise, broil, grill
123B	Rib, short ribs, trimmed	amount as specified	braise, broil, grill
123C	Rib, short ribs	amount as specified	braise, broil, grill
124	Rib, back ribs	amount as specified	braise, broil, grill
125	Chuck, armbone	88–118	braise, roast
126	Chuck, armbone, boneless (3-way)	70–90	braise, roast
126A	Chuck, armbone, boneless, clod-out	57–77	braise, roast
158	Round	71–95	roast, braise, simmer, broil, sauté, grill
158A	Round, diamond-cut	76–102	roast, braise, simmer, broil, pan-fry, sauté
159	Round, boneless	53–71	roast, braise, simmer, broil, pan-fry, sauté
160	Round, shank off, partially boneless	57–76	roast, braise, simmer, broil, pan-fry, sauté
161	Round, shank off, boneless	51–71	roast, braise, simmer, broil, pan-fry, sauté
163	Round, shank off, 3-way, boneless	50–66	roast, braise, simmer, broil, pan-fry, sauté
164	Round, rump and shank off	48–64	roast, braise, simmer, broil, pan-fry, sauté
165	Round, rump and shank off, boneless	43–57	roast, braise, simmer, broil, pan-fry, sauté
165A	Round, rump and shank off, boneless, special	46–60	roast, braise, simmer, broil, pan-fry, sauté
165B	Round, rump and shank off, boneless, special, tied	46–60	roast, braise
166	Round, rump and shank off, boneless, tied	43–57	roast, braise
166A	Round, rump partially removed, shank off, boneless, tied	52–70	roast, braise

TABLE 5-2 BEEF CHART *(continued)*

NAMP Item Number	Product/Cut	Weight Range (Pounds)	Suggested Cooking Method
166B	Round, rump and shank partially removed, handle on	52–70	roast, braise, simmer, broil, pan-broil, pan-fry, sauté
167	Round, knuckle	9–13	braise
167A	Round, knuckle, peeled	8–12	braise
167B	Round, knuckle, full	12–16	braise
169	Round, top (inside)	17–23	braise, roast
170	Round, bottom (gooseneck)	23–31	stew, braise, roast
170A	Round, bottom (gooseneck), heel out	20–28	roast, braise, simmer, broil, pan-broil, pan-fry, sauté
171	Round, bottom (gooseneck), untrimmed	21–29	roast, braise, simmer, broil, pan-broil, pan-fry, sauté
171A	Round, bottom (gooseneck) untrimmed, heel out	20–28	roast, braise, simmer, broil, pan-broil, pan-fry, sauté
171B	Round, outside round	10–16	roast, braise, simmer, broil, pan-broil, pan-fry, sauté
171C	Round, eye of round	3–up	roast, braise, simmer, broil, pan-broil, pan-fry, sauté
172	Loin, full loin, trimmed	37–52	sauté, pan-fry, broil, grill
172A	Loin, full loin, diamond cut	42–57	sauté, pan-fry, broil, pan-broil, grill
173	Loin, short loin	24–35	sauté, pan-fry, broil, pan-broil, grill
174	Loin, short loin, short-cut	20–30	sauté, pan-fry, broil, pan-broil, grill
175	Loin, strip loin	14–22	sauté, pan-fry, broil, pan-broil, grill
176	Loin, strip loin, boneless	10–14	sauté, pan-fry, broil, pan-broil, grill
179	Loin, strip loin, short-cut	10–14	sauté, pan-fry, broil, pan-broil, grill
180	Loin, strip loin, short-cut, boneless	7–11	sauté, pan-fry, broil, pan-broil, grill
181	Loin, sirloin	19–28	sauté, pan-fry, broil, pan-broil, grill
182	Loin, sirloin butt, boneless	14–19	sauté, pan-fry, broil, pan-broil, grill
183	Loin, sirloin butt, boneless, trimmed	10–15	sauté, pan-fry, broil, pan-broil, grill
184	Loin, top sirloin butt	10–14	sauté, pan-fry, broil, pan-broil, grill
185	Loin, bottom sirloin butt	6–8	sauté, pan-fry, broil, pan-broil, grill
185A	Loin, bottom sirloin butt, flap	3–up	sauté, pan-fry, broil, pan-broil, grill
185B	Loin, bottom sirloin butt, ball tip	3–up	sauté, pan-fry, broil, pan-broil, grill
185C	Loin, bottom sirloin butt, tri-tip	3–up	sauté, pan-fry, broil, pan-broil, grill
185D	Loin, bottom sirloin butt, tri-tip, defatted	3–up	sauté, pan-fry, broil, pan-broil, grill
186	Loin, bottom sirloin butt, trimmed	3–5	sauté, pan-fry, broil, pan-broil, grill
189	Loin, full tenderloin	5–7	sauté, pan-fry, broil, pan-broil, grill
189A	Loin, full tenderloin, side muscle on, defatted	4–6	sauté, pan-fry, broil, pan-broil, grill
189B	Loin, full tenderloin, side muscle on, partially defatted	4–6	sauté, pan-fry, broil, pan-broil, grill
190	Loin, full tenderloin, side muscle off, defatted	3–up	sauté, pan-fry, broil, pan-broil, grill
190A	Loin, full tenderloin, side muscle off, skinned	3–up	sauté, pan-fry, broil, pan-broil, grill
191	Loin, butt tenderloin	2–4	sauté, pan-fry, broil, pan-broil, grill
192	Loin, short tenderloin	3–up	sauté, pan-fry, broil, pan-broil, grill
193	Flank steak	1–up	braise, sauté, pan-fry, grill
134	Beef bones	amount as specified	simmer
135	Diced beef	amount as specified	braise, stew, simmer, sauté
135A	Beef for stewing	amount as specified	braise, stew, simmer, sauté
136	Ground beef	amount as specified	bake, broil, pan-broil, pan-fry, braise, sauté
136A	Ground beef and vegetable protein product	amount as specified	roast, pan-fry, sauté
136B	Beef pattie mix	amount as specified	roast, pan-fry, sauté

"Organic" and "natural" beef have not yet been clearly defined by the USDA. The terms are currently used in accordance with standards set by individual groups. "Organic" and "natural" claims do not necessarily mean that meats are free of antibiotics, steroids, or growth hormones, although that is the implication and the ultimate goal.

Aged beef was once more readily available and had greater consumer acceptance than it enjoys today. Aging is traditionally done to a number of meats, including beef, venison, and game birds. The meat is allowed to hang, uncovered, in a controlled environment such as a meat locker. The temperature and humidity are carefully monitored. Enzymes present in the meat begin to break down the meat fibers. This gives the meat a pronounced "high" flavor and increases tenderness, but at the same time, it reduces the overall yield. Some butchers still age meats, and will work with individuals to custom age meats to exact specifications.

Restaurants that feature beef, such as steak or chop houses, are an institution. Even if your restaurant only features one or two entrées based on beef, you cannot take shortcuts with this all-American commodity. Take the time to do your homework. Learn which cuts react best to which cooking methods. Get a good working knowledge of average yields from the cuts you feature on your menu. Consider the ways to maximize yield and profit without cutting into the customer's perception of dollar value. For more information refer to Table 5-2.

The Beef Primals

Primal and market cuts of beef are shown in Figures 5-8 to 5-14.

Chuck This large portion of the animal contains some of its most-exercised muscles. As a general rule, this means that cuts from the chuck will be best when prepared by one of the moist or combination cooking methods. Long, slow cooking brings out the flavor of these cuts, while softening any toughness.

In addition to cuts and steaks for braising, stewing meat and ground beef are often prepared from the chuck.

Rib The rib contains many of the most-prized roasts and steaks. These cuts are tender and well

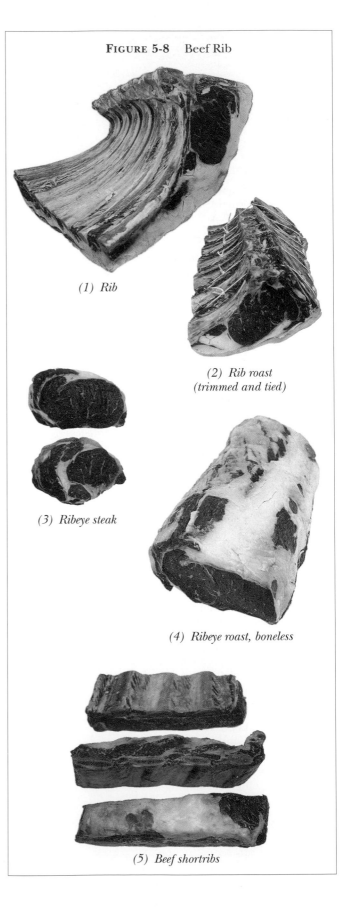

FIGURE 5-8   Beef Rib

(1) Rib

*(2) Rib roast
(trimmed and tied)*

(3) Ribeye steak

(4) Ribeye roast, boneless

(5) Beef shortribs

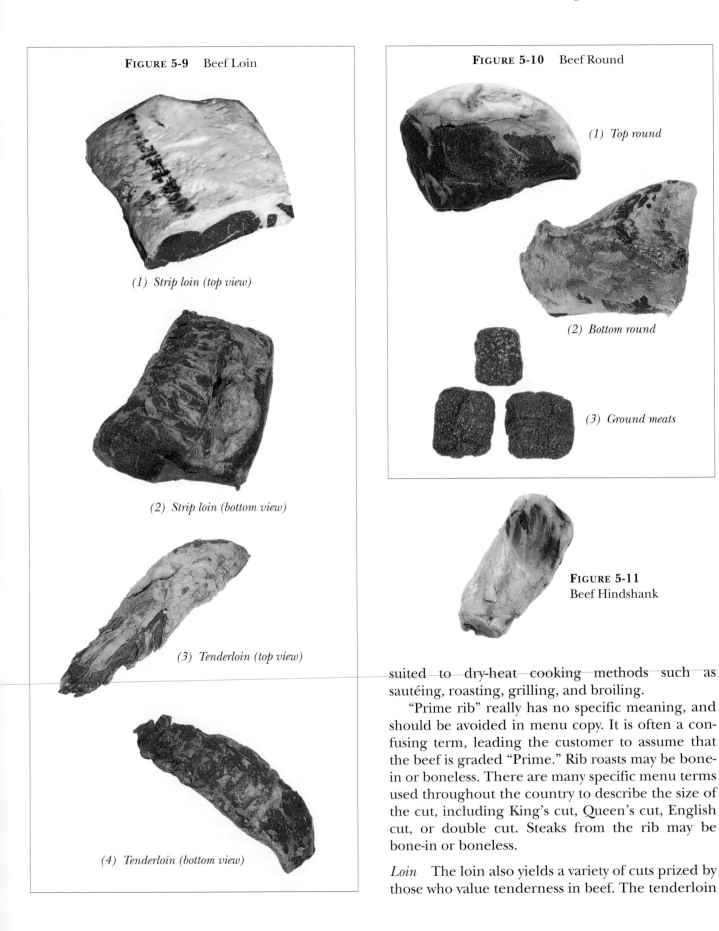

FIGURE 5-9 Beef Loin

(1) Strip loin (top view)

(2) Strip loin (bottom view)

(3) Tenderloin (top view)

(4) Tenderloin (bottom view)

FIGURE 5-10 Beef Round

(1) Top round

(2) Bottom round

(3) Ground meats

FIGURE 5-11
Beef Hindshank

suited to dry-heat cooking methods such as sautéing, roasting, grilling, and broiling.

"Prime rib" really has no specific meaning, and should be avoided in menu copy. It is often a confusing term, leading the customer to assume that the beef is graded "Prime." Rib roasts may be bone-in or boneless. There are many specific menu terms used throughout the country to describe the size of the cut, including King's cut, Queen's cut, English cut, or double cut. Steaks from the rib may be bone-in or boneless.

Loin   The loin also yields a variety of cuts prized by those who value tenderness in beef. The tenderloin

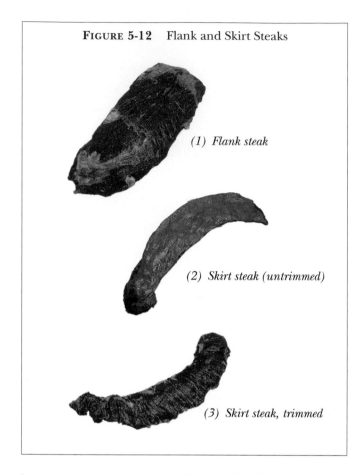

FIGURE 5-12   Flank and Skirt Steaks

(1) Flank steak

(2) Skirt steak (untrimmed)

(3) Skirt steak, trimmed

is one very important subprimal fabricated from the loin. Some terms often used in conjunction with cuts from the tenderloin include *chateaubriand, tournedos,* medallions, *filet mignon,* and tenderloin tips.

Roasts from the loin may be referred to as strip loins or New York strips. A variety of steaks are also available by fabricating the loin, or may be purchased by specification from your purveyor, allowing you to indicate weight and fat trim.

Round   This section of the animal produces a range of cuts. Some are best when braised, stewed, or simmered, while others, if handled properly, can be roasted with great success. These cuts are generally less tender than those from the rib and the loin, but there are instances when a top round or even a carefully roasted bottom round may make more sense than an expensive cut from the rib or loin. Roast beef sandwiches can be prepared from

chateaubriand: a classic French dish made by grilling a cut from the center of the tenderloin, served with an accompanying sauce and vegetable garnish.

FIGURE 5-13
Brisket

any properly cooked cut of meat. Since economics dictate that the lower your food cost the greater your margin of profit, you may want to do some tests before deciding that bottom rounds are only for pot roast.

Good-quality, lean ground meats are made from the round as well.

Shank   Both the hindshank and the foreshank are typically used for braising or stews. Shank meat is also ground and used in the clarification of consommés. (See pages 299-302 for more information.)

Flank and Skirt Steak   These cuts have become increasingly popular as more restaurants serve grilled and broiled flank and skirt steak, and as the American love affair with "barbecued" meats shows no signs of fading.

Both steaks are found along the very edge of the rib and loin portion of the animal. The fibers, though long and relatively coarse, are even. There is enough intramuscular fat to assure that the meat stays tender, as long as it is carefully sliced and not overcooked.

Brisket   Brisket may be found fresh or corned. Fresh brisket is often favored for pot roasts and other braises. It responds well to slow cooking in a sauce. Corned beef has been brined and cured with spices. It is traditionally prepared by simmering, with or without its root vegetable accompaniments. Sliced corned beef is a favorite sandwich meat.

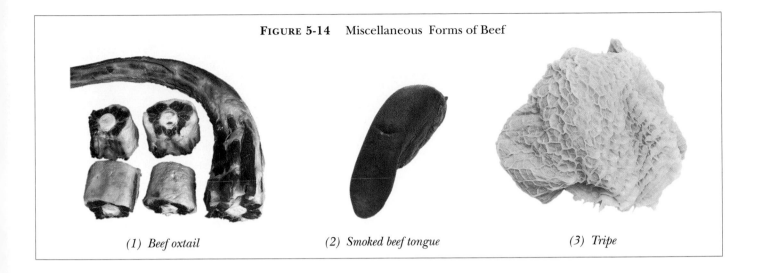

FIGURE 5-14 Miscellaneous Forms of Beef

(1) Beef oxtail   *(2) Smoked beef tongue*   *(3) Tripe*

Miscellaneous Cuts of Beef

Oxtail This intensely flavored cut is excellent in stews, soups, and braises. It may be purchased whole or as cross cuts.

Heart Fresh heart can be prepared in the same way that any muscular cut is handled—by braising or stewing. Though not a common cut of meat in many U.S. restaurants, it does have a high level of respect in many ethnic cuisines.

Liver Beef liver is darker and more deeply flavored than other livers. It, like heart, is not commonly found in many restaurants or homes. However, aficionados of liver and onions, liver pies and puddings, and other dishes can be found in this country and in others where variety meats are accorded a more welcome place on the table.

Tongue Tongue is available fresh, smoked, or cured. Japan and other Asian countries esteem tongue highly, making it more difficult to obtain in this country than it used to be. This cut is best prepared by simmering in a flavored court bouillon or broth, and is often served "pickled" or with sharply flavored sauces. Sliced tongue sandwiches are a deli specialty, where its leanness and unique texture shine.

brine: a solution of salt, water, and seasonings used to preserve foods.

cure: to preserve food by salting, smoking, and/or drying.

Tripe Tripe is the edible lining of the first and second stomachs of a cow. The type of tripe most often found is referred to as "honeycomb" tripe. One of the most famous recipes for this meat is *tripes à la mode de Caen*, which is a long-cooked, braise, finished with Calvados, an apple brandy produced in Normandy.

Veal

Considered by some to be the finest meat available, veal is more an offshoot of the dairy industry than a commodity raised specifically as veal. Dairy cows must be bred in order to produce milk. Once the calves are born, they are generally separated from their mothers and raised to a specific age. The practices used in raising veal for slaughter have been cause for concern among many individuals. This issue is outside the scope of this book, and is more a matter for individual conscience.

Fine veal is known as "milk-fed" or "nature-fed." Calves who never receive grain, grass, or more adult feed have finely textured meat with a pale pink color. Because the overall ratio of meat to bone is less than it would be in a full-grown heifer or steer, there are proportionately fewer cuts of veal.

Veal, like beef, may be split into two parts, known as the fore and hind quarters. Alternatively, it may be cut into a foresaddle and a hindsaddle, which is accomplished by splitting the carcass at a point between the eleventh and twelfth ribs.

TABLE 5-3 VEAL CHART

NAMP Item Number	Product/Cut	Weight Range (Pounds)	Suggested Cooking Method
304	Foresaddle, 11 ribs	44–86	roast, pan-fry
306	Hotel rack, 7 ribs	9–14	roast, pan-fry
307	Rack, ribeye	3–5	roast, pan-fry
308	Chuck, 4 ribs	40–70	braise, roast
309	Chuck, square-cut	20–36	braise, roast
309B	Chuck, square cut, boneless	19–33	braise, roast
309D	Chuck, square-cut, neck off, boneless, tied	18–32	braise, roast, pan-fry
310	Chuck, shoulder clod	4–7	braise, roast, pan-fry
310A	Chuck, shoulder clod, special	4–7	braise, roast
310B	Chuck, shoulder clod roast	4–7	braise, roast, pan-fry
310C	Chuck, Scotch tender	$\frac{1}{2}$–1	braise
311	Chuck, square-cut, clod out, boneless, tied	18–32	braise, roast
312	Foreshank	2–4	braise, simmer
313	Breast	6–10	braise, roast
314	Breast with pocket	6–10	braise, roast
330	Hindsaddle, 2 ribs	50–88	braise, roast, pan-fry, broil, grill
331	Loin	10–18	braise, roast
332	Loin, trimmed	8–14	braise, roast, pan-fry, broil, grill
344	Loin, strip loin, boneless	3–6	braise, roast, pan-fry, broil, grill
344A	Loin, strip loin, boneless, special	2–5	braise, roast, pan-fry, broil, grill
346	Loin, butt tenderloin	1–1 $\frac{1}{2}$	roast, pan-fry, broil, grill
346A	Loin, butt tenderloin, skinned	$\frac{1}{2}$–1	roast, pan-fry, broil, grill
347	Loin, short tenderloin	$\frac{1}{2}$–1	roast, pan-fry, broil, grill
334	Leg	40–70	roast, braise, pan-fry, broil
335	Leg, boneless, roast ready, tied	15–26	roast, braise
336	Leg, shank off, boneless, roast ready, tied	11–19	roast, braise
337	Hindshank	2–4	braise, simmer
338	Shank, osso buco	1–3	braise, simmer
341	Back, 9 ribs, trimmed	15–25	braise, roast, pan-fry
348	Leg, TBS, 4 parts	24–32	pan-fry, sauté, broil, grill
348A	Leg, TBS, 3 parts	16–24	pan-fry, sauté, broil, grill
349	Leg, top round, cap on	8–12	roast, braise, pan-fry, sauté, broil
349A	Leg, top round, cap off	6–8	roast, braise, pan-fry, sauté, broil
395	Veal for stewing	amount as specified	stew, simmer
396	Ground veal	amount as specified	roast, pan-fry, sauté

Veal Primals and Market Forms

The primal cuts for veal are the shoulder (chuck), rack (rib), loin, and leg. Organ meats (**offal**) from veal are highly prized, especially the sweetbreads, liver, calf's head, and brains. A number of primal and market cuts are shown in Figures 5-15 to 5-21. Refer also to Table 5-3 for additional information.

FIGURE 5-15   Veal Shoulder Roast

FIGURE 5-16   Veal Hindshank

Shoulder (Chuck)   Cuts from this primal may be handled in the same way that beef chuck cuts are used. Stew meat and ground meat are commonly fabricated from less-desirable cuts, or the trim from roasts used for braises.

Veal Shank   The veal hindshank is most commonly available, though it may be possible to procure the foreshank as well. The hindshank is generally meatier, and typically braised. *Osso bucco* is one of the most famous dishes made from the shank. There are many regional variations on this dish.

Rib   The rib may be roasted whole (bone-in or as a boneless rolled roast). Portion-size cuts from the rib are referred to as "chops." The rib bones may be left attached and are generally "frenched."

Loin   The loin of veal is one of the most-expensive and prized portions of the veal. Chops, medallions, and roasts are all easily prepared from the loin. Tenderloins of veal may also be fabricated from this cut.

Leg   The leg yields numerous cuts, perhaps the most familiar of which is the cutlet. Veal cutlets fabricated from the top round have the best texture and cook the most evenly. It is possible to make cutlets from other areas of the leg, including the bottom round. Some butchers may even make them from the chuck, but they are not suitable for sautéing or pan-frying.

Veal legs may be purchased whole and then broken down into their various components in-house. This offers the chef a good bit of flexibility, but re-

FIGURE 5-17   Veal Rack

FIGURE 5-18   Veal Loin

quires some knowledge of meat-cutting techniques. The general instruction given is to follow the natural seams in the meat, which separate one large muscle group from another. The meat is cut and scraped from the bone. If an operation is capable of butchering a leg of veal, the initial cost per pound is less than when smaller roasts or portion-size cuts are purchased. There is also a greater opportunity to control costs through the use of lean trim and bones in other preparations.

---

sweetbreads: the thymus gland.

frenched: the bone has been scraped free of all meat, cartilage, and sinew.

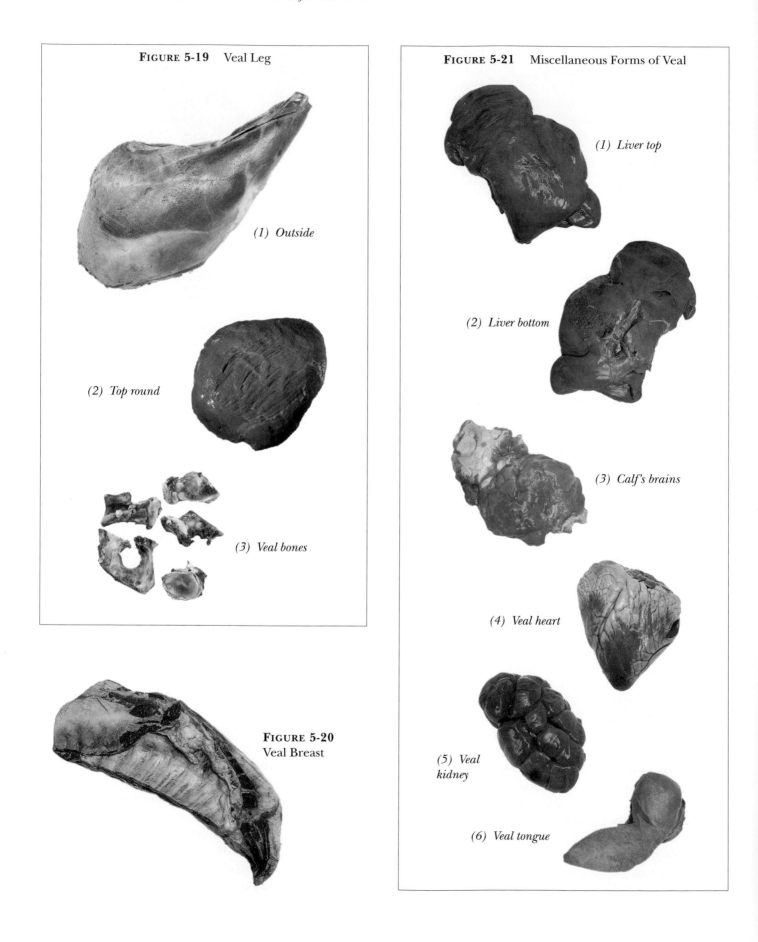

FIGURE 5-19   Veal Leg

(1) Outside

(2) Top round

(3) Veal bones

FIGURE 5-20
Veal Breast

FIGURE 5-21   Miscellaneous Forms of Veal

(1) Liver top

(2) Liver bottom

(3) Calf's brains

(4) Veal heart

(5) Veal kidney

(6) Veal tongue

There are many names for cutlets, and they vary from one cuisine to another: scallops (English term), *scaloppine* (Italian term), *escalope* (French term) are some of the more familiar. A cutlet that has been pounded and then cooked is sometimes referred to on the menu as a *paillard*.

Breast Veal breast is often prepared as a bone-in roast or as a rolled-and-tied boneless roast. There are also boned, butterflied, stuffed, and rolled preparations. Long cooking methods, such as braising, are best for this cut.

Organ Meats/Variety Meats Veal or calf's liver, tongue, and bones are among those most familiar and frequently used in American kitchens. Sweetbreads, brains, and heart can also be found. A relatively small proportion of the public is interested in these specialty items. However, menus that draw from regions of the world where such cuts have greater acceptance than in this country may find that the clientele they serve will order them.

Many of these items are so popular in other countries that it has become increasingly difficult to find them in the United States.

Cooking methods for these cuts vary: Sweetbreads are generally poached and then prepared in a sauce or used as a garnish in forcemeats. Brains may be cooked *à la meunière* or prepared, as in a classic French dish, with scrambled eggs. Tongue is generally simmered until tender, then sliced; it may also be pickled or smoked. Heart is braised. Veal bones and feet are excellent for preparing stocks and foundation sauces.

Pork

Pigs were once raised by city dwellers and farmers alike. These animals tended not to require penning or extensive acreage. They would forage for feed. Those days are gone, at least in this society. We have rules and codes regarding how livestock is raised, slaughtered, and butchered. These regulations have as their primary goal the protection of the public health.

Today, pork is among the most popular meats sold in the United States, despite growing concerns over health issues related to meats perceived as high in fat and cholesterol. Pigs have been specifically bred over many generations in order to produce leaner meat cuts. They are slaughtered and butchered in facilities that handle no other type of meat, to prevent the spread of disease and infection, such as trichinosis. (See page 40 for more information.) Chefs and consumers alike are more conscious of how to handle pork to avoid food-borne illnesses. While beef remains the number one favorite meat in restaurants across the country, pork continues to grow in popularity as dishes that showcase its special qualities take their place on menus. Barbecued spareribs, tender chops and cutlets, and a range of smoked and cured meats are common menu items today.

Pigs were once commonly slaughtered in the late fall. The meat was used to make a number of items that were specially handled to assure that they would last through the winter, providing some meat during the colder months. These traditional processed, cured, and brined pork cuts are still popular today.

We continue to enjoy such items, primarily because we like the taste. This change in emphasis, from food-storage needs to simple enjoyment, has encouraged some modification in processing methods, resulting in hams, sausage, bacon, and other items that contain fewer additives and preservatives.

Purchasing agents, chefs, and consumers alike will seldom see the inspection stamps or grading shields often found on beef, veal, or lamb. There are several reasons for this. The inspection stamp is applied to the carcass before it is cut into wholesale and retail cuts. With pork, trimming and cutting generally removes the stamp. Quality grades are less frequently assigned to pork than other meats. Packers will often use their own grading system, instead of paying for federal graders to be on hand. This does not necessarily mean that you cannot be certain that various cuts of pork will have good quality. The grading systems used by major packers are clearly defined and are generally reliable.

Pork Primals and Market Forms

The pork carcass, once split into two halves along the backbone, is divided in a slightly different

---

à la meunière: fish that has been seasoned, floured, and sauteed in butter. (See pages 350-355 for more information)

TABLE 5-4 PORK CHART

NAMP Item Number	Product/Cut	Weight Range (Pounds)	Suggested Cooking Method
401	Fresh ham	17–26	roast, braise, simmer, broil, pan-fry
401A	Fresh ham, short shank	17–26	roast, braise, simmer, broil, pan-fry
402	Fresh ham, skinned	17–26	roast, braise, simmer, broil, pan-fry
402A	Fresh ham, skinned, short shank	17–26	roast, braise, simmer, broil, pan-fry
402B	Fresh ham, boneless, tied	8–12	roast, braise
402C	Fresh ham, boneless, trimmed, tied	8–12	roast, braise
402D	Fresh ham, outside, tied	6–12	roast, braise
402E	Fresh ham, outside, trimmed, tied	6–up	roast, braise
403	Shoulder	12–20	roast, braise, simmer, broil, pan-broil, pan-fry
404	Shoulder, skinned	12–20	roast, braise, simmer, broil, pan-broil, pan-fry
405A	Shoulder, picnic, boneless	4–8	roast, braise, simmer
405B	Shoulder, picnic, cushion, boneless	amount as specified	roast, braise, simmer
406	Shoulder, Boston butt	4–up	roast, braise, simmer, broil, pan-fry
406A	Shoulder, Boston butt, boneless	4–up	roast, braise, simmer, broil, pan-fry
407	Shoulder butt, cellar-trimmed, boneless	3–7	roast, braise, simmer, broil, pan-fry
408	Belly	12–18	sauté, pan-fry, simmer
409	Belly, skinless	9–13	sauté, pan-fry, simmer
410	Loin	14–22	roast, braise, pan-fry
411	Loin, bladeless	14–22	sauté, pan-fry, simmer
412	Loin, center cut, 8 ribs	6–10	roast, braise, pan-fry

manner from most other meats. Instead of a primal rib, the loin is cut long. This is done to maximize the number of cuts possible from the prized loin. However, chops cut from the "rib" end are generally indicated as rib chops. Those from the leg end may be referred to a "sirloin" chops. Various primals and market cuts are shown in Figures 5-22 to 5-26. Refer also to Table 5-4 for additional information.

The Shoulder or Butt   Roasts, stew meat and ground pork are often made from this primal and the subprimals it produces. The ratio of fat to lean meat is somewhat higher than in other portions on the animal. This makes it highly desirable for use in sausages and other items prepared by the charcutière. For more information, refer to Chapter 11 and recipes that can be found in Part IV, Chapter 27 of this book.

There are many regional names given to cuts from the shoulder, including daisy ham, picnic ham (or butt). Because of the greater abundance of fat in these cuts, it is possible to roast them with some success. However, they are generally best for stewing and braising.

FIGURE 5-22
Boston Butt

charcutière: the cook who prepares items such as terrines, sausages, and pâtés.

TABLE 5-4 PORK CHART *(continued)*

NAMP Item Number	Product/Cut	Weight Range (Pounds)	Suggested Cooking Method
412A	Loin, center cut, 8 ribs, chine bone off	5–9	roast, braise, pan-fry, sauté, grill
412B	Loin, center cut, 8 ribs, boneless	4–6	roast, braise, pan-fry, sauté, grill
412C	Loin, center cut, 11 ribs	7–11	roast, braise, pan-fry, sauté, grill
412D	Loin, center cut, 11 ribs, chine bone off	6–10	roast, braise, pan-fry, sauté, grill
412E	Loin, center cut, 11 ribs, boneless	5–7	roast, braise, pan-fry, sauté, grill
413	Loin, boneless	8–12	roast, braise, pan-fry, sauté, grill
413A	Loin, boneless, tied	8–12	roast, braise
413B	Loin, boneless, tied, special	8–12	roast, braise
414	Loin, Canadian back	4–6	roast, braise, pan-fry
415	Tenderloin	1–up	roast, braise, pan-fry, sauté, grill
415A	Tenderloin, side muscle off	1–up	roast, braise, pan-fry, sauté, grill
416	Spareribs	2 ½–5 ½	braise, smoke, broil, grill
416A	Spareribs, St. Louis style	2–3	braise, smoke, broil, grill
416B	Spareribs, breast bones	½–¾	braise, smoke, broil, grill
417	Shoulder hocks	¾–up	braise, simmer
418	Trimmings	amount as specified	braise, simmer
420	Pig's feet, front		simmer
421	Neck bones	amount as specified	simmer
422	Loin, back ribs	1 ½–2 ¼	braise, broil, grill
423	Loin, country-style ribs	3–up	braise, broil, grill
435	Diced pork	amount as specified	braise, simmer, saute
496	Ground pork	amount as specified	roast, sauté, pan-fry

FIGURE 5-23 Pork Loin

(1) Pork loin

(2) Center cut pork chops

(3) Pork chops from arm, center, and leg section

(4) Pork tenderloin (bottom view)

FIGURE 5-24   The Ham

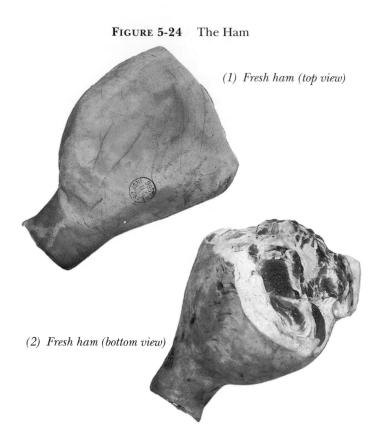

(1) Fresh ham (top view)

(2) Fresh ham (bottom view)

FIGURE 5-25   Spareribs

The Loin   This is the second largest primal cut from the pig. It is intentionally cut longer than the loins for beef, veal, or lamb. The loin is often roasted, bone-in or boneless. One rather impressive cut produced from the rib portion of the loin is a crown roast of pork. This is occasionally prepared for banquet service. The roast may be stuffed before it is roasted.

Cuts from the loin include chops of various thickness. The composition of the chop varies greatly from one end of the loin to the other. Boneless cutlets are also prepared from the loin. They are generally sautéed, grilled, or broiled. Thick chops are often stuffed and baked. Chops from the shoulder end of the loin may be braised.

The tenderloin, a prized subprimal of the loin, is widely available. Noisettes and medallions are often fashioned from the tenderloin. These cuts are sautéed, grilled, or broiled.

A boneless smoked loin (sometimes referred to in the United States as Canadian bacon) is also popular. One of its classic uses is as a component of eggs Benedict. (See below for more information about bacon, salt pork, and other cured pork products.)

The Ham (Leg)   This primal cut is often referred to as the ham, regardless of whether or not it has been cured. Fresh pork roasts or hams are quite different in flavor and texture from cured hams.

Ham steaks (available fresh, cured, or smoked) are also available, and are popular breakfast items as well as having a place on lunch and dinner menus.

Cured or smoked hams occasionally are fully cooked and ready-to-eat. These items may often benefit from simmering, or they may be roasted to enhance tenderness and flavor. Others, including such hams as prosciutto and Smithfield, need not be cooked after curing. They are often simply sliced thinly and used "as is." Or they may be used as a special flavoring ingredient in pasta dishes, appetizers, or other preparations.

Stew meat and ground pork are also cut from lean trim produced when smaller cuts are fabricated from this primal.

Spareribs   Spareribs are similar to beef short ribs, breast of veal, and breast of lamb. This cut has more bone than meat, but it is immensely popular throughout the country. Other cuisines have also developed trademark preparations that feature this particular cut. Spareribs are sold whole or cut into portions. Baby-back ribs and country-style ribs are also available.

Cured Pork and Pork "By-Products"   It has often been said that you can use everything on the pig except the oink. Even in our society, where we tend to prefer recognizable cuts such as roasts, chops, and

---

eggs Benedict: poached eggs with a toasted English muffin, sliced Canadian bacon, and hollandaise.

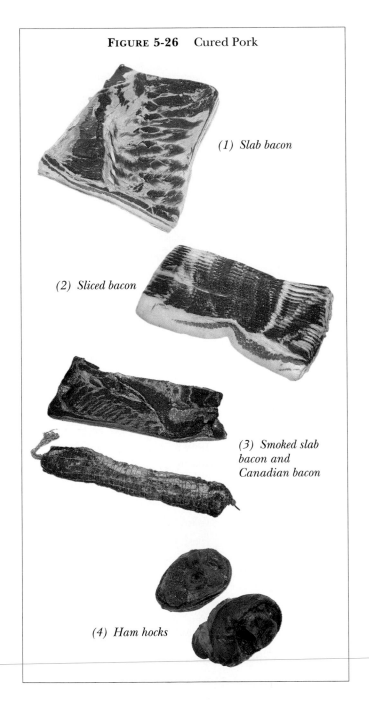

FIGURE 5-26 Cured Pork

(1) Slab bacon

(2) Sliced bacon

(3) Smoked slab bacon and Canadian bacon

(4) Ham hocks

along the animal's back. It is referred to as clear fat to distinguish it from the belly, sometimes known as "streak of lean," an apt description of bacon's composition. Jowl bacon is not well-suited for cooking as strips, but is excellent for use as a cooking or flavoring ingredient.

Ham hocks, pig's feet and knuckles, and even snouts are used to produce a variety of regional and ethnic dishes. These items are available fresh, cured, and smoked. They are often simmered, and are traditionally paired with "peasant" foods including beans and greens, for soups and stews.

Liver, heart, and kidneys are sometimes available, but their use is limited both by availability and consumer acceptance.

Lamb and Mutton

Lamb has grown in popularity over the last several years, and the impression that it will have a "sheepy" flavor is fading fast because of improved methods for breeding, raising, and feeding sheep. Improved breeding techniques mean that the availability of lamb is no longer limited only to the spring (the traditional time for "lambing" or "dropping young").

Because the lamb is slaughtered when still quite young, it is almost completely tender, and most cuts can be cooked by any method. Spring lamb and hot-house lamb are not fed grass or grain because once the lamb begins to eat grass, the flesh loses some of its delicacy. As the animal ages, the flesh will darken in color, take on a slightly coarser texture, and have a much more pronounced flavor. Sheep slaughtered under the age of a year may still be labeled lamb; if slaughtered after that, however, they must be labeled yearling. Sheep slaughtered after two years of age must be labeled mutton.

Like veal, lamb is also cut into a foresaddle and hindsaddle and may also be cut into sides. The major lamb cuts are: rib (known also as rack), square-cut shoulder, breast, shank, loin, and leg. Various lamb cuts are shown in Figures 5-27 to 5-30 and described in Table 5-5.

steaks, we enjoy a number of specialty items produced from the pig.

Bacon is made by curing and/or smoking the belly. This classic breakfast item may be sold as slab bacon, with or without the rind, or sliced. Special types of bacon are produced by different cuisines, including *pancetta* among others.

Fatback, used for larding, barding, and lining pâté and terrine molds, comes from the "clear fat"

larding: the insertion of long, thin strips of fat into a dry cut of meat to make it more succulent during cooking.

barding: to cover an item with slabs of fat so that it bastes itself as it cooks.

TABLE 5-5 LAMB CHART

NAMP Item Number	Product/Cut	Weight Range (Pounds)	Suggested Cooking Method
204	Rack	5–9	roast, grill, broil, pan-fry
204A	Rack, roast-ready, single	2–4	roast, grill, broil, pan-fry
204B	Rack, roast-ready, single, frenched	2–4	roast, grill, broil, pan-fry
204C	Rack, roast-ready, single, frenched, special	1 ½–3 ½	roast, grill, broil, pan-fry
206	Shoulders	19–27	roast, grill, broil, pan-fry
207	Shoulders, square-cut	13–19	roast, grill, broil, braise, pan-fry
208	Shoulder, square-cut, boneless, tied		roast, braise
209	Breast	7–11	braise, simmer, broil, grill
209A	Ribs, Denver-style	5–9	braise, simmer, broil, grill
210	Foreshank	2–3	braise, simmer
230	Hindsaddle	27–38	roast, braise, grill, sauté
231	Loins	8–12	roast, grill, broil, pan-fry, sauté
232	Loins, trimmed	5–9	roast, grill, broil, pan-fry, sauté
232A	Loins, short-cut, trimmed	3–7	roast, grill, broil, pan-fry, sauté
232B	Loins, double, boneless, tied	2–5	roast
233	Legs	19–27	roast, braise, grill, broil, pan-broil, pan-fry, sauté
233A	Leg, lower shank off, single	9–14	roast, grill, broil, pan-fry
233B	Leg, boneless, tied	8–13	roast
233C	Leg, shank off, single	4–7	roast
233E	Leg, hind shank	1–up	roast, braise
233F	Leg, hind shank, heel on	1–up	roast, braise
234	Leg, lower shank off, partially boneless	6–9	roast, braise
234A	Leg, shank off, single, partially boneless	8–11	roast, braise
234B	Leg, shank off, boneless, tied	8–11	roast, braise
236	Back, trimmed	11–15	braise, pan-fry
238	Hindsaddle, long-cut, trimmed	29–41	roast, grill, broil, pan-fry, sauté
295	Lamb for stewing	amount as specified	stew, braise, simmer
295A	Lamb for kebobs	amount as specified	roast, broil, grill
296	Ground lamb	amount as specified	roast, pan-fry
240	Leg, ¾, single	7–11	roast
241	Leg, steamship	6–10	roast
245	Sirloin, boneless	2–4	pan-fry, sauté

Venison and Large, Furred Game

Fallow deer (a farm-raised deer) produces a lean, tasty meat with less fat and cholesterol than beef. The loin and the rib are quite tender and can be suitable for most cooking techniques, especially roasting, grilling, and sautéing. The haunch and legs are more exercised, and are best when prepared by moist-heat or combination techniques. (See Figures 5-31 to 5-33.)

Depending upon the area of the country, other types of game—including wild boar, elk, and bear—

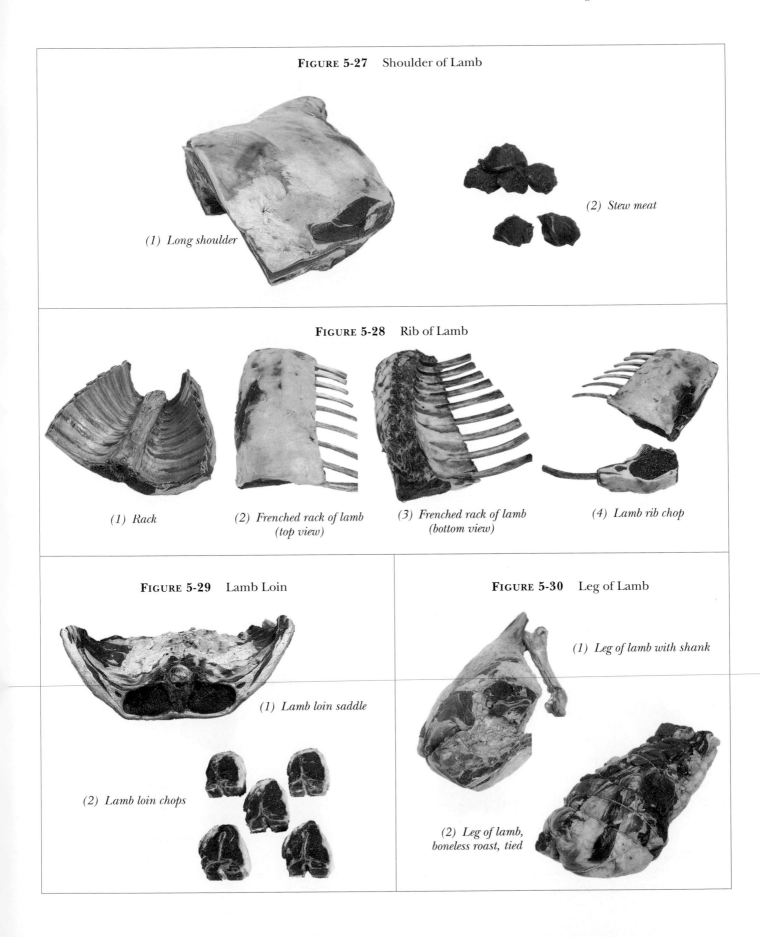

FIGURE 5-27 Shoulder of Lamb

(1) Long shoulder

(2) Stew meat

FIGURE 5-28 Rib of Lamb

(1) Rack

(2) Frenched rack of lamb (top view)

(3) Frenched rack of lamb (bottom view)

(4) Lamb rib chop

FIGURE 5-29 Lamb Loin

(1) Lamb loin saddle

(2) Lamb loin chops

FIGURE 5-30 Leg of Lamb

(1) Leg of lamb with shank

(2) Leg of lamb, boneless roast, tied

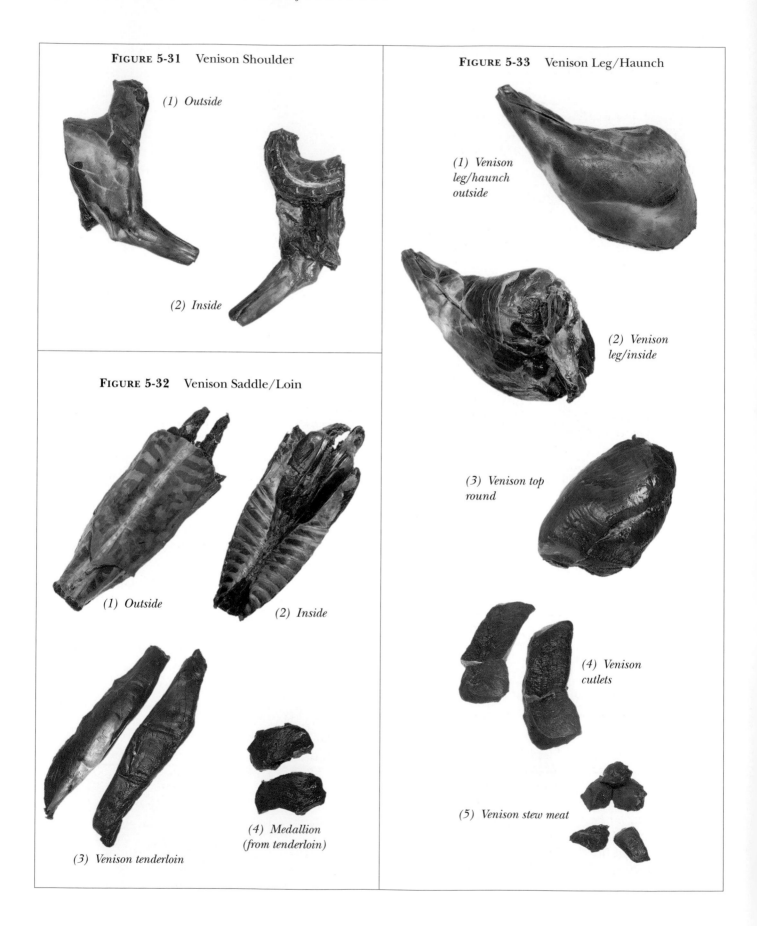

FIGURE 5-31   Venison Shoulder

(1) Outside

(2) Inside

FIGURE 5-32   Venison Saddle/Loin

(1) Outside

(2) Inside

(3) Venison tenderloin

(4) Medallion (from tenderloin)

FIGURE 5-33   Venison Leg/Haunch

(1) Venison leg/haunch outside

(2) Venison leg/inside

(3) Venison top round

(4) Venison cutlets

(5) Venison stew meat

may also be available. The same general rules that determine how to cook a red meat cut will work for these meats:

- Cuts from less-exercised portions of the animal may be prepared by any technique and are frequently paired with dry-heat methods, such as grilling or roasting.

- Well-exercised areas of the animal, such as the leg (or haunch), shank, and shoulder are best when cooked by moist-heat or combination methods. These cuts are also used for preparing pâtés and other charcuterie items.

Rabbit

Rabbit, raised domestically, is available throughout the year. The loin meat is delicate in flavor and color, and has a tendency to dry out if not handled carefully. Traditional preparation methods include roasting, braising, and "jugging," which preserves the meat by cooking and storing it in fat. The loin and legs are often prepared by two separate techniques—the loin is roasted or sautéed and the legs, which are more exercised, are cooked by stewing or braising. (See Figure 5-34.)

Poultry and Game Birds

As better rearing methods have been perfected, chicken, once reserved for special occasions, and other poultry have become commonplace in restaurants and homes. Poultry production is now a big business, with breeding, care, and feeding all scientifically controlled.

Today, chicken, turkey, and game birds can be found sold as **free-range,** and/or "organic." Just as these terms may not have a precise meaning when applied to beef, they are equally unclear in relation to the methods used to raise poultry. Some chefs are inclined to prefer birds raised in a free-range environment. There is a greater likelihood that these birds have been allowed at least some exercise in a lot, rather than spending their entire lives in a cage. They may be allowed to forage for some of their feed but, most likely, a commercial operation of any size will need to more carefully regulate the

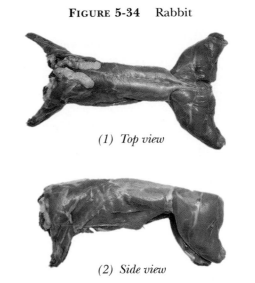

FIGURE 5-34   Rabbit

(1) Top view

(2) Side view

care and feeding of birds intended for sale to the public. This means that feed formulas will be prepared, and certain health precautions including immunizations and treatment with antibiotics are necessary. Organically raised birds may be free of chemically produced growth enhancers or steroids, but it is important to ask questions about any product you buy that is sold to you as either "natural" or "organic."

Poultry, like other meats, must undergo a mandatory inspection for wholesomeness. It may be graded as USDA A, B, or C. The following factors determine the grade: shape of the carcass; ratio of meat to bone; freedom from pinfeathers, hair, and down; and number (if any) of tears, cuts, or broken bones.

After post-mortem inspection, the birds are plucked, cleaned, chilled, and packaged. (See Figures 5-35 and 5-36.) They can be purchased whole or in parts. The younger the bird, the more tender its flesh. As birds age, their flesh toughens, and the cartilage in the breast hardens. The windpipe and bill of ducks and geese will also harden.

Poultry is classified by size and age (maturity). (See Table 5-6.)

Chicken

Chicken is usually available as broilers, fryers, or roasters. Very small chicken, or baby chicken, is sometimes available, and may be referred to as

TABLE 5-6 POULTRY CLASSIFICATION

Name	Description	Weight
Rock Cornish game hen	Very tender, suitable for all cooking techniques	¾–2 pounds
Broiler	Very tender, suitable for all cooking techniques	1 ½–2 pounds
Fryer	Very tender, suitable for all cooking techniques	2 ½–3 ½ pounds
Roaster	Very tender, suitable for all cooking techniques	3 ½–5 pounds
Stewing hen*	Mature female bird, requires slow, moist cooking	3 ½–6 pounds
Capon	Very tender, usually roasted or poêléed	5–8 pounds
Young hen or tom turkey	Very tender, suitable for all cooking techniques	8–22 pounds
Yearling turkey	Fully mature but still tender, usually roasted	10–30 pounds
Broiler or fryer duckling	Very tender, usually roasted, but suitable for most techniques	2–4 pounds
Roaster duckling	Tender, usually roasted	4–6 pounds
Young goose or gosling	Tender, usually roasted	6–10 pounds
Guinea hen or fowl	Related to pheasant; tender, suitable for most techniques	¾–1 ½ pounds
Squab (domestic pigeon that has not begun to fly)	Light, tender meat, suitable for sauté, roast, grill; as bird ages, the meat darkens and toughens	under 1 pound

*Note: Very mature turkeys, ducks, and geese are also available, though not listed here; they are tough, with hardened cartilage and windpipes.

poussin. These birds are sold whole or as parts. They may be roasted, grilled, broiled, baked in pieces, sautéed, pan-fried, or deep-fried.

Stewing hens or fowls are more mature and are best simmered, stewed, or braised. They are excellent for soups.

Chicken feet and cock's combs, though difficult to obtain, are traditional elements in stocks and soups, providing excellent flavor and body.

Chicken livers, gizzards, hearts, backs, and necks are also sold and have various applications in the kitchen. *Schmaltz,* or rendered chicken fat, is also available, and is an important component in kosher cooking.

Cornish Game Hen/Rock Cornish Game Hen

These birds are the result of careful breeding. They are small, relatively plump birds. There is more breast meat, in relation to their overall size and composition, than dark or leg meat.

Turkey

Benjamin Franklin made a strong case for endorsing the turkey as the national bird for the United States. This large bird has gained in popularity over the years, and turkey products are finding their way onto the menu year-round, instead of only at Thanksgiving.

Turkeys are classified as either young hen or tom, or mature hen or tom birds. In general, the meat-to-bone ratio is best at weights over 12 pounds.

Turkey is increasingly available as parts: breast with neck and back attached, boneless breast meat, legs only, even portion-cut scallops or cutlets. Turkey has a more distinct flavor than chicken. The

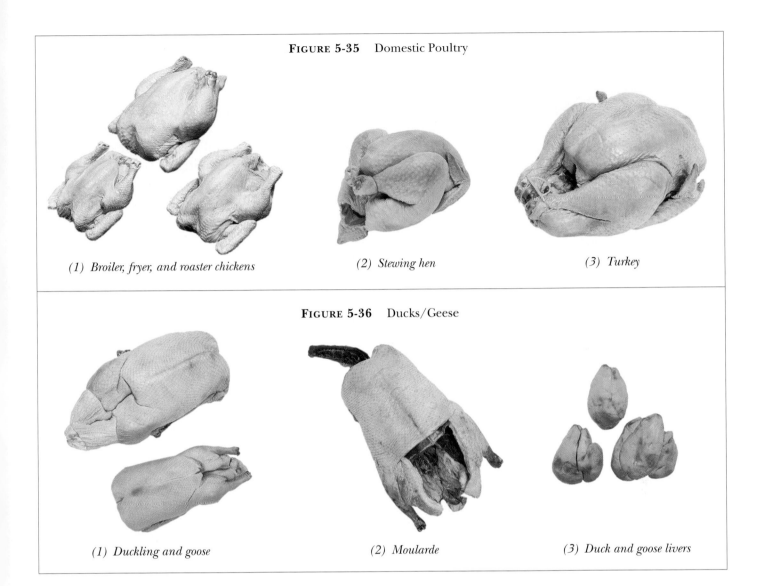

FIGURE 5-35   Domestic Poultry

(1) Broiler, fryer, and roaster chickens   *(2) Stewing hen*   *(3) Turkey*

FIGURE 5-36   Ducks/Geese

(1) Duckling and goose   *(2) Moularde*   *(3) Duck and goose livers*

traditional turkey club or sandwich remains popular on all menus.

Wild turkey is infrequently available through special purveyors. It must meet certain health and safety standards in order to be sold legally in restaurants. If you are unsure, contact your local health department for more information.

Ducks and Geese   Ducklings (ducks under one year of age) are generally roasted. Full-grown ducks may be roasted, but are also braised, stewed, or made into confit. Peking, Long Island, moularde, and muscovy duck constitute the breeds commonly found in this country.

It is possible to purchase duck parts, including breasts, legs, and liver. The breast is often sautéed, grilled, or pan-seared. Legs are typically slow roasted or braised. The fattened liver of the moularde duck known as **foie gras** is produced commercially in this country, making it more readily available as a fresh product. Foie gras shrinks when cooked, so great care should be taken to sauté it correctly. It is also used in a variety of sausages, gratins, and other charcuterie preparations.

Geese are referred to a goslings when young. These birds are generally suited to roasting. Geese over one year old may be better stewed or braised.

---

confit: meat cooked and preserved in its own fat.

FIGURE 5-37   Game Birds (Pheasant, Squab, and Quails)

Wild Game Birds

Traditionally, chefs could obtain most game birds only during the hunting season, usually late fall and early winter. Today, game birds are raised on farms year-round. However, many game birds, especially those allowed "free range," will still be at their best from October through December or January. Game birds are technically "wild" species. This means that while they may be farm-raised, their characteristics are usually not reproductively controlled. (See Figure 5–37.)

Young fowl should have soft, smooth, pliable skin. The breastbone cartilage should be flexible, as it is for domestic fowl. The flesh should be tender, with a slight "gamy" taste. The types of game birds most often used today in cooking are the following:

Quail   The smallest of the game birds, these are traditionally spit-roasted, poêléed, or poached.

Snipe/Woodcock   The snipe is available in three sizes: large, common, and small, and traditionally has been considered by gourmets to be one of the finest of all game birds.

Wild Duck   Teal, a small duck, is considered a delicacy. As wild duck ages, the flesh may take on a fishy or oily taste.

Pheasant   One of the meatiest of all game birds, pheasant may be roasted or braised. Domestically raised pheasant will not have a pronounced gamy flavor.

Fish and Shellfish

Fish were once plentiful and inexpensive, but due to various factors, including nutritional concerns, pollution of fishing beds, and the search for variety, demand has begun to outstrip supply. At this time, regulations have been passed by a number of countries, restricting commercial fishing to an ever smaller percentage of such renowned fishing waters as the Grand Banks and St. George's Bay. No one can be certain how long it will take for the great fishing banks to replenish themselves, if in fact they ever do.

What this means to most chefs and consumers is that longtime menu favorites, including cod, tuna, bluefish, true striped bass, and red snapper, are increasingly unavailable. **Aquaculture,** or fish farming, is growing in importance as it becomes an increasingly reliable source of fresh fish. Today, hybrid striped bass, trout, salmon, halibut, snails, tilapia, catfish, oysters, mussels, and clams are more easily found because they are farm raised.

Fish's dietary importance has gained a great deal of credibility. Americans, who traditionally have favored red meats both at home and when they eat out, are ordering fish entrées more often. The chef should be familiar with many fish, including underutilized varieties, which can be excellent alternatives to species that are no longer available due to overfishing or because their habitats have become polluted.

Fish Basics

The chef should select absolutely fresh fish of the best quality. The first step in this process is assessing the purveyor or market. The fishmonger should properly handle, ice, and transport the fish and should be able to answer any questions regarding the fish's origin and its qualities: lean or oily, firm-

---

pôelé: a method in which items are cooked in their own juices in a covered pot.

fishmonger: a dealer in fish.

FIGURE 5-38 Checking Fish

(1) Looking at the fins and tail.

(2) Feeling the skin.

(3) Checking the gills.

(4) Checking the belly.

textured or delicate, appropriate for moist-heat methods or able to withstand a grill's heat.

Purchasing

Fish can be transported rapidly from the source to the consumer, but to ensure that fish is of the best quality, the chef should apply as many of the following tests as possible. If a fish smells fresh and looks fresh, but has a slight browning of the gills, it may still be acceptable. If a fish smells bad, no matter how clear the eyes or firm the flesh, reject it. (See Figure 5-38.)

1. *Smell the fish.* It should have a fresh, clean "sea" aroma, appropriate to the fish. Very strong odors are a clear indication that the fish is aging or was improperly handled or stored.

2. *Feel the skin.* The skin should feel slick and moist. The scales, if any, should be firmly attached.

3. *Look at the fins and tail.* They should be moist, fresh, flexible, and full, and should not appear ragged or dry.

4. *Press the flesh.* It should feel firm and elastic. There should be no visible fingerprint when you lift your finger away.

5. *Check the eyes.* Eyes should be clear and full. As the fish ages, the eyes will begin to lose moisture and sink back into the head. (Note: The wall-eyed pike's eyes *should* appear milky.)

6. *Check the gills.* They should have a good red to maroon color, with no traces of gray or brown, and should be moist and fresh looking. The exact shade of red will depend on the fish type.

7. *Check the belly.* There should be no sign of "belly burn," which occurs when the guts are not removed promptly; the stomach enzymes begin to eat the flesh, causing it to come away from the bones. There should be no breaks or tears in the flesh either.

8. *Check live shellfish for signs of movement.* Lobster and crab should move about. Clams, mussels, and oysters should be tightly closed. As they age, they will start to open. Any shells that do not snap shut when tapped should be discarded; the

shellfish are dead. If a bag contains many open shells the delivery should be rejected.

Storage

Ideally, the chef should purchase only the amount of fish needed for a day or two at most, and should store it properly as described below. When the purveyor is only able to make deliveries once or twice a week, then proper storage becomes a critical concern. (See Figure 5-39.)

Under proper storage conditions, fish and shellfish can be held for several days without losing any appreciable quality. When the fish arrives, the following things should be done:

1. *Check the fish carefully for freshness and quality.* The fish may be rinsed at this point; scaling and fabricating can be delayed until closer to service time.

2. *Place the fish on a bed of shaved or flaked ice in a perforated container.* Stainless steel is preferred.

Round fish should be belly down, flat fish on its side. The belly cavity should be filled with shaved ice as well.

3. *Cover with additional shaved or flaked ice.* Cubed ice can bruise the fish's flesh. It also will not conform as closely to the fish. Shaved or flaked ice makes a tighter seal around the entire fish. This prevents undue contact with the air, slowing the loss of quality and helping to extend safe storage life. The fish may be layered, if necessary.

4. *Set the perforated container inside a second container.* In this way, as the ice melts, the water will drain away. If fish is allowed to sit in a pool of water, some flavor and texture loss will occur. The longer it sits, the greater the loss of quality.

5. *Re-ice fish daily.* Even when properly iced, the fish will gradually lose some quality. To slow this loss down, remove the fish from its storage containers. Repack the fish in clean ice, in clean pans or containers. Whenever possible, perform this task in a refrigerated area.

FIGURE 5-39   Storing/Icing

(1) Pans for storing.

(2) Icing fish. They should be positioned in the ice as if they were swimming.

FIGURE 5-40   Dressed or Pan-dressed Fish

(1) Pan-dressed trout.

(2) Pan-dressed flounder.

Clams, mussels, and oysters should be stored in the bag in which they were delivered, but should not be iced. They last better at a temperature range from 35° to 40°F (2° to 4°C). The bag should be closed tightly and lightly weighted to keep the shellfish from opening up.

Scallops out of the shell and fish purchased as fillets should be stored in metal or plastic containers set on or in ice. They should not be in direct contact with the ice, however, because as it melts much of the flavor and texture of the scallops or fish will be leached away.

Crabs, lobsters, and other live shellfish should be packed in seaweed or damp paper upon delivery. They can be stored directly in their shipping containers at 39° to 45°F (4° to 7°C) until they are to be prepared, if a lobster tank is not available. Do not allow fresh water to come in direct contact with lobsters or crabs during storage, as it will kill them.

Frozen fish, including glazed, whole fish (fish repeatedly coated with water and frozen so that the ice builds up in layers, coating the entire fish) and frozen shrimp, should be stored at –20 to 0°F (–29° to –18°C) until they are ready to be thawed and cooked. (Storage at –10°F/–2°C is ideal and will greatly extend shelf life.)

Do not accept any frozen fish with white frost on its edges. This indicates freezer burn, the result of improper packaging or thawing and refreezing of the product.

Market Forms Butchering fresh fish is relatively simple, and many restaurant chefs prefer to do this, retaining the bones and head for stocks or fumet. As with meats, however, butchering fish can result in great waste and expense if fabricating skills are not up to par. Fish are too expensive to be cut up carelessly, and the extra money spent on buying fish fillets may balance out the money lost through waste. Fish may be purchased frozen, smoked, pickled, or salted in addition to the market forms shown in Figures 5-40 and 5-41. Table 5-7 also includes helpful purchasing information.

A description of basic cuts and butchering techniques, instructions for shucking clams and oysters, and other fish fabrication techniques can be found in Chapter 6.

Categories

There are many different fish species and even greater numbers of names for these fish, not all of which may be of culinary importance. The name by which a fish will be sold depends upon the region. However, basic groupings can be used to sort fish and shellfish. Once these groupings are explained, appropriate selection becomes a much easier matter.

The skeletal structure of finfish can also be used as the initial way to separate fish types into more readily understandable subjects. There are three basic skeletal types. (See Figure 5-42, for two types.)

1. **Round fish,** such as trout, bass, perch, salmon; these have a backbone along the upper edge with two fillets on either side. A round fish has one eye on each side of its head.

2. **Flat fish,** such as the various flounders and Dover sole; these have a backbone that runs

(continued on page 137)

FIGURE 5-41   Market Forms of Fish

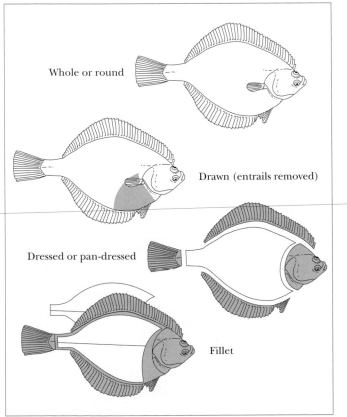

Whole or round

Drawn (entrails removed)

Dressed or pan-dressed

Fillet

fumet: a fish stock made with white wine and aromatics. (See page 247 for information.)

FIGURE 5-42   Skeletal Structure of Fish

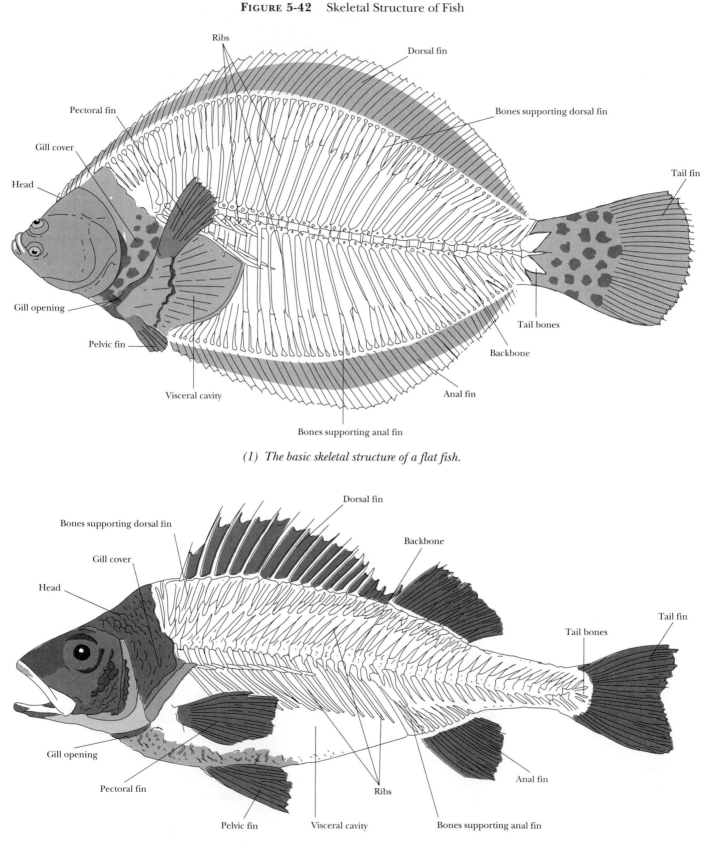

(1) The basic skeletal structure of a flat fish.

(2) The basic skeletal structure of a round fish.

TABLE 5-7 MARKET FORMS OF COMMON FISH

Common Name	Common Market Forms	Characteristics	Location
Fin Fish			
Barracuda	round, dressed, steaks, fillet	moderate fat, firm textured	salt water, Pacific
Bluefish	round, drawn, fillet	fat soft, strong tasting	salt water, Atlantic and Gulf
Bass	all	moderately fatty, fairly firm, smooth-textured	salt water, Atlantic and Pacific
Butterfish	round, drawn, fillet	fatty, soft, mild	salt water, Atlantic and Pacific
Catfish	round, dressed	moderately fatty, firm, sweet	primarily fresh water or farmed except hogfish which is saltwater
Chub	dressed, smoked	fat, smooth, firm texture, strong taste	fresh water, northern lakes
Cod	all, salted, smoked, dried	lean, firm white flesh, mild-flavored	salt water, Atlantic (New England)
Croaker	round, dressed, fillet, steaks	fine, sweet flesh	salt water
Cusk	drawn, dressed, whole, fillet	lean white, mild taste	salt water, Atlantic
Drum	round, drawn, fillet, steaks	lean, fine, sweet tasting (except white sea bass—stronger flavor, coarse texture)	salt water
Flounder	dressed, fillet	lean, delicate, mild taste	salt water, Atlantic
Grouper	all	lean, firm white flesh, mild taste	salt water, Atlantic and Gulf
Haddock	fillet, sticks	lean, firm white flesh, mild taste	salt water, Atlantic
Hake	fillet	lean, firm white flesh mild flavor	salt water, Atlantic, and northern Pacific
Halibut	all	lean, fine-textured, delicate flavor	salt water, Atlantic, and northern Pacific
Herring, sea	round	fairly fat, soft-textured	salt water, Atlantic and Pacific
Herring, lake	round, dressed, smoked	fatty, smooth, firm texture, salty and oily taste	fresh water, northern lakes
Mackerel, Spanish	round, dressed	high fat, soft flesh, oily	salt water, Florida coast and Gulf of Mexico
Mackerel, king	all	high fat, firm flesh	salt water
Lingcod	dressed, fillet	lean, firm, mild, sweet flavor	salt water, Pacific
Mullet	round, dressed, fillet	moderate fat, firm flesh, nutty flavor	salt water, South Atlantic and Gulf
Perch, white or yellow	dressed, fillet	lean, firm, sweet flavor	fresh water, northern lakes and rivers
Perch, ocean	fillet	fat, firm, well-flavored flesh	salt water, Atlantic
Pickerel	dressed, fillet	lean, firm, bony flesh	fresh water, northern lakes and rivers
Pike, blue	round, fillet		
Pike, wall-eye	dressed, fillet	lean, firm, sweet	fresh water, northern lakes and rivers
Pollock	fillet	lean, firm, mildly sweet-flavored	salt water, Atlantic
Pompano	dressed, round	moderate fat, firm texture, full flavor	salt water, south Atlantic and Gulf
Sablefish, black cod	dressed, steaks, smoked	high fat, finely grained, buttery flavor	salt water, north Pacific
Salmon, Atlantic	dressed, steaks	moderately fat, firm flesh distinctive rich flavor	salt water, only salmon from the Atlantic

(Table continued on following page)

TABLE 5-7 MARKET FORMS OF COMMON FISH *(continued)*

Common Name	Common Market Forms	Characteristics	Location
Salmon, chum	drawn, dressed, steaks, fillet	lowest fat content of all salmon	salt water, Pacific
Salmon, king	drawn, dressed, steaks, fillet	high fat, soft texture, rich flavor	salt water, Pacific, Alaska
Scrod	all	white, lean, and firm	salt water, Pacific and Atlantic
Shellfish			
Abalone	meat in shell	lean, rubbery, sweet flavor	coast of California, Mexico, and Japan
Clams, butter	shell—100# sack, shucked—100–250/gal	small, sweet, hard shell	Puget sound
Clams, quahog	Bushel—11# EP, 80# sack, shucked—100–250/gal	large, hard shell	East coast
Clams, littleneck	60# bushel	small, usually eaten "on the half shell"	East and West coast
Clams, razor	80# box, 16 EP /bushel	soft shelled	West coast
Clams, soft	45# bushel, shucked— 200–700/gal, 16# EP/bushel	soft shelled	East and West coast
Conch	15# EP/bushel	tough, should be pounded to be tenderized	southern, Florida, Gulf and Caribbean
Crabs, blue, hardshell	5# EP/bushel	sweet, succulent meat	Atlantic and Gulf coast
Crabs, blue, soft shell	3# EP/doz	sweet, succulent meat, blue crabs that have shed their shells	Atlantic and Gulf coast
Crabs, rock	5# EP/bushel	firm, sweet, succulent, claw meat	Atlantic, North Carolina to Texas
Crabs, Dungeness	all	sweet, succulent meat	Pacific coast
Crabs, king	legs only	firm, sweet, succulent meat	north Pacific
Lobsters	whole	firm, sweet meat	Atlantic
Lobsters, spiny	tails only	firm, stringy meat, not as sweet as Maine lobster	Tropics, Australlia, South Africa
Mussels	45–55#/bushel, 10# EP/bushel	slightly tough, sweet flavor	Atlantic, Pacific, and Mediterranean
Oysters, Eastern	80#/bushel, shucked— 150–200/gal (bluepoint)	range from bland to salty, from tender to firm; superior to Pacific oyster	Atlantic
Oysters, Pacific	80#/sack, 64–240/gal shucked	range from bland to salty, from tender to firm	Pacific coast
Oysters, Olympia	120# sack, 1600–1700/gal	range from bland to salty, from tender to firm	Puget Sound
Scallops, bay	shucked—500/gal	sweet, succulent meat, sweeter than sea scallops	East coast
Scallops, sea	shucked—150/gal	sweet and moist, but less tender, more chewy than bay	
Sea urchins	5# EP/bushel	edible roe, served briefly cooked or raw	salt water, moderate climate throughout the world
Shrimp	see Table 5-8		
Squid	5–6/#	light, extremely firm flesh	salt water, moderate climate throughout the world
Snails	imported as tinned; live from CA farms	dense, chewy	California (farm-raised)

through the center of the fish to create four quarter fillets, two upper and two lower or two full fillets (one from top, one from bottom). Both eyes are on the same side of the head.

3. *Nonbony fish,* such as ray, skate, sharks, and monkfish, which have cartilage rather than bones. For simplicity, these fish have been grouped with other round fish in the following section.

Shellfish can also be broken into distinct categories, also based on their skeletal structure:

1. **Mollusks** (soft-bodied shellfish covered by a shell of one or more pieces), which are of two types:

   • **Univalves** (single-shelled), such as abalone, snails, conch, and sea urchins.

   • **Bivalves** (two shells joined by a hinge), such as clams, mussels, oysters, and scallops.

2. **Crustaceans** (jointed exterior skeletons or shells), such as lobster, shrimp, and crayfish.

3. **Cephalopods,** such as squid and octopus. The name translates as "head-footed," and is a reflection of the fact that the tentacles and arms are attached directly to the head.

Within these fairly broad categories are a wide range of flavors and textures. Some fish are naturally lean; others are more oily; some have extremely delicate and subtle flavors; others are robust and meaty.

The best way to pair a fish with a cooking technique is to consider the flesh. For example, oily fish such as bluefish and mackerel are often prepared by dry-heat techniques such as grilling or broiling. Fish with moderate amounts of fat such as salmon and trout, work well with any technique, with the possible exception of deep-frying. Very lean fish, such as sole or flounder, are most successfully prepared by poaching, sautéing, pan-frying, or deep-frying.

Knowing how to work with fish and shellfish is a skill that takes time and experience to truly master. There are some classic preparations, however, that combine certain fish with specific techniques.

Commonly Available Fish

Round Fish

Anchovy   The most common form for the anchovy is the canned fillet packed in oil, with or without capers. In addition, they are sold in paste form or as smoked fillets. They may also be occasionally available fresh. The salted and oil-packed fillet is a classic component in Caesar salad.

Bass   Black sea bass feed primarily on shrimp, crabs, and mollusks. It has firm, well-flavored flesh that can be prepared by all cooking techniques. Considered to hold a close resemblance to a Mediterranean fish called the sea bream, black sea bass generally weigh

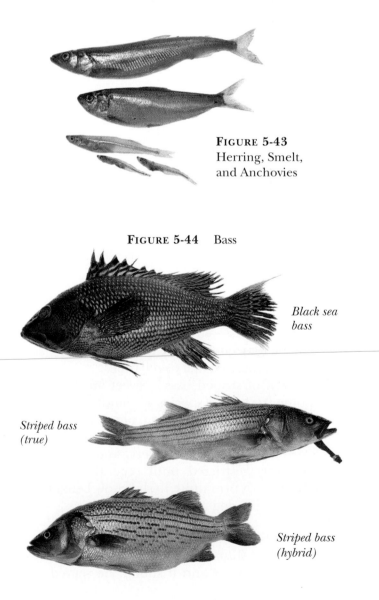

FIGURE 5-43
Herring, Smelt, and Anchovies

FIGURE 5-44   Bass

Black sea bass

Striped bass (true)

Striped bass (hybrid)

FIGURE 5-45   Catfish

FIGURE 5-46   Cod/Haddock

FIGURE 5-47   Eel

FIGURE 5-48   Grouper

FIGURE 5-49   John Dory

FIGURE 5-50   Mackerel

FIGURE 5-51   Monkfish

FIGURE 5-52   Permit

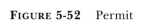

FIGURE 5-53   Pike

from 1 to 3 pounds, but may be larger in the fall. Other so-called bass—striped bass, sea bass, pike, and red snapper, for example—are not necessarily related by family, but share culinary similarities.

The flesh of striped bass is sweet and relatively firm. Some freshwater species are landlocked in the United States, but those fished from clean saltwater tend to have the best texture and flavor. Striped bass can tolerate polluted waters, and its sale has been severely restricted until recently. A hybrid striped bass with firm white flesh is now being farm-raised and is growing in popularity.

Bluefish   A fish with a relatively strong flavor and oily flesh, bluefish should be drawn as soon as possible after it is caught and it should be served very

fresh. Young bluefish generally have an excellent flavor, as they feed on mollusks and shrimp. The flesh has a loose, flaky texture and is excellent broiled or grilled. The strip of dark-colored flesh in the fillet is often removed because it has a more pronounced flavor and tends to hold any pollutants or contaminants that may be present. Bluefish has become more difficult to find as its habitat becomes increasingly polluted. There may be restrictions on its availability in some areas.

Catfish   Catfish are farmed and marketed under carefully controlled conditions. Catfish should be skinned before cooking and are commonly sold as skinless fillets. The flesh is delicately flavored, lean, and very firm in texture. This fish can be prepared by any cooking technique; a traditional preparation is coating in cornmeal and pan-fried. (See Figure 5-45.)

Cod   Cod has a lean, white flesh. Within the cod family there are a number of distinct species, each with different identifying marks. Atlantic cod, haddock, cusk, whiting, hake, and pollock are all members of the cod family. Severe restrictions have been imposed throughout the Grand Banks and St. George's Bay making shortages likely. (See Figure 5-46.) Cod may be poached, used in chowder, or steamed. It is also available salted (known as *baccala*). The traditional Scottish dish, *finnan haddie*, is split, smoked haddock, a species of cod.

Dolphin Fish (Mahi Mahi)   Dolphin fish is different from dolphin, the mammal. It often appears on menus with its Hawaiian name, mahi mahi, to avoid any confusion. This fish, harvested from the Pacific and Atlantic Oceans, has firm flesh with a sweet, delicate flavor. It can be prepared by all cooking techniques and is excellent in *ceviche*. The skin should be removed before cooking.

Eel   Eel has a rich, oily flesh. Eels spawn in the Sargasso Sea, which is part of the North Atlantic, and then begin the journey back to either Europe or America. They are available live, whole, skinned, in fillets, smoked, and jellied. (See Figure 5-47.) One of the most famous eel dishes is a French stew known as *matelote*.

Groupers   There are several kinds of grouper, all members of the sea bass family. (See Figure 5-48.) One of the most commonly available is red grouper. Grouper has lean, firm, white flesh that is best when sautéed, pan-fried, steamed, or shallow-poached. The skin should be removed before cooking.

Haddock (see Cod)

John Dory   John Dory, also known as *San Pedro*, is identified by the large "thumbprint of Saint Peter" on either side of its body. This fish is well known in the Mediterranean and the Bay of Biscay, although it can be found as far north as Norway. There is a slightly different American John Dory as well. The white flesh is very delicate and may be poached or grilled whole or filleted. The proportion of fillet to whole fish is low, but the bones can be used to pro-

duce a good fumet. John Dory is commonly used in *bouillabaisse*. (See Figure 5-49.)

Mackerel   This is an oily, soft-textured fish, once regularly sold salted. Spanish and king mackerel are both considered fish of good eating quality, but the Spanish mackerel is conceded to be the better. The flesh flakes easily when cooked. Mackerel is best when prepared by dry-heat cooking techniques and is commonly broiled. (See Figure 5-50.)

Monkfish   This fish has been known by a number of names, including angler fish, goosefish, lawyer fish, and belly fish. The French name is *lotte*. Monkfish has a firm, dense texture and sweet taste. Suitable for any cooking technique, it is commonly used in fish stews. (See Figure 5-51.)

Perch   Perch and its close relative, the wall-eyed pike (below), has a lean and delicate flesh. The best perch are harvested from the fresh waters of lakes and reservoirs. Small perch may be deep-fried and served whole; large fish are cut into fillets and pan-fried, steamed, or shallow-poached.

Permit   This warm-water fish is found from North Carolina to the Gulf of Mexico. It is a larger relative (averaging 9 pounds) of the more popular pompano. When purchasing, select the smaller permits, which have better flavor. It can be poached, baked, or broiled. (See Figure 5-52.)

Pike   Most famous for its use in *quenelles de brochet*, wall-eyed pike has sweet, white, firmly textured flesh that is relatively lean but stands up well to dry-heat techniques. It is also commonly poached or used to prepare mousses or terrines. (See Figure 5-53.) It should not be confused with pickerel, a fish of virtually no culinary importance.

Pompano   Considered by some as one of the finest saltwater fish, pompano is becoming increasingly

---

ceviche: raw fish marinated in citrus juice (usually lime).

bouillabaisse: a French seafood stew.

quenelles de brochet: fish forcemeat dumplings.

mousse: a dish made by folding whipped egg whites and/or cream into a flavored base; may be sweet or savory.

FIGURE 5-54   Pompano

FIGURE 5-55   Puffer

FIGURE 5-56   Salmon

FIGURE 5-57   Shark/Swordfish Steaks

FIGURE 5-58   Snapper

(1) Red snapper

(2) Vermillion snapper

FIGURE 5-60   Tilapia

FIGURE 5-59   Tautog

(1) Hybrid

(2) Lake Victoria/original

expensive. Pompano has firm, well-flavored flesh and is often broiled or prepared *en papillote*. Most pompano comes from the Gulf of Mexico. (See Figure 5-54.)

Puffer   This fish (see Figure 5-55) is named for its ability to inflate to a size that makes it impossible for the puffer's predators to devour it. It is a warm-water fish, but is found as far north as New York and southern Newfoundland. Also known as blower or northern swellfish, the American variety of this fish is considered less dangerous than the Japanese species, *fugu*. To prepare, cut off the head and peel back the skin. The meat with the backbone, can be fried whole or filleted and pan-fried. Because of the prickly scales, wear gloves when skinning this fish.

Salmon   This firm, moderately oily fish has a distinctively colored flesh, ranging from light pink to a deep orange-pink or red. A number of different species, including cohoe, king, and Atlantic, are

available. The Atlantic species is commonly farm-raised.

Salmon may be prepared using virtually any technique. Some of the more popular presentations are poached, baked in pastry *(coulibiac)*, and grilled. Salmon is available fresh, smoked, or cured as *gravad lox*. Salmon shares flavors, textures, and culinary treatments with trout. (See Figure 5-56)

Shad   Shad usually enter the rivers of the Atlantic coast from the Gulf of St. Lawrence to northern Florida during the months of May to December. The flesh of both sexes, which is sweet and white but extremely bony, and the roe of the female are

---

en papillote: a cooking method in which foods are wrapped in paper and allowed to "steam." (See pages 378-380 for more information.)

gravad lox: a Scandinavian specialty made from cured raw salmon. (See pages 419-420, for more information.).

highly regarded. A traditional preparation method for shad and shad roe is to sauté or pan-fry them with bacon. A classic technique for preparing this fish is known as "planking."

Shark Mako and blue shark are very popular, and other types of shark, including yellow-tip and black-tip, are becoming important in the marketplace, especially as overfishing of the mako depletes supplies. Shark sometimes may be sold to the unwary as swordfish. Check the pattern of the strip of the dark-colored flesh to be sure you are receiving what was ordered. (See Figure 5-57.) The flesh of shark is sweet and relatively firm and moist, but the skin is extremely tough. Shark is commonly made into steaks and grilled, broiled, or sautéed.

Skate/Ray The flesh of the skate or ray is sweet and firm and has been compared to scallops. It is sold as wings, which should be skinned prior to sautéing, although they may be poached with the skin on and are easier to skin after poaching. One famous presentation method is to sauté the skate and serve it with *beurre noir*.

Snappers There are a number of different snappers. One of the most popular is red snapper (see Figure 5-58). True red snapper comes from the Gulf of Mexico and adjacent Atlantic waters. Among other desirable snapper species are vermillion, silk, mutton, mangrove, gray, beeliner, pink, and yellowtail. The flesh is firm, moist, and finely textured. Almost any preparation technique can be used; snapper is often prepared en papillote or baked.

Swordfish Swordfish has an extremely firm texture with a unique flavor. Commonly cut into steaks and grilled, swordfish has a lot of characteristics similar to shark. Swordfish's darker strip of flesh has a Y-shaped pattern, which is one way to distinguish it from shark, with its round pattern. The distinction between swordfish and mako shark steaks is clearly illustrated in Figure 5-57.

Tautog This fish (see Figure 5-59) is found from Nova Scotia to South Carolina, but predominantly from Cape Cod to the Delaware Bay. Its white flesh is dry and delicate. It is suitable for grilling and bak-

beurre noir: black butter sauce.

ing and is firm enough to to be used in fish chowder.

Tilapia A popular freshwater fish in Asian cuisine, tilapia is now being farm-raised extensively in the United States. (See Figure 5-60.) The undesirable muddy taste once associated with this fish is not apparent in farm-raised species. It can be poached, steamed, or grilled.

Tilefish/Golden Bass This fish has an off-white, flaky flesh and delicate flavor. Tilefish can be cooked by any technique and is occasionally smoked.

Trigger Fish Trigger fish is a tropical or subtropical fish, occasionally harvested in cooler climates. (See Figure 5-61.) It is sold as turbot in the Bahamas, Bermuda, and Florida. The tough skin should be removed before cooking. The firm flesh is best when poached or sautéed.

Trout Along with catfish, salmon, oysters, mussels, and clams, trout are farm-raised in large quantities. (See Figure 5-62.) Nearly all trout sold in restaurants today come from commercial hatcheries. Rainbow trout is the most readily available type of trout. It is excellent when pan-fried in a manner similar to catfish, roasted, or poached. *Truite au bleu* is a famous trout preparation; freshly caught trout is poached in a vinegar court bouillon until the blue color is barely set. Smoked trout is also widely available.

Tuna Tuna's flesh is similar to that of swordfish in texture; meaty and firm. Its flavor is unique, and the color of its flesh ranges from a deep pinkish-beige to a dark maroon. A member of the mackerel family, tuna has the distinctive strip of dark-colored flesh along its back. Tuna is often roasted or cut into steaks and grilled. (See Figure 5-63.) Also pop-

FIGURE 5-61
Trout

FIGURE 5-62
Tuna

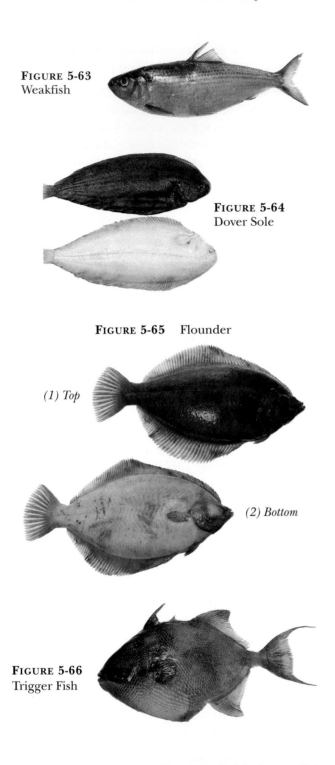

FIGURE 5-63
Weakfish

FIGURE 5-64
Dover Sole

FIGURE 5-65   Flounder

(1) Top

(2) Bottom

FIGURE 5-66
Trigger Fish

Its lean and flaky flesh makes it a popular fish for grilling and pan-frying. The spotted squeteague is most abundant in North Carolina and the southern states. (See Figure 5-64.)

Flat Fish

Dover Sole   One of the only true soles is the Dover sole, a flat fish with a compact, oval shape and firmly textured, delicately flavored flesh. Dover sole was so highly esteemed that hundreds of different dishes were devised to feature it in the classical repertoire. Dover sole is available fresh or frozen. Note that although many species of flounder have been dubbed "sole," they should not be confused with Dover sole. (See Figure 5-65)

Flounder   Flounder is often sold in the United States under the market name of "sole": lemon sole, gray sole, white sole are all forms of flounder, a flat, disk-shaped fish with both eyes on the same side of its head. (See Figure 5-66.) Plaice, another flounder species, is often sold as dab, sand dab, roughback. Flounder is generally quite delicate, with a tendency to flake readily. It is particularly suited to shallow-poaching and steaming and is also commonly cut into "fingers" and deep-fried. Readily available whole, flounder is also sold cut into quarter fillets and skinned.

Halibut   Halibut has firm, white meat with a delicate flavor. The halibut can grow to be quite large and may be cut into steaks or fillets. A halibut of 10 to 40 pounds is considered market-size; they can grow to be over 200 pounds. This fish is now being farm-raised, as over-fishing has greatly reduced its availability. (See Figure 5-67.)

Turbot   A disk-shaped fish esteemed for its snowy-white, moist, finely textured flesh, turbot may grow large enough to cut into steaks or fillets. It is generally steamed or poached to highlight its delicacy and whiteness. This fish, although a northern Atlantic species, is being successfully farm-raised in Chile.

---

vitello tonnato: cold roast veal served with a sauce of puréed tuna, anchovies, capers, lemon juice, and olive oil.

Niçoise salad: a salad containing tuna fish, olives, anchovies, green beans, potatoes, and hard-cooked eggs.

ular is canned tuna—albacore (white) or light meat, packed in either oil or water. Canned tuna is often indicated in recipes such as *vitello tonnato* and Niçoise salad.

Weakfish   The weakfish is harvested in the United States from Massachusetts to Florida. It is also marketed as squeteaque, drum, croaker, and sea trout.

FIGURE 5-67   Halibut

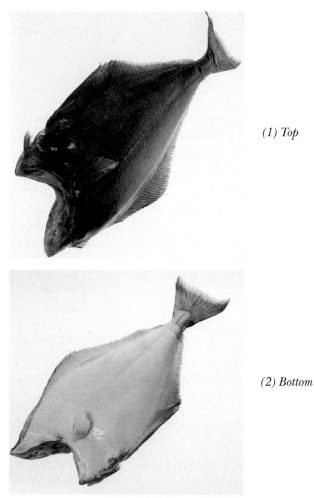

(1) Top

(2) Bottom

Shellfish

Univalves

Abalone The abalone has one shell and a suction cup that attaches firmly to rocks; it must be pried loose. Available from California, state law prohibits the exportation of live abalone, so most of the country must rely on frozen or canned abalone. The meat, which is cut into steaks and pounded before sautéing or grilling, becomes extremely tough if overcooked. Advances in raising aquacultured abalone may help increase its availability.

Conch True conch comes from the Caribbean and is more accurately classified as a gastropod—a large class of mollusk. Conch is sold out of the shell and may be available ground. It is used in salads, ceviche, chowders, and fritters. Further north, the whelk, which is much smaller and grayish in color, is sold as conch, although it is more accurately categorized as a sea snail.

Snails Fresh snails, or *escargots*, are imported from France. They average 32 snails per pound and are classically served in their shells with a garlic compound butter as an appetizer. Fresh snails are far superior to canned snails, and are increasingly available from farms in this country. (See Figure 5-68.)

Bivalves

Clams Clams are available in the shell, shucked (sometimes frozen), and canned. Clams sold "live" should definitely be checked for tightly closed shells, to make sure they are alive. They should have a sweet briny smell.

Clams, like oysters, may be marketed by the name of the bed from which they were taken and

---

compound butter: butter flavored with garlic, herbs or other seasonings. (See page 335, for more information.)

FIGURE 5-68
Land Snails

FIGURE 5-69   Clams

FIGURE 5-70
Mussels

FIGURE 5-71   Oysters

FIGURE 5-72   Scallops

local preferences for species will vary. (See Figure 5-69.) The following terms are commonly applied to clams:

- *Littlenecks* (1 to 1½ inches) are small hardshell clams often eaten raw on the half shell.

- *Topnecks* (1½ to 2-inches) and

- *Cherrystones* are the next largest size and are also commonly eaten raw.

- *Quahogs* are a hardshell variety that grow to be more than 3 inches in diameter. They are most often used for chowder or fritters.

- *Pacific littleneck* clams, also known as *manilla clams*, are found on the Pacific coast and are generally steamed.

- *Soft-shell* clams, or *"steamers,"* are generally steamed or used in fritters.

Mussels   Most commercially available mussels are farm-raised and are sold live in the shell. (See Figure 5-70.) Mussels are commonly prepared *à la marinière* (steamed with wine, garlic, and lemon) or as the major component of Billi-bi soup (a velouté soup garnished with mussels), although there are a great many other preparations.

Mussels steamed and served in the shell should be debearded first. (See page 288, for more information.)

Oysters   Oysters are sold live in the shell or shucked. (See Figure 5-71.) As with clams, they are generally marketed by the name of the beds from which they were harvested, and local preference for particular species will vary greatly. Some of the most famous presentations include raw on the half shell,

---

velouté soup: a soup prepared from thickened broth finished with a mixture of cream and egg yolks.

oyster stew, oyster omelets, and oysters Rockefeller, a dish that includes spinach and Pernod.

Scallops Three species of scallop are of commercial importance: bay scallops, sea scallops, and calico scallops. Sea scallops can become quite large (2 to 3 inches in diameter); bay and calico scallops are smaller. True bay scallops (northern) are generally considered superior in quality to calicos.

Most scallops are sold shucked (See Figure 5-72.) Occasionally, shucked scallops with the roe attached may be found. Even less frequently, they are sold still in the shells, though farm-raised scallops in the shell are increasingly available.

Coquilles St. Jacques is customarily thought of as a cream-based scallop gratin; it is also the name for scallop in French, and refers to the fact that St. James wore the shell of the scallop as his personal emblem.

Crustaceans

Crab Common kinds of crab include blue, Dungeness, king, and spider. Blue crab, which is found on the Atlantic Coast, especially around the Chesapeake Bay, is sold live, or as pasteurized or canned meat. (See Figure 5-73.)

From the spring through late summer, when the crab molts, blue crab are sold as "soft-shelled crabs," which are commonly pan-fried or sautéed. Hardshelled crab may be boiled or steamed. The meat may be removed and used in a variety of preparations, including one of the most famous, crab cakes.

She-crab soup is made from the roe and meat of female crabs, identifiable by their broad "aprons."

Dungeness crab is common on the Pacific Coast. King crab and spider crab are valued mainly for their legs, although the whole crab can be used. Spider crab is common to the Adriatic and the Mediterranean. Only one claw per stone crab, measuring at least 2¾ inches, can be harvested, however, in order to help save the species. Fishermen simply twist off the claws (which grow back) and return the crab to the sea. Legs and claws are cooked and frozen on the ship in most cases and the claw may be cracked (especially in the case of stone crab).

Pernod: a licorice-flavored liqueur.

FIGURE 5-73 Crustaceans

(1) Clockwise from left: Dungeness, American lobster, Crayfish, Shrimp (head on) Shrimp, Blue crab.

(2) Spider crab

Jonah crab is a larger relative of the stone crab. It is found only from Nova Scotia to Florida. The meat of the crab is excellent for crab cakes.

Crayfish Freshwater crayfish is widely available year-round because it can be farmed. Crayfish may be purchased live or precooked and frozen (whole, or tail meat only). Crayfish are used extensively in Creole and Cajun cooking and are also a classic garnish. *Etouffé* and *jambalaya* are two of the most popular crayfish dishes.

Lobster American lobster is highly prized worldwide; it is available live or cooked and canned. The meat is firm and succulent. The female may contain an egg sac, known as the roe. It is considered a delicacy; however, lobsters with egg sacs on the body's exterior cannot be legally harvested. Both sexes possess the green tomalley, or liver, another prized part.

To determine the sex of the lobster, feel the appendages where the tail meets the body. In the female they will be soft and feathery, whereas in the male they are rigid. The female's tail or abdomen is generally broader.

Other types of lobster include the rock lobster (rock lobster is the market name for spiny lobster), Dublin prawn, and lobsterette.

Shrimp　Shrimp is probably one of the most popular crustaceans. Shrimp are most commonly available frozen, as they are often processed and flash-frozen either on the boat or as soon as boats are unloaded at shore in order to preserve flavor and quality. Fresh shrimp are highly perishable, but they may be available in some regions of the United States, notably the Gulf of Mexico and Chesapeake Bay regions, and there are both saltwater and freshwater species. The flesh has a sweet flavor and a firm, almost crisp texture.

Shrimp are sold according to the number in a pound, known as the "count." The count ranges include 3 per pound; 10 to 15; 21 to 25; 26 to 30; 31 to 35; and on up to over 100 per pound. (See Table 5-8.)

Some common presentations include cold "cocktails," deep-fried, baked, sautéed, and grilled.

Cephalopods

Octopus　Octopus is firmly textured with a sweet "marine" flavor. It is generally sold fresh, and cleaned of its ink and beak, but may also come

FIGURE 5-74　Cephalopods

(1) Cuttlefish

(2) Octopus

frozen. Octopus may be prepared in a number of dishes, including *ceviche*, chowders, and salads. (See Figure 5-74.)

Squid　Squid is one of the most widely available forms of seafood. It is an established part of Mediterranean and Asian cuisines and is gaining popularity in the United States. Squid are available in a range of sizes; small squid are frequently

TABLE 5-8　SHRIMP SIZE AND COUNT

Commercial Name	Type I: Raw, Chilled or Frozen, Not Peeled	Peeled, Deveined	Type II: Cooked, Chilled or Frozen, Peeled, Deveined
Colossal	15 or fewer	10 or fewer	30 or fewer
Extra jumbo	16–20	20–25	31–40
Jumbo	21–25	26–31	41–60
Extra large	26–30	32–38	61–90
Large	31–35	39–44	91–125
Medium large	36–42	45–53	126 up
Small	51–60	64–75	
Extra Small	61 and over	76 and over	

Commercial names apply to Type I only.

SEA URCHINS

Though they are a delicacy in Japan, sea urchins are infrequently seen on American menus. They are round, hard-shelled marine animals with sharp spines covering their entire surface. A piece of the shell must be cut away with scissors to expose the roe. The roe is then customarily scooped out with a spoon and eaten raw. Sea urchin is also found throughout the Mediterranean region, where it is often cooked lightly, shelled, and placed on a wedge of French bread with a squeeze of lemon juice.

stuffed and cooked whole in a sauce, whereas large squid are cut into rings, fried, and served with a spicy sauce. There are many different presentations, however, because squid are suited to most cooking techniques. Squid over nine inches long are too tough for culinary use.

Miscellaneous Items

Caviar "Caviar" is defined by the FDA as the salted roe from the sturgeon. It is available fresh (it must be refrigerated carefully) or pasteurized and canned. Two terms that are often associated with packaged caviar relate the amount of salt included; "malasol" indicates little salt and "sol" is saltier.

Fresh caviar "grains" or individual eggs, should be bright, shiny, and whole. The four varieties (ranging from the most expensive and desirable to the least expensive) are: beluga (has a large grain and is light in color), ship (medium grain, also light in color), sevruga (small grain and dark colored), and osetra (also small grained and dark). The best quality caviar is served perfectly plain. Lesser-quality (but still good) caviar is traditionally served with toast or blinis and lemon, hard-boiled eggs, and finely chopped onions.

Roe from other kinds of fish are sometimes also sold as "caviar," usually with the fish's name included on the label: salmon, lumpfish, or mullet, for example.

Frogs' Legs These are the hind legs of frogs that are usually farm-raised. Frogs' legs are sold in pairs. One classic dish is frogs' legs sautéed *à la provençale.*

à la provençal: with garlic, tomatoes, and olive oil.

compote: fresh or dried fruit that is cooked in a liquid, sometimes sweetened or flavored with spices or liqueur.

Fruits and Vegetables

Fruits

For the chef, the term "fruits" means a fresh product that is sweet. They are customarily used in sweet dishes, such as pies, puddings, preserves, ice creams, and dessert sauces. They are also delicious stewed or candied, and even poached or baked whole. Other spots held by fruits on the menu are as a plate of fresh seasonal fruits, fruit salads, or fruit soups. They are the classic end to most meals, with or without a plate of cheese. Table 5-9 provides general information about basic fruits.

Historically, fruits have been used as ingredients in savory dishes as well as sweet ones. You can find recipes both old and new that pair a variety of fresh and dried fruits with meat, poultry, and fish. There are several reasons that these pairings have such enduring popularity. Fruits can be an excellent foil for richly flavored or oily foods. Rhubarb, for instance, is traditionally served with mackerel. Dried fruits find their way into compotes, stuffings, and sauces served with game meats, pork, and even some cuts of beef. Applesauce is served with crisp, buttery potato pancakes. The bright flavors of citrus fruits and grapes are frequently used in combination with poultry, veal, or fish preparations.

Apples

Apples are perhaps America's favorite fruit. According to surveys from the International Apple Institute, apples account for nearly 14 percent of all tree fruits (including both fruit and nuts) sold in this country. The most commonly available varieties consist of Golden and Red Delicious, MacIntosh, Granny Smith, and Rome Beauty. Examples of popular varieties of apples are displayed in Figure 5-75. There are, however, thousands of other vari-

TABLE 5-9 GENERAL FRUIT INFORMATION

Fruit type	Grades Available	Pack, Count, and/or Weight	Yield %	Available Forms
Apples	U.S. Extra Fancy, U.S. No. 1, No. 2	Carton/box (variable count, cell-packed or loose, 34–43#)	76%	Fresh, (see Table 5-10), sliced, frozen, dried, canned
Apricots	U.S. No. 1, No.2	Lug (22#)	80%	Fresh, dried (sulphured, unsulphured)
Bananas	U.S. No. 1, No. 2	Box (40#: average count for No. 1 grade is 115 each)	75%	Fresh, dried
Berries	U.S. No. 1	Basket ($\frac{1}{2}$ pint, pint, or quart); Flats (12 baskets, 10#)	90 to 100%	Fresh (see Table 5-11), dried, IQF frozen frozen in syrup
Cherries	U.S. No. 1	Lugs, 20# California lugs, 18#; Flats, 12#	80%	Fresh, dried, frozen, canned
Citrus, U.S. fruits	U.S. Fancy, No. 1, Combination, or No. 2	Case (count varies by variety from 32 to 100)	65% (varies by use)	Fresh (see Table 5-12), frozen juice concentrate
Figs	U.S. No. 1	Case (35 ea.)	80%	Fresh, dried, IQF frozen
Grapes	U.S. Fancy, Extra No. 1, No.1	Lug/carton (weight ranges: 12, 17, or 23#)	93%	Fresh (see Table 5-13), dried (raisins)
Kiwi	U.S. Fancy, No. 1, No. 2	Case, (39 each)	89%	Fresh
Mango	No Federal grades	Case (12 each)	62%	Fresh, purée
Melons	U.S. No. 1, Commercial, No. 2	Case (5 each)	65 to 70%	Fresh (see Table 5-14)
Nectarines	U.S. Extra No. 1, No. 1	Case (25#)	87%	Fresh, IQF frozen
Papayas	U.S. No. 1, No. 2	Carton/flat (8 to 14 each)	84%	Fresh, purée
Peaches	U.S. Extra Fancy No. 1, Fancy No. 2	Lug/case (35#)	75%	Fresh, IQF frozen slices, frozen in syrup, canned, halves, or slices
Pears	U.S. Extra Fancy No. 1, Fancy No. 2	Case (40 to 90 each, by variety)	87%	Fresh (see Table 5-15), dried, canned, sliced, IQF frozen slices
Persimmons	No Federal grades	Flat (11–13#, 25 each)	85%	Fresh
Pineapples	U.S. Fancy No. 1, No. 2	Case (5 each)	62%	Fresh, canned (sliced, crushed, chunks), juice
Plums	U.S. No. 1	Lug/case (28#)	78%	Fresh (see Table 5-16)
Pomegranates	No Federal grades	Case (24 each)	58%	Fresh
Rhubarb	U.S. No. 1	Case (20#); Box (5#); Bulk (varies)	90%	Fresh, IQF pieces

eties grown in orchards throughout the country. A little searching can result in a find that may make your apple tart uniquely flavorful.

Different varieties of apples have particular characteristics. Some are best for eating out of hand or in other preparations where they are left fresh and uncooked. Many apples will begin to turn brown once they come in contact with air. Dousing them in water that has a little lemon juice added will help prevent browning, but may not be desirable if a truly pure apple taste is important. Other types are considered best for pies and baking. These fruits tend to retain a recognizable shape and some texture even when baked. Still oth-

FIGURE 5-75   Apples

(1) Red Delicious (whole), Golden Delicious, Rome Beauty

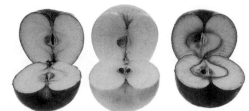

(2) Rome Beauty, Golden Delicious, Red Delicious (cut)

ers are selected for their ability to cook down into a rich, smooth purée for applesauce. The best apple cider is usually made from a blend of apples chosen to give the finished drink a full, well-balanced flavor.

Apple varieties are considered both summer fruits (at their best for only a short season) and winter fruits (which can be held in cold storage for many months without significant loss of quality). This makes it possible to get good fresh apples throughout the year. Climatic conditions, such as temperature and humidity are carefully controlled in apple storage warehouses to pace the ripening process. In this way, the rate at which apples produce **ethylene gas** can be controlled to prevent spoilage.

Dried apples, prepared applesauce, apple juice (bottled or frozen concentrate), cider, spiced or plain pie fillings, and a host of prepared items made from apples can be purchased.

This quintessentially North American fruit is found in thousands of recipes, from soups to breads to classic apple pie. They can be found in

---

ethylene gas: a natural plant gas that promotes the ripening process.

TABLE 5-10   APPLE VARIETIES

Variety*	Description	Peak Season/Fresh	Uses
Crabapple	Very small, tart, red with blush of yellow or white	Fall	In sauces, pickles, as relish
Golden Delicious	Golden skin with freckling. Flesh is sweet, juicy, and crisp	September to May	All-purpose fruit. Stays white after cutting longer than other varieties
Granny Smith	Green skin and white-light green flesh. Extremely crisp and finely textured flesh; tart	April to July	All-purpose fruit
Greening	Green skin. Firm flesh with mild, sweet-tart flavor	October to March	Used for pies, sauces, baked; can be frozen
Jonathan	Bright red, flecked with yellow-green. Tender flesh, semi-tart	September to January	Eating out-of-hand; used for pies, sauces, can be frozen
McIntosh	Primarily red, streaked with yellow or green. Flesh is very white; crisp	September to June	Eating out-of-hand; used for sauces, cider, can be frozen
Northern Spy	Firm texture, juicy, sweet-tart taste	October to November	Excellent in pies
Red Delicious	Bright red speckled with yellow. Flesh is a yellow-white, with firm texture and sweet taste	September to June	All-purpose
Rome Beauty	Bright red skin. Flesh is firm with a milk tart-sweet flavor	October to June	Baking
Winesap	Bright red skin with some yellow green. Flesh is firm, tart-sweet, aromatic	October to June	Eating out-of-hand; used for pies, sauces, baking, can be frozen

*There are many varieties of apples available only within smaller regions. These apples share eating and cooking characteristics with those described here. If you have any questions, ask your purveyor or other reputable source for the best use for a particular variety.

FIGURE 5-76　Berries

(1) Blackberries, raspberries, strawberries, and blueberries

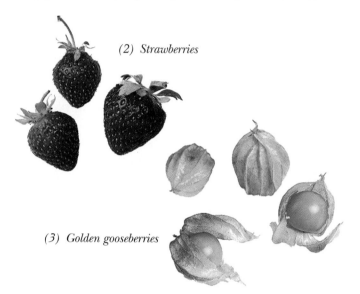

(2) Strawberries

(3) Golden gooseberries

puddings, savory and sweet dishes, sauces and salads. See Table 5-10 to determine which varieties are best for eating out of hand, cooking, and baking.

Berries

Strawberries, raspberries, blueberries, and blackberries are so seasonal that for most people, they mean that spring has arrived or that summer is at its height. Some varieties can be found virtually any time of the year, but it only takes one bite to convince most people that locally grown berries, picked that day, outshine any foreign import.

They tend to be highly perishable (with the exception of cranberries) and are susceptible to bruising, mold, and overripening in fairly short order. Inspect all berries and their packaging carefully before you accept them. Juice-stained cartons or juice leaking through the carton is a clear indication that the fruit has been mishandled or is old. Once berries begin to turn moldy, the entire batch goes quickly.

Cranberries are almost always cooked. Other berries can be featured as fresh fruit, used as a flavoring, purée, or sauce in a number of dishes. They

TABLE 5-11　BERRIES

Variety	Description	Peak Season/Fresh	Uses
Blueberry	Blue/purple with dusty silver-blue "bloom"	Late summer	Eaten fresh, in baked goods, jams, dried, as flavoring for vinegar
Boysenberry	Hybrid of various types of raspberry, with similar flavor and texture		Eaten fresh, jams and jellies, made into wine or syrup
Cranberry	Shiny red berry, some with white blush; dry and sour	Fall	Generally cooked, although there are some raw chopped relishes; sauces, jellies, in breads, dried
Currant	May be red, black, or white. Red is generally sweetest, black is very dark	Midsummer	Generally cooked for use in relishes, jams, jellies, wines, cordials, or syrups
Elderberry	Small purple-black berry		Jams, jellies, wines, or cordials
Gooseberry	Smooth skin (some with papery husk still attached. May be green, golden, red, purple or white. Some have fuzzy skins		Used crushed in "fools" or in compotes, relishes, jams, jellies
Mulberry	Resembles but is unrelated to raspberry; juicy with slightly musty aroma	Midsummer	Wines, syrups, cordials
Raspberry	Actually clusters of tiny fruits (drupes), each containing a seed. May have "hairs" on surface. May be red, black, or white. Sweet, juicy fruit. Cloudberry and dewberry are types of raspberries	Two seasons: early summer, late summer	Eaten fresh, used in baked items, syrups, purées/sauces, cordials, syrups, to flavor vinegars
Strawberry	Red shiny, heart-shaped berry, seeds on exterior	Late spring into early summer	Eaten fresh, shortcakes, baked goods, as purée, jams, jellies

may also be used to flavor vinegars, marinades, or dressings. When fresh berries are out of season, frozen berries are often a perfectly fine substitute. Dried berries can be used to great advantage in winter fruit compotes, stuffings, breads, or other sweet and savory dishes. Some classic dishes that use berries include strawberry shortcake, fresh berry cobblers, pies, jams, jellies, and ice creams. (See Figure 5-76 and Table 5-11.)

Citrus Fruits

Citrus fruits are characterized by their thick skins, which contain aromatic oils, and their seg-

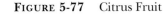

FIGURE 5-77 Citrus Fruit

(1) Blood orange   *(2) Lemon and lime*   *(3) White grapefruit*   *(4) Pink grapefruit*

TABLE 5-12 CITRUS VARIETIES

Variety	Description	Uses
Navel orange	Orange skin, relatively smooth; seedless	Eating fresh, juice, zest (zest may be candied)
Temple orange	Orange skin, slightly pebbled texture. Juicy, slightly tart flavor	Eating fresh
Seville orange	Sour flavor	Marmalade
Blood orange	Orange skin with blush of red; pockets of dark red/maroon pigmented flesh. Aromatic	Eating fresh, juicing, in sauces, as flavoring ingredient
Tangerine	Orange, lightly pebbled to smooth skin, loosely attached to fruit. Usually has many seeds. Juicy, sweet-tart flavor	Eating fresh, juice
Mandarin	Deep-orange, smooth skin with "nipple" on one end. Skin loosely attached to flesh, seedless	Eating fresh
Meyers lemon	Relatively large lemon with sweet juicy flesh.	Juice, flavoring, baked items, zest (zest may be candied)
Lemon	Yellow green to deep yellow skin; extremely tart flesh	Juice, flavoring, zest (zest may be candied)
Persian lime	Dark green, smooth skin. Flesh is tart, seedless	Juice, flavoring, zest (zest may be candied)
Key lime	Light green	Juice, flavoring (most famous use is Key lime pie)
Red grapefruit	Yellow flesh, possible red blush. Flesh is deep red, seedless, mellow sweet-tart flavor	Eating fresh, juice
White grapefruit	Yellow flesh, sometimes with green blush. Flesh is pale yellow; seedless varieties available	Eating fresh, juice, flavoring, zest (zest may be candied)
Ugli fruit	Hybrid citrus, with wrinkled yellow-green skin, pink-yellow flesh, seedless	Eating fresh
Juice orange	Orange skin, mottled with green; extremely juicy, smooth sweet flavor	Juice

FIGURE 5-78 Specialty Fruit

(1) Mango

(2) Kumquats

(3) Kiwi

(4) Dates

(5) Figs

(6) Pomegranate

(7) Persimmon

(8) Bananas

FIGURE 5-79   Pineapple

mented flesh, which is extremely juicy. Grapefruits, lemons, limes, oranges, and tangerines are the most common citrus fruits. They range in flavor from the sweetness of oranges to the tartness of lemons. Four common citrus fruits are shown in Figure 5-77. See Table 5-12 for additional informatio about citrus fruits.

Oranges come in three basic varieties: thin-skinned, thick-skinned, and bitter. Thin-skinned or-

anges have smooth skin that is somewhat difficult to peel. They are usually plump and sweet, which makes them ideal for juicing. Varieties include the small Valencia and the blood orange (with orange skin and red pulp). Thick-skinned oranges include the navel, which is large, seedless, and easy to peel, and consequently makes the best eating orange. Bitter oranges like Seville and Bigarade are used almost exclusively for making marmalade. Bigarade sauce—a classic hollandaise-style sauce—is flavored with the juice and rind of the Bigarade orange.

Grapefruits have yellow skin with an occasional rosy blush where the sun hits them. They are juicy and tart-sweet and are available with either white (actually yellow) or pink flesh. Pink grapefruits are generally slightly sweeter than white varieties.

Specialty Fruits   A wide variety of fruits fall into this category. Bananas are almost always picked green and allowed to ripen en route from the plantation to the ultimate buyer. Included in this category are also dates, figs, kiwis, mangos, papayas, plantains, pomegranates, carambolas (also known as star fruit), and passion fruit. (See Figures 5-78 and 5-

TABLE 5-13 GRAPE VARIETIES

Variety	Description	Peak Season/Fresh	Uses
Thompson seedless	Green, with thin skin, seedless	Year-round	Table grape, also dried as raisins
Concord	Thick skin, which may be deep purple, red, or white. Skin "slips" easily from flesh	Late summer, fall	Juices, jams, jellies, syrups, preserves
Black	Deep-purple skin, usually with seeds	Summer (may be available sporadically at other times, especially winter)	Table grape
Red Emperor	Light to deep red, occasionally with green streaking. Thin, tightly adhering skin with seeds.	Summer (available year-round, as imported item)	Table grape
Champagne	Small grape, red to light purple, seedless	Late summer	Table grape

FIGURE 5-80 Grapes

(1) Red table

(2) White/seedless

(3) Purple/black   *(4) Champagne*

79.) Pineapples will not ripen after picking and should, ideally, be picked for shipping only when fully ripe.

Grapes Grapes, either with seeds or seedless, are juicy fruits that grow in clusters on vines. Technically, they are berries, but because they include so many varieties and have so many different uses, they are grouped separately. (See Figure 5-80.) Of the many kinds available for both eating and wine making, two of the most popular are Californian or Thompson Seedless, which are appropriate for both cooking and eating out of hand, and Napoleon Red, a good table variety. Grapes are dried to form raisins, and they can be purchased throughout the year.

There are some classic dishes that make use of grapes as an ingredient. The most famous is sole Véronique, a poached fillet of sole in a cream sauce garnished with peeled seedless grapes. For the most part, they are used in fruit platters, as an accompaniment to cheese plates, or in salads. (See Table 5-13.)

Melons Melons are fragrant, succulent fruits, most of which are related to squash and cucumbers. They also come in many varieties and range from the size of an orange to that of a watermelon. The four major types are cantaloupes, watermelons, winter melons (honeydew, casaba, crenshaw), and muskmelons. (See Figure 5-81.)

The ability to determine when a melon is ripe is one that eludes some people. Depending upon the type, you will look for a variety of different signs. Cantaloupe melon should have a "full slip." This means that the melon ripened on the vine and grew away from the stem, leaving no rough edge. Unripe cantaloupes usually have a scarred or rough end. Some melons may become slightly soft at the stem end, though for other melons that could indicate that they are over-the-hill. Aroma is

TABLE 5-14 MELON VARIETIES

Variety	Description	Peak Season/Fresh	Signs of Maturity
Cantaloupe	Netting or veining over surface of skin; flesh is smooth, orange, juicy, and fragrant	Summer	Full slip; coarse netting, ground color is yellow to buff, has pleasant melon aroma
Casaba	Skin is light green to yellow green	Early fall	Smooth, velvety feel to skin. Melon aroma
Cranshaw	Salmon-colored, very fragrant flesh	Early fall	Rich melon aroma, slight softening near stem
Gallia	Green flesh that tastes and smells like cantaloupe	Early summer	
Honeydew	Green flesh, juicy	Summer	Velvety to slightly sticky feel of skin. Skin is yellow with no greenish cast
Muskmelon	Deeply ridged melon with bright orange, aromatic flesh	Mid-to-late summer	Ground color is yellow to buff (not green). Full slip
Persian	Dark green skin with yellow marking, flesh is yellow-orange	Summer	Heavy for size, some yielding when pressed
Watermelon	Large, oblong-shape melon with red or yellow flesh. Some seedless varieties	Mid-to-late summer	Underside of fruit should have some color, not dead white

FIGURE 5-81   Melons

(1) Watermelon

(2) Honeydew

(3) Cantaloupe

(4) Muskmelon

(5) Casaba

(6) Cranshaw

FIGURE 5-82   Peaches, Nectarines, and Apricots

(1) Apricot   *(2) Peach and nectarine*   *(3) White peach*

one of the best keys to determining ripeness. (See Table 5-14.)

Stone Fruits   Peaches, nectarines, apricots, plums, and cherries are often referred to as "stone fruits." This means that they have one large, central pit, or "stone." They typically come into peak season throughout late spring and summer growing seasons. Stone fruits need to be handled delicately because their flesh has a tendency to bruise easily. Stone fruits are used in jams, preserves, shortcakes, pies, cobblers, as well as in savory dishes. In addition to their fresh form, these fruits are also commonly available as canned, frozen, and dried commodities. Fruit brandies, wines, and cordials flavored with peaches, cherries, and plums are produced in many countries around the world.

Peaches   Sweet and juicy, having a distinctively fuzzy skin, they come in many varieties. All peaches fall into one of two categories—clingstone or freestone. Clingstone peaches have flesh that clings to the pit, whereas the flesh of freestone peaches separates easily. Peach flesh comes in a range of color, from white to creamy yellow to yellow-orange to red, with a whole host of combinations possible.

Nectarines   They are similar in shape, color, and flavor to peaches, and they are classified similarly as either clingstone or freestone. They have smooth skin and their flesh may closely resemble the flesh of plums in texture in some varieties.

Apricots   They resemble peaches in some ways. They have slightly fuzzy skin but are smaller, with somewhat drier flesh. They range in color from yellow to golden-orange and some have rosy patches

Plums   Plums can be anywhere in size from as small as an apricot to as large as a peach. Their col-

FIGURE 5-83   Plums

(1) Santa Rosa   *(2) Black Friar*

TABLE 5-15   PLUM VARIETIES

Variety	Description	Peak Season/Fresh	Uses
Santa Rosa	Red, with light-yellow flesh	Fall	Eating fresh
Black Friar	Dark-purple with silvery bloom, deep red to purple flesh	Fall	Eating fresh
Damson	Small, with red to light-purple skin, green flesh	Fall	Eating fresh, preserves, conserved, pies
Greengage	Green skin, with yellow-green flesh	Fall	Eating fresh
Prune	Small, purple skin with green flesh, flesh is relatively dry, and pit comes cleanly away	Fall	Eating fresh, dried as prunes. Also known as "prune plum"

FIGURE 5-84   Pears

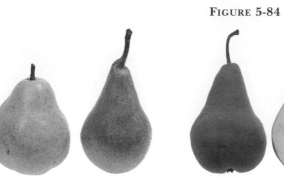

(1) *Bartlett and green (unripe) Bosc*

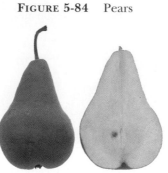

(2) *Ripe Bosc*

(3) *Seckle and Red Bartlett*

TABLE 5-16 PEARS

Variety	Description	Peak Season/Fresh	Uses
Bartlett	Green skin, turning yellow as fruit ripens, some red varieties	Fall	Eating fresh, poached
Bosc	Long neck, dark russeted skin, brown when ripe	Late fall	Eating fresh, poached, baked
d'Anjou	Green skin, becoming yellow as it ripens, may have brown scarring	Fall	Eating fresh, poached, baked
Seckel	Small pear, green skin with red blush, crisp flesh	Fall	Eating fresh
William	Long neck, yellow skin, strong perfume	Fall	Preserves, used to flavor cordial "Poire William"

ors range from green, to red, to purple, with various shades in-between. (See Figure 5-83.) When ripe, they are sweet and juicy, and some have sour skins that contrast nicely with their succulent flesh. Cooking plums are generally drier and more acidic than dessert plums, but both types can be eaten raw. Greengage, a sweet plum with green skin and flesh, is a popular dessert variety. Damson, which has purple skin with a silver-blue bloom (faint blush on the skin), is probably the most well-known cooking plum. (See Table 5-15.)

Cherries Cherries are grown in numerous varieties and come in many shades of red, from the light crimson of Queen Anne to the almost black Bing. They vary in texture from hard and crisp to soft and juicy, and flavors run the gamut from sweet to sour. Cherries are available in a number of different forms. They may be found fresh throughout their growing season, and are also sold canned or dried. Fillings for Danish, pies, and other pastries can also be found, as well a cherry syrups. Cherry-

flavored *kirschwasser,* a clear cordial, is often used in bake shops and kitchens.

Pears Pears are to the French what apples are to the Americans. They also come in many varieties, although fewer than apples. The most commonly available are Bartlett, Bosc, d'Anjou, and Seckel. (See Figure 5-84.) The flesh of pears is extremely fragile. Because they are usually picked for shipping before they have ripened, it is sometimes difficult to find perfectly ripe pears in the market. They will become softer after picking but will not actually continue to ripen. For this reason, pears are often poached whole or used in a sorbet to

FIGURE 5-85   Rhubarb

compensate for their underdeveloped flavor. (See Table 5-16.)

Rhubarb Although technically a vegetable, rhubarb has been classified here as a fruit because of the way it is used. Known as "pie plant," it grows in long stalks with broad, somewhat curly leaves. Only the reddish-green stalks are eaten. The leaves should not be ingested because they contain a high concentration of a toxic compound known as oxalic acid. Rhubarb is crisp and very sour, so it is usu-

---

oxalic acid: A chemical compound found in plants, such as rhubarb leaves, spinach, and sorrel. Some foods have levels concentrated enough to be poisonous.

ally cooked and sweetened. In addition to being served as a dessert, it is classically combined with rich, oily fish, such as mackerel or bluefish. (See Figure 5-85.)

Vegetables

Vegetables include a number of foods, even some that might be botanically classified as "fruits." Tomatoes, for example, are really fruits. Their culinary application is the guiding principle for placing them in this section, rather than the previous one.

As we continue to explore other cuisines, and to reexamine some of the traditional dishes from vari-

TABLE 5-17 GENERAL VEGETABLE INFORMATION

Vegetable by Type	Grades Available	Pack/Weight and/or Count	Yield %	Available Forms
Artichoke, globe	U.S. No. 1, No. 2	½ carton (20#, 18, 24, 48 or 60 count)	40%	Fresh, frozen (hearts) marinated, canned in brine
Asparagus	U.S. No. 1, No.2	Case/pyramid (30#)	varies	Fresh, (green, white), canned, frozen, pieces
Avocados	U.S. No. 1; U.S. Combination; U.S. No. 2	Case (36 count)	50%	Fresh, purée, canned, frozen
Beans	U.S. Fancy No.1; U.S. Combination; U.S. No. 2	Case (varies by type)	varies	Fresh (see Table 5-25), frozen, canned
Beets	U.S. No. 1; U.S. No. 2	Case, (25# carton: 24-bunch count)	75%	Fresh (see Table 5-27), frozen, canned
Broccoli	U.S. Fancy; U.S. No. 1; U.S. No. 2	Case (14 bunches)	65%	Fresh, frozen: pieces, spears, chopped
Brussels sprouts	U.S. No. 1; U.S. No. 2	Flat (12 pints)	75%	Fresh
Cabbage	U.S. . No. 1; U.S. Commercial	Case (varies by type)	75%	Fresh (see Table 5-18)
Carrots	U.S. Extra No. 1; U.S. No. 1; U.S. No. 1 Jumbo; U.S. No. 2	Case (varies by type)	85%	Fresh
Cauliflower	U.S. No. 1	Case (12 heads)	58%	Fresh, frozen: florets
Celeriac	U.S. No. 1	Case (12#)	75%	Fresh
Celery	U.S. Extra; U.S. No. 1; U.S. No. 2	Carton (weight and count varies)	75%	Fresh
Corn (sweet)	U.S. Fancy; U.S. No. 1; U.S. No. 2	Case, crate, or bag	48%	Fresh, frozen kernels, canned kernels
Cucumbers	U.S. Fancy; U.S. Choice; U.S. Extra No. 1; U.S. No. 1 Small; U.S. No. 1 Large	Carton, bushel, or LA lug (count and weight varies)	93% (peeled) or 68% (peeled & seeded)	Fresh (see Table 5-20)
Eggplant	U.S. Fancy; U.S. No. 1; U.S. No. 2	Case (count and weight varies)	81%	Fresh (see Table 5-20)
Fennel	U.S. No. 1	Case (24 each)	45%	Fresh

(Table continued on following page)

TABLE 5-17 GENERAL VEGETABLE INFORMATION *(continued)*

Vegetable by Type	Grades Available	Pack/Weight and/or Count	Yield %	Available Forms
Greens (cooking)	(Varies by type)	Case (weight varies)	average of 65%	Fresh (see Table 5-19)
Kohlrabi	No Federal grades	Case (24#)	58%	Fresh
Lettuces	(Varies by type)	Case, flat (weight varies)	average of 70%	Fresh (see Table 5-21)
Mushrooms	(Grading for domestic only) U.S. No. 1; U.S. No. 2	Basket (3#); case or flat (weight varies), or bulk, by #	average of 95%	Fresh (see Table 5-22), dried, canned Frozen, sliced
Onions (cured/dry)	U.S. No. 1, Export; Commerical; U.S. No. 1; U.S. No. 1 Picklers; U.S. No. 2	Bag (25 to 50#)	85%	Fresh (see Table 5-23)
Onions (green/fresh)	U.S. No. 1; U.S. No. 2	Case (48 bunches)	90%	Fresh
Parsnip	U.S. No. 1; U.S. No. 2	Case (12#)	80%	Fresh, frozen
Peas	U.S. No. 1; U.S. Fancy	Case or bunch (weight varies)	varies by type	Fresh (see Table 5-25), frozen, canned
Peppers, sweet	U.S. Fancy; U.S. No. 1; U.S. No. 2	Case (weight varies)	average of 80%	Fresh
Peppers, chili	No Federal grades	Case or bulk by #	85%	Fresh (see Table 5-24)
Potatoes	(Varies by type)	Case or bag (weight varies)	varies by use	Fresh (see Table 5-26) Frozen, canned
Squash (summer)	U.S. No. 1; U.S. No. 2	Case (count and weight varies)	80%	Fresh (see Table 5-20)
Squash (winter)	U.S. No. 1; U.S. No. 2	Case (count and weight varies)	75%	Fresh (see Table 5-20), frozen, pieces, canned
Tomatoes	U.S. No. 1; U.S. Combination; U.S. No. 2; U.S. No.3	Case (count and weight varies)	100% (varies by use)	Fresh (see Table 5-28), canned, dried
Turnips	U.S. No. 1; U.S. No. 2	Case (25#)	80%	Fresh
Rutabagas	U.S. No. 1; U.S. No. 2	Case (50#)	80%	Fresh

ous regions in our own country, we are becoming more adventurous in our selection of vegetables to serve either as side dishes, or on their own, as appetizers, salads, and entrées. Table 5-17 provides general information about basic vegetable types.

Avocados These egg- or pear-shaped vegetables have green to black leathery skin, which can be smooth or bumpy. (See Figure 5-86.) Avocado flesh is buttery smooth, delicately flavored, green near the skin, and yellow toward

FIGURE 5-86 Avocado

the center. Cut surfaces can be treated with lemon or lime juice to prevent browning.

Haas avocados have dark, pebbly skin and a more-pronounced pear shape than other varieties. Florida varieties are smoother and brighter green in color. If avocados are not ripe when you purchase them, hold them at room temperature (around 70°F/21°C) until they soften. Use ripe avocados as soon as possible, and avoid refrigerating them. If they must be stored in the refrigerator, allow them enough time to warm slightly before

RIPENING AN AVOCADO

When you know you are going to need an avocado tomorrow and your entire supply is still rock hard, there is a trick known to speed the ripening process:

Place it in a paper bag with a banana peel overnight.

serving them, so that their full flavor is allowed to develop.

Cabbage Family The cabbage family *(brassicas)* includes broccoli, Brussels sprouts, cauliflower, kale, kohlrabi, collard greens, and many kinds of cabbage. (See Figure 5-87.) All have a similar flavor. Turnips and rutabagas are also members of the brassica family, but they are more commonly thought of as root vegetables. Various cooking

FIGURE 5-87   Cabbages

(1) Green, Napa, and red cabbages   *(2) Red, cut*   *(3) Bok choy, Savoy*

(4) Kohlrabi, broccoli, broccoli rabe, cauliflower   *(5) Brussels sprouts*

TABLE 5-18 CABBAGE VARIETIES

Variety	Description	Peak Season/Fresh	Quality Indicators
Broccoli	Usually dark green, some have purple cast	Summer. Also available year-round through imports	Flowers are tight, stems ends not split; leaves firm.
Broccoli rabe (also broccoli raab, rapini)	Stemmed, green, with small florets, leafy	Summer to fall	No yellowing of flowers, leaves firm and stems bright white to light green.
Brussels Sprouts	Small, round, cabbage-shaped, light green	Late fall to winter. Can be found year-round from storage or imports	Leaves firmly attached, stem ends bright.
Cabbage, bok choy	Loose head, deep-green glossy leaves and green-to-white stems	Summer into fall. Available year-round	Stems should be fresh and firm, leaves unwithered.
Cabbage, celery	Long, heading cabbage with light, yellow, green color	Summer into fall. Available year-round	Free from browning of withering of leaves. Relatively heavy for size.

(Table continued on following page)

TABLE 5-18 CABBAGE VARIETIES *(continued)*

Variety	Description	Peak Season/Fresh	Quality Indicators
Cabbage, green	Tight, round, heading cabbage. Color may range from light to medium green	Late summer to fall. Available year-round	May have loose "wrapper leaves" that should be firm, unwithered. Free from browning or bore holes. Heavy for size. Early varieties are less tight. Winter or storage cabbage are more firmly packed.
Cabbage, red	Tight, round heading cabbage ranging from deep purple to maroon. Stems on individual leaves are white, giving marbled appearance when cut	Late summer to fall. Available year-round	May have loose wrapper leaves with greenish cast. Head should be very glossy with creamy-white veining.
Cabbage, Savoy	Moderately tight round heading cabbage. Leaves are textured, giving a "waffled" appearance	Summer to fall	Color can range from moderate to light green, but should appear fresh. Loose "wrapper" leaves should be firm.
Cauliflower	Snowy-to creamy-white flowering head with green leaves	Late summer to fall. Available throughout the year in most areas	No evidence of yellowing, browning, or opened flowers. Wrapper leaves should be firmly attached, no wilting.
Kohlrabi	Round, turnip-shaped bulb with stems and leaves attached; also known as cabbage turnip	Early summer, periodically throughout the year	Bulbs should be firm, no evidence of cracking. Leaves should be firm and green, no evidence of yellowing.

greens are shown in Figure 5-88 and described in Table 5-19.

Cooking Greens Chefs across the country are beginning to make use of the wide variety of cooking greens. A resurgence of interest in authentic regional dishes from this country and other cuisines around the world is partly responsible. Another important factor is the public's awareness of the po-

tent vitamin and mineral "cocktails" they deliver. Cooking greens can be eaten raw, as long as they have been harvested while still quite young. In fact, many mesclun mixes include one or two of these greens. Still, as the name implies, the most common way to serve greens is as a cooked dish.

Cooking greens have a rather limited shelf life, and should be used as soon after they are purchased as possible. Some types are perfect for quick

FIGURE 5-88 Cooking Greens

(1) Collards, dandelion, beet green, turnip, arugula (from bottom left, clockwise)   *(2) Ruby chard*   *(3) Swiss chard*   *(4) Spinach*

TABLE 5-19 COOKING GREENS

Variety	Description	Peak Season/Fresh	Uses
Beet greens	Flat leaf, red ribbing	Year-round, especially summer into fall	Steamed, sautéed (especially with garlic), braised
Collards	Large, flat, rounded leaves	Fall	Steamed, sautéed (especially with garlic), braised
Dandelion greens	Narrow leaves with deep teeth on edges	Spring	Steamed, sautéed (especially with garlic), braised
Kale	Ruffled leaves	Late fall	Steamed, sautéed (especially with garlic), braised, soups
Mustard greens	Deeply scalloped, narrow leaves	Summer	Steamed, sautéed (especially with garlic), braised
Spinach	Leaves may be deeply lobed or flat, depending upon variety; deep green	Year-round	Steamed, sautéed (especially with garlic), braised, served raw in salads
Swiss chard	Deeply lobed, glossy leaves, dark green, stems and ribs may be white or deep ruby	Fall	Steamed, sautéed (especially with garlic), braised
Turnip greens	Broad flat leaves with coarse texture, green	Summer into fall	Steamed, sautéed (especially with garlic), braised

stir-fries. Others are best when treated to a long slow simmer, with or without the addition of ham hocks, bacon, or other smoked pork items. (See Table 5–19 and Figure 5-88.)

Cucumbers, Squash, and Eggplant Cucumbers and the many squash varieties are members of the gourd family. Eggplants share many similarities with the gourd family, though they are botanically unrelated. All have fairly tough rinds, thick flesh, and flat, oval seeds. Summer squash (zucchini, yellow, crookneck, pattypan) are picked when they are immature to ensure a delicate flesh, tender seeds, and thin edible skins. Winter squash (acorn, butternut, hubbard, pumpkin, spaghetti) are characterized by their inedible rind and seeds. (See Figures 5-89 and 5-90 and Table 5-20.)

Cucumbers are a common ingredient in salad bowls, crudité platters, and as part of uncooked sauces or soups, such as salsa or gazpacho. They can also be served cooked, or as a part of a creamed soup.

Eggplant is a member of the nightshade family, which includes potatoes, tomatoes and many poisonous plants as well. It comes in a range of shapes and sizes from the slender, glossy black Japanese varieties, to very large specimens. Although many people swear by their own technique for removing the bitterness from eggplant, the best advice is to choose eggplant that are mature, but not overlarge by type. Roasted eggplant is used in numerous dishes, ranging from a Middle Eastern dip to a luscious soup. It is wonderful grilled, pan-fried, braised, or stewed. Ratatouille, a famous French vegetable stew, makes liberal use of eggplant.

Lettuces Salads have long been one of the most neglected parts of many menus. Today's chef has more options regarding the type and quality of greens featured in the salad bowl than at any other time, however. (See Figure 5-92.) Guests at your restaurant are growing less and less likely to be satisfied with a wedge of iceberg and Thousand Island dressing.

Some lettuces are better "keepers" than others. Special mixes can be purchased, some with the addition of edible flowers, such as nasturtiums, chrysanthemums, or pansies. (See Table 5-21.)

Mushrooms Mushrooms are a type of fungus. Some varieties are edible and delicious, some are edible but of little culinary consequence. Still others are toxic, producing a host of unpleasant effects ranging from cramps and headaches to death. Knowing

crudité: raw seasonal vegetables, often served with a dip, as an appetizer.

FIGURE 5-89   Cucumber and Summer Squash

(1) English/seedless,
slicing, and Kirby
cucumbers (top to bottom)

(2) Yellow squash and zucchini

(3) Chayote

(4) Zucchini with blossom

(5) Baby pattypan

FIGURE 5-90   Winter Squash

(1) Spaghetti squash

(2) Hubbard, mini-pumpkins, cheese squash

(3) Acorn squash

(4) Butternut squash

TABLE 5-20 CUCUMBER, SQUASH, AND EGGPLANT VARIETIES

Variety	Description	Uses
Cucumbers		
Slicing	Long, narrow, green, occasionally with pale-green or yellow underside	Salads, pickling, relishes, uncooked sauces
Kirby	Short, chubby cylinder with green skin, deep ridges, warts	Eating fresh, pickles
English/burpless	Long, even cylinder with some ridging, no seeds	Salads, crudités
Squash, Summer		
Pattypan	Yellow (may be mottled or streaked with green) flattened ball shape	Generally steamed, sautéed, pan-fried
Chayote	Pear-shape, green, with deep ridging between halves	Steamed, sautéed, stir-fried, stuffed, pan-fried
Crookneck	Yellow skin with bent narrow neck	As for pattypan
Yellow	Yellow, elongated pear shape	As for pattypan
Zucchini	Green, with flecks of yellow, cylinder shape. Golden variety is deep yellow with green at stem end	As for pattypan, also in breads, fritters
Squash, Winter		
Acorn	Dark green (some varieties may have orange blush or be virtually all orange) with deep ridges and acorn shape	Baked, puréed, simmered, glazed with honey or maple syrup, soups
Butternut	Tan, orange, or light brown skin, elongated pear shape	Baked, puréed, simmered, glazed with honey or maple syrup, soups
Hubbard	Dusty green, very warty	Baked, puréed, simmered, glazed with honey or maple syrup, soups
Pumpkin	Deep orange with deep ridges	Baked, puréed, simmered, glazed with honey or maple syrup, soups, pies, breads
Spaghetti	Yellow, "zeppelin" shape	Steamed or roasted, flesh may be served with herbs, sauces, etc.
Eggplant		
Purple (standard)	May have rounded or elongated pear shape, deep glossy purple/black skin. Green leaves attached	Stewed, braised, roasted, grilled
Japanese	Long, narrow, cylinder shape with deep glossy purple black shape	Stewed, braised, roasted, grilled
White	May be long or round (egg shape) Some are streaked with purple	Stewed, braised, roasted, grilled

your purveyor is of great importance when you have wild mushroom varieties on the menu. Extreme caution should be exercised when accepting any mushrooms from a forager. Remember that certain wild mushrooms can be toxic, even fatal. Domestically raised mushrooms include familiar white or button mushrooms, as well as exotic varieties, including shiitakes and oyster mushrooms. There are other varieties that are not yet successfully farm-raised, and are offered to either the purveyor or the chef by professional "foragers." (See Figure 5-92.)

Most mushrooms are completely edible, but if the stem is tough (such as shiitakes) or has a sticky skin it should be trimmed away. Many wild mushrooms are available dried as well as fresh. Dried versions of morels, shiitakes, and wood ears are sometimes preferred for certain dishes, as they deliver an even more intense flavor than when fresh. (See Table 5-22.)

(Continued on page 167)

TABLE 5-21 LETTUCE VARIETIES

Variety	Description	Flavor
Arugula	Tender leaves, rounded "teeth"	Pungent, peppery, becoming very biting as it ages
Belgian endive	Tight, oblong head, white leaves with some yellow or green at tips	Slightly bitter; often prepared as a braised. vegetable, in addition to use as salad item.
Boston lettuce (butterhead)	Soft, tender leaves. Heading lettuce	Mild, delicate flavor. May also be braised as vegetable.
Curly endive	Heading lettuce; sharp "teeth" on curly leaves. Interior leaves light yellow	Slightly to very bitter.
Escarole	Heading lettuce, with scalloped edges on leaves	Slightly to very bitter. Often served as cooking green, in soups, stews.
Iceberg lettuce	Tight heading lettuce with pale-green leaves	Very mild
Leaf lettuce	May be green or red-tipped. Loose heading lettuce with tender leaves	Usually mild, becoming bitter with age.
Oak leaf lettuce	Deep scalloping on leaves, tender	Nutty flavor
Mâche	Loose bunches, very tender leaves, rounded	Very delicate flavor
Radicchio	Heading form of endive, deep-red to purple leaves with white veining	Bitter
Watercress	Bunching green, with rounded scallops on leaves	Peppery

FIGURE 5-91 Lettuces

(1) Iceberg, Boston, and Romaine

(2) Red/green leaf

(3) Arugula   *(4) Mesclun mix*

FIGURE 5-92 Mushrooms

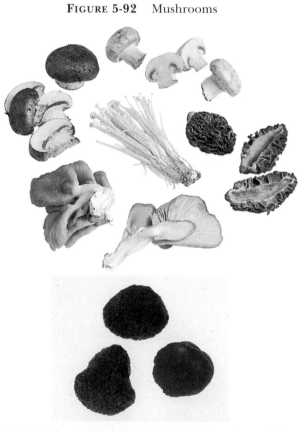

(clockwise from top: cultivated white, morel, oyster, cremini, enoki; below: truffles)

TABLE 5-22 MUSHROOM VARIETIES

Variety	Description	Peak Season/Fresh	Uses
White	Standard white-to-buff-colored mushroom	Year-round	Raw or cooked, marinated, in sauces, soups, stews
Boletus (also bolete)	Rounded golden cap, bulbous stem	Fall	Raw or cooked, marinated, in sauces, soups, stews; may be dried
Cèpe (also Cep)	Type of boletus	Fall	Raw or cooked, marinated, in sauces, soups, stews
Chanterelles	Golden to apricot (black and ivory sometimes available)	Fall	Raw or cooked, marinated, in sauces, soups, stews
Cremini	Round cap, buff to brown	Year-round	Raw, cooked, sauces
Enoki (enokidake)	White to buff, long slender stalk-like mushrooms	Year-round	Salads, Asian dishes, soups and consommés as garnish
Lobster mushroom	Deep red, mottled color	Fall	Sautéed, used in some sauces
Morels	Cone-shaped cap, deeply pitted, hollow stem and cap	Early spring	Sauces, in cream sauce, may be dried
Porcini	Type of boletus		Raw or cooked, marinated, in sauces, soups, stews; may be dried
Portobello	Large tan-to-brown caps, opened from stem, like a parasol	Fall	Sautéed or grilled
Oak mushroom	Creamy to silvery gray cluster of shell-shaped mushrooms, very delicate	Year-round (farm-raised)	Sautéed, used in some sauces, ragouts, etc.
Oyster mushroom	See Oak mushroom		
Shiitake	Parasol-shaped with light-brown cap, tough stems (usually cut away before cooking)	Year-round	Sautéed or grilled; frequently dried
Straw mushrooms	Conical cap, usually gray to nearly black with white "fringe" and slender stems	Year-round	Sautéed, used in some sauces, ragouts, etc.
Truffles	Ball-shaped fungus, may be black or white	Black, fall; white, spring into summer	Sautéed, used in some sauces, ragouts; sold canned, as essence, or as truffle-flavored oil, fresh

TRUFFLES

Worthy of a special mention here are truffles, which are perhaps, the most singularly costly item of produce you can buy. Truffles are a rounded, knobby, rough-skinned variety of mushroom. The finest specimens are considered by many to be black truffles from France. White truffles from Italy are also highly prized, although many other regions all over the world produce truffles of reputed lesser quality.

Truffles grow underground at the base of oak trees, and are found with the help of specially trained dogs or pigs, which are used to sniff them out.

Despite their dusty and nondelicate appearance, truffles give off a heady, earthy aroma and flavor. Black truffles are always cooked and there are a wide variety of classic recipes that call for them. Raw white truffles are traditionally served thinly shaved over risotto and other rice and pasta dishes.

Fresh truffles are often stored in dry rice. The rice absorbs their aroma and should be used when the truffles are gone. Canned truffles and truffle essence are also available.

TABLE 5-23 ONION VARIETIES

Variety	Description	Uses
Boiling onions	Small round onions with white skin	Stews, soups, compotes
Cippolini onions	Small round, flattened onions with yellow papery skin	Baked, grilled, casserole
Garlic (standard, elephant)	Bulb, with white or red-streaked papery skin, encasing individual cloves, also covered with papery skin	Flavoring ingredient; may be roasted into purée
Leeks	Long, fresh onion with white root end gradually becoming a dark green at tops	Grilled, steamed, serve "à la grecque" or other cold preparation. Used extensively in soups, stews, and sauces; main ingredient or flavoring
Pearl onions	Small, oval onions. May be white or red.	Boiled, pickled, or brined. Often served in stews and braises
Ramps	Wild leeks, small white stem ends with flat green tops	Stewed or sautéed
Red onions	Small, round flattened onions with red papery skin. Flesh is red and white	Eaten raw in salads, grilled, in compotes or marmalades
Scallions (green onions)	Fresh onions, with white root ends becoming green at tops. Entire plant is used, except for roots	Eaten raw as crudité, in salads, as ingredient in uncooked sauces
Shallots	May be cloves bunched together or single shallots, with light-brown papery skin. Flesh is white/purple	Used primarily as flavoring ingredient
Spanish onions	Large onions with yellow to yellow-brown skin. Flesh is milder than yellow onion	Used as an aromatic or ingredient in soups, stews, sauces, braises. Basic component of mirepoix
Sweet onions (Walla Walla, Vidalia, Maui)	Generally has flattened shape. Skin varies by type from white to tan. Flesh is very sweet	Eaten raw in salads, grilled, sautéed
Yellow onions	Moderate size, with yellow brown, papery skin. Pungent flesh	Used as an aromatic or ingredient (see Spanish onions)
White onions	Moderate size, with white, papery skin	Used as an aromatic or ingredient (see Spanish onions)

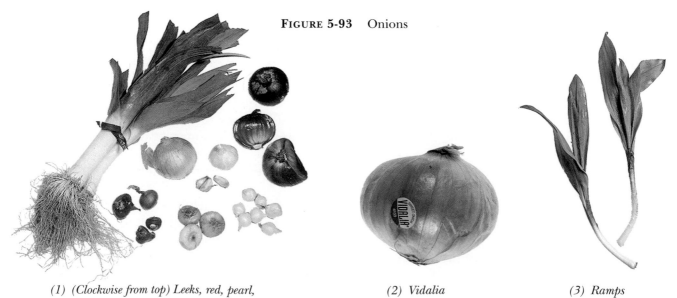

FIGURE 5-93   Onions

(1) (Clockwise from top) Leeks, red, pearl, cippolini, shallots, Spanish, and garlic

(2) Vidalia

(3) Ramps

Onion Family Onions and their relations belong to the *allium,* or lily, family. All varieties share a pungent flavor and aroma. It is hard to imagine a kitchen without a good supply of this basic item. Garlic, shallots, dry, and green onions are used in so many dishes, and in so many guises, that they are quite rightly considered indispensable. (See Figure 5-93.)

Onions are part of that most fundamental aromatic combination—mirepoix. Garlic is called for in so many preparations that it is nearly taken for granted. Roasted, chopped, or slivered, it can be found as a topping for flatbreads, a flavoring for sauces, or the main ingredient in soups or sauces. Over the last several years, sweet onions have become widely available at certain times of the year. These varieties are often featured either raw or as grilled, baked, or broiled dishes.

Onions fall into two main categories, reflecting the state in which they are used: cured (dried) and fresh (green). Dry onions should be stored in a relatively cool, dry area of the kitchen in the bags or boxes in which they are received. (See Table 5-23.) Fresh onions should be stored under refrigeration. One additional member of this family that has not been included here is chives. They are discussed with other fresh herbs in the section that follows.

Peppers, Bell Bell, or sweet, peppers are named for their shape and come in many colors—green, red, yellow, even creamy white and purple-black. All peppers start out green, but special varieties will ripen into rich vibrant colors. Sweet peppers have similar flavors, though red and yellow varieties tend to be sweeter than green peppers. Still, it is generally acceptable to substitute one color for another. The only big difference in most dishes will be appearance.

Bell peppers are hollow, except for whitish ribs and a core with a cluster of small seeds. Usually both ribs and core are removed before use. One of the most popular ways to prepare sweet peppers is to roast them and toss them with a good-quality oil, fresh herbs, and cracked peppercorns. They are featured in sauces such as coulis, in antipastos, as the topping for grilled breads or pizzas, and in salads.

Look for firm peppers when examining a delivery or the offerings in the local farmer's market. The skin should be tight and glossy, with no puckering or wrinkling. The flesh should be thick and crisp. Depending upon the variety, the color may be mottled or streaked and the pepper may be more or less deeply ridged. Peppers will keep well for several days, but if a few peppers in a box begin to soften or develop brown spots, check the entire box immediately and use all acceptable peppers as soon as possible. Once peppers start to lose quality, they go quickly.

Peppers, Chili Chili peppers (*chiles* in Spanish) are related to bell peppers, but they are usually smaller and contain spicy, volatile oils. There are numerous books devoted to chili peppers, and a whole host of fresh and dried chilies are available throughout the entire country. (See Figure 5-94.) The hotter the peppers, the more important it is to handle them carefully. Use sensible precautions when working with such powerhouses as habaneros or banana chilies—wear gloves, wash and rinse your cutting surface and knives, and avoid contact with sensitive tissues, such as the eyes. (See pages 227-229 for more information.)

Chilies are available fresh, canned, dried (whole, flaked, and ground), and smoked. Fre-

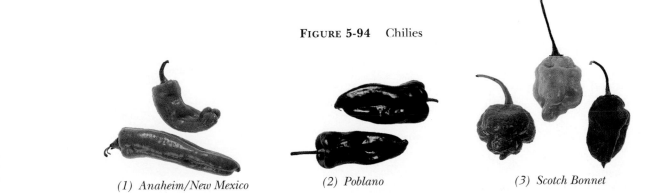

FIGURE 5-94 Chilies

(1) Anaheim/New Mexico   *(2) Poblano*   *(3) Scotch Bonnet*

TABLE 5-24 CHILI PEPPER VARIETIES*

Variety	Description	Forms
Anaheim (also New Mexico)	Tapered deep-green chili, glossy	Fresh, dried
Banana (also Hungarian wax)	Small tapered chili, pale yellow to yellow green. Considered one of the hottest peppers	Used in sauces, stews, may be pickled
Habanero (also Scotch bonnet)	Ball-shaped, wrinkled pepper, about the size of cherry pepper. Possibly the hottest pepper	Used in sauces, bottled condiments, as dried flakes
Jalapeño	Compact tapered chili, may be deep green, or red	Chipotle (roasted, usually packed in adobo sauce); pickled; canned whole or chopped)
Poblano (also ancho, pasilla)	Very-deep green to black, tapered and flattened shape. Relatively mild	Often used for stuffing
Serrano	Tiny, skinny, dark green, and very hot	May be used in place of jalapeños, or use jalapeños in their place

*Peak season occurs during the summer months, but are generally available fresh throughout the year.

quently, smoked chilies are given another name. Popular varieties include anaheim, ancho/poblano, jalapeño, and serrano. (See Table 5-24.)

Pod and Seed Vegetables These vegetables include fresh legumes, such as peas, beans, and bean sprouts, as well as corn and okra. All are best eaten

DRIED CHILI NOMENCLATURE

Dried chilies are often given different names to distinguish them from fresh chilies, as the following list illustrates:

Fresh	Dried (*and smoked)
poblano	ancho
poblano	mulato
jalapeño	chipotle*
jalapeño	mora or morita*
New Mexico green	New Mexico, or California
New Mexico red	pasado (roasted and peeled, then dried)
chilaca	pasilla
serrano	chilie seco, or serano seco

* Chili is also smoked.

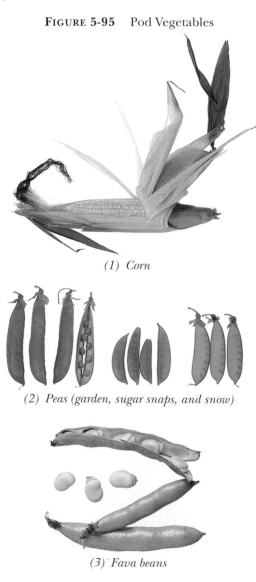

FIGURE 5-95   Pod Vegetables

(1) Corn

(2) Peas (garden, sugar snaps, and snow)

(3) Fava beans

TABLE 5-25 PEA AND BEAN VARIETIES

Variety	Description	Peak Season/Fresh	Uses
Beans, Edible Pods			
Green beans	Long green beans, slender, with even, matte color	Mid-to late summer	As side dish, pickled, may be fresh or frozen
Haricot verts	Smaller and more slender than regular regular beans, velvety skin	Mid-to late summer	Side dish
Romano	Similar in color to regular beans, but wider and more flattened with more developed flavor	Mid-to late summer	As for regular beans, often braised with ham or bacon
Burgundy/purple	Similar in shape to regular beans, but with deep purple to maroon skin that turns green as it is cooked	Mid-to late summer	As for regular beans
Beans, Inedible Pods*			
Fava	Pods are long, large, and light green, beans are a delicate green color, almost kidney shaped	Spring to early summer	Cooked, puréed, may be cooked and eaten cold. Large beans must be peeled before eating
Cranberry	Pods are white streaked with red, beans are mottled with red	Midsummer	Cooked, puréed, soups, braised
Borlotti	Pods are green to buff, beans are creamy white	Early to midsummer	Cooked, puréed, soups, braised
Flageolot	Pods are green, beans are a light green	Midsummer	Cooked, puréed, soups, braised
Black-eyed pea	Pods are green often mottled with brown, beans are round, tan, with black "eye"	Throughout summer and into fall	Cooked, puréed, soups, braised; Hoppin' John is most famous dish
Peas			
Garden pea/ petit pois	Pods are tapered, rounded, and should "squeak" when rubbed together, peas are round, light-drab green when raw	Early spring to summer	Steamed, stewed (petits pois à la Française), chilled, puréed, in soups
Snow pea	Pods are flat, drab green when raw	Early spring to summer	Steamed, stir-fried
Sugar snap	Pods are deeper green than garden or snow peas	Early spring to summer	Steamed, stir-fried

*All beans in this section are available fresh and also dried.

young and fresh, when they are at their sweetest and most tender. Once picked, they begin to convert their natural sugars into starch. Garden peas and sweet corn are especially prone to flavor loss. There is a perceptible difference in the quality of these items within only hours of picking. They can lose their sweetness as soon as a day after being harvested. After a few days, they become mealy.

If possible, purchase pod and seed vegetables from local growers to minimize lag time between picking and serving. Peas, beans, and corn are also available in dried form, as discussed later in this chapter.

Some fresh peas and beans are eaten whole, when the pods are still fleshy and tender—for example, sugar snap peas, snow peas, green beans, and wax beans. In other cases, the peas or beans

FIGURE 5-96 Potatoes

(clockwise from top left: Red Bliss, Sweet potato, Yams, Russet, Chef's, and Russet)

TABLE 5-26 POTATO VARIETIES

Variety	Description	Peak Season/Fresh	Uses
Chef's potato	Firm, smooth, relatively round with white to light tan skin, shallow eyes. Available in range of sizes (chef can specify)	Year-round (fresh in late summer into fall)	The younger the potato, the waxier it is. Used for salads, purées, soups, and other dishes. Tends to be too moist for baking
Red potato	Firm, smooth, relatively round with light-pink to dark-red skin, shallow eyes. Available in range of sizes (chef can specify)	Year-round (fresh in late summer into fall)	The younger the potato, the waxier it is. Used for salads, purées, soups, and other dishes. Excellent for oven-roasting.
Russet/Idaho	Oblong, with brown, russeted skin	Year-round (fresh in late summer into fall)	Best for baking and for frying
Purple/Caribe	Deep-purple skin with purple flesh	Midsummer	Salads, home-fries, other preparations to showcase color and flavor
Yukon gold/ Yellow Finn	Brown, tan, or red skin with buttery golden flesh	Year-round (fresh in late summer into fall)	Baked, puréed, casseroles, salads
Irish	Relatively round, but generally "misshapen," deep eyes	Late summer	Boiling
Salt	Small, no more than 1 inch in diameter	Year-round (fresh in late summer into fall)	Boiling, steaming
New potatoes	Same as chef's, but no more than 1–1½ inches in diameter	Early summer	Steaming, oven-roasting with herbs
Bliss potatoes	Same as red, but no more than 1–1½ inches in diameter	Early summer	Steaming, oven-roasting with herbs
Sweet potatoes	Light to deep-orange skin with deep orange, moist flesh, may be rounded or tapered, dense texture, quite sweet	Year-round (fresh in late summer into fall)	Roasted, boiled, puréed, used in casseroles, soups
Yam	Tan to light-brown russeted skin with pale to deep yellow flesh, dryer and less sweet than sweet potato	Year-round (fresh in late summer into fall)	Roasted, boiled, puréed, used in casseroles, soups

(such as limas, scarlet runners, and black-eyed peas) are removed from their inedible pods. (See Figure 5-95 and Table 5-25.)

Potatoes The popularity of potatoes has swung like a pendulum. They have gone from being America's favorite side dish, to an item that weight-watchers and sophisticates shunned as too filling and pedestrian, back to the limelight as a terrific source of various nutrients. Today, you can choose from a wide variety of special potatoes, as well as the more familiar favorites, to establish a repertoire of potato dishes that belong in virtually every category of the menu. (See Figure 5-96 and Table 5-26.)

This sweet, subtly flavored tuber was originally grown in South America. The potato was at first thought to be poisonous by the Europeans. After a long period of distrust, they were both finally established as standard items in cuisines around the world. A French physician, Antoine-August Parmentier, was perhaps most responsible for changing the public opinion. Without his efforts, some classic dishes developed by French chefs might still be undiscovered.

Sweet potatoes and yams, unrelated botanically to each other, are also not closely related to the white potato. Still, they are covered here, since they are handled in the same basic way in the kitchen. Sweet potatoes tend to be a little moister and more deeply colored than yams. Yams have a more understated flavor than sweet potatoes, but both are noticeably sweeter than white potatoes.

While potatoes are among the vegetables referred to as "winter" vegetables, they do require proper storage in order to retain quality. Potatoes

TABLE 5-27 VARIETIES OF ROOTS AND TUBERS

Variety	Description	Peak Season/Fresh	Uses
Beets			
Baby	Small, red ball-shaped	Throughout summer and into fall (greens are available from mid-spring)	Cooked, served hot, in salads, glazed
Red	Medium to large deep red/maroon root vegetable. May be sold w/ or w/out tops	Throughout summer and into fall (greens are available from mid-spring)	Cooked, served hot, in salads, glazed, pickled, in soup (borscht)
Golden	Small, yellow to golden-orange ball-shaped	Throughout summer and into fall	Cooked, served hot, in salads, glazed (do not bleed)
Turnips			
Purple-topped or white	White, similar in shape to beets, with purple "blush" on stem end	Late fall into early winter months, throughout winter from storage	Cooked, as vegetable side dish
Rutabagas/ Swedes	Large, ball-shaped vegetable, usually coated with wax	Late fall into early winter months, throughout winter from storage	Cooked, as vegetable side dish, often puréed
Radish			
Red	Small, ball-shaped or slightly elongated root vegetable, may be cherry red, striped, white, or specialty colors (purple, orange, etc.) (may be sold in cello packs or with green tops)	Early spring and fall crops (available throughout the year from storage or imports)	Salads, crudité platter
Daikon	Carrot-shaped, white radish with mild radish flavor	Late summer and early fall (available year round)	Cooked, raw, grated as garnish
Salsify Oyster Plant			
White	Similar in appearance to parsnip	Fall into winter	Cooked as side vegetable, often creamed
Black	Long, stick-shaped, dark-black matte skin	Fall into winter	Cooked as side vegetable, often creamed

FIGURE 5-97 Roots and Tubers

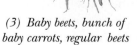

(1) Carrots (baby, horse, and fresh)   *(2) Radish*   *(3) Baby beets, bunch of baby carrots, regular beets*   *(4) Black salsify*   *(5) Parsnips*

HOW THE JERUSALEM ARTICHOKE GOT ITS NAME

The Jerusalem artichoke used to grow wild throughout the midwestern United States and in Canada. The tubers send up shoots producing bright yellow, above ground flowers, which resemble daisies. It is, in fact, a member of the sunflower family of plants. English settlers borrowed from French the lovely name *girasol* for this flower, which translates as "turns toward the sun." One can only assume that over time they had difficulty remembering or pronouncing the name, and it evolved into the similar sounding and easier to remember word, "Jerusalem."

In the seventeenth century, the famous explorer Champlain, (after whom the lake is named), mentioned in his journal, "roots cultivated by the Indians, which have the flavour of the artichoke." This flavor association stuck and the two concepts were indelibly paired, producing: "Jerusalem artichoke."

should be kept dry, away from excess heat or sunlight, and in a well-ventilated area.

Roots and Tubers   Roots and tubers serve as nutrient reservoirs for their plants. Consequently, they are rich in sugars, starches, vitamins, and minerals. Popular root vegetables include beets, carrots, celeriac, parsnips, radishes, rutabagas, and turnips. (See Figure 5-97.) Salsify, a relatively unfamiliar root to most Americans, is also part of this group. It may be white or black, and has a flavor some consider similar to oysters, others to asparagus, and still others compare to artichoke hearts.

Tubers are enlarged, bulbous roots capable of generating a new plant. In addition to potatoes, described above, this category includes Jerusalem arti-

chokes, an ironic name for a vegetable that is not native to Jerusalem and which is not technically an artichoke. (See How the Jerusalem Artichoke Got Its Name.)

Roots and tubers should be stored dry and unpeeled. If they come with greens still attached, the greens should appear fresh at the time of purchase

FIGURE 5-99   Tomatoes

(1) Slicing, plum (Roma), and cherry

(2) Yellow, green zebra, and Big Boy

(3) Tomatillo

FIGURE 5-98 Fennel and Celery

TABLE 5-28 TOMATOES

Variety	Description	Peak Season/Fresh	Uses
Beefsteak	Large, deep red, deeply ridged, juicy	Late summer	Serve fresh in salads, sandwiches
Cherry tomatoes	Small red or yellow tomatoes that grow in clusters. Yellow version is low acid	Mid- to late summer	Salads, crudité platters
Currant (or cranberry) tomatoes	Very small red or yellow tomatoes that grow in clusters. Yellow version is low acid	Mid- to late summer	Specialty items, usually served fresh
Pear tomatoes	Pear-shaped, small red or yellow tomatoes	Mid- to late summer	Usually served fresh in salads or crudité
Plum tomatoes (Roma)	Egg-shaped tomato, red with relatively greater proportion of flesh	Late summer	Sauces, purées, soups, and other cooked dishes
Yellow slicing tomatoes	Large, round, smooth-skinned tomatoes; low acid	Mid- to late summer	Sliced fresh in salads and other uncooked preparations
Tomatillos	Small, green, round berry, tastes like a green tomato, with a light-green-to-brown papery husk	Mid- to late summer	Usually cooked before used in sauces (e.g. pico de gallo*e*)

and cut off as soon thereafter as possible. When they are properly stored, most roots and tubers will retain good quality for several weeks. (See Table 5-27.)

Shoots and Stalks This family consists of plants that produce shoots and stalks. Globe artichokes, asparagus, celery, and fennel are examples. Globe artichokes are thistles. Asparagus is part of the growth cycle of a fern. The stalks or stems should be firm, fleshy, and full, and should have no evidence of browning or wilting. (See Figure 5-98.)

Tomatoes These succulent "vegetables" are actually berries. They are grown in hundreds of varieties, in colors from green to yellow to bright red. Basic types include small, round cherry tomatoes, oblong plum tomatoes, and large beefsteak tomatoes. All have smooth, shiny skin, juicy flesh, and small, edible seeds. Most tomatoes grown commercially are picked green-ripe and allowed to ripen in transit. Many chefs prefer to find locally grown varieties whenever possible, since vine-ripened tomatoes have especially rich flavors and juiciness.

Recently, growers have been able to produce several special varieties of tomatoes for the market, including special low-acid golden varieties of both slicing and cherry tomatoes. Heirloom species can also be found occasionally.

There are no hard and fast rules about which tomatoes work best under which circumstances, but there is a certain etiquette. Slicing tomatoes,

including deeply ridged beefsteaks and other varieties, are favored for use in salads and other uncooked preparations. Plum, or Roma, tomatoes with their relatively drier flesh are preferred for sauces and purées. (See Figure 5-99 and Table 5-28.)

Herbs

Herbs are the leaves of aromatic plants and are used primarily to add flavor to foods. (See Table 5-29 for basic information on each of the most common culinary herbs.)

Selection

Most herbs are available both fresh and dried, although some (thyme, bay leaf, rosemary) dry more successfully than others. Aroma is a good indicator of quality in both fresh and dried herbs. Crumble a few leaves between your fingers and smell them. A weak or stale aroma indicates old and less-potent herbs. Fresh herbs also may be judged by appearance. They should have good color (usually green), fresh-looking leaves and stems, and no wilt, brown spots, sunburn, or pest damage. (See Figure 5-100.)

Proper Use

Herbs can be used to flavor numerous preparations. They should enhance and balance, not over-

TABLE 5-29 CULINARY HERBS

Variety	Description	Peak Season/Fresh	Uses/Affinities
Basil	Leaves are pointed, green. Purple varieties, large or small-leafed varieties available, also specialty types with cinnamon, clove, and other flavors	Summer/year-round	Flavoring for sauces, pesto, dressings, infusing oils, vinegars etc. Also available in dried-leaf form. Chicken, fish, and pasta dishes
Bay leaf	Smooth, rigid leaf	Summer	Available dried year-round. Used to flavor soups, stews, stocks, sauces, and grain dishes
Chervil	Similar in shape to parsley, with finer leaves, licorice flavor	Summer	Component of fines herbes often used in "pluches" to garnish dishes. Egg, chicken, shellfish, dishes
Cilantro	Similar in shape to parsley, with pronounced, unique flavor	Mid to late summer	Component of Asian and South/Central American dishes; flavoring for salsa and other uncooked sauces
Dill	Feathery shape with strong aroma	Late summer	Fresh is used to flavor sauces, stews, braises (especially Central and Eastern European dishes). Seeds used in pickles
Marjoram	Small, rounded leaves with a flavor similar to oregano	Throughout summer	Used in Greek, Italian, and Mexican dishes. Especially suitable for vegetable dishes
Mint	Pointed, textured leaves. Size varies by type, as does particular flavor	Throughout summer	Used to flavor sweet dishes, beverages, as a *tisane* and in some sauces. Mint jelly is traditional with lamb
Oregano	Small, oval leaves	Throughout summer	Used with a variety of sauces, with poultry, beef, veal, lamb, and vegetables
Parsley	Feathered leaves; may be curly or flat	Year-round	Component of fines herbes and of bouquet garni. Flavoring for sauces, soups, dressings, and other dishes. Garnish
Rosemary	Leaves shaped like pine needles with a pine aroma and flavor	Year-round	Large branches used as skewers. Popular in Middle Eastern dishes, grilled foods, and in marinades. Dried is nearly as intense in flavor as fresh
Sage	Large leaves, may be furry or velvety. Sage-green color	Summer	Popular as flavoring in stuffings, sausages, and some stews. Dried, rubbed sage also available
Savory	Summer savory has flavor similar to thyme. Winter savory is more like rosemary	Summer and fall	Used in salads, stuffings, sauces
Tarragon	Narrow leaves with pronounced licorice flavor	Summer	Another component of fines herbes. Used with chicken, fish, veal, and egg dishes
Thyme	Very small leaves. Varieties available with special flavors (nutmeg, mint, lemon, etc.)	Summer	Part of bouquet garni. Dried leaves may occasionally be used in place of fresh. Used to flavor soups, stocks, stews, and braises

Figure 5-100 Herbs

(1) Thyme

(2) Curly and flat parsley

(3) Dill

(4) Sage

(5) Mint

(6) Cilantro

(7) Basil

(8) Oregano

(9) Rosemary   *(10) Tarragon*

Certain herbs have a special affinity for certain foods. Guidelines stating which herbs are most effectively paired with which foods are not cast in stone, but following them can familiarize the chef with the way herb–food combinations work and can serve as a springboard for future experimentation.

Fresh herbs should be minced or cut in chiffonade as close to serving time as possible. They are usually added to a dish toward the end of the cooking time, to prevent the flavor from cooking out. Dried herbs are usually added early in the process. For uncooked preparations, fresh herbs should be added well enough in advance of serving to give them a chance to blend with the other elements.

Storage To store fresh herbs, wrap them loosely in damp paper or cloth. If desired, the wrapped herbs may then be placed in plastic bags to help retain freshness and reduce wilting of leaves, and should be stored at 35 to 45°F (2 to 7°C). Some herbs, especially watercress, cilantro, and parsley, may be held by trimming the stems and placing the bunch in a jar of water. Wrap damp towels around the leaves to prevent wilting.

power, a dish's flavors. Only occasionally, and with a purpose, should the herb's flavor be dominant. When used with discretion, herbs can transform the taste of plain foods into something special. Overuse or inappropriate use can cause, at best, a dish that tastes of nothing but herbs and, at worst, a culinary disaster.

chiffonade: cut into fine strips. (See page 219 for more information.)

Foodservice operations that grow herbs may have an excess at certain times of the season. These may be used for making compound butters, pestos, and flavored vinegars and oils.

Dairy, Cheese, and Egg Identification

A concentrated source of many nutrients—especially protein and calcium—dairy products and eggs hold a prominent place on menus. Milk and milk products are not only used as beverages but as ingredients in many dishes. Béchamel sauce, for example, is based on milk. Cream, crème fraîche, sour cream, and yogurt are used to finish sauces, to prepare salad dressings, and in many baked goods.

Cheese may be served as is, perhaps as a separate course with fruit, or as part of another dish. Fondue, raclette, and Welsh rarebit are classic dishes from around the world that feature cheese.

Eggs appear on menus throughout the day—from morning breakfast dishes to dessert soufflés served at midnight. The unique composition of eggs makes them useful in the preparation of numerous sauces, especially emulsified sauces, such as hollandaise and mayonnaise. (See pages 332 and 680 for more information)

Purchasing and Storage

Although dairy products and eggs are two separate kinds of products, freshness and wholesomeness are important for both. Both are also highly perishable. For these reasons, careful purchasing and storage procedures are extremely important.

Table 5-30 provides information regarding holding temperatures and the average shelf life of eggs and various dairy products. Milk and cream containers customarily are dated to indicate how long

---

fondue: a traditional Swiss dish of melted cheese, white wine, and seasonings, and served with bread.

raclette: a dish prepared by heating cheese in front of an electric unit or, originally, a fire. As the cheese melts, it is scraped away and served with boiled potatoes.

Welsh rarebit: a traditional dish from the British Isles made by simmering cheddar cheese with beer and seasonings; it is typically served over toast points.

curdle: the separation of solids and liquids in milk.

TABLE 5-30 PROPER STORAGE TIMES AND TEMPERATURES OF DAIRY PRODUCTS AND EGGS

Product	Storage Time	Temperature
Milk, fluid, pasteurized (whole, low-fat, skim, other unfermented)	1 week	35–40°F/2-4°C
Milk, evaporated		
Unopened	6 months	60–70°F/16–21°C
Opened	3–5 days	35–40°F/2–4°C
Milk, sweetened, condensed		
Unopened	2–3 months	60–70°F/16–21°C
Opened	3–5 days	35–40°F/2–4°C
Milk, nonfat dry		
Unopened	3 months	60–70°F/16–21°C
Reconstituted	1 week	35–40°F/2–4°C
Buttermilk, fluid	2–3 weeks	35–40°F/2–4°C
Yogurt	3–6 weeks	35–40°F/2–4°C
Cream		
Table or whipping	1 week	35–40°F/2–4°C
Ultrapasteurized	6 weeks	35–40°F/2–4°C
Whipped, pressurized	3 weeks	35–40°F/2–4°C
Ice cream	4 weeks	−10–0°F/ −23− −18°C
Butter	3–5 days	35°F/2°C
Margarine	5–7 days	35°F/2°C
Cheese, unripened, soft	5–7 days	35–40°F/2–4°C
Cheese, ripened, soft, semisoft	5–7 days	35–40°F/2–4°C
Cheese, ripened, hard	2–3 months	35–40°F/2–4°C
Cheese, very hard	2–3 months	35–40°F/2–4°C
Cheese foods	2–3 weeks	35–40°F/2–4°C
Cheese, processed		
Unopened	3–4 months	60–70°F/16–21°C
Opened	1–2 weeks	35–40°F/2–4°C
Eggs, whole, in shell	5–7 days	33–38°F/1–3°C
Eggs, whole, fluid	2–3 days	29–32°F/−1–0°C
Eggs, frozen	1–2 months	−10–0°F/ −23− −18°C
Eggs, dried	1–2 months	40°F/4°C

Adapted from Eva Medved, *Food Preparation and Theory*, which was adapted from various USDA publications.

---

the contents will remain fresh enough to use. Because the freshness period will vary, you should never combine, or "marry," milk and cream from separate containers, to avoid contamination.

When used in hot dishes, milk or cream should be brought to a boil before being added to other ingredients. If milk curdles, it should not be used. Unfortunately, detecting spoilage by simply smelling or tasting unheated milk is often impossible.

When considering storage arrangements for dairy products, flavor transfer is a particular concern. Storing all milk, cream, and butter away from foods with strong odors is preferable, when feasible. Cheeses should be carefully wrapped, both to maintain moistness and to prevent the odor from permeating other foods and vice versa.

Eggs should be refrigerated and the stock rotated to assure that only fresh, wholesome eggs are served. The chef should inspect eggs carefully upon delivery, making sure that shells are clean and free of cracks. Eggs with broken shells should be discarded because of the high contamination risk.

Dairy Products

Milk Milk is invaluable in the kitchen, whether it is served as a beverage or used as a component in dishes. U.S. federal regulations govern how milk is produced and sold, to assure that it is clean and safe to use.

Most milk sold in the United States has been pasteurized. In **pasteurization,** the milk is heated to 145°F (63°C) for 30 minutes, or to 161°F (72°C) for 15 seconds in order to kill bacteria or other organisms that could cause infection or contamination. Milk products with a higher percentage of milkfat are heated to either 150°F (65°C) for 30 minutes or to 166°F (74°C) for 30 seconds for **ultrapasteurization.**

The **date stamp** on milk and cream cartons is 10 days after the date of pasteurization. For example, if milk was pasteurized on October 10, the date on the carton would read October 20. If the product has been properly stored and handled, it should still be fresh and wholesome on the stamped date.

Milk is also generally **homogenized,** which means that it has been forced through an ultrafine mesh at high pressure in order to break up the fat globules it contains. This fat is then dispersed evenly throughout the milk, preventing it from rising to the surface. Milk may also be fortified with vitamins A and D. Lowfat or skim milk is almost always fortified, because removing the fat also removes fat-soluble vitamins.

TABLE 5-31 FORMS OF MILK AND CREAM

Form	Description	Type of Container
Milk		
Whole	Contains no less than 3% milkfat	Bulk, gallon, half-gallon, quart, pint, ½ pint
Low-fat	Usually contains 1 or 2% milkfat and is generally labeled accordingly	Same as whole milk
Skim	Contains less than 0.1% milkfat	Same as whole milk
Powdered or dry	Milk from which water is completely removed. Made from either whole or skim milk and labeled accordingly	50# bulk, 24 oz. bulk
Evaporated	Milk that has been heated in a vacuum to remove 60% of its water. May be made from whole or skim milk and is labeled accordingly	14.5 oz., 10 oz., or 6 oz. cans
Condensed	Evaporated milk that has been sweetened	Same as above
Cream		
Heavy or Whipping	Must contain at least 35% milkfat. Light whipping cream is occasionally available, containing 30 to 35% fat	Quarts, pints, ½ pints
Light	Contains between 16 and 32% fat	Same as heavy cream
Half-and-half	Contains between 10.5 and 12% fat. Used as a lightener for coffee	Same as heavy cream and in portion sizes

State and local government standards for milk are fairly consistent. Milk products are carefully inspected before and after production. Farms and animals (cows, sheep, and goats) are also inspected, to assure that sanitary conditions are upheld. Milk that has been properly produced and processed is labeled "grade A."

FIGURE 5-101   Milk and Cream

Milk comes in various forms and is classified according to its percentage of fat and milk solids. (See Table 5-31 and Figure 5-101.)

Cream   Milk, as it comes from the cow, goat, or sheep, contains a certain percentage of fat, known alternately as **milkfat** or **butterfat.** Originally, milk was allowed to settle long enough for the cream, which is lighter than the milk, to rise to the surface. Today, a centrifuge is used to spin the milk. The cream is quickly forced to separate and can be easily drawn off, leaving the milk behind.

Cream, like milk, is homogenized and pasteurized, and may also be stabilized to help extend shelf life. Some chefs prefer cream that has not been stabilized or ultrapasteurized because they believe it will whip to a greater volume. Two forms of cream are used in most kitchens: heavy (whipping) cream and light cream. Half-and-half, a combination of whole milk and cream, does not contain enough milkfat to be considered a true cream. Its milkfat content is approximately 10.5 percent. (See Table 5-31.)

Ice Cream   In order to meet government standards, any product labeled as ice cream must contain a certain amount of milkfat. For vanilla, it is no less than 10 percent milkfat. For any other flavor, the requirement is 8 percent. Stabilizers can make up no more than 2 percent of ice cream. Ice creams that contain less fat should be labeled "ice milk."

Premium-brand ice cream may contain several times more fat than is required by these standards. The richest ice creams have a custard base (a mix-

ture of cream and/or milk and eggs), which gives them a dense, smooth texture. It should readily melt in the mouth. When the ice cream is allowed to melt at room temperature, there should be no separation. The appearance of "weeping" in melting ice cream indicates an excessive amount of stabilizers.

Other frozen desserts similar to ice cream are sherbet, sorbet, granité, frozen yogurt, and frozen tofu. Sherbet does not contain cream, and so it is far lower in butterfat than ice creams. It does contain a relatively high percentage of sugar in order to achieve the correct texture and consistency during freezing. Some sherbets will contain a percentage of either eggs or milk, or both.

Although the word "sherbet" is the closest English translation of the French word "sorbet," sorbets are commonly understood to contain no milk.

Granités, the simplest forms of "ices," are basically flavored syrups that are allowed to freeze. Once solid, they are scraped to produce large crystals or flakes.

Frozen yogurts and tofu often contain stabilizers and a high percentage of fat. They may be lower in total fat than ice cream or even fat-free, but some brands are still high in calories due to a high sugar content.

Test a variety of these products to determine which brand offers the best quality for the best price.

Refer to Chapter 12 for information about preparing frozen desserts.

FIGURE 5-102   Butter and Cream Cheese

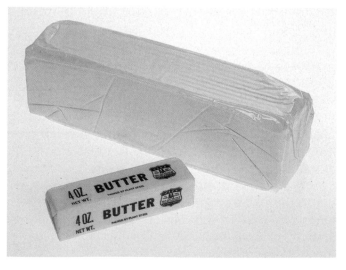

Butter Anyone who has accidentally overwhipped cream has been well on the way to producing butter. Historically, butter was churned by hand. Today it is made mechanically by mixing cream that contains between 30 and 45 percent milkfat at a high speed. Eventually, the milkfat clumps together, separating out into a solid mass, leaving a fluid referred to as buttermilk. The solid mass is butter.

The best-quality butter has a sweet flavor, similar to very fresh heavy cream. If salt has been added, it should be barely detectable. The color of butter will vary depending upon the breed of cow and time of year, but is usually a pale yellow. The cow's diet will vary from season to season, affecting the color and flavor of the butter.

The designation "sweet butter" indicates only that the butter is made from sweet (as opposed to sour) cream. It does not mean necessarily that the butter is unsalted. If unsalted butter is desired, be sure that the word "unsalted" appears on the package.

Salted butter may contain no more than a maximum of 2 percent salt. This added salt will aid in extending butter's shelf life. It may also mask a slightly "old" flavor or aroma. Old butter will take on a faint cheesy flavor and aroma, especially when heated, as it is for cooking and baking. As it continues to deteriorate, the flavor and aroma can become quite pronounced, and extremely unpleasant, much like sour or curdled milk.

The best-quality butter, labeled "grade AA," is made from sweet cream. It has the best flavor, color, aroma, and texture. Grade A butter also is of excellent quality. Both grades AA and A contain a minimum of 80 percent fat. Grade B may have a slightly acidic taste, as it is made from sour cream. (See Figure 5-102.)

Fermented and Cultured Milk Products Yogurt, sour cream, crème fraîche, and buttermilk are all produced by inoculating milk or cream with a bacterial strain or **culture** that causes fermentation to begin. The **fermentation** process thickens the milk and gives it a pleasantly sour flavor. A variety of these products are illustrated in Figure 5-103.

Yogurt is made by introducing the proper culture into milk (whole, lowfat, or skim may be used). Available in a variety of container sizes, yogurt can be purchased plain or flavored with different fruits, honey, coffee, or other ingredients.

FIGURE 5-103 Crème Fraîche, Cottage Cheese, Ricotta, and Yogurt

Sour cream is a cultured sweet cream that contains about 16 to 22 percent fat. It comes in containers of various sizes, beginning with a half-pint. Low, reduced, and nonfat versions of sour cream are also available.

Crème fraîche is similar to sour cream but has a slightly more rounded flavor, with less bite. It is often preferred in cooking, since it curdles less readily than sour cream in hot dishes. This product is made from heavy cream with a butterfat content of approximately 30 percent. This high butterfat content accounts for its higher cost.

Although crème fraîche is available commercially, many operations make their own. They heat heavy cream, add a small amount of buttermilk, and allow the mixture to ferment at room temperature until thickened and slightly soured.

Buttermilk, strictly speaking, is the by-product of churned butter. Despite its name, it contains only a very small amount of butterfat. Most buttermilk sold today is actually skim milk to which a bacterial strain has been added. Usually sold in pints or quarts, buttermilk is also available as a dried powder for baking uses.

TABLE 5-32 FRESH CHEESE

Type/Milk Used	Shape and Color	Flavor	Texture
Bucheron (raw goat's)	Log, white	Slightly tangy	Soft, creamy
Chèvre (general) (goat's)	Block, pyramid, button, wheel, log	Mild to tangy (depending on age), may be flavored with herbs or peppercorns	Soft to crumbly (depending on age)
Cottage (whole or skim cow's*)	Curds, white	Mild	Soft, moist
Cream (whole cow's, plus cream)	Block, white	Mild, slightly tangy	Soft, cream
Feta (sheep's, goat's, or cow's)	Block, white	Tangy, salty	Soft, crumbly
Fromage blanc (whole or skim cow's)	Soft, white	Mild, tangy	Soft, slightly crumbly
Mascarpone (whole cow's milk/cream)	Soft, pale yellow	Buttery, slightly tangy	Soft, smooth
Montrachet (raw goat's)	Log, white	Slightly tangy	Soft, creamy
Mozzarella (whole or skim cow's, buffalo's)	Irregular sphere, white	Mild, sometimes smoked	Tender to slightly elastic (depending on age)
Neufchâtel (whole or skim cow's**)	Block, white	Mild, slightly tangy	Soft, creamy
Ricotta (whole, skim, or low-fat cow's***)	Soft curds, white	Mild	Soft, moist to slightly dry, grainy

* Cream may be added to finished curds.
**May have added cream.
***May have added whey.

Cheese

The variety of cheeses produced throughout the world is extensive, ranging from mild fresh cheeses (pot cheese or cottage cheese) to strongly flavored, blue-veined cheeses (Roquefort or Gorgonzola) to hard grating cheeses (Parmesan or Romano). Cheeses are used in many dishes and require careful handling and selection. Some cheeses are excellent for cooking, while others will become a hopelessly stringy mass when subjected to heat. Selecting the right cheese for the intended effect is important, because cheese can be quite expensive.

In general, the procedure for making cheese is this: Milk is combined with the appropriate starter (generally rennet, a natural enzyme extracted from the stomachs of cows), which causes milk solids to coagulate into curds. The liquid left after **curds** are formed is known as the **whey.**

The curds are then processed in various ways, depending on the type of cheese desired. They may be drained and used immediately, as fresh cheese, or they may be pressed, shaped, inoculated with a special mold, and aged. Whey is also used to make some cheeses, notably ricotta.

Cheese is made from a variety of different milks—cow's milk, goat's milk, sheep's milk, even buffalo's milk. The type of milk used will determine the ultimate flavor and texture of the cheese.

Natural cheeses are considered "living" in much the same way that wine is considered living. The cheese will continue to grow, developing or aging to maturity (ripening), and finally spoiling (overripening). Processed or pasteurized cheeses and cheese foods, on the other hand, do not ripen and their character will not change.

Cheeses may be grouped according to the type of milk from which they are made, their texture, age, or ripening process. The terms used are:

• Fresh cheese

• Soft, or rind-ripened cheese

• Semi-soft cheese

FIGURE 5-104   Aged Goat Cheese cone, Fresh Goat Cheese cylinder, Pont l'Evêque, Herbed Boursin, Pepper Boursin, and Brie (clockwise from top)

FIGURE 5-105   Bel Paese, Gruyère, Jarlsberg, Gouda, Morbier, and Colby Cheeses

TABLE 5-33   SOFT AND RIND-RIPENED CHEESES

Type/Milk Used	Shape and Color	Flavor	Texture
Brie (pasteurized, whole or skim cow's, goat's, sometimes cream)	Disk, light yellow	Buttery to pungent	Soft, smooth, with edible rind
Camembert (raw or pasteurized whole cow's, goats)	Disk, light yellow	Slightly tangy	Soft, creamy, with edible rind
Explorateur (whole cow's and cream)	Wheel, pale yellow	Rich, mild	Soft and creamy
Limburger (whole or low-fat cow's)	Block, light yellow, brown exterior	Very strong flavor and aroma	Soft, smooth, waxy
Pont-l'Evêque (whole cow's)	Square, light yellow	Piquant, strong aroma	Soft, supple, with small holes and edible golden-yellow crust

- Hard cheese
- Grating cheese
- Blue-veined cheese

These cheeses are shown in Figures 5-104 to 5-108.

Fresh Cheese

Fresh cheeses include cottage cheese or fresh goat's cheese, mozzarella, fromage blanc, ricotta, and quark. These cheeses are moist and very soft. They have a flavor that is generally termed "mild," but fresh cheese made from goat's or sheep's milk may seem strong to some tastes. (See Table 5-32.)

Soft or Rind-ripened Cheese

Soft cheeses, such as Brie or Camembert, usually have a surface mold. This soft, velvety skin is often edible, though some people find it too strong to

TABLE 5-34 SEMI-SOFT CHEESES

Type/Milk Used	Shape and Color	Flavor	Texture
Bel Paese (whole cow's)	Wheel, light yellow	Mild, buttery	Semi-soft, creamy, waxy
Brick (whole cow's)	Block, light yellow	Mild to pungent (depending on age)	Semi-soft, elastic, with many tiny holes
Edam (whole or part-skim cow's)	Loaf or sphere (may be coated with wax)	Mild to tangy (depending on age)	Hard, may be slightly crumbly with tiny holes
Fontina (whole cow's or sheep's)	Wheel, medium yellow	Nutty flavor, strong aroma	Hard
Harvarti (cream-enriched cow's)	Loaf or wheel, medium yellow	Buttery (may be flavored with dill or caraway	Semi-soft, creamy, with small holes
Morbier (whole cow's)	Wheel, light yellow with edible ash layer	Mild	Semi-soft, smooth
Monterey Jack (whole cow's)	Wheel or block, light yellow	Mild to pungent (may be flavored with jalapeño peppers)	Semi-soft to very hard (depending on age)
Muenster (whole cow's)	Wheel or block, light yellow (rind may be orange)	Mild to pungent (depending on age)	Semi-soft, smooth, waxy with small holes
Port-Salut (whole or low-fat cow's)	Wheel or cylinder, white with russet exterior	Buttery, mellow to sharp	Semi-soft, smooth
Taleggio (raw cow's)	Square, light yellow	Creamy	Semi-soft with holes

enjoy. The cheese ripens from the outside to the center. When fully ripe, a soft cheese should be nearly runny, with a full flavor. (See Table 5-33.)

Semi-soft Cheese

Semi-soft cheeses are more solid than soft cheeses but do not grate easily. They can be sliced, however. An inedible wax rind is used to coat the cheese, in order to preserve moisture and extend shelf life. Edam, Muenster, and Port-Salut are among the better-known semi-soft cheeses. These cheeses are allowed to age for specified periods of time, though not quite as long as hard or grating cheeses. (See Table 5-34.)

Hard Cheeses (Cheddar-type)

Hard cheeses, such as Gruyère, Cheshire, and Cheddar, have a drier texture than semi-soft

(Continued on page 185)

FIGURE 5-106   Vermont Cheddar, Swiss/Jarlsberg, Emmenthaler, Appenzell, and Provolone (clockwise from left, and center)

TABLE 5-35 HARD AND CHEDDAR-TYPE CHEESES

Type/Milk Used	Shape and Color	Flavor	Texture
Cantal (whole cow's)	Cylinder, light yellow	Mild to sharp, slightly nutty	Hard
Cheddar (whole cow's)	Wheel, light or medium yellow	Mild to sharp (depending on age)	Hard
Cheshire (whole cow's)	Cylinder, light or medium yellow (may have blue marbling)	Mellow to piquant	Hard
Derby (whole cow's)	Cylinder, honey colored	Mild (may be flavored with sage)	Firm
Double Gloucester (whole cow's)	Large wheel, bright yellow-orange, colored with annatto	Full flavored	Firm, smooth, creamy
Emmenthaler (Swiss); (raw or pasteurized, part-skim cow's)	Wheel, light yellow	Mild, nutty	Hard, smooth, shiny with large holes
Gjetost (whole cow's and goat's)	Small block, light brown	Butter, caramel, slightly tangy	Hard
Gouda (whole cow's)	Wheel (may be coated with wax)	Mild, creamy, slightly nutty	Hard, smooth, may have tiny holes
Jarlsberg (whole cow's)	Wheel, light yellow	Sharp, nutty	Hard with large holes
Manchego (whole sheep's)	Cylinder, light yellow	Full and mellow	Semisoft to firm (depending on age) with holes
Provolone (whole cow's)	Pear, sausage, round, other, light yellow to golden-brown	Mild to sharp (depending on age), may be smoked	Hard, elastic

TABLE 5-36 GRATING CHEESES

Type/Milk Used	Shape and Color	Flavor	Texture
Asiago (whole or part-skim cow's)	Cylinder or flat block, light yellow	Mild to sharp	Semi-soft to hard (depending on age)
Parmigiano Reggiano/Parmesan (part-skim cow's)	Cylinder, light yellow	Sharp, nutty	Very hard, dry, crumbly
Ricotta salata (whole sheep's)	Cylinder, off-white	Pungent	Hard
Romano, pecorino (whole sheep's, goat's, or cow's)	Cylinder	Very sharp	Very hard, dry, crumbly
Sapsago (buttermilk, whey, and skim cow's)	Flattened cone, light green	Piquant, flavored with clover leaves	Very hard, granular

FIGURE 5-107 Sapsago, Parmigiano-Reggiano, and Pecorino Romano Cheeses

FIGURE 5-108 Roquefort, Gorgonzola, and Maytag Blue Cheeses

TABLE 5-37 BLUE CHEESES

Type/Milk Used	Shape and Color	Flavor	Texture
Bleu/Blue (whole cow's or goat's)	Cylinder, white with blue-green veins	Piquant, tangy	Semi-soft, possibly crumbly
Blue Brie (whole cow's, goat's with added cream)	Wheel, white with patches of blue	Rich, piquant, but mild for blue	Soft, creamy
Bleu de Bresse (whole cow's or goat's)	Wheel, light yellow with blue veins	Piquant but mild for blue	Soft, creamy, slightly crumbly
Danish Blue (whole cow's)	Blocks, drums, white	Strong, sharp, salty	Firm, crumbly
Fourme D'Ambert (whole cow's)	Cylinder, medium yellow with blue-green marbling and reddish yellow rind	Sharp, pungent	Semi-soft, crumbly
Gorgonzola (whole cow's and/or goat's)	Wheel, medium yellow with blue marbling	Tangy, piquant	Semi-soft, dry for blue
Maytag Blue (whole cow's)	Cylinder, medium yellow with blue marbling	Strong, salty	Hard, crumbly
Roquefort (raw sheep's)	Cylinder, white with blue-green marbling	Sharp, pungent	Semi-soft, crumbly
Stilton (whole cow's)	Cylinder, medium yellow with blue-green marbling	Piquant, but mild for blue	Hard, crumbly

cheeses, and a firm consistency. They will slice and grate easily. (See Table 5-35.)

Cheddar cheese, though it originated as a farmhouse cheese in England, is extremely popular in the United States. In fact, its popularity is so widespread that some people refer to it as American cheese. Be aware, however, that the sliced processed cheese also known as American cheese is not the same product.

An aged version of Monterey Jack cheese, known as Dry Jack, is produced in this country and is gaining in popularity.

Grating Cheeses

Parmesan, Romano, and Sapsago cheeses are typically grated or shaved rather than cut into slices because of their crumbly texture. The best-quality Parmesan is imported from the Reggiano region of Italy. It is used as a table or grating cheese.

Domestically produced versions of these cheeses are available, as are blends of Parmesan and Romano. These cheeses are almost inescapably linked in the public mind with pasta dishes, and may actually be referred to as "pasta cheese." (See Table 5-36.)

Blue-veined Cheeses

Blue-veined cheeses, such as Roquefort and Gorgonzola, have consistencies that range from smooth and creamy to dry and crumbly. Their blue veining is the result of injecting a special mold into the cheese before ripening. (See Table 5-37.)

Eggs

Eggs are one of the kitchen's most important items. From mayonnaise to meringues, soups to sauces, appetizers to desserts, they are prominent on any menu. Today's consumer is well aware of the potential for foodborne illness through eggs. Therefore, we will look first at basic rules for safe handling here.

- All eggs in the shell should be free from cracks, leaking, or obvious holes.

- Eggs should be cooked to a minimum of 165°F (74°C) to kill the salmonella bacteria. Fried eggs

FIGURE 5-109   Flat of Eggs

or poached eggs with runny yolks should be prepared only at customer request.

- Any foods containing eggs must be kept within safe temperatures throughout handling, cooking, and storage. Cooling and reheating must be done quickly over direct heat.

The egg is composed of two parts: the white and the yolk. Each is able to play a number of important culinary roles. Whole eggs are used as the main component of many breakfast dishes and can be prepared by scrambling, frying, poaching, baking, or in custards. Eggs are also used to glaze baked goods, and add nourishment, flavor, and color. Despite concerns over safe handling, the egg remains one of the most adaptable and functional ingredients in the chef's larder. (See Figure 5-109.)

Egg Whites

The white consists almost exclusively of protein and water. The protein is known as "albumen." Its ability to form a relatively stable foam is crucial to the development of proper structure in many

---

mousseline: a very light forcemeat based on white meat or seafood combined (see pages 408-409).

items: angel food cakes, soufflés, meringues. They are a key ingredient in clarifying stocks and broths to produce consommés. Egg whites may replace some or all of other binders used in some force-meats, especially mousselines made from fish, poultry, or vegetables.

Egg Yolks

The yolk also has the ability to foam. This function, plus its ability to form emulsions, make egg yolks crucial to the preparation of items including mayonnaise, hollandaise, and génoise. Yolks are also responsible for providing additional richness to foods, as when they are included as a liaison in sauces or soups. The yolk contains protein and, in addition, significant amounts of fat and a natural emulsifier called lecithin.

Grading, Sizes, and Market Forms

Eggs are graded by the U.S. Department of Agriculture (USDA) on the basis of external appearance and freshness. The top grade, AA, indicates that the egg is fresh, with a white that will not spread unduly once the egg is broken. The yolk should ride high on the white's surface. The yolk is anchored in place by two twisted white membranes known as the chalazae.

Eggs come in a number of sizes: jumbo, extra-large, large, medium, small, and pee wee.

The color of eggshells range from creamy white to brown to speckled, depending on the kind of hen. There are some who insist that brown eggs taste better than white eggs, but this is only an opinion. Flavor differences are more a result of quality and care of the hens, and the handling of their eggs, than eggshell color.

Younger hens produce smaller eggs, which are often regarded to be of a better quality than larger eggs. Medium eggs are best for breakfast cookery, where the cooked egg's appearance is important. Large and extra-large eggs are generally used for cooking and baking, where the whole egg's appearance is less critical.

---

génoise: a sponge cake (see pages 440-442).

liaison: a mixture of egg yolks and cream used to thicken and enrich sauces and soups.

Eggs are also sold in several processed forms: bulk, or fluid, whole eggs (which sometimes includes a percentage of extra yolks to obtain a specific blend), egg whites, and egg yolks. Pasteurized eggs are used in preparations such as salad dressings, eggnog, or desserts where the traditional recipe may have indicated that the eggs should be raw. These products generally are available in liquid or frozen form.

Dried, powdered eggs are also sold and may be useful for some baked goods or in specific circumstances. For instance, on shipboard, it may not be possible to properly store fresh eggs for the duration of a voyage.

Egg substitutes may be entirely egg free or may be produced from egg whites, with dairy or vegetable products substituted for the yolks. These substitutes are important for people who require a reduced-cholesterol diet.

Nonperishable Goods Identification

The term "nonperishable goods" is somewhat misleading. Although the staple items covered in this section do have long shelf lives, most of them are of the best quality when they are relatively fresh. A broad spectrum of nonperishable goods, also known as "dry goods," forms part of any foodservice operation's basic day-to-day needs. The following products are discussed:

- grains, meals, and flours
- dried legumes
- dried pastas and noodles
- oils and shortenings
- vinegars and condiments
- dried herbs and spices
- salt and pepper
- extracts and other flavorings
- nuts and seeds
- dried fruits and vegetables
- sugars, syrups, and other sweeteners
- chocolate
- coffee, tea, and other beverages
- thickeners
- prepared, canned, and frozen foods

TABLE 5-38 GRAINS, MEALS, FLOURS, & OTHER STARCHES

Name	Purchase Form	Major Uses or Dishes
Wheat		
Whole	Unrefined or minimally processed whole kernels	Side dish
Cracked	Coarsely crushed, minimally processed kernels	Side dish, hot cereal
Bulgur	Hulled, cracked hard or soft wheat; parboiled and dried	Side dish, salad (tabbouleh)
Semolina	Polished wheat kernel (bran and germ removed), whole or ground	Pasta, flour, couscous (below)
Couscous	Semolina pellets, often parcooked	Side dish (often served with stew of same name)
Farina	Polished, medium–grind wheat cereals	Breakfast cereal
Bran	Separated outer covering of wheat kernel; flakes	Added to baked goods; prepared cereals, and other foods to increase dietary fiber
Germ	Separated embryo of wheat kernel; flakes	Added to baked goods and cereals to boost flavor and nutrition
Wheat flour (whole or graham)	Finely ground, whole kernels	Baked goods
All-Purpose	Finely ground, polished kernels; usually enriched; may be bleached	Baked goods, thickener, other kitchen uses
Bread	Finely ground, polished hard wheat kernels; usually enriched; may be bleached	Bread dough
Cake	Very finely ground, polished soft wheat kernels; usually enriched and bleached	Cakes and other delicate baked goods
Pastry	Very finely ground, polished soft wheat kernels; usually enriched and bleached	Pastry and other delicate baked goods
Self-rising	Very finely ground, polished soft wheat kernels to which baking powder and salt have been added; usually enriched and bleached	Cakes and other baked goods not leavened with yeast
Rice		
Brown	Hulled grains, bran intact; short, medium, or long grain; may be enriched	Side dish, other
White	Polished grains, usually enriched, long or short grain	Long grain: side dish, other. Short grain: pudding
Converted	Parcooked, polished grains, may be enriched	Side dish, other
Basmati	Delicate, extra, long grain, polished	Side dish including pilaf
Arborio	Short grain, polished	Risotto

(Table continued on following page)

TABLE 5-38 GRAINS, MEALS, FLOURS, & OTHER STARCHES *(continued)*

Name	*Purchase Form*	*Major Uses or Dishes*
Wild	Long, dark-brown grain not related to regular rice	Side dish, stuffings, other
Glutinous	Round, short grain, very starchy; black (unhulled) or white (polished)	Sushi, other Oriental dishes
Rice flour	Very finely ground polished rice	Thickener
Corn		
Hominy	Whole, hulled kernels; dry or canned	Side dish including succotash, in soup or stew
Grits	Cracked hominy	Side dish, hot cereal, baked goods
Meal	Medium-fine ground, hulled kernels; white or yellow	Baked goods, coating, polenta
Masa harina	Corn processed with lime to remove hull, medium ground; dry, dough, raw or cooked tortillas	Tortillas and other Mexican dishes
Cornstarch	Very finely ground, hulled kernels	Thickener, coating
Barley		
Pot or Scotch	Coarse, whole kernels; ground (barley meal)	Side dish, hot cereal, soups; meal: baked goods
Pearl	Polished, whole kernels; ground (barley flour)	Side dish, hot cereal, soups; flour: baked goods
Oats		
Oats, whole	Groats or berries	Cereal, stuffing
Oatmeal	Steel cut, rolled, flakes, quick-cooking, instant	Cereal, cakes, cookies, quickbreads
Oat bran	Separated outer covering of grain, flakes	Added to cereals and baked goods for dietary fiber
Others		
Arrowroot	Fine, starchy powder made from a tropical root	Thickener
Buckwheat	Whole, coarsely cracked groats (kashi), flour	Whole: side dish; flour: pancakes, baked goods
Filé	Fine, starchy powder made from sassafras leaves	Thickener (especially in Creole dishes such as gumbo)
Millet	Whole, flour	Side dish, flat breads
Rye	Cracked, flour (whole berries available)	Cracked: side dish; flour: baked goods
Sorghum	Whole, flour, syrup	Porridge, flat breads, beer, syrup and molasses

Purchasing and Storage

Well-organized kitchens maintain a parstock of dry goods. This assures that there is enough of an item to prepare all menu offerings, as well as any items for special events or unusually busy weekends, from what is on hand. There should also be a slight overstock in case of an unusually busy weekend or for other contingencies. Excessive overstock, however, can monopolize valuable storage space. Non-

FIGURE 5-110   Grains, etc.

(1) Flour group (clockwise from top left: bread, graham, unbleached all-purpose, cornmeal, (center) semolina)

(2) Oat group (from top: steel cut, rolled, groats)

(3) (Top) Buckwheat groats, (Bottom left) millet, (Bottom right) pearl barley

(4) Wheat group (clockwise from top left: germ, berries, bulgur, cracked)

(continued on following page)

perishable goods may be purchased in bulk, by the case, or in single units.

Inspect all dry goods as they arrive, just as carefully as you would produce, meats, and fish, to ensure that the delivery matches the order. Check bags, boxes, cans, or other containers to make sure they are intact and clean and that they are not dented, broken, or in any way below standard.

Store dry goods in an area that is properly dry, ventilated, and accessible. All goods should be

FIGURE 5-110　Grains, etc. *(continued)*

(5) Starches (rice flour, wheat starch, glutinous wheat flour)

(6) Wild rice and basmati brown rice

FIGURE 5-111　Dried Legumes

placed above floor level, on shelving or pallets. Some nonperishable items, such as whole grains, nuts and seeds, and coffee (if it is not vacuum-packed) are best stored under refrigeration, or even in the freezer.

Grains, Meals, and Flours

This broad category extends from whole grains such as rice and barley to ground cornmeal and pastry flour. Grains are of great importance to many cuisines. Wheat and corn are of primary importance in Western countries, such as the United States and Canada. Rice is fundamental to many Eastern cuisines. In fact, in many Eastern countries, the word for rice is the same as that for food. Other cultures rely upon grains such as oats, rye, and buckwheat.

Whole grains are grains that have not been milled. They tend to have a shorter life span than milled grains and, therefore, should be purchased in amounts that can be used in a relatively short period of time—two to three weeks.

Milled grains have had the germ, bran, and/or hull removed, or have been polished. When the whole grain is milled, it is essentially crushed into successively smaller particles. Although processed, or milled, grains tend to last longer, some of their nutritive value is lost during processing.

Milled grains that are broken into coarse particles may be referred to as "cracked." If the milling process continues, meals and cereals (cornmeal, farina, cream of rice) are formed. Finally, the grain may be ground into a fine powder, the form we know as flour. (See Table 5-38 and Figure 5-110.)

Various methods are used for milling: crushing between metal rollers, grinding between stones, or cutting with steel blades in an action similar to that of a food processor. Grains ground between stones are called "stone-ground"; they may be preferred in some cases, because they retain more of their nutritive value due to a lower temperature during this milling process than in others.

Dried Legumes

These foodstuffs, seeds from pod-producing plants, have many uses in the contemporary

(Continued on page 193)

TABLE 5-39 DRIED BEANS, LENTILS, AND PEAS

Name	Description	Purchase Form	Uses
Beans			
Adzuki	Small, reddish-brown with white ridge on one side, slightly sweet flavor	Dried	Asian dishes
Black/Turtle	Shiny, brownish-black, medium sized, rounded kidney shape	Dried, canned	Mexican dishes
Black-eyed pea	Cream-colored with black patch around hilum, medium-sized, kidney-shaped	Dried, canned, fresh	Caribbean, soul food, and Southern dishes (including Hoppin' John)
Cannelini	Medium-sized, white, smooth, long, kidney-shaped, a type of haricot	Dried, canned	Soups, Italian dishes
Chick pea	Medium-sized, acorn-shaped, light tan to brown	Dried, canned	Middle Eastern and Mediterranean dishes, salads
Fava/Broad bean	Large, flat, green (fresh) to brown (dried)	Fresh; dried: large, baby	Mediterranean dishes (including *falafel*)
Flageolet	Medium-sized, smooth, flat oval, green or white, a type of haricot	Dried	Stews, soups, with roast lamb
Kidney	Long, curved kidney shape, pink to maroon	Dried, canned	Mexican dishes, chili, salads
Lentils	Small, green, brown, yellow, orange, dark green (puy)	Dried, canned soups	Soups, stews, side dishes, purées
Lima	Medium-sized, flat, white light green	Canned, frozen	Side dishes, including succotash
Mung	Small, round, green or yellow	Fresh or dried; whole, skinless, split, sprouted	Asian dishes
Navy	Small, smooth, rounded, white, a type of haricot	Dried, canned	Soups, baked beans
Pigeon pea	Small, nearly round, off-white with orange-brown mottling	Dried, canned	African, Indian, and Caribbean dishes
Pinto	Medium-sized, kidney-shaped mottled pink	Dried, canned	Latin American dishes including refried beans, Italian *pasta e fagioli*
Soissons	Medium-sized, oval, white, a type of haricot	Dried	Cassoulet
Soy	Medium-sized, rounded, black or yellow	Fresh or dried: salted, fermented, soy sauce, other (see below)	Asian dishes
Bean Products			
Bean paste, soy	Thick sauce of fermented soybeans, flour, and salt	Bottled or canned, whole or ground beans	Asian dishes
Bean paste, hot	Soybean paste with crushed chili peppers	Bottled or canned	Asian dishes
Bean paste, sweet/red	Puréed red beans and sugar	Bottled or canned	Sweet Asian dishes (such as dumplings)
Miso	Japanese soybean paste	Foil pouches, jars	Japanese soups and sauces
Tofu (soybean curd)	Off-white, soft, curdled bean protein	Cakes, packed in water or pressed	Asian dishes
Peas	Dried: Green or yellow, smooth or wrinkled	dried, split or whole, canned, fresh	purées, soups.

TABLE 5-40   DRIED PASTA AND NOODLES (PATES SECHES, PASTA SECCA)

Name (Italian/English)	Description (Shape, Base Flour)	Major Dish(es)
Acini di pepe/ Peppercorns	Tiny, pellet-shaped; wheat flour	Soups
Anelli/Rings	Medium-small, ridged, tubular pasta cut in thin rings; wheat flour	Soups
Arrowroot Vermicelli	Very thin, Chinese noodles; arrowroot starch dough enriched with egg yolks	Asian dishes
Canneloni/Large Pipes	Large cylinders; wheat flour	Stuffed with cheese or meat, sauced, and baked
Capellini/Hair	Very, fine, solid, cylindrical; the finest is *capelli d'angelo* (angel's hair); wheat flour	With oil, butter, tomato, seafood, or other thin sauce; soup
Cavatappi/Corkscrews	Medium-thin, hollow, ridged pasta twisted into a spiral and cut into short lengths; wheat flour	With medium and hearty sauces
Cellophane Noodles	Very thin, transparent noodles; in bunches or compressed bundles; mung bean starch mung bean starch	Asian dishes: fried crisp for garnish, boiled for lo mein
Conchiglie/Shells	Large or medium, ridged shell shape; *conchigliette* are small shells; wheat flour	Filled with meat or cheese and baked; conchigliette: soups
Cresti di Gallo/ Cocks' Combs	Ridged, hollow, elbow-shaped noodles with a ruffled crest along one edge; wheat flour	With hearty sauces
Ditali/Thimbles	Narrow tubes cut in short lengths; *ditalini* are tiny thimbles; wheat flour	With medium-texture sauces, soups
Egg Flakes	Tiny, flat squares; wheat flour	Soups
Egg Noodles	Usually ribbons in varying widths; may be cut long or short, packaged loose or in compressed bundles; may have spinach or other flavorings; wheat flour dough enriched with egg yolks	Buttered casseroles, some sauces, puddings (sweet and savory)
Elbow Macaroni	Narrow, curved tubes cut in short lengths (about 1 inch); wheat flour	Macaroni and cheese, casseroles, salads
Farfalle/Butterflies	Flat, rectangular noodles pinched in center to resemble butterfly or bow; may have crimped edges; *farfallini* are tiny butterflies; wheat flour	With medium or hearty sauces; baked, soups
Fedeli or Fidelini	Very fine ribbon pasta, similar to capellini; wheat flour	With oil, butter, or light sauce
Fettucini	Long, flat, ribbon-shaped, about $1/4$-inch wide; wheat flour	With medium-hearty, rich sauces (*e.g.* alfredo)
Fiochetti/Bowties	Rectangles of flat pasta curled up and pinched slightly in the center to form bow shapes; wheat flour	With medium and hearty sauces sauces
Fusilli/Twists	Long, spring- or corkscrew-shaped strands; thicker than spaghetti; wheat flour	With tomato and other medium-thick sauces
Lasagne	Large, flat noodles about 3-inches wide; usually with curly edges; wheat flour	Baked with sauce, cheese, and meat or vegetables
Linguine	Thin, slightly flattened, solid strands, about $1/8$-inch wide; wheat flour	With oil, butter, marinara, or other thin sauces
Maccheroni/Macaroni	Thin, tubular pasta in various widths; may be long like spaghetti or cut into shorter lengths	With medium-hearty sauces
Mafalde	Flat, curly-edged, about $3/4$-inch wide; sometimes called lasagnette or malfadine; wheat flour	Sauced and baked
Manicotti/Small Muffs	Thick, ridged tubes; may be cut straight or on an angle; wheat flour	Filled with meat or cheese and baked

(Table continued on facing page)

TABLE 5-40 DRIED PASTA AND NOODLES (PATES SECHES, PASTA SECCA) *(continued)*

Name (Italian/English)	Description (Shape, Base Flour)	Major Dish(es)
Mostaccioli/ Small Mustaches	Medium-size tubes with angle-cut ends; may be ridged (rigati); wheat flour	With hearty sauces
Orecchiette/Ears	Smooth, curved rounds of flat pasta; about 1/2-inch in diameter; wheat flour	With oil-and-vegetable sauces or any medium sauce; soups
Orzo	Tiny, grain-shaped; wheat flour	Soups, salads, pilaf
Pastina/Tiny Pasta	Miniature pasta in any of various shapes, including stars, rings, alphabets, seeds/teardrops	Soups, side dish, or cereal
Penne/Quills or Pens	Same as mostaccioli	With hearty sauces
Rice Noodles	Noodles in various widths (up to about 1/8 inch); rice sticks are long, straight ribbons; rice vermicelli is very thin; rice flour	Asian dishes
Rigatoni	Thick, ridged tubes cut in lengths of about 1 1/2 inches	With hearty sauces; baked
Rotelle/Wheels	Spiral shaped; wheat flour	With medium or hearty sauces
Rotini/Cartwheels	Small, round, 6-spoked wheels; wheat flour	With hearty sauces; soups
Soba (Japanese)	Noodles the approximate shape and thickness of fedeli or taglarini; buckwheat flour	Asian dishes, including soups, hot and cold noodle dishes
Somen (Japanese)	Long, thin, noodles; made from wheat flour	Asian dishes, including soup
Spaghetti/Little Strings	Solid, round strands ranging from very thin to thin; very thin spaghetti may be labeled spaghettini; wheat flour	With oil, butter, marinara, seafood, or other thin sauces
Tagliarini	Ribbon pasta cut about 1/8-inch wide; wheat flour	With rich, medium-hearty sauces
Tagliatelli	Same as fetuccini; may be mixed plain and spinach noodles, called *paglia e fieno* (straw and hay)	With rich, hearty sauces
Tubetti /Tubes	Medium-small (usually about as thick as elbow macaroni), tubular, may be long or cut in lengths of about an inch; tubettini are tiny tubes	With medium and hearty sauces; soups
Udon (Japanese)	Thick noodles, similar to somen; wheat flour	Asian dishes
Vermicelli	Very fine cylindrical pasta, similar to capellini; wheat flour	With oil, butter, or light sauce
Ziti/Bridegrooms	Medium-size tubes; may be ridged (rigati); may be long or cut in approximately 2-inch lengths (ziti tagliate); wheat flour	With hearty sauces; baked

kitchen. Although in theory they have a lengthy shelf life, as do most nonperishable items, **legumes** are best when used within six months of purchase. In some cases, they may be dried versions of beans and peas that are also available fresh, canned, or frozen.

Store dried legumes in a cool, dry, well-ventilated area. Before using, discard any beans or peas that appear moldy, damp, or wrinkled. It should be noted that as beans age they will take longer to cook. (See Table 5-39 and Figure 5-111.)

Dried Pasta and Noodles

Dried pasta is a valuable "convenience food." It stores well, cooks quickly, and comes in an extensive array of shapes, sizes, and flavors. This range of shapes and flavors provides a base for a number of preparations, from a simple spaghetti dish to Asian and Middle Eastern specialties.

Pasta and noodles are made from a number of different flours and grains. Good-quality dried pas-

durum semolina: a coarsely ground flour made from durum wheat, which is high in the elastic-like protein gluten.

FIGURE 5-112   Pasta

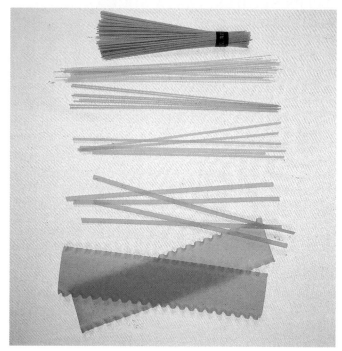

(1) (from top: soba, cappelini, spaghetti, linguini, fettucini, lasagne)

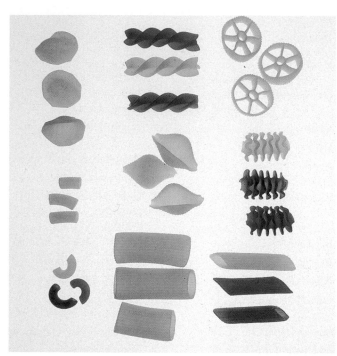

(2) Special and flavored pastas (top row: orechietti, fusilli, pin wheels; middle: tubetti, shells, radiatore; bottom: elbow, rigatoni, penne)

(3) Extruded types (clockwise from top left: orzo, elbow, tubettini, orrechietti)

tas from wheat flour are customarily made from durum semolina. Many pastas are flavored or colored with vegetables, such as spinach, peppers, or tomatoes. (See Table 5-40 and Figure 5-112.)

Oils and Shortenings

Oils are produced by pressing a high-oil-content food, such as olives, nuts, corn, avocados, and soy-

beans. The oil then may be filtered, clarified, or hydrogenated in order to produce an oil or shortening that has the appropriate characteristics for its intended use.

The hydrogenation process allows the oil to remain solid at room temperature, when it is known as **shortening.** A shortening labeled "vegetable shortening" is made from vegetable oil, whereas one labeled just "shortening" may contain animal products.

Several different oils and shortenings are required in every kitchen. Oils for salads and other cold dishes should be of the best possible quality, with a perfectly fresh flavor. First pressings of olive oil or nut oils are often chosen for these purposes, because of their special flavors.

Cooking oils may have a neutral flavor; those used for frying should have a high smoking point as well. Shortenings used for baking should also be neutral in flavor.

Oils and shortenings should be stored in dry storage away from extremes of heat and light. (See Tables 5-41 and 5-42; Figure 5-113.) For more information about cooking oils and fats, refer to Chapter 9.

Table 5-41 FATS AND OILS

Name	Description/Uses
Butter-flavored oils/ Shortenings	Vegetable oils (usually blended) flavored with real or artificial butter flavor for use on griddles. Hydrogenated shortening used for baked goods, pastries.
Canola oil (Rapeseed oil)	A light, golden-colored oil, similar to safflower oil. Low in saturated fat. Extracted from the seeds of a variety of turnip (the same plant as the vegetable, broccoli rabe). Used in salads and cooking, mostly in the Mediterranean region and India; also used in margarine and blended vegetable oils.
Coconut oil	A heavy, nearly colorless oil extracted from fresh coconuts. Used primarily in blended oils and shortenings, and in prepared, processed, packaged foods.
Corn oil	A mild-flavored refined oil. It is medium-yellow colored, inexpensive, and versatile
Cottonseed oil	This pale-yellow oil is extracted from seed of the cotton plant. Used for frying.
Frying fats	Blended oils or shortenings (usually based on processed corn or peanut oils) designed for high smoke point and long fry life. May be liquid or plastic at room temperature.
Grapeseed oil	This light, medium-yellow, aromatic oil is a by-product of wine making. It is used in salads and some cooking and in the manufacture of margarine.
Lard	Solid animal fat. May be treated to neutralize flavor.
Olive oil	Oil varies in weight and may be pale-yellow to deep-green depending on fruit used and processing. Cold-pressed olive oil, is superior in flavor to refined. Oil from the first pressing, called "virgin" oilve oil is the most flavorful. Also classified according to acidity: extra virgin, superfine, fine, virgin, and pure, in ascending degree of acidity. "Pure" olive oil, and that labeled just "olive oil" may be a combination of cold-pressed and refined oil; suitable for cooking.
Oil sprays	Vegetable oils (usually blended) packaged in pump or aerosol sprays for lightly coating pans, griddles.
Peanut oil	A pale-yellow refined oil, with a very subtle scent and flavor. Some varieties are darker, with a more pronounced peanut flavor. These are used primarily in Asian cooking.
Safflower oil	A golden-color oil with a light texture. Made from a plant that resembles the thistle. Usually refined.
Salad oil	Mild flavored vegetable oils blended for use in salad dressings, mayonnaise, etc.
Sesame oil	Two types: a light, very mild, Middle Eastern type and a darker Asian type pressed from toasted sesame seeds. Asian sesame oil may be light or dark brown. The darker oil has a more pronounced sesame flavor and aroma. Asian sesame oil has a low smoke point so it is used primarily as a flavoring rather than in cooking.
Shortening/Baking fat	Blended oil solidified using various processes, including whipping in air and hydrogenation. Designed for plasticity and mild flavor. May have real or artificial butter flavor added. Usually emulsified to enable absorption of more sugar in baked goods. May contain animal fats unless labeled "vegetable shortening."
Soybean oil	A fairly heavy oil with a pronounced flavor and aroma. More soybean oil is produced than any other type. Used in most blended vegetable oils and margarines.
Sunflower oil	A light, odorless and nearly flavorless oil pressed from sunflower seeds. Pale yellow and versatile.
Vegetable oil	Made by blending several different refined oils. Designed to have a mild flavor and a high smoke point.
Walnut oil	A medium-yellow oil with a nutty flavor and aroma. Cold-pressed from dried walnuts. More perishable than most other oils; should be used soon after purchase. Used primarily in salads. (Other nut oils include almond, hazelnut, and peanut above.)

TABLE 5-42   MELTING AND SMOKING POINTS OF SELECTED FATS

Name	Uses	Approximate Melting Point	Smoking Point*
Butter, whole	Baking, cooking	95°F/36°C	300°F/150°C
Butter, clarified	Cooking	95°F/36°C	300°F/150°C
Coconut oil	Coatings, confectionary, shortening	75°F/24°C	350°F/175°C
Corn oil	Frying, salad dressings, shortening	12°F/−11°C	450°F/230°C
Cottonseed oil	Margarine, salad dressings, shortening	55°F/13°C	420°F/215°C
Frying fat	Frying	105°F/40°C	465°F/240°C
Lard	Baking, cooking, specialty items	92°F/33°C	375°F/190°C
Olive oil	Cooking, salad dressings	32°F/0°C	375°F/190°C
Peanut oil	Frying, margarine, salad dressings, shortening	28°F/−2°C	440°F/225°C
Safflower oil	Margarine, mayonnaise, salad dressings	2°F/−17°C	510°F/265°C
Shortening, vegetable	Baking, frying, shortening	115°F/46°C	325°F/165°C
Soybean oil	Margarine, salad dressings, shortening	−5°F/−20°C	495°F/257°C
Sunflower oil	Cooking, margarine, salad dressings, shortening	2°F/−17°C	440°F/225°C

*The smoke point of any oil will be reduced after it is used for cooking. Temperatures are approximate.

FIGURE 5-113   Oils and Vinegars

(1) Top row: vinegars; bottom row: oils

(2) Infused oils

(3) Virgin olive oils

(4) Nut oils

TABLE 5-43 SPICES

Product	Uses/Affinities	Product	Uses/Affinities
Allspice	Braises, forcemeats, fish, pickles, desserts	**Ginger**	Fresh: Asian dishes, curries, braises; ground dry: Some desserts and baked goods
Anise	Desserts and other baked goods, liqueur		
Caraway	Rye bread, pork, cabbage, soups, stews, some cheeses, liqueur (*kummel*)	**Horseradish**	Sauces (for beef, chicken, fish), egg salad, potatoes, beets
Cardamom	Curries, some baked goods, pickling	**Juniper**	Marinades, braises (especially game), sauerkraut, gin, and liqueurs
Cayenne	Sauces, soups, most meats, some fish, and poultry	**Mace**	Some forcemeats, pork, fish, spinach, other vegetables, pickles, desserts, and baked goods
Celery seed	Salads (including cole slaw), salad dressings, soups, stews, tomatoes, some baked goods		
Chili powder	Chili and other Mexican dishes, curries	**Mustard**	Pickling, meats, sauces, cheese and eggs, prepared mustard
Cinnamon	Desserts, some baked goods, sweet potatoes, hot beverages, curries, pickles, and preserves	**Nutmeg**	Sauces, cream soups, veal, chicken aspics, spinach, mushrooms, potatoes, other vegetables, custards, baked goods
Cloves	Stocks, sauces, braises, marinades, curries, pickling, desserts, some baked goods	**Paprika**	Braises and stews (including goulash), sauces, garnish
Coriander seeds	Curries, some forcemeats, pickling, some baked goods	**Pepper**	Stocks, sauces, meats, vegetables, many other uses
Cumin	Curries; chili and other Mexican dishes	**Saffron**	Poultry, seafood, rice dishes, sauces, soups, some baked goods
Dill seeds	Pickling, sauerkraut		
Fennel seeds	Sausage, fish and shellfish, tomatoes, some baked goods, marinades	**Star anise**	Asian dishes, especially pork and duck
Fenugreek	Curries, meat, poultry, chutney	**Turmeric**	Curries, sauces, pickling, rice

Vinegars and Condiments

Vinegars and most **condiments** are used to introduce sharp, piquant, sweet, or hot flavors into foods. They may be used as an ingredient or served on the side, to be added according to a guest's taste. A well-stocked kitchen should include a full range of vinegars, mustards, relishes, pickles, olives, jams, and other condiments. In general, vinegars and condiments should be stored in the same manner as oils and shortenings.

Dried Herbs and Spices

Many of the fresh herbs discussed earlier in this chapter, are also available in dried form. Some herbs, such as rosemary, sage, and bay leaves, dry successfully, whereas others will retain very little flavor.

Dried herbs are often stored incorrectly, which compounds the problem of flavor loss. They are frequently stored on the top shelf over the range, are kept for too long, and are purchased in overly large quantities. A chef should buy only the amount of dried herbs that can be used within two or three months, and should store them away from heat. Herbs that have a musty or "flat" aroma should be discarded. If at all possible, the chef should try to find fresh herbs.

Spices are aromatics produced primarily from the bark and seeds of plants. Most spices' flavors are quite intense and powerful. Spices are nearly always sold in dried form and may be available whole or ground. In addition, the chef may use spice blends, such as curry powder, quatre épices, chili powder, and pickling spice.

Whole spices will keep longer than ground spices, although most spices will retain their potency for about six months if they are properly stored. They should be kept in sealed containers in a cool, dry spot, away from extreme heat and direct

quatre épices: a combination of four spices, pepper, nutmeg, ginger, cinnamon, or cloves.

TABLE 5-44   SALT AND PEPPER

Name	Description
Salt	
Rock salt	An unrefined, coarse salt not added directly to foods but used in some ice cream machines.
Table salt	All-purpose salt made by grinding refined rock salt into fine crystals. May be fortified with iodine and treated with magnesium carbonate to prevent clumping.
Sea salt	Made by allowing sea water to evaporate, leaving behind salt crystals. Available refined or unrefined, in whole crystals or ground. In its unrefined state, it may be known as *sel gris,* French for "gray salt."
Kosher salt	Pure refined rock salt, also known as "coarse salt" or "pickling salt." Because it does not contain magnesium carbonate, it will not cloud items to which it is added. Kosher salt is required for "koshering" foods that must meet Jewish dietary guidelines.
Curing salt	A blend of 94 percent salt and 6 percent sodium nitrite. Used in a variety of charcuterie items, especially those to be cold-smoked. Usually dyed pink to differentiate it from other salts. Saltpeter, which is potassium nitrate, is occasionally used in place of curing salt.
MSG (monosodium glutamate)	A flavor enhancer, without a distinct flavor of its own. Associated with the "Chinese Food Syndrome," MSG causes severe allergic reactions in some people.
Pepper	
Black peppercorns	Available as whole berries, cracked, or ground. The Telicherry peppercorn is one of the most prized. Mignonette or shot pepper is a combination of coarsely ground or crushed black and white peppercorns.
White peppercorns	Black peppercorns are allowed to ripen and then husks are removed. May be preferred for pale or lightly colored sauces. Available in same form as black peppercorns.
Green peppercorns	Unripe peppercorns that are packed in vinegar or brine; also available freeze-dried (they must be reconstituted in water before use).
Cayenne	A special type of chili, originally grown in Cayenne in French Guiana. The chili is dried and ground into a fine powder. The same chili is used to make hot pepper sauces.
Chili flakes	Dried, whole red chili peppers that are crushed or coarsely ground.
Paprika	A powder made from dried sweet peppers (pimientos). Available as mild, sweet, or hot. Hungarian paprikas are considered superior in flavor.

light. Check spices from time to time to be sure they are still potent, discarding any that have lost their flavor or have become stale or musty smelling. For optimum flavor, purchase whole spices and grind them as close as possible to the time they are to be used. (See Table 5-43 and Figure 5-114.)

Salt and Pepper

Salt was once one of the most prized of all seasonings. The expression "below the salt" shows its importance as an indicator of class differences. The nobles, who sat at the head of the table ("above the salt") were allowed to use salt. The lesser folk, sitting "below the salt," relied on herbs to flavor their food. Salt is today readily available in numerous forms (see Table 5-44).

Pepper was at one time the single most expensive seasoning in the world. Today, most kitchens require a number of different peppers for differ-

ent uses. Not all of the peppers listed in Table 5-44 are related botanically; however, they all have a pungent, fiery flavor and aroma. Freshly ground pepper is preferable, and should be used when possible.

Bulk stores of salt and pepper should be held in dry storage, away from moisture. In very humid weather when salt tends to cake together, mixing a few grains of rice in with the salt will help to prevent this. Whole peppercorns will retain their flavor indefinitely, releasing it only when crushed or ground. Check ground or cracked pepper for pungency if its age is in question.

Extracts and Other Flavorings

The chef uses a variety of flavorings for cooking and baking. They may be either **extracts,** which are alcohol-based, or **emulsions,** which are oil-based. Herbs, spices, nuts, and fruits are used to prepare

FIGURE 5-114   Dried Herbs and Spices

(1) Peppercorns (clockwise from top left: green, black, ground cayenne, red)

(2) Powdered seasonings and blends (from top right: ground mustard, ground coriander, ground cumin, poultry seasoning)

(3) Powdered seasonings and blends (top left to right) turmeric, cardamom, (center) curry powder, (bottom left to right) paprika, Old Bay

(4) Seeds (clockwise from top: mustard, celery, dill, fennel)

(5) Saffron

(6) Herbs and spices (clockwise from top left: parsley flakes, pickling spice, bay leaves, cloves)

(7) Spices (clockwise from top left: nutmeg, cinnamon, star anise, mace)

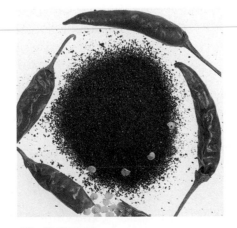

(8) Chili powder

both extracts and emulsions. Common flavors include vanilla, lemon, mint, and almond.

Alcohol-based extracts can lose their potency with prolonged exposure to air, heat, or light. To preserve flavor, store in tightly capped dark jars or bottles away from heat or direct light. Oil-based emulsions are more stable, but should also be stored in cool, well-ventilated areas in tightly capped jars or bottles to preserve freshness and flavor.

Wines, Cordials, and Liqueurs

A general rule of thumb for selecting wines, cordials, and liqueurs for use in cooking and baking is this: If it is not suitable for drinking, it is not suitable for cooking.

Among the common selections for use in the kitchen are brandies and cognacs, champagne, dry red and white wines, port, sauternes, sherry, stouts, ales, beers, and sweet and dry vermouth. For baking purposes, the chef should keep on hand bourbon, cassis, fruit brandies, gin, Kahlua, rum, and Scotch. Items listed for the kitchen can, of course, be used in the bakeshop, and vice versa.

Purchase wines and cordials that are affordably priced and of good quality. Table wines (burgundies, chablis, and chardonnays, for example) lose their flavor and become acidic once opened, especially when subjected to heat, light, and air. To preserve flavor, keep them in closed bottles or bottles fitted with pouring spouts, and refrigerate when not needed. Fortified wines (madeiras, sherries, and ports, for example) are more stable than table wines and can be held in dry storage if there is not enough room to refrigerate them. The same advice also applies to cordials, cognacs, and liqueurs.

Nuts and Seeds

With the exception of the peanut, which grows underground in the root system of a leguminous plant, nuts are the fruits of various trees. They are available in the following forms—in the shell, roasted, shelled, blanched, sliced, slivered, chopped, and as butters.

---

fortified wines: wines to which brandy or another spirit has been added to increase alcohol content.

FIGURE 5-115   Nuts and Seeds

(top row left to right) Black sesame, almonds, pine nuts, (2nd row) pecans, macademia, pistachios, (3rd row) pumpkin seeds, hazelnut/filberts, sunflower seeds, (bottom) Brazil nuts, cashews, walnuts

Nuts have a number of culinary uses, adding a special flavor and texture to dishes. They are relatively expensive and should be stored carefully to keep them from becoming rancid. Nuts that have not been roasted or shelled will keep longer. Shelled nuts may be stored in the freezer or cooler, if space allows. In any case, they should be stored in a cool, dry, well-ventilated area and checked periodically to be sure they are still fresh.

Some of the seeds used in the kitchen are considered spices (celery or fennel seed, for example), and others, including sesame seeds and poppy seeds, are covered in Table 5-45. Seeds are usually available whole or as a paste and should be stored in the same manner as nuts. (Also see Figure 5-115.)

Dried Fruits and Vegetables

The United States processes over one billion pounds of dried fruit per year. Federal and state standards

TABLE 5-45 NUTS AND SEEDS

Name	Description	Purchase Form
Almond	Teardrop-shape seed of a fruit that resembles the apricot. Pale-tan, woody, shell. Bitter and sweet types available. Bitter require cooking; sweet may be used raw or cooked	Whole in shell; shelled: whole, blanched, slivered, ground, almond paste, other products
Brazil	Large, oval nut; grows in clusters of segments. Each segment is a hard, wrinkled, three-sided, brown seed containing the rich nut	Whole in shell; shelled
Cashew	Kidney-shape nut that grows as the appendage of an apple-like fruit, which is not usually eaten. It is always sold hulled, as its skin contains irritating oils similar to those in poison ivy	Shelled: raw or toasted
Chestnut	Fairly large, round-to teardrop-shape nut; hard, glossy, dark-brown shell	Raw (whole in shell); canned: whole in water or syrup, puréed
Coconut	Melon-sized fruit that grows on a type of palm. The "nut," its woody, brown "seed," is covered with hairy fibers and surrounds a layer of rich, white nutmeat. The inside of the nut is hollow and contains thin, white juice (coconut water)	Whole in shell, flaked (may be sweetened), coconut cream, other products
Hazelnut	Small, nearly round nut; shiny, hard shell with matte spot where cap was attached. Nutmeat rich and delicately flavored	Whole in shell; shelled: whole, chopped
Macadamia	Nearly round, rich, sweet nut native to Australia	Shelled and roasted in coconut oil
Peanut	Seed grows inside a fibrous pod among the roots of a leguminous plant	Whole in shell; shelled: whole, skinned; raw or roasted; peanut butter
Pecan	Medium-brown, smooth, glossy, oval shaped shell. Two-lobed nutmeat has a rich flavor	Whole in shell; shelled: halved, chopped
Pine nut	Tiny, cream-colored, elongated kernel is the seed of a Mediterranean pine. Fairly perishable	Shelled: raw or toasted
Pistachio	Cream-colored shell; green nutmeat with distinctive, sweet flavor	Whole in shell: roasted, usually salted, natural or dyed red; occasionally shelled, chopped
Poppy seeds	Tiny, round, blue-black seeds with a rich, slightly musty flavor	Whole
Pumpkin seeds	Flat, oval, cream-colored seeds with semi-hard hull and soft, oily interior	Whole in shell; shelled: raw or toasted
Sesame seeds	Tiny, flat, oval seeds; may be black (unhulled) or tan (hulled); oily with rich, nutty flavor	Whole: hulled or unhulled; paste (tahini)
Sunflower seeds	Small, somewhat flat, teardrop-shape seeds; oily, light tan seed with woody, black and white shell; grown primarily for oil	Whole in shell; shelled
Walnut	Mild, tender, oily nutmeat; grows in convoluted segments inside hard, light-brown shell. White walnuts, or butternuts, and black walnuts are North American varieties. Butternuts are richer and black walnuts stronger in flavor	Whole in shell; shelled: halved, chopped; pickled (whole)

Figure 5-116   Dried Fruits and Vegetables

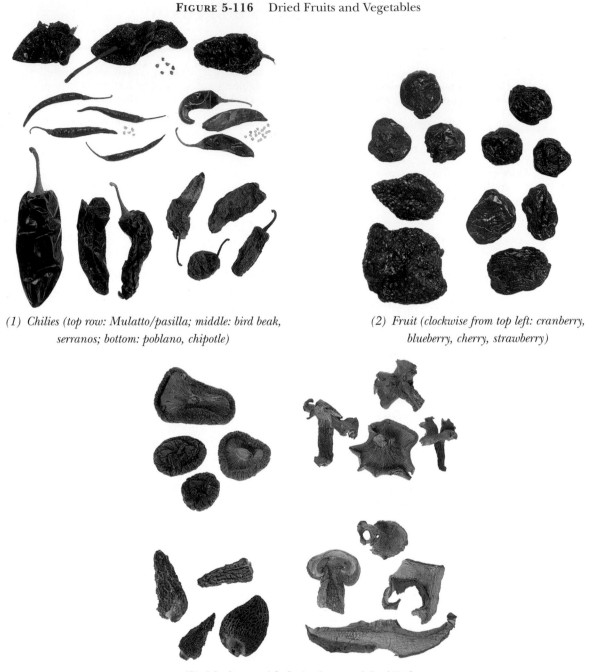

(1) Chilies (top row: Mulatto/pasilla; middle: bird beak, serranos; bottom: poblano, chipotle)

(2) Fruit (clockwise from top left: cranberry, blueberry, cherry, strawberry)

(3) Mushrooms (clockwise from top left: shiitake, chanterelle, porcini/cèpe, morel)

have been established for some (but not all) types of dried or low-moisture fruits and vegetables. Because the fruit is allowed to fully mature before being harvested and dried, there is greater potential for damage and defects. Low-moisture fruits and vegetables (raisins, sun-dried tomatoes, and so on) are somewhat perishable and should be refrigerated or carefully stored. Purchase no more than a one-month supply. Vacuum- or chemically-dried vegetables such as mushrooms, are not as perishable, but should be carefully stored in a cool, dry area. There is a great variety in the price and quality of dried fruits and vegetables. You will need to experiment to determine the best quality available. (See Figure 5-116.)

TABLE 5-46 SUGARS, SYRUPS, AND OTHER SWEETENERS

Name	Description	Purchase Form
Sugar		
Brown	Granular, refined sugar with some impurities left in or some molasses added; light to medium brown; moister than white sugar; slight molasses flavor	Bulk, bags, boxes
Muscovado	Granular, brown sugar, which has undergone little processing; soft and moist; dark brown with pronounced molasses flavor	Bulk, bags
Demerara	Partially refined sugar in large crystals, golden-brown, dissolves slowly	Bulk, boxes
Turbinado	Coarse granular sugar that is slightly more refined than demarara sugar; golden	Bulk, boxes
White, coarse/preserving	Pure, refined sugar in large crystals; dissolves slowly	Bulk boxes
White, Granulated	Pure, refined sugar in small, evenly sized crystals	Bulk, bags, individual packets
White, superfine/bar	Pure, refined sugar in very small crystals; dissolves quickly	Bulk, bags, boxes
Confectioners, 10X	Very finely powdered, pure refined sugar; usually mixed with a small amount of cornstarch to prevent clumping	Bulk, bags, boxes
White, lump/cube	Pure, refined, granulated sugar pressed into small cubes or tablets	Boxes
Syrup		
Corn	Liquified sugar extracted from corn; less sweet than sugar (types: light-pale yellow and dark-deep amber)	Bulk, jars
Maple	Liquified sugar made from the concentrated sap of the sugar maple, golden brown	Bulk, jars (jugs)
Treacle	A liquid by-product of refining, not widely used in the United States, light or dark, flavor resembles molasses	Bulk, jars
Flavored	Sugar or other syrup with added flavoring (common types: cassis-black currant, grenadine-pomegranate, maple)	Bulk, jars, individual packets
Molasses	Thick, dark-brown liquid by-product of sugar refining; rich flavor but less sweet than sugar (types: sulfured, unsulfured, blackstrap)	Bulk, jars
Honey	Thick, pale-straw to deep-brown liquid (creamed honeys are moist and granular) may be packaged with honeycomb, whole or in pieces; sweeter than sugar	Bulk, jars

Sugars, Syrups, and Other Sweeteners

Once a symbol of wealth and prosperity, sugar is now so commonplace and inexpensive that it takes a good deal of effort to avoid using it. Sugar is extracted from plant sources (sugar beet or sugar cane) and then refined into the desired form. Syrups (maple syrup, corn syrup, molasses, and honey) are also derived from plants.

Table sugar has a number of important roles in the kitchen and bakeshop, in addition to being commonplace on the table to sweeten beverages.

Syrups and other sweeteners, such as honey and sugar substitutes, may also be necessary, depending on a particular kitchen's menu and the guests' needs. (See Table 5-46 and Figure 5-117.)

Chocolate

Chocolate is produced from beans, known as cocoa beans, which grow in a pod on the cacao tree. For the ancient Aztecs, cocoa beans served not only to produce drinks and as a component of various sauces, but also as currency. Today the word "chocolate" is usually associated with sweets—cakes, candies, and other desserts—although it is also used in a variety of savory entrées, such as *mole poblano,* a chocolate chicken dish of Mexican origin.

The chocolate extraction process is lengthy, and has undergone a great deal of refinement since the days of the Aztecs. The first stage involves crushing the kernel into a paste, called **chocolate liquor**. The liquor is then further ground to give it a smoother,

FIGURE 5-117 Sugars and Syrups

FIGURE 5-118 Chocolates and Cocoa

(2) Syrups (from left: maple, pancake, honey, karo, light)

finer texture, and sweeteners and other ingredients may be added. The liquor may be pressed, causing cocoa butter to be forced out. The cocoa solids that are left are ground into **cocoa powder.** The remaining cocoa butter may be combined with chocolate liquor to make eating chocolates or it may be flavored and sweetened to make **white chocolate.** (See Table 5-47 and Figure 5-118.) Cocoa butter also has numerous pharmaceutical and cosmetic uses.

Chocolate should be stored well wrapped, in a cool, dry, ventilated area. Under most conditions it should not be refrigerated, since this could cause moisture to condense on the surface of the choco-

late. If the weather is hot and humid, however, it may be preferable to refrigerate or freeze the chocolate to prevent loss of flavor. Sometimes stored chocolate develops a white coating, or **bloom.** The bloom merely indicates that some of the cocoa butter has melted and then recrystallized on the surface. Chocolate with a bloom can still be safely used. If properly stored, chocolate will last for several months. Cocoa powder should be stored in tightly sealed containers in a dry place. It will keep almost indefinitely.

Coffee, Tea, and Other Beverages

A good cup of coffee or tea is often the key to a restaurant's reputation; it is one of the last impressions made on customers before they leave the restaurant. The chef should identify brands and blends that best serve the establishment's specific needs. Whereas some operations prefer to select whole coffee beans, others may be better served by buying preground, portioned, and vacuum-packed coffee. Many restaurants serve brewed, decaffeinated coffee, and some offer espresso and cappuccino, regular and decaffeinated.

Teas come in many varieties, including decaffeinated and herbal teas. Most are blends and

TABLE 5-47 CHOCOLATE AND RELATED PRODUCTS

Type	Description	Purchase Form
Chocolate liquor	The chocolate-flavored portion of chocolate; obtained by grinding and liquefying chocolate nibs	(See chocolate, unsweetened)
Cocoa butter	The vegetable fat portion of chocolate; removed for cocoa; added for chocolate	Plastic at room tempertaure
Cocoa	Chocolate from which all but 10–25% of the cocoa butter has been removed	Powder, unsweetened
Cocoa, dutch process	Chocolate from which all but 22–24% of the cocoa butter has been removed; treated with alkali to reduce its acidity	Powder, unsweetened
Cocoa, breakfast	Cocoa (above) with at least 22% cocoa butter	Powder, unsweetened
Cocoa, low-fat	Cocoa (above) with less than 10% cocoa butter	Powder, unsweetened
Cocoa, instant	Cocoa (above) that has been precooked, sweetened (usually about 80% sugar), and emulsified to make it dissolve more easily in liquid; may have powdered milk added	Powder
Chocolate, unsweetened (bitter/baking)	Solid chocolate made with about 95% chocolate liquor and 5% cocoa butter	Blocks or bars
Chocolate, bittersweet	Solid chocolate made with 35–50% chocolate liquor, 15% cocoa butter, and 35–50% sugar; interchangeable with semisweet chocolate; may have added ingredients, such as nuts, fillings, stabilizers, emulsifiers, and/or preservatives	Blocks, bars, chunks, and chips
Chocolate, semisweet	Solid chocolate made with about 45% chocolate liquor, 15% cocoa butter, and 40% sugar; interchangeable with bittersweet chocolate; may have added ingredients. (See above)	Blocks, bars, chunks, and chips
Chocolate, sweet	Solid chocolate made with 15% chocolate liquor, 15% cocoa butter, and 70% sugar; may have added ingredients. (See above)	Blocks, bars, chunks, and chips
Chocolate, milk	Solid chocolate made with 10% chocolate liquor, 20% cocoa butter, 50% sugar, and 15% milk solids; may have added ingredients. (See above)	Blocks, bars, chunks, and chips
Chocolate, coating (couverture)	Solid chocolate made with 15% chocolate liquor, 35% cocoa butter, and 50% sugar; high fat content makes it ideal for coating candy, pastries, and cakes	Blocks, bars, chunks, and chips
Confectionary coating	Solid, artificial chocolate made with vegetable fat other than cocoa butter; usually contains real chocolate flavoring in chocolate-flavored types; other flavors available	Blocks, bars, chunks, and chips
Chocolate, white	Solid chocolate made with cocoa butter or other vegetable fats, sugar, milk solids, and vanilla flavoring; contains no chocolate liquor; may contain artificial yellow color and/or other added ingredients. (See above)	Blocks, bars, chunks, and chips
Chocolate syrup	Chocolate or cocoa, sugar and/or other sweeteners, water, salt, other flavorings	Thick liquid
Chocolate sauce	Same as chocolate syrup but thicker; may have added milk, cream, butter, and/or other thickeners	Thick liquid
Carob	A dark-brown, somewhat chocolate-like flavoring produced from the carob bean; unsweetened carob is somewhat sweet, so it requires less added sugar than chocolate (about $3/4$ usual amount)	Blocks, bars, chunks, powder

FIGURE 5-119   Coffee/Tea

(1) Coffee beans (clockwise from top left: full city [medium-roast], dark [French] roast, Espresso [Italian] roast, light-roast)

(2) Tea varieties (clockwise from top left: spiced, black, herbal [tisane], green)

are available in single-serving bags or in loose form.

Although coffee and tea generally keep well, they will lose a lot of flavor if stored too long or under improper conditions. Whole roasted beans or opened containers of ground coffee should be kept cool, ideally, refrigerated. Teas should be stored in cool, dry areas, away from light and moisture.

Prepared mixes (powdered fruit drinks or cocoa mixes, for example) also should be kept moisture-free. Frozen juices and other beverages should remain solidly frozen until needed. Canned juices should be kept in dry storage. Remember to rotate stock, and check all cans, boxes, and other containers for leaks, bulges, or mold. (See Figure 5-119.)

Leaveners

Leaveners are used to give foods a light, airy texture. Chemical leaveners, such as baking soda (sodium bicarbonate) and baking powder (a combination of baking soda, cream of tartar, and talc),

work rapidly in the presence of moisture and heat. Baking powder is usually double-acting, which means that an initial reaction occurs in the presence of moisture, when liquids are added to dry ingredients, and a second in the presence of heat, as the item bakes in the oven.

Yeast also leavens foods through the process of fermentation, which produces alcohol and carbon dioxide gas. The gas creates a number of small air pockets which give yeast products such as breads their distinctive texturte. The alcohol burns off during baking.

Chemical leaveners should be kept perfectly dry. Dried yeast can be held for extended periods, but fresh yeast has a short shelf life of only a few weeks under refrigeration.

---

puff pastry: a pastry dough made by layering in butter through a series of folding and rolling steps. (See pages 446-449, for more information.)

brioche: a rich yeast bread with butter and eggs.

phyllo dough: a lean dough stretched into extremely thin sheets. These sheets are often layered, creating a flaky, almost brittle, texture after baking.

TABLE 5-48 COMMON CAN SIZES

Can Size (Industry Term)	Approximate Net Weight or Fluid Measure	Approximate Cups Per Can	Number of Portions	Principal Products
No. 10	6–7 lb 5 oz	12–13	25	Institutional size for fruits, vegetables
No. 5 Squat	4–4 ¼ lb	8	16–20	Institutional size for canned fish, sweet potatoes
No. 3 Cyl	46 or 51 fl oz	5 ¼	10–12	Fruit and vegetable juices, condensed soups
No. 2 ½	26–30 oz	3 ½	5–7	Fruits, some vegetables
No. 2	18 or 20 oz	2 ½	5	Juices, fruits, ready-to-serve soups
No. 303	1 lb	2	4	Fruits, vegetables, ready-to-serve soups
No. 300	14–16 oz	1 ¾	3–4	Some fruits and meat products
No. 1 (Picnic)	10 ½–12 oz	1 ¼	2–3	Condensed soups
8 oz	8 oz	1	2	Ready-to-serve soups, fruits, vegetables

Note: When substituting one can for another size, one No. 10 can is approximately equivalent to:
   7 No. 303 (1 lb) cans
   5 No. 2 (1 lb 4 oz) cans
   4 No. 2 ½ (1 lb 13 oz) cans
   2 No. 3 (46 to 50 oz) cans

FIGURE 5-120   Prepared and Miscellaneous Foods

(1) Wonton wrappers

(2) Tahini paste

(3) Seaweed wrappers and rice paper wrappers

(4) Truffles

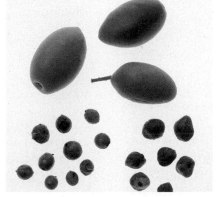

(5) Green peppercorns, olives, capers

(6) Can sizes

Thickeners

Thickeners are used to give a liquid a certain amount of viscosity. The process of forming an emulsion is one way to thicken a liquid, as is the process of reduction. In addition, various thickening ingredients can be used. These include the following:

- *Arrowroot* is a starchy root from a tropical tuber of the same name that is ground and highly refined. A lesser amount of arrowroot than of cornstarch may be used to achieve the same degree of thickening.

- *Cornstarch* is a refined, finely ground corn flour.

- *Filé gumbo powder* is made from the leaves of the sassafras tree and is used in Cajun and Creole cookery.

- *Gelatin* is a protein that, when properly combined with a liquid, will cause the liquid to gel as it cools. It is available in powdered form and in sheets.

Thickeners should be stored in tightly sealed containers in dry storage. They will keep almost indefinitely.

Prepared, Canned, and Frozen Foods

The use of convenience foods in professional kitchens today depends upon the requirements and capabilities of the kitchen, the quality of the convenience foods available, and the chef's judgment. (See Figure 5-120.) It may make sense, for example, to purchase prepared and frozen doughs (puff pastry, brioche, phyllo dough). Other frozen items frequently used are corn, peas, and spinach. As highly skilled food engineers develop appropriate methods of producing high-quality prepared foods, more products are becoming available. Everything from special breads to custom-made sauces is currently on the market, with new products and lines being developed all the time.

Canned products also have valid uses in the contemporary kitchen. Depending upon the season, some canned items may be of better quality than below standard fresh produce. An obvious example is canned tomatoes, which are often superior to out-of-season fresh tomatoes. Quality, determined by good taste, yield, price, and color, will vary from product to product. (See Table 5-48.)

Other convenience foods that may have a place in the kitchen include mayonnaise and prepared bases. In all cases, remember to choose products that are of good quality.

For storage purposes, frozen goods should be kept solidly frozen until they are needed. Canned goods should be rotated on the shelves to assure that the "first in" is the "first out" (FIFO rule).

Summary

As a chef, you must be able to understand how the seasonality, availability, and storage requirements of raw ingredients called for on the menu impact your purchasing plan. This chapter provides an extensive list of raw ingredients you should understand thoroughly in order to make the most effective possible use of the raw ingredients you buy. Throughout your career, you should continue to develop the following abilities and skills:

- Identifying restaurant and retail cuts of meat and appropriate purchasing specifications.

- Understanding how poultry and game birds are classified.

- Identifying the market forms of fish and shellfish, as well as their point of origin and purchasing specifications.

- Matching a variety of meats, poultry, and seafood with appropriate cooking methods.

- Understanding the procedure for purchasing, receiving, and storing fresh fruits, vegetables, and herbs.

- Properly selecting good-quality dairy, cheese and eggs, and receiving and storing them correctly.

- Categorizing and identifying the flavors and textures of a wide range of cheeses.

- Establishing criteria for purchasing the necessary and appropriate nonperishable, frozen, and convenience foods required by your individual foodservice operation and its menu.

SELF-STUDY QUESTIONS

1. Name the three highest USDA grades for beef, veal, and lamb. What are the USDA quality grades for pork?

2. Name some factors that will affect the tenderness of a cut of meat.

3. Name the quality standards for poultry applied by a USDA inspector.

4. Name at least two differences between game birds and domesticated poultry.

5. Describe the cooking technique best suited to each type of poultry.

6. What are the steps for checking the quality and freshness in fish?

7. Describe the correct setup for storing whole fish, fish fillets, and shellfish.

8. Why is shaved ice preferred to cubes for icing down fish?

9. Name five members of the onion family.

10. Name and describe the four varieties of caviar.

11. Name one fruit that will not continue to ripen after it is picked, and one fruit that will.

12. Name the two categories of peaches and nectarines and explain the difference between them.

13. What is the difference between roots and tubers?

14. What guidelines should be followed for the correct storage and use of fresh herbs?

15. Name the six categories used to group cheeses and give at least two characteristics of each one.

16. How are yogurts, buttermilk, sour cream, and crème fraîche produced?

17. Name three functions of the egg yolk in cooking.

18. Why should nuts be stored in a cool place, even under refrigeration if possible?

19. Name at least ten different flours, grains, or meals, and give their major uses or the name of a specific dish associated with them.

20. Give the melting and smoking points for the following fats and oil:

    - clarified butter

    - sunflower oil

    - lard

    - corn oil

ACTIVITIES

- Ask your local butcher for a tour of the facility. Note whether or not meats are received pre-cut, as "hung" or boxed meat, and if aged meats are available.

- Take a tour of your school's storeroom or, if possible, volunteer your time to work there for one day. Make a list of all the ingredients you see that are not familiar and research how they are used.

- Buy a variety of apples and conduct your own tasting. Take note of the size, color, crispness, and the acidity or sweetness of each apple.

- Get a sample menu from a local restaurant. Draw up a basic inventory list using the following categories:

  - meat/poultry/fish

  - fruits/vegetables/herbs

  - dairy/eggs/cheese

  - nonperishable/dry goods

  - frozen/canned/convenience foods

aged beef
ante-mortem
aquaculture
bivalve
boxed meat
cephalopod
chocolate liquor
cocoa powder
condiment
Cryovac®
culture
curds

cutability
date stamp
emulsion
ethylene gas
extracts
fermentation
flat fish
foie gras
free-range
government inspection
hanging meat
homogenized

kosher meat
legume
marbling
milkfat/butterfat
milled grains
mollusk
natural cheese
offal
oil
pasteurization
post-mortem
primal cuts

quality grading
round fish
shortening
subprimals/retail cuts
ultrapasteurization
univalve
USDA
vinegar
whey
white chocolate
whole grains
yield grade

III

Cooking in the Professional Kitchen

*This is an industry with tremendous
opportunity and I'd like to help as many
young people get involved with it as
possible. But you can't just look for the
glory. You can't see the pot at the end of
the rainbow and expect it to be yours,
because it's not going to be given to you.
You have to work hard. You have to earn it.*

—PATRICK CLARK,
EXECUTIVE CHEF, TAVERN ON THE GREEN

*As soon as you hear the term "chef," certain associations immediately spring to mind. You can
see the flashing knife and the steam rising like a cloud from a pot of soup. You can feel the
velvety texture of a perfect sauce, hear the crackle of foods as they first hit a hot pan.*

*These are the sights, sounds, and textures of cooking in the professional kitchen. Whether
you are a novice or an old hand, there is a sense of excitement and magic whenever you begin to
work. Finding a perfect groove, fitting your rhythms with those of the dining room, tackling the
day's work—these are the fundamentals of cooking in the professional kitchen.*

Throughout this part of the book, the basic cooking methods will be thoroughly explained. Mise en place covers such things as the basic knife cuts, the preparation of aromatic combinations, including mirepoix, sachet d'épices, and bouquet garni. Other tasks that you will perform—preparing stocks; cutting up poultry, meats, and fish; cleaning salad greens; or grinding spice blends, for instance—are also found in this chapter. A good mise en place is the point from which a good day's work flows.

The chapter devoted to soups covers a variety of basic soup preparation methods. From broths to consommés, purées to bisques, cold soups to specialty soups, all can be found in this chapter.

Sauces are often regarded as a chef's highest technical challenge. It is true that a silken cream sauce, a light but rich hollandaise, and a complex yet translucent brown sauce is no mean feat. The ability to consistently produce sauces that meet high standards of excellence is the hallmark of the skilled artisan.

Chapters 9 and 10 define and illustrate the cooking methods used for meats, fish, poultry, grains and pastas, dry and fresh vegetables, fruits, and eggs. Matching the right food with the right technique is the first step. Completing the process with attention to each detail—assembly of mise en place, advance preparation of foods and equipment, care in maintaining the highest standards of safety and cleanliness, cooking just to the exact moment of doneness, and preparing all sauces and garnishes required—is the fulfillment of your responsibility as a chef.

The basic dry-heat techniques include grilling, roasting, poêléing, sautéing, pan-frying, and deep-frying. Foods are cooked either through direct radiant heat, contact with a hot pan, or in hot fats. These foods are typically intensely flavored. Many have a crisp exterior texture that offers an interesting contrast.

Moist-heat and combination cooking methods have different attributes, varying according to the method you select, and the food you are preparing. Steaming, poaching, simmering, stewing, and braising are all examples of these techniques.

Two other areas in the kitchen are also explained in this part of the book: charcuterie and baking. These special pursuits may often form the particular focus of a chef's career. Whether or not you intend to become a charcutière, any professional must know the correct way of preparing pâtés, sausages, terrines, and other items produced in the cold kitchen. Likewise, the procedure for preparing breads, cakes, simple pastries and cookies, and kitchen desserts ought to be a part of your professional repertoire, even if you have no inclination to become a pâstissière.

Once the food has been cooked perfectly, the final task that remains is to prepare the plate for the guest. It is in completing this last detail that you apply the finishing touches. The placement of each element, the combinations of colors, textures, and even heights on a plate, the appearance of the plate itself, and the addition of a garnish tell the guest immediately that you have done your job carefully and with pride.

6

Mise en Place

There's a real key time in your life to devote yourself to something. I mean 125 percent every day, seven days a week, It's a brief period of time—four, five, or six years after school—when you are religiously, fanatically applying yourself with absolute confidence that whatever else, it's going to work. Know that if you're sincere your efforts, things will come that you couldn't have even dreamed.

—CHARLIE TROTTER,
EXECUTIVE CHEF AND OWNER, CHARLIE TROTTER'S

Mise en place *is a French phrase that translates as "to put in place." For the true professional, it means far more than simply assembling all the ingredients, pots and pans, plates, and serving pieces needed for a particular period. Mise en place is also a state of mind. Someone who has truly grasped the concept is able to keep many tasks in mind simultaneously, weighing and assigning each its proper value and priority. This assures that the chef has anticipated and prepared for every situation that could logically occur during a service period.*

The techniques, terms, basic preparations (or appareils), and skills covered in this chapter represent only the most basic elements of mise en place, gathered together for easy reference. They include knife skills, common seasoning and flavoring combinations, and techniques for mixing, shaping, and cooking a variety of ingredients and preparations, ranging from meat fabrication to stocks and court bouillons. Each of the cooking techniques explained throughout this book will impart its own lessons on the meaning of mise en place.

CHAPTER OBJECTIVES

- Understand a variety of basic knife cuts, including a few decorative cuts.

- Peel and/or cut a variety of specific vegetables.

- Work properly with a variety of dried fruits, vegetables, and beans.

- Prepare and use a number of thickeners.

- Prepare and use a number of aromatic and flavoring combinations.

- Explain the categories of stocks, broths, and court bouillons and describe the correct methods of preparing, storing, and using them.

- Execute a number of basic cooking techniques, including:

  - rendering and clarifying fats
  - preparing foams and folding them into a base
  - preparing parchment cones and liners
  - separating eggs
  - tempering ingredients
  - straining sauces

- Fabricate a variety of cuts of beef, veal, lamb, pork, and game into serving preparations, including:

  - tying a roast
  - butterflying
  - frenching
  - pounding
  - boning
  - cleaning and trimming

- Fabricate poultry, into the following preparations:

  - trussing
  - cutting whole birds into portions
  - preparing suprêmes

- Fabricate a variety of fish and shellfish into serving preparations, including:

  - scaling, trimming, and gutting
  - pan-dressing
  - shucking mollusks
  - filleting
  - peeling and deveining

Knife Skills

Knife skills include basic and advanced cuts that are used every day to prepare vegetables and other ingredients. Some of these cuts are quite familiar. Others are more unusual and may even require specialized tools or equipment. Some ingredients (onions, peppers, tomatoes, and leeks, for example) may demand special handling or preparation prior to cutting. These advance preparation steps will be discussed in the next section of this chapter.

The information and skills required to select, maintain, store, and sharpen knives and other cutting tools are discussed in Chapter 4, "Equipment Identification."

Holding the Knife

It is important to be comfortable with your knife as you work. There are several different ways a knife can be held. The way you hold the knife will be determined in part by the way your knife and your

FIGURE 6-1   Three Knife Grips

(1) Grasping the handle with thumb along spine of the blade.

(2) Grasping the handle with thumb along side of the blade.

(3) Grasping the handle with the thumb and two fingers along either side of the blade.

hand fit one another. The grip you choose will also be determined according to the task at hand. Delicate cutting or shaping techniques will call for greater control, involving the fingertips more than the fist. Coarser chopping and cutting tasks require a firmer grip and more leverage. The three basic grips used with a chef's knife are as follows:

1. Grip the handle with all four fingers and hold the thumb gently but firmly on top of the blade.

2. Grip the handle with four fingers and hold the thumb firmly against the side of the blade.

3. Grip the handle with three fingers, resting the index finger flat against the blade on one side, and holding the thumb on the opposite side to give additional stability and control for finer cuts.

See Figure 6-1 for examples of these holds.

The Guiding Hand

The guiding hand, the hand not holding the knife, is used to hold the object being cut (see Figure 6-2). This is done to prevent the food from slipping as you cut it. It also makes it easier to control the size of the cut or slice you are making. Your fingertips hold the object, with the thumb curved behind them and the fingertips tucked under slightly, so that your knuckles curl out over your fingertips. The knife blade then rests against your knuckles, preventing your fingers from being cut.

FIGURE 6-2
The Guiding Hand

As you make successive cuts, your fingertips should move back, maintaining a grip and controlling the width of each cut that is made.

Basic Knife Cuts

The basic cuts include:

- Coarse chopping and mincing
- Mincing
- Shredding (chiffonade)
- Julienne and bâtonnet
- Dicing
- Paysanne or fermière
- Lozenge
- Rondelle
- Oblique, or roll cut

Your aim, whenever you cut something, should always be to cut the food into pieces of uniform shape

FIGURE 6-3   Basic Vegetables Cuts and Dimensions

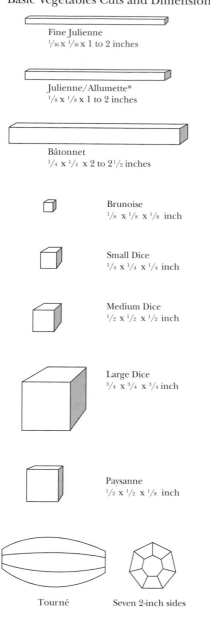

Fine Julienne
¹/₁₆ x ¹/₁₆ x 1 to 2 inches

Julienne/Allumette*
¹/₈ x ¹/₈ x 1 to 2 inches

Bâtonnet
¹/₄ x ¹/₄ x 2 to 2¹/₂ inches

Brunoise
¹/₈ x ¹/₈ x ¹/₈ inch

Small Dice
¹/₄ x ¹/₄ x ¹/₄ inch

Medium Dice
¹/₂ x ¹/₂ x ¹/₂ inch

Large Dice
³/₄ x ³/₄ x ³/₄ inch

Paysanne
¹/₂ x ¹/₂ x ¹/₈ inch

Tourné   Seven 2-inch sides

*Allumette normally refers only to potatoes.

and size. Unevenly cut items give an impression of carelessness that can spoil the dish's look. An even more important consideration is that foods of different sizes and shapes won't cook evenly. The basic cuts are illustrated in Figure 6-3. They are also discussed in the following pages, with step-by-step methods. It should be noted that the dimensions indicated in Figure 6-3 are recommended guidelines and may be modified if necessary. It is important that you be completely familiar with these cuts and able to execute them properly.

Peeling Vegetables and Fruits

Many vegetables and fruits should be peeled before they are cut. Swivel-bladed peelers are commonly used, since they cut only very thin strips from the outside of the vegetable. A paring knife can be used to either scrape or cut away the skin as well. Thicker or tougher skins may require a chef's knife to cut them away—winter squash, pineapples, rutabagas, or celeriac, for example. Figure 6-4 illus-

FIGURE 6-4   Basic Peeling Techniques

(1) Using a paring knife to scrape carrots.

(2) Using a swivel-bladed peeler.

(3) Using a chef's knife to remove heavy peels.

trates three basic peeling techniques. Special peeling techniques are explained in the next section.

Coarse Chopping

This method (see Figure 6-5) is often used for such items as mirepoix which will not be part of the finished presentation. They are normally strained out of the dish and discarded before service. The method for **coarse chopping** is as follows:

FIGURE 6-5
Coarse Chopping

FIGURE 6-6
Mincing Parsley

FIGURE 6-7
Cutting Belgian
Endive into
Chiffonade

1. Trim the root and stem ends and peel the vegetables if necessary.

2. Slice or chop the vegetables at nearly regular intervals until the cuts are relatively uniform. This need not be a perfectly neat cut, but all the pieces should be roughly the same size so that they cook evenly.

Mincing

This is a very fine, even cut (see Figure 6-6) that is especially appropriate for herbs and other flavoring ingredients such as garlic and shallots (See also pages 223-225 later in this chapter). Usually, the guiding hand is used to hold the item being cut just until a very coarse **mince** is achieved. As the fineness of the mince becomes greater, the guiding hand is often used to hold the tip of the knife's blade in position. The method is as follows:

1. Gather herbs or roughly chopped garlic or shallots into a pile on a cutting board and position the knife above the pile.

2. Keeping the tip of the blade against the cutting board, raise and lower the knife's heel firmly and rapidly, repeatedly chopping through the herbs or vegetables.

3. Continue chopping until the desired fineness is attained.

Chiffonade/Shredding

The **chiffonade** cut is used for leafy vegetables and herbs (see Figure 6-7). The result is a finely shredded product, often used as a garnish or bed for larger items. The method is as follows:

1. When cutting tight heads of greens, such as Belgian endive or head cabbage, core the head and cut it in half if it is large, to make cutting easier. For greens with large, loose leaves, roll individual leaves into tight cylinders before cutting. For smaller leaves, stack several leaves on top of one another.

2. Use a chef's knife to make very fine, parallel cuts to produce fine shreds. A box grater or mandoline can also be used to cut items such as cabbages or head lettuce, if you prefer.

FIGURE 6-8   Cutting Julienne Potatoes

(1) Squaring off the potato to make it stable on cutting surface.

(2) Cutting even slices, ⅛-inch thick.

(3) Stacking slices and cutting at ⅛-inch intervals to make julienne.

FIGURE 6-9
Cutting Julienned Potatoes into Small Dice

(The trimmings can be used, as appropriate, for stocks, soups, purées, or any preparation where shape is not important.)

2. Slice the vegetable lengthwise, using parallel cuts of the proper thickness.

3. Stack the slices, aligning the edges, and make parallel cuts of the same thickness through the stack. To make bâtonnet, the cuts should be thick. To make a fine julienne, the cuts should be very thin.

Dice

Dicing is a cutting technique that produces a cube shape (see Figure 6-9). Different preparations require different sizes of **dice.** The names given to different-sized dice are ***brunoise,*** small, medium, and large dice. The method is as follows:

1. Trim and cut the vegetable as for julienne or bâtonnet.

2. Gather the julienne or bâtonnets and cut through them crosswise at evenly spaced intervals.

Paysanne/Fermière

Paysanne or **fermière** cuts resemble the thin, square wooden tiles used in the game of Scrabble® (see Figure 6-10). They are often used for vegetables that are to garnish soups, stews, and braises. Although the size may vary, depending on the vegetable being cut and its intended use, a cut of ½-inch square and ¼-inch thick is customary. The method is as follows:

1. Trim and cut the vegetable as for bâtonnet.

Julienne and Bâtonnet

Julienne and **bâtonnet** cuts are long and rectangular (see Figure 6-8). Related cuts are the standard *pommes frites* and *pommes pont neuf* (both are names for French fries) and the **allumette** or matchstick. The differences between these cuts is the size of the final product. The method is as follows:

1. Trim the vegetable so that the sides are straight, which will make it easier to produce even cuts.

FIGURE 6-10
Paysanne Cut
Made from
Bâtonnet Potatoes

2. Make even, thin, crosswise cuts in the bâtonnets, at roughly ¼-inch intervals.

Lozenge/Diamond

The **lozenge** cut (see Figure 6-11) is similar to the paysanne. Instead of cutting battonet, the vegetable is sliced thinly and then cut into strips of the appropriate width, as shown. The method is as follows:

1. Trim and slice the vegetable thinly.

2. Cut the slices into strips of the desired width.

3. Make an initial bias cut to begin the process. This will leave some trim that should be reserved for use in preparations that do not require a neat, decorative cut.

FIGURE 6-11
Lozenge Cut from
Carrots

4. Continue to make bias cuts, parallel to the first one.

Rondelles/Rounds

This cut is one of the simplest. (See Figure 6-12.) The shape is the result of cutting a cylindrical vegetable, such as a carrot or cucumber, crosswise. The basic **rondelle** shape, a round disk, can be varied by cutting the vegetable on the bias to produce an elongated or oval disk, or by slicing it in half for half-moons. If the vegetable is scored with a channel knife, flower shapes are produced. The method is as follows:

FIGURE 6-12
Rondelle Cut
Variations:
Straight
(foreground);
Diagonal
(center); Halved
Cut on Diagonal
(backround)

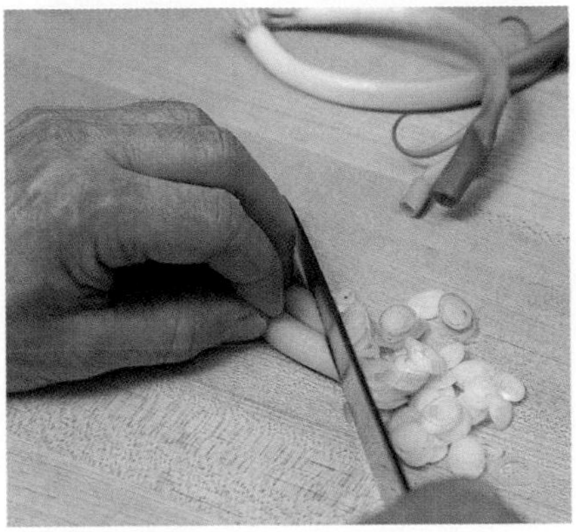

1. Trim and peel the vegetable if necessary.

2. Make parallel slicing cuts through the vegetable at even intervals.

Diagonal/Bias Cut

The **diagonal** cut is often used to make vegetables ready for stir-fries and other Asian-style dishes (see Figure 6-13). Because it exposes a greater surface area of the vegetable, employing this cut shortens cooking time. The method is as follows:

FIGURE 6-13
Diagonal/Bias
Cut

1. Place the peeled or trimmed vegetable on the work surface.

2. Make a series of even parallel cuts on the bias.

You can create numerous special cuts using such tools as a Japanese "turner," an apple peeler, mouli cutters or mandolines, ripple cutters, and box graters. Be sure to read any instructions that come with special cutters and use all the safety guards that are available.

A swivel-bladed peeler can also be used to create special cuts, such as curled or shaved Parmesan to top carpaccio or Caesar salads. Parisienne scoops (melon ballers) can also be used to prepare balls of varying sizes.

Fluting

Fluting (see Figure 6-14) takes some practice to master, but the result makes an attractive garnish. It is customarily used on mushrooms. The method is as follows:

FIGURE 6-14   Fluting Mushrooms

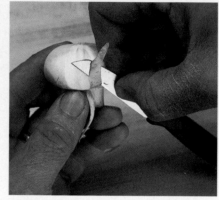

(1) Hold the mushroom between the thumb and forefinger of the guiding hand. Place the blade of a paring knife at an angle against the mushroom cap center. Begin cutting a groove, drawing the blade smoothly over the cap.

(2) Rotate the knife toward the cap edge, to cut a shallow groove. At the same time the knife blade is cutting, the guiding hand turns the mushroom in the opposite direction. Continue cutting grooves around the cap.

(3) Turn the mushroom slightly and repeat the cutting steps. Continue until the entire cap is fluted. The trimmings should be pulled away. Trim away the stem.

Fanning

Fanning (see Figure 6-15) cut uses one basic, easy-to-master cut to produce complicated-looking garnishes. It is used on both raw and cooked foods, such as pickles, strawberries, peach halves, zucchini, avocados, and other somewhat pliable vegetables and fruits. The method is as follows:

FIGURE 6-15
Cutting a
Cornichon "Fan"

Leaving the stem end intact, make a series of parallel vertical slices through the item. Spread the cut item into a fan shape.

FIGURE 6-16
Oblique or
Roll Cut

FIGURE 6-17
Turning
(*Tournéing*)
Carrots

Oblique or Roll Cut

The **oblique** cut is used primarily with long, cylindrical vegetables such as parsnips, carrots, and celery (see Figure 6-16). The method is as follows:

1. Place the peeled vegetable on a cutting board. Make a diagonal cut to remove the stem end.

2. Hold the knife in the same position and roll the vegetable 180 degrees (a half-turn). Slice through it on the same diagonal, forming a piece with two angled edges.

3. Repeat until the entire vegetable has been cut.

Turned (Tournéed) Vegetables

Turning vegetables (*tourner* in French) requires a series of cuts that simultaneously trim and shape the vegetable (see Figure 6-17). The shape may be likened to a barrel or football. **Tourné** vegetables are traditionally given different names, depending on their size. *Printanière* (the size of a large marble) and *jardinière* (the size of a quail's egg) are two of the more common names for turned cuts. The method is as follows:

1. Peel the vegetable, if desired.

2. Cut into pieces of manageable size. Cut large round or oval vegetables, such as beets and potatoes, into quarters, sixths, or eighths (depending on their size), to form pieces slightly larger than 2 inches. Cut cylindrical vegetables, such as carrots, into 2-inch pieces.

3. Using a paring or tourné knife, carve the pieces into barrel or football shapes. The faces should

be smooth, evenly spaced, and tapered so that both ends are narrower than the center.

Advance Preparation Techniques for Certain Vegetables

The number of ingredients that need to be on hand for a smooth service period will vary. Some menus will require an extensive mise en place setup, including tomato concassé, minced herbs, roasted peppers, plumped sun-dried tomatoes, and other ingredients. The steps involved in preparing foods for cutting or other applications are discussed by type below.

Onions

Onions are among the most indispensable ingredients in any kitchen. They can be cut into a variety of shapes and sizes. It is best to cut onions as close as possible to the time you need them; as cut onions sit, they take on a strong, sulfurous odor.

Aromatic combinations that include onions are explained in the section, "Basic Aromatic and Flavoring Combinations," later in this chapter.

Peeling and Dicing an Onion

Because onions grow in layers, they require a special cutting technique. The method is as follows:

---

tomato concassé: tomato which has been peeled, seeded and diced. (See page 226 for greater detail.)

FIGURE 6-18   Peeling and Dicing an Onion

(1) Peel away the skin, leaving root end intact.

(2) Halve the onion from end to end.

(3) Make a series of parallel cuts, leaving root end intact.

(4) Make horizontal cuts parallel to work surface

(5) Cut through onion, producing even dice.

1. Use a paring knife to remove the stem end. Peel off the skin and underlying layer, if it contains brown spots. Trim the root end but leave it intact.

2. Halve the onion lengthwise through the root. Lay it cut-side down and make a series of evenly spaced, parallel, lengthwise cuts with the tip of a chef's knife, again leaving the root end intact. The closer the cuts, the finer the dice will be.

3. Make two or three horizontal cuts parallel to the work surface, from the onion's stem end toward the root end, but do not cut all the way through.

4. Make even, crosswise cuts with a chef's knife, all the way through, from stem to root end.

See Figure 6-18 for photos illustrating the method for peeling and dicing an onion.

Garlic and Shallots

Minced shallots and garlic are required in many preparations—for example, they are used as a component in the aromatic bed for shallow-poached items, or in the reduction used to flavor emulsion sauces. It is important to have enough prepared to last through a service period. To prevent bacterial growth, store uncooked minced shallots or garlic covered in oil under refrigeration.

Garlic and shallots can be purchased already chopped, but many chefs feel strongly that these ingredients should be cut and used as close as possible to cooking time. The method for preparing minced garlic is as follows (see Figure 6-19):

1. To loosen the skin, crush the garlic clove between the knife blade's flat side and the cutting board, using the heel of the hand. Peel off the skin and remove the root end and any brown spots. (This technique is also indicated whenever you need crushed garlic).

2. Chop or mince the clove fairly fine. If desired, sprinkle the garlic with salt before mincing. This makes mashing easier by providing abrasion and absorbing excess juice and oil. Large quantities of garlic and shallots can be minced in a food processor.

FIGURE 6-19 Peeling and Mincing Garlic

(1) Break the skin, using the flat side of a chef's knife.

(2) Pull away the skin.

(3) Chop the cloves into progressively smaller dice.

FIGURE 6-20 Mincing Shallots

FIGURE 6-21 Mashing Garlic to a Paste

See Figure 6-20 for photos illustrating the method for mincing shallots.

To mash garlic to a paste hold the knife at an angle and use the cutting edge to mash the garlic against the cutting board. Repeat this step until the garlic is mashed to a paste. See Figure 6-21 for an illustration of this technique.

The technique used to mince shallots is similar to that for onions.

Hold the blade almost flat to mash the garlic to a paste.

Roasting Garlic and Shallots

The flavor of garlic and shallots becomes rich, sweet, and smoky after roasting. This technique is quite popular, and roasted garlic can be found as a component of marinades, glazes, and vinaigrettes, as well as a spread for grilled breads. The method is as follows:

1. Place the unpeeled head of garlic or shallot bulbs in a small pan or sizzler platter. Some chefs like to place them on a bed of salt. The salt holds the heat, roasting the garlic quickly and producing a drier texture in the finished product.

2. Roast at a moderate temperature until the garlic or shallots are quite soft. Any juices that run from the garlic or shallots should be brown. The aroma should be sweet and pleasing, with no hints of harshness or sulfur.

Leeks

One of the biggest concerns when working with leeks is removing every trace of dirt. A leek grows in layers, trapping grit and sand between each layer. Careful rinsing is essential (see Figure 6-22).

The stringy roots of a leek should be trimmed away, but its end should be left intact. Most of the dark green leaves are cut away as well. The leek is then slit along its length, leaving the root end still

---

sizzler platter: a metal cooking platter, often used to hold food items under a broiler, or to finish partially cooked items in an oven.

FIGURE 6-22
Cleaning Leeks
Under Running
Water

intact, if desired. Rinse under running water until there is no dirt remaining.

Tomatoes

Fresh and canned tomatoes are used in a number of dishes. When using fresh tomatoes, you will often be called upon to prepare *concassé*. This term indicates that the tomato has been peeled, seeded, and then chopped. Canned whole tomatoes may also be seeded and chopped, but they are normally already peeled before canning.

Roasting is another advance preparation technique that can be used. While the flavor is deeper and more intense than that of fresh or canned tomatoes, it is not so rich as that of sun-dried tomatoes. For directions regarding the proper use of sun-dried tomatoes (and other dried fruits and vegetables), refer to pages 235-236 in this chapter.

Preparing Tomato Concassé

Tomato concassé is required to prepare or garnish a number of different sauces and dishes. It

may be made in advance, but make only enough to last through a single service period. Once peeled and chopped, tomatoes will begin to lose some of their flavor and texture. The same blanching and peeling method used for tomatoes is also used for chestnuts, almonds, peaches and apricots. The method is as follows:

1. Cut an "X" into the bottom of the tomato. Some chefs also like to cut out the stem at this point. Others prefer to wait until the tomato has already been blanched.

2. Bring a pot of water to a rolling boil. Drop the tomatoes into the water. After 10 to 30 seconds (depending on the tomatoes' age and ripeness), remove them with a slotted spoon, skimmer, or spider. Immediately plunge them into very cold or ice water. Pull away the skin.

3. Halve each tomato crosswise at its widest point and gently squeeze out the seeds. (Plum tomatoes are more easily seeded by cutting lengthwise.)

4. Coarsely chop or cut the flesh into dice or julienne, as desired.

See Figure 6-23 for a step in the method for preparing tomato concassé.

Roasting Tomatoes

Roasted tomatoes (sometimes referred to as "oven-dried") can be made by either halving or slicing ripe tomatoes (see Figure 6-24). They can be used to replace sun-dried tomatoes in some dishes. The method is as follows:

1. Core the tomato and cut it into halves or slices.

2. Coat lightly with oil, and add seasonings and

FIGURE 6-23
Submerging
Tomatoes in Ice
Water to Stop
Cooking

FIGURE 6-24
Roasted Tomatoes

aromatics as desired. Salt, pepper, fresh or dried herbs, plain or infused oils, chopped garlic, or shallots are all good choices.

3. Roast the tomatoes at a moderate temperature until they are browned and have a rich "roasted" aroma.

Sweet Peppers and Chilies

Peppers and chilies are used in dishes from cuisines as diverse as those of Central and South America, Japan and other Asian countries, Spain, and Hungary. As the interest in chilies and peppers has grown, many special varieties, both fresh and dried, have become available. For more information about working with dried chilies, refer to pages 236 later in this chapter.

Seeding and Cutting Peppers

Make a cut around the stem end of the pepper and then halve the pepper from top to bottom. Pull or cut away the seeds. If you are working with very hot chilies, you may want to use plastic gloves to protect your skin.

Chilies retain a good deal of their heat in the seeds, ribs, and blossom ends. You can control the degree of heat by adjusting how much, if any, of these parts of the chili you add to a dish.

You can make very regular julienne or dice by "filleting" the pepper before cutting. Cut away the top and bottom of the pepper. Cut the pepper from top to bottom and open it out flat to create an even rectangle. Slice away the flesh from the skin, if desired, and then cut into neat julienne or dice. Reserve any edible scraps to use in coulis or to flavor broths, stews, or court bouillons.

See Figure 6-25 for photos illustrating the method for seeding and filleting peppers.

Roasting and Peeling Peppers

There are four basic methods for peeling peppers. The first method does not involve roasting the pepper, so its sweet, fresh flavor is not changed. The remaining three versions actually cook the pepper. Roasting or grilling peppers makes it easy to remove their skin, and also gives them a special flavor. See Figure 6-26 for photos illustrating methods of roasting and peeling peppers.

Peeling with a Swivel Peeler This method is used when peeled, raw peppers are needed.

1. Section the pepper with a knife, cutting along the folds to expose the unpeeled skin.

2. Remove the core, seeds, and ribs and peel with a swivel peeler.

FIGURE 6-25 Seeding and Filleting Peppers and Chilies

(1) Cut away both ends, halve, and cut away seeds and stems. Reserve trim for other uses.

(2) Cut flesh away from skin before dicing, a process known as "filleting."

(3) Wear gloves to protect skin when working with chilies.

FIGURE 6-26 Roasting and Peeling Peppers

(1) Turn peppers in a gas flame until charred.

(2) Wrap in plastic to allow skin to steam.

(3) Remove skin, using a paring knife if necessary.

(4) Roast large batches in a very hot oven on a sheet pan.

(5) Once charred, cover with an inverted roasting pan to steam.

(6) Blister peppers by dropping into hot oil.

Charred Peppers This technique is used to roast and peel small quantities.

1. Hold the pepper over the flame of a gas burner with tongs or a kitchen fork or place the pepper on a grill. Turn the pepper and roast it until the surface is evenly charred.

2. Place in a plastic or paper bag or under an inverted bowl to steam the skin loose.

3. When the pepper is cool enough to handle, remove the charred skin, using a paring knife if necessary.

Oven- or Broiler-Roasted Peppers This method is used for larger quantities.

1. Halve the peppers and remove stems and seeds. Place cut-side down on an oiled sheet pan.

2. Place in a very hot oven or under a broiler. Roast or broil until evenly charred.

3. Remove from the oven or broiler and cover immediately, using an inverted sheet pan. This will steam the peppers, making the skin easier to remove.

4. Peel, using a paring knife as necessary.

Deep-Fried Peppers This is a quick method for blistering small quantities.

1. Using tongs or doubled frying baskets to submerge the peppers in oil that has been heated to 325°F (165°C).

2. Deep-fry the peppers for about a minute, until they are blistered all over. The peppers usually will not brown dramatically.

3. Remove from the deep fat, drain, and let cool.

4. Peel away the skin, using a paring knife if necessary.

Mushrooms

Fresh mushrooms may require some careful cleaning before they are sliced or minced. Whenever practical, the preferred method is to use a clean cloth or soft brush to wipe away any dirt. Large quantities can be very quickly rinsed in cold water, then drained well on layers of absorbent toweling. Avoid any prolonged contact with water as you clean or hold mushrooms, however. They absorb liquids quickly, and an excess of moisture will cause them to deteriorate rapidly.

Some mushrooms should have the stems removed. Shiitakes, for example, have very tough, woody stems that should not be served. The stems should be cut away from the cap and discarded (see Figure 6-27).

Sliced and minced mushrooms will begin to weep almost as soon as they are cut. When you need cut mushrooms (as a garnish for a sauce, to sauté or grill, or to prepare duxelles), try to cook them as soon as possible after they are cut. Avoid cutting more than you need at a given time.

Leafy Greens

Salad greens, cooking greens, and herbs are often quite sandy and gritty. Removing all traces of dirt from them is a very important part of the mise en place for the pantry and hot line. Greens that are raised hydroponically, prepared mesclun mixes, and pre-rinsed spinach may need only a quick plunge or rinse with cool water. Other leafy greens should be cleaned as follows:

1. Fill a sink with cool water. Separate or loosen heading greens and dip them into the water. Plunging them in and out of the water will loosen the sand.

2. Lift them out of the water and then drain the sink. Repeat the process until there are no signs of grit remaining in the water.

3. Once rinsed, allow the greens to drain briefly and, if necessary, spin them dry using a salad spinner.

To remove the core from iceberg or Boston lettuce, gently rap or push the core down onto a work surface. This will generally break the core away from the leaves. For tighter heads, you may need to use a paring knife to cut out the core.

Loose heads and "bunching" greens such as Romaine or frisée will separate into individual leaves easily. Trim the coarse ribs or stem ends away if necessary. Spinach stems can be pulled away easily.

Refer to Figure 6-28 for photos illustrating preparation of leafy greens.

Fresh Herbs

The procedure for refreshing or rinsing herbs is the same as that described above for leafy greens. Many chefs feel that mincing or cutting fresh herbs with a knife is an acceptable practice, as long as it is not done too far in advance. Others, however, prefer to tear or snip herbs to avoid bruising them. Figure 6-29 illustrates the different methods for preparing fresh herbs.

FIGURE 6-27
Removing Tough Stems from Shiitake Mushrooms

Citrus Fruits

Citrus fruits, including oranges, lemons, limes, and grapefruit, are used to add flavor and color to dishes. They are also served as a functional garnish for some dishes—for instance, a slice of lime with a Cuban-style black bean soup or a wedge of lemon with a broiled fish.

---

functional garnish: free-standing ingredient or combination of ingredients served with a dish, meant to be eaten. There should be a logical connection between the garnish and the main item.

FIGURE 6-28   Preparing Greens

(1) Rinsing lettuces in cold water (Romaine and Boston lettuces are shown here).

(5) Pulling out the core.

(2) Draining excess water away from greens.

(6) Rinsing leafy greens (spinach shown here).

(3) Removing tough cores from Romaine lettuce leaves.

(7) Draining in a colander.

(4) Rapping core of iceberg lettuce on work surface to loosen it.

(8) Removing heavy stems.

(Figure 6-28 continued on facing page)

FIGURE 6-28 Preparing Greens *(continued)*

(9) Salad greens ready to spin dry.

(10) Greens after spinning, ready to dress.

FIGURE 6-29 Working with Fresh Herbs

(1) Mincing parsley with scissors.

(2) Tearing basil into small pieces by hand.

Although citrus fruits keep well, be sure that the fruit you select is not bruised or softened. Before juicing citrus fruits, you should allow them to come to room temperature, if possible. Roll the fruit under the palm of your hand on a cutting board or other work surface before juicing to break some of the membranes. This helps to release more juice. Remember to strain out seeds and pith before using the juice, either by covering the citrus fruit with cheesecloth before squeezing it, or by straining the juice. There are numerous special tools to juice citrus fruits including reamers, extractors, and electric juicers.

Zesting Citrus Fruit

The zest, the outer portion of a citrus fruit's peel or rind, is used to add color, texture, and flavor to various preparations. The zest includes *only* the skin's brightly colored part, which contains much of the fruit's flavorful and aromatic volatile oils. It does not include the underlying white pith,

which has a bitter taste. See Figure 6-30 for photos illustrating the method for zesting citrus fruit. The method is as follows:

1. Use a paring knife, swivel-bladed peeler, or zester to remove only the peel's colored portion.

2. If julienned or grated zest is called for, use a chef's knife to cut or mince the zest. Grated zest can also be prepared using the fine holes of a box grater.

Chestnuts

To peel chestnuts, cut an "X" with a paring knife in the flat side of the nut. Then, they can be either boiled or roasted just until the skin begins to pull away. Work in small batches, keeping the chestnuts warm, and pull and cut away the tough outer skin.

Cooked chestnuts can be left whole, puréed, sweetened, or glazed.

FIGURE 6-30   Zesting Citrus

(1) Using a zester.

(2) Using a vegetable peeler to remove strips.

(3) Cutting strips into julienne.

See Figure 6-31 for photos illustrating the method for roasting and peeling chestnuts.

Eggplant

Eggplant is available in a range of shapes and colors, from small white balls to enormous purple-black specimens. For the best results, whether you intend to roast, pan-fry, or grill eggplant, be sure

FIGURE 6-31   Roasting Chestnuts

(1) Chestnuts ready to come out of the oven.

(2) Peeling chestnuts.

the vegetable is properly handled. Eggplant will discolor once cut, so be sure to work quickly.

Salting Eggplant

Large eggplants can become bitter, as can large cucumbers and summer squash. To reduce bitterness, many chefs believe that eggplant (as well as cucumbers and summer squash) should be salted as follows:

1. Slice the ends from the eggplant and discard. Slice the eggplant as required by recipe or desired result.

2. Scatter salt liberally over the eggplant, tossing the slices to coat them evenly.

3. Place the eggplant in a colander or perforated hotel pan, and (optional) weight the eggplant to help expel its juices. Generally speaking, a few hours is sufficient to draw off any bitterness.

4. Rinse the eggplant well to remove the salt, dry thoroughly, and then proceed with cooking.

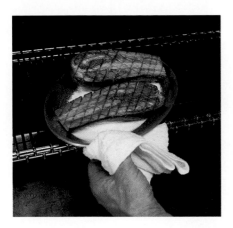

FIGURE 6-32
Roasting Eggplant

Roasting Eggplant

Eggplant responds well to roasting (see Figure 6-32). The flesh becomes extremely soft with an appetizing flavor and aroma. To prepare the eggplant for roasting, proceed as follows:

1. Slice the eggplant in half from stem to blossom end.

2. Score it in a diamond pattern, cutting through most of the flesh, but leaving the skin intact.

3. If desired, rub the cut surface with some olive oil.

4. Roast the eggplant cut-side down in a moderate oven until softened but not browned.

5. Turn the eggplant cut-side up and continue to roast until the flesh is very soft. It is now ready to

purée, if desired. The flesh can be strained after puréeing for a very smooth texture. This is especially recommended for larger eggplant, that may be stringy.

Corn

Sweet corn should be husked and the silk removed just before cooking. To remove the kernels, hold the ear upright and cut down the rows. To "milk" the corn, proceed as follows:

1. Score the rows of kernels with a knife.

2. Use the back of a knife, spoon, or butter curler to scrape out the flesh.

See Figure 6-33 for photos illustrating the method for removing corn kernels and milking corn.

Potatoes

When you peel or cut potatoes, the exposure to air will cause them to discolor quickly. To prevent this, place the cut potatoes in a container of cool water. If you will be frying the potatoes, you must take the time to blot them dry on absorbent toweling. This will dramatically reduce the splattering that occurs when the potatoes come in contact with hot oil. It will also prolong the life of the oil in deep-fat fryers, since excess moisture encourages fats and oils to break down more quickly.

Baked potatoes can blow apart in the oven, if they are not pierced. Piercing them with the tip of a par-

FIGURE 6-33   Cutting Kernels from the Cob and Milking Corn

(1) Use a chef's knife to cut kernels away, before or after cooking.

(2) To "milk" corn, first score rows with a knife.

(3) Use the back of the knife to scrape out the pulp and milk.

FIGURE 6-34   Preparing Potatoes

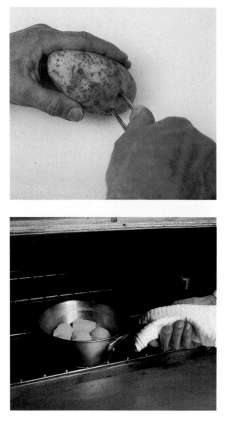

(1) Pierce with a kitchen fork before baking, to allow steam to vent.

(2) Dry boiled or steamed potatoes after draining for best texture and flavor.

FIGURE 6-35   Preparing an Artichoke

(1) Trim away both ends of the artichoke.

(2) Use scissors to cut away the barbs from ends of leaves.

ing knife or kitchen fork allows the steam to escape before enough pressure builds up to cause an explosion. Baking potatoes on a bed of salt or rubbing the skin lightly with oil are methods recommended by some chefs to encourage the development of a crisp skin and delicate, fluffy interior.

Whenever potatoes are boiled or steamed, it is a good idea to dry them briefly before serving them, or going on to make purées, salads, or hash browns. This drives off any excess moisture, improving both flavor and texture. To dry potatoes, place them in a pot or on a sheet pan, and then into the oven or over low heat until the potatoes look dry and "mealy."

See Figure 6-34 for photos illustrating the method for piercing and drying potatoes.

Artichokes

Artichokes are related to thistles and need to have the hairy "choke" removed before they are served. This can be done before or after cooking. Either spread the leaves open and scoop out the purple

and white leaves, or cut the artichoke in half and then remove the choke.

To "turn" the artichoke bottom, cut away the leaves and stem, and scoop out the choke. This will leave a dish-shaped portion of the artichoke, referred to as the bottom. If the artichoke was not cooked before the leaves and choke are cut away, submerge the bottom immediately in lightly acidulated water or rub it with lemon juice to prevent discoloration.

To prepare a whole artichoke for service, trim away the sharp tips of the leaves and the stem as follows:

1. Use a sharp knife to cut away the very top and the stem of the artichoke. Rub the cut surface with lemon to prevent discoloration.

2. Use kitchen shears to snip off the barbs that remain on the leaves. (The choke, visible in Figure 6-35 as the light purple area near the center of

---

acidulated water: a mixture of water and lemon juice.

FIGURE 6-36
Pulling Away Strings from Snow Peas

FIGURE 6-37   Coring an Apple

(1) Use an apple corer to remove core.

(2) The apple is ready to stuff, bake, or poach.

the vegetable, can be scooped out now if desired.)

3. (Optional) Use twine to hold the artichoke's shape. A piece of lemon will give additional protection against any discoloration. Or, lemon slices or juice can be added to the cooking water.

Snow and Sugar Snap Peas

Snow and sugar snap peas have a rather tough string that runs along one seam. This string should be removed before the peas are cooked. Snap off the stem end and pull (see Figure 6-36). The string will come away easily.

Asparagus

Very slender young asparagus may need no further preparation than simply a trim to remove the lowest end of the stalk, and a quick rinse. However, it is often a good idea to trim the stalk a little further up and peel the stem partially to remove the "fingernails," which can be a little tough and unpleasant to eat.

As asparagus matures, the stem becomes tough. To remove the woody portion, you can bend the stem gently until it snaps. Use a special asparagus peeler or swivel-bladed peeler. Peeling the stem part-way up not only enhances palatability, it also makes it easier to cook the asparagus evenly, so that the stem and tips are done at the same time.

Asparagus may be tied into loose bundles to make it easier to remove them from boiling water when they are properly blanched or cooked. Don't tie them too tightly, or make the bundles more than

a few inches in diameter. Otherwise, the center stalks will not cook properly.

Apples

Apples, as well as pears, peaches, and bananas, will discolor when they are exposed to air. To prevent this, toss them in acidulated water. There shouldn't be so much acid that it overwhelms the flavor of the fruit, however.

To remove the core from apples before baking or slicing them, you can use an apple corer, as shown in Figure 6-37.

Working with Dried Fruits and Vegetables

Dried fruits and vegetables have always been an important part of many cuisines. Drying foods makes them suitable for long-term storage. It also concentrates flavors. Today, there are still some vegetables and fruits that are only briefly available as fresh ingredients—morel mushrooms, for instance. Throughout the rest of the year, they are only available in a preserved form.

We also enjoy the special flavors of dried chilies, mushrooms, tomatoes, and fruits such as apples, cherries, and raisins, even though we may often be able to purchase those same ingredients fresh. To get the most from these ingredients, recipes may often call for "plumped" or rehydrated dried fruits, vegetables, and mushrooms. The method is as follows:

1. Check the dried ingredient first. Remove any obvious debris or seriously blemished, moldy specimens.

2. Place it in a bowl or other container and add enough boiling or very hot liquid (water, wine, fruit juices, or broth can all be used) to cover.

3. Let the dried ingredient steep in the hot water for several minutes, until softened and plumped as shown in Figure 6-38.

4. Pour off the liquid, reserving it if desired for use in another preparation. If necessary, the liquid can be strained through a coffee filter or cheese-cloth to remove any debris.

Dried chilies may be toasted in the same manner as dried spices, nuts, and seeds, by tossing them in a dry skillet over moderate heat. They may also be passed repeatedly through a flame until toasted and softened. The pulp and seeds can then be scraped from the skin, or the whole chili may be used, according to recipe direction.

FIGURE 6-39
Beans Before Soaking (on right) and After (on left)

Soaking Beans

Most beans, with a few notable exceptions (lentils, split peas, and black-eyed peas), are easier to prepare and produce a better-quality finished dish if they are allowed to soak. The skins soften slightly, allowing for more rapid and even cooking. Figure 6-39 shows the change in volume after soaking. (For information about beans and soaking times, refer to the bean cookery table in Appendix 2.)

Rinse and sort beans first to remove dirt, stones, and moldy specimens. There are two methods commonly used, the long- and quick-soak methods.

The Long-Soak Method

1. Place the rinsed and sorted beans in a container and add enough cool water to cover them by a few inches.

2. Let the beans soak for the suggested time period; this will vary, depending on the bean, from 4 to 24 hours.

3. Drain the beans and cook as directed.

Quick-Soak Method

1. Place the rinsed and sorted beans in a pot, and add enough water to cover by a few inches. Bring the water to a simmer.

2. Remove the pot from direct heat and cover. Let the beans steep for 1 hour.

3. Drain and continue cooking as directed by recipe.

FIGURE 6-38
Dried Fruits Before Plumping (background) and After (foreground)

Making Bread Crumbs

Bread crumbs may be "dry" or "fresh." Fresh bread crumbs (known as **mie de pain**) are prepared by grating or processing a finely textured bread, such as 1- or 2-day-old hard rolls. Dry bread crumbs can be prepared from slightly stale bread that has been additionally dried or toasted in a warm oven.

Bread crumbs are used as a binder, topping, crust, and as part of the standard breading mise en place. (See Chapter 9, page 368, for more information about standard breadings).

Making Croutons

Croutons are commonly used as a garnish for soups and salads. Large croutons, known as rusks, are made to act as the base for sautéed or grilled meats, a reflection of an earlier dining practice, when plates were actually slabs of bread, intended for consumption once they had been well dampened with juices and sauces from the meal.

To prepare croutons, cut bread (crusts removed or not, as desired) into the desired size. You may want to rub or toss the cubes or slices lightly with oil or clarified butter. Seasonings such as salt and pepper, chopped herbs and garlic, or grated Parmesan cheese may also be added.

There are a few different ways to finish croutons. You may bake them in a moderate oven until lightly browned (see Figure 6-40). Turn them from time to time and check them frequently to avoid scorching. Smaller quantities may be tossed in a dry or lightly oiled skillet. Deep-fried croutons will not hold long and tend to become quite oily.

Good croutons should be light in color, relatively greaseless, and appropriately seasoned.

Toasting Nuts and Seeds

Toasting nuts, seeds, and spices improves their flavor, as long as they are not allowed to scorch. To toast small quantities, use a dry skillet (cast iron is an excellent choice, but other materials will also work well). Heat it over direct heat and add the nuts, seeds, or spices (see Figure 6-41). Toss or stir frequently, stopping just as a good color and aroma are achieved. Remove the nuts, seeds, or spices from the hot pan and place them in a cool container, spreading into a thin layer to stop any further browning.

Large quantities can be toasted in a moderate oven. Spread the nuts, seeds, or spices out on a dry sheet pan and toast just until a pleasant aroma is apparent. The oils in nuts, seeds, and spices can scorch quickly, so be sure to check frequently. Stir them often to encourage even browning. Be sure to transfer nuts and spices toasted in the oven to a cool container also, so that they do not become scorched from residual heat in the pan.

FIGURE 6-41   Toasting Pine Nuts

(1) Pine nuts in a dry skillet, just starting to brown.

FIGURE 6-40
Preparing Croutons in the Oven

(2) Tossing the nuts to ensure even browning.

Additional Basic Mise en Place and Appareil

In addition to properly peeled, trimmed and cut vegetables and fruits, the chef must also have other ingredients on hand. Mixtures of ingredients that are themselves used as components in a dish are referred to as **appareils.** Thickeners, aromatic combinations, batters, basic stocks, sauces, stuffing mixtures, and marinades are all properly termed appareils.

Thickeners

Thickeners are added to liquids to give a sauce, soup, stew, or braise additional body. The type of thickener you choose will have a definite effect on the overall characteristics of the finished dish. Some thickeners, such as roux and gelatin, require meticulous care in order to achieve the best results. Others, including beurre manié and slurries, are less demanding in terms of the length of time required for preparation, as well as the "trickiness" of properly incorporating them into a liquid. Recipes for specific thickeners can be found in Part IV, Chapter 13.

Slurries

A **slurry** is a starch (arrowroot, cornstarch, or rice flour) dissolved in a cool liquid. The mixture should have the consistency of heavy cream (see Figure 6-42). The method is as follows:

1. Blend the starch thoroughly with one to two times its volume of cold liquid. If the slurry has been standing for a while before you use it, be sure to stir it well before mixing it into the hot liquid, as the starch tends to settle.

2. Bring the hot liquid to a simmer or low boil.

3. Gradually add the slurry, stirring or whisking constantly to prevent lumping and scorching.

4. Bring the liquid back to a boil and cook just until the sauce reaches the desired thickness and clarity.

Sauces, soups, and other dishes thickened with slurries have limited holding periods. Be sure to check them periodically for quality if they must be held in a steam table. Since slurries work quickly, it

FIGURE 6-42 Making a Slurry Using Wine

(1) Adding wine (a burgundy used here) to arrowroot.

(2) The properly diluted arrowroot, ready to use.

is best to thicken items in batches throughout service whenever possible.

Beurre Manié

A French term meaning "kneaded butter," **beurre manié** is a mixture of equal amounts (by weight) of softened whole butter and flour. Sometimes called "uncooked roux," it is used to quickly thicken sauces and stews. Beurre manié produces a thin to medium consistency and a glossy texture. It is traditionally used in vegetable dishes (peas *bonne femme,* for example) and fish stews (known as *matelotes*). The method is as follows:

1. Allow the butter to soften until it is pliable but not melted—it should still be cool and "plastic."

2. Add an equal weight of flour and work to a smooth paste. Use a wooden spoon when working with small amounts; the friction of the wood against the bowl helps to work the butter and flour together quickly. When making large

quantities, use an electric mixer with a paddle attachment.

3. If the beurre manié will not be used right away, store it, tightly wrapped, in the refrigerator.

Roux

This thickener is prepared by cooking together a fat and a flour. **Roux** is often prepared in advance in large quantities for use as needed. Butter is the most commonly used fat, but chicken fat, vegetable oils, or fats rendered from roasts may also be used. Different fats will have a subtle to dramatic influence on the flavor of the finished dish.

The standard proportion of fat to flour is one to one by weight, but depending on the type of fat and flour used, this proportion may need to be adjusted slightly. Cooked roux should be moist but not greasy. A common description is "like sand at low tide." There are four basic types of roux, differing in thickening strength, aroma, and color—the longer a roux is cooked, the less powerful its thickening ability, the nuttier its aroma, and the darker its color.

- White roux: barely colored, chalky.
- Pale or blond roux: golden straw color, with a slightly nutty aroma.
- Brown roux: deep brown, with a deep nutty aroma.
- Dark brown or "black" roux: very dark brown to black, with a strong charred, almost burned aroma.

Preparing a Roux The method for preparing a roux is as follows:

1. Melt the butter or other fat in a pan over moderate to low heat.

2. Add the flour and stir until smooth.

3. If necessary, add a small amount of flour to achieve the proper consistency.

4. Cook, stirring constantly, to the desired color. Roux should be glossy in appearance.

5. If the roux will not be used right away, cool and store it, tightly wrapped, in the refrigerator.

FIGURE 6-43   Preparing Roux

(1) Adding flour to heated clarified butter.

(2) Cooking over moderate heat.

(3) Proper texture.

(4) Blond, brown, and dark brown rouxs.

See Figure 6-43 for photos illustrating the method for preparing a roux.

Large quantities of roux may be made in the oven in a rondeau or brazier. The fat is melted and the flour added as in the previous method. The pan is then placed in a moderate (350 to 375°F/175 to 190°C) oven and cooked to the desired color. It should be stirred occasionally during the cooking time.

A so-called "dry roux" may be prepared by gently toasting flour in the oven. This type of roux is often associated with certain Creole and Cajun dishes.

Combining Roux with Liquid The method for combining a roux with liquid is as follows:

1. Be sure that the roux and liquid temperatures are different—hot liquid and cold roux or cold liquid and hot roux—to help prevent lumping. Add one to the other gradually and whip constantly to work out lumps.

2. Gradually return the soup or sauce to a boil, whisking occasionally.

3. Reduce the heat and simmer, stirring occasionally, for at least 20 minutes, to cook out the taste of the flour.

To test for the presence of starch, press a small amount of the sauce to the roof of the mouth with your tongue. It should not feel gritty or gluey. If it does, continue cooking until the starch is completely cooked out.

Liaison

A **liaison** is a mixture of egg yolks and cream that is used to both thicken and enrich sauces and soups. A liaison also adds flavor to a sauce or soup and gives it a smooth texture and golden color.

The basic ratio in a liaison is three parts cream to one part egg yolk, by weight. Sour cream or crème fraîche may be substituted for the heavy cream. A combination of 8 ounces (240 milliliters) heavy cream and three egg yolks is sufficient to thicken and enrich 24 ounces (720 milliliters) of liquid.

Liaisons are never added directly to boiling liquids because the heat could cause the yolks to scramble. To avoid this, some of the hot liquid is added to the liaison to raise its temperature gradually. This process is known as "tempering." For a more detailed description of tempering, refer to the section on basic techniques on page 258 later in this chapter.

Gelatin

Gelatin is used to stabilize foams and thicken liquid-based mixtures that will be served cold. Approximately 2 ounces (75 grams) of any type of gelatin will thicken about 1 gallon (3.75 liters) of liquid. More gelatin will be required if the liquid contains sugar or acidic ingredients, which inhibit gelling. The method for preparing gelatin to add to other foods is as follows:

1. Soak the gelatin in cool liquid before using. This process, called "blooming," allows the gelatin to soften and to begin absorption of the liquid.

2. Melt the dissolved gelatin crystals. This may be done by placing the gelatin–liquid mixture over a warm water bath or by heating it in a microwave oven on a low-power setting. If the gelatin is to be combined with a hot liquid, it may be tempered with some or all of that liquid to melt the crystals.

3. Combine the dissolved gelatin with the liquid. Stir well to disperse throughout the mixture. Chill until the mixture is set.

Pâte à Choux

Pâte à choux, or cream puff paste, is the base for such desserts as profiteroles, éclairs, and Paris-Brest. It is also combined with puréed potatoes in savory dishes such as pommes dauphines and as a base for savory soufflés. A step-by-step illustration of the procedure for making pâte à choux appears in Chapter 12. The recipe for pâte à choux can be found in Part IV, Chapter 30.

---

profiteroles: a small puff made from pâte à choux.

éclair: an oblong pastry made from pâte à choux.

Paris-Brest: a ring of pâte à choux, topped with almonds, filled with a flavored cream. Named for a bicycle race run between Paris and Brest, and shaped to resemble a bicycle tire.

pommes dauphines: potato purée combined with pâte à choux, shaped, rolled in bread crumbs, and deep-fried.

SALT AND PEPPER MIX

These two ingredients are so much a part of the final seasoning adjustment made to many dishes that they sometimes are considered a "given." To make it simple to use salt and pepper on the line, many line cooks like to have a mixture ready, either in a small bowl or shaker, to add to dishes.

The ratio of salt to pepper most commonly recommended is four parts salt to one part ground pepper, by volume. This ratio can be changed if kosher or sea salts are used, since they have a different flavor and degree of saltiness than ordinary table salt.

Basic Aromatic and Flavoring Combinations

Various seasoning and flavoring ingredients, ranging from single items to more complicated mixtures, are used in many different preparations. Classic seasoning combinations include mirepoix, matignon, marinades, oignon piqué, and oignon brûlé. These combinations of aromatic vegetables, herbs, and spices are meant to enhance and support, not dominate, a dish's flavors. Recipes for these mixtures can be found in Part IV, Chapter 13.

Spice Blends

You can purchase spice blends such as curry powder, garam masala, blackening spices, and chili powders already prepared. However, for customized blends and the freshest flavor, you may prefer to make your own. If desired, the spices can be lightly toasted in a skillet, just until they start to give off an aroma.

They can be ground using a mortar and pestle, or in a spice grinder or coffee grinder reserved specifically for use with spices (see Figure 6-44).

Mirepoix

A combination of chopped aromatic vegetables, customarily onion, carrot, and celery, **mirepoix** is used to flavor stocks, soups, braises, and stews (see

FIGURE 6-44 Preparing Spice Blends

(1) By hand using a mortar and pestle.

(2) Using a spice grinder.

Figure 6-45). The basic ratio of ingredients is two parts onion, one part carrot, and one part celery, by weight. When the mirepoix is not part of the finished dish, the vegetables, except the onions, do not have to be peeled.

The size of the cut will depend on how the mirepoix is to be used. For preparations with short cooking times, such as fish fumet, the mirepoix should be sliced or chopped small. For preparations with more than an hour of cooking time, such as brown stock, the vegetables may be cut into larger pieces or even left whole.

Other ingredients may be added to the mirepoix, depending on the needs of a specific recipe.

garam masala: an Indian spice mix consisting of up to 12 dried spices, typically including black pepper, cinnamon, cloves, coriander, cumin, cardamom, chilies, fennel, mace, and nutmeg.

mortar and pestle: a traditional tool consisting of a bowl and a grinding stick used to grind or pulverize spices, herbs and other items for culinary, medicinal, and cosmetic priparations.

fish fumet: stock made from fish bones, wine, and aromatics.

FIGURE 6-45   White Mirepoix; Finely Cut Regular Mirepoix; and Coarsely Cut Regular Mirepoix

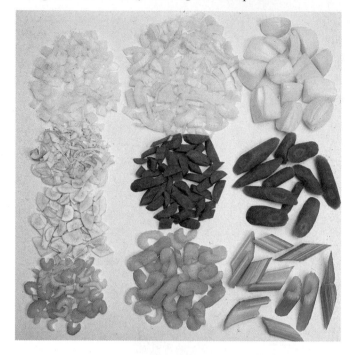

Leeks are often used in place of all or part of the onion. Other root vegetables, such as parsnips, may be used in addition to, or in place of, the carrots. Bacon and ham are also sometimes included.

White Mirepoix

This combination replaces the carrots with parsnips. This is done to be sure that the finished sauce, stock, or soup will have a pale ivory or white color. Leeks may be used in combination with, or in place of, onions.

Matignon

Sometimes referred to as "edible mirepoix," **matignon** is a combination of aromatic vegetables intended as part of the finished dish. Consequently, the vegetables are peeled and cut in uniform dice. Diced ham or bacon is also included to enhance the flavor.

Matignons are commonly used in poêléed dishes, such as poêléed capon. The ratio of ingredients in a matignon generally is two parts carrot, one part celery, one part leek, one part onion, one part mushroom (optional), and one part pork product (ham or bacon). Various herbs and spices may be included as desired.

Bouquet Garni

Another combination of herbs and vegetables used to flavor stocks and other savory preparations is the **bouquet garni,** the French term for "bouquet of herbs." A bouquet garni is a combination of fresh vegetables and herbs that typically contains fresh thyme, parsley stems, a celery stalk, and a bay leaf, tied into a bundle.

When a bouquet garni has contributed adequate flavor (determined by tasting), it should be removed from the preparation and discarded. If a long end is left on the string used to tie up the bouquet garni, it can be attached to the pot handle. Then, it is easy to pull out the bouquet garni when you are ready to remove it.

See Figure 6-46 for photos illustrating mise en place and assembly for bouquet garni.

Sachet d'Epices

A standard **sachet d'épices,** French for "bag of spices," contains parsley stems, dried thyme, bay leaf, and cracked peppercorns in a cheesecloth bag as shown in Figure 6-47. As with the bouquet garni, it should be removed and discarded after enough flavor has been released into the stock or other preparation.

Oignon Piqué and Oignon Brûlé

Both the *oignon piqué* (pricked or studded onion) and *oignon brûlé* (burnt onion) are flavoring ingredients based on whole, halved, or quartered onions (see Figure 6-48). An oignon piqué is made by studding an onion with a whole clove and a bay leaf. It is used to flavor béchamel sauce and some soups.

An oignon brûlé is made by peeling an onion, halving it crosswise, and charring the cut edges on a flat top or in a skillet or griswold. Oignon brûlé is used in some stocks and consommés to provide a golden brown color.

Marinades

Originally, **marinades** were intended to both preserve and tenderize tough meats. These intensely flavored combinations were used to disguise the fla-

FIGURE 6-46 Preparing Bouquet Garni

(1) Mise en place.

(2) Assemble by enclosing herbs in leek leaves.

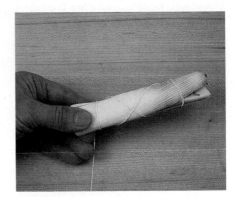

(3) Tied into a bundle, ready to use.

FIGURE 6-47 Preparing a Sachet d'Epices

FIGURE 6-48 Oignon Piqué and Brûlé

(1) Mise en place in foreground, completed sachet in background.

(2) Folding spices and herbs into cheesecloth.

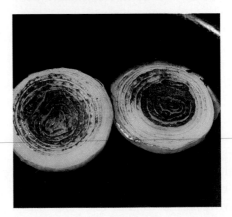

(1) An onion is studded with bay leaf and cloves to prepare oignon piqué.

(2) An onion is charred in a dry skillet to prepare oignon brûlé.

vor of meats that had become "high"—meats we might no longer consider suitable or safe to serve to our guests. In contemporary kitchens, they are more often used to add flavor to naturally tender meats, fish, and vegetables.

The three components of marinades are oils, acids, and aromatics (spices, herbs, and vegeta-

bles). Oils are used primarily to protect and preserve foods, either as they marinate or during cooking. Acids, such as vinegar, yogurt, wine, and citrus juices, change the food's texture. In some cases, acid will make foods firmer, as happens when fish is marinated in lime juice to make ceviche. In others, it will break down connective fibers making foods seem more tender, as happens when beef is marinated in red wine for several days to make sauerbraten.

There are four different types of marinades, made from the three basic types of ingredients:

• Oil and acid marinades

• Oil and aromatic marinades

• Acid and aromatic marinades

• Dry marinades and rubs

Recipes for a variety of marinades can be found in Part IV, Chapter 13.

Liquid Marinades

Liquid marinades are used to soak foods before or after cooking, or as a means of cooking foods chemically, by denaturing the proteins in a food. Marinades made from oils and acids are typically used to add flavor and some moisture to foods. They are prepared using the same ratio of oil to acid as a classic vinaigrette—three parts oil to one part acid. These marinades are often used as a preliminary step when grilling foods. Oil and spice marinades are used for the same purpose. Marinades that include acids and spices, and no oil, are used to flavor foods, as well as to chemically cook them as happens when preparing ceviche.

The ingredients should be selected according to the marinade's intended use. Select the oil, if any, and the acid carefully, plus the desired seasonings and aromatics. Almost any oil can be used, depending on the desired effect. Commonly used acidic ingredients include vinegar, fruit juice, wine, and beer. Aromatics or other flavoring combinations such as a mirepoix may be included.

Some marinades are cooked before use, others are not. In some cases, the marinade is used to flavor an accompanying sauce, or may itself become a dipping sauce.

To use a liquid marinade, the chef should:

1. Prepare the items to be marinated and place them in a hotel pan large enough to hold the ingredients comfortably.

---

sauerbraten: a traditional German dish of marinated braised beef. Often served with dumplings, potatoes, or noodles.

FIGURE 6-49   A Marinade for Fish

2. Add the marinade and turn the ingredient(s) to coat evenly (see Figure 6-49).

3. Marinate for the length of time indicated by the recipe, type of main product, or desired result.

Dry Marinades and Rubs

A dry marinade is a mixture of salt, crushed or chopped herbs, spices, and occasionally other aromatics, such as citrus zest. In some cases, the marinade is mixed with oil to make a paste. The marinade is rubbed over the food—usually meats and fish—and the coated item is then allowed to stand, under refrigeration, to absorb the marinade's flavors.

Dry marinades may be referred to as "rubs." Once the ingredients have been properly blended, they are packed or rubbed onto the surface of the food. They may be left on the food during cooking to develop a richly flavored crust. Alternately, they may be scraped away before cooking. One classic use for a dry marinade is the preparation of gravad lax, detailed in Chapter 11. Barbecued beef dishes and tandoori chicken are examples of other dishes that may be prepared using a dry rub (see Figure 6-50).

FIGURE 6-50 A Tandoori Rub for Chicken

Duxelles

A *duxelles* is a mixture of finely chopped and sautéed mushrooms that also includes shallots and white wine. Duxelles may be "dry" or of a sauce consistency. It may be used as a flavoring, stuffing, or coating. It should be moist enough to hold together but not runny. The recipe for duxelles may be found in Chapter 13 on page 471.

Pesto and Other Herb Pastes

Pesto is a mixture of an herb and an oil, puréed into a smooth, thick paste. Italy, specifically Genoa, claims to have first developed this sauce. A French version, known as *pistou*, is traditionally added to a vegetable soup.

Pesto customarily contains basil and oil and may also contain grated cheese, garlic, nuts, or seeds, depending on the individual recipe. Contemporary renditions may replace some or all of the basil with cilantro, oregano, or other herbs.

---

tandoori chicken: an Indian chicken preparation made by marinating the chicken in a spice rub; traditionally cooked in a tandoori oven.

Sun-dried tomatoes, olives, and other ingredients are sometimes used in herb pastes or spreads that are made in a similar fashion as pesto.

Pesto and other herb pastes may be used as a sauce for pasta and other foods, as a soup garnish, or as a dressing or sauce ingredient.

Traditionally, pestos and similar herb pastes were made with a mortar and pestle. Some people still feel that this is the best way to prepare them. For large quantities, it may be more efficient to use a food processor, however. Pestos can discolor quickly. You may want to pour a thin layer of oil on top of the pesto to prevent contact with the air from turning it brown or black.

Persillade

Persillade is a mixture of bread crumbs, minced parsley, and garlic used as a coating for roasted and grilled items. It protects the meat, seals in the juices, and provides textural contrast. Usually, a small amount of melted butter or oil is rubbed into the persillade to help the ingredients adhere better. *Persillé* is the French term used to describe items coated with this appareil.

Stocks, Broths, and Court Bouillons

Escoffier noted in the first chapter of his classic work *Le Guide Cuilinaire,* the following basic culinary preparations:

- Stocks and broths used for soups

- Brown and white stocks used for sauces and thickened gravies

- **Fumets** and essences used to flavor the so-called "small sauces"

Not much has changed with regard to these basic items. Although circumstances may force a chef to use shortcuts, such as prepared stock bases, it is still preferable to prepare stocks in-house from fresh and wholesome ingredients.

Stocks are flavorful liquids produced by simmering bones, meat trimmings, vegetables, and other aromatic ingredients in water. Stocks are further categorized as white stock or brown stock, both of which are discussed below. They are used as the foundation for soups, stews, and sauces. They are not served "as is," however. Recipes for a variety of stocks, essences, and **court bouillons** can be found in Part IV, Chapter 13.

See Figure 6-51 for examples of various stocks, broths, and fumet.

Categories and Types of Stocks

White Stock

White stocks are made from the meaty bones and trim from veal, beef, poultry, some types of game, and fish. The bones are frequently blanched in order to remove any impurities that might cloud or discolor the finished stock. Ordinary white stock is classically prepared from veal meat and bones, with the addition of poultry carcasses.

A white beef stock (sometimes referred to as a "neutral stock") is often prepared by first simmering the stock at a higher temperature than would be used for most stocks for several minutes. The aim is to produce a stock with a nearly neutral flavor. It is often favored for use in vegetable soups or bean dishes. White beef stock can contribute a significant body to these dishes, while still allowing the flavor of the primary ingredient to predominate.

See Figure 6-52 for mise en place for white chicken and beef stocks.

Brown Stock

One of the most commonly called-for stocks in the classic and contemporary repertoire of any kitchen is likely to be brown veal stock (*fond de veau brun*). Brown stocks are prepared by first cooking meaty bones and meat trim to a deep brown color, as well as the mirepoix and a tomato product, before they are simmered. This changes both the flavor and color of the finished stock. Brown stocks are especially valuable in sauce cookery, as they are used as the foundation for brown sauce, jus lié, demi-glace, and pan gravies.

---

blanched bones: bones that have been quickly boiled to remove impurities before they are used to make a stock. (See page 249 for greater detail.)

FIGURE 6-51   A Variety of Stocks and Broths

(1) White beef stock (left), chicken stock (center), and brown veal stock (right).

(2) Court bouillon (left), fish stock (center), and fish fumet (right).

(3) Remouillage (left) and broth (right).

(4) Estouffade (left) and glace de viande (right).

FIGURE 6-52 Mise en Place for White Stocks

(1) White beef stock.

(2) Chicken stock.

See Figure 6-53 for mise en place for brown stock.

Remouillage

The word translates as a "rewetting," which is a good way to understand the procedure for making **remouillage.** Bones used to prepare a "primary stock" are reserved after the first stock is strained away from the bones. The bones are then covered with water, and a "secondary stock" is prepared.

FIGURE 6-53
Mise en Place for
Brown Veal Stock

REMOUILLAGE

Some chefs argue that, if the first stock was made properly and simmered for the correct amount of time, there will be little if anything left in the bones to provide either flavor or body in the remouillage. Others feel that this second generation of stock can be used as the basis for other broths or as the cooking liquid for braises and stews. The food being prepared will provide the majority of the flavor in the finished sauce, and a first-rate stock can be reserved for use in dishes where its role is more significant.

Broth (or Bouillon)

Broths and **bouillons** share many similarities with stocks. They are prepared in essentially the same fashion: Meaty bones (or in some cases, the entire cut of meat, bird, or fish) are simmered in water (or remouillage or a prepared stock) along with a variety of vegetables and other aromatic ingredients. For a more detailed discussion of broth preparation, refer to Chapter 7.

Many meatless dishes are prepared with a vegetable broth. Some chefs may refer to this preparation as a vegetable stock. For the purposes of this book, vegetable broth will be used, rather than stock. Those stocks made from meat or fish bones will reach a state of clarity and body through the extraction of proteins found in bones and meat. Vegetable broths vary greatly in the degree of body and clarity that they may achieve.

Fumet (or Essence)

The most common **fumet** is one prepared by sweating fish bones along with vegetables such as leeks, mushrooms, and celery, then simmering these ingredients in water, perhaps with the addition of a dry white wine. The end result is generally not as clear as a stock, but it is highly flavored. Fumets and essences can be prepared from such ingredients as

jus lié: meat juice or stock thickened lightly with arrowroot or cornstarch.

demi-glace: a mixture of equal portions of brown stock and brown sauce that has been reduced by half.

FIGURE 6-54
Mise en Place for
Fish Fumet

ESTOUFFADE

The classic formula for *estouffade* set down by Escoffier is virtually identical to what was then known as a brown stock. There are some differences to note, however. Estouffade is prepared by simmering together browned meaty veal bones, a piece of fresh or cured pork, and the requisite vegetables and other aromatics.

Contemporary kitchens tend to prepare a brown stock that does not include pork. Today, estouffade is less widely used as a basic preparation, although it is still regarded as a classic preparation.

wild mushrooms, tomato, celery or celery root, ginger, and so forth. These essences, nothing more than highly flavored infusions made from especially aromatic ingredients, can be used to introduce flavor to other preparations, such as consommés or broths and a variety of small sauces.

See Figure 6-54 for mise en place for fish fumet.

Court Bouillon

A "short broth" is often prepared as the cooking liquid for fish or vegetables. The basic components of a **court bouillon** include aromatic vegetables and herbs, water, and an acid such as vinegar, wine, or lemon juice. See Figure 6-55 for an example of a court bouillon. A court bouillon may be prepared as part of the cooking process, or it may be prepared in large batches and used as required, in much the same manner as stocks and broths are prepared.

Ratios for Stocks

Beef, Veal, Poultry, Game, or Special Stocks (e.g., Pork or Turkey)　For every gallon of stock, use 8 pounds of bones, 6 quarts of water, 1 pound of mirepoix, and 1 sachet d'épices or bouquet garni.

Fish Stock or Fumet　For every gallon of finished stock, use 11 pounds of bones, 5 quarts of water, 1 pound of mirepoix, and 1 standard sachet d'épices or bouquet garni.

When you use these ratios, you will produce stocks that meet all the criteria of a good-quality

product: flavor, clarity, aroma, body, and color. This is not to insist that there are no exceptions or modifications that may not also be appropriate, depending on an individual operation's needs. For instance, if veal bones are either unavailable or their cost makes stock production more expensive than it is worth, the chef may then look to other means to reach the desired end: A quantity of lean trim from meats, or a combination of compatibly flavored meats, may be used to replace some of the bones.

A lesser quantity of bones may be used, resulting in a weaker stock. That stock can then be fortified with a commercially prepared base. These are possible responses to a situation that may be beyond the chef's control. It is still best to use the correct ratio and the suggested ingredients, without resorting to bases and the like, of course. Maintaining the proper balance between bones and liquid is crucial if the

FIGURE 6-55
Court Bouillon

chef is going to produce an excellent-quality stock. The standards used in most kitchens are as follows:

Preparing Stocks

Mise en Place

1. Assemble all ingredients and preparations required for stocks.

The basic elements of any stock are:

- Cool water
- The major flavoring component
- Aromatics and other flavoring ingredients

In some restaurants, stock-making goes on constantly, with brown stocks being left to simmer all night in steam kettles, and white stocks prepared during all shifts as space becomes available on the stove top or in a steam kettle. Wholesome trim from meats such as veal, poultry, pork, beef, and game are reserved (separately) to be included in stocks. The same is true of trim from vegetable preparation: Leeks, onions, carrot, celery, parsnip, turnips, tomatoes, mushrooms, and other aromatic vegetables are often cut to a very special size and shape when they will be part of a finished dish presented to a customer. Unused portions or trim are saved to add to stocks.

It is important that all usable trim be wholesome. Storage containers should be clearly labeled, properly covered, and stored in the refrigerator. Before you add trim of any type to a stock, check it carefully. There is no way to remove the taste of a spoiled ingredient once it is added to the stock.

Major flavoring ingredients for stocks will vary from one formula to another. Some items that are considered aromatics in one recipe may be the principle component of a court bouillon or vegetable broth. There are several steps that may be required to prepare the major flavoring ingredients. Bones and vegetables are usually cut into an appropriate size. These ingredients may also be roasted or blanched as necessary. The steps for blanching and browning are discussed below.

Large bones from veal, beef, or game animals should be cut into short lengths, about 2 to 3 inches. This will allow the flavor and body to be easily extracted. Bones can usually be purchased precut, and in larger metropolitan areas they are often available fresh. If you do much of your own butchering, you will need to cut the bones using a bandsaw or heavy cleaver. Bones from poultry or fish should also be cut into smaller pieces using cleavers, kitchen shears, or knives.

In addition to the traditional mirepoix, sachet d'épices or bouquet garni, a number of different ingredients may be added to give special flavors or aromas to stocks, court bouillons, and essences, such as wines, spices, herbs, vinegars, and a variety of other vegetables. These should be prepared in advance and added only as necessary to contribute the desired flavor.

2. Assemble all equipment necessary for preparing stocks.

Pots used for stocks are usually taller than they are wide. Some have spigots that can be used to remove the finished stock without disturbing the bones. Steam-jacketed kettles are often used to produce large quantities of stock. Court bouillons, fumets, and essences that do not have long simmering times are prepared in rondeaus or other wide shallow pots. Tilting kettles are used when available for large-scale production.

Ladles or skimmers should be on hand to remove floating debris from the stock as it simmers. Sieves, colanders, or other strainers are used to separate bones and vegetables from the stock. The necessary containers for cooling and storing the stock should also be on hand.

Advance Preparation for Bones

Blanching Bones White stocks are made from bones that have been blanched prior to the start of the process. Blanching assures that any impurities that could cloud the stock or give it a too-strong flavor are first cooked out. The technique is almost universal when working with bones that are received in the kitchen frozen or packed in ice:

1. Place the bones in a large pot and add enough cool water to cover them by several inches.

2. Bring the water to a full boil and skim away any scum that rises to the surface.

3. Drain away or pour off the cooking liquid, and rinse the bones to remove any scum that may have been trapped by the bones themselves.

4. The bones are now properly blanched and ready to use.

Browning Bones and Mirepoix Brown stocks are made by first browning bones and mirepoix and, if required by recipe, tomato paste or purée. This step starts the process of developing the stock's flavor. Allow sufficient time for ingredients to roast properly for the best end product.

Although the steps below explain the procedure for roasting bones, the same steps are used to roast vegetables if you are preparing a roasted vegetable broth:

1. Rinse the bones if necessary and dry them well to remove any excess moisture.

   Taking the time to do this will shorten the time required to properly brown the bones. If bones go into the oven when they are wet or still frozen, they will steam before the browning process begins. No one can say for sure that there is a distinct and measurable loss of flavor, but certainly it will increase the time the bones need to spend in the oven, as well as increasing the amount of energy required to cook them.

2. Heat a roasting pan in a hot oven and add the bones in an even layer.

   Some chefs feel that adding a layer of oil in the pan is a good idea to help spur the browning process. However, since there is usually a fair amount of fat left on the meaty trim or scraps, this is not absolutely critical.

3. Roast the bones until they are a rich brown color (see Figure 6-56).

   The amount of time required will vary, depending on whether or not the bones had time to defrost and dry, how many bones are packed into the pan, and the heat of the oven.

   For small quantities, it may be a good idea to heat some oil in a large rondeau over direct heat, add the bones and cook them on the top

FIGURE 6-56
Bones and Aromatics Properly Roasted for a Brown Stock

of the range. This is not recommended for large quantities, but it is a good way to quickly prepare smaller amounts.

4. Add the mirepoix and tomato product to the pan and continue roasting until all the vegetables are browned properly.

   Although some chefs feel that the best-quality stocks are achieved by first removing the bones and beginning the stock-making process, then browning the vegetables later on in the same roasting pan, others consider the time-saving technique of adding the mirepoix and tomato directly to the bones as they roast to be a fair tradeoff. The recipes in this book follow the first course, where bones and mirepoix are roasted in separate stages.

5. Transfer the bones from the roasting pan to the stockpot.

6. Deglaze the roasting pan to retain as much of the flavor released as drippings in the final stock as possible.

Method

Since stocks are so basic to so many dishes prepared in the professional kitchen, strict adherence to all sanitary and safety standards mush be observed at all times. This means that all equipment must be clean, including cutting boards and knives.

---

deglaze: adding a liquid to a cooking pan to dissolve drippings (fond) into a pan sauce.

Temperature control, particularly during cooling and storage, is also of vital importance.

There are some specific differences between the method for stocks and the method used to prepare court bouillons and fumets. Those distinctions will be noted as appropriate throughout the steps below:

1. Combine the bones (blanched or browned, if necessary) with cold water and bring the water slowly to a boil.

This slow rise to cooking temperature will allow any blood or impurities which might cloud the finished stock, to be released into the water, where they will coagulate and then rise to the surface. Once they have risen to the surface, they can readily be skimmed away. It is this careful and consistent skimming of stocks as they develop that determines how clear the finished stock will be.

Apart from the aesthetics of a clear limpid stock as opposed to a cloudy one, remember that the same impurities which leave a stock cloudy are the elements that will "turn" most quickly, spoiling and souring a stock. The clearer the stock, the longer its effective shelf life.

Fumets and essences, in contrast, often call for the flavoring ingredient(s) to be allowed to sweat to begin a rapid release of flavor. Once that has happened, the remainder of the liquid ingredients are added and brought slowly to a simmer.

2. Add the flavoring ingredients at the correct point.

The right time to add mirepoix to a simmering stock (except for fish stocks and fumets) is about 1 hour before the end of cooking time. This will allow plenty of time for the best flavor to be extracted, but not so much time that the flavor will be broken down and destroyed.

Spices and herbs will generally release their flavor sufficiently to flavor a stock within 15 to 30 minutes.

There are a number of other ingredients that might be added to stocks as they simmer to give them a special, distinctive flavor. Wines or essences of highly aromatic ingredients (wild mushrooms, celery, tomatoes, or gingerroot, for instance) can also be added close to the end of cooking time. Refer to specific recipes, both those in this book and others you may collect throughout your training and work experience, for guidance.

Since fumets, essences, and court bouillons do not have extended cooking times., all the ingredients are normally added at once and remain in the preparation throughout cooking.

3. Simmer the stock long enough to fully develop flavor, body, clarity, color, and aroma.

- Brown or white veal stock normally requires 6 to 8 hours of simmering time.
- White beef stock may be simmered for 8 to 10 hours.
- White and brown poultry stocks (including chicken, duck, turkey, pheasant, and so forth) should be allowed a minimum of 3 hours of simmering time.
- Fish stock, fumets and essences are properly cooked within 30 minutes to an hour.

Smell and taste the stock as it develops so that you can begin to learn the stages that a stock goes through as it develops, as well as to gauge when it has reached its peak. Once the stock reaches that peak, its quality will begin to decline, flavors will deaden and become flat, and even the color of the stock may be adversely affected if it is allowed to simmer for too long.

4. Properly strain, cool, and store the stock, if it is not intended for immediate use.

The need to handle all foods carefully has been stressed in Chapter 2, "Food and Kitchen Safety." The correct procedure for handling finished stocks is this:

(a) Strain the finished stock through the spigot, if available. Otherwise, ladle the stock out of the pot, disturbing the bones as little as possible to retain the stock's clarity. Once you have gotten as much stock as possible by ladling, drain the remaining bones and stock in a colander, collecting any stock in a bowl. This stock will not be as clear as that which you handled more carefully, but it is

FIGURE 6-57   Preparing Chicken Stock

(1) Adding cold water to generously cover bones.

(2) Water at proper level in relation to bones.

(3) Skimming surface to remove impurities.

(4) Adding mirepoix.

(5) Cooking at a simmer.

(6) At the end of cooking time, some loss of volume is apparent.

(7) Straining through cheesecloth.

(8) Cooling in an ice water bath.

(9) Placed in storage container, covered, labeled, and dated.

still useful for preparing grain pilafs, thick soups, and other dishes where clarity is not as important as flavor.

(b) Cool the stock as explained in Chapter 2 and check it with a thermometer to determine when it has cooled sufficiently. Generally, a temperature of around 40°F(4°C) is desirable. At that point, the stock can be transferred to plastic storage containers, which frees the cooking vessels for more appropriate uses.

(c) Stocks should also be clearly labeled with their name and the date they were prepared. If you still have some stock in the walk-in or refrigerator, be sure to store the fresh stock behind the older stock so that the next person searching for stock will naturally reach for the older product first.

See Figure 6-57 for photos illustrating the method for preparing chicken stock.

Basic Cooking Techniques

Instead of explaining the most basic cooking techniques each time they appear in a method or recipe, they are outlined in this section for easy reference.

Rendering and Clarifying Fats

Occasionally, the fat from ducks, geese, or pork may be required for such dishes as confit. Salt pork, another example, should be gently **rendered,** or melted down, so that the fat can be used to smother the aromatic vegetables used in the preparation of soups, stews, and braises. Properly **clarifying** a roast's fat and drippings is essential for the preparation of a good pan gravy. The method is as follows:

1. Cube the fat, if necessary.

2. Place the fat in a sauteuse. Add about ½ inch of water to the uncooked fats if there are no drippings present.

3. Cook over low heat until the water evaporates and the fat is released. (This is the actual clarifying process.)

4. Remove the cracklings, if any, with a slotted spoon (they may be reserved for garnish).

5. Use the clarified fat or store it under refrigeration. The concentrated drippings should remain once the clarified fat is poured away. Deglaze these drippings with stock, wine, or water and use them to prepare a pan gravy. See the discussion on pan gravies in Chapter 9.

Clarifying Butter

Clarified butter is pure butterfat. Ghee is clarified butter that has been simmered longer to highly clarify the butterfat. Drawn butter is clarified butter served with boiled or steamed seafood.

The purpose of clarifying butter is to allow the chef to cook with butter at a higher temperature than would be possible with whole butter. The milk solids in whole butter scorch easily and lower its smoking point.

Because it has some butter flavor, clarified butter is often used for sautéing, sometimes in combination with a vegetable oil to further raise the smoking point. It is also commonly used to make roux.

When whole butter is clarified, some of its volume is lost during skimming and decanting. One pound (450 grams) of whole butter yields approximately 12 ounces (340 grams) of clarified butter. The process of clarifying butter is as follows:

1. Melt the butter in a heavy saucepan over moderate heat.

2. Continue to cook over low heat until the butterfat becomes very clear and the milk solids drop to the bottom of the pot.

3. Skim the surface foam as the butter clarifies.

4. Pour or ladle off the butterfat into another container, being careful to leave all the liquid in the pan bottom. Discard the liquid.

---

pilaf: a technique for cooking grains in which the grain is sautéed briefly in butter, then simmered in stock or water with various seasonings.

cracklings: crunchy pieces of animal fat left after rendering.

decant: to carefully pour off a liquid into a separate container in order to separate it from its sediment.

FIGURE 6-60 Whipping Egg Whites

(1) A thick foam has formed.

(2) Soft peaks.

(3) Stiff peaks.

(4) Egg whites are beginning to dry out; they are over whipped.

FIGURE 6-61 Whipping Heavy Cream

(1) Cream is beginning to thicken.

(2) Soft peaks are forming.

(3) Firm peaks are forming.

(4) Cream is overwhipped.

Whipping Cream

To whip cream, follow the same general technique as for whipping egg whites. The cream should be cold when it is whipped. Chilling the bowl and beaters or whip in advance also aids in achieving the greatest volume. For best results, sugar and other flavorings should be added after the cream is whipped to at least a soft peak.

Like egg whites, cream can be overbeaten. Overbeaten cream first develops a grainy texture. Eventually, lumps will form and, if whipping continues, the cream will turn to butter.

See Figure 6-61 for photos illustrating the method for whipping cream.

Folding Foams into a Base Appareil

The purpose of folding foams into base mixtures is to produce light, delicately textured finished items. Soufflés, mousses, and Bavarian creams are examples of items lightened by incorporating a foam. Folding is a gentle mixing method and is performed as follows:

1. Have the base appareil in a large bowl to accommodate the folding motion. Stir or beat this mixture to soften it, especially if it has been refrigerated for any length of time.

2. Add about one-third of the beaten egg whites or cream and fold in, using a circular motion, going from the side to the bottom of the bowl and back up to the surface.

3. Add the remaining whipped item in one or two additional stages, folding just until blended.

See Figure 6-62 for photos illustrating the method for folding whipped items into a base appareil.

Tempering

Tempering is a term used to describe the method of incorporating an egg-and-cream liaison in a hot liquid (see Figure 6-63). It is also the term used for the careful heating of chocolate or fondant for dipping. The process reduces the temperature extremes present in the food or the appareils so that the finished item remains smooth.

FIGURE 6-62   Folding Ingredients Together

(1) Add the foam (whipped cream shown here) to the base (pastry cream shown here).

(2) Use a folding motion to gently incorporate.

(3) Cream is blended into pastry cream properly.

Tempering as it relates to chocolates and fondant is explained in Chapter 12. The method for tempering a liaison is outlined below:

1. Place the liaison in a container and blend until smooth. Placing a towel under the bowl will stabilize it and prevent it from skidding.

Italian buttercream: an icing or frosting made by combining an Italian meringue with softened butter and/or shortening.

Bavarian cream: cream made by combining a custard with whipped cream and additional flavorings such as chocolate, liqueur, or fruit. It is stabilized with the addition of gelatin.

FIGURE 6-66   Cutting Parchment Lids

(1) Fold a rectangle of parchment paper in half, and then into a triangle.

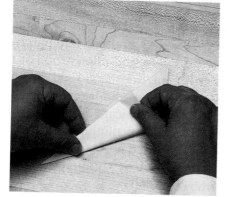

(2) Continue folding the paper into smaller triangles.

(3) Position the tip of the triangle over the center of the pan, and trim the wider end to fit.

(4) The completed lid. Note that the tip was also cut away to create a hole for steam to escape as foods cook.

FIGURE 6-67   Cutting Parchment Lids or Liners for Ring Molds

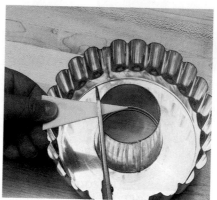

(1) Fold the paper as shown in Figure 6-64. Position the tip of the triangle in the center of the ring mold, and trim as shown.

(2) The proper trimmed liner or lid is ready.

whole lambs, or entire veal legs. Band saws and other special tools may be required for some types of butchering. The simple meat fabrication techniques presented in this section for use with beef, veal, lamb, pork, poultry, and game are probably well within the abilities of most chefs, however.

There are definite advantages to fabricating items on the premises. Purveyors may not always be able to cut meat exactly to specification or they may be unsure of the exact definition of a particular menu term. For example, they may be familiar with the term "cutlet," but not have a clear idea of what a paillard is. For this reason, the ability to cut paillards, medallions, noisettes, and other "menu cuts" is a skill worth mastering. It also allows you to control portion size and be sure that each portion meets your standards for quality.

You can generally make use of at least some of the "clean trim" generated by fabrication for other kitchen items (soups, sauces, stocks, salads, and forcemeats, to name a few). The aim is to keep the amount of trim meat to a minimum, however.

Cutting and Pounding Cutlets

When used in reference to meat, the term **cutlet** means a thin boneless cut of meat that may come from the loin, the tenderloin, or any other sufficiently tender cut, such as the top round. Chicken and turkey cutlets are also common. They are made from the breast, in most cases, although it is possible to prepare cutlets from the thighs of large birds.

Cutlets are often pounded to an even thickness over their entire surface so that they can be rapidly sautéed or pan-fried. Place the cutlet between two pieces of parchment or plastic wrap and then gently pound the meat using a meat pounder, mallet, or (in their absence) the side of a cleaver or even the bottom of a skillet or pot. Work from the center of the cut outward.

See Figure 6-68 for photos illustrating the method for cutting and pounding of veal cutlets.

Preparing Paillards

A **paillard** (derived from the French term for a straw bed) is a pounded cutlet that is grilled, sautéed, or pan-fried. Veal and poultry paillards are commonly found on French-style menus.

Preparing Emincé

This French word translates as "minced." It is not the same cut as minced herbs or garlic, however. Meats cut into **éminc**é are prepared by first trimming a boneless piece of meat to remove all fat, gristle, or sinew. It is then cut into long strips that have the same diameter as that of the finished cut. Then, slices are made so that each piece is relatively uniform, usually around ¼ inch thick, 1 to 1½ inches wide, and up to 3 inches long (see Figure 6-69).

This cut is generally used with meats that are to be sautéed. This means that the cuts appropriate for preparing éminc é should come from tender portions of the animal: the loin, tenderloin, and top round, for instance.

Trimming a Tenderloin

The tenderloin is one of the most expensive cuts, whether from veal, beef, venison, or pork. Great care must be taken when trimming a tenderloin to prevent unnecessary loss.

FIGURE 6-68   Preparing Cutlets

(1) Cutting portions from a fully trimmed piece of veal.

(2) Pounding cutlets, a step necessary to prepare cutlets, paillards, and other menu items.

Your knife should be very sharp. Stop as often as necessary to hone the blade with a steel. Pull away the heavy covering of fat, if it is still on the meat. Use the tip of a boning knife to work the blade under the elastin, also referred to as silverskin. This membrane will shrink and pucker during cooking, causing the meat to cook unevenly. It is extremely tough and unpleasant to bite into as well. Angle the blade as you cut away the silverskin so that it is removed, but the meat is left intact.

The "chain" is also cut away from a tenderloin of beef, since it contains mainly fat and relatively little usable meat.

See Figure 6-70 for photos illustrating the method for trimming a tenderloin. Note also the number of 6-ounce portions available from a properly trimmed tenderloin.

Shaping Medallions

Cuts from the boneless loin or the tenderloin of beef, veal, lamb, pork, or venison may be known by a variety of menu terms. **Medallions,** noisettes, and

FIGURE 6-69 Cutting Emincé

(1) Small pieces are cut from the a piece of boneless meat, well trimmed to remove fat, sinew, gristle, and silverskin.

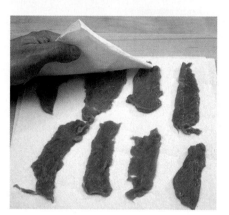

(2) Blot the pounded émincé dry before cooking.

grenadine are among the most common. Some specific menu terms generally associated only with the beef tenderloin include tournedos and chateaubriand.

These cuts may vary in size depending upon the cut you wish to serve. To give them a uniform appearance and to aid in even cooking, you can gently shape medallions or similar cuts by the following technique:

1. Dampen a piece of cheesecloth large enough to wrap completely around the medallion, and gather the edges, twisting them until the cheesecloth fits snugly.

2. Use the flat of your knife blade to hold the meat in place as you continue to twist, tightening the cheesecloth around the meat to make it into an even disk.

See Figure 6-71 for photos illustrating the method for shaping a medallion.

Tying a Roast

This is one of the simplest and most frequently required types of meat fabrication. The chef uses this technique to ensure that the roast will be evenly cooked and that it will retain its shape after roasting. This technique is often one of the most frustrating to learn. For one thing, knot tying is not always an easy thing to do. There are no awards given for neatness, however. As long as the string is taut enough to give the roast a compact shape without tying the meat too tightly, the result will be fine. There is one trick to keep in mind that will make initial attempts easier: Leave the string very long so that it will wrap easily around the entire diameter of the meat. In the second technique, the string is left attached to the spool, and is only cut when the entire roast is tied.

Both of the techniques illustrated here are appropriate for tying boneless or bone-in roasts. The choice of technique is largely a matter of personal preference; some chefs find one method easier than the other. See Figures 6-72 and 6-73 for two ways to tie a roast.

Cleaning a Skirt Steak

Skirt steaks have become a more familiar item on many menus today. They may be purchased already cleaned, but cleaning them is an easy process. The basic procedure is demonstrated in the accompanying photos.

See Figure 6-74 for photos illustrating the method for cleaning a skirt steak.

Frenching a Rack of Lamb

Frenching is one of the more complicated covered in this chapter, although once it is understood, it is not especially difficult to master. Trimmed and frenched racks or chops can be ordered from a meat purveyor if desired, but you will be able to exercise greater control over the trim loss if you are able to do this yourself.

This same technique can be used to french individual chops of lamb, veal, or pork, as well as the

(continued on page 266)

---

silverskin: the tough connective tissue (elastin) that surrounds certain muscles.

chain: trim from a beef tenderloin.

FIGURE 6-70   Trimming and Portioning a Beef Tenderloin

(1) Lift up the fat cap, pulling up with your hand and using the flat of the blade to hold the tenderloin steady.

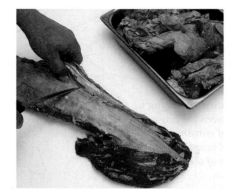

(2) Remove the chain from the tenderloin.

(3) The chain is completely removed from the tenderloin.

(4) Cutting away the silverskin. Angle the blade upward slightly so that only the silverskin is cut away.

(5) The fully trimmed loin cut into 6-ounce portions.

FIGURE 6-71   Shaping a Medallion

(1) Wrap the meat in a single layer of cheesecloth rinsed in cold water.

(2) Gather the cheesecloth and twist it slightly to begin to shape the meat.

(3) The shaped medallion is in the foreground.

Working with Variety Meats

There are a number of terms used to refer to organ meats, as well as such cuts as the heart, tongue, or stomach. Variety meats, offal, *abats*, and "innards" are all in use, depending upon the area of the country or the cuisine. In recent years, exports of tongue, liver, kidneys, lungs, sweetbreads, and other variety meats to foreign countries, have reduced supplies in this country. These cuts have been difficult for the ordinary consumer to find for

some time. Restaurants and butchers are just as likely to find them in short supply.

If you do have a clientele who appreciates these items, considered delicacies throughout many of the world's cuisines, be sure to give them the correct care and advance preparation.

Sweetbreads

Sweetbreads are the thymus glands of young animals. In some species, this gland gradually atro-

FIGURE 6-77   Boning and Butterflying a Breast of Veal

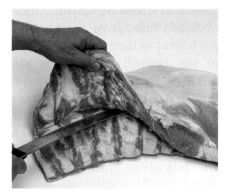 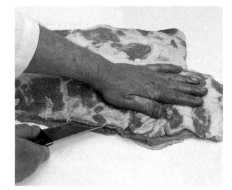 

(1) Lay the breast bone-side down and cut along the bones to free the meat.

(2) Continue cutting, pulling the meat back as you work, until the bones are cut away.

(3) Lay the boned breast on a work surface, and make a horizontal cut through the meat, leaving one length intact.

FIGURE 6-78   Trimming and Boning a Pork Loin

(1) Remove the excess fat covering the edge of the loin to expose the tips of the rib bones.

(2) Make smooth strokes along the bones to free the meat. Pull the meat away to make it easy to see.

(3) When all the meat is freed from one side of the bones, turn the loin over and free the meat from the other side. Here the tenderloin is being gently cut from the bones.

FIGURE 6-79   Boning a Leg of Veal

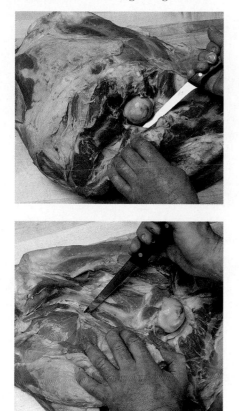

(1) Locate the ball joint and cut around it to loosen the meat.

(2) Cut carefully along the natural seams in the meat to separate the muscle groups.

phies with age, all but disappearing. The meat has a moderately delicate texture and is quite rich.

To prepare sweetbreads for use, you must first remove all traces of blood by allowing them to soak in several changes of fresh cool water.

The next step is to blanch them in a court bouillon. This loosens the outer membrane, which needs to be peeled away and discarded. After they are peeled, sweetbreads can be pressed to give them a firmer, more appealing texture in certain preparations.

See Figure 6-80 for photos illustrating the method for preparing sweetbreads.

Liver

Calves liver is often featured on menus, smothered with onions and bacon or in pâtés and terrines. Pork, lamb, and some types of game liver may also be used.

To prepare liver for sautéing or braising, you will need to first remove any veins, sinew, gristle, or silverskin before cooking. The membrane pulls away easily, as shown in Figure 6-81.

Kidneys

Steak and kidney pies are still popular in Britain. Other cuisines also feature recipes that call for kidneys. To be sure that the finished recipe does not have an unpleasant taste, kidneys should be cleaned.

Split the kidneys in half and cut out the artery and fat. In some recipes, there may be instructions to blanch the kidneys or soak them in buttermilk to remove any lingering taste of urine.

See Figure 6-82 for photos illustrating how to split and clean kidneys.

Tongue

Tongue is a muscle meat that can be quite tough unless it is gently simmered in a flavorful broth or bouillon until it is very tender. Allowing the tongue to cool in the liquid will bolster its flavor. Once cooled, the tongue should be carefully peeled to remove the skin. Then, it can be used in a variety of ways: as the garnish for a sauce or soup or as part of a boiled dinner or stew. It may also be served on its own.

See Figure 6-83 for photos illustrating the method for peeling tongue.

Removing Marrow

Marrow—the soft, inner substance of bone—is often used as a garnish for a variety of sauces, soups, as well as in dumplings and other dishes. The bones should first be sawed into reasonable lengths to make it easier to remove the marrow. The bones are then rinsed or soaked in cool running water until all traces of blood have been eliminated and the water runs clear. The marrow can then be removed from the bone.

See Figure 6-84 for photos illustrating the method for removing bone marrow.

Poultry Fabrication

All kinds of poultry, including chicken, squab, duck, pheasant, and quail, are of great importance to most restaurants. Always popular and readily available, poultry, for the most part, is among the least costly of meats used for entrées and other menu items. Throughout this section, the fabrica-

FIGURE 6-80 Cleaning and Pressing Sweetbreads

(1) Once the sweetbreads have been properly blanched and cooled, pull away the heavy membrane.

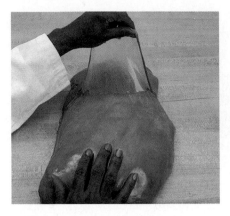

FIGURE 6-81 Cleaning Liver by Pulling Away the Membrane

(2) Wrap the sweetbreads in clean cheesecloth and roll them up. Tie the ends with string.

FIGURE 6-82 Cleaning Kidneys

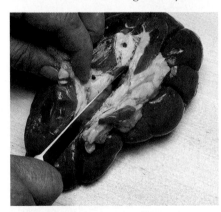

(1) Make a cut through the center of the kidneys, dividing them into two equal pieces.

(3) Place the wrapped sweetbreads in a terrine or other container and top with a flat item, such as a clean length of board as used here.

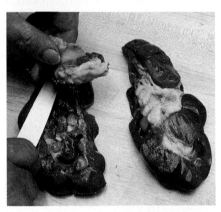

(2) Lift away the kidney fat and use the tip of a sharp knife to cut it away from the kidneys.

(4) Top the board with a weight. Refrigerate. As the weight pushes out the excess moisture, the sweetbreads will take on a firm, compact texture and shape.

tion techniques are demonstrated on a chicken, the bird most commonly used in restaurants. These techniques can be applied to the fabrication of virtually all poultry types.

The younger the bird, the easier it is to cut up. They are usually much smaller and their bones are not completely hardened. The size and breed of the bird will also have some bearing on how easy or difficult it will be to fabricate. Chickens are gener-

FIGURE 6-83   Peeling Tongue

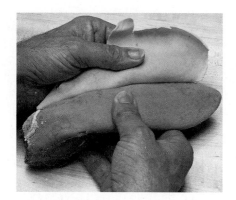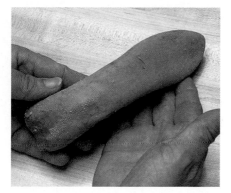

(1) Use the tip of a knife to trim the skin from the underside. Lift it away from the tongue as the cuts are made to make it easier to see what you are doing.

(2) The skin will peel away easily from the tongue's top.

(3) The completely peeled tongue is shown.

FIGURE 6-84   Removing Marrow from Bones

(1) Place the marrow bones in a container and cover with cold water. Add salt to help draw away any excess blood and other impurities.

(2) After the marrow bones have soaked for a few hours, push the marrow out using the thumb.

(3) The marrow is completely freed.

ally simpler to cut up, for example, than pheasant. The tendons and ligaments in chickens are less well developed, except in the case of free-range birds, which move freely about an enclosed yard or pen.

Although the procedure for boning a duck, for instance, is very similar to that used in boning a Cornish game hen, carcass shapes do differ from breed to breed. A duck has shorter legs and a long, barrel-shaped chest. The game hen, since it is small, will require smaller, more delicate cuts than a turkey. A quail, one of the smallest birds, requires all of a chef's skill and care to avoid mangling the tiny morsels of meat that cling to delicate bones.

The bones and trim remaining after fabrication can be used in a variety of ways: the wings used for hors d'oeuvres, any lean trim for forcemeat preparation, and the bones for making stock.

When working with any type of poultry, the chef should keep all tools and work surfaces scrupulously clean because of the potential for cross-contamination. Follow all of the proper procedures described in Chapter 2 for working with potentially hazardous foods. The following standards must be adhered to strictly:

• Keep poultry iced and under refrigeration when it is not being fabricated or prepared for cooking.

• Be sure that the cutting board has been thoroughly cleaned and sanitized before and after using it to cut up poultry.

FIGURE 6-85   Trussing a Bird

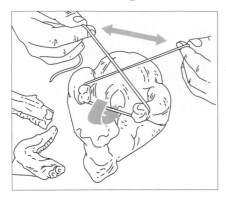

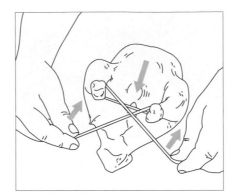

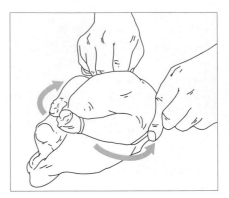

(1) Cut away the first two wing joints. Pass the middle of a long piece of string underneath the joints at the end of the drumstick, and cross the ends of the string to make an "X" as shown.

(2) Pull the ends of the string down toward the tail and begin to pull the string back along the body.

(3) Pull both ends of the string tightly across the joint that connects the drumstick and the thigh and continue to pull the string along the body toward the bird's back, catching the wing underneath the string.

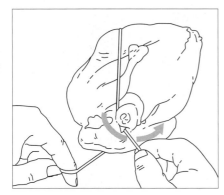

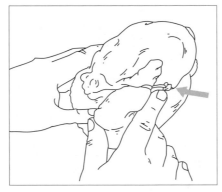

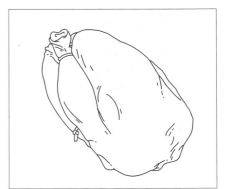

(4) Pull one end of the string securely underneath the backbone at the neck opening.

(5) Tie the two ends of the string with a secure knot.

(6) A properly trussed bird.

- Clean and sanitize knives, poultry shears, and sharpening steel before and after cutting poultry.

- Store poultry in clean, leak-proof containers, and do not place poultry above any cooked meats. If the poultry drips on the food below it, the food will become contaminated. For added safety, it is a good idea to place a drip pan underneath the container holding the poultry.

The essential tools for cutting up poultry are a clean work surface, a boning knife, and a chef's knife. Some chefs are comfortable using poultry shears to cut through joints and smaller bones. Others may prefer to use a cleaver.

Trussing Birds for Roasting Whole

Roast chicken, turkey, duck, and geese are familiar and popular items. The advance preparation techniques required can vary. Some chefs prefer to leave birds untrussed, in the belief that this permits birds to cook quickly and evenly. Others prefer to truss birds, in order to produce roasted birds that are moist, with a classic appearance.

Since the wing tips are generally not served, they may be cut away before **trussing.** Then the bird is ready for trussing either with or without a trussing needle. There are some alterations to these basic techniques that you may learn. The aim of trussing is to produce a neat, compact shape. Figure 6-85

FIGURE 6-86   Removing the Wing Tips and Backbone

 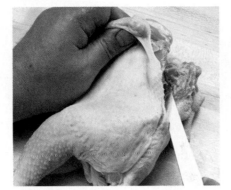

(1) Cut away the first two wing joints. These wing tips may be reserved for use in stock.

(2) Lay the chicken on one side. Make a cut along one side of the backbone, working from the neck to the tail.

(3) Turn the bird onto its other side. Make another cut along the backbone, this time cutting from the tail toward the neck.

demonstrates one of a number of acceptable ways to truss poultry.

Halving a Bird

Cutting a bird into halves is an especially important technique for use on smaller birds, such as Cornish game hens and broiler chickens, that are to be prepared by grilling. If the bones are left intact during grilling, they provide some protection against scorching and help to control shrinkage. This technique is also important when birds are roasted whole, but served as semi-boneless halves.

The first step is often removing the wing tips. Then the bird is cut down along the backbone using either a boning knife, a chef's knife, or poultry shears. The wing tips and backbone should be saved to use when you prepare stock.

See Figure 6-86 for photos illustrating the method for removing the wingtips and backbone.

Removing the Keel Bone

Once the backbone has been cut away, the keel bone is also removed. Lay the bird out flat, bones facing up. Make an incision just at the top of the keel bone to release it. Then bend the bird so that the keel bone pops out, as shown in Figure 6-87.

---

trussing needle: a large needle, specially designed for trussing poultry.

Cut down the length of the breast to finish dividing the bird into halves.

Preparing a Halved Bird to Grill or Broil

Birds that are to be grilled can be given an attractive shape by completing the process shown in Figure 6-88. Here, the chef has removed the end of the drumstick using the heel of the chef's knife. Then, a slit is cut into the skin over the thigh. The end of the drumstick is inserted, creating a neat, compact halved bird that is easy to handle.

Quartering a Bird

Instead of leaving the bird halved, you can continue the cutting process to produce quarters: two leg pieces and two breast pieces. Simply make a cut between the legs and the breast, at the point where the thigh meets the breast, as shown in Figure 6-89.

Removing the Legs from a Whole Bird

Instead of first removing the backbone, you may opt to remove the legs first. This can be done before or after the wing tips are removed. Make a cut in the skin where the leg and the breast join. Then, bend the leg away from the breast, popping the leg away and exposing the ball joint. Cut through the joint to remove the leg.

The leg can then be separated into two pieces: the drumstick and the thigh. Turn the leg so that

FIGURE 6-87   Removing the Keel Bone and Halving a Bird

(1) Open the bird out flat, with the skin side facing down. Notch the breast on one side of the keel bone to made it easier to pop out of the bird.

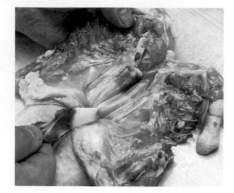

(2) Pull the keel bone away from the chicken completely. The bone may separate into two portions; be sure that it is all removed.

(3) Cut the bird in half through the breast.

FIGURE 6-88   Preparing Halved Birds to Grill or Broil

(1) Use the heel of the chef's knife to cut away the end of the drumstick.

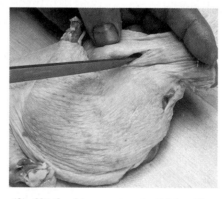

(2) Slit the skin covering the thigh with a boning knife tip.

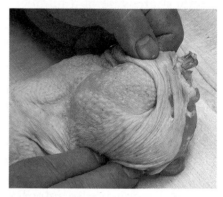

(3) Insert the end of the drumstick into the slit to hold the leg securely in place during cooking.

you can see a line of fat running over the joint. Use it as a guide to mark the spot where you can easily cut through the joint.

See Figure 6-90 for photos illustrating the method for removing the legs from a whole bird.

Cutting a Bird in Eighths

When a bird is cut into eighths, the chef then has two drumsticks, two thighs, two wing portions, and two breast portions (see Figure 6-91). Broiler or fryer chickens to be pan-fried or deep-fried are usually cut into eighths so that they will cook evenly and thoroughly before their exterior becomes charred. This is also a popular way to cut up poultry for baking, stewing, braising, or barbecuing.

Boneless, Skinless Chicken Breasts

The breast meat can be cut away from the rib cage before or after the legs are removed. Make a cut along the breast bone, and then carefully cut the meat away from the rib bones. If the wings are still attached, cut through the joint where the wings join the breast.

Be sure to remove the wishbone, if you haven't already. This is removed by either cutting or pushing the bones cleanly away from the meat.

Pull the skin away from the breast, and you have completed the process. If desired, the "tenderloin" can be removed from the breast. It is attached by a thin filament, and should pull cleanly away from the breast meat. If necessary, use a par-

FIGURE 6-89   Cutting a Bird into Quarters

FIGURE 6-90   Removing the Legs from a Whole Bird

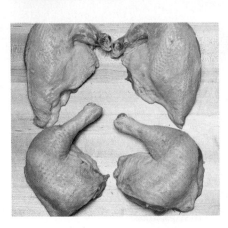

(1) Make a diagonal cut to separate the breast from the leg.

(1) Lay the chicken on its back on a flat work surface. Using a sharp knife, make a cut between the leg and the breast.

(2) The quartered chicken.

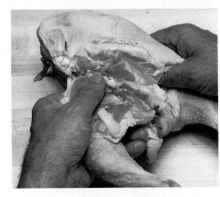

(2) Bend the leg away from the body and press fingertips into the back of the joint to pop the joint loose. Continue to cut the leg away from the breast.

ing knife or the tip of a boning knife to completely sever it. The tenderloin has a tendon running through it which can be removed easily by holding the tendon steady with a towel. Press a knife blade at an angle so that the tendon is trapped but not cut, and push the knife away from the hand holding the tendon down, until the entire piece comes out.

See Figure 6-92 for photos illustrating the method for boning and skinning chicken breasts.

(3) Make a cut completely around the end of the drumstick to sever the flesh, tendons, and skin from the bone.

Preparing Suprêmes

A **suprême** is a semi-boneless poultry breast, usually from a chicken, pheasant, partridge, or duck. One wing joint, often frenched, is left attached to the breast meat. The preferred cooking techniques include sautéing, shallow poaching, and grilling.

To prepare a suprême, cut the breast away from the rib cage as you would for a boneless skinless breast. Cut away the wing tips, leaving one section still attached. Use the heel of your chef's knife to french the bone.

FIGURE 6-91   A Chicken Cut into Eighths

FIGURE 6-92   Boneless Skinless Breasts

(1) Make a cut along one side of the breastbone to free the breast from the rib cage.

(2) Pull the meat away from the bones as the cut is made so that as little meat as possible is left on the bones.

(3) Make a cut through the joint that attaches the wing to the rib cage. At this point, the chicken breast may be made into suprêmes, or the wings and skin may be completely removed.

(4) Boneless, skinless chicken breasts.

FIGURE 6-93   Making a Suprême

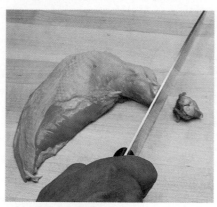

(1) Cut away the first two wing joints. Then use the heel of a chef's knife to cut the end of the remaining wing joint.

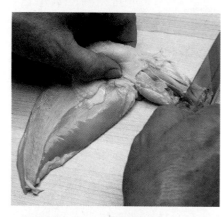

(2) Scrape the meat away from the wing bone, leaving as little meat as possible on the bone.

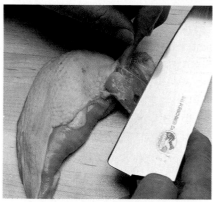

(3) Cut the meat away from the wing bone.

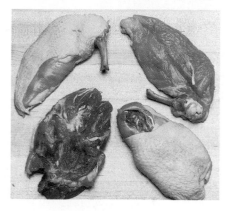

(4) The finished suprême.

FIGURE 6-94   Boning a Chicken Leg

(1) Cut around the end of the drumstick.

(2) Cut along the natural seams in the meat to expose the drumstick and thighbones. Use the knife tip to cut the meat away from the bone.

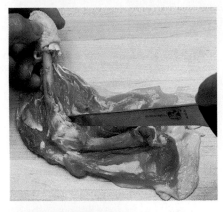

(3) When the bones are completely exposed from the top, run the point of the knife blade underneath them to free them from the meat.

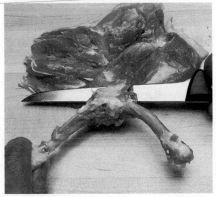

(4) Pull the leg bones away from the meat. Cut the joint that joins the thighbone and the drumstick bone away from the meat. The leg is now completely boneless.

See Figure 6-93 for photos illustrating the method for preparing suprêmes.

Boning a Poultry Leg

A boneless leg can be prepared in a number of ways, or it may be cut into strips to use for stir-fries and other dishes. First, make a cut around the end of the drumstick to sever the tendons. Use the tip of a boning knife to cut along the bones, freeing the meat. Then, lift away the bones, cutting through the tendons holding the joint between the drumstick and the thigh.

See Figure 6-94 for photos illustrating the method for boning a poultry leg.

Disjointing a Rabbit

Rabbit is often considered to be similar to chicken, both in terms of its flavor and its relative simplicity to disjoint. The loin and rib sections tend to be drier than the legs, in much the same way that the chicken breast can be drier than the legs. By first removing the legs and shoulder, as demonstrated in

FIGURE 6-95   Disjointing a Rabbit

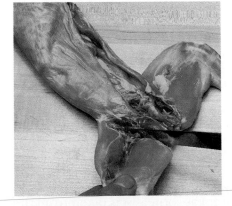

(1) Pull the leg away from the body and then cut through the meat and the joint to separate the leg from the loin.

(2) Pull the shoulder away from the body. Cut through the breast and the joint to completely separate the foreleg from the body.

Figure 6-95, two different cooking methods can be applied to one rabbit—moist heat for the legs, dry heat for the loin—to achieve the most satisfactory results. Or the rabbit can be stewed in pieces.

Fish and Shellfish Fabrication

The days of inexpensive fish in great abundance are probably gone. Overfishing of certain species, pollution, and increased demand have made some types of fish difficult or impossible to find. It is, therefore, especially important to make use of this valuable resource in the most profitable way. If whole fish can be cleaned and cut up in-house, with as little trim loss as possible, and if the trim can be put to good use in a mousseline, a filling, canapés, or soups, then fish can still be considered an excellent value.

Fish and shellfish fabrication includes such techniques as scaling, gutting, and cutting round and flat fish into steaks and fillets. Although the more fabrication the chef can do, the more money can be saved, the flip side of this consideration is that if a poor job is done, there will be more waste. If the chef does not have the ability, time, or proper storage space, buying prepared fillets and steaks or shucked oysters and clams is more cost-effective.

The techniques shown here are not exceptionally difficult, nor do they require much special equipment. A fish scaler, a sharp flexible filleting knife, needlenose pliers, and a clam and oyster knife are the customary tools.

Gutting a Fish

Fish may be gutted as soon as it is taken from the water, right on the fishing boat. If you receive fish that has not been gutted yet, you should do this as soon as possible. The gut, or viscera, contains enzymes that can begin to break down the flesh rapidly, leading to spoilage. This step may be performed right after the fish has been scaled or, if fish is to be stored on ice, the scales can be allowed to remain until right before cooking. The methods for

---

canapé: an hors d'oeuvre consisting of a small piece of bread or toast, garnished with a savory spread or topping.

FIGURE 6-96   Gutting a Round Fish

(1) Slit the belly of the fish to expose the viscera.

(2) Pull out the viscera.

(3) Rinse the cavity thoroughly under cold running water.

gutting both round and flat fish are shown in Figures 6-96 and 6-97.

Scaling and Trimming Fish

Many types of fish, although not all, have scales. Whenever scales are present, the first step in fabricating the fish is to remove them. Scales are difficult to see if they are adhering to flesh rather than to skin.

FIGURE 6-97   Gutting a Flat Fish

(1) Make a cut as shown.

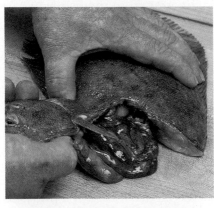

(2) Pull away the head and viscera by hooking your thumb in the head.

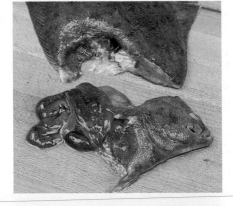

(3) The head and viscera, completely removed.

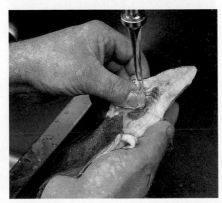

(4) Rinse the cavity thoroughly under cold running water.

FIGURE 6-98   Scaling and Trimming Fish

(1) Work in a sink under running water. Hold the fish gently by the head to keep it steady and work from the tail to the head.

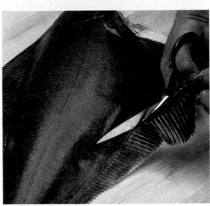

(2) Use scissors to cut fins away.

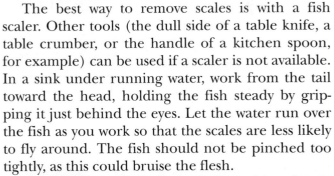

The best way to remove scales is with a fish scaler. Other tools (the dull side of a table knife, a table crumber, or the handle of a kitchen spoon, for example) can be used if a scaler is not available. In a sink under running water, work from the tail toward the head, holding the fish steady by gripping it just behind the eyes. Let the water run over the fish as you work so that the scales are less likely to fly around. The fish should not be pinched too tightly, as this could bruise the flesh.

The fins and tail can be cut away at this point, or you may prefer to wait until the fish has been gutted.

See Figure 6-98 for photos illustrating the method for scaling and trimming fish.

Pan-Dressed Fish

Pan-dressed fish are those which have been scaled, gutted, and trimmed. In some cases, the head and tail may be removed before cooking. This is not an ironclad rule, however. Depending upon the established practice in your kitchen, or the requirements of a particular dish, you may opt to leave the head

FIGURE 6-99   A Pan-Dressed Trout

and tail on during both cooking and presentation to the guest.

Pan-dressed fish are served as a single portion and their weight is usually no more than 12 ounces after they have been gutted, scaled, and trimmed. Pan-frying and grilling are the most-often used techniques for preparing a pan-dressed fish. You may want to add an aromatic filling, such as fresh sprigs of herbs, lemon slices, or scallions to give the fish additional flavor as it cooks.

See Figure 6-99 for photos of a pan-dressed trout.

Filleting a Fish

Fillets are one of the most popular cuts of fish. They should be completely boneless. The skin may or may not be removed, depending upon the type of fish. Typical cooking methods for fillets include sautéing, broiling, grilling, baking, and poaching. Once fish fillets have been formed, they can be used to prepare paupiettes, tranches, or goujonettes. These cuts are demonstrated in Figures 6-106 through 6-108, and in further discussion on pages 281-284.

Round fish, such as salmon, yield two fillets, one from either side. The common approach, for right-handed chefs, is to hold the scaled and gutted fish so that it appears to be swimming away to the right. The second fillet is a little more difficult to remove than the first. See Figure 6-100 for photos illustrating the method for filleting salmon.

Once the fillet is cut away from the fish, you can remove the skin. Be careful that you avoid placing the flesh side down on the cutting surface. There may be some scales or other trim that you would rather not have to rinse or blot away from the fillet. See Figure 6-101 for photos illustrating the method for skinning salmon fillets.

Some fish, such as salmon, have a number of bones in the fillet, known as pin bones. These are located by gently running your finger down the fillet. Use needlenose pliers or sturdy tweezers to pull them out of the fish. See Figure 6-102 for a photo illustrating the method for removing pin bones.

Flat fish can be cut into two fillets—one from the dark and one from the white side. They can also be made into quarter fillets to make four separate pieces. Figure 6-103 shows how to prepare fillets and quarter fillets from a flounder. The technique for removing the skin from a flounder fillet is shown in Figure 6-104.

FIGURE 6-100   Filleting Salmon

(1) Make a cut behind the head, and run the knife down the length of the fish, working from head to tail on the first side.

(2) Turn the fish to the second side and work from the tail to the head.

(3) Trim away the belly bones.

FIGURE 6-101   Skinning Salmon Fillets

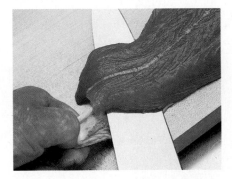

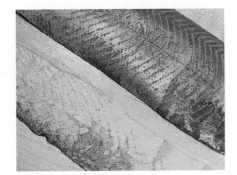

(1) Lay the fillet near the edge of the work surface. Run the blade of a chef's knife between the skin and the flesh, angling the blade downward slightly.

(2) Use a sawing motion, and hold the skin taut to make it easier to remove.

(3) The completely skinned fillet. Note how clean and smooth the flesh is on the skin side.

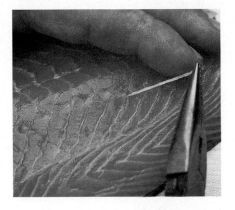

FIGURE 6-102
Removing Pin
Bones from a
Salmon Fillet

Dover sole is handled in a special way. Many chefs like to skin the fish before filleting. The skin is freed from the tail, using a filleting knife, and then it is simply pulled away. See Figure 6-105 for photos illustrating the method of skinning Dover sole.

Tranche

A *tranche* is simply a slice of the fillet. It is made by holding the knife at an angle while cutting to expose more surface area and give the piece of fish a larger appearance. A tranche can be cut from any relatively large fillet of fish; for example, salmon, halibut, or tuna are often cut into tranches. Though this cut is normally associated with sautéed or pan-fried preparations, it is perfectly acceptable to grill or broil a tranche.

See Figure 6-106 for a photo illustrating cutting a tranche.

Goujonette

The name for this cut is derived from the French name for small fish, *goujon*. **Goujonettes** are small strips cut from a fillet, often breaded or dipped in batter, and then deep-fried. This cut has approximately the same dimensions as an adult's index finger. Goujonettes are normally cut from lean white fish, such as sole or flounder, and may be served with a piquant sauce, such as remoulade or tartar sauce.

See Figure 6-107 for a photo illustrating cutting a goujounette.

Paupiette

A *paupiette* is a thin, rolled fillet, often filled with a forcemeat or other stuffing. It should resemble a large cork or spiral. Paupiettes are generally made from lean fish, such as flounder or sole, although they may also be made from some moderately fatty fish, such as trout or salmon. The most common preparation technique for paupiettes is shallow-poaching.

See Figure 6-108 for a photo illustrating a paupiette.

Cutting Steaks

Steaks are simply cross-cuts of the fish and are relatively easy to make. The fish is gutted, scaled,

---

tartar sauce: a cold sauce prepared with mayonnaise, capers, anchovies, and mustard.

FIGURE 6-103   Filleting Flounder

(1) Make the initial cut as shown.

(2) Continue cutting, lifting the flesh away as you work.

(3) Turn the fish and continue cutting to make a fillet.

(4) To make quarter fillets, first cut down the center of the fish.

(5) Make cuts from the center working outward.

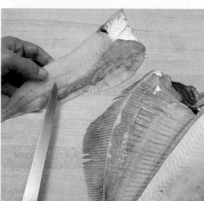

(6) Trim the fillet.

(7) Remove the final quarter fillet.

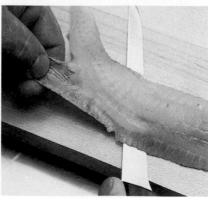

FIGURE 6-104
Skinning
Flounder Fillets

FIGURE 6-105   Trimming and Peeling Dover Sole

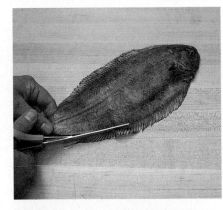

(1) Cut away the fins.

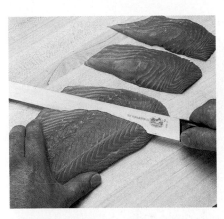

FIGURE 6-106
Cutting a
Tranche from
Salmon Fillets

(2) Make an initial cut to loosen the skin.

FIGURE 6-107
Cutting
Goujonettes from
Flounder Fillets

(3) Pull the skin away before filleting the fish, if desired.

FIGURE 6-108
Preparing
Paupiettes

(4) The Dover sole shown here is ready to be breaded and deep-fried for the classic "Colbert" presentation.

FIGURE 6-109
Cutting Salmon
Steaks

FIGURE 6-110 Cutting Halibut Steaks

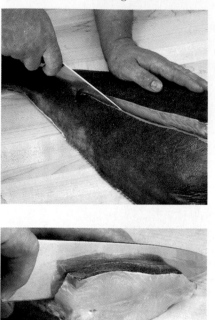

(1) Cutting a halibut in half as the first step in preparing steaks.

(2) Cutting the steaks from halibut.

and trimmed of its fins. The size of the steak is determined by the thickness of the cut. There are a few flat fish large enough to cut into steaks—halibut, and turbot are two examples.

See Figures 6-109 and 6-110 for photos illustrating the method for cutting steaks from round and flat fishes.

Working with Shellfish

Shrimp

Shrimp may be peeled, deveined, and occasionally butterflied before cooking.

Peeling and Deveining Shrimp

Shrimp can be cooked in the shell, before peeling and deveining. For many preparations, however, recipes clearly state that shrimp are to be cleaned before cooking. And, in other instances, these operations may be performed after cooking the shrimp.

The greatest advantage to peeling and deveining raw shrimp before cooking is that the shrimp are easy to present to the guest, with no messy peeling required at the table. Reserved raw shrimp shells can be used to make a flavorful stock or sauce. There are specific tools available that will lift away the shell and make an incision along the back of the shrimp, pulling away the vein, but a sharp paring knife is all you need.

See Figure 6-111 for photos illustrating the method for peeling and deveining shrimp.

Butterflying Shrimp

To butterfly a shrimp, use a small sharp knife, such as a paring knife, to cut into the shrimp at the same point where the vein was removed. Cut into the shrimp deeply enough to allow the sides to flatten out, but don't cut all the way through the shrimp.

FIGURE 6-111 Peeling and Deveining

(1) Pulling away the shell.

(2) Cutting along the back vein.

(3) Removing the intestinal tract.

FIGURE 6-112 Working with Cooked Lobsters

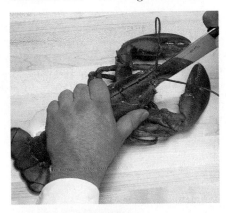

(1) Halving a cooked lobster.

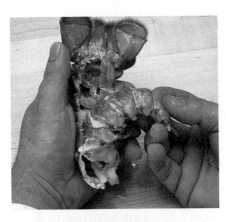

(5) Releasing the meat from the shell.

(2) The halved lobster.

(6) To remove flesh from the claw, you can crack it with a mallet, or

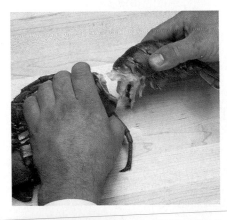

(3) Pulling the tail away from the body.

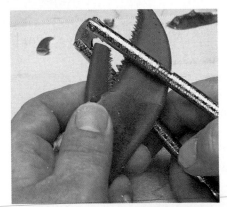

(7) Use a nutcracker to break the shell, or

(4) Cutting the shell away with kitchen shears.

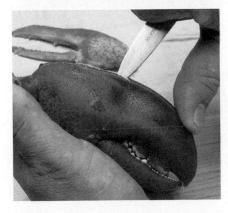

(8) Cut through the shell with the tip of a paring knife.

Lobster

Lobster can be handled in a number of ways before cooking. Some chefs prefer to simply plunge the live lobster into a pot of boiling water. Others believe that it is more humane to kill the lobster first. This is generally accomplished by inserting the tip of a knife into the back of the lobster, just behind the head. This is done to sever the spinal nerve, killing the lobster before cooking it. (See Chapter 10, Moist-Heat and Combination Cooking Methods, page 387, for more information.) Because lobsters have relatively simple nervous systems, you may see that the lobster continues to move. Keep the bands on the claws to avoid being pinched until the lobster is cooked or stops moving completely.

Working with Cooked Lobster

It is easier to remove the meat from a lobster that has been partially or fully cooked. Cook the lobster by steaming, boiling, or baking. The lobster need not be completely cooked. It is only important that the flesh has begun to firm slightly.

Techniques for halving a lobster and removing the tail and claw meat are shown in Figure 6-112.

Crayfish

Crayfish share many similarities with lobster, but they are much smaller. Crayfish are especially popular in Cajun and Creole dishes. Like shrimp, they may be simply boiled or steamed and peeled after cooking when the meat is easy to remove from the shell. It is relatively simple to remove the vein from the crayfish before cooking, though this may be done afterward, if preferred.

See Figure 6-113 for photos illustrating how to clean crayfish.

Crab

Blue crab, like lobster, are purchased live. You may prefer to kill them before cooking, as you would do for lobster. Once crabs are cooked, the meat is often removed from the shell. It must be examined carefully, or "picked," to remove any bits of shell or cartilage that remain. This step is important for tinned or frozen crab meat, as well as that which you cook and clean yourself.

Cleaning a Soft-Shelled Crab

A seasonal favorite, soft-shelled crabs are considered a great delicacy. They are not especially difficult to clean once their various parts are identified. Soft-shelled crabs are commonly prepared by sautéing or pan-frying, and the shell may be eaten along with the meat.

See Figure 6-114 for photos illustrating the method for cleaning a soft-shelled crab.

FIGURE 6-113 Working with Crayfish

(1) Twist the middle fan of the tail and pull out the intestinal tract, before cooking.

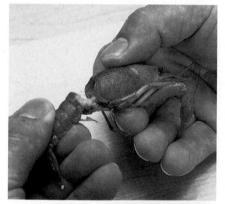

(2) Once cooked, pull the tail away and

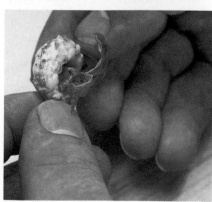

(3) Pull the shell away from the meat.

FIGURE 6-114 Cleaning a Soft-Shelled Crab

(1) Peel back the pointed shell and scrape away the gill filament on each side.

(2) Cut off the head and carefully squeeze out the green bubble behind the eyes.

(3) Bend back the apron and twist to remove it and the intestinal vein at the same time.

(4) The cleaned crab.

FIGURE 6-115 Cleaning and Opening Oysters

(1) Scrub the oyster well under running water.

(2) Wear a mesh glove to protect your hands. Insert the tip of the oyster knife into the hinge of the shell.

(3) Release the flesh from the shell.

FIGURE 6-116   Opening Clams

(1) Use the tip of the knife to release the meat from the top shell.

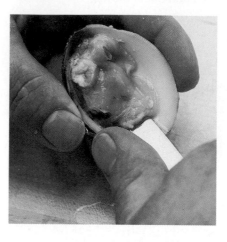

(2) Run the knife under the clam meat to loosen. This clam can now be served "on the half shell."

Mollusks

Cleaning and Opening Clams and Oysters

Freshly shucked oysters and clams are required for such classic dishes as oysters Rockefeller or clams casino. Although shucked oysters and clams are available, you may prefer to open them yourself to assure freshness in chowders, gumbos, and other dishes. The practice of serving clams and oysters on the half shell is an important aspect of some establishments.

Clean all **mollusks** (clams, oysters, and mussels) well by scrubbing them under running water to remove all dirt. Check them carefully. Live clams and oysters will have tightly closed shells. Any that are open, or that feel "heavy," are either dead or close to death, or full of silt. Discard them.

To protect your hands, you may with to use a wire mesh glove and/or side towels. Clam and oyster knives should be used, as shown in Figures 6-115 and 6-116.

Cleaning and Debearding Mussels

Mussels are rarely served raw, but the method for cleaning them before steaming and poaching is similar to that used for clams. Unlike clams and oysters, mussels have a dark, shaggy beard that is normally pulled away before cooking.

---

oysters Rockefeller: baked or broiled oysters on the half shell, topped with a mixture of spinach, butter, bread crumbs, and seasonings, including Pernod.

clams casino: baked or broiled clams on the half shell, topped with a sautéed mixture of bacon, onion, and red and green bell peppers.

FIGURE 6-117   Cleaning and Debearding Mussels

(1) Scrub well under running water.

(2) Pull the beard away.

(3) The cleaned and debearded mussel

See Figure 6-117 for photos illustrating the method for cleaning and debearding mussels.

Cephalopods

This group includes squid, octopus, and cuttlefish. There are some ethnic terms used for these shellfish that may be equally familiar to you and your guests—for instance, *calamari* or *scungilli* are Italian terms. These shellfish are not difficult to prepare, but they do need some advance preparation to remove the ink sac and quill.

When properly fabricated and cooked, they are tender, sweet, and flavorful with a distinctive texture. The mantle can be cut into rings to sauté, pan-fry, or deep-fry; or it may be left whole to grill or braise, with or without a stuffing. If desired, the ink sac can be saved and used to tint various dishes, such as pasta *(calamares en su tinta)* and rice *(arroz negro)*.

Cleaning Squid and Octopus

Pull away any skin that remains on the mantle and tentacles. Rinse carefully, and pull out the "quill" from the mantle. Cut the tentacles away from the body if desired, by cutting just behind the eye. To remove an octopus's beak, use the tip of a knife or pop it out with your fingers.

See Figure 6-118 for photos illustrating the method for cleaning squid and Figure 6-119 for cleaning octopus.

FIGURE 6-118   Cleaning Squid

(1) Pull the mantle and tentacles apart under running water.

(2) Pull off the skin from the mantle.

(3) Pull out the quill.

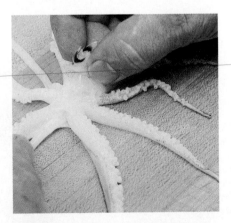

(4) Cut the tentacles away from the head by cutting just above the eye. If desired, the ink sac may be reserved.

(5) Open out the tentacles and pull out the beak.

FIGURE 6-119   Cleaning Octopus

(1) Use the tip of a filleting knife to cut around the eye and lift it from the octopus.

(2) Peel the skin away from the body by pulling firmly.

(3) Pull the suction cups away from the tentacles.

FIGURE 6-120   Cleaning a Sea Urchin

FIGURE 6-121   Skinning an Eel

(1) Wear gloves to protect your hands and cut off the shell's top with scissors.

(1) Use a sharp filleting knife to make an incision completely around the fish just behind the fins nearest the head.

(2) The urchin, cleaned and ready to serve. (Note that you may prefer to shave off the spines before opening and serving.)

(2) Hold the head securely with one hand and pull the skin away. Hold the skin with a kitchen towel to prevent slipping.

Miscellaneous Items

Cleaning a Sea Urchin

Sea urchins are a spiny marine fish that may not be available in all areas of the country. They are considered a delicacy in many cuisines, especially French and Japanese. When working with these creatures, the chef should always wear thick rubber gloves to protect his or her hands. Scrape or cut away the spines, which can be quite painful if they pierce the skin. This may be done before cleaning, if desired.

See Figure 6-120 for photos illustrating the method for cleaning a sea urchin.

Skinning an Eel

This is not one of the easiest of tasks, because the eel's skin is firmly attached. It may take several attempts to accomplish the job. The skin must be removed before cooking because it is tough and slippery. The best-known preparation for eel is *matelote,* an eel stew.

See Figure 6-121 for photos illustrating the method for skinning an eel.

Summary

Mise en place is the foundation of all kitchen operations. Any well-schooled chef should be able to produce such commonly used items as mirepoix, bouquet garni, and roux with ease and speed. Assembling properly trimmed steaks, filleted fish, perfectly cleaned salad greens, and minced herbs is as much a part of the chef's daily work as is the preparation of sauces and garnishing of finished plates. Gaining proficiency and speed in the following areas is essential:

- Using a knife properly to produce a wide range of cuts.

- Preparing all types of vegetables appropriately for their intended use and/or cooking method.

- Preparing dried ingredients for use.

- Preparing and properly using a range of thickeners.

- Preparing and properly using aromatic and flavoring combinations.

- Making stocks, broths, and court bouillons.

- Performing a variety of basic techniques such as whipping, folding, and preparing bain maries.

- Fabricating meats, poultry, and fish for service with as little waste as possible.

SELF-STUDY QUESTIONS

1. Name cuts of meat that may be frenched and explain how this is done.

2. Define mise en place.

3. Name the three basic knife grips. Why might you opt to use a different grip from one cutting tasks to another?

4. What is meant by the guiding hand? Describe how the guiding hand is held during cutting tasks.

5. Name seven basic cuts used to prepare vegetables. Give the approximate dimensions for each.

6. Name several decorative cuts and food items with which they are commonly used.

7. Describe the process for cleaning a leek.

8. How is tomato concassé prepared?

9. How many different ways are there to roast a pepper?

10. Describe the correct method for cleaning leafy greens.

11. Explain the long-soak method for beans.

12. Name five different types of thickeners used in the professional kitchen.

13. What is the difference between a bouquet garni and a sachet d'épices?

14. Name the four different types of marinades.

15. Define dry duxelles and give two uses for it.

16. Define each of the following terms:

   - neutral stock   - remouillage

   - fumet   - estouffade

   - court bouillon

17. What are the basic ratios and cooking times for:

   - beef stock   - veal stock

   - poultry stock   - fish fumet

18. How and why are bones blanched? Browned?

19. How are stocks properly cooled and stored?

20. What is clarified butter? Ghee?

21. What steps can you take to achieve the greatest stability and volume for whipped egg whites?

22. Name three different types of meringue.

23. Why should a liaison be tempered? How is this properly done?

24. What is a cutlet of veal? How is it fabricated?

25. Give two reasons for tying a meat roast.

26. What are sweetbreads and how are they prepared for cooking?

27. Name four standards for working safely with poultry as it is fabricated.

28. Define poultry suprême and describe the method for preparing it.

29. When should a fish be gutted? How is this done?

30. Define pan-dressed fish.

31. Name and describe three cuts that can be prepared from a fish fillet.

32. How are mussels prepared for cooking?

33. How can lobsters be killed just before boiling or steaming?

ACTIVITIES

- Prepare a pale roux and use it to thicken a broth to a good consistency. Make note of how much was used and how the flavor and texture were changed. Now make a slurry and bring a second batch of broth to a similar consistency. Compare the flavor, texture, and quantities of thickener used. Keep both mixtures hot for half an hour, then retest them. Note your observations.

- Whip cold egg whites by hand in a copper bowl. Whip room-temperature egg whites by hand in a copper bowl. How long did each method take?

- Prepare: (1) a chicken breast suprême, and (2) a boneless, skinless breast. Cook each breast separately using the recipe Chicken Provençal, on page 556. Which do you prefer. Why?

- Prepare the Vegetable Stock recipe on page 483 using vegetables that have been cut into large dice. Prepare the same recipe using vegetables that have been sliced thin, adhering to cooking time. Compare the flavor and color. Which do you prefer? Why?

- Whip heavy cream by hand through each of the various peak stages. Note the point at which it begins to turn into butter.

KEYWORDS

allumette
appareil
bâtonnet
beurre manie
bouquet garni
broth
brunoise
butterflying meats
chiffonade (shredding)
clarifying
coarse chopping
court bouillon
cutlet
diagonal cut

dice
emincé
estouffade
fermiere
  (farmer's style cut)
fillet
fine brunoise
Frenching
fumet (essence)
goujonette
julienne
liaison
lozenge (diamond cut)
marinade

marrow
matignon
medallion
mie de pain
mince (mincing)
mirepoix
oblique (roll cut)
oignon brûlé
oignon piqué
paillard
pan-dressed
paupiette
paysanne
  (peasant style cut)

remouillage
render
rondelle (rounds)
roux
sachet d'epice
slurry
steak
stock
suprêmes
temper
tomato concassé
tourné
tranche
truss

Lunch menus frequently rely on a typically American institution: soup and sandwich, and two important variations on that theme: soup and quiche or soup and salad. It is hard to imagine a lunch menu that has no soup offering. The "soup du jour" has become such a standard that people expect to see it on the menu, or hear about it from their server.

Soups can be hearty, as is the case with many regional specialties: chowders, gumbos, or thick vegetable or bean soups. They can also be smooth and suave: cream of mushroom, broccoli, or celery. Light broths and consommés tend to do well on dinner menus, when (it is hoped) diners will select a soup that will whet, not overwhelm, their appetite for a more substantial entrée.

The season will have a great deal to do with which soups fit the menu best. In fall, corn chowders, pumpkin bisques, and other soups made from the fullness of the harvest are appropriate. In winter, a filling, steaming

bowl of goulash soup or borscht is appealing. Soups in spring can capitalize on tender fresh vegetables, such as asparagus, green peas, sorrel, and lettuces. In summer, the refreshing, bright flavors and textures of cold soups (gazpacho, vichyssoise, cold fruit soups) are an attractive contrast to the season's heat.

For all these reasons, it is important for the chef to fully master the techniques used to prepare a wide variety of soups. That means learning the fundamentals necessary to produce several distinct styles of soups:

- *Broths*
- *Consommés*
- *Clear vegetable soups*
- *Cream soups and velouté soups*
- *Purée soups*
- *Bisques*
- *Special soups (including international and regional)*
- *Cold soups*

CHAPTER OBJECTIVES

- Describe the basic techniques for preparing the following kinds of soup:
  - broths
  - consommés
  - clear vegetable soups
  - cream and velouté soups
  - purée soups
  - bisques
  - special soups
  - cold soups

- Identify quality products used to make soup and the standards used to assess a soup's overall quality.

- Understand how to select an appropriate garnish for a soup and how to properly heat it.

- Describe the soup service guidelines.

- Apply the proper cooling, storing, and reheating procedures for all types of soup.

The skills involved in making soups include the proper preparation of excellent-quality basic flavoring and aromatic combinations (covered in Chapter 6) such as stocks, mirepoix, bouquet garni, and sachet d'épices. A review of any techniques or preparations that are unfamiliar is suggested before undertaking the actual preparation of a particular soup.

For many soups, the fundamental technique and the basic ratio of liquid to principle ingredient

(and thickener, if necessary) are all the chef needs in order to produce a wide variety of soups. Once these techniques and ratios are learned, a quick survey of the ingredients on hand, due to arrive from the purveyor, or available in the farmer's market can act as the inspiration for the "soup du jour." Recipes, which can be found in Part IV, Chapter 14, offer concrete examples and classic renditions of soups that should be part of any chef's repertoire.

Basic Soup-Making Techniques

Broths

A **broth** is a clear soup made from meats, poultry, fish, or vegetables. Broths can be used in many of the same applications as a stock: as the basis of other soups, sauces, stews, and braised dishes. Unlike stocks, however, broths are flavorful enough to be served "as is."

A perfectly made broth should be translucent, amber to golden brown in color. When you take a spoonful into your mouth, you should sense a perceptible body, as well as a rich, deep, and well-balanced flavor. The aroma of the finished broth should be such that it immediately stimulates the appetite.

In order to produce a broth that has all these characteristics, the chef needs to observe the basic rules of broth preparation:

- Proper selection of ingredients

- Careful monitoring of the broth as it develops

- Safe handling procedures throughout cooking, cooling, reheating, and service.

Mise en Place

1. Assemble all ingredients necessary for making the broth.

The best broths are made from the most flavorful meats, fish, vegetables, and aromatics. This means that you should select from among the ingredients detailed in Table 7-1. Generally speaking, meat cuts should be selected from more-exercised parts of the animal. The more fully developed the muscle, the more pronounced the flavor. The same is true of poultry broths. In this case, stewing hens or mature game birds are the best choice. They have a deeper flavor than younger birds.

Fish should also be carefully selected. Freshness is of tremendous concern, as is the relative leanness or oiliness of the fish. Generally speaking, it is best to use lean, white-fleshed fish, such as sole, halibut, cod, or flounder. Richer or more oily fish tend to lose their fresh savor when the delicate oils found in the fish

TABLE 7-1 SELECTING INGREDIENTS FOR BROTH

Main item	Possible choices
Beef	Shank, chuck, bottom round, oxtail, short ribs/flanken. *Note that a portion of veal shank/shin may also be added.*
Veal	Shank/shin, chuck, bottom round, calves' head.
Pork	Hocks (fresh or smoked), meaty ham bones, Boston butt.
Lamb	Shank, leg, shoulder.
Poultry	Stewing hens, necks and backs (meaty portions), legs.
Fish	Lean white fish, including cod, halibut, hake, flounder, pike.
Shellfish	Shrimp, lobster, clams, mussels.
Vegetables	Carrots, onions, parsnips, leeks, mushrooms, tomatoes, celery, celeriac, garlic, shallots, fennel, broccoli stems. Others as deemed appropriate by recipe or intended use.

are subjected to high temperatures for even short periods. Shellfish are generally cooked in a small amount of liquid while still in their shells to produce excellent broths. They must be strained very carefully to remove all traces of grit or sand.

Vegetable broths are made from any reasonable combination of vegetables. A selection of wholesome trim from a variety of vegetables (carrots, celery, fennel, onions, leeks, parsnips, tomatoes, broccoli stems, lettuce leaves, for instance) can be combined to make a broth, or a specific recipe can be followed. There are no real hard-and-fast rules about which vegetables to use in preparing a vegetable broth, beyond this simple advice: Do not use any vegetable you would otherwise consign to the compost bucket.

When you select the best ingredients for a broth, you are well on the way to producing the best-quality product. It is equally important to remember that a ratio exists between flavoring ingredients and liquid in order to get a broth that is deep, complex, full-bodied, and flavorful. To produce 1 gallon of broth, you will need:

- 8 to 10 pounds of meat or poultry to 6 quarts of cold water, or

Mirepoix should be finely cut so that it can become part of the network created as the consommé comes to a simmer and the meat's proteins begin to adhere into a large mass, without being so large and heavy that they fall out of the formed **raft.** A variety of aromatic vegetables such as onions, carrots, celery, parsnips, mushrooms, and leeks are typically selected. Other special items are used as appropriate to achieve a special flavor.

Herbs and spices are also included in the clarification mixture for supporting or starring roles in the big flavor picture. Garlic, cloves, sprigs or stems of tarragon, parsley, chervil, dill, thyme, or other fresh herbs, bay leaf, peppercorns, gingerroot, juniper berries, star anise, and lemongrass are among the many options chefs feature in contemporary renditions of consommé.

An oignon brûlé or oignon piqué is also commonly included in the ingredients selected for flavoring or coloring a consommé.

There are hundreds of classically codified garnishes for consommés, ranging from humble items such as neatly diced root vegetables, to the esoteric edible gold leaf featured in a recipe found in Escoffier's *Le Guide Culinaire.*

Contemporary chefs have extended the range of possibilities even further. They draw on influences as diverse as Eastern Asian cuisines, Caribbean dishes, or Italian provincial cooking styles. No matter what the garnish selected may be, it is important to remember the following guidelines:

- The garnish itself should be as well prepared as the consommé.

- Vegetable cuts should be neat and precise.

- Royales should be delicately set, soft, and supple in the mouth.

- The seasoning selected for the garnish should serve to enhance the flavor of the consommé, not distract from it.

2. Assemble all necessary equipment for preparing consommés.

Equipment needs for consommé are the same as those described for broths. Review the information earlier in this chapter on page 298.

Method

1. Blend the ingredients for the clarification and add the broth. (See Figure 7-1 for photos illustrating the method for preparing a consommé.)

Mix all the ingredients directly in the pot until the mixture is fairly homogenous. Gradually add the cold broth. Stir the broth into the clarification mixture until evenly blended.

If you need to speed up the process, heat the broth to a simmer, reserving ¼ the total volume of the cold stock to temper the clarification.

2. Bring the consommé slowly to a boil.

Continue to stir the consommé frequently as it comes to a boil. As the temperature rises, the clarification ingredients will begin to adhere into a large, soft mass known as a raft. Once the raft begins to form, stop stirring the consommé, to allow the raft to come together.

3. When the raft has formed, establish a gentle, even simmer.

As the raft coagulates into a mass, it will rise to the surface of the broth. Since the raft traps the heat, in much the same way that a lid on a pot traps the heat, it is important to adjust the heat to establish a gentle simmer. Many chefs will break a small hole in the raft, just large enough for a ladle to pass through. This helps to prevent the consommé from coming to a rapid boil. It also makes it possible to baste the raft as the consommé is cooking.

Adjust the heat so that you have a number of small bubbles breaking on the surface. If there is a strong simmering or boiling action, the raft might break apart before it has properly cleared and flavored the consommé. On the other hand, if the cooking speed is too slow, there may not be sufficient convection within the pot to carry impurities from the bottom of the pot to the top, where they can be trapped by the raft. The raft may actually sink below the surface of the consommé before cooking time is completed.

---

coagulate: the action of proteins as they stiffen, usually due to the application of either heat or acid.

FIGURE 7-1 Preparing Consommé

(1) The stock and clarification are thoroughly blended.

(2) The consommé is breaking through the raft. An oignon brûlé gives additional color and flavor.

(3) The raft has risen to the top.

4. Continue to simmer the consommé until it has fully developed.

The goal is to produce a consommé that is very rich and smooth, with an even, well-balanced flavor and crystal clarity. Recipes will specify a cooking time, generally 1 to 1½ hours. When the raft begins to sink slightly, if we assume that this event happens after a reasonable cooking time rather than because the heat was not adjusted properly, the consommé is most likely properly simmered.

But, the only way to be sure that the consommé has cooked long enough is to taste it occasionally as it cooks. Once you taste the consommé at different stages, you will be able, with continued practice, to recognize when it has reached a peak of flavor and body. When the consommé is properly cooked, check it again for seasoning and make any necessary adjustments at this point, before straining the soup. Remember to pour a small amount into a soup bowl or plate to assess its clarity as well.

5. Strain the finished consommé carefully.

The finished consommé should be strained through a bouillon strainer or a cheesecloth-lined strainer or colander. or carefully rinsed cheesecloth. If cheesecloth is used, be sure that it has been properly prepared as follows: Rinse it first in very hot water to remove any loose fibers or items that may have been left on the surface of the cheesecloth during its own processing.

(4) The finished consommé.

Then, once the water runs perfectly clear, rinse it with cold water. Rinsing is important not only to remove fibers that could cloud the soup, it also helps the cheesecloth to adhere to the strainer or colander.

Avoid breaking up the raft as you strain the consommé. Allow the liquid to drain out of the pot or steam kettle through a spigot, if there is one. Otherwise, carefully enlarge the opening in the raft, then use a ladle to dip the consommé out of the pot. Don't pour the consommé and raft into a strainer, since it will release back into the consommé some of the impurities you have worked so hard to cook out.

The consommé is now ready for service or to be properly cooled and stored, following the procedures outlined in Chapter 2.

Refer to Part IV, Chapter 14 for specific consommé recipes.

Clear Vegetable Soups

Clear **vegetable soups** are based on clear broth or stock. The vegetables are cut into an appropriate and uniform size and the soup is simmered until all ingredients are tender. Meats, grains, and pastas are frequently included to give additional body. Vegetable soups may also be made from a single vegetable, as is done when preparing onion soup. Clear vegetable soups should have a full flavor and be somewhat thicker than broths. Because additional ingredients are cooked directly in the broth, these soups will lack the clarity of broth or consommé. Croutons are a common garnish, and they may be an integral part of the preparation, as for French onion soup *gratiné*.

Mise en Place

1. Assemble and prepare all ingredients and appareils necessary.

   Trim, peel, and cut vegetables as required by type and recipe. Since the vegetables that are cooked in the soup are also part of the finished dish, it is important the cuts are neat and uniform. In this way, you can be certain they will cook uniformly and maintain an attractive appearance.

   Some vegetable soups also include meat or fish. Some include a combination—for example, *pot au feu*, which typically includes beef and chicken. Trim and cut meats, poultry, or fish properly. Poultry may be trussed and cooked whole, rather than cut into pieces. A likely scenario is that meats cooked separately will be diced or julienned, and then returned to the soup near the end of cooking time as a garnish. Be sure that any gristle or excess fat is trimmed from the cooked meat, that fish is completely boned, and the skin has been removed from poultry.

   Any beans to be included in the soup can be either cooked directly in the soup, or cooked separately and added near the end of cooking

FIXING A CLOUDY CONSOMMÉ

Completely cool down the cloudy consommé. Repeat the entire process using the cloudy consommé as your base stock, but this time do not use any meat in the raft, and simmer for only ten minutes after the raft has formed. Carefully strain and check for better results.

time. Whole grains, pastas, rice, or other similar ingredients can also be either cooked directly in the soup, or cooked separately and added during the final minutes of cooking time.

A variety of broths, good-quality stocks, and other liquids, including water, vegetable essences, or juices, are used as the liquid base for vegetable soups. Refer to specific recipes for exact amounts. As always, be sure to test the quality of any broth or stock that has been stored under refrigeration by bringing a small quantity to a boil, and then tasting it to be sure that it smells and tastes fresh and wholesome.

When you are preparing large quantities of soup, it is helpful to bring the broth to a simmer over low heat while preparing the other ingredients. This will reduce overall cooking time, since the soup arrives at the correct cooking temperature more quickly.

Prepare a sachet d'épices or bouquet garni as required by the recipe. In addition to the traditional ingredients, you may opt to include a variety of other herbs, herb stems, spices, dried or fresh mushrooms and chilies to achieve a particular flavor in the finished soup.

There are several garnishes typically paired with vegetable soups. In addition to croutons, pesto, grated cheese, even beaten eggs can be added to vegetable soups just before they are served. Purées of red peppers, chilies, tomato, or sorrel may also be added at the last moment for a dash of color and flavor.

Fortified wines (for example, a splash of sherry added to a French onion soup), vinegar (added at the last moment to borscht), or citrus

---

gratiné: browned in an oven or under a salamander.

juices (lime juice added to a Cuban-style black bean soup) are all common choices for last minute flavor adjustments.

2. Assemble all equipment necessary for cooking.

Most vegetable soups are prepared from start to finish in a single pot. The pot should usually be taller than it is wide to allow the soup to cook gently and evenly at a constant simmer. Review additional information about equipment for cooling and storing soups in Chapter 2.

Method

1. Sweat the aromatic vegetables.

Onions, garlic, leeks, carrots, celery, and parsnips are often included as the basic flavoring ingredients of a vegetable soup. Cooking them gently in a small amount of oil, butter, or rendered salt pork begins the process of releasing their flavors into the soup. Note that some tender vegetables, such as broccoli florets, asparagus tips, and other delicate types, are not generally allowed to sweat. They will be added at staggered intervals, according to individual cooking times.

2. Add the stock, broth, or water and bring the soup slowly to a boil.

A slow simmer is the best cooking speed for most soups. The vegetables and meats will release the best flavor, and the appearance of vegetables will be more attractive when cooked at a simmer. A hard boil tends to cook foods to shreds.

Skim the surface as needed throughout preparation. The scum that is thrown by the ingredients in the soup needs to be removed for the best finished quality.

3. Add any remaining ingredients at appropriate intervals.

Depending on the style of soup you are preparing, additional ingredients, such as chicken pieces, beef brisket, dense vegetables, grains, or legumes, may be added at the same time as the liquid. Keep in mind the overall cooking time of the soup, as well as that required by individual ingredients. Or, refer to recipes for more guidance.

Sachet d'épices and bouquet garni are generally added so that they will cook just long enough to release flavor into the soup. Overcooking these ingredients can deaden their flavor.

Delicate vegetables, such as green peas, kernel corn, asparagus tips, or tomatoes, are added near the end of cooking time. Meats, vegetables, pastas, or grains that have been cooked separately are also usually added in the last few minutes of cooking time.

4. Cook until all ingredients are fully cooked and tender and the soup's flavor is developed.

It is important to taste the soup frequently as it cooks. This will allow you to make adjustments if necessary during cooking time. It will also tell you when the soup has reached a peak of flavor. Be sure to follow all safe food-handling practices: Use tasting spoons, and never use the same spoon to taste a soup twice.

5. The soup is now ready for final seasoning, garnishing, and service. Or, it may be properly cooled and stored, following the procedures outlined in Chapter 2.

See Part IV, Chapter 14, for specific vegetable soup recipes.

Cream Soups and Velouté Soups

According to classic definition, a **cream soup** is based on a béchamel sauce—milk thickened with roux—and is finished with heavy cream. A **velouté soup** is based on a light velouté sauce—a stock thickened with roux—and is finished with a liaison of heavy cream and egg yolks. Contemporary menu writers no longer draw a sharp distinction between the two, and in modern kitchens chefs frequently substitute a velouté base for the béchamel in cream soups. True velouté soups are less frequently prepared in professional kitchens today than they once were. This is true partly because the addition of a li-

---

borscht: a traditional soup made from beets, served hot or cold and garnished with a dollop of sour cream.

sweat: to cook an item in a covered pot with a small amount of fat until it softens and releases moisture.

aison should be done at the last minute. Also, soups finished with a liaison are richer and higher in calories than many guests prefer.

The major flavoring ingredient for cream and velouté soups is simmered in the velouté or béchamel until it is tender. The solids are strained out and, in some cases, puréed and returned to the soup. A second straining is often suggested to develop the velvety-smooth texture associated with excellent cream soups. The finished soup should have the thickness of heavy cream.

A garnish is usually included just prior to service. The garnish is frequently diced meat or vegetables that reflect the major flavoring ingredient. For example, cream of broccoli soup may be garnished with lightly blanched broccoli florets.

Mise en Place

1. Assemble and prepare all ingredients and appareils necessary.

   Trim, peel, and cut vegetables according to type and recipe requirements. It is less important that the cuts be as neat and uniform for cream soups as they are for vegetable soups, since they are most likely going to be puréed. However, it is still important that the cuts be relatively uniform in size so that they will cook evenly. Peel away any tough vegetable stems before using them in soups.

   Cream soups based on chicken or fish are typically made from very richly flavored broths or essences. The poultry or fish is then usually added as a garnish at the end of cooking time, or just before the soup is served.

   The mirepoix should be cut into relatively small dice, to allow its flavors to be released properly into the soup. If a very pale or ivory-colored cream soup is the goal, use a white mirepoix. Other aromatic combinations, including sachet d'épices or bouquet garni, are also used in many cream soup recipes.

   A full-bodied broth or stock should be available, or a light velouté. In some cases, milk or a light béchamel is appropriate. Refer to specific recipes for guidance. If broth or milk is used instead of velouté or béchamel, you will also need a sufficient quantity of prepared roux or flour to thicken the soup.

Finishing ingredients, final flavoring and seasonings, and garnishes should be assembled and ready to add at the appropriate point. Fresh sweet cream is the most common finishing ingredient. Liaisons and flavored creams (scented with ginger or other aromatics) are also frequently employed.

2. Assemble all equipment necessary for cooking.

   It is best to avoid aluminum pots when you are making cream soups, since the action of spoons and whips against the pot could cause the soup to take on a grayish cast. It is also best to choose a pot that is of relatively heavy gauge. Because of the presence of starches in the roux or velouté, or in the major flavoring ingredients, cream soups are far more susceptible to scorching than clear soups. If available, a flame-diffuser or other similar device should be used to prevent hot spots from developing.

   Wooden spoons, ladles, and skimmers are generally required throughout the cooking process. In order to finish the soup properly, you will additionally need strainers and cheesecloth. Puréeing equipment is also necessary: food mills, blenders, burr mixers, or food processors.

   Review equipment needs for cooling and storing soups in Chapter 2.

Method

1. Sweat the aromatic vegetables. (See Figure 7-2 for photos illustrating the method for preparing a cream soup.)

   In addition to a standard or white mirepoix, you may also need to sweat various other vegetables that will act as the major flavoring of the soup: celery, mushrooms, or tomatoes for example. This should be done gently over low heat in a small amount of oil, butter, or stock until the vegetables begin to release their juices.

---

liaison: combination of egg yolks and heavy cream or sour cream.

flame-diffuser: a utensil placed over a burner to disperse the flame and the heat.

FIGURE 7-2   Preparing a Cream Soup (Cream of Broccoli Soup)

(1) Removing broccoli stems to purée.

(2) Returning puréed broccoli to soup.

(3) Finished soup garnished with blanched broccoli florets.

Be careful not to undercook the vegetables, since this step is of great importance in determining the quality of the finished soup. On the other hand, avoid overcooking them. They should not begin to brown at all, but rather remain light in color, cooked just until they are softened and aromatic.

2. Add the liquid base for the soup, and bring it to a gentle simmer.

If you have a prepared velouté or béchamel, add it now and proceed with soup preparation in Step 3. Or, add the broth, stock, or milk and bring the soup to a full boil. Then, using a whip, gradually incorporate the correct amount of roux to get the desired consistency. The roux should be cooler than the liquid. Remember to stir or whip constantly as it is incorporated to smooth out any lumps.

At the same time that you add the liquid base, add other ingredients as appropriate, such as peeled broccoli, asparagus stems, or carrots. Working over low heat, bring the soup just up to a simmer.

3. Add the additional ingredients at appropriate intervals.

The time at which certain ingredients are added to the soup will depend on their individual cooking requirements. Tender new peas will become gray and pasty if allowed to cook for too long. A sachet d'épices left in the soup too long may lose its fresh flavor.

4. Simmer the soup gently until it has developed the appropriate flavor, body, and texture.

Skim the surface as needed during cooking time to remove any impurities that could affect the finished soup's flavor. Pulling the pot slightly to the side of the burner will cause the impurities to collect on one side of the pot, where they can be more easily skimmed away.

Taste the soup often as it develops. You can remove the soup from the heat once all the ingredients are very tender and the soup has good flavor.

Stir frequently to prevent scorching. If there is a slight hint of sticking or scorching, immediately transfer the soup to a cool clean pot. Check it again for any scorched taste. If there is none, you can continue cooking the soup. However, if the soup has a burnt aroma or flavor, it is generally beyond repair.

5. Strain the solids from the soup.

For vegetable cream soups, the solids are frequently puréed and returned to the soup. Gradually reincorporate them, adding just enough to achieve the right consistency and flavor. These soups can be strained once more, after the puréed ingredients are reincorporated, for an even smoother consistency.

Cream of chicken or fish soups are generally just strained once to remove all solids.

6. The soup is now ready to be finished, seasoned, and garnished, or it may be properly cooled and stored, following the procedures outlined in Chapter 2.

To finish a cream soup, bring the cream to a simmer and then add it to the soup. Remember that the right amount of cream, liaison, or sour cream will produce a soup that is delicately flavored, suave, and perfectly smooth. Too much cream will detract from the major flavor of the soup, masking the original taste.

Make any additional adjustments to the soup's consistency or flavor once the cream has been added. If it is too thick, add broth or water. Recheck carefully for flavor, and make additional corrections to the seasoning as needed.

If the cream soup you have prepared is going to be served cold, be sure that it is completely chilled before adding cold cream. Check the flavoring and consistency again once the soup has chilled. Foods often need to be more strongly seasoned when they are served cold, since cooling tends to subdue flavors, even that of salt and pepper.

Refer to Part IV, Chapter 14, for individual cream soup recipes.

Purée Soups

Purée soups are slightly thicker than cream soups and have a somewhat coarser texture. They are often based on dried peas, lentils, or beans, or on starchy vegetables such as potatoes, carrots, and squashes.

One of the most frequent complaints about purée soups is that they are served too thick. Remember, the consistency of any soup must be such that it can be eaten easily from a spoon. The spoon should not be able to stand upright in the soup. Observing the relationship between the flavoring ingredient and the liquid should assure that the soup has a pleasing, robust flavor, without becoming watery or too starchy during cooking and reheating.

Mise en Place

1. Assemble and prepare the ingredients.

A great many purée soups are based on dried beans: Great Northerns, navy beans, lentils, black beans, and split peas are all favorites. Some beans should be soaked for several hours before cooking. This allows the beans to absorb some liquid, shortening the overall cooking time for the soup, as well as ensuring that they cook evenly.

Other purée soups are made from starchy vegetables such as squash, potatoes, carrots, or turnips. These will normally require peeling and dicing. Since they are puréed before they are served, neatness is not critical. Relative uniformity of size is, however, to allow all the ingredients to cook properly, and at about the same speed.

Water, broth, or stock are the most commonly used base liquids. Carefully check broths or stocks for freshness before using them in a soup. Bring a small amount to a boil and taste it. If there is any evidence of souring, or off and musty odors, do not use it.

Many purée soups will call for a bit of rendered salt pork, smoked ham, bacon, or other cured pork products. In some instances, you should blanch these ingredients first to remove any excess salt. Cover them with cool water, bring the water to a simmer, and then drain and rinse the pork product. Alternatively, you can use a ham-based broth to impart a similar flavor.

Onions, garlic, carrots, celery, mushrooms, and tomatoes are all commonly found in purée soups. Other vegetables are also suggested by specific recipes, such as sweet peppers. They may be puréed during final preparation of the soup, or they may be left as is, to act as a garnish for the soup. Consult specific recipes for preparation and cutting instructions.

A variety of ingredients may be used to season purée soups: chilies, dried mushrooms, diced meats, hot sauces, citrus zests or juices, and vinegars. Garnishes include croutons, diced meats, salsas, dollops of sour cream, and so forth.

2. Assemble all equipment necessary for cooking.

Equipment requirements for purée soups are similar to those for cream soups. Review the information earlier in this chapter on page 304.

Method

1. Sweat the aromatic vegetables.(See Figure 7-3 for photos illustrating method for preparing a purée soup.)

   If the recipe calls for a pork product such as minced salt pork or bacon, it should be rendered to release the fat over low heat. Then add the onions, garlic, shallots, leeks, or other aromatic vegetables called for by the recipe. Cook them over low heat, until a rich aroma develops. It is often appropriate to allow aromatics for a purée soup to cook long enough to take on a rich golden hue. Remember that this should be done over moderate heat to avoid developing a harsh flavor. It can take anywhere from 20 to 30 minutes to properly cook these aromatics.

2. Add the liquid and any additional ingredients required at this point. Bring the soup to a gentle simmer.

   Because most purée soups are made from starchy ingredients, it is generally best to start them in a cool liquid. Beans, potatoes, squash, and other similar ingredients should therefore be added at the same time that the liquid base is added to the soup pot.

3. Add additional ingredients at the correct point and continue to simmer until all the ingredients are soft enough to purée easily.

   Purée soups, like all others, should be skimmed throughout cooking time. They also need to be stirred frequently, and to have their cooking speed and temperature carefully monitored.
   Another critical consideration to keep in mind is that the relative dryness of the ingredients featured in purée soups makes it difficult to predict how much liquid might be needed to keep the soup at the correct consistency. If a batch of beans are old, for instance, they will require up to one-third more liquid to cook properly than younger, moister beans. If the soup looks thick as it simmers, it may need additional broth, stock, or water.
   Add the sachet d'épices or bouquet garni approximately 1 hour before the end of the cooking time and remove it once the soup has extracted the right amount of flavor.

FIGURE 7-3   Preparing a Purée Soup (Senate Bean Soup)

(1) Adding beans to cold liquid to simmer.

(2) Beans and vegetables simmering.

(3) Returning partially puréed soup to pot.

Stir the soup frequently to prevent scorching. If there is a slight hint of sticking or scorching, immediately transfer the soup to a cool clean pot. Check it again for any scorched taste. If there is none, continue cooking the soup.

4. Purée the soup.

   Some soups, such as Senate bean soup, are only partially puréed. About half the ingredients are left whole to provide textural contrast. Others may be completely puréed. Depending on the quantity of soup you are making and the desired result, you may use a food mill, vertical chopping machine, food processor, blender, or burr mixer. (See Figure 7-4).

Some chefs like to control the texture and consistency of the finished soup by straining out the solids, puréeing them until smooth, and then gradually reincorporating the liquid portion of the soup. It may not be necessary to incorporate all this liquid, or it may be necessary to add a little more broth or water.

5. The soup is now ready to garnish and serve, or it may be properly cooled and stored.

Purée soups can be garnished and seasoned in a variety of ways. The relatively subtle flavor of many purée soups makes them good candidates for highly flavored seasonings and garnishes. It is important not to overdo it, however.

Croutons, diced meats, chopped herbs, and other items are typically used. Toasted or deep-fried tortillas are often used with bean soups. Consult specific recipes in this book or others for inspiration.

Refer to Part IV, Chapter 14, for individual purée soup recipes.

Bisques

Bisques, traditionally based on crustaceans such as shrimp, lobster, or crayfish, share characteristics with both purée and cream soups. Lobster, shrimp, and/or crayfish shells are seared in hot oil. Then they are simmered in stock or a fish fumet, along with aromatic vegetables. Rice is the classic thickener. Contemporary renditions often opt for roux in order to achieve a smoother texture and greater stability. A prepared velouté may also be used.

Bisques should have about the same thickness as cream soups and are usually garnished with small pieces of the appropriate shellfish or a combination of shellfish. A dash of sherry may also be added at the last moment.

A vegetable-based bisque is prepared in the same manner as a purée soup. If the vegetable does not contain enough starch to act as a thickener, rice, roux, or a starchy vegetable such as potatoes

FIGURE 7-4 Using an Immersion Blender

Using an immersion blender, or "burr" mixer, to purée a pumpkin soup.

may be used to provide additional thickness. After the vegetables are tender, the soup is puréed until a smooth, velvety texture is reached.

Mise en Place

1. Assemble and prepare all ingredients.

Coarsely chop the shellfish and/or shells. It may be a good idea to rinse them in cool water, but allow enough time for them to drain adequately.

A fish fumet or broth is often used to prepare a shellfish bisque and should be checked before use if it has been stored. Bring a small amount to a boil and taste it for any sour or off odors. Or, a prepared fish-based velouté may be used to prepare a bisque, in which case, no additional thickener need be prepared.

Peel, trim, and chop any vegetables to be used in the bisque. Mirepoix is generally included. Other ingredients used to add flavor and color include tomato paste, brandy, and dry white wine.

Rice or a prepared roux should be on hand to thicken the soup as needed as it simmers.

Cream is a common finishing ingredient for most bisques, although some recipes may call for a liaison of cream and egg yolks for additional richness and a golden hue. Diced poached pieces of shrimp, lobster, crayfish, or other appropriate shellfish are also traditionally used to garnish a bisque

2. Assemble all equipment necessary for cooking.

The requirements for bisque are identical to those of cream soup; review the information earlier in this chapter on page 304.

FIGURE 7-5 Preparing a Lobster Bisque

(1) Searing lobster in hot oil.

(2) Adding the tomato paste to cook out (pinçage).

(3) Garnishing finished bisque with diced cooked lobster meat.

Method

1. **Sear** the shells in oil or clarified butter. (See Figure 7-5 for photos illustrating method for preparing a bisque.)

   The shells are responsible for developing the flavor of a good bisque, so it is important that they be cooked until they turn a deep red or pink. Stir them frequently to cook well on all sides.

2. Add the aromatic vegetables and allow them to sweat.

   Cook the onions, garlic, shallots, leeks, or other aromatic vegetables called for along with the seared shells. This should be done over moderate heat to avoid developing a harsh flavor. It can take anywhere from 20 to 30 minutes to properly cook these aromatics.

3. Add the tomato paste and cook until it takes on a deep rust color.

   This process, known as *pinçage,* cooks the tomato paste down so it will contribute a deep, rich flavor that is not excessively sweet. Otherwise, the tomato paste could give the soup a raw flavor.

4. Add the brandy and cook it out.

   This step also continues the process of developing a complex, refined flavor base for the finished bisque. Flaming the brandy will quickly reduce it and burn off the raw alcohol, leaving behind the brandy's flavor essence.

5. Add the liquid and additional appropriate ingredients and bring the soup to a simmer.

   At this point, add the fumet or broth (or the prepared velouté, if available), along with a sachet d'épices or bouquet garni, if required. Bring the liquid up to a simmer and, if you are not using velouté, add the thickener at this point. Rice is simply stirred into the soup; roux (which should be cooler than the stock) is added carefully and whipped into the soup to prevent lumping.

   Wine and additional herbs or other aromatics are generally added at this point. Remember to taste the bisque as it simmers, and remove the sachet or bouquet once the best flavor has been transferred into the soup.

6. Simmer the bisque until it is well flavored and has a good consistency.

   Bisques take an average of about 1 hour to cook properly. At that point, all ingredients should be relatively tender, so they will purée easily, except, obviously, the shells.

   Bisques should be skimmed throughout cooking time. Stir them frequently and be sure to monitor the heat. Bisques, like any other soup with starchy ingredients, can scorch quickly if left untended for even a few minutes.

   Taste the soup (using tasting spoons and cups and following safe food-handling proce-

---

poach: a method in which items are cooked gently in a simmering liquid.

dures) so that you can make modifications during cooking time. Add additional liquid if necessary to maintain the proper balance between liquids and solids as the soup cooks.

7. Strain and purée the soup.

All the solids strained from the soup, including the shells, should be puréed until a very smooth paste forms. This mixture is then added back to the liquid portion of the soup. Then, the entire soup should be strained once more through a cheesecloth-lined sieve or colander, or a bouillon strainer.

If you are using cheesecloth, remember that it must be thoroughly rinsed in hot water to remove any fibers or traces of lint. Squeeze or wring the cheesecloth, pressing the solids left behind to extract as much flavor as possible.

8. The bisque is now ready to garnish and serve, or it may be cooled and properly stored.

If you will be serving the soup immediately, add the simmering cream or a tempered liaison, along with any other desired or suggested finishing, seasoning, or garnishing ingredients. See recipes for specific suggestions.

Refer to Part IV, Chapter 14, for individual bisque recipes.

Special Soups

This category of soups includes a number of regional and ethnic specialties that do not fit neatly into any of the basic soup categories outlined previously in this chapter. Despite the fact that they are not strictly defined as either purées, vegetable soups, or bisques, the basic techniques used to prepare them do fall within the principles detailed above. A number of recipes for regional and international soups can be found in Part IV, Chapter 14.

A brief and general definition for some of these soups follows: **Chowders** almost invariably contain potatoes; **minestrone** contains beans and pasta; **gumbos** are made with a dark roux, okra, and/or gumbo filé; in a **garbure**, some or all of the ingredients are puréed, or starchy ingredients may be in-

cluded so that the finished soup will, therefore, have more body than a clear vegetable soup.

Cold Soups

Cold soups may be prepared in a variety of ways. Some, such as **vichyssoise**, are simply cream soups that are served cold. Others, such as chilled cantaloupe soup or **gazpacho**, are based on a purée of raw or cooked ingredients that has been brought to the correct consistency by adding a liquid such as a fruit or vegetable juice. Recipes for cold soups can be found in Part IV, Chapter14.

Soup Service Guidelines

Soup is often the first dish served to a guest in a restaurant. A well-prepared soup will make a positive initial impression. Soups should always be carefully presented—hot soups hot and cold soups cold—in serving dishes that have been properly heated or chilled.

Remember that the greater the surface area of a hot soup that is exposed to the air, the more quickly the soup will cool. This is the reason that consommés and other broth-style soups are traditionally served in cups rather than the flatter, wider plates or bowls used for cream soups and purées.

Try, as much as possible, to plate all soups, but especially consommé, only when the waiter is in the kitchen, ready to pick up the order. That way, soups will not lose heat as they sit on the line waiting for pick up. Remember that the waitstaff wants foods to come out of the kitchen as perfectly as possible too. Their work depends on yours.

If waiters are responsible for plating soups themselves, be sure that their soup station has adequate space for keeping bowls and plates hot, and that all appropriate garnishes are available and at the correct temperature.

Take the time to explain to anyone involved in serving soups the importance of keeping hot soups very hot, and taking them quickly from the kitchen to the guest. Show all waiters or line cooks the way that a soup should look when it is served to the guest: garnishes, additional elements to pass or serve on the side or at table side (grated cheeses, fine oils, etc.).

Reheating Soups

Reheat small quantities of soup over direct heat throughout service, if at all possible. Thick soups should be reheated carefully, allowing them sufficient time to "soften" over low heat before bringing them up to a simmer.

Learn the best way to make use of the equipment available for service to determine how to get foods to the optimal service temperature. This aspect of foodservice requires some thought and attention to detail. Getting soups through the danger zone (see Chapter 2) quickly is important to keeping them wholesome. Maintaining soups at high temperatures for extended periods of time often compromises their flavor, aroma, and texture.

Check the temperature of soups held in a steam table. If they consistently fall short of at least 180°F (82°C), then adjust the thermostat on the steam table, have it repaired, or learn to compensate by quickly bringing individual servings up to temperature over direct heat or in a microwave. While this may seem awkward or time-consuming, it is a definite improvement over having disgruntled customers send back their soup.

Final Seasoning and Consistency Adjustments

Check the consistency and seasoning of all soups before sending them out to the patron. Storage under refrigeration, as well as holding in a steam table, has the effect of weakening a soup's flavor. And thick soups, especially those made from beans or potatoes, tend to get thicker the longer they sit. Be sure that you take the time to make all necessary adjustments. Add broth or water to thin a soup that is too thick. Add herbs, salt, pepper, condiments, fortified wines, or other seasonings to bring the flavors back to life. If nothing seems to work, then discard the soup and replace it with a fresh batch.

Garnishes

Large **garnishes**, such as dumplings, spring rolls, or wontons, should not be so large that they overwhelm the soup cup or plate selected for service. It is equally important that they not be too difficult for the guest to eat. If your garnish is not soft enough to cut through with the edge of a soup spoon, then it might be a good idea to rethink its use.

Occasionally, garnishes for soups are prepared and cooked separately. They are generally added to the soup cup individually, so that they will not cloud the consommé you have worked so hard to prepare, for instance. Since service temperature is extremely important for all thin soups, remember to also bring the garnish to service temperature before adding it to the soup. There are several ways to do this:

- Heat the garnish in a small quantity of broth, consommé, or water, and hold it in a steam table.

- Cut delicate items into shapes that will allow the heat of the soup to heat them quickly and thoroughly. (If they are small and relatively thin, they will not cause the soup's temperature to drop too severely.)

- Keep large items like wontons, dumplings, or quenelles warm and lightly moistened in a steam table.

Summary

Soup is a staple component of virtually every menu. Applying the proper preparation and handling techniques for all types of soup is a skill that every good chef must develop. In this chapter we have outlined the ways to develop good judgment to aid in the success of any soup-making endeavor, which include:

- Understanding the basic techniques for preparing, straining, cooling, and reheating broths, consommés, clear vegetable soups, cream soups, purée soups, bisques, special soups, and cold soups.

- Selecting quality products and handling them appropriately to make the best soup possible.

- Selecting the appropriate garnish and determining its size and the best methods for heating.

- Following soup service guidelines to be sure that the guest receives wholesome, delicious soups that are attractively presented at the correct temperatures.

SELF-STUDY QUESTIONS

1. What is clarification? What are the principles and procedures used in preparing a consommé?

2. What is the correct consistency for most thick soups?

3. What is the difference between a stock and a broth?

4. Explain the difference between a bisque and a cream soup.

5. Name three items used to thicken soups and describe how each is used.

6. Name the quality standards for a properly made consommé.

7. What is the proper procedure for plating soups?

8. What is the optimum size for a soup garnish?

9. Name two classic garnishes for consommé.

10. What type of poultry is the best for making a poultry broth? Why?

11. What are the indications that a consommé is developing flavor?

ACTIVITIES

- Heat a thin soup and a thick soup to a full boil. Place a serving of each in heated cups. Keep track of how long it takes for each one to cool below 165°F (74°C). What conclusions can you draw?

- Make a broth using a frying chicken and another using a stewing hen or fowl. Compare the flavors. Which do you prefer? Why?

- Prepare the Cream of Broccoli soup recipe on page 493. At step 5, divide the soup into two batches. Finish batch one with cream. Leave the second batch unfinished. Cool both batches separately. Place them in labeled storage containers, and refrigerate overnight. The next day, reheat both soups and add cream to the unfinished batch. Adjust the seasoning for both and taste, comparing flavor, texture, and color. Which do you prefer? Why?

KEYWORDS

bisque	consommé	gazpacho	pot au feu	temper
broth	cream soup	gumbo	purée soup	vegetable soup
chowder	garbure	minestrone	raft	velouté soup
clarification	garnish	pinçage (pincé)	sear	

8
Sauces

You don't need to flood a plate with sauce just for good looks. Too much sauce ruins a dish. A few teaspoons is all you need—really, that's it!

—Jasper White, Chef and Proprietor,
Restaurant Jasper

Sauces are often considered one of the greatest tests of a chef's skill. Whether they are classics, such as sauce suprême, or contemporary, such as red pepper coulis, good sauces demand the highest technical expertise. The successful pairing of a sauce with a food demonstrates an understanding of the food and an ability to judge and evaluate a dish's flavors, textures, and colors. Understanding the nuances of pairing a particular sauce with a food is something that develops throughout a chef's career, as lessons are learned about how and why certain combinations have become enduring classics. Uncovering the principles behind these pairings will form the foundation for developing a sensitivity to sauces in particular and the skill and artistry of cooking in general.

Sauces are not just an afterthought—they serve a particular function in a dish's composition. It is in learning to understand why a certain sauce will or will not work with a particular dish that the process of developing culinary judgment begins. Particular sauce combinations endure because the composition is well balanced in all areas: taste, texture, and eye appeal. Some examples of sauces that are classically combined with particular foods will help to illustrate this point.

Sauce suprême is made by reducing a chicken velouté with chicken stock and finishing it with cream. Correctly made, this ivory-colored sauce has a deep chicken flavor and a velvety texture. When served with chicken meat, the sauce's subtle color, smooth flavor, and creamy texture complement the chicken and help to intensify the meat's flavor. The addition of cream to the sauce serves to "round out" the flavors.

Sauce Robert is prepared by finishing demi-glace with mustard and a garnish of julienned cornichons. Its sharp flavors are traditionally paired with pork to cut the meat's richness. The contrast of both flavor and texture produces an effect that is pleasing, but not startling, to the palate. This pungent, flavorful sauce brings out the pork's flavor but might overwhelm a more delicate meat, such as veal.

Naturally leaner foods, such as poultry or fish, are often prepared by quick cooking methods: grilling,

sautéing, shallow poaching, or steaming. These methods are well suited to these tender cuts but, unlike slower moist heat methods, they add no additional moisture. That is why grilled steaks are commonly served with a compound butter or an emulsion sauce such as a béarnaise. The same rationale applies to serving beurre blanc with a delicate white fish that has been shallow poached. These sauces are rich, buttery, creamy preparations that add a layer of suavity and succulence to foods that, left unsauced, might seem dry or bland.

Contemporary dishes take a different approach to counteracting any potential dryness that could result from dry heat methods. Various hot and cold compotes, relishes, chutneys, or marmalades may be substituted for the classic choices.

Lightly coating a sautéed medallion of lamb with a jus lié gives the lamb a glossy finish that contributes more eye appeal to the entire plate. Pooling a red pepper coulis around a grilled swordfish steak gives the dish a degree of visual excitement by adding an element of color. Brushing ribs or chicken breasts with a barbecue sauce also enhances the look of the finished dish, glazing the item with color and flavor.

Here are some of the points to consider when selecting the appropriate sauce:

CHAPTER OBJECTIVES

- Explain the function of a sauce in relation to the other components of a dish.

- Select a suitable sauce for the style of service the cooking technique applied to the main ingredient.

- Name all the grand sauces and derivatives for each.

- Identify some contemporary and miscellaneous sauces.

- Describe and outline the techniques used to make sauces

- Explain how sauces are properly reheated, held, and plated.

The Sauce Should Be Suitable for the Style of Service In a banquet setting, or for any situation where large quantities of food must be served rapidly and at their flavor peak, it is usually best to rely on the traditional grand sauces or a contemporary sauce that shares some of the same characteristics. One of a the fundamental benefits of all grand sauces is that they may be prepared in advance and held in large quantities at the correct temperature. In an à la carte kitchen, this advantage is less important.

The sauce should be suitable for the main ingredient's cooking technique A cooking technique that produces flavorful drippings *(fond)*, such as roasting or sautéing, should logically be paired with a sauce that makes use of those drippings. Beurre blancs are suitable for foods that have been shallow poached, because the cooking liquid *(cuisson)* can become a part of the sauce instead of being discarded.

The sauce's flavor should be appropriate for the flavor of the food with which it is paired Make sure the flavor of the sauce does not overpower the flavor of the main ingredients and vice versa. Although a delicate cream sauce complements the flavor of Dover sole, it would be overwhelmed by the flavor of grilled tuna steak. By the same token, a sauce flavored with rosemary would completely overpower a delicate fish, but nicely complement lamb.

The Grand Sauces

Demi-glace, velouté, béchamel, tomato, and (in at least some instances) hollandaise are often referred to as the **grand sauces** or "mother sauces." A sauce is typicallly considered to be a grand sauce if it can meet the following basic criteria: It can be prepared in large batches, and then flavored, finished, and garnished in great variety, producing the hundreds and thousands of so-called "small sauces." This principle was still considered revolutionary in Carême's time. Escoffier's codification of sauces was considered a major advance.

Some chefs argue that because hollandaise cannot be made in advance in a large quantity and stored, and it is not intended as a base sauce used to prepare a variety of derivative sauces, it does not qualify as a grand sauce. Others feel that it should be counted as one of the grand sauces. Not only do they feel that this sauce can be used to prepare derivatives, but it also demonstrates the basic technique to yield a variety of other sauces.

Contemporary Sauces

The broad category of contemporary sauces includes jus lié, beurre blanc, coulis, compound butters, and a variety of miscellaneous sauces, such as relishes, salsas, and compotes. The primary factors distinguishing contemporary sauces from the grand sauces are the following:

- They usually take less time to prepare.
- They are more likely to be specifically tailored to a given food or technique.
- They have a lighter color, texture, and flavor than some of the grand sauces.
- They are more likely to be thickened and finished using emulsions, modified starches, or reduction and less likely to contain roux.

Techniques for Classic and Contemporary Sauces

Brown Sauce (Sauce Espagnole)

The classic method of preparing a **brown sauce**, as written by Carême, is a lengthy and involved process that calls for Bayonne ham, veal, and partridges. The contemporary version has been greatly simplified and the cooking time reduced.

Brown sauce, though rarely served on its own in today's restaurants, it is still an important preparation. It is used to prepare demi-glace, and may be used to prepare derivative sauces or gravies. It is believed that this is one of the sauces that arrived with Catharine of Aragon and the chefs in her entourage when she married Henry VIII.

Mise en Place

1. Assemble the ingredients and preparations necessary to prepare brown sauce.

Bayonne ham: a wine-cured ham produced in Bayonne, France.

The four basic elements of this sauce are:

- Brown veal stock or estouffade
- Mirepoix, cut into large dice
- Tomato purée
- Brown roux

The stock is directly responsible for the ultimate success of this sauce. It must be of excellent quality, with a rich appealing flavor and aroma. The flavor should be well balanced with no strong notes of mirepoix, herbs, or spices that might overwhelm the finished sauce. On the other hand, if the stock has a weak flavor, the sauce will be similarly lacking in taste.

The addition of mirepoix to the sauce is made at the chef's discretion. If there is sufficient flavor in the stock, then it may be unnecessary.

If tomato purée is unavailable, tomato paste, chopped tomatoes, or plain tomato sauce may be substituted. Be sure to allow whatever tomato product you select sufficient time to cook out properly.

Brown roux contributes to the flavor, color, and texture of the finished sauce. Some chefs like to make this particular roux in the oven to prevent it from developing a bitter taste.

2. Assemble and prepare the equipment necessary for preparing brown sauce.

Brown sauce is generally prepared in a saucepan or pot that is taller than it is wide. You will also need a whip to incorporate the roux into the stock (or visa versa), kitchen spoons or skimmers to skim the developing sauce, tasting spoons, fine strainers, and containers to hold the finished sauce. Additional containers are necessary for both cooling and storing the sauce.

Method

1. Sweat the mirepoix in a little oil or clarified butter until juices are released and the onions are translucent.

Sweating implies that aromatic vegetables are being cooked gently over low heat, usually in a covered pot, to encourage them to begin releasing their flavor. This is an important step in flavor development and should be given enough time.

2. Add the tomato purée and sauté until caramelized.

Allowing the tomato to "cook out" reduces any excessive sweetness, acidity, or bitterness, which might affect the finished sauce. It also encourages the development of a deep rich note that, while it should remain a subtle influence, still has a role to play in the sauce's overall flavor and aroma. This process is referred to in French as *pinçage*, a culinary term which indicates that an ingredient (usually tomatoes) is browned in fat.

3. Add brown stock to the mirepoix, bring it to a boil, and gradually incorporate the brown roux.

In order for roux to properly thicken the sauce, it is important that the stock be at a boil as the roux is incorporated. Once the roux has been whipped into the stock, allow the stock to return once more to a full boil. This allows the starches in the flour to expand quickly, beginning the process of thickening almost immediately.

Stir or whip the sauce constantly while adding the roux a little at a time. There will be a tendency for the roux to form lumps and fall to the bottom of the pot. To counteract this, keep the sauce in motion.

The correct ratio of roux to stock for a sauce is 12 ounces of roux to 1 gallon of stock. Because of the long simmering time of this stock, it is acceptable to slightly reduce the amount of roux. If too much roux is added, be sure to adjust the consistency early on in the cooking process by adding additional stock or water. In that way, the sauce's natural reduction will allow the best possible flavor to develop, despite any miscalculation with regard to roux.

4. Simmer the sauce for approximately 2 to 3 hours, skimming the surface throughout the cooking time.

Once the roux has been fully incorporated, reduce the heat to establish a slow, gentle simmer. A cooking time of up to 3 hours allows the starchy taste and feel of the roux to completely cook out of the sauce. It also permits all the flavors to properly develop.

Skim the surface of the sauce frequently throughout simmering time. Pulling the pot slightly off the center of the burner will allow the natural convection of the simmering liquid to throw the impurities to one side of the pot. This makes it easier to skim away the scum.

The flour present in the roux may easily settle on the bottom of the pot. Be sure to stir carefully with a wooden spoon from time to time during cooking to prevent the flour from sticking and scorching.

Taste the sauce frequently as it develops, so that you can stop cooking at the moment that the sauce has the best flavor, texture, and color. It should have a deep rich flavor and aroma, a lustrous sheen, some translucence, and a well-balanced taste. Hold a small amount of the sauce on your tongue, pressed against the roof of your mouth. If the sauce is properly cooked, there should be no tacky or gluey sensation.

Remember that this sauce is often reduced further, so don't add extra seasonings now.

5. Strain the sauce through a sieve.

At this point, the sauce is ready for use in other preparations, or it may be properly cooled and stored for later use. Refer to proper cooling techniques in Chapter 2.

See Part IV, Chapter 15, for the Brown Sauce recipe.

Demi-Glace

It is important to learn the procedure for making a **demi-glace,** a highly flavored, glossy sauce, even though in contemporary kitchens a jus de veau lié is often used in its place. The name "demi-glace" translates literally as "half-glaze." There are a number of **derivatives** based on demi-glace that have an important place in the chef's repertoire, some of which can be found in Table 8-1.

A demi-glace of excellent quality will have several characteristics. Demi-glace should have a full, rich flavor. The sauce is prepared from equal quantities of good brown sauce and brown veal stock (or estouffade). The flavor should be that of roasted veal. The aromatics, mirepoix, and tomatoes used in the base preparations should not overpower the main flavor of the finished sauce, but should contribute to a well-balanced taste.

Demi-glace should have a deep brown color. When properly simmered, skimmed, and reduced, demi-glace is translucent and highly glossy. Because of the reduction and also the use of roux in the brown sauce, demi-glace has noticeable body, although it should never feel tacky in the mouth. It is at the correct consistency when it evenly coats the back of a spoon (a condition known as **nappé**).

A meatless version of demi-glace is a great boon to those trying to achieve the greatest possible flavor for a vegetarian entrée. Its preparation is similar to that outlined for jus de veau lié, found later in this chapter. It is made by preparing a vegetable stock, simmering it with roasted vegetables and aromatics, and then thickening the demi-glace with arrowroot.

Mise en Place

1. Assemble the ingredients and preparations necessary for demi-glace.

Only two base preparations are required for demi-glace:

- Brown veal stock or estouffade
- Brown sauce (sauce espagnole)

No additional seasonings or aromatics are called for. Both the brown sauce and stock have already been flavored. The reduction of this sauce intensifies those flavors significantly.

2. Assemble the equipment necessary for preparing demi-glace.

The shape of the pan, as well as its gauge, are of some importance. A pan that is wider than it is tall will encourage even, rapid reduction by bringing more of the sauce into contact with the source of the heat. The greater surface area also encourages the sauce to reduce. If necessary, have some smaller pots on hand to hold the sauce as it continues to reduce.

---

jus de veau lié: cooked veal juices thickened with arrowroot to make a sauce.

TABLE 8-1 DEMI-GLACE DERIVATIVES

Sauce	Garnish	Sauce	Garnish
Bercy	Shallots, pepper, white wine, butter, diced marrow, parsley	**Périgueux**	Truffle essence, chopped truffles, Madeira
Bordelaise	Red wine reduction, glace de viande, poached marrow	**Périgourdine**	Foie gras purée, sliced truffles
Charcutière	Robert sauce, julienne of cornichons	**Piquante**	Reduction of white wine, vinegar, shallots, strained and garnished with gherkins, chervil, tarragon, pepper
Chasseur	Mushrooms, shallots, white wine, tomato concassé	**Poivrade**	Reduction of red wine marinade, peppercorns, butter
Chateaubriand	Shallots, thyme, bay leaves, mushrooms white wine, butter, tarragon, parsley	**Porto**	Reduction of port with shallots, thyme, lemon and orange juice and zest, salt, cayenne
Diable	White wine reduction, pepper mignonette, shallots, cayenne	**Robert**	White wine, onions, mustard, butter
Diane	Poivrade sauce with cream	**Romaine**	Pale caramel dissolved with vinegar, demi-glace and game stock, garnished with toasted pignolis, plumped sultanas and currants
Estragon	Tarragon		
Financière	Madeira sauce with truffle essence		
Fines Herbes	White wine, fines herbes, lemon juice		
Lyonnaise	Onions fried in butter, deglazed with white wine and vinegar; add demi-glace, strain	**Solférino**	Shallots, maître d'hôtel butter, tomato essence, cayenne, lemon
Madère/Madeira	Madeira wine	**Zingara**	Tomatoes, mushroom julienne, truffles, ham, tongue, cayenne, Madeira
Moscovite	Poivrade sauce with an infusion of juniper berries, toasted sliced almonds, currants, Marsala		

A fine strainer and cheesecloth are also necessary for the preparation of this sauce, as well as the usual containers for holding, cooling, or storing. Tasting spoons, skimmers or ladles, and kitchen spoons should also be available.

Method

1. Combine equal parts of the brown veal stock and brown sauce in a heavy-bottomed pot and bring to a boil, then reduce the heat slightly to maintain a simmer.

   A moderate cooking speed is important, to avoid scorching the sauce as it reduces. Keep an eye on this sauce as it develops, and rely on not only your eyes but also your nose to act as a watch-keeper. Depending on the quantity of demi-glace being prepared, you may want to begin transferring the sauce into successively smaller pots. This will have the effect of preventing the sauce from scorching as it cooks.

FIGURE 8-1   Reducing Demi-Glace

(1) The sauce is ready to begin reducing. Note that it pours freely from the spoon.

(2) The sauce has reduced by half. The color has changed and the sauce is noticeably thicker.

Pull the pot slightly off the center of the heat source to encourage any impurities and fat that might remain in either the brown sauce or stock to collect on one side of the pot. Skim them away as they collect. This helps to produce a sauce that is extremely translucent and glossy.

2. Simmer until the sauce is reduced to half its original volume.

The photos in Figure 8-1 show demi-glace as it begins to reduce and then when it is fully reduced. When demi-glace has the correct consistency, it will feel slightly tacky when you take a small amount into your mouth. This is acceptable. To test another way, pour a small amount of the demi-glace onto a plate. Blow on the sauce. A rose pattern that remains in the sauce should develop. (Remember to discard this test portion. Do not reintroduce it to the pot.)

3. Strain, using either the wringing or milking techniques (see Figures 8-2 and 8-3).

The sauce is now ready to serve, or to use to prepare various derivatives, or it may be properly cooled and stored, following the techniques described in Chapter 2.

FIGURE 8-2   The Wringing Method for Straining Sauces

(1) The rinsed cheesecloth is draped over a bowl and the sauce is poured into it.

(2) Two people gather up the cheesecloth, each twisting in the opposite direction from the other.

(3) Continue until all the sauce has been wrung from the cheesecloth.

FIGURE 8-3   The Milking Method for Straining Sauces

(1) Drape rinsed cheesecloth over a pot or bowl. Pour the sauce into the lined pot, with two people holding onto the corners of the cloth, as shown.

(2) Lift one corner at a time, alternating from one side to another. The other corners should be held steady. Notice that the upper left corner has been lifted.

(3) The upper right corner has been lifted. Continue alternating corners until the sauce is strained through the cheesecloth into the container.

FIGURE 8-4 Adding Fortified Wine

Add Madeira to demi-glace at the last minute for the best flavor.

See Part IV, Chapter 15, for the demi-glace recipe.

Preparing Demi-Glace Derivatives

There are a number of recipes for sauces derived from demi-glace included Chapter 15. The three main ways of finishing demi-glace to create a variety of special sauces are:

- Finishing with a fortified wine
- Reduction
- Finishing with butter *(monté au beurre)*

Fortified wines, such as port (see Figure 8-4), Madeira, marsala, or sherry, are frequently used to give a sauce a special flavor. Because these wines are so intensely flavored, it is not recommended that

they be allowed to reduce. Instead, the appropriate quantity of wine is added to the reduced sauce and blended in. Then, the sauce is served as soon as possible for the best flavor.

Reduction sauces are made by using a wine or other flavorful liquid (brandies, cognacs, juices, or essences) to deglaze a sauté pan, along with the specified aromatic or garnishing ingredients. (This may also be done independently of the sautéing process, as in the case of preparing a large batch of a special sauce for banquet service.) In some cases, especially when garnish or flavoring ingredients such as mushrooms, shallots, or tomatoes are added, they are allowed to sauté briefly to bring out their flavors. The wine, if not already added, is added at this point and allowed to reduce to intensify the flavor. Demi-glace is added to the sauce. The sauce simmers briefly, usually about 5 to 10 minutes, so that the flavors can develop fully. Then, the final seasoning adjustments are made.

See Figure 8-5 for photos illustrating the method for preparing chasseur sauce.

Finishing with butter is a step that can be employed either on its own, or as a finishing step for fortified wine sauces or reduction sauces. Whole, unsalted butter is diced and kept firm. It is swirled into the sauce, emulsifying and thickening the sauce. It is important to remember that the pan should be kept in motion the entire time that the butter is blending into the sauce.

Figure 8-6 shows butter being used to finish a chasseur sauce. This final addition of butter gives

FIGURE 8-5 Preparing Chasseur Sauce

(1) Wine is added to sautéed mushrooms.

(2) The wine is cooking away (reducing) over high heat.

(3) Demi-glace is added to the sauce chasseur. All garnish and flavoring ingredients have been reduced and cooked completely.

FIGURE 8-6
Adding Butter to
Sauce Chasseur
(*Monté au Beurre*).

the sauce a slightly more opaque appearance as well as blending all its flavors into one, rich harmonious taste.

Jus Lié

Jus lié, frequently referred to simply as "jus," is a thickened sauce made from stock (usually brown veal stock, although other stocks may be used). Some chefs prefer a relatively strict interpretation of this term. To them, it should be nothing more than either a stock or drippings from a roast lightly thickened with arrowroot.

Other chefs use it as a replacement for the classic grand sauce, demi-glace. Although similar to a demi-glace in appearance and use, jus lié requires less cooking time because it contains a modified starch (arrowroot, for example) as a thickener. It also has a greater degree of clarity, translucence, and sheen, but a less deep and complex flavor and a somewhat lighter texture and color. It may be used in the preparation of many other sauces, in the same way that demi-glace is employed. Jus lié is often used to deglaze pans and create sauces that are specifically tailored to sautés or roasts. It may be flavored or finished using any of the methods described above for demi-glace.

Another way in which jus lié can be varied is to introduce the flavor of a special spice or herb. For example, sprigs of rosemary or tarragon may be added to the jus lié as it develops. This would rarely be done as a step in preparing demi-glace, since the object of demi-glace is to produce a foundation sauce where a single, pronounced flavor might be inappropriate for some uses. Since jus lié does not require the lengthy simmering called for with demi-glace, it is more appropriate to make smaller, more customized batches.

Jus de veau lié indicates that the sauce was made with a brown veal stock as its base. It is possible to use an array of other base stocks, to further vary the range of possibilities with jus lié. Brown stocks based on poultry, game, pork, or even vegetable stocks are often used to make jus lié in kitchens today.

Mise en Place

1. Assemble the ingredients and preparations necessary to prepare jus lié.

   The four basic elements of jus lié are:

   - Brown stock
   - Mirepoix, cut into large dice
   - Tomato purée
   - Arrowroot, diluted in a cold liquid (slurry)

   The stock is directly responsible for the ultimate success of this sauce. It must be of excellent quality, with a rich appealing flavor and aroma. The flavor should be well balanced with no strong notes of mirepoix, herbs, or spices that might overwhelm the finished sauce. On the other hand, if the stock has a weak flavor, the sauce will be similarly lacking in taste. Jus lié is prepared with a brown stock: veal, chicken, game, pork, or vegetable.

   The addition of mirepoix to the sauce is made at the chef's discretion. If there is sufficient flavor in the stock, then it may be unnecessary.

   If tomato purée is unavailable, tomato paste, chopped tomatoes, or plain tomato sauce may be substituted. Be sure to allow whatever tomato product you select sufficient time to cook out properly.

   There are a number of possible additions to the basic list. Wine (a dry table wine, red or white according to the desired result) is a frequent addition. It may be added to the sauce as it simmers, or it may be used in place of water to dilute the arrowroot. Mushroom trimmings, herbs (whole sprigs or stems), ginger, garlic, shallots, or dried fruits and vegetables may also be added to the sauce as it develops. Many chefs also like to add a quantity of well-browned meaty bones or lean trim meat.

2. Assemble and prepare the equipment necessary for preparing jus lié.

Jus lié is generally prepared in a saucepan or pot that is wider than it is tall. This is the most effective means of extracting flavors fully and quickly into the finished sauce. You will also need kitchen spoons or skimmers to skim the developing sauce, tasting spoons, fine strainers, and containers to hold the finished sauce. Additional containers are necessary for both cooling and storing the sauce.

FIGURE 8-7
Adding diluted arrowroot to prepare jus de veau lié.

Method

1. Sweat the mirepoix in a little oil or clarified butter until juices are released and onions are golden. (See page 318 for information on sweating)

   This is an important step in flavor development and should be given enough time. It is best to let the mirepoix develop a deep golden color.

   An alternative to sweating the vegetables is to roast them. This eliminates the need to add extra fat to the sauce.

2. Add the tomato purée and sauté until caramelized.

   Allowing the tomato to "cook out" reduces any excessive sweetness, acidity, or bitterness, which might affect the finished sauce. It also encourages the development of the sauce's overall flavor and aroma. If you are roasting the vegetables to brown them, add the tomato purée to the roasting pan at the same time.

3. Add brown stock to the mirepoix, bring it to a boil, and simmer over low heat for 4 to 6 hours.

   In order for the sauce to develop the richest flavor possible, it is important that it be allowed to simmer long enough.

   Skim the surface of the sauce frequently throughout simmering time. Pulling the pot slightly off the center of the burner will allow the natural convection of the simmering liquid to throw the impurities to one side of the pot. This makes it easier to skim away the scum.

   Taste the sauce frequently as it develops, so that you can stop cooking at the moment that the sauce has developed its full characer. It should have a deep rich flavor and aroma, a lustrous sheen, some translucence, and a well-balanced taste.

4. Add the slurry to the simmering sauce, and continue to cook for another 2 to 3 minutes.

   The arrowroot (or cornstarch) should lightly thicken the sauce, so that it will coat the back of a spoon. Add the slurry gradually, so that you don't inadvertently overthicken the sauce. (See Figure 8-7).

5. Strain the sauce through a sieve. At this point, the sauce is ready for use in other preparations, or it may be properly cooled and stored for later use. Refer to proper cooling techniques in Chapter 2.

   See Part IV, Chapter 15, for recipes for jus lié.

Velouté

This sauce, used to prepare numerous white sauces, has a name that translates from French as "velvety, soft, and smooth to the palate." A truly excellent **velouté** should meet several criteria. The flavor of a velouté should reflect the stock used in its preparation: white veal, which will be nearly neutral in flavor; chicken; or fish. It is thickened with an appropriate amount of pale roux (see Table 8-2).It should have a pale ivory color, with absolutely no hint of gray. Although a velouté will never be transparent, it should be translucent, lustrous, and have a definite sheen. Velouté should be perfectly smooth, with no hint of graininess. The sauce should have a noticeable body, thick enough to coat the back of a spoon, yet still easy to pour from a ladle.

The number of sauces that can be derived from velouté is second only to those derived from demiglace. Some of the classic small sauces made from velouté are listed in Table 8-3. Additionally, veloutés are also used to prepare soups, as we have seen in Chapter 7.

Mise en Place

1. Assemble the necessary ingredients and preparations to prepare velouté.

The basic required items to prepare a velouté are:

- White stock (veal, chicken, fish, or vegetable)
- Pale roux
- Optional seasoning or flavoring ingredients as desired

Mushroom trimmings (about 5 ounces per gallon of velouté) are occasionally added for additional flavor, if they are available. A sachet d'épices or bouquet garni may also be included. If used, add these ingredients at the point indicated in the method below.

The amount of roux required varies according to the desired consistency of the finished velouté. A medium consistency is used for most sauces. A light consistency is required for soups. A heavy consistency is used for a binder, such as would be required to prepare a croquette. See Table 8-2 for the correct ratio of roux to liquid.

A broth or stock can also be thickened with an arrowroot or cornstarch slurry to create a lighter sauce. This will eliminate the additional fat found in traditional roux-thickened veloutés. This sauce has a more limited shelf-life, however, and does not stand up well to being held in a steam table.

TABLE 8-2 RATIOS FOR LIGHT, MEDIUM, AND HEAVY VELOUTÉ AND BÉCHAMEL

Consistency	Roux	Liquid
Light	10–12 ounces	1 gallon
Medium	12–16 ounces	1 gallon
Heavy	18–20 ounces	1 gallon

TABLE 8-3 VELOUTÉ DERIVATIVES

Sauce	Base stock	Garnish
Albufera	Veal	Suprême sauce with meat glaze and pimento butter
Allemande	Veal	Mushrooms
Anchois	Fish	Normande sauce, anchovy butter, minced anchovy fillets
Aromates	Veal	Infusion of thyme, basil, marjoram, chives, shallots, pepper, garnished with chervil, blanched tarragon, lemon juice
Aurore	Veal/fish	Suprême sauce flavored with tomato
Bercy	Fish	Shallots, butter, white wine, parsley
Bonnefoy	Veal	Tarragon
Bretonne	Veal/fish	Julienned leeks, celery, onions, mushrooms, all cooked in butter
Chivry	Chicken	Infusion of chervil, parsley, tarragon, chives, pimpernel, white wine, strained, chive butter added
Crevettes	Fish	Shrimp butter
Curry	Veal	Onions, apple, curry powder, coconut milk, strained, cream added
Diplomate	Fish	Normande sauce, lobster butter, garnished with lobster and truffles
Hongroise	Veal	Suprême sauce, onions, paprika, white wine
Huîtres	Fish	Normande sauce, oyster juice, poached oysters
Ivoire	Veal	Suprême sauce, pale meat glaze
Joinville	Fish	Crayfish and shrimp coulis, julienne of truffles
Livonienne	Fish	Julienne of truffles and carrots, parsley
Normande	Fish	Mushroom/oyster essence, yolks, butter, cream
Ravigote	Veal	Reduction of white wine and vinegar, shallot butter, garnished with chervil, chives, tarragon
Suprême	Chicken	Reduced with heavy cream
Vin Blanc	Fish	Shallots, butter, fines herbes

FIGURE 8-8   Preparing Velouté

(1) The pot is slightly off the center of the burner, and a kitchen spoon is used to push the impurities to one side.

(2) Lifting the scum from the surface of the sauce.

(3) Straining the sauce. Note the skin that has formed.

(4) The texture, color, and sheen of a finished velouté.

2. Assemble the necessary equipment to prepare velouté.

When selecting a pot, avoid aluminum pans, which might cause the finished velouté to take on a grayish cast. Wooden spoons are less likely to impart an off color to this delicately colored sauce. Remember that you will also need tasting spoons, a skimmer, a fine sieve or cheesecloth for straining, and storage or service containers for the finished sauce.

Method

1. Bring the stock to a simmer. Gradually whip in the roux.

In order for roux to properly thicken the sauce, it is important that the stock be at a boil as the roux is incorporated. Once the roux has been whipped into the stock, allow the stock to return once more to a full boil. This allows the starches in the flour to expand quickly, beginning the process of thickening almost immediately.

Stir or whip the sauce constantly while adding the roux a little at a time. There will be a tendency for the roux to form lumps and fall to the bottom of the pot. To counteract this, keep the sauce in motion.

If you are making the roux as part of the sauce-making procedure, it can be prepared directly in the pot you are using. Then add the stock gradually to the roux. The stock should be cooler than the roux, but it does not have to be cold. To make the process go more efficiently, bring the stock to a simmer, then remove it from the heat as you make the pale roux. Add the stock gradually, whipping constantly, to work out all lumps from the sauce.

2. Bring to a full boil, then reduce the heat to establish a simmer.

Once the roux has been fully incorporated and a true boil reached, reduce the heat until a slow, gentle simmer is established. If you plan to add extra flavoring ingredients, they should be added now. A cooking time of at least 30 min-

---

croquette: mixtures of pureed meat or vegetables, bound with velouté, coated, and deep fried.

utes (some chefs prefer to simmer up to 1 hour) will effectively cook away any residual starches in the roux's flour. It also permits any impurities that might affect the final flavor, texture, and appearance of the sauce to be thrown to the surface where they can be skimmed away.

Pulling the pot slightly off the center of the burner will allow the natural convection of the simmering liquid to throw the impurities to one side of the pot. As you can see in Figure 8-8, the chef has placed the pot properly. Then a kitchen spoon is used to first push these impurities to one side and then lift them from the surface of the sauce.

Stir the sauce carefully, using a wooden spoon. Make sure that the spoon scrapes the bottom of the pot, releasing any buildup before it scorches.

Taste the sauce frequently as it develops, so you can stop cooking at the moment that the sauce has the best flavor, texture, and color. It should have the distinct flavor of the stock you have selected. The aroma and taste will have a very slight nuttiness from the addition of roux. Any optional additions, such as mushroom trimmings or a bouquet garni, should serve to enhance the overall flavor of the sauce.

A good-quality velouté should have a discernable body and aroma, a lustrous sheen, some translucence, and a well-balanced taste. Hold a small amount of the sauce on your tongue, pressed against the roof of your mouth. If the sauce is properly cooked, there should be no tacky or gluey sensation.

3. Strain the sauce through a fine sieve.

As the sauce simmers, it will almost inevitably develop a thick skin on its surface, as well as a heavy, gluey layer on the bottom and sides of the pot. Straining the sauce at this point removes any of these impurities. For a truly velvety texture, use either the wringing or milking method to strain the sauce once more through cheesecloth. (See Figures 8-2 and 8-3.) The sauce is now ready to be served or it may be properly cooled and stored for later use, following the steps outlined in Chapter 2.

See Part IV, Chapter 15, for the recipe for velouté.

Béchamel

According to legend, the Marquis Louis de Béchameil (noted for his financial acumen) was responsible for the development of this classic sauce. Whether or not it was he, this sauce has become a permanent part of the basic repertoire of sauces. Originally, a béchamel sauce was made by adding cream to a relatively thick velouté sauce, thinning and finishing it. Today, it is made by thickening milk with a white roux and simmering it with aromatics.

When properly prepared, **béchamel** should have a creamy flavor, reflecting its base liquid—milk. There should be no taste of roux remaining if the sauce has been allowed to simmer for a sufficient time. Béchamel should have the color of heavy cream—slightly ivory. Although béchamel is essentially opaque, the finished sauce will have a definite sheen. It should be perfectly smooth, with no graininess.

Béchamel and velouté may both be prepared with light, medium, or heavy consistencies. (Refer to Table 8-2 for ratios of roux to liquid.) Light béchamel can be used as the basis for cream soups. Medium béchamel is used as a sauce. Heavy béchamel can be used as a binder for fillings, stuffings, or baked macaroni dishes.

The number of derivative or small sauces made with béchamel is not as extensive as that for either demi-glace or velouté. There are some classic sauces that should be part of your repertoire, however. Table 8-4 gives the basic garnishes required for béchamel-based sauces.

Mise en Place

1. Assemble the ingredients and preparations necessary for béchamel.

Relatively few ingredients are required to make a good béchamel sauce. They are:

- Milk
- White roux, prepared with oil
- Aromatics

Be sure to check the milk's quality before beginning the process. When milk is very cold, it is often easy to miss the early signs of souring. It is also nearly impossible to tell if the milk has absorbed odors from other foods in the reach-in or walk-in. Bring a small amount to a boil and check it carefully. The milk should smell sweet and have a smooth appearance, with no curdling evident.

If you prefer to make the roux as part of the overall process, you will need to have vegetable oil and all-purpose flour on hand, instead of a prepared roux. This technique is illustrated in Figure 8-9.

The selection of aromatics can make a distinct difference in the finished sauce. In Figure 8-9, the béchamel is being prepared with diced onions that have been allowed to sweat. Some chefs prefer to use an oignon piqué (a whole or halved onion that has been studded with whole cloves and a piece of bay leaf). Even if you do not use a oignon piqué, you may want to add a whole clove or two, a piece of bay leaf, or even a sprig of fresh thyme to give extra depth to the flavor of this sauce. A final addition of grated nutmeg is considered essential by many. Be wary, however, since nutmeg has a strong flavor and cannot be removed from the sauce once you have put it in.

TABLE 8-4 BÉCHAMEL DERIVATIVES

Sauce	Garnish
Aomard à l'Anglaise	Anchovy essence, cayenne, diced lobster
Bohémienne	Served cold, made into mayonnaise, finished with tarragon vinegar
Cardinal	Fish stock, truffle essence, cream, lobster butter
Céleri	Celery hearts cooked in white consommé, onion pierced with clove, strained, cream sauce mixed in
Crème	Cream, lemon juice
Ecossaise	Thin béchamel with julienned hard-boiled egg white and finely crumbled hard-boiled yolks
Mornay	Butter, grated Gruyère and Parmesan
Oeufs à l'Anglaise	Diced hard-boiled egg, nutmeg
Shrimp	Fish stock, shrimp, butter
Soubise	Chopped onions, puréed

2. Assemble the equipment necessary to prepare béchamel.

When selecting a pot, avoid aluminum pans, which might cause the finished velouté to take on a grayish cast. A pot that is relatively heavy is important for this sauce, since it, more than any other, is likely to scorch as it simmers.

Wooden spoons are less likely to impart an off color to this delicately colored sauce. Remember that you will also need tasting spoons, a skimmer, a fine sieve or cheesecloth for straining, and storage or service containers for the finished sauce.

Method

1. Sweat the minced onion in a small amount of oil. (See Figure 8-9 for photos illustrating the method for preparing béchamel.)

Since you want the finished sauce to have a distinctly white color, be sure that the onion is allowed to sweat in a covered pot over low heat until it softens and becomes translucent. There should be no browning, but the onion should be fully cooked, so that it will not give a sulfurous aroma to the finished sauce.

2. Add the flour to the onion and prepare a white roux.

Stir the flour into the onions until it is evenly blended and allow the roux to cook over low heat for several minutes. This will begin to remove the raw flavor from the flour. It also imparts an understated nutty aroma to the finished sauce. For a perfectly white or very pale sauce, do not allow the roux to become even slightly golden at this stage.

If you have a prepared roux on hand, then this step is not necessary. Instead, you would proceed as described for velouté. Add the milk to the smothered onions and bring it to a boil and gradually whip in the roux.

3. Gradually add the milk to the roux and bring the sauce to a simmer.

As always when working with roux and a liquid, be sure that they are not the same temperature. If you intend to make the roux, as illustrated in

FIGURE 8-9   Preparing Béchamel Sauce and a Mornay Derivative

(1) The flour for the roux is being cooked along with the diced onions.

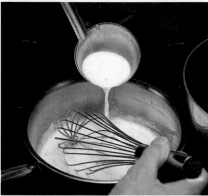

(2) Adding the cool milk to the roux gradually.

(3) Adding grated Gruyère to strained béchamel for Mornay sauce.

(4) The finished Mornay sauce.

the accompanying photographs, the milk can be brought to a simmer, then pulled off the heat to cool while preparing the roux. If you do use oignon piqué, it can be added to the milk as it comes to a simmer, then allowed to steep in the milk as it rests off the heat.

Use a whip or wooden spoon to gradually mix together the liquid and roux. Add any additional ingredients you have selected—thyme, bay leaf, cloves, or oignon piqué now.

Simmer the sauce for 30 minutes to 1 hour. Scorching is even more of a concern with béchamel than any other sauce. Not only will the starches in the flour try to settle out, so will the milk solids. Use a flame diffuser, if you have one, to help prevent scorching.

Follow the same skimming procedure as for velouté and remember to taste the sauce as it develops. As soon as the taste of the flour is no longer evident, the sauce has cooked enough.

4. Add the grated nutmeg to taste before straining the sauce.

For many chefs, nutmeg is an indispensable component of béchamel. Remember, however, that it should only be added if it will not interfere with the intended flavor of the finished sauce. Nutmeg is a powerful flavoring and should be added judiciously, a little at a time.

5. The sauce is now ready for service, or it may be cooled and stored properly as explained in Chapter 2.

See Part IV, Chapter 15, for the recipe for béchamel sauce.

Tomato Sauce

Tomato sauce was a relative late-comer to the society of grand sauces, since tomatoes had first to arrive in Europe from the New World. Once there, they had to overcome the serious prejudice against them. Many people actually feared that they were poisonous. Still, once assimilated (most likely at some point in the nineteenth century), tomatoes became critical in not only this sauce, but also, as you have seen, as a flavoring ingredient in other sauces.

Although the number of derivative sauces made from a basic tomato sauce are not as great as for demi-glace, béchamel, or velouté, it is an important sauce in any kitchen. There are several approaches to making tomato sauce. In some versions, olive oil is used as the only cooking fat. For others, rendered salt pork or bacon is required. Some recipes call for the use of roasted veal or pork bones; others are made strictly from tomatoes and vegetables. Refer to Table 8-5 for a listing of some typical tomato sauces.

Tomato sauce is frequently served as an accompaniment to crisp fried foods, vegetable dishes, pastas, or certain sautéed foods. It has a distinctive texture, less smooth and refined than the sauces we have discussed to this point.

Tomato sauce should have a deep, rich tomato flavor, with no trace of bitterness, excess acidity, or sweetness. Any of the optional ingredients selected to flavor the sauce should provide underpinnings for the flavor of tomatoes. Once the sauce is properly made, it is perfectly acceptable to add garnishing, finishing, or seasoning ingredients that will lend a special flavor, of course.

Tomato sauce will be opaque, but proper simmering, puréeing, and straining will lend it some sheen. This sauce should be slightly more coarse than any other of the grand sauces because of the degree of texture that remains even after puréeing and straining the tomatoes. The sauce should be relatively smooth, thick enough to coat the back of a spoon, and thin enough to pour easily.

Mise en Place

1. Assemble the ingredients and preparations necessary for tomato sauce.

Because of the number of different recipes for tomato sauce, there is a wide range of ingredients and preparations that might be required. Review the recipe or formula you have selected and use that as a guide. The basic components are outlined below:

- Plum tomatoes (fresh or canned)
- Tomato purée (fresh or canned)
- Ground salt pork, oil, or clarified butter
- Stock: veal, chicken, beef, pork, or vegetable as desired

TABLE 8-5 TOMATO SAUCES

Tomato	Garnish
Chaudfroid	Aspic jelly
Meat	Cooked ground beef, veal, and/or pork
Nantua	Mirepoix sautéed with crayfish butter, white wine, cognac, fresh tomatoes, fish velouté, cayenne
Portugaise	Fried onions, concassé, salt, pepper, thin tomato sauce, meat glaze, garlic, parsley
Provençale	Sliced mushrooms, oil, salt, pepper, sugar, garlic, parsley

- Aromatic vegetables, cut into a medium dice
- Sachet d'épices or bouquet garni
- Additional or optional flavoring or seasoning items

Plum tomatoes, sometimes referred to as Romas, are generally preferred for tomato sauces, since they have a relatively good ratio of flesh to skin and seeds. When fresh tomatoes are at their peak, it may be a good idea to use them exclusively. At other times of the year, good-quality canned tomatoes are preferred. Fresh tomatoes should be chopped. Canned tomatoes may be whole, puréed, or a combination of the two. In some cases, you may want or need to add tomato paste for additional flavor and texture as well.

Roasted bones of veal or pork or browned lean trimmings of these meats are sometimes included in a tomato sauce. One classic tomato sauce, Bolognese, includes a good quantity of beef and is considered a *ragu* (stew) by most Italians. The presence of meat is not an absolute requirement for all tomato sauces, however. A *marinara* sauce, the foundation of many dishes found throughout various regions of Italy, is described in many traditional renditions as a simple, quickly prepared sauce made of olive oil, garlic, onions, and chopped tomatoes.

Some recipes may call for a standard mirepoix as the aromatic vegetable component. Others may rely more simply on garlic and onions. Let your recipe or your palate be your guide.

A variety of herbs and spices pair well with tomatoes. This makes it easy to "customize" a sauce to suit a particular need. You might want to use only basil for a sauce destined to accompany a dish of pasta. Or, you may want to introduce a more exotic flavoring to serve with a Middle Eastern-style stuffed vegetable entrée.

2. Assemble the equipment necessary for preparing tomato sauce.

Tomatoes are high-acid foods, so it is best to select a pot that is nonreactive, such as stainless steel or anodized aluminum. The gauge of the pot is important also. Because of the high sugar content of tomatoes, you need to establish even heat with as few hot spots as possible so the sauce won't scorch.

A food mill or sieve is used to purée the sauce. For a very smooth texture, you may then wish to use a blender, food processor, or immersion blender as a final step.

Method

1. Heat the oil, butter, or ground salt pork in a pot over low heat. Then, add the aromatic vegetables and allow them to sweat.

The onions should become translucent, and juices should begin to be released from all the vegetables. It is acceptable to cook the onions to a rich golden brown, especially if you need to develop a sweet flavor to counteract any excess acidity present in the tomatoes.

2. Add the remaining ingredients and bring to a simmer.

Add the tomatoes along with any stock or broth required by the recipe. Any vegetables or flavoring ingredients not already added to the saucepan should be added now.

3. Simmer the sauce until the flavor is fully developed and strain.

Depending on whether the tomatoes are fresh or canned as well as the type of sauce you are preparing, there may be distinct differences in cooking times. The drier the tomatoes, the more quickly the sauce will complete cooking.

Stir frequently throughout cooking and check the flavor occasionally. It may be necessary to correct a harsh or bitter flavor by sweating a small

FIGURE 8-10 Preparing Tomato Sauce

(1) The sauce has simmered and is ready to purée.

(2) Using a food mill to purée the sauce.

(3) This portion of the purée should be scraped from the food mill and stirred into the sauce.

(4) Finishing a puréed tomato sauce with chopped fresh oregano, basil, and parsley.

amount of additional chopped onion and carrots separately and adding them to the sauce. If the flavor is weak, add a small amount of reduced tomato paste or purée. A too-sweet sauce may be corrected by adding more tomatoes, stock, or water.

Strain the sauce through a colander or coarse sieve once it has reached the desired flavor. Remove and discard any bones and the sachet or bouquet, if you have used them. Press well on the solids remaining in the colander to extract all the juices.

4. Purée the sauce through a food mill fitted with a fine disk.

Using a food mill is the best way to produce a sauce with the correct consistency. If you prefer a really smooth sauce, purée the sauce a second time using a food processor, blender, or immersion blender.

5. The sauce is ready to serve now or it may be properly cooled and stored as explained in Chapter 2.

See Figure 8-10 for photos illustrating the method for preparing tomato sauce. Refer to Part IV, Chapter 15, for tomato sauce recipes.

Coulis

Before the codification of sauces into the grand sauces and their derivatives, any sauce would most likely have gone by the name of **coulis.** Certain soups were also known as coulis, especially those based on game and game birds.

Today, coulis generally indicates a sauce that is essentially a purée of a vegetable, such as red peppers, broccoli, or tomatoes. In fact, the method of preparation is quite similar to that described for a tomato sauce, explained above: Aromatic vegetables and herbs are allowed to sweat; the major flavoring ingredient is added along with a liquid such as broth, stock, vegetable or fruit juices, or water. The sauce is then simmered until tender enough to purée.

A coulis may be finished with cream or butter, flavored or garnished with a variety of ingredients, such as chopped fresh herbs, julienne, or dice of the main flavoring ingredient, and so forth. Refer

FIGURE 8-11   Preparing Red Pepper Coulis

(1) The diced peppers, ready to cook.

(2) The finished, puréed coulis, being flavored with fresh herbs.

to the coulis recipe found in Part IV, Chapter 15, for specific information about mise en place, ingredients, and method.

See Figure 8-11 for photos illustrating the method for preparing red pepper coulis.

Hollandaise

This sauce was named in a recognition of the high quality of butter and other dairy products produced in Holland. Since the largest proportion of a **hollandaise** is butter, the sauce will succeed or fail according to not only the skillful balance between egg yolks, reduction, and butter, but also the quality of the butter itself.

Hollandaise belongs to a group of sauces known as **emulsion sauces.** An emulsion is formed when one substance is suspended in another—in this case, melted or clarified butter is suspended in partially cooked egg yolks. It is fragile because it is not a true mixture and could separate easily into its distinct components. In other words, it could "break." Other examples of emulsion sauces include mayonnaise, beurre blancs, vin blancs, and vinaigrettes.

Hollandaise should be a pale lemon color with a satin-smooth texture and appearance. The hollandaise-style sauces described in Table 8-6 may have slightly different colors. Sauce choron, for instance, contains tomato purée, which will give the finished sauce a pale orange color.

Mise en Place

1. Assemble the ingredients and preparations necessary for hollandaise. To prepare a hollandaise you will need:

- Unsalted butter, melted or clarified, and warm
- Egg yolks
- Reduction
- Water
- Fresh lemon juice
- Additional or optional seasoning, flavoring, or garnish ingredients

Opinions differ on whether to use clarified or melted whole butter. Some chefs feel that clarified butter results in a more stable sauce. Others prefer melted whole butter. Then some of the milk solids can be blended into the sauce, giving it a creamier flavor. Whichever approach you take, remember that the best results are achieved when the butter and properly cooked egg yolks are at the same temperature.

The reduction for a hollandaise is prepared as outlined in step 1 of the method for hollandaise below. It consists of water and/or dry white wine, white wine vinegar, minced shallots, and cracked peppercorns.

The seasonings and consistency adjustments needed for this sauce are generally quite simple: Freshly squeezed lemon juice, salt, finely ground white pepper, and a bit of water, if necessary.

2. Assemble all equipment necessary to prepare a hollandaise.

As shown in Figure 8-12, hollandaise is frequently prepared by mixing the sauce in a bowl set over a pot of simmering water. A small saucepan is necessary to make the reduction, and a small fine strainer to strain the finished reduction (if desired). If necessary, the finished sauce can be strained through rinsed cheesecloth.

A whip is used to incorporate the butter and a ladle is necessary to add the butter to the egg yolks in a gradual stream. Once the sauce is prepared, it may be kept warm directly in the container used to prepare it, or it may be transferred to a clean bain-marie or wide-necked vacuum bottle.

Method

1. Make the reduction and add a small amount of water to cool it. Transfer the reduction (strained, if desired) to a stainless steel bowl. (See Figure 8-12 for photos illustrating the method for preparing a hollandaise.)

Cook the ingredients for the reduction over moderate heat until the liquid is almost completely cooked away (au sec). This initial reduction of water and/or wine, vinegar, shallots, and cracked peppercorns gives the sauce a certain brightness of flavor. Without it, the combination of egg yolks and butter would result in a sauce that is almost deadeningly rich.

The reduction must be cooled down to avoid overcooking the egg yolks. Be careful not to add too much water, however. Usually, a teaspoon or

TABLE 8-6 WARM BUTTER EMULSION SAUCES (HOLLANDAISE-STYLE)

Sauce	Garnish
Bavaroise	Reduction of pepper, horseradish, thyme, bay leaves, parsley, vinegar, crayfish, garnish with crayfish tails
Béarnaise	Tarragon and chervil
Choron	Béarnaise sauce with tomato
Foyot	Béarnaise sauce with meat glaze
Maltaise	Blood orange
Mousseline	Whipped cream
Noisette	Brown butter
Paloise	Mint
Rubens	Reduction of white wine, mirepoix, and fish stock, strain, add crayfish butter, anchovy sauce

Figure 8-12 Preparing Hollandaise

(1) Egg yolks in a bowl with strained reduction.

(2) Whipping the egg yolks over simmering water until thickened and frothy.

(3) A clean side towel is used to steady the bowl while the butter is incorporated.

(4) Butter is added in a thin stream while the chef is whipping constantly.

(5) Hollandaise at the proper consistency. Note the ribbons left in the sauce by the whip.

(6) A broken hollandaise.

so is enough to moisten and cool the reduction sufficiently. To avoid the need to strain the sauce later, strain the reduction now into the bowl or pot you will use to prepare the sauce.

The stainless steel bowl can be replaced with the top of a double boiler, if you have one. Some chefs may prefer to make the sauce directly in the pan used for the reduction, working carefully over direct heat. This calls for extreme care and attention throughout cooking to avoid scrambling the eggs. It is also a good idea to use a pan that is not made of a reactive metal such as aluminum, that might cause the sauce to become a little gray.

2. Add egg yolks to the reduction and whip over barely simmering water until they are thickened and frothy.

A successful hollandaise is most easily prepared when the egg yolks are cooked to exactly the right point—thickened and frothy but still very liquid. They should be very warm, but not hot enough to scramble. The yolks will increase in volume as they cook.

If they seem to be getting too hot and begin coagulating slightly around the sides and bottom of the bowl or pot, remove the bowl or pan from the heat. Set it on a cool surface and continue to whip until the mixture has cooled very slightly. Then continue cooking the sauce over simmering water.

Be sure that the water is just barely simmering. There should be no visible signs of boiling, just plenty of steam rising from the surface.

TIPS TO RESCUE A BROKEN HOLLANDAISE

The butter and eggs should be at about the same temperature for the best results during mixing the sauce. If the eggs are cooler than the butter, it could cause the sauce to take on a curdled appearance since the egg yolks might further cool the butter. If that happens, continue to whip the sauce over the simmering water until the sauce loses its oily, curdled appearance before adding more butter.

If the butter is a great deal hotter than the eggs (or if the water is allowed to come to a boil under the sauce), then it is possible that the eggs might begin to overcook. In that case, the sauce will develop a "scrambled-eggs" appearance. To counteract this, immediately add a little cold water to the sauce and remove it from the heat. Set the bowl on a cool surface, such as a stainless steel work table, and continue to whip until the sauce looks smooth once more. If it does not become smooth, you will need to strain the sauce before continuing with its preparation.

3. Add warm butter gradually in a thin stream, whipping constantly. Season to taste as desired.

You will need both hands free to whip and ladle the butter into the egg yolks. Therefore, it is a good precaution to stabilize the bowl over the simmering water. Drape a clean side towel between the bottom of the bain-marie and the bowl to steady it, if you have not already done so.

Add the butter a little at a time, whipping constantly as it is incorporated. The sauce will begin to thicken as more butter is blended in. Continue adding butter and whipping until the sauce is thickened and all the butter is incorporated. Figure 8-12 shows the sauce as it develops.

Add salt, pepper, or lemon juice to taste as the sauce is nearly finished. Lemon juice will lighten the sauce's flavor and texture, but do not let it become a dominant taste. Add just enough to lift the flavor. If the sauce is too thick, you may want to add a little warm water to regain the desired light texture.

You may also want to strain the sauce at this point through cheesecloth or a fine sieve, especially if the reduction was not already strained. If care is taken throughout preparation, straining the sauce should be unnecessary, however.

4. The sauce is now ready to serve. Keep it warm (at around 160°F/70°C).

Hollandaise is a delicate sauce in more ways than one. Not only is it easy to break the emulsion by letting the sauce become too warm, it is also easy to inadvertently create a situation that might encourage the growth of pathogens (e.g., the salmonella bacteria) that could cause a food-borne illness. The quantity of egg yolks and butter (both potentially hazardous foods) in the sauce makes it a likely target. Be sure that any containers you transfer the cooked sauce into are perfectly clean. Stainless steel bain-maries or vacuum bottles with wide necks are good choices.

Keep all spoons and ladles used to serve the sauce meticulously clean and never reintroduce a used tasting spoon, bare fingers, or other sources of cross-contamination into the sauce.

Hollandaise should never be held longer than 2 to 3 hours. Discard any unused hollandaise after that point.

See Part IV, Chapter 15, for the recipe for hollandaise sauce.

Beurre Blanc

There are many stories about how, when, and by whom, beurre blanc was first made. One such story makes the claim that a renowned female chef in France created the sauce. According to Mapie, the Countess de Toulouse-Lautrec, in her book *La Cuisine de France*, Mme. Clémence first created the sauce as an accompaniment to salmon and other freshwater fish that abounded in the Loire River.

Beurre blanc, like hollandaise, is a sauce in which butter forms an emulsion with a reduction. Traditionally, the reduction consists of the cooking liquid (*cuis-*

son) used to prepare shallow-poached dishes. These poaching liquids often contain wine, which makes this sauce similar in nature to a *sauce vin blanc* (see below). It is also possible to prepare a reduction separately, as for hollandaise. Occasionally, a quantity of reduced heavy cream is added to this sauce to stabilize it, so that it can be held during a service period.

Mise en Place

1. Assemble the ingredients and preparations necessary for beurre blanc. To make beurre blanc, you should have:

FIGURE 8-13
Whipping Butter into Beurre Blanc

   - Whole unsalted butter, diced and chilled

   - Reduction

   - Reduced heavy cream (optional)

   - Additional seasoning, flavoring, or garnish ingredients, as needed

   Just as the quality of the butter is critical to the success of a hollandaise, it is equally important to a beurre blanc. Unsalted butter is best, since the presence of extra salt is not necessarily desirable. You can always add salt to taste later on. Check the butter carefully for a rich, sweet, creamy texture and aroma.

   The reduction for a beurre blanc may include a variety of ingredients. Those ingredients most commonly used include an acid such as a dry wine, vinegar, or citrus juice; minced shallots, garlic, or ginger; chopped herbs including tarragon, basil, chives, or chervil; the cooking liquid used to poach fish or chicken (especially when the court bouillon contains wine or vinegar); cracked peppercorns; diced tomatoes; saffron; and possibly other ingredients as indicated in a specific recipe. Be sure that the reduction is allowed to cook to the proper consistency—syrupy but not dry.

   If cream is used to stabilize this sauce, it should be reduced separately. Carefully simmer the cream (do not let it boil over) until it is thickened and takes on a rich, ivory-yellow color.

   The seasonings and consistency adjustments needed for this sauce are generally quite simple: freshly squeezed lemon juice, salt, finely ground white pepper, and a bit of water, if necessary.

2. Assemble all equipment necessary to prepare a beurre blanc.

   A *sauteuse* is generally used to prepare a beurre blanc, since the greater the surface of the pan in direct contact with the heat, the easier it is to prepare this sauce quickly. Be sure that the pan is made of a nonreactive metal. Bi-metal pans, such as copper or anodized aluminum lined with stainless steel, are excellent choices for this sauce. The ingredients used in the reduction are typically left in the sauce, adding texture and garnish, so it is unnecessary to strain it after cooking.

   A whip may be used to incorporate the butter in the sauce, but many chefs prefer to use the motion of the pan, swirling it over the burner or flat top, to incorporate the butter. Once the sauce is prepared, it may be kept warm directly in the container used to prepare it, or it may be transferred to a clean bain-marie or wide-necked vacuum bottle.

Method

1. Make the reduction and add a small amount of cream, if desired.

   This initial reduction of cooking liquids, wine, and/or vinegar, shallots, and cracked peppercorns gives the sauce most of its flavor. Allow all the ingredients to reduce over fairly brisk heat until enough of the liquid has cooked away to create a consistency similar to syrup.

   Add a little reduced cream at this point, if desired. Don't overdo the cream, however, since the sauce should have the flavor of fresh sweet butter, not heavy cream.

TROUBLESHOOTING BEURRE BLANC

If the sauce appears to be separating, and the butter is becoming oily rather than creamy, it has gotten too hot. Immediately pull the pan away from the heat and set it on a cool surface. Continue to add chilled butter a little at a time, whipping until the mixture regains the proper appearance (see Figure 8-13). Then continue to incorporate the remainder of the butter over low heat.

If the butter takes a very long time to become incorporated into the sauce, you may need to increase the heat under the pan very slightly. If the sauce appears broken, you may be able to save it by blending in a little additional reduced cream or chilled butter.

2. Add chilled diced butter to the reduction and incorporate over low heat until the sauce is the correct consistency.

Temperature control is the key to preparing this sauce. The cooking temperature should be quite low. The butter should be a little cooler than room temperature. Some chefs prefer to have the butter slightly softened, but this requires extra vigilance to be sure that the sauce won't break as it is prepared. Melted or runny butter will rarely produce a good sauce.

Beurre blanc is blended either with a fork, a whip, or by keeping the pan in constant motion as the butter is added a little at a time. The action is quite similar to that used for finishing a sauce with butter.

3. The sauce is now ready to serve. Keep it warm (at around 160°F/70°C). In many operations, beurre blanc is considered an *à la minute* sauce. This means that it is not generally held throughout service. If you are intending to prepare a large batch and hold it, use the same techniques described for hollandaise.

See Part IV, Chapter 15, for the recipe for beurre blanc.

Sauce Vin Blanc

Sauce vin blanc can often cause a great deal of confusion. Indeed, it is one of the few sauces that has three distinctly different preparation methods. Since all three methods rely on techniques already described for other sauces, notably velouté, hollandaise, and beurre blanc sauces, we will look at them quickly and refer to more detailed explanations of method as necessary.

Method 1 for Sauce Vin Blanc A poaching liquid containing wine (usually for the fish being served with this sauce), is reduced and then this reduction is used as the basis for a hollandaise sauce: Egg yolks are cooked with the reduction and melted or clarified butter is gradually whipped into the yolks.

Method 2 for Sauce Vin Blanc The poaching liquid (as described in method 1) is reduced along with an equal quantity of fish velouté. The sauce is then finished by adding egg yolks and cooking until the sauce thickens slightly. Diced chilled butter is worked into the sauce, using the same technique as for beurre blanc. According to both Escoffier and *Larousse Gastronomique*, this method is best for use as a glaze.

Method 3 for Sauce Vin Blanc A hollandaise is prepared in the usual manner, and then reduced poaching liquid used to prepare fish is added to the hollandaise. The sauce is then strained.

Compound Butters

These flavored butters may be considered as a kind of sauce used to finish grilled or broiled meats, fish, poultry, or game. **Compound butters** may be flavored with a wide variety of ingredients, including herbs, nuts, citrus zest, garlic, shallots, ginger, and vegetables.

They are easy to prepare and can be stored, wrapped in parchment and/or plastic, for several days without loss of quality. They may also be frozen for extended storage.

In addition to their use as the "sauce" for grilled or broiled foods, they can also be used to flavor grain dishes, pasta, or as a finishing ingredient in other sauces. Boiled or steamed vegetables may be tossed in compound butter just before service. One classic dish, chicken Kiev, calls for a compound butter to be well chilled, shaped into fingers, and then rolled into a chicken breast. Thus, when the breaded and fried chicken breast is cut open, the "sauce" is released.

Mise en Place

1. Assemble the ingredients necessary for compound butter.

   You will need to refer to specific recipes or your own inspiration for the exact ingredients and ratios. The recipe found in Part IV, Chapter 15, will give a general sense of the quantity of flavoring ingredients 1 pound of butter can accommodate as well as the wide range of possible flavoring options.

   The butter used must be perfectly fresh. Let the butter soften to room temperature, or use the paddle attachment of a mixer to soften it. As noted, unsalted butter is preferred, but you can use salted butter if that is all you have on hand. Just use extra caution when adding the final seasonings.

   Many compound butters are flavored with chopped fresh herbs. There are a host of other options: rendered bacon, puréed and reduced tomatoes or bell peppers, roasted garlic, lemon juice and zest, and so on.

2. Assemble the necessary equipment for compound butter.

   Small batches of compound butter are mixed in a bowl with a wooden spoon, larger batches are prepared in a mixer with a paddle attachment. Parchment paper is necessary to roll the compound butter after mixing.

Method

1. Prepare the flavoring agents or according to individual recipes.

   This sauce is not cooked, so be sure that any item that needs cooking is properly prepared and well chilled before it is worked into the butter.

2. Incorporate the flavoring agents into the softened butter working by hand with a spoon, or with a mixer or food processor.

   Be sure that all ingredients are thoroughly incorporated and evenly distributed throughout the butter.

3. Roll the butter into a cylinder in parchment paper or pipe it into individual rosettes. Thoroughly chill the butter before service.(See Figure 8-14 for photos illustrating the method for preparing compound butter.)

   Butters that are rolled into cylinders can be sliced into medallions before they are used to top broiled items. Rosettes are often added at the last moment and allowed to melt delicately from the heat of the food. The idea is that the rosette will still retain enough of its shape to act as a pleasing and functional garnish on the plate.

FIGURE 8-14 Rolling a Compound Butter into a Cylinder

(1) Using the edge of a pan to tighten compound butter into an even cylinder.

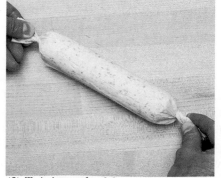

(2) Twisting ends of the parchment paper.

(3) Slicing the chilled compound butter for service.

Miscellaneous Sauces

Several other items are commonly found on contemporary plated dishes that fill in for traditional sauces, though they may not themselves fit the classic definition of a sauce.

- Broths, essences, and juices

- Pilafs, risottos, ragouts, and stews

- Barbecue sauces and glazes

- Compotes, marmalades, conserves, and chutneys

- Salsas (see Figure 8-15) and other "raw sauces"

- Cold emulsion sauces (mayonnaise, vinaigrettes, and marinades)

- Infused oils

A quick look through some menus today will make it apparent that demi-glace sauce and its derivatives are more and more giving way to preparations as diverse as bean ragouts, compotes, chutneys, relishes, and vegetable stews.

Though not true sauces, these items do fulfill some of the classic functions of sauces: They add flavor, moisture, texture, and color to other items on a plate. Beyond that, they also allow the chef greater freedom to accomplish other things. Turning to a sauce alternative, such as those discussed here, allows the chef to breathe new life into old standards by introducing new flavors or preparations from other ethnic cuisines.

Salsas, broths, stews, compotes, and vinaigrettes served instead of butter-based or finished sauces also makes it easy for chefs to lighten the overall calorie and fat content of a dish without leaving guests wondering where the flavor and excitement went. Selecting these sauce alternatives in place of a hollandaise or sauce vin blanc encourages you to increase the variety of grains, legumes, fruits, and vegetables offered to the guest, without belaboring the shift toward a more nutritional focus. Some of these same issues were initially addressed in Chapter 3.

One new "sauce" gaining favor in contemporary restaurants is a broth. The broth (or, as it may also be known on menus, fumet or essence) should be extremely flavorful. It is still light in body, although some broths may have a light purée added for color

FIGURE 8-15
Salsa: A Sauce Alternative

and flavor. The broth is often used as a pool beneath the food being served. It is not intended to turn every main course into a soup, however. An example might be a rich salmon broth flavored with a purée of fresh peas. A piece of pan-seared or grilled salmon would be served on a puddle of that broth. Juices, made from vegetables, fruits, or herbs, are also popular.

Cold vinaigrettes may be used as a sauce for hot sautéed items or as a marinade. Relishes and compotes based on fruits and/or vegetables may be served hot or cold. An example is a **confit** of red onion, consisting of onions stewed in butter and finished with a small amount of honey and vinegar. Another example is a dried-fruit compote, composed of dried fruits stewed in wine, stock, or a combination of the two.

Rice and other grains, such as bulgur and barley, are prepared by the pilaf or risotto method and used as a bed for other foods. Beans and other dried legumes, such as lentils, may be stewed and served in lieu of a standard sauce. Recipes for some of these sauces can be found in Part IV of this book, as well as in numerous other books and magazines.

Serving Sauces

Reheating Sauces

As you have seen, most of the grand sauces and some contemporary sauces can be prepared in advance, then cooled and stored. When you are ready to serve them, you will need to reheat the sauce quickly and safely. This is most easily accomplished over direct heat, although in the case of some very delicate cream sauces, you may prefer to use a double boiler.

Once the sauce is at the correct temperature, check it carefully for the best possible flavor, aroma, texture, color, and appearance. Make any necessary adjustments to the sauce either now or after the sauce has been finished according to need.

Holding a Finished Sauce

Some sauces are suitable for holding in a steam table during service. As noted, they must be brought as quickly as possible through the danger zone and up to service temperature. Then, they are generally transferred to clean bain-maries and placed in a hot water bath.

Those sauces that have been thickened with a starch will be prone to developing a skin if they are left uncovered. Some chefs like to top the sauce with clarified butter. This creates an airtight seal that prevents a skin from forming on the surface of the sauce. Others prefer to use a fitted cover for the bain-marie or a piece of parchment paper cut to fit directly onto the surface of the sauce. Plastic wrap can also be used.

Emulsion sauces, such as hollandaise-type sauces and beurre blancs, need special care. They may not hold up in a steam table, since temperatures could be high enough to cause the sauce to break. Find another warm spot in the kitchen, or use a vacuum bottle (preferably one with a wide neck). Be sure that any emulsified sauces left over after service are discarded to avoid foodborne disease.

Plating and Presentation

Sauces can add flavor, moisture, and texture to a dish. They also serve to enhance its visual appeal. Some of the principles used in applying sauces to foods are outlined below:

- Maintain the temperature of the sauce. Be sure that hot sauces are extremely hot, warm emulsions sauces are as warm as possible without danger of breaking, and cold sauces remain cold until they come in contact with hot foods. The temperatures of the sauce, the food being sauced, and the plate should all be carefully monitored.

- If the food being served has a crisp or otherwise interesting texture, it is generally best to pool the sauce beneath the food, spreading it in a layer directly on the plate. If an item could benefit from a little cover or the sauce has more visual appeal than the item being sauced, spoon or ladle it evenly over the top of the food.

- Use common sense when you determine portion sizes for sauces. There should be enough for the guest to enjoy the flavor of the sauce with each bite, but not so much that the dish looks swamped. Not only does this disturb the balance between the items on the plate, it also makes it difficult for the waiter to carry the food from the kitchen to the guest's table without at least some of the sauce running onto the rim, or worse, over the edge of the plate.

- Sauces should be artfully applied to foods, but they should never look as if they were "touched" or labored over. Foods should appear fresh and as natural as possible.

Summary

Sauces are often the yardstick by which a chef's skill is measured. Learning the proper preparation techniques for the five grand sauces will stand you in good stead for future experimentation and invention. Good sauce techniques go beyond preparation, however. A chef must know how to also properly store, reheat, hold, and serve sauces. Throughout this chapter we have looked at the fundamental skills required to make several basic sauces, as well as their variations. Beyond the classic grand sauces we have examined the ways in which contemporary menu items are served, with a host of non-traditional sauces, including broths, essences, salsas, vinaigrettes, and stews. You should continue to enhance your knowledge and skill in the following sauce-making areas as you develop your career as a chef:

- Identifying a suitable sauce for the style of service and the cooking method used to prepare the main ingredient

- Understanding the nuances of pairing a sauce with food

- Developing mastery of the components and cooking techniques required by each of the grand sauces, as well as their derivatives

- Understanding the quality indicators of each sauce

- Knowing how to properly serve, reheat, hold, and plate sauces

- Expanding your repertoire of modern sauce ideas

SELF-STUDY QUESTIONS

1. Why should stock return to a full boil immediately after incorporating the roux when preparing velouté?

2. What are the three ratios of roux to stock for light velouté? medium? heavy? Name the appropriate application(s) for each consistency.

3. Why is skimming a sauce throughout its cooking time important? How is this process made easier?

4. What are the characteristics of an excellent-quality demi-glace?

5. Explain two methods used for straining a sauce through cheesecloth.

6. Name three ways to prepare demi-glace derivatives.

7. Define the term *nappé*.

8. How and why should milk's quality be tested before using it to make a béchamel?

9. What are the basic components of a tomato sauce?

10. What distinctions can be made between contemporary and grand sauces?

11. List three emulsion sauces and describe how an emulsion is formed.

12. Describe how to make a reduction and why it is important in a hollandaise sauce.

13. How long can hollandaise be held safety?

14. What qualities should the following sauces have when properly prepared:

    - velouté
    - tomato
    - jus lié

    - béchamel
    - hollandaise
    - beurre blanc

15. What is a compound butter and how is it used?

ACTIVITIES

- Make the beurre blanc recipe on page 522 as described, using reduced heavy cream. Taste it and take note of its consistency. Make the beurre blanc again omitting the heavy cream. Taste and note its consistency. Hold both sauces in similar containers at the appropriate temperature. Note whether and/or when either sauce "breaks."

- Prepare a hollandaise according to the recipe on page 521. Deliberately break the sauce, and use one of the recommended techniques to save it (page 335).

- Prepare a velouté thickened with roux, as directed in the recipe on page 484. Thicken a comparable amount of stock with an arrowroot or cornstarch slurry, using enough to make a sauce with the same consistency. Place both sauces in a steam table and observe the quality of each at $1/_2$ hour intervals over a 3-hour span. Record your observations.

KEYWORDS

béchamel	cuisson	hollandaise	sweating
beurre blanc	demi-glace	jus lié	tomato sauce
brown sauce	derivatives	modified starch	velouté
compound butter	emulsion sauce	*monté au beurre*	
confit	fond	nappé	
coulis	grand sauce	sauce vin blanc	

9

Dry-Heat Cooking Methods

*One must cook a piece of meat a thousand
times before one begins to truly understand it*

—ANDRE SOLTNER

*The cooking methods explained in this chapter are known collectively as the dry-heat
methods. They include: grilling, broiling, and barbecuing; roasting and baking;
poêléing; sautéing (and variations); pan-frying; deep-frying.*

*The dry heat techniques discussed in this chapter can produce a range of results.
Grilled and broiled items should have a highly flavored exterior, smoky and slightly
charred. Their interiors should be evenly moist and juicy. Roasted foods should develop
a rich roasted aroma, a well-developed color and texture. Sautéed and stir-fried foods
should also develop the appropriate degree of browning; their textures will vary
according to the food being prepared, but in general, they remain resilient but tender
enough to produce a pleasing effect when eaten. Pan-fried and deep-fried items have a
tender interior and a crisp exterior.*

Understanding how these techniques actually cook the food makes it clear that the reason for selecting a particular cooking medium depends on the desired result. In sautéing, for example, the butter or oil chosen for a preparation contributes flavor as well as pan lubrication. Pan-fried and deep-fried foods tend not to depend upon the flavor of the cooking oil to develop a particular effect. In fact, oils that are nearly neutral in flavor and have high smoking points are best.

Certain kinds or cuts of meat, poultry, and fish are best prepared using certain techniques. Consider the food's characteristics: What is the texture—firm, delicate, dense? Are there bones? Is the food naturally lean or oily? What is the size, shape, and thickness of the food?

Because dry heat does not have a tenderizing effect, any food prepared by one of these cooking methods must be naturally tender or should be prepared in a way that will introduce additional moisture. This can be done by barding or marinating foods, for example, which are techniques also outlined in this chapter.

No matter what food you are preparing or which dry-heat cooking technique you intend to use, two abilities are of great importance: selecting the proper cuts, shapes, and sizes of foods for grilling, roasting, sautéing, or frying; and being adept at gauging the exact point at which foods are perfectly cooked—a skill acquired only through experience.

CHAPTER OBJECTIVES

- Explain the following dry-heat techniques:
  - grilling, broiling, barbecuing
  - roasting and baking
  - poêléing
  - sautéing, and two variations
  - pan-frying
  - deep-frying
- Understand what cuts of meat, poultry, and fish are best suited for which dry-heat cooking techniques.
- Describe how to make gravies and jus liés for roasted items.
- Describe how to make sauces for sautéed foods.
- Explain standard breading procedure.
- Understand how to select and maintain frying oil.

The Dry-Heat Cooking Methods

Grilling, Broiling, and Barbecuing

Broiling, barbecuing, and **pan-broiling** are all forms of grilling. The difference between the methods lies in the source of the heat.

Grilled foods are cooked by radiant heat from a source located below the food. They should have a smoky, slightly charred flavor resulting from the flaring of the juices and fats that are rendered out as the item cooks. The drippings that might have collected or reduced in a sauté pan are actually reducing directly on the food's surface. This creates an intensely flavored exterior.

Hardwoods such as grapevines, mesquite, hickory, or apple are frequently used to introduce a special flavor. Branches of herbs may also be allowed to smolder on the fire to lend their distinct flavor.

Broiled foods are generally considered to be those cooked by a heat source located above the food. The broiler is used to perform other types of cooking, however, and this can result in a little confusion.

Frequently, delicate items such as lean white fish are first brushed with butter and then placed on a heated sizzler platter before being placed on the rack below the heat source. This is not broiling in the strictest sense of the word; it is actually closer to baking. Items prepared in this manner may still be

FIGURE 9-1 Salmon Gratin

Salmon is cooked with glaçage and then browned in a broiler or salamander.

referred to as "broiled" on a menu. Similarly, the broiler or a salamander can be used to prepare glazed or "gratinéed" foods, such as stuffed tomatoes, sole Véronique with glaçage, or a salmon gratin (see Figure 9-1).

Barbecuing is also a term that can cause confusion. In some parts of the country, it signifies a food that has been basted repeatedly with a barbecue sauce during grilling. In others, it refers to pit- or spit-roasted items. On some menus, it may have little if anything to do with either a pit, spit, or grill. A "barbecued beef sandwich" may simply be roasted beef that has been thinly sliced and simmered in a barbecue sauce.

Pan-broiled foods are cooked on top of the stove in a heavy cast-iron or other warp-resistant metal pan over intense heat. Any fat or juices released during cooking are removed as they accumulate; otherwise the result is a sauté or a stew. Special pans made to simulate a grill's effect may be used. These pans have thick ridges that hold the food up and away from any juices or fat that might collect.

---

sole Véronique: fillet of soul poached in white wine and served with white sauce and garnished with seedless white grapes. ("Véronique" refers to the grape garnish.)

glaçage: a combination of hollandaise sauce, velouté, and whipped heavy cream.

gratin (gratinée): browned under a salamander or broiler.

Mise en Place

1. Assemble all ingredients and preparations used for grilling.

There are relatively few items necessary to create good grilled foods. Refer to either Chapter 5 or specific recipes for additional guidance in selecting:

- Meats, fish, poultry, breads, vegetables, fruits
- Oils for lubricating both the food and the grill's rods
- Seasonings and flavorings
- Additional and optional items, as desired

Foods should be cut thinly enough to allow them to cook properly without excessive exterior charring. Cut them into the appropriate size. Trim away any fat, silverskin, and gristle from meats. Pound or butterfly meats and fish to even their thickness, if appropriate. Some foods are cut into strips, chunks, or large dice and then threaded on skewers (see Figure 9-2).

FIGURE 9-2 Preparing Skewered Items

(1) Be sure to soak wooden skewers first.

(2) Note that some space is left between items to allow even, rapid cooking.

The oil you select can be neutral in flavor. Or, depending upon the item you are grilling, you may wish to incorporate a flavored oil to add a special taste.

Salt and pepper are, of course, the mainstay seasonings. But, remember that marinades may be used to introduce additional flavor or moisture. Some marinades are also intended to improve the texture of foods that might otherwise become too soft to handle easily on the grill (see Figure 9-3).

There are numerous ways to enhance the flavor, texture, and color of foods being grilled. A protective coating of melted butter and bread crumbs, known as *à l'anglaise,* may be applied to foods, for example. Or a glaze or barbecue sauce can be added.

2. Assemble and prepare all equipment necessary for grilling.

Grills and broilers should be carefully maintained (see Figure 9-4). The rods should be scoured or brushed well between service periods. Rub the rods lightly with a vegetable oil to season them before preheating the grill.

Remember that it is best to establish temperature **zones** on the grill (see Figure 9-5). Learn which is the "hot" area and which is "cool." Developing a system for placing foods on the grill, whether by food type or by range of doneness, will help speed your work on the line.

Some restaurants have special procedures so that potential problems created by foods that might drip through the grill can be avoided. For instance, cheese may not be applied to burgers while still on the grill. Instead, the burger might be cooked to just a few degrees less than requested, and then transferred to a sizzler platter. The sliced cheese is used to top the burger, and a quick pass under a broiler or salamander completes the cooking process. A special zone on the grill may have to be established for foods brushed with barbecue sauce to prevent a flavor transfer from the sauce to all the other grilled items.

Hand racks for delicate items, or those that might be awkward to turn easily, should be similarly cleaned between uses. A light brushing or

FIGURE 9-3   Marinated Foods for Grilling

(1) Vegetables in a marinade prior to cooking.

(2) Marinated flank steak and zucchini being grilled.

FIGURE 9-4   Preparing the Grill

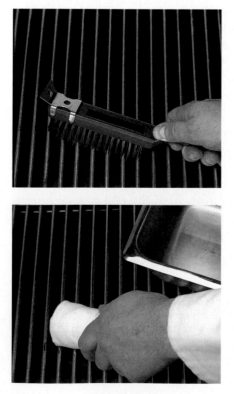

(1) Scrub grill well to remove any burned-on particles.

(2) Rub the grill lightly with oil.

FIGURE 9-5 Zones on a Grill

Mentally divide the grill so that you avoid flavor transfers. Cook the foods at their best temperatures.

FIGURE 9-6 Placing Fish in a Hand Grill

(1) Brush the fish's skin (red snapper shown) lightly with oil to prevent tearing.

(2) Close the hand grill, and position the metal collar so it is securely fastened.

FIGURE 9-7 Grilling Chicken Paillards

(1) Using tongs, dip the chicken in plain or seasoned oil, and allow the excess to drain away before placing it on the grill.

(2) Grill on the first side until the edges begin to change color.

FIGURE 9-8 Releasing Fish from Hand Grill

Use a spatula to gently release the fish from the grill without tearing the skin. A black bass is shown.

coating of oil will help prevent the skin of delicate fish or poultry from sticking and tearing. Be sure that the collar on the handle is well secured once the food has been properly positioned (see Figure 9-6).

Tongs, offset spatulas, flexible spatulas, and sizzler plates are almost universally required at the grill station (see Figures 9-7 and 9-8). You should also have a collection of spoons, brushes, or other utensils for serving sauces and applying glazes, marinades, or barbecue sauces. Hot serving plates should also be on hand so that the food can be quickly and correctly plated and served to the guest.

Method

1. Place the food on the grill to start cooking and **mark** it.

It does make a difference which side of the food goes onto the grill first. The best-looking, or "presentation," side always goes face down on the grill first. Once the item is turned to the second side, it should not usually be turned again.

Most patrons expect to see the familiar cross-hatch marks on grilled food at a restaurant. While it is certainly possible to grill foods correctly without giving them the trademark "grid," it is not difficult to do. It has the added advantage of "releasing" the food from the grill before the presentation side sticks and tears.

To mark foods on a grill or broiler, gently work the spatula under the food and give it a quarter turn. Let it continue to cook on the first side another minute or two before turning the food completely over.

2. Turn once to cook on second side.

Since most foods cooked by grilling or broiling are relatively thin and tender, they should not require much more cooking time, once they have been turned. Thicker cuts, or those that must be cooked to a higher internal doneness

FIGURE 9-9   Applying Barbecue Sauce

Brush the meat after it has been partially cooked for the best results.

may need to move to the cooler portion of the grill, so that they don't develop a charred exterior. Or, they may be removed from the grill altogether and allowed to finish cooking in the oven.

For banquets, it may be helpful to quickly mark foods on the grill, just barely cooking the outer layers. Then, they can be laid out on sheet

FIGURE 9-10   Degrees of Doneness in Red Meats

(1) Very rare.

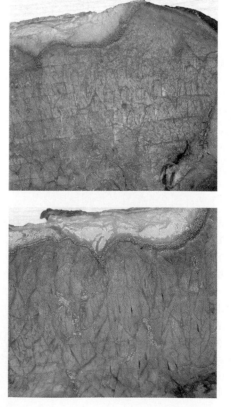

(3) Medium.

(2) Rare.

(4) Medium-well.

or hotel pans, and finished in the oven. This allows you to greatly expand the potential output of your grill. Exercise vigilant attention to chilling the food quickly if it is to be held for any appreciable amount of time.

If you are using a barbecue sauce or glaze, it is usually a good idea to apply several thin coats, rather than one heavy coat (see Figure 9-9). Brush barbecue sauce on the top of the food and turn it repeatedly, until a good shiny glaze or crust has developed. The more light coats, the better the finished color, flavor, and appearance of the food.

3. Finish to desired doneness and serve at once.

Most red meats, some fish, and duck breasts may be prepared to a range of doneness. Most other foods are cooked through. In either case, a deft touch and a sixth sense about when a food is properly cooked is a great boon to a grill chef. Rely on a combination of previous experience and sensory data—the way food looks, feels, and smells—to guide you. Figure 9-10 shows red meats cooked to different degrees of doneness.

Roasting and Baking

Spit-roasting was one of the earliest cooking methods. This technique involves placing the food on a rod that is turned either manually or with a motor (see Figure 9-11). The radiant heat, given off by a fire or gas jets, cooks the item in much the same manner as grilling or broiling. Constant turning assures that the food cooks evenly and develops a good crust on all sides. The tradition of serving roasted and grilled foods on toasted bread or a croûton began when pieces of bread were placed below the cooking food to trap escaping juices. In contemporary kitchens, drip pans are placed under the spit, as shown in Figure 9-12.

Roasting, as it is most commonly performed today, however, is more similar to baking than it is to the original form of roasting.

Roasted foods are cooked through contact with dry, heated air held in the closed environment of an oven. As the outer layers of a food become heated, its natural juices begin to heat and pene-

FIGURE 9-11 Spit-Roasting Chickens

trate the food more deeply. The rendered juices, or pan-drippings, are the foundation for sauces and pan gravies.

The flavor and aroma of a roasted food should contribute to an overall sensation of fullness, richness, and depth. This is due in part to the nature of the food and in part to the browning process. Roasted foods should have a rich color, ranging from delicate gold to the nearly black color of a perfectly roasted rib of beef. The proper development of color has a direct bearing on the flavor. Items that are too pale lack not only eye appeal but also the depth of flavor associated with properly roasted foods.

FIGURE 9-12 Spit-Roasting Setup

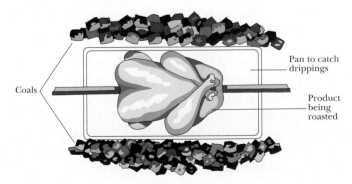

Pan to catch drippings

Coals

Product being roasted

FIGURE 9-13   Smoke-Roasting

(1) Corn is being smoke-roasted in a hotel pan setup.

(2) Chicken is given a light "smoking" using disposable pans and a rack.

FIGURE 9-14
Roasted Bones for
Jus de Veau Lié

Baking is the term associated with most portion-size foods that are cooked according to the techniques outlined for roasting, including pork chops, potatoes, and squash. Still, this is not an ironclad definition. Garlic is roasted, hams are baked, and potatoes cooked in their skins are baked while those peeled and added to the roast's drippings or coated with oil are said to be "oven-roasted."

Smoke-roasting is an adaptation of roasting that allows foods to take on a rich, smoky flavor. The food cooks in a smoke bath, in a tightly closed roasting pan or smoking setup such as that shown in Figure 9-13. This can be done over an open flame or in the oven.

Unlike a smoked item made in traditional charcuterie operations, the food does not have to be brined and cured before smoking. There are limitations and drawbacks, however. Smoke-roasting does not preserve foods. Any food left too long in the smoke bath can develop an acrid, unappetizing aroma and taste.

In some cases, roasting is used as a preliminary step in other preparations. For example, bones are often roasted for stocks (see Figure 9-14). Mirepoix and tomato products are also roasted in many types of brown stocks.

Mise en Place

1. Assemble all ingredients and preparations used for roasting:

   • Main item: meat, fish, poultry, vegetable, or fruit

   • Barding, larding, or other flavoring/moisturizing ingredients

   • Stuffings, coatings, crusts, and seasoning mixtures

   • Stock or brown sauce and other items required (bones, mirepoix, tomato product, and deglazing liquid)

   Select the appropriate meat cuts from the rib and loin areas for the best results. The more tender cuts from the legs of certain animals, such as top round, are also excellent when roasted. Young whole birds may be roasted, as may whole fish. Whole chickens may be cut into pieces and "baked."

   Vegetables and fruits are also roasted or baked, the terminology varying according to custom. Vegetables cooked whole and in their skins should be pierced or scored. This allows the steam to escape as the food cooks. If this step is

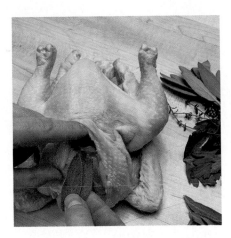

FIGURE 9-15
Stuffing Herbs
Under a
Chicken's Skin

FIGURE 9-16
Using Flavored
Bread Crumbs to
Coat Tenderloin
Steaks

omitted, you may find that you have exploding potatoes and squash shrapnel to clean up.

A layer of fat or poultry skin is traditionally allowed to remain. It is felt that this bastes foods naturally, as they roast. For additional flavor during roasting, herbs or aromatic vegetables may be used to stuff the cavity, or they may be inserted just under the skin (see Figure 9-15).

Barding—tying thin sheets of fatback, bacon, or caul fat—and **larding**—inserting small strips of fatback into a food—have been the traditional preparation techniques for roasted foods that are naturally lean. Venison, wild boar, game birds, and certain cuts of beef or lamb may be candidates. These same techniques, sometimes using different products, are still used today. Rather than larding a roast with fatback, today you may find a roast has been studded with slivers of garlic. Or a "robe" of shredded potatoes may be applied in place of the bacon.

---

fatback: unsmoked and unsalted fresh pork fat, taken from the fat layer that runs along the animal's back.

Foods such as chicken breasts, chops, squash, tomatoes, peppers, or apples are sometimes stuffed before roasting (see Figures 9-17 and 9-18). These stuffings should be properly prepared. Remember that adding a hot stuffing to a cold food could result in food poisoning. Keep all foods at the correct temperature at each stage of preparation.

Some vegetables are halved and baked, such as the squash shown in Figure 9-19. It is often a good idea to baste and season these items before and during cooking.

Mirepoix is used to flavor the jus or pan gravy for roasted items. It should be cut into a size that allows it to brown properly. If it will be added during roasting, take the overall cooking time into account. The longer a roast cooks, the larger the cut should be. If you will be adding the mirepoix at the last moment, cut it small, so that it will brown properly in a much shorter amount of time. To complete the pan gravy or jus, a rich stock or brown sauce should be on hand. Pan gravy calls for flour to make a roux,

KEEPING ROASTS LEAN AND MOIST

Today, with an increased concern over the amount of fat in diets, every trace of visible fat or skin is often removed in an effort to keep foods as "fat-free" as possible. If the natural protection of fat or skin is removed, then foods might become dry and lose flavor. In that case, an alternative "skin" should be added, in the form of coatings or crusts (see Figure 9-16). You should be aware, however, that fat released from skin or fat layers as foods roast does not penetrate far into the meat. Since it does provide some protection from the drying effects of an oven without dramatically increasing the amount of fat in a serving, you may opt to leave it in place during roasting and then remove the fat or skin before the item is served.

Figure 9-17   Preparing Stuffed Pork Chops

(1) Cutting a pocket in the chop.

(2) Chops are secured by skewers or tying with twine .

(3) The stuffed chops.

Figure 9-18   Baking Apples

Apples may be peeled, cored, stuffed, and flavored before baking in cider

Figure 9-19   Baking Squash

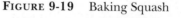

(1) Brushing the cut side of the squash with butter.

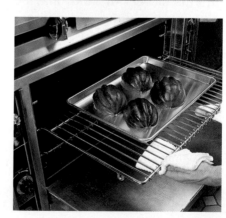

(2) Place cut side down on the baking sheet before baking.

while a jus is usually thickened with arrowroot or cornstarch.

2. Assemble all equipment necessary for preparation and service.

Roasting pans or baking sheets should be the right size and shape to hold the food correctly. There should be enough room for air to circulate freely, but not so much that any juices that render from the food are likely to scorch.

The less that comes between the food and direct contact with the heated air, the more successfully the food will roast. To that end, you may want to set foods on roasting racks, beds of mirepoix, or even bones. Or you may prefer to set the foods directly on very shallow roasting or baking pans. The food should remain uncovered. Covering the pan will trap the steam that escapes from the meat. Roasting pans that are too deep for the

food will also create a steam bath that could affect the finished quality of the dish.

You may also need butcher's twine or skewers, instant-reading thermometers, and a kitchen fork. You will need an additional pan to hold the roasted food while you make a sauce from the pan drippings. Strainers and skimmers or ladles are necessary to prepare the sauce. A carving board and extremely sharp carving knife should be nearby for final service.

Method

1. Sear the food as appropriate and baste throughout cooking time.

   Searing is an initial step for certain foods. This may be done by cooking small items in a little hot oil or other fat over direct heat. Or, you may opt to begin the roasting process at a very high temperature, then reduce the heat once the food takes on a good color. Chefs often prefer to allow a deep color to develop gradually over the course of roasting larger items, rather than searing them. They feel that avoiding extreme temperatures produces a food that is moister and has lost less volume during cooking. As long as the finished dish has a rich and appealing color, it matters little which approach you take.

   Roasted and baked foods may be basted as they cook. The fats and juices released by the food itself are the traditional basting liquid. Vegetables or fruit may call for a special basting liquid, prepared separately. A marinade, glaze, flavored or plain butter, or fruit juices are possible choices.

   Adjust the temperature of the oven if necessary throughout the roasting period. Or, if you typically have ovens preset to specific temperatures, be prepared to move foods from one oven to another. Some foods roast best at high temperatures for very short periods. Others may need an initial period at high temperature, then a more extended period at moderate to low temperatures. Failure to watch the cooking speed and to regulate the temperature accordingly will result in foods that are uneven in color, taste, and texture.

2. Cook foods to the correct doneness, and allow them to rest briefly.

   Meats, fish, poultry, and game are generally cooked to a specified internal temperature. An instant-reading thermometer is the most accurate gauge (see Figure 9-20). Other tests, including the "skewer" test, touch, or fork-tenderness may also be used for meats and other foods.

FIGURE 9-20
Determining Doneness with an Instant-Reading Thermometer

FIGURE 9-21
Checking Juices from a Roast Chicken for Doneness

To test whole roasted birds for doneness, pierce them at the point where the thigh is thickest (see Figure 9-21). The juices should run nearly clear. Any juices that have accumulated in the cavity should no longer have a red or pink hue.

Allow a **resting period** of a few minutes for small items or up to 15 or 20 minutes for larger foods. While this might seem to run counter to the constant refrain that hot foods should be served hot, it is an important step in properly roasting foods. This resting period once foods come out of the oven allows the food's temperature to equalize and allows the natural juices to redistribute themselves. This benefits the texture, aroma, moisture, and flavor of the foods. It also plays a key role in carryover cooking, which should be considered the final stage of cooking (see next page).

3. Prepare the pan gravy or jus, if desired (see Figure 9-22). Steps in preparing gravies follow.

---

fork-tender: food offers little or no resistance when pierced with a fork.

FIGURE 9-22   Preparing a Pan Gravy

(1) Add flour to released drippings and cook to form a roux.

(2) Add the stock and simmer until thickened.

(3) Strain the gravy to remove mirepoix.

4. Carve (optional) and serve with appropriate sauce and garnish.

Carryover Cooking

Carryover cooking refers to the fact that the heat retained by foods, even after they come out of the oven, is enough to continue "cooking" the food. The internal temperature will rise, and this can change the degree of doneness dramatically.

The larger the item, the greater the amount of heat it will retain and the more its internal temperature will rise. A Cornish game hen or quail may show an increase in its internal temperature of 5 to 10 degrees. A top round of beef's temperature may increase as much as 15 degrees; the temperature for a steamship round of beef can go up by as much as 20 degrees. In order to achieve the correct doneness, the main item should be removed from the oven when the internal temperature is lower than the desired service temperature by an amount that corresponds to the anticipated carryover cooking.

Preparing Jus or Pan Gravy for Roasted Foods

The sauce made from the accumulated drippings is frequently referred to as a **jus** or **pan gravy.** When the jus made from drippings is thickened with arrowroot or cornstarch, it may be referred to as **jus lié.** If a sauce is made with a roux incorporating the fat rendered from a roast, it is usually called pan gravy.

For both jus and gravy, add the mirepoix to the rendered fat and drippings in the roasting pan (if the drippings are not scorched). They may be added during the roasting period, or they can be allowed to brown in the drippings after the roast has been removed as follows: Place the roasting pan over direct heat. Cook the mirepoix until it is browned, the fat is clarified, and the drippings are reduced.

To make a pan gravy, pour off the excess fat, leaving only enough to prepare an adequate amount of roux. Add flour to the roasting pan for pan gravy, and stir it well. Cook this roux for a few minutes. Gradually add an appropriate stock to the pan, being sure to stir it continuously to work out all the lumps in the roux.

Simmer the gravy until it is well flavored and properly thickened. This will usually take 15 to 20 minutes. Strain the gravy. Adjust the seasoning if necessary, and skim any fat floating on the surface before serving. Hold pan gravies in a steam table as you would any sauce, taking the necessary precautions to keep a skin from forming: Cover with a layer of clarified butter, a piece of parchment, or a tight-fitting cover.

For jus, add stock to the reduced drippings and mirepoix. Making a roux is unnecessary. Simmer for the same amount of time as you would a regular gravy. Skim the jus as it cooks to remove fat from the surface. Then, just before you are ready to strain the sauce, it may be thickened with an arrowroot or cornstarch slurry if desired.

Carving

Once the food is properly roasted and rested, it must be carved correctly to make the most of the item. Some meats, poultry, and fish are cut into serving-sized portions before they are cooked. In other instances, it is more appropriate to prepare a large roast or an entire bird or fish. The rib roast of beef, leg of lamb, and whole duck are considered prototypes for the carving techniques used with all other items. For example, a ham would be carved in the same manner as a leg of lamb because they are similar in structure.

Standing Rib Roast

This carving method could also be used for a rack of veal or venison or a crown roast of lamb or pork (see Figure 9-23).

FIGURE 9-23   Carving a Rib Roast

(1) Make cuts parallel to the cutting board until you reach the bone.

(2) Use the tip of the knife to release the cut from the bone.

FIGURE 9-24   Carving a Leg of Lamb

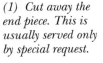

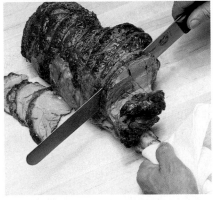

(1) Cut away the end piece. This is usually served only by special request.

(2) The initial cuts are made vertically, until the bone is reached.

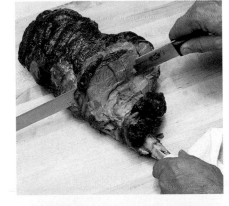

(3) Angle the knife as you continue cutting, so that cuts stay properly sized.

(4) Reverse the angle to get the most cuts.

FIGURE 9-25   Carving a Roasted Duck

(1) Cut through the skin to expose the thigh joint.

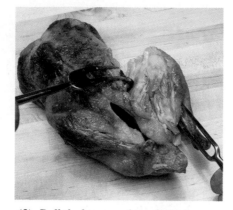

(2) Pull the leg away from the body completely.

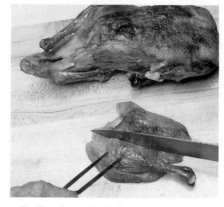

(3) Cut through the leg to separate it into thigh and drumstick.

(4) Cut the breast over the breastbone.

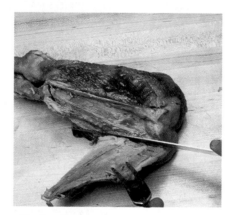

(5) Cut the meat away from the bones.

cutting away from the bone to make even slices.

3. When the slices become very large, begin to cut the meat at a slight angle, first from the left side, then from the right side, alternating until the leg is entirely sliced.

Birds

Although a duck is used to demonstrate these carving techniques, they could be applied to any bird (see Figure 9-25).

1. Lay the rib roast on its side.

    Using a sharp meat slicer, make parallel cuts from the outer edge toward the bones. (In the case of a crown roast, the cut begins at a point between the rib bones to make the cut to your desired thickness.)

2. Use the knife tip to cut the slice of meat or chops away from the rest of the rib, rack, or roast and serve it.

Leg of Lamb

1. To steady the leg, hold the shank bone firmly in one hand with a clean side towel. Make parallel cuts from the shank end down to the bone (see Figure 9-24).

2. Continue cutting slices of meat from the leg,

1. Use a knife tip to cut through the skin at the point where the leg meets the breast. Use the tines of a kitchen fork to gently press the leg away from the body. A properly roasted bird's leg will come away easily.

2. Use one kitchen fork to hold the breast steady. Insert another kitchen fork at the joint between the drumstick and the thigh. Pull and twist the fork to separate the leg away from the body. Repeat for the other leg.

3. Cut the legs into two pieces each through the joint between the thigh and the drumstick.

4. Cut through the skin on the breast on either side of the breastbone to begin to remove the breast meat.

5. Use the tines of a kitchen fork to gently pull the breast meat away from the rib cage. Make short, smooth strokes with the knife tip to cut the meat cleanly and completely away.

Poêléing

Poêléing, a technique most often associated with white meats and game birds, is sometimes known as "butter-roasting." Foods are liberally basted with butter then allowed to cook in their own juices in a covered vessel on a bed of aromatic vegetables known as a **matignon.** The matignon then becomes a garnish served as part of the sauce. Stock or jus, sometimes thickened, is often used to prepare a sauce from the pan drippings.

Because the food's surface is not browned as deeply as it would be in roasting, the flavor tends to be more delicate. An initial searing, or removing the cover during the final cooking stage, will allow the surface of the poêléed item to brown slightly. In general, poêléed items should have a less-pronounced color than that of roasted items. The surface should appear moist. Poêléed items should be tender and moist. They should develop only a slight crust, which offers some contrast in textures.

Mise en Place

1. Assemble all ingredients and preparations used for poêléing.

- Main item: lean white meats

- Matignon

- Butter (melted)

- Stock or a prepared jus for sauce

- Thickener if necessary

Veal, chicken, capon, and small game are often prepared by this method. The addition of butter, as well as the matignon, furnishes additional moisture during cooking. As in other dry-heat techniques, the meats should be trimmed of excess fat. They are also frequently tied to help retain their shape and to promote even cooking.

FIGURE 9-26 Poussin Poêlé

(1) The matignon is allowed to sweat in butter.

(2) Cover the pot when ready to go in the oven. The birds have been basted with additional butter.

(3) Poêlé, covered, in the oven.

(4) Add a thickener to the sauce after it has been degreased.

Other ingredients may be required to prepare a variety of stuffings, fillings, or garnishes. Refer to specific recipes for guidance.

2. Assemble all equipment necessary for preparation and service.

The equipment necessary for poêléing is similar to that for roasting with one special additional piece required: a tight-fitting cover. If there is no cover available, then cover a baking or roasting pan tightly with aluminum foil. Note that the pan used for poêléing is often deeper than typically used when roasting. Glazed or unglazed casseroles or baking dishes are often used, as well.

Method

1. Sear or **seize** the main item. See Figure 9-26 for photos illustrating the method for poêléing.

Cook the main item on all sides in the hot oil, just until the surface begins to turn color. Seizing as this is known, is done to begin the development of flavor. Remove the main item. Whether or not the food should be allowed to just lightly stiffen or to take on a rich golden hue is a decision made according to the desired end result.

2. Sweat or smother the matignon in batter.

Cook the matignon in melted whole butter over medium heat, stirring frequently until the onions are translucent. This is a crucial step in the development of flavor for the finished dish, especially for the sauce made from the pan drippings. The matignon will be a part of this sauce, so it is important that it be properly cooked. Replace the pan's cover to encourage the correct flavor development.

3. Baste with additional butter (optional), cover and cook in oven until properly cooked.

The same tests for doneness applied to roast meats are used for poêléed dishes. An instant-reading thermometer, inserted in the thickest part of the meat or the thigh of birds is the surest method. It should be used in conjunction with other evaluations, such as the correct color of the food's exterior. Juices running from meats or the cavity of birds should be nearly clear. The bird's leg should move freely when wiggled. If the leg pulls away or falls away, then the bird is overcooked. There should be a pleasing and appropriate aroma as well. Remember to allow a sufficient margin for carryover cooking as the meat rests.

4. Prepare the sauce as you would a pan gravy or jus. Carve the item if necessary, and serve.

Remove the main item from the cooking vessel and set it aside to rest. Place the pan over high heat and add the stock or jus. Simmer until it is well flavored and slightly reduced. Pull the pan slightly off-center to allow the fat to collect on one side; skim.

Thicken the stock or jus with an arrowroot or cornstarch slurry. Add any additional ingredients to finish or garnish the sauce. Adjust the seasoning to taste.

Sautéing

The object of **sautéing** foods is to produce a flavorful exterior with the best possible texture and color. The proper color and texture will vary, of course, depending upon the food you are sautéing. Red meats and game should have a deep-brown exterior. White meats, such as veal, pork, and poultry, should have a golden or amber exterior. Lean white fish will be pale gold when sautéed as skinless fillets, whereas steaks of firm fish, such as tuna, will take on a darker color. Onions can be sautéed to a variety of stages: limp and translucent, crisp and deep brown, or a rich mahogany with a melting texture.

Because sautéing is a rapid technique and does not have the tenderizing effect of some of the moist-heat methods described in Chapter 10, any food to be sautéed must be naturally tender. This technique cooks food rapidly in a small amount of fat over relatively high heat. The juices released during cooking form the base for a sauce made in the same pan and served with the sautéed item.

The sauce serves three purposes:

• It recaptures the food's flavor that has been released into the pan during cooking.

- It introduces additional flavor (an important factor because tender foods often have a subtle flavor).

- It counteracts any dryness resulting from the sautéing process.

Mise en Place

1. Assemble all ingredients and preparations used for sautéing:

   - Main item: boneless meat, poultry, eggs, fish; vegetable, or fruit

   - Marinades, stuffings, or special seasonings

   - Flour for dredging

   - Cooking fat or oil

   - Base sauce or stock

   - Additional ingredients for finishing or garnishing the sauce

Cut the main item into an appropriate size. Trim away the fat, silverskin, and gristle from meats. For poultry suprêmes and fillets of fish, remove the skin and bones. Pound or butterfly the meats to achieve an even thickness.

Vegetables and fruits are generally sliced, but this should be a decision made with respect to the nature of the food itself. For instance, you would certainly slice or chunk pineapple before sautéing it, but you may not need to do so with small button mushrooms.

Marinades, stuffings, or special seasonings may also be required by specific recipes. Marinades should be allowed a sufficient amount of time to add the correct degree of flavor. Stuffings must be properly prepared, allowed to cool if necessary, then incorporated correctly, and secured, so that they do not escape during cooking.

Dredging or dusting the item with flour is another common advance preparation technique. This is generally recommended for meat cut into strips (*émincé*) and for chicken and fish. If you wish, seasoning can be added to the flour. One particular application of sautéing, *à la meunière,* requires flour-dusted fish and meats (see

FIGURE 9-27 Dredging Trout with Flour

(1) Coat first one side and then the other of a pan-ready trout with flour.

(2) Shake off any excess flour before sautéing.

Figure 9-27). Otherwise, dusting is optional, and many chefs feel that it is not always desirable.

The cooking medium must be able to reach relatively high temperatures without breaking down or smoking. Clarified butter, neutral-flavored oil, olive oil, or rendered fats such as bacon, goose fat, or lard are often used.

A base sauce (demi-glace, jus lié, essences, broths, or a coulis, for instance) is usually necessary. There are a number of possible ingredients you may need to have on hand to flavor or finish the sauce. Wine, stock, cognac or liqueur, fortified wine, or water is often used to deglaze the pan first.

Additional aromatic ingredients, such as shallots, mushrooms, capers, tomatoes, or peppers, might be required. Butter may be used to finish the sauce; it should be whole butter, diced and either chilled or softened to room temperature.

For additional suggestions, refer to specific recipes in Part IV of this book, or other classic and contemporary recipe collections.

2. Assemble all equipment necessary for preparation and service.

A sauté pan may be referred to as a sauteuse or sautoir. It may also be referred to, depending upon the size, shape, and material used to make the pan, as a griswold (cast iron), bi-metal (copper lined with tin or stainless steel), or rondeau (if they are quite large).

Bear in mind that certain materials are better at conducting heat quickly with quick reaction to changes in temperature, while others offer a more constant heat that does not react to change as quickly. There are benefits to both types of pans, and you will learn quickly which pan works best in which situation and with which food.

The quantity of food you will be sautéing should be taken into account when selecting a pan. It is important that the pan be an appropriate size, to avoid overcrowding. If too much is put into the pan, the temperature will drop quickly and a good crust will not form on the food. Equally important, the pan must not be too large. This can cause the drippings to scorch, rendering them unsuitable for the sauce.

A selection of small tools, holding containers, and serving pieces are also necessary. Spatulas, tongs, spoons (slotted and solid metal spoons, wooden spoons, and tasting spoons), sizzler platters or sheet pans, bain-maries and steam tables for holding sauce, and strainers should be close at hand.

Method

1. Place food into preheated oil and let it cook until browned or golden (see Figures 9-28, 9-29, and 9-30).

The cooking medium (e.g., butter or oil) helps assure an even heat transfer from the pan to the item. The amount you add to the pan will depend upon the type of food being prepared. The more natural marbling or fat present in the food, the less fat you need to add. Well-seasoned or nonstick pans may not require any fat beyond that which is already present in the food.

Red meats and/or very thin meat pieces will sauté best when fat is at, or nearly at, the smok-

FIGURE 9-28   Trout à la Meunière

(1) Add fish to a pan with preheated oil, clarified butter, or a mixture of both.

(2) Turn the trout when the first side is golden brown. Note the use of both an offset spatula and a flexible spatula for greater control.

(3) Pour off the clarified butter, add fresh whole butter, and allow it to cook until lightly browned.

(4) Add the lemon juice and parsley.

FIGURE 9-29   Swiss-Style Shredded Veal

(1) Sauté the veal émincé in a sauté pan sized to hold the meat comfortably. Do not overcrowd or the color and flavor will not develop.

(2) Remove the veal once it has a good color on both sides.

(3) After the sauce is finished (made directly in the pan) return the veal to coat with the sauce and briefly reheat.

FIGURE 9-30   Sautéed Pork with Winter Fruits

(1) Pork medallions are sautéed until browned. Note the color change on the unturned piece, which indicates that it is ready to be turned.

(2) Deglaze the sauté pan with stock.

(3) Add the garnishing ingredients to the sauce.

ing point. Less-intense heat is required for white meats, fish, shellfish, most vegetables, fruits, and eggs.

Both the pan and the cooking medium must be allowed to reach the correct temperature before the main item is added. This assures that as soon as the food hits the hot pan, the cooking process begins. The juices released by the food should cook down quickly, coating and glazing the food, as well as forming a rich fond, used to flavor the sauce.

It is important that the best-looking side of the food (the side you want facing up to the customer), should go down onto the heated pan first. Do not crowd the food, and avoid overlapping pieces. Direct contact with the pan is critical to the proper development of color and flavor.

2. Turn the item(s) once.

Sautéed foods should be thin enough to cook properly after only a few minutes on each side. Turning foods repeatedly during cooking can disturb the process of flavor development. There are exceptions to this general piece of wisdom, however. Stir-frying is one such instance. Sautéed vegetables and fruits may repeatedly be tossed or turned as they cook. Common sense and experience will guide you. For even more specific details, refer to recipes, at the back of this book or elsewhere.

Very thin pieces of meat are generally cooked completely on top of the stove, over high heat. Larger cuts of meat that must be cooked through (veal, chicken, and pork, for example), may need to have the heat beneath them lowered slightly during the final phases of sautéing. Another option is to finish them in the oven, either in the sauté pan or in a baking dish, sizzler platter, or sheet pan.

Determining doneness for sautéed foods is an imprecise science. It might seem helpful to indicate that a strip loin steak, for example, will be cooked to medium rare in 6 to 7 minutes. Such an instruction ignores some crucial factors which will alter the actual cooking time however: the intensity of the heat beneath the pan, the pan's material, the number of meat pieces in the pan, how well aged the meat is, the conditions under which the meat was raised and/or harvested, and so on. In general, the thinner, moister, and more delicate the food, the more quickly it will cook.

3. Remove the food from the pan while preparing the sauce (if any), add the appropriate flavoring or garnishing ingredients, and serve at once on heated plates.

Sautéed foods will not, as a rule, hold as much heat as roasted items. They will, however, continue to cook a little once removed from the pan, as a result of carryover cooking. Be sure to allow a slight margin, so that foods are not overdone by the time you are ready to put them on a plate.

Making Sauces for Sautéed Foods

The basic technique for making a sauce that incorporates the fond in sauté pans is this:

1. Remove any excess fat or oil.

2. Add aromatic ingredients or garnish items that need to be cooked, such as garlic, shallots, mushrooms, ginger, and so forth.

3. Deglaze the pan, releasing the reduced drippings from the pan.

Wines, cognac, water, or broths can be used for this step. Whatever liquid is added should be reduced; this means that fortified wines should be reserved until later, since their flavors are best when not allowed to reduce.

4. Add the base sauce (brown sauce, demi-glace, jus de veau lié, for example). Other ingredients intended to add flavor, texture, and color can be added along with the base sauce, as appropriate.

5. Add garnish and finishing ingredients. Cream, butter, purées of vegetables or herbs, or fortified wines are added last.

In many cases, chefs opt to return the main item (a chicken breast or veal scallop, for example) to the finished sauce briefly. This glazes and coats the item, and reheats it very gently. The sauce may be ladled directly onto the plate, forming a shallow pool, and the sautéed item is placed on the sauce. Or, the sauce may be ladled over the food. Be sure that any stray spots or drips are carefully wiped from the plate using a clean cloth wrung out in hot water.

Variations on the Basic Sautéing Technique

Scrambled eggs, omelets, and stir-frys, are quite similar in execution to a classic sauté technique. They require high heat, relatively small amounts of cooking fats, and are quickly prepared. The selection and preparation of ingredients and equipment is very important.

Scrambling Eggs and Preparing Omelets According to Escoffier: "In a few words, what is an omelet? It is really a special type of scrambled egg enclosed in a coating or envelop of coagulated egg and nothing else." **Scrambled eggs** and **omelets** are made by whisking together the eggs so that the yolks and whites are evenly blended. They are then cooked over gentle heat, keeping the pan and the eggs in motion constantly, until the eggs begin to form a soft, thickened mass. The photos in Figure 9-31 show the various stages of scrambling eggs. The classic rolled omelet (see Figure 9-32) is also shown.

FIGURE 9-31 Scrambling Eggs

(1) Add the beaten eggs to a pan, preheated over moderate heat.

(2) Keep the eggs in constant motion, so that soft curds form slowly.

(3) At this point the eggs are almost fully scrambled.

FIGURE 9-32 Making a Rolled Omelet

(1) Stop stirring the eggs when they reach a softly set state (see Figure 9-31(3)) and allow a skin to form. Then, release the eggs from the skillet by jarring the handle.

(2) Roll the omelet out of the pan onto a heated plate.

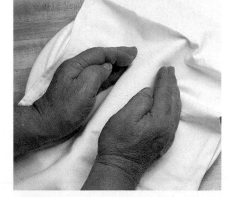

(3) If desired, shape the omelet using a clean towel or napkin.

(4) Lightly "glaze" the omelet with butter for added sheen.

Stir-Frying Generally associated with Asian styles of cooking and successfully borrowed by innovative Western chefs, **stir-frying** shares many similarities with sautéing. A wok is the traditional tool for stir-frying, constructed and shaped specially for this cooking technique. The wok concentrates heat in the bottom of the pan. The sides of the pan conduct varying degrees of heat, creating zones that allow a variety of foods to be prepared in a single pan, without overcooking or undercooking any single item.

Foods must be cut properly, usually into small strips, dice, or shreds. They are added to the pan in sequence, with foods requiring the longest cooking time added first, and those that cook very quickly or are simply included for flavor and texture added at the last moment.

Rather than turning the food once, you should keep stir-fried foods constantly in motion. Push them up to the sides of the wok out of the most intensely heated part of the pan. This makes room for items to be added to the bottom of the wok in their turn.

Sauces are frequently part of stir-fried dishes. They are generally combinations of intensely flavored liquids and oils such as soy sauce and sesame oil, occasionally thickened with a small amount of arrowroot or cornstarch slurry.

Pan-Frying

The object of **pan-frying** is to produce a flavorful exterior with a crisp, brown crust, which acts as a barrier to retain juices and flavor. Because the product itself is not browned, the flavor will be different than if the item had been sautéed. The proper color depends upon the type of item, the coating that is used and, to a certain extent, the item's thickness. The color of relatively thin and delicate meats, fish, shellfish, and poultry should be golden to amber. Thicker pieces may take on a deeper color, resulting from longer cooking time. In all cases, the product should not be extremely pale. As with sautéing, a lack of color indicates that improper heat levels or the incorrect pan size were used.

Only naturally tender foods should be pan-fried and, after cooking, the product should still be tender and moist. Excessive dryness means the food was allowed to overcook, was cooked too far in advance and held too long, or was cooked at a temperature higher than required.

Although this technique shares similarities with sautéing, there are some important differences. While a sautéed item is often lightly dusted with flour and quickly cooked over high heat in a small amount of oil, a pan-fried food is usually coated with batter or breaded and cooked in a larger amount of oil over less-intense heat. The product is cooked more by the oil's heat than by direct con-

FIGURE 9-33   Southern-Fried Chicken

(1) Chicken is marinated in seasoned milk or buttermilk and then coated with flour.

(2) Add the pieces in a single layer to hot oil. Turn periodically until the chicken is evenly browned and fully cooked.

(3) Make a roux using some of the cooking oil.

(4) Add stock to make a gravy and simmer, then finish with cream if desired.

FIGURE 9-34   Wiener Schnitzel

(1) Breaded cutlets are pan-fried in hot oil and turned carefully.

(2) Note the color of the properly cooked schnitzel, as well as the quantity of oil used for pan-frying.

tact with the pan. In pan-frying, the hot oil seals the food's coated surface, thereby creating a more defined crust. Because few juices are released in the pan and a larger amount of oil is involved, any accompanying sauce is typically made separately, although there are some classic exceptions.

Mise en Place

1. Assemble all ingredients and preparations used for pan-frying:

   • Main item: meat, poultry, fish, vegetable

   • Breadings, batters, or other coatings

   • Oil

   • Stuffings, marinades, or seasoning mixtures

   • Ingredients for sauce or gravy

   Cut the food you are pan-frying into an appropriate size. A whole chicken, for instance, may be cut into eighths. Pork loins can be made

into cutlets, which are pounded to an even thickness. Veal is prepared in a similar fashion for scaloppine or wiener schnitzel (see Figure 9-34). Trim away any fat, silverskin, or gristle on meat. Remove the skin and bones for poultry suprêmes and fillets of fish, if necessary or desired. Zucchini, eggplant, and green tomatoes are usually sliced.

Items for **standard breading** include flour (with seasoning added if desired), milk and/or beaten eggs, and bread crumbs. Read more about the standard breading procedure on page 366. Batters, such as beer batter, are prepared according to the formula or recipe being used. They should be held at the correct temperature, if they are made in advance. Refer to recipes for guidance.

The oil for pan-frying should have the ability to reach high temperatures without breaking down or smoking. Vegetable oils, olive oil, and shortenings are all appropriate. Rendered animal fats have a place in certain regional and ethnic dishes. You should understand that many people have not grown up with these dishes on their daily table, however. Today's guest may find that chicken fried in lard tastes too heavy. Oils with particular flavors, especially olive oil or rendered bacon, pork, or goose fats, should be selected with an understanding that they will influence the flavor of the finished dish.

Fillings, stuffings, or sauces are all commonly a part of the pan-frying technique. Some dishes will call for a sauce made separately. For at least one classic dish, Southern-fried chicken, the gravy is made directly in the pan used to fry the food (see Figure 9-33).

2. Assemble all equipment necessary for preparation and service:

   • Pan

   • Tongs, kitchen fork, skimmer, spider

   • Holding or finishing pans

   • Setup to blot/drain after frying

   • Heated plates

---

wiener schnitzel: pan-fried breaded veal cutlets Viennese-style (served with butter, lemon, and parsley).

STANDARD BREADING PROCEDURE

This process, while optional, is a common way to prepare foods for pan-frying. If it is done correctly, the finished item will have an even coating that is extremely crisp, golden, and delicious.

Breading needs a little time to firm up before it is pan-fried for the best possible results. If you bread an item, then immediately put it into hot oil, there is a good chance that the breading will fall away. Not only will this have a negative impact on the dish's finished texture, it will also make the cooking oil break down quickly. Then, subsequent batches cooked in the same oil will blacken without cooking properly.

1. Dry the main item well, then hold it in one hand (left hand if you are right-handed, and right hand if you are left-handed) and dip it in flour. Shake off any excess flour, and transfer the food to the container of egg wash.

2. Switch hands, pick up the food and turn it if necessary to coat it on all sides. Transfer it to the container of bread crumbs. Use your dry hand to pack bread crumbs evenly around the food. Shake off any excess, then transfer the food to a holding tray.

3. Let the food rest under refrigeration for about 1 hour or longer before pan-frying.

4. Discard any unused flour, egg wash, or bread crumbs. The presence of juices, drippings, or particles of the food you just coated will contaminate these products, making them unsafe for use with other foods. Even sifting the flour or crumbs or straining the egg wash will not be sufficient to prevent cross-contamination and eliminate the potential for food poisoning.

The pan must be large enough to avoid overcrowding. If the pan is crowded, the oil's temperature will drop quickly and a good seal will not form. If this happens, the food may absorb the oil and the breading can become soggy or even fall away in places.

Method

1. Heat oil to correct temperature for food being cooked.

   In general, there should be enough cooking oil in the pan to allow the food to swim in the oil. As a rule of thumb, add enough oil so that it comes one-quarter to one-half the way up the sides of the food; the thinner the main item, the less oil is required.

   The pan and the cooking oil must reach the correct temperature before you add the food. Otherwise, the development of the crust will be slowed, and it may never achieve the desired color and texture. When a faint haze or slight shimmer is noticeable, the oil is usually hot enough.

2. Add food to hot oil and keep oil and/or food in motion.

   Getting all surfaces of pan-fried foods evenly browned and crisped requires that the food be in direct contact with the hot oil (see Figures 9-34 and 9-35). If foods are crowded, then they may not develop good colors and textures.

   If there is not enough oil in the pan, the food may stick to the pan and tear, or the coating may come away. Keep the oil and the food gently in motion, either by using tongs to carefully move the food around in the pan, or by using an easy circular motion to keep the oil in the pan moving.

   When pan-frying a large quantity of food in batches, remember to skim away any loose particles between batches. Add more fresh oil, or replace all of the oil, to keep the level constant and to prevent smoking or foaming.

3. Brown items on the first side, then turn them.

   Once a good crust and a pleasing color develops on the first side, turn the food. Continue to

FIGURE 9-35   Potato Pancakes

(1) The prepared batter is dropped by spoonfuls into heated oil. A cast iron skillet is often used for its ability to produce crisp crusts.

(2) Turn the cakes carefully to avoid splashing.

cook until a rich golden color develops on the second side. If the food is the right size and shape, it will be completely cooked at this point (see Figure 9-36). Foods that can finish cooking in the pan over direct heat should be watched carefully. If they are becoming too brown, turn the heat down.

4. Finish in pan or uncovered in oven.

FIGURE 9-36
Pan-Frying Batter-
Coated Zucchini
Slices

Some foods, because they are thick, include bones, or a stuffing, may need to finish cooking in the oven. If they do need to go into the oven, be sure that they are left uncovered to prevent steam from softening the crisp coating you have developed. Ideally, they should be placed on a rack.

5. Sauce and serve the food while it is still very hot.

Deep-Frying

In this technique, foods are cooked by being completely submerged in hot fat. Foods prepared by **deep-frying** are almost always given a coating—a standard breading, a batter such as a tempura or beer batter or, in some instances, a simple coating of flour alone. The coating acts as a barrier between the fat and the product and also contributes flavor and texture contrast. One notable exception is potatoes.

As with the other dry-heat methods that use cooking fats and oils, the foods must be naturally tender and of a shape and size that allow them to cook quickly without becoming tough or dry. Poultry, fish, and potatoes are among the most commonly selected foods for deep-frying. Vegetables, coated with breading or a tempura batter, are also popular choices. Cooked foods are often finely chopped, bound with a heavy béchamel or velouté, shaped into croquettes and then deep-fried.

Mise en Place

1. Assemble all ingredients and preparations used for deep-frying:

- Main item being prepared: meat, poultry, fish, vegetable
- Batters, breading, coatings (optional)
- Oil
- Separately prepared sauce

Cut the item into the appropriate size. Foods should be fairly thin, with a uniform size and shape so that they can cook rapidly and evenly. Remove the skin (especially from fish), as desired or as indicated in the recipe. Remove any gristle, fat, and silverskin or any inedible shells. Cut the food into chunks or fingers, or butterfly and pound it, depending upon the food's nature and the desired result.

Breading may be applied up to one hour in advance of deep-frying and chilled to allow the breading to firm. Batters or plain flour coatings should be applied immediately before cooking.

The cooking medium must be able to reach a high temperature without smoking or breaking down. Have available a neutral-flavored oil with a high smoking point. A rendered fat, such as lard, may be used to create a special flavor or effect, as in certain regional dishes. The careful se-

FAT AND OIL SELECTION AND MAINTENANCE

The ultimate quality of fried foods depends to a great extent on the proper selection and care of frying oils. Both fats and oils may be used as a cooking medium for deep-frying, although vegetable oil is most commonly used. Fats and oils differ in specific properties such as flavor, color, or smoking point, but they are all basically the same compound. They contain fatty acids, flavor compounds, and glycerin. The amount of saturated, monounsaturated, or polyunsaturated fats in an oil or shortening gives it a particular set of characteristics. For deep-fat frying, the ideal oil is one with a neutral flavor and color and a high smoking point (around 425°F/218°C).

If fried foods taste heavy, oily, or strongly of another food, it means that the oil was not properly handled. If the color has not developed properly, it may mean that the oil was not hot enough, or that too many items were added at once. With the exception of tempura, which should be light gold in color, most deep-fried foods should have a strong golden color.

Another possibility is that the oil is old, or has started to break down through extended use or improper care. Or, the oil may have been used to cook a strongly flavored food such as fish.

A properly deep-fried food's texture is moist and tender on the interior, with a crisp, delicate crust. If the crust has become soggy, the food may have been held too long after cooking or the coating may have been applied too heavily. In addition to selecting the proper oil, there are other measures you can take to help prolong the product's life. Follow these steps to get the best from your frying oil:

- Store oils in a cool, dry area and keep them away from strong lights, which leach vitamin A.

- Use a high-quality oil.

- Prevent the oil from coming in contact with copper, brass, or bronze, because these metals hasten breakdown.

- When frying moist items, dry them as thoroughly as possible before placing them in oil, because water breaks down the oil and lowers the smoking point.

- Do not salt products over the pan, because salt breaks down the oil.

- Fry items at the proper temperature. Do not overheat the oil.

- Turn off the fryer after using it and cover when it is not used for long periods of time.

- Constantly remove any small particles (such as loose bits of breading or batter) from the oil during use.

- Filter the kettle's entire contents after each shift, if possible, or at least once a day. After the oil has been properly filtered, replace 20 percent of the original volume with fresh oil, to extend the life of the entire amount.

- Discard the oil if it becomes rancid, smokes below 350°F (176°C), or foams excessively. As oil is used, it will darken; if it is a great deal darker than when it was fresh, it will brown the food too rapidly. The food may appear properly cooked but actually be underdone.

lection and maintenance of cooking oils for deep-fat frying is critical.

In addition to the usual salt-and-pepper seasoning mixture, spice blends, marinades, stuffings, or fillings are also commonly used to add interest to fried foods.

2. Assemble all equipment necessary for preparation and service:

- Frying kettle or fryolator
- Basket, spider, skimmer
- Tongs
- Set up to blot/drain after frying
- Container to finish in oven or hold warm
- Serving pieces

Electric or gas deep-fryers are excellent choices if you do a great deal of deep-frying, since they maintain even temperatures. They are also put together in such a way that it is relatively easy to clean them and care for the oil properly. If you fry many different types of foods, it is generally a good idea to reserve different fryers to handle different foods. This will help prevent flavor transfer. No one wants an apple fritter to taste like a piece of fish.

If you do not have a free-standing fryer, deep kettles or pots, such as stock pots, can be used. A thermometer will help control temperatures. Once the correct frying temperature is reached, adjust the heat so that the temperature remains relatively constant.

A collection of other equipment, baskets, spiders, tongs, and containers lined with absorbent toweling are all important.

Method

1. Place prepared items directly into hot oil.

When foods are added to hot oil, the oil will lose temperature for a brief time. The more food added, the lower the temperature will drop and the longer it will take to come back to the proper level. This period of time is known as "recovery time."

FIGURE 9-37
Vegetable Tempura Prepared by the Swimming Method

FIGURE 9-38
Breaded Shrimp Prepared by the Basket Method

There are three distinct approaches to introducing foods to the hot oil. The method chosen depends upon the food, any coating it may or may not have, and the intended result.

Swimming Method In the swimming method of frying, used for tempura and other batter-coated items (see Figure 9-37), the food is gently lowered into hot oil using tongs. Then, it falls to the bottom of the fryer. As it cooks, it "swims" back to the surface. It may be necessary to turn it once it reaches the surface, to allow it to brown evenly. It is then removed with a skimmer.

Basket Method The foods are placed in a basket that is lowered into the hot oil, and then they are lifted out in the basket once properly cooked. This method is generally used for breaded items (see Figure 9-38) and French fries.

Double-basket Method Certain types of food, in order to develop a good color, need to be fully submerged in hot oil for a fairly long time. Foods that would tend to rise to the surface too rapidly are placed in a basket, which is lowered into the hot oil, and are then held under the oil's surface by the bottom of a second basket. A variation on this method is used to produce nests from julienned potatoes with two ladels.

2. Cook foods to the proper color and doneness.

Some foods are fried in two stages. The first stage, known as blanching, gives foods a preliminary cooking at a lower temperature. This is typically done for French fries. During the initial cooking, the food cooks evenly but the surface does not brown completely. Then, once they are properly blanched, they are finished just at the time of service by submerging them in oil heated to a higher temperature.

Foods that are properly fried may rise to the surface, indicating that they are fully cooked. Or, you may rely on their appearance. A deep golden brown is appropriate (see Figures 9-39 and 9-40). Cutting foods into small pieces, or blanching them, or using precooked items, as for croquettes, are all ways to assure that fried foods are fully cooked.

If it is necessary, some foods, such as chicken pieces, can be partially cooked by deep-frying, and then allowed to finish in the oven. To prevent the crust from becoming too soggy or oily during this finishing, place the food on a rack in a sheet pan. That way, any excess oil will drain away, and no steam that could dampen the crust will develop.

---

lorette potatoes: puréed potatoes combined with pâté à choux and deep-fried.

FIGURE 9-39   Lorette Potatoes

(1) The lorette appareil is piped into shapes on parchment strips.

(2) The strip is lowered into the hot oil and the lorette potatoes release from the parchment.

(3) The properly cooked lorette potatoes.

FIGURE 9-40   Making Souffléd Potatoes

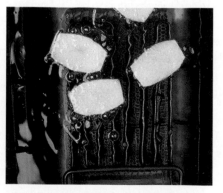

(1) Thinly sliced and shaped potatoes are placed in hot oil.

(2) The potatoes are beginning to "soufflé."

(3) Golden-brown souffléd potatoes being removed from the fryer.

3. Drain or blot foods and serve them while very hot.

   Fried foods retain their best quality for only a short time. The best approach is to drain them briefly, salt or season as desired, and then serve at once. Sometimes foods may be held for very short periods in a warm oven or under a heat lamp, but the shelf life of any fried food is short.

Summary

Once you have developed the following skills and abilities, you can begin the process of refining and creating virtually endless variations employing dry-heat cooking methods:

- Understanding how to properly grill, broil, and barbecue, roasting and baking, poêléing, sautéing (and variations), pan-frying, and deep-frying.

- Selecting the cuts of meat, poultry, fish and vegetables which are best suited for each type of dry-heat cooking method.

- Understanding how to make a sauce for sautéed food as well as pan-gravies or jus for roasts.

- Knowing how to select the proper cooking vessel and the amount of fat for pan-frying and deep-frying.

- Understand how to select and maintain frying oil.

SELF-STUDY QUESTIONS

1. What is meant by zones on a grill? Why is it important to establish zones?

2. List three characteristics of properly grilled food.

3. Briefly describe pan-broiling.

4. What is the purpose of marinating broiled or grilled items before cooking them?

5. Describe the spit-roasting method.

6. What is the difference between roasting and baking?

7. What is carryover cooking? How can it affect the quality of a roasted item?

8. What are the two major factors in successfully using dry-heat techniques without fats or oils?

9. What are the major differences between sautéing and pan-frying?

10. Name three reasons for dryness in pan-fried foods.

11. What is the difference between jus lié and pan gravy? Describe the method for making each sauce.

12. What meats are best suited for pôêléing? Briefly describe the poêléing method.

13. Name two cooking techniques derived from sautéing.

14. What are the stages of development of sautéed onions?

15. How does the size of a sauté pan and the amount of cooking oil affect the quality of a finished sautéed food?

16. Describe standard breading procedure.

17. List at least six practices that should help to maintain your frying oil.

18. List three possible reasons that fried food might taste heavy, oily, or have the strong flavor of another food.

- Deep-fry a batch of French fries using the proper two-stage procedure. Deep-fry another batch in only one stage. Compare the time it takes for each batch to develop the desired golden color. Does the oil behave differently with each batch? Taste and evaluate the two results. Which batch do you prefer? Why?

- Sauté two boneless skinless chicken breasts, one in a sauté pan with oil, the other in a nonstick pan without fat. Note how long it takes each to cook. Is there a difference in color between the two finished products? Taste and evaluate both. Is one more tender and moist? Is there a noticeable difference in flavor? Which do you prefer? Why?

- Roast two rump roasts in a 350° F (177° C) oven to an internal temperature of 111° F (44° C). Take both roasts out of the oven. Carve one of them immediately, making note of: 1) the ease or difficulty of carving, 2) the amount of juice lost during carving, 3) the doneness of the meat.

  Now take an internal temperature reading of the resting roast. Continue taking readings every 5 minutes until the temperature has peaked and starts dropping again. Then carve the roast and evaluate it using the same three criteria above. What are your conclusions?

KEYWORDS

à l'anglaise	grilling	pan gravy	smoke-roasting
à la meunière	jus	poêléing	spit-roasting
baking	jus lié	resting period	standard breading
barbecuing	larding	roasting	stir-frying
barding	mark	sautéing	zones
broiling	omelet	scrambled eggs	
carryover cooking	pan-broiling	searing	
deep frying	pan-frying	seize	

10
Moist-Heat and Combination Cooking Techniques

*Give us this day our daily taste…Raise up
among us stews with more gravy than we
have bread to lot it with…*

—ROBERT FARRAR CAPON

*The moist-heat techniques—steaming, poaching, simmering, and boiling—result in
products that have a distinctly different flavor, texture, and appearance from those
prepared with dry-heat methods. The foods prepared by these methods are generally
subtly flavored with a simple, straightforward appeal. These techniques typically
require the use of naturally tender meats, poultry, or fish, and vegetables and fruits.
The proper selection of a flavorful liquid adds an important dimension to many of
these preparations. Careful monitoring of cooking temperatures and times and the
ability to determine doneness are also critical to a mastery of moist-heat methods.*

Stewing and braising are known as "combination" methods because foods are usually given a preliminary preparation, such as the initial searing of a pot roast or blanching of veal for a blanquette, before the principal cooking technique is applied. A properly prepared braise or stew has a complexity and flavor concentration that is simply not possible with other cooking techniques. The dish's finished consistency should be smooth, suave, and meltingly tender, because of the slow cooking needed to soften the main item's tough connective tissues. Braising

and stewing are frequently regarded as "peasant" techniques, often associated with regional or home-style cooking.

The successful execution of these techniques depends on the proper choice of main ingredients and careful attention to proper technique throughout each step of preparation and service, as do all cookery methods. Contemporary renditions of classic dishes, such as a navarin made with lobster instead of mutton, are clear examples that no cooking technique need become outmoded.

CHAPTER OBJECTIVES

- Name the mise en place and methods for the following moist-heat cooking techniques:

  -steaming
  -poaching
  -stewing
  -braising
  -simmering
  -boiling

- Identify the kinds and cuts of food best suited to each of these techniques

- Determine the proper doneness of items cooked with moist-heat and combination techniques

- Name some variations on moist-heat techniques used to prepare eggs, various grains, legumes, vegetables, and fruits

Steaming and Its Variations

There are any number of foods that can be prepared by steaming or one of the techniques based on steaming. The cooking methods covered in this section include:

- Steaming

- Preparing foods *en papillote*

- Shallow-poaching

- Pan-steaming

All of these techniques cook foods by surrounding them with a vapor bath. In some cases, the food is suspended above a simmering or boiling liquid or stew. Foods prepared en papillote rely on the moisture naturally present in the food or introduced through the use of sauces or ingredients,

such as mushrooms or tomatoes, which have high moisture contents. Shallow-poaching and pan-steaming call for the food to be cooked directly in a small amount of liquid in a covered pan. The cover traps steam, cooking the portion of the food that is not submerged in the poaching liquid.

Steaming

Steaming is an efficient and highly effective way to prepare naturally tender foods. It is unfortunate that, to many minds, steaming has become synonymous with the bland foods suggested by diet plans for patients on a low-fat, low-cholesterol, and low-sodium regime. It is true that this technique lends itself to healthful cooking. But that does not mean

---

navarin: a lamb stew garnished with root vegetables, notably turnips.

that steamed foods are, or need to be, tasteless and uninteresting.

Foods that are steamed include such standard offerings as steamed lean fish, vegetables, poultry breasts, and some fruits. It also includes more exotic and unusual fare such as tamales or dim sum. (See Figure 10-1.) The success or failure of any steamed food rests upon the same criteria that are applied to sautéed or roasted foods. Is the dish moist, flavorful, and appealing from both a visual and textural stance? Are the flavors fully developed? Have the accompanying seasonings, garnishes, and sauces been selected with care and prepared with the same attention to detail as the main item?

Steamed foods are cooked by surrounding them with a vapor bath in a closed cooking vessel. Tiered aluminum or bamboo steamers, small inserts, couscoussières, gas or electric pressure or convection steamers can all be used to steam foods. The food should not come in direct contact with the liquid used to create the steam, and the container should stay closed until the food is properly cooked.

To add more interest to steamed foods, they may be stuffed, wrapped in aromatic leaves, marinated, or sauced. There is no excuse for serving uninteresting steamed vegetables, when the judicious application of some simple seasonings can make all the difference.

Overcooking foods in a steamer is a common problem. Once foods have gone from properly cooked to overdone, they become as dry and unappealing as a roast that was left untended for too long. Properly steamed foods do not generally lose much of their original volume, remaining exceptionally plump, moist, and tender. Just as a roast will continue to cook even after it is removed from the oven, so will steamed fish or poultry after being removed from a steamer. This makes timing of great importance.

Mise en Place

1. Assemble all ingredients and preparations used for steaming:

---

tamale: a cormeal-based dough, used to fill banana leaves or dried corn husks, steamed.

dim sum: a variety of appetizer-sized dumplings steamed, fried, or boiled.

FIGURE 10-1 Making Dim Sum

(1) Filling the dough wrappers.

(2) Arranging the dim sum in a steamer.

(3) The steamer is set over simmering water.

(4) The steamed dumplings with a dipping sauce.

- Main ingredient(s)
- Steaming liquid
- Additional or optional items for flavoring, finishing, and garnishing
- Sauce or items necessary to prepare sauce

Items to be steamed should be naturally tender and of a size and shape that will allow them to cook in a short amount of time. Cut the main item into the appropriate size, if necessary. Foods, especially meats, should be boned, trimmed, butterflied, pounded, or ground as appropriate.

Fish is generally made into fillets, though there are some classic presentations of whole steamed fish. Leave shellfish in the shells, unless otherwise indicated (scallops are customarily removed from the shell, for example).

Poultry breasts are often made into suprêmes, or boneless skinless pieces.

Vegetables and fruits should be handled as appropriate by type. Remove tough skins that could slow down cooking. Cut them into even, regular shapes, so that they will all finish cooking at the same time.

Relatively few grains are appropriate for steaming, with two notable exceptions. Couscous, not a true grain, is often steamed over a flavorful stew, or prepared on its own over simmering water (see Figure 10-2). Short grain rice may also be steamed. The length of time required to steam raw rice is considerable, however.

Any liquid may be used for steaming. Water is most commonly used. If you want to serve the steaming liquid as a flavorful broth along with the steamed food, you may prefer to select from other more highly flavored items: broths, stocks, wine, beer, or court bouillon. Adding aromatic ingredients to the liquid will also boost the flavor of the liquid, as well as adding flavor to the food being steamed. Herbs, spices, citrus rinds, gingerroot, garlic, or mushrooms could be added.

Stuffings or fillings, marinades, or wrappers can all be used in preparing steamed foods. Refer to recipes in Part IV, or in other resources for specific suggestions.

FIGURE 10-2   Steaming Couscous

(1) The top of the couscoussière is filled with couscous and set over a simmering stew.

(2) Steam is being released and clumps are being broken up by stirring with a kitchen fork.

2. Assemble all equipment necessary for cooking and serving:

- Steamer, steamer insert, or other equipment for steaming
- Steamer racks, pans, or inserts
- Tongs, spoons, spatulas
- Serving pieces

The quantity of food being steamed will guide you to the correct equipment (see Figure 10-3(1)). Small amounts of food can be steamed using a small insert. Larger quantities, or foods that require different cooking times, are better prepared in tiered steamers. Remember that it is important to allow enough room for steam to circulate completely around foods as they cook. This will encourage even, rapid cooking.

Convection or pressure steamers are good choices for steaming large quantities of foods.

FIGURE 10-3 Steaming Vegetables

(1) A small steamer with broccoli florets.

(2) A steamer insert ready to go into a pressure or convection steamer.

They allow the chef to steam foods in appropriate batch sizes throughout a meal period, or to handle the more intense demands of a banquet or institutional feeding situation.

In addition to steamers, you will also need to have on hand the necessary tools for handling foods, transferring them from the steamer to serving pieces, containers to hold sauces, and spoons, ladles, and other serving utensils.

Method

1. **Bring the liquid to a full boil in a covered vessel.**

   Add enough liquid to the bottom of the steamer to last throughout the entire cooking time. Each time you need to add more liquid to the pot, you will lower the cooking temperature, and affect the overall time necessary to prepare steamed foods.

   If you should need to open the lid during cooking time, remember to tilt the lid away from your face and hands, so the steam will not burn you.

2. **Add the main item to the steamer on a rack in a single layer.**

   To ensure even cooking, foods should be placed in a single layer, not touching one another, so that the steam can circulate completely. Foods may be placed on plates or in shallow dishes on the rack in order to collect any juices that might escape.

3. **Replace the lid and allow the steam to build up again.**

   It is a good idea to adjust the heat to maintain an even, moderate cooking speed. Liquids do not need to be at a rolling boil in order to produce steam. Rapid boiling may cause the liquid to cook away too quickly.

   Once the food is in the steamer and the cover has been replaced, avoid removing the lid unnecessarily. The drop in temperature can be significant. This makes it a little more difficult to gauge how long foods need to cook, so it may be a good idea to refer to tables of standard cooking times. Most recipes include information about how long specific foods take to steam to the correct doneness. Still, it is important to check the foods, starting at the earliest point at which they might be done.

4. **Steam the main item to the correct doneness.**

   Steamed foods should be cooked until they are just done. Since steaming is used as a preliminary cooking technique in many cases, remember to stop cooking earlier for parcooked foods. Foods that are to be puréed once steamed should be cooked until they are easy to pierce with a kitchen fork or paring knife, so they will mash easily. In general, check steamed foods for doneness by applying the tests described in the sidebar on page 378, taking texture, color, consistency, shape, and aroma into account.

5. **Serve the food immediately on heated plates with an appropriate sauce, as desired or as indicated by the recipe.**

DETERMINING DONENESS FOR MOIST-HEAT METHODS

Steamed, poached, and simmered/boiled foods should be plump, moist, tender to the bite, and *just* cooked when these moist heat methods are used as the primary cooking method. Excessive cooking will cause the food to take on an inappropriate texture. Vegetables that should have been just barely tender may become soft enough to mash, and they may well lose their best color. Foods meant to be puréed, however, should be cooked until they no longer offer any resistance when pierced or cut. In some cases, it will be possible to mash them with a fork or spoon. The terms used to refer to the different stages of doneness include:

- **Blanched**—foods are cooked just long enough to set colors or make them easy to peel.

- **Parcooked**—foods are cooked to partial doneness, as might be appropriate for vegetables or grains to be finished by sautéing or stewing.

- **Al dente** or tender-crisp—foods are cooked until they can be bitten into easily, but still offer a slight resistance and sense of texture. There should be no audible crunch, and foods should not fly off the plate when a guest tries to cut them.

- **Fully cooked**—foods are quite tender, though they should still retain their shape and color.

Any juices from poultry should be nearly colorless. Meats and poultry should offer a little resistance when pressed with a fingertip and should take on an evenly opaque appearance.

The flesh of fish and shellfish will lose its translucency when properly cooked, taking on a nearly opaque appearance.

Mussels, clams, and oysters will open when properly cooked and the edges of the flesh should curl.

Shrimp, crab, and lobster should have a bright pink or red color.

Vegetables and fruits should have a good color, with no dulling or graying evident. They should be tender to the bite, if they are being served directly from the steamer.

Grains should be fluffy and tender to the bite. Beans should be tender enough to mash easily, yet still retain their shape.

Cooking Foods en Papillote

In this variation of steaming, the main item and accompanying ingredients are encased in parchment paper and cooked in a hot oven. The main item may rest on a bed of herbs, vegetables, or sauce. The combination of these ingredients and their natural juices serves as the sauce. The steam created by the food's natural juices cooks the food. As the steam volume increases, the paper puffs up.

Foods that have been properly prepared **en papillote** will demonstrate the same characteristics of flavor, appearance, and texture as other steamed foods.

Mise en Place

1. Assemble all ingredients and preparations used for en papillote:

- Main item(s)

- Broth or sauce

- Additional or optional flavoring, seasoning, or garnishing items

In addition to the preparation techniques for steaming, there is an optional first step. Thicker meat cuts may be seared in advance to ensure that they will be adequately cooked during the relatively short cooking times associated with this technique, as well as to provide additional color and flavor.

Vegetables can be included to provide moisture for steam. They also add color, flavor, and texture. Cut the vegetables into a fine julienne or dice. Sweat or blanch the vegetables, if necessary, to ensure that they will cook in the same amount of time as the main item.

Prepare herbs and spices according to type. Some herbs may be left in sprigs; others are cut into a chiffonade or minced. Have prepared sauces, reduced heavy cream, wine, or citrus juices on hand if your recipe calls for them.

2. Assemble all equipment necessary for cooking and serving:

- Parchment paper
- Sizzler platters or baking sheets
- Serving pieces

Method

1. Assemble the packages.

The method for cutting the parchment and making the individual packages is shown in Figure 10-4. Cut the parchment into a heart shape large enough to allow the food and any additional ingredients to fit comfortably without overcrowding. The paper needs to have enough "give" to expand during cooking. Oil or butter the paper on both sides to prevent it from burning.

Place a bed of aromatics, vegetables, or sauce (if you are using these optional components) on one half of the heart and top it with the main item.

Fold the empty half of the heart over the main item and fold and crimp the edges of the paper to form a tight seal.

2. Place the bag on a preheated sizzler platter and put it in a very hot oven.

The oven temperature may need to be carefully monitored, since delicate foods such as fish fillets can be overcooked quickly at a high temperature. A thicker cut may be best if cooked slowly at a moderate temperature and "puffed" in a very hot oven.

Foods prepared en papillote should be cooked until they are just done. This is difficult to gauge without experience, since you cannot apply the senses of sight and touch in determining done-

FIGURE 10-4 Snapper en Papillote

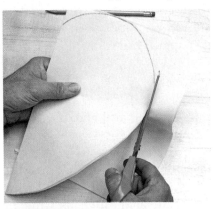

(1) Preparing the parchment heart.

(2) Arranging the ingredients on the oiled paper.

(3) Folding, crimping, and sealing the package.

(4) The fully cooked snapper being opened.

ness. If the item has been cut to the correct size or if it has been partially cooked before being placed en papillote, it should be done when the bag is very puffy and the paper is brown.

Shallow-Poaching

Shallow-poaching, like sautéing and grilling, is an à la minute technique suited to foods that are cut into portion-size or smaller pieces. This method cooks foods using a combination of steam and a liquid bath. The food is partially submerged in a liquid that often contains an acid, such as wine or lemon juice, and aromatics, such as shallots and herbs. The pan is loosely covered to capture some of the steam released by the liquid during cooking. The captured steam cooks the portion of the food not directly in the liquid.

In shallow-poaching, a significant amount of flavor is transferred from the food to the cooking liquid. This cooking liquid (or *cuisson*) is frequently used as the base for a sauce served with the main item. Adding acids, such as wine or lemon juice, to the cooking liquid gives the finished sauce a bright flavor. Those same ingredients also make it easier for butter to be emulsified in the sauce, thus a beurre blanc is often the sauce of choice.

Mise en Place

1. Assemble all ingredients and preparations used for shallow-poaching:

   - Main ingredient(s)

   - Liquid

   - Additional or optional items for flavoring, finishing, and garnishing

   - Items necessary to prepare the sauce

   Items to be shallow-poached should be naturally tender and of a size and shape that will allow them to cook in a short time. Remove the skin and bones from poultry and game birds to make them into suprêmes. Remove the skin and bones from fish to prepare fillets. The fillets may be rolled or folded to form **paupiettes.** The "meat" side of the fish should be on the outside. Remove shellfish from its shell, if desired.

The liquid should contribute flavor to the food as well as to the sauce prepared from the cooking liquid. Chose rich broths or stocks, and add wine, vinegar, and/or citrus juice.

Cut shallots, garlic, or gingerroot finely or mince them. Other ingredients you wish to serve along with the sauce as a garnish should be cut neatly into strips, dice, julienne, or chiffonade. These ingredients are often allowed to smother or parcook in advance of shallow-poaching the main item. This is done to develop the best possible flavor, as well as to make certain that all of the ingredients in the finished dish are fully cooked at the same time.

The sauce you prepare may be a beurre blanc, sauce vin blanc, or simply the reduced cooking liquids served as a broth.

If you need butter for a beurre blanc, it should be diced and kept cool. Sauce vin blanc may require a velouté, egg yolks, and/or butter. Refer to specific recipes for additional suggestions or guidance.

2. Assemble all equipment necessary for cooking and serving:

   - Sauté pan, or other suitable cooking vessel

   - Parchment or loose-fitting lid

   - Serving pieces as needed: strainers, whip, tongs, etc.

   Select the pan or baking dishes carefully for shallow-poached dishes. If there is too much space left around the food, then you will need to add a significant quantity of poaching liquid. This will have several adverse effects: It will make it easier to overcook the food; sauce preparation will take longer, since you will have more liquid to reduce, cooking speed can be more difficult to control properly and there could be a lack of flavor in both the main item and the sauce.

Parchment is generally used to loosely cover the pan as the food cooks. It traps enough of the steam to cook the unexposed part of the food, but not so much that the cooking speed acceler-

FIGURE 10-5   Shallow-Poaching Fillet of Sole

(1) The sole is placed in a pan of the correct size and lightly covered with parchment.

(2) Adding velouté to the reduced cooking liquid to prepare a sauce vin blanc.

ates. Maintaining a gentle, low cooking temperature is the best way to produce the most delicious results.

Method

1. Add the ingredients to the pan. (The method for shallow-poaching is shown in Figure 10-5.)

   Although not always essential, a coating of butter is generally spread in an even layer in a cold pan or baking dish. Then, the aromatic ingredients (shallots, garlic, vegetables, herbs, or mushrooms) are added in an even layer. They may be allowed to smother lightly in the butter at this point, or they may have been cooked separately. If they can cook completely in the time it takes to properly cook the main item and prepare sauce, they can be added raw.

2. Add the main item and the cooking liquid.

   Set the main item on top of the aromatics, and then pour in the liquid. It is not necessary in most cases to have already heated the liquid. For large items, it may be helpful, however. Be careful that it is not at a full boil, however.

   The liquid's level should be no higher than halfway up the item; generally, less liquid is required.

3. Bring the liquid to a bare simmer over direct heat.

   The liquid is typically brought up to the correct cooking speed over direct heat. There may be some occasions when it is preferable to perform the entire cooking operation in the oven, however. The quantity of food being prepared and available equipment will dictate where it is most logically done. Do not allow the liquid to boil at any time. A rapid boil will cook the food too quickly, affecting the quality of the dish. Fish might easily break apart or poultry and game suprêmes may toughen if they are not cooked at the correct temperature—never more than 170°F (75°C).

4. Lightly cover the sauté pan with parchment paper and finish cooking the main item either over direct heat or in a moderate oven.

   Acceptable results can be achieved by finishing the cooking over direct heat; however, the heat in an oven, which is more even and gentle, is preferable. In addition, finishing shallow-poaching in the oven makes burner space available for other purposes. Shallow-poached foods should be cooked until they are just done. Apply the tests outlined above for moist-heat methods.

5. Transfer the main item to a holding dish. Moisten it with a small amount of the cooking liquid. Cover the item and keep it warm while completing the sauce.

6. Prepare a sauce from the cooking liquid.

7. Ladle the sauce over the food and serve it while still very hot.

Making a Sauce from the Cooking Liquid

Allow the cooking liquid to reduce rapidly over direct heat until it is thickened. This concentrates the flavors and will form the foundation for the sauce.

Add the additional ingredients for the sauce, including any seasoning or garnish ingredients. Butter is often added for a beurre blanc. Keep the pan in motion as the butter is added, a little at a time. Velouté or béchamel may be required for a vin blanc sauce.

Finishing ingredients, such as liaisons, must be added carefully so that they cook properly. It is usually safest to add egg yolk and cream liaisons away from direct heat. With experience, however, many chefs find it possible to add these delicate ingredients without any problem over direct heat.

For additional information about beurre blanc or sauce vin blanc, refer to Chapter 8, "Sauces". For additional suggestions and recommendations to prepare sauces for shallow-poached items, refer to specific recipes, either in Part IV of this book or other sources.

Pan-steaming

Pan-steaming cooks foods by placing them directly in a liquid, such as water, broth, or court bouillon. There should not be so much water that the food is completely submerged, however. This technique is most often used to prepare vegetables.

The mise en place for ingredients and equipment is similar to that required for shallow-poaching, with the following difference: A tight-fitting lid is essential in order to pan-steam foods fully and quickly. Speed is one of this technique's most valuable assets.

The amount of liquid required is determined by the texture of the food being pan-steamed. For denser foods, such as carrots or turnips, you may need more liquid. Delicate items, including new peas or asparagus tips, may require relatively little liquid.

Mise en Place

1. Assemble all ingredients for pan-steaming.

   Refer to the information for both shallow-poaching and steaming (above). Since the liquid used in pan-steaming is often discarded, water is the most ordinary choice. The addition of aromatics, such as chopped shallots or additional minced vegetables is common.

Once foods are pan-steamed, the liquid may be drained away and a little cream or butter added to finish the dish. These are optional ingredients.

2. Assemble all equipment necessary for cooking and serving.

   Apart from the usual serving pieces, the only requirement for pan-steaming is a sautoir or rondeau with a tight-fitting lid. It is important to select a pan that can comfortably hold the food being pan-steamed without crowding. Remember that the food should be added to the pan in a single, even layer (see Figure 10-6).

Method

1. Bring the liquid to a boil in a pan.

   If you are adding any special aromatics, they should be added to the liquid as it comes to a boil so that they can release their flavors.

2. Add the food being pan-steamed in a single layer.

   Some foods, such as peas, may be allowed to pile up in the pan but, in general, there should be only enough food added so that the liquid comes up about one-quarter to one-third of the depth of the food, with enough head room between the top of the food and the lid to allow steam to build up.

3. Cover the pan and cook until the food is properly done.

FIGURE 10-6
Pan-Steaming
Cauliflower

Refer to the tests for doneness in moist-heat methods outlined on page 378.

The Submersion Techniques

Poaching, simmering, and boiling are techniques that call for a food to be completely submerged in a liquid that is kept at a constant, moderate temperature. The distinction between each technique is only a slight difference in cooking temperatures.

At the low end of the temperature range, from around 160 to 185°F (70° to 82°), foods are considered "poached." There should be relatively little flavor lost from the food to the cooking liquid. At the middle range, from 185 to 200°F (82 to 85°C), foods may be referred to as either simmered or "boiled." Simmering temperatures encourage a greater transfer of flavor from the food being prepared into the liquid. It is important to monitor these temperatures in order to properly cook foods such as less-tender cuts of meat, stewing hens, and some vegetables. This is the same approximate temperature necessary to make rich broths or stocks, where the goal is producing a richly flavored liquid.

Boiling, done either at or close to a true boil (212°F/100°C), is best for grains, beans, pasta, and some vegetables. Often foods are referred to as boiled when it might be more accurate to say that they are simmered. Very often, the distinction is simply made according to the accepted usage. Boiled eggs, New England boiled dinners, and boiled potatoes are all truly simmered. Simmering and boiling will be considered together as one basic cooking technique however, since they are used with the same types of foods.

The major areas of concern with all of these methods are proper development of flavor, color, and texture in the finished dish, a proper balance between the main ingredients and any aromatic, seasoning or flavoring ingredients, and careful monitoring of cooking temperature and speed. As you become more comfortable with these skills, you will be able to produce perfectly poached, boiled, and simmered foods that have full, satisfying flavors, textures, aromas, and colors.

The desired degrees of doneness, and terms used to refer to those stages include all of those previously described for moist-heat methods on page 378. In addition, some foods are cooked when they are **fork tender.** This means they are cooked to a point at which they slide from a kitchen fork easily when lifted or pierced.

Poaching

Poached foods are often naturally tender. Eggs, fruits, chickens, and fish all respond well to this technique, for example.

Poaching is done within a temperature range of 160 to 185°F (70 to 82°C). The surface of a poaching liquid should show some motion, sometimes called "shivering," but no air bubbles should break the surface.

Mise en Place

1. Assemble all ingredients and preparations used for poaching:

- Main ingredient(s)
- Liquid
- Additional or optional items for flavoring, finishing, and garnishing
- Items necessary to prepare sauce

Many different foods are poached: chicken, fish, eggs, fruits, and occasionally meats. Even though the cooking method is fairly gentle, it is often a good idea to give some items a little added protection. Prepare whole fish by wrapping it in cheesecloth to protect it from breaking apart during cooking. Stuff poultry or meats, if desired, and truss or tie them to help retain their shape.

The poaching liquid should be appropriate to the food and well flavored in order to compensate for any flavor lost during cooking. It is important to use good-quality stocks, broths, or court bouillons, and enough aromatic ingredients, such as herbs, wines, spices, and vegetables, to produce a full, pleasing flavor in both the finished product and any sauce prepared from the poaching liquid.

Poached items may also be served with a pungent sauce prepared separately, as with tradi-

FIGURE 10-7   Poaching Salmon

(1) The salmon is set on a poaching rack to protect it from breaking up during cooking.

(2) The court bouillon's temperature should now be reduced to ensure the correct cooking speed.

(3) The salmon in the poaching liquid. Thermometer now reads 160°F (70°C).

(4) Removing the center bone from the poached salmon.

tional "boiled" beef served with a horseradish sauce.

2. Assemble all equipment necessary for cooking and serving:

- Poacher or other appropriately sized pot
- Ladles or skimmers
- Holding containers to keep foods warm (optional)
- Carving boards and slicers (optional)
- Instant-reading thermometer

The pot used for poaching should be selected with attention to the size and shape of the food being prepared. The pot should hold the food, the liquid, and aromatics comfortably, with enough room to allow the liquid to expand as it heats. There should also be enough space so that the surface can be skimmed if necessary throughout cooking. Racks or trivets may be necessary to protect the food from sticking to the bottom of the pot during cooking. Specially designed fish poachers can be used if available.

An instant-reading thermometer can be used both to gauge doneness and to monitor the temperature of the cooking liquid. It can be difficult to see the difference between a liquid at a perfect poaching temperature and one that is a degree or two away from a slow boil. The difference to the food's quality can be quite dramatic, however.

Method

1. Combine the food to be poached with the liquid and bring to the correct cooking temperature. (The method for poaching salmon is shown in Figure 10-7.)

Some foods are allowed to start off in cool water. Others are placed into water that is already at poaching temperature. The choice is made according to the needs of the item itself, as well as the overall cooking time. Eggs, for instance, should be started in water already at about 160 to 170°F (70 to 75°C) (see Figure 10-8). Dense fruits, such as pears, might be allowed to come

FIGURE 10-8   Poaching Eggs

(1) Adding the eggs to heated water.

(2) Stopping the cooking to hold for later service.

(3) Blotting the egg after it is reheated, to remove excess water.

up to temperature along with the cooking liquid, to ensure that they are evenly and fully cooked. (See Figure 10-9.)

Be sure that the item is completely submerged in the liquid. This is especially important for poultry. If a part of the food is above the level of the cooking liquid, cooking will be uneven, and the finished product will probably not have the proper color or texture.

2. Maintain the desired cooking speed throughout the poaching process.

Make sure the liquid does not boil. The temperature should be checked periodically with an instant-reading thermometer and the heat adjusted as necessary. If a cover is used on a fish poacher, the cooking speed must be monitored regularly. Covering a pot creates pressure, which causes the liquid's temperature to become higher. Setting the lid just slightly ajar may be a good precaution to prevent boiling.

As is true for shallow-poached items, it is sometimes desirable to complete poaching in the oven, once the proper cooking temperature has been reached over direct heat. Common sense will tell you which items can be placed in the oven and which should remain on top of the stove. For instance, it would be difficult and dangerous to lift a large pot full of hot liquid off the stove and place it into the oven.

Skim the surface of the liquid throughout the cooking time, if necessary. This will help the

dish to develop appropriate and attractive colors, as well as keeping the broth from becoming too cloudy.

3. Carefully remove the main item to a holding container and moisten it with some of the liquid to prevent it from drying out while the sauce is being prepared.

Poached foods should be cooked just until the food is set and a safe internal temperature is reached. Refer to the information on page 378 concerning degrees of doneness and tests for determining when a food is properly poached.

If a poached or simmered item is to be served cold, it may be desirable to slightly undercook it. Then, the pot can be removed from the heat and the food allowed to cool in the

FIGURE 10-9
Poaching Pears in
Red Wine

poaching liquid. The liquid will retain enough heat to complete the cooking process and the item will reabsorb some of the flavors lost to the cooking liquid.

Once it has reached room temperature, the item and the broth should be carefully cooled and stored for later use. The liquid is customarily used in a sauce or as the basis of another dish.

4. Serve the food at the appropriate temperature with the necesary sauces and garnish.

Observe the standard rules of thumb regarding service of foods: hot foods hot, on hot plates; cold foods cold, on chilled plates. Depending upon the food itself, you may need to carve, disjoint, slice, or portion the food before plating it.

Simmering and Boiling

Simmered foods are often referred to as being **boiled**; however, this is not an accurate description of the cooking speed. In fact, the liquid's temperature should be kept as close to a boil as possible without ever reaching a true boil. A vigorous boil causes most meats, fish, and poultry to become tough and stringy. The temperature should be high enough to allow connective tissues to soften, however. Usually the required cooking time is deliberately extended to allow even well-exercised cuts of meat to become tender to the bite.

Dried beans and grains, meals, and some vegetables are more often boiled. The few additional degrees are necessary to soften the tough fibers and coatings that make these foods such excellent candidates for extended storage. Boiling both rehydrates and cooks the food, changing the texture from dry and hard into something agreeable to the palate.

Mise en Place

1. Assemble all ingredients and preparations used for simmering and boiling:

   - Main ingredient(s)
   - Liquid
   - Additional or optional items for flavoring, finishing, and garnishing

   - Items necessary to prepare sauce

Some items to be simmered are naturally tender. Wrap whole fish in cheesecloth to protect it from breaking apart during cooking. Stuff meats or poultry, if desired. Proper tying or trussing of the item will ensure that its natural shape is preserved.

Most dried beans and some grains may require an initial soaking to begin softening them. This can be done in one of two ways. The long soak method requires covering the item with cool water and leaving it to soak for several hours. The quick-soak method calls for beans to be combined with cold water, brought up to a boil, and allowed to steep in the hot water for about 1 hour. In either case, they should be drained before beginning the actual boiling process.

The liquid used for simmering should be appropriate to the food and well flavored in order to compensate for any flavor lost during cooking. It is important to use good-quality stocks and enough aromatic ingredients, such as herbs, wines, spices, and vegetables, to produce a full, pleasing flavor in both the finished product and any sauce prepared from the liquid. Boiled foods are often prepared in plain or salted water.

Boiled foods are often served with a pungent sauce prepared separately—pasta served with a tomato sauce, for instance. Others are simply dressed with butter and seasoned.

2. Assemble all equipment necessary for cooking and serving:

   - Poacher or other pot
   - Ladles or skimmers
   - Strainers or colanders
   - Holding containers to keep foods warm or to hold once cooled (optional)
   - Carving boards and slicers (optional)
   - Instant-reading thermometer

The pots used for simmering and boiling should be selected with attention to the size and shape of the food being prepared. They should hold the food, the liquid, and any aromatics comfortably, with

Moist-Heat and Combination Cooking Techniques

enough room to allow the liquid to expand as it heats. There should also be enough space so that the surface can be skimmed if necessary throughout cooking. A tight-fitting lid is necessary for some types of simmering and boiling, such as pilafs (see page 389). The method for boiling lobsters is shown in Figure 10-10.

Method

1. **Combine the food to be simmered or boiled with the liquid and bring to the correct cooking temperature.**

   Some foods are allowed to start off in cool water—potatoes or heavily salted or brined meats, for instance. Others, such as pastas or vegetables, are added to a liquid that is already at the correct temperature. This allows the liquid to return to the correct temperature quickly after the item is added to ensure proper cooking.

   In general, the amount of liquid in the pot should be sufficient to keep the item completely submerged throughout cooking time. Grains and beans will absorb significant amounts of liquid as they cook. Add more water or stock if necessary to keep the pot from cooking dry. By the end of cooking time, there may be no free liquid at all. For more specific details, refer to the recipes in Part IV.

2. **Maintain the proper cooking temperature throughout the simmering or boiling process.**

   Maintain an even cooking temperature throughout cooking time. Skim the surface of the liquid to remove any impurities, if necessary. This will help the dish to develop appropriate and attractive colors, as well as keeping any broth from becoming too cloudy—an important point if the broth is to be used as a sauce or served separately.

   The tests for doneness will vary from one food type to another. Polenta for instance, should pull cleanly away from the sides of the pot. Risotto should be creamy. Rice pilafs should be fluffy and separate easily into distinct grains. Pasta is cooked al dente, the point at which it is tender enough to bite into easily, although it

FIGURE 10-10 Boiling Lobsters

(1) Killing the lobster.

(2) Adding the lobster to rapidly boiling water.

(3) The color is beginning to change.

(4) Removing the cooked lobster to a holding container.

FIGURE 10-11
Carving Boiled
Corned Beef

FIGURE 10-12   Cooking Pasta

(1) Salt is being added to boiling water.

should not be mushy. Meats should be fork tender. Refer to the sidebar on page 378 for more information.

3. Carefully remove the main item as appropriate.

The food is ready to finish as desired, or it may be properly cooled and stored for later service. Figure 10-11 shows boiled corned beef being carved.

(2) Add the pasta and separate the strands to prevent clumps from forming.

Special Boiling Methods

Pasta

Pasta is traditionally cooked in boiling or near-boiling water. (See Figure 10-12.) Most chefs like to add salt to the water. If it is added, there should be enough so that the taste of salt is just barely discernible.

Add dry or fresh pasta to simmering or boiling water. Stir the pasta with a fork to separate the strands. If this step is ignored, the pasta will clump together as it cooks. Fresh pasta should be cooked at a slightly slower speed than dried pasta to keep it from falling apart. Filled pastas, such as tortellini and ravioli, should be cooked at a bare simmer so that they do not separate.

Once the pasta has cooked sufficiently, drain it immediately, and then process as necessary. If it is to be served right away, combine it with any sauce or garnish ingredients suggested by the recipe. To hold pasta for later service, drain it in a colander, rinse it with or submerge it in cool water, and allow it to drain well again. If desired, you can rub a little oil through the pasta to help keep the pieces separated.

(3) Draining the pasta in a colander.

(4) Rinsing the pasta with cold water to stop cooking.

FIGURE 10-13   Making Spaetzle

(1) Using a spaetzle board and a spatula.

(2) Using a spaetzle-maker.

(3) Using a ricer.

To reheat pasta that has been cooled, drop it into simmering water long enough to reheat. Then drain it well before combining it with sauces or garnish.

Spaetzle

Spaetzle is a kind of soft noodle made from a batter which is added to water or broth at a lazy simmer. Three techniques for shaping spaetzle are shown in Figure 10-13. The recipe can be found in Part IV, Chapter 22.

Pilaf

Pilafs are grain dishes that should be light, fluffy, and relatively dry. To achieve this, it is important to observe the correct ratio of grain to liquid. For specific information, refer to the chart included in Appendix 2. Figure 10-14 shows the proper method for preparing rice pilaf.

Any aromatic vegetables you will be including, such as onions or leeks, should be smothered in fat or oil first. Then the grain is added and stirred until it is completely coated with oil. Next the correct amount of liquid is added and brought to a simmer. Herbs, spices, or other seasonings can also be added at this point. To prevent the grain from becoming sticky, it is not stirred once a simmer is reached.

At this point, the pot should be covered. The pilaf can be finished either over direct heat or in the oven. When properly cooked, the grains should separate easily when fluffed with a fork.

Polenta and Other Cereals

Polenta (see Figure 10-15), and other cereals, are prepared as follows: Bring the liquid to a simmer. Gradually add the cereal, stirring constantly so that lumps don't form. Many traditionalists feel that polenta should be added so slowly that you can see through the stream as it is poured into the pot. Others like to add a handful at a time.

Once the cereal is added, it is generally stirred constantly as it returns to a simmer. Some cereals require less stirring (oatmeal or farina, for instance); others demand constant stirring (polenta and grits). Continue to cook, stirring as needed, until the correct consistency and doneness is reached. Polenta is properly cooked when the cereal forms a mass that pulls away from the sides of the pot.

Risotto

Risotto, like pilaf, demands careful attention to ratios between grain and liquid. Unlike pilaf, risotto cannot be successfully prepared with a wide variety of grains. Instead, a round grain rice, such as arborio, is generally specified. This rice has the best properties for preparing a creamy dish, since the starch is released more readily during cooking.

FIGURE 10-14   Making Rice Pilaf

(1) Onions are allowed to cook until the flavor is developed.

(2) The rice is added and stirred until coated with oil.

(3) The stock and aromatics are added and brought to a simmer before the pot is covered and cooking finished.

(4) The rice has absorbed all of the stock and is ready to serve.

FIGURE 10-15   Preparing Polenta

(1) Add the cornmeal gradually to simmering water. Stir constantly with a wooden spoon throughout cooking time.

(2) The polenta is at the correct consistency.

(3) Spread the polenta into an even layer and cool to use later.

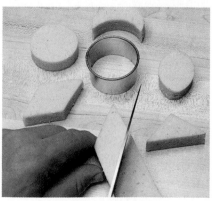

(4) Polenta can be cut into a variety of shapes, then grilled, pan-fried, baked, or broiled before serving.

Aromatic vegetables, spices (e.g. saffron), and rice are given a preliminary sauté in oil or butter, as is done for pilaf. However, rather than adding all of the liquid at once and coming immediately to the correct cooking speed, the liquid is added in smaller quantities, usually in thirds. The risotto is stirred constantly as each addition is absorbed by the grain. For the final addition of liquid, some recipes call for wine. This should not be added earlier, since the acids in wine could prevent the grain from softening properly. Figure 10-16 shows the method for preparing risotto. Figure 10-17 shows a fully cooked saffron risotto in the pot.

The Combination Cooking Methods

Braising

This technique is considered appropriate for foods that are portion-sized or larger, or cuts from more-exercised areas of large animals, mature whole birds, or large fish. Relatively little liquid (stock or jus) is used in relation to the main item. A bed of mirepoix, which should be peeled if it is to be served, also introduces additional moisture and flavor during **braising**.

One of braising's benefits is that less-tender cuts of meat become tender as the moist heat gently penetrates the meat and causes tough connective tissues to soften. Another bonus is that any flavor from the item is released into the cooking liquid, and becomes the accompanying sauce; thus, virtually all flavor and nutrients are retained.

Tender foods, even delicate fish and vegetables, can also be braised. To properly braise these kinds of foods, use less cooking liquid, and cook the food at a lower temperature and for a shorter time.

The first step for most braises is to sear the main item in a small amount of hot fat in a rondeau or brazier over direct heat on the stove top. This develops the proper flavor and color. Braised vegetables, however, are usually blanched before they are braised. Mirepoix is then allowed to lightly brown or sweat in the braising vessel and the cooking liquid is added and brought to a simmer. Once these steps are completed, the pot is usually covered and placed in a moderate oven.

FIGURE 10-16   Making Risotto

(1) Adding heated stock gradually to the short grain rice.

(2) Stiring the risotto constantly as it absorbs successive additions of stock and broth, to develop the correct, creamy consistency.

FIGURE 10-17 A Properly Cooked Saffron Rissotto

Braising in the oven tends to result in a better product because it avoids the danger of scorching foods as they cook for prolonged periods over an open flame. Air is a less-efficient conductor than metal—the result is a gentler transfer of heat in the oven. There is also less chance of inadvertently overcooking (and thereby toughening) the item. Finally, burner space is kept open for other needs.

If the entire braising operation is to be done on the stove top, certain precautions must be taken. The cooking speed must be carefully regulated because the liquid can easily become too hot. If this happens, the portion of the main item covered by

FIGURE 10-18   Braising Beef

(1) The meat has been seared on all sides, and is being removed from the pan.

(2) Allowing the tomatoes to "cook out" after the mirepoix has already been sautéed.

(3) Adding the broth and sachet to the pan and bringing the liquid to a simmer.

(4) The meat is returned to the pan, ready to braise until fork-tender.

the liquid will cook more quickly than any exposed areas and could become tough or stringy. Scorching could also be a problem.

Braised foods should have an intense flavor as the result of slow, gentle cooking. The main item's natural juices, along with the braising liquid, become concentrated, providing both a depth of flavor and a full-bodied sauce.

If a braised food does not have a robust flavor, it may have been undercooked or perhaps was allowed to braise at too high a temperature for an insufficient time. Another possibility is that the main item was not seared properly, with inadequate time allowed for browning the product before liquids were introduced. Finally, if the lid was not removed from the pot during the final stage of cooking, the sauce may not have reduced properly and a glaze may not have been allowed to form on the main item's surface.

Braised foods should have a deep color appropriate to the type of food being prepared. They should retain their natural shape, although a significant amount of volume is lost during cooking.

To maintain the proper shape throughout the cooking time, the main item can be trussed or tied. Braised foods should be extremely tender, almost to the point at which they can be cut with a fork. They should not, however, fall into shreds; this would indicate that the main item has been overcooked.

Mise en Place

1. Assemble all ingredients for braising:

   - Main item(s)
   - Cooking fat or oil (optional in some cases)
   - Braising liquid
   - Additional or optional flavoring, seasoning, or garnishing items
   - Thickener for sauce (optional in some cases)

   Foods to be braised are traditionally more mature, less tender, and more flavorful than foods prepared by dry-heat and moist-heat techniques. Tender foods, especially fish, should be cooked the minimum amount of time necessary to achieve the best flavor. Trim away all fat, silverskin, and gristle on the main item. Marinate red meats and poultry, if desired; truss or tie. Stuff whole fish with an aromatic filling and then wrap it in lettuce leaves or other coverings to help maintain shape and prevent it from breaking apart during cooking, if desired. Dredge the main item in flour. This will help to thicken the sauce during cooking.

A mirepoix used in braising should be peeled if it is to be puréed and used in the sauce. Cut the vegetables into an appropriate size, depending on the cooking time required for the main item.

Use a white mirepoix for "white" braises. Use a well-flavored stock or jus appropriate to the main item's flavor. Broths, essences, or vegetable juices may be used.

Prepare a sachet d'épices or bouquet garni, including spices, herbs, and other aromatic ingredients, as desired or required by the recipe.

Braised items often include some sort of pork product. Have available ham, bacon, or salt pork according to recipes. Blanch these ingredients to remove excess salt, if necessary.

Tomatoes are included frequently in braised dishes. They act as a tenderizer to break down the tough tissues of less tender meats and also give the finished dish additional flavor and color.

Vegetable garnishes may be added for color, flavor, and texture to the dish as it braises. They should be added in a timely fashion, so that they will finish cooking at the same time as the main item.

Various thickeners may be used to prepare a sauce from the braising liquid (see Figure 10-19). Prepare an arrowroot or cornstarch slurry and add it to the sauce at the end of the cooking time; prepare a roux and add it to the braised item at the start of the cooking time; or purée the mirepoix and return it to the sauce.

3. Assemble all equipment necessary for cooking and serving.

- Deep pot with lid (or other cooking vessel)
- Kitchen fork to test doneness
- Carving knife, if necessary

FIGURE 10-19   Finishing the Sauce for Braised Foods

(1) Transfer the braising liquid to another pot if necessary, and reduce it over direct heat. Skim the surface to degrease.

(2) Add a thickener (diluted arrowroot is used here) to give the sauce additional body if necessary.

- Equipment as needed to finish sauce

Method

1. Sear the main item in hot oil or blanch in a liquid.

   This initial searing helps the item develop color and flavor. White meat and poultry should be seared only to the point at which the skin begins to turn color. Red meats should be seared to a deep brown color. Fish may not require an initial searing. Blanch vegetables by boiling or steaming.

2. Remove the main item and add the mirepoix.

   For white meats, fish, poultry, and game birds, sweat the mirepoix until the onions are translucent. For red meats and large game, sweat until the onions are golden-brown. The mirepoix furnishes both moisture and flavor. If you will be including it in the finished sauce, cut it evenly and neatly to the desired shape and size. If a roux is being used as a sauce thickener, it may be added at this point.

3. Add the appropriate amount of liquid.

There should be just enough liquid to keep the main item moistened throughout the cooking time and to produce an adequate amount of sauce to serve with the finished dish. The more tender the product, the less liquid will be required, because the cooking time will be shorter and there will be less opportunity for the liquid to reduce properly. In general, the liquid should be adequate to cover the main item only by one-third. Bring the liquid to a simmer over direct heat.

4. Return the main item, cover the pot, and place it in a moderate oven.

The more tender the item, the lower the oven's temperature should be. Covering the pot allows the steam to condense on the lid and fall back onto the main item, moistening the food's exposed surfaces. The main item should be turned from time to time during cooking to keep all surfaces evenly moistened with the braising liquid.

5. Add the sachet d'épices or bouquet garni and vegetable garnish at the appropriate times, to ensure proper flavor extraction and cooking.

6. Remove the lid during the final portion of the cooking time.

This will cause the braising liquid to reduce adequately so that the sauce will have the proper consistency and flavor. Also, if the main item is turned frequently after the lid has been removed and is thus exposed to hot air, a glaze will form on its surface, providing a glossy sheen and a good flavor.

7. Remove the main item from the braising liquid when it is properly cooked.

Properly braised foods are fork-tender. This means that they will slide easily from a kitchen

FIGURE 10-20
Adding Herbs to Braised Endive Wrapped with Bacon

fork inserted at the food's thickest part. For foods that are portion size or smaller, check for doneness by "cutting" them with the side of a fork.

8. Place the pot over direct heat and continue to reduce the sauce to develop its flavor, body, and consistency.

This additional reduction fortifies the flavor of the sauce and provides an opportunity to skim away any surface fat. Add additional garnish or finishing ingredients at this point, as appropriate or proceed with the optional step of straining.

9. Strain the sauce.

If mirepoix is strained out, it may be puréed and returned to the sauce if it is still flavorful. Otherwise, simply strain it out of the sauce and discard it along with the sachet d'épices or bouquet garni. Return the sauce to the heat and bring it to a boil. Add an arrowroot or cornstarch slurry to lightly thicken the sauce, if desired. Add any final finishing or garnishing ingredients (see Figure 10-20). Adjust the seasoning with salt and pepper.

10. Carve or slice the main item and serve it on heated plates with the sauce and an appropriate garnish.

Stewing

Stewing is a gentle cooking method in which the main item is cut into bite-size pieces and is allowed to cook slowly in a liquid over low heat.

GLOSSARY OF BRAISES AND STEWS

This is a partial list of *braises* featured in different cuisines:

Daube A daube is a braise customarily made from red meats (often beef) and includes red wine. The main item is often marinated beforehand. The name is derived from the French pot used to prepare a daube, the *daubière,* which has an indentation in the lid to hold hot pieces of charcoal.

Estouffade This is a French term used to refer to the braising method and the dish itself.

Pot Roast This common American term for braising is also the name of a traditional braised dish.

Swissing This is a braising technique often associated with portion-size meat cuts. The main item is repeatedly dredged in flour and pounded to tenderize the flesh.

This is a partial listing of the *stews* featured in different cuisines.

Blanquette This white stew is traditionally made from white meats (veal or chicken) or lamb, and is garnished with mushrooms and pearl onions. The sauce is always white and is finished with a liaison of egg yolks and heavy cream (see Figure 10-19).

Bouillabaisse This is a Mediterranean-style fish stew combining a variety of fish and shellfish.

Fricassée Fricassée is a white stew, often made from veal, poultry, or small game (rabbit, for example).

Goulash (gulyas) This stew originated in Hungary and is made from beef, veal, or poultry, seasoned and colored with paprika, and generally served with potatoes and dumplings.

Navarin This is a stew traditionally prepared from mutton or lamb, with a garnish of root vegetables, onions, and peas. The name probably derives from the French word for turnips, *navets,* which is the principle garnish.

Ragout A French term for stew, this translates literally as "restores the appetite."

Matelote This is a special type of fish stew, typically prepared with eel, although other fish may be used. Other fish stews that are served as main courses include bouillabaisse, cioppino, and bourride.

The amount of liquid used in relation to the amount of the item varies from one stew to another. Some stews call for very little additional liquid; others may call for proportionately more liquid than the main item. A stew's basic components do not substantially differ from those of a braise.

The technique for stewing is also nearly identical to that for braising, although a few optional steps in stewing allow the cook to vary the results. For example, initial blanching of veal or chicken, instead of searing, results in a pale, almost ivory-colored fricassée. Because the main item is cut into small pieces (see Figure 10-21), the cooking time for stewing is shorter than for braising.

Mise en Place

1. Assemble all ingredients for stewing:

   - Main item(s)

   - Cooking fat or oil (optional in some cases)

   - Cooking liquid

   - Additional or optional flavoring, seasoning, or garnishing items

   - Thickener for sauce (optional in some cases)

   Meats, poultry, and fish should be trimmed, cut into small pieces, and seasoned. It may be appropriate to dust these items with flour. Peel and cut fruits and vegetables as necessary. Beans

FIGURE 10-21   Vegetable Stew

(1) Vegetables are undercooked at an early stage.

(2) Vegetables are tender and fully cooked. The final seasonings are being added now.

and grains may require soaking or parcooking.

Select the appropriate cooking liquid according to the foods you are stewing or the recipe's recommendation. Water, broth, stock, vegetable and fruit juices, or milk may be used.

Refer to the recipes in Part IV for seasoning, garnishing and finishing ingredients.

2. Assemble all equipment necessary for cooking and serving:

• Deep pot with lid (or other cooking vessel)

• Kitchen fork to test doneness

• Equipment as needed to finish sauce

Method

1. Sear the main item in hot oil or blanch it by placing it in a pot of cold stock or water and bringing the liquid to a boil.

Searing the main item assists in developing color and flavor. In order to develop a good color, the main item should not be added to the pot in quantities so large that the pieces are touching one another. If they are touching, the pan's temperature will be lowered significantly, hindering proper coloring. Instead, the item should be seared in batches, and each batch should be removed when it has developed a good color. The main item is generally dredged in flour prior to searing, to assist in lightly thickening the cooking liquid.

Blanching is done to improve the color and flavor of certain types of stews. Skimming the surface of the blanching liquid removes any im-

purities that could give the stew a gray color or off flavor. Once the boil is reached, drain the main item.

2. Remove the main item from the pot and add the mirepoix.

Lightly brown the mirepoix or, for stews that should remain pale in color, sweat it until the vegetables begin to release their juices and become translucent.

3. Return the main item to the mirepoix in the pot; add the appropriate cooking liquid and bring it to a simmer.

Some stews call for only a small amount of liquid, relying on the main item's natural juices to provide moisture. This is especially true for stews made from naturally tender foods such as fish or shellfish. Other stews may include proportionately more liquid than main item. See specific recipes for guidance.

4. Cover the pot and place it in a moderate oven, or cook it over direct heat on the stove top.

5. Add the aromatics and vegetable garnish, if necessary or desired, at the appropriate time to ensure proper cooking and extraction of flavor.

6. Stew the food until a piece of the main item is tender to the bite.

Because the main item is cut into small pieces, it is possible and advisable to test for doneness by

FIGURE 10-22   Veal Blanquette

(1) Adding hot stock to blanch the veal. A carrot, bouquet garni, and an oignon piqué are added as the aromatics.

(2) The finished stew, with a final addition of chopped parsley.

biting into the food rather than applying the fork-tender test.

7. Finish the stew by adding any additional thickeners or liaison, garnish ingredients, or final seasoning adjustments.

8. Serve the stew on heated plates with the sauce and the appropriate garnish.

Summary

The moist heat and combination cooking methods detailed in this chapter, combined with the dry heat methods in Chapter 9, are the basic techniques used to build numerous specific recipes. Just as a painter must learn the basics of form and color, a chef must fully master these fundamentals of the kitchen. Once you have all these methods firmly within your grasp, you can begin the process of refining and creating virtually endless variations. You need to gain skill and confidence in all of the cooking methods described in Chapter 9 as well as in the following areas:

- Steaming and its variations:
  -preparing foods
  -shallow-poaching
  -pan-steaming

- The submersion techniques:
  -poaching
  -simmering
  -boiling

- The combination cooking methods:
  -stewing
  -braising

- The ability to accurately determine the proper degree of doneness

- The preparation of sauces derived directly from the application of the moist-heat or combination cooking methods.

SELF-STUDY QUESTIONS

1. What foods are best suited to the simmering technique?

2. Describe the correct sequence for shallow-poaching a piece of fish.

3. Explain why foods prepared en papillote are considered steamed.

4. What are some of the differences between poaching and simmering?

5. Why are boiled foods often served with a sharp or piquant sauce?

6. What types of foods are generally braised? Why?

7. Describe proper doneness for the following items:
   -blanched vegetables
   -pasta
   -parcooked potatoes
   -fork-tender meats
   -fully cooked fish fillet

8. Why is shallow poaching considered an à la minute technique?

9. When cooking *en papillote*, what can be done to thicker cuts of meat and vegetables to ensure proper cooking?

10. Why do steamed foods generally contain a greater portion of nutrients than foods cooked by other moist-heat methods?

11. What are the differences and similarities between simmering and boiling?

12. What is a pilaf? Explain how it is made.

13. What are three possible explanations for an absence of flavor in a braise?

14. Name four different kinds of stews.

ACTIVITIES

- Individually cook three equal-size pieces of salmon in the Vinegar Court Bouillon recipe on page 484, at the following temperatures: 165°F (74°C), 190°F (88°C), and 212°F (100°C). Record the cooking times required to reach an internal temperature of 150°F (66°C), the appearance, and the texture of each piece of salmon. Now taste each one. Which do you prefer? Why?

- Using the recipe for Poached Eggs on page 655, poach an egg. Prepare a second batch of poaching liquid without the vinegar and poach a second egg in it. What differences, if any, do you observe in cooking, appearance, texture, and flavor between the two eggs?

- Compare the cooking time, flavor, texture, and color of broccoli that has been steamed and broccoli that has been boiled. Which do you prefer? Why?

KEYWORDS

al dente	fork-tender	poaching	steaming
blanched	fully cooked	risotto	stewing
boiling	pan-steaming	shallow-poaching	
braising	par-cooked	simmering	
en papillote	pilaf	spaetzle	

11
Charcuterie and Garde-Manger

A slice or two of saucisson

Will give the palate tone...

STEPHEN GWYNN,
FROM HAIL SAUSAGE!

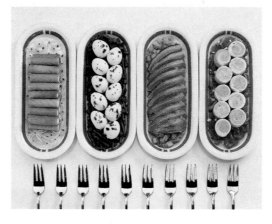

In its strictest interpretation, the term charcuterie *refers to items made from a pig. These
include sausages, smoked hams, bacon, pâtés, terrines, and head cheeses. Translated from the French, the word literally means "cooked flesh."*

*Garde-manger's original reference was to the kitchen's pantry or larder section, where
foods were kept cold. Various preparations completed in this "cold kitchen" came to be
known as part of the garde-manger repertoire. Over time, because of the similarities in
their products, the seemingly separate areas of charcuterie and garde-manger have become
closely joined. In this chapter, the various responsibilities of the garde-manger and
charcuterie kitchen areas and the types of items they produce will be covered.*

This chapter will touch on only a small number of the vast array of items that fall within the scope of the charcuterie and garde-manger stations. These "cold kitchen" areas hold the primary responsibility for several courses on the standard menu, as well as for various special events, including buffets and receptions.

The garde-manger station, or pantry, is generally given responsibility for the preparation of all cold appetizers, including cold salads, soups, and any first course items to be served cold. This might include chilled seafood cocktails, mixed green or composed salads, vinaigrettes, and other special cold preparations. While the pantry station may not necessarily be responsible for the actual production of sausages, pâtés, terrines, smoked meats, and fish, it is often called upon to plate and present these items for regular service or buffets. Recipes and preparation notes for salads and salad dressings can be found in Part IV, Chapter 25.

Information about selecting and preparing greens and other ingredients is contained in Chapters 5 and 6. Appetizer and hors d'oeuvre recipes may be found in Part IV, Chapter 26.

The subject of this chapter is focused primarily on the preparation of forcemeats, as well as a few additional charcuterie items, including gravad lox and cold daubes.

Pâtés, sausages, terrines, and galantines allow the chef to make full use of all food items brought into the kitchen, whether as the foundation for a mousseline forcemeat or as the garnish for a pâté.

Due to the dramatic change in eating style among contemporary diners, there is a reduced emphasis on rich, high-fat terrines and other classic cold delicacies. This does not mean that the role of the cold kitchen has been greatly diminished. It simply challenges chefs to update classic preparations, making them lighter and more appealing to modern tastes.

CHAPTER OBJECTIVES

- Describe the basic duties of the garde-manger station.
- Identify the components and preparation techniques for a variety of forcemeats, including:
  - straight
  - country-style
  - mousseline
  - gratin
  - emulsified
- Explain the purpose of thickeners and binders in forcemeat preparations and name several different types
- Describe the purpose and method for using pâté dough in forcemeat preparations
- Understand the use and purpose of aspic gelée in forcemeat preparations
- Describe a number of garde-manger and charcuterie specialties, including:
  - quenelles
  - country-style pâté
  - pâté en croûte
  - terrines
  - sausages
  - galantines
- Explain different curing methods, as well as special ingredients used to produce cured and smoked foods

FIGURE 11-1   A Selection of Specialties

(1) Clockwise from top left: kielbasi, stuffed derma, jambonneau, head cheese, lieberkaese, rolled pressed pig's head. Kiszka, a polish blood sausage, is in the center.

(2) Clockwise from top left: bacon, English bacon, tasso, smoked loin of pork.

Background

The need to preserve foods of all sorts to last over long periods of time has been felt throughout the world and throughout time. Fruits, grains, and vegetables have been dried and stored in virtually every culture. Methods for preserving meats, fish, and poultry, always among the most-prized and difficult-to obtain food items, have also been developed.

Preparations as diverse as pemmican and jerky, prepared by Native Americans, to dried Chinese-style sausages, presumably one of the earliest of all sausages made, to gravlax (also referred to as "gravad lox") from Scandinavia, to the *boudin noir* made throughout France, have been relished for centuries. This chapter owes a large debt to the methods employed by French charcutières over the

---

pemmican: dried meat that has been pounded to a paste, mixed with fat and berries, and shaped into small cakes.

jerky: sun-dried strips of beef that are also sometimes smoked

boudin noir: blood sausage.

(3) Fresh sausages (clockwise from top): Tuscan, merguez, Mexican chorizo, and hot Italian.

(continued on next page)

FIGURE 11-1 A Selection of Specialties *(continued)*

(4) Semidry sausages (clockwise from top): salami, hard-smoked salami, Lyonerwurst, Swiss pantli.

(5) A selection of smoked and cooked sausages.

years, so most of the terminology will bear a distinctly Gallic stamp. See Figure 11-1 for a selection of charcutèrie and garde-manger specialties.

The history of charcuterie extends back to the workers' guilds at the end of the Middle Ages, when the charcutières were granted a charter allowing them to sell products from the pig, including cooked items. Since those times, the role of the charcutière has expanded greatly. Sausages, pâtés, and terrines today are made from a wide range of ingredients, including poultry, fish, shellfish, and vegetables. In contemporary kitchens, especially large ones, there may still be a separate area for the preparation and production of charcuterie and garde-manger items. Smaller kitchens may rely on outside purveyors for some or all of these products, or they may incorporate their production into other kitchen areas.

Historically, charcuterie and garde-manger products provided a way of preserving meat over the winter by using spices and herbs, fats, smoking, and curing with salt. The use of salts, spices, and fats was noticeably more liberal than is the case today, but not because tastes were so radically dif-

ferent. These ingredients all have the ability to aid in preserving foods by slowing or preventing various types of spoilage or foodborne illness.

Salts dry out foods, creating an environment that is not suitable to many types of pathogens. Salt combined with nitrites or nitrates is even more effective. It is no longer such a great necessity that ingredients such as curing salts, saltpeter, or pot ash be added to foods to prevent the growth of botulism. Introducing curing salts or lavish quantities of other types of salt is more often a matter of personal preference today, an option exercised in order to obtain a specific color or flavor in the finished dish.

The addition of what might be seen as excessive spices to foods also had a function beyond simple flavoring: it was a way to mask the taste of foods that became increasingly "high" or "gamey" as the months wore on. Fat was also used liberally for its preservative effect by limiting the amount of exposure to air a food will have. In addition, it added flavor and moisture, and gave a sense of fullness and satisfaction to those who ate foods cooked or preserved in fats. Now that refrigeration is available, the flavoring in

FIGURE 11-2 Mise en Place for Contemporary and Classic Charcuterie Items

garde-manger and charcuterie products is somewhat lighter and less fat is used, but the resulting products should still be rich and well-flavored. Figure 11-2 illustrates mise en place for charcuterie items.

Forcemeats

One of the basic components of charcuterie and garde-manger items is a preparation known as a **forcemeat.** In the following sections, five distinct forcemeat styles are explained and a variety of items prepared from forcemeats is also discussed.

A forcemeat is a lean meat-and-fat emulsion that is established when the ingredients are forced together by grinding, sieving, or puréeing. Depending on the grinding and emulsifying methods and the intended use, the forcemeat can have a smooth consistency or be heavily textured and coarse. In either case, the combined ingredients must be more than just a mixture—they must form an emulsion so that it will hold together properly when sliced and have a rich and pleasant taste and feel in the mouth.

Forcemeats are used in the hot kitchen, as well as in the cold kitchen. They can be found as fillings or stuffings for a variety of dishes, ranging from mousseline spread on a fish fillet to gratin forcemeat used to stuff mushroom caps. Two additional uses of forcemeat in the contemporary kitchen are shown in Figure 11-3.

Basic Forcemeat Types

Forcemeats may be used for quenelles, sausages, pâtés, terrines, and galantines or to prepare stuffings for other items (a salmon forcemeat may be used to fill a paupiette of sole, for example). There are five basic styles of forcemeat, each with its own particular texture:

- Straight forcemeats combine pork and pork fat with another dominant or flavoring meat in equal parts, through a process of progressive grinding and emulsification. The meats and fat are cut into strips,

paupiette: a fillet or scallop of fish or meat that is rolled up around a stuffing and poached.

FIGURE 11-3 Forcemeats in the Hot Kitchen

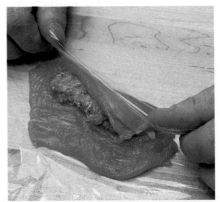

(1) Filling a chicken breast.

(2) Preparing filled pastas with Forcemeat, such as the cappelletti shown here.

seasoned, cured, rested, progressively ground, and then processed with a binder, such as egg.

- A country-style forcemeat is rather coarse in texture. It is traditionally made from pork and pork fat with a percentage of liver and other garnish ingredients.

- In a gratin forcemeat, some portion of the dominant meat is seared and cooled before it is ground. The term *gratin* means "browned" and does not imply that cheese is included in the recipe.

- Mousseline is a very light forcemeat based on white meats (veal or poultry) or fish. The inclusion of cream and eggs gives a mousseline its characteristic light texture and consistency.

- Emulsified forcemeats (also referred to as 5/4/3 forcemeats) combine meat, fat, and seasonings into a very finely textured forcemeat. Careful temperature control must be maintained throughout the mixing of this forcemeat. The basic mixture is five parts meat/four parts fat/three parts ice. This forcemeat is used for frankfurters, bockwurst, and knockwurst.

Basic Preparation Guidelines

1. Maintain proper sanitation and temperature at all times.

All necessary ingredients and tools used in preparing any forcemeat must be scrupulously clean and well chilled at all times. If the forcemeat is to be a true emulsion, it must be kept quite cold throughout its preparation so that the proteins and fats can combine properly.

Ingredients should be refrigerated until they are ready to be used and, if necessary, held over a container of ice to keep the temperatures low during actual preparation.

Maintaining the correct temperature is important for more than the proper formation of an emulsion. These foods are often highly susceptible to contamination, due to the amount of handling they receive, their increased contact with equipment, and greater exposure to air.

Pork, poultry, seafood, and dairy products can begin to lose their quality and safety rapidly when they rise above 40°F (4°C). If the forcemeat seems to be approaching room temperature, it is too warm. Work should be stopped and all ingredients and equipment refrigerated. Work may be resumed only after everything is below 40°F (4°C) once more.

2. Grind foods properly.

The technique used to prepare most forcemeats is known as **progressive grinding.** The following procedures should be observed:

- Cut all solid foods into dice or strips that will fit easily through the grinder's feed tube.

- Do not force the foods through the feed tube with a tamper. If they are the correct size, they will be drawn easily by the **worm.**

- Be sure that the blade is sharp. Meats should be cut cleanly, never mangled or mashed, as they pass through the grinder.

- For all but very delicate meats (fish or some types of organ meats, for example), begin with a die that has large or medium openings. Continue to grind through progressively smaller dies until the correct consistency is achieved.

- Remember to chill ingredients and equipment between successive grindings.

- When using a food processor to finish grinding the meat, be sure that the blade is very sharp and the meat is not overprocessed.

- Mousseline or other very delicate forcemeats may be pushed through a sieve (tamis) for the smoothest possible texture.

Special Preparations and Ingredients

There are a number of other preparations frequently used in the production of forcemeat products. They are panadas or binders, pastry dough for items prepared "en croûte," aspic gelée, and curing salt.

Thickeners and Binders   Binding ingredients or mixtures (often referred to as **panadas**) are added to forcemeats once the meat(s) has been properly ground. This is done to assure that pâtés, terrines, and other finished items do not fall apart or crumble when sliced. Whenever a panada is required, it should comprise no more than 20 percent of the forcemeat's total volume, not including garnish ingredients. The kind of **binder** used will vary, depending on the type of meat, fish, or vegetable used in the forcemeat. The three types most often called for are bread panada, flour panada, or pâte à choux. Panadas may also be based on rice and potatoes, although these are less frequently used. In some forcemeats, heavy cream or a liaison of heavy cream and eggs may act as a thickener.

Bread panadas are made as follows: Cubed bread is combined with milk, in an approximate ratio of one part bread to one part milk. The bread cubes and milk are allowed to soak until the bread has absorbed the milk. If necessary, the bread may be squeezed to remove any excess milk before the panada is added to the forcemeat.

A flour panada is essentially a very heavy béchamel. A roux is prepared and milk added, in an approximate ratio of one part roux to one part milk. Three to four egg yolks per pound of béchamel may also be added. The panada must be chilled completely before it is combined with the forcemeat.

Pâte à choux is sometimes used as a binder for forcemeats as well. The recipe and directions for preparing pâte à choux are found in Chapter 30. The pâte à choux must also be completely chilled before it is added to the forcemeat.

Pâté Dough **Pâté dough** is by necessity a stronger dough than a normal pie dough, although its preparation technique is identical to that used for more delicate pastry doughs. (Refer to Part IV, Chapter 30.) Other flours, herbs, ground spices, or lemon zest may be added to change the dough's flavor. Instructions for lining a mold with pâté dough are included in the step-by-step illustrations of preparing a pâté en croûte later in this chapter.

Aspic Gelée **Aspic gelée** is a well-seasoned, highly gelatinous, perfectly clarified stock. It is frequently strengthened by adding a quantity of gelatin (either sheets or granular gelatin may be used). The aspic is applied to foods to prevent them from drying out, preserving their moisture and freshness.

When properly prepared, aspic should set firmly but still melt in the mouth. The recipe and ratios for aspic are included in Part IV, Chapter 27. Aspic gelée made from white stock will be clear, with practically no color. When the base stock is brown, the result is amber or brown in color. Other colors may be achieved by adding an appropriate spice, herb, or vegetable purée.

Curing Salt **Curing salt,** also known as tinted curing mix (TCM), is a special compound that combines salt with sodium nitrate. It is tinted a very bright pink color so that it will not be inadvertently confused with other salts. It is typically referred to as "TCM" in forcemeat recipes. The ratio is 94 percent salt and 6 percent nitrite. Its primary function is to prevent botulism in forcemeat items such as sausages that are to undergo lengthy smoking at extremely low temperatures. Today it is most often used to produce a pink color found desirable in sausages, pâtés, and other items.

Straight Forcemeat

A **straight forcemeat** is a basic forcemeat that can be used to prepare a variety of items, including sausages, pâtés, terrines, and galantines, illustrated later in this chapter.

Mise en Place

1. Assemble all ingredients and preparations necessary for a straight forcemeat. The main components are:

- Dominant or theme meat
- Fat
- Panada or other binder
- Seasoning, flavoring, and garnish

"Dominant meat" need not necessarily mean pork. It might just as easily be veal, beef, lamb, game, poultry, fish, shellfish, or even a combination of meats. The ratio of dominant meat to other ingredients will vary, depending on the desired result (see the specific recipes which can be found in Part IV, Chapter 27).

Cut the meat into cubes or strips. Combine it with spices and/or a marinade, if desired. Chill

FIGURE 11-4 Preparing Straight Forcemeat

(1) Marinating the meats and fat.

(2) First stage: Grinding through a coarse die.

(3) Second stage: Grinding through a medium die.

(4) Third stage: Puréeing with egg in a food processor.

(5) Adding the garnish.

Forcemeats, especially those to be served cold, should have a full flavor. Salt and/or curing salt, in addition to acting as a preservative, as discussed earlier, is one of the most common flavorings used in seasoning a forcemeat. Ground pepper (black or white), green peppercorns, various ground seeds and spices, and spice blends, fresh herbs, liqueurs and cordials can also be used to season forcemeats.

A variety of garnishes may be included to provide additional texture, flavor, or color. The choices include diced meats (usually the same as the dominant meat), vegetables (dices, purées, juliennes), herbs and spices, nuts, and dried fruits.

Aspic may be used to coat charcuterie items once they are cooked and completely cooled. Although aspic adds visual appeal by giving sheen and luster, its basic function is to protect the product from moisture loss during storage.

Method

it well before proceeding with grinding or mixing.

Pork fat is traditionally used for most straight forcemeats. It should be cut into cubes or strips, then chilled until needed. Chilled heavy cream may be more appropriate for delicately flavored forcemeats based on white meats, poultry, or fish.

Different forms of binders can be used, depending on the type of forcemeat. In some cases, the proteins naturally present in the dominant meat may bind the forcemeat sufficiently to permit the cooked forcemeat to be sliced neatly after it is cooked. In other cases, it may be necessary to add a panada, additional eggs, or sometimes a combination of binders to prevent the slices from crumbling.

1. Have all ingredients and equipment at the correct temperature, under 40°F (4°C). See Figure 11-4 for photos illustrating method for preparing straight forcemeat.

2. Combine the dominant meat, fat, and (if appropriate) the garnish ingredients with a marinade and refrigerate them.

Marinating the meat and fat will allow you to get as much flavor as possible into the finished product. The marinade may be complex, including wines, spices, and herbs, or it may be relatively simple, including nothing more than cognac or port. Refer to specific recipes.

3. Run the meats and fat through a meat grinder, using a die with large openings (coarse die).

The degree of fineness of the finished forcemeat is determined by the number of successive grindings, as well as the opening size of the die used on the grinder. Be sure that you start with the largest hole and proceed through progressively fine grindings until the desired texture is achieved. Hold the ingredients over ice or refrigerate them before continuing.

4. Place the ground meat in a food processor and add the panada. Process the mixture to a smooth consistency.

Not always essential, this final "grinding" or puréeing step, shown in the accompanying illustration, gives the finished item a smooth texture and encourages it to hold together well when sliced. To test the forcemeat's quality, prepare a test quenelle as explained later in this chapter. Make any necessary adjustments to correct the consistency or seasoning.

5. Gently fold the garnish into the forcemeat by hand, working over ice. The forcemeat is now ready to use for a variety of applications.

Refer to Chapter 27 for specific recipes.

Country-Style Forcemeat

Mise en Place

For a description of essential and optional components required by a **country-style forcemeat,** refer to the mise en place for straight forcemeat on page 405.

FIGURE 11-5 Preparing Country-Style Forcemeat

(1) Pushing the liver through a drum sieve.

(2) Adding the liver and panada (cream and eggs) to the meat.

Method

1. Prepare all meats, fat, and garnish ingredients as indicated by the recipe. See Figure 11-5 for photos illustrating the method for preparing country-style forcemeat.

Cut the meats and fat into dice or strips. Marinate the ingredients if desired or appropriate. Keep them chilled at all times.

2. Grind the meats once through a coarse die and again through a medium die, and hold over ice or keep them refrigerated.

3. Push the liver through a sieve (tamis) to remove all sinews, membranes, and fibers.

4. Gently work the sieved liver and panada into the ground meats and fat by hand.

Do this over ice to keep all ingredients at the correct temperature. Prepare a test quenelle to check consistency and seasoning as explained later in this chapter. Any garnish should be added after making any necessary adjustments. The forcemeat is now ready to be used in a variety of applications.

Refer to Part IV, Chapter 27, for specific recipes.

Gratin Forcemeat

Mise en Place

Review information for straight forcemeat earlier in this chapter on pages 405-406.

The dominant meat used to flavor a **gratin forcemeat** is quickly seared before being marinated, to give this forcemeat its distinctive flavor. Livers are often used today, but rabbit, veal, game birds, and pork would all be equally appropriate as the theme meat.

Method

1. Sear the theme meat first to give it the proper flavor. See Figure 11-6 for photos illustrating the method for preparing gratin forcemeat.

   Allow the meat to cool completely before proceeding with the method.

2. Grind the other meats (which have been cut into dice or strips of the appropriate size), pork fat, and cooked meat first through a coarse die and then through a medium or fine die. Hold the ground mixture over ice or refrigerate it between grindings.

3. Stir the panada into the ground meats, working over ice.

   To test the forcemeat's quality, prepare a test quenelle as explained later in this chapter. Make any necessary adjustments to correct the consistency or seasoning. The forcemeat is now ready to be used in a variety of applications.

   Refer to Part IV, Chapter 27, for specific recipes.

Mousseline Forcemeat

Mise en Place

Mousseline forcemeat is used to prepare a number of items, including quenelles, terrines, and

FIGURE 11-6   Preparing Gratin Forcemeat

(1) Cooking chicken livers with spices and aromatics.

(2) Adding cream to the ground meats while working over ice.

stuffings. Review the information for essential and optional components in the mise en place for straight forcemeat on pages 405-406.

Method

1. Cut the meat into dice, and keep it very cold until it is time to prepare the forcemeat. See Figure 11-7 for photos illustrating the method for preparing mousseline forcemeat.

2. Grind the meat to a paste in a cold food processor.

   If eggs are included, add them at this time, and pulse the machine on and off to incorporate them into the meat. Do not overwork the meat.

3. With the machine running, add cold heavy cream in a thin stream.

   Once the cream is incorporated, add aspic gelée in the same manner, if desired or necessary. The

FIGURE 11-7   Preparing Mousseline Forcemeat

(1) Grinding the chicken in a food processor.

(2) Adding the cream with the machine running.

(3) The correct consistency before pushing the forcemeat through a drum sieve.

(4) Pushing the forcemeat through a drum sieve.

forcemeat should be very smooth, but not rubbery. Add seasonings according to recipes or desired result at this point.

4. Push the forcemeat through a drum sieve with a rigid plastic scraper to remove any sinews and membranes that may remain. This assures the correct texture.

   Work with only a small quantity of the forcemeat at a time, keeping the remainder over ice or refrigerated. To test the forcemeat's quality, prepare a test quenelle as explained later in this chapter. Make any necessary adjustments to correct the consistency or seasoning.

5. The forcemeat is ready to be used at this point as a stuffing or to prepare sausages, terrines, or quenelles.

   Refer to Part IV, Chapter 27, for specific recipes.

Emulsion, Forcemeat

Mise en Place

A typical **emulsion forcemeat** will always contain five parts meat, four parts fat, and three parts ice, hence, the name "5/4/3." See Figure 11-8 for the mise en place for an emulsion forcemeat. Refer to the mise en place for straight forcemeat on page 405 for additional information regarding essential and optional components.

Method

1. Cut all meats and fat into dice or strips. Hold the meats and fat separately and keep them very cold.

   See Figure 11-9 for photos illustrating the method for preparing an emulsifion forcemeat.

2. Add curing salt to the meat only; do not add it to the fat.

3. Grind the meats separately through the fine die once.

   Place them in the bowl of a chopping machine or a food processor. Add the ice along with the

FIGURE 11-8   Mise en Place for an Emulsion Forcemeat

(1) Adding a curing mix.

(2) Grinding the meats through a fine die.

(3) Grinding jowl fat through a fine die.

FIGURE 11-9   Preparing an Emulsion Forcemeat

(1) Combining the meats with ice and spices in the bowl of a chopper.

(2) Chopping the meat until it reaches a temperature of 40°F (4°C).

(3) Adding the ground fat to the mixture.

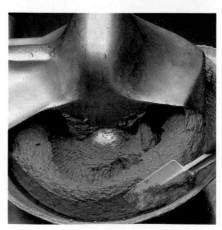

(4) The correct consistency.

spices and other ingredients and blend the mixture until it reaches 40°F (4°C) for the second time. The temperature will drop below 40°F (4°C) and then gradually begin to rise again. When it has reached 40°F (4°C) once more, then proceed with the next step. It is important that the temperature be correct in order for the emulsion to form.

4. Grind the fat through a fine die.

   Add this to the meat mixture. Continue to blend the mixture until it reaches a temperature of 58°F (14°C).

5. Make a quenelle to test for binding and taste, and adjust these accordingly.

This forcemeat can be used in a variety of preparations: Stuff the mixture into casings and hot-smoke them (see the information later in this chapter about smoking). These sausages are usually smoked only until they have a good color; they must be poached to an internal temperature of 155°F (68°C) and then prepared as desired, (e.g., grilled) or cooled before service.

Garde-Manger and Charcuterie Specialties

This section includes step-by-step instructions for preparing a number of different items produced in the garde-manger kitchen, including various forcemeat-based preparations such as quenelles, sausages, pâté en croûte, galantines, and items such as daubes and cured salmon.

Quenelles

Quenelles are poached dumplings made from a forcemeat. Any forcemeat can and should be checked for flavor, texture, color, and consistency by preparing a test quenelle. This is, in fact, an excellent safeguard against producing sausages, terrines, or pâtés that have poor quality.

A mousseline forcemeat, shaped into a quenelle and gently poached, is often served as an appetizer or a garnish for soups. There are many ways to form a quenelle. Different techniques are described in the method that follows. A richly flavored stock or court bouillon is used as the poaching liquid. Properly prepared quenelles should be light and tender, with a good flavor.

Method

1. Prepare the forcemeat and keep it chilled until it is time to poach the quenelles.

2. Bring the poaching liquid to 150°F (65°C).

   The liquid must not be at a rolling boil; this could cause the quenelles to fall apart as they cook. Cooking quenelles at high temperatures will give a false impression of the forcemeat's quality. Even an excellent mousseline can become rubbery if improperly cooked.

3. Shape the quenelles.

   There are many ways to do this, one of which employs spoons. The spoons are first dipped in cold water; an appropriate amount of the forcemeat is scooped up with one of the spoons, and the second spoon is used to smooth and shape the mixture. The quenelle is pushed from the spoon into the poaching medium. Other shaping methods include using ladles or piping the mixture through a plain-tipped pastry bag. One method for preparing quenelles from a forcemeat is illustrated in Figure 11-10.

FIGURE 11-10
Preparing Quenelles from a Forcemeat

4. Poach the quenelles in the poaching liquid.

   The cooking time will vary, depending on the diameter of the quenelles. They should be completely cooked through when broken open.

5. When making a test quenelle, be sure to test it at serving temperature.

   If the forcemeat is to be served cold, let the sample cool completely before tasting it. Make any necessary adjustments to the forcemeat. If it has a rubbery or tough consistency, add heavy cream; if it does not hold together properly, additional panada or egg whites may be necessary. Adjust the seasoning and flavoring ingredients as needed.

   See Part IV, Chapters 26 and 27, for specific recipes.

Pâté de Campagne, or Country-Style Pâté

Pâté de campagne is made from a country-style forcemeat. Many traditional garnishes may be added, including nuts, marinated meats, or dried fruits. Traditionally, the mold for a pâté de campagne would be lined with sheets of fatback. Contemporary versions may call for other liners, including romaine lettuce leaves, leek leaves, or plain plasic wrap.

Method

1. Line the mold completely with thin slices of fatback. There should be a 2- to 3-inch overhang on all sides. See Figure 11-11 for photos illustrating the method for preparing pâté de campagne, or country-style pâté.

2. Add the garnished country-style forcemeat to the lined mold and press it down with a spatula to remove any air pockets.

3. Fold the overhanging fatback onto the top of the pâté to completely encase the forcemeat.

4. Lay various herbs and spices over the top of the pâté, if desired. Place the lid on the mold or cover tightly with foil. Cook the pâté in a bain-

FIGURE 11-11   Pâté de Campagne, or Country-Style Pâté

(1) Filling a lined mold.

(2) Folding the fatback overhang.

(3) The pâté is shown without its cover, to illustrate the water's height in relationship to the terrine.

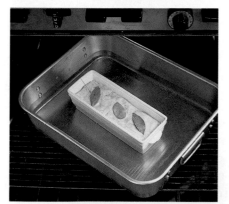

(4) Adding aspic to the cooled pâté.

marie in order to maintain the correct temperature. This will yield a product that is smooth, moist, and flavorful.

5. After the pâté has cooked to the correct internal temperature, allow it to cool to room temperature. Pour off all the fat and liquid that may have collected in the mold. Pour aspic gelée into the mold to fill it to the top. Then chill it completely before slicing.

Refer to Part IV, Chapter 27, for specific pâté recipes.

Pâté en Croûte

This is a more elaborate style of pâté in which the mold is lined with a pastry crust. The procedures for lining the mold, baking the pâté, cutting the chimney, and filling the pâté with aspic are explained here. Various forcemeats, including straight and country-style, may be used to prepare a **pâté en croûte.** Some chefs like to use elaborate inlays and garnishes to create decorative effects, especially for competitions and display pieces.

Method

1. Prepare the forcemeat as necessary, according to the type. Keep the forcemeat and garnish cold until it is time to fill the mold.

2. Line the mold.

   Roll out sheets of dough to approximately ⅛-inch thick. Cut the sheets to fit the mold: Measure the mold's bottom and sides and lightly score the dough. The corners may be cut out, and will eventually be pinched together as a seam, or the excess can be pinched away when the pastry is laid into the mold. An overhang of about 2 inches on the sides and ends of the pâté is necessary.

   A second piece, known as the cap piece, should be measured out large enough to completely cover the top of the mold and extend down into the mold about 2 to 2½ inches.

   The method for measuring dough for pâté en croûte is illustrated in Figure 11-12.

FIGURE 11-12   Measuring Dough for Pâté en Croûte

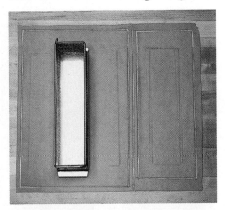

(1) Measure cutting lines as shown. Allow sufficient dough to create a generous overhang.

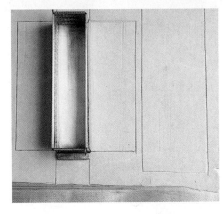

(2) The excess dough can be cut out of the corners if desired by making cuts as shown here.

3. Lay the pieces into the mold and press them into place.

   If a single large rectangle has been used, fit the dough gently into the corners and use a ball of scrap dough to press out any air pockets. If the pieces have been cut to fit, lay them in the mold and press them into place.

4. Use egg wash to "glue" the dough together in the corners and pinch the seams closed or pinch away the excess in the corners.

   Save dough scraps to make the chimney and any desired decorations. The method for lining the mold with dough is illustrated in Figure 11-13.

5. Line the bottom and sides of the dough-lined mold with sheets of fatback, thinly sliced prosciutto, or other sliced meats.

6. Garnish the forcemeat as desired, if the garnish has not already been folded in. Add the forcemeat to the lined mold and press out any air pockets with a spatula, smoothing the surface.

FIGURE 11-13   Lining the Mold with Dough

(1) Laying pieces of dough into the mold and forming seams.

(2) Using egg wash to "glue" the seams closed.

(3) Lining the pastry dough with thin fatback sheets.

FIGURE 11-14   Filling and Capping the Pâté

(1) Filling the prepared mold.

(2) Trimming the excess dough.

(3) Freeing the dough from the mold sides.

(4) Putting the cap piece in place.

7. Fold the fatback, prosciutto, or other sliced meat over the top of the forcemeat. Then fold over the pastry dough sheets and trim the top layers with scissors so that the edges just meet. Pull the pâté away from the mold's edges with a spatula.

At this point, some chefs prefer to invert the pâté mold. This bottom piece of the mold should be removed and replaced over the top, so that the bottom of the pâté becomes the top crust. This eliminates the need for a cap piece.

8. Add the cap piece to seal the pâté, and tuck the edges down into the mold.

The method for filling and capping the pâté is illustrated in Figure 11-14.

9. Cover the pâté with aluminum foil and bake it (see Figure 11-15) until it is half-done (about 45 minutes). Remove the pâté from the oven and remove the foil.

The dough should have just begun to lose its moist appearance. Egg wash can be brushed onto the dough now with less danger of surface appearing cracked or checkered.

10. Using round cutters, cut one or two vent holes in the pastry to allow steam to escape.

Use aluminum foil rolled into a tube to keep the hole from closing during the final baking. This "chimney" will allow steam to escape and prevent the crust from rupturing. Cut a ring of pastry to go around the opening at the base of the "chimney." Add any decorative pieces of pastry dough, as desired, using egg wash to secure them to the top crust.

11. Complete baking in a 350°F (170°C) oven to an internal temperature of 150°F (65°C) for meat and 145°F (63°C) for fish and vegetables.

12. Remove the pâté from the oven and let it cool for about 1 hour. Drain away any cooking liquid. Fill the mold with aspic, pouring the liquid through the holes that have been cut in the crust.

13. Chill the pâté thoroughly before slicing and serving. Excessive shrinkage or gaps between

FIGURE 11-15 Baking Pâté en Croûte

(1) Covering the pâté with foil before the first stage of baking.

(2) Cutting a hole in the crust and brushing with egg wash.

(3) Filling the cooled pâté with aspic.

(4) A sliced pâté en croûte.

the pastry and the pâté itself usually means that the pâté has been baked too long or in an oven that was too hot.

See Part IV, Chapter 27 for an example of a pâté en croûte recipe.

Terrines

Like pâtés, **terrines** are loaves of straight, country-style, or gratin forcemeats baked in a mold. The difference is that terrines are placed in a covered earthenware mold, called a terrine, and cooked in a hot-water bath. While pâtés are traditionally unmolded before they are served, terrines have customarily been served directly in the mold used to prepare them. The strict interpretation of a terrine has been somewhat modified for contemporary service however; today they are usually unmolded and sliced. To vary the presentation the mold can be filled with two forcemeats of different colors—for example, layers of a forcemeat flavored and colored with green herbs could be alternated with layers of a forcemeat flavored and colored with saffron.

Method

1. Prepare a forcemeat as desired or according to the recipe. Chill it until it is time to fill the mold.

   Meat and game terrines may be made from straight or country-style forcemeats. Fish, chicken, and vegetable terrines may be prepared from mousseline forcemeats.

2. Prepare any garnishes as desired or necessary. Keep them refrigerated until they are ready to be used.

3. Prepare the mold. Line it first with plastic wrap and then with a "liner" ingredient, such as: thin sheets of fatback, blanched vegetables, blanched romaine leaves, or thin slices of ham or smoked fish.

4. Fill the mold, adding the garnish as described for pâtés.

5. Fold all liners over the mold's surface.

6. Cover the terrine with its lid.

7. Place the terrine in a deep baking dish or roasting pan. Set the pan on the rack of a 300°F (150°C) oven. Add enough boiling water to come up nearly to the level of the top of the forcemeat.

8. Bake the terrine to an internal temperature of 150°F (65°C) for meats and 140°F (60°C) for fish.

   Regulate the temperature of the oven throughout cooking time. The waterbath's temperature should remain at approximately 160°F (70°C).

9. Remove the terrine from the bath and allow it to cool. Weight the terrine and refrigerate it overnight.

   To weight terrines, remove the lid and cover the terrine with foil or plastic. Fit a press plate over the surface, or use a board cut to the mold's dimensions and set a 2-pound (900-gram) weight on the board.

10. If desired, fill the mold with aspic once it has been cooled and the weight has been removed. Chill the terrine thoroughly before slicing and serving it.

See Part IV, Chapter 27 for specific terrine recipes.

Sausages

There are almost countless types of sausages. Many of them are indelibly associated with the cultures from which they originated. Sausages popular in France include such classics as *andouilles, boudins blancs* and *noirs, saucisson,* and *crepinettes.* Dishes that feature sausages include venerable favorites such as *cassoulet* and *choucroute.* In the British Isles, sausages are equally important; *haggis* is popular in Scotland, bangers in England, and white puddings are made in Wales. Spain and Portugal produce *chorizo* and *linguiça.* In Italy, *cotechino, salamis* (both dried and smoked), and *pepperoni* find their way into sauces, soups, baked dishes, and breads. Germany and Switzerland make a prodigious quantity of sausages,

FIGURE 11-16 Filling Sausage Casings and Tying Them into Links

(1) Filling the casing with forcemeat.

(2) Tying the sausages into even links.

FIGURE 11-17 Twisting Sausage into Links

(1) Using fingers to press the sausage into even links.

(2) Twisting the links to keep them separate; no twine is used here.

including *bratwurst, knockwurst, leberwurst,* and *landjaeger.*

Sausage meat may be used either in bulk (loose) form or to fill natural or synthetic casings, which are then usually formed into links. From this point, they may be used fresh (poached, grilled, fried, or baked) or, if appropriate, they may be dried and smoked or cured. Smoked or cured sausages generally do not require additional cooking. The following method describes the procedure for filling sausage casings using a sausage-stuffing machine. The same general guidelines apply to hand stuffing. See Figure 11-1 (3) and (4) for examples of sausages.

Method

1. Prepare and garnish the forcemeat as desired or required by the recipe used. (The method for filling sausage casings and tying them into links is illustrated in Figure 11-16, and that for twisting sausage into links in Figure 11-17.)

2. Rinse the casings thoroughly in tepid water to remove the salt and to make them more pliable.

3. Be sure that all parts of the sausage stuffer that will come in contact with the forcemeat are clean and chilled.

4. Tie a double knot in the casing end. Depending on the type of casing, as well as the type of sausage, the casing may be cut into appropriate lengths.

5. Gather the casing over the nozzle of the sausage stuffer.

6. Support the casing as the forcemeat is expressed through the nozzle and into the casing.

7. If the sausage is to be made into links, use either of the following methods:

Press the casing into links at the desired intervals and then twist the link in alternating directions for each link; or, tie the casing with twine at the desired intervals.

8. At this point, fresh sausages may be cooked or stored under refrigeration. Other types of sausage may undergo additional curing, smoking, or drying.

See Part IV, Chapter 27, for specific sausage recipes.

Galantines

The term **galantine** derives from an Old French word, *galin,* meaning "chicken." Originally, galantines were made exclusively from poultry and game birds by filling the birds' skin with a foremeat and tying them to resemble the birds' natural shape. Today, however, they are made from a wide range of products, including fish, shellfish, and meats. The skin, if available, is still used as a casing to hold the forcemeat.

Method

1. Remove the skin, keeping it as intact as possible. (See Figure 11-18 for photos illustrating the method for preparing a galantine, specifically a chicken galantine.)

   Make an incision through the skin down the middle of the back and pull the entire skin away from the bird. Use a small knife to help loosen it, if necessary.

2. Bone out the dominant meat, reserving intact any pieces that will be used for garnish.

   All other meat should be cut into dice or strips of the appropriate size to prepare the forcemeat. The bones and any nonusable trim should be used to prepare a rich stock to poach the galantine.

3. Trim the skin to form a large rectangle.

   Lay out the skin or other casing for the galantine on a large cheesecloth square. Mound the forcemeat

FIGURE 11-18   Preparing a Chicken Galantine

(1) Mise en place.

(2) Filling and rolling the galantine.

(3) Tying the galantine.

(4) Placing the galantine on a rack before poaching it.

down the rectangle's center and position any garnish (the tenderloin or diced, marinated breast meat, for example) as desired. Use the cheesecloth to roll the galantine into a tight cylinder.

4. Tie the ends with butcher's twine and use a strip of cheesecloth to secure it at even intervals in order to maintain the shape of the cylinder.

5. Place the galantine on a perforated rack and then lower it into a simmering stock.

   Be sure that the galantine is completely submerged. Maintain the liquid at a constant 150–155°F (65–67°C) even simmer throughout the cooking time—generally 1 to 1½ hours or until an internal temperature of 150°F (65°C) for meats and 140°F (60°C) for fish has been reached.

6. Let the galantine cool in the cooking liquid.

   (If cheesecloth or plastic wrap has been used, remove the casing.) Rewrap the galantine in fresh plastic wrap, reroll it to form a tight cylinder, and refrigerate it.

7. Unwrap the galantine before slicing and serving it.

Refer to Part IV, Chapter 27, for individual galantine recipes.

Cured and Smoked Items

Before they are used in other charcuterie preparations, many foods undergo a cure. Curing is especially important as the first step for items that are to be smoked. Meat, fish, and sausage cures and brines often call for curing salt (tinted curing mix or TCM). Today its use may be optional for all but items smoked or air-cured for long periods at low temperatures.

Cures may be wet or dry. In a **dry cure** a mixture of salts, spices, and herbs is packed around the item to be cured. Ratios and curing times vary according to recipe. In a **wet cure** the food is completely immersed in a brine, which is a combination of water, salt, spices, and other flavorings. Ratios of brine ingredients and curing times also vary according to

recipe, depending largely on the nature and size of the item.

After the food has been properly cured or brined, it is allowed to air-dry, making it more receptive to smoke. Smoking flavors foods and preserves their colors. A variety of smoking methods can be used. Even kitchens too small to have a commericial smoker can produce foods with a smoked flavor.

Smoking takes place in an enclosed structure—a smokehouse—where smoke from hardwood chips (hickory, mesquite, apple, for example) circulates freely and reaches all sides of the product. Depending on the nature of the items, they may be hung from the ceiling or placed on racks. The smokehouse temperature and the time needed for smoking depend on the product's nature and the desired outcome. The common ways of smoking are cold smoking, hot smoking, and smoke-roasting or pan-smoking.

Cold smoking is done at a temperature of less than 100°F (37°C). The food should take on a smoky flavor and color but will not be fully cooked during the process. It is usually necessary to complete the cooking of the product before it is served. This method is commonly used for smoked salmon, landjaeger, classic French garlic sausage, and all other hard-salami sausage types. Cold smoking will give the food a smoky flavor and darker color.

Hot smoking, at temperatures above 145°F (63°C), will fully cook the food. Smoke roasting is not a traditional smoking method, but it offers a wide range of possibilities for smaller kitchens with no access to a smokehouse. (For more information about smoke-roasting or pan roasting, see Chapter 9.)

See Part IV, Chapter 26, for specific smoked and cured item recipes.

Cured Salmon

Cured salmon is commonly referred to as **gravad lox** or **gravlax.** This dish of Swedish origin, is essentially raw salmon marinated in a dry cure of salt, sugar, and dill. Numerous interpretations of this dish can be found today, some made with tequila and cilantro, others with vodka and caraway. It is the classic accompaniment to bagels and cream cheese.

FIGURE 11-19   Preparing Cured Salmon

(1) Coating salmon fillets with a dry cure spice mixture.

(2) Wrapping the salmon tightly in cheesecloth.

(3) Draining away the drippings.

(4) Unwrapping the salmon and scraping away the cure.

FIGURE 11-20   Slicing and Serving Cured Salmon

(1) Slicing the salmon thinly on the diagonal.

(2) Preparing a mayonnaise.

Method

1. Coat trimmed salmon fillets with a dry-cure-and-herb mixture. Wrap them tightly in cheesecloth, place them in a hotel pan, and weight them with a press plate. Allow the salmon to cure for several hours or days, according to the recipe. The method for preparing cured salmon is illustrated in Figure 11-19. Slicing and serving gravad lox is illustrated in Figure 11-20.

2. Drain away any drippings that have accumulated in the pan and reserve them to make a mayonnaise-style sauce to serve with the cured salmon.

3. Unwrap the salmon and scrape away the cure. Slice the salmon very thinly on the diagonal to serve.

See Part IV, Chapter 26 page for a gravad lox recipe.

FIGURE 11-21   Preparing a Daube

FIGURE 11-21   Preparing a Daube

(1) Simmering the meats.

(2) Lining the mold with plastic wrap.

(3) Filling the mold with meats and aspic.

(4) Sealing by folding back the overhanging plastic wrap.

Daube

A **daube,** when prepared by a charcutière, is a cold preparation of a variety of meats, usually including the tongue, head, and feet of veal and/or pork. The hot version of the dish is also known as a daube—a rich, slowly cooked braise. The cold version is slowly simmered, like the hot version. Then it is chilled until the proteins of the meat set the cooking liquid into a gel firm enough to slice. Head cheese and similar cold meat in aspic preparations are made in much the same manner as the daube described here.

Method

1. Gently simmer the meats in an aromatic broth enriched with vegetables and herbs. Once the meats are tender, trim and cut them into julienne or dice. (See Figure 11-21 for photo illustrating the method for preparing a daube.)

2. Line the mold, usually an earthenware terrine, with plastic wrap. Leave enough overhang to ensure that the mold can be fully sealed.

3. Place the prepared meats, along with the desired herbs and other garnishes, in the mold. An aspic, made by clarifying and enriching the stock used to simmer the meats, is added to completely fill the mold.

4. Fold back the overhanging plastic wrap over the top of the mold to seal the daube, and refrigerate the entire dish until the aspic is firmly set.

5. Once the daube is thoroughly chilled, it is ready to be sliced and served.

Summary

This chapter has introduced the classic methods used to create a wide range of charcuterie and garde-manger items. As tastes change and the trend toward lighter food styles is reflected on menus, it is a challenge for today's chefs to update classic preparations, making them lighter and more appealing to modern tastes.

FIGURE 12-2   Preparing Molds

(1) Coating soufflé molds.

(2) Lining mold with acetate.

baked in pans that have been liberally greased (usually with a hydrogenated shortening or a blend of shortening and flour) and lined with parchment paper.

To coat a pan with sugar or flour, use the technique shown in Figure 12-2. Shake a handful of sugar into the pan and spread it around to coat all surfaces. To release the excess sugar, rap the pan sharply on a work surface and shake it out.

Angel food cakes are baked in ungreased tube pans. An exception to the general rule of greasing pans, this is critical in producing tall cakes. The batter must be able to adhere to the pan sides in order to give the cake stability until it is fully baked and cooled.

Parchment may be called for as a liner for delicate items. Delicate cookies, muffins, or loaf cakes may be baked in pans or tins that have been lined with parchment or fluted paper liners. Frozen desserts or molded items can be chilled in molds lined with acetate sheets (see Figure 12-2). Mixers, kneading equipment, sheeters, and proof boxes are also important pieces of equipment when baking is

done frequently and on a large scale. Special equipment may be required to prepare large quantities of Kaiser rolls or other specialty items, such as bagels.

Selecting and Preparing Ovens

The final quality of baked goods depends on baking them at the right temperature and in the appropriate oven. In all cases, the oven should be fully preheated to the correct temperature.

Items that will rise during baking, such as vol-au-vents made from puff pastry or éclairs made from pâte à choux, should be prepared in standard ovens. The oven must not be overloaded because the air will not be able to circulate evenly in a crowded space. For even baking and browning in a conventional oven, the racks should be inserted in the oven's center. It may be necessary to rotate or rearrange the pans for even baking.

Some cakes, muffins, and cookies may be baked in a convection oven, the advantage being that larger batches may be baked in a single load. The forced movement of air allows each item to bake evenly.

Yeast-Raised Breads

The earliest breads were nothing like the light, airy breads we know today. Leavened bread did not become possible until the Egyptians, using the wheat that flourished in the fertile Nile River valley, discovered why some of their baked dough seemed to have a different texture.

Few foods appeal so directly to the guest as bread. As more specialty or **artisanal** bakeshops open up around the country, Americans are re-learning the pleasures of good breads. Whole grains, organically grown flours, hearth-style ovens, and old-fashioned techniques are gaining favor. If you are able to produce breads on-site, so much the better.

Several factors should be kept in mind when deciding whether or not to bake breads on the premises. The first is the amount of space available—there should be room to accommodate each stage of the process. Second, there should be adequate and appropriate baking equipment, with enough oven space to avoid competing against other kitchen needs.

Although baking is meticulous work, requiring careful measuring and proper handling of doughs, the rewards can be significant, especially if quality baked goods are not readily available through a reliable purveyor.

Mixing Yeast Doughs

Yeast breads are divided into two categories: **lean doughs** and **rich doughs** (see Figure 12-3). A lean dough, the type used to prepare hard rolls or pizza dough, can be produced with only flour, yeast, and water. In fact, that is the formula for a classic French baguette. This dough can be varied by including additional ingredients, such as spices, herbs, special flours, and/or dried nuts and fruits. These additions will not greatly change the basic texture. Breads made from lean dough tend to have a chewier texture, more bite, and a crisp crust. Hard rolls, French- and Italian-style breads, and whole-wheat, rye, and pumpernickel breads are considered lean.

A rich dough, such as brioche or challah, is produced by the addition of tenderizing ingredients, such as sugars or syrups, butter or oil, whole eggs or egg yolks, milk or cream. When these fats or sugars are introduced, they give the bread a cake-like texture after baking. The doughs are usually softer and a little more difficult to work with during kneading and shaping than lean doughs.

Mise en Place

1. Assemble and prepare all ingredients.

Select the appropriate flour for the type of bread being prepared. Yeast doughs made with low-gluten flours (rye, oat, pumpernickel) usually also include some wheat flour, to introduce the necessary gluten for proper rise and texture.

The liquid most often used for lean doughs is water. Milk is used for most rich doughs.

Salt controls the yeast's activity and, with the exception of sodium-free breads, it is an essen-

---

brioche: a rich yeast dough traditionally baked in a fluted pan with a distinctive topknot of dough.

challah: a traditional Jewish yeast bread, rich with eggs and usually shaped into a braid.

FIGURE 12-3   A Selection of Breads

(1) Lean dough breads.

(2) Rich dough and quick breads.

tial component. It also helps to give bread the correct texture and flavor.

As with any baked item, it is important to scale all ingredients correctly. An additional concern with yeast-raised doughs is that the temperature of the ingredients must be carefully monitored. The liquid ingredient's temperature is usually the easiest to manipulate during the mixing stage. The overall temperature of the dough and the bakeshop will affect the way that the dough behaves during all phases of mixing, proofing, shaping, and the final rise.

2. Assemble all the necessary equipment.

The equipment required for preparing yeast doughs will vary depending upon the size of the

FIGURE 12-4   Mixing Yeast Dough

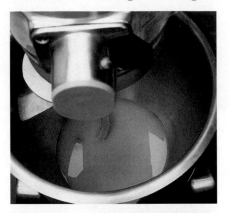

(1) Dissolving fresh yeast in water.

(2) Dry ingredients are added to yeast mixture.

(3) The dough has formed a shaggy mass.

(4) Properly kneaded dough.

batch you intend to make. A variety of bowls, a scale, a drum sieve (or tamis), a bench scraper, a clean working surface (wood is traditional), a mixer with a dough hook, clean cloths to cover the dough as it rises, molds to use during rising, pans or a hearth stove, and a correctly pre-heated stove are all important.

Other tools that may be necessary, or simply helpful, include a proofing box, a dough or in-stant-reading thermometer, and a dough "di-vider" used to separate scaled dough into rolls, if available.

Method

There are a few points at which the chef or baker can vary the method for preparing yeast doughs (see Figure 12-4), and these will be de-scribed throughout the method below.

1. Blend fresh yeast with some or all of the liquid and mix until it is evenly blended. Instant dry yeast should be thoroughly blended with the dry ingredients before adding liquids.

   If it is necessary, you may want to "proof" the yeast as described earlier to be sure that it is vig-orous. Remember that temperature control is important at this stage and throughout the bread-baking process.

   Sourdough starters may be used to replace all or some of the yeast.

   A **sponge** is often prepared by combining the yeast and liquid with a portion of the flour and allowing it to ferment until the mixture is light and spongy. This additional step in mixing is often recommended to produce a good texture when using low-gluten flours such as rye or oat or for a slower, more controlled cool rise.

2. Add all the remaining ingredients—except the salt—to the yeast mixture. Once all the dry in-gredients have been added, then add the salt on top of them. This will prevent the salt from killing the yeast.

3. Mix on low speed until the dough starts to "catch." It should look like a shaggy mass at this point. Scrape down the bowl's sides and bottom once or twice so that the dough will mix evenly.

FIGURE 12-5 First Rise for Dough

(1) Shaped dough before the first rise.

(2) Dough has risen and is ready to punch down.

5. Remove the dough to a clean bowl that has been lightly oiled. Cover the dough with plastic wrap or a clean cloth and let it rise (see Figure 12-5).

It is a good idea to take the temperature of the dough at this point so that you can make any adjustments necessary for a slow rise. Generally speaking, a slow rise at around 78°F (26°C) results in a better finished item.

As the dough rises, it will grow in volume. To test the dough to see if it has risen sufficiently, press your finger into the dough. The hole should remain visible. The dough should not spring back in place.

Doughs should be allowed to rise sufficiently so the finished bread will have the correct texture. Dough that has not risen sufficiently (considered underfermented) will have a coarse texture and poor volume after it is baked. Underproofed breads often have a dull appearance and a tight texture. Dough that has risen too much due to overfermentation may have a sour taste, sometimes described as "yeasty" or as tasting like beer.

6. When the dough has risen sufficiently, punch it down (see Figure 12-6).

Press the dough down in a few places. This will gently expel the carbon dioxide, even out the overall temperature, and redistribute the yeast evenly. It also introduces a fresh supply of oxygen, essential to continued yeast activity.

7. Remove the dough to a prepared work surface.

A clean wooden surface is often used to work with doughs. Use a bench knife to cut the dough

4. Increase the mixing speed to medium and continue to knead until the dough develops a smooth appearance and feels springy when touched.

Proper **kneading** is essential to the full development of the gluten. Gluten is what provides the dough enough strength and elasticity to allow it to rise properly. As the yeast feeds on the sugars in the flour, it gives off gas, which when trapped by the dough, causes the dough to rise. If the dough could not expand, it would not rise. If the dough is either underkneaded or overkneaded, the finished product will have a coarse texture, full of large tunnels and holes.

Kneading is generally done directly in the mixing machine using a dough hook. Small batches may be kneaded by hand. If you are kneading a dough by hand, be sure to allow plenty of time. It is difficult to overknead when you are supplying the power. When using a machine be sure to adhere to recommended kneading times.

FIGURE 12-6 Punching Down Dough

into pieces of the correct size. Use a scale to be most accurate.

If you are making individual loaves, each piece should be enough for one loaf. If you are making rolls and will be using a dough divider,

scale the dough into a piece known as a "press." The press is then divided in a dividing machine into pieces adequate to make a single roll.

At this point, you will gently round the dough into smooth balls before the dough is given a second rise (see Figure 12-7), sometimes referred to as "bench proofing."

FIGURE 12-7
Rounding Off
Dough

Shaping Doughs

Properly shaping the dough helps to achieve an attractive appearance; but, more important, proper shaping will ensure that the items bake evenly.

Use a slapping action to punch the dough into a rectangle of an even thickness. Once the dough is flattened, fold it in half and flatten it once more. Now grasp both ends of the dough and gently stretch it. Lift the ends up from the work table and allow the dough's weight to stretch itself out.

FIGURE 12-8   Shaping Baguettes

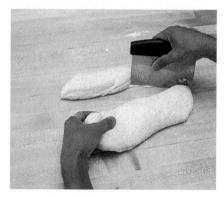

(1) Dividing the dough into pieces.

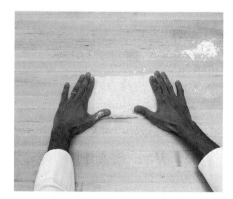

(2) Stretching the dough.

(3) Rolling into a baguette.

(4) Sealing the seams and stretching the baguette.

(5) The baguette is ready to go into bread form.

(6) Docking baguettes.

FIGURE 12-9 Shaping Round Loaves

(1) Dough is allowed to rise after rounding. A special basket is used to give crust additional interest.

(2) Docking the bread.

(3) Baking in a hearth oven.

FIGURE 12-10 Preparing Ciabatta

(1) Forming ciabatta into cylinders.

(2) Brushing ciabatta with olive oil.

(3) Baked ciabatta.

For some breads, such as baguettes or pan loaves, you will now fold the dough into thirds, and then begin the process of rolling each loaf or roll (see Figure 12-8). Use the heel of your palm to firmly seal the seams as the dough is rolled into a cylinder. Hard rolls are often prepared in the same way as long loaves. They should be transferred to prepared pans.

For round loaves (see Figure 12-9), shaped in molds or linen-lined baskets, stretch the dough as described above, and then round it off once more, rather than folding it into thirds and rolling it into a cylinder. Once the dough is rounded, place it into prepared molds.

For flatbreads, such as ciabatta (see Figure 12-10), the dough is formed very gently into a rectangle. Then, you will lift it onto a prepared pan or sheet, and flatten or dimple it with your fingertips.

The dough is then typically brushed with olive oil or a sauce (as for pizza). Herbs or other flavoring ingredients may be added at this point as well.

The Final Rise (Pan-Proofing) The shaped dough is allowed to rise once more. Some breads should be allowed to complete this second rise in a steam-filled proof box, while others react best to being left to rise on the table or in their forms, covered, but not in a proof box.

Docking Breads and Rolls After shaping, many products will need to be **docked,** meaning that the dough's surface is punctured so that the steam that builds up inside the product during baking will not cause it to split or rupture in an uncontrolled manner. The surface may be simply slashed with a sharp blade. Round loaves may be punctured with a wooden skewer or towel.

FIGURE 12-11
Cooling on a
Rack

Baking Yeast Breads

Once the dough has risen for the final time, it should be baked at the appropriate temperature. Doneness is determined by examining the item. Look for a rich color on the exterior, both top and bottom crusts. Thumping the item on the bottom to check for a hollow sound is not always effective, although it is a commonly used test.

Cooling and Storing Yeast Breads

Once the bread or rolls have been baked, they should be allowed to cool on a rack before they are cut or wrapped for storage (see Figure 12-11). If you do hold baked goods, remember that it is not always the best idea to wrap them in a completely airtight fashion. The character of some whole grain and dark rye breads develops more slowly than others and a few days at room temperature, covered but not tightly wrapped, actually will enhance the product. Crisp crusts do not stand up well to plastic wraps, which tend to trap moisture.

Quick Breads, Cakes, and Other Batters

Quick breads differ from yeast breads in that they use chemical leaveners rather than organic ones and thus do not require a rising period. Muffins, biscuits, and scones are examples of quick breads that have a place on the breakfast menu as well as in the breadbasket at lunch or dinner. These simple baked items allow the chef to offer freshly made breads and cakes without requiring the time needed for yeast doughs.

There are four basic methods for preparing the batters used to create cakes, muffins, and quick-breads:

- The straight mixing method calls for all ingredients to be combined at once and blended into a batter.

- The creaming method is used to prepare products with more refined crumb and texture—pound cakes, butter cakes, and most drop cookies. A fat is creamed together with sugar. Eggs, other liquids, and flavoring extracts are added in stages. The last step is blending the dry ingredients into the batter.

- The two-stage method is used to prepare cakes that contain a very high percentage of sugar. The dry ingredients are first blended with all of the shortening and half of the liquid until smooth, then the remaining wet ingredients are gradually added.

- The foaming method, which produces the lightest texture, is used for genoise (sponge cakes), angel food, and chiffon cakes. Eggs and sugar are beaten until very light, and flour is carefully folded into the batter.

The Straight Mixing Method

The **straight mixing method** is used when making such popular items as pancakes, popovers, cornsticks, bran muffins, pumpkin bread, and carrot cake. Once the basic technique is understood, they are simple to produce, requiring little special equipment.

All ingredients are combined at once in this method and blended into a batter. The important thing to remember is that the batter should not be overworked; unlike yeast doughs, these batters should be mixed as briefly as possible to ensure a light, delicate texture in the finished item.

Mise en Place

1. Assemble all ingredients required for the batter.

   Specific recipes may indicate the use of one or a combination of different flours according to the desired result. The flour should be carefully weighed, then properly sifted.

A variety of liquids may be used in preparing a batter. Milk, buttermilk, water, oil, the moisture from vegetables, such as zucchini, and other liquids can all be appropriate, according to the recipe. The liquid should be properly measured, either by weight or by volume; both methods of measure will be accurate in most instances.

The leavener for most quick breads and many other batters is a chemical leavener: either baking soda, baking powder, or a combination of the two. It may be appropriate to measure by volume rather than weight when the leavener is used in very small amounts. A teaspoon or tablespoon measure may be more accurate than a scale at these small measures. The leavener should be sifted with the flour, the salt, and any other dry ingredients required by the recipe.

The amount and type of fat used in a dough will determine its final texture. Refer to the specific recipe for directions to prepare the shortener. In some cases, it may need to be melted and cooled; for others, it should be left cold, but still smooth and pliable.

There is virtually an unlimited number and variety of flavoring ingredients that can be used in batters: cocoa, chopped nuts, grated vegetables, berries, citrus zest, and spices and herbs, for example. Refer to the specific recipe for information regarding the advanced preparation of these ingredients.

Method

1. Sift together all of the dry ingredients, and have them ready.

   A standard procedure is to sift the flour, leavener, and other dry ingredients through a drum sieve directly into a bowl or onto parchment. This makes it easy to pick up the dry ingredients and add them to the rest of the batter.

2. Combine all the liquid or pourable ingredients (eggs, milk or buttermilk, oil or melted butter, for example) in a mixing bowl. Blend them well to achieve a relatively uniform mixture.

3. Combine the dry ingredients with the liquid ingredients all at once.

   Mix the ingredients by hand or in a mixer with a paddle attachment, just until the dry ingredients are moistened. The appearance and consistency of the batter will differ from product to product.

4. Scale off the batter into prepared baking pans. Use paper liners, if available, to line pans and muffin tins, or butter the pans and dust them with flour.

5. Bake the batter at the appropriate temperature until it is baked through.

   When properly baked, the item's surface should spring back when pressed with a fingertip, and a skewer inserted near the center should come away clean.

   During baking, muffins and quick breads should rise to create a dome-shaped upper crust. The crust may develop a crack. The edges may become slightly darker than the center, but they should not shrink too far away from the pan's sides.

6. Remove the item from the oven, then cool it on racks before serving and/or storing.

   The texture should be even throughout the product's interior, with a cake-like crumb. Quick breads should be moist but not wet or unduly heavy.

The Creaming Method

Creaming together fat and sugar produces an exceptionally fine crumb and a dense, rich texture that holds up well and slices evenly. Pound cakes are the primary example of the results of the **creaming method.** Many cookies are also made by creaming, although the ingredient proportions differ—cakes have less butter and more eggs, whereas cookies usually have greater amounts of butter and sugar.

A leavener, such as baking powder or baking soda, is not always required for pound cake and cookies. However, use of a leavener will result in

FIGURE 12-12   Creaming Method

(1) Combine butter and sugar.

(2) Add eggs.

(3) Blend.

(4) Add sifted dry ingredients.

(5) Alternate with liquid ingredients.

(6) Finished batter.

lighter, less-dense products. Refer to the specific recipes for guidelines.

Mise en Place

Refer to the basic mise en place for the straight mixing method, earlier in this chapter.

Method

1. Combine the room temperature butter (or other shortening) and sugar and blend them together until the mixture is smooth, light, and creamy (see Figure 12-12).

   This is generally done in a mixer, using a paddle attachment. Scrape down the bowl's sides and bottom as needed throughout mixing to be sure that the mixture is evenly creamed together. It should be light in both color and tex-ture and relatively smooth. Do not undermix at this stage, because the final texture will depend upon this step. If you have begun with cold butter, you may need to allow some extra mixing time to allow the friction of the paddle and the sugar to gently warm and soften the butter.

2. Gradually add the eggs, which should be at room temperature.

   If either the eggs or the butter mixture are too cool, the batter may appear curdled, like a broken hollandaise. If this should happen, continue to mix, without adding more eggs, until the mixture looks completely smooth again. If your kitchen or bakeshop is exceptionally cold, you may need to allow the batter to heat up very slightly over warm water before returning it to the mixing machine for further beating. Conversely, if the room is very warm, have eggs cool when they are added.

3. Once the eggs are incorporated, gradually add the sifted dry ingredients, alternating with the liquid ingredients in stages.

Continue to mix until the batter is very smooth. It is not necessary to divide the dry and liquid ingredients into exact thirds, but they should be added, alternately, to the batter in three batches.

Scrape down the bottom and sides of the bowl to be sure that the finished batter is perfectly blended. The finished batter should be extremely smooth and light, with no trace of lumps.

If you are adding fruits, nuts, or other ingredients, they should be incorporated according to the recipe or formula you have selected.

4. Pour the batter into pans that have been greased and floured or lined with parchment paper.

Bake the batter until the cake springs back when pressed lightly with a fingertip and the edges have begun to shrink from the pan's sides. Tests for doneness may vary from one type of item to another, but in general a wooden skewer inserted near the center of the item should come out clean.

5. Remove the cake from the oven and the pan, and cool it properly before serving and/or storing.

Specific items may require special handling at this point, but a general rule is this: Allow the cake, muffin, or quick bread to cool briefly while still in the pan, then unmold it onto a rack and allow it to continue to cool to room temperature.

The crust of these products is usually slightly darker than the interior. The higher proportion of eggs, butter, and sugar causes this browning action. The cake should rise evenly, without a noticeable center hump or dip. If the cake has been properly mixed, it should not have tunnels or air pockets.

At this point, many items may be given a glaze, frosting, or other coating. Figure 12-13 shows a pound cake being glazed.

FIGURE 12-13 Glazes

(1) Brushing pound cake with apricot glaze.

(2) Ladling on confectioners' sugar glaze.

The Two-Stage Method

The **two-stage method** is used to prepare what are referred to as **high-ratio cakes.** This means that the weight of the sugar given in the recipe is either equal to or greater than the weight of the flour. In order for these cakes to be successfully prepared, it is necessary to use an emulsified shortening.

A high-ratio cake has a tender texture, a fine crumb, and excellent keeping qualities. The sugar acts as a moisturizing agent, and prevents the cake from becoming stale and dry too rapidly.

Mise en Place

Refer to the basic mise en place for the straight mixing method, earlier in this chapter.

Method

1. Place all of the sifted dry ingredients in the bowl of a mixer.

2. Add all of the shortening and approximately half of the liquid to the dry ingredients, and mix them using the paddle attachment, at a low speed. The batter should be smoothly blended but stiff and fairly thick.

3. Combine the eggs with the remaining liquid ingredients and blend them into the batter using the whip attachment. Add this mixture to the batter in two or three parts and whip until smooth.

Mix the batter well between additions and remember to scrape the sides and bottom of the bowl in order to blend the batter smoothly. This process should usually be accomplished in 3 minutes of actual mixing time.

The characteristics of the finished baked item will depend a great deal on how the batter is handled during mixing. Overmixing can result in cakes that have a rapid initial rise, only to collapse as they continue baking. Undermixed batters may not rise evenly, or they may develop large tunnels or air pockets.

4. After all of the wet ingredients have been incorporated, increase the speed of the mixer to medium and mix the batter for another 3 minutes.

It is important to scrape the bowl down repeatedly during this process. This is the only way to be certain that the batter is properly and fully blended.

5. Scale the batter as desired and place it into prepared pans. Bake the cake at an appropriate temperature, usually 350°F (175°C).

These cakes are baked until the surface of the cake springs back when it is lightly pressed with a fingertip. The top crust should be lightly browned, with an even, uncracked surface. The texture and crumb throughout the cake should be quite fine and very even, with no evidence of air pockets or tunnels. When properly prepared and baked, the taste of the cake should reflect the dominant flavoring ingredients (butter, vanilla, or chocolate, for instance).

Cool the cake completely before going on to fill, frost, or decorate.

The Foaming Method

A foam of whole eggs, yolks, or whites provides the structure for genoise, angel food cake, and chiffon cakes, and some special small cakes or cookies, such as madeleines and ladyfingers. These extremely delicate cakes are also quite resilient; in some cases, cakes made by the **foaming method** may be rolled, as in the French classic holiday dessert, *bûche de Noël*.

There are two versions of the foaming method. In one method, used for **genoise,** the eggs and sugar are heated before they are beaten into a foam. In the other, used for **angel food** and **chiffon cakes,** a basic meringue is prepared using just egg whites. In the method outlined below, requirements for angel food and chiffon cakes are given as variations of the genoise technique.

The foaming method is also used for preparing meringue, a mixture made of egg whites and sugar beaten until thickened. Recipes for meringues can be found in Part IV, Chapter 30, and the technique for making meringues can be found in Chapter 6.

Mise en Place

Refer to the basic mise en place for the straight mixing method earlier in this chapter for a discussion of ingredients and equipment.

If you are using egg whites as the foundation of a cake, be sure that they are completely free of all traces of yolk.

Method

1. Combine the eggs (whole, yolk, or whites) with sugar in a bowl. Place the bowl over a hot-water bath and heat it to approximately 100°F (38°C) whipping constantly.

This is done to completely dissolve the sugar, increase the volume, and develop a finer grain.

---

madeleine: a small cookie, baked in a special scallop-shell shaped pan.

lady finger: a spongy cookie, shaped like a finger and used to accompany other desserts, such as ice cream. Also an integral component in some desserts.

Use a whip to blend together the sugar and eggs (see Figure 12-14).

For angel food and chiffon cakes, especially those made with only egg whites, it may be preferable to omit this stage and start by whipping the room-temperature whites into a thick foam and then gradually incorporating the sugar.

2. Remove the mixture from the heat and beat it with the whip attachment until the eggs form a stable foam that has tripled in volume.

Mixing time is generally 15 minutes on third speed and five minutes on second speed. The mixture should form a ribbon as it falls from the whip.

3. Gently fold in the sifted dry ingredients.

This can be done by hand, using a spatula or whisk, or at a low speed using the whip attachment. Do not overwork the batter at this point, as the foam could start to deflate, resulting in a flat, dense product.

4. Add any flavorings or additional ingredients.

If butter or chocolate is required, it should be melted and slightly cooled. Add it after the dry ingredients have been properly incorporated. These ingredients should be warm enough to liquefy, to ensure that they are evenly distributed throughout the batter.

Be sure that any garnish ingredients added to the batter, such as nuts or chips, are small enough to stay suspended in the batter as it bakes.

5. Immediately pour the batter into prepared pans. Bake until the surface springs back when lightly pressed with a fingertip and the cake has begun to shrink from the pan's sides.

6. Remove the cake from the oven and let it cool. Some cakes should be allowed to remain in the pan as they cool to help them retain the correct structure once they are unmolded. Others need to be removed from the pans and allowed to cool on cooling racks.

These cakes should rise evenly during baking. When they are properly baked, they will begin to shrink away from the pan's sides. When cut, the

FIGURE 12-14   Foaming Method

(1) Combine eggs and sugar in bowl.

(2) Beating mixture with whip.

(3) Folding in sifted dry ingredients.

(4) Finished genoise sponge cake.

cake should have no large tunnels or air pockets. Cakes prepared by the foaming method are often more spongy than other cakes, although they do have a discernible crumb.

Angel food and chiffon cakes are the most spongy of these types. The limited amount of fats (e.g., butter) used gives these cakes a slightly dry texture, which is why they often are flavored and moistened with simple syrup. Even though there is a large proportion of eggs in foamed cakes, there should not be a marked egg flavor.

Biscuits, Scones, and Soda Breads

Although biscuits, scones, and soda breads are also considered quick breads, the techniques for preparing their batters are different from the straight mix method used for muffins and batter-type breads. Some biscuits, for example, are prepared by a creaming mixing method, while others are prepared by a technique similar to that used for pie dough.

These items are generally referred to as "doughs," rather than batters. The texture of the finished baked good will vary, depending upon both the mixing mithod used and the ingredients called for in the recipe. Some biscuits, are light and cakey, such as shortcake biscuits made with eggs and buttermilk, mixed by a creaming method. Other biscuits are flakier, because the shortening is rubbed, not creamed, into the dough. These biscuits will separate easily into layers once baked. Refer to specific recipes for additional guidance.

Pastry Doughs for Pies and Pastries

All chefs should be able to prepare and work with a variety of doughs including flaky and mealy pie doughs; blitz puff pastry; roll-in doughs such as classic puff pastry, croissant, and Danish doughs; phyllo dough and pâte à choux. These doughs are certainly not retained for exclusive use in the bakeshop. They are used as components in such savory dishes as cheese straws or pot pies. Phyllo dough is frequently used to make savory strudels and turnovers, and such special items as spanako-pita or beurrecks.

Cookies, including shortbreads and tuiles, are important elements in many of the more elaborate plated desserts and cakes you might want to offer on your dessert menu. You may want to use them to decorate cakes you purchase from elsewhere, if you do not make the majority of your own desserts. This is one way to make sure that your dessert menu is not exactly the same as the restaurant down the street.

Basic Pie Dough

Basic pie dough is often called 3–2–1 dough, because it is composed of three parts flour, two parts fat, and one part water (by weight). When properly made, the crust is flaky and crisp. This dough is also referred to a **pâte brisée.**

Pie dough may be referred to as either "flaky" or "mealy." The difference has to do with how the fat or shortening is incorporated into the flour. When the shortening is allowed to remain in large pieces, the finished pie dough will separate easily into layers, hence the descriptive term, flaky. When the fat is worked more thoroughly into the flour, the result will be a pie crust with a very small flake. It will be more similar to a shortbread or cookie dough, with a short fine grain referred to as mealy.

Mise en Place

1. Assemble all ingredients.

   Many formulas suggest the use of pastry flour to keep the dough tender. Since it has a tendency to clump together, pastry flour must be properly sifted. Special flours may also be used to prepare a variety of pastry doughs and cookies, according to the specific recipe. In some instances, notably the dough for linzertortes, the flour is partially replaced by ground toasted nuts.

   The type of fat selected will have an effect on the finished item. Lard is a traditional choice among some chefs. Hydrogenated vegetable shortenings are also a common choice, and they should be chilled for best results. Butter is often used for its flavor. If you do use butter, remember that it contains a small but significant quantity of moisture (water). You

FIGURE 12-15 Pie Dough

(1) Combining flour and fat.

(2) Flaky pie dough.

(3) Mealy pie dough.

should adjust the recipe slightly to account for that. Cream cheese or sour cream may be required in some doughs. They contain a good deal of fat, which will affect the amount of other fats used in the dough. The amount of fat in the overall formula should be decreased if these ingredients are used.

The liquid used in pie doughs is customarily water, but milk or cream may also be used for very tender crusts. In some cases, the liquid should be very cold to achieve the proper flaky texture in the finished item. It is a good idea to completely dissolve the salt in the liquid to ensure that it will be evenly distributed throughout.

When sugar is added to the dough, it will also have an effect, changing not only the flavor but also the texture and color of the baked dough. This dough is known as *pâte sucrée*. Eggs give doughs a golden color and a firmer texture. Refer to the formulas in Part IV of this book for specific quantities.

2. Assemble all equipment necessary.

This type of dough can be prepared by hand or in a mixer with a paddle or dough hook. In addition to a variety of bowls, you will also need a rolling pin, pastry cutters, crimpers, knives or scissors, a brush to apply egg wash, and pie or tart pans.

Method

1. Combine the flour and the fat.

Cut the fat into the dough either by hand, by using a mixer with a paddle attachment, or with a pastry knife (see Figure 12-15). For flaky pie dough, leave the fat pieces rather large, about the size of marbles. For mealy pie dough, continue to blend the mixture until it resembles a coarse meal and has begun to take on a slightly yellow color.

2. Add the cold water all at once; mix it quickly into the flour-and-fat mixture.

Keep mixing just until a shaggy mass forms. It is not necessary to create a completely homogeneous dough at this point. In fact, for flaky pie dough, you may be startled at first to see large lumps of shortening or butter still visible. This is desirable, and not a matter for concern.

3. Gather the dough into a smooth ball and chill it until it is firm.

You may have to knead the dough very briefly by hand to get it gathered into a smooth ball. A few turns ought to be sufficient. Any more and you may warm the dough too much. Proper chilling allows the dough to relax and also firms up the fat.

FIGURE 12-16 Rolling Pie Crust

(1) Roll with pin in one direction on a diagonal.

(2) Switch hands and roll in the opposite direction.

FIGURE 12-17 Lining a Pie Plate with the Bottom Crust

(1) Transferring bottom pie crust into pan.

(2) A scrap of dough is used to gently press the dough into the pan's corners.

4. Turn the chilled dough onto a floured work surface. Scale the dough into the correct size.

   As a general rule, you will need about one ounce of pie dough for every inch of the pan's diameter, plus an additional ounce or two to allow for an adequate overhang. If the dough is extremely cold and hard, you may need to give it a little time to soften very slightly.

5. Using even strokes, roll the dough into the desired thickness and shape.

   Turn it occasionally to produce an even shape and to keep it from sticking to the work surface (see Figure 12-16).

   Dust the working surface very lightly with flour, if necessary, as you work. Try to avoid adding a lot of flour. This will affect the quality of the baked dough. Work from the center toward the edges, rolling in different directions. Try not to let the rolling pin run off the edges of the dough.

Preparing Pies and Tarts

Although pies and tarts are alike in terms of the doughs and fillings that are used, there are some differences. Pies are generally double-crusted (having top and bottom crusts) and are baked in a relatively deep pan with sloping sides to accommodate large amounts of filling. Tarts are usually prepared in thin, straight-sided pans, often with removable bottoms. Tarts (and tartlets) most often have a single crust and are not as deep as pies.

Lining a Pie Plate or Tart Mold

The dough should be rolled out in a circle that is large enough to fit into the pan, covering the bottom and sides, with an inch or so of overhang (see Figure 12-17). Brush away all flour from the upper surface, then fold the dough in half, and brush away any excess flour on the bottom.

With the dough still folded in half or draped over the rolling pin, transfer the dough to a pan and fit it gently into the pan's corners. Use a ball of scrap dough to press out any air pockets. Trim away the excess dough. At this point, the pie is ready to fill, or you may want to bake the crust "blind." Both procedures are outlined below.

Baking Blind

The procedure for preparing a prebaked pie shell is known as **baking blind.** The dough is prepared, rolled out, and fitted into the pan. The dough is pierced in several places with the tines of a fork (known as docking) to prevent blisters from forming in the dough as it bakes.

The pastry is then covered with parchment paper and an empty pie pan is set on top of the paper (this is known as double panning). Or, the pie or tart may be filled with pie weights, dry beans, or uncooked rice. The dough is baked in a moderate oven until it is set, appears dry, and has a light golden color.

Once the shell is baked, it may be coated with melted chocolate or an apricot glaze to prevent the crust from becoming soggy. This also adds additional flavor to the finished pie or tart. Be sure however, that the flavor you introduce is appropriate to the particular item.

Fillings for Pies and Tarts

Most fruit fillings and some custard fillings for American-style pies are added to the pie crust before baking. Some special tarts (a jam-filled linzertorte, for instance) are also filled before baking.

Other pies and tarts are made by first prebaking the crust and then adding a filling. Cream fillings, such as a pastry cream, Bavarian or a mousse, are usually added to prebaked crusts. Fresh-fruit or cream-filled tarts are also generally made with prebaked crusts.

Fruit-filled pies and tarts may be uncooked or cooked, depending upon the type of fruit you are using—fresh, frozen, or dried. Thickeners may be added to the fruit to tighten the filling, giving it additional body and making the finished product easier to slice into portions. Toasted bread crumbs may also be used to trap the juices and prevent the bottom crust from becoming soggy.

Topping Pies and Tarts

Many pies and tarts will receive a topping of some sort. There are many possibilities, including a standard top crust, a lattice top, or a crumb topping. Other topping choices include meringues, whipped cream, or glazes.

To make a top crust, roll out the dough in the same manner as for the bottom crust. You will need slightly less dough for the top layer than the bottom, however. Cut slashes or a circular vent in the top crust to allow steam to escape. Egg wash the edge of the bottom layer or brush it lightly with water or milk to help seal the bottom and top crusts together. Pinch or cut away any excess dough and, finally, turn the edges and crimp or flute to seal.

Brush the top crust very lightly with egg wash if desired, or sprinkle it with sugar. You may opt to decorate the pie with cutouts made from scraps of dough. Brush both the tops and bottoms of these decorations with egg wash also so that they will stick well.

Lattice tops are made by cutting even strips of pie dough, and arranging them in a basketweave pattern. For the most evenly spaced lattice, you can use the method demonstrated in Figure 12-18.

Another common pie topping is a meringue, which is piped onto the pie in a decorative pattern or simply mounded and peaked. Meringues are quickly browned in a very hot oven. If properly applied, they should not lift away from the filling, nor should there be visible moisture beads on the meringue's surface.

Fresh-fruit tarts are generally brushed with a glaze, such as apricot, to enhance their appearance and extend their shelf life.

Baking Pies and Tarts

Filled and trimmed pies and tarts should be placed on sheet pans and baked at a high temperature until the dough is browned. To enhance the finished product's appearance, milk or an egg

FIGURE 12-18   Preparing a Lattice Top

(1) Cut even strips of pie dough.

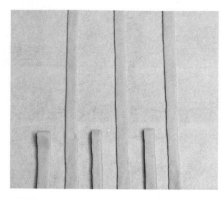

(2) Lay out vertical strips, folding back- every other one.

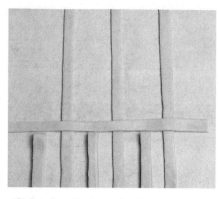

(3) Lay in a horizontal strip.

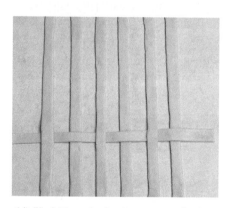

(4) Unfold vertical strips to create lattice. Repeat until all horizontal strips are interwoven

(5) The lattice is ready to transfer to the filled pie.

(6) The cherry pie is ready to bake.

wash may be brushed on the dough in the final 15 minutes of baking to make a shiny, darker, and perhaps golden (if egg yolk is used) surface.

Roll-In Doughs

Danish, croissant, and **puff pastry doughs** are used to prepare a number of special pastries. These are considered by many to be among the most technically advanced and time-consuming doughs to prepare correctly. Proper mixing methods, rolling techniques, and temperature control are important in order to produce **roll-in (or laminated) doughs** that are flaky and delicate after baking. Pastries based on these doughs, especially those made from puff pastry, are often referred to as French pastries.

The techniques for preparing these three doughs are similar. Danish and croissant doughs use yeast, but puff pastry (*pâte feuilletée*) does not include an added leavener. In all three, the dough is layered with butter (referred to as a "roll-in") in such a manner that several layers are produced after the dough is properly folded and rolled.

Blitz puff pastry is mixed using a method similar to that used in preparing pie dough. The dough is rolled and folded using the same technique used with the traditional roll-in doughs.

Phyllo dough, though itself not considered a roll-in dough, is also discussed here. A very lean dough is prepared, kneaded, and stretched into very thin sheets. Before the dough is used, it is brushed with melted butter. The effect is similar to that created by the layers of butter in roll-in doughs.

Excellent-quality doughs can be purchased, usually as frozen sheets. This makes is possible to create special Danish and other pastries, especially in

FIGURE 12-19 Positioning the Roll-In and Marking the Turns

(1) Rolling dough into rectangle.

(2) Removing excess flour from dough.

(3) Roll-in encased in dough.

(4) Marking the number of turns completed.

(5) Refrigerating the dough before continuing to roll out.

operations where space is too limited to support full-scale pastry production. To use the frozen doughs, allow the dough to thaw in the refrigerator before rolling, cutting, shaping, and baking.

Mise en Place

1. Assemble all ingredients necessary to prepare the dough.

The ingredients for puff pastry are few: butter or shortening, flour, and water. Croissant and Danish doughs are both made from a yeast-raised dough. All three require a roll-in, made from butter or shortening blended with a little flour.

The proper mixing methods for the basic roll-in dough components have been discussed in earlier sections of this chapter. Blitz puff pastry is made in the same way as flaky pie dough. It does not include a separately prepared roll-in.

2. Assemble all equipment necessary.

These doughs and roll-in can be mixed by hand or by using a mixer. A work surface, rolling pin, knives, or special cutters are also required. Sheet trays are necessary, as is an adequate refrigerator.

Method for Doughs with Separate Roll-Ins

1. Working on a floured surface, roll the prepared dough out into a rectangle, about ½-inch thick. It should be cool but not stiff. Use a brush to remove any excess flour from the dough (see Figure 12-19).

2. Roll out the roll-in between two pieces of parchment paper to form a rectangle that will cover two-thirds of the dough; it should be the same approximate thickness (½-inch) and consistency as the dough.

3. Position the roll-in on the dough so that one-third of the dough is uncovered and there is a one-half-inch border on the other three sides. Fold the uncovered third of the dough over the roll-in. Next, fold the opposite third on top of

FIGURE 12-20   Blitz Puff Pastry

FIGURE 12-20   Blitz Puff Pastry

(1) Combining ingredients for dough.

(2) Blending into rough dough.

(3) Gathering dough into ball.

(4) Rolling dough into rectangle.

the dough. The dough should appear stacked in the five layers, with alternating layers of dough and roll-in. Use your fingertips to weld the seams together.

Once the roll-in has been encased in the dough, it is rolled out and given a three- or letter-fold (refer to the descrtiption of these folds below). This initial fold is then followed with the recommended number of three or four folds. Be sure to brush away any excess flour from the dough.

FIGURE 12-21
Initial Three-Fold (Letter-Fold) Blitz

FIGURE 12-22   Blitz Puff Pastry

(1) Book-fold blitz.

(2) Repeating book-fold.

HANDLING ROLL-IN DOUGHS

To work with these doughs after they are completely prepared, or with purchased frozen doughs that have been gently thawed, observe the following guidelines.

- Keep the dough chilled, taking out only the amount to be worked with at a given time. If the dough is too warm, the finished product will not have the desired flakiness.

- Use a sharp knife when shaping or cutting the dough. Clean cuts will ensure that the baked item rises evenly. This is especially important for high, straight-sided items such as vol-au-vent and *bouchée*.

- Do not run the roller over the dough's edge; this will destroy the layers.

- Chill puff-pastry items before baking them. This keeps the layers of dough and roll-in separate, ensuring the best rise and flakiness in the finished product.

- Save puff-pastry scraps. They can be piled together and rolled out to use for items such as *Napoléons* where a substantial rise is not necessary.

Left on the dough, this flour might interfere with proper layer formation.

Method for Blitz Puff Pastry

Combine all of the ingredients as you would for pie dough and blend into a rough dough. Turn the dough onto a floured surface, gather into a ball, and dust lightly with flour (see Figure 12-20).

Rolling, Folding, and Shaping the Finished Dough

It is essential to completely chill the dough between the rolling out and folding stages. If the dough is worked long enough for the butter (or other fat) to become warm, it will be absorbed into the dough, instead of remaining in a separate layer. This will reduce the number of layers and could give the finished product a rubbery or gummy texture.

1. Roll dough out into a rectangle, and fold into thirds (a letter-fold—see Figure 12-21). If the dough has warmed up, stop at this point and let it firm in the refrigerator.

2. Turn dough so the longest edge is parallel to the edge of the work surface. Roll the dough out again into a rectangle, and make a "book-fold" as follows (see Figure 12-22):

Fold the narrow edges of the rectangle inward until they meet in the center of the rectangle. Now fold the rectangle in half again, as shown in the accompanying photographs. Repeat the book-fold another three or four times, allowing the dough sufficient time to chill and firm up again between rolling out the dough and folding it.

Once the dough has received all the necessary turns, it should be allowed to rest under refrigeration overnight before the final rolling, shaping, and baking.

Handling Method for Phyllo Dough

This dough should be thawed under refrigeration if necessary. Keep the dough covered lightly with plastic wrap and dampened towels as you work with it. Otherwise, it can become brittle and shatter. Melted butter, bread crumbs, or a combination of both are spread evenly over the dough to keep the layers separate as they bake. This creates a flaky finished product. A brush or spray bottle is generally used to apply the butter or oil in an even coat.

Fillings for Pastries

There are a number of fillings that are appropriate for pastries made from Danish, croissant, and

FIGURE 12-23   Pâte à Choux

(1) Pâte à choux in progress.

(2) Ready to come off the heat.

(3) Adding eggs gradually.

(4) Working the dough.

(5) Piping dough onto sheet pan.

puff-pastry doughs, including fresh or cooked fruits, chocolate, custards and other creams, jams, and savory ingredients, such as cheese or sliced ham.

Nut- and seed-paste fillings can be purchased, as in the case of almond paste and poppy seed paste.

It is generally best to allow filled and shaped pastry doughs some time to firm or chill again before they are baked. For the best results, bake the pastries at the correct temperature; usually parchment-lined baking sheets are used.

Pâte à Choux

Pâte à choux may be considered a "cooked dough." It is made by heating a combination of water, butter, and flour, and then mixing in eggs. When properly prepared and baked, it will expand during baking, creating a delicate shell with an essentially hollow center. Pâte à choux is soft enough so that

the chef can use a pastry bag to pipe it into different shapes. Among the most common shapes are cream puffs, profiteroles, and éclairs.

Mise en Place

1. Assemble and prepare all ingredients.

   This includes the basic components: water, or a combination of water and milk, butter or shortening, eggs, and flour. Sugar, ground spices, or grated cheese may also be added, according to specific recipes.

2. Assemble all equipment.

   The dough is mixed in a pan over direct heat. The eggs can be incorporated with a spoon or a mixer fitted with a paddle attachment. Pastry bags or parchment cones are used to pipe out the pâte à choux onto parchment-lined sheet pans.

Method

1. Bring the liquid and butter to a full boil. Add the flour and cook it until the mixture pulls away from the pan, forming a ball (see Figure 12-23).

2. Place the dough in the bowl of a mixer. Use the paddle attachment to mix it for a few minutes,

allowing the dough to cool slightly. This will prevent the dough's heat from cooking the eggs as they are worked into the mixture. (Small batches can be simply removed from the heat and left in the pot.)

3. Add the eggs gradually, in three or four additions, working the dough until it is smooth each time. Scrape down the bowl's sides and bottom as necessary. Continue to do so until all the eggs are incorporated. Mix the dough just until a smooth heavy paste forms. Do not overmix.

4. The dough is ready to use at this point. It should be piped or dropped onto sheet pans lined with parchment paper, according to the desired result.

To properly bake pâte à choux, begin the baking process at a high temperature (375 to 400°F/190 to 204°C). Reduce the heat to 250°F (120°C) once the pâte à choux begins to take on color. Continue to bake the items until they are golden brown, and there are no visible beads of moisture on their exteriors.

Remove the items from the oven as soon as they are fully baked. Slash eclairs, cream puffs, and other large items with a sharp knife to allow the steam to escape. This will ensure that the shells remain crisp.

If the item is to be filled, slice it open and pull away any loose dough from the interior. Spoon or pipe the filling into the shell. Glaze or sauce as desired.

Creams, Bavarians, and Mousses

Vanilla Sauce

This sauce has also been included in the creams section of this chapter, since it is the foundation of many other dessert items, including ice cream, mousses, Bavarians, and a buttercream. A baked custard is based on the same ingredients, combined in the same ratio as a **vanilla sauce.** Instead of stirring the sauce as it cooks over direct heat, a custard is placed in an appropriate mold and baked in a bain-marie until it is firmly set. As a dessert sauce, it is a classic accompaniment to soufflés and other hot desserts, such as steamed puddings.

Mise en Place

1. Assemble all ingredients for the sauce.

Differences do exist between various vanilla sauce formulas. Some recipes may include whole milk, whereas others will call for heavy cream, light cream, or a combination of cream and milk. Some recipes use only egg yolks; others use whole eggs or a ratio of whole eggs to egg yolks.

Vanilla sauce can be flavored by adding a number of other ingredients, including liqueurs, cordials, chocolate, or fruits.

2. Assemble all equipment necessary to prepare the sauce.

Since this is a delicate sauce that can curdle easily if it is allowed to overheat, select a heavy-gauge pot, a double-boiler, or a bain-marie. The sauce should be prepared in a nonreactive pot, such as stainless steel, to prevent it from becoming even slightly gray. Wooden spoons are suggested for stirring the sauce as it cooks. A fine chinois or cheesecloth is used to strain the sauce into a clean container. Prepare an ice or cold water bath to quickly cool the sauce once it is cooked, if necessary.

Method

1. Combine the eggs with half of the sugar in a stainless steel bowl. Blend them well, using a whip (see Figure 12-24).

2. Combine the milk with half of the sugar in a large pot and heat it just to the boiling point. If you are using a vanilla bean to flavor the sauce, it should be added now, to steep in the milk as it heats. Be sure to keep an eye on the milk as it heats because there is a likelihood that it will boil over as it nears the boiling point.

3. Temper the egg and sugar mixture with the hot milk; return it to the pot. Continue to cook the sauce over low heat until it begins to thicken. Stir the sauce constantly to prevent it from overcooking. The sauce should never come to a boil, because egg yolks and whites coagulate well

FIGURE 12-24 Vanilla Sauce

(1) Blend eggs and sugar, and heat milk or cream.

(2) Tempering egg-and-sugar mixture with hot milk.

(3) Adding the remainder of the egg mixture.

(4) Creating soft "gel" that will coat wooden spoon.

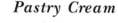

(5) Adding desired flavoring.

below the boiling point. The idea is to create a soft gel that will coat the back of a wooden spoon. The sauce's temperature should not go above 180°F (82°C).

4. Add any desired flavoring ingredients at this point. For specific suggestions, refer to the recipes in Part IV, Chapter 29, of this book.

5. Once the sauce has reached the correct consistency, strain it immediately through a fine chinois or cheesecloth into a bain-marie or other container. Cool the sauce as quickly as possible in an ice water bath if it is not to be served immediately. Wrap or cover tightly, if the cream is to be stored for any length of time.

Pastry Cream

Pastry cream (*crème pâtissière*) is often required for the production of Napoléons, éclairs, and Boston cream pie. It may also be used as a soufflé base or to prepare steamed puddings.

Mise en Place

1. Assemble all ingredients required for pastry cream.

The basic ingredients are quite similar to those used to prepare vanilla sauce: eggs, milk, sugar, and flavoring. In addition, a thickener, such as flour or cornstarch may be required in some formulas.

2. Assemble all equipment required for pastry cream. Refer to the information regarding vanilla sauce above.

Method

1. Mix the flour, half of the sugar, and the whole eggs together in one bowl and blend them to a smooth consistency (see Figure 12-25).

2. Bring the milk and the remaining sugar to a boil. If a vanilla bean is used to flavor the sauce, it may be added at this point.

FIGURE 12-25 Pastry Cream

(1) Mixing flour, sugar, and eggs.   *(2) Passing the whip through the cream.*   *(3) Adding whole butter.*

3. Use part of the milk mixture to temper the egg mixture.

Be sure to blend it thoroughly at this point, so that there will not be any lumps of starch in the finished pastry cream. Return the tempered eggs to the pot and continue to cook the mixture until it reaches a full boil. Stir or whip the pastry cream constantly while it cooks. It will become very thick; when the whip passes through the cream, the wires will leave traces.

4. After removing the pastry cream from the heat, add flavorings and whole butter.

Remove the cream to a clean bowl and cool it quickly over an ice bath if it will not be used right away. Some chefs sprinkle sugar on the cream's surface to prevent the formation of a skin; others dot it with additional butter or place a sheet of plastic wrap or parchment paper directly on the surface.

Preparing Dessert Soufflés

Classic **dessert soufflés** are made by combining a pastry cream (plain or flavored) with beaten egg whites. This mixture is then baked in a hot oven until the soufflé expands and is just barely cooked. As an alternative to a pastry cream base, a purée of cooked or raw fruits may be used, as demonstrated in the method for an apricot soufflé (see Figure 12-26).

The soufflé should rise evenly, without requiring a collar. Because soufflés are fragile, they must be served immediately upon removing them from the oven. This means that both the kitchen and wait-staff need to be completely prepared with a total mise en place—including all sauces, garnishes, serving pieces, and a tray—so that there is no delay in taking the finished soufflé to the guest. Careful timing and clear communication are critical.

Bavarian Creams

These delicate creams are made by stabilizing a vanilla sauce with gelatin, and then lightening the mixture with whipped cream and beaten egg whites (see Figure 12-27). They may be used on their own or as a filling for a variety of pastries, tortes, pies, and cakes.

Bavarian creams are incredibly versatile and lend themselves well to a wide range of flavors. Among the possible flavorings are various fruits (raspberries, bananas, and mangoes, to name a small sampling), chocolate, nuts, and many liqueurs, such as Grand Marnier or Kahlúa.

Mousse

Although quite similar to a Bavarian, a **mousse** (see Figure 12-28) usually does not contain

Figure 12-26   Preparing Apricot Soufflé

(1) First addition of beaten whites to puréed apricots.

(2) Blending purée and whites with a whip.

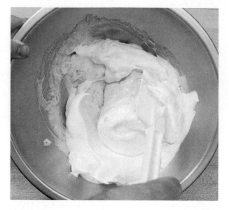

(3) Folding final additions of egg whites in with a rubber spatula.

(4) Level the top of filled soufflé molds.

(5) Run your thumb around the dish's rim to promote an even rise during baking.

Figure 12-27   Bavarian Cream

(1) An alternate folding sequence is to add the purée to the beaten whites.

(2) Folding gently until mixture appears homogeneous.

FIGURE 12-28 White Chocolate Mousse

(1) Cooking eggs.

(2) Adding syrup.

(3) Folding in melted chocolate.

(4) Filling mold.

(5) Finished plated dessert.

Flavoring ingredients are added, and then the mousse is lightened with whipped cream. A well-prepared mousse may often become the signature dessert for a restaurant. The presentation may be varied by using different containers, such as tuile cups, hollowed fruits, or special molds or glasses.

Buttercreams

There are four varieties of **buttercream**—Italian, French, German, and Swiss—distinguished by slight variations in ingredients. Most versions follow one of two basic methods:

gelatin as a stabilizer. For the best texture in the finished mousse, the eggs and sugar are beaten to a foam over a hot water bath. They should be allowed to reach at least 165°F (74°C) to be sure that the finished mousse will remain wholesome. The cooked eggs are then beaten until they form ribbons.

- A pastry cream or vanilla sauce is prepared, flavored, and allowed to cool. Softened butter is whipped into this base.

FIGURE 12-29 Preparing Italian Buttercream

(1) The meringue is whipped to full volume.

(2) Add softened butter to the meringue.

(3) The finished buttercream.

- The second method requires a syrup made by heating sugar and water. The hot syrup is beaten into eggs (whole, yolks, or whites) to make a meringue or foam, and then softened butter is added gradually, as shown in the step-by-step photos for Italian buttercream (see Figure 12-29).

Refer to the recipes for buttercreams in Part IV of this book.

Sauces and Glazes

The sauces described here are used to add flavor, moisture, and eye appeal to various desserts. In addition to their role as dessert adornment, they are also used as a basic component or ingredient in other items, as we have already seen in the previous discussion of vanilla sauce. Other sauces and glazes include chocolate sauce, sugar-based items, such as simple syrup, butterscotch and caramel, and various fruits sauces. Sabayons and fruit curds are also included here.

Chocolate Sauce

The success of any chocolate sauce or glaze sauce depends primarily on the chocolate's quality. Chocolate must be melted carefully to prevent it from scorching or becoming grainy. Any liquid that is to be added should also be incorporated carefully. A small amount of water can cause chocolate to seize or stiffen.

There are numerous formulas for chocolate sauces and syrups. **Ganache,** made by heating chocolate with cream and butter, can also be used as a sauce, a glaze, or to prepare truffles. Once shaped, truffles can be rolled in cocoa powder or dipped in chocolate.

Fondant

Fondant is basically a sugar-and-water syrup that has been cooked to the correct temperature, cooled, and worked repeatedly until it is smooth, creamy, opaque, and thick. Although it is made in some bakeshops, good-quality fondant can be purchased from purveyors.

For use as a glaze, fondant must be heated to approximately 105°F (40°C) and poured evenly over the product. The product may also be dipped directly into the fondant. The fondant provides a protective coating. This is especially useful for cakes that need to be held or that could dry out easily—petits fours, for example.

Syrups and Glazes

Simple syrup (see Figure 12-30) is make by cooking together sugar and water, along with any flavorings you like, until the sugar is completely dissolved. This preparation is then used to moisten layer cakes or genoise, or it may be used to poach fruits. It has many uses, and can be prepared in quantity and held under refrigeration for extended periods.

Glazes made from preserves or jellies are often brushed onto fresh fruit tarts or tartlets to give the fruit a sheen. The glazes also help to prevent the darkening of fruits that might discolor in the presence of air. The jelly or preserves should be heated gently to a liquid state, and then strained if necessary to remove seeds or fibers. The glaze should be applied lightly with a pastry brush.

There are other glazes that may be used with baked items. Many are made by stirring together confectioner's sugar with some water and possibly a flavoring, such as an extract or concentrated fruit purée. These should be room temperature, or possibly warm, so that they flow easily when applied to the baked item.

Fruit Sauces

These sauces may be made from a variety of fruits, which may be fresh, frozen, or dried. Some of the most popular fruit sauces include fresh berry coulis, such as raspberry or strawberry, and compotes, made by simmering dried fruits, such as apricots, currants, and raisins.

Fresh berry sauces or puréed fruit compotes can be used as a base for flourless soufflés, as noted above. They may also be used to flavor Bavarian creams, buttercreams, and other fillings and frostings.

FIGURE 12-30
Cooking Simple Syrup

Caramel/Butterscotch Sauces

These sauces are based on a richly flavored sugar syrup that has been allowed to cook to a deep, golden color. If no additional ingredients are added to the caramelized syrup, the mixture can be used to coat the mold for a classic dessert—*crème caramel*. To make a smooth caramel sauce, cream and butter are often added. Butterscotch sauce contains these same ingredients plus a small amount of an acid, such as apple-cider vinegar, to provide its distinctive flavor.

Sabayon (Zabaglione)

This fragile sauce is one of the few dessert sauces that cannot easily be made ahead and held. It is a delicate foam of egg yolks, sugar, and wine, customarily Marsala. The mixture is whipped constantly as it cooks over simmering water until it becomes thick and light.

Sabayon may be flavored as desired. If chocolate is added, the sauce will lose some of its airiness. For this reason, melted chocolate should be stirred in at the very end of the preparation time. Traditionally, a sabayon is served over peeled and sliced fresh fruit or on its own, with delicate cookies. It may also be stabilized with gelatin and used in the same manner as a Bavarian cream.

Fruit Curds

Curds are made in much the same manner as a hollandaise sauce. Egg yolks are cooked together with sugar and a fruit juice or purée over low heat or in a bain-marie. Softened butter is added, and the sauce is allowed to cook until thickened. Unlike a hollandaise, **fruit curds** may be allowed to reach a gentle simmer. Once prepared, the sauce should be cooled rapidly, and kept refrigerated if it will not be used immediately.

This sauce may be used on its own or folded together with whipped cream. It is also used to fill tarts and other pastries.

Frozen Desserts

Frozen desserts have always been extremely popular. The actual production of some of these desserts requires no special equipment beyond the usual assortment of cooking utensils. Granité and frozen soufflés, are "still-frozen." This means that the basic mixture is prepared, placed in a mold, and then allowed to freeze. The presence of various ingredients such as sugar and alcohol ensures that the end result will be smooth, light, and not rock-hard. Whipped cream and beaten egg whites will naturally introduce enough air to prevent the frozen soufflés and mousses from becoming too hard.

Other frozen desserts such as ice creams, gelatos, and sherbets, are made in an ice cream freezer that churns the base mixture to produce a smooth creamy product. This means that the mixture is agitated as it is cooled, incorporating additional air so that the end result is light and smooth, making it easy to eat with a spoon.

Frozen Soufflés and Mousses

Frozen soufflés, parfaits, and mousses are made by preparing a mousse or Bavarian cream (as outlined in the section covering creams), and using it to fill an appropriate mold or other container. It is then "still-frozen" until it becomes solid. To give the appearance of a classic hot soufflé, a parchment collar may be attached to the container, so that the mousse or Bavarian appears to have "risen" above the rim of the dish. A frozen soufflé or mousse is often allowed to "temper" briefly in the refrigerator before it is served.

Ice Cream and Gelato

Ice creams and gelato may be made in various ways and with different equipment. Essentially, a vanilla sauce is prepared, flavored, and then chilled. Once it is cooled, it is placed in an ice cream freezer along with appropriate flavorings and garnishes. The freezer is chilled to temperatures below 32°F (0°C), and a paddle churns the custard as it freezes. Gelato is an Italian specialty. It is generally lower in fat than many ice creams, and may be prepared with or without the addition of eggs.

Sorbets and Sherbets

Sorbets are based on liquids, such as fruit juices, wine, or coffee. The liquid is sweetened and may be combined with milk or cream (especially for sherbets) and, in some cases, egg whites. The base mixture is then frozen in the same manner as ice cream. The result is a frozen dessert with a texture similar to that of ice cream. The far-lower percentage of butterfat and absence of egg yolks, however, gives sorbets and sherbets a more "icy" texture.

Sorbets that are not heavily sweetened and do not contain cream or milk frequently are served between a formal meal's courses as an *intermezzo* ("between the work") to cleanse the palate.

Granité

Granité (or *granita* in Italian) is a special type of frozen dessert. In these "icy" preparations, the base mixture is prepared in the same manner as for a sorbet, although it customarily does not contain any milk, cream, or eggs. The mixture is placed in the freezer and allowed to still-freeze until service. At that time, the granité is scraped to produce large flakes or granules.

Simple Cookies, Candies, and Confections

The practice of offering a small confection at the end of a meal lends a special touch to a guest's dining experience. Truffles, petits fours, and other simple candies can be a mark of distinction between your establishment and others.

Candy making, especially fine chocolates, is demanding and can be quite expensive. The two confections shown here are simple to prepare, however, even in restaurants where special equipment may not always be on hand:

- Candied citrus peels may be dipped in chocolate.
- Flavored fondant may be shaped using a special mat then dipped in chocolate and simply decorated.

There are many other examples and recipes you may find suitable for your needs and level of skill.

Preparing Cookies, Petits Fours, and Other Small Pastries

The range of items known as cookies is so large that no single definition is appropriate. They typically contain a high percentage of sugar, so the oven temperature must be regulated during baking. Convection ovens, with their constant flow of even heat, are especially good for baking many kinds of cookies.

Cookies are often served at receptions, as part of a dessert buffet, or with ice cream or sorbet. An assort-

FIGURE 12-31   Various Cookies and Petits Fours

FIGURE 12-32 Tuiles

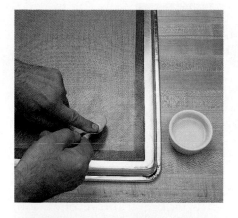

(1) Drop the batter onto a prepared baking sheet.

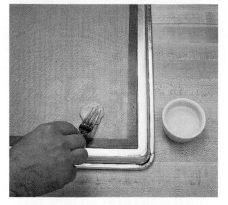

(2) Use the back of a spoon to spread out the batter.

(3) Remove the tuiles from the baking sheet when the edges are browned.

(4) To shape tuiles, lay in a mold and press down while they are still very hot.

ment of cookies might be presented at the end of a meal, as an appealing "extra." In general, these cookies should be bite-size. Cookies may be elaborate, with frostings and fillings, or plain (see Figure 12-31). Some cookies—tuiles for example—are used as shells for various fillings (see Figure 12-32).

Tempering Chocolate for Coating

The process of preparing chocolate for glazing or coating items is known as **tempering.** Chocolate contains two distinct types of fat, which melt at different temperatures. In order to ensure that the chocolate will melt smoothly and harden evenly with a good shine, it must be handled carefully.

Method

1. Chop the chocolate coarsely with a chef's knife and place it in a stainless steel bowl. Place the bowl over very low heat or barely simmering water, making sure that no moisture comes in contact with the chocolate. Stir the chocolate occasionally as it melts to keep it at an even temperature throughout (see Figure 12-33.)

2. Continue to heat the chocolate until it reaches a temperature of between 105 to 110°F (40 to 43°C). Use an instant-reading thermometer for the most accurate results.

3. Remove the chocolate from the heat. Add a large piece of unmelted chocolate and stir it in until the temperature drops to 87 to 92°F (30 to 33°C). This temperature should be kept constant all during the time you are working with

(5) Dark chocolate mousse in tuiles.

FIGURE 12-33   Tempering Chocolate

FIGURE 12-34   Fondant

(1) Chopping chocolate coarsely.

(1) Preparing fondant for candies.

(2) Testing temperature of chocolate.

(2) Molding fondant.

(3) Dipping candied orange peel into the chocolate.

(3) Dipping the fondant into the chocolate.

(4) Decorating chocolate-dipped fondant.

FIGURE 12-35   Parchment Cones

(1) Folding parchment on the diagonal.

(2) Making a pivot point.

(3) Rolling into funnel shape.

(4) Sealing the filled cone.

(5) Creating small opening.

purées, or melted chocolate and then molded or shaped as desired. Once cooled, fondant confections can be dipped in chocolate and decorated, as shown in Figure 12-34.

Special Tools and Techniques for Decorating Pastries and Cakes

the chocolate. If the chocolate drops below 85°F (29°C) while you are working with it, it will be necessary to repeat the steps described here to retemper it. If the chocolate scorches or becomes grainy, it can no longer be used. If any moisture comes in contact with the chocolate as it is being tempered, it will seize (or stiffen).

Tempered chocolate will coat the back of a spoon with an even layer and then harden into a shiny shell. Items can be either dipped directly into the tempered chocolate with a dipping fork, or placed on a rack over a clean sheet tray and the chocolate poured over them.

Preparing Candies from Fondant

Fondant for candies should be heated to 160°F (70°C). Then it can be flavored with extracts,

There are two basic tools used to create cakes and tortes that are readily available in virtually any kitchen or bakeshop—pastry bags and parchment cones.

Parchment Cones

Parchment cones are used to decorate pastries with delicate designs of chocolate, fondant, or special piping gels. To prepare a cone, complete the following steps (see Figure 12-35):

1. Fold a sheet of parchment paper on the diagonal, slightly overlapping. Do not form a perfect triangle. Use a nonserrated knife to cut through the fold.

2. Hold the uneven corner between the thumb and forefinger of one hand. Use the other

thumb and forefinger to make a "pivot point" by holding the parchment at the diagonal's midpoint.

3. Roll the parchment into a funnel shape, keeping the point closed as the paper is rolled. This may require some practice. It is important to keep the paper taut as it is rolled.

4. When the entire triangle has been rolled into a cone, fold the point on the top so that it is on the interior of the cone.

5. Hold the cone so that the tip is pointing downward, and fill the cone no more than half full. Do not add too much, or it will ooze out of the top. Fold the outer points in toward the cone's center and fold the last corner over the top of the other points, sealing the cone completely.

6. Hold the cone so that the tip is resting on a cutting surface and use scissors or a sharp knife to nick away a small amount of the paper, creating a small opening. The deeper the cut, the larger the opening and the larger the lines of piping will be.

When working with a parchment cone, make sure that the seam is on the side of the cone away from you. This will keep the seam from buckling open as you pipe.

Parchment cones are used to create a variety of finely worked designs or filigree work. To prepare decorative filigree, use the method shown in Figure 12-36:

Secure a stencil to the back of a sheet pan, near the center of the pan. Position a parchment sheet over the stencil so that it can be used as a guide for piping the chocolate. The parchment can then be easily slid to a clean spot once the initial design is completed, until the desired amount of designs have been traced onto the sheet. Use your fingers to gently pinch the top of the cone, expressing the chocolate out through the tip. Use the fingertips of your other hand to steady the cone.

Pastry Bags and Tips

Pastry bags are important throughout the kitchen for a number of different applications. To properly

FIGURE 12-36
Filigree Pattern to Make Ornaments

FIGURE 12-37 Pastry Bags

(1) Filling pastry bag.

(2) Hand position for piping.

(3) Caring for pastry bag.

fill, use, and care for a bag, use the following procedures (see Figure 12-37):

1. Select the desired tip and position it securely in the pastry bag's opening. A coupler makes it easy to change tips as you work.

2. Fold down the bag's top to create a cuff, then transfer the buttercream or other preparation to the bag with a spatula or spoon. Support the bag with your free hand while filling it.

3. Unfold the bag's cuff, and use one hand to gather together and twist the top of the bag. Press on the bag first to expel any air pockets. Once these have been removed, the bag is ready to use. With one hand, press the buttercream down and out of the bag. Use the other hand to support and guide the bag.

   When the design is finished, first release the pressure on the bag, then gently twist the tip while simultaneously lifting it cleanly away from the rosette or other design. This will prevent the formation of tails and threads that could spoil the effect.

4. Remove all the excess buttercream or other filling or frosting from the bag and wash it carefully inside and out with warm, soapy water after each use. Let the bag air dry before storing it to keep it in good condition, safe, and sanitary between uses.

Various effects can be created using a selection of tips. In Figure 12-38, rows 1 and 2 show a border design and individual rosettes made with a plain opening. Rows 3 and 4 show the same technique using a plain tip with a smaller opening. Rows 5 and 6 show the effect of two different-sized leaf tips. Rows 7 and 8 show rosettes made with a star tip and a shell border from the same tip. A number of other tips are available.

Assembling and Decorating Tortes

The elaborate wedding cakes, tortes, and other fancy cakes prepared by bakeshops have a definite place. They are not included here, however, since they represent a very specific type of pastry work. Instead, we will look at the ways that a restaurant

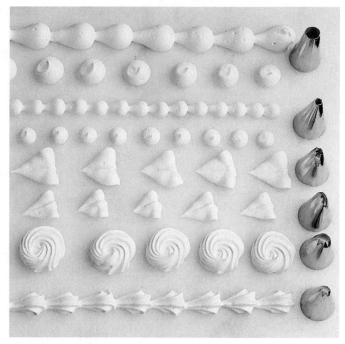

FIGURE 12-38 Various Tips and Their Effects

can produce beautiful, simple, high-quality cakes and tortes.

1. Prepare all the basic components and have them at the correct temperature. Some will need to be warmed or held at room temperature in order to spread properly. Others may need to be held under refrigeration.

2. To separate a cake into layers, use a knife with a long blade to cut the cake horizontally. Be sure to use the entire blade to make the cut. Trim the cake's edges, if necessary, and brush away any loose crumbs.

3. Moisten the layers with simple syrup or brush them with melted jam or preserves. Place the first layer on a cake circle, or in the bottom of a round mold.

   If desired, you can cut additional pieces to line the walls of the mold. This will give the finished cake a neat, attractive appearance, as well as making it easier to decorate later on.

4. Spread the filling evenly on each layer, building the cake as you go. You may use a Bavarian cream, or a mousse, pastry cream, or custard.

FIGURE 12-39 Tortes

(1) Assembling torte—splitting layers.

(2) Building torte.

(3) Brushing layers with melted jam or preserves.

(4) Adding filling.

(5) Glazing torte.

Add garnish or flavoring ingredients, such as poached or fresh fruit, as you work.

The amount of filling spread between each layers will vary, depending upon the type you select. However, as a general rule, its thickness should not exceed that of the cake layer.

5. Once the final layer has been added and smoothed off, a glaze or topping should be applied evenly. If the glaze is at the correct consistency, it is easy to spread it by tilting it, as shown in Figure 12-39, or with a spatula.

After the cake is filled and glazed, it can be refrigerated to firm up if necessary before any additional frostings or decorations are applied. A traditional approach to frosting a cake is shown in Figure 12-40.

Set the assembled cake on a turntable. Spread an even layer of icing on the cake's top and sides. Use level, even strokes to smooth it out. Hold the palette knife parallel to the cake's edge and turn the cake into the palette knife to even the coating on the sides. Smooth the top surface once more. Occasionally dip the palette knife into hot water for the smoothest finish.

DECORATING TIPS FOR TORTES AND CAKES

- Use a cake comb to create a decorative edge.
- Use fine cake crumbs, or sliced or chopped nuts to create an edge for the cake. Gently press them along the cake's bottom. Scatter the crumbs evenly over the top of the cake, if desired.
- Very lightly score the cake's top by pressing the edge of a palette knife into the icing to mark the slices. Place decorations, such as chocolate circles and whipped cream or buttercream rosettes, so that each slice will have a share of the decoration.

FIGURE 12-40   Frosting Cake

(1) Adding icing.

(2) Using cake comb to create decorative edge.

(3) The finished cake.

Summary

The restaurant experience is often begun with bread and finished with dessert. Both ends of the meal are framed by the impressions left from baking and pastry products. This is a very important dimension to your culinary education, and one in which considerable practice and patience are required to develop proficiency. Throughout your education and afterwards, you should work toward refining the following skills:

- Selecting, measuring, and preparing ingredients and equipment carefully, as called for by each recipe.

- Executing a variety of mixing methods properly to ensure a high quality finished product.

- Developing an ability to produce a good selection of sauces, creams, fillings, and glazes to enhance the appeal and perceived value of baked goods and desserts on your menu.

SELF-STUDY QUESTIONS

1. Why is scaling ingredients so important?

2. What are the three types of leaveners? Give examples of each and explain how they function.

3. Why are flour and eggs considered strengtheners?

4. What happens to starch when it is heated during the baking process?

5. Besides sweetening and flavoring, what other function does sugar serve?

6. Why do we refer to yeast as a "living" organism?

7. How and why is yeast proofed?

8. What is gelatin and how is it used?

9. Why is sifting important?

10. List four reasons for punching down dough.

11. How is gluten developed in a dough? Why is it important to the quality of bread?

12. Name the four basic methods for preparing batters.

13. Describe the two-stage mixing method.

14. What is the common foundation for the following items: ice cream, mousse, Bavarian, buttercream?

15. Describe the procedure for tempering chocolate and the results this process achieves.

ACTIVITIES

- Go to a local bakeshop and look over their products. See if you can identify the variety of breads, cakes, and other confections they may have available.

- Using a one-cup standard dry measure, scale out the following types of flour: all-purpose, cake, bread, rye, whole wheat, and cornmeal. Carefully weigh each cup of flour and record your results. Repeat the process at least twice more. What conclusion can you draw about the accuracy of volume versus weight measurement? Now sift each flour, scale out one cup measures of each kind of flour again and weigh them. Compare your results to the unsifted weights and explain.

KEYWORDS

angel food cake
artisanal
baking blind
basic pie dough
  (*pâte brisée*)
Bavarian cream
blitz puff pastry
bloom
buttercream
carmelization
chemical leaveners
chiffon cake
creaming method
croissant dough
crumb

Danish dough
dessert soufflé
dock
foaming method
fondant
frozen desserts
fruit curd
ganache
gelatin
genoise (sponge cake)
granita/granité
high-ratio cake
kneading
lean dough
leaveners

mousse
organic leavener
parchment cone
pastry cream
  (*creme patissière*)
pastry bag
pâte á choux
peel
phyllo dough
physical leavener
proof
puff pastry dough
rich dough
roll-in (laminated) dough
sabayon

scaling
shorteners
sifting
simple syrup
sourdough
sponge
straight mixing
  method
strengtheners
sweeteners
tempering
thickeners
two-stage method
vanilla sauce
yeast

IV

The Recipes

*The discovery of a new dish does more for
the happiness of mankind than the
discovery of a new star.*
—*Brillat-Savarin*

13

Mise en Place and Stock Recipes

Each day, for each menu item, you will need to prepare the basic ingredients and mixtures used to season, flavor, and garnish foods.

The recipes in this chapter include the following categories:

- *Vegetable combinations, such as mirepoix and matignon*
- *Thickeners, such as roux*
- *Aromatics and spice blends*
- *Marinades*
- *Stocks, broths, essences, fumets, and court bouillons*

These recipes can be scaled to produce the quantities you require.

White mirepoix (left) and regular mirepoix (middle and right) have been cut into varying degrees of fineness.

Mirepoix should be cut into an appropriate size, depending upon overall cooking time.

White mirepoix is used for white or light-colored stocks, soups, sauces, stews, and braisers.

TECHNIQUE:
Mirepoix (pages 241-242)
Cleaning leeks (pages 225-226)
Peeling and cutting vegetables (pages 218-223)

Mirepoix

Yield: 1 pound (450 grams)

Onions, chopped	*8 ounces*	*225 grams*
Carrots, chopped	*4 ounces*	*115 grams*
Celery, chopped	*4 ounces*	*115 grams*

1. Cut the vegetables into an appropriate size based on the cooking time of the dish.

2. Add mirepoix to the recipe as directed.

White Mirepoix

Yield: 1 pound (450 grams)

Onions, chopped	*4 ounces*	*115 grams*
Leeks, chopped	*4 ounces*	*115 grams*
Celery, chopped	*4 ounces*	*115 grams*
Parsnips, chopped	*4 ounces*	*115 grams*
Mushroom trimmings (optional)	*2 to 3 ounces*	*60 to 85 grams*

1. Cut the vegetables into an appropriate size, based on the cooking time of the dish.

2. Add mirepoix to the recipe as directed.

Matignon is generally indicated for poêléed items and braised vegetables.

TECHNIQUE
Matignon (page 242)
Poêléing (pages 357-358)

Matignon

Yield: 1 pound (450 grams)

Onions, small dice	*4 ounces*	*115 grams*
Carrots, small dice	*4 ounces*	*115 grams*
Celery, small dice	*4 ounces*	*115 grams*
Mushrooms, small dice	*2 ounces*	*60 grams*
Bacon or ham, small dice or minced	*2 ounces*	*60 grams*
Whole butter	*1 ounce*	*30 grams*

1. Cut all the vegetables and the bacon or ham into a neat, small dice and combine.

2. Sweat in whole butter, or use as directed in specific recipes.

Dry Duxelles

Yield: Approximately 1 pound (450 grams)

Clarified butter	*3 ounces*	*85 grams*
Shallots, minced	*2 ounces*	*60 grams*
Mushrooms, chopped fine	*1¹/₂ pounds*	*680 grams*
Parsley, chopped	*1 tablespoon*	*1 tablespoon*
Salt to taste	*¹/₂ teaspoon*	*¹/₂ teaspoon*
Pepper to taste	*¹/₄ teaspoon*	*¹/₄ teaspoon*

1. Heat butter in a small sauté pan.

2. Add the shallots and sweat.

3. Add the mushrooms to the pan and cook until they are browned and dry.

4. Add parsley; add salt and pepper to taste.

VARIATION

Duxelles Sauce: Add enough demi-glace and tomato purée for a good sauce consistency. Add chopped parsley just before serving.

Replace domestic mushrooms with wild varieties for special preparations.

It is believed that duxelles are so named because they were created by Chef La Varenne while working in the household of Marquis d'Uxelle.

Add dry bread crumbs and a little tomato sauce for a vegetable stuffing.

TECHNIQUE
Clarifying butter (page 253)
Shallots (pages 224-225)
Mincing herbs (page 219)

Basic Roux

Yield: 2 pounds (900 grams)

Clarified butter or oil	*1 pound*	*450 grams*
Flour	*1 pound*	*450 grams*

1. Heat the clarified butter or oil in a rondeau over moderate heat.

2. Add the flour all at once. Stirring constantly, cook over low heat until the roux is a very pale ivory, about 8 minutes.

VARIATIONS

White Roux: Always use oil to maintain the color. Cook as directed above.

Blonde/Pale Roux: Cook the roux for an additional 2 to 3 minutes, until roux becomes golden in color.

Brown Roux: Continue to cook the roux until it is browned and has a pronounced nutty aroma.

Add the flour all at once to the heated butter or oil.

Brown and black roux are used extensively in Acadian/Creole cuisine; in gumbos, stews, and gravies.

TECHNIQUE
Clarifying butter (page 253)
Roux (pages 239-240)

Beurre Manié

Yield: 6 ounces (170 grams)

Butter	*3 ¹/₂ ounces*	*100 grams*
Flour	*2 ¹/₂ ounces*	*70 grams*

Beurre manié is used to thicken vegetable stews (petits pois à la française) and matelotes.

1. Allow the butter to soften until pliable.

2. Add the flour and, using a wooden spoon, work to a smooth paste. (An electric mixer may be used for larger quantities.)

3. Use immediately or wrap tightly and refrigerate.

Bouquet Garni

Bouquet Garni

Yield: 1 each

Celery, whole stalk, trimmed	*4 ounces*	*115 grams*
Parsley stems	*3 or 4 each*	*3 or 4 each*
Thyme sprig	*1 each*	*1 each*
Bay leaf	*1 each*	*1 each*
Leek leaves	*2 or 3 each*	*2 or 3 each*

1. Halve the celery stalk crosswise. Sandwich herbs between celery pieces and fold leek leaves around the herbs and celery.

2. Tie the bundle securely with butcher's twine.

Savory, sage, rosemary, or other fresh herbs may be used in addition to or in place of the ingredients called for in the bouquet garni, depending on the recipe or desired result.

One sachet or bouquet garni is enough to flavor 1 gallon (3.75 liters) of liquid.

TECHNIQUE
Bouquet Garni (page 242)
Cleaning leeks (pages 225-226)
Garlic (pages 224-225)

Sachet d'Epices

Yield: 1 each

Parsley stems	*3 or 4 each*	*3 or 4 each*
Thyme leaves	*¹/₂ teaspoon*	*¹/₂ teaspoon*
Bay leaf	*1 each*	*1 each*
Peppercorns, cracked	*¹/₂ teaspoon*	*¹/₂ teaspoon*
Garlic clove, crushed (optional)	*1 each*	*1 each*

Place all ingredients on a piece of cheesecloth approximately 4 inches square. Gather up the edges and tie with butcher's twine, leaving a long tail of string to tie to the stockpot handle.

To make it easy to pull a sachet out of a soup or stew once it has added flavor, leave the string tail extra long and tie it to the handle.

Cloves, dill, tarragon stems, juniper berries, star anise, allspice, and other herbs and spices may be included in a sachet, according to the recipe or desired result.

TECHNIQUE
Sachet d' Epices (page 242)

Fines Herbes

Yield: 4 ounces (115 grams)

Chervil leaves, chopped	*1 ounce*	*30 grams*
Chives, chopped	*1 ounce*	*30 grams*
Parsley leaves, chopped	*1 ounce*	*30 grams*
Tarragon leaves, chopped	*1 ounce*	*30 grams*

Combine all herbs. Use according to specific recipes.

VARIATION

Herbes de Provence: Combine basil, fennel seed, lavender, marjoram, rosemary, sage, savory, and thyme for this classic blend from the south of France.

Fines herbes is a classic combination of fresh herbs.

Add burnet, marjoram, savory, lovage, or watercress.

TECHNIQUE
Fresh herbs (page 229)

Basic Meat Marinade

Yield: 8 fluid ounces (240 milliliters)

Add other herbs as desired—sage, rosemary, parsley, and tarragon are all good choices.

Wild game such as bear, boar, or elk should be allowed to marinate at least 12 hours, up to 36 hours, before cooking.

Vegetable oil	*7 fluid ounces*	*200 milliliters*
Worcestershire sauce	*1 fluid ounce*	*30 milliliters*
Thyme, fresh, chopped	*1 bunch*	*1 bunch*
Garlic cloves, minced	*8 each*	*8 each*
Pepper, coarse ground	*2 teaspoons*	*2 teaspoons*

Combine all the ingredients. Pour the marinade over the meat. Refrigerate until ready to cook the meat.

Technique
Garlic (pages 224-225)
Marinades (pages 242-245)

Fish Marinade

Yield: 8 fluid ounces (240 milliliters)

The acids in a marinade balance the oil for a good flavor.

Olive oil	*6 fluid ounces*	*180 milliliters*
Lemon juice	*2 ounces*	*60 milliliters*
Garlic cloves, minced	*2 each*	*2 each*
Salt	*1 teaspoon*	*1 teaspoon*
Pepper, coarse ground	*1 teaspoon*	*1 teaspoon*

Mix together all the ingredients. Pour over the fish. Refrigerate until ready to cook.

Substitute grapefruit or tangerine juice in this marinade if you prefer.

Marinate fish under refrigeration from 30 minutes up to 2 hours.

VARIATION

White Wine Marinade: Replace the lemon juice with a dry white wine or white vermouth. Substitute shallots for the garlic.

Technique
Garlic (pages 224-225)
Marinades (pages 242-245)

Red Wine Marinade

Yield: 1 pint (480 milliliters)

Red wine	*8 fluid ounces*	*240 milliliters*
Olive oil	*6 fluid ounces*	*180 milliliters*
Lemon juice	*2 fluid ounces*	*60 milliliters*
Garlic cloves, minced	*3 each*	*3 each*
Salt	*1 teaspoon*	*1 teaspoon*
Pepper, coarse ground	*1 teaspoon*	*1 teaspoon*

Combine all ingredients. Pour over the meat and refrigerate until ready to cook.

Red wine.

Use this marinade for sauerbraten or other marinated and braised red meat dishes.

TECHNIQUE
Garlic (pages 224-225)
Marinades (pages 242-245)

Teriyaki Marinade

Yield: 1 pint (480 milliliters)

Soy sauce	*6 fluid ounces*	*180 milliliters*
Corn or peanut oil	*6 fluid ounces*	*180 milliliters*
Dry sherry	*3 fluid ounces*	*90 milliliters*
Honey	*1 ounce*	*30 grams*
Garlic cloves, minced	*2 each*	*2 each*
Gingerroot, grated	*$^1/_4$ ounce*	*10 grams*
Orange zest (optional)	*2 tablespoons*	*2 tablespoons*

1. Combine all ingredients. Blend well.

2. Pour over meats, shellfish, or poultry. Marinate under refrigeration for up to 8 hours.

Star anise cloves and/or cinnamon may be added.

Brush or baste foods with this marinade as they cook.

TECHNIQUE
Citrus zest (page 231)
Marinades (pages 242-245)

477

The mise en place for brown veal stock.

The mirepoix can be browned with the bones in step 2. A larger cut of mirepoix can be used if this procedure is followed.

TECHNIQUE
Browning bones (page 250)
Stocks (pages 246-250)
Cooling and storing stocks (pages 251-253)

RECIPES
Mirepoix (page 472)
Sachet d'Epices (page 475)

Brown Veal Stock (Jus de Veau)

Yield: 1 gallon (3.75 liters)

Veal bones, including knuckles and trim	*8 pounds*	*3.6 kilograms*
Oil, as needed	*4 fluid ounces*	*120 milliliters*
Cold water	*6 quarts*	*5.75 liters*
Mirepoix	*1 pound*	*450 grams*
Tomato paste	*6 fluid ounces*	*180 milliliters*
Sachet d'Epices	*1 each*	*1 each*
Salt (optional)	*to taste*	*to taste*

1. Rinse the bones and dry them well. Preheat the oven to 400°F (205°C).

2. Brown the bones in a roasting pan coated with oil in the oven.

3. Combine the bones and water.

4. Bring the stock to a boil over low heat.

5. Simmer for a total of about 6 hours, skimming the surface as necessary.

6. Brown the mirepoix and tomato paste; add to the stock after the stock has simmered for about 5 hours. Deglaze the reduced drippings with water and add to the stock. Add sachet (and salt, if used).

7. Simmer an additional hour.

8. Strain the stock.

VARIATION

Brown Game Stock (**Jus de Gibier**): Replace the veal bones with an equal weight of venison bones and lean trim (or bones of other game animals). Include fennel seeds and/or juniper berries in the sachet, if desired.

Glace de Viande

Yield: 4 to 8 fluid ounces (120 to 240 milliliters)

Brown Veal Stock	1 quart	1 liter

1. Place the stock in a heavy gauge pot over moderate heat.

2. Bring to a simmer and let reduce until volume is halved, then transfer to a smaller pot.

3. Continue to reduce, transferring to successively smaller pots until very thick and syrupy.

VARIATIONS

Glace de Gibier: Substitute brown or white game stock for brown veal stock.

Glace de Volaille: Substitute brown or white chicken stock for brown veal stock.

Glace de Poisson: Substitute fish stock or fumet for brown veal stock.

The glace has reduced by about half.

Yeild will vary depending on cooking time and desired consistency.

RECIPE
Brown Veal Stock (page 476)

Veal Stock

Yield: 1 gallon (3.75 liters)

Veal bones, cut into 3-inch lengths	8 pounds	3.6 kilograms
Cold water	6 quarts	5.75 liters
Mirepoix	1 pound	450 grams
Sachet d'Epices	1 each	1 each
Salt (optional)	to taste	to taste

1. Blanch the bones, if desired. Drain and rinse.

2. Combine the bones and water.

3. Bring the stock to a boil over low heat.

4. Skim the surface as necessary.

5. Simmer the stock for a total of 6 hours.

6. Add mirepoix and sachet in the last hour of simmering. Add salt if desired.

7. Strain the stock. Cool and store.

This stock was originally called "ordinary stock."

TECHNIQUE
Stocks (pages 246-250)
Cooling and storing stocks (pages 251-253)

RECIPES
Mirepoix (page 472)
Sachet d'Epices (page 475)

White Beef Stock

Yield: 1 gallon (3.75 liters)

Beef bones, cut into 3-inch lengths	*8 pounds*	*3.6 kilograms*
Cold water	*6 quarts*	*5.75 liters*
Mirepoix	*1 pound*	*450 grams*
Sachet d'Epices	*1 each*	*1 each*
Salt (optional)	*to taste*	*to taste*

1. Blanch the bones if desired. Drain and rinse.
2. Combine the bones and water.
3. Bring the stock to a boil over low heat.
4. Skim the surface as necessary.
5. Simmer the stock for a total of 8 hours. Add more water if necessary.
6. Add mirepoix, sachet, and salt (if used) in the last hour of simmering.
7. Strain the stock. Cool and store.

Veal shank or feet are sometimes added to bolster this stock's body.

This stock is a good choice for preparing vegetable or bean soups.

TECHNIQUE
Stocks (pages 246-250)
Cooling and storing stocks (pages 251-253)

RECIPE
Mirepoix (page 472)
Sachet d'Epices (page 475)

Chicken Stock

Yield: 1 gallon (3.75 liters)

Chicken bones, cut into 3-inch lengths	*8 pounds*	*3.6 kilograms*
Cold water	*6 quarts*	*5.75 liters*
Mirepoix	*1 pound*	*450 grams*
Sachet d'Epices	*1 each*	*1 each*
Salt (optional)	*to taste*	*to taste*

1. Blanch the bones if desired. Drain and rinse.
2. Combine the bones and water.
3. Bring the stock to a boil over low heat.
4. Skim the surface as necessary.
5. Simmer the stock for a total of 4 to 5 hours.
6. Add the mirepoix, sachet, and salt (if used) in the last hour of simmering.
7. Strain the stock. Cool and store.

(Continued on facing page)

Cooling stock in a cold water bath.

For a very rich stock, substitute stewing hens.

TECHNIQUE
Stock (pages 246-250)
Cooling and storing stocks (pages 251-253)

RECIPES
Mirepoix (page 472)
Sachet d'Epices (page 475)

VARIATIONS

Brown Chicken Stock: Rinse the bones and dry them. Brown the bones in a roasting pan in the oven. Combine them with the water and bring to a boil over low heat. Simmer for about 4 hours. Brown the mirepoix and up to 4 ounces (115 grams) tomato paste in the roasting pan; add to the stock. Deglaze the pan with water and add to the stock. Simmer an additional hour.

Asian-style Chicken Stock: Add gingerroot, lemongrass, scallions, and fresh or dried chilies to the sachet.

Turkey Stock: Replace chicken bones with meaty turkey bones.

Fish Fumet

Yield: 1 gallon (3.75 liters)

Oil	*4 fluid ounces*	*120 milliliters*
Fish bones	*11 pounds*	*5 kilograms*
White Mirepoix	*1 pound*	*450 grams*
Mushroom trimmings	*10 ounces*	*285 grams*
Cold water	*1 gallon*	*3.75 liters*
White wine	*1 quart*	*1 liter*
Bouquet Garni	*1 each*	*1 each*
Salt (optional)	*to taste*	*to taste*

1. Heat the oil; add the bones and mirepoix.

2. Sweat the bones and mirepoix.

3. Add the mushroom trimmings.

4. Add water, wine, and bouquet garni; bring to simmer.

5. Simmer for 35 to 40 minutes, skimming the surface as necessary. Add salt if desired.

6. Strain the stock. Cool and store.

VARIATION

Shellfish Fumet: Substitute an equal amount of shrimp, crab, or lobster shells for the fish bones.

Mise en place for fish fumet.

The fumet is prepared using the "sweating method."

TECHNIQUE
Stocks (pages 246-250)
Cooling and storing stocks (pages 251-253)

RECIPES
White Mirepoix (page 472)
Bouquet Garni (page 474)

Preparing a sachet d'èpices.

This stock is prepared when clarity is important (for consommé, broth, etc.).

Add the fish's head only if it is extremely fresh.

Be sure to remove all traces of visceral blood from the bones.

TECHNIQUE
Stocks (pages 246-250)
Cooling and storing stocks
  (pages 251-253)

RECIPES
White Mirepoix (page 472)
Sachet d'Epices (page 475)

Fish Stock

Yield: 1 gallon (3.75 liters)

Fish bones, trimmings	*11 pounds*	*5 kilograms*
Cold water	*5 quarts*	*4.75 liters*
White Mirepoix	*1 pound*	*450 grams*
Sachet d'Epices	*1 each*	*1 each*
Mushroom trimmings (optional)	*10 ounces*	*285 grams*
Salt (optional)	*to taste*	*to taste*

1. Combine all ingredients.

2. Bring the mixture to a simmer over low heat.

3. Skim the surface as necessary.

4. Simmer for 30 to 40 minutes. Add salt if desired.

5. Strain the stock. Cool and store.

VARIATION

Shellfish Stock: Sear 11 pounds (5 kilograms) of shrimp, crab, or lobster shells until bright red. Add all the remaining ingredients (omitting the fish bones) and proceed with the recipe.

Vegetable Stock

Yield: 1 gallon (3.75 liters)

Vegetable oil	2 fluid ounces	60 milliliters
Onions, sliced	4 ounces	115 grams
Leeks, green and white parts, chopped	4 ounces	115 grams
Celery, chopped	2 ounces	60 grams
Green cabbage, chopped	2 ounces	60 grams
Carrots, chopped	2 ounces	60 grams
Turnip, chopped	2 ounces	60 grams
Tomato, chopped	2 ounces	60 grams
Garlic cloves, crushed	3 each	3 each
Cold water	4 $\frac{1}{2}$ quarts	4.25 liters
Sachet d'Epices, *plus*	1 each	1 each
Fennel seeds	1 teaspoon	1 teaspoon
Whole cloves	3 each	3 each

1. Heat the oil.

2. Add the vegetables and sweat them for 3 to 5 minutes.

3. Add water and sachet and simmer for 30 to 40 minutes.

4. Strain the stock. Cool and store.

VARIATION

Roasted Vegetable Stock: Roast the vegetables in a large pan, turning to make sure all sides are evenly roasted. Combine them with the water and simmer for 30 to 40 minutes. If desired, fresh or dried chilies may be roasted with the other vegetables.

Crushing garlic.

This stock can be used in any recipe calling for stock, particularly when a meatless version is preferred.

TECHNIQUE
Stocks (pages 246-250)
Cooling and storing stocks
   (pages 251-253)

RECIPE
Sachet d'Epices (page 475)

Court bouillon is also the name of a savory fish stew featured in Acadian cuisine. It has a broth base containing aromatic vegetables and regional fish (snapper is most commonly used), thickened with brown roux and served over steamed rice.

If desired, include coriander and fennel seeds in the court bouillon.

TECHNIQUE
Court Bouillon (page 248)
Poaching (pages 383-386)

White Wine Court Bouillon

Yield: 1 gallon (3.75 liters)

Cold water	2 ¹/₂ quarts	2.4 liters
White wine	2 ¹/₂ quarts	2.4 liters
Salt (optional)	2 teaspoons	2 teaspoons
Carrots, sliced	12 ounces	340 grams
Onions, sliced	1 pound	450 grams
Thyme leaves, dried	pinch	pinch
Bay leaves	3 each	3 each
Parsley stems	1 bunch	1 bunch
Peppercorns	¹/₂ ounce	15 grams

1. Combine all ingredients except the peppercorns.

2. Simmer for 50 minutes.

3. Add the peppercorns and simmer for an additional 10 minutes.

VARIATION

Red Wine Court Bouillon: Replace half of the white wine with an equal amount of dry red wine.

Court bouillon is used to poach fish and vegetables.

TECHNIQUE
Court Bouillon (page 248)
Poaching (pages 383-386)

Vinegar Court Bouillon

Yield: 1 gallon (3.75 liters)

Cold water	5 quarts	4.75 liters
White wine vinegar	¹/₂ pint	240 milliliters
Salt (optional)	2 teaspoons	2 teaspoons
Carrots, sliced	12 ounces	340 grams
Onions, sliced	1 pound	450 grams
Thyme leaves, dried	pinch	pinch
Bay leaves	3 each	3 each
Parsley stems	5 to 6 each	5 to 6 each
Peppercorns	¹/₂ ounce	15 grams

1. Combine all ingredients except the peppercorns.

2. Simmer for 50 minutes.

3. Add the peppercorns and simmer for an additional 10 minutes.

14
Soup Recipes

Soups are an important part of most menus. They may be served as a separate course, or as a combination luncheon item: soup and salad, soup and quiche, or soup and sandwich. Some soups are even good as a main course.

Be sure to check the seasoning and flavor of all soups before they are served, especially if you reheat batches of soup. Bring hot broth-based soups to a full boil over direct heat. Cream soups and veloutés need careful handling to prevent them from breaking. Do not allow them to boil, but bring them up to at least 180°F (82°C).

The recipes in this chapter have been grouped as follows:

- *Broths and Consommés*
- *Cold Soups*
- *Vegetable Soups*
- *American Regional Soups*
- *Cream Soups*
- *International Soups*
- *Purée Soups*
- *Asian Soups*
- *Bisques*

Adding different garnishes to a perfectly prepared broth gives you great flexibility in preparing special soups for your menu.

Use chicken, diced or julienned, as a garnish, or try one of the garnishes suggested in the variations.

TECHNIQUE
Broth (pages 297-299)
Cooling and storing food (pages 45-47)
Serving soup (page 311)

RECIPES
Chicken Stock (page 480)
Mirepoix (page 472)
Sachet d'Epices (page 475)
Spaetzle (page 649)

Double Chicken Broth

Yield: 1 gallon (3.75 liters)

Stewing hen	*6 pounds*	*2.7 kilograms*
Chicken Stock	*1 ¹/₂ gallons*	*5 ³/₄ liters*
Mirepoix	*1 pound*	*450 grams*
Chopped tomatoes	*8 ounces*	*225 grams*
Sachet d'Epices	*1 each*	*1 each*
Garlic clove, sliced	*1 each*	*1 each*
Salt to taste	*1 teaspoon*	*1 teaspoon*
Pepper to taste	*¹/₂ teaspoon*	*¹/₂ teaspoon*

1. Bring the stewing hen and stock to a simmer, skim the surface, and simmer very gently for 2 hours.

2. Add the mirepoix and tomatoes and simmer for ¹/₂ hour.

3. Add the sachet and garlic; simmer for an additional ¹/₂ hour.

4. Degrease, remove the chicken, and strain thoroughly.

5. Adjust the seasoning with salt and pepper to taste and garnish as desired.

V A R I A T I O N S

Chicken Broth with Garden Vegetables: Garnish each portion with finely diced, blanched vegetables (carrots, celery, leeks, peas, turnips) and diced, cooked chicken.

Chicken Broth with Barley: Garnish with diced, cooked vegetables and 1 tablespoon of cooked barley per portion.

Chicken Broth with Spaetzle: Garnish with plain, herbed, or spinach spaetzle.

Chicken Noodle Soup: Cook egg noodles (broad or fine) in the broth. Garnish with assorted blanched or cooked vegetables.

Beef Broth

Yield: 1 gallon (3.75 liters)

Beef hindshank	*8 pounds*	*3.6 kilograms*
Cold water	*1 1/2 gallons*	*5 3/4 liters*
Mirepoix	*1 pound*	*450 grams*
Tomatoes, chopped	*8 ounces*	*225 grams*
Sachet d'Epices	*1 each*	*1 each*
Garlic clove, sliced	*1 each*	*1 each*
Salt to taste	*1 teaspoon*	*1 teaspoon*
Pepper to taste	*1/2 teaspoon*	*1/2 teaspoon*

Hindshank is a flavorful cut.

1. Bring the beef shank and water to a simmer, skim the surface, and simmer very gently for 3 hours.

2. Add the mirepoix and tomatoes; simmer for 1/2 hour.

3. Add the sachet and garlic, and simmer for an additional 1/2 hour.

4. Degrease, remove the beef shank, and strain thoroughly. Cool and store if desired.

5. Adjust the seasoning with salt and pepper to taste; garnish as desired.

VARIATIONS

Beef Broth with Garden Vegetables: Garnish each portion with finely diced, blanched vegetables (carrots, celery, leeks, peas, turnips) and diced, cooked beef.

Beef Broth with Barley: Garnish with diced, cooked vegetables and 1 tablespoon of cooked barley per portion.

Beef Broth with Spaetzle: Garnish with plain, herbed, or spinach spaetzle.

For a deeper flavor, roast the mirepoix or add 1/2 oignon brûlé.

Use lean beef, diced or julienned, as a garnish, or try one of the garnishes suggested in the variations.

TECHNIQUE
Broth (pages 297-299)
Cooling and storing food (pages 45-47)
Serving soup (page 311)
Oignon brûlé (page 242)

RECIPES
Mirepoix (page 472)
Sachet d'Epices (page 475)
Spaetzle (page 649)

The "raft" is beginning to form.

Add celeriac and turnips to the clarification if desired.

TECHNIQUE
Consommé (pages 299-302)
Oignon brûlé (page 242)
Cooling and storing food (pages 45-47)
Serving soup (page 311)

RECIPES
White Beef Stock (page 480)
Mirepoix (page 472)
Sachet d'Epices (page 475)

Beef Consommé

Yield: 1 gallon (3.75 liters)

Clarification		
Oignon brûlé	*1 each*	*1 each*
Mirepoix	*1 pound*	*450 grams*
Beef shank, ground	*3 pounds*	*1.3 kilograms*
Egg whites, beaten	*10 each*	*10 each*
Tomatoes, chopped	*12 ounces*	*340 grams*
White Beef Stock	*5 quarts*	*4.75 liters*
Sachet d'Epices, *plus*	*1 each*	*1 each*
Whole cloves	*1 each*	*1 each*
Allspice berries	*2 each*	*2 each*
Kosher salt to taste	*1 teaspoon*	*1 teaspoon*
White pepper to taste	*1 teaspoon*	*1 teaspoon*

1. Mix the ingredients for the clarification and blend with stock. Mix well.

2. Bring the mixture to a slow simmer, stirring frequently until raft forms.

3. Add the sachet and simmer for 45 minutes, or until the appropriate flavor and clarity are achieved. Baste raft occasionally.

4. Strain the consommé and cool and store if desired. Adjust the seasoning with salt and white pepper to taste before serving.

VARIATIONS

Beef Consommé Julienne: Garnish with a julienne of vegetables, blanched until tender.

Beef Consommé Paysanne: Garnish with paysanne-cut vegetables, blanched until tender.

Beef Consommé Printanière: Garnish with tourné vegetables, blanched until tender.

Beef Consommé with Wild Mushrooms: Garnish with sliced wild mushrooms that have been steamed or lightly stewed.

Fish Consommé

Yield: 1 gallon (3.75 liters)

Clarification

Fish (whiting or pike), ground	*3 pounds*	*1.3 kilograms*
Egg whites, beaten	*8 each*	*8 each*
Leeks, rough julienne	*4 ounces*	*115 grams*
Celery, rough julienne	*4 ounces*	*115 grams*
Parsley stems	*5 to 6 each*	*5 to 6 each*
White wine	*1 pint*	*480 milliliters*
Lemons, juiced	*2 each*	*2 each*
Fish Stock	*5 quarts*	*4.75 liters*
Sachet d'Epices	*1 each*	*1 each*
Salt to taste	*1 teaspoon*	*1 teaspoon*
Ground white pepper to taste	*¹/₂ teaspoon*	*¹/₂ teaspoon*

Pike is a high-protein fish, a good choice for clarifying consommé.

1. Mix the ingredients for the clarification and blend with fish stock. Mix well.

2. Bring the mixture to a slow simmer, stirring frequently until raft forms.

3. Add the sachet and simmer for 45 minutes, or until the appropriate flavor and clarity are achieved. Baste raft occasionally.

4. Strain the consommé; adjust the seasoning with salt and white pepper to taste. Cool and store if desired.

VARIATIONS

Asian Fish Consommé: Flavor with lemongrass, chili pods, or gingerroot, and serve with spring rolls or wontons.

Fish Consommé with Seafood and Fresh Dill: Garnish with small-diced, cooked seafood (shrimp, lobster, crab, scallops) and chopped, fresh dill.

Fish Consommé with Quenelles: Garnish each portion with small quenelles made from fish mousseline forcemeat.

The quantity of fish in the clarification can be reduced by 1 pound (450 grams) and still produce acceptable results.

Instead of adding the garnish directly to the soup, it should be served with individual portions.

TECHNIQUE
Consommé (pages 299-302)
Cooling and storing food (pages 45-47)
Serving soup (page 311)

RECIPES
Fish Stock (page 482)
Sachet d'Epices (page 475)

Add a garnish of shiitakes and chervil at service, if desired.

The recipes for crêpes, used in the garnish of the Chicken Consommé Celestine, is found on page 665.

TECHNIQUE
Consommé (pages 299-302)
Oignon brûlé (page 242)
Cooling and storing food (pages 45-47)
Serving soup (page 311)

RECIPES
White Mirepoix (page 472)
Chicken Stock (page 480)
Sachet d'Epices (page 475)

Chicken Consommé

Yield: 1 gallon (3.75 liters)

Clarification		
White Mirepoix, chopped	*1 pound*	*450 grams*
Chicken, lean, ground	*3 pounds*	*1.3 kilograms*
Egg whites, beaten	*10 each*	*10 each*
Tomatoes, chopped	*12 ounces*	*340 grams*
Oignon brûlé	*1 each*	*1 each*
Chicken Stock, cold	*5 quarts*	*4.75 liters*
Standard Sachet d'Epices, *plus*	*1 each*	*1 each*
Whole clove	*1 each*	*1 each*
Allspice berries	*2 each*	*2 each*
Kosher salt to taste	*1 teaspoon*	*1 teaspoon*
White pepper to taste	*$^1/_2$ teaspoon*	*$^1/_2$ teaspoon*

1. Mix the ingredients for the clarification and blend with chicken stock. Mix well.

2. Bring the mixture to a slow simmer, stirring frequently until raft forms.

3. Add the sachet and simmer for 45 minutes, or until the appropriate flavor and clarity are achieved. Baste raft occasionally.

4. Strain the consommé; adjust the seasoning with salt and white pepper to taste.

VARIATIONS

Chicken Consommé with Julienned Vegetables: Garnish each portion with blanched, julienned leeks, carrots, celery, and potatoes; include a fine julienne of cooked chicken breast, if desired.

Chicken Consommé Paysanne: Garnish each portion with blanched paysanne-cut leeks, turnips, carrots, celery, and potatoes.

Chicken Consommé with Quenelles: Garnish with small quenelles made of chicken mousseline forcemeat.

Chicken Consommé with Garden Vegetables: Garnish with fresh peas, tomato concassé, and other garden vegetables cut into brunoise, if desired.

Chicken Consommé Celestine: Garnish each portion with julienned strips of a plain or herb-flavored crêpe.

American Bounty Vegetable Soup

Yield: 1 gallon (3.75 liters)

Beef shank, sliced 3 inches thick	*3 pounds*	*1.3 kilograms*
White Beef Stock	*1 gallon*	*3.75 liters*
Leeks, white only, thinly sliced	*4 ounces*	*115 grams*
Onions, small dice	*8 ounces*	*225 grams*
Carrots, peeled, small dice	*4 ounces*	*115 grams*
Celery, small dice	*4 ounces*	*115 grams*
Turnips, peeled, small dice	*6 ounces*	*170 grams*
Green cabbage, chiffonade	*4 ounces*	*115 grams*
Clarified butter, as needed	*2 ounces*	*60 grams*
Garlic cloves, minced	*3 each*	*3 each*
Sachet d'Epices	*1 each*	*1 each*
Potatoes, small dice	*4 ounces*	*115 grams*
Lima beans	*4 ounces*	*115 grams*
Corn kernels, fresh or frozen	*4 ounces*	*115 grams*
Tomato concassé	*4 ounces*	*115 grams*
Salt to taste	*1 teaspoon*	*1 teaspoon*
Pepper to taste	*1/2 teaspoon*	*1/2 teaspoon*
Nutmeg, ground, to taste	*1/4 teaspoon*	*1/4 teaspoon*
Parsley, flat leaf, chopped	*1/4 cup*	*1/4 cup*

Select a colorful variety of vegetables and prepare them properly.

1. Simmer the beef shank in the stock until the meat is very tender. Strain and degrease the broth.

2. When the meat is cool enough to handle, cut it into neat dice and reserve for garnish.

3. Sweat the leeks, onions, carrots, celery, turnips, and cabbage in clarified butter until limp.

4. Add garlic and sauté until aroma is apparent.

5. Add the reserved beef broth and sachet; simmer for approximately 10 minutes.

6. Add the potatoes, beans, corn, and tomato concassé. Continue to simmer for another 20 minutes.

7. Adjust the seasoning with salt, pepper, and nutmeg to taste.

8. Garnish with parsley.

Some chefs prefer the flavor of chicken broth in this soup.

Garnish the soup with croutons.

TECHNIQUE
Vegetable Soup (pages 302-303)
Tomato concassé (page 226)
Chiffonade (page 219)
Clarifying butter (page 253))
Serving soup (page 311)
Cooling and storing food (pages 45-47)

RECIPE
White Beeef Stock (page 480)
Sachet d'Epices (page 475)

Black-eyed peas are traditional, but use other beans or peas if you prefer.

Replace the ditalini with other types of pasta: vermicelli, tubettini, or spaghetti. Break long strands of pasta into shorter lengths before cooking them.

To bolster the flavor, add up to 4 ounces (115 grams) of tomato paste.

TECHNIQUE
Paysanne (pages 220-221)
Chiffonade (page 219)
Garlic (page 224-225)
Tomato concassé (page 226)
Cooking pasta (pages 388-389)
Special soups (page 310)
Serving soup (page 311)
Cooling and storing food (pages 45-47)

RECIPE
Chicken Stock (page 480)

Minestrone

Yield: 1 gallon (3.75 liters)

Salt pork, ground	*2 ounces*	*60 grams*
Olive oil	*2 fluid ounces*	*60 milliliters*
Onions, paysanne	*1 pound*	*450 grams*
Celery, paysanne	*8 ounces*	*225 grams*
Carrots, paysanne	*8 ounces*	*225 grams*
Green peppers, paysanne	*8 ounces*	*225 grams*
Green cabbage, chiffonade	*8 ounces*	*225 grams*
Garlic cloves, minced	*3 each*	*3 each*
Tomato concassé	*1 ¹/₂ pounds*	*680 grams*
Chicken Stock	*1 gallon*	*3.75 liters*
Chickpeas, cooked	*4 ounces*	*115 grams*
Black-eyed peas, cooked	*6 ounces*	*170 grams*
Ditalini, cooked	*6 ounces*	*170 grams*
Salt to taste	*1 teaspoon*	*1 teaspoon*
Pepper to taste	*¹/₂ teaspoon*	*¹/₂ teaspoon*
Parmesan cheese, grated	*5 ounces*	*140 grams*

1. Render the salt pork in the oil. Do not brown.

2. Add the onions, celery, carrots, peppers, cabbage, and garlic and sweat until the onions are translucent.

3. Add the tomato concassé and stock.

4. Simmer until the vegetables are tender. Do not overcook them.

5. Add the chickpeas, black-eyed peas, and ditalini. Simmer the soup until all ingredients are hot.

6. Adjust the seasoning with salt and pepper to taste.

7. Garnish with grated Parmesan cheese just prior to service.

Onion Soup Gratiné

Yield: 1 gallon (3.75 liters)

Onions, thinly sliced	3 pounds	1.3 kilograms
Clarified butter	2 ounces	60 grams
Calvados (optional)	4 fluid ounces	120 milliliters
White Beef Stock	1 gallon	3.75 liters
Salt to taste	1 teaspoon	1 teaspoon
Pepper to taste	$\frac{1}{2}$ teaspoon	$\frac{1}{2}$ teaspoon
Croutons or rusks	1 per portion	1 per portion
Gruyère cheese, grated	$1\frac{1}{4}$ pounds	570 grams

Cutting onions.

1. Sauté the onions in clarified butter until browned. Add a little butter, if necessary, to prevent burning.

2. Deglaze the pan with the Calvados; add the stock.

3. Simmer until the onions are tender and the soup is properly flavored.

4. Adjust the seasoning with salt and pepper to taste.

5. Garnish each portion with a crouton. Top generously with grated Gruyère and brown under a salamander or broiler, or bake in a moderate oven until lightly browned.

VARIATIONS

White Onion Soup: Gently cook the onions in butter or oil until they are limp but not colored, over low heat. If desired, up to 6 ounces (170 grams) of flour may be added as a thickener.

Other stocks, including white stock, chicken stock, or combinations of stocks, can be used to prepare a good onion soup. Each will have a different flavor and color.

White wine is often used instead of Calvados in this soup. Or, if preferred, some apple juice may be used.

Sherry may be used to finish the soup just before it is served, if desired.

You will need approximately 20 croutons for 20, 6-fluid ounce (180-milliliter) servings.

TECHNIQUE
Croutons (page 237)
Serving soup (page 311)
Cooling and storing food (pages 45-47)

RECIPE
White Beef Stock (page 480)

Cut the onions into small dice for this soup.

A garbure is a traditional French soup that typically includes cabbage, potatoes, and an assortment of root vegetables.

TECHNIQUE
Vegetable soup (pages 302-303)
Dicing vegetables (page 220)
Serving soup (page 311)
Tomato concassé (page 226)

RECIPE
Chicken Stock (page 480)

Potage Garbure

Yield: 1 gallon (3.75 liters)

Salt pork, ground	*4 ounces*	*115 grams*
Olive oil	*2 fluid ounces*	*60 milliliters*
Onion, small dice	*8 ounces*	*225 grams*
Carrots, small dice	*12 ounces*	*340 grams*
Leeks, small dice	*12 ounces*	*340 grams*
Chicken Stock	*3 quarts*	*3 liters*
Turnips, small dice	*12 ounces*	*340 grams*
Potatoes, small dice	*12 ounces*	*340 grams*
Green cabbage, small dice	*12 ounces*	*340 grams*
Zucchini, small dice	*12 ounces*	*340 grams*
Tomato concassé, small dice	*1 pound*	*450 grams*
Salt to taste	*1 teaspoon*	*1 teaspoon*
Pepper to taste	*$^1/_2$ teaspoon*	*$^1/_2$ teaspoon*

1. Render the salt pork. Add the olive oil and heat.

2. Sauté onions, carrots, and leeks in olive oil and salt pork, add chicken stock and bring to a simmer. Cook for 10 minutes.

3. Add turnips, potatoes, cabbage, and zucchini; simmer 10 minutes longer.

4. Add tomato concassé, salt, and pepper to soup and simmer 10 minutes; adjust seasoning.

Cream of Broccoli Soup

Yield: 1 gallon (3.75 liters)

Onions, chopped	*8 ounces*	*225 grams*
Celery, chopped	*4 ounces*	*115 grams*
Leeks, chopped	*4 ounces*	*115 grams*
Broccoli stems, chopped	*3 pounds*	*1.3 kilograms*
Butter	*3 ounces*	*85 grams*
Chicken Velouté	*3 quarts*	*3 liters*
Chicken Stock	*12 fluid ounces*	*360 milliliters*
Salt to taste	*1 teaspoon*	*1 teaspoon*
Pepper to taste	*½ teaspoon*	*½ teaspoon*
Heavy cream, heated	*1 pint*	*480 milliliters*
Broccoli florets, blanched	*1 pound*	*450 grams*

Adding the purée to the soup base gives greater control of the flavor and consistency of the finished soup.

1. Sweat the onions, celery, leeks, and broccoli stems in butter.

2. Add the stock and velouté and cook until all ingredients are tender.

3. Purée the solids until they are completely smooth. Return the purée to the soup and simmer slowly for 10 minutes.

4. Adjust the seasoning with salt and pepper to taste.

5. Add hot cream immediately before service.

6. Strain through either a cheesecloth or chinois.

7. Garnish to order with broccoli florets before serving.

This basic recipe can be used to prepare numerous variations, including those following the main recipe.

TECHNIQUE
Cream Soup (pages 303-306)
Cooling and storing food (pages 45-47)
Serving soup (page 311)

RECIPES
Chicken Stock (page 480)
Chicken Velouté (page 517)

VARIATIONS

Cream of Asparagus (**Crème Argenteuil**): Replace the broccoli with an equal weight of asparagus stems. Garnish with blanched asparagus tips.

Cream of Lettuce (**Crème Choisy**): Replace the broccoli with an equal weight of shredded lettuce (Romaine, Boston, etc.). Garnish with a chiffonade of fines herbes.

Cream of Celery (**Crème Céleri**): Replace the broccoli with an equal weight of celery or celeriac. Garnish with diced, blanched celery.

Cream of Cauliflower (**Crème DuBarry**): Replace the broccoli with an equal weight of cauliflower. Garnish with blanched cauliflower florets.

Use a stewing hen for the most flavorful soup.

This soup is also known as Purée à la Reine, *or Queen's Soup.*

Use a thin chicken velouté (page 517) to prepare this soup, if you prefer. In that case, omit the onion, carrots, celery, butter, flour, and bay leaf.

TECHNIQUE
Dicing vegetables (page 220)
Cream soup (pages 303-306)
Cooling and storing food (pages 45-47)
Serving soup (page 311)

RECIPE
Chicken Stock (page 480)

Cream of Chicken Soup

Yield: 1 gallon (3.75 liters)

Onions, medium dice	*8 ounces*	*225 grams*
Celery, medium dice	*4 ounces*	*115 grams*
Carrots, medium dice	*4 ounces*	*115 grams*
Butter	*9 ounces*	*250 grams*
Flour	*7 ounces*	*200 grams*
Chicken Stock, heated	*1 gallon*	*3.75 liters*
Bay leaf	*1 each*	*1 each*
Chicken breasts, diced	*3 1/4 pounds*	*1.5 kilograms*
Milk, heated	*24 fluid ounces*	*720 milliliters*
Half and half, heated	*12 fluid ounces*	*360 milliliters*
Salt to taste	*1 teaspoon*	*1 teaspoon*
Pepper to taste	*1/2 teaspoon*	*1/2 teaspoon*

1. Sauté the onions, celery, and carrots in butter until tender.

2. Add the flour to make a roux; cook for 8 to 10 minutes.

3. Add the stock gradually, stirring until thickened and smooth.

4. Add the bay leaf and chicken; simmer for 30 minutes.

5. Remove the chicken and purée it. Return to the soup.

6. Add the milk and half and half. Simmer 10 minutes and strain through a fine sieve.

7. Adjust the seasoning with salt and pepper to taste.

Cream of Tomato Soup

Yield: 1 gallon (3.75 liters)

Bacon, diced	*2 ounces*	*60 grams*
Oil as needed	*2 ounces*	*60 grams*
Carrots, diced	*8 ounces*	*225 grams*
Celery, diced	*8 ounces*	*225 grams*
Onions, diced	*8 ounces*	*225 grams*
Garlic cloves, minced	*2 each*	*2 each*
Flour	*6 ounces*	*170 grams*
Chicken Stock	*2 quarts*	*2 liters*
Tomatoes, chopped	*2 pounds*	*900 grams*
Tomato purée	*24 fluid ounces*	*720 milliliters*
Pepper to taste	*$1/2$ teaspoon*	*$1/2$ teaspoon*
Parsley stems	*4 each*	*4 each*
Bay leaf	*1 each*	*1 each*
Clove, whole	*1 each*	*1 each*
Light cream, hot	*$1 1/2$ pints*	*720 milliliters*

Use fresh tomatoes when they are in season.

1. Render the bacon in the oil. Add carrots, celery, onions, and garlic, reduce heat and sweat about 8 to 10 minutes. Add flour and blend well to make a roux. Cook about 3 to 4 minutes.

2. Add stock and blend well. Add chopped tomatoes, tomato purée, and pepper; simmer about 30 minutes. Add the parsley stems, bay leaf, and clove; continue to simmer another 30 minutes. Strain well.

3. Blend hot cream into strained base soup. Adjust consistency and seasoning.

VARIATION

Cream of Tomato with Rice: Add 1 pound (450 grams) of cooked long grain white rice to the tomato soup immediately prior to serving, or garnish individual portions of soup with 3 tablespoons of cooked rice.

Roasted Tomato Soup: Slice the fresh tomatoes and roast them at 400°F (205°C) until browned before adding them to the soup.

Use Vegetable Stock (page 483) and omit the bacon to make a meatless version of this soup.

TECHNIQUE
Cream soup (pages 303-306)
Cooling and storing food (pages 45-47)
Serving soup (page 311)

RECIPE
Chicken Stock (page 480)

Straining the soup.

The quality of the cheese plays a distinct role in this soup. Select an aged Cheddar for the best results.

Add the cheese just before serving the soup; it may take on a curdled appearance if held too long.

Use a prepared velouté (page 517) and begin this soup at step 4, if desired.

Replace the wine with a lager beer, if you prefer.

TECHNIQUE
Clarifying butter (page 253)
Cream soup (pages 303-306)
Cooling and storing food (pages 45-47)
Cutting peppers (page 227)

RECIPES
White Mirepoix (page 472)
Chicken Stock (page 480)

Cheddar Cheese Soup

Yield: 1 gallon (3.75 liters)

White Mirepoix	12 ounces	340 grams
Garlic cloves, minced	2 each	2 each
Clarified butter	4 ounces	115 grams
Flour	4 ounces	115 grams
Chicken Stock	3 quarts	3 liters
Cheddar cheese, grated	2 pounds	900 grams
White wine	8 fluid ounces	240 milliliters
Dry mustard	2 tablespoons	2 tablespoons
Heavy cream	1 pint	480 milliliters
Tabasco to taste	1/2 teaspoon	1/2 teaspoon
Worcestershire sauce to taste	1/2 teaspoon	1/2 teaspoon
Salt to taste	1/2 teaspoon	1/2 teaspoon
White pepper to taste	1/4 teaspoon	1/4 teaspoon
Green peppers, julienne, blanched	4 ounces	115 grams
Red peppers, julienne, blanched	4 ounces	115 grams

1. Sweat the mirepoix and garlic in the butter until it is limp.

2. Add the flour to make a roux and cook out for 5 minutes.

3. Add the stock gradually, whipping to work out lumps, and simmer for 45 minutes.

4. Add the Cheddar cheese and wine (reserving 2 tablespoons to dilute the mustard) and continue to heat the soup gently until cheese melts. Do not allow the soup to boil.

5. Blend the dry mustard and wine. Add this mixture along wih the cream. Heat gently for 2 to 3 minutes, and adjust consistency with stock if necessary. Season to taste with Tabasco and Worcestershire sauces, salt, and pepper. Strain the soup.

6. Add the peppers to the soup or use them to garnish individual portions.

Purée of Split Pea

Yield: 1 gallon (3.75 liters)

Bacon, finely chopped	*6 slices*	*6 slices*
Vegetable oil	*2 fluid ounces*	*60 milliliters*
Onions, chopped	*12 ounces*	*340 grams*
Celery, chopped	*4 ounces*	*115 grams*
Garlic, crushed	*1 tablespoon*	*1 tablespoon*
Chicken Stock	*1 gallon*	*3.75 liters*
Potatoes, large dice	*1 pound*	*450 grams*
Green split peas	*1 ½ pounds*	*680 kilograms*
Smoked ham hocks	*1 pound*	*450 grams*
Bay leaves	*2 each*	*2 each*
Salt to taste	*1 teaspoon*	*1 teaspoon*
Cracked black peppercorns	*½ teaspoon*	*½ teaspoon*

A soup service set up for banquets.

1. Render the bacon in the oil.

2. Add the onions and celery and sauté until the onions become transparent.

3. Add the garlic and sauté until an aroma develops; do not brown.

4. Add the stock, potatoes, split peas, ham hocks, and bay leaves and bring to a simmer. Allow the soup to simmer for 90 minutes or until the peas are very tender.

5. Remove the ham hocks and bay leaves.

6. Purée the soup until smooth. Adjust consistency with additional stock if necessary.

7. Dice the lean meat from the ham hock and return it to the soup.

8. Bring the soup back to a boil. Adjust the seasoning with salt and pepper to taste.

A pale roux may be incorporated into the stock in step 4. This will give the soup greater stability if it must be held on a steam table.

For a heartier version, purée half of the soup in step 4 and return the purée with the meat in step 7.

Garnish individual portions at service with croutons that have been fried in butter and garlic.

TECHNIQUE
Cooling and storing food (pages 45-47)
Serving soup (page 311)

RECIPE
Chicken Stock (page 480)

VARIATIONS

Yellow Split Pea Soup: Replace the green split peas with yellow split peas.

Vegetarian Split Pea Soup: The chicken stock can be replaced with vegetable stock, if desired. Omit the ham hocks and bacon.

Add the beans to the soup and simmer.

Garnish individual portions at service time with croutons.

For a meatless version, replace the chicken stock with vegetable stock and omit the ham hocks. Replace the bacon fat with vegetable oil.

Another method for preparing this soup is as follows: Simmer the beans with the stock and ham hocks for 1 hour. Add the potatoes, oignon piqué, and sachet; continue to simmer until they are very tender. Remove and discard the oignon piqué and sachet. Purée half of the soup and recombine. Sweat the vegetables in bacon fat, lard, or oil. Add them to the soup, with the diced ham, at service time.

TECHNIQUE
Soaking beans (page 236)
Oignon piqué (page 242)
Purée soup (pages 306-308)
Cooling and storing food (pages 45-47)
Serving soup (page 311)

RECIPES
Chicken Stock (page 480)
Sachet d'Epices (page 475)

Senate Bean Soup

Yield: 1 gallon (3.75 liters)

Navy beans, dried	*1 ½ pounds*	*680 grams*
Chicken Stock	*1 gallon*	*3.75 liters*
Smoked ham hocks	*2 each*	*2 each*
Vegetable oil	*2 ounces*	*60 milliliters*
Onions, medium dice	*6 ounces*	*170 grams*
Carrots, medium dice	*6 ounces*	*170 grams*
Celery, medium dice	*6 ounces*	*170 grams*
Garlic cloves, minced	*2 each*	*2 each*
Oignon piqué (optional)	*1 each*	*1 each*
Sachet d'Epices	*1 each*	*1 each*
Chef's potatoes, large dice	*1 pound*	*450 grams*
Tabasco, to taste	*1 teaspoon*	*1 teaspoon*
Salt, to taste	*1 teaspoon*	*1 teaspoon*
Pepper, to taste	*½ teaspoon*	*½ teaspoon*

1. Soak the beans overnight. Drain.

2. Combine the beans, stock, and ham hocks. Simmer for 2 hours. Strain this broth. Dice meat from ham hocks and reserve.

3. Heat the oil. Add the onions, carrots, and celery; sweat for 4 to 5 minutes, or until the onions are translucent. Add the garlic; sauté it until an aroma is apparent.

4. Add the beans, broth, oignon piqué, sachet, potatoes, and ham hocks; simmer until the beans and potatoes are tender.

5. Remove and discard the oignon piqué and the sachet.

6. Purée half of the soup. Recombine the purée and reserved ham with the remaining soup. Adjust the consistency with additional broth or water if necessary.

7. Return the soup to a simmer and adjust the seasoning with Tabasco, salt, and pepper to taste.

Shrimp Bisque

Yield: 1 gallon (3.75 liters)

Shrimp shells	1 ½ pounds	680 grams
Onions, minced	1 pound	450 grams
Butter	2 ounces	60 grams
Garlic cloves, minced	2 each	2 each
Paprika	3 tablespoons	3 tablespoons
Tomato paste	2 ounces	60 grams
Brandy	3 fluid ounces	90 milliliters
Shellfish Velouté	3 quarts	3 liters
Heavy cream, heated	1 quart	1 liter
Shrimp, peeled and deveined	26 ounces	750 grams
Salt to taste	½ teaspoon	½ teaspoon
Pepper to taste	¼ teaspoon	¼ teaspoon
Old Bay Seasoning to taste	½ teaspoon	½ teaspoon
Tabasco to taste	¼ teaspoon	¼ teaspoon
Worcestershire sauce to taste	½ teaspoon	½ teaspoon
Dry sherry	4 fluid ounces	120 milliliters

Add cooked diced shrimp meat to garnish the finished soup.

TECHNIQUE
Bisque (pages 308-310)
Cooling and storing food (pages 45-47)
Serving soup (page 311)
Peeling and deveining shrimp (page 284)

RECIPE
Shellfish Velouté (page 517)

1. Sauté the shrimp shells and onions in butter.

2. Add the garlic, paprika, and tomato paste. Cook out for a few minutes.

3. Add the brandy and deglaze. Let the brandy reduce until dry.

4. Add the velouté. Simmer for 45 minutes. Strain the bisque through a fine chinois or cheesecloth.

5. Return the bisque to a simmer. Add the heavy cream.

6. Dice the shrimp, sauté, and add to the bisque, simmering gently for 5 minutes. Adjust the seasoning to taste with salt, pepper, Old Bay Seasoning, Tabasco, and Worcestershire sauce.

7. Add the sherry immediately before serving.

VARIATION

Lobster Bisque: Replace shrimp shells and shrimp with lobster shells and lobster tail meat.

Cucumbers are a basic part of gazpacho.

Serve individual portions garnished with chopped herbs or scallions and croutons. Add a pinch of clove to the croutons when frying them for additional flavor.

Gazpacho has a short refrigeration shelf-life. The tomatoes will sour very quickly. It is best when prepared on a daily basis.

TECHNIQUE
Tomato concassé (page 226)
Working with peppers (page 227)
Serving soup (page 311)
Croutons (page 237)

Chilled Gazpacho

Yield: 1 gallon (3.75 liters)

Tomato concassé	2 ½ pounds	1.15 kilograms
Cucumbers, peeled, seeded, and diced	10 ounces	285 grams
Onions, small dice	10 ounces	285 grams
Green peppers, small dice	10 ounces	285 grams
Red peppers, small dice	10 ounces	285 grams
White bread, cubed	8 ounces	225 grams
Olive oil	6 fluid ounces	180 milliliters
Red wine vinegar	4 fluid ounces	120 milliliters
Salt to taste	1 teaspoon	1 teaspoon
White pepper to taste	½ teaspoon	½ teaspoon
Garnish		
Tomato, small dice	2 ounces	60 grams
Red pepper, small dice	2 ounces	60 grams
Green pepper, small dice	2 ounces	60 grams
Cucumber, small dice	2 ounces	60 grams
Croutons	8 ounces	225 grams

1. Combine all ingredients except the garnish; chill the soup and let it rest overnight.

2. Purée the soup and strain if desired.

3. Garnish each portion or serve garnish ingredients on the side.

New England-Style Clam Chowder

Yield: 1 gallon (3.75 liters)

Cherrystone clams, washed	*20 each*	*20 each*
Water	*1 quart*	*1 liter*
Salt pork, minced to a paste	*4 ounces*	*115 grams*
Onions, minced	*4 ounces*	*115 grams*
Celery, fine dice	*4 ounces*	*115 grams*
Flour	*3 1/2 ounces*	*100 grams*
Potatoes, small dice	*12 ounces*	*340 grams*
Milk, scalded	*1 quart*	*1 liter*
Heavy cream, scalded	*12 fluid ounces*	*360 milliliters*
Salt to taste	*1/2 teaspoon*	*1/2 teaspoon*
White pepper to taste	*1/2 teaspoon*	*1/2 teaspoon*
Tabasco to taste	*1/2 teaspoon*	*1/2 teaspoon*
Worcestershire sauce to taste	*1/2 teaspoon*	*1/2 teaspoon*

Chowder clams are also known as "quahogs."

Clams must be alive at the time they are cooked. For more information on selecting clams, see Chapter 5.

TECHNIQUE
Washing clams (page 288)
Special soups (page 310)
Cooking and storing food (pages 45-47)
Serving soup (page 311)

1. Steam the clams in water in a covered pot until they open.

2. Strain the broth through a filter or cheesecloth and reserve it.

3. Pick, chop, and reserve the clams.

4. Render the salt pork in the soup pot; add the onions and celery and sweat until they are translucent.

5. Add the flour; cook to make a blond roux.

6. Add reserved broth and milk gradually and incorporate it completely, working out any lumps that might form.

7. Simmer for 30 minutes, skimming the surface as necessary.

8. Add the potato to the soup and simmer until tender.

9. Add the reserved clams and cream.

10. Adjust the seasoning to taste with salt, white pepper, Tabasco, and Worcestershire sauce.

Shocking tomatoes before peeling and cutting into concassé.

Manhattan-Style Clam Chowder

Yield: 1 gallon (3.75 liters)

Chowder clams, washed	*30 each*	*30 each*
Water	*1 quart*	*1 liter*
Salt pork, minced to a paste	*3 ounces*	*85 grams*
Onions, medium dice	*8 ounces*	*225 grams*
Carrots, medium dice	*4 ounces*	*115 grams*
Celery, medium dice	*8 ounces*	*225 grams*
Leeks, white only, medium dice	*4 ounces*	*115 grams*
Green peppers, medium dice	*4 ounces*	*115 grams*
Garlic, mashed to a paste	*1 teaspoon*	*1 teaspoon*
Tomato concassé	*1 pound*	*450 grams*
Bay leaf	*1 each*	*1 each*
Thyme sprig	*1 each*	*1 each*
Oregano sprig	*1 each*	*1 each*
Potatoes, medium dice	*12 ounces*	*340 grams*
Salt to taste	*1 teaspoon*	*1 teaspoon*
White pepper to taste	*1/2 teaspoon*	*1/2 teaspoon*
Tabasco to taste	*1/2 teaspoon*	*1/2 teaspoon*
Worcestershire sauce to taste	*1/2 teaspoon*	*1/2 teaspoon*
Old Bay Seasoning to taste	*1/2 teaspoon*	*1/2 teaspoon*

The recipe for Manhattan-Style Clam Chowder has a tomato broth base. New England-Style Clam Chowder has a creamy base and no tomatoes at all.

Clams must be alive at the time they are cooked. For more information on selecting clams, see Chapter 5.

TECHNIQUE
Cleaning clams (page 288)
Cleaning leeks (pages 225-226)
Mashing garlic to a paste (page 225)
Special soups (page 310)
Cooling and storing food (pages 45-47)
Serving soup (page 311)

1. Steam the clams in water in a covered pot until they open.

2. Pick, chop, and reserve the clams. Strain and reserve the clam broth.

3. Render the salt pork in the soup pot.

4. Sweat the onions, carrots, celery, leeks, and green peppers in the rendered salt pork until limp.

5. Add the garlic; sauté until an aroma is apparent.

6. Add the reserved clam broth, tomato concassé, bay leaf, thyme, and oregano; simmer for 30 minutes.

7. Add the potatoes; simmer until they are tender.

8. Remove the herbs and discard.

9. Degrease the soup. Add the clams and adjust the seasoning to taste with salt, white pepper, Tabasco, Worcestershire sauce, and Old Bay Seasoning.

Corn Chowder

Yield: 1 gallon (3.75 liters)

Salt pork, ground	*4 ounces*	*115 grams*
Onions, small dice	*6 ounces*	*170 grams*
Celery, small dice	*6 ounces*	*170 grams*
Green peppers, small dice	*4 ounces*	*115 grams*
Red peppers, small dice	*4 ounces*	*115 grams*
Flour	*4 ounces*	*115 grams*
Chicken Stock	*2 quarts*	*2 liters*
Corn kernels	*2 pounds*	*900 grams*
Potatoes, small dice	*2 pounds*	*900 grams*
Bay leaf	*1 each*	*1 each*
Heavy cream, scalded	*1 pint*	*480 milliliters*
Milk, scalded	*1 pint*	*480 milliliters*
Salt to taste	*1/2 teaspoon*	*1/2 teaspoon*
White pepper to taste	*1/2 teaspoon*	*1/2 teaspoon*
Tabasco to taste	*1/2 teaspoon*	*1/2 teaspoon*
Worcestershire sauce to taste	*1 teaspoon*	*1 teaspoon*

1. Render the salt pork.

2. Sweat the onions, celery, and peppers in the rendered salt pork.

3. Add the flour and cook to make a blond roux.

4. Add the chicken stock gradually, whipping to work out lumps. Bring the soup to a simmer. Cook for 30 to 40 minutes.

5. Purée half of the corn and add it to the soup with the potatoes.

6. Add the whole corn kernels and bay leaf and simmer until the corn and potatoes are tender.

7. Combine the heavy cream and milk; add to the soup.

8. Remove and discard the bay leaf.

9. Adjust the seasoning with salt, white pepper, Tabasco, and Worcestershire sauce, to taste.

Fresh corn gives this soup a rich, sweet flavor.

Substitute evaporated milk for the heavy cream in the recipe for a lower cholesterol soup.

TECHNIQUE
*Cutting corn kernels from the cob
  (page 233)*
Special soups (page 310)
Cooling and storing food (pages 45-47)
Serving soup (page 311)

RECIPE
Chicken Stock (page 480)

Use smoked ham hocks, as shown here, neck bones, or other smoked pork cuts to make a broth. This broth can then be used to prepare beans, soups, stews, or sauces.

Eliminate the cream if desired. Replace salt pork with 1 fluid ounce (30 milliliters) vegetable oil.

If collards are unavailable, escarole, dandelion, turnip, and kale may be used.

TECHNIQUE
Blanching vegetables (page 378)
Cooling and storing food (pages 45-47)
Serving soup (page 311)

RECIPES
Chicken Stock (page 480)
Sachet d'Epices (page 475)

Ham Bone and Collard Greens Soup

Yield: 1 gallon (3.75 liters)

Salt pork	*4 ounces*	*115 grams*
Onions, small dice	*8 ounces*	*225 grams*
Celery, small dice	*4 ounces*	*115 grams*
Flour	*5 ounces*	*140 grams*
Chicken Stock	*3 quarts*	*3 liters*
Ham hock	*2 each*	*2 each*
Sachet d'Epices	*1 each*	*1 each*
Collard greens, chopped, blanched	*2 pounds*	*900 grams*
Heavy cream	*8 fluid ounces*	*240 milliliters*

1. Render the salt pork.

2. Sweat the onions and celery.

3. Add the flour and make a roux. Cook out for several minutes.

4. Add the chicken stock gradually, whipping to work out any lumps.

5. Add the ham hock and sachet; simmer until tender.

6. Cut collard greens into small dice or chiffonade and add to soup. Simmer until tender.

7. Remove hocks and sachet. Remove meat from hocks and dice.

8. Finish with heavy cream and garnish with diced reserved ham hock meat.

Seafood Gumbo

Yield: 1 gallon (3.75 liters)

Shrimp, 31 to 35 count	2 pounds	900 grams
Crabs, cut in half	10 each	10 each
Mirepoix	1 ½ pounds	680 kilograms
Butter	4 ounces	115 grams
Fish Stock	1 gallon	3.75 liters
Seafood seasoning	1 tablespoon	1 tablespoon
Bacon, chopped	6 slices	6 slices
Onions, fine dice	4 ounces	115 grams
Celery, fine dice	2 ounces	60 grams
Green peppers, fine dice	2 ounces	60 grams
Garlic, minced	2 tablespoons	2 tablespoons
Thyme, dried	2 teaspoons	2 teaspoons
Basil, dried	2 teaspoons	2 teaspoons
Oregano, dried	2 teaspoons	2 teaspoons
Marjoram, dried	2 teaspoons	2 teaspoons
Bay leaf	1 each	1 each
Brown Roux	8 ounces	225 grams
Tomato concassé	8 ounces	225 grams
Okra, sliced ½-inch thick	1 pound	450 grams
Vegetable oil, as needed	1 fluid ounce	30 milliliters
Basic Boiled Rice	8 ounces	225 grams
Worcestershire sauce to taste	½ teaspoon	½ teaspoon
Tabasco to taste	2 dashes	2 dashes
Cayenne pepper to taste	⅛ teaspoon	⅛ teaspoon
Salt to taste	½ teaspoon	½ teaspoon

1. Peel and devein the shrimp. Dice the shrimp. Reserve the shells and meat separately.

2. Sauté shrimp shells, crabs, and mirepoix in butter until shells turn bright red.

3. Add stock and seafood seasoning. Simmer for 45 minutes, then strain. Reserve this broth.

4. Pick crabmeat from shells. Reserve.

5. Render bacon until limp, not browned. Add onions, celery, green peppers, garlic, and spices; sauté until onions are lightly browned.

6. Add stock and bring to a simmer.

(Recipe continued on next page)

Deveining shrimp.

Gumbo is a term derived from one of the African words for okra. Gumbos are generally thickened with one or a combination of the following: roux, filé powder, or okra.

Instead of preparing a separate broth, it is fine to use a previously prepared shellfish broth. Reserve shells from this recipe for use in broths, soups, or fumets.

Instead of adding the rice directly to the soup, it can be added to individual portions. Use about 2 tablespoons cooked rice per portion.

TECHNIQUE
Peeling and deveining shrimp (page 284)
Tomato concassé (page 226)
Cooling and storing food (pages 45-47)
Serving soup (page 311)

RECIPES
Mirepoix (page 472)
Fish Stock (page 482)
Brown Roux (page 473)
Basic Boiled Rice (page 643)

7. Thicken soup with roux; add tomato concassé and seasonings.

8. Sauté okra in oil until softened and add to soup.

9. Simmer the soup until okra is tender; add rice.

10. Dice shrimp, sauté, and add to soup. Adjust seasonings.

Serving borscht from a tureen.

There are numerous recipes for borscht throughout Eastern Europe. This version is adapted from a Polish-style soup. Other renditions are meatless, served cold, or puréed and finished with yogurt.

TECHNIQUE
Julienne (page 220)
Tomato concassé (page 226)

RECIPES
White Beef Stock (page 480)
Sachet d'Epices (page 475)

Borscht

Yield: 1 gallon (3.75 liters)

Butter	*2 ounces*	*60 grams*
Onions, julienne	*3 ounces*	*85 grams*
Leeks, julienne	*4 ounces*	*115 grams*
Green cabbage, julienne	*3 ounces*	*85 grams*
Celery, julienne	*3 ounces*	*85 grams*
Beets, fresh, julienne	*2 1/2 pounds*	*1.15 kilograms*
Tomato concassé	*8 ounces*	*225 grams*
White Beef Stock	*1 gallon*	*3.75 liters*
Beef brisket, cooked, julienne	*1 pound*	*450 grams*
Duck breast, cooked, julienne	*8 ounces*	*225 grams*
Sachet d'Epices, *plus*	*1 each*	*1 each*
Fennel seed	*1/4 teaspoon*	*1/4 teaspoon*
Clove, whole	*1 each*	*1 each*
Red wine vinegar	*6 fluid ounces*	*180 milliliters*
Salt	*1 teaspoon*	*1 teaspoon*
Pepper	*1/2 teaspoon*	*1/2 teaspoon*
Garnish		
Sour cream	*11 fluid ounces*	*330 milliliters*
Dill sprigs, fresh	*as needed*	*as needed*

1. Heat the butter; add onions, leeks, cabbage, celery, and beets. Sweat.

2. Add the tomatoes, stock, beef, duck, and sachet. Simmer 30 minutes or until all ingredients are fully cooked.

3. Adjust seasoning to taste with vinegar, salt, and pepper. Top each portion with sour cream and sprinkle with dill.

Mansahari Mirchi Soup—Mulligatawny Soup

Yield: 1 gallon (3.75 liters)

Fresh green chilies, seeded and chopped	6 each	6 each
Coriander, ground	2 tablespoons	2 tablespoons
Turmeric, ground	4 teaspoons	4 teaspoons
Cumin, ground	1½ teaspoons	1½ teaspoons
Nutmeg, ground	1 teaspoon	1 teaspoon
Clove, ground	½ teaspoon	½ teaspoon
Black pepper, ground	½ ounce	15 grams
Garlic cloves	5 each	5 each
Gingerroot, grated	4 teaspoons	4 teaspoons
Onions, chopped	4 each	4 each
Ghee (clarified butter)	1 ounce	30 grams
Lamb, medium dice	2 pounds	900 grams
Salt to taste	½ teaspoon	½ teaspoon
Tomato paste	6 ounces	170 grams
White Beef Stock	3 quarts	3 liters
Carrots, small dice	4 each	4 each
Granny Smith apples, peeled, small dice	4 each	4 each

Fresh green chilies are chopped and added to this soup.

1. Using a food processor, grind all chilies, spices, garlic, and gingerroot into a fine paste.

2. Sauté onions in ghee until golden brown; add spice paste and lamb and sauté for 5 minutes.

3. Add salt, tomato paste, and stock; simmer until meat is almost cooked.

4. Add carrots and apples; simmer soup until everything is tender.

VARIATION

Chicken Mulligatawny: Chicken can replace lamb in this soup. Add cooked white or brown rice before serving.

"Mulligatawny" derives from a word meaning "pepper water" and is from the southern part of India.

Cardamom, fenugreek, garam masala, curry powder, and/or cinnamon can also be added. Finish the soup with a bit of unsweetened coconut milk, if desired.

TECHNIQUE
Chopping chilies (page 227)
Grinding spices (241)
Ghee (clarified butter) (page 253)
Vegetable soups (pages 302-303)
Cooling and storing food (pages 45-47)
Serving soup (page 311)

RECIPE
White Beef Stock (page 480)

509

Lean lamb cubes for Scotch Broth.

The method in this recipe is a traditional approach to making this soup. Instead of blanching the lamb, you may prefer to "sweat" it in 2 fluid ounces (60 milliliters) of oil. Add the vegetables to the lamb and smother. Then add the broth and barley, and simmer. The flavor will be slightly different.

Add a bouquet garni (page 474) during simmering, if desired.

Use a lamb broth to replace white beef stock if desired.

TECHNIQUE
Blanching meats (in method for stewing) (pages 397-399)
Cutting vegetables (pages 217-223)
Vegetable soup (pages 302-303)
Cooling and storing food (pages 45-47)
Serving soup (page 311)

RECIPE
White Beef Stock (page 480)

Scotch Broth

Yield: 1 gallon (3.75 liters)

Lamb, medium dice	*2 pounds*	*900 grams*
White Beef Stock	*3 quarts*	*3 liters*
Barley	*8 ounces*	*225 grams*
Salt to taste	*½ teaspoon*	*½ teaspoon*
Carrots, brunoise	*4 ounces*	*115 grams*
Turnips, brunoise	*4 ounces*	*115 grams*
Onions, brunoise	*4 ounces*	*115 grams*
Leeks, brunoise	*4 ounces*	*115 grams*
Celery, brunoise	*4 ounces*	*115 grams*
Savoy cabbage, diced	*4 ounces*	*115 grams*
Pepper to taste	*to taste*	*to taste*
Parsley, chopped	*as needed*	*as needed*

1. Blanch the lamb in simmering water for 5 minutes. Drain.

2. Combine meat, stock, barley, and salt in a soup pot. Simmer for 45 minutes.

3. Add the carrots, turnips, onions, leeks, celery, and cabbage to the soup and simmer until all ingredients are very tender.

4. Adjust seasoning to taste with salt and pepper; finish with chopped parsley.

Chicken Egg Drop Soup

Yield: 1 gallon (3.75 liters)

Oil, vegetable or peanut	*1 tablespoon*	*1 tablespoon*
Ginger, minced	*1 tablespoon*	*1 tablespoon*
Scallions, sliced thin	*2 ounces*	*60 grams*
Asian-style Chicken Stock	*3 quarts*	*3 liters*
Cornstarch, as needed	*2 ounces*	*60 grams*
Eggs, beaten	*8 to 10 each*	*8 to 10 each*
Salt to taste	*2 teaspoons*	*2 teaspoons*
White pepper to taste	*1 teaspoon*	*1 teaspoon*
Egg shade color, diluted (optional)	*$^1/_4$ teaspoon*	*$^1/_4$ teaspoon*
Garnish		
Green scallions, chopped	*2 ounces*	*60 grams*

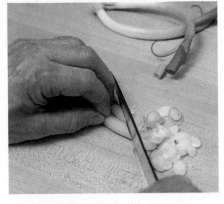

Cut the scallions on the bias.

1. Heat oil, add ginger and scallions, and stir-fry. Add chicken stock and bring to a boil.

2. Combine cornstarch and some water or cold stock to make a slurry. Add half to the soup, stirring constantly; return to a boil. Check consistency, and add more of the slurry if desired.

3. Stir in eggs, and add seasonings and color (optional).

4. Garnish individual portions with scallion greens.

Egg shade is a food coloring. Its use is optional, but it is traditionally added to particular recipes, such as this one, to provide a rich golden color.

TECHNIQUE
Slurries (page 238)
Serving soup (page 311)
Cooling and storing food (pages 45-47)

RECIPE
Asian-style Chicken Stock (page 480)

Wonton wrappers of various sizes and shapes.

The method for filling and folding wontons is similar to that for preparing tortellini. Fold in half to make a triangle and overlap two points.

Wontons can be cooked, shocked in cold water, and held for service. Place wontons in a cup, then add hot soup.

TECHNIQUE
Blanching vegetables (page 380)
Serving soup (page 311)
Cooling and storing food (pages 45-47)

RECIPE
Asian-style Chicken Stock (page 480)

Wonton Soup

Yield: 1 gallon (3.75 liters)

Wonton wrappers (thin skin)	*2 packs*	*2 packs*
Eggs, beaten lightly	*2 each*	*2 each*
Wonton stuffing		
Ground pork	*1 pound*	*450 grams*
Chinese cabbage, chopped	*8 ounces*	*225 grams*
Scallions, chopped	*4 each*	*4 each*
Ginger, minced	*$1/_2$ tablespoon*	*$1/_2$ tablespoon*
Soy sauce	*2 tablespoons*	*2 tablespoons*
Salt	*1 teaspoon*	*1 teaspoon*
White pepper	*$1/_2$ teaspoon*	*3 grams*
Sesame oil	*2 tablespoons*	*2 tablespoons*
Chicken Stock	*8 fluid ounces*	*240 milliliters*
Soup		
Asian-style Chicken Stock	*1 gallon*	*3.75 liters*
Black soy sauce	*2 tablespoons*	*2 tablespoons*
Salt to taste	*1 teaspoon*	*1 teaspoon*
Pepper to taste	*$1/_2$ teaspoon*	*$1/_2$ teaspoon*
Garnish		
Ham, fine julienne	*4 ounces*	*115 grams*
Eggs	*4 each*	*4 each*
Spinach or watercress, blanched for 30 seconds, rough cut	*12 ounces*	*340 grams*

1. To make the wontons, combine all ingredients for the stuffing and mix together. Place $1/_2$ teaspoon stuffing on each wonton wrapper, brush edges with egg wash, and fold.

2. Sauté scallions and ginger in oil. Add chicken stock and bring to a boil. Add soy sauce, salt, and pepper.

3. Cook wontons in boiling, salted water for 2 minutes, drain, and add to soup.

4. Add garnish to individual portions.

CHAPTER

15

Sauce Recipes

This chapter contains recipes for the grand sauces and many classic variations. In addition, you will find recipes for contemporary sauces such as vegetable coulis. The recipes are grouped as follows:

- *Basic Brown Sauces and Derivatives*
- *Velouté Sauce and Derivatives*
- *Béchamel Sauce and Derivatives*
- *Tomato Sauces*
- *Warm Butter Sauces*
- *Compound Butter*
- *Coulis and Vegetable Sauces*
- *Barbecue Sauce*

As you read through the entrée recipe chapters which follow, however, you will also find additional sauces contained within an individual recipe. Look at the various cold sauces in Chapters 24 and 26, as well.

Straining the sauce.

Another method for preparing this sauce is as follows: Add half of the stock to the browned mirepoix and tomato. Thicken the other half of the stock with all of the roux. Combine and simmer.

TECHNIQUE
Adding roux to a sauce (page 240)
Straining sauces (page 321)
Cooling and storing foods (pages 45-47)

RECIPES
Mirepoix (page 472)
Brown Veal Stock (page 478)
Pale Roux (page 473)
Sachet d'Epices (page 475)

Brown Sauce (Sauce Espagnole)

Yield: 1 gallon (3.75 liters)

Mirepoix	*1 pound*	*450 grams*
Vegetable oil, hot	*3 fluid ounces*	*90 milliliters*
Tomato paste	*4 ounces*	*115 grams*
Brown Veal Stock, hot	*1 ½ gallons*	*5.75 liters*
Pale Roux	*12 ounces*	*340 grams*
Sachet d'Epices	*1 each*	*1 each*

1. Brown the onions from the mirepoix in the hot oil; add the remainder of the mirepoix and continue to brown.

2. Add the tomato paste; cook out for several minutes.

3. Add the brown stock; bring up to a simmer.

4. Whip the roux into the stock. Return to a simmer and add the sachet.

5. Simmer for approximately 1 hour; skim the surface as necessary.

6. Strain through cheesecloth. Cool and store properly.

Demi-Glace

Yield: 1 quart (1 liter)

Brown Veal Stock	*2 quarts*	*2 liters*
Brown Sauce	*2 quarts*	*2 liters*

1. Reduce the stock by one-third.

2. Add the brown sauce; continue to reduce to 1 quart. Skim the surface as necessary.

3. Strain the sauce. Cool and store properly.

VARIATIONS

Marsala Sauce: Combine 1 quart (1 liter) of demi–glace with 3 tablespoons of shallots and ¼ teaspoon of cracked peppercorns and reduce over moderate heat. Add 3 fluid ounces (90 milliliters) of Marsala to the sauce. The sauce is ready to serve as is, or it may be finished with cold butter to order.

Madeira Sauce: Reduce 1 quart (1 liter) of demi-glace by ¼. Add 8 fluid ounces (240 milliliters) of Madeira. Finish the sauce to order with cold butter.

(Recipe continued on facing page)

Fines Herbes Sauce: Combine 10 fluid ounces (300 milliliters) of dry white wine with 1 ounce (30 grams) minced shallots, 6 parsley stems, 1½ tablespoons each of chopped chervil, tarragon, and chives; reduce over medium heat by ½. Add 1 quart (1 liter) demi-glace and continue to reduce until the sauce coats the back of a spoon. Add fresh lemon juice to taste. At service add 1 teaspoon each chopped fines herbes (page 475) and cold butter per portion.

Mushroom Sauce: Sauté 2 ounces (60 grams) of shallots and 8 ounces (225 grams) of mushroom trimmings in butter until the juices have cooked away. Add 2 sprigs of thyme, a bay leaf, and 4 fluid ounces (120 milliliters) of burgundy; reduce by half. Add 1 quart (1 liter) demi-glace and reduce until the sauce coats the back of a spoon. Degrease and strain the sauce. Add 12 ounces (340 grams) sautéed, sliced mushrooms to finish the sauce.

Robert Sauce: Sauté 14 ounces (400 grams) minced onion in clarified butter. Add 1 pint (480 milliliters) of white wine and reduce by ¾. Add 1 quart (1 liter) demi-glace and reduce. Dissolve 2 teaspoons dry mustard in a little warm water and add to the sauce. Finish with butter at service.

Bordelaise Sauce: Combine 1 ounce (30 grams) shallots, 2 thyme sprigs, a bay leaf, and ½ teaspoon whole peppercorns with 1 pint (480 milliliters) dry red wine; reduce by half. Add 1 quart (1 liter) demi-glace and reduce the sauce until it coats the back of a spoon. Finish the sauce with 4 ounces (115 grams) diced poached bone marrow, lemon juice to taste, 1 tablespoon glace de viande (page 479), and 3 ounces (140 grams) butter.

Chasseur Sauce: Sauté 10 ounces (285 grams) thickly sliced mushrooms in a combination of clarified butter and olive oil. Add 1 ounce (30 grams) shallots, and a finely minced garlic clove; sauté briefly. Add 3 ounces (85 grams) tomato paste and sauté. Add 8 fluid ounces (240 milliliters) of dry white wine and 3 fluid ounces (90 milliliters) of brandy. Reduce by half. Add 1 quart (1 liter) demi-glace and 8 ounces (240 grams) tomato concassé. Reduce to a sauce consistency. Finish the sauce with 2 tablespoons glace de viande (page 479), 1 tablespoon each chopped parsley and tarragon, and 2 ounces (60 grams) cold butter.

Chateaubriand Sauce: Combine 1 pint (480 milliliters) dry white wine, 2 minced shallots, 3 thyme sprigs, 4 ounces (115 grams) mushroom trimmings, and a bay leaf; reduce by half. Add 1 quart (1 liter) demi-glace and simmer briefly. Strain the sauce and finish with 1 tablespoon chopped tarragon and 3 ounces (85 grams) of maître d'hôtel butter (page 522).

This demi-glace has cooked sufficiently to coat a spoon.

Often, jus de veau lié, or other types of lié sauces, are used to replace demi-glace in contemporary cooking.

TECHNIQUE
Demi-glace (pages 319-322)
Cooling and storing foods (pages 45-47)

RECIPES
Brown Veal Stock (page 478)
Brown Sauce (page 514)

Adding diluted arrowroot to thicken jus de veau lié.

Add various fresh herbs or spices to the jus (either loose or in a sachet or bouquet garni) to give the sauce a particular flavor.

Another way to customize a jus is to add an essence or fumet made from such ingredients as tomatoes, celery, or mushrooms.

TECHNIQUE
Roasting bones (page 250)
Slurries (page 238)
Straining sauces (page 321)
Cooling and storing food (pages 45-47)

RECIPES
Brown Veal Stock (page 478)
Mirepoix (page 472)
Sachet d'Epices (page 475)

Jus de Veau Lié

Yield: 1 gallon (3.75 liters)

Brown Veal Stock	*4 ¹/₂ quarts*	*4.25 liters*
Veal bones and trim, roasted	*4 pounds*	*1.8 kilograms*
Mirepoix, caramelized	*1 pound*	*450 grams*
Sachet d'Epices	*1 each*	*1 each*
Arrowroot or cornstarch, diluted with cold water or dry wine	*1 ounce*	*30 grams*

1. Combine all the ingredients except the arrowroot and bring to a simmer.

2. Simmer for a minimum of 2 ¹/₂ to 3 hours, skimming the surface as necessary to extract full body and flavor from the bones and trim.

3. Strain the sauce, pressing well. Return the strained sauce to the heat and bring to a full boil. Whisk in diluted arrowroot or cornstarch to thicken the sauce enough to coat the back of a wooden spoon. Cool and store properly.

VARIATIONS

Jus de Volaille Lié: Replace the brown veal stock with a brown chicken stock and replace the veal bones and trim with an equal weight of chicken bones and trim.

Jus de Canard Lié: Replace the brown veal stock with a brown duck stock and replace the veal bones and trim with an equal weight of duck bones and trim.

Velouté

Yield: 2 quarts (2 liters)

Veal Stock	2 ¹/₂ quarts	2.5 liters
White Roux	8 ounces	225 grams
Salt to taste	¹/₂ teaspoon	¹/₂ teaspoon
Pepper to taste	¹/₄ teaspoon	¹/₄ teaspoon

1. Bring the stock to a boil.

2. Whip the roux into the stock; work out all the lumps.

3. Simmer for 30 to 40 minutes, skimming the surface as necessary.

4. Season with salt and pepper to taste and then strain the sauce. Cool and store properly.

VARIATIONS

Chicken Velouté: Prepare velouté substituting chicken stock for veal stock.

Fish Velouté: Prepare velouté substituting fish stock or fumet for white veal stock.

Shellfish Velouté: Prepare velouté substituting shellfish stock for veal stock.

Vegetarian Velouté: Prepare velouté substituting vegetable broth for veal stock.

Dill Sauce: Sweat 4 ounces (115 grams) minced onions in clarified butter. Add 1 quart (1 liter) velouté and simmer until the sauce coats the back of a spoon. Finish the sauce with 10 ounces (285 grams) sour cream and 3 tablespoons chopped fresh dill. Season to taste with salt and pepper.

Suprême Sauce: Combine 1 quart (1 liter) chicken velouté and 8 fluid ounces (240 milliliters) heavy cream and simmer until reduced to a good sauce consistency. Season with salt and pepper to taste.

Shrimp Sauce: Sauté 2 pounds (900 grams) shrimp shells in butter until red. Add 1 tablespoon minced shallots and 2 minced garlic cloves and sauté until the aroma is apparent. Add 1 tablespoon sweet Hungarian paprika to deglaze the pan. Add 1 quart (1 liter) heavy cream and 1 ¹/₂ quarts (1.5 liters) fish velouté and simmer until the sauce coats the back of a spoon. Season to taste with salt and pepper.

Straining the sauce is a critical step in order to produce the best texture in the finished sauce.

There are a number of optional aromatics that can be added to this sauce as it simmers to give it a special flavor: bay leaf, thyme, mushroom trimmings, or a sachet. However, if the sauce is to be further reduced or flavored to make a special sauce, it is best to keep this base as plain as possible.

Some chefs prefer to add the stock to the roux. See Chapter 6 for information on working with roux.

TECHNIQUE
Velouté (pages 324-327)
Cooling and storing food (pages 45-47)

RECIPES
Veal Stock (page 480)
White Roux (page 473)

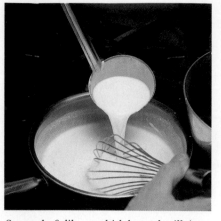

Some chefs like to whisk heated milk into the roux, working gradually to avoid lumps.

You may see some older versions of the béchamel recipe that call for the addition of an oignon piqué as the sauce simmers. However, leaving an onion whole in the sauce as it cooks could cause it to sour in a relatively short period of time. You may prefer to add just the bay leaf and clove as it simmers; or simply a thyme sprig, as some chefs prefer.

.

TECHNIQUE
Béchamel (pages 327-329)

RECIPE
White Roux (page 473)

Béchamel

Yield: 2 quarts (2 liters)

Milk	*2 ¹/₂ quarts*	*2.5 liters*
White Roux	*8 ounces*	*225 grams*
Onions, fine dice, smothered in clarified butter	*2 ounces*	*60 grams*
Salt to taste	*¹/₂ teaspoon*	*¹/₂ teaspoon*
White pepper to taste	*¹/₄ teaspoon*	*¹/₄ teaspoon*
Nutmeg, ground to taste	*¹/₄ teaspoon*	*¹/₄ teaspoon*

1. Scald the milk (do not boil) and pour it over the roux. Bring to a boil.

2. Add the smothered onions.

3. Simmer for 30 minutes.

4. Adjust the seasoning to taste with salt, white pepper, and nutmeg.

5. Strain through a double thickness of cheesecloth. Cool and store properly.

VARIATIONS

Cheddar Cheese Sauce: Add 1 pound (450 grams) grated aged Cheddar cheese to 2 quarts (2 liters) of simmering béchamel. Combine 2 fluid ounces (60 milliliters) of dry white wine with 1 tablespoon dry mustard and add to the sauce. Stir until the cheese is melted and the sauce is very smooth. Season with salt and pepper to taste.

Cream Sauce: Combine 1 quart (1 liter) béchamel with 8 fluid ounces (240 milliliters) heated heavy cream. Simmer until the sauce coats the back of a spoon. Season to taste with salt and pepper.

Heavy Béchamel: A heavy béchamel is often used as a binder for croquettes and similar preparations. Increase the amount of roux to 12 ounces (340 grams) per gallon (3.75 liters).

Mornay Sauce: Combine béchamel with 1 quart (1 liter) poaching liquid. Simmer until reduced to 2 quarts (2 liters). Add 8 ounces (225 grams) each of Gruyère and Parmesan cheese to the sauce. Finish with up to 2 ounces (60 grams) of cheese, if desired.

Marinara Sauce

Yield: 2 quarts (2 liters)

Olive oil	*1 fluid ounce*	*30 milliliters*
Onions, small dice	*8 ounces*	*225 grams*
Garlic cloves, minced	*4 each*	*4 each*
Tomato concassé	*7 pounds*	*3.5 kilograms*
Tomato purée	*20 fluid ounces*	*600 milliliters*
Oregano, fresh, chopped	*1 tablespoon*	*1 tablespoon*
Basil, fresh, chopped	*¹/₂ cup*	*¹/₂ cup*

1. Sweat the onions in the olive oil until they are translucent.

2. Add the garlic and sauté it until an aroma is apparent.

3. Add the tomato concassé, tomato purée, and oregano to the onions.

4. Simmer the mixture to achieve a heavy consistency.

5. Add the basil and adjust the seasoning to taste. Serve at once or cool and store properly.

Basil and oregano are added at the last moment.

This is a classic accompaniment to light pastas and fried seafood dishes such as fried calamari.

For a spicier sauce, add a few red pepper flakes.

Canned tomatoes should be used when good fresh tomatoes are not available.

TECHNIQUE
Mincing garlic (page 227)
Tomato concassé (page 226)
Fresh herbs (page 229)

Use coarsely ground lean meat.

The classic "spaghetti sauce" loved by children and adults; this sauce also works well with lasagna and heavier pasta dishes. See pasta recommendations in Table 5-40.

TECHNIQUE
Mincing onions (page 219)
Mincing garlic (page 225)
Cooling and storing food (page 45-47)

Meat Sauce

Yield: Approximately 2 quarts (2 liters)

Olive oil	*2 tablespoons*	*2 tablespoons*
Garlic cloves, minced	*2 each*	*2 each*
Onion, minced	*3 ounces*	*85 grams*
Chuck, ground (or combination of ground veal and chuck)	*2 ¹/₂ pounds*	*1.15 kilograms*
Tomato purée	*1 quart*	*1 liter*
Tomato paste	*1 ¹/₂ ounces*	*45 grams*
Salt to taste	*1 teaspoon*	*1 teaspoon*
Pepper to taste	*¹/₂ teaspoon*	*¹/₂ teaspoon*
Basil, fresh, chopped	*1 tablespoon*	*1 tablespoon*
Oregano, fresh, chopped	*1 tablespoon*	*1 tablespoon*
Thyme, fresh, chopped	*1 tablespoon*	*1 tablespoon*

1. Heat the olive oil in a large skillet.

2. Add the garlic and onion and sauté them until the onions are tender and light and brown.

3. Add the ground meat. Sauté the mixture, stirring it with a wooden spoon to break up any lumps, until the meat is browned, about 5 minutes.

4. Add the tomato purée and 2 tablespoons (30 grams) of the tomato paste. Mix well.

5. Season the sauce to taste with the salt and pepper. Add the herbs.

6. Degrease the sauce if necessary.

7. Adjust the seasoning or consistency with additional tomato paste if necessary. Serve at once or cool and store properly.

Hollandaise Sauce

Yield: 20 ounces (600 milliliters)

Reduction		
Cider vinegar	*2 fluid ounces*	*60 milliliters*
Black peppercorns, cracked	*¹/₂ teaspoon*	*¹/₂ teaspoon*
Water	*4 fluid ounces*	*120 milliliters*
Egg yolks	*6 each*	*6 each*
Clarified butter, warm	*12 ounces*	*340 grams*
Lemon juice	*2 teaspoons*	*2 teaspoons*
Salt to taste	*¹/₂ teaspoon*	*¹/₂ teaspoon*
Pepper to taste (optional)	*¹/₄ teaspoon*	*¹/₄ teaspoon*

Cook the yolks until they are frothy and have reached the same temperature as the butter.

1. Combine the vinegar and peppercorns; reduce until the liquid has almost cooked away. Cool the reduction slightly.

2. Add hot water to the reduction. (The reduction may be strained at this point, if desired.)

3. Add the reduction to the egg yolks. In a stainless steel bowl, whip over simmering water until the yolks ribbon and triple in volume. They should have a light consistency.

4. Gradually add the warm clarified butter, whipping constantly.

5. Add the lemon juice, and adjust the seasoning to taste with salt and pepper.

6. Strain through a cheesecloth, if necessary, to remove any pieces of cooked egg. Serve at once.

When making hollandaise, the butter may be increased slightly; consider a ratio of 2 to 3 ounces (60 to 85 grams) of butter per egg yolk.

TECHNIQUE
Hollandaise (pages 332-335)
Separating eggs (page 254)
Clarifying butter (page 253)
Straining sauces (page 321)

VARIATIONS

Maltaise Sauce: Finish the hollandaise with zest and juice from a blood orange.

Mousseline Sauce: Add unsweetened whipped heavy cream to the sauce just before service. Use about 2 tablespoons of whipped cream per portion.

Creole Mustard Sauce: Add Dijon, Creole, and/or a mild prepared mustard to the finished hollandaise.

Choron Sauce: Make reduction of 1 ounce (30 grams) chopped shallots, 12 cracked black peppercorns, 3 tablespoons dried tarragon leaves, 4 fluid ounces (120 milliliters) each of tarragon vinegar and dry white wine, reduce until nearly dry. Moisten the reduction with 2 fluid ounces (60 milliliters) of water and strain. Use this reduction in the hollandaise recipe above. Finish the sauce with 1 ¹/₂ ounces (45 grams) of tomato purée.

Royal Glaçage: Combine equal parts of a warm hollandaise sauce, warm velouté, and heavy cream (whipped to soft peaks). Use this mixture to coat items to be glazed in a broiler.

Tarragon is the herb that gives this sauce its special flavor.

A pinch of cayenne is added for a classic presentation.

If your kitchen often prepares Béarnaise or other warm-butter sauces that are based on a reduction, you may want to prepare reductions separately, in advance.

TECHNIQUE
Separating eggs (page 254)
Clarifying butter (page 253)
Straining sauces (page 321)

Béarnaise

Yield: 20 fluid ounces (600 milliliters)

Reduction		
Shallots, chopped	*1 tablespoon*	*1 tablespoon*
Black peppercorns, cracked	*½ teaspoon*	*½ teaspoon*
Tarragon leaves, dried	*1 tablespoon*	*1 tablespoon*
Tarragon vinegar	*3 fluid ounces*	*90 milliliters*
Dry white wine	*3 fluid ounces*	*90 milliliters*
Water	*4 fluid ounces*	*120 milliliters*
Egg yolks	*6 each*	*6 each*
Clarified butter, warm	*12 ounces*	*340 grams*
Tarragon leaves, coarsely chopped	*2 tablespoons*	*2 tablespoons*
Chervil pluches, coarsely chopped	*1 tablespoon*	*1 tablespoon*
Salt to taste	*½ teaspoon*	*½ teaspoon*

1. Combine the shallots, peppercorns, dried tarragon, vinegar, and wine. Reduce until nearly dry.

2. Add the water to the reduction; strain if desired.

3. Combine the reduction and the egg yolks in a stainless steel bowl. Whip over a bain-marie until the yolks form ribbons and triple in volume. They should be light in consistency.

4. Add the clarified butter gradually, whipping constantly. Strain if necessary to remove any cooked egg particles.

5. Add the chopped tarragon and chervil; adjust the seasoning to taste with salt. Serve at once.

Lemon Beurre Blanc

Traditionally, a beurre blanc does not contain cream. However, the cream serves as a stabilizer here. The more the cream is reduced, the greater its stabilizing effect, and therefore the longer it will last during service.

Yield: 1 ½ pints (720 milliliters)

Shallots, minced	*2 ounces*	*60 grams*
Dry white wine	*8 fluid ounces*	*240 milliliters*
Lemon juice	*3 fluid ounces*	*90 milliliters*
Cider vinegar	*3 fluid ounces*	*90 milliliters*
Heavy cream (optional)	*8 fluid ounces*	*240 milliliters*
Butter, softened	*1 ½ pounds*	*680 grams*
Salt to taste	*½ teaspoon*	*½ teaspoon*
Pepper to taste	*¼ teaspoon*	*¼ teaspoon*
Lemon zest	*1 tablespoon*	*1 tablespoon*

(Recipe continued on facing page)

1. Reduce the cream by half.

2. Combine the shallots, wine, lemon juice, and vinegar. Reduce until nearly dry.

3. Add the reduced heavy cream and continue to reduce slightly.

4. Gradually whisk in the butter.

5. Adjust the seasoning to taste with salt and pepper. Serve at once.

TECHNIQUE
Beurre Blanc (pages 336-337)

Maître d'Hôtel Butter

Yield: 1 1/4 pounds (570 grams)

Butter, softened	*1 pound*	*450 grams*
Parsley, finely chopped	*1/2 bunch*	*1/2 bunch*
Lemon juice	*2 to 3 tablespoons*	*2 to 3 tablespoons*
Salt to taste	*1/2 teaspoon*	*1/2 teaspoon*
Pepper to taste	*1/4 teaspoon*	*1/4 teaspoon*

1. Combine all the ingredients.

2. Pipe into rosettes, using a pastry bag, or roll in parchment paper.

3. Refrigerate or freeze until needed.

Use the edge of a hotel pan to shape the compound butter.

VARIATIONS

Basil Butter: Replace the parsley with chopped fresh basil. Add grated Parmesan cheese and minced garlic to taste. For best flavor, sweat the garlic in olive oil or butter, and cool before adding to the butter.

Sun-Dried Tomato-and-Oregano Butter: Add about 3 tablespoons of minced fresh oregano in addition to the parsley. Add 2 ounces (60 grams) of minced sun-dried tomatoes.

Rosemary-and-Ginger Butter: Replace the parsley with about 2 to 3 tablespoons of minced fresh rosemary leaves; add 1 tablespoon of grated fresh gingerroot (or more to taste). If desired, add soy or tamari sauce to replace the lemon juice.

Cilantro-and-Lime Butter: Replace the parsley with chopped cilantro leaves. Replace the lemon juice with fresh lime juice. Add dried red pepper flakes to taste, if desired.

This is one of the most commonly prepared compound butters. It can be held under refrigeration for several days, but be sure to check it carefully for any souring as a result. It is best held in the freezer.

When serving this butter with grilled meat or fish, consider adding 1 to 2 tablespoons of prepared mustard to the blend

TECHNIQUE
Compound butters (pages 338-339)
Fresh herbs (page 229)

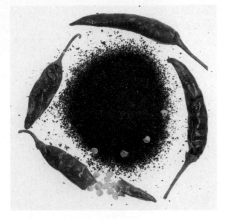

Chilies, in whole, dried, and solid forms.

The sauce can be finished with butter for added richness.

Almost any whole dried chilies can be used in place of, or in addition to, the chili powder. To use dried chilies, first roast the chilies in a skillet for 3 or 4 minutes. Soak them in boiling water, seed, and then purée them. The purée can be added to the sauce with the stock. Strain the sauce in the final step.

RECIPE
Chicken Stock (page 480)

Red Chili Sauce

Yield: 1 quart (1 liter)

Vegetable oil	*3 tablespoons*	*3 tablespoons*
Onions, finely chopped	*3 ounces*	*85 grams*
Garlic cloves, minced	*2 each*	*2 each*
Oregano	*1/2 teaspoon*	*1/2 teaspoon*
Cumin, ground	*2 teaspoons*	*2 teaspoons*
Chili powder	*4 ounces*	*115 grams*
Chicken Stock	*1 1/4 quarts*	*1.2 liters*
Salt to taste	*1/2 teaspoon*	*1/2 teaspoon*

1. Sweat the onions in the oil. Add the garlic and cook 30 seconds more. Add the oregano and the cumin and continue to cook. Add the chili powder and cook briefly, stirring constantly. Do not let mixture burn.

2. Add the stock, whisking to remove any lumps. Simmer for about 30 minutes and reduce to sauce consistency. Strain if desired. Adjust seasoning. Serve at once or cool and store properly.

VARIATIONS

Red Chili Sauce with Tomatoes: For a sweeter sauce, replace 1 pint (480 milliliters) of the stock with 10 ounces (285 grams) of tomato concassé. Increase the onions to 6 ounces (170 grams).

Chipotle Chili Sauce: For a smoky flavor, add 2 or 3 chipotle peppers and Adobo sauce (depending on desired heat) to the cooking sauce.

Red Pepper Coulis

Yield: 2 quarts (2 liters)

Red peppers, roasted and chopped	*3 pounds*	*1.3 kilograms*
Olive oil	*2 fluid ounces*	*60 milliliters*
Shallots, chopped	*1 ounce*	*30 grams*
White wine	*8 fluid ounces*	*240 milliliters*
Chicken Stock	*1 pint*	*480 milliliters*
Salt to taste	*1/2 teaspoon*	*1/2 teaspoon*
Pepper to taste	*1/4 teaspoon*	*1/4 teaspoon*

(Recipe continued on facing page)

1. Sweat the peppers in the olive oil until they are tender; remove the peppers and purée. Reserve the oil used to sweat the peppers.

2. Sweat the shallots in the reserved oil.

3. Deglaze with wine.

4. Add the stock; reduce by half. Purée the sauce. Adjust the consistency.

5. Adjust the seasoning with salt and pepper to taste. Serve at once or cool and store properly.

This sauce can be finished in a number of ways: add a small amount of heavy cream or crème fraîche, additional chopped fresh herbs, or a julienne of other bell peppers (red, green, yellow, etc.).

TECHNIQUE
Coulis (page 332)
Roasting and peeling peppers (page 227)
Mincing shallots (pages 224-225)

RECIPE
Chicken Stock (page 480)

Tomato Coulis

Yield: 2 quarts (2 liters)

Olive oil	2 fluid ounces	60 milliliters
Onions, minced	8 ounces	225 grams
Garlic, minced	1/2 ounce	15 grams
Tomato paste	8 fluid ounces	240 milliliters
Red wine	12 fluid ounces	360 milliliters
Tomato concassé	2 1/2 pounds	1.5 kilograms
Chicken Stock	1 quart	1 liter
Basil sprigs	2 each	2 each
Thyme sprig	1 each	1 each
Bay leaf	1 each	1 each
Pepper to taste	1/4 teaspoon	1/4 teaspoon

1. Heat the olive oil; sauté the onions until they are tender. Add the garlic; sauté it briefly. Add the tomato paste; caramelize it lightly.

2. Add the red wine, tomato concassé, stock, basil, thyme, and bay leaf. Simmer the mixture for approximately 45 minutes. Remove and discard the herbs.

3. Run the mixture through a food mill with a coarse plate. Adjust the consistency if necessary.

4. Finish the sauce with pepper to taste. Serve at once or cool and store properly.

The sauce is ready to purée.

Roasted garlic and roasted red peppers may be included in this purée for a more intense flavor.

TECHNIQUE
Tomato concassé (page 226)
Puréeing sauces (page 332)
Coulis (page 332)
Cooling and storing foods (pages 45-47)

RECIPE
Chicken Stock (page 480)

Wear gloves to protect skin when working with chilies.

Additional seasonings for barbecue sauce include, but are not limited to: bourbon, rum, molasses, honey, maple syrup, ketchup, cocktail sauce, A-1 Steak Sauce, mustard, cumin, cracked black peppercorns, oregano, chipotle or other chilies, additional vinegars, and infused oils.

TECHNIQUE
Chilies (page 227)
Garlic (pages 224-225)

RECIPES
Chicken Stock (page 480)
White Beef Stock (page 480)

Barbecue Sauce

Yield: 1 quart (1 liter)

Butter	*1 tablespoon*	*1 tablespoon*
Onions, chopped	*4 ounces*	*115 grams*
Garlic, minced	*1 tablespoon*	*1 tablespoon*
Chili powder	*2 tablespoons*	*2 tablespoons*
Jalapeño chilies, minced	*1 tablespoon*	*1 tablespoon*
Coffee, brewed	*4 fluid ounces*	*120 milliliters*
Worcestershire sauce	*4 fluid ounces*	*120 milliliters*
Tomato paste	*4 ounces*	*115 grams*
Apple cider vinegar	*2 fluid ounces*	*60 milliliters*
Brown sugar	*2 ounces*	*60 grams*
Apple cider	*2 tablespoons*	*2 tablespoons*
Chicken or White Beef Stock	*as needed*	*as needed*

1. Heat the butter in a saucepan over medium heat. Add the onion and garlic. Sauté them for 2 or 3 minutes until an aroma is apparent.

2. Add the chili powder and jalapeños. Sauté the mixture for another 30 to 45 seconds.

3. Add the coffee, Worcestershire sauce, tomato paste, vinegar, brown sugar, and cider. Simmer the sauce for 20 minutes, or until it is somewhat thickened. Serve or use at once, or cool and store properly.

16

Meat Entrées

There are numerous possibilities when it comes to devising the menu selections for entrées. The recipes here, plus those in the following four chapters, offer a wide range of options. You will find them arranged both by the type of meat and cooking method.

- *Beef*
- *Veal*
- *Lamb*
- *Pork*
- *Game*
- *Variety Meats*
- *Ground Meats*

Please look at the selections in Chapter 20, International Entrées, for additional options.

Beef Stroganoff is traditionally served over egg noodles or spaëtzle.

Two ounces (60 grams) of tomato paste may be added to the cooked onions if desired. Sauté briefly to develop flavor.

TECHNIQUE
Trimming a tenderloin (page 261)
Preparing émincé (page 261)
Sautéing (pages 358-362)

RECIPE
Jus de Veau Lié (page 514)

Beef Stroganoff

Yield: 10 servings

Tenderloin of beef cut into émincé, or beef tips	4 pounds	1.8 kilograms
Vegetable oil, as needed	3 fluid ounces	90 milliliters
Mushrooms, sliced	1/2 pound	225 grams
Butter	2 ounces	60 grams
Onions, minced	8 ounces	225 grams
Jus de Veau Lié	1 pint	480 milliliters
Sour cream	8 fluid ounces	240 milliliters
Dijon mustard	1 tablespoon	1 tablespoon
Lemon juice	1 tablespoon	1 tablespoon
Salt to taste	1/2 teaspoon	1/2 teaspoon
Pepper to taste	1/2 teaspoon	1/2 teaspoon

1. Sauté beef in hot oil to desired doneness. Remove meat and keep warm.

2. Sauté mushrooms in butter for 2 to 3 minutes and remove.

3. Sauté onions in butter until translucent. Add jus and simmer 10 minutes. Add sour cream to pan, stirring constantly. Reduce until proper consistency is reached.

4. Add mustard, lemon juice, and adjust seasoning to taste with salt and pepper.

5. Reheat meat and mushrooms in sauce (do not boil meat in sauce).

Carving a beef rib roast.

Roast Prime Rib au Jus

Yield: 10 servings

Beef, rib roast	8 pounds	3.6 kilograms
Salt to taste	1 teaspoon	1 teaspoon
Pepper, coarse-ground, to taste	1 teaspoon	1 teaspoon
Mirepoix, medium dice	8 ounces	225 grams
Brown Veal Stock	1 1/2 quarts	1.5 liters
Arrowroot, diluted, as needed	1/2 ounce	15 grams

(Recipe continued on facing page)

1. Rub roast with salt and pepper; tie the roast.

2. Place roast on a wire rack in a roasting pan.

3. Roast in a 300 to 315°F (150 to 157°C) oven, until the roast reaches an internal temperature of 100°F (35°C); add mirepoix.

4. Remove roast when it has reached an internal temperature of 125°F (50°C); allow to rest.

5. To make jus, clarify fat in a roast pan, then discard all fat.

6. Add stock and simmer until reduced by one-half; degrease.

7. Strain through a fine chinoise, and adjust seasonings.

8. Remove string, slice meat against the grain, and serve with jus.

TECHNIQUE
Tying a roast (page 262)
Roasting (page 349)
Carving (pages 355-357)
Slurries (page 238)

RECIPES
Mirepoix (page 472)
Brown Veal Stock (page 478)

Broiled Sirloin Steak with Mushroom Sauce

Yield: 10 servings

Sirloin steaks	*10 each*	*10 each*
Salt to taste	*1/2 teaspoon*	*1/2 teaspoon*
Black pepper, fresh-ground, to taste	*1/4 teaspoon*	*1/4 teaspoon*
Vegetable oil	*as needed*	*as needed*
Mushroom Sauce	*1 1/2 pints*	*720 milliliters*

1. Season steak with salt and pepper; brush with oil.

2. Broil in hot broiler to desired doneness.

3. Turn steak at 45-degree angles during broiling to achieve grill marks.

4. Serve with chili butter and other accompaniments.

Add demi-glace to the mushrooms to prepare the sauce.

The steaks for this recipe are cut to the desired size, according to preference or individual restaurant standards.

TECHNIQUE
Cutting Steaks (page 226)
Broiling (pages 344-349)

RECIPE
Mushroom Sauce (page 514)

Mash the garlic clove between the work surface and the flat edge of the blade.

Cut the steaks into 6- to 8-ounce (170- to 225-gram) portions, depending on use.

Increase the garlic in the sauce if desired. You may also want to add capers and sliced cornichons.

Although the sauce may be prepared in advance, broil the steaks to order.

TECHNIQUE
Marinades (pages 242-245)
Cutting Steaks (page 266)
Tomato Concassé (page 226)
Grilling (pages 344-349)

Strip Steak "Provençale"

Yield: 10 servings

Marinade

Dry white wine	8 fluid ounces	240 milliliters
Garlic cloves, mashed	1 tablespoon	1 tablespoon
Bay leaves	2 each	2 each
Black peppercorns, cracked	1 teaspoon	1 teaspoon
Rosemary leaves	2 teaspoons	2 teaspoons
Beef strip loin steaks	10 each	10 each
Olive oil as needed	3 fluid ounces	90 milliliters

Sauce

Olive oil	2 fluid ounces	60 milliliters
Mushrooms, sliced	16 ounces	450 grams
Tomato concassé	16 ounces	450 grams
Niçoise olives, pitted and sliced	30 each	30 each
Scallions, sliced	4 each	4 each
Salt to taste	1/2 teaspoon	1/2 teaspoon
Pepper to taste	1/2 teaspoon	1/2 teaspoon

1. Combine all ingredients for the marinade, pour over the steak, and marinate at least 1 hour.

2. Drain steak, brush with olive oil, and place on the grids of a preheated hot broiler or grill.

3. Mark and turn steak at a 45-degree angle; mark and turn over; finish cooking to proper degree of doneness.

4. Sauté mushrooms in olive oil until almost dry. Add the tomato concassé and heat through.

5. Add remaining marinade, olives, and scallions; reduce until desired sauce consistency is reached. Season with salt and pepper to taste.

6. Portion sauce on a plate and arrange steak on top.

London Broil

Yield: 10 servings

Flank steak	4 pounds	1.8 kilograms
Marinade		
Vegetable oil	4 fluid ounces	120 milliliters
Salt to taste	$^1/_2$ teaspoon	$^1/_2$ teaspoon
Pepper to taste	$^1/_4$ teaspoon	$^1/_4$ teaspoon
Paprika	2 teaspoons	2 teaspoons
Jus de Veau Lié or Demi-glace	20 fluid ounces	600 milliliters

1. Trim the flanks and remove all skin, membrane, and fat, if necessary.

2. Pour marinade over steaks and marinate under refrigeration for 2 to 3 hours or overnight.

3. Broil 3 to 5 minutes on each side.

4. Cut in very thin diagonal slices across the grain.

5. Return the jus or demi-glace to a boil and serve the sliced steak with 2 ounces (60 mililliters) per portion.

Flank steak

Flank steaks usually range from $1^1/_2$ to 3 pounds (680 grams to 1.3 kilograms). You will needed 2 to 3 for 10 servings. Use any extra for salads and sandwiches.

Minced shallots, garlic, chopped cilantro, or other fresh herbs may be added to the marinade.

London Broil is also often served with mushroom sauce (page 514) or sauce bordelaise (page 514).

TECHNIQUE
Grilling (pages 344-349)
Marinades (pages 242-245)

RECIPES
Jus de Veau Lié (page 516)
Demi-glace (page 514)

The dish is ready to go into the oven to finish braising.

The traditional version of this dish would be larded with strips of salt pork marinated in brandy.

"Lardons" are very short bâtonnet cuts of salt pork. They are often blanched in boiling water to reduce saltiness, as well as to render out some fat.

TECHNIQUE
Braising (pages 391-394)
Tying a roast (page 262)
Carving (pages 355-357)

RECIPES
Mirepoix (page 472)
Red Wine Marinade (page 477)
Demi-Glace (page 514)
Brown Veal Stock (page 478)
Sachet d'Epices (page 475)

Braised Beef Bourguignonne

Yield: 10 servings

Boneless bottom round or chuck	*4 pounds*	*1.8 kilograms*
Salt to taste	*1/2 teaspoon*	*1/2 teaspoon*
Pepper to taste	*1/2 teaspoon*	*1/2 teaspoon*
Oil	*as needed*	*as needed*
Salt pork, cut into *lardons*	*4 ounces*	*115 grams*
Mirepoix	*8 ounces*	*225 kilograms*
Flour	*2 ounces*	*60 grams*
Tomato purée	*6 fluid ounces*	*180 milliliters*
Red Wine Marinade	*1 pint*	*480 milliliters*
Demi-Glace	*1 pint*	*480 milliliters*
Brown Veal Stock	*1 quart*	*1 liter*
Sachet d'Epices	*1 each*	*1 each*

1. Trim, tie, and season the meat. Place in a pan with the marinade; cover and marinate for 2 hours, turning occasionally. Drain and reserve marinade.

2. Fry the lardons in hot oil until brown on all sides; remove and reserve. Sear the meat on all sides; remove.

3. Add the mirepoix and sauté until brown.

4. Add the flour; cook it out for 3 to 4 minutes.

5. Add the tomato purée and cook it out for 2 minutes.

6. Return the meat to the pan; add the marinade, stock, demi-glace, and sachet. Bring the liquid to a simmer. Cover the pan and braise the meat until it is fork tender, about 2 to 3 hours.

7. Remove the meat and keep it warm. Degrease the sauce and strain it. Simmer the sauce to reduce it, if necessary. Adjust the seasoning with salt and pepper. Return the fried lardons.

8. Slice and serve the meat with the sauce.

VARIATION

Beef Stew à la Bourguignonne: Cut the meat into large pieces (2 to 3 inches/5 to 7.5 centimeters). Marinate and prepare as directed above. Add blanched pearl onions and butter mushrooms if desired.

Chili con Carne

Yield: 15 servings

Pinto or kidney beans, dried	*1 pound*	*450 grams*
Beef shank, meat only, diced	*4 pounds*	*1.8 kilograms*
Salt to taste	*1/2 teaspoon*	*1/2 teaspoon*
Pepper to taste	*1/2 teaspoon*	*1/2 teaspoon*

(Recipe continued on facing page)

Onions, minced	10 ounces	285 grams
Red peppers, chopped	4 ounces	115 grams
Green peppers, chopped	4 ounces	115 grams
Anaheim peppers, chopped	2 ounces	60 grams
Vegetable oil	as needed	as needed
Garlic cloves, mashed to a paste	3 each	3 each
Chili powder, mild	1 ounce	30 grams
Cumin, ground	1 ounce	30 grams
Oregano, dried	1/2 ounce	15 grams
Tomato purée	3 fluid ounces	90 milliliters
Brown Veal Stock	1 pint	480 milliliters
Beer	12 fluid ounces	360 milliliters
Tomato concassé	1 1/2 pounds	680 grams
Garnish		
Onions, chopped	4 ounces	115 grams
Cilantro, chopped	3 tablespoons	3 tablespoons
Cheddar or Jack cheese, grated	8 ounces	225 grams

Use a variety of dried chilies to make your own chile powder.

1. Soak the beans overnight. Drain. Cover with water and cook until tender.

2. Season the beef with the salt and pepper.

3. Sweat the onions in hot oil. Add the red, green, and Anaheim peppers and cook until almost tender. Add the garlic and cook it until an aroma is apparent.

4. Add the meat. Sauté it until lightly seared.

5. Add the spices and sauté briefly. Add the tomato purée, beef stock, and beer. Mix them together with the meat.

6. Bring the chili to a simmer; cover the pan and braise the meat on the stove in a moderate oven until it is very tender to the bite.

7. Add the tomato concassé and the cooked beans; heat the chili thoroughly. Adjust the consistency. Adjust the seasoning with salt and pepper to taste.

8. Garnish each serving with chopped onions, grated cheese, and chopped cilantro.

VARIATIONS

Cincinnati Chili: *Include one or more of the following: cinnamon, allspice, nutmeg, ginger, clove, mace, coriander, cardamom, or mustard to taste.*

Two-way: *Serve the chili over spaghetti.*

Three-way: *Spaghetti, chili, Cheddar cheese.*

Four-way: *Spaghetti, chili, Cheddar cheese, chopped onions.*

Five-way: *Beans, spaghetti, chili, Cheddar cheese, chopped onions.*

Use pinto, kidney, black beans, or a combination of any cooked beans. Different types of beans should be cooked separately as they cook at different times and black beans will color other beans.

Chipotle, ancho, or other chilies may be added.

Serve over rice or with cornbread.

TECHNIQUE
Stewing (pages 394-397)
Soaking beans (page 236)
Working with chilies (page 227)
Mashing garlic to a paste (page 225)
Tomato concassé (page 226)

RECIPE
Brown Veal Stock (page 478)

Carving corned beef.

This is traditionally served with horseradish sauce.

Corned beef remaining from this dish can be used to prepare red flannel hash, page 667, or reuben sandwiches, page 686

TECHNIQUE
Simmering (pages 386-388)
Carving (pages 355-357)

RECIPE
White Beef Stock (page 480)

Corned Beef with Cabbage and Boiled Vegetables

Yield: 12 to 14 servings

Corned beef brisket, trimmed	1 each	1 each
Water or White Beef Stock	2 quarts	2 liters
Green cabbage, cut into wedges	3 heads	3 heads
Carrots, 3-inch pieces, cut on the bias	2 pounds	900 grams
Turnips, peeled, halved or quartered	2 pounds	900 grams
Onions, small whole	2 pounds	900 grams
Beets, small	2 pounds	900 grams
Potatoes, small, peeled, halved, or quartered	24 each	24 each

1. Split the brisket along the natural seam into two pieces.
2. Cover the meat with water or stock, bring to a boil, and simmer until meat is tender (approximately 3 hours).
3. Cook beets with skins on until tender, in boiling water; reserve water, peel, cut, return to cooking liquid, and keep warm.
4. Cook remaining vegetables in corned beef stock until tender; keep warm.

Boiled dinners appear in numerous cuisines. This version could be made with a combination of fish or cured meats.

A sharp sauce, such as the one here, is typical. You might prefer to offer a selection of condiments such as mustards or horseradish.

TECHNIQUE
Simmering (pages 386-388)
Peeling tongue (page 269)

RECIPES
White Beef Stock (page 480)
Sachet d'Epices (page 475)
Béchamel (page 518)

New England Boiled Dinner

Yield: 25 servings

Corned beef brisket	10 pounds	4.5 kilograms
Beef tongue	2 pounds	900 grams
White Beef Stock	1 gallon	3.75 liters
Sachet d'Epices	1 each	1 each
Vegetable garnish, per serving		
Red Bliss potatoes	50 each	50 each
Green cabbage, cut into wedges	50 each	50 each
Pearl onions	50 each	50 each
Carrots, tourné	50 each	50 each
Parsnips, tourné	50 each	50 each
Rutabaga, tourné	50 each	50 each
Beets, tourné	50 each	50 each
Green beans, cut in 2-inch lengths	5 ounces	140 grams

(Recipe continued on facing page)

Horseradish Sauce

Béchamel	1 ¹/₂ quarts	1.5 liters
Heavy cream	12 fluid ounces	360 milliliters
Horseradish, grated to taste	6 ounces	170 grams

1. Place the beef and tongue in a pot with enough cold stock to cover them. Bring the stock to a slow simmer.

2. Add the sachet; continue to simmer the liquid gently for approximately 3 hours or until the meats are very tender. Remove the meats; keep them warm and moist.

3. Cook the vegetables separately in the stock or reserved cooking liquid.

4. Combine the ingredients for the sauce and heat the mixture.

5. Peel the tongue. Slice the meats and serve them with the vegetables and sauce.

Veal Scaloppine Marsala

Yield: 10 servings

Veal top round or loin	3 pounds	1.3 kilogram
Flour, seasoned	as needed	as needed
Butter	3 ounces	85 grams
Shallots, minced	4 each	4 each
Marsala, dry	10 fluid ounces	300 milliliters
Jus de Veau Lié	10 fluid ounces	300 milliliters
Butter	4 ounces	115 grams
Salt to taste	¹/₂ teaspoon	¹/₂ teaspoon
Pepper to taste	¹/₄ teaspoon	¹/₄ teaspoon

Adding marsala to finish the sauce.

1. Cut veal into scaloppine. Flatten veal with a mallet to an even thickness.

2. Dredge veal in flour and sauté on both sides in butter until lightly browned.

3. When veal is done, remove from pan and keep warm.

4. Add shallots to pan and sauté until translucent.

5. Add wine and reduce to one-half.

6. Add jus and reduce until sauce consistency is reached.

7. Remove from heat and finish with butter. Season.

8. Serve sauce over the veal.

Cut the scaloppini into 2-ounce (60-gram) portions.

TECHNIQUE
Cutting and pounding cutlets (page 261)
Sautéing (pages 358-362)

RECIPES
Jus de Veau Lié (page 516)

V A R I A T I O N S

Pork Scaloppine Marsala: Cut pork tenderloins into 2-ounce (60-gram) portions and prepare in the same manner.

Chicken Marsala: Lightly pound boneless, skinless breasts (¹/₂ per portion) to an even thickness. Prepare as for veal.

The veal is allowed to reheat briefly in the sauce.

The traditional accompaniment to this dish is roësti potatoes, page 640.

DRY-SAUTÉ TECHNIQUE

1. Heat pan, remove from heat, and spray with vegetable oil; wipe out excess.

2. Place pan back on heat; add meat.

3. Allow meat to sauté until moisture appears on its surface; stir to loosen.

4. When meat is done, remove; finish cooking process.

TECHNIQUE
Sautéing (pages 358-362)
Preparing émincé (page 261)

RECIPE
Demi-Glace (page 514)

Swiss-Style Shredded Veal

Yield: 10 servings

Veal top round	*3 pounds*	*1.3 kilograms*
Salt to taste	*¹/₂ teaspoon*	*¹/₂ teaspoon*
Pepper to taste	*¹/₄ teaspoon*	*¹/₄ teaspoon*
Vegetable oil as needed	*2 fluid ounces*	*60 milliliters*
Flour as needed	*3 ounces*	*85 grams*
Shallots, minced	*¹/₂ ounce*	*15 grams*
Mushrooms, sliced	*1 pound*	*450 grams*
Dry white wine	*5 fluid ounces*	*150 milliliters*
Demi-Glace	*10 ounces*	*285 grams*
Brandy	*1 fluid ounce*	*30 milliliters*
Lemon juice to taste	*1 teaspoon*	*1 teaspoon*

1. Cut the veal into émincé; blot dry and season with salt and pepper.

2. Heat the oil in a sauteuse; dredge the veal and sauté until just cooked through. Remove the veal and keep warm. Pour off any excess oil.

3. Add shallots and mushrooms to the pan. Sauté until the mushroom juices cook away.

4. Deglaze the pan with white wine.

5. Add the demi-glace, heavy cream, and any juices released by the veal. Simmer until reduced to a good sauce consistency. Degrease if necessary.

6. Add the brandy; flame. Season the sauce to taste with lemon juice, salt, and pepper.

7. Return the veal to the pan and reheat briefly. Do not allow the sauce to boil. Serve.

Veal Cordon Bleu

Yield: 10 servings

Veal top round	*3 pounds*	*1.3 kilograms*
Ham, cut very thin	*6 ounces*	*170 grams*
Gruyère, cut very thin	*6 ounces*	*170 grams*
Flour	*as needed*	*as needed*
Egg wash	*as needed*	*as needed*
White bread crumbs, fresh	*as needed*	*as needed*
Oil	*as needed*	*as needed*
Butter	*1 ounce*	*30 grams*
Shallots, minced	*2 ounces*	*60 grams*
Mushrooms, small, sliced	*6 ounces*	*170 grams*
White wine	*4 fluid ounces*	*120 milliliters*
Jus de Veau Lié	*1 1/2 pints*	*720 milliliters*
Heavy cream	*4 fluid ounces*	*120 milliliters*
Parsley, chopped	*1 tablespoon*	*1 tablespoon*
Salt to taste	*1/2 teaspoon*	*1/2 teaspoon*
Pepper to taste	*1/4 teaspoon*	*1/4 teaspoon*

Pounding veal cutlets.

The term cordon bleu *has its origins in a society of knights established by Henri III of France in 1578.*

This dish is one of many taught to students at the Cordon Bleu cooking schools.

TECHNIQUE
Cutting and pounding cutlets (page 261)
Making bread crumbs (page 237)
Pan-frying (pages 364-367)

RECIPE
Jus de Veau Lié (page 516)

1. Cut the veal into 5- to 6-ounce (140- to 170-gram) cutlets. Flatten veal cutlets with a meat mallet.

2. Place ham and cheese together; fold in thirds.

3. Place ham roll in center of the veal cutlet, fold meat around the ham, and chill.

4. Dredge the veal in flour, dip in egg wash, and roll in bread crumbs. Allow to rest in the refrigerator for 30 to 60 minutes.

5. Pan-fry veal in oil until well browned on both sides, about 3 minutes on each side. Transfer to a rack on a sheet pan.

6. Finish veal in a 350°F (175°C) oven, until an internal temperature of 150°F (66°C) is reached.

7. To make sauce, sauté shallots in butter, add mushrooms, and continue to sauté.

8. Add wine and reduce by one-half, add jus, and simmer 15 to 20 minutes.

9. Finish with heavy cream, add parsley and season. Portion sauce on a plate; slice veal in 3 pieces on the bias; fan out on sauce.

Allow the matignon to cook long enough to develop flavor.

Poêléing is sometimes referred to as "butter-roasting."

TECHNIQUE
Poêléing (pages 358-360)
Butterflying meats (page 266)
Fresh herbs (page 224)
Mashing garlic (page 225)

RECIPES
Matignon (page 472)
Brown Veal Stock (page 476)

Veal Shoulder Poêlé

Yield: 10 servings

Veal shoulder roast	*4 pounds*	*1.8 kilograms*
Rosemary, fresh, chopped	*¼ teaspoon*	*¼ teaspoon*
Basil, fresh, chopped	*½ teaspoon*	*½ teaspoon*
Thyme, fresh, chopped	*½ teaspoon*	*½ teaspoon*
Marjoram, fresh, chopped	*½ teaspoon*	*½ teaspoon*
Garlic cloves, mashed to a paste	*2 each*	*2 each*
Salt to taste	*½ teaspoon*	*½ teaspoon*
Pepper to taste	*¼ teaspoon*	*¼ teaspoon*
Bacon slices, diced	*3 each*	*3 each*
Butter	*½ ounce*	*15 grams*
Matignon, fine dice	*4 ounces*	*115 grams*
Dry white wine	*8 fluid ounces*	*240 milliliters*
Bay leaves	*2 each*	*2 each*
Brown Veal Stock	*8 fluid ounces*	*240 milliliters*
Cornstarch as needed	*1 tablespoon*	*1 tablespoon*

1. Trim and butterfly the roast.

2. Mix chopped herbs and garlic together. Spread them over the veal, shape into a roast, and tie. Season with salt and pepper.

3. Render bacon in butter, add matignon and sauté lightly.

4. Place veal in pot on top of matignon and baste with some of the fat.

5. Cover pot and pôelé in 300°F (150°C) oven, basting every 20 minutes; remove lid for the last 30 minutes to allow veal to brown.

6. Check for doneness; meat should have an internal temperature of 140°F (60°C) and be tender when pierced with a fork. When done, remove veal and keep warm.

7. Add wine, bay leaves, and stock to pan; simmer 20 minutes. Degrease if necessary.

8. Thicken with diluted cornstarch, reduce more if necessary.

9. Degrease sauce and season with salt and pepper to taste.

10. Slice the veal and serve with the sauce.

Veal Blanquette

Yield: 10 servings

Veal breast, boned, cut in a large dice	*4 pounds*	*1.8 kilograms*
Water, cold	*as needed*	*as needed*
Veal Stock	*2 quarts*	*2 liters*
Sachet d'Epices	*1 each*	*1 each*
White Roux	*4 ounces*	*115 grams*
Mushroom caps (fluted if desired)	*1 ¹/₂ pounds*	*680 grams*
Butter	*1 ounce*	*30 grams*
Lemon juice as needed	*2 tablespoons*	*2 tablespoons*
Egg yolks	*2 each*	*2 each*
Heavy cream	*8 fluid ounces*	*240 milliliters*
Pearl onions	*20 each*	*20 each*
Salt to taste	*¹/₂ teaspoon*	*¹/₂ teaspoon*
Pepper to taste	*¹/₄ teaspoon*	*¹/₄ teaspoon*

The finished blanquette.

TECHNIQUE
Stewing (pages 394-397)
Liaisons (page 240)

RECIPES
Veal Stock (page 480)
Sachet d'Epices (page 475)
White Roux (page 473)

1. Cover the veal with cold water and blanch it. Drain and rinse the veal.

2. Combine the veal with the stock; simmer the veal until it is tender, about 1¹/₂ hours. Add the sachet during the final half-hour of cooking time. Remove and discard the sachet and reduce the stock briefly.

3. Combine the roux with the stew; simmer the mixture until it is thickened.

4. Stew the mushrooms and pearl onions in butter until they are tender. Add the lemon juice, salt, and pepper to taste; reserve.

5. At service, heat the blanquette to just below a boil. Combine the egg yolks and cream for a liaison. Temper the mixture and add it to the blanquette. Simmer the sauce until it is thickened, but do not boil it.

6. Add the reserved mushrooms and pearl onions. Adjust the seasoning with salt and pepper to taste.

VARIATIONS

Chicken Blanquette: Substitute 4 pounds (1.8 kilograms) of chicken for the veal. Include fresh thyme in the sachet.

Lamb Blanquette: Substitute 4 pounds (1.8 kilograms) lamb for the veal. Include fresh rosemary in the sachet.

The roast may be boneless, if preferred.

Boulangère refers to dishes baked in the baker's oven, not necessarily dishes involving bread, as might be expected. Traditionally, in France, on wash day (usually Monday), villagers would prepare their dinner and leave it at the local boulangerie to be baked off in the oven. This tradition of having special wash-day meals seems to be common throughout the world.

If desired, stud the lamb with rosemary leaves along with the garlic.

TECHNIQUE
Roasting (page 349)
Tying a roast (page 262)
Carving (pages 355-357)

RECIPES
Brown Veal Stock (page 478)
Jus de Veau Lié (page 516)
Mirepoix (page 472)

Roast Leg of Lamb Boulangère

Yield: 16 servings

Lamb leg, tied	10 pounds	4.5 kilograms
Salt to taste	1 teaspoon	1 teaspoon
Pepper to taste	1 teaspoon	1 teaspoon
Garlic cloves, slivered	2 each	2 each
Idaho potatoes, sliced $^1/_8$-inch thick	4 pounds	1.8 kilograms
Onions, sliced thin	1 pound	450 grams
Brown Veal Stock, hot, as needed	20 fluid ounces	600 milliliters
Jus de Veau Lié, hot	1 quart	1 liter

1. Season the lamb with salt and pepper to taste; stud it with the slivered garlic.

2. Roast the lamb for $1^1/_2$ hours. Remove from pan; pour off grease.

3. Layer the sliced potatoes and onions in the roasting pan. Season the layers with salt and pepper to taste. Add enough stock to moisten well.

4. Place the lamb on the potatoes. Continue to roast to an internal temperature of 130 to 135°F (55 to 57°C). The potatoes should be tender.

5. Let the leg rest before carving it.

6. Serve the sliced lamb on a bed of potatoes. Serve it with the hot jus.

Roast Leg of Lamb with Mint Sauce

Yield: 10 servings

Salt herbs (see note)	2 tablespoons	2 tablespoons
Lamb leg, boneless, rolled and tied	6 pounds	2.7 kilograms
Garlic cloves, mashed to paste	3 each	3 each
Mirepoix, medium dice	4 ounces	115 grams
Brown Veal Stock	1 $^1/_2$ quarts	1.5 liters
Salt to taste	$^1/_2$ teaspoon	$^1/_2$ teaspoon
Mint, chopped	1 tablespoon	1 tablespoon
Arrowroot or cornstarch, diluted	as needed	as needed

For salt herbs, combine 2 tablespoons of salt with 1 tablespoon each of rosemary and thyme, 3 bay leaves, and 1 teaspoon of pepper. Let rest 12 hours before using.

(Recipe continued on facing page)

1. Combine all ingredients for spice mixture; grind to a fine powder in a blender.

2. Rub roast with seasoning mixture and garlic paste; marinate overnight.

3. Rub roast with oil; place on a wire rack in a roast pan.

4. Roast in a 325 to 350°F (160 to 175°C) oven, to an internal temperature of 110°F (40°C); add mirepoix.

5. Remove roast at 135°F (55°C); allow to rest.

6. To make mint sauce, clarify fat in roasting pan, then discard all fat.

7. Add mirepoix, stock, and mint; simmer until reduced by one-third; degrease.

8. Thicken with arrowroot, strain through a fine chinoise, and adjust seasonings.

9. Remove string, slice meat against the grain, and serve with jus.

Mediterranean in origin, mint is an aromatic herb which complements the flavor of the lamb.

Grilled Lamb Chops with Mint Sauce

Yield: 10 servings

Double lamb rib chops	*20 each*	*20 each*
Olive oil, as needed	*2 fluid ounces*	*60 milliliters*
Salt, to taste	*1/2 teaspoon*	*1/2 teaspoon*
Pepper, to taste	*1/4 teaspoon*	*1/4 teaspoon*
Jus de Veau Lié	*20 fluid ounces*	*600 milliliters*
Vegetables, brunoise, blanched (carrot, celery, leek, onion)	*1 1/4 pounds*	*570 grams*
Mint leaves, chiffonade	*1 ounce*	*30 grams*

This could be prepared as a rack, to serve two, if you prefer.

TECHNIQUE
Cutting steaks and chops (page 266)
Frenching a rack of lamb (page 262)
Basic knife cuts (pages 217-223)

RECIPE
Jus de Veau Lié (page 516)

1. Pound the lamb chops lightly to shape them to an even thickness.

2. Season with salt and pepper. Brush the chops with oil; grill the chops to desired doneness. Hold the chops on a sizzler platter.

3. Heat the jus to reduce it slightly. Add the brunoise vegetables and chiffonade of mint. Adjust the seasoning with salt and pepper.

4. Serré the chops with the sauce and serve.

Use stew meat from the leg or shoulder.

Additional vegetables such as fresh peas, parsnips, and rutabagas might be added. Roasted garlic, rosemary, thyme, or other seasonings could also be included.

TECHNIQUE
Stewing (pages 394-397)
Basic Knife cuts (pages 217-223)
Fluting (page 220)
Tomato concassé (page 226)

RECIPES
Brown Veal Stock (page 476)
Brown Sauce (page 514)
Sachet d'Epices (page 475)

Lamb Stew

Yield: 10 servings

Lamb, cubed	*4 pounds*	*1.8 kilograms*
Vegetable oil, as needed	*4 fluid ounces*	*120 milliliters*
Onions, chopped	*6 ounces*	*170 grams*
Tomato paste	*2 ounces*	*60 grams*
Brown Veal Stock or red wine	*8 fluid ounces*	*240 milliliters*
Brown Sauce	*20 fluid ounces*	*600 milliliters*
Sachet d'Epices	*1 each*	*1 each*
Carrots, tourné	*20 each*	*20 each*
Potatoes, tourné	*20 each*	*20 each*
Celery, tourné	*20 each*	*20 each*
Turnips, tourné	*20 each*	*20 each*
Mushroom caps (fluted if desired)	*20 each*	*20 each*
Tomato concassé	*8 ounces*	*225 grams*
Salt to taste	*1/2 teaspoon*	*1/2 teaspoon*
Pepper to taste	*1/2 teaspoon*	*1/2 teaspoon*

1. Brown the lamb on all sides in hot oil.

2. Remove meat, add onions, and sauté until translucent.

3. Add tomato paste; sauté 2 to 3 minutes.

4. Add stock, sauce, and sachet; bring to a simmer.

5. Add meat; cover.

6. Braise in 350°F (175°C) oven until fork-tender.

7. About 20 minutes before done, add carrots, potatoes, celery, and turnips.

8. About 5 minutes before done, add mushrooms and tomato concassé.

9. When finished, degrease the sauce.

10. Adjust consistency and seasonings with salt and pepper to taste.

Braised Lamb Shanks

Yield: 10 servings

Lamb shanks, well-trimmed	*10 each*	*10 each*
Salt to taste	*1/2 teaspoon*	*1/2 teaspoon*
Pepper to taste	*1/4 teaspoon*	*1/4 teaspoon*
Vegetable oil as needed	*4 fluid ounces*	*120 milliliters*
Mirepoix	*1 pound*	*450 grams*
Garlic cloves, mashed to a paste	*3 each*	*3 each*
Tomato paste	*1 ounce*	*30 grams*
Dry white wine (optional)	*1 pint*	*480 milliliters*
Brown Sauce	*2 quarts*	*2 liters*
Sachet d'Epices	*1 each*	*1 each*

Allow the mirepoix and tomato paste to cook long enough to develop their flavors.

1. Season the lamb with the salt and pepper. Sear it in hot oil on all sides and remove it.

2. Add the mirepoix to the same oil and caramelize it.

3. Add the garlic, tomato paste, and wine; reduce the sauce.

4. Add the brown sauce and reduce it slightly.

5. Add the lamb shanks and sachet and adjust the seasoning with salt and pepper to taste. Cover the pan and braise the lamb until it is fork tender, about 1 1/4 hours.

6. Remove the lamb shanks. Strain the sauce, degrease it, adjust the consistency, and return the meat to the sauce.

VARIATION

Lamb Shanks Printanière: Garnish the lamb with tournéed carrots, turnips, potatoes, glazed pearl onions, peas, and green beans. The vegetables and lamb should be prepared separately.

Select lamb shanks that average 1 pound (450 grams) each.

If you wish, prepare a brown lamb sauce as directed on page 514, using a brown lamb stock.

TECHNIQUE
Braising (pages 391-394)
Mashing Garlic to a Paste (page 225)

RECIPES
Mirepoix (page 472)
Brown Sauce (page 514)
Sachet d'Epices (page 475)

Add dried and fresh fruits to the sauce.

Dry-sautéeing is explained in a note on page 536.

Pork chops, venison, game birds, duck, turkey, or goose will all work well with this sauce.

To make pumpkin pasta, sauté 4 ounces (115 grams) of puréed pumpkin until it is reduced to 3 ounces (85 grams). Cool and add to Basic Pasta Dough, page 648.

TECHNIQUE
Sautéing (page 358-362)
Basic knife cuts (pages 217-223)
Working with dried fruits and vegitables (pages 235-236)

RECIPES
Chicken Stock (page 480)
Demi-Glace (page 514)

Sautéed Medallions of Pork with Warm Fruits

Yield: 10 servings

Pork loin, trimmed	*4 pounds*	*1.8 kilograms*
Red Delicious apples, tourné or large dice	*5 ounces*	*140 grams*
Bartlett pears, tourné or large dice	*4 ounces*	*115 grams*
Dry white wine	*1 quart*	*1 liter*
Cherries, dried	*1 ³/₄ ounces*	*50 grams*
Dried apricots	*3 ¹/₂ ounces*	*100 grams*
Chicken Stock, hot	*1 quart*	*1 liter*
Demi-Glace	*1 quart*	*1 liter*
Apple brandy	*1 ³/₄ fluid ounces*	*50 milliliters*
For service		
Pumpkin pasta	*1 ¹/₂ pounds*	*680 grams*
Haricots verts, steamed	*1 ¹/₄ pounds*	*570 grams*

1. Cut the pork into 2-ounce (60-gram) medallions. Shape them in cheese-cloth.

2. Poach the apple and pear in the white wine until tender. Let cool in the poaching liquid.

3. Reconstitute the dried fruits in stock. Strain and reserve the stock.

4. At service, season the pork and sauté it in a properly seasoned or a non-stick sauté pan. Remove the pork from the pan and keep it warm.

5. Deglaze the pan with a small amount of the reserved stock. Add the fruits and heat well. Add the demi-glace and the brandy and flame the sauce to burn off some of the alcohol.

6. Return the pork to the sauté pan to coat lightly with the sauce.

7. Serve the pork on a bed of pumpkin pasta with the haricots verts. Coat the pork with the sauce and garnish with the fruit.

Pan-fried Breaded Pork Cutlets

Yield: 10 servings

Pork loin, trimmed	*4 pounds*	*1.8 kilograms*
Flour	*as needed*	*as needed*
Salt to taste	*$1/2$ teaspoon*	*$1/2$ teaspoon*
Pepper to taste	*$1/4$ teaspoon*	*$1/4$ teaspoon*
Oregano	*1 teaspoon*	*1 teaspoon*
Egg wash	*6 fluid ounces*	*180 milliliters*
Bread crumbs, dry	*as needed*	*as needed*
Vegetable oil	*8 fluid ounces*	*240 milliliters*
Lard	*8 ounces*	*225 grams*
Lemon wedges	*10 each*	*10 each*

1. Cut the pork loin into cutlets and pound them to an even thickness.

2. Season the flour with salt, pepper, and oregano.

3. Dredge the cutlets in flour and dip in egg wash.

4. Dredge in dry bread crumbs; allow cutlets to rest 30 minutes in refrigerator.

5. Pan-fry the cutlets in oil and lard until lightly browned. Drain on absorbent paper.

6. Serve with a lemon wedge.

Cutting chops from a pork loin.

The pork cutlets should weigh 4 to 5 ounces (115 to 140 grams) each.

Other dried herbs may be used to season the flour or the bread crumbs.

If you prefer, you may delete the lard and fry the pork cutlets in vegetable oil only.

TECHNIQUE
Cutting and pounding cutlets (page 261)
Pan-frying (pages 364-367)
Making bread crumbs (page 237)

545

Thyme and rosemary add flavor to the jus.

For additional flavor in the jus lié save the bones from the pork loin and use them as a rack to roast the loin.

Tomato paste may be added to mirepoix and browned if a darker gravy is desired. One ounce (30 grams) should be sufficient.

TECHNIQUE
Roasting (page 349)
Tying a Roast (page 262)
Slurries (page 238)
Carving pages 355-357)

RECIPES
Mirepoix (page 472)
Brown Veal Stock (page 478)

Pork Roast with Jus Lié

Yield: 10 servings

Pork loin roast, boneless	*3 1/2 pounds*	*1.3 kilograms*
Salt to taste	*1/2 teaspoon*	*1/2 teaspoon*
Black peppercorns, coarse-ground	*1/2 teaspoon*	*1/2 teaspoon*
Garlic cloves, mashed to paste	*2 each*	*2 each*
Rosemary sprigs	*1 each*	*1 each*
Thyme sprigs	*2 each*	*2 each*
Vegetable oil as needed	*3 fluid ounces*	*90 milliliters*
Mirepoix, medium dice	*4 ounces*	*115 grams*
Dry white wine (optional)	*4 fluid ounces*	*120 milliliters*
Bay leaves	*2 each*	*2 each*
Brown Veal Stock	*1 quart*	*1 liter*
Arrowroot as needed, diluted	*2 tablespoons*	*2 tablespoons*
Salt to taste	*1/2 teaspoon*	*1/2 teaspoon*
Pepper to taste	*1/4 teaspoon*	*1/4 teaspoon*

1. Season pork loin with salt, pepper, garlic, herbs, and spices; tie. Sear the pork in the oil until browned.

2. Place pork loin on a rack in a roasting pan. Add the mirepoix.

3. Roast at 325°F (160°C) to an internal temperature of 160°F (80°C); remove roast and allow to rest. This should take 30 to 45 minutes.

4. To make stock, clarify fat from drippings in the roasting pan; pour off all fat.

5. Deglaze pan with wine, add stock and bay leaves, and simmer until reduced by half; degrease.

6. Mix arrowroot and water, and whisk into simmering sauce; return to a simmer.

7. Strain through a fine chinoise and adjust seasonings.

8. Remove string, slice pork against the grain, and serve with jus lié.

Broiled Pork Chop

Yield: 10 servings

Pork chops, thick-cut	*10 each*	*10 each*
Salt to taste	*1/2 teaspoon*	*1/2 teaspoon*
Pepper to taste	*1/4 teaspoon*	*1/4 teaspoon*
Vegetable oil	*as needed*	*as needed*
Maître d'Hotel Butter	*10 ounces*	*285 grams*

(Recipe continued on facing page)

1. Season pork chops and dip in oil.

2. Broil on medium heat broiler until done.

3. Turn at 45-degree angles during broiling to achieve grill marks.

4. Serve with a slice of compound butter.

VARIATION

Teriyaki-Style Pork Chop: Marinate the chops in the Teriyaki Marinade, page 434. Brush the chops with the marinade as they broil.

Use a marinade or a spice blend to give a special flavor to the chops, if desired. Or, use one of the variations for the Maître d' Hotel Butter, on page 522.

TECHNIQUE
Broiling (pages 344-349)
Cutting steaks and chops (page 266)

RECIPE
Maître d'Hotel Butter (page 522)

Pork Goulash

Yield: 10 servings

Pork shoulder, boneless	*3 pounds*	*1.3 kilograms*
Hungarian paprika	*3 tablespoons*	*3 tablespoons*
Vegetable oil or lard	*3 fluid ounces*	*90 milliliters*
Salt to taste	*1/2 teaspoon*	*1/2 teaspoon*
Pepper to taste	*1/4 teaspoon*	*1/4 teaspoon*
Onions, diced	*3 pounds*	*1.3 kilograms*
Garlic cloves, minced	*2 each*	*2 each*
Dry white wine	*8 fluid ounces*	*240 milliliters*
Brown Veal Stock	*1 pint*	*480 milliliters*
Jus de Veau Lié	*1 pint*	*480 milliliters*
Sachet d'Epices, *plus*	*1 each*	*1 each*
Caraway seeds	*1 teaspoon*	*1 teaspoon*
Marjoram leaves, chopped	*1/2 teaspoon*	*1/2 teaspoon*
Savory leaves, chopped	*1/2 teaspoon*	*1/2 teaspoon*
Lemon zest	*1 teaspoon*	*1 teaspoon*
Sour cream	*8 ounces*	*240 milliliters*

1. Cut the pork into large cubes. Rub pork with paprika and season with salt and pepper.

2. Brown pork in hot oil or lard; remove.

3. Add onions, cover, and sweat lightly. Add garlic and cook briefly

4. Add wine and deglaze; reduce slightly.

5. Return pork, add stock and sachet; bring to a simmer.

6. Cover and braise at 350°F (175°C) until meat is tender, about 1 1/4 hours.

7. When meat is done, degrease and check consistency of sauce. Remove sachet and discard.

8. Add lemon zest and adjust seasonings with salt and pepper to taste.

9. Serve each portion garnished with sour cream.

Add some lemon zest as a final flavoring ingredient.

Goulash is traditionally served with spaetzle or bread dumplings.

You may replace the pork with beef or veal.

Placing the caraway seeds, marjoram, and savory in the sachet will make a smoother sauce.

TECHNIQUE
Braising (pages 391-394)
Basic knife cuts (pages 217-223)
Fresh herbs (page 229)
Zesting citrus fruits (page 231)

RECIPES
Brown Veal Stock (page 478)
Jus de Veau Lié (page 516)
Sachet d'Epices (page 475)

Rabbit, ready to disjoint.

Stewed Rabbit with Prunes

Yield: 10 servings

Rabbits	*3 to 4 each*	*3 to 4 each*
Flour	*6 ounces*	*170 grams*
Lard	*2 ounces*	*60 grams*
Shallots, minced	*2 ounces*	*60 grams*
Mirepoix, fine dice	*1 ¹/₂ pounds*	*680 grams*
White wine	*12 fluid ounces*	*360 milliliters*
Brown Sauce	*12 fluid ounces*	*360 milliliters*
Salt to taste	*¹/₂ teaspoon*	*¹/₂ teaspoon*
Pepper to taste	*¹/₄ teaspoon*	*¹/₄ teaspoon*
Thyme sprig	*1 each*	*1 each*
Bay leaves	*2 each*	*2 each*
Arrowroot, diluted	*as needed*	*as needed*
Prunes, pitted	*1 pound*	*450 grams*
Red currant jelly	*6 ounces*	*170 grams*

This recipe could be prepared with a chicken cut into eighths, if you prefer.

The loin pieces of the rabbit (or chicken breast) will cook more quickly than the legs. Be sure to check them periodically and remove them once they are fully tender.

TECHNIQUE
Disjointing a rabbit (pages 277-278)
Braising (pages 391-394)
Slurries (page 238)

RECIPES
Mirepoix (page 472)
Brown Sauce (page 514)

1. Clean the rabbits thoroughly. Remove all sinews and tendons. Cut each rabbit into pieces. Reserve the trim meat and bones.

2. Dredge the rabbit pieces in flour. Shake off the excess.

3. Sauté the rabbit in hot lard in a brazier until it is light brown. Remove it and keep it warm.

4. Add the shallots and mirepoix to the pot along with the reserved trim meat and bones. Sauté briefly.

5. Add the wine, brown sauce, salt, pepper, and herbs with the reserved rabbit. Bring the mixture to a boil.

6. Cover the pot and braise the rabbit in a 300°F (150°C) oven until it is tender. Remove the rabbit, moisten with a little braising liquid, and keep warm.

7. Strain and skim the sauce. Return to the heat, simmer, and degrease.

8. Adjust the sauce consistency with the diluted arrowroot if necessary.

9. Add the prunes and currant jelly and simmer the sauce for 5 minutes. Adjust the seasoning to taste.

10. Serve the rabbit with the sauce.

Roast Venison with Mustard Sauce

Yield: 10 servings

Venison roast, from loin or leg, boneless, tied	*4 pounds*	*1.8 kilograms*
Salt, to taste	*¹/₂ teaspoon*	*¹/₂ teaspoon*
Pepper, to taste	*¹/₂ teaspoon*	*¹/₂ teaspoon*
Vegetable oil, as needed	*2 fluid ounces*	*60 milliliters*
Jus de Veau Lié	*1 ¹/₄ pints*	*600 milliliters*
Heavy cream, reduced	*8 fluid ounces*	*240 milliliters*
White wine	*2 fluid ounces*	*60 milliliters*
Creole mustard	*2 ounces*	*60 grams*

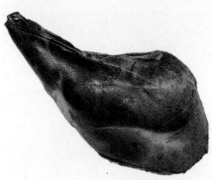

The leg of venison is often referred to as the haunch.

1. Season the roast with the salt and pepper. Sear it on all sides in hot oil.

2. Roast at about 140°F (60°C) to the desired doneness.

3. Let the roast rest for 15 minutes before carving it.

4. To prepare the sauce, heat the rendered juices over direct heat. Pour off the fat.

5. Deglaze the roasting pan with the white wine; stir it well to release the fond. Add the jus and simmer.

6. Strain the sauce into a saucepan. Add the heavy cream and mustard; simmer until it has reduced.

7. Adjust the seasoning to taste with salt and pepper.

8. Carve the roast; serve each portion with approximately 2 ounces (60 milliliters) of sauce.

Serve the roast with spaetzle or noodles. Braised red cabbage would work well with this.

TECHNIQUE
Roasting (page 349)
Carving (pages 355-357)

RECIPE
Jus de Veau Lié (page 516)

VARIATIONS

Roast Venison with Garlic Glaze: Mix together 1 part glace de viande and 2 parts puréed roasted garlic. Spread the glaze on the roast during the final part of roasting. Serve with mushroom sauce, page 514.

Roast Venison with Marsala Sauce: Serve with marsala sauce, page 514.

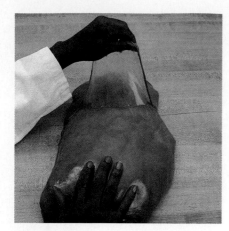

Cleaning liver.

A good portion size for this dish is 6 to 8 ounces (170 to 225 grams).

This dish may be garnished with crisp fried onions.

A tossed green salad is a good accompaniment to this dish.

TECHNIQUE
Sautéing (pages 358-362)
Basic knife cuts (pages 217-223)

Calf's Liver with Bacon Cream Sauce

Yield: 10 servings

Bacon Cream Sauce		
Bacon, diced	1 ¼ pounds	570 grams
Onions, chopped fine	10 ounces	285 grams
Heavy cream	40 fluid ounces	1.2 liters
Calves' livers, sliced	4 pounds	1.8 kilograms
Salt to taste	½ teaspoon	½ teaspoon
Pepper to taste	¼ teaspoon	¼ teaspoon
Vegetable oil or rendered bacon fat	as needed	as needed

1. Sauté the bacon until it is crisp; remove and drain it. Strain the bacon fat and reserve.

2. Sauté the onions in the strained bacon fat until they are lightly browned, drain the excess fat, and add the cooked bacon.

3. Add the heavy cream and reduce to sauce consistency. Keep the sauce hot until needed.

4. Season the liver with the salt and pepper.

5. Sauté the liver in the oil or rendered bacon fat until it is medium-rare and browned on both sides.

6. Serve the liver with 2 ounces (60 grams) of sauce per serving.

Braised Oxtails

Yield: 12 servings

Oil as needed	2 fluid ounces	60 milliliters
Oxtails, trimmed, cut in pieces	10 pounds	4.5 kilograms
Mirepoix	1 pound	450 grams
Dry red wine	1 quart	1 liter
Thyme, ground	1 teaspoon	1 teaspoon
Bay leaf	2 each	2 each
Peppercorns	1 teaspoon	1 teaspoon
Garlic cloves, minced	3 each	3 each
Parsley stems	4 each	4 each
Tomato purée	6 fluid ounces	180 milliliters
Brown Veal Stock, as needed	1 quart	1 liter
Garnish		
Carrots, tourné, cooked	48 each	48 each
Celeriac, tourné, cooked	48 each	48 each
White turnip, tourné, cooked	48 each	48 each
Rutabaga, tourné, cooked	48 each	48 each
Onion rings, fried	6 each	6 each

Oxtail.

1. Heat a large rondeau, add a small amount of oil, and sear oxtails until browned on all sides; remove and reserve.

2. Add mirepoix and caramelize. Add tomato purée; cook out for 2 to 3 minutes. Add wine, reduce by one-half, and add aromatics; return oxtails.

3. Add enough stock to cover meat halfway. Bring to a simmer, cover, and braise in a 300°F (150°C) oven until tender, turning occasionally during cooking.

4. When meat is tender, remove, cover, and keep warm. Strain and degrease sauce, and reserve fat.

5. Heat the carrots, celeriac, and turnips in reserved fat.

6. Serve the oxtails surrounded by the garnish and coated with the sauce. Top with onion rings.

To prepare onion rings, slice quartered onions thinly and separate them. Dredge in flour, shake off any excess, and deep-fry until crisp and deep brown.

TECHNIQUE
Braising (pages 391-394)
Basic knife cuts (pages 217-223)

RECIPES
Mirepoix (page 472)
Brown Veal Stock (page 478)

Use freshly ground meat for the best flavor.

Tomato purée, fennel seeds, rosemary, and basil are other seasoning ingredients that might be added.

When combining the ingredients, handle them gently. Be careful not to overmix or compress the mixture.

A combination of ground beef, pork, and veal may be used.

To hold the meatballs for service, dish them into a hotel pan and cover with hot stock or refrigerate.

TECHNIQUE
Basic knife cuts (pages 217-223)
Making bread crumbs (page 237)

Italian Meatballs

Yield: 10 servings

Onions, finely chopped	1 pound	450 grams
Celery, finely chopped	6 ounces	170 grams
Oil	2 fluid ounces	60 milliliters
Garlic, minced	2 teaspoons	2 teaspoons
Bread crumbs, fresh	6 ounces	170 grams
Milk, cold	10 fluid ounces	300 milliliters
Ground beef	4 $\frac{1}{2}$ pounds	2 kilograms
Eggs	3 each	3 each
Parmesan cheese, grated	1 ounce	30 grams
Parsley, finely chopped	$\frac{1}{2}$ ounce	15 grams
Oregano, minced	1 teaspoon	1 teaspoon
Salt to taste	$\frac{1}{2}$ teaspoon	$\frac{1}{2}$ teaspoon
Pepper to taste	$\frac{1}{4}$ teaspoon	$\frac{1}{4}$ teaspoon

1. Sauté onions and celery in oil. Add the garlic and sweat. Cool.

2. Combine bread and milk in large mixing bowl; mix well. Add the remaining ingredients, including the onions, and blend thoroughly.

3. Form into balls and roast at 350°F (175°C) for about 30 minutes.

VARIATIONS

Swedish Meatballs: Use ground veal; omit oregano. Season with nutmeg and serve in a cream sauce with leeks.

Italian Meat Loaf: Place mixture in a loaf pan and bake for about 1$\frac{1}{2}$ hours at 350°F (175°C).

Meat Loaf

Yield: 10 servings

White bread, small dice	6 ounces	170 grams
Milk as needed	8 fluid ounces	480 milliliters
Ground beef	3 $\frac{1}{2}$ pounds	1.6 kilograms
Onions, minced, sautéed	10 ounces	285 grams
Ketchup	6 ounces	180 grams
A-1 Steak Sauce	10 fluid ounces	300 milliliters
Salt to taste	$\frac{1}{2}$ teaspoon	$\frac{1}{2}$ teaspoon
Pepper to taste	$\frac{1}{4}$ teaspoon	$\frac{1}{4}$ teaspoon
Eggs	3 each	3 each
Bread crumbs, fresh	6 ounces	170 grams

(Recipe continued on facing page)

1. Place cubed bread into a mixing bowl. Add milk to soak the bread. Squeeze out and discard excess milk.

2. Add the remaining ingredients and mix gently.

3. Place in loaf pan or form into shape in a roasting pan.

4. Bake in a 350°F (175°C) oven until meat loaf is firm and evenly browned, approximately 1¹/₂ hours.

VARIATIONS

Asian Meat Loaf: Replace the A-1 Steak Sauce with 2 fluid ounces (60 milliliters) of soy sauce; add diced water chestnuts; replace half the bread with cooked rice.

Italian Meat Loaf: Substitute 1¹/₂ pounds (680 grams) sweet or hot Italian sausage for 1¹/₂ pounds (680 grams) ground beef. Add ¹/₂ ounce (15 grams) of chopped parsley.

For an American classic, serve with mashed potatoes and buttered peas and carrots. Or offer meat loaf sandwiches on white bread.

Glaze the meat loaf with ketchup in the final 20 minutes of roasting.

Lay parcooked bacon over the top of the meat loaf in the final 30 minutes of roasting.

This is a basic meat loaf. Additional seasonings, such as chopped parsley, oregano, sautéed garlic or green peppers, and chili powder can be included in the preparation.

TECHNIQUE
Basic knife cuts (pages 217-223)
Making bread crumbs (page 237)

Roast Beef Hash

Yield: 10 servings

Onions, chopped fine	6 ounces	170 grams
Celery, chopped fine	3 ounces	85 grams
Vegetable oil as needed	2 ounces	60 milliliters
Potatoes, cooked and diced	2 pounds	900 grams
Roast beef, cooked and chopped	2 pounds	900 grams
Salt to taste	¹/₂ teaspoon	¹/₂ teaspoon
Pepper to taste	¹/₄ teaspoon	¹/₄ teaspoon

1. Sauté onions and celery in oil in a hot skillet until tender.

2. Add the potatoes and roast beef and heat thoroughly. Season with salt and pepper to taste.

3. Allow a crust to form on the bottom. Turn the hash and allow a crust to form on the second side.

4. Cut into wedges and serve.

Cutting onions for the hash.

Hash may be prepared in advance, portioned and fried and placed on a sheet pan. Immediately prior to service, heat in the oven and top with poached egg.

Any beef or other meat may be substituted for the roast beef. This is a good use of wholesome usable trim from roasted meats.

TECHNIQUE
Basic knife cuts (pages 217-223)
Making bread crumbs (page 237)

17
Poultry Entrées

It was once a sign of great prosperity to be able to provide a meal that included chicken. Today, this enormously adaptable bird is prepared in almost endless ways. In this chapter, you will find chicken recipes for

- *Sautéed and Pan-Fried*
- *Roasted*
- *Grilled and Broiled*
- *Braised and Stewed*

In addition you will find recipes for:

- *Game Birds*
- *Turkey*

Remember to review the options in Chapter 20 as well.

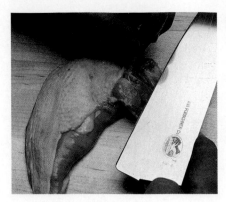

French the wing bone, as shown here.

Chicken suprêmes are semi-boneless breasts with one wing bone (usually frenched) still attached.

Dishes referred to as "provençal" typically include olive oil, garlic, and herbs. Provence is a region of France along the Mediterranean.

TECHNIQUE
Preparing suprêmes (pages 275-277)
Tomato concassé (page 226)
Chiffonade (page 219)

Chicken Provençal

Yield: 10 servings

Chicken suprêmes	*10 each*	*10 each*
Salt to taste	*$^1/_2$ teaspoon*	*$^1/_2$ teaspoon*
Pepper to taste	*$^1/_4$ teaspoon*	*$^1/_4$ teaspoon*
Flour as needed	*3 ounces*	*85 grams*
Vegetable oil as needed	*3 fluid ounces*	*90 milliliters*
Butter	*5 ounces*	*140 grams*
Garlic cloves, minced	*3 each*	*3 each*
White wine	*10 fluid ounces*	*300 milliliters*
Tomato concassé	*1 $^3/_4$ pounds*	*800 grams*
Black olives, sliced or julienned	*4 ounces*	*115 grams*
Anchovy fillets, mashed to a paste	*3 each*	*3 each*
Basil, chiffonade	*2 tablespoons*	*2 tablespoons*

1. Season the chicken suprêmes with salt and pepper. Dredge them lightly with the flour, shaking off excess.

2. Heat the vegetable oil in a sauté pan and sauté the chicken breasts until golden brown and cooked through. Remove the breasts from the pan and keep warm.

3. Pour off excess fat from the sauté pan; add the butter. Return the pan to the heat. Add the garlic to the melted butter and sauté it briefly.

4. Deglaze the pan with the wine, stirring well to release all of the drippings. Add the tomato concassé, olives, and anchovy paste. Bring this mixture to a simmer and cook it for a few minutes or until the flavor is developed.

5. Return the chicken breasts along with any released juices to the sauté pan and toss to coat the chicken with the sauce.

6. Serve the chicken with the sauce on a heated plate. Garnish with the basil.

VARIATION

Chicken Breast with Olives, Capers, and Herbs: You may elect to use different olives in this dish, introduce some capers, or add other herbs, either in addition to or as a replacement for the basil. Oregano, marjoram, chives, chervil, and thyme are all good choices.

Chicken Suprêmes with Fines Herbes Sauce

Yield: 10 servings

Chicken suprêmes	*10 each*	*10 each*
Salt to taste	*¹/₂ teaspoon*	*¹/₂ teaspoon*
Pepper to taste	*¹/₄ teaspoon*	*¹/₄ teaspoon*
Flour (optional)	*3 ounces*	*85 grams*
Clarified butter as needed	*2 ounces*	*60 grams*
Shallots, minced	*2 tablespoons*	*2 tablespoons*
Dry white wine	*12 fluid ounces*	*360 milliliters*
Chicken Stock	*12 fluid ounces*	*360 milliliters*
Glace de Volaille	*3 ounces*	*90 milliliters*
Heavy cream	*6 fluid ounces*	*180 milliliters*
Fines Herbes	*2 ounces*	*60 grams*

1. Blot chicken suprêmes to dry. Season well. Dredge in flour, if desired.

2. Sauté the chicken in the clarified butter until cooked through. Remove and keep warm.

3. Degrease the pan. Add the shallots and sauté them until they are translucent.

4. Deglaze the pan with the white wine; reduce until nearly dry.

5. Add the stock and glace.

6. Add the cream; reduce the sauce until thickened.

7. Add the fines herbes and adjust the sauce's consistency by additional reduction if necessary. Serve the sauce over the chicken.

Fines herbes is a French term for a classic herb combination of tarragon, parsley, chive, and chervil.

TECHNIQUE
Preparing suprêmes (pages 275-277)
Sautéing (pages 358-362)
Clarifying butter (page 253)

RECIPES
Chicken Stock (page 480)
Glace de Volaille (page 479)
Fines Herbes (page 475)

Turn chicken pieces as they cook.

The traditional accompaniments are whipped potatoes and biscuits.

Southern Fried Chicken may also be served cold with potato salad and cole slaw.

TECHNIQUE
Pan-frying (pages 364-367)
Cutting a bird in eighths (page 274)

Southern Fried Chicken with Country-Style Gravy

Yield: 8 servings

Chickens (fryers)	*4 each*	*4 each*
Salt as needed	*1 teaspoon*	*1 teaspoon*
Pepper as needed	*1 teaspoon*	*1 teaspoon*
Buttermilk	*1 quart*	*1 liter*
Dijon mustard	*4 ounces*	*115 grams*
Tarragon leaves, chopped	*1 tablespoon*	*1 tablespoon*
Flour as needed	*8 ounces*	*225 grams*
Vegetable oil	*1 pint*	*480 milliliters*
Milk	*24 fluid ounces*	*720 milliliters*

1. Cut chicken in eighths, trim, and season well with salt and pepper to taste.

2. Combine buttermilk, mustard, and tarragon. Add chicken pieces and turn until coated evenly. Let chicken pieces marinate for at least 4 hours, up to overnight.

3. Remove the chicken from the buttermilk and let it drain.

4. Roll the chicken in flour until well coated.

5. Heat the oil in a rondeau. Add the chicken pieces without crowding. Cook, turning occasionally, until well browned and cooked through.

6. Remove the chicken from the oil; drain on absorbent toweling.

7. Pour off most of the oil from the pan, leaving about 2 ounces (60 milliliters) in the pan. Add 2 ounces (60 grams) of flour to make a roux. Cook the roux for 5 to 6 minutes.

8. Add the milk, stirring well to remove all lumps. Let this gravy simmer at least 15 minutes. Adjust seasoning with salt and fresh ground pepper.

9. Serve the chicken with the gravy.

VARIATION

Chicken-Fried Steak with "Cream" Gravy: Substitute 8 steaks (shell, top round, or chuck) for the chicken. The steaks should weigh 4 to 5 ounces (115 to 140 grams) per portion. Marinate the steaks in buttermilk (omit the mustard and tarragon) or "swiss" the steaks by flouring and pounding them until tender. Fry them as directed above. The gravy is prepared in the same manner, with plenty of salt and fresh ground pepper. Serve with mashed potatoes.

Roast Chicken with Pan Gravy

Yield: 10 servings

Chickens, wing tips removed	*5 each*	*5 each*
Salt to taste	*³/₄ teaspoon*	*³/₄ teaspoon*
White pepper to taste	*¹/₂ teaspoon*	*¹/₂ teaspoon*
Thyme sprigs	*5 each*	*5 each*
Rosemary sprigs	*5 each*	*5 each*
Garlic cloves, bruised	*5 each*	*5 each*
Bay leaves	*5 each*	*5 each*
Chervil sprigs	*10 each*	*10 each*
Vegetable oil as needed	*2 fluid ounces*	*60 milliliters*
Mirepoix, diced	*8 ounces*	*225 grams*
Flour	*2 ounces*	*60 grams*
Chicken Stock, hot	*1 pint*	*480 milliliters*
Tomato paste (optional)	*¹/₂ ounce*	*15 grams*

Check doneness by piercing the thigh.
Juices should run clear.

1. Season chicken, and place thyme, rosemary, garlic, bay leaves, and chervil in the cavity of each bird.

2. Rub skin with oil; truss chickens with twine.

3. Place chicken, breast side up, on a rack in a roasting pan.

4. Roast at 375°F (190°C) until the thigh meat registers an internal temperature of 165°F (72°C). Add the mirepoix after the chicken has roasted 30 to 40 minutes.

5. Remove chicken and mirepoix and allow the chicken to rest.

6. Clarify fat in the roasting pan; discard all but 3 ounces (90 milliliters).

7. Add flour, cook out roux, incorporate stock, and whisk until smooth.

8. Simmer gravy until proper consistency and flavor is reached; degrease thoroughly.

9. Strain the gravy through a fine chinoise and season to taste.

10. Carve the chicken into portions and serve with gravy.

Serve with whipped potatoes or roasted potatoes seasoned with garlic and rosemary.

TECHNIQUE
Trussing birds for roasting whole (pages 272-273)
Roasting (page 349)
Preparing pan gravy (pages 354-355)

RECIPES
Chicken Stock (page 480)
Mirepoix (page 472)

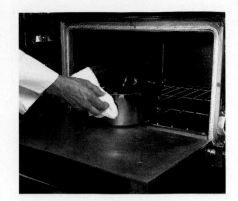

Finish poêléing in the oven.

Finish the sauce by thickening with an arrowroot slurry if desired.

TECHNIQUE
Poêléing (pages 358-360)
Trussing birds for roasting whole (pages 272-273)
Tomato concassé (page 226)
Preparing artichokes (Pages 234-235)

RECIPES
Chicken Stock (page 480)
Jus de Volaille Lié (page 516)
Matignon (page 472)

Poêlé of Capon with Tomatoes and Artichokes

Yield: 10 servings

Capon (12 pounds)	*1 each*	*1 each*
Salt to taste	*1 teaspoon*	*1 teaspoon*
Pepper to taste	*$^1/_2$ teaspoon*	*$^1/_2$ teaspoon*
Fresh herbs as available or desired	*1 bunch*	*1 bunch*
Matignon	*8 ounces*	*225 grams*
Butter as needed	*2 ounces*	*60 grams*
Chicken Stock or Jus de Volaille Lié	*1 quart*	*1 liter*
Arrowroot	*2 teaspoons*	*2 teaspoons*
Tomato concassé	*8 ounces*	*225 grams*
Artichoke bottoms, poached and sliced	*8 ounces*	*225 grams*
Parsley, chopped	*2 tablespoons*	*2 tablespoons*
Chives, chopped	*2 tablespoons*	*2 tablespoons*
Chervil, chopped	*2 tablespoons*	*2 tablespoons*
Tarragon, chopped	*2 tablespoons*	*2 tablespoons*

1. Season the bird with the salt and pepper and stuff the cavity with a bundle of the fresh herbs. Truss the bird.

2. Sweat the matignon in butter. Place the capon on the matignon. Brush liberally with butter. Cover it in a casserole and poêlé the bird in a moderate oven (350°F/175°C) for approximately 2 hours, or until the thigh registers 165°F (72°C). Remove the cover during the final half-hour of cooking time to brown the skin.

3. Remove the capon and allow it to rest while completing the sauce. Place the casserole on direct heat and bring the liquid to a boil; let it reduce slightly.

4. Add the stock or jus and bring the mixture to a boil.

5. Dilute the arrowroot and add it to the stock to thicken the stock lightly. Add the tomato concassé, artichoke bottoms, and chopped herbs. Adjust the seasoning to taste. Skim the excess butter from the surface as necessary.

6. Carve the capon and serve it with the sauce.

VARIATIONS

Poêlé Poussins: Substitute poussins (baby chickens) or squab for the capon. Use one or two per portion, depending upon the bird's size.

Poêlé of Rabbit with Prunes: Substitute approximately 5 rabbits for the capon. Each rabbit will make 2 servings. Substitute 1 pound (450 grams) of prunes plumped in cognac for the tomatoes and artichokes.

Grilled Paillards of Chicken with Sun-Dried Tomato and Oregano Butter

Yield: 10 servings

Chicken paillards	*10 each*	*10 each*
Oil	*2 fluid ounces*	*60 milliliters*
Salt to taste	*1 teaspoon*	*1 teaspoon*
Pepper to taste	*¹/₂ teaspoon*	*¹/₂ teaspoon*
Lemon juice	*2 teaspoons*	*2 teaspoons*
Oregano, fresh, chopped	*2 teaspoons*	*2 teaspoons*
Sun-Dried Tomato and Oregano Butter	*1 tablespoon*	*1 tablespoon*

The paillards are ready to turn.

1. Trim and lightly pound the chicken paillards. Combine the oil, salt, pepper, lemon juice, and oragano, and brush the mixture on the chicken.

2. Grill the chicken until it is cooked through.

3. Top each paillard with a rosette or a slice of the flavored butter and serve it immediately.

The term "paillard" originally meant straw mattress. Today, its culinary application refers to boneless cuts of meat that have been pounded to an even thickness. They are typically grilled or sautéed.

RECIPE
Sun-Dried Tomato and Oragano Butter (page 522)

VARIATIONS

Grilled Chicken Sandwich: Serve the chicken on a sliced baguette or club roll. Garnish the sandwich as desired.

Grilled Chicken with Basil and Fresh Mozzarella: Grill the chicken as indicated in the recipe, substituting chopped, fresh basil for the oragano in the marinade. Omit the flavored butter. Top each grilled paillard with a fresh basil leaf and a slice of fresh mozzarella. Place the chicken under a broiler briefly before serving.

Grilled Chicken Fajitas: Add ground cumin and chili powder to the marinade. Slice the chicken breasts on a diagonal. Serve them with steamed flour tortillas, salsa, chopped onions, tomato, lettuce, and other condiments as desired. Omit the flavored butter.

A chicken, cut up for the fricassée.

Chicken Fricassée

Yield: 10 servings

Chickens, whole	*2 each*	*2 each*
Salt to taste	*¹/₂ teaspoon*	*¹/₂ teaspoon*
Pepper to taste	*¹/₄ teaspoon*	*¹/₄ teaspoon*
Vegetable oil	*4 fluid ounces*	*120 milliliters*
Onions, diced	*1 pound*	*450 grams*
Garlic cloves, minced	*2 each*	*2 each*
Flour	*2 ounces*	*60 grams*
Dry white wine	*8 fluid ounces*	*240 milliliters*
Chicken Stock	*1 pint*	*480 milliliters*
Bay leaves	*2 each*	*2 each*
Thyme leaves	*1 teaspoon*	*1 teaspoon*
Heavy cream	*8 fluid ounces*	*240 milliliters*
Carrots, diced and blanched	*1 pound*	*450 grams*
Leeks, diced and blanched	*1 pound*	*450 grams*

This dish has the best flavor when prepared with a stewing hen. Increase the cooking time to 1 ¹/₂ hours.

Fricassée refers to a white stew typically made from poultry or veal.

TECHNIQUE
Stewing (pages 394-397)
Cutting a bird in eighths (page 274)
Basic knife cuts (pages 217-223)

RECIPE
Chicken Stock (page 480)

1. Cut chickens into pieces. Rinse and blot dry. Season well with the salt and pepper.

2. Heat the oil and sauté the chicken until it stiffens slightly, but does not brown. Remove and reserve.

3. Add the onions and garlic to the pan; cover and sweat.

4. Add the flour to the pan and cook, stirring frequently, for about 5 minutes.

5. Add the wine, stock, bay leaves, and thyme. Bring to a simmer and return the chicken along with released juices.

6. Cover the pan and braise the chicken until it is fork-tender, about 35 to 45 minutes.

7. To finish the sauce, remove the chicken and keep warm. Strain the sauce and degrease. Add the heavy cream and simmer until the sauce has thickened slightly. Add the carrots and leeks. Adjust the seasoning.

8. Return the chicken to the sauce, simmer about 2 minutes and serve.

Chicken Pot Pie

Yield: 10 servings

Chicken, white and dark meat, cooked	2 pounds	900 grams
Pearl onions, cooked	20 each	20 each
Mushrooms caps, sautéed	20 each	20 each
Carrots, cubed, blanched	4 each	4 each
Potatoes, parisienne	4 each	4 each
Green peas	8 ounces	225 grams
Chicken Velouté	1 1/2 quarts	1.4 liters
Puff Pastry	2 sheets	2 sheets
Egg wash	as needed	as needed

1. Cut the chicken into large bite-size pieces. Divide evenly and place into 10 portion-size casserole or soup bowls; add the vegetables.

2. Pour the velouté over the chicken and vegetables.

3. Roll out the puff pastry 1/4-inch thick. Cut a circle slightly larger than the casserole. Lay it over the casserole, seal, and brush with egg wash.

4. Bake at 425°F (220°C) until crust is done and chicken is heated thoroughly.

Fluting mushroom caps.

Other vegetables such as turnips, rutabagas, and green beans may be added. You may season the velouté with fresh herbs if desired.

RECIPES
Chicken Velouté (page 517)
Butter Puff Pastry (page 738)

Tournéing carrots.

Henry VIII is credited with saying, "A chicken in every pot." This was the celebrated monarch's way of expressing his wish for his subjects' well-being and prosperity.

TECHNIQUE
Poaching (pages 382-384)
Tourné or battonet (page 220)
Trussing (pages 272-273)
Basic Knife Cuts (pages 217-223)

RECIPES
Chicken Stock (page 480)
Bouquet Garni (page (474)

Poule au Pôt (Chicken with Vegetables)

Yield: 10 servings

Chickens, whole	*5 each*	*5 each*
Chicken Stock, as needed	*2 ¹/₂ quarts*	*2.4 liters*
Bouquet Garni	*1 each*	*1 each*
Vegetable garnish		
Carrots, tourné or bâttonet	*30 pieces*	*30 pieces*
Pearl onions	*30 pieces*	*30 pieces*
Celery, bâttonet	*30 pieces*	*30 pieces*
Parsnips, tourné or bâttonet	*30 pieces*	*30 pieces*
Peas	*10 ounces*	*285 grams*
Fennel, bâtonnet	*30 pieces*	*30 pieces*
Mushrooms	*20 each*	*20 each*
Salt to taste	*¹/₂ teaspoon*	*¹/₂ teaspoon*
Pepper to taste	*¹/₄ teaspoon*	*¹/₄ teaspoon*
Fresh herbs, as available or **desired, chopped**	*2 ounces*	*60 grams*

1. Truss the chicken.

2. Cover the chicken with cold stock. Bring the stock to a simmer. Add the bouquet garni. Poach the chicken until it is tender and cooked through. Skim the surface as necessary throughout the poaching procedure.

3. Cook the vegetables separately (in additional stock, if available) until they are tender. Refresh and hold them.

4. At service, portion the chicken and serve it with the broth and vegetables heated in the broth. Add the salt, pepper, and chopped, fresh herbs, if desired.

Roast Duckling with Sauce Bigarade

Yield: 10 servings

Ducklings	*5 each*	*5 each*
Salt to taste	*$^1/_2$ teaspoon*	*$^1/_2$ teaspoon*
Pepper to taste	*$^1/_4$ teaspoon*	*$^1/_4$ teaspoon*
Parsley stems	*15 each*	*15 each*
Thyme sprigs	*5 each*	*5 each*
Bay leaves	*5 each*	*5 each*
Sauce Bigarade		
Sugar	*$^3/_4$ ounce*	*20 grams*
Water	*1 tablespoon*	*1 tablespoon*
White wine	*1 fluid ounce*	*30 milliliters*
Cider vinegar	*1 fluid ounce*	*30 milliliters*
Blood orange juice	*3 fluid ounces*	*90 milliliters*
Demi-Glace	*1 quart*	*1 liter*
Brown Veal Stock	*1 pint*	*480 milliliters*
Blood orange, zest, julienned and blanched	*1 each*	*1 each*
Blood orange, segment, flesh only	*1 each*	*1 each*

Blood oranges.

1. Place ducklings, breast side up, on a rack. Season with salt and pepper. Place the parsley stems, thyme, and bay leaves into the cavity.

2. Roast the ducklings until the thigh has an internal temperature of 140°F (60°C). Remove the ducklings from the pan, and let cool. Split and partially debone the ducklings.

3. Degrease the pan and reserve the drippings.

4. To prepare the gastrique: Combine the sugar and water. Caramelize carefully.

5. Add the wine, vinegar, and orange juice, and reduce by half.

6. Add the demi-glace and stock; bring sauce to a boil.

7. Add the pan drippings. Reduce the heat and simmer until the mixture is reduced to 1 quart (1 liter). Strain through a cheesecloth. Reserve.

8. At service, brush the duckling halves with a small amount of the sauce and reheat them until they are crisp in a very hot oven (450°F/230°C).

9. Reheat approximately 2 ounces (60 milliliters) of sauce per serving and finish it with the blanched orange zest and orange segments. Pool the sauce on a plate and place the duckling on the sauce.

A gastrique is defined by Larousse Gastronomique as a mixture of vinegar and sugar cooked until nearly dry and used to flavor fruit sauces, such as the one here.

If blood oranges are not available, substitute tangerines or juice oranges and adjust the flavor with lemon or lime juice.

TECHNIQUE
Roasting (page 349)
Zesting citrus fruit (page 231)

RECIPES
Demi-Glace (page 514)
Brown Veal Stock (page 178)

565

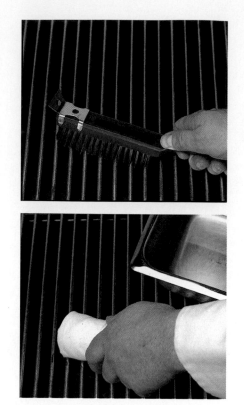

Preparing the grill.

Serve the sliced duck breast with dauphinoise potatoes (page 639).

Another way to serve this duck is as part of a composed salad on a bed of mixed greens.

TECHNIQUE
Grilling (pages 344-349)
Marinades (pages 242-245)

Marinated Grilled Duck Breast

Yield: 10 servings

Duck breasts, boned and halved	*10 each*	*10 each*
Marinade		
Soy sauce	*8 fluid ounces*	*240 milliliters*
Water	*8 fluid ounces*	*240 milliliters*
Sesame oil, dark	*$^1/_2$ ounce*	*15 grams*
Hoisin sauce	*$^1/_2$ ounce*	*15 grams*
Ginger, coarsely chopped	*1 tablespoon*	*1 tablespoon*
Garlic, minced	*1 tablespoon*	*1 tablespoon*
Salt, to taste	*$^1/_2$ teaspoon*	*$^1/_2$ teaspoon*
Pepper, to taste	*$^1/_4$ teaspoon*	*$^1/_4$ teaspoon*

1. Trim the duck breasts if necessary; place in a hotel pan.

2. Combine all of the ingredients for the marinade and pour the mixture over the duck. Turn the breasts to coat evenly. Let marinate in the refrigerator for several hours or overnight.

3. Grill the duck until it has cooked to the desired doneness. Brush with marinade during the grilling.

4. At service, slice the breast on the diagonal and serve.

Roast Turkey with Chestnut Stuffing

Yield: 12 servings

Turkey, whole	*15 pounds*	*6.75 kilograms*
Salt to taste	*1/2 teaspoon*	*1/2 teaspoon*
Pepper to taste	*1/4 teaspoon*	*1/4 teaspoon*
Mirepoix	*1 pound*	*450 grams*
Chestnut stuffing		
Onions, minced	*4 ounces*	*115 grams*
Bacon fat	*4 ounces*	*115 grams*
Bread cubes, dried	*1 1/2 pounds*	*680 grams*
Chicken Stock, hot	*4 fluid ounces*	*120 milliliters*
Egg, beaten	*1 each*	*1 each*
Parsley, chopped	*2 tablespoons*	*2 tablespoons*
Salt to taste	*1/2 teaspoon*	*1/2 teaspoon*
Pepper to taste	*1/2 teaspoon*	*1/2 teaspoon*
Sage, rubbed	*1 teaspoon*	*1 teaspoon*
Chestnuts, roasted and chopped	*8 ounces*	*225 grams*
Flour	*3 ounces*	*85 grams*
Turkey Stock	*1 1/2 quarts*	*1.5 liters*

The chestnuts are ready to peel.

1. Season the outside of the turkey with the salt and pepper. Place it on a rack in a roasting pan. Roast it at 425°F (220°C) for 15 minutes. Reduce the heat to 350°F (175°C) and roast the turkey to an internal temperature of 165°F (72°C). Add the mirepoix when the turkey has roasted for about 3 hours.

2. To make the stuffing, sauté the onion in bacon fat until tender.

3. Combine the bread cubes, stock, and eggs; add to the onion.

4. Add the parsley, salt, pepper, sage, and chestnuts. Mix them well.

5. Place the stuffing in a buttered hotel pan and cover it with parchment paper. Bake the stuffing at 350°F (175°C) for 45 minutes.

6. Pour off most of the fat from the roasting pan. Let the drippings reduce over direct heat until syrupy.

7. Add the flour, stir well to combine, and cook out for 5 to 6 minutes. Add the broth and whisk to remove any lumps. Simmer for 20 minutes; strain, degrease, and adjust the seasoning.

8. Let the turkey stand 20 minutes before carving it. Serve it with pan gravy and the chestnut stuffing.

If desired, add 4 ounces (115 grams) sautéed celery to the stuffing. The egg may be omitted. Add more chicken stock to bind the mixture. Thyme, rosemary, and oregano may be added for additional seasoning.

A rich chicken stock or double chicken broth may be substituted for the turkey stock.

TECHNIQUE
Roasting chestnuts (pages 231-232)
Roasting (page 349)

RECIPES
Mirepoix (page 472)
Chicken Stock (page 480)
Turkey Stock (page 480)

Sauté until a good color develops on the first side; turn the fish once.

Some chefs prefer to add the lemon juice and the parsley to the browned butter, creating a slightly thickened sauce to pour over the trout.

This technique may be applied to most pan-dressed fish or fillets cut from larger fish.

Meunière-style means "in the manner of the miller's wife."

TECHNIQUE
Sautéeing (pages 358-362)
Pan-dressed fish (pages 279-280)
Clarifying butter (page 253)
Dredging trout with flour (page 359)

Trout Meunière

Yield: 10 servings

Trout, pan-dressed	10 each	10 each
Lemon juice as needed	1 lemon	1 lemon
Salt to taste	½ teaspoon	½ teaspoon
Pepper to taste	¼ teaspoon	¼ teaspoon
Flour for dredging	2 ounces	60 grams
Clarified butter	2 ounces	60 grams
Lemon slices, skinless, seedless	20 each	20 each
Lemon juice	2 fluid ounces	60 milliliters
Parsley, chopped	3 tablespoons	3 tablespoons
Butter, whole	6 ounces	170 grams

1. Season trout with lemon juice, salt, and pepper; dredge in flour.

2. Sauté in clarified butter over moderate heat until lightly browned and cooked through, about 8 to 10 minutes.

3. When trout is done, remove to a serving platter and keep warm.

4. Sprinkle with lemon juice and parsley.

5. Wipe out pan and add whole butter. Heat butter until lightly browned and pour over fish. Garnish trout with lemon slices.

Pan-Fried Halibut with Puttanesca Sauce

Yield: 10 servings

Halibut fillets, skinless	*4 pounds*	*1.8 kilograms*
Salt to taste	*1/2 teaspoon*	*1/2 teaspoon*
Pepper to taste	*1/4 teaspoon*	*1/4 teaspoon*
Flour as needed	*3 ounces*	*85 grams*
Egg wash as needed	*8 fluid ounces*	*240 milliliters*
Bread crumbs, fresh	*4 ounces*	*115 grams*
Almonds, slivered and coarse-chopped	*6 ounces*	*170 grams*
Vegetable oil as needed	*6 fluid ounces*	*180 milliliters*
Puttanesca Sauce		
Olive oil as needed	*2 tablespoons*	*2 tablespoons*
Garlic cloves, mashed to a paste	*3 each*	*3 each*
Anchovy paste	*1 tablespoon*	*1 tablespoon*
Red pepper flakes	*1/4 teaspoon*	*1/4 teaspoon*
White wine	*6 ounces*	*170 grams*
Capers, roughly chopped	*2 tablespoons*	*2 tablespoons*
Tomato concassé	*1 1/2 pounds*	*680 grams*
Black olives, pitted	*3 ounces*	*85 grams*
Lemon juice as needed	*2 teaspoons*	*2 teaspoons*
Parsley, chopped	*1 ounce*	*30 grams*

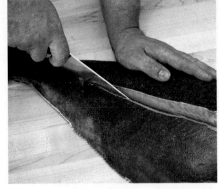

Filleting the halibut.

Coarse-ground pecans or walnuts may be used instead of almonds.

Puttanesca sauce is reputed to have first been devised by the prostitutes of Naples. It is a quickly made sauce of pungent, salty ingredients.

TECHNIQUE
Pan-frying (pages 364-367)
Halibut fillets (pages 280-281)
Makng bread crumbs (page 237)
Tomato concassé (page 226)
Mashing garlic (page 225
Basic knife cuts (pages 217-223)

1. Portion the fillets at approximately 6 ounces (170 grams) each. Season the halibut with salt and pepper.

2. Dredge the fish in the flour, dip in the egg wash, and coat with a combination of the bread crumbs and almonds. Allow to rest, refrigerated, at least 30 minutes.

3. Pan-fry the halibut in hot vegetable oil. Finish in a 325°F (165°C) oven, if necessary.

4. For the sauce, heat the olive oil; add the garlic, anchovy paste, and red pepper flakes; sauté briefly.

5. Add the wine and reduce the mixture. Add the capers and tomato concassé. Cook until the liquid is reduced slightly. Adjust the seasoning with the salt, pepper, and lemon juice. Add the parsley.

6. Pool the sauce on a heated plate. Arrange the halibut on the sauce and serve.

Preparing goujonettes.

You may prefer to deep fry the fish and shellfish.

Other breadings that might be used include cornmeal, cracker or corn flake crumbs, or flour and ground nut mixes.

Cocktail sauce and lemon slices may be preferred by some customers.

TECHNIQUE
Pan-frying (pages 364-367)
Goujonettes (page 281)
Working with shellfish (pages 284-289)
Standard breading (page 366)

RECIPE
Tartar Sauce (page 682)

Fisherman's Platter

Yield: 10 servings

Fish, cut in goujonettes	*1 1/4 pounds*	*570 grams*
Oysters, shucked	*20 each*	*20 each*
Little Neck clams, shucked	*20 each*	*20 each*
Shrimp, 16 to 20 count, peeled, deveined, and butterflied	*20 each*	*20 each*
Sea scallops, muscle tabs removed	*10 ounces*	*285 grams*
Salt to taste	*1/2 teaspoon*	*1/2 teaspoon*
Pepper to taste	*1/4 teaspoon*	*1/4 teaspoon*
Lemon juice to taste	*4 fluid ounces*	*120 milliliters*
Flour as needed	*4 ounces*	*115 grams*
Egg wash as needed	*6 fluid ounces*	*180 milliliters*
Bread crumbs, fresh	*8 ounces*	*225 grams*
Vegetable oil as needed	*1 pint*	*480 milliliters*
Tartar Sauce	*1 pint*	*480 milliliters*

1. Season the fish and shellfish with the salt, pepper, and lemon juice.

2. Bread the fish and shellfish. Refrigerate for at least 30 minutes.

3. Pan-fry them until they are cooked through.

4. Drain the fish and shellfish briefly on absorbent paper.

5. Serve the fish immediately with the Tartar or Rémoulade Sauce.

Flounder Stuffed with Crabmeat with Lemon Beurre Blanc

Skinning a flounder fillet.

Yield: 10 servings

Stuffing

Shallots, minced	2 each	2 each
Scallions, minced	2 each	2 each
Butter	1 ounce	30 grams
Flour	1 ½ ounces	45 grams
White wine	8 fluid ounces	240 milliliters
Heavy cream	8 fluid ounces	240 milliliters
King crabmeat, roughly chopped	14 ounces	400 grams
Parsley, chopped	1 tablespoon	1 tablespoon
Salt to taste	½ teaspoon	½ teaspoon
Pepper to taste	¼ teaspoon	¼ teaspoon
Flounder fillet	10 each	10 each
Flour	2 ounces	60 grams
Salt to taste	½ teaspoon	½ teaspoon
Pepper to taste	¼ teaspoon	¼ teaspoon
Eggs, beaten	5 each	5 each
Vegetable oil	6 ounces	170 milliliters
Lemon Beurre Blanc	20 ounces	600 milliliters

Other fish suitable for this dish include halibut, trout, and grouper.

If you prefer a dish that is not quite so rich, serve the stuffed flounder with a vegetable coulis such as those found on pages 522 and 523.

TECHNIQUE
Pan-frying (pages 364-367)
Basic knife cuts (pages 217-223)
Filleting a flat fish (pages 280-281)

RECIPE
Lemon Beurre Blanc (page 522)

1. To make stuffing, sauté shallots and scallions in butter.

2. Add flour; cook 1 minute.

3. Add wine, cream, and crabmeat; bring to a boil, and cook until mixture is thick, stirring occasionally.

4. Add parsley; season and chill.

5. Portion the flounder at about 5 ounces (140 grams) per portion. Spread stuffing on fillet and roll up, completely encasing the filling.

6. Dip fish in seasoned flour; shake off excess. Dip fish in egg, brown in oil, and finish in a 350°F (175°C) oven 8 to 10 minutes.

7. Serve with lemon beurre blanc.

Cutting the fillets away from the bones.

This fish can also be served with French fries and malt vinegar as you would for a classic "fish and chips."

TECHNIQUE
Deep-frying (pages 367-371)
Filleting flounder (pages 280-281)

RECIPE
Marinara sauce (page 519)

Flounder à la Orly

Yield: 10 servings

Flounder fillets	*4 pounds*	*1.8 kilograms*
Salt to taste	*1/2 teaspoon*	*1/2 teaspoon*
Pepper to taste	*1/4 teaspoon*	*1/4 teaspoon*
Lemon juice to taste	*1 fluid ounce*	*30 milliliters*
Beer Batter		
All-purpose flour	*5 ounces*	*140 grams*
Baking powder	*2 tablespoons*	*2 tablespoons*
Sugar	*1 tablespoon*	*1 tablespoon*
Salt	*1/2 teaspoon*	*1/2 teaspoon*
Pepper	*1/4 teaspoon*	*1/4 teaspoon*
Beer (lager)	*12 fluid ounces*	*360 milliliters*
Flour as needed	*4 ounces*	*115 grams*
Parsley sprigs	*20 each*	*20 each*
Marinara Sauce	*20 fluid ounces*	*600 milliliters*
Lemon wedges	*10 each*	*10 each*

1. Portion the flounder at 6 ounces (170 grams). Season fillets with salt, pepper, and lemon juice.
2. Combine the flour, baking powder, sugar, salt and pepper in a bowl. Add the beer and stir until a batter forms.
3. Dredge the fish in flour and shake off excess.
4. Dip in batter.
5. Deep-fry at 350°F (175°C) until lightly browned.
6. Drain on absorbent paper.
7. Deep-fry parsley sprigs at 350°F (175°C) until crisp, 45 seconds; drain.
8. Serve fried fish with marinara sauce; garnish with lemon wedge and fried parsley.

Deep-Fried Breaded Shrimp

Yield: 10 servings

Shrimp, peeled and deveined	*3 1/2 pounds*	*1.6 kilograms*
Flour as needed	*4 ounces*	*115 grams*
Egg wash as needed	*6 fluid ounces*	*180 milliliters*
Bread crumbs, fresh, white	*4 ounces*	*115 grams*
Salt to taste	*1/2 teaspoon*	*1/2 teaspoon*
Tartar Sauce	*1 pint*	*480 milliliters*

(Recipe continued on facing page)

1. Bread the shrimp according to the standard breading procedure: First, dip them into the flour and shake off any excess. Then, coat the shrimp with the egg wash. Finally, evenly coat the shrimp with the bread crumbs.

2. Place the shrimp in a fryer basket and lower them into a deep fryer set at 375°F (190°C).

3. Deep-fry the shrimp until they are evenly browned and thoroughly cooked. Lift the basket and allow the excess oil to drain back into the fryer. Drain the shrimp very briefly on absorbent toweling, and season them to taste with salt as desired.

4. Serve the shrimp on a heated plate with Rémoulade or Tartar Sauce, or as desired.

VARIATION

Popcorn Shrimp: Season very small shrimp with a seasoning blend such as barbecue spice blend or chili powder. Bread and fry; serve as an appetizer with a fruit chutney.

Another option is to dip the shrimp in a beer batter and fry. See facing page for Beer Batter recipe.

TECHNIQUE
Deep-frying (pages 367-371)
Cleaning shrimp (page 284)
Standard breading procedure (page 366)
Making bread crumbs (page 237)

RECIPE
Tartar Sauce (page 682)

Deep-Fried Sole Anglaise

Yield: 10 servings

Dover sole fillets, skinless	3 ¹/₂ pounds	1.6 kilograms
Salt to taste	¹/₂ teaspoon	¹/₂ teaspoon
Pepper to taste	¹/₄ teaspoon	¹/₄ teaspoon
Lemon juice to taste	1 fluid ounce	30 milliliters
Flour as needed	2 ounces	60 grams
Egg wash	6 fluid ounces	180 milliliters
Bread crumbs, fresh	4 ounces	115 grams
Parsley sprigs	20 each	20 each
Lemon wedges	10 each	10 each
Tartar Sauce	1 pint	480 millimeters

1. Portion the sole into 5-ounce (140-gram) servings. Season sole with salt, pepper, and lemon, and dredge in flour.

2. Dip the pieces of fish in the egg wash, drain, and dredge in bread crumbs.

3. Deep-fry at 350°F (175°C) until lightly browned. Drain on absorbent paper.

4. Deep-fry parsley sprigs until crisp, about 45 seconds; drain on paper.

5. Serve fish garnished with lemon wedge and fried parsley.

Pullling the skin away from Dover sole.

Five ounces (140 grams) is a sufficient portion size.

Traditional accompaniments include cole slaw (page 673), French fries, and hush puppies.

TECHNIQUE
Deep-frying (pages 367-371)
Filleting a fish (pages 280-281)
Standard breading procedure (page 366)
Making bread crumbs (page 237)

RECIPE
Tartar Sauce (page 682)

Cutting salmon steaks.

The steaks should weigh approximately 6 ounces (170 grams).

TECHNIQUE
Broiling (pages 344-349)
Cutting fish Steaks (pages 281-282)
Making bread crumbs (page 237)
Placing fish in a hand grill (page 347)

RECIPE
Rosemary-and-Ginger Butter (page 522)

Broiled Salmon Steaks

Yield: 10 servings

Salmon steaks	*10 each*	*10 each*
Salt to taste	*1/2 teaspoon*	*1/2 teaspoon*
Pepper to taste	*1/4 teaspoon*	*1/4 teaspoon*
Lemon juice to taste	*1 fluid ounce*	*30 milliliters*
Vegetable oil	*4 fluid ounces*	*120 milliliters*
Bread crumbs, fresh	*8 ounces*	*225 grams*
Rosemary-and-Ginger Butter	*5 ounces*	*140 grams*

1. Season salmon steak with salt, pepper, and lemon juice.

2. Dip in oil and dredge in bread crumbs.

3. Place in hand grill and broil in medium-heat broiler, turning when golden brown. Cooking time is 6 to 8 minutes.

4. Serve with compound butter.

Use any lean, flaky white fish that is available: cod, haddock, halibut, turbot, or flounder.

TECHNIQUE
Broiling (pages 344-349)
Working with shellfish (page 284)
Clarifying butter (page 253)
Filleting a fish (pages 280-281)
Making bread crumbs (page 237)

RECIPE
Tartar Sauce (page 682)

Broiled Seafood Platter

Yield: 10 servings

Hake fillets	*2 pounds*	*900 grams*
Shrimp, peeled, deveined, butterflied	*20 each*	*20 each*
Oysters, shucked, on the halfshell	*20 each*	*20 each*
Clams, shucked, on the halfshell	*30 each*	*30 each*
Sea scallops	*20 each*	*20 each*
Salt to taste	*1/2 teaspoon*	*1/2 teaspoon*
Pepper to taste	*1/2 teaspoon*	*1/2 teaspoon*
Lemon juice to taste	*2 fluid ounces*	*60 milliliters*
Clarified butter	*2 ounces*	*60 grams*
Bread crumbs, dry	*3 ounces*	*85 grams*
Lemon wedges	*10 each*	*10 each*
Tartar Sauce	*1 pint*	*480 milliliters*

1. Season fish and seafood with salt, pepper, and lemon juice. Dip in oil, dredge in bread crumbs, and place on a sizzler platter. (The oysters and clams may be returned to their shells, if desired.)

2. Top the seafood with additional bread crumbs and drizzle with butter.

3. Broil on medium heat in the broiler until browned and cooked (approximately 6 minutes). Serve at once.

Broiled Stuffed Lobster

Yield: 10 servings

Lobsters, split and cleaned	5 each	5 each
Stuffing		
Butter	2 ounces	60 grams
Onions, minced	10 ounces	285 grams
Celery, minced	5 ounces	140 grams
Red peppers, minced	1 ½ ounces	45 grams
Green peppers, minced	1 ½ ounces	45 grams
Bread crumbs, fresh	8 ounces	225 grams
Lemon wedges	20 each	20 each
Butter, drawn	10 fluid ounces	300 grams

Kill the lobster before cooking it.

1. Place lobsters on a grill rack, shell side up. Grill until the shells are red. Remove from the rack.

2. Melt the butter in a sauté pan. Sweat the vegetables. Remove from the heat. Add the bread crumbs and spoon the mixture into each cavity. (Do not place it over the tail meat.)

3. Place lobsters on a sheet pan and finish in a 400°F (205°C) oven.

4. Crack the claws but leave the meat inside. Serve the lobster with lemon wedges and drawn butter.

Lobsters should be about 1 to 1½ pounds (450 to 685 grams) each.

TECHNIQUE
Broiling (pages 344-349)
Clarifying butter (page 253)
Making bread crumbs (page 237)
Basic knife cuts (pages 217-223)

Saffron is the thread-like stamen of a crocus.

Puff pastry sheets may be used in place of phyllo. Increase the baking time until the pastry reaches a light golden brown.

TECHNIQUE
Filleting a fish (pages 280-281)
Preparing a mousseline forcemeat (page 408)
Tomato concassé (page 226)
Basic knife cuts (pages 217-223)
Making bread crumbs (page 237)

RECIPES
Duxelles (page 473)
Fish Velouté (page 517)

Salmon Baked in Phyllo with Saffron Sauce

Yield: 10 servings

Salmon fillet	*3 ½ pounds*	*1.6 kilograms*
Salt to taste	*½ teaspoon*	*½ teaspoon*
Pepper to taste	*¼ teaspoon*	*¼ teaspoon*
Egg white, chilled	*1 each*	*1 each*
Heavy cream, chilled	*2 fluid ounces*	*60 milliliters*
Tarragon leaves, chopped	*½ teaspoon*	*½ teaspoon*
Basil leaves, chopped	*½ teaspoon*	*½ teaspoon*
Salt	*¼ teaspoon*	*¼ teaspoon*
Duxelles	*10 ounces*	*285 grams*
Phyllo dough sheets	*10 each*	*10 each*
Clarified butter as needed	*3 ounces*	*85 grams*
Bread crumbs, dry	*3 ounces*	*85 grams*
Saffron Sauce		
Dry white wine	*2 fluid ounces*	*60 milliliters*
Saffron threads, crushed	*1 pinch*	*1 pinch*
Fish Velouté	*1 pint*	*480 milliliters*
Tomato concassé	*5 ounces*	*140 grams*
Chives, chopped	*as needed*	*as needed*

1. Cut the salmon into 5-ounce (140-gram) pieces. Reserve all trim for the mousseline filling. You will need 5 ounces (140 grams). Chill the fish thoroughly.

2. Make a mousseline as follows: Purée the salmon in the chilled bowl of a food processor to a smooth paste. Add the egg white, cream, herbs, and salt. Pulse the machine off and on, until the ingredients are all just incorporated. Keep chilled until needed.

3. Spread the forcemeat on the salmon and top with the duxelles.

4. Wrap the salmon in the phyllo (brush with butter, scattering bread crumbs between each sheet) and bake in a 400°F (205°C) oven for 20 minutes. Salmon should have an internal temperature of 150°F (65°C) and pastry should be a golden brown.

5. To prepare the sauce, heat the wine and steep the saffron in it. Add it to the velouté and simmer until the sauce is a deep golden color and reduced to a good consistency. Add the tomato concassé and the chives. Pool the sauce on heated plates and serve the salmon on top of the sauce.

Cioppino

Yield: 10 servings

Olive oil	1 fluid ounce	30 milliliters
Onions, diced fine	6 ounces	170 grams
Scallions, diced	2 bunches	2 bunches
Green peppers, diced	2 each	2 each
Fennel, diced	5 ounces	140 grams
Garlic cloves, minced	5 each	5 each
Fish fumet	1 quart	1 liter
Tomato concassé	6 pounds	2.7 kilograms
Tomato purée	4 fluid ounces	120 milliliters
Dry white wine	8 fluid ounces	240 milliliters
Bay leaves	2 each	2 each
Pepper, to taste	$1/4$ teaspoon	$1/4$ teaspoon
Salt, to taste	$1/2$ teaspoon	$1/2$ teaspoon
Little Neck clams	20 each	20 each
Crabs, disjointed	3 each	3 each
Shrimp, 21 to 25 count, peeled and deveined	20 each	20 each
Swordfish, diced	$1 1/4$ pounds	570 grams
Basil, chopped	3 tablespoons	3 tablespoons
Croutons, garlic-flavored	10 each	10 each

1. Heat the oil in a soup pot. Add the onions, scallions, peppers, and fennel. Sauté until the onions are translucent.

2. Add the garlic and sauté it until an aroma is apparent. Add the white wine and reduce by half.

3. Add the fish fumet, tomato concassé, tomato purée, white wine, and bay leaves. Cover the pot and simmer the mixture slowly for about 45 minutes. Add a small amount of water, if necessary. Cioppino should be more of a broth than a stew.

4. Remove and discard the bay leaves.

5. Add the whole clams and crabs. Simmer for about 10 minutes. Add the shrimp and swordfish; simmer them until the fish is just cooked through.

6. Add the chopped basil; adjust the seasoning to taste with salt and pepper. Ladle the cioppino into heated bowls and garnish each bowl with a crouton.

Cioppino, as it was originally prepared in San Francisco, probably featured a large selection of fish and shellfish.

This fish stew and others like it are derived from dishes prepared by fishermen returning to shore. The selection of seafood would vary from day to day.

To prepare the croutons, spread 10 slices of Italian bread with an olive oil/garlic mixuure. Toast in the oven until crisp.

TECHNIQUE
Stewing (pages 394-397)
Dicing (page 220)
Mincing (page 219)
Tomato concassé (page 226)
Working with shellfish (pages 284-289)
Basic knife cuts (pages 217-223)

RECIPE
Fish Fumet (page 481)

Removing seeds and stems from peppers.

The okra may be left whole if it is very small. Slice larger okra about 1/2 inch (1 centimeter) thick.

It is thought that the term jambalaya *has its origins in the French word for ham (*jambon*), an important ingredient in any good version of this dish.*

Chickpeas can be cooked following the method for Basic Boiled Beans (page 646). Refer to the table on Bean Cookery in Appendix 2 for additonal information.

TECHNIQUE
Simmering (pages 386-388)
Basic knife cuts (pages 217-223)
Cleaning shrimp (page 284)

RECIPE
Fish Stock (page 482)

Shrimp Jambalaya

Yield: 10 servings

Salt pork, minced	*6 ounces*	*170 grams*
Onions, diced	*6 ounces*	*170 grams*
Green pepper, diced	*6 ounces*	*170 grams*
Red pepper, diced	*6 ounces*	*170 grams*
Celery, diced	*6 ounces*	*170 grams*
Ham, diced	*8 ounces*	*225 grams*
Garlic cloves, minced	*5 each*	*5 each*
Long-grain rice	*8 ounces*	*225 grams*
Salt to taste	*2 teaspoons*	*2 teaspoons*
Tabasco to taste	*several drops*	*several drops*
Thyme leaves	*1 teaspoon*	*1 teaspoon*
Fish Stock	*3 pints*	*1.5 liters*
Chick peas, cooked and drained	*8 ounces*	*225 grams*
Olives, ripe, pitted	*3 ounces*	*85 grams*
Tomato concassé	*1 1/2 pounds*	*680 grams*
Shrimp, peeled and deveined	*2 1/4 pounds*	*1 kilogram*
Okra	*20 each*	*20 each*
Parsley, chopped	*3 tablespoons*	*3 tablespoons*

1. Render the salt pork until it is lightly browned.

2. Add the onions, peppers, celery, ham, and garlic; cook them over high heat until an aroma is apparent.

3. Add the rice; cook until the rice is coated with the rendered fat. (It should appear shiny.) Add the salt, Tabasco, thyme, and stock. Bring the mixture to a boil.

4. Add the chickpeas, olives, and tomato concassé. Cover the pot and cook the mixture over low heat for 20 minutes, or until the rice is nearly tender.

5. Add the shrimp; cover the pot again and cook the jambalaya until the shrimp are barely cooked through and the rice is tender.

6. Sauté the okra quickly and add it to the jambalaya. Adjust the seasoning to taste with salt, pepper, and Tabasco.

7. Garnish with chopped parsley.

Fillet of Snapper en Papillote

Yield: 10 servings

Red snapper fillets	*4 pounds*	*1.8 kilograms*
Salt to taste	*½ teaspoon*	*½ teaspoon*
Pepper to taste	*¼ teaspoon*	*¼ teaspoon*
Clarified butter	*2 ounces*	*60 grams*
Fish Velouté	*1 pint*	*480 milliliters*
Dry white wine	*4 fluid ounces*	*120 milliliters*
Shallots, minced	*2 tablespoons*	*2 tablespoons*
Scallions, sliced	*5 ounces*	*140 grams*
Mushrooms, sliced	*5 ounces*	*140 grams*

1. Cut the fillets into 6-ounce (170-gram) portions; season well with salt and pepper.

2. Optional: Heat the clarified butter in a sauteuse. Quickly sear the fish on both sides until stiffened. Remove from the pan.

3. Cut 10 pieces of parchment into heart shapes large enough to enclose the fillets. Brush lightly with oil or butter.

4. Place the velouté on one side of each parchment heart. Place the fish on top. Sprinkle with the wine, shallots, and scallions. Shingle the mushrooms on top.

5. Fold the paper over and seal the sides tightly.

6. Place each bag on a hot, buttered sizzler platter. Shake it to prevent burning.

7. Finish in a hot oven (400 to 425°F/205 to 220°C) for 5 to 8 minutes. Serve immediately.

When the paper is cut, the wonderful aroma of the dish is released.

The vegetable garnish can be varied according to the season: peas in early summer, tomatoes and squash in the fall. For an elegant spring entrée, use asparagus tips and morels.

If you cook the fish in clarified butter (step 2), be sure you cool the fish properly before storing them (see pages 45-47).

TECHNIQUE
*Cooking foods en papillote
  (pages 378-380)
Filleting a fish (pages 280-281)
Carifying butter (page 253)
Basic Knife cuts (pages 217-223)*

RECIPE
Fish Velouté (page 517)

The steaks are ready to poach.

TECHNIQUE
Poaching (pages 383-386)

RECIPE
Court Bouillon (page 484)
Bouquet Garni (page 474)
Green Mayonnaise (page 680)

Cold Poached Salmon Steaks with Green Mayonnaise

Yield: 10 servings

Salmon, whole	*4 pounds*	*1.8 kilograms*
Court Bouillon as needed	*1 quart*	*1 liter*
Bouquet Garni	*1 each*	*1 each*
Lemons, sliced	*3 each*	*3 each*
Green Mayonnaise	*20 fluid ounces*	*600 milliliters*

1. Cut the salmon into 10 steaks and blot dry. Place on a fish-poacher rack.

2. Bring the court bouillon, bouquet garni, and lemon slices to a bare simmer.

3. Lower the salmon into the court bouillon. Monitor the cooking speed carefully, maintaining a poaching temperature of 155°F (67°C).

4. Cook the salmon just until it is barely cooked through (internal temperature should be 150°F/65°C); the flesh should still hold together. Allow it to cool in the court bouillon.

5. Remove the salmon from the court bouillon. Chill thoroughly and serve with mayonnaise.

Poached Sole Vin Blanc

Yield: 10 servings

Sole fillets	*4 pounds*	*1.8 kilograms*
Salt to taste	*¹/₂ teaspoon*	*¹/₂ teaspoon*
Pepper to taste	*¹/₄ teaspoon*	*¹/₂ teaspoon*
Butter as needed	*1 ounce*	*30 grams*
Shallots, minced	*¹/₄ ounce*	*15 grams*
Dry white wine	*4 fluid ounces*	*120 milliliters*
Fish Stock	*8 fluid ounces*	*240 milliliters*
Fish Velouté or Béchamel	*20 fluid ounces*	*600 milliliters*
Egg yolks, beaten	*3 each*	*3 each*
Butter, diced	*2 ounces*	*30 grams*

Use a parchment lid to cover the fish as it cooks.

1. Portion the sole at 6 ounces (170 grams) each. Season the sole with the salt and pepper and fold into thirds.

2. Butter a pan; sprinkle with the shallots. Place the sole on the bed of shallots. Add the wine and stock.

3. Bring the liquid to a bare simmer over direct heat.

4. Cover the sole with buttered parchment paper; finish it in a 350°F (175°C) oven.

5. Remove the sole and keep it warm.

6. Reduce the cooking liquid and add the velouté; simmer until reduced to a good sauce consistency.

7. Temper the yolks with the hot sauce; return the sauce to the heat and cook until thickened. Do not boil the sauce.

8. Finish the sauce with the butter, season to taste, and coat the fish with the sauce.

Vin blanc sauce may be prepared in three different ways. After the fish is properly poached, you may:

(1) reduce the cooking liquid and add it to prepared velouté,
(2) reduce the cooking liquid and use it to replace the standard reduction for hollandaise sauce, or
(3) prepare a hollandaise (without a reduction), gradually incorporating the reduced cooking liquid.

TECHNIQUE
Shallow-poaching (pages 382-384)
Filleting a fish (pages 280-281)
Mincing (page 219)
Cutting parchment lids (page 259)
Tempering (page 257)
Separating eggs (page 254)

RECIPES
Fish Stock (page 482)
Fish Velouté (page 517)
Béchamel (page 518)

Green grapes add a delicate flavor to the dish.

"Veronique" generally appears in the title of any dish served with a white sauce or glaçage, garnished with peeled, seedless grapes.

TECHNIQUE
Filleting a fish (page 280-281)
Preparing a mousseline forcemeat
(page 408)
Shallow-poaching (pages 382-384)
Paupiettes (page 281)
Mincing (page 219)
Chopping (page 219)
Separating eggs (page 254)
Whipping/cream (page 257)
Broiling (pages 344-349)
Glaçage (page 345)
Beurre Manié (pages 238-239)

RECIPES
Fish Fumet (page 481)
Hollandaise Sauce (page 521)

Paupiettes of Sole Véronique

Yield: 10 servings

Sole fillets	*4 pounds*	*1.8 kilograms*
Egg white	*1 each*	*1 each*
Heavy cream	*4 fluid ounces*	*120 milliliters*
Salt to taste	*1/2 teaspoon*	*1/2 teaspoon*
Pepper to taste	*1/4 teaspoon*	*1/4 teaspoon*
Shallots, minced	*1 tablespoon*	*1 tablespoon*
Parsley stems, chopped	*8 each*	*8 each*
Dry white wine	*4 fluid ounces*	*120 milliliters*
Fish Fumet	*5 fluid ounces*	*150 milliliters*
Beurre Manié	*2 ounces*	*60 grams*
Heavy cream, whipped	*4 fluid ounces*	*120 milliliters*
Hollandaise Sauce	*4 fluid ounces*	*120 milliliters*
Green grapes, peeled, 3 to 4 per order	*10 ounces*	*285 grams*

1. Trim the fillets and portion at 6 ounces (170 grams) per serving. Refrigerate them. Save all the trim for the filling.

2. To prepare the mousseline filling: Purée the diced trim in a food processor. Add egg white to the purée and process until it is just blended. Work in the heavy cream by hand over an ice bath; season the mixture to taste with salt and pepper.

3. Divide the filling evenly between the fillets and roll them in paupiettes.

4. Butter a sauteuse and add the shallots and parsley stems. Arrange the paupiettes in the sauteuse.

5. Add the wine and fumet; cover the fish with buttered parchment paper. Bring the liquid to a simmer over direct heat and finish the fish in a moderate oven. Remove the paupiettes and keep them warm while finishing the sauce.

6. Return the sauteuse to the heat and thicken the cooking liquid with the beurre manié. Remove the pan from the heat. Add the heavy cream and hollandaise; mix them in thoroughly and adjust the seasoning to taste to make glaçage.

7. Place the paupiettes on a sizzler platter. Coat each portion completely with 2 fluid ounces (60 milliliters) of glaçage. Brown them under a salamander or broiler.

8. Serve the fish immediately with heated grapes.

Boiled Lobster with Drawn Butter

Yield: 10 servings

Lobsters	*10 each*	*10 each*
Butter, drawn	*20 ounces*	*570 grams*
Lemon wedges	*as needed*	*as needed*
Parsley sprigs (optional)	*10 each*	*10 each*

1. Plunge the live lobsters head-first into a large pot of boiling, salted water.

2. When the water returns to a boil, simmer the lobster for 6 to 8 minutes for a 1-pound lobster (larger lobsters may take up to 20 minutes, depending on their weight). Do not overcook or the flesh will become tough.

3. Serve the lobster immediately with lemon wedges and drawn butter.

4. Garnish with parsley sprigs.

The lobster is properly cooked.

When lobster meat must be removed from the shell for another use, cool the cooked lobster in cold running water. (This makes handling easier and prevents further cooking.)

TECHNIQUE
Boiling lobsters (page 387)
Drawn butter (page 253)

Removing the mussel's beard.

Cut the cod fillet into 2-ounce (60-gram) portions.

TECHNIQUE
Steaming (pages 374-378)
Working with shellfish (pages 284-289)
Filleting a fish (pages 280-281)
Leeks (page 225)
Basic knife cuts (pages 217-223)

RECIPE
Chicken Stock (page 480)

New England Shore Dinner

Yield: 10 servings

Onions, small dice	*10 ounces*	*285 grams*
Butter	*3 ounces*	*85 grams*
Garlic cloves, minced	*3 each*	*3 each*
Thyme leaves	*1 teaspoon*	*1 teaspoon*
Bay leaves	*2 each*	*2 each*
Chicken Stock as needed	*1 pint*	*480 milliliters*
Corn on the cob, husked and quartered	*3 each*	*3 each*
Lobsters, quartered	*3 each*	*3 each*
Clams, topneck	*20 each*	*20 each*
Mussels, cleaned	*20 each*	*20 each*
Red Bliss potatoes, cooked	*10 each*	*10 each*
Cod fillet	*1 ¼ pounds*	*570 grams*
Leeks, split	*5 each*	*5 each*
Boiling onions, parcooked	*5 each*	*5 each*
Sea scallops	*5 ounces*	*140 grams*
Zucchini, thick bâtonnet	*2 each*	*2 each*
Parsley, chopped	*2 teaspoons*	*2 teaspoons*

1. Sweat the onion in the butter. Add the garlic and sauté until the aroma is apparent.

2. Add the thyme, bay leaves, and stock; simmer the liquid.

3. Arrange the following ingredients in a flameproof casserole. Bottom layer: corn, lobster, clams, mussels, potatoes. Top layer: cod, leeks, boiling onions, scallops, zucchini.

4. Cover and steam all of the ingredients over direct heat or in a 350°F (175°C) oven until the seafood is cooked through, about 20 to 25 minutes.

5. Arrange the fish, seafood, and vegetables on a heated platter, or serve it directly from the casserole.

19

Vegetarian Entrées

An increasing number of individuals are looking for vegetarian options on the menu. In this chapter you will find recipes in the following groups:

- *Egg and Crêpe Dishes*
- *Nut, Bean, and Tofu Dishes*
- *Vegetable Burgers*
- *Roulades and Strudels*
- *Pasta*
- *Vegetable Stews*
- *Tex-Mex Specialties*

In addition, you may wish to adapt recipes from chapters devoted to vegetable, potato, rice, and grain dishes, breakfast recipes, and salads and sandwiches (Chapters 21 and 25).

Cleaning spinach.

Use smaller leaves for bite-sized rolls suitable for appetizer portions or canapés.

If desired, 6 ounces (170 grams) of duxelles (page 473) can be added to the mix. Ricotta cheese may replace some of the required cheese.

TECHNIQUE
Chopping garlic (pages 224-225)
Cooking grains (barley) (Appendix 2)
Toasting nuts (page 237)
Making bread crumbs (page 237)

RECIPE
Vegetable Stock (page 483)

Stuffed Spinach Rolls

Yield: 10 servings

Spinach leaves (large)	*40 each*	*40 each*
Garlic cloves, chopped	*3 each*	*3 each*
Butter	*1 tablespoon*	*1 tablespoon*
Walnuts, toasted and chopped	*6 ounces*	*170 grams*
Bread crumbs, fresh	*2 ounces*	*60 grams*
Pepper, to taste	*¼ teaspoon*	*¼ teaspoon*
Parmesan cheese, grated	*10 ounces*	*285 grams*
Mozzarella cheese, grated	*10 ounces*	*285 grams*
Barley, cooked	*12 ounces*	*340 grams*
Chives, chopped	*1 teaspoon*	*1 teaspoon*
Thyme, dried	*½ teaspoon*	*½ teaspoon*
Scallions, chopped	*2 each*	*2 each*
Vegetable Stock	*8 fluid ounces*	*240 milliliters*

1. Blanch spinach leaves carefully in boiling water. Drain well and spread out, ready to use.

2. Sweat the garlic lightly in butter, add the walnuts, bread crumbs, and a little pepper to taste. Allow to cool completely.

3. Add the bread crumbs mixture, chives, thyme, and scallions with the cheeses; stir just enough to blend the ingredients together. Do not overmix.

4. Take 2 spinach leaves and lay them out flat on a board. Place a spoonful of the cheese mix onto the spinach leaves.

5. Fold the sides of the spinach leaf in toward the center first, then roll up the spinach leaf into a roll, keeping it reasonably taut.

6. Place the spinach rolls into a greased gratin dish (2 per portion). Add enough vegetable stock to just cover the bottom of the pan. Cover with a tight-fitting lid and shallow-poach for a few minutes over medium-high heat on the range until the stock has disappeared. Serve at once.

Falafel

Yield: 10 servings

Chickpeas, soaked overnight	*1 pound*	*450 grams*
Garlic cloves, coarsely chopped	*3 each*	*3 each*
Large onions, coarsely chopped	*1 each*	*1 each*
Parsley, flat-leaf	*¼ bunch*	*¼ bunch*
Cumin, toasted	*1 tablespoon*	*1 tablespoon*
Coriander, toasted	*1 tablespoon*	*1 tablespoon*
Cayenne to taste	*¼ teaspoon*	*¼ teaspoon*
Salt to taste	*1 tablespoon*	*1 tablespoon*
Baking soda	*1 teaspoon*	*1 teaspoon*
Water	*4 fluid ounces*	*120 milliliters*

1. Drain the chickpeas and rinse. Grind beans, garlic, onions, and parsley through a fine die or grinder.

2. Add spices and mix.

3. Dissolve salt and baking soda in water. Add to chickpea mixture and mix.

4. Mold into flat round disks.

5. Heat oil to 350°F (175°C). Deep-fry falafel until golden brown. Drain and serve.

Tahini paste.

Falafels are traditionally served in pitas with lettuce, tomato, onions, and a tahini sauce.

*To make a **Mediterranean Sampler Plate:** Include humus b'tahini, baba ghannouj, pita triangles, and stuffed grape leaves (page 696).*

TECHNIQUE
Deep-frying (pages 367-371)
Soaking beans (page 236)
Basic knife cuts (pages 217-223)
Toasting nuts and seeds (page 237)

Grilled Marinated Tofu with Fresh Tomato Salsa

Yield: 10 servings

Tofu, drained and pressed	*36 ounces*	*1 kilogram*
White wine	*6 fluid ounces*	*180 milliliters*
Vegetable oil	*1 tablespoon*	*1 tablespoon*
Salt	*¼ teaspoon*	*¼ teaspoon*
Pepper	*½ teaspoon*	*½ teaspoon*
Rosemary sprigs	*2 each*	*2 each*
Fresh Tomato Salsa	*20 ounces*	*570 grams*

1. Cut tofu into 2-inch (5-centimeter) cubes.

2. Combine wine, oil, salt, pepper, and rosemary to make a marinade. Add the tofu.

3. Allow to marinate for about 30 minutes.

4. Remove the tofu from marinade and thread on skewers.

5. Mark the tofu squares on the grill.

6. Serve with salsa on the side.

Remember to soak the skewers if you are using wooden ones.

To press tofu, place it in a pan between several layers of cheesecloth. Top with a board or a second hotel pan. Weight with canned goods or weights (5 pounds/2.25 kilograms) for several hours.

TECHNIQUE
Grilling (pages 344-349)
Marinades (pages 242-245)

RECIPE
Fresh Tomato Salsa (page 690)

Carrots give these burgers a "meaty" color and texture.

Garnish with yogurt seasoned with lemons and roasted garlic cloves. Top with alfalfa sprouts.

The burger can also be served as a sandwich or a Kaiser roll topped with melted cheese, lettuce, and tomato.

TECHNIQUE
Basic knife cuts (pages 217-223)
Pan-Frying (pages 364-367)

Vegetable Burger

Yield: 10 servings

Carrots, ground	*1 1/2 pounds*	*680 grams*
Celery, ground	*4 ounces*	*115 grams*
Onions, ground	*4 ounces*	*115 grams*
Red pepper, ground	*2 ounces*	*60 grams*
Green pepper, ground	*2 ounces*	*60 grams*
Walnuts, ground	*3 ounces*	*85 grams*
Mushrooms, finely chopped	*8 ounces*	*225 grams*
Scallions, finely chopped	*8 ounces*	*225 grams*
Eggs	*2 each*	*2 each*
Tabasco to taste	*1/4 teaspoon*	*1/4 teaspoon*
Salt to taste	*1/2 teaspoon*	*1/2 teaspoon*
Pepper to taste	*1/4 teaspoon*	*1/4 teaspoon*
Sesame oil to taste	*1/2 teaspoon*	*1/2 teaspoon*
Cracker or matzoh meal as needed to bind	*2 ounces*	*60 grams*

1. Mix together the carrots, celery, onions, and peppers. Press out any excess liquid. Add walnuts, mushrooms, scallions, eggs, Tabasco, and seasonings.

2. Add enough cracker meal to make a firm mixture. Form into patties (6 ounces/170 grams).

3. Roll in additional cracker meal, if desired, then pan-fry both sides to golden brown. Finish cooking in a 350°F (175°C) oven, about 30 minutes.

Vegetable Strudel

Yield: 10 servings

Snow peas, julienned and blanched	*8 ounces*	*225 grams*
Carrots, julienned and blanched	*8 ounces*	*225 grams*
Yellow squash, julienned	*8 ounces*	*225 grams*
Zucchini, julienned	*8 ounces*	*225 grams*
Yellow pepper, julienned	*8 ounces*	*225 grams*
Red pepper, julienned	*8 ounces*	*225 grams*
Ricotta cheese	*8 ounces*	*225 grams*
Garlic cloves, roasted	*6 each*	*6 each*
Salt to taste	*½ teaspoon*	*½ teaspoon*
Basil, shredded	*3 tablespoons*	*3 tablespoons*
Phyllo, large sheets	*5 each*	*5 each*
Vegetable oil or melted butter	*2 fluid ounces*	*60 milliliters*
Bread crumbs, fresh	*4 ounces*	*115 grams*
Tomato Coulis	*20 fluid ounces*	*600 milliliters*

1. Combine all vegetables with roasted garlic, salt, and pepper to taste and mix well. Gently fold in the basil.

2. Stack the phyllo sheets, brushing them with oil or melted butter, and dusting with bread crumbs between each layer.

3. Spread the vegetable mixture evenly along one edge of the sheets. Roll the sheets into a log. Brush the top with a little butter.

4. With a serrated knife, score lines where you will cut the strudel after it is baked.

5. Place seam-side down on a parchment-lined sheet pan, and bake at 400°F (200°C) about 15 to 20 minutes, or to an even golden brown.

6. Slice the strudel, and place it in a pool of heated coulis.

Vary the vegetables according to the season.

Authentic strudel dough is made by stretching a ball of dough carefully into a delicate, almost translucent sheet. This recipe calls for machine-made phyllo dough.

TECHNIQUE
Roasting and baking (page 349)
Basic knife cuts (pages 217-223)
Blanching vegetables (page 378)
Roasting garlic (page 225)
Working with phyllo (page 446)
Making bread crumbs (page 237)

RECIPE
Tomato Coulis (page 525)

Dust the work surface with flour; this is a sticky dough.

Escarole-Feta Turnovers

Yield: 10 servings

Cream Cheese Pastry		
Cream cheese, softened	*8 ounces*	*225 grams*
Butter, softened	*8 ounces*	*225 grams*
Flour	*20 ounces*	*570 grams*
Salt	*1 teaspoon*	*1 teaspoon*
Milk	*as needed*	*as needed*
Olive oil	*1 tablespoon*	*1 tablespoon*
Garlic cloves, minced	*2 each*	*2 each*
Escarole, rinsed and chopped	*1 1/2 pounds*	*680 grams*
Sun-dried tomatoes, rehydrated, diced	*5 each*	*5 each*
Scallions, chopped	*3 each*	*3 each*
Feta cheese, crumbled	*8 ounces*	*225 grams*
Salt to taste	*1/2 teaspoon*	*1/2 teaspoon*
Pepper to taste	*1/4 teaspoon*	*1/4 teaspoon*
Egg wash	*as needed*	*as needed*

1. Blend the cream cheese and butter. Cut in the flour and add the salt. Mix until the butter is pea-sized. Form into a ball and chill while preparing the filling.

2. Heat the olive oil, sauté the garlic, and add the escarole. Cover and steam. Add the sun-dried tomatoes and scallions. Drain. Cool. Add the feta cheese. Season to taste with salt and pepper.

3. Roll out the dough and cut it into 6-inch (15-centimeter) squares. Place a portion of the filling in the center; fold over to create a triangle. Seal with egg wash, and crimp edges. Brush surface with egg wash. Bake at 325°F (165°C) until golden brown, approximately 30 minutes.

VARIATIONS

Vegetable Curry Turnover: Heat 2 tablespoons olive oil; add 4 ounces (115 grams) chopped onions and 2 mashed garlic cloves. Cover and sweat. Add 2 tablespoons curry powder. Cook briefly. Add 1/2 pound (225 grams) each of blanched, chopped cauliflower, broccoli, potatoes, and peas. Toss to blend. Add 8 fluid ounces (225 milliliters) vegetable stock or 4 fluid ounces (115 milliliters) coconut milk and cook out. Fill as above.

Roasted Pepper with Gorgonzola Turnover: Prepare roasted pepper salad and chill. Add 8 ounces (225 grams) crumbled gorgonzola. Use this to fill the pastry as directed above.

Basic pie crust dough or puff pastry dough may be substituted for the cream cheese pastry.

Serve the turnovers with any of the tomato sauces or vegetable coulis suggested in Chapter 15. Prepared mango chutney and toasted coconut would work well with the Vegetable Curry Turnover variation.

TECHNIQUE
Preparing pastry crusts (pages 442-444)
Cleaning leafy greens (page 229)
Basic knife cuts (pages 217-223)
Working with dried fruits and vegetables (pages 235-236)

Vegetable Lasagna

Yield: 10 servings

Eggplant, peeled, $^1/_8$-inch slices	*2 pounds*	*900 grams*
Flour as needed	*4 ounces*	*115 grams*
Egg wash	*5 ounces*	*140 grams*
Bread crumbs, dry	*6 ounces*	*170 grams*
Vegetable oil as needed	*6 fluid ounces*	*180 milliliters*
Zucchini	*1 pound*	*450 grams*
Yellow squash	*1 pound*	*450 grams*
Mushrooms, sliced	*1 pound*	*450 grams*
Garlic cloves, minced	*3 each*	*3 each*
Salt to taste	*$^1/_2$ teaspoon*	*$^1/_2$ teaspoon*
Pepper to taste	*$^1/_2$ teaspoon*	*$^1/_2$ teaspoon*
Ricotta cheese	*1 pound*	*450 grams*
Eggs, beaten	*2 each*	*2 each*
Parmesan cheese, grated	*8 ounces*	*225 grams*
Mozzarella, grated	*12 ounces*	*340 grams*
Marinara Sauce	*1 quart*	*1 liter*

Yellow squash and zucchini.

1. Coat eggplant with flour, egg wash, and bread crumbs using standard breading procedure.

2. Pan-fry eggplant in very hot oil and drain well.

3. Slice zucchini and yellow squash lengthwise into $^1/_8$-inch thick slices to make "lasagna noodles." Blanch, shock, and drain well. Reserve.

4. Sauté mushrooms, add the garlic, and season to taste. Drain off excess liquid.

5. Mix ricotta, eggs, and half of the Parmesan.

6. In a baking pan, place a thin layer of tomato sauce, a layer of eggplant, then the ricotta mixture, zucchini, yellow squash, mushrooms and mozzarella. Repeat the process until all ingredients are used, ending with a layer of eggplant and marinara sauce. Cover the pan.

7. Bake at 350°F (175°C) until all ingredients are thoroughly cooked, about one hour. Remove cover, top with the remaining Parmesan and place back in the oven to bake another 15 to 20 minutes. Allow to rest about 15 minutes before cutting.

For a spicier finish, add up to 1 tablespoon red chili flakes to the tomato sauce.

If you pefer, you may grill or blanch the eggplant rather than bread and fry it.

Include other vegetables, as available: sautéed onions, red and green peppers (roasted or blanched), blanched broccoli, Swiss chard, or spinach are all good choices.

Prepared lasagna noodles may also be added.

TECHNIQUE
Pan-frying (pages 364-367)
Standard breading procedure (page 366)
Basic knife cuts (pages 217-223)
Blanching vegetables (page 378)

RECIPE
Marinara Sauce (page 519)

Swiss Chard

To prepare crêpes for this dish, use the recipe on page 665, adding 2 tablespoons of minced fresh parsley.

Canneloni is prepared in this manner in the Piedmont region of Italy. The traditional filling includes veal, prosciutto, and Parmesan. Elsewhere, canneloni are pasta sheets filled with tomato sauce and mozzarella.

TECHNIQUE
Cleaning leafy greens (page 229)
Basic knife cuts (pages 217-223)
Toasting nuts and seeds (page 237)

RECIPES
Crêpes (page 665)
Cream Sauce (page 518)

Canneloni with Swiss Chard and Walnuts, Piedmont Style

Yield: 10 servings

Swiss chard, rinsed, stems removed	2 pounds	900 grams
Butter	2 ounces	60 grams
Onions, minced	4 ounces	115 grams
Brandy	2 fluid ounces	60 milliliters
Heavy cream	1 fluid ounce	30 milliliters
Walnuts, toasted	3 ounces	85 grams
Gruyère cheese, grated	1 ounce	30 grams
Egg, beaten well	1 each	1 each
Salt to taste	1 teaspoon	1 teaspoon
Pepper to taste	$^1/_2$ teaspoon	$^1/_2$ teaspoon
Nutmeg, ground to taste	$^1/_8$ teaspoon	$^1/_8$ teaspoon
Crêpes	20 each	20 each
Cream Sauce	8 fluid ounces	240 milliliters
Egg yolk, beaten	1 each	1 each

1. Blanch the Swiss chard in rapidly boiling salted water. Drain, squeeze dry, and coarsely chop.

2. Melt the butter in a skillet. Add the shallots and allow them to sweat.

3. Add the brandy and flame. Add the cream and reduce slightly. Add the Swiss chard and cook over medium heat for 5 minutes.

4. Away from the heat, mix in the walnuts, Gruyère, and beaten egg. Add salt, pepper, and nutmeg to taste. Let this mixture cool and keep refrigerated until needed.

5. Add the filling to the crêpes and roll into canneloni. Place in a baking pan or individual gratin dishes.

6. Blend the cream sauce and egg yolk and ladle over the canneloni.

7. Bake at 375°F (190°C) for about 20 to 30 minutes, or until heated throughly. Serve at once.

Eggplant Parmesan

Yield: 10 servings

Eggplant, peeled, ¹/₂-inch slices	*2 pounds*	*900 grams*
Flour as needed	*4 ounces*	*115 grams*
Egg wash	*5 ounces*	*140 grams*
Bread crumbs, dry	*6 ounces*	*170 grams*
Vegetable oil as needed	*4 fluid ounces*	*120 milliliters*
Salt to taste	*¹/₂ teaspoon*	*¹/₂ teaspoon*
Pepper to taste	*¹/₂ teaspoon*	*¹/₂ teaspoon*
Marinara Sauce	*1 quart*	*1 liter*
Mozzarella cheese, grated	*12 ounces*	*340 grams*
Parmesan cheese, grated	*4 ounces*	*115 grams*

1. Bread eggplant using the standard breading procedure. Preheat the oven to 375°F (190°C).

2. Pan-fry eggplant until golden, and drain well. Season with salt and pepper.

3. Pour a thin layer of marinara sauce into a gratin dish, then top with the eggplant slices. Cover with additional sauce. Top with mozzarella cheese.

4. Cover and bake in the oven for 15 minutes. Remove the cover and bake for an additional 6 to 8 minutes to brown the cheese. Serve with Parmesan cheese.

Add fresh herbs to the tomato sauce, if you wish.

Prepare the eggplant parmesan in a hotel pan or in individual gratin dishes.

TECHNIQUE
Pan-frying (pages 364-367)
Standard breading procedure (page 366)

RECIPE
Marinara Sauce (pag 519)

Macaroni and Cheese

Yield: 10 servings

Macaroni, uncooked	*2 ¹/₄ pounds*	*1 kilogram*
Salt	*¹/₂ teaspoon*	*¹/₂ teaspoon*
Cheddar Cheese Sauce	*1 quart*	*1 liter*
Bread crumbs, fresh (optional)	*6 ounces*	*170 grams*

1. Bring a large pot of salted water to a boil on the stove. Add the macaroni and return to a boil. Cook the pasta al dente, 7 to 9 minutes. Do not over-cook.

2. Drain the pasta and shock. Mix the pasta with the sauce.

3. Pour into a gratin or hotel pan. If desired, sprinkle bread crumbs over the surface. Bake at 300°F (175°C) until heated through and the surface is crisp. Lower the temperature if necessary. The cheese will separate if baked at too high a temperature.

Use a good quality, aged cheddar for the richest flavor.

Other cheeses may be blended with the Cheddar cheese: Monterey Jack, fontina, or Swiss. Grate some over the surface near the end of baking time.

Other ingredients may be precooked and included with the macaroni and cheese. Try blanched broccoli florets, peas, diced red and green peppers, chopped onions, and canned tuna.

Other pasta shapes can replace the macaroni: rotini, fusilli, and shells all work well.

TECHNIQUE
Cooking pasta (pages 388-389)

RECIPE
Cheddar Cheese Sauce (page 518)

Serve the chili with cornbread.

Serve over brown rice with cornbread, or as a filling for burritos and enchiladas.

Twelve fluid ounces (360 milliliters) of beer may replace part of the vegetable stock.

If chipotles are not available, use diced, fresh jalapeños or add any dried red chilies. Remove dried chilies at the end of cooking time.

Chopped carrots, zucchini, celery, or jicama may be added in step 2.

You may use Red Chili Sauce (page 524) as the base of the chili if you prefer.

TECHNIQUE
Stewing (pages 394-397)
Soaking beans (page 236)
Bean cookery table (Appendix 2)
Basic knife cuts (pages 217-223)
Tomato concassé (page 226)

RECIPE
Vegetable Stock (page 483)

Vegetarian Chili

Yield: 10 servings

Pinto beans, soaked	*1 pound*	*450 grams*
Black beans, soaked	*1 pound*	*450 grams*
Kidney beans, soaked	*8 ounces*	*225 grams*
Chickpeas, soaked	*8 ounces*	*225 grams*
Vegetable oil	*as needed*	*as needed*
Onions, chopped	*1 pound*	*450 grams*
Red peppers, diced	*6 ounces*	*170 grams*
Green peppers, diced	*6 ounces*	*170 grams*
Oregano leaves, chopped	*1 tablespoon*	*1 tablespoon*
Cumin, seed, to taste, ground	*2 tablespoons*	*2 tablespoons*
Chili powder	*1 ounce*	*30 grams*
Garlic cloves, minced	*3 each*	*3 each*
Green chilies, roasted, peeled, and seeded (or canned)	*3 each*	*3 each*
Chipotles, finely chopped	*3 each*	*3 each*
Adobo sauce, from canned chipotles	*2 tablespoons*	*2 tablespoons*
Tomato concassé, juice reserved	*1 1/2 pounds*	*680 grams*
Vegetable Stock, or water, as needed	*1 quart*	*1 liter*
Salt to taste	*1/2 teaspoon*	*1/2 teaspoon*
Pepper to taste	*1/4 teaspoon*	*1/4 teaspoon*
Lime juice to taste	*1 fluid ounce*	*30 milliliters*

1. Cook the beans separately in boiling salted water until very tender. Drain and reserve.

2. Heat the oil in a large rondeau. Add onions and sweat. Add the red and green peppers. Cook until soft.

3. Add the oregano, cumin, and chili powder; cook for a minute. Do not let the spices burn. Add the garlic and cook briefly. Add the green chilies, chipotles, and Adobo sauce.

4. Add the tomato concassé with any juices and stock. Simmer approximately 30 minutes. Add the beans; continue to simmer to a good stew-like consistency. Adjust the seasoning to taste with salt, pepper, and lime juice.

20

International Entrées

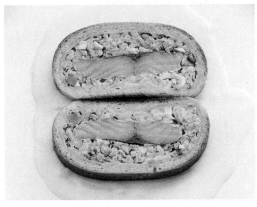

The constant interchange of recipes, ingredients, and cooking styles from one group to another has made it difficult to draw strict lines around any single cuisine. There are "international" recipes to be found throughout this book, many of which are so familiar that they are no longer regarded as foreign.

As the availability of special ingredients favored in Asian, Latin American, Caribbean, Mediterannean, and Middle Eastern cuisines has increased, so has the appearance of those dishes on many menus throughout this country. Add to that the increased awareness of the potential health benefits associated with ethnic cuisines, and it is easy to understand the growing demand on the part of your guests for a broader spectrum of offerings from around the world.

The recipes in this chapter are loosely grouped as follows:

- *Europe: Beef*
- *Europe: Veal*
- *Europe: Lamb*
- *Europe: Poultry*
- *Europe: Fish*
- *Europe: Mixed*

- *Latin: Beef*
- *Latin: Pork*
- *Latin: Poultry*
- *Latin: Fish*

- *Asia: Beef*
- *Asia: Pork*
- *Asia: Lamb*
- *Asia: Poultry*
- *Asia: Fish*

Stew meat.

There are many goulash recipes, with each region of Central Europe favoring its own style. Serve goulash with bread dumplings (page 651) or broad egg noodles. Garnish with heavy cream and chopped dill.

Goulash is best when it is prepared a day in advance to allow the flavors to "marry."

TECHNIQUE
Braising (pages 391-394)
Basic knife cuts (pages 217-223)
Zesting citrus (page 231)

RECIPE
White Beef Stock (page 480)

Beef Goulash

Yield: 10 servings

Onions, sliced or diced	*2 pounds*	*900 grams*
Lard or oil	*2 ounces*	*60 grams*
White wine vinegar	*1 fluid ounce*	*30 milliliters*
Sweet Hungarian paprika	*4 tablespoons*	*4 tablespoons*
Marjoram, powdered	*1 teaspoon*	*1 teaspoon*
Garlic cloves, minced	*3 each*	*3 each*
Lemon zest	*1 teaspoon*	*1 teaspoon*
Salt to taste	*¹/₂ teaspoon*	*¹/₂ teaspoon*
White Beef Stock	*1 quart*	*1 liter*
Tomato paste	*4 ounces*	*115 grams*
Beef shank, boneless, cut in large cubes	*5 pounds*	*2.25 kilograms*

1. Sauté the onions in lard or oil until they are brown.

2. Add the vinegar, spices, garlic, lemon zest, and salt; cook over moderate heat until nearly dry.

3. Add the stock and tomato paste and bring the mixture to a simmer.

4. Add the beef shank, cover the pan, and braise it until fork-tender, approximately 1¹/₂ hours. Degrease the sauce and adjust the seasoning with salt and pepper to taste.

Sauerbraten

Yield: 10 servings

Marinade

Dry red wine	8 fluid ounces	240 milliliters
Red wine vinegar	8 fluid ounces	240 milliliters
Water	2 quarts	2 liters
Onions, sliced	2 each	2 each
Whole black peppercorns	8 each	8 each
Juniper berries	10 each	10 each
Bay leaves	2 each	2 each
Whole cloves	2 each	2 each
Salt to taste	2 teaspoons	2 teaspoons
Vegetable oil	3 fluid ounces	90 milliliters
Mirepoix, diced	1 pound	450 grams
Tomato paste	4 ounces	115 grams
Flour	2 ounces	60 grams
Brown Veal Stock	3 quarts	3 liters
Gingersnaps, pulverized	3 ounces	85 grams
Beef bottom round	4 pounds	1.8 kilograms

Sear the meat on all sides.

1. Trim the beef to remove any gristle or silverskin.

2. Combine all the ingredients for the marinade and bring the mixture to a boil. Cool it to room temperature.

3. Season the beef with salt and place it in the marinade; marinate it under refrigeration for 3 to 5 days, turning it twice per day.

4. Remove the meat from the marinade. Strain and reserve the marinade; reserve the onions and herbs separately.

5. Bring the strained marinade to a boil and skim off the scum.

6. Heat the oil in a brazier. Add the beef and sear it on all sides. Remove the meat and reserve it.

7. Add the mirepoix and reserved onions and herbs from the marinade. Let them brown lightly.

8. Add the tomato paste and cook out for several seconds.

9. Deglaze the pan with the strained marinade and reduce the liquid by half.

10. Add the flour and combine the mixture thoroughly.

11. Add the brown stock, whip out any lumps, and bring to a simmer. Return the meat to the pan, cover it and braise until fork-tender.

12. Remove the meat and reduce the sauce. Degrease thoroughly.

13. Add the gingersnaps and cook the sauce for 10 minutes, until the gingersnaps dissolve. Strain the sauce through cheesecloth.

14. Carve the meat into 4- to 5-ounce (115- to 40-gram) portions and serve with the sauce.

Braising may be done in the oven at 300°F (150°C) or on the stove top.

"Fork-tender" means that meats will slide easily from a kitchen fork when lifted, or that they can be "cut" with a fork.

TECHNIQUE
Braising (pages 391-394)
Marinades (pages 242-245)

RECIPES
Mirepoix (page 472)
Brown Veal Stock (page 478)

Fresh sage is layered between veal and prosciutto.

Saltimbocca means "to jump in the mouth," an apt name for this quickly prepared sauté.

Although not essential, some people like to add a small slice of cheese to the veal along with the prosciutto and sage. Use mozzarella or smoked provolone.

TECHNIQUE
Sautéing (pages 358-362)
Cutting and pounding cutlets (page 261)

RECIPES
Demi-Glace (page 514)
Jus de Veau Lié (page 516)

Veal Saltimbocca

Yield: 10 servings

Veal top round	*4 pounds*	*1.8 kilograms*
Prosciutto, thinly sliced	*5 ounces*	*140 grams*
Sage leaves	*10 each*	*10 each*
Flour as needed	*4 ounces*	*115 grams*
Clarified butter as needed	*1 3/4 ounce*	*50 grams*
Demi-Glace or Jus de Veau Lié	*20 fluid ounces*	*600 milliliters*
Salt to taste	*1/2 teaspoon*	*1/2 teaspoon*
Pepper to taste	*1/2 teaspoon*	*1/2 teaspoon*
Marsala	*10 fluid ounces*	*300 milliliters*

1. Cut the veal into 2- to 3-ounce (60- to 85-gram) scaloppine. To assemble the saltimbocca, pound the veal, lay a piece of prosciutto amd a sage leaf on one side of the veal, and fold in half. Secure the veal with a toothpick. Season with salt and pepper.

2. Dredge the veal in the flour; shake off excess.

3. Heat the butter in a sauté pan. Add the veal and sauté on both sides.

4. Remove the veal from the pan and keep warm.

5. Pour off the butter from the pan. Add the demi-glace or jus and bring the sauce to a simmer; reduce by about one-fourth. Finish the sauce with the Marsala; adjust seasoning to taste with salt and pepper.

6. Pool the sauce on a heated plate and place the veal in the pool of sauce. Remove the toothpicks.

This dish must be served while it is extremely hot. In fact, the butter should still be bubbly when the dish is presented to the guest.

Rolled anchovies are another classic garnish for this dish.

TECHNIQUE
Pan-frying (pages 364-367)
Cutting and pounding cutlets (page 261)
Standard breading (page 366)
Making bread crumbs (page 237)

Wiener Schnitzel

Yield: 10 servings

Veal top round	*3 1/2 pounds*	*1.6 kilograms*
Salt to taste	*1/2 teaspoon*	*1/2 teaspoon*
Pepper to taste	*1/4 teaspoon*	*1/4 teaspoon*
Flour as needed	*4 ounces*	*115 grams*
Eggs, whole	*4 each*	*4 each*
Milk	*4 fluid ounces*	*120 milliliters*
Bread crumbs, dry	*12 ounces*	*340 grams*
Vegetable oil as needed	*3 to 4 ounces*	*90 to 120 milliliters*
Whole butter	*3 ounces*	*85 grams*
Lemon wedges or slices	*10 each*	*10 each*
Parsley sprigs	*10 each*	*10 each*

(Recipe continued on facing page)

1. Cut the veal into cutlets of about 5 to 6 ounces (140 to 170 grams). Pound them to an even thickness. Season well with salt and pepper.

2. Bread the veal cutlets: Dredge in flour, dip in egg wash (made by blending eggs and milk), and coat in bread crumbs. Refrigerate the cutlets until firm.

3. Pan-fry the cutlets in the hot oil until golden brown on both sides and cooked through. Shake the pan occasionally to keep the cutlets moving.

4. Heat the butter in a separate pan until hot and foamy.

5. Serve the cutlet topped with foaming butter and garnished with a lemon wedge and parsley.

VARIATION

Holstein Schnitzel: Top the Wiener Schnitzel with a soft-cooked fried egg.

Ossobuco alla Milanese

Yield: 10 servings

Veal hindshank.

Veal shanks	*10 each*	*10 each*
Salt to taste	*¹/₂ teaspoon*	*¹/₂ teaspoon*
Pepper to taste	*¹/₄ teaspoon*	*¹/₂ teaspoon*
Flour as needed	*3 ounces*	*85 grams*
Vegetable oil as needed	*2 fluid ounces*	*60 milliliters*
Dry white wine	*8 fluid ounces*	*240 milliliters*
Tomato paste	*6 ounces*	*170 grams*
Brown Sauce	*2 quarts*	*2 liters*
Gremolata		
Garlic cloves, minced	*2 each*	*2 each*
Lemon zest	*2 tablespoons*	*2 tablespoons*
Parsley, flat-leaf, chopped	*2 tablespoons*	*2 tablespoons*
Anchovy fillets, chopped	*5 each*	*5 each*

A veal shank generally weighs 1 to 3 pounds (450 grams to 1.3 kilograms). Use one small shank per portion. Cut larger shanks into crosscuts and serve 1 to 1 ¹/₂ pounds (450 to 680 grams) per portion.

In Milan, ossobuco is served with risotto, one of the rare occasions in Italy that risotto is served as a side dish.

For additional flavor, sauté 8 ounces (225 grams) of mirepoix and 2 cloves of minced garlic in the pan before deglazing it with wine. Prior to service, strain the sauce and reduce to proper consistency.

TECHNIQUE
Braising (pages 391-394)

RECIPE
Brown Sauce (page 514)

1. Season the meat with the salt and pepper; dredge in the flour, and sear on all sides in hot oil. Remove the meat and reserve.

2. Degrease the pan and deglaze it with the wine; reduce the wine by three-quarters.

3. Add the tomato paste and sauté briefly. Add the brown sauce; return the meat to the pan and bring the sauce to a simmer.

4. Cover the pan and braise the meat until it is fork-tender, approximately 2 to 3 hours. Remove the meat to moisten and keep it hot.

5. Return the pan to the heat and reduce the sauce to the proper thickness. Adjust seasoning to taste with salt and pepper. Degrease well.

6. Combine all of the ingredients for the gremolata.

7. Serve the ossobuco with the sauce and top with the gremolata.

Simmering lamb in stock.

Irish Stew is a "white" stew, made in virtually the same manner as a fricassée or blanquette. As you might imagine, the stew is not finished with the rich liason of egg yolks and cream. The final result is a simple, basic stew, given its body by the addition of a good selection of starchy vegetables.

Pearl onions may be used instead of chopped onions.

Serve with Irish Soda Bread.

TECHNIQUE
Stewing (pages 394-397)
Basic knife cuts (pages 217-223)

RECIPES
White Veal Stock (page 480)
Bouquet Garni (page 474)

Irish Stew

Yield: 10 servings

Lamb shoulder	*4 pounds*	*1.8 kilograms*
White Veal Stock	*1 1/2 quarts*	*1.5 liters*
Bouquet Garni	*1 each*	*1 each*
Onions, large dice	*1 pound*	*450 grams*
Potatoes, large dice	*1 pound*	*450 grams*
Celery, large dice	*1/2 pound*	*225 grams*
Carrots, large dice	*1/2 pound*	*225 grams*
Parsnips, large dice	*1/2 pound*	*225 grams*
Turnips, large dice	*1/2 pound*	*225 grams*
Salt to taste	*1/2 teaspoon*	*1/2 teaspoon*
White pepper to taste	*1/2 teaspoon*	*1/2 teaspoon*
Parsley, chopped	*1 tablespoon*	*1 tablespoon*

1. Combine the lamb and stock and bring to a simmer. Skim the surface throughout cooking time as necessary. Continue to cook over low heat for an hour; maintain a very gentle simmer.

2. Add the bouquet garni and the vegetables. Simmer slowly for another 1 to 1½ hours or until all of the ingredients are fork-tender.

3. Season to taste with salt and pepper and add parsley.

4. Serve in heated crocks or shallow soup plates.

VARIATION

Shepherd's Pie: Place a portion of stew in a crock or individual casserole. Top with duchesse potatoes. Brush the potatoes lightly with egg wash. Bake until browned.

Roast Chicken with Walnut Sauce
(Kotmis Satsivi)

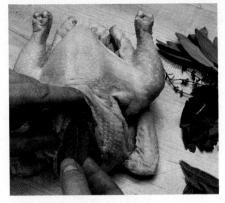

Stuff herbs under the skin to provide
additional flavor if desired.

Yield: 10 servings

Broiler chickens	*5 each*	*5 each*
Butter, melted	*3 ounces*	*85 grams*
Salt to taste	*1/2 teaspoon*	*1/2 teaspoon*
Pepper to taste	*1/4 teaspoon*	*1/4 teaspoon*
Walnut Sauce		
Onions, minced	*4 ounces*	*115 grams*
Butter, unsalted	*1 ounce*	*30 grams*
Red wine vinegar	*2 fluid ounces*	*60 milliliters*
Garlic, minced	*3 tablespoons*	*3 tablespoons*
Cloves, ground	*1/4 teaspoon*	*1/4 teaspoon*
Cinnamon, ground	*3/4 teaspoon*	*3/4 teaspoon*
Cayenne, ground	*3/4 teaspoon*	*3/4 teaspoon*
Bay leaf	*1 each*	*1 each*
Saffron threads, crushed	*3/4 teaspoon*	*3/4 teaspoon*
Red wine	*4 fluid ounces*	*120 milliliters*
Chicken Stock	*1 1/2 quarts*	*1.5 liters*
Brown Roux	*5 ounces*	*140 grams*
Walnuts, roasted and chopped	*10 ounces*	*285 grams*
Parsley, chopped	*1/4 ounce*	*2 grams*

*Broiler chickens average about 1 1/2
pounds (680 grams). You may wish to
substitute Cornish game hens in this dish.*

TECHNIQUE
Roasting (page 349)
Trussing poultry (pages 272-273)
Basic knife cuts (pages 217-223)
Toasting nuts and seeds (page 237)
Fresh herbs (page 229)

RECIPES
Chicken Stock (page 480)
Brown Roux (page 473)

1. Truss the chickens, brush with butter, and season with salt and pepper.

2. Roast on a rack in a 375°F (190°C) oven to an internal temperature of 160°F (70°C); baste occasionally with drippings.

3. Remove chickens and reserve pan drippings.

4. To make the sauce: Sauté onions in butter until translucent, add vinegar, and reduce until almost dry.

5. Add garlic, cloves, cinnamon, cayenne, bay leaf, and saffron; sauté 2 to 3 minutes.

6. Add red wine, reduce by half, add stock and pan drippings, and bring to a simmer. Degrease the sauce.

7. Thicken with roux; simmer 20 minutes, and add walnuts, parsley, and adjust seasonings to taste with salt and pepper.

8. Cut chicken into halves or quarters. Serve one half or 2 quarters of chicken per serving with 2 ounces (60 grams) of the sauce.

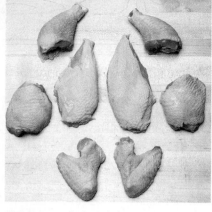

Chicken cut into eighths.

There are many versions of this dish, made from the hunter's catch—game birds or rabbits prepared as a satisfying stew garnished with mushrooms and herbs. Frying chickens average about 2 1/2 pounds (1 kilogram).

TECHNIQUE
Braising (pages 391-394)
Cutting a bird into eighths (page 274)
Basic knife cuts (pages 217-223)
Tomato concassé (page 226)
Zesting citrus fruits (page 231)

RECIPE
Brown Sauce (page 514)

Chicken Cacciatore

Yield: 10 servings

Chicken, fryers	*5 each*	*5 each*
Salt to taste	*1/2 teaspoon*	*1/2 teaspoon*
Pepper to taste	*1/4 teaspoon*	*1/4 teaspoon*
Flour as needed	*4 ounces*	*115 grams*
Olive oil	*2 fluid ounces*	*60 milliliters*
Onions, medium dice	*10 ounces*	*285 grams*
White wine	*5 fluid ounces*	*150 milliliters*
Mushrooms, sliced	*1 pound*	*450 grams*
Tomato concassé	*10 ounces*	*285 grams*
Garlic cloves, minced	*3 each*	*3 each*
Lemon zest, grated	*2 teaspoons*	*2 teaspoons*
Brown Sauce	*30 fluid ounces*	*900 milliliters*

1. Cut the chickens into eight pieces.

2. Season the chicken with salt and pepper and dredge it in the flour.

3. Sauté the chicken in the olive oil until it is lightly browned. Remove and reserve it.

4. Sauté the onion in the same oil.

5. Add the mushrooms, tomato concassé, garlic, and lemon zest. Sauté until the mushrooms have begun to release their juices.

6. Deglaze the pan with the wine and reduce the liquid.

7. Add the brown sauce and return the chicken pieces. Bring the sauce to a simmer.

8. Cover and braise in a 300°F (150°C) oven until fork-tender. Remove the chicken. Degrease the sauce. Serve 4 pieces per order, coated with the sauce.

Salmon in Brioche (Coulibiac)

Yield: 10 servings

Brioche dough

Yeast, instant	*1 ounce*	*30 grams*
Milk, warm	*24 fluid ounces*	*720 milliliters*
Flour	*2 pounds*	*1 kilogram*
Eggs, beaten	*2 each*	*2 each*
Salt	*1 teaspoon*	*1 teaspoon*
Nutmeg, ground	*pinch*	*pinch*
Butter, melted	*2 1/2 ounces*	*70 grams*

Filling

Butter	*1 ounce*	*30 grams*
Onions, minced	*4 ounces*	*115 grams*
Mushrooms, minced	*4 ounces*	*115 grams*
Lemon juice to taste	*2 teaspoons*	*2 teaspoons*
Basic Boiled Rice	*8 ounces*	*225 grams*
Hard-Cooked Eggs, chopped	*3 each*	*3 each*
Vesiga, soaked and chopped (see notes)	*8 ounces*	*225 grams*
Salmon fillets	*3 pounds*	*1.3 kilograms*
Salt to taste	*1/2 teaspoon*	*1/2 teaspoon*
Pepper to taste	*1/2 teaspoon*	*1/2 teaspoon*

1. To prepare the brioche, dissolve yeast in milk.

2. Add one-half of the flour, mix together and rest in a warm place for 15 minutes.

3. Add the eggs, salt, nutmeg, and butter to the yeast mixture; mix well.

4. Add the remaining flour, and mix until a smooth dough is formed.

5. Proof dough 20 minutes (covered), press flat and chill until firm (about 15 minutes).

6. Roll out dough and cut into two fish shapes 12 inches (30 centimeters) long.

7. Heat the butter and sauté the onions and mushrooms until tender. Remove from the heat and cool.

8. Combine all of the remaining ingredients for the filling. Season to taste with salt and pepper.

9. Spread a layer of the filling on one piece of dough. Place the salmon fillet on the filling. Top the salmon with the remaining filling and cover with the second piece of dough.

10. Decorate with fins, eyes, and scales sculpted from the remaining dough; brush with egg wash.

11. Bake in a 350°F (175°C) oven to an internal temperature of 145°F (60°C); rest 15 minutes before slicing.

Coulibiac, served with a cream sauce.

Vesiga is a traditional component of coulibiac. It is the dried spinal cord of the sturgeon. If you are using dried vesiga, it must be soaked in cool water for 5 to 6 hours, then simmered in fish stock for 3 to 4 hours. It should then be chopped before it is added to the rice mixture. Although traditional, vesiga may be omitted if it is unavailable.

TECHNIQUE
Roasting and baking (page 349)
Making yeast doughs (pages 430-434)
Basic knife cuts (pages 217-223)
Filleting a round fish (pages 280-281)

RECIPES
Basic Boiled Rice (page 643)
Hard-Cooked Eggs (page 654)

Removing the quill from squid.

Use a very rich, clear broth or fumet for the consommé if you prefer.

TECHNIQUE
Stewing (pages 394-397)
Basic knife cuts (pages 217-223)
Peeling and deveining shrimp (page 282)
Cleaning and debearding mussels (page 289)
Preparing squid (page 289)

RECIPE
Fish Consommé (page 489)

Shellfish Soup Flavored with Fennel and Saffron (Zuppa di Pesce alla Modenese)

Yield: 10 servings

Butter	1 ounce	30 grams
Fennel, julienne	3 ounces	85 grams
Celery root, julienne	2 ounces	60 grams
Leeks, julienne	4 ounces	115 grams
Carrots, julienne	4 ounces	115 grams
Saffron threads, crushed	$1/2$ teaspoon	$1/2$ teaspoon
Fish Consommé, hot	$1\,3/4$ quarts	1.6 liters
Sea bass fillet	20 ounces	570 grams
Shrimp, peeled and deveined	20 each	20 each
Littleneck clams, washed	20 each	20 each
Mussels, cleaned, debearded	30 each	30 each
Squids, cleaned, cut in thin slices	2 each	2 each
Salt to taste	$1/2$ teaspoon	$1/2$ teaspoon
Pepper to taste	$1/4$ teaspoon	$1/4$ teaspoon
Croutons, large	20 each	20 each
Parsley, chopped	2 tablespoons	2 tablespoons

1. Heat the butter. Sauté fennel, celery, leek, and carrot in butter until limp.

2. Add saffron to the hot consommé and allow to infuse for 5 minutes.

3. Cut the sea bass into 2-ounce (60-gram) portions. Arrange the fish and shellfish on the fennel mixture.

4. Carefully pour the consommé over the fish, and simmer gently, covered, until the fish is cooked. Season to taste with salt and pepper.

5. Serve the fish stew with croutons and sprinkle with chopped parsley.

Paella

Yield: 10 servings

Pork, lean, diced	*24 ounces*	*680 grams*
Chicken legs, cut into thighs and drumsticks	*2 pounds*	*900 grams*
Olive oil	*5 fluid ounces*	*150 milliliters*
Garlic cloves, chopped	*3 each*	*3 each*
Onions, small dice	*8 ounces*	*225 grams*
Red peppers, small dice	*8 ounces*	*225 grams*
Green peppers, small dice	*8 ounces*	*225 grams*
Rice, short-grain	*10 ounces*	*285 grams*
Saffron, crushed	*1 teaspoon*	*1 teaspoon*
Salt	*½ teaspoon*	*½ teaspoon*
Chicken Stock, hot	*1 ½ pints*	*720 milliliters*
Clams, cleaned	*20 each*	*20 each*
Mussels, cleaned	*20 each*	*20 each*
Shrimp, peeled and deveined	*20 each*	*20 each*
Chorizo, cooked and sliced	*8 ounces*	*225 grams*
Tomato concassé, small dice	*8 ounces*	*225 grams*
Carrots, small dice	*4 ounces*	*115 grams*
Green peas	*4 ounces*	*115 grams*
Niçoise olives, pitted	*6 ounces*	*170 grams*
Green olives, pitted	*6 ounces*	*170 grams*
Scallions, sliced	*4 ounces*	*115 grams*
Lemons, cut into wedges	*4 each*	*4 each*

Separating the thigh and drumstick.

There are many variations of this traditional Spanish dish. Garnish with strips of roasted red peppers and serve it directly in a paella pan for an authentic presentation.

TECHNIQUE
Basic knife cuts (pages 217-223)
Cleaning clams (page 288)
Cleaning and debearding mussels (pages 288-289)
Peeling and deveining shrimp (page 284)
Tomato concassé (page 226)

RECIPE
Chicken Stock (page 480)

1. Brown the chicken and pork in the olive oil. Remove and reserve.

2. Sauté the garlic, onions, and peppers in the reserved oil.

3. Add the rice, saffron and salt. Stir until the rice is coated with oil.

4. Add the stock and bring the mixture to a boil. Cover the pan and place it in a 400°F (205°C) oven; cook the rice mixture for 8 minutes.

5. Place the clams and mussels on top of the rice. Check the rice periodically and add more stock or water if necessary. Replace the cover and return the pan to the oven for 5 minutes.

6. Add the shrimp, chorizo, tomato concassé, carrots, and peas. Return the pan to the oven and cook the paella until the shrimp is cooked through and all ingredients are very hot.

7. Garnish the paella with the olives and scallions. Drizzle with the juice of 2 lemons. Cover the paella pan and allow the paella to rest for 10 minutes. Wedge the remaining lemons and serve with the paella.

Herbs and spices play an important role in this dish.

Cassoulet is a classic dish from the south of France. As with other traditional dishes, ingredients vary from region to region and from season to season. The one common ingredient is white beans. Mutton is often used, though goat is not unheard of in France.

This recipe is essentially a combination of three separate preparations: duck confit, bean stew, and braised meats. These components are combined and baked.

Although the whole process can take several days when done correctly, it is well worth the effort and is a popular item on any menu.

Select a duck that weighs approximately 6 pounds (2.75 kilograms).

Cassoulet

Yield: 12 to 14 servings

Confit

Kosher salt	2 ounces	60 grams
Curing salt	$1/4$ teaspoon	$1/4$ teaspoon
Pepper, ground	$1/4$ teaspoon	$1/4$ teaspoon
Juniper berries, crushed	2 each	2 each
Bay leaf, crushed	1 each	1 each
Garlic, chopped	$1/2$ teaspoon	$1/2$ teaspoon
Duck, cut in 6 pieces	1 each	1 each
Duck fat, rendered, as needed	1 pint	480 milliliters

Bean stew

Chicken Stock	3 quarts	3 liters
Navy beans, dried, soaked overnight	2 pounds	900 grams
Garlic sausage	1 pound	450 grams
Slab bacon, bâttonet	1 pound	450 grams
Onions, whole	2 each	2 each
Garlic, chopped	1 ounce	30 grams
Bouquet Garni	1 each	1 each

Meat stew

Pork loin, cut into large cubes	$1 1/2$ pounds	680 grams
Lamb shoulder, or leg, cut into large cubes	$1 1/2$ pounds	680 grams
Olive oil	3 fluid ounces	90 milliliters
White Mirepoix	1 pound	450 grams
Salt to taste	$1/2$ teaspoon	$1/2$ teaspoon
Garlic, mashed to a paste	$1/2$ teaspoon	$1/2$ teaspoon
White wine	3 fluid ounces	90 milliliters
Tomato concassé	8 ounces	225 grams
Sachet d'Epices	1 each	1 each
Demi-Glace	1 pint	480 milliliters
Brown Stock, as needed	1 quart	1 liter
Salt to taste	$1/2$ teaspoon	$1/2$ teaspoon
Pepper to taste	$1/2$ teaspoon	$1/2$ teaspoon
Bread crumbs, fresh	12 ounces	340 grams
Parsley, chopped	2 tablespoons	2 tablespoons

(Recipe continued on facing page)

1. To prepare the confit: Mix all the seasonings, coat the duck with the mixture, and place it in a container with a weighted lid. Press the duck for 72 hours under refrigeration.

2. Brush off the excess seasoning mixture and stew the bird in the duck fat until it is very tender.

3. When ready to use the confit, scrape away excess fat and broil the duck on a rack until the skin is crisp. Debone and slice the duck.

4. To prepare the beans: Bring the chicken stock to a boil and add the beans.

5. Add the bacon and return to a boil; cook for 30 minutes.

6. Add the sausage, onions, garlic, and bouquet garni; return the mixture to a boil and cook it until the sausage reaches a 150°F (65°C) internal temperature and the bacon is fork-tender.

7. Remove the sausage, bacon, onion, and bouquet garni. Reserve the sausage and bacon.

8. Continue to cook the beans until they are tender but still hold their shape. Strain the beans and reserve; reduce the stock.

9. To prepare the meats: Sear the pork and lamb in hot olive oil until they are brown. Remove and reserve them.

10. Degrease the pan and sauté the mirepoix. Add the garlic and salt.

11. Deglaze the pan with the white wine.

12. Add the tomato concassé, sachet, demi-glace, and brown stock. Bring the sauce to a boil; return the meat to the sauce.

13. Cover the pan and braise the meat in an oven at 300°F (150°C) until fork-tender.

14. Remove the meat and reduce the braising liquid. Adjust the seasoning and strain the sauce. Combine the reduced braising liquid with the bean stock.

15. Peel the sausage and slice it.

16. Cut the bacon in $1/4$-inch (.5-centimeter) slices.

17. Layer the sausage, bacon, pork, and lamb into individual casseroles. Cover with the beans and duck confit.

18. Pour the combined braising liquid and bean stock over all and sprinkle it with the bread crumbs and parsley.

19. Bake the cassoulet in a moderate oven (350°F/175°C) until it is heated through and a good crust has formed, about 45 to 50 minutes.

TECHNIQUE
Braising (pages 391-394)
Stewing (pages 394-397)
Cured items (Confit) (page 419)
Soaking beans (page 236)
Basic knife cuts (pages 217-223)
Mashing garlic to a paste (page 225)
Tomato concassé (page 226)
Making bread crumbs (page 237)
Fresh herbs (page 229)

RECIPES
Chicken Stock (page 480)
Bouquet Garni (page 474)
White Mirepoix (page 472)
Sachet d'Epices (page 475)
Demi-Glace (page 514)
Brown Stock (page 480)

Butterfly the flank steak to hold the filling.

MATAHAMBRE translates literally as kill-the-hunger. A traditional element in most stuffings is spinach. While this recipe indicates serving the meat while warm, many traditional recipes call for the braised steak to be weighted and sliced after it has chilled thoroughly.

TECHNIQUE
Braising (pages 391-394)
Marinades (pages 242-245)
Basic knife cuts (pages 217-223)
Fresh herbs (page 229)
Making bread crumbs (page 237)
Cutting corn from the cob (page 233)
Butterflying meats (page 266)
Tying a roast (page 262)
Carving (pages 355-357)

RECIPES
Hard-Cooked Eggs (page 654)
Demi-Glace (page 514)
Brown Veal Stock (page 478)
Sachet d'Epices (page 475)

Braised Stuffed Flank Steak (Matahambre)

Yield: 10 servings

Flank steaks, trimmed	4 pounds	1.8 kilograms
Salt to taste	1/2 teaspoon	1/2 teaspoon
Pepper to taste	1/4 teaspoon	1/4 teaspoon
Marinade		
Garlic cloves, mashed	4 each	4 each
Cilantro, chopped	2 tablespoons	2 tablespoons
Basil, chopped	2 tablespoons	2 tablespoons
Olive oil	1 pint	480 milliliters
Red wine vinegar	8 fluid ounces	240 milliliters
Stuffing		
Bread crumbs, fresh	8 ounces	225 grams
Hard-cooked eggs, chopped	3 each	3 each
Corn kernels	6 ounces	170 grams
Spinach leaves, blanched, squeezed dry, and chopped	1 pound	450 grams
Carrots, cut lengthwise, parboiled	3 each	3 each
Onions, sliced	4 ounces	115 grams
Cilantro, chopped	1 ounce	30 grams
Olive oil	4 fluid ounces	120 milliliters
Red wine	10 fluid ounces	300 milliliters
Demi-Glace	1 quart	1 liter
Brown Veal Stock	1 quart	1 liter
Sachet d'Epices, *plus* oregano leaves	1 each	1 each

1. Butterfly the steak, slitting it horizontally in the direction of the grain. Season to taste with salt and pepper.

2. Combine all of the ingredients for the marinade. Add the meat and marinate it under refrigeration for 24 hours. Drain the meat and dry it.

3. Mix the bread crumbs and eggs and spread a layer over the opened butterflied steak. Sprinkle the corn kernels over the breading.

4. Place the spinach on the breading mixture. Add a layer of carrots.

5. Sprinkle the onions, cilantro, salt, and pepper on top.

6. Roll the flank steak in jelly-roll fashion and tie it with butcher's twine.

7. Brown the steak rolls evenly in hot oil.

8. Deglaze the pan with wine. Add the demi-glace, stock, and sachet; braise the meat until it is fork-tender.

9. Reduce the sauce, degreasing as necessary. Adjust the seasoning and strain it.

10. Carve the steak rolls crosswise. Serve them with the sauce.

Chicken Mole (Mole Poblano de Pollo)

Yield: 10 servings

Sesame seeds	*3 ounces*	*85 grams*
Almonds, chopped	*1 ounce*	*30 grams*
Chili powder	*2 ounces*	*60 grams*
Anise seeds	*1 teaspoon*	*1 teaspoon*
Cinnamon, ground	*½ teaspoon*	*½ teaspoon*
Oregano, dried	*1 teaspoon*	*1 teaspoon*
Chicken breasts, boneless	*10 each*	*10 each*
Peanut oil	*4 fluid ounces*	*120 milliliters*
Onions, fine dice	*8 ounces*	*225 grams*
Garlic cloves, mashed to paste	*6 each*	*6 each*
Green peppers, fine dice	*8 ounces*	*225 grams*
Jalapeño peppers, chopped fine	*10 each*	*10 each*
Corn tortilla, toasted and chopped	*1 each*	*1 each*
Tomato concassé	*1 pound*	*450 grams*
Chicken Stock	*1 pint*	*480 milliliters*
Mexican chocolate, chopped	*4 ounces*	*115 grams*
Salt to taste	*½ teaspoon*	*½ teaspoon*
Pepper to taste	*¼ teaspoon*	*¼ teaspoon*

Nuts and seeds, as well as chilies and chocolate, make up a good mole.

1. Toast the sesame seeds, almonds, chili powder, anise, cinnamon, and oregano in a dry skillet until very aromatic. Remove and set aside. Brown the onions; add the garlic, peppers, and jalapeños and sauté for a few minutes.

2. Return the seasonings and sauté the mixture briefly. Add the tortilla and tomato concassé. Sauté until nearly dry. Allow the sauce to cool, then purée until smooth.

3. Sear the chicken in oil in a braising pan. Deglaze the pan with the stock and add the puréed sauce. Blend until smooth.

4. Add the chicken and bring to a boil. Cover the pan and braise the chicken in a moderate oven 325°F (165°C) until tender. Remove the chicken and keep it warm.

5. Adjust the consistency of the sauce by simmering to reduce. Add the chocolate, simmer the sauce, and adjust the seasoning with salt and pepper to taste.

6. Pour the sauce over the chicken and reheat it in the oven. Garnish it with additional toasted sesame seeds if desired.

It is said that mole poblano was first created by nuns in Mexico in anticipation of a visit by the bishop. Originally prepared with turkey, it is still served with turkey at fiestas in Mexico, especially at Christmas and weddings.

The term mole *comes from the Nahuatl word for "concoction." As with most sauces, mole varies from region to region in Mexico, each immensely proud of their variation. A mix of chilies (fresh and dried), seeds (sesame, pumpkin), nuts and breads can be included. Chocolate is a well-known ingredient but not required in all versions. If Mexican chocolate is not available, use bittersweet chocolate and a touch of sugar and cinnamon.*

TECHNIQUE
Braising (pages 391–394)
Preparing boneless chicken breasts
 (pages 274–275)
Basic knife cuts (pages 217–223)
Toasting nuts and seeds (page 237)
Working with chilies (page 227)
Tomato concassé (page 226)

RECIPE
Chicken Stock (page 480)

Trimming the tenderloin.

Yakitori is a favorite restaurant offering throughout Japan, in which foods are first brushed with teriyaki sauce and then quickly grilled. The highly prized and extremely tender Matsuzaka and Kobe beef would be used in Japan, but a good quality tenderloin works very well also.

This would make about 25 tasting portions as part of a combination platter.

TECHNIQUE
Grilling (pages 344-349)
Trimming a tenderloin (page 261)
Basic knife cuts (pages 217-223)
Slurries (page 238)

RECIPE
Chicken Stock (page 480)

Beef Yakitori

Yield: 10 servings

Beef tenderloin, trimmed	3 ½ pounds	1.6 kilograms
Vegetable oil, as needed	2 fluid ounces	60 milliliters
Sesame oil	2 fluid ounces	60 milliliters
Teriyaki Sauce		
Japanese soy sauce	3 fluid ounces	90 milliliters
Sugar	1 ounce	30 grams
Shire-mirin	1 fluid ounce	30 milliliters
Scallions, minced	2 ounces	60 grams
Ginger, minced	½ teaspoon	½ teaspoon
Garlic, minced	½ teaspoon	½ teaspoon
Chicken Stock	8 fluid ounces	240 milliliters
Rice vinegar	1 tablespoon	1 tablespoon
Sake (rice wine)	2 tablespoons	2 tablespoons
Cornstarch, diluted in water	2 teaspoons	2 teaspoons

1. Trim the beef and cut it into 2-ounce (60-gram) pieces.

2. To make the sauce, combine the soy sauce, sugar, mirin, scallions, ginger, garlic, and stock. Bring to a simmer, and cook 10 minutes. Season to taste with salt and pepper. Add vinegar, sake, and adjust thickening with cornstarch.

3. Rub oil on beef and grill to medium-rare.

4. Serve the hot sauce with beef on heated plates.

Chinese-Style Barbecued Spareribs

Yield: 10 servings

Pork spareribs.

Marinade

Hoisin sauce	*4 fluid ounces*	*120 milliliters*
Bean sauce	*4 fluid ounces*	*120 milliliters*
Applesauce	*4 ounces*	*115 grams*
Ketchup	*8 fluid ounces*	*240 grams*
Soy sauce	*4 fluid ounces*	*120 milliliters*
Sake	*8 fluid ounces*	*240 milliliters*
Peanut oil	*4 fluid ounces*	*120 milliliters*
Ginger, minced	*2 tablespoons*	*2 tablespoons*
Scallions, minced	*6 each*	*6 each*
Garlic cloves, minced	*6 each*	*6 each*
Sugar	*2 ounces*	*60 grams*
Salt	*1 tablespoon*	*1 tablespoon*
Spareribs, trimmed	*10 racks*	*10 racks*
Honey	*8 fluid ounces*	*240 milliliters*

1. Combine all of the ingredients for the marinade.

2. Score the ribs with a sharp knife. Place the ribs in the marinade. Marinate them for at least 4 hours.

3. Place the ribs in a smoker at 425°F (220°C) for 30 minutes. Reduce the heat to 375°F (190°C). Smoke the ribs for 50 minutes more.

4. Brush the honey on the ribs during the last 5 minutes. Slice the ribs between the bones and serve.

Although stir-frying most often comes to mind as the basic Chinese cooking method, slowly roasted foods prepared in a smoker are also very popular.

To serve as an appetizer, cut the racks into 2- to 3-ounce (60- to 85-gram) portions.

TECHNIQUE
Smoked foods (page 419)
Marinades (pages 242-245)
Basic knife cuts (pages 217-223)

Cutting the meat.

Substitute other meats for the pork: beef, lamb, or chicken.

Include vegetables such as broccoli florets, julienned carrots, or snow peas, if desired.

TECHNIQUE
Stir-frying (page 363)
Slurries (page 238)

RECIPE
Chicken Stock (page 480)

Stir-Fried Pork

Yield: 10 servings

Pork loin, boneless	3 ½ pounds	1.6 kilograms
Scallions	1 bunch	1 bunch
Cornstarch	1 tablespoon	1 tablespoon
Oyster sauce	1 fluid ounce	30 milliliters
Sugar	2 teaspoons	2 teaspoons
Soy sauce	½ fluid ounce	15 milliliters
Water	1 fluid ounce	30 milliliters
Vegetable oil	1 fluid ounce	30 milliliters
Garlic cloves, minced	2 each	2 each
Dry sherry	1 fluid ounce	30 milliliters
Chicken Stock	12 fluid ounces	360 milliliters
Salt to taste	½ teaspoon	½ teaspoon

1. Cut pork into strips or shreds. Reserve.

2. Split scallions and cut into 1-inch (2.5-centimeter) sections.

3. Mix cornstarch, oyster sauce, sugar, soy sauce, and water into a paste.

4. Heat oil, add garlic, and stir-fry. Add pork, and stir-fry for 3 more minutes.

5. Add sherry wine and remaining soy sauce; stir-fry for 1 to 2 minutes. Add stock and bring to a boil.

6. Add reserved cornstarch paste and return to a boil, just until the juices are thickened.

7. Add scallions and season. Serve at once.

Pakistani-Style Lamb Patties

Yield: 10 servings

Onions, minced	*2 ounces*	*60 grams*
Vegetable oil	*1 fluid ounce*	*30 milliliters*
Garlic cloves, minced	*8 each*	*8 each*
Bread crumbs, fresh	*2 ounces*	*60 grams*
Lamb, lean, ground	*3 pounds*	*1.3 kilograms*
Pine nuts, toasted	*3 ounces*	*85 grams*
Eggs, beaten	*2 or 3 each*	*2 or 3 each*
Tahini paste	*1 ounce*	*30 grams*
Parsley, chopped	*3 tablespoons*	*3 tablespoons*
Salt to taste	*¹/₂ teaspoon*	*¹/₂ teaspoon*
Pepper to taste	*¹/₄ teaspoon*	*¹/₄ teaspoon*
Coriander, ground	*1 teaspoon*	*1 teaspoon*
Cumin, ground	*2 tablespoons*	*2 tablespoons*
Fennel seed, ground	*1 teaspoon*	*1 teaspoon*
Gingerroot, grated	*2 tablespoons*	*2 tablespoons*

1. Sauté the onions in hot oil until they are translucent.

2. Add the garlic and sauté it briefly. Remove the mixture from the heat and allow it to cool.

3. Soak the bread crumbs in water. Squeeze out any excess moisture.

4. Combine the bread crumbs, onions, and garlic.

5. Add the lamb, pine nuts, beaten eggs, tahini, parsley, salt, pepper, and spices. Mix together gently but thoroughly.

6. Shape the mixture into patties and chill.

7. Grill or broil the patties to the desired doneness.

Grind the meat as close to the time of service as possible.

These patties are often served with a variety of relishes and marinated salads. For the fullest flavor, toast whole spices in a dry skillet and then grind as directed on page 241.

TECHNIQUE
Grilling (pages 344-349)
Basic knife cuts (pages 217-223)
Grinding meats (page 104)
Making bread crumbs (page 237)

Steaming couscous.

Substitute Jerusalem artichokes for white truffles.

Couscous is actually a pasta rather than a grain. It is made from durum semolina.

Harissa is a prepared hot sauce.

TECHNIQUE
Stewing (pages 394-397)
Basic knife cuts (pages 217-223)
Basic bean cooking table (Appendix 2)
Preparing artichokes (pages 234-235)

RECIPE
Chicken Stock (page 480)

Couscous with Lamb Stew

Yield: 10 servings

Lamb, shoulder or leg, cut in large cubes	*2 pounds*	*900 grams*
Onion, diced	*8 ounces*	*225 grams*
Garlic cloves, chopped	*8 each*	*8 each*
Saffron threads, crushed	*pinch*	*pinch*
Gingerroot, grated	*1 tablespoon*	*1 tablespoon*
Cloves, ground	*dash*	*dash*
Cumin, ground	*1 teaspoon*	*1 teaspoon*
Coriander, ground	*1 teaspoon*	*1 teaspoon*
Nutmeg, ground	*1/2 teaspoon*	*1/2 teaspoon*
Turmeric, ground	*3 tablespoons*	*3 tablespoons*
Bay leaves	*2 each*	*2 each*
Olive oil	*3 fluid ounces*	*90 milliliters*
Chicken Stock	*1 quart*	*1 liter*
Carrots, large dice	*8 ounces*	*225 grams*
Turnips, large dice	*4 ounces*	*115 grams*
Chicken legs	*4 each*	*4 each*
Couscous	*1 pound*	*450 grams*
Salt to taste	*1/2 teaspoon*	*1/2 teaspoon*
Zucchini, large dice	*8 ounces*	*225 grams*
Green peppers, large dice	*8 ounces*	*225 grams*
Chickpeas, cooked	*8 ounces*	*225 grams*
Tomatoes, peeled, wedged	*1 pound*	*450 grams*
Artichoke bottoms, quartered	*10 each*	*10 each*
Lima beans, cooked	*2 ounces*	*60 grams*
Arabic white truffles, (if available), sliced	*4 ounces*	*115 grams*
Garnish		
Almonds, sliced and toasted	*2 ounces*	*60 grams*
Raisins or currants	*2 ounces*	*60 grams*
Harissa	*2 fluid ounces*	*60 milliliters*
Parsley, chopped, as needed	*2 ounces*	*60 grams*

1. In the lower pan of a couscousière, sauté the lamb with the onion, garlic, and spices in the olive oil. Cover with the stock and simmer until the lamb is nearly cooked.

2. Add the carrots, turnips, and chicken legs and stew over low heat for 15 minutes.

(Recipe continued on facing page)

3. Rinse and soak the couscous in warm water for 90 seconds and place it in the top pan of the couscousière.

4. Steam the couscous over the simmering stew for 20 minutes.

5. Remove the top pan and season the couscous with salt to taste. Reserve warm while finishing the stew.

6. Add the zucchini and green peppers to the lower pan and cook the stew for 4 minutes.

7. Add the chickpeas, tomatoes, artichoke bottoms, lima beans, and truffles and return the stew to a boil. Adjust the seasonings to taste.

8. Mound the couscous on a heated plate or platter and place the meat stew in the center of the mound. Serve the garnishes separately.

Tandoori-Style Chicken

Yield: 10 servings

Chicken breast, boneless skinless	*10 each*	*10 each*
Yogurt	*8 ounces*	*225 grams*
Water	*1 fluid ounce*	*30 milliliters*
Saffron threads, crushed	*1/2 teaspoon*	*1/2 teaspoon*
Cumin, ground	*1 tablespoon*	*1 tablespoon*
Cardamom, ground	*1 tablespoon*	*1 tablespoon*
Coriander, ground	*1 tablespoon*	*1 tablespoon*
Gingerroot, minced	*2 ounces*	*60 grams*
Garlic cloves, minced	*4 each*	*4 each*
Cayenne, ground, to taste	*1/2 teaspoon*	*1/2 teaspoon*
Lime juice to taste	*2 teaspoons*	*2 teaspoons*

1. Trim the chicken breasts.

2. Mix the yogurt, water, spices, seasonings, and lime juice together.

3. Place the chicken in the yogurt mixture and marinate for 12 hours.

4. Remove and grill the chicken breasts until cooked through.

Allow the chicken to marinate before grilling.

TECHNIQUE
Grilling (pages 344-349)
Marinades (pages 242-245)
Preparing poultry suprêmes (pages 275-277)

Select a god variety of vegetables for color and flavor.

TECHNIQUE
Deep-frying (pages 367-371)
Basic knife cuts (pages 217-223)
Fresh herbs (page 229)

Hot and Sour Fish with Vegetables

Yield: 10 servings

Sole fillets	4 pounds	1.8 kilograms
Salt to taste	$^1/_2$ teaspoon	$^1/_2$ teaspoon
Pepper to taste	$^1/_4$ teaspoon	$^1/_4$ teaspoon
Batter		
Cold water	24 fluid ounces	720 milliliters
Baking powder	3 tablespoons	3 tablespoons
Flour	1 pound	450 grams
Sesame oil	2 fluid ounces	60 milliliters
Hot and Sour Sauce		
Peanut oil as needed	2 fluid ounces	60 milliliters
Garlic cloves, minced	2 each	2 each
Assorted vegetables, fine dice	1 pound	450 grams
Tomato paste	4 ounces	115 grams
Water	12 fluid ounces	360 milliliters
Fish sauce	2 tablespoons	2 tablespoons
Sugar	1 tablespoon	1 tablespoon
Worcestershire sauce	1 tablespoon	1 tablespoon
Red wine vinegar	1 fluid ounce	30 milliliters
Red chili pepper flakes	1 teaspoon	1 teaspoon
Soy sauce	1 tablespoon	1 tablespoon
Cilantro, chopped fine	2 tablespoons	2 tablespoons
Oil (for deep-frying)	1 pint	480 milliliters

1. Cut the fish into portions (5 to 6 ounces/140 to 170 grams).

2. Combine all of the ingredients for the batter; mix until smooth. Chill until needed.

3. To make the sauce: Heat the oil in a wok; add the garlic and vegetables; stir-fry briefly.

4. Add tomato paste, water, fish sauce, and sugar; mix together.

5. Add remaining ingredients for the sauce. Simmer 15 to 20 minutes, and adjust consistency with water if necessary. Keep hot for service.

6. To fry the fish: Season lightly with salt and pepper, dip fish in batter, deep-fry in 350°F (175°C) oil until golden brown, and drain on absorbent paper. Serve with hot sauce.

Shrimp in Chili Sauce

Yield: 10 servings

Shrimp	*3 ¹/₂ pounds*	*1.6 kilograms*
Chili Sauce		
Gingerroot, minced	*2 ounces*	*60 grams*
Garlic, minced	*2 ounces*	*60 grams*
Scallion, minced	*2 ounces*	*60 grams*
Chili bean paste	*1 ounce*	*30 grams*
Tomato ketchup	*12 fluid ounces*	*360 milliliters*
Rice vinegar	*2 fluid ounces*	*60 milliliters*
Soy sauce	*2 fluid ounces*	*60 milliliters*
Oil as needed	*3 fluid ounces*	*90 milliliters*
Gingerroot, minced	*1 tablespoon*	*1 tablespoon*
Garlic, minced	*1 tablespoon*	*1 tablespoon*
Scallions, shredded	*1 bunch*	*1 bunch*
Baby corn, drained	*8 ounces*	*225 grams*
Straw mushrooms	*8 ounces*	*225 grams*
Snow peas	*1 pound*	*450 grams*
Sliced scallions	*3 ounces*	*85 grams*
Dry sherry	*2 fluid ounces*	*60 milliliters*
Sugar to taste	*2 ounces*	*60 grams*
Chicken or Shellfish Stock	*4 fluid ounces*	*120 milliliters*
Cornstarch slurry	*1 tablespoon*	*1 tablespoon*
Sesame oil, to finish	*1 tablespoon*	*1 tablespoon*

1. Peel and devein shrimp and set aside.

2. Combine the ingredients for the sauce and bring to a boil.

3. Heat the remaining oil in a wok; add ginger, garlic, and scallion; stir-fry until aromatic.

4. Add shrimp, corn, straw mushrooms, and snow peas, stir-fry until shrimp is just cooked.

5. Add the chili sauce and mix together; add sesame oil and sliced scallions. Check seasonings and serve.

Deveining shrimp.

TECHNIQUE
Stir-frying (page 363)
Basic knife cuts (pages 217-223)
Slurries (page 238)
Peeling and deveining shrimp (page 284)

RECIPES
Chicken Stock (page 480)
Shellfish Stock (page 480)

21

Vegetable Side Dishes

Vegetables deserve as much care and attention as any other element on the plate. Remember to prepare all vegetables properly before cooking. Techniques for peeling, rinsing, trimming, and cutting a selection of basic and unique vegetables can be found on pages 217 to 236.

You may wish to adapt some of the recipes here to expand your meatless-menu options. Herein, recipes are grouped as follows:

- *Green Vegetables*
- *White Vegetables*
- *Red and Yellow Vegetables*
- *Braises and Stews*
- *Grilled Vegetables*
- *Mixed Vegetables*
- *Asian Vegetable Dishes*

Steamed vegetables have an increased appeal for those who prefer low-fat and low-calorie foods. Don't neglect seasonings, however.

Peeling broccoli and asparagus stems removes inedible skins and helps ensure even cooking.

Cauliflower, carrots, or peeled asparagus may all be cooked in this manner. Adjust cooking time as necessary.

TECHNIQUE
Steaming (pages 374-378)

Steamed Broccoli

Yield: 10 servings

Broccoli, peeled	*2 pounds*	*900 grams*
Water	*6 fluid ounces*	*180 milliliters*
Salt to taste	*1/2 teaspoon*	*1/2 teaspoon*
Pepper to taste	*1/4 teaspoon*	*1/4 teaspoon*

1. Arrange the broccoli on a steamer rack so that the pieces are not crowded.

2. Bring the water to a full boil in the bottom of the steamer.

3. Add the broccoli to the steamer, replace the lid, and steam the vegetable for 5 to 7 minutes or until tender. Season the broccoli with salt and pepper to taste.

VARIATION

Steamed Cauliflower: Clean 2 pounds (900 grams) of cauliflower and cut into florets. Steam as above.

Add a small amount of reduced heavy cream in place of the butter.

Add chopped fresh mint just before serving.

For a summer side dish, cool the peas, toss lightly with sour cream, and add chopped peanuts.

TECHNIQUE
Pan-steaming (page 382)

RECIPE
Hollandaise Sauce (page 521)

Pan-Steamed Peas

Yield: 10 servings

Peas, fresh, shelled	*2 pounds*	*900 grams*
Water, boiling	*6 fluid ounces*	*180 milliliters*
Butter	*2 ounces*	*60 grams*
Salt to taste	*1/2 teaspoon*	*1/2 teaspoon*
Pepper to taste	*1/4 teaspoon*	*1/4 teaspoon*

1. Place the peas in a shallow sauteuse with $1/4$ inch (.5 centimeter) of boiling water. Cover the pan.

2. Pan-steam the peas over high heat for about 2 to 3 minutes, shaking the pan occasionally. Drain away excess water and return pan to the heat.

3. Remove the cover and add the butter, salt, and pepper. Toss the peas to coat them evenly.

VARIATION

Pan-Steamed Asparagus: Trim the asparagus and peel the stem ends. Place the stalks in a pot. Fill the pot up about $1/2$ inch (1 centimeter) with boiling water. Pan-steam for about 3 to 4 minutes or until just tender. Do not overcook. Serve immediately with hollandaise sauce, melted butter, or lemon-butter.

French-Style Peas (Petits Pois à la Française)

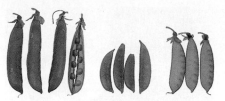

Three varieties pf peas.

Yield: 10 servings

Pearl onions	*2 ounces*	*60 grams*
Butter	*2 ounces*	*60 grams*
Peas, fresh, shelled	*1 ¼ pounds*	*560 grams*
Chicken or Vegetable Stock	*4 fluid ounces*	*120 milliliters*
Salt to taste	*½ teaspoon*	*½ teaspoon*
Pepper to taste	*¼ teaspoon*	*¼ teaspoon*
Boston lettuce, shredded	*12 ounces*	*340 grams*
Beurre Manié	*as needed*	*as needed*

1. Smother the pearl onions in the fresh butter without browning them.

2. Add the peas and stock. Season the stock with salt and pepper. Cook the mixture quickly, covered, for a few minutes. Add the lettuce.

3. Add the beurre manié gradually in small pieces until the mixture is thickened. Season to taste with salt and pepper.

VARIATION

Petits Pois à la Fermière: Add 4 ounces (115 grams) of sbaby carrots with the onions.

The lettuce should be added as close to serving time as possible. You may reduce the amount of lettuce if desired.

A bouquet garni of parsley and chervil may be added with the stock.

You may want to finish this dish by adding 2 to 4 ounces (60 to 115 grams) of crisp-cooked crumbled bacon.

TECHNIQUE
Stewing (pages 394-397)

RECIPES
Chicken Stock (page 480)
Vegetable Stock (page 483)
Beurre Manié (page 474)

Peeling roasted peppers.

Include green and yellow peppers for additional color.

If desired, drain off most of the oil before proceeding with step 3. The drained oil should be reserved and refrigerated, as it is now infused with shallots and can be used to season other sauces or vinaigrettes.

TECHNIQUE
Sautéing (pages 358-362)
Basic knife cuts pages 217-223)
Asparagus preparation (page 235)

Asparagus with Roasted Pepper and Shallot Chips

Yield: 10 servings

Asparagus, trimmed and peeled	2 pounds	900 grams
Olive oil	2 fluid ounces	60 milliliters
Shallots, peeled and thinly sliced	3 ounces	85 grams
Red peppers, roasted, diced or bâtonnet	4 ounces	115 grams
Salt to taste	1 teaspoon	1 teaspoon
Pepper, coarse grind, to taste	1/2 teaspoon	1/2 teaspoon
Oregano leaves, chopped	2 teaspoons	2 teaspoons

1. Slice the asparagus on the bias into 2-inch (5-centimeter) pieces. Steam or boil until tender. Drain immediately.

2. Heat the oil in a skillet over medium heat. Add the shallots and sauté until the slices are crisp and browned. Remove with slotted spoon and blot on absorbent toweling.

3. Add the asparagus, red peppers, and salt and pepper to taste to the olive oil and sauté, tossing frequently until heated. Add the oregano and heat another minute.

4. Serve with shallot chips scattered over the top of the asparagus and red pepper mixture.

Make smaller pancakes for canapés; top with herbed cream cheese and diced roasted red pepper.

This Scandinavian-style pancake is typically served with lingonberry jam as an appetizer. It may also be served as a side dish to accompany roasted or sautéed veal or poultry.

Plättar pans are special cast-iron griddles used to prepare these pancakes.

TECHNIQUE
Pan-frying (pages 364-367)

Spinach Pancakes

Yield: 20 servings

Milk	12 fluid ounces	360 milliliters
Butter, melted	1 ounce	30 grams
Flour	5 ounces	140 grams
Eggs	4 each	4 each
Sugar	1/2 teaspoon	1/2 teaspoon
Spinach, steamed, squeezed dried, and puréed	1 pound	450 grams
Salt to taste	1 teaspoon	1 teaspoon
Pepper to taste	1/2 teaspoon	1/2 teaspoon
Nutmeg, ground (optional)	to taste	to taste

1. Combine the milk, butter, flour, eggs, and sugar to form a batter.

2. Add the spinach and season the batter with salt, pepper, and nutmeg to taste.

3. Pan-fry the pancakes in plättar pans or on a griddle until done. Serve them immediately.

Pan-Fried Zucchini

Yield: 10 servings

Zucchini, trimmed and sliced	*2 pounds*	*900 grams*
Flour as needed	*2 ounces*	*60 grams*
Beer Batter	*1 pint*	*480 milliliters*
Olive oil	*as needed*	*as needed*
Salt to taste	*1/2 teaspoon*	*1/2 teaspoon*
Black pepper to taste	*1/4 teaspoon*	*1/4 teaspoon*

Pan-fried zucchini

1. Dredge the zucchini in flour. Evenly coat the zucchini slices (or sticks) with the batter and add them to hot oil in a single layer. Do not crowd them.

2. Pan-fry the zucchini on the first side for approximately 1 minute or until golden brown. Turn and complete the cooking on the second side.

3. Remove the zucchini from the hot oil and blot briefly on absorbent paper toweling.

4. Season zucchini slices with salt and pepper. Serve at once.

The recipes for beer batter is included in the recipe for flounder à la Orly (page 574).

This recipe makes a nice accompaniment to broiled or fried fish. It also makes a popular appetizer. Serve them on their own with tomato coulis dip or a seasoned mayonnaise, or on an appetizer plate with broccoli and cheddar fritters.

Other vegetables can be batter-dipped and fried. Experiment with mushrooms, broccoli florets, and carrots battonnet.

TECHNIQUE
Pan-frying (pages 364-367)

Pan-steaming cauliflower.

Polonaise is a French term referring to a dish prepared in the Polish style, in this case a vegetable served with a garnish of bread crumbs, parsley, and chopped, hard-boiled eggs.

TECHNIQUE
Boiling (pages 386-388)
Steaming (pages 374-378)
Making bread crumbs (page 237)

RECIPE
Hard-Cooked Eggs (page 654)

Cauliflower Polonaise

Yield: 10 servings

Cauliflower, cut into florets	*2 pounds*	*900 grams*
Water	*as needed*	*as needed*
Butter	*3 ounces*	*85 grams*
Bread crumbs, fresh	*3 ounces*	*85 grams*
Hard-cooked eggs, chopped	*2 each*	*2 each*
Parsley, chopped	*2 tablespoons*	*2 tablespoons*
Salt to taste	*½ teaspoon*	*½ teaspoon*
White pepper to taste	*½ teaspoon*	*½ teaspoon*

1. Boil or pan-steam the cauliflower until it is tender. If necessary, refresh and reheat at service time.

2. Brown the butter lightly in a sautoir. Add the bread crumbs and cook until golden brown.

3. Remove them from the heat; add the chopped egg and parsley and mix well. Season to taste with salt and pepper.

4. Sprinkle the crumb mixture over individual portions of the heated cauliflower.

VARIATION

Asparagus Polonaise: Substitute 2 pounds (900 grams) of peeled asparagus for the cauliflower. The asparagus should be cooked through but slightly firm.

Additional optional ingredients include caramelized onions, roasted garlic, and boiled potatoes, to be pushed through the food mill with the parsnips and pears. Butter may be used in place of the heavy cream.

The purée goes well with game and other winter dishes.

TECHNIQUE
Boiling (pages 386-388)

Parsnip and Pear Purée

Yield: 10 servings

Parsnips, peeled, diced	*1 ½ pounds*	*675 grams*
Bartlett pears, diced	*¾ pound*	*340 grams*
Heavy cream, heated	*4 fluid ounces*	*120 milliliters*
Salt	*to taste*	*to taste*
White pepper, ground	*to taste*	*to taste*

1. Boil the parsnips and pears separately in boiling water.

2. The parsnips and pears should be very hot. Push them through a fine sieve or food mill.

3. Add the hot heavy cream gradually and blend the mixture to a smooth, light purée. Season the purée with salt and pepper to taste.

Boiled Carrots

Yield: 10 servings

Carrots, trimmed and cut into even pieces	*2 pounds*	*900 grams*
Water, boiling, salted	*3 quarts*	*3 liters*

1. Add the carrots to the boiling water. If necessary, return the cover to the pot to allow the water to return to boil as quickly as possible.

2. Boil the carrots for 4 to 7 minutes (depending upon the thickness of the cut). Remove them from the water. Serve at once, seasoned as desired, or drain, shock, and reserve.

VARIATIONS

Boiled Green Vegetables: Peel, trim, and cut according to type. Add vegetables to boiling water. Cook uncovered to keep green color.

Boiled Red and Yellow Vegetables: The lid may be left in place to encourage best development of color.

Boiled White Vegetables: Add an acid (lemon juice or vinegar)for the whitest vegetables.

Baby carrots, horse carrots, and bunch carrots with greens still attached.

Use this recipe as a guide for boiling vegetables. It can serve more as a method than a recipe. Cooking times will vary according to the density of the vegetable.

For more information about simmering and boiling, and blanching and parcooking vegetables, see page 380.

Boiled vegetables may be tossed with compound butter, lemon juice, fresh herbs, soy sauce, or a number of other seasonings, depending on desired results.

TECHNIQUE
Boiling (pages 386-388)

Glazed Carrots

Yield: 10 servings

Butter	*3 ounces*	*85 grams*
Carrots, oblique, bâtonnet, or sliced	*2 pounds*	*900 grams*
Sugar (optional), to taste	*1 tablespoon*	*1 tablespoon*
Salt to taste	*1/2 teaspoon*	*1/2 teaspoon*
White pepper to taste	*1/4 teaspoon*	*1/4 teaspoon*
Chicken Stock	*12 fluid ounces*	*360 milliliters*

1. Melt the butter and add the carrots.

2. Cover the pan and lightly sweat the carrots.

3. Add the sugar, salt, pepper, and stock.

4. Cook, covered, at low heat until the carrots are almost done.

5. Remove the cover and allow the liquid to reduce to a glaze.

VARIATION

Glazed Carrots and Parsnips: Substitute 1 pound (459 grams) of peeled parsnips for half of the carrots.

If carrots are cooked before a glaze is formed, remove them with a slotted spoon and reduce the liquid. Return the carrots to the pan to finish the process.

RECIPE
Chicken Stock (page 480)

627

"Milking" the corn.

Although leeks and chervil are not essential to this dish, they do provide additional flavor.

Frozen corn may be used if necessary. In that case, you may want to increase the amount of reduced heavy cream.

TECHNIQUE
Stewing (pages 394-397)

Creamed Corn

Yield: 10 servings

Corn on the cob, husked	*10 each*	*10 each*
Leeks, white, fine dice	*6 ounces*	*170 grams*
Heavy cream	*1 pint*	*480 milliliters*
Salt to taste	*1/2 teaspoon*	*1/2 teaspoon*
Pepper to taste	*1/2 teaspoon*	*1/2 teaspoon*
Nutmeg, ground, to taste	*1/8 teaspoon*	*1/8 teaspoon*
Chervil, chopped	*1 tablespoon*	*1 tablespoon*

1. Cut the kernels from the cobs. Scrape well to release all milk. Cook over low heat for about 5 minutes.

2. Combine the leeks and the heavy cream; reduce the cream by half.

3. Season the leeks with the salt, pepper, and nutmeg if desired.

4. Add the corn to the reduced cream and leek mixture; stew the corn until it is tender and liquid has reduced.

5. Add the chopped chervil.

Use honey or maple syrup to replace brown sugar.

Red wine may be used to replace some of the water in the compote. This will help retain the bright cranberry color.

TECHNIQUE
Roasting and baking (pages 349-350)
Zesting citrus (page 231)

Baked Acorn Squash with Cranberry-Orange Compote

Yield: 12 servings

Butter, melted	*6 ounces*	*170 grams*
Brown sugar	*4 ounces*	*115 grams*
Acorn squash, halved, seeded	*3 each*	*3 each*
Salt to taste	*1/2 teaspoon*	*1/2 teaspoon*
Pepper to taste	*1/4 teaspoon*	*1/4 teaspoon*
Cranberry-Orange Compote		
Cranberries	*1 pound*	*450 grams*
Orange juice	*6 fluid ounces*	*180 milliliters*
Water as needed	*4 fluid ounces*	*120 milliliters*
Sugar as needed	*2 tablespoons*	*2 tablespoons*
Orange zest, blanched	*2 ounces*	*60 grams*

1. Heat the butter and brown sugar together in a saucepan to make a glaze. Brush it on the squash. Reserve the remainder of the glaze.

(Recipe continued on facing page)

2. Bake the squash halves in a moderate oven, cut side down, until they are almost tender. Baste them periodically with the reserved glaze. When almost tender, turn over, prick flesh, and baste with remaining glaze. Finish cooking with cut side up.

3. Combine the cranberries, orange juice, and water to barely cover the berries. Add the sugar to taste. Simmer the berries over medium heat until they are softened and thickened, approximately 10 minutes. Add the orange zest.

4. To serve, cut the squash into wedges; spoon the hot cranberry compote over the squash.

Braised Red Cabbage

Yield: 10 servings

Onions, medium dice	*4 ounces*	*115 grams*
Granny Smith apples, diced	*8 ounces*	*225 grams*
Vegetable oil, or rendered bacon fat	*1 ¹/₂ fluid ounces*	*45 milliliters*
Water	*8 fluid ounces*	*240 milliliters*
Red wine	*2 fluid ounces*	*60 milliliters*
Red wine vinegar	*2 fluid ounces*	*60 milliliters*
Sugar	*1 ounce*	*30 grams*
Red currant jelly	*2 ounces*	*60 grams*
Cinnamon stick	*1 each*	*1 each*
Whole clove	*1 each*	*1 each*
Bay leaf	*1 each*	*1 each*
Juniper berries	*3 each*	*3 each*
Red cabbage, chiffonade	*2 pounds*	*900 grams*
Arrowroot	*¹/₂ teaspoon*	*¹/₂ teaspoon*
Salt to taste	*¹/₂ teaspoon*	*¹/₂ teaspoon*
Pepper to taste	*¹/₂ teaspoon*	*¹/₂ teaspoon*

Add a little acid (vinegar, wine, or lemon juice) and keep the pot covered as you braise red cabbage to keep it from turning blue or green.

1. Slowly sweat the onions and apples in the oil or bacon fat.

2. Add water, wine, vinegar, sugar, and jelly. Check the flavor; it should be tart and strong.

3. Place the cinnamon stick, clove, bay leaf, and juniper berries in a sachet.

4. Add the cabbage and sachet. Cover the pan and braise the mixture until the apples are tender, checking occasionally to make sure the liquid does not completely evaporate.

5. When the cabbage and apples are cooked, remove the sachet. Mix the arrowroot with cold water or wine. Use this to thicken the cooking liquid slightly if necessary. Adjust the seasoning with salt and pepper to taste.

Some chefs prefer to thicken the cabbage with raw grated potatoes rather than arrowroot. If this approach is used, add 1 medium potato, grated, to the cabbage in step 4.

Preparing ratatouille.

Use a light tomato purée or tomato juice to replace some or all of the stock.

Add herbs as available or desired; oregano, marjoram, and thyme would all be suitable.

Add a bouquet garni or sachet during cooking time if desired.

TECHNIQUE
Stewing (pages 394-397)
Basic knife cuts (pages 217-223)
Tomato concassé (page 226)

RECIPES
Chicken Stock (page 480)
Vegetable Stock (page 483)

Ratatouille

Yield: 10 servings

Garlic, minced	1 tablespoon	1 tablespoon
Olive oil	1 fluid ounce	30 milliliters
Shallots, minced	1 tablespoon	1 tablespoon
Red onions, small dice	3 ¹/₂ ounces	100 grams
Tomato paste	1 ounce	30 grams
Chicken or Vegetable Stock	12 fluid ounces	360 milliliters
Yellow squash, seeded, small dice	3 ¹/₂ ounces	100 grams
Zucchini, seeded, small dice	8 ounces	225 grams
Green peppers, small dice	3 ounces	85 grams
Eggplant, peeled, medium dice	6 ounces	170 grams
Mushrooms, quartered or sliced	12 ounces	340 grams
Tomato concassé	6 ounces	170 grams
Salt to taste	¹/₂ teaspoon	¹/₂ teaspoon
White pepper to taste	¹/₂ teaspoon	¹/₂ teaspoon
Basil, chopped	2 tablespoons	2 tablespoons

1. Sauté the garlic in the oil. Add the shallots and sauté until they are soft.

2. Add the red onions and sauté until soft.

3. Add the tomato paste and sauté the mixture briefly.

4. Combine the remaining vegetables and stew, covered, until the vegetables are very tender.

5. At service time, season the ratatouille to taste with salt, pepper, and chopped basil.

Grilled Vegetables

Yield: 10 servings

Vegetables, assorted, according to season	2 1/4 pounds	1 kilogram
Marinade		
Vegetable oil	*1 pint*	*480 milliliters*
Soy sauce	*5 fluid ounces*	*150 milliliters*
Lemon juice	*1 fluid ounce*	*30 milliliters*
Garlic, minced	*1 tablespoon*	*1 tablespoon*
Fennel seeds, whole	*1/2 teaspoon*	*1/2 teaspoon*
Salt to taste	*1 teaspoon*	*1 teaspoon*
Pepper to taste	*1 teaspoon*	*1 teaspoon*

Marinating vegetables before grilling.

1. Slice the vegetables into pieces thick enough to withstand the grill's heat. If necessary, parcook or blanch the vegetables prior to grilling them.

2. Combine all the ingredients for the marinade. Coat the vegetables evenly with the marinade. Let any excess drain completely away from the vegetables.

3. Place the vegetables on a hot grill; grill them on both sides (the time will vary depending upon the type of vegetable and thickness of the cut), turning each once to create crosshatch marks, if desired.

4. Complete the cooking on the second side. Brush with the marinade throughout cooking time.

VARIATION

Mediterranean-Style Grilled Vegetables: Select a good variety of vegetables. Cut them into slices about 3/4 inch (1 centimeter) thick, leaving them rather large. Grill as directed, using an infused oil for the marinade, then cut into strips and toss with plumped raisins, toasted pine nuts, and capers. Drizzle with additional olive oil. Serve at room temperature.

Vegetables that grill well include eggplant, zucchini, summer squash, onions, tomatoes, Belgian endive, potatoes, squashes, radicchio, and radishes.

Include gingerroot, scallions, chilies, rice wine vinegar, fresh herbs, or other seasonings in the marinade, if you desire.

For other marinade suggestions, see pages 476 and 477.

TECHNIQUE
Grilling (pages 344-349)

Trim the stems from shiitake.

TECHNIQUE
Stir-frying (page 363)
Basic knife cuts (pages 217-223)
Slurries (page 238)

RECIPE
Chicken Stock (page 480)

Broccoli and Shiitake Mushrooms in Garlic Sauce

Yield: 10 servings

Broccoli, peeled, cut into small pieces	2 pounds	900 grams
Shiitake mushrooms	12 ounces	340 grams
Garlic sauce		
Garlic, mashed to a paste	1 tablespoon	1 tablespoon
Oil as needed	1 tablespoon	1 tablespoon
Sherry	2 fluid ounces	60 milliliters
Rice vinegar	2 fluid ounces	60 milliliters
Soy sauce	2 fluid ounces	60 milliliters
Hot bean paste	1 tablespoon	1 tablespoon
Sugar	1 ounce	30 grams
Chicken Stock	1 pint	480 milliliters
Cornstarch diluted in cold water	1 ounce	30 grams
Peanut oil	2 fluid ounces	60 milliliters
Ginger, minced	1 tablespoon	1 tablespoon
Garlic, minced	2 tablespoons	2 tablespoons
Scallions, chopped	3 each	3 each
Red pepper, julienne or shredded	1/2 pound	225 grams

1. Blanch broccoli in boiling water, shock, and drain (do not overcook).

2. Trim the stems from the shiitake and slice the caps.

3. To make the sauce: Sweat the garlic in a little oil. Combine all ingredients, bring to a boil, and thicken with cornstarch slurry to medium consistency.

4. Heat the oil, add the ginger, garlic, and scallions, stir-fry until aromatic. Add red pepper, broccoli, and shiitake caps and stir-fry until tender. Add sauce and bring to the simmer. Serve at once.

Hot and Spicy Eggplant

Yield: 10 servings

Japanese eggplant	*2 1/4 pounds*	*1 kilogram*
Sauce		
Hot bean paste	*2 teaspoons*	*2 teaspoons*
Rice vinegar	*1 fluid ounce*	*30 milliliters*
Sugar	*2 teaspoons*	*2 teaspoons*
Soy sauce	*2 fluid ounces*	*60 milliliters*
Chicken Stock	*1 pint*	*480 milliliters*
Oyster sauce	*1 fluid ounce*	*30 milliliters*
Sesame oil	*2 teaspoons*	*2 teaspoons*
Cornstarch slurry as needed	*2 teaspoons*	*2 teaspoons*
Oil (as needed to stir-fry)	*2 fluid ounces*	*60 milliliters*
Ginger, minced	*1 teaspoon*	*1 teaspoon*
Garlic, minced	*1 teaspoon*	*1 teaspoon*
Scallion, chopped	*1 tablespoon*	*1 tablespoon*
Preserved vegetables, fine dice	*2 ounces*	*60 grams*
Green peppers, fine dice	*4 ounces*	*115 grams*
Red peppers, fine dice	*4 ounces*	*115 grams*
Salt as needed	*1/2 teaspoon*	*1/2 teaspoon*

1. Halve the eggplant, score the flesh, and roast at 350°F (175°C) for 10 minutes, or until tender. Cut the eggplant into strips and reserve.

2. To make the sauce: Combine all ingredients except the cornstarch slurry and bring to a boil.

3. Thicken sauce with slurry, adding just enough to thicken the sauce to a coating consistency.

4. To finish the eggplant, heat the oil in a wok, add ginger, garlic, scallion, and preserved vegetables; stir-fry until aromatic.

5. Add peppers and stir-fry until tender; add eggplant and sauce, stir-fry until well mixed, check seasoning and add sesame oil to taste.

Roasted eggplant.

This dish may be served as a meatless entrée. Accompany it with additional sauce and serve with steamed rice and additional vegetables.

TECHNIQUE
Stir-fry (page 363)
Steaming (pages 374-378)
Slurries (page 238)
Basic knife cuts (pages 217-223)
Roasting eggplant (page 233)

RECIPE
Chicken Stock (page 480)

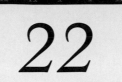

22

Potato, Grain, and Pasta Dishes

*The recipes in this chapter make excellent side dishes to accompany
entrée selections. Some can be adapted to make entrées—some
meatless, some with fish, chicken, or meats. Pastas and risottos can be
portioned into suitable appetizers or selections on an hors d'oeuvre
buffet. The recipes have been grouped as follows:*

- *Boiled Potatoes*
- *Baked Potatoes*
- *Potato Casseroles*
- *Pan-Fried and Sautéed Potatoes*
- *Potato Purées*
- *Deep-Fried Potatoes*
- *Rice—Boiled and Pilafs*

- *Risotto*
- *Cornmeal Dishes*
- *Other Grains*
- *Beans*
- *Pasta*
- *Dumplings*

Adding chopped parsley.

Hold the potatoes in water to prevent discoloration until it is time to cook them.

TECHNIQUE
Boiling (tourné) (pages 386-388)
Basic knife cuts (pages 217-223)

Boiled Parslied Potatoes

Yield: 10 servings

Potatoes, tournéed	*2 ¹/₄ pounds*	*1 kilogram*
Butter	*2 ounces*	*60 grams*
Parsley, chopped	*3 tablespoons*	*3 tablespoons*
Salt to taste	*¹/₂ teaspoon*	*¹/₂ teaspoon*
Pepper to taste	*¹/₄ teaspoon*	*¹/₄ teaspoon*

1. Place the potatoes in a pot with enough cold water to cover them by about 2 inches (5 centimeters). Gradually bring the water to a simmer over an open burner. Simmer the potatoes until they are easily pierced with the tip of a paring knife.

2. Drain the potatoes. Return them to the pot and let them dry briefly over very low heat until no more steam rises from the potatoes, or spread them out on a sheet pan and dry them in a low oven.

3. Heat the butter in a sauteuse over medium heat. Add the potatoes; roll and toss them to coat evenly with butter; heat them through.

4. Add the parsley, salt, and pepper. Toss the potatoes to coat. Serve them immediately.

VARIATION

Potatoes with Lemon and Thyme: Boil potatoes as directed. Roll in hot butter to finish and season with lemon juice and chopped thyme leaves.

Baked Idaho Potatoes with Fried Onions

Yield: 10 servings

Idaho potatoes	*10 each*	*10 each*
Sour cream	*10 fluid ounces*	*300 milliliters*
Chives, minced	*2 tablespoons*	*2 tablespoons*
Onions, large, sliced thin	*1 each*	*1 each*
Flour	*2 ounces*	*60 grams*
Cornstarch	*2 ounces*	*60 grams*
Salt to taste	*1 teaspoon*	*1 teaspoon*
White pepper to taste	*¹/₂ teaspoon*	*¹/₂ teaspoon*

1. Pierce the potatoes with a kitchen fork or knife. Bake in a 425°F (220°C) oven for about 1 hour, or until very tender and cooked through.

2. Blend the sour cream and chives and reserve for service.

3. Separate the onion slices into rings.

4. Combine the flour, cornstarch, salt, and pepper. Add the onion and toss to coat well.

5. Deep-fry the onions in 375°F (190°C) oil until very crisp. Drain on toweling.

6. To serve, pinch or cut open the potato, place a dollop of sour cream with chopped chives on the flesh and top with onions.

Pierce potatoes before baking.

Idaho or russet potatoes are a high starch variety. They become mealy and fluffy after baking.

Some chefs rub potatoes with either oil or coarse salt to develop a crisp skin.

TECHNIQUE
Roasting and baking (pages 349-350)
Deep-frying (pages 367-371)

Baked Stuffed Potatoes

Yield: 10 servings

Idaho potatoes	*10 each*	*10 each*
Butter, softened	*2 ounces*	*60 grams*
Salt to taste	*¹/₂ teaspoon*	*¹/₂ teaspoon*
Pepper to taste	*¹/₄ teaspoon*	*¹/₄ teaspoon*
Egg yolk	*1 each*	*1 each*
Cream or milk, hot, as needed	*4 fluid ounces*	*120 milliliters*
Parmesan cheese (optional)	*2 ounces*	*60 grams*

1. Bake the potatoes until they are tender as directed above.

2. Remove the tops of the potatoes by slicing them lengthwise. Scoop out the potato pulp.

3. Rice the pulp while very hot and mix with the butter, salt, and pepper. Work in the egg yolk and hot cream or milk.

4. Pipe the potato mixture back into the shells.

5. Sprinkle the potatoes with Parmesan. Return them to the oven until they are heated through and lightly browned on top.

These potatoes may be known as "Pommes au Four," Potatoes Jackson, or Twice-Baked Potatoes.

Add grated cheese (Cheddar, Gruyère, Parmesan, or fresh goat cheese) to the filling.

TECHNIQUE
Roasting and baking (pages 349-350)

Use a good-flavored hard cheese in this dish.

Idaho potatoes will release enough starch as they cook to thicken the milk and cream. However, you may prefer to make this dish using a prepared Mornay Sauce (see page 518).

To make Scalloped Potatoes, slice potatoes directly into a baking dish containing the milk and seasonings. Spread into an even layer; bake at 350°F (175°C) for 1 to 1 1/2 hours or until a crust forms.

TECHNIQUE
Making bread crumbs (page 237)

Potatoes au Gratin

Yield: 10 servings

Idaho potatoes, peeled and sliced 1/8-inch (.25-centimeter) thick	2 1/4 pounds	1 kilogram
Milk, cold	1 pint	480 milliliters
Heavy cream, hot	1 pint	480 milliliters
Salt to taste	1/2 teaspoon	1/2 teaspoon
Pepper to taste	1/4 teaspoon	1/4 teaspoon
Nutmeg, ground, to taste	pinch	pinch
Gruyère cheese, grated	5 ounces	140 grams
Parmesan cheese, grated	4 ounces	115 grams
Bread crumbs, fresh	3 ounces	85 grams
Butter	3 ounces	85 grams

1. Add the potatoes to the milk and bring it to a boil. Simmer until the potatoes are parcooked.

2. Add the cream and season the potatoes to taste with the salt, pepper, and nutmeg.

3. Layer the potatoes in a buttered hotel pan, alternating them with the grated cheeses. Finish with cheese on top. Sprinkle with bread crumbs and dot with butter.

4. Bake the gratin in a slow oven (300 to 325°F/150 to 165°C), loosely covered, until the potatoes are cooked, about 30 to 45 minutes. Remove the cover and bake until the cheese is browned and a crust has formed.

5. Let the potatoes rest for at least 15 minutes before cutting into portions and serving.

Dauphinoise Potatoes

Yield: 10 servings

Milk, scalded and cooled	*24 fluid ounces*	*720 milliliters*
Eggs, beaten	*2 each*	*2 each*
Salt to taste	*1/2 teaspoon*	*1/2 teaspoon*
Pepper to taste	*1/4 teaspoon*	*1/4 teaspoon*
Nutmeg, ground (optional)	*pinch*	*pinch*
Butter, softened	*1 ounce*	*30 grams*
Garlic clove, crushed	*1 each*	*1 each*
Potatoes, peeled, sliced thin	*2 1/4 pounds*	*1 kilogram*
Gruyère cheese, grated	*5 ounces*	*140 grams*

1. Combine the milk, eggs, salt, pepper, and nutmeg. Heat the mixture but do not boil it; it should thicken slightly.

2. Butter a hotel pan and rub it with the crushed garlic clove.

3. Layer the potatoes in the hotel pan. Add the milk and the egg mixture. Top it with the grated cheese.

4. Cover and bake the potatoes in a bain-marie at 300°F (150°C) until they are tender, about 1 1/2 hours. Uncover them and let the cheese brown lightly. Let them rest 15 minutes before cutting and serving.

Waxy potaoes hold their shape well in casseroled dishes.

Add sliced truffles to the potatoes as they are layered into the pan.

Hash Brown Potatoes

Yield: 10 servings

Vegetable oil	*as needed*	*as needed*
Potatoes, peeled and cooked, small or medium dice or shredded	*2 1/4 pounds*	*1 kilogram*
Salt to taste	*1/2 teaspoon*	*1/2 teaspoon*
Pepper to taste	*1/4 teaspoon*	*1/4 teaspoon*
Parsley, chopped	*2 teaspoons*	*2 teaspoons*

1. Heat the oil in a griswold. Add the potatoes and season them with the salt and pepper.

2. Cook the potatoes until they are heated through, stirring occasionally.

3. Allow the potatoes to brown well on the bottom; turn the entire cake and brown it on the other side. Garnish with parsley and serve.

VARIATIONS

Lyonnaise Potatoes: Sauté 8 ounces (225 grams) of sliced onions before adding the potatoes.

O'Brien Potatoes: Sauté 4 ounces (115 grams) each of red and green peppers before adding the potatoes.

Homefries are made by cooking raw diced potatoes as directed for hash browns. The skillet should be covered to "steam" them, then removed so they will brown properly.

TECHNIQUE
Pan-frying (pages 364-367)

Pan-frying the pancakes.

Potato pancakes are often served with braised meats. Serve sour cream or applesauce with them.

The cooking method for potato pancakes is illustrated on page 640.

TECHNIQUE
Pan-frying (pages 364-367)

Potato Pancakes

Yield: 10 servings

Potatoes, peeled	*2 1/4 pounds*	*1 kilogram*
Onions, trimmed	*1 pound*	*450 grams*
Lemon juice, to taste	*1 fluid ounce*	*30 milliliters*
Eggs	*2 each*	*2 each*
Salt, to taste	*1/2 teaspoon*	*1/2 teaspoon*
Pepper, to taste	*1/4 teaspoon*	*1/4 teaspoon*
Bread flour	*1 ounce*	*30 grams*
Matzo meal, as needed	*1 ounce*	*30 grams*
Vegetable oil	*4 fluid ounces*	*120 milliliters*

1. Grind or grate the potatoes and onions together; toss them with the lemon juice to prevent discoloration.

2. Place the grated potatoes and onions in a cheesecloth; squeeze out the liquid. Place them in a stainless steel bowl.

3. Add all the remaining ingredients, except the oil.

4. Heat 1/4 inch (.50 centimeter) of the oil in a griswold.

5. Drop the potato batter into the hot oil by level serving spoons. When the pancakes are lightly browned, turn them and brown the other side. Finish them in a 375°F (190°C) oven until they are brown and crisp.

This is often served with Swiss-Style Shredded Veal (page 536).

TECHNIQUE
Pan-frying (pages 364-367)

Roësti Potatoes

Yield: 10 servings

Yukon Gold or yellow Finn potatoes	*2 1/4 pounds*	*1 kilogram*
Clarified butter as needed	*3 ounces*	*85 grams*
Salt to taste	*1/2 teaspoon*	*1/2 teaspoon*
Pepper to taste	*1/4 teaspoon*	*1/4 teaspoon*
Butter, whole	*2 ounces*	*60 grams*

1. Parcook the potatoes until they are slightly underdone. (Cool and store them under refrigeration until needed.) Peel and coarsely grate the potatoes.

2. Heat a well-seasoned sauté pan and add a small amount of the clarified butter.

3. Place the potatoes in the heated pan with the remaining clarified butter. Season with salt and pepper, and dot the outside edge with whole butter.

4. Cook the potatoes until they are golden brown and form a cake. Turn the entire cake, dot the edge with the whole butter, and cook the other side until golden brown and heated through.

Mashed Potatoes (Pommes Purée)

Yield: 10 servings

Potatoes, peeled and sliced thin	2 ^{1}/$_4$ pounds	1 kilogram
Milk, heated	12 fluid ounces	360 milliliters
Butter, melted	4 ounces	115 grams
Salt to taste	1 teaspoon	1 teaspoon
Pepper to taste	^{1}/$_2$ teaspoon	^{1}/$_2$ easpoon

1. Cook the potatoes until they are very tender. Drain and return them to the heat to dry.

2. Purée the potatoes through a food mill while they are still very hot.

3. Add the heated milk and butter and whip until smooth and light. Season with salt and pepper to taste.

VARIATIONS

Duchesse Potatoes: Replace the milk with 4 egg yolks. Add a few grains of nutmeg if desired. This is often used as a border for other items such as Coquilles St. Jacques.

Buttermilk Whipped Potatoes: Use buttermilk to replace the milk. Add 2 to 3 tablespoons of minced chives with the salt and pepper. (Do not heat buttermilk.)

Roasted Garlic Mashed Potatoes: Add 1 to 2 whole heads of roasted garlic to the potatoes when they are being puréed.

Sweet Potato Purée: Substitute roasted and puréed sweet potatoes for the white potatoes; use cooking liquid to replace half the milk. Season with honey, maple syrup, cinnamon, nutmeg, and salt and pepper as desired.

Dry the potatoes before puréeing them.

For the best flavor and texture, be sure that all the ingredients are very hot when they are combined.

TECHNIQUE
Boiling (pages 386-388)

Separating eggs.

Add ground nuts to the bread crumbs if desired.

TECHNIQUE
Deep-frying (pages 367-371)
Making bread crumbs (page 237)

Croquette Potatoes

Yield: 10 servings

Idaho potatoes	*2 pounds*	*900 grams*
Parmesan cheese, grated (optional)	*4 ounces*	*115 grams*
Butter, softened	*2 ounces*	*60 grams*
Egg yolks	*3 each*	*3 each*
Salt to taste	*1/2 teaspoon*	*1/2 teaspoon*
Pepper to taste	*1/4 teaspoon*	*1/4 teaspoon*
Flour	*3 ounces*	*85 grams*
Bread crumbs, dry	*4 ounces*	*115 grams*

1. Cook the potatoes until they are very tender. Drain and dry them.

2. Purée the potatoes while they are very hot.

3. Add the cheese, butter, and egg yolks, mixing them well, and season the appareil with salt and pepper.

4. Shape the croquettes as required.

5. Dredge the croquettes in flour and coat with bread crumbs. Deep-fry them in 375°F (190°C) oil until they are golden brown. Serve them immediately.

French fries can be cut into a variety of shapes from straw or match stick to "pont-neuf" or steak fries.

TECHNIQUE
Deep-frying (pages 367-371)

French-Fried Potatoes

Yield: 10 servings

Idaho potatoes	*2 1/4 pounds*	*1 kilogram*
Vegetable oil or frying fat	*as needed*	*as needed*
Salt to taste	*1 teaspoon*	*1 teaspoon*

1. Cut the potatoes into the desired shape, rinse them in cold water, and dry them thoroughly.

2. Add the potatoes in batches to oil heated to 325°F (165°C). Blanch for 2 minutes.

3. Drain well and transfer the potatoes to pans lined with absorbent paper.

4. Finish the potatoes in 375°F (190°C) oven until they are golden brown and cooked through. Drain them well, season, and serve immediately.

Rice Pilaf

Yield: 10 servings

Onion, diced	1 ¹/₂ ounces	45 grams
Butter	1 ounce	30 grams
Long-grain white rice	14 ounces	400 grams
Chicken or Vegetable Stock, hot	28 fluid ounces	840 milliliters
Bay leaf	1 each	1 each
Thyme sprigs	2 each	2 each
Salt to taste	¹/₂ teaspoon	¹/₂ teaspoon
Pepper to taste	¹/₄ teaspoon	¹/₄ teaspoon

1. Sweat the onion in butter.

2. Add the rice and stir it to coat with the butter.

3. Add the hot stock, bay leaf, thyme sprigs, and salt and pepper to taste.

4. Bring the liquid to a boil. Cover the pot and transfer it to a moderate oven (350°F/175°C) and cook for 18 to 20 minutes until the liquid is absorbed and the rice is tender.

5. Use a kitchen fork to separate the grains of rice and to release the steam.

The pilaf is fully cooked.

An average portion of cooked rice served as a side dish is about 3 ounces (85 grams).

This technique can be used to prepare other grains. Refer to the table in Appendix II.

TECHNIQUE
Pilaf (page 389)

RECIPES
Chicken Stock (page 480)
Vegetable Stock (page 483)

Basic Boiled Rice

Yield: 10 servings

Water	2 quarts	2 liters
Salt to taste	¹/₂ teaspoon	¹/₂ teaspoon
Long-grain white rice	10 ounces	285 grams

1. Bring the water and salt to a rolling boil.

2. Add the rice in a thin stream, stirring it with a fork to prevent the grains from clumping as they are added. When the water returns to a boil, reduce the heat to a simmer.

3. Simmer the rice for approximately 15 minutes, or until the grains are tender. Drain the rice immediately; let steam dry.

This method is sometimes referred to as the "pasta" method. The result is a fluffy cooked grain.

To use this recipe to prepare other grains, refer to the table in Appendix II.

TECHNIQUE
Boiling (pages 386-388)

Add the hot stock gradually.

Arborio rice is a round-grain rice that cooks to the ideal "creamy" consistency. Although other grains may be prepared in this manner, the end result will not be exactly the same.

TECHNIQUE
Risotto (pages 389-391)

RECIPE
Chicken Stock (page 480)

Basic Risotto

Yield: 10 servings

Onions, diced	*2 ounces*	*60 grams*
Butter	*3 ounces*	*85 grams*
Arborio rice	*14 ounces*	*420 grams*
Chicken Stock, hot	*2 pints*	*1 liter*
Dry white wine	*8 fluid ounces*	*2.25 milliliters*
Parmesan cheese, grated	*3 ounces*	*85 grams*
Salt, to taste	*1/2 teaspoon*	*1/2 teaspoon*
Pepper, to taste	*1/4 teaspoon*	*1/4 teaspoon*

1. Sweat the onions in half of the butter.

2. Add the rice and mix it thoroughly with the butter. Cook it, stirring, until a toasted aroma develops.

3. Add 1/3 of the stock, stirring the rice frequently until the rice has absorbed the stock. Add the remaining stock in 2 more additions, stirring constantly. Add the wine and stir in the same manner. Cook the risotto until the rice is al dente and most of the liquid is absorbed. The texture should be creamy.

4. Add the grated Parmesan cheese and the remaining butter. Season to taste with salt and pepper.

VARIATION

Saffron Risotto: Add 1/2 teaspoon of saffron threads to the onions as they sauté.

The method for preparing Polenta is found on pages 342 to 343.

Polenta may be served directly from the pot as a "soft polenta."

TECHNIQUE
Special boiling methods (Polenta) (page 389)

Basic Polenta

Yield: 20 servings

Water	*2 1/2 quarts*	*2.5 liters*
Salt	*1 tablespoon*	*1 tablespoon*
Yellow cornmeal, coarse	*1 pound*	*450 grams*
Butter	*2 ounces*	*60 grams*

1. Bring the water to a boil in a heavy pot. Add the salt.

2. Add the cornmeal to the boiling water in a thin stream, stirring constantly.

3. Cook the polenta over moderate heat, stirring constantly for about 35 minutes or until it pulls away from the sides of the pot.

4. Pour the polenta into a lined sheet pan. Cool thoroughly.

5. Cut the polenta into the desired shape. Bake, sauté, pan-fry, or grill to reheat.

Garlic Cheese Grits

Yield: 10 servings

Water, salted to taste	*2 quarts*	*2 liters*
Regular grits	*12 ounces*	*340 grams*
Butter	*6 ounces*	*170 grams*
Cheddar cheese, sharp, grated	*12 ounces*	*340 grams*
Milk	*12 fluid ounces*	*360 milliliters*
Eggs, lightly beaten	*4 each*	*4 each*
Garlic cloves, minced	*2 each*	*2 each*
Worcestershire sauce	*1 teaspoon*	*1 teaspoon*
Tabasco	*1/2 teaspoon*	*1/2 teaspoon*
Cayenne pepper	*pinch*	*pinch*
Salt, to taste	*2 teaspoons*	*2 teaspoons*
Pepper, to taste	*1/4 teaspoon*	*1/4 teaspoon*

1. Bring the water to a rolling boil. Stir in grits; simmer about 30 minutes or until thick. Remove from heat and stir in butter and 10 ounces (300 grams) of cheese until melted.

2. Combine milk, eggs, garlic, Tabasco, Worcestershire sauce, and cayenne. Add mixture to grits. Add salt and pepper to taste.

3. Pour into buttered dish and top with remaining cheese.

4. Bake in 350°F (175°C) oven until firm, about 1 hour. Let set for 10 minutes before slicing and serving.

There are both yellow and white grits.

To make souffléed grits, separate the eggs. Add the yolks in step 2. Beat the whites to medium peaks and fold into the grits just before pouring into a baking dish.

Prepare in individual timbales or soufflé dishes.

TECHNIQUE
Polenta and other cereals (page 389)
Mincing garlic (pages 224-225)

Couscous

Yield: 10 servings

Couscous	*1 pound*	*450 grams*
Salt to taste	*1/2 teaspoon*	*1/2 teaspoon*
Olive oil	*as needed*	*as needed*

1. Soak the couscous for about 5 minutes in enough warm water to cover, then drain it in a colander.

2. Set the colander over a pot of simmering water; cover the pot and let the couscous steam for 3 to 4 minutes. Uncover the pot and stir the couscous with a fork to break up any lumps. (Rinse the couscous at this point if it is not the precooked variety, and continue to steam it for another 5 minutes.)

3. Fluff the couscous with a fork, and season it to taste with salt. Drizzle a small amount of olive oil over the couscous, if desired.

Couscous can also be prepared by cooking it directly in simmering water or broth. The recipe for Couscous with Lamb Stew in found on page 616.

The method for preparing couscous is illustrated on page 645.

TECHNIQUE
Steaming (pages 374-378)

Bulgur wheat.

To prepare this recipe as a breakfast dish, use skim milk instead of stock.

TECHNIQUE
Boiling (pages 386-388)
Working with dried fruits and vegetables (pages 235-236)

RECIPES
Chicken Stock (page 480)
Vegetable Stock (page 483)

Bulgur with Dried Cherries and Apples

Yield: 10 servings

Chicken or Vegetable Stock or water	*1 quart*	*1 liter*
Bulgur wheat	*10 ounces*	*285 grams*
Salt	*¹/₂ teaspoon*	*¹/₂ teaspoon*
Dried cherries, plumped	*2 ounces*	*60 grams*
Dried apples rings, coarsely chopped	*5 each*	*5 each*

1. Bring the stock or water to a boil.

2. Add the bulgur and stir well. Reduce the heat to low and simmer for about 3 to 4 minutes. Remove the pan from the heat.

3. Fold in the salt, cherries, and apples, using a fork. Cover the pan and allow to rest for about 10 minutes before serving.

This recipe may be used to prepare most types of beans. Refer to the table in Appendix II for the approximate cooking times.

Use a pork broth or ham stock if available.

TECHNIQUE
Boiling (pages 386-388)
Soaking beans (page 236)

RECIPE
Chicken Stock (page 480)
Bouquet Garni (page 474)

Basic Boiled Beans

Yield: 10 servings

Onion, chopped	*1 each*	*1 each*
Vegetable oil	*1 fluid ounce*	*30 milliliters*
Beans, soaked overnight in water to cover	*12 ounces*	*340 grams*
Fresh ham hocks (optional)	*1 each*	*1 each*
Chicken Stock, as needed to cover	*3 quarts*	*3 liters*
Bouquet garni	*1 each*	*1 each*

1. Sweat the onions in oil.

2. Add the beans, ham hock, stock to cover, and bouquet garni; simmer the beans until they are done.

3. (Optional) Remove half of the beans and purée them. Return them to the pot and mix the purée with the whole beans.

Refried Beans

Yield: 10 servings

Pinto beans, soaked overnight	*12 ounces*	*340 grams*
Chicken or Vegetable Stock, as needed to cover	*3 quarts*	*3 liters*
Onions, chopped fine	*8 ounces*	*225 grams*
Garlic cloves, minced	*3 each*	*3 each*
Cumin seeds, ground	*1 teaspoon*	*1 teaspoon*
Chili powder	*2 teaspoons*	*2 teaspoons*
Bacon fat or lard	*6 ounces*	*170 grams*
Tomato concassé	*3 ounces*	*225 grams*
Salt to taste	*1/2 teaspoon*	*1/2 teaspoon*
Pepper to taste	*1/4 teaspoon*	*1/4 teaspoon*
Monterey Jack cheese, grated	*5 ounces*	*140 grams*

1. Cook the beans in the stock until they are very soft.

2. Sauté the onions, garlic, cumin, and chili powder in the bacon fat; add the tomato concassé, and cook the mixture for 2 minutes.

3. Add the cooked beans and continue to cook the mixture, mashing the beans with a spoon as they cook.

4. Season the beans to taste with salt and pepper. Top the beans with grated Monterey Jack cheese before serving, and heat them briefly under a salamander or broiler.

Beans before (right) and after (left) soaking.

Adding the chili powder and cumin seed to the hot oil in step 2 helps to more fully release their flavor.

TECHNIQUE
Boiling (pages 386-388)
Soaking beans (page 236)
Making spice blends (page 241)
Tomato concassé (page 226)

RECIPES
Chicken Stock (page 480)
Vegetable Stock (page 483)

Lentil ragout, ready to serve.

To use this ragout as a sauce, add white wine (5 fluid ounces/150 milliliters) and Jus de Veau Lié or Demi-Glace (6 fluid ounces/180 milliliters) and simmer to reach a good sauce consistency.

TECHNIQUE
Stewing (pages 394-397)
Basic knife cuts (pages 217-223)
Zesting citrus (page 231)

RECIPES
Chicken Stock (page 480)
Sachet d'Epices (page 475)

Lentil Ragout

Yield: 10 servings

Slab bacon, finely diced	2 ounces	60 grams
Onions, fine dice	8 ounces	225 grams
Leeks, fine dice	6 ounces	170 grams
Carrots, fine dice	6 ounces	170 grams
Celery, fine dice	5 ounces	140 grams
Garlic, minced	1 tablespoon	1 tablespoon
Tomato paste	2 ounces	60 grams
French lentils	12 ounces	340 grams
Chicken Stock, as needed	3 pints	1.5 liters
Sachet d'Epices, *plus*		
Caraway seeds	$^{1}/_{4}$ teaspoon	$^{1}/_{4}$ teaspoon
Lemon peel	1 strip	1 strip
Sherry wine vinegar	1 fluid ounce	30 milliliters
Salt to taste	1 teaspoon	1 teaspoon
White pepper to taste	$^{1}/_{2}$ teaspoon	$^{1}/_{2}$ teaspoon

1. Render bacon; add onion, leeks, carrots, celery, and garlic; sauté.

2. Add tomato paste; sauté for several seconds to concentrate the flavor.

3. Add lentils, stock, and sachet; simmer until lentils are tender (about 30 minutes).

4. Remove sachet and discard. Adjust the seasoning to taste with vinegar, salt, and pepper.

The original pastas were made from barley, rye, or spelt flours. Later, when wheat was introduced to Italy, wheat (especially hard wheats) became more common.

Fresh pasta is used to make both flat and filled pastas.

TECHNIQUE
Kneading dough (pages 439-442)

Basic Pasta Dough

Yield: 1 $^{1}/_{2}$ pounds (680 grams)

Semolina or bread flour	1 pound	450 grams
Eggs	6 each	6 each
Salt	pinch	pinch
Water as needed	2 fluid ounces	60 milliliters

1. Combine all the ingredients in a large bowl and knead the mixture until it is smooth.

2. Cover the dough and allow to rest for 1 hour before rolling and shaping.

VARIATIONS

Spinach Pasta: Add 6 ounces (170 grams) of puréed raw spinach. Add additional flour as needed for consistency.

(Recipe continued on facing page)

Tomato Pasta: Sauté 2 to 3 ounces (60 to 85 grams) of tomato paste to concentrate the flavor. Let it cool and add with the eggs.

Fresh Herb Pasta: Add 2 to 4 tablespoons of finely chopped fresh herbs to basic dough.

Pumpkin, Beet, or Carrot Pasta: Sauté 3 to 4 ounces (85 to 115 grams) of cooked, puréed pumpkin, beet, or carrot until dry. Cool and add with the eggs.

Draining cooked pasta.

Basic Boiled Pasta

Yield: 10 servings

Water	4 quarts	4 liters
Salt to taste	1 tablespoon	1 tablespoon
Pasta, fresh or dried	1 pound	450 grams

1. Bring the water and the salt to a rolling boil in a large pot.

2. Add the pasta to the water and stir it well to separate the strands. Let the pasta cook until it is tender but not soft.

3. Drain the pasta at once. Add desired sauce or garnish at this point, according to the specific recipe.

Fresh pastas may cook in less than 3 minutes; dried pastas may take up to 8 minutes or longer, depending upon the size and shape of the noodle.

If the pasta is to be held, plunge it into an ice-water bath to stop the cooking. Drain immediately and drizzle a small amount of vegetable oil over pasta; toss to prevent from sticking together.

The method for cooking, draining, and cooling pasta is illustrated on pages 388-389.

Spaetzle Dough

Yield: 10 servings

Eggs	4 each	4 each
Milk	6 fluid ounces	180 milliliters
Salt to taste	$^1/_2$ teaspoon	$^1/_2$ teaspoon
Pepper to taste	$^1/_4$ teaspoon	$^1/_4$ teaspoon
Nutmeg, ground (optional)	to taste	to taste
Flour	12 ounces	340 grams
Butter	as needed	as needed

1. Combine the eggs, milk, and seasonings in a large bowl; mix well.

2. Work in the flour by hand.

3. Let the dough rest for 10 minutes.

4. Using a spaetzle machine (or other shaping technique), drop the dough into a large pot of boiling, salted water. Simmer until done.

5. Remove the spaetzle with a spider, shock in cold water; drain well.

6. Sauté the spaetzle in whole butter, season to taste with salt and pepper, and serve.

The methods for preparing spaetzle are explained and illustrated on page 389.

This soft dumpling is frequently used to garnish soups. In that case, it should not be sautéed in butter.

TECHNIQUE
Spaetzle (page 389)

Dumplings arranged in a steamer.

Serve with the dipping sauce for Shrimp Tempura or other dipping sauce.

TECHNIQUE
Boiling (pages 386-388)
Steaming (pages 374-378)
Pan-frying (pages 364-367)
Making dim sum (page 375)

Chinese Dumplings (Fried, Steamed, or Boiled)

Yield: 20 pieces

Dough

Flour	*1 pound*	*450 grams*
Water, hot	*8 fluid ounces*	*240 milliliters*

Filling

Pork, ground	*12 ounces*	*340 grams*
Chinese cabbage	*8 ounces*	*225 grams*
Scallions, chopped	*2 ounces*	*60 grams*
Gingerroot, minced	*1 teaspoon*	*1 teaspoon*
Soy sauce	*¹/₂ fluid ounce*	*15 milliliters*
Sesame oil, dark	*¹/₂ fluid ounce*	*15 milliliters*
Egg white	*1 each*	*1 each*
Salt to taste	*¹/₂ teaspoon*	*¹/₂ teaspoon*
White pepper to taste	*¹/₄ teaspoon*	*¹/₄ teaspoon*

1. Mix the flour and water. Let the dough set for 30 minutes. Divide the dough into ¹/₂-ounce (15-gram) portions and roll out into thin circles for individual dumpling skins.

2. Combine all the filling ingredients. Mix well. Check the consistency and seasoning of the filling by sautéing a small amount.

3. Place 1 tablespoon of filling on each dumpling skin and seal the edges tightly.

4. Boil the dumplings in boiling water, or steam until cooked through, about 8 minutes. Or, pan-fry the dumplings on one side only until golden brown and cooked through. Serve them immediately.

Bread Dumplings

Yield: 40 pieces

Onions, fine dice	*8 ounces*	*225 grams*
Butter	*4 ounces*	*115 grams*
Rolls, hard, day old, **small dice**	*2 pounds*	*900 grams*
Milk	*1 pint*	*480 milliliters*
Eggs	*10 each*	*10 each*
Parsley, fresh, chopped	*1 ounce*	*30 grams*
Salt to taste	*$^1/_2$ teaspoon*	*$^1/_2$ teaspoon*
White pepper, ground to taste	*$^1/_4$ teaspoon*	*$^1/_4$ teaspoon*
Nutmeg, ground (optional)	*to taste*	*to taste*
Flour	*8 ounces*	*225 grams*

1. Sauté the onions in the butter until they are lightly browned; cool.

2. Moisten the rolls with the milk. Let them sit for 30 to 40 minutes.

3. Combine the rolls and milk with the cooled onions, eggs, parsley, salt, pepper, and nutmeg.

4. Stir in the flour.

5. Let the mixture rest for 30 minutes, covered. Add additional egg-and-milk mixture if the bread is very dry.

6. Shape the mixture into 2-inch (5-centimeter) dumplings by hand or shape in cheesecloth as for a galantine.

7. Poach the dumplings in boiling salted water for 15 minutes or to an internal temperature of 160°F (70°C). Hold them in the same water until ready to serve.

Wrapping the dumpling in cheesecloth.

TECHNIQUE
Poaching (pages 383-386)

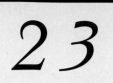

23

Breakfast Recipes

Breakfast is considered by some to be one of the most difficult and thankless meals to master. There are endless varieties of egg preparations alone. The chef must have the skill to quickly meet each early-morning patron's specific request. Although these are considered breakfast items, many of these items may also be served at brunch, lunch, or dinner. Quiche, in particular, is often paired with salad at lunch, or baked in tartelette pans and served as canapés. Muffins, Danish, bagels, and fresh breads prepared on the premises are also excellent breakfast items. Smoked salmon service information and other crêpe recipes may be found in Chapter 26, and sausages may be found in Chapter 27.

The recipes are arranged as follows:

- *Boiled and Poached Eggs*
- *Fried Eggs and Omelets*
- *Baked Eggs and Quiches*
- *Soufflés*
- *Cereals*
- *Pancakes and Other Batters*
- *Breakfast Meats*

Medium to large eggs are the preferred size for breakfast cookery.

If the eggs are used directly from the refrigerator, temper them by letting them sit in warm water for a few minutes before cooking them.

TECHNIQUE
Boiling (pages 386-388)

Soft-Cooked Eggs

Yield: 10 servings

Eggs   *20 each   20 each*

1. Place the eggs in boiling water. Time the cooking from the point that the boiling resumes. For coddled eggs in the shell, cook for 2 to 5 minutes. For soft eggs in a glass, cook for 4 minutes. For soft eggs, cook for 5 minutes.

2. Shock the eggs in cold water for 2 to 3 seconds. Serve them warm.

Hard-cooked eggs can be eaten as is, or pickled, made into egg salad (page 676) or deviled eggs (page 691). These are also chopped and used as a garnish for numerous items.

Hard-cooked eggs are less likely to develop a green ring around the yolk if they are cooled and peeled immediately after cooking.

TECHNIQUE
Boiling (pages 386-388)

Hard-Cooked Eggs

Yield: 10 servings

Eggs, cold   *20 each   20 each*

1. Place the eggs in a pot. Fill the pot with enough cold water to cover the eggs.

2. Bring the water to a gentle boil and immediately lower the temperature to a simmer. Begin timing the cooking at this point.

3. Cook small eggs for 12 minutes, medium eggs for 13 minutes, large eggs for 14 to 15 minutes, and extra large eggs for 15 minutes.

4. Serve the eggs hot in the shell (2 per portion), or cool them quickly in cool water and peel as soon as possible for cold preparations.

Poached Eggs

Yield: 10 servings

Eggs	20 each	20 each
Water	as needed	as needed
Distilled white vinegar	as needed	as needed

1. In a large, shallow pot, bring a mixture of water and vinegar to 200°F (95°C). (See notes.)

2. Break the eggs into cups one at a time, being careful not to break the yolks.

3. Slide the eggs into the simmering water and simmer them until they are done, 3 to 4 minutes. (Poached eggs should feel soft when touched; if they feel hard, they are overcooked.)

4. Remove the eggs carefully with a skimmer and drop into ice water to stop the cooking process if necessary.

5. Remove the eggs from the cold water and trim any excess white to make them even.

6. For service, reheat the poached eggs in slightly salted, 120 to 140°F (50 to 60°C) water. Remove the eggs with a skimmer, dry, and serve.

Slide the cracked egg into barely simmering water.

Use a ratio of 1 quart (1 liter) of water to 1 tablespoon of vinegar.

TECHNIQUE
Poaching (page 383-386)

VARIATIONS

Poached Eggs Mornay: Brush toast with butter, top with the poached eggs, nappé with mornay sauce, sprinkle with grated cheese, and gratiné.

Poached Eggs with Mushrooms: Fill tartlets with creamed mushrooms, top with poached eggs, and nappé with hollandaise sauce.

Eggs Benedict: Brush toasted English muffins with butter and top with heated slices of Canadian bacon, poached eggs, and hollandaise sauce.

Poached Eggs Farmer-Style: Brush toast with butter and top with a peeled tomato slice, boiled ham, creamed mushrooms, and poached eggs.

Poached Egg Parmesan: Slice an eggplant into rounds, bread it using the standard breading procedure, and deep-fry. Top each eggplant slice with ricotta cheese and a peeled tomato slice. Season them with salt and pepper. Heat in a 350°F (175°C) oven for 5 minutes. Place poached eggs on top of the tomatoes. Top with a slice of Provolone cheese and sprinkle with Parmesan. Brown under a broiler.

Egg "sunny side up."

TECHNIQUE
Clarifying butter (page 253)

Fried Eggs

Yield: 10 servings

Eggs	*20 each*	*20 each*
Butter, clarified, or oil or bacon fat, rendered, as needed	*4 fluid ounces*	*120 milliliters*

1. Break the eggs into a bowl without damaging the yolks.

2. Heat the clarified butter in a pan until it is very hot but not smoking. Slide the eggs into the pan and reduce the heat to medium-low or low.

3. When the egg whites have set, tilt the skillet, allow the fat to collect at the side of the pan, and baste the eggs with the fat as they cook. This is known as "sunny-side up." Or, add a small amount of water and cover the pan to steam the eggs. Or, turn over the eggs near the end of their cooking time and cook them to the desired doneness (20 to 30 seconds more for "over-light," 1 minute more for "overhard").

VARIATION

Huevos Rancheros: Spoon salsa over a crisp fried corn tortilla. Top with 2 poached eggs and grated Monterey Jack cheese. Serve with refried beans (page 647) on the side or spread directly on the tortilla. Finish with sour cream and chopped cilantro.

Scrambled Eggs

Yield: 10 servings

Eggs	*20 each*	*20 each*
Salt to taste	*¹/₂ teaspoon*	*¹/₂ teaspoon*
Pepper to taste	*¹/₂ teaspoon*	*¹/₂ teaspoon*
Butter as needed	*3 ounces*	*85 grams*

1. Break eggs into a bowl. Whip them well and season to taste immediately before cooking.

2. Heat the butter in a pan over low heat. Add the beaten eggs; stir them with a wooden spoon until they are soft and creamy. A bain-marie can be used for an even smoother texture.

Scrambling eggs.

V A R I A T I O N S

(all additions are per-portion amounts)

Scrambled Eggs Greek-Style: Slice small eggplants lengthwise into ¹/₂-inch (1.25-centimeter) slices. Season them with salt and sauté them in oil. Sauté 1 ounce (30 grams) of tomato concassé with garlic to taste; season with salt and pepper. Place the scrambled eggs on top of eggplant slices; top the eggs with the tomato concassé.

Scrambled Eggs Hunter-Style: Sauté ³/₄ ounce (20 grams) of diced bacon. Add 2 beaten eggs and ¹/₂ teaspoon of chopped chives, and scramble. Sauté ¹/₄ teaspoon of minced shallots and 3 ounces (85 grams) of sliced mushrooms in butter. Season them with salt and place on top of the eggs.

Scrambled Eggs with Bratwurst: Season peeled tomato slices with garlic, salt, and pepper and sauté them in butter on both sides. Top the tomatoes with the scrambled eggs and cooked bratwurst.

Scrambled Eggs with Smoked Salmon: Heat 1 tablespoon (15 grams) of butter. Add 1 finely crushed juniper berry and 1 ounce (30 grams) of smoked salmon, julienned. Add 2 beaten eggs and 1 teaspoon of chopped chives and scramble. Serve with toast.

Scrambled Eggs Gratiné: Top the scrambled eggs with mornay sauce, sprinkle them with grated cheese, and brown them lightly under a broiler.

Garnish with grated cheese, crumbled bacon, diced ham, leftover meats, fish, or poultry, if desired. (See also the recommended garnishes for poached eggs, page 655.)

For buffet service, scrambled eggs may be precooked in small batches. Add heavy cream, milk, or broth; this prevents the egg from stiffening too fast.

TECHNIQUE
Scrambling eggs (page 362)

A perfectly cooked omlet.

"In a few words, what is an omelet? It is really a special type of scrambled egg...and nothing else."—Escoffier

TECHNIQUE
Preparing omelets (pages 362-363)

Plain Rolled Omelet

Yield: 10 servings

Eggs	*30 each*	*30 each*
Salt to taste	*$1/_2$ teaspoon*	*$1/_2$ teaspoon*
Pepper to taste	*$1/_4$ teaspoon*	*$1/_4$ teaspoon*
Butter as needed	*4 ounces*	*115 grams*

1. Beat the eggs well; season with salt and pepper.

2. Heat the butter in an omelet pan over high heat, tilting the pan to coat the entire surface.

3. Pour the egg mixture into the pan and scramble with a fork or wooden spoon. Move the pan and utensil at the same time until the egg mixture has coagulated slightly (at this point, add the filling if desired).

4. Let the egg mixture finish cooking without stirring.

5. Tilt the pan and slide a fork or a spatula around the lip of the pan, under the omelet, to be sure it is not sticking. Slide the omelet to the front of the pan and use a fork or a wooden spoon to fold it inside to the center.

6. Turn the pan upside down, rolling the omelet onto the plate seam side down. The finished omelet should be oval-shaped, with little or no color.

VARIATIONS

(all additions are per-portion amounts)

Enchilada Omelet: Fill the omelet with 1 ounce (30 grams) each diced red, yellow, and green peppers, and jalapeño jack cheese. Serve with guacamole and salsa on the side. Wrap in a flour or corn tortilla or serve tortillas on the side.

Herb Omelet: Sprinkle the omelet with 2 to 3 teaspoons of finely chopped fresh herbs before rolling it.

Jelly Omelet With Cream Cheese: Fill the omelet with 2 tablespoons jelly, chutney, or other fresh fruits. Add 2 tablespoons mascarpone or cream cheese blended with sweetened sour cream.

Cheese Omelet: Fill the omelet with 1 ounce (30 grams) of grated or diced cheese, alone or with other items. (Possible combinations include sun-dried tomatoes and goat's milk cheese, Gorgonzola and walnuts, cream cheese and olives, sautéed leeks and Gruyère.)

Omelet Florentine: Fill the omelet with 1 $1/_2$ ounces (45 grams) of blanched spinach leaves sautéed with shallots and seasoned with salt and nutmeg.

Western Omelet: Fill the omelet with 1 ounce (30 grams) each of diced sautéed ham, red and green peppers, and onions. Add cheese, if desired.

Spanish Omelet: Fill the omelet with 2 ounces (60 grams) tomato concassé or sauce, and 1 ounce (30 grams) each of diced onions and green peppers.

Frittata (Farmer-Style Omelet)

Yield: 10 servings

Bacon, lean, diced	*12 ounces*	*340 grams*
Onions, minced	*10 ounces*	*285 grams*
Potatoes, cooked and diced	*10 ounces*	*285 grams*
Eggs	*20 each*	*20 each*
Salt to taste	*¹/₂ teaspoon*	*¹/₂ teaspoon*
Pepper to taste	*¹/₄ teaspoon*	*¹/₄ teaspoon*

1. Cook the bacon in a skillet until it is crisp.

2. Add the onions and sauté for 1 minute.

3. Add the potatoes and sauté until they are lightly browned.

4. Meanwhile, beat the eggs with the salt and pepper. Pour them over the ingredients in the skillet and stir gently.

5. Reduce the heat to low, cover the skillet, and cook until the eggs are nearly set. (Finish cooking the frittata in a 325°F/165°C oven if necessary.)

6. Remove the cover and place the skillet under a broiler to brown the eggs lightly. Cut the frittata into wedges and serve.

Potatoes have an important role in this dish.

Frittatas (tortillas in Spanish cuisine) are often cut into small pieces and served hot or cold as tapas.

Two fluid ounces (60 milliliters) of oil or butter may replace the bacon. Or, use sausage instead.

Other cooked vegetables such as peas, diced carrots, and asparagus may be added, as well as herbs such as oregano, parsley, and thyme.

Baked Eggs

Yield: 10 servings

Butter as needed	*2 ounces*	*60 grams*
Filling (see note)	*1 pound*	*450 grams*
Eggs	*20 each*	*20 each*
Salt to taste	*¹/₂ teaspoon*	*¹/₂ teaspoon*
Pepper to taste	*¹/₄ teaspoon*	*¹/₄ teaspoon*

1. Warm ramekins; brush insides with butter.

2. Place the filling in the ramekins. Top each with an egg, season with salt and pepper, and top with a small piece of whole butter.

3. Set the ramekins in a prepared bain-marie filled with boiling water and cover with a lid or vented aluminum foil. Cook in a preheated 350 to 375°F (175 to 190°C) oven until done, about 6 to 8 minutes. The egg whites should be stiff and the yolks should be soft. Serve in the ramekins.

Possible fillings for baked eggs include ratatouille, ragoûts, sautéed and diced chicken livers, sautéed mushrooms, and/or other vegetables; duxelles; hash browns, succotash, and flannel hash; refried beans with salsa, cheeses, tomato concassé, and sautéed spinach with garlic.

Other filling suggestions can be found with poached-egg garnishes (page 655) and omelet fillings (page 658).

TECHNIQUE
Bain-marie (pages 258-259)

Shirred Eggs

Yield: 10 servings

Butter, melted, as needed	2 ounces	60 grams
Eggs	20 each	20 each
Salt to taste	$^1/_2$ teaspoon	$^1/_2$ teaspoon
Pepper to taste	$^1/_4$ teaspoon	$^1/_4$ teaspoon
Heavy cream, hot	5 fluid ounces	150 milliliters

1. Brush a gratin dish or flameproof ramekins with melted butter.

2. Break the eggs into gratin dish or ramekins; cook them over low to medium heat on stove top for 1 to 2 minutes or until their underside has set.

3. Season the eggs, add the heavy cream, and bake the eggs in a 350°F (175°C) oven until they are done (4 to 5 minutes).

Prepared mustard, curry powder, or grated cheese may be added to the cream before pouring it over the eggs. Fillings and garnishes such as those recommended for omelets may also be added. These eggs can be prepared individually or in a larger gratin for buffet service.

Quiche Lorraine

Yield: One 9-inch tart

Slab bacon, lean, chopped	*8 ounces*	*225 grams*
Butter or oil	*as needed*	*as needed*
Heavy cream or crème fraîche	*12 fluid ounces*	*360 milliliters*
Eggs	*3 each*	*3 each*
Salt	*½ teaspoon*	*½ teaspoon*
Pepper	*½ teaspoon*	*½ teaspoon*
Gruyère cheese (optional), grated	*6 ounces*	*115 grams*
Pie Crust, 9-inch, baked blind	*1 each*	*1 each*

Use a scrap of dough to press the crust into the pan's corners.

1. Sauté the bacon in butter or oil until it is browned. Remove the bacon with a slotted spoon; drain.

2. Whisk together the heavy cream or crème fraîche and eggs to make a custard. Season to taste with salt and pepper.

3. Scatter the drained bacon and cheese evenly over the crust. Add the custard mixture gradually, stirring it with a fork to distribute the filling ingredients evenly.

4. Set the quiche pan on a baking dish and bake it in a 350°F (175°C) oven until a knife blade inserted in the quiche's center comes out clean, about 40 to 45 minutes. Serve the quiche hot or at room temperature.

Quiche may be baked without a pastry crust as follows: Butter a shallow casserole or baking dish. Sprinkle it with grated Parmesan cheese if desired. Spread the filling ingredients over the casserole bottom. Pour the egg mixture over the flavorings. Bake the quiche in a bain-marie until a knife inserted near its center comes clean.

Sautéed onions may be added to the Quiche Lorraine or any of its variations.

V A R I A T I O N S

Spinach Quiche: Include 12 ounces (340 grams) of spinach, well rinsed, blanched, squeezed dry, and chopped coarsely. Reduce the bacon to 4 ounces (115 grams). Lightly season with nutmeg.

Quiche Provençale: Substitute 12 ounces (340 grams) of reduced ratatouille for the bacon and cheese. Gratinée with cheese at service, if desired.

Vegetable Quiche: Substitute 1 pound (450 grams) of finely diced sautéed vegetables (snow peas, snap peas, green peas, asparagus, zucchini, yellow squash, carrots, etc.) for the bacon and cheese.

Southwestern Quiche: Include 8 ounces (225 grams) of julienned green chilies. Omit the bacon. Use Monterey Jack and Cheddar cheese. Add diced jalapeño peppers, or salsa, if desired. The pie crust recipe may be amended by replacing the flour with a blend of equal parts masa harina and flour.

TECHNIQUE
Baking blind (page 445)

RECIPE
Pie Crust (3-2-1) (page 736)

Folding beaten egg whites into the base.

Soufflés serve many functions as brunch items, side dishes, appetizers, and entrées.

In some instances, cayenne may be preferred in place of nutmeg.

Fresh, chopped herbs would also be excellent in the soufflé.

Savory Cheese Soufflé

Yield: 10 servings

Butter	*2 ounces*	*60 grams*
Flour	*2 ounces*	*60 grams*
Milk	*1 ¼ quarts*	*1.2 liters*
Egg yolks	*15 each*	*15 each*
Butter	*as needed*	*as needed*
Parmesan cheese, grated	*3 ounces*	*85 grams*
Gruyère or Emmentaler cheese, grated	*3 ounces*	*85 grams*
Salt, added to taste	*½ teaspoon*	*½ teaspoon*
Black pepper, ground to taste	*½ teaspoon*	*½ teaspoon*
Nutmeg, ground	*to taste*	*to taste*
Egg whites	*10 each*	*10 each*

1. To make the soufflé base: Prepare a light roux with the butter and flour.

2. Gradually add the milk, whipping out any lumps after each addition. Simmer the mixture for 15 minutes, stirring frequently. Remove the sauce from the heat.

3. Beat the egg yolks in a small bowl. Temper the yolks with hot sauce, and add them to the sauce. Reserve the base in a large bowl. (Soufflé base may be prepared up to this point and refrigerated or frozen for later use.)

4. Butter a 2-quart (2-liter) soufflé dish or 10 individual dishes. Sprinkle the sides and bottom with some Parmesan cheese. Tap the dish(es) on the counter to shake off any excess cheese; reserve the remaining Parmesan.

5. Stir in the Gruyère or Emmentaler cheese, salt, pepper, and nutmeg into the reserved soufflé base.

6. Whip the egg whites to soft peaks. Fold the whites into the base, half at a time.

7. Spoon the soufflé batter into the prepared molds to within ½ inch (1.5 centimeters) of the rim. Wipe the rim carefully to remove any batter. Tap the soufflé(s) gently on the counter to settle the batter.

8. Sprinkle the soufflé top(s) with the remaining Parmesan cheese.

9. Place the soufflé(s) in the bottom third of a preheated 425°F (220°C) oven and bake until puffy and a skewer inserted in their centers comes out relatively clean (14 to 18 minutes for individual soufflé(s), 30 to 35 minutes for a single large soufflé).

VARIATIONS

Herb Soufflé: Pesto, prepared mustard, tarragon, parsley, chives, chervil, or curry may be added to taste.

(Recipe continued on facing page)

Spinach Soufflé: Add 4 ounces (115 grams) of blanched, squeezed, coarsely chopped spinach, 4 ounces (115 grams) of minced, sautéed onions or leeks, and 4 ounces (115 grams) of sautéed chopped mushrooms. Kale or watercress may be substituted for the spinach.

Seafood Soufflé: Add 8 ounces (225 grams) of cooked, diced seafood with 1 teaspoon chopped, fresh tarragon; 1 to 2 teaspoons dry sherry, 4 ounces (115 grams) of green peas, and 2 tablespoons (10 grams) of chopped sun-dried tomatoes. Omit the nutmeg.

Vegetable Soufflé: Add 4 ounces (115 grams) of reduced vegetable coulis or purée. Roasted red peppers, green peas, roasted eggplant, pumpkin or squash, potato, or sweet corn all make good choices. Omit the nutmeg. Season with fresh herbs.

Cream of Wheat

Yield: 10 servings

Water	3 quarts	3 liters
Salt	1 teaspoon	1 teaspoon
Cream of wheat	7 ounces	200 grams

1. Bring the water to a rolling boil. Add salt.
2. Add the cream of wheat in a stream, stirring to prevent lumping.
3. Continue to cook over low to medium heat for 15 to 20 minutes until the cereal has become thick and creamy.

VARIATIONS

Farina: Cooking time is 5 to 20 minutes.

Grits, quick-cooking: Cooking time is 5 minutes.

Grits, regular: Cooking time is 15 to 20 minutes.

Oatmeal, rolled: Cooking time is 10 minutes.

Buckwheat: Cooking time is 15 minutes.

Hominy, whole: Cooking time is 30 minutes.

Add dried fruits, chopped, toasted nuts, raisins, and ground spices as desired, or top with granola.

Cereals may be cooked in a mix of milk and water for a creamier texture, or finish with cream.

Serve with a small pitcher of milk or cream and brown sugar or syrup.

TECHNIQUE
Simmering (pages 386-388)

Use a variety of flours and meals for multi-grain pancakes.

For an extra-rich version, use light cream to replace part of the milk.

Seasonal fruits such as blueberries, raspberries, and parcooked dried apples (dusted with cinnamon) all make excellent additions. Add more sugar if necessary. If using frozen berries, it is not necessary to thaw them first, but you should make a test pancake using only about 2 1/2 pints (1.2 liters) of the milk before adding the remainder.

Chopped toasted nuts provide additional texture.

Basic Pancakes

Yield: 10 servings

Flour	24 ounces	680 grams
Salt	2 teaspoons	2 teaspoons
Sugar	6 ounces	170 grams
Baking soda	1 tablespoon	1 tablespoon
Baking powder	2 tablespoons	2 tablespoons
Milk or buttermilk	3 pints	1.5 liters
Eggs, lightly beaten	6 each	6 each
Butter, melted	3 ounces	85 grams
Vegetable oil	as needed	as needed

1. Sift together the flour, salt, sugar, baking soda, and baking powder into a large mixing bowl.

2. In a separate bowl, whisk together the milk, eggs, and some of the melted butter.

3. Add the wet ingredients to the dry. Add the remaining butter. Stir with a wooden spoon to combine. The batter will be slightly lumpy.

4. Brush the griddle or skillet lightly with the oil; heat the oil until it is moderately hot.

5. Drop the batter onto the griddle, using a 2-ounce (60-milliliter) ladle, leaving about 1 inch (2.5 centimeters) of space between the pancakes.

6. Cook the pancakes until the undersides are brown, the edges begin to dry, and bubbles begin to break the surface of the batter, about 3 to 5 minutes.

7. Turn the pancakes and cook them until the second side is brown. Repeat using the remaining batter.

8. Serve the pancakes immediately or keep them warm, uncovered, in a slow oven. Do not hold the pancakes longer than 30 minutes, or they will become tough.

VARIATIONS

Pigs in a Blanket: Make 5-inch (12-centimeter) pancakes and roll each pancake around a precooked link sausage. Serve 2 to 3 on a plate with maple syrup.

Silver Dollar Pancakes: Thin batter with a bit more milk. Make pancakes about 2 to 3 inches (4 to 5 centimeters) in diameter. Serve 6 to 8 on a plate.

Whole-Grain Pancakes: Substitute buckwheat flour, whole wheat flour, or oatmeal for 3/4 cup of the white flour.

Johnny Cakes: Substitute cornmeal for half of the flour. Add cooked corn kernels if desired.

Cottage Cheese Pancakes: Add 1 1/2 pints drained cottage cheese to the mixture.

Souffléed Pancakes: Separate eggs and add yolks to batter. Whip egg whites to medium peaks and fold into batter just before cooking.

Crêpes

Yield: 20 servings (2 per serving)

Eggs	*3 each*	*3 each*
Milk	*10 fluid ounces*	*300 milliliters*
Butter, melted	*1 ounce*	*30 grams*
Flour	*4 ounces*	*115 grams*
Salt	*¹/₂ teaspoon*	*¹/₂ teaspoon*
Vegetable oil	*as needed*	*as needed*

Tilt the pan and roll it to produce very thin, even crêpes.

1. Combine all ingredients except the oil in the bowl of a food processor or blender and blend for 30 seconds. Scrape down the sides of the bowl and process another minute, until the batter is very smooth. Or, mix the liquid ingredients with a wire whip. Add the flour and salt and beat until smooth.

2. Adjust the consistency with water or flour; the batter should be the consistency of heavy cream.

3. Let the batter rest, refrigerated, for 30 minutes.

4. Heat a crêpe pan over medium-high heat. Brush it lightly with oil.

5. Ladle about 3 tablespoons of batter in the center of the pan. Tilt the pan to swirl the batter over the surface to the edges.

6. Cook the crêpe until the edges are brown and the underside is golden. Flip and cook 1 minute more. Slide the crêpe onto a plate.

7. Repeat the procedure with the remaining batter. Stack the finished crêpes slightly off-center so they will be easier to separate.

8. To serve the crêpes, fill them, if desired, and roll them or fold them in quarters or in a pocket-fold.

Crêpes can be used for sweet or savory dishes. They may be filled with meat and vegetable mixtures or with sweet items such as fresh berries and whipped cream. Refer to Chapter 29 for other dessert ideas.

For savory crêpes, you may, replace part or all of the milk with beer.

Heavy cream can be substituted for ¹/₄ cup (60 milliliters) of the milk for a more tender crêpe.

VARIATIONS

Whole-Grain Crêpes: Substitute 2 ounces (60 grams) whole-grain flour (wheat, rye, buckwheat) for half of the all-purpose flour.

Herbed Crêpes: Add 3 to 4 tablespoons of finely chopped fresh herbs to the batter.

Wild Rice Crêpes: Add up to 3 ounces (75 grams) of cooked, drained wild rice to the batter.

Spinach Crêpes: Add 1 ounce (30 grams) of cooked, squeezed, and finely chopped spinach leaves, 3 thinly sliced scallions, and a pinch of nutmeg to the batter.

Buttermilk Crêpes: Replace 8 fluid ounces (240 milliliters) of the milk with buttermilk.

Cornmeal Crêpes: Substitute 2 ounces of cornmeal or masa harina for half of the flour. Add up to 4 ounces (115 grams) of crushed corn kernels if desired.

The batter for waffles is simple to make and can be prepared up to one day in advance and held in the refrigerator.

Serve with warmed maple syrup and butter or fresh fruit and whipped cream.

Waffles

Yield: 12 servings

All-purpose or cake flour, sifted	*8 ounces*	*225 grams*
Salt	*1 teaspoon*	*1 teaspoon*
Sugar	*2 ounces*	*60 grams*
Baking powder	*1 ¹/₂ tablespoons*	*1 ¹/₂ tablespoons*
Egg yolks	*4 each*	*4 each*
Milk	*12 fluid ounces*	*360 milliliters*
Butter, melted	*4 ounces*	*115 grams*
Egg whites, room temperature	*4 each*	*4 each*

1. Sift together the flour, salt, sugar, and baking powder in a large mixing bowl.

2. In a separate bowl, beat together the egg yolks, milk, and melted butter.

3. Add the wet ingredients to the dry. Stir with a wooden spoon just to combine. The batter will be slightly lumpy.

4. Preheat the waffle iron. Lightly oil.

5. Whip the egg whites to soft peaks and fold into the batter in two parts.

6. Ladle the batter onto the waffle iron. Close the iron and cook the waffles until they are crisp, golden, and cooked through.

Dust the French toast with powdered sugar if desired.

Traditional accompaniments are syrup or honey and butter. Add toasted chopped nuts to the syrup, or substitute a warm fruit compote for the syrup.

The amount of bread this will coat will depend on size of slice and freshness of bread.

TECHNIQUE
Pan-frying (pages 364-367)

French Toast

Yield: 1 ¹/₄ quarts (1.25 liter);
enough for approximately 7 servings

Milk	*1 quart*	*1 liter*
Eggs	*8 each*	*8 each*
Sugar as needed	*2 ounces*	*60 grams*
Cinnamon, ground (optional)	*pinch*	*pinch*
Nutmeg, ground (optional)	*pinch*	*pinch*
Salt	*pinch*	*pinch*
Bread, sliced, day-old: wheat, French, challah, or other	*21 pieces*	*21 pieces*

(Recipe continued on facing page)

1. Combine the milk, eggs, sugar, cinnamon, nutmeg, and salt and mix them into a smooth batter. Keep this batter refrigerated until needed.

2. Heat a skillet (use a nonstick pan or lubricate the skillet with a small amount of vegetable oil or butter to prevent sticking) over moderate heat.

3. Dip the bread into the batter, coating the slices evenly. Fry the slices on one side until evenly browned; then turn them and brown the other side.

4. Serve three pieces of the French toast per serving at once.

Red Flannel Hash

Yield: 10 servings

Butter	*2 ounces*	*60 grams*
Onions, minced	*6 ounces*	*170 grams*
Carrots, minced	*4 ounces*	*115 grams*
Green peppers, minced	*4 ounces*	*115 grams*
Corned beef, cooked and minced or ground	*1 pound*	*450 grams*
Chef's potatoes, grated, cooked	*8 ounces*	*225 grams*
Beets, cooked, peeled, grated	*8 ounces*	*225 grams*
Scallions, minced	*4 ounces*	*115 grams*
Parsley, fresh, chopped	*1 ounce*	*30 grams*
Thyme leaf, fresh, chopped	*1 tablespoon*	*1 tablespoon*
Salt to taste	*$^1/_2$ teaspoon*	*$^1/_2$ teaspoon*
Pepper to taste	*$^1/_4$ teaspoon*	*$^1/_4$ teaspoon*
Vegetable oil	*as needed*	*as needed*

1. Heat the butter over medium heat in a sauté pan. Add the onions, carrots, and peppers; cook until they are translucent and tender. Remove the vegetables from the pan and place them in a large bowl.

2. Combine all the remaining ingredients (except for the vegetable oil) with the cooked onions and peppers and mix until evenly combined.

3. Heat the oil in a griswold over high heat. Add the hash mixture and press it into an even layer in the pan. Turn the heat down; cook the hash until a good crust has formed on the bottom.

4. Turn the hash and cook it until a crust has formed on the second side and the hash is thoroughly heated. Cut the hash into wedges and serve it at once.

Beets and carrots give red flannel hash its distinctive color.

An optional cooking method is to combine the ingredients and place them into an oiled hotel pan. The hash can be cooked in a hot oven until it is heated through and a crust has formed on the top. This is a convenient way to prepare hash for buffet service.

A traditional presentation is topped with poached or fried eggs.

Ketchup may be offered on the side.

TECHNIQUE
Pan-frying (pages 364-367)
Basic knife cuts (pages 217-223)

Preparing the gravy.

You may substitute a prepared béchamel for the roux and milk if desired.

Chipped or air-dried beef may be very salty, so adjust seasoning accordingly.

If you like, add 5 chopped hard-cooked eggs to the chipped beef before service.

TECHNIQUE
Sautéing (pages 358-362)

Creamed Chipped Beef

Yield: 10 servings

Chipped beef, coarse chop	*12 ounces*	*340 grams*
Butter	*4 ounces*	*115 grams*
Onions, chopped (optional)	*5 ounces*	*140 grams*
Flour	*2 ounces*	*60 grams*
Milk	*1 quart*	*1 liter*
White pepper to taste	*¹/₄ teaspoon*	*¹/₄ teaspoon*
Salt to taste	*¹/₂ teaspoon*	*¹/₂ teaspoon*
Bread slices, toasted and halved	*20 each*	*20 each*

1. Sauté the beef in some the butter until the edges curl. Remove the beef.

2. Add the onions and sweat (optional); add the flour and make a pale roux. Whisk in the milk, stirring constantly so it doesn't lump. Cook until the sauce thickens. Add the beef. Season to taste with salt and pepper. Serve on toasted bread slices.

VARIATION

Sausage Gravy: Replace beef with 12 ounces (340 grams) of ground sausage. Render the fat from the sausage and substitute some of the fat for the butter to make the roux if desired.

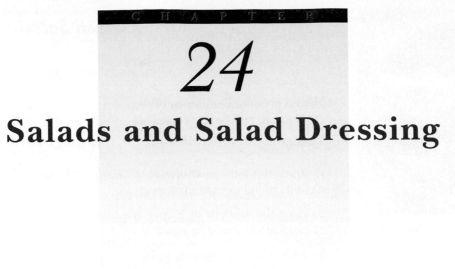

24

Salads and Salad Dressing

The salad recipes that are included in this chapter range from those appropriate for a first course or side dish to entrées. Almost all can be served as a main course with a few modifications. Although many have suggested dressings or accompaniments, you may always consider other dressings, ingredients, and presentations. Other salad recipes may be found in Chapter 26, Hors d'Oeuvres and Appetizers.

The recipes have been grouped in the following order:

- *Green Salads*
- *Composed Salads*
- *Vegetable Salads*
- *Meat and Fish Salads*
- *Potato Salads*
- *Grain and Pasta Salads*
- *Vinaigrettes*
- *Mayonnaise and Creamy Dressings*

Keep lettuce well chilled until ready for service.

Optional vegetable garnishes: sliced or shredded carrots or radishes; halved, quartered, or sliced tomatoes; raw or blanched green beans; peas, broccoli or cauliflower florets; crumbled, diced, or shredded cheese (goat, Cheddar, Swiss, blue, etc.); croutons; roasted pepper strips; sun-dried tomatoes; olives.

TECHNIQUE
Preparing greens (page 229)

RECIPES
Basic Vinaigrette (page 678)

Wilted green salads are popular lunch options. Or, serve this as a side dish with a grilled or roasted entrée.

TECHNIQUE
Preparing greens (page 229)
Rendering fats (page 253)
Mashing garlic (pages 224-225)
Basic knife cuts (pages 217-223)

RECIPES
Hard-Cooked Eggs (page 654)

Mixed Green Salad

Yield: 10 servings

Mixed greens: Romaine, bibb, Boston, red leaf, green leaf	*30 ounces*	*840 grams*
Vinaigrette or other dressing	*10 fluid ounces*	*300 milliliters*

1. Rinse the lettuces thoroughly. Drain well and spin dry. Keep the lettuce well chilled until ready for service.

2. Place the amount of lettuce required (2 to 3 ounces/60 to 85 grams per portion) in a mixing bowl.

3. Add sufficient dressing to lightly coat the leaves. Toss the salad gently to coat evenly.

4. Mound the lettuce on chilled salad plates and garnish as desired.

Wilted Spinach Salad with Warm Bacon Vinaigrette

Yield: 10 servings

Warm Bacon Vinaigrette		
Bacon, diced	*8 ounces*	*225 grams*
Shallots, minced	*1 1/2 ounces*	*45 grams*
Garlic cloves, mashed	*2 each*	*2 each*
Brown sugar	*4 ounces*	*115 grams*
Cider vinegar	*3 ounces*	*85 grams*
Vegetable oil	*5 to 6 fluid ounces*	*150 to 180 milliliters*
Salt to taste	*1 teaspoon*	*1 teaspoon*
Black peppercorns, cracked	*1 teaspoon*	*1 teaspoon*
Spinach, stemmed, torn	*1 1/2 pounds*	*680 grams*
Eggs, hard-cooked and chopped	*5 each*	*5 each*
Mushrooms, sliced	*6 ounces*	*170 grams*
Red onion, sliced into thin rings	*1 each*	*1 each*
Croutons, as needed	*4 ounces*	*225 grams*

1. To make the vinaigrette: Render the bacon. Remove the diced bacon from

(Recipe continued on facing page)

the pan and reserve. Add the shallots and garlic to the bacon fat and sweat. Blend in the brown sugar to melt. Whisk in the cider vinegar and then oil. Season to taste with salt and pepper. Bring to a simmer.

2. Add the spinach to the hot dressing; toss until just wilted. Transfer to a plate. Top with eggs, mushrooms, onion rings, croutons, and reserved bacon.

Chef Salad

Yield: 10 servings

Assorted salad greens, rinsed	*2 pounds*	*900 grams*
Smoked ham, boneless, sliced	*1 pound*	*450 grams*
Chicken breasts, cooked and sliced	*10 each*	*10 each*
Tomatoes, peeled and quartered	*10 each*	*10 each*
Cucumber, sliced	*1 each*	*1 each*
Carrots, sliced	*1 each*	*1 each*
Eggs, hard-cooked and quartered	*10 each*	*10 each*
Salami, sliced very thin, rolled tightly	*30 each*	*30 each*
Cheddar cheese, julienne	*10 ounces*	*285 grams*
Gruyère cheese, julienne	*10 ounces*	*285 grams*
Chives, chopped	*2 tablespoons*	*2 tablespoons*

1. Place the greens in a chilled bowl or arrange them on a chilled plate.

2. Arrange the chicken, vegetables, eggs, salami, and cheeses on the lettuce.

3. Top with the chopped chives.

4. Serve a dressing on the side or drizzled over the salad.

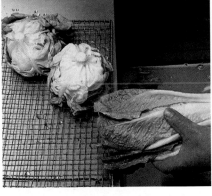

A variety of leafy greens may be used to prepare chef salad

Serve this salad with a choice of dressings: Vinaigrette, page 678 Catalina, page 679, Blue Cheese, page 682, Ranch-Style, page 681.

TECHNIQUE
Preparing greens (page 229)
Basic knife cuts (pages 217-223)
Tomatoes (pages 226-227)

RECIPE
Hard-Cooked Eggs (page 654)

671

Removing the core from iceburg lettuce.

Tortilla shells can be purchased already prepared. To make them, used nested frying baskets to deep-fry flour or corn tortillas at 375°F (190°C) until crisp. Drain and cool before filling.

TECHNIQUE
Basic knife cuts (pages 217-223)
Preparing greens (page 229)
Deep-frying (pages 367-371)

RECIPE
Fresh Tomato Salsa (page 690)

TECHNIQUE
Basic knife cuts (pages 217-223)
Slurries (page 238)

RECIPE
Chicken Stock (page 480)

Taco Salad

Yield: 10 servings

Ground beef	2 ¹/₂ pounds	1.15 kilograms
Taco Sauce (below)	1 pint	480 grams
Iceberg lettuce, chiffonade	2 pounds	900 grams
Tortilla bowls, fried, corn or flour	10 each	10 each
Black beans, cooked	12 ounces	340 grams
Pinto beans, cooked	12 ounces	340 grams
Tomatoes, diced	10 ounces	285 grams
Red onions, diced	1 each	1 each
Sour cream	5 fluid ounces	150 milliliters
Cheddar or Monterey Jack cheese, shredded	10 ounces	285 grams
Black olives, sliced	20 each	20 each
Fresh Tomato Salsa	20 ounces	680 grams

1. Brown ground beef. Drain well, and combine with taco sauce.

2. Lay a bed of lettuce in the bottom of the tortilla bowl. Top with beans, tomatoes, onions, sour cream, cheese, olives, and salsa.

Taco Sauce

Yield: 1 pint (480 milliliters)

Onion, small dice	1 ounce	30 grams
Garlic cloves, minced	2 each	2 each
Vegetable oil	2 fluid ounces	60 milliliters
Oregano, ground	2 teaspoons	2 teaspoons
Cumin, ground	1 tablespoon	1 tablespoon
Chili powder	1 tablespoon	1 tablespoon
Chicken Stock	8 fluid ounces	240 milliliters
Tomato purée	6 fluid ounces	180 milliliters
Cornstarch slurry	as needed	as needed

1. Sweat onions and garlic in oil.

2. Add spices and cook briefly.

3. Add stock and tomato purée and simmer. Thicken with cornstarch slurry, if needed. Chill well before using in salads.

Coleslaw

Yield: 10 servings

Sour cream	*6 fluid ounces*	*180 milliliters*
Basic Mayonnaise	*2 fluid ounces*	*60 milliliters*
Cider vinegar	*2 fluid ounces*	*60 milliliters*
Dry mustard	*1 tablespoon*	*1 tablespoon*
Sugar	*1 1/2 ounces*	*45 grams*
Celery seed	*2 teaspoons*	*2 teaspoons*
Salt to taste	*1/2 teaspoon*	*1/2 teaspoon*
Pepper to taste	*1/4 teaspoon*	*1/4 teaspoon*
Green cabbage, shredded	*1 1/2 pounds*	*680 grams*
Carrots, shredded	*6 ounces*	*170 milliliters*

1. Mix the sour cream, mayonnaise, vinegar, mustard, sugar, and celery seed together in a large bowl until smooth. Add salt and pepper to taste.

2. Add the cabbage and carrots and toss until evenly coated.

Use a variety of cabbages for a special effect.

Coleslaw has been an American dish since the late 1700s. The name derives from the Dutch koolsla, *meaning "cabbage salad."*

RECIPE
Basic Mayonnaise (pagge 680)

Carrot and Raisin Salad

Yield: 10 servings

Water	*8 fluid ounces*	*240 milliliters*
Sugar	*1 ounce*	*30 grams*
Salt to taste	*1/4 teaspoon*	*1/4 teaspoon*
Lemon juice	*1 tablespoon*	*1 tablespoon*
Raisins	*5 ounces*	*140 grams*
Carrots, grated	*1 1/2 pounds*	*680 grams*
Basic Mayonnaise	*3 fluid ounces*	*90 milliliters*
Catalina Dressing	*3 fluid ounces*	*90 milliliters*

RECIPE
Basic Mayonnaise (page 680)
Catalina Dressing (page 679)

1. Combine water with the sugar, salt, and lemon juice and bring to a boil. Pour over the raisins and steep until the raisins are plump. Drain and cool.

2. Mix raisins and carrots with the two dressings. Chill.

If preparing the apples in advance, toss the cubed apples in acidulated water to prevent discoloration.

Waldorf salad, a staple in many hotel dining rooms, was created in 1896 by Oscar Tschirky, maître d'hôtel of the Waldorf-Astoria Hotel in New York City.

TECHNIQUE
Preparing greens (page 229)

RECIPE
Basic Mayonnaise (page 680)

Add spice blends (curry, chili powder, barbecue spice, or fines herbes) to the mayonnaise if desired.

Additional garnish items include toasted walnuts, halved seedless grapes, or chopped red or green onions.

TECHNIQUE
Basic knife cuts (pages 217-223)

RECIPE
Basic Mayonnaise (page 680)

Waldorf Salad

Yield: 10 servings

Apples, peeled, cored, and cubed	1 ¼ pounds	570 grams
Celery, large dice	6 ounces	170 grams
Basic Mayonnaise	3 fluid ounces	90 milliliters
Lettuce leaves (Boston or bibb)	20 each	20 each
Walnuts, chopped coarsely	2 ounces	60 grams

1. Combine the apples, celery, and mayonnaise; chill.

2. Serve on a bed of lettuce. Top with walnuts.

Chicken Salad

Yield: 2 quarts (2 liters)

Chicken meat, cooked, cubed	4 pounds	1.9 kilograms
Basic Mayonnaise	1 pint	480 milliliters
Celery, minced	1 ½ pounds	680 grams
Salt to taste	1 teaspoon	1 teaspoon
Pepper to taste	½ teaspoon	½ teaspoon
Poultry seasoning	to taste	to taste

1. Combine all ingredients, mix well, and adjust seasoning.

Ham Salad

Yield: 2 quarts (2 liters)

Smoked ham, fine dice, or ground	*4 pounds*	*1.8 kilograms*
Basic Mayonnaise	*1 pint*	*480 milliliters*
Sweet relish	*2 to 3 ounces*	*60 to 85 grams*
Prepared mustard	*1 to 2 ounces*	*30 to 60 grams*

1. Mix all ingredients together and adjust seasoning.

Serve as a sandwich on rye bread with lettuce, tomato, and Swiss cheese.

TECHNIQUE
Basic knife cuts (pages 217-223)

RECIPE
Basic Mayonnaise (page 680)

Tuna Salad

Yield: 2 quarts (2 liters)

Tuna, canned, drained	*2 1/2 pounds*	*1 kilogram*
Basic Mayonnaise	*10 ounces*	*285 grams*
Celery, chopped fine	*4 ounces*	*115 grams*
Onion, minced	*4 ounces*	*115 grams*
Garlic powder	*to taste*	*to taste*
Worcestershire sauce	*2 teaspoons*	*2 teaspoons*
White pepper to taste	*1/2 teaspoon*	*1/2 teaspoon*
Salt to taste	*1/2 teaspoon*	*1/2 teaspoon*
Dry mustard	*1/2 teaspoon*	*1/2 teaspoon*

1. Drain tuna thoroughly; flake and place in large bowl.

2. Add mayonnaise, celery, onion, seasonings, and mustard; mix well.

Chopped celery adds texture to tuna salad.

Use this salad to stuff cherry tomatoes or profiteroles as an hors d'oeuvre or canapé.

TECHNIQUE
Basic knife cuts (pages 217-223)

RECIPE
Basic Mayonnaise (page 680)

Eggs that are not farm-fresh are easier to peel.

Use this salad to make sandwiches on whole-grain bread with lettuce, tomato, and onion for a lunch menu classic.

TECHNIQUE
Basic knife cuts (pages 217–223)

RECIPES
Hard-Cooked Eggs (page 654)
Basic Mayonnaise (page 680)

Egg Salad

Yield: 2 quarts (2 liters)

Eggs, hard-cooked, chopped fine	*24 each*	*24 each*
Basic Mayonnaise	*10 ounces*	*300 milliliters*
Celery, minced	*6 ounces*	*170 grams*
Onion, minced	*3 ounces*	*85 grams*
White pepper to taste	*1/2 teaspoon*	*1/2 teaspoon*
Salt to taste	*1/2 teaspoon*	*1/2 teaspoon*
Garlic powder to taste	*1/2 teaspoon*	*1/2 teaspoon*
Dijon mustard to taste	*1 tablespoon*	*1 tablespoon*

1. Mix all ingredients together. Keep chilled.

Chopped fresh herbs (parsley, chives, or tarragon) may be added to taste in step 2.

TECHNIQUE
Basic knife cuts (pages 217–223)

RECIPES
Hard-Cooked Eggs (page 654)
Basic Mayonnaise (page 680)

Potato Salad

Yield: 10 servings

Red Bliss potatoes	*2 1/4 pounds*	*1 kilogram*
Eggs, hard-cooked, chopped	*4 each*	*4 each*
Onions, diced	*5 ounces*	*140 grams*
Celery, diced	*5 ounces*	*140 grams*
Dijon mustard to taste	*1 ounce*	*30 grams*
Basic Mayonnaise	*1 pint*	*480 milliliters*
Worcestershire sauce to taste	*1/2 teaspoon*	*1/2 teaspoon*
Salt to taste	*1/2 teaspoon*	*1/2 teaspoon*
Pepper to taste	*1/4 teaspoon*	*1/4 teaspoon*

1. Place the potatoes in a pot. Cover with cold salted water and bring to a simmer. Cook until the potatoes can be easily pierced. Drain and dry. When they are cool enough to handle, slice or dice. (Peel them first if desired.)

2. Combine vegetables and eggs in a bowl. Mix the mustard with the mayonnaise and Worcestershire sauce to taste.

3. Gently toss with the potatoes. Adjust seasoning. Chill.

German Potato Salad

Yield: 10 servings

Potatoes, all-purpose or Yukon Gold	2 1/4 pounds	1 kilogram
Bacon, diced	4 ounces	115 grams
Onions, diced	8 ounces	225 grams
White wine vinegar	4 fluid ounces	120 milliliters
Vegetable oil	4 fluid ounces	120 milliliters
Salt to taste	1/2 teaspoon	1/2 teaspoon
Pepper to taste	1/4 teaspoon	1/4 teaspoon
Dijon mustard	2 tablespoons	2 tablespoons
Chicken Stock, heated	1 pint	480 milliliters
Chives, snipped	2 ounces	60 grams

1. Cook the potatoes in simmering water until tender. Drain.

2. Sauté the bacon until it is nearly cooked. Add and sweat the onion; then drain off the excess fat.

3. Add the vinegar, oil, salt, pepper, mustard, stock, and chives to the bacon and simmer. Pour the dressing over the hot sliced potatoes. Serve the salad warm.

Add diced sausage to this salad, or serve it as an accompaniment to grilled or pan-broiled knockwurst (or other sausages):

TECHNIQUE
Basic knife cuts (pages 217-223)
Rendering (page 253)

RECIPE
Chicken Stock (page 480)

Macaroni Salad

Yield: 10 servings

Elbow macaroni, cooked, cooled	2 pounds	900 grams
Celery, chopped	5 ounces	140 grams
Onions, fine dice	4 ounces	115 grams
Green pepper, diced (optional)	4 ounces	115 grams
Red pepper, diced (optional)	2 ounces	60 grams
Garlic cloves, mashed	2 each	2 each
Basic Mayonnaise as needed	12 ounces	360 milliliters
Salt to taste	1 teaspoon	1 teaspoon
Pepper to taste	1/2 teaspoon	1/2 teaspoon

1. Combine all ingredients with just enough mayonnaise to bind.

2. Season to taste with salt and pepper.

Use different pasta shapes in this salad.

Add shredded cheese (Cheddar, Monterey Jack, or Pepper Montarey Jack) if desired.

TECHNIQUE
Cooking pasta (pages 388-389)
Basic knife cuts (pages 217-223)
Mashing garlic (page 225)

RECIPE
Basic Mayonnaise (page 680)

Flavored oils and vinegars add variety to a basic vinaigrette.

Vinaigrettes may separate out into their individual components as they sit. Whisk well to recombine the dressing before adding it to a salad.

Oil choices include:
- *Corn or vegetable*
- *Peanut*
- *Sesame (light)*
- *Safflower*
- *Extra-virgin olive*
- *Hazelnut*
- *Walnut*
- *Avocado*

Vinegar options include:
- *Wine (white or red)*
- *Herb-infused (tarragon, etc.)*
- *Cider*
- *Balsamic*
- *Citrus juices (lemon, lime, orange, or grapefruit)*

Fresh herbs to add include:
- *Parsley*
- *Chives*
- *Basil*
- *Tarragon*
- *Rosemary*
- *Cilantro*

Basic Vinaigrette

Yield: 1 quart (1 liter)

Vegetable oil	*24 fluid ounces*	*720 milliliters*
Vinegar	*8 fluid ounces*	*240 milliliters*
Salt	*to taste*	*to taste*
Pepper	*to taste*	*to taste*
Coleman's mustard (optional)	*$^1/_2$ teaspoon*	*$^1/_2$ teaspoon*
Herbs, chopped (optional)	*2 tablespoons*	*2 tablespoons*
Sugar (optional)	*$^1/_4$ teaspoon*	*$^1/_4$ teaspoon*

1. Combine all of the ingredients and whip them until they are thoroughly blended.

2. Taste the vinaigrette and adjust the seasoning with additional salt, pepper, or sugar.

VARIATION

Balsamic Vinaigrette: Use balsamic vinegar (6 fluid ounces/180 milliliters) and increase the oil to 26 fluid ounces (780 milliliters). Extra-virgin olive oil or a nut oil (walnut, hazelnut, or almond) would be a good choice.

Lemon Parsley Vinaigrette: Use lemon juice to replace the vinegar. Add 2 to 3 tablespoons chopped flat-leaf parsley.

Catalina Dressing

Yield: 1 quart (1 liter)

Eggs	2 each	2 each
Dark brown sugar	4 ounces	115 grams
Cider vinegar	4 fluid ounces	120 milliliters
Paprika oil (see note)	4 fluid ounces	120 milliliters
Allspice, ground	$^1/_8$ teaspoon	$^1/_8$ teaspoon
White pepper, ground to taste	$^1/_4$ teaspoon	$^1/_4$ teaspoon
Garlic powder	$^1/_4$ teaspoon	$^1/_4$ teaspoon
Onion powder	$^1/_4$ teaspoon	$^1/_4$ teaspoon
Salt	$^1/_2$ teaspoon	$^1/_2$ teaspoon
Dijon mustard	2 teaspoons	2 teaspoons
Vegetable oil	24 fluid ounces	720 milliliters

1. Combine all of the ingredients except the vegetable oil; blend well.

2. Gradually incorporate the vegetable oil in a thin stream.

3. Adjust the seasoning if necessary.

To make paprika oil, heat 6 ounces (180 milliliters) of oil until hot; add 1 ounce (30 grams) of paprika. Remove it from the heat and allow it to steep for 10 to 12 hours before using it in this dressing.

One egg yolk can emulsify up to 8 ounces (240 milliliters) of oil.

Basic mayonnaise is a key ingredient in many cold salads and sandwiches.

Basic Mayonnaise

Yield: 1 quart (1 liter)

Egg yolks	*3 each*	*3 each*
White wine vinegar	*1 fluid ounce*	*30 milliliters*
Water	*1 fluid ounce*	*30 milliliters*
Dry mustard	*2 teaspoons*	*2 teaspoons*
Vegetable, olive, or peanut oil, as desired to achieve flavor	*24 fluid ounces*	*720 milliliters*
Salt to taste	*¹/₂ teaspoon*	*¹/₂ teaspoon*
Pepper to taste	*¹/₂ teaspoon*	*¹/₂ teaspoon*
Lemon juice to taste	*1 fluid ounce*	*30 milliliters*

1. Combine the yolks, vinegar, water, and mustard in a bowl. Mix them well with a balloon whip until the mixture is slightly foamy.

2. Gradually add the oil in a thin stream, constantly beating with the whip, until the oil is incorporated and the mayonnaise is thick.

3. Adjust the flavor with salt, pepper, and lemon juice.

4. Refrigerate the mayonnaise immediately. Use as desired.

VARIATIONS

Green Mayonnaise: Finely chop 4 ounces (115 grams) of spinach. Squeeze it in cheesecloth to extract the juice. Add the juice to the mayonnaise. Add additional chopped fresh herbs to taste.

Herb Mayonnaise: Add 1 to 2 ounces (30 to 60 grams) of Fines Herbes (page 475).

Green Goddess Dressing

Yield: 1 quart (1 liter)

Spinach leaves	*2 ounces*	*60 grams*
Watercress leaves	*2 ounces*	*60 grams*
Parsley leaves, fresh	*1 tablespoon*	*1 tablespoon*
Tarragon leaves, fresh	*1 tablespoon*	*1 tablespoon*
Garlic clove, mashed to a paste	*1 each*	*1 each*
Vegetable oil	*4 fluid ounces*	*120 milliliters*
Basic Mayonnaise	*12 fluid ounces*	*360 milliliters*
Prepared mustard	*1 tablespoon*	*1 tablespoon*
Salt to taste	*¹/₂ teaspoon*	*¹/₂ teaspoon*
Pepper to taste	*¹/₂ teaspoon*	*¹/₂ teaspoon*
Lemon juice to taste	*1 fluid ounce*	*30 milliliters*

(Recipe continued on facing page)

1. Purée the spinach, watercress, parsley, tarragon, and garlic with the oil in a food processor.

2. Combine the purée with the mayonnaise and mustard.

3. Add the salt, pepper, and lemon juice to taste.

4. Refrigerate the dressing immediately.

TECHNIQUE
Preparing greens (page 229)
Herbs (page 229)

RECIPE
Basic Mayonnaise (page 680)

Ranch-Style Dressing

Yield: 1 quart (1 liter)

Sour cream	*12 ounces*	*360 milliliters*
Basic Mayonnaise	*12 ounces*	*360 milliliters*
Buttermilk	*8 fluid ounces*	*240 milliliters*
Lemon juice	*1 fluid ounce*	*30 milliliters*
Red wine vinegar	*2 fluid ounces*	*60 milliliters*
Garlic cloves, mashed to a paste	*2 each*	*2 each*
Worcestershire sauce	*1 1/2 fluid ounces*	*45 milliliters*
Parsley, chopped	*1 tablespoon*	*1 tablespoon*
Chives, chopped	*1 tablespoon*	*1 tablespoon*
Shallots, chopped	*1 tablespoon*	*1 tablespoon*
Dijon mustard	*1 tablespoon*	*1 tablespoon*
Celery seed	*1 teaspoon*	*1 teaspoon*

1. Combine all ingredients well.

2. Store under refrigeration until needed.

Ranch-style dressing makes a good dip for a crudité platter.

TECHNIQUE
Basic knife cuts (pages 217-223)

RECIPE
Basic Mayonnaise (page 680)

Roquefort, Gorgonzola, and Maytag blue cheeses.

If you prefer a chunky-style dressing, reserve 4 ounces (115 grams) of the cheese and crumble it into the dressing after it has been blended.

TECHNIQUE
Mashing garlic (page 225)

RECIPE
Basic Mayonnaise (page 680)

Blue Cheese Dressing

Yield: 1 quart (1 liter)

Blue cheese, crumbled	*12 ounces*	*340 grams*
Basic Mayonnaise	*1 pint*	*480 milliliters*
Sour cream	*8 ounces*	*225 grams*
Buttermilk	*6 fluid ounces*	*180 milliliters*
Milk	*3 fluid ounces*	*90 milliliters*
Lemon juice	*1 tablespoon*	*1 tablespoon*
Worcestershire sauce to taste	*1 1/2 fluid ounces*	*45 milliliters*
Garlic, mashed to a paste	*1/4 teaspoon*	*1/4 teaspoon*
Salt to taste	*1/2 teaspoon*	*1/2 teaspoon*
Pepper to taste	*1/4 teaspoon*	*1/4 teaspoon*

1. Combine all of the ingredients; mix them to a smooth consistency.

2. Adjust the seasoning to taste.

3. Chill the dressing until it is needed.

Some people prefer this sauce to rémoulade. It may be served with fried or broiled fish.

TECHNIQUE
Basic knife cuts (pages 217-223)

RECIPE
Basic Mayonnaise (page 680)
Hard-Cooked Eggs (page 654)

Tartar Sauce

Yield: approximately 1 quart (1 liter)

Basic Mayonnaise	*1 quart*	*1 liter*
Sweet pickle relish, drained	*8 ounces*	*240 grams*
Capers, drained and chopped	*2 ounces*	*60 grams*
Hard-Cooked Eggs, chopped	*2 each*	*2 each*
Salt to taste	*1/2 teaspoon*	*1/2 teaspoon*
White pepper to taste	*1/2 teaspoon*	*1/2 teaspoon*
Worcestershire sauce to taste	*1/2 teaspoon*	*1/2 teaspoon*
Tabasco to taste	*2 to 3 dashes*	*2 to 3 dashes*

1. Combine all of the ingredients and stir until they are evenly blended.

2. Chill the sauce thoroughly.

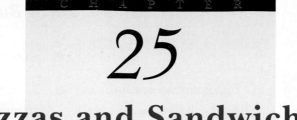

25

Pizzas and Sandwiches

The recipes that follow run the gamut from coffee shop classics to vegetarian pizzas. Along with traditional sandwiches and pizzas, other snack and "street" food from around the world may be found in this chapter. Although specific breads and ingredients are suggested, almost all can be varied to suit your needs. Most can be served as appetizers, entrées, or afternoon or late night snacks. Chapter 19 includes sandwich recipes; tuna salad and similar salad spreads may be found in Chapter 24; other spreads and finger foods may be found in Chapter 26. Many of the recipes in the entrée chapters can be adapted, as well; consider meatball subs, fried fish fillet sandwiches, and roast turkey clubs.

The recipes are organized as follows:

- *Coffee Shop and Deli Standards*
- *Grilled Hot Sandwiches*
- *Tex-Mex and Caribbean Foods*
- *Pizza*
- *Cold Sandwiches*

Freshly ground chicken

Use other cheeses such as Cheddar or Jack if preferred. Consider a portion size of $^1/_2$ ounce (15 grams).

Ground turkey may be substituted for the chicken.

TECHNIQUE
Pan-frying (pages 364-367)
Basic knife cuts (pages 217-223)
Making bread crumbs (page 237)

RECIPE
Dry Duxelles (page 473)

Chicken Burgers

Yield: 10 servings

Chicken meat, ground	2 $^1/_2$ pounds	1.15 kilograms
Bread crumbs, fresh	6 ounces	170 grams
Duxelles, cooked dry, cooled	1 pound	450 grams
Mixed herbs, chopped: chives, oregano, basil, rosemary	2 tablespoons	2 tablespoons
Salt to taste	1 teaspoon	1 teaspoon
White pepper to taste	$^1/_2$ teaspoon	$^1/_2$ teaspoon
Provolone cheese, sliced	10 ounces	285 grams
Kaiser rolls	10 each	10 each
Butter, melted, as needed	4 ounces	115 grams

1. Gently mix chicken, bread crumbs, duxelles, herbs, salt, and pepper.
2. Form into patties.
3. Lightly butter a griddle. Brown the patties. Finish in a 350°F (175°C) oven.
4. Prior to service, top with provolone cheese and return to oven to melt.
5. Slice roll, leaving bread hinged. Brush with melted butter, then grill.
4. Place chicken on grilled roll; serve open-faced.

TECHNIQUE
Basic knife cuts (pages 217-223)

RECIPE
White Beef Stock (page 480)

Sloppy Joes

Yield: 10 servings

Vegetable oil as needed	2 fluid ounces	60 milliliters
Onions, chopped	8 ounces	225 grams
Celery, chopped fine	4 ounces	115 grams
Garlic cloves, minced	2 each	2 each
Ground beef	3 pounds	1.3 kilograms
Tomato concassé	8 ounces	225 grams
Ketchup	1 pint	480 milliliters
White Beef Stock	1 pint	480 milliliters
Worcestershire sauce	2 tablespoons	2 tablespoons
Dry mustard	2 teaspoons	2 teaspoons
Cayenne	$^1/_4$ teaspoon	$^1/_4$ teaspoon
Salt to taste	$^1/_2$ teaspoon	$^1/_2$ teaspoon
Pepper to taste	$^1/_2$ teaspoon	$^1/_2$ teaspoon
Kaiser rolls	10 each	10 each

(Recipe continued on facing page)

1. Heat the oil in a sauce pan. Add the onions and celery; sweat about 5 minutes. Add the garlic and continue to sweat for 2 minutes.

2. Add the ground beef and cook until no longer pink. Drain off excess grease.

3. Stir in the tomato, ketchup, beef stock, Worcestershire sauce, and mustard. Simmer about 30 minutes, stirring occasionally. Check consistency. Season to taste with salt and pepper.

4. Split open the roll and grill. Serve the beef mixture on the grilled roll.

VARIATIONS

Southwestern-Style Sloppy Joes: Add 4 ounces (115 grams) chopped, roasted New Mexico chilies, add 1 jalapeño pepper. Substitute tomato sauce for the ketchup. Season with chili powder, cumin, and oregano. Top with beans and cheese. Serve on a roll or a crisp corn tortilla.

Italian-Style Sloppy Joes: Substitute Italian sausages for some of the hamburger. Add oregano, green peppers, and mushrooms. Use tomato sauce. Serve on Italian bread and top with Parmesan cheese.

Barbecued Beef Sandwich

Yield: 10 servings

Beef brisket, fresh	4 pounds	1.8 kilograms
Barbecue Sauce	20 fluid ounces	600 milliliters
Hoagie or kaiser roll	10 each	10 each
Butter, melted, as needed	4 ounces	115 grams

1. Place brisket on rack, roast in 325°F (160°C) oven until fork tender, about 5 hours.

2. Cool, trim off excess fat. Slice or shred. Mix with barbecue sauce, reheat in 350°F (175°C) oven or on stove top.

3. Slice roll, leaving bread hinged. Brush with melted butter, then grill.

4. Place barbecued beef on grilled roll, serve open-faced.

Use a spice rub on the brisket if you wish.

TECHNIQUE
Roasting (page 349)
Carving (pages 355-357)

RECIPE
Barbecue Sauce (page 526)

Allow approximately five hours at 325°F (160°C) to roast a four-pound corned beef brisket.

If time allows, prepare the dressing a day in advance.

Although classically served grilled, this sandwich may be served cold.

TECHNIQUE
Pan-frying (pages 364-367)

RECIPE
Basic Mayonnaise (page 680)

Reuben Sandwich

Yield: 10 servings

Russian Dressing

Basic Mayonnaise	20 fluid ounces	600 milliliters
Chili sauce, prepared	6 fluid ounces	180 milliliters
Horseradish, prepared	1 1/2 ounces	40 grams
Onions, minced, blanched	2 ounces	60 grams
Worcestershire sauce	1 1/2 teaspoons	1 1/2 teaspoons
Salt to taste	1/2 teaspoon	1/2 teaspoon
Pepper to taste	1/4 teaspoon	1/4 teaspoon
Rye bread, slices	20 each	20 each
Swiss cheese, sliced thin	10 ounces	285 grams
Corned beef brisket, cooked, sliced	2 pounds	900 grams
Sauerkraut, prepared	20 ounces	570 grams
Butter, room temperature, as needed	4 ounces	115 grams

1. Mix together the ingredients for the dressing.

2. On one slice of bread, layer the cheese, Russian dressing, a thin layer of corned beef, the sauerkraut, more corned beef, and a second slice of cheese and Russian dressing. Top with a bread slice.

3. Butter both sides of sandwich. Pan-fry until golden brown. If necessary, finish in oven to melt the cheese and heat through.

Additional garnishes include chopped cilantro, chopped red onions, and sliced black olives.

This basic taco filling may also be used to fill burritos, enchiladas, or quesadillas. Serve with Red Chili Sauce, page 524.

TECHNIQUE
Sautéing (pages 358-362)
Tomato concassé (page 226)
Preparing greens (page 229)

RECIPE
Taco Sauce (page 672)

Beef Tacos

Yield: 10 servings

Ground beef	2 1/2 pounds	1.15 kilograms
Taco Sauce	1 pint	480 milliliters
Taco shells, heated	20 each	20 each
Cheddar or Monterey Jack cheese, shredded	10 ounces	285 grams
Iceberg lettuce, shredded	2 pounds	900 grams
Tomato concassé	2 1/2 pounds	680 grams

1. Brown ground beef. Drain well, combine with taco sauce.

2. Place 2 ounces of the beef mix in each taco shell. Top with grated cheese, lettuce, and tomatoes.

Grilled Vegetable Pizza

Yield: 10 servings

Basic Pizza Dough	*3 1/2 pounds*	*1.6 kilograms*
Marinade		
Olive oil, extra-virgin	*6 fluid ounces*	*180 milliliters*
Balsamic vinegar	*2 fluid ounces*	*60 milliliters*
Garlic, minced	*1 teaspoon*	*1 teaspoon*
Basil, chopped	*2 teaspoons*	*2 teaspoons*
Thyme, chopped	*2 teaspoons*	*2 teaspoons*
Oregano, chopped	*2 teaspoons*	*2 teaspoons*
Parsley, chopped	*2 teaspoons*	*2 teaspoons*
Salt to taste	*1/2 teaspoon*	*1/2 teaspoon*
Pepper to taste	*1/4 teaspoon*	*1/4 teaspoon*
Green peppers, halved	*2 each*	*2 each*
Red peppers, halved	*2 each*	*2 each*
Onions, thick-sliced	*2 each*	*2 each*
Fennel, quartered	*1 each*	*1 each*
Yellow squash, sliced	*2 each*	*2 each*
Zucchini, sliced	*2 each*	*2 each*
Goat cheese, crumbled	*20 ounces*	*570 grams*
Parmesan cheese, grated	*10 ounces*	*285 grams*

1. When pizza dough has doubled in bulk, punch down, measure out into 4-ounce (115-gram) portions.

2. Place on a plastic-wrap-covered tray. Refrigerate until needed. Allow one hour for the second rise.

3. Combine olive oil, balsamic vinegar, garlic, herbs, salt, and pepper for the marinade. Toss vegetables with vinaigrette and grill until tender. Allow to cool.

4. When vegetables are cooled, cut into appropriate sizes if necessary.

5. Roll pizza dough into disks. Top with vegetables, goat cheese, and Parmesan. Bake in a 450°F (230°C) oven until done.

The started dough must be refrigerated overnight. On the day of service, let dough sit at room temperature.

Other vegetables that may be grilled include eggplants, radishes, and tomatoes.

TECHNIQUE
Marinades (pages 242-245)
Grilling (pages 344-349)
Basic knife cuts (pages 217-223)

RECIPE
Basic Pizza Dough (page 648)

CIA Club

Yield: 10 servings

Basic Mayonnaise as needed	*6 fluid ounces*	*180 milliliters*
Bread slices, lightly toasted	*30 each*	*30 each*
Red leaf lettuce leaves	*20 each*	*20 each*
Turkey, cooked, sliced thin	*20 ounces*	*570 grams*
Ham, cooked, sliced thin	*20 ounces*	*570 grams*
Tomato slices	*20 each*	*20 each*
Bacon, cooked, cut in half	*15 strips*	*15 strips*

1. Spread mayonnaise on one slice of toast.

2. Layer in this order: lettuce, turkey, ham, toast, more mayonnaise on both sides, more lettuce, tomato, and bacon. Top with toast that has mayonnaise spread on the underside.

3. Secure with a frilled toothpick. Cut into 4 wedges. Garnish with pickles and olives.

For a party, buffet, or reception presentation, select a large round country loaf, split it horizontally, and layer the ingredients as described in this recipe, omitting the middle slice of bread. Secure with club frills, arranging as many portions as desired, and cut the sandwich into wedges.

Create your own signature club by adding other ingredients: salami, pastrami, avocados, alfalfa sprouts, cheese, or Green Goddess Dressing, page 680.

RECIPE
Basic Mayonnaise (page 680)

A variety of cured meats may be featured in this sandwich.

"Philly" Hoagie (Italian Combo)

Yield: 10 servings

Submarine roll	*10 each*	*10 each*
Dressing		
Olive oil	*6 fluid ounces*	*180 milliliters*
Vinegar	*3 fluid ounces*	*90 milliliters*
Oregano, chopped	*1 tablespoon*	*1 tablespoon*
Smoked ham, sliced thin	*1 ¹/₂ pounds*	*680 grams*
Sweet cappicola, imported, sliced thin	*10 ounces*	*285 grams*
Genoa salami, sliced thin	*10 ounces*	*285 grams*
Provolone, sliced	*20 ounces*	*570 grams*
Iceberg lettuce, shredded	*10 ounces*	*285 grams*
Tomato slices	*30 each*	*30 each*
Onion slices	*30 each*	*30 each*

1. Slice roll open, leaving it hinged. Brush inside of roll with dressing.

2. Arrange ham, cappicola, salami, and provolone on roll. Top with shredded lettuce. Place 3 slices of tomato on top of lettuce. Top with onions and additional dressing.

Prepare the dressing a day in advance to "marry" the flavors.

Hot pickled peppers may be sliced and added to the dressing. Season the dressing with salt and pepper.

Serve with quartered garlic pickle on the side.

26

Hors d'Oeuvres and Appetizers

Hors d'oeuvres and appetizers are one of the menu categories that most often needs an infusion of fresh ideas. The appeal of small dishes with brilliant flavors and an intriguing presentation is universal. Some guests may look to the first course selections as a way to sample a wide range of dishes without becoming "bogged down" with a larger menu item.

This catering style is enhanced with a special tasting menu, often composed of the chef's selections for the night, and is composed to make the best use of whatever is best from the market.

Wear gloves to protect your skin when working with chilies.

Increase the amount of lime juice or tomatoes, as desired.

TECHNIQUE
Tomato concassé (page 226)
Working with chilies (page 227)
Basic knife cuts (pages 217-223)

Fresh Tomato Salsa

Yield: 10 servings

Tomato concassé	*8 ounces*	*225 grams*
Jalapeño peppers, seeded, minced	*$1/_2$ ounce*	*15 grams*
Red onion, peeled, minced	*2 ounces*	*60 grams*
Cilantro, fresh, chopped	*3 tablespoons*	*3 tablespoons*
Lime juice	*1 tablespoon*	*1 tablespoon*

1. Combine all ingredients and mix well.

2. Refrigerate for several hours to let flavors combine.

3. Check seasoning before serving.

Serve as soon as possible. If this must be held, place plastic wrap directly on surface to prevent discoloration.

Lime juice may be used in place of the lemon juice. For very hot, spicy foods, increase the amount of lime juice. Tomato concassé may also be added.

TECHNIQUE
Mashing garlic to a paste (page 225)

Guacamole

Yield: 10 servings

Avocados, sliced	*8 ounces*	*225 grams*
Garlic clove, mashed to a paste	*1 each*	*1 each*
Scallions, chopped fine	*1 ounce*	*30 grams*
Jalapeño peppers, seeded, chopped fine	*1 tablespoon*	*1 tablespoon*
Lemon juice	*1 tablespoon*	*1 tablespoon*

1. Mash avocado to a paste.

2. Add remaining ingredients and blend.

Deviled Eggs

Yield: 20 pieces

Hard-Cooked Eggs, peeled	10 each	10 each
Basic Mayonnaise	6 fluid ounces	180 milliliters
Mustard, prepared	1 tablespoon	1 tablespoon
Salt to taste	$1/2$ teaspoon	$1/2$ teaspoon
Pepper to taste	$1/2$ teaspoon	$1/2$ teaspoon
Cayenne pepper	to taste	to taste

1. Slice the eggs in half lengthwise. Separate the yolks from the whites. Reserve the whites separately.

2. Rub the yolks through a sieve into a bowl or food processor. Add the mayonnaise, mustard, salt, and pepper. Mix or process the ingredients into a smooth paste.

3. Pipe (using a star tip) or spoon the yolk mixture into the cavities of the egg whites.

VARIATIONS

Deviled Eggs with Tomato: Add tomato concassé to the yolk mixture. Add a small amount of fresh or dried herbs (basil, oregano, sage, thyme) and $1/2$ teaspoon of sautéed minced garlic or shallots to the tomatoes, if desired.

Deviled Eggs with Greens: Add 1 teaspoon per yolk of blanched, puréed spinach, watercress, sorrel, lettuce, or other greens to the yolk mixture.

Deviled Eggs with Vegetables: Add small dice of cooked, raw, and/or marinated vegetables, such as celery, carrot, red onion, peppers, fennel, mushrooms (wild or cultivated), tomato, green beans, peas, corn, and eggplant.

Deviled Eggs with Peppers: Purée roasted sweet bell peppers (red or green), pimientos, and/or hot chilies. Add 2 to 3 fluid ounces (60 to 90 milliliters) of purée (to taste) per 10 yolks.

Deviled Eggs with Cheese: Add up to 2 ounces (60 grams) of grated hard or soft cheese. Purée the filling well in a food processor.

Deviled Eggs with Fish or Shellfish: Add approximately 4 ounces (115 grams) of finely diced fish or shellfish (also any vegetables desired; see above) to the yolk mixture. Or, make a paste of fish by puréeing it with butter, mayonnaise, or heavy cream. Use smoked fish (especially small pieces or trimmings), shrimp, fresh-cooked or canned tuna, salmon, crab, or lobster.

The eggs may be separated and the filling mixed in advance, but if they are not to be served immediately, the whites and the yolks should be held separately until as close as possible to service.

Garnishes may include chopped parsley, snipped chives, sliced scallion tops, dill sprigs, pimiento strips, chopped olives, caviar, or shredded carrots. Spices may include toasted cumin seeds (ground after toasting), oregano, paprika, cayenne, or crushed red pepper flakes.

Substitute softened butter or compound butter, sour cream, puréed cottage cheese, softened cream cheese, yogurt, or crème fraîche.

TECHNIQUE
Pastry bags and tips (pages 462-463)

RECIPES
Hard-Cooked Eggs (page 654)
Basic Mayonnaise (page 680)

Spring roll wrappers (right) and wonton wrappers (left).

Use 4 pounds (1.8 kilograms) of ground or shredded pork instead of the shrimp, if you prefer.

To make a flour paste to seal the spring rolls, mix flour with enough cold water to reach the consistency of a thin pancake.

Serve with prepared duck sauce or other dipping sauces.

TECHNIQUE
Basic knife cuts (pages 217-223)
Working with dried fruits and vegetables
(pages 235-236)
Deep-frying (pages 367-371)

Shrimp Spring Roll

Yield: 80 pieces

Filling

Oil	*4 fluid ounces*	*120 milliliters*
Gingerroot, minced	*2 tablespoons*	*2 tablespoons*
Scallions, chopped	*14 ounces*	*400 grams*
Shrimp, peeled, deveined, and chopped	*3 pounds*	*1.3 kilograms*
Bamboo shoots, shredded	*10 ounces*	*285 grams*
Black fungus, soaked, roughly cut	*1 ¹/₂ ounces*	*40 grams*
Chinese cabbage, shredded	*3 pounds*	*1.3 kilograms*
Bean sprouts	*2 pounds*	*900 grams*
Mushrooms, thinly sliced	*1 pound*	*450 grams*
Black soy sauce	*4 fluid ounces*	*120 milliliters*
Sesame oil	*2 fluid ounces*	*60 milliliters*
Salt	*1 tablespoon*	*1 tablespoon*
White pepper	*2 teaspoons*	*2 teaspoons*
Cornstarch	*3 ounces*	*85 grams*
Water	*4 fluid ounces*	*120 milliliters*
Spring roll sheets	*80 pieces*	*80 pieces*
Flour	*5 ounces*	*140 grams*

1. To make the filling: heat the oil in a wok. Stir-fry gingerroot and scallions in oil for a few minutes.

2. Add shrimp, bamboo shoots, and black fungus. Stir-fry until shrimp is tender.

3. Add cabbage, bean sprouts, mushrooms, and scallions; stir-fry until all vegetables are cooked.

4. Add soy sauce, sesame oil, salt, and pepper; mix together.

5. Drain away the excess liquid; mix in cornstarch that has been dissolved in water, return this mixture to vegetables; cook until cornstarch has thickened.

6. Remove the filling mixture from the heat, cool thoroughly.

7. Place 1 full tablespoon of filling on each spring roll sheet, brush edges of sheet with flour-water paste, roll, and seal.

8. Deep-fry in 350°F (175°C) hot fat until golden brown, drain on absorbent paper.

Gravad Lox

Yield: 2 fillets

Kosher salt	7 ounces	200 grams
Dark brown sugar	1 pound	450 grams
White peppercorns, cracked	³/₄ ounce	20 grams
Dill, freshly chopped	2 bunches	2 bunches
Lemons, juiced	2 each	2 each
Olive oil	1 fluid ounce	30 milliliters
Brandy	³/₄ fluid ounce	25 milliliters
Salmon fillets, cleaned	2 each	2 each

1. Combine the salt, sugar, peppercorns, and dill to make the dry cure.

2. Combine the lemon juice, olive oil, and brandy. Brush this mixture on the salmon fillets.

3. Pack the cure evenly on the salmon fillets and wrap them tightly.

4. Place the wrapped fillets in a pan and weight them. Marinate the salmon under refrigeration for 2 to 3 days.

5. Unwrap the salmon and scrape off the cure.

6. Slice the salmon thinly on the bias to serve it.

Apply the cure mix evenly.

Use aquavit or vodka to replace the brandy, if desired.

Serve with bagels and cream cheese as a brunch or breakfast offering.

TECHNIQUE
Preparing gravad lox (pages 419-420)
Filleting a round fish (pages 280-281)

Broiled Shrimp with Garlic and Aromatics

Yield: 10 servings

Bread crumbs, dry	8 ounces	225 grams
Garlic cloves, minced	3 each	3 each
Parsley, chopped	1 teaspoon	1 teaspoon
Oregano, chopped	1 teaspoon	1 teaspoon
Butter, melted	12 ounces	340 grams
Salt to taste	¹/₂ teaspoon	¹/₂ teaspoon
Pepper to taste	¹/₄ teaspoon	¹/₄ teaspoon
Shrimp, 31/35 count, tail intact and butterflied	30 each	30 each

TECHNIQUE
Cleaning shrimp (pages 284 285)
Making bread crumbs (page 237)
Basic knife cuts (pages 217-223)
Broiling (pages 344-349)

1. Combine the bread crumbs, garlic, parsley, oregano, and three-quarters of the butter. Adjust the seasoning to taste with the salt and pepper.

2. Arrange the shrimp on gratin dishes (3 per portion) and brush with the remaining butter.

3. Place 1 to 2 teaspoons each of the bread crumb mixture on the shrimp and broil under a salamander until very hot and cooked through. Serve at once.

Mussels.

Marinière, or "in the mariner's style," refers to quickly prepared dishes made out of the fresh daily catch, often steamed in wine with aromatics, as here.

TECHNIQUE
Cleaning mussels (pages 288-289)
Steaming (pages 374-378)

Moules Marinière

Yield: 10 servings

Mussels, scrubbed and debearded	*80 each*	*80 each*
Dry white wine	*12 fluid ounces*	*360 milliliters*
Shallots, minced	*4 ounces*	*115 grams*
Bay leaf	*1 each*	*1 each*
Black peppercorns, cracked	*1/2 teaspoon*	*1/2 teaspoon*
Thyme sprig	*1 each*	*1 each*
Garlic cloves, minced	*6 each*	*6 each*
Butter, softened	*6 ounces*	*170 grams*
Parsley, chopped	*1 tablespoon*	*1 tablespoon*
Chives, chopped	*1 tablespoon*	*1 tablespoon*

1. Scrub and debeard mussels; discard any that remain open.

2. Combine the wine, shallots, bay leaf, peppercorns, thyme, and garlic. Bring to a simmer.

3. Add the mussels; cover the pot, and steam until the shells open.

4. Remove the mussels and keep warm while finishing the sauce.

5. Strain the steaming liquid, whisk in the butter, add parsley and chives and season to taste with additional pepper.

6. Serve the sauce ladled over the mussels; serve eight mussels per order.

Other shellfish or flaky firm fish may be prepared in this manner also.

The proper selection and care of frying oils may be found on page 368.

TECHNIQUE
Cleaning and shucking clams (pages 288-289)
Deep-frying (pages 367-371)

RECIPE
Tartar Sauce (page 682)

Clam Fritters

Yield: 10 servings

Flour	*7 ounces*	*200 grams*
Baking powder	*1 tablespoon*	*1 tablespoon*
Salt	*1/4 teaspoon*	*1/4 teaspoon*
White pepper	*1/4 teaspoon*	*1/4 teaspoon*
Clams, chopped, juices reserved	*10 ounces*	*285 grams*
Reserved clam juice	*6 fluid ounces*	*180 milliliters*
Milk	*4 fluid ounces*	*120 milliliters*
Tartar Sauce	*1 pint*	*480 milliliters*

1. Combine all the dry ingredients.

2. Combine all the wet ingredients, including the chopped clams.

3. Combine the wet and dry ingredients.

4. Drop the mixture by spoonfuls into 375°F (190°C) oil.

5. Fry the fritters until they are golden brown. Serve them with Tartar sauce.

Black Bean Cakes

Yield: 10 servings

Black beans, soaked overnight	14 ounces	400 grams
Vegetable Stock, to cook beans	28 fluid ounces	840 milliliters
Onions, minced	3 ounces	85 grams
Garlic, minced	1 tablespoon	1 tablespoon
Vegetable oil as needed	1 ounce	30 grams
Jalapeño peppers, minced	1 each	1 each
Chili powder	$^3/_4$ teaspoon	$^3/_4$ teaspoon
Cumin, ground	$^3/_4$ teaspoon	$^3/_4$ teaspoon
Cardamom, ground	$^3/_4$ teaspoon	$^3/_4$ teaspoon
Cilantro, chopped	1 teaspoon	1 teaspoon
Salt	$^1/_2$ teaspoon	$^1/_2$ teaspoon
Lime juice	1 teaspoon	1 teaspoon
Egg white, beaten	1 each	1 each
Cornmeal, for dusting	4 ounces	115 grams
Clarified butter	1 $^1/_2$ ounces	40 grams
Garnish		
Yogurt, drained	1 $^1/_2$ ounces	40 grams
Sour cream	1 $^1/_2$ fluid ounces	45 milliliters
Fresh Tomato Salsa	8 ounces	225 grams

1. Cook presoaked black beans in vegetable stock until tender, let stock reduce at the end of cooking.

2. Purée two-thirds of the beans, recombine the purée with the whole beans.

3. Sauté the onion, garlic, and peppers in oil, add herbs, spices, and salt; sauté until aromatic. Let this mixture cool. Add to bean mixture and blend.

4. Add lime juice and egg white, form into patties.

5. Dust patties in cornmeal; pan-fry in clarified butter.

6. Mix the sour cream and yogurt together. Serve with salsa as garnish.

A variety of beans or dried peas could be used in this dish.

To drain yogurt, place it in a cheesecloth-lined colander. Place it in a bowl. Let it drain for 12 to 24 hours.

'

Diced red and green peppers, blanched corn, rice, and other cooked beans may be incorporated into these cakes.

TECHNIQUE
Soaking beans (page 236)
Basic knife cuts (pages 217-223)
Pan-frying (pages 364-367)

RECIPES
Vegetable Stock (page 483)
Fresh Tomato Salsa (page 690)

Toasting pine nuts in a skillet.

These are a common component in Greek salads, falafel plates, and Mediterranean-style sampler plates.

TECHNIQUE
Basic knife cuts (pages 217-223)
Tomato concassé (page 226)
Toasting nuts and seeds (page 237)
Braising (pages 391-394)

RECIPE
Vegetable Stock (page 483)

Stuffed Grape Leaves

Yield: 10 servings

Garlic, chopped	*1 ounce*	*30 grams*
Onions, fine dice	*12 ounces*	*340 grams*
Olive oil	*4 fluid ounces*	*120 milliliters*
Rice, uncooked	*12 ounces*	*340 grams*
Tomato concassé	*1 ½ pounds*	*680 grams*
Salt to taste	*½ teaspoon*	*½ teaspoon*
Pepper to taste	*¼ teaspoon*	*¼ teaspoon*
Parsley, chopped	*1 ounce*	*30 grams*
Pine nuts (optional), toasted	*1 ounce*	*30 grams*
Grape leaves, rinsed	*50 each*	*50 each*
Vegetable Stock or water, to cover	*1 quart*	*1 liter*
Lemon juice	*3 fluid ounces*	*90 milliliters*

1. Sweat garlic and onion in oil until tender and translucent.

2. Add uncooked rice, stir to coat with oil.

3. Add tomato, salt, and pepper. Combine and heat through.

4. Remove from pan, mix in parsley and pine nuts. Cool and reserve.

5. Place grape leaves in saucepan with water to cover. Bring to a boil, blanch until softened.

6. Spread each leaf open on a flat surface. Place 1 tablespoon of rice mixture in the center of each leaf, then roll like an egg roll.

7. Place a rack on the bottom of a braising vessel. (This will prevent the stuffed grape leaves from sticking.) Place the rolls, side-by-side but un-crowded, on top of the rack.

8. Cover with stock or water and lemon juice. Use a weighted plate to keep them submerged, and under pressure. Braise on stove top for 1 hour. Cool overnight. Serve chilled.

27

Sausages, Pâtés, and Terrines

The recipes included are found as breakfast items, appetizers, hors d'oeuvres, and buffet and reception standards. Others may be served as entrées and some are used as fillings or stuffing for foods such as chicken breasts or pasta. Before preparing these recipes, you may wish to review the techniques, described in the text in Chapter 11. There are also recipes within the entrée recipe chapters and Chapter 26 which require forcemeats. With experience, you can make variations and substitutions as desired. Once you are familiar with the technique, you will be able to create dishes to suit your needs.

Adding the cream to the forcemeat.

An average moould will hold 3 pounds
(1.3 kilograms) and yield 24 slices.

TECHNIQUE
Country-style forcemeat (pages 407-408)
Pâte de campagne or
Country-style pâté (pages 412-413)

RECIPE
Pâte Spice (page 701)

Country-Style Pâte (Pâté de Campagne)

Yield: approximately 3 pounds (1.36 kilograms)

Pork butt, diced	2 ¹/₂ pounds	1.15 kilograms
Pork liver, cleaned and diced	¹/₂ pound	230 grams
Onion, chopped fine	4 ounces	115 grams
Garlic cloves, minced	2 each	2 each
Parsley sprigs, chopped fine	5 each	5 each
Flour	2 ¹/₂ ounces	70 grams
Eggs	2 each	2 each
Salt	¹/₄ ounce	20 grams
White pepper	¹/₂ teaspoon	¹/₂ teaspoon
Pâte Spice	pinch	pinch
Brandy	1 fluid ounce	30 milliliters
Heavy cream	4 fluid ounces	120 milliliters
Fatback, sliced thin	as needed	as needed

1. Grind 1 pound (450 grams) of the pork butt with the pork liver, onion, garlic, and parsley through the medium and then fine die of a grinder.

2. Grind the remainder of the pork butt through a coarse die. Combine the fine- and coarse-ground meats in a large bowl. Working over an ice bath, stir in the remainder of the ingredients, except the fatback, until they are just blended. Make a test quenelle to check for seasoning and consistency.

3. Use the fatback to line a pâté mold. Bake in a water bath at 325°F (160°C) to an internal temperature of 150°F (65°C).

A number of herbs and spices may be used
to vary the flavor of this forcemeat,
according to the discretion of the chef or
the needs of a specific recipe.

This may be used to prepare pâtés,
terrines, and as a stuffing for poultry.

TECHNIQUE
Gratin forcemeat (page 408)

Chicken Liver Gratin-Style Forcemeat

Yield: approximately 2 pounds (900 grams)

Vegetable oil	1 fluid ounce	30 milliliters
Chicken livers, cleaned	10 ounces	285 grams
Onions, minced	4 ounces	115 grams
Shallots, minced	2 ounces	60 grams
Bay leaf	1 each	1 each
Thyme leaves, dried	1 teaspoon	1 teaspoon
Salt to taste	2 teaspoons	2 teaspoons
Pepper to taste	¹/₄ teaspoon	¹/₄ teaspoon
Lean pork, cubed	10 ounces	285 grams
Pork fat, cubed	10 ounces	285 grams
Eggs	2 each	2 each
Curing salt (optional)	¹/₄ teaspoon	¹/₄ teaspoon

(Recipe continued on facing page)

1. Heat a small amount of oil in a sauté pan. Add the livers, onions, shallots, bay leaf, thyme leaves, salt, and pepper. Cook the livers over low heat until they are done, but do not allow them to take on any color.

2. Refrigerate the liver mixture to chill it thoroughly.

3. Grind the liver mixture, lean pork, and pork fat through a coarse die, then again through a medium or fine die.

4. Place the ground meats in the chilled bowl of a food processor. Process them with the eggs and curing salt until a smooth paste is formed.

5. Make a test quenelle to check the forcemeat for consistency and seasoning. Make any necessary adjustments. Keep the forcemeat chilled until it is ready to use for various charcuterie and garde-manger items.

Chicken Mousseline Forcemeat

Yield: approximately 1 ³/₄ pounds (750 grams)

Chicken breast, boneless, cubed	*1 pound*	*450 grams*
Egg	*1 each*	*1 each*
Heavy cream, chilled	*10 fluid ounces*	*300 milliliters*
Salt to taste	*2 teaspoons*	*2 teaspoons*
White pepper to taste	*¹/₄ teaspoon*	*¹/₄ teaspoon*
Fresh herbs, chopped (dill, parsley, tarragon, etc., as desired or available)	*2 tablespoons*	*2 tablespoons*

1. Grind the chicken through the fine die of a grinder and place it in the chilled bowl of a food processor.

2. Process the chicken with the egg until it is a smooth paste, but do not allow it to exceed 40°F (4°C).

3. Add the heavy cream, salt, pepper, and fresh herbs. Pulse the machine on and off just until the ingredients are blended.

4. Make a test quenelle by poaching it in simmering water or stock to test for consistency and seasoning. Make any necessary adjustments. Keep the forcemeat chilled until ready to use for quenelles, stuffing, or other charcuterie and garde-manger items.

The mousseline at the proper consistency.

This recipe can be prepared in the bowl of a standard food processor. It may be scaled up according to need.

Substitute fish or shellfish for the chicken to make a fish mousseline.

TECHNIQUE
Mousseline forcemeat (page 408)

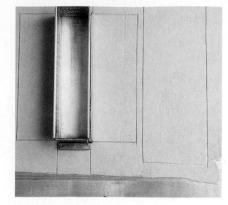

Measuring pâté dough.

The flavor of this dough can be varied by adding ground spices and herbs, lemon zest, or grated cheese. Rye or whole wheat flour or cornmeal may be used to replace up to one-third of the bread flour for a different flavor, texture, and appearance.

This will yield enough dough for one pâté en croûte.

TECHNIQUE
Making pastry doughs (pages 442-444)

Pâté Dough

Yield: 2 pounds (900 grams)

Bread flour, sifted	20 ounces	580 grams
Powdered milk (optional)	1 3/4 ounces	35 grams
Baking powder	1/4 ounce	7 grams
Salt	1/2 ounce	15 grams
Shortening	3 1/2 ounces	100 grams
Butter	2 1/2 ounces	70 grams
Milk or water	8 to 10 fluid ounces	240 to 300 milliliters
Eggs	2 each	2 each
Lemon juice or vinegar	1/2 fluid ounce	15 milliliters

1. Combine the flour, powdered milk, baking powder, and salt in a food processor. Mix the ingredients well until the mixture resembles a coarse meal.

2. Transfer the mixture to a mixer bowl. Incorporate the shortening, butter, milk, eggs, and lemon juice or vinegar with a dough hook. If the dough seems too dry, add up to 1 fluid ounce (30 milliliters) of additional water.

3. Let the dough rest for 1 hour before rolling it out.

If desired, you may add dried mushrooms (cèpes, bolétes, chanterelles, or porcini) to this mixture. One ounce (30 grams) should be adequate.

TECHNIQUE
Making spice blends (page 241)

Pâté Spice

Yield: 13 ounces (370 grams)

Whole white peppercorns	1 1/2 ounces	45 grams
Coriander, ground	3 ounces	85 grams
Thyme	1 3/4 ounces	50 grams
Basil	1 3/4 ounces	50 grams
Cloves	3 ounces	85 grams
Nutmeg	1 1/2 ounces	45 grams
Bay leaf	1/2 ounce	15 grams
Mace	3/4 ounce	20 grams

Combine all of the ingredients and grind them, using a mortar or blender.

Aspic Gelée

Yield: 1 gallon (3.75 liters)

Clarification

Oignon brûlé	*1 each*	*1 each*
Mirepoix	*1 pound*	*450 grams*
Ground beef	*3 pounds*	*1.35 kilograms*
Egg whites, beaten	*10 each*	*10 each*
Tomato concassé	*12 ounces*	*340 grams*
Stock	*1 gallon*	*3.75 liters*
Sachet d'Epices	*1 each*	*1 each*
Kosher salt	*1 teaspoon*	*1 teaspoon*
Gelatin powder	*4 ounces*	*115 grams*

1. Mix the ingredients for the clarification and blend with stock. Mix well.

2. Bring the mixture to a slow simmer, stirring frequently until raft forms.

3. Add the sachet and simmer for 45 minutes or until the appropriate flavor and clarity are achieved. Baste raft occasionally.

4. Strain the consommé; adjust the seasoning with salt and white pepper to taste.

5. Soften the gelatin in cold water, then melt over simmering water. Add to the cooled clarified stock. Refrigerate until needed. Warm as necessary for use.

A step in clarifying aspic gelée

The method for clarifying stock is virtually identical to the clarification of a consommé.

Use an appropriate stock, depending upon the intended use. For example, prepare a lobster stock and use ground fish for the clarification if the aspic is to be used to coat a seafood item.

The classic method for preparing an aspic gelée calls for a very strong and extremely gelatinous stock to be made by adding veal shank and calves' feet to a standard stock as it simmers. The high percentage of cartilage in the shank and feet will act in the same way as powdered gelatin does.

TECHNIQUE
Consommés (pages 299-302)
Working with gelatin (page 405)
Oignon brûlé (page 242)

RECIPE
Sachet d'Epices (page 475)

Mise en place for sausage.

Be sure that the ingredients and equipment remain cool (below 40°F/4°C) throughout preparation.

TECHNIQUE
Straight forcemeat (pages 405-407)
Sausages (pages 416-418)

Andouille Sausage

Yield: 7 ½ pounds (3.4 kilograms)

Pork butt, boned and cubed	6 ¼ pounds	2.8 kilograms
Cayenne, ground	2 ½ tablespoons	2 ½ tablespoons
Salt	2 ¼ ounce	80 grams
Curing salt (T.C.M.)	¼ ounce	7 grams
Thyme, ground	¾ teaspoon	¾ teaspoon
Mace, ground	1 teaspoon	1 teaspoon
Cloves, ground	¼ teaspoon	¼ teaspoon
Allspice, ground	1 teaspoon	1 teaspoon
Marjoram	2 teaspoons	2 teaspoons
Onions, chopped	1 ¼ pounds	570 kilograms
Garlic, minced	1 ¼ ounces	40 grams
Sheep casing, rinsed	as needed	as needed

1. Spread the meat over a sheet pan.

2. Combine the spices in a bowl; then sprinkle them over the meat. Incorporate well.

3. Grind the meat, onions, and garlic using a fine die.

4. Make a test quenelle to check for seasoning and consistency.

5. Stuff the meat into the sheep casing. Tie or twist it off at 8-inch (20-centimeter) intervals.

6. Cold-smoke the sausages for 12 to 14 hours.

7. Cook them using the desired method.

Breakfast-Style Sausage

TECHNIQUE
Straight forcemeat (pages 405-407)
Sausages (pages 416-418)

Yield: 6 pounds (2.75 kilograms)

Pork butt, diced	5 pounds	2.25 kilograms
Jowl fat, diced, frozen	1 pound	450 grams
Salt to taste	2 tablespoons	2 tablespoons
Bell's Poultry Seasoning	pinch	pinch
Dextrose	¾ ounce	20 grams
Ginger, ground	pinch	pinch
Water, cold	1 pint	480 milliliters
Sheep casing, rinsed	as needed	as needed

(Recipe continued on facing page)

1. Spread the meat and fat over a sheet pan.

2. Mix the spices in a bowl, then sprinkle them over the meat and fat. Incorporate well.

3. Grind the meat and fat, using first a coarse, then a medium or a fine die.

4. Mix the meat in a mixer fitted with a paddle attachment for approximately 60 seconds. Add the cold water while mixing.

5. Make a test patty, pan-fry it, and taste it to check the seasoning consistency, which should be adjusted as necessary.

6. Stuff the mixture into the sheep casing.

7. Twist off the casing at approximately $4^1/_2$-inch (12-centimeter) intervals.

8. Cook the sausages, using the desired method (pan-fry, bake, etc.).

Italian-Style Sausage

Yield: 11 pounds (5 kilograms)

Pork (approximately 25 percent fat),		
diced	*10 pounds*	*4.5 kilograms*
Pepper, coarse-ground	*1 ounce*	*30 grams*
Salt	*3 tablespoons*	*3 tablespoons*
Sweet Hungarian paprika	*$^1/_4$ ounce*	*7 grams*
Fennel seed	*$1^1/_2$ ounces*	*40 grams*
Dextrose	*1 ounce*	*30 grams*
Cold water	*1 pint*	*480 milliliters*
Hog casing, rinsed	*as needed*	*as needed*

Freshly ground meat for sausage.

1. Combine the diced meat, spices, and dextrose on a sheet pan. Toss to coat evenly.

2. Grind the meat, using a coarse, then medium, then fine die.

3. Mix the meat, using a mixer fitted with a paddle attachment for 30 seconds on slow speed. Add the water while mixing.

4. Mix the meat for 30 seconds more on fast speed.

5. Make a test quenelle or patty to check for seasoning and consistency.

6. Stuff the mixture into the hog casing.

7. Tie the casing at $4^1/_2$-inch (12-centimeter) intervals.

8. Cook the sausages using the desired method.

TECHNIQUE
Straight forcemeat (pages 405-407)
Sausages (pages 416-418)

VARIATION

Hot Italian Sausage: Add the following spices: ground coriander ($^1/_2$ ounce/15 grams), Spanish and Hungarian paprikas ($^3/_4$ ounce/20 grams each), crushed red pepper flakes ($1^3/_4$ ounces/75 grams) and 2 teaspoons cayenne.

Tying sausage into links.

Spanish chorizo is usually stuffed in casings. Mexican chorizo is often left in bulk.

To make a smoked sausage, place sausage on lined sheet trays and refrigerate uncovered overnight. Then cold-smoke for 12 to 14 hours. If not smoking, curing salt is optional.

TECHNIQUE
Straight forcemeat (pages 405-407)
Sausages (pages 416-418)
Cured and smoked items (page 419)

Fresh Chorizo

Yield: 12 pounds (5.5 kilograms)

Pork butt, ground fine	*2 pounds*	*900 grams*
Pork, lean, ground coarse	*6 pounds*	*2.7 kilograms*
Jowl fat, ground fine	*4 pounds*	*1.8 kilograms*
Curing salt (T.C.M.)	*¹/₂ ounce*	*15 grams*
Onion powder	*¹/₂ teaspoon*	*¹/₂ teaspoon*
Cumin, ground	*3 tablespoons*	*3 tablespoons*
Spanish paprika	*³/₄ ounce*	*20 grams*
Dextrose	*²/₃ ounce*	*18 grams*
Cayenne, ground	*2 ¹/₂ tablespoons*	*2 ¹/₂ tablespoons*
Garlic powder	*2 teaspoons*	*2 teaspoons*
Red peppers, crushed	*1 teaspoon*	*1 teaspoon*
Vinegar	*2 ¹/₂ fluid ounces*	*75 milliliters*
Nonfat dried milk	*3 ounces*	*85 grams*
Cold water	*6 fluid ounces*	*180 milliliters*
Hog or sheep casing, rinsed	*as needed*	*as needed*

1. Combine all of the ingredients except the water and casing. Mix them together in a mixer fitted with a paddle attachment. Add the water while mixing.

2. Stuff the mixture into the casing. Twist or tie off the casing at 3- to 4-inch (8- to 10-centimeter) intervals.

3. Cook the sausages using the desired method.

Duck Pâté en Croute

Yield: 2 pounds (900 grams)

Forcemeat

Duck (4 ¹/₂ pounds/2 kilograms)	*1 each*	*1 each*
Brine	*1 pint*	*480 milliliters*
Pork fat, cubed	*7 ounces*	*200 grams*
Orange zest, grated	*2 tablespoons*	*2 tablespoons*
Sage, chopped	*1 tablespoon*	*1 tablespoon*
Tarragon, chopped	*2 tablespoons*	*2 tablespoons*
Juniper berries, crushed	*6 each*	*6 each*
Curing salt (T.C.M.)	*¹/₂ teaspoon*	*¹/₂ teaspoon*
Shallots, minced	*1 ounce*	*30 grams*
Garlic cloves, minced	*2 each*	*2 each*

(Recipe continued on facing page)

Oil as needed	2 fluid ounces	60 milliliters
Red port	2 fluid ounces	60 milliliters
Madeira	2 fluid ounces	60 milliliters
Orange, juice only	1 each	1 each
Glace de Viande	1 ounce	30 grams
Duck livers, cleaned	4 ounces	120 grams
Bacon fat	1 ounce	30 grams
Egg	1 each	1 each
Apricots, quartered	1 ounce	30 grams
Dried cherries, soaked in Triple Sec	1 ounce	30 grams
Pistachio nuts, peeled	2 ounces	60 grams
Triple Sec, as needed	3 fluid ounces	90 milliliters
Pâté Dough, rolled thin, covered, chilled	1 recipe	1 recipe
Ham, thin sliced, for lining dough	4 ounces	115 grams
Gelatin, powdered (optional)	½ teaspoon	½ teaspoon
Egg albumen (optional)	½ teaspoon	½ teaspoon
Aspic Gelée, as needed	6 ounces	170 grams

1. Bone duck, clean leg and thigh meat; cube.

2. Trim breasts, submerge in brine, cure for 4 hours.

3. Combine cubed leg meat, pork fat, orange zest, sage, tarragon, berries, and salt; marinate refrigerated for 1 hour.

4. Sauté shallots and garlic in oil, add wines and orange juice, reduce by half, add glace, cool and add to marinating meat.

5. Sauté chicken livers in hot bacon fat, drain on paper towels, cool.

6. Grind marinated meat once through a coarse die and again through a medium die; purée in food processor; add egg, process until smooth.

7. Fold in cooked livers, drained apricots, cherries, peeled pistachio nuts, and 2 fluid ounces (60 milliliters) of reserved Triple Sec.

8. Oil the pâté pan, line it with dough; line dough with thin sliced ham.

9. Place half of the forcemeat in the mold.

10. Drain duck breasts, rinse, pat dry, sprinkle with gelatin powder and egg albumen, and set on top of forcemeat.

11. Fill mold with remaining forcemeat.

12. Fold over dough, paint with egg wash, add top, and bake to an internal temperature of 150°F (65°C).

13. Fill with aspic when pâté has cooled between 90 to 100°F (30 to 35°C).

Adding aspic to cooled pâté en croûte.

To make the **Brine**, combine 1 pint (480 milliliters) water with 1 ounce (30 grams) salt, 1 teaspoon curing salt (T.C.M.), 2 teaspoons pickling spice, and 1 garlic clove. Bring to a boil; strain and cool.

Serve two 2-ounce (60 gram) slices per portion for an appetizer.

Chicken livers may be used if duck liver is not available.

Curing salt is added in a ratio of 4 ounces per 100 pounds (115 grams per 45.5 kilograms).

TECHNIQUE
Straight forcemeat (pages 405-407)
Pâté en croûte (pages 413-416)

RECIPE
Glace de Viande (page 479)
Pâté Dough (page 701)
Aspic Gelée (page 702)

Filling the terrine mold.

Keep all ingredients and equipment very cool throughout each stage of grinding and processing.

The procedure for making a test quenelle is explained on pages 411-412.

Once a terrine is cooled and weighted overnight, you may wish to fill the mold with Aspic Gelée (page 702).

TECHNIQUE
Country-style forcemeat (pages 407-408)
Terrines (page 416)

Country Terrine

Yield: 1 terrine

Brandy	*2 fluid ounces*	*60 milliliters*
Bay leaves, crushed	*6 each*	*6 each*
Sage, chopped	*1 tablespoon*	*1 tablespoon*
Thyme, chopped	*1 tablespoon*	*1 tablespoon*
Savory, chopped	*1 tablespoon*	*1 tablespoon*
Salt to taste	*2 teaspoons*	*2 teaspoons*
Pepper to taste	*1/2 teaspoon*	*1/2 teaspoon*
Dijon mustard	*1 ounce*	*30 grams*
Garlic cloves, minced, sweated	*5 each*	*5 each*
Chicken livers, cleaned and seared	*3 ounces*	*90 grams*
Sugar	*1 tablespoon*	*1 tablespoon*
Curing salt (T.C.M.)	*1/2 teaspoon*	*1/2 teaspoon*
Chicken meat, cubed	*12 ounces*	*340 grams*
Pork meat, lean, cubed	*6 ounces*	*170 grams*
Fatback, cubed	*6 ounces*	*170 grams*
White bread, crusts removed	*2 ounces*	*60 grams*
Milk	*2 fluid ounces*	*60 milliliters*
Egg	*1 each*	*1 each*
Tabasco to taste	*2 to 3 drops*	*2 to 3 drops*
Ham, medium dice	*6 ounces*	*170 grams*
Pistachio nuts, whole, peeled	*4 ounces*	*115 grams*
Truffle, small dice	*1 each*	*1 each*
Bacon, sliced	*3/4 pound*	*340 grams*

1. Combine the brandy and bay leaves. Bring to a boil and let steep until cool. Strain.

2. Add the strained brandy, the sage, thyme, savory, salt, pepper, Dijon mustard, the sweated garlic, seared chicken livers, sugar, and the curing salt to the cubed meat and fat.

3. Grind the meat through the large die of the grinder, reserve half of the ground mixture for the garnish. Grind the remainder through the medium die.

4. Soak the bread in the milk and then squeeze out the excess. Add the medium-ground meat and egg to the soaked white bread; purée in a food processor.

5. Combine all ingredients (except the bacon) by hand over an ice bath; make a test quenelle.

6. Line a terrine mold with plastic wrap, then with sliced bacon. Fill terrine, bake in a 160°F (70°C) water bath to an internal temperature of 150°F (65°C).

7. Let cool to 110°F (43°C) and press overnight with a 2-pound (900-gram) weight.

Chicken Galantine

Yield: 5 ½ pounds (3 kilograms)

Panada

Eggs	2 each	2 each
Brandy	3 tablespoons	45 milliliters
Pâté Spice	1 teaspoon	1 teaspoon
Flour	3 ounces	85 grams
Salt to taste	1 tablespoon	1 tablespoon
White pepper to taste	½ teaspoon	½ teaspoon
Heavy cream	8 fluid ounces	240 milliliters
Roasting chicken, boned, wing tips removed, skin removed intact	1 each	1 each
Pork butt, 1-inch cubes, chilled, as needed	2 pounds	900 grams
Madeira	6 fluid ounces	180 milliliters
Ham or cooked tongue, small dice	4 ounces	120 grams
Black truffles, chopped fine	2 tablespoons	2 tablespoons
Pistachios, blanched, peeled, and chopped coarse	4 ounces	120 grams
Chicken Stock	as needed	as needed

1. Prepare the panada: Mix the eggs with brandy, spice, flour, salt, and pepper.

2. Bring the heavy cream to a boil. Remove it from the heat.

3. Temper the egg mixture with the hot cream. Return the tempered egg mixture to the heat and cook it until it is thickened. Chill thoroughly.

4. Weigh the leg and thigh meat from the chicken. Add an equal amount of pork butt, or enough for approximately 4 pounds (1.8 kilograms) of meat. Grind the chicken leg and thigh meat and pork twice, using a coarse then a fine die. Chill.

5. Cut the chicken breast meat into ½- to ¾-inch (1-centimeter) cubes. Season it to taste. Marinate the meat in the Madeira under refrigeration.

6. Drain the chicken breast; add the Madeira and panada to the ground meat mixture. Blend well.

7. Fold the ham, truffles, and pistachios into the forcemeat by hand, working over an ice bath. Mix well.

8. Gently fold in the reserved chicken breast over ice.

9. Roll the galantine securely in the reserved skin and cheesecloth.

10. Poach the galantine, in enough simmering stock to cover it, to an internal temperature of 160°F (70°C).

11. Cool the galantine in the stock in a hotel pan. Refrigerate it overnight. Remove the galantine from the stock and wrap it in new cheesecloth to firm its texture. Chill overnight. To serve the galantine, unwrap and slice it.

Galantine ready to poach.

The method for preparing a Galantine is explained on page 418. The photographs in Figure 11-18 show how to roll and wrap a galantine.

TECHNIQUE
Panadas (page 404)
Galantines (page 418)

RECIPES
Pâté Spice (page 701)
Chicken Stock (page 480)

28

Breads

Filling your bread basket with an array of muffins, rolls, and breads is a good way to make your restaurant different from your competitors. The selection in this chapter includes such favorites as blueberry and corn muffins, popovers, and zucchini bread. These "quick" breads are prepared with chemical leaveners.

The eggs are properly blended into creamed sugar mixture.

The batter can be made up and stored in a tightly sealed container for up to 48 hours. You can also scale into muffin pans and freeze. Raisins and nuts or seeds may be added for variety. If you do bake off directly from the freezer, adjust baking time by 10 minutes. Some chefs recommend thawing them first.

Batters with acidic ingredients cannot be prepared in advance.

TECHNIQUE
Creaming mixing method
  (pages 437-439)
Scaling (page 429)
Sifting dry ingredients (page 429)

Baking muffins and biscuits at a higher temperature will give a quicker, higher rise, without drying out the product.

This recipe may be used to make any type of fruit or nut muffin by substituting the desired ingredients for the blueberries.

Blueberries may react with certain chemical leaveners, giving them a greenish appearance. Baking powder, rather than baking soda, is preferred for more appealing color.

TECHNIQUE
Creaming mixing method
  (pages 437-439)
Sifting dry ingredients (page 429)

Basic Muffins

Yield: 6 dozen

Sugar	*1 pound, 5 ounces*	*600 grams*
Butter	*12 ounces*	*340 grams*
Shortening (emulsified)	*5 ounces*	*140 grams*
Salt	*³/₄ ounce*	*25 grams*
Eggs	*1 pound, 2 ounces*	*500 grams*
Bread flour	*2 ¹/₂ pounds*	*1.15 kilograms*
Baking powder	*2 ounces*	*60 grams*
Milk	*2 pounds*	*900 grams*

1. Cream together the sugar, butter, shortening, and salt for 2 minutes.

2. Gradually add the eggs, scraping sides of bowl occasionally and, when incorporated, mix on speed 2 (if using a 3-speed mixer) for 2 minutes. (You will need to increase mixing speed if using a 4-speed mixer.)

3. Add the remaining ingredients on low speed for 1 minute, scrape bowl, and then mix on speed 2 for 2 more minutes.

4. Scale 2 ounces (60 grams) of batter for each 1 dozen muffins if using a regular-size cupcake pan or 3 ounces (85 grams) for a muffin pan.

5. Bake at 425°F (220°C) for 11 to 13 minutes if using a cupcake pan, 16 to 18 minutes if using a muffin pan, or until golden brown on top and firm to the touch.

Blueberry Muffins

Yield: 4 dozen

Confectioners' sugar	*1 pound*	*450 grams*
Shortening	*8 ounces*	*225 grams*
Butter	*8 ounces*	*225 grams*
Salt	*¹/₂ ounce*	*15 grams*
Eggs	*1 pound*	*450 grams*
Milk	*1 pound*	*450 grams*
Cake flour	*1 ³/₄ pounds*	*800 grams*
Baking powder	*1 ounce*	*30 grams*
Bran	*8 ounces*	*225 grams*
Blueberries	*1 pound, 6 ounces*	*625 grams*

(Recipe continued on facing page)

1. Cream together the sugar, shortening, butter, and salt.

2. Gradually add the eggs, scraping sides of bowl occasionally.

3. Gradually add some of the milk.

4. Sift together the flour and the baking powder (two times), mixing in until smooth. Alternate dry ingredients with milk.

5. Gently fold in the blueberries.

6. Scale 1 pound, 14 ounces (850 grams) of batter for each 1 dozen muffins and divide evenly into prepared muffin cups.

7. Bake at 425°F (220°C) for 20 minutes or until light brown on top.

Corn Muffins

Yield: 3 dozen

Sugar	*1 pound*	*450 grams*
Shortening	*8 ounces*	*225 grams*
Salt	*$\frac{1}{2}$ ounce*	*15 grams*
Eggs	*8 ounces*	*225 grams*
Milk	*1 $\frac{1}{2}$ pounds*	*680 grams*
Cornmeal	*1 pound*	*450 grams*
Pastry flour	*1 $\frac{1}{2}$ pounds*	*680 grams*
Baking powder	*1 $\frac{1}{2}$ ounces*	*40 grams*

Add fresh corn kernels to the batter, if desired.

1. Cream together the sugar, shortening, and salt.

2. Gradually add the eggs, scraping sides of bowl occasionally.

3. Gradually add the milk and then the cornmeal, mixing until incorporated.

4. Sift together the flour and the baking powder twice and add to the mixture, mixing in until smooth.

5. Scale 2 pounds (900 grams) of batter for each 1 dozen muffins and divide evenly into prepared muffin cups.

6. Bake at 425°F (220°C) for 20 minutes or until light brown on top.

VARIATION

Cornbread: Prepare batter as directed above, and scale into small loaf pans (for individual loaves) or small cast iron skillets or pans.

For a savory muffin, add cheddar cheese, diced jalapeño or New Mexico green chilies, and/or whole corn kernels. Reduce the sugar by 20 to 30% if desired.

TECHNIQUE
*Creaming mixing method
(pages 437-439)*

Bran Muffins

Yield: 4 dozen

Add approximately 1 pound (450 grams) of nuts, or chopped fresh or dry fruit.

TECHNIQUE
Creaming mixing method (pages 437-439)
Sifting dry ingredients (page 429)

Sugar	1 pound	450 grams
Shortening	8 ounces	225 grams
Salt	$^1/_2$ ounce	15 grams
Eggs	1 pound	450 grams
Milk	1 pound	450 grams
Bran	8 ounces	225 grams
Bread flour	1 $^1/_2$ pounds	680 grams
Baking powder	1 $^1/_2$ ounces	40 grams
Honey	4 ounces	115 grams
Molasses	4 ounces	115 grams

1. Cream together the sugar, shortening, and salt.

2. Gradually add the eggs, scraping sides of bowl occasionally.

3. Gradually add the milk and then the bran, mixing until incorporated.

4. Sift together the flour and the baking powder twice and add to the mixture, mixing in until smooth.

5. Add in the honey and molasses.

6. Scale 2 pounds (900 grams) of batter for each 1 dozen muffins and divide evenly into prepared muffin cups.

7. Bake at 400°F (205°C) for 20 minutes or until light brown on top.

Zucchini Bread

Yield: 9 loaves

Fresh zucchini makes a delicious bread. Remove all seeds and grate.

Zucchini, large	5 pounds	2.25 kilograms
Sugar	4 $^1/_2$ pounds	2 kilograms
Eggs	1 $^1/_2$ pounds	680 grams
Baking powder	1 $^1/_4$ ounces	38 grams
Baking soda	$^3/_4$ ounce	115 grams
Salt	1 ounce	30 grams
Cloves, ground	$^1/_4$ ounce	115 grams
Cinnamon, ground	$^1/_4$ ounce	8 grams
Oil	1 $^1/_2$ pounds	680 grams
Bread flour	3 pounds	1.3 kilograms
Pastry flour	8 ounces	225 grams
Pecans	1 pound	450 grams

(Recipe continued on facing page)

1. Trim zucchini, split, remove seeds, and grate.

2. Combine all ingredients and zucchini and mix with a whip for 5 minutes on high speed, scraping bowl often.

3. Scale 1 pound, 14 ounces (400 grams) into prepared loaf pans.

4. Bake in a 350°F (175°C) oven for 45 minutes to 1 hour.

Muffins may also be made from this batter.

TECHNIQUE
Straight mixing method (pages 436-437)
Sifting dry ingredient (page 429)

Banana Nut Bread

Yield: 13 loaves

Cake flour	*3 pounds*	*1.3 kilograms*
Shortening (emulsified)	*2 1/2 pounds*	*1.15 kilograms*
Orange zest	*1/2 ounce*	*15 grams*
Sugar	*5 pounds*	*2.25 kilograms*
Cake flour	*2 pounds*	*900 grams*
Salt	*2 1/2 ounces*	*70 grams*
Baking powder	*3 1/4 ounces*	*95 grams*
Bananas, ripe	*5 pounds*	*2.25 kilograms*
Honey	*1 1/4 pounds*	*570 grams*
Eggs	*3 pounds*	*1.3 kilograms*
Pecans or walnuts, chopped	*1 pound*	*450 grams*
Vanilla extract	*1 1/2 ounces*	*40 grams*

Bananas.

1. Combine cake flour, shortening, and orange zest in 20-quart bowl with paddle; mix on second speed for 2 minutes, then add sugar.

2. Sift together the remaining flour, salt, and baking powder; add to bowl along with the bananas and honey; mix on first speed for 3 minutes, scraping bowl often.

3. Gradually add eggs on first speed and when all the eggs have been incorporated, mix for 5 minutes on second speed.

4. Add nuts and vanilla.

5. Scale 1 pound, 12 ounces (340 grams) of batter into prepared loaf pans and bake at 350°F (175°C) for 45 to 60 minutes or until done.

Emulsified shortening helps extend the shelf life of the bread.

TECHNIQUE
Zesting citrus fruits (page 231)
Two-stage mixing method
   (pages 439-440)

Biscuits

Yield: 5 dozen (3 ounces/85 grams)

If desired, make 4 dozen large (4 ounce/115 gram) biscuits, or about 10 dozen (1 ¹/₂ ounce/40 gram) mini biscuits.

TECHNIQUE
Straight dough mixing method
(pages 436-437)
Scaling (page 429)

Whole eggs	8 each	8 each
Buttermilk	as needed	as needed
Bread flour	3 pounds	1.3 kilograms
Pastry flour	3 pounds	1.3 kilograms
Salt	1 ¹/₂ ounces	40 grams
Baking powder	8 ounces	225 grams
Sugar	12 ounces	340 grams
Butter	1 pound	450 grams

1. Place eggs in a 2-quart measure, add enough buttermilk to fill to top.
2. Use straight dough-mixing method for 4 minutes; use speed two.
3. Roll dough to ¹/₂-inch thickness; let relax. Cut with round cutter.
4. Place biscuits on a sheet pan.
5. Brush with egg wash and bake at 425°F (220°C) for 20 to 22 minutes or until golden brown.

VARIATION

Flaky Biscuits: Sift the dry ingredients; working fat by hand as with a pie dough, blend in eggs and buttermilk just until blended. Bake at 450°F (225°C) for about 15 minutes.

Scones: Add 1 ¹/₂ pounds (680 grams) of plumped currants to above recipe.

Popovers

Yield: 2 dozen

This same formula may be used to prepare Yorkshire pudding. See variation for information.

TECHNIQUE
Straight mixing method (pages 436-437)

Butter as needed	8 ounces	225 grams
Eggs	6 each	6 each
Milk	1 pint	480 milliliters
Butter, melted	3 ounces	90 milliliters
All-purpose flour, sifted	8 ounces	225 grams
Salt	1 teaspoon	1 teaspoon

1. Generously butter popover pans or 4-ounce (115-gram) ramekins. Place on a sheet pan. Place the pan in a preheated 425°F (220°C) oven.
2. Whisk together the eggs, milk, and melted butter. Beat them until the mixture is frothy.
3. Combine the flour and salt in a separate bowl. Beat in the liquid gradually. Continue to beat the mixture until it is smooth and well blended.
4. Spoon the batter into prepared ramekins or popover pans. They should be about three-quarters full. Return to oven; reduce the heat to 375°F (190°C) and bake the popovers, undisturbed, for 50 minutes.
5. Remove the popovers from the oven. For crisp popovers, slit the side of each popover to allow the steam to escape, then return them to the oven until the tops are firm, crisp, and brown, about 10 minutes.

(Recipe continued on facing page)

Yorkshire Pudding: Prepare batter as directed above. Bake in popover pans or ramekins with drippings from roast beef.

Pain de Campagne

Yield: approximately 3 pounds (1.3 kilograms) dough

Cornmeal	*as needed*	*as needed*
Water	*18 fluid ounces*	*40 milliliters*
Compressed yeast	*¹/₂ ounce*	*15 grams*
Extra-virgin olive oil	*2 fluid ounces*	*60 milliliters*
Hard wheat flour (10 to 11% protein)	*1 ³/₄ pounds*	*850 grams*
Salt	*¹/₂ ounce*	*15 grams*

This basic formula can be varied to produce a wide range of results.

1. Line baking sheets with parchment. Scatter with cornmeal.
2. Combine the water, yeast, and oil until dissoved.
3. Add the flour and salt. Mix the dough until smooth and elastic.
4. Cover the bowl and allow the dough to ferment for 75 minutes.
5. Punch down and scale as desired. Round off dough.
6. Set dough on prepared sheet pan and proof for 1 hour.
7. Press the dough down to flatten; shape as desired.
8. Pan proof an additional 30 minutes.
9. Bake at 425°F (220°C) for approximately 30 minutes.

V A R I A T I O N S

The recipe makes about 5 loaves (10 ounces/285 grams per loaf), or 2 ¹/₂ dozen rolls (1 ¹/₂ ounces/15 grams per roll).

Hard Rolls: Use dough press to scale dough, or cut 1 ¹/₂ ounces (45 grams) per hard roll. Round off and do an initial pan proofing of 1 hour. Flatten each ball of dough into a rectangle and roll up to shape into hard roll, pressing seams closed. Pan proof for 1 hour after shaping. Score, pan proof another 30 minutes, and bake at 450°F (230°C) for 20 minutes.

Baguettes: Scale dough at 14 ounces (400 grams) per baguette. After initial pan proof, flatten and stretch dough into a long rectangle. Roll into a baguette, pressing seams closed. Pan proof for 1 hour after shaping. Score baguettes in several places with a diagonal slash. Pan proof another 30 minutes, and bake at 450°F (230°C) for 30 minutes.

Pizza Dough: Scale at 10 ounces (285 grams) per pizza. Flatten after initial pan proof, stretching and shaping into a disc. Pan proof another 30 minutes before adding toppings. Bake at 450°F (230°C) for 25 to 30 minutes in a pizza oven or directly on the hearth. (For appetizer or individual pizzas, scale dough at 6 ounces/170 grams per pizza.)

TECHNIQUE
Yeast-raised breads (pages 430-436)

Foccacia: Scale the dough at 10 ounces (285 grams) per foccacia. Brush with additional oil and top as desired with one or more of the following: chopped onions, chopped olives, and/or rosemary or other herbs. To shape foccacia, press balls of dough flat, and stretch slightly. Baking time is approximately 30 minutes at 450°F (230°C).

Ciabatta: Increase the water to 22 fluid ounces (660 milliliters). Omit the olive oil. Shape the dough into rectangles rather than rounds. Pan proof time for step 6 is increased to 90 minutes. Bake at 450°F (230°C) (with steam, if possible) for 30 minutes.

This basic formula can be varied to produce a wide range of results.

Scale pieces at 2 pounds (900 grams) for small loaves; 3 pounds (1.3 kilograms) for large loaves or Pullman loaves; 3 pounds (1.3 kilograms) is also one "press" if you are using a dough divider for rolls. One press makes 3 dozen rolls.

TECHNIQUE
Mixing yeast doughs (pages 431-434)

Multigrain Bread

Yield: about 12 pounds (5.5 kilograms) dough

Cornmeal	*4 ounces*	*115 grams*
Clear flour	*5 pounds*	*2.5 kilograms*
Bran	*8 ounces*	*225 grams*
Oatmeal	*8 ounces*	*225 grams*
Cracked wheat	*8 ounces*	*225 grams*
Wheat flour	*4 ounces*	*115 grams*
Molasses	*1 ounce*	*30 grams*
Sugar	*10 ounces*	*285 grams*
Shortening	*6 ounces*	*170 grams*
Milk powder	*6 ounces*	*170 grams*
Salt	*2 ounces*	*60 grams*
Yeast	*6 ounces*	*170 grams*
Water	*4 ¹/₂ pounds*	*2 kilograms*

1. Line baking sheets with parchment. Scatter with cornmeal.
2. Combine the cornmeal, clear flour, bran, oatmeal, cracked wheat, and wheat flour.
3. Add the remaining ingredients. Mix the dough until smooth and elastic.
4. Cover the bowl and allow the dough to ferment for 75 minutes.
5. Punch down and scale as desired. Round off dough.
6. Set dough on prepared sheet pan and proof for 1 hour.
7. Press the dough down to flatten, shape as desired.
8. Pan proof an additional 30 minutes.
9. Bake at 425°F (°220°C) for approximately 30 minutes.

Cottage Dill Bread

Yield: about 12 1/2 pounds (6 kilograms)

Cottage cheese	3 pounds	1.3 kilograms
Sugar	4 1/2 ounces	125 grams
Onions, minced	1 1/2 ounces	40 grams
Butter, soft	3 ounces	85 grams
Salt	1 ounce	30 grams
Dill, chopped	1 ounce	30 grams
Baking soda	1 ounce	30 grams
Eggs	6 ounces	170 grams
Horseradish	pinch	pinch
Yeast	5 ounces	140 grams
Water	12 ounces	340 grams
Bread flour	5 1/4 pounds	2.4 kilograms

1. Combine all of the ingredients, except the flour, and blend. Add the flour and mix until a nice dough forms.

2. Scaling instructions: 3 pounds (1.3 kilograms) per press for loaves and rolls of specific size.

3. After baking, brush with butter and sprinkle with a pinch of salt.

Fresh dill brings a wonderful flavor to this bread.

TECHNIQUE
Mixing yeast doughs (pages 431-434)

Raisin Bread

Yield: 16 to 17 loaves (18 ounces/500 grams each)

Yeast	8 ounces	225 grams
Milk	2 quarts	2 liters
Eggs	8 ounces	225 grams
Sugar	14 1/2 ounces	410 grams
Bread flour	6 1/2 pounds	2.9 kilograms
Cinnamon	1/2 ounce	15 grams
Salt	2 1/2 ounces	70 grams
Shortening	1 1/4 pounds	570 grams
Raisins	5 1/2 pounds	2.5 kilograms

1. Place the milk and the yeast in a bowl and stir to dissolve.

2. Add all the other ingredients, mixing on low speed until the flour is incorporated.

3. Mix for 10 to 12 minutes on second speed or until the dough is developed. Turn into an oiled bowl to keep the dough from forming a skin; place in a warm area to rise.

4. When dough has doubled in size, punch down and scale into 18-ounce (500-gram) pieces. Bench rest for 15 to 20 minutes, then shape into a loaf.

5. Give a final proof then bake in a 380°F (193°C) oven for 35 minutes or until done.

To make swirl pattern, scale the dough and stretch it out. Spread the cinnamon and raisins over the dough, roll up and seal.

TECHNIQUE
Mixing yeast doughs (pages 431-434)

717

Positioning the roll-in on the dough.

This recipe can also be used for coffee cake.

TECHNIQUE
Mixing yeast doughs (pages 431-434)
Roll-in dough (page 446-450)

Danish

Yield: about 12 pounds (5.5 kilograms)

Yeast	*8 ounces*	*225 grams*
Milk	*2 pounds*	*900 grams*
Sugar	*10 ounces*	*285 grams*
Salt	*1 1/2 ounces*	*40 grams*
Butter	*8 ounces*	*225 grams*
Egg yolks	*1 pound*	*450 grams*
Pastry flour	*1 1/2 pounds*	*680 grams*
Bread flour	*3 pounds*	*1.3 kilograms*
Cardamom, mace, or nutmeg, ground	*1/4 ounce*	*8 grams*
Butter	*3 pounds*	*1.3 kilograms*

1. Dissolve yeast in milk directly in the mixing bowl. Use the straight dough-mixing method, mixing for 8 minutes.

2. Roll butter between two pieces of bread-floured parchment paper, filling two-thirds of the length of the paper.

3. Place dough on a bread-floured sheet pan; refrigerate for 30 minutes.

4. Remove dough and roll out to the size of a sheet pan (approximately 1/2-inch thick).

5. Place the rolled butter (butter and dough should be 65°F/(18°C)) on two-thirds of the dough; fold in thirds to layer in butter; seal.

6. Turn the dough 90 degrees, roll out; make a 3-fold.

7. Refrigerate 30 minutes, roll out again and do a second 3-fold.

8. Refrigerate 30 minutes, roll out again and do the last 3-fold.

9. Cut into segments to make up danish. Bake at 375 to 400°F (190 to 205°C).

V A R I A T I O N S

Coffee Cake: Scale coffee cakes at 10 ounces (285 grams) each. Individual Danishes are scaled from 1 1/2 to 3 ounces (45 to 85 grams).

Croissants

Yield: 9 dozen

Milk	*3 pints, 3 ounces*	*1.5 liters*
Yeast	*5 ounces*	*140 grams*
Salt	*1 $\frac{1}{2}$ ounces*	*40 grams*
Sugar	*4 $\frac{1}{2}$ ounces*	*125 grams*
Butter, soft	*8 ounces*	*225 grams*
Bread flour	*5 $\frac{1}{4}$ pounds*	*2.4 kilograms*
Roll-in		
Butter, unsalted	*3 $\frac{3}{4}$ pounds*	*1.7 kilograms*
Bread flour	*4 ounces*	*115 grams*

Allow the dough to firm in the refrigerator for best result.

1. Combine first set of ingredients and mix for 2 $\frac{1}{2}$ minutes at medium speed.

2. Place dough in a rectangular shape on table and let rest while mixing roll-in butter.

3. Combine the roll-in butter and flour, using a paddle on "pulse" first speed until butter is chopped up; then switch to second speed only until butter is smooth and firm with no lumps. Roll the butter in flour to two-thirds the size of the dough.

4. Roll rectangular dough to the size of a sheet pan and place the rolled butter on the dough so that two-thirds of the dough is covered.

5. Lock butter into the dough by way of a 3-fold (the dough will have 5 layers, 3 of dough, 2 of butter), seal the ends and sides, and turn 90 degrees.

6. Roll out immediately to a rectangle twice the size of a sheet pan, brush off extra flour, give a 3-fold, turn 90 degrees, roll to fit the sheet pan, cover, and rest in the refrigerator for 20 to 30 minutes.

7. Repeat step 6 two more times. Brush the dough with melted shortening (not too warm) to seal the sides and top of dough.

8. Mark the dough with three indentations to indicate the number of 3-folds that have been done, wrap in plastic and refrigerate overnight.

9. The next day, roll out the dough, cut to fit croissant-cutter width and roll-up to make crescents. Egg wash, proof, egg wash again before baking, and bake at 380°F (193°C) for 28 minutes, or until medium golden brown.

Dough has to be made up to 1 day in advance and allowed to rest overnight in the refrigerator.

Dough can be frozen for up to 3 weeks; beyond that the yeast loses its potency. Frozen dough should be taken out of the freezer and placed in the refrigerator to thaw 1 day before using.

TECHNIQUE
Mixing yeast doughs (pages 431-434)
Roll-in dough (pages 446-450)

29
Kitchen Desserts

Kitchen desserts are those that can easily be prepared without a separate bakery or pastry shop on the premises. Many classic desserts, such as soufflés or crêpes, are among the offerings found here.

Even if you can purchase prepared tortes and cakes, you may turn to this chapter in order to find a number of sauce recipes that you may use to customize the desserts you are serving your guests.

The recipes have been grouped as follows:

- *Puddings*
- *Creams and Custards*
- *Soufflés and Other Egg Desserts*
- *Frozen Desserts*
- *Fruits*
- *Dessert Sauces*

Varieties of chocolate.

Chocolate Pudding

Yield: 50 servings (3 to 4 ounces/85 to 115 grams each)

Milk	*9 quarts*	*8.5 liters*
Sugar	*2 1/4 pounds*	*1 kilogram*
Salt	*pinch*	*pinch*
Vanilla bean (optional)	*1 each*	*1 each*
Cornstarch	*13 1/2 ounces*	*385 grams*
Cocoa powder	*13 1/2 ounces*	*385 grams*
Eggs	*1 pound, 13 ounces*	*820 grams*
Butter	*9 ounces*	*255 grams*

1. Combine milk, 8 ounces (225 grams) of the sugar, and salt; bring to a boil.

2. Split the vanilla bean (if used) and add to the hot milk. Allow to steep 15 minutes off the heat.

3. Sift remaining sugar, cornstarch, and cocoa powder together; mix in the eggs.

4. Add some of the hot milk to the egg mixture to temper it. Mix well; return egg mixture to remaining hot milk.

5. Bring to a second boil, remove from the heat, stir in butter.

6. Pour into prepared molds. Chill thoroughly.

Use 1 tablespoon of good-quality vanilla extract instead of the vanilla bean if you prefer. Add it with the butter in step 4.

If you use a vanilla bean, remove it from the milk, rinse it, pat dry, and use it to scent sugar.

TECHNIQUE
Tempering a liaison (page 257)

Chocolate Mousse in Tuiles

Yield: 10 servings

Chocolate, semisweet	*10 ounces*	*285 grams*
Butter	*1 1/2 ounces*	*40 grams*
Egg yolks, pasteurized	*5 each*	*5 each*
Sugar	*2 ounces*	*60 grams*
Egg whites, pasteurized	*5 each*	*5 each*
Dark rum or vanilla to taste	*1 fluid ounce*	*30 milliliters*
Heavy cream, whipped	*8 fluid ounces*	*240 milliliters*
Tuiles	*20 each*	*20 each*

1. Combine chocolate and butter; melt over a water bath.

2. Whip egg yolks and half the sugar to full volume.

3. Whip egg whites and the remaining sugar to full volume.

4. Fold egg whites into egg yolks.

Pasteurized eggs are used to prevent any potential problems with foodborne disease.

TECHNIQUE
Creams, Bavarians, and mousses (pages 453-454)

RECIPE
Tuiles (page 743)

(Recipe continued on facing page)

5. Fold butter–chocolate mixture into egg–sugar mixture.

6. Add rum or vanilla and fold in whipped cream.

7. Scoop or pipe into tuiles at time of service. Serve 2 tuiles per serving.

VARIATION

White Chocolate Mousse : Substitute white chocolate for the semi-sweet chocolate. To make this mousse with whole eggs, use 10 eggs. Combine them with the sugar and whip over a hot water bath until the eggs reach 165°F (74°C). Transfer the bowl to a mixer and beat until cool. Then fold in melted chocolate and, finally, whipped cream.

Bread and Butter Pudding

Yield: 15 servings

Custard

Milk	1 quart	1 liter
Eggs, beaten	6 each	6 each
Egg yolks, beaten	3 each	6 each
Sugar	6 ounces	170 grams
Vanilla extract	1 teaspoon	1 teaspoon

Bread

Bread, leftover	1 ½ pounds	680 grams
Butter, melted	3 ounces	85 grams
Raisins	4 ounces	115 grams

1. To make the custard: Combine all ingredients and mix well.

2. To prepare the bread: Cut in cubes, drizzle with butter, and toast in the oven.

3. Combine custard, bread, and raisins; fill buttered custard cups.

4. Bake in a water bath in a 325°F (165°C) oven for 45 minutes or until custard is set.

Use other dried fruits to replace the raisins.

TECHNIQUE
Creams, Bavarians, and mousses
(pages 453-454)
Water baths (pages 258-259)

Fresh berries may be varied according to seasonal availability.

TECHNIQUE
Tempering a liaison (page 257)

RECIPE
Raspberry Sauce (page 732)

Rice Pudding with Fresh Raspberries

Yield: 15 servings

Rice	*6 ounces*	*170 grams*
Milk	*54 fluid ounces*	*1.6 liters*
Golden raisins	*8 ounces*	*225 grams*
Nutmeg, ground	*¼ teaspoon*	*¼ teaspoon*
Cinnamon, ground	*¼ teaspoon*	*¼ teaspoon*
Salt	*¼ teaspoon*	*¼ teaspoon*
Sugar	*6 ounces*	*170 grams*
Egg yolks	*3 each*	*3 each*
Vanilla extract	*½ ounce*	*15 grams*
Raspberries, fresh	*1 pound, 7 ounces*	*650 grams*
Raspberry Sauce	*17 fluid ounces*	*520 milliliters*

1. Combine rice, milk, nutmeg, cinnamon, salt, and half the sugar; simmer, covered, until rice is cooked and milk is absorbed.

2. Blend the yolks with the remaining sugar. Temper and add to the rice. Bring up to a bare simmer. Remove from the heat.

3. Combine raisins and vanilla.

4. Serve on plates with raspberries and raspberry sauce.

Crème Caramel

This dessert is also referred to as flan.

The dissolved caramel that appears when turning out the custards is actually the sauce for this dessert.

Crème caramel and crème brûlée may also be prepared in larger dishes or hotel pans. The presentation is less dramatic but sometimes more practical for buffets or "family-style" seating.

TECHNIQUE
Creams, Bavarians, and mousses
(pages 453-454)

Yield: 14 servings (4 ounces/115 grams each)

Caramel		
Sugar	*8 ounces*	*225 grams*
Lemon juice, fresh	*few drops*	*few drops*
Water	*3 fluid ounces*	*90 milliliters*
Custard		
Milk	*1 quart*	*1 liter*
Sugar	*8 ounces*	*225 grams*
Vanilla bean	*1 each*	*1 each*
Egg yolks	*4 each*	*4 each*
Eggs, beaten	*6 each*	*6 each*

1. Butter the sides of ramekins.

2. Combine the sugar, lemon juice, and water for the caramel and cook to a rich brown; carefully divide among the bottoms of ramekins.

(Recipe continued on facing page)

3. Bring milk and 4 ounces (115 grams) of sugar to a boil; remove from heat. (If using a vanilla bean steep it in the hot milk mixture.)

4. Combine the egg yolks and the remaining sugar; stir well to combine.

5. Temper together the eggs with hot milk. Do not return to the heat.

6. Divide the custard mixture among the ramekins.

7. Place the cups in a bain-marie; bake at an oven temperature of 325°F (165°C).

8. Bake for approximately 35 minutes or until the custard has set.

9. Refrigerate overnight before turning out and serving.

English Trifle

Yield: 6 servings

Currant jelly	*1 ¹/₂ ounces*	*40 grams*
Sponge cake, soaked, cubed	*3 ounces*	*85 grams*
Vanilla Sauce	*12 fluid ounces*	*360 milliliters*
Sherry or rum	*1 ¹/₄ fluid ounces*	*37.5 milliliters*
Marinated fruits	*6 ounces*	*170 grams*
Vanilla Sauce	*12 fluid ounces*	*360 milliliters*
Whipped cream, for decoration	*6 ounces*	*170 grams*
Chocolate decoration	*6 pieces*	*6 pieces*

1. Place currant jelly in the bottom of each 4-ounce (120-gram) glass.

2. Alternate layers of sponge cake brushed with sherry, fruit, and vanilla sauce.

3. Top with vanilla sauce.

4. Before serving, pipe with a rosette of whipped cream on top and decorate with chocolate decoration.

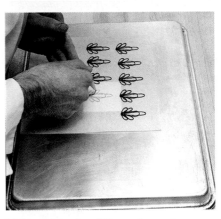

Making chocolate filigree decorations.

Select seasonal fruits and poach them if necessary. Combine them with simple syrup and rum or sherry. Marinate several hours. Drain before adding to trifle.

TECHNIQUE
Whipping cream (page 257)

RECIPES
Vanilla Sponge Cake (page 750)
Vanilla Sauce (page 731)

Dessert soufflé with a sauce.

Flavorings to add to this soufflé (per portion) include fresh fruits (1 ounce/30 grams), cordials like Kahlua, Tia Maria, Grand Marnier, Amaretto (1 tablespoon), ground toasted nuts (hazelnut, almond, macadamia, 1 tablespoon), and melted chocolate (1 ounce/30 grams).

TECHNIQUE
Preparing dessert soufflé (page 453)

Hot Dessert Soufflé

Yield: 40 servings

Milk	*1 quart*	*1 liter*
Vanilla bean, split lengthwise	*1 each*	*1 each*
Egg yolks	*8 ounces*	*225 grams*
Sugar	*1 pound*	*455 grams*
All-purpose flour	*6 ounces*	*170 grams*
Arrowroot	*2 tablespoons*	*2 tablespoons*

1. To make the base: Bring the milk to a boil with vanilla bean, and allow to steep for 15 minutes off the heat.

2. Combine egg yolks and sugar, whip until light; sift flour and arrowroot together and add to egg mixture.

3. Temper egg yolk mixture with some of the hot milk, stir constantly, add back to the remaining milk.

4. Bring to a boil, stirring constantly; whip until cool.

For one soufflé:

Base from above (3 tablespoons)	*1 ¹/₂ ounces*	*40 grams*
Egg whites, whipped to stiff peaks	*2 each*	*2 each*
Flavorings, as desired	*to taste*	*to taste*

1. Add flavorings to base.

2. Stir one-third of the egg whites into base.

3. Fold in remaining egg whites.

4. Fill prepared molds three-quarters full and bake at 400°F (200°C) for 20 minutes.

Use any of a variety of molds to create a signature frozen parfait dessert. The presence of whipped cream will prevent the parfait from freezing solid.

TECHNIQUE
Bavarians, creams, and mousses (pages 453-454)

Basic Parfait

Yield: 20 servings

Egg yolks	*15 ounces*	*425 grams*
Sugar	*8 ounces*	*225 grams*
Heavy cream, whipped	*1 quart*	*1 liter*
Flavoring: fruit purée, hazelnut paste	*10 ounces*	*285 grams*

1. Combine egg yolks and sugar, warm over a water bath, and whip until thickened.

2. Fold in whipped cream and flavoring.

3. Fill molds, freeze, and dip in hot water to unmold if desired.

4. Set on a plate; garnish edge with whipped cream rosettes.

Soufflé Glacé

Yield: 16 servings

Egg yolks	15 each	15 each
Sugar	14 ounces	400 grams
Egg whites	5 each	5 each
Heavy cream	1 quart	1 liter
Grand Marnier	4 fluid ounces	120 milliliters

1. Using parchment paper or aluminum foil, make a 1-inch collar around 4-ounce (120-milliliter) soufflé molds.

2. Whip egg yolks with half of the sugar, and whip egg whites with the remaining half of the sugar.

3. Whip heavy cream.

4. Fold egg whites into egg yolks.

5. Fold whipped cream into egg mixture; fold in Grand Marnier.

6. Fill soufflé molds to top of collar; freeze.

7. When frozen, remove collar, and decorate as desired; serve.

VARIATION

Frozen Orange Soufflé: Cut 8 oranges in half; remove the pulp and trim the bottoms so the orange sits flat. Make collars for the oranges. Garnish each portion with orange segments, chocolate ornaments, whipped cream, and mint leaves.

Blood oranges, when available, would make a dramatic dessert

TECHNIQUE
Frozen desserts (pages 457-458)
Whipping egg whites and Ccream
  (pages 254-257)
Folding (page 257)

Whole eggs give this ice cream its rich color and flavor

This ice cream may also be known as frozen custard. The egg yolks give it a rich golden hue.

Ripening (step 4) allows flavors to fully develop and ensures a good texture.

TECHNIQUE
Frozen desserts (pages 457-458)
Tempering a liaison (page 257)

RECIPE
Vanilla sauce (page 731)

French Ice Cream

Yield: approximately 1 gallon (3.75 liters)

Milk	1 ½ quarts	1.5 liters
Heavy cream	1 ½ pints	720 milliliters
Sugar	1 pound	450 grams
Corn syrup	1 pound	450 grams
Eggs	20 each	20 each
Sugar	8 ounces	225 grams

1. Boil together the milk, heavy cream, 8 ounces (225 grams) of the sugar, and the corn syrup.

2. Make a liaison of the eggs and the remaining sugar, mixing well, then temper it with one-third of the boiling milk.

3. Bring the liquid back to a boil and cook until the mixture coats the back of a spoon.

4. Strain and cool over ice. Ripen overnight in the refrigerator.

5. Process in ice cream freezer. Freezing times may vary according to the equipment being used.

VARIATIONS

Chocolate Ice Cream: Add 4 ounces (120 grams) of sweet chocolate and 4 ounces (120 grams) of bitter chocolate to the base recipe for chocolate flavor.

Caramel Ice Cream: Caramelize 8 ounces (225 grams) of sugar. Add the boiled milk and corn syrup to the pan to dissolve the caramel. Proceed with the recipe from step 2.

Coffee Ice Cream: Add powdered instant coffee (to taste) to the hot milk in step 1.

The classic test to see if the syrup for a sorbet is properly sweetened is this: Float a well-washed raw whole egg in the syrup (step 2). If the exposed surface area of the egg is about the size of a nickel, the syrup is good. If a greater area is exposed, it is too sweet; add water. If the egg is submerged or sinks, add sugar.

TECHNIQUE
Frozen desserts (pages 457-458)

Lemon Sorbet

Yield: approximately 3 quarts (3 liters)

Water	1 ¾ quarts	1.7 liters
Sugar	18 ounces	500 grams
Lemon juice, strained	8 ounces	225 grams
Egg white, whipped	1 each	1 each

1. Combine water and sugar, until sugar is totally dissolved.

2. Add lemon juice; cool to room temperature and check flavor and density.

3. Add egg white to syrup base, blending well.

4. Freeze in an ice cream freezer according to manufacturer's directions.

Wine Sorbet: Replace some of the water with white wine.

Orange Sorbet: Replace the lemon juice with orange juice.

Fruit Sorbet: Replace the lemon juice with fruit purée, and replace the water with the liquid the fruit may have been poached in (apple, pear, other firm fruits).

Fresh Peach Granità

Yield: 15 to 20 servings

Sugar	*6 ounces*	*170 grams*
Peaches, peeled, diced	*3 pounds*	*1.3 kilograms*
Lemon juice	*1 teaspoon*	*1 teaspoon*
Water	*1 pint*	*480 milliliters*

1. Combine the sugar and peaches and let sit for 2 hours.

2. Purée the peaches and syrup. Strain. Add all remaining ingredients. Pour into shallow pan.

3. Place in freezer, stir mixture every 15 to 30 minutes. Or, scrape the mixture once frozen to loosen "grains."

4. Serve with fresh fruit and champagne.

VARIATION

Sour Cherry: Use 3 pounds (1.3 kilograms) pitted, puréed sour cherries.

White peaches have a wonderful aroma.

Serve in a chanpagne flute or coupe with a splash of champagne.

Garnish with fresh or poached fruit, mint leaves, and a drizzle of a cordial such as Framboise or Midori.

Serve a sampler of 2 or more flavors.

TECHNIQUE
Frozen desserts (pages 457-458)

Poached Pears

Yield: 6 servings

Pears	*6 each*	*6 each*
Simple Syrup	*1 1/2 quarts*	*1.5 liters*
Filling		
Almond paste	*6 ounces*	*170 grams*
Sugar	*4 ounces*	*115 grams*
Hazelnuts, toasted, ground	*4 ounces*	*115 grams*

1. Peel, core, and trim the pears.

2. Bring the simple syrup to a simmer. Poach pears until tender; cool.

3. For filling: Combine all ingredients, mix together, and adjust consistency with poaching liquid as necessary.

4. Cut out each pear with circular cutter; stuff with filling.

5. Serve with a sauce or garnish as desired.

TECHNIQUE
Poaching (pages 383-386)

RECIPE
Simple Syrup (page 734)

Pears are good choices for a winter dessert.

Use prepared frozen puff pastry, if preferred.

RECIPE
Butter Puff Pastry Dough (page 738)

Individual Warm Fruit Tartlettes

Yield: 10 servings

Butter Puff Pastry Dough	1 ¼ pounds	570 grams
Cookie crumbs	3 ½ ounces	100 grams
Fresh fruit, poached, cleaned, sliced	1 ½ pounds	680 grams
Cinnamon sugar	2 tablespoons	2 tablespoons
Apricot jam, melted and strained	3 ounces	85 grams
Almonds, sliced and toasted	2 ounces	60 grams

1. Roll the dough thin, line greased tartlette molds, and trim edges.

2. Sprinkle cookie crumbs on top of dough.

3. Arrange fruit in tartlettes and sprinkle with cinnamon sugar.

4. Bake in a 350°F (175°C) oven about 30 minutes or until fruit and dough are cooked.

5. Cool slightly, brush with apricot jam, and garnish with sliced almonds.

Fresh Banana Fritters

Yield: about 1 ½ pints (720 milliliters)

Batter		
Eggs	2 each	2 each
Sugar	1 ounce	30 grams
White wine	6 fluid ounces	180 milliliters
Apple juice	6 fluid ounces	180 milliliters
Salt	pinch	pinch
Lemon rind, blanched, chopped	½ teaspoon	½ teaspoon
Orange rind, blanched, chopped	½ teaspoon	½ teaspoon
All-purpose flour, sifted	12 ounces	340 grams
Bananas, cut into pieces	2 pounds	900 grams

TECHNIQUE
Deep-frying (pages 367-371)
Straight mixing method (pages 436-437)

1. To make the batter, combine eggs and sugar, and whip lightly.

2. Add wine, apple juice, salt, and rinds.

3. Add flour; blend until smooth.

4. To use, dip fruit in batter; deep-fry at 350°F (175°C) until golden brown and drain on absorbent paper.

5. Serve with fruit sauce or whipped cream as desired.

(Recipe continued on facing page)

VARIATIONS

Strawberry Fritters: Dip hulled strawberries into heated and strained strawberry preserves, roll in chopped almonds or toasted coconut, then dip in batter. Fry as directed above.

Apple Fritters: Cut chunks or rings from cored, peeled apples.

Vanilla Sauce

Yield: 3 pints (1.5 liters)

Milk	*1 pint*	*480 milliliters*
Heavy cream	*1 pint*	*480 milliliters*
Vanilla bean	*1 each*	*1 each*
Sugar	*4 ounces*	*115 grams*
Egg yolks	*9 ounces*	*255 grams*
Sugar	*4 ounces*	*115 grams*

1. Heat milk, heavy cream, vanilla bean, and half of the sugar until it boils. Remove the vanilla bean and reserve for other uses.

2. Combine egg yolks and the remaining sugar, then temper with part of the boiling milk while stirring constantly.

3. Pour liaison into the remaining milk and return to the heat.

4. Stirring constantly, cook slowly to stage of nappé or 180°F (80°C).

5. Remove immediately from stove and strain through a chinois, directly into a bain-marie in an ice bath.

Vanilla sauce should coat the back of a wooden spoon.

This sauce is also known as custard sauce and sauce anglaise. It can be made over a water bath for more control of the heat source.

Add good-quality vanilla extract to the sauce in step 3 if you do not wish to use a vanilla bean. One tablespoon will flavor this recipe adequately.

TECHNIQUE
Creams, Bavarians, and mousses
(pages 453-454)

Use lemons or limes for this fruit curd.

The butter amount can be increased if a firmer consistency is desired.

This mixture can be used for a number of preparations, such as lemon tartlettes, or fillings for cakes and French pastries.

Serve with spicy cakes as a filling or sauce.

Serve with biscuits or breakfast breads as a spread.

TECHNIQUE
Creams, Bavarians, and mousses (pages 453-454)
Zesting citrus (page 231)

Lemon Curd

Yield: 24 ounces (680 grams)

Sugar	*10 ounces*	*285 grams*
Eggs	*7 ounces*	*200 grams*
Lemon juice	*2 fluid ounces*	*60 milliliters*
Lemon, peeled, grated	*1/2 each*	*1/2 each*
Butter, diced	*5 ounces*	*140 grams*

1. Whisk together the sugar, eggs, and lemon juice and peel over boiling water until mixture is thick and has reached 165°F (70°C). Do not boil.

2. Add the butter a few pieces at a time. Simmer briefly. Cool properly and store.

VARIATIONS

Lemon Mousse: Fold in enough beaten egg whites and whipped cream to make a mousselike consistency. Pipe into molds and refrigerate.

Orange Curd: Substitute orange juice and orange zest for the lemon.

Lime Curd: Substitute lime juice and lime zest for the lemon.

Raspberry Sauce

Yield: 12 ounces (340 grams)

Sugar	*2 3/4 ounces*	*80 grams*
Burgundy wine	*3 fluid ounces*	*90 milliliters*
Raspberry purée (fresh)	*7 fluid ounces*	*210 milliliters*

1. Combine all ingredients, simmer 3 minutes, and strain.

2. Let cool; use 1 to 1 1/2 ounces (15 grams) per serving.

VARIATION

Blackberry or Blueberry Sauce: Substitute blackberries or blueberries, pureed, and strained, for the rasberry purée.

To purée fresh berries, place them in a blender or food processor. A fine sieve can be used to strain out seeds if desired.

TECHNIQUE
Sauces and glazes (pages 456-457)

Chocolate Sauce

Yield: 30 fluid ounces (900 milliliters)

Heavy cream	*1 pint*	*480 milliliters*
Honey	*2 ounces*	*60 grams*
Vanilla extract	*to taste*	*to taste*
Chocolate, melted	*13 ounces*	*370 grams*

1. Combine heavy cream and honey, bring to a boil, remove from heat.

2. Add vanilla and chocolate, let cool.

Alternative preparation: Mix 1 quart (1 liter) vanilla sauce with 12 ounces (340 grams) of semisweet chocolate; add chocolate when sauce is hot. Let cool and serve.

Under most conditions, chocolate should not be refrigerated, since this could cause moisture to condense on the surface.

TECHNIQUE
Sauces and glazes (pages 456-457)

Chocolate Ganache

Yield: 25 ounces (700 grams)

Sugar	*2 ounces*	*60 grams*
Heavy cream	*1 quart*	*1 liter*
Butter	*2 ounces*	*60 grams*
Chocolate, semisweet, chopped	*2 pounds*	*900 grams*
Liqueur (optional)	*2 fluid ounces*	*60 milliliters*

1. Combine sugar, cream, and butter; heat to a boil, and remove from heat.

2. Add chocolate, stir until chocolate is melted. Cool. When cool, add liquor.

VARIATIONS

Truffles: Let the ganache cool. Scoop out ¹/₄ ounce (7 grams) of ganache and roll. Coat by rolling in cocoa powder or dipping in chocolate.

Chocolate Glaze: Warm the ganache and use it to glaze cakes and small pastries.

Soft Ganache: Increase the cream to 40 fluid ounces (1.5 liters). Decrease chocolate by 4 ounces (115 grams).

Vary the flavor by using different types of chocolate: semisweet and bitter combinations; white chocolate; and liquors.

TECHNIQUE
Sauces and glazes (pages 456-457)

Caramel Sauce

Yield: 1 ¹/₂ quarts (1.5 liters)

Be very careful whenever you work with sugar. The sugar can "explode" when you add liquid, so do it away from the heat and keep your face and hands clear of the pan to prevent burns.

TECHNIQUE
Sauces and glazes (pages 456-457)

Sugar	8 ounces	225 grams
Water	2 fluid ounces	60 milliliters
Milk or heavy cream	1 quart	1 liter
Egg yolks	6 ounces	170 grams

1. Melt sugar until it is a caramel color; add the water; stir until smooth and caramel sugar is melted.

2. Add milk and eggs; cook until the sauce coats the back of a spoon. Serve warm.

Cooking simple syrup.

To make coffee-flavored syrup, add prepared coffee syrup or diluted powdered instant coffee, or espresso to taste.

TECHNIQUE
Syrups and glazes (page 456)

Simple Syrup

Yield: 1 quart (1 liter)

Water	1 quart	1 liter
Sugar	8 ounces	225 grams
Lemons, juiced	3 each	3 each
Oranges, juiced	3 each	3 each

1. Bring water and sugar to a boil.

2. Cool.

3. Flavor with lemon and orange juices and refrigerate until needed.

30

Cakes and Pastries

Elaborate pastries and cakes are often thought of as a serious challenge. They tend to involve the preparation of more than one component, as when you may be called upon to prepare a cookie base, a genoise, a bavarian filling, and a buttercream or frosting.

The recipes in this chapter have been grouped as follows:

- *Pastry Doughs*
- *Cookies*
- *Fillings*
- *Meringues*
- *Frostings and Buttercreams*
- *Basic Cakes*
- *Cheesecakes*

It is important to use pastry flour and to work the dough as little as possible.

This is sometimes called a 3-2-1 dough, because it's made from 3 parts flour, 2 parts shortening, and 1 part water.

TECHNIQUE
Basic pie dough (page 492)
Lining a pie plate (pages 444-445)
Baking blind (page 445)

Pie Crust Dough

Yield: five 2-crust pies

Butter or shortening	*2 pounds*	*900 grams*
Pastry flour	*3 pounds*	*1.3 kilograms*
Salt	*1 ounce*	*30 grams*
Cold water	*1 pound*	*450 grams*

1. Break shortening into flour to form large nuggets the size of walnuts.

2. Dissolve salt in water.

3. Add cold liquid to flour and shortening and mix just enough to form a dough.

4. Use 1 ounce (30 grams) of dough for each inch of pie pan size.

5. Bake at 425°F (220°C) for 35 minutes, or until done if you need a prebaked pie shell.

6. For pies made with an unbaked shell, follow through step 4 and then fill with amount recipe calls for.

As with many basic formulas, the types of ingredients (butter, or shortening, etc.) used in pâte à choux can be varied depending on its intended use. Be aware, however, that these changes will provide different results, such as the quick browning that is caused when milk is used rather than water.

TECHNIQUE
Pâte à choux (pages 450-451)
Pastry bags and tips (pages 462-463)

Pâte à Choux

Yield: 5 pounds (2.25 kilograms)

Water	*1 pound*	*450 grams*
Milk	*1 pound*	*450 grams*
Butter, cut in pieces	*8 ounces*	*225 grams*
Shortening, cut in pieces	*8 ounces*	*225 grams*
Salt	*¼ ounce*	*8 grams*
Sugar	*¼ ounce*	*8 grams*
Bread flour	*1 ½ pounds*	*680 grams*
Eggs, adjust consistency	*1 pint*	*480 milliliters*

1. Combine liquid, butter, shortening, salt, and sugar. Bring to a rolling boil.

2. Add flour all at once, stirring constantly, until mixture forms a ball and pulls away from the sides of the pan.

3. Place mixture into a mixing bowl on second speed for 2 minutes to cool slightly.

4. Slowly add eggs in 3 to 4 additions, mixing well between each addition to form a medium-stiff paste.

5. Fill a pastry bag and pipe out as needed for what you are making.

6. Bake at 380 to 400°F (190 to 200°C) for 10 minutes until the structure has attained a little color, then reduce temperature to 250°F (120°C) until the moisture has evaporated, approximately 30 minutes.

Short Dough for Crust (Pâte Sucre)

Yield: 6 pounds (2.75 kilograms)

Butter	*2 pounds*	*900 grams*
Shortening	*1 pound*	*450 grams*
Sugar	*1 pound*	*450 grams*
Eggs	*6 ounces*	*170 grams*
Vanilla extract	*$^1/_2$ fluid ounce*	*15 milliliters*
Cake flour	*2 pounds*	*900 grams*
Bread flour	*1 pound*	*450 grams*
Baking powder	*$^1/_2$ ounce*	*15 grams*
Salt	*$^1/_2$ ounce*	*15 grams*

1. Cream the butter, shortening, and sugar in 12-quart (20-liter) mixer with paddle on first speed, 8 to 10 minutes.

2. Slowly blend in eggs and vanilla in 3 additions.

3. Sift dry ingredients together once only.

4. Blend in dry ingredients just enough to incorporate and make a smooth dough.

5. Chill dough until firm enough to roll out. Dough can be made in advance and stores well in a refrigerator.

6. Prebake either partially, at 350 to 375°F (175 to 190°C) for 15 to 20 minutes until firm but no color, or bake fully, depending on need.

Creaming sugar and shortenings.

This dough is also known as pâte sucre. It is commonly used for tarts.

TECHNIQUE
*Creaming mixing method
  (pages 437-439)
Sifting (page 429)
Scaling (page 429)
Baking blind (page 445)*

Positioning the roll-in on the dough.

TECHNIQUE
Roll-in doughs (pages 446-450)
Preparing ingredients and equipment
(pages 429-430)

Butter Puff Pastry Dough

Yield: 12 pounds (5.5 kilograms)

Dough

Cake flour	12 ounces	340 grams
Bread flour	3 1/4 pounds	1.5 kilograms
Butter	8 ounces	225 grams
Water	2 1/2 pounds	1.15 kilograms
Salt	1/4 ounce	8 grams

Roll-In

Butter, cool	4 1/2 pounds	2 kilograms
Bread flour	12 ounces	340 grams
Cake flour	4 ounces	115 grams

1. To make the dough: Sift cake and bread flours together.

2. Rub the butter into the mixed flours.

3. Add water and salt, and knead into a smooth dough. Allow to relax in the refrigerator.

4. To make the roll-in: Combine butter with the bread and cake flour, knead until smooth, and roll into an 18-by-18-inch square; cool slightly; do not allow it to become brittle and cold.

5. To assemble: Roll dough into a rectangle the same width as the butter mix but one-third longer.

6. Place butter on two-thirds of the dough, leaving one-third exposed.

7. Fold the exposed third of the dough over the middle butter-covered third of dough and fold the remaining third of fat-covered dough over the exposed dough. This will produce a 3-fold. Roll to original size, seal edges, and turn 90 degrees.

8. Rest dough 20 to 30 minutes between folding and rolling.

9. Roll, book-fold, and turn dough 4 times, resting between each rolling.

Blitz Puff Pastry

Yield: 10 pounds (2.25 kilograms)

Bread flour	*2 pounds*	*900 grams*
Pastry flour	*2 pounds*	*900 grams*
Butter, diced	*4 pounds*	*1.8 kilograms*
Salt	*1 ounce*	*30 grams*
Water	*1 quart*	*1 liter*

1. Combine the flours in a large bowl.

2. Cut the butter into the flour very lightly. The pieces of butter should be quite large.

3. Combine the salt and the water and stir until dissolved.

4. Add the water to the dough and mix just until it catches.

5. Refrigerate the dough briefly if necessary, then roll it out into a rectangle.

6. Make three 4-folds, rolling out and refrigerating the dough between each fold.

7. Cut and shape the dough as desired.

This dough is ready for its folds.

TECHNIQUE
Roll-in doughs (pages 446-450)
Preparing ingredients and equipment (pages 429-430)

Regular Cookie Dough

Yield: 6 pounds (2.75 kilograms)

Sugar	*1 pound*	*450 grams*
Butter	*2 pounds*	*900 grams*
Eggs	*6 ounces*	*170 grams*
Flavoring	*1/2 ounce*	*40 grams*
Cake flour	*3 pounds*	*1.3 kilograms*

1. Combine sugar and butter. Cream together.

2. Add eggs and flavoring. Cream together.

3. Add flour and mix just long enough to combine; do not overmix.

4. Chill.

5. Bake at 385°F (195°C). (Baking time depends on the product you are making.)

Add various extracts or citrus zests to achieve the desired flavor.

This cookie dough may be known as a 1-2-3 dough because it is composed of 1 part sugar, 2 parts butter, and 3 parts flour. This ratio produces a delicate cookie with a good texture. Using confectioners sugar in the special formula produces a dough that does not spread as it bakes.

TECHNIQUE
Creaming mixing method (pages 437-439)
Preparing ingredients and equipment (pages 429-430)

Piping cookies out.

A round cookie can be garnished with cherries or nuts, added before baking.

Sandwich two cookies together with jam and dip in tempered chocolate.

TECHNIQUE
*Creaming mixing method
    (pages 437-439)
Preparing ingredients and equipment
    (pages 429-430)*

Spritz Cookies

Yield: 30 dozen cookies

Sugar	2 ¼ pounds	1 kilogram
Butter	2 ¼ pounds	1 kilogram
Vanilla extract	¼ ounce	8 milliliters
Lemon extract	¼ ounce	8 milliliters
Salt	1 ounce	30 grams
Butter or shortening	26 ounces	735 grams
Eggs	9 ounces	255 grams
Milk	9 fluid ounces	270 milliliters
Pastry flour	3 ¾ pounds	1.7 kilograms
Bread flour	1 ¼ pounds	570 grams
Milk powder	3 ounces	85 grams

1. Cream together sugar, butter, vanilla, lemon, salt, and butter.
2. Add eggs gradually.
3. Add milk.
4. Sift together pastry and bread flours and milk powder.
5. Fold flour mixture into butter, mix just until incorporated. Do not overmix.
6. Pipe out cookies into desired shapes on parchment-lined sheet pans.
7. Bake in a 380°F (190°C) oven for 14 minutes or until light brown on edges.

Instead of using chips, coarsely chop semisweet, milk, or white chocolate.

Use walnuts, hazelnuts, or macadamia nuts instead of pecans.

TECHNIQUE
*Creaming mixing method
    (pages 437-439)
Preparing ingredients and equipment
    (pages 429-430)*

Chocolate Chip

Yield: 10 dozen cookies

Sugar	1 ½ pounds	680 grams
Brown sugar	1 ½ pounds	680 grams
Butter	1 pound	450 grams
Butter or shortening	1 pound	450 grams
Salt	½ ounce	15 grams
Baking soda	1 ounce	30 grams
Eggs	1 ½ pounds	680 grams
Pastry flour	3 pounds	1.3 kilograms
Chocolate chips	4 pounds	1.8 kilograms
Pecans, chopped	12 ounces	340 grams

(Recipe continued on facing page)

1. Combine sugars, butter, shortening, salt, and baking soda; cream together.

2. Add eggs slowly.

3. Add pastry flour. Mix until just combined; do not overmix. Add chocolate chips and nuts, mix just enough to combine.

4. Portion onto parchment-lined sheet pans by dropping from a spoon or using a portion scoop, $1\,^1/_2$ ounces (45 grams) each cookie.

5. Bake in a 350°F (175°C) oven for 15 to 17 minutes or until golden brown on edges.

Hermit Cookies

Yield: 7 $^1/_2$ dozen cookies

Sugar	$1\,^1/_2$ pounds	680 grams
Shortening	8 ounces	225 grams
Butter	4 ounces	115 grams
Molasses	6 ounces	170 grams
Salt	$^3/_8$ ounce	12 grams
Allspice, ground	$^1/_4$ ounce	8 grams
Cinnamon, ground	$^1/_4$ ounce	8 grams
Eggs	6 ounces	170 grams
Water	5 fluid ounces	150 milliliters
Cake flour	$2\,^1/_2$ pounds	1.15 kilograms
Baking soda	$^3/_4$ ounce	20 grams
Raisins	1 pound	455 grams

These are a type of bar cookie. The addition of raisins and molasses makes them stay fresher longer.

TECHNIQUE
Preparing ingredients and equipment (pages 429-430)

1. Cream together the sugar, shortening, butter, molasses, salt, and spices.

2. Gradually add the eggs.

3. Gradually add the water.

4. Sift together the cake flour and baking soda; add to the mixture, and mix until smooth.

5. Add raisins.

6. Scale into 12-ounce (340-gram) units and roll into a circular tube $1^1/_2$ inches (4 centimeters) in diameter.

7. Bake for 18 to 20 minutes at 360 to 375°F (180 to 190°C). Allow cookies to cool slightly before slicing into bars.

Melting chocolate.

TECHNIQUE
Melting chocolate (pages 459-461)
Preparing ingredients and equipment
(pages 429-430)

Fudge Brownie

Yield: 1 sheet pan

Bitter chocolate	1 ¹/₂ pounds	680 grams
Butter	2 ¹/₄ pounds	1 kilogram
Eggs	30 ounces	850 grams
Sugar	4 ¹/₂ pounds	2 kilograms
Vanilla extract	1 fluid ounce	30 milliliters
Cake flour	1 ¹/₂ pounds	680 grams
Pecans or walnuts	18 ounces	510 grams

1. Melt chocolate and butter carefully over a water bath; do not exceed 110°F (43°C).

2. Combine eggs, sugar, and vanilla; beat until lemon-colored.

3. Add chocolate–butter mixture to eggs, tempering the eggs first.

4. Gently fold in flour.

5. Fold in 1 pound (450 grams) of nuts, pour into sheet pan. Sprinkle remaining nuts on top.

6. Bake at 350°F (175°C) for 40 minutes until done or until brownie is firm to touch on top.

Cake Brownie

Yield: 1 sheet pan

These two formulas will produce brownies with distinctly different textures.

Make brownie sundaes by topping a brownie with ice cream and fudge sauce.

Use the corners and edges (diced) as a garnish for ice cream.

TECHNIQUE
Preparing ingredients and equipment
(pages 429-430)

Sugar	2 pounds	900 grams
Butter	2 pounds	900 grams
Baking powder	4 ounces	115 grams
Salt	4 ounces	115 grams
Corn syrup	1 pound	450 grams
Eggs	2 pounds	900 grams
Baking soda	³/₄ ounce	20 grams
Bread flour	2 pounds	900 grams
Cocoa powder	8 ounces	225 grams
Water	27 fluid ounces	810 milliliters
Pecans	1 pound	450 grams

1. Cream together sugar, butter, baking powder, salt, and corn syrup.

2. Add eggs slowly and mix until incorporated.

3. Sift together dry ingredients.

4. Add dry ingredients alternately with water.

5. Add pecans.

6. Pour into sheet pans, bake at 375°F (190°C) for 35 minutes or until done. Cut to the desired size.

Tuiles

Yield: 6 ¹/₂ dozen cookies

Confectioners sugar, sifted	9 ounces	255 grams
Bread flour, sifted	6 ounces	170 grams
Almonds, toasted and crushed	10 ounces	285 grams
Egg whites	4 ounces	115 grams
Eggs	6 ounces	170 grams
Vanilla extract	¹/₂ teaspoon	¹/₂ teaspoon
Butter, melted	3 ounces	85 grams

1. Combine sugar, flour, and almonds together.

2. Add egg whites, eggs, flavoring, and melted butter; scrape down the bowl well.

3. Spoon ¹/₂ ounce (15 grams) for each cookie onto a flat sheet pan that has been buttered and floured.

4. Flatten with fork (to prevent fork from sticking to dough, dip into water each time).

5. Bake at 380°F (190°C) for 8 minutes or until pale brown at the edges.

6. Immediately remove from sheet pan and place bottom up into a trough-shaped mold.

7. Store in airtight container.

Shaping the tuiles while still warm.

Grated orange or lemon zest can be used for flavor.

TECHNIQUE
Preparing cookies, petits fours, and other small pastries (page 458)
Preparing ingredients and equipment (pages 429-430)
Toasting nuts and seeds (pages 47-52)

Pastry Cream

Yield: 3 pounds (1.3 kilograms)

Milk	1 quart	1 liter
Sugar	8 ounces	225 grams
Butter	3 ounces	85 grams
Cornstarch	3 ounces	85 grams
Eggs	6 to 8 each	6 to 8 each
Flavorings, as required	as needed	as needed

1. Combine milk with half of the sugar and the butter, bring to a boil.

2. Combine remaining sugar with cornstarch, add eggs and mix until smooth.

3. Temper egg mixture, add to milk, return to a boil.

4. Remove from heat, add butter mixture and flavorings.

5. Pour into a hotel pan, cover, and refrigerate. Use as needed.

TECHNIQUE
Pastry cream (pages 452-453)
Cooling and storing foods (pages 47-52)

Folding in whipped cream.

You may add a wide variety of flavorings to this cream: espresso, nut extracts, chopped nuts, fruit purées, lemon curd, and cordials and liqueurs.

This recipe makes enough to fill two 10-inch (25-centimeter) cakes.

TECHNIQUE
Bavarians, creams, and mousses (pages 453-454)
Whipping cream (page 257)

Vanilla Bavarian Cream

Yield: 4 1/2 pounds (2 kilograms)

Vanilla Sauce	*1 quart*	*1 liter*
Gelatin	*1 ounce*	*30 grams*
Water	*8 fluid ounces*	*240 milliliters*
Flavorings	*to taste*	*to taste*
Heavy cream	*1 quart*	*1 liter*

1. Prepare the vanilla sauce.

2. Soften the gelatin in the water.

3. Add the softened gelatin to the warm vanilla sauce. Stir until the gelatin is completely melted.

4. Cool the mixture over an ice bath to about 70°F (21°C).

5. Whip the cream to medium peaks.

6. Fold the whipped cream into the vanilla sauce.

7. Use as desired to fill cakes or mold and chill.

A classic home-style version of this pie is made by cutting the apples and tossing them together with a mixture of the sugar, spices, and cornstarch or flour. Dot the fruit with a little butter for extra richness, if you wish.

TECHNIQUE
Basic pie dough (page 442)
Preparing pies and tarts (pages 444-446)

RECIPE
Pie Crust Dough (page 736)

Apple Pie

Yield: five 10-inch (25-centimeter) pies

Water	*1 1/2 quarts*	*480 milliliters*
Sugar	*14 ounces*	*400 grams*
Cinnamon, ground	*1/2 ounce*	*15 grams*
Nutmeg, ground	*1/4 ounce*	*8 grams*
Lemon extract	*1/4 teaspoon*	*1/2 teaspoon*
Water	*8 ounces*	*225 grams*
Cornstarch	*4 3/4 ounces*	*135 grams*
Apples, peeled, cored, sliced	*7 1/2 pounds*	*3.3 kilograms*
Pie Crust Dough	*1 recipe*	*1 recipe*

(Recipe continued on facing page)

1. Bring water, all but 2 ounces (60 grams) of sugar, spices, and lemon to a boil in a stainless steel pot.

2. Combine water, cornstarch, and remaining sugar; mix together.

3. Add cornstarch mixture to boiling liquid, stirring constantly; bring to a second boil.

4. Remove from heat, gently fold in fruit, and cool. Scale 2 pounds (900 grams) in each shell, add top or lattice crust; bake for 40 to 50 minutes in a 375°F (190°C) degree oven until done.

5. Roll out dough and line 5 pie plates.

Pumpkin Pie

Yield: nine 10-inch (25-centimeter) pies

Granulated sugar	1 pound	450 grams
Light brown sugar	1 pound	450 grams
Salt	1 ounce	30 grams
Cinnamon	1 ounce	30 grams
Ginger, ground	1/4 ounce	7 grams
Nutmeg, ground	1/4 ounce	7 grams
Bread flour	4 ounces	115 grams
Corn syrup	1 1/2 pounds	680 grams
Pumpkin (solid pack)	7 pounds	3.15 kilograms
Milk	8 pounds	3.6 kilograms
Eggs, beaten	1 quart	1 liter
Pie Crust Dough	1 recipe	1 recipe

1. Mix the sugars, salt, and spices.

2. Stir in the flour.

3. Add the syrup, pumpkin, and milk. Let rest overnight.

4. Blend in eggs.

5. Roll out pie dough and fit into pans.

6. Scale filling at approximately 2 pounds (900 grams) per pie.

7. Bake at 400°F (205°C) for about 45 minutes, or until filling is set but still soft.

You can purchase a pumpkin pie spice blend, or make your own.

Allowing the filling to rest overnight (step 3) lets the flavors fully develop.

TECHNIQUE
Basic pie dough (page 442)
Preparing pies and tarts (pages 444-446)

RECIPE
Pie Crust Dough (page 736)

Preparing the crust.

Toast the pecans in advance for more flavor, or top each pie with a circle of whole pecans which will toast while the pie is baking.

TECHNIQUE
Basic pie dough (page 442)
Preparing pies and tarts (pages 444-446)

RECIPE
Pie Crust Dough (page 736)

Pecan Pie

Yield: six 10-inch (25-centimeter) pies

Pie Crust Dough	*1 recipe*	*1 recipe*
Sugar	*6 ounces*	*170 grams*
Bread flour	*6 ounces*	*170 grams*
Corn syrup	*9 pounds*	*4 kilograms*
Eggs	*3 pounds*	*1.3 kilograms*
Vanilla extract	*1 1/2 fluid ounces*	*45 milliliters*
Salt	*1 1/2 ounces*	*40 grams*
Butter, melted	*10 ounces*	*285 grams*
Pecans	*36 ounces*	*950 grams*

1. Prepare unbaked fluted shells (single crust) and set aside.

2. Combine sugar and flour, then add the corn syrup.

3. Add eggs, vanilla, and salt; mix until incorporated.

4. Stir in melted butter.

5. Divide pecans evenly among the pies.

6. Portion 8 ounces (115 grams) of filling for each pie; pour on top of pecans and bake for 40 minutes at 400°F (200°C) or until filling sets and crust browns.

Lemon Meringue Pie

Make sure that the meringue covers the top of the pie, touching the crust so that weeping and shrinking will not occur.

TECHNIQUE
Basic pie dough (page 442)
Preparing pies and tarts (pages 444-446)

RECIPE
Regular Meringue (page 748)
Pie Crust Dough (page 736)

Yield: four 10-inch pies

Pie Crust Dough	*1/2 recipe*	*1/2 recipe*
Water	*2 quarts*	*2 liters*
Sugar	*2 pounds*	*900 grams*
Salt	*1/2 ounce*	*15 grams*
Lemon juice	*10 fluid ounces*	*300 milliliters*
Lemon rind	*2 ounces*	*60 grams*
Cornstarch	*6 ounces*	*170 grams*
Egg yolks	*8 ounces*	*225 grams*
Butter	*4 ounces*	*115 grams*
Regular Meringue	*1 recipe*	*1 recipe*

(Recipe continued on facing page)

1. Prepare pie dough, roll out, and bake blind.

2. Combine 3 pints (1.4 liters) of water, 1 pound (450 grams) of sugar, the salt, lemon juice, and rind; bring to a boil.

3. Combine 1 pound (450 grams) of sugar and cornstarch, mix together.

4. Combine egg yolks and 1 pint (480 milliliters) of water, add to sugar/cornstarch mixture, mix until blended and reserve.

5. When the lemon juice/water comes to a boil, temper into cornstarch/egg-yolk mixture, put back on the heat and return to boil; remove from heat immediately.

6. Stir in butter, scale 26 ounces (735 grams) into prebaked pie shells and let cool.

7. Using a pastry bag with a #8 or #9 plain tip or a pallet knife, divide regular meringue between 4 pies and swirl into a nice pattern. Dust with powdered sugar and brown off in a 425°F (215°C) oven.

Cherry Pie

Yield: fifteen 10-inch (25-centimeter) pies

Pie Crust Dough	*3 recipes*	*3 recipes*
Cherry juice	*1 1/2 pounds*	*680 grams*
Sugar	*3 pounds*	*1.3 kilograms*
Salt	*1/2 ounce*	*15 grams*
Clear gel	*1 pound*	*450 grams*
Cherries, frozen, thawed, juice reserved	*10 1/2 pounds*	*4.75 kilograms*
Lemons, juiced	*3 each*	*3 each*

1. Prepare unbaked fluted shells and set aside.

2. Combine 9 pounds (4 kilograms) of cherry juice, the sugar, and salt and bring to a boil.

3. Dissolve clear gel in the remaining cherry juice; slowly add to boiling mixture.

4. Bring cherry mixture back up to a boil and cook for 5 minutes until mixture becomes clear; remove from heat.

5. Using a wooden spoon, gently fold in well-drained cherries and lemon juice; cool.

6. Scale 2 pounds (900 grams) of filling for pie, add a top or lattice crust and bake for 1 hour at 400 to 425°F (205 to 220°C) until done and crust browns.

If filling is not sweet enough, more sugar can be added.

TECHNIQUE
Preparing pies and tarts (pages 444-446)

RECIPE
Pie Crust Dough (page 736)

Egg whites are frothy.

This meringue is used to prepare toppings for pies. It is sometimes known as "common" meringue.

TECHNIQUE
Making meringues (page 255)
Separating eggs (page 254)

Regular Meringue

Yield: 3 pounds (1.35 kilograms)

Egg whites	*1 pound*	*450 grams*
Sugar	*2 pounds*	*900 grams*

1. Place the egg whites in a bowl of appropriate size and composition.
2. Beat the egg whites to a frothy stage.
3. Add the sugar and continue beating until soft peaks form.
4. For a hard meringue, continue whipping until hard peaks form.

This meringue is prepared as the first step of an Italian buttercream.

TECHNIQUE
Making meringues (page 255)
Separating eggs (page 254)

Italian Meringue

Yield: 3 ¹/₂ pounds (1.8 kilograms)

Sugar	*2 pounds*	*900 grams*
Water	*8 fluid ounces*	*240 milliliters*
Egg whites	*1 pound*	*450 grams*

1. Combine the sugar and water in a sauce pan over moderate heat and bring the mixture to 238°F (114°C).
2. Place the egg whites in a bowl of appropriate size and composition; beat them to the soft-peak stage.
3. Add the sugar mixture to the egg whites in a thick, steady stream while continuing to whip until the desired consistency is reached.

Swiss Meringue

Yield: 3 pounds (1.35 kilograms)

Egg whites	*1 pound*	*450 grams*
Sugar	*2 pounds*	*900 grams*

1. Place the egg whites and sugar in a bowl of appropriate size and composition.

2. Beat the egg whites and sugar together, holding the bowl over a bain-marie until the mixture reaches 100 to 110°F (35 to 45°C).

3. Beat the egg whites and sugar together to the soft- or the stiff-peak stage as desired.

TECHNIQUE
Making meringue (page 255)
Separating eggs (page 254)

Cream Cheese Icing

Yield: 6 pounds (2.75 kilograms)

Cream cheese	*2 pounds*	*900 grams*
Pastry Cream	*4 pounds*	*1.8 kilograms*
Flavoring	*as needed*	*as needed*

1. Cream the cheese until smooth, soft, and free from lumps.

2. Mix with the pastry cream until blended.

3. Use for filling and icing; refrigerate as needed.

This ia a good icing for carrot cakes or spice cakes.

Vanilla, almond, or lemon extract could be added to taste, if desired.

TECHNIQUE
Creaming mixing method
  (pages 437-439)

RECIPE
Pastry Cream (page 743)

Italian Buttercream

Yield: about 6 pounds (2.75 kilograms)

Sugar	*22 ounces*	*625 grams*
Water	*7 fluid ounces*	*210 milliliters*
Egg whites	*1 pound*	*450 grams*
Butter	*4 pounds*	*1.8 kilograms*
Flavoring	*as needed*	*as needed*

1. Combine 12 ounces (340 grams) of the sugar and the water in a heavy sauce pan and cook to 240°F (115°C).

2. Place the egg whites in a mixing bowl and beat to medium-stiff peaks with the remaining 10 ounces (285 grams) of sugar.

3. In a slow steady stream add boiling sugar to whipped whites.

4. Continue to whip until mixture has cooled to room temperature.

5. Whip in butter by adding in small quantities.

6. Flavor as desired.

Adding butter to meringue.

TECHNIQUE
Buttercreams (pages 455-456)

Combine yolks with sugar.

To make a Bûche Noël, fill the roulade with a chocolate-flavored buttercream and roll up into a log. Frost with chocolate buttercream made to look like a log and decorate with meringue mushrooms.

TECHNIQUE
Foaming mixing method (page 440-442)
Preparing ingredients and equipment
    (pages 429-430)

Sponge Roulade

Yield: 1 sheet pan

Egg yolks	*8 ounces*	*225 grams*
Sugar	*5 ounces*	*60 grams*
Egg whites	*8 ounces*	*225 grams*
Cake flour, sifted	*6 ounces*	*170 grams*

1. Whip egg yolks and 2 ounces (60 grams) of sugar.

2. Whip egg whites and 3 ounces (95 grams) of sugar to a medium peak.

3. Fold beaten egg whites into beaten yolks.

4. Sift cake flour twice and fold in.

5. Spread carefully on parchment paper-lined sheet pans.

6. Bake in a 425°F (220°C) oven for 10 to 15 minutes or until done.

7. Immediately after baking, move the sponge onto a cold sheet pan. Keep from drying out.

TECHNIQUE
Foaming mixing method (page 440-442)
Preparing ingredients and equipment
    (pages 429-430)

Vanilla Sponge Cake

Yield: five 10-inch (25-centimeter)
or eight 8-inch (20-centimeter) cakes

Eggs	*3 3/4 pounds*	*1.7 kilograms*
Sugar	*30 ounces*	*850 grams*
Cake flour	*22 ounces*	*625 grams*
Cornstarch	*8 ounces*	*225 grams*
Butter, melted	*10 ounces*	*285 grams*
Vanilla extract	*1/2 ounce*	*15 grams*

1. Combine eggs and sugar in a mixing bowl; heat to 110°F (45°C) over a double-boiler.

2. Sift flour and cornstarch together twice.

3. Whip eggs until foam is 3 times original volume and starts to recede from the sides of the bowl.

4. Fold in flour/cornstarch mix; fold in butter and vanilla.

5. Bake in a 375°F (190°C) oven for 30 minutes or until top is firm to touch.

Chocolate Sponge Cake

Yield: five 10-inch (25-centimeter)
or eight 8-inch (20-centimeter) cakes

Eggs	3 3/4 pounds	1.7 kilograms
Sugar	30 ounces	850 grams
Cake flour	9 ounces	700 grams
Cocoa powder	5 ounces	140 grams
Baking soda	1/2 teaspoon	1/2 teaspoon
Butter, melted	5 ounces	140 grams

1. Combine eggs and sugar in a mixing bowl, heat to 110°F (45°C) over a double-boiler.

2. Sift flour, cocoa powder, and baking soda together 3 times.

3. Whip eggs until foam is 3 times original volume and starts to recede from the sides of the bowl.

4. Fold in flour mixture; fold in butter.

5. Divide into five 10-inch cake pans that have been greased on the sides and lined with parchment paper circles on the bottom.

6. Bake in a 375°F (190°C) oven for 30 minutes or until golden brown.

VARIATION

Chocolate Nut Sponge: Add 20 percent of the flour weight in finely ground nuts and reduce the flour weight by 10 percent.

Ratios in these recipes equal 2 parts egg, 1 part sugar, 1 part flour.

TECHNIQUE
Foaming mixing method (pages 440-442)
Preparing Ingredients and Equipment
(pages 429-430)

The batter is ready to bake.

TECHNIQUE

Creaming mixing method
    pages 437-439)
Scaling (page 429)
Preparing ingredients and pans
    (pages 429-430)
Zesting citrus (page 231)

Pound Cake

Yield: 2 cakes

Butter	*1 ¼ pounds*	*1.9 kilograms*
Sugar	*1 ½ pounds*	*680 grams*
Lemon rind, grated	*1 ounce*	*30 grams*
Salt	*¼ ounce*	*115 grams*
Cake flour	*1 ¾ pounds*	*800 grams*
Baking powder	*¾ ounce*	*115 grams*
Eggs	*2 pounds*	*900 grams*

1. Cream together butter, sugar, lemon rind, and salt.

2. Sift together cake flour and baking powder.

3. Add eggs alternately with flour mixture in three stages with flour on low speed.

4. Fill into greased pans with a paper on the bottom.

5. Scaling instructions: 1 ¾ pounds of batter (800 grams) per loaf pan; bake at 340°F (170°C).

High-Ratio Cake, White

Yield: fifteen, 10-inch (25-centimeter) cakes

Scale 3 pounds (1.3 kilograms) for a half-sheet cake; fill ¾ full for cupcakes; use 24 ounces (680 grams) for each 10-inch (25-centimeter) pan.

TECHNIQUE

Two-stage mixing method
    (pages 439-440)
Sifting dry ingredients (page 429)
Preparing pans (pages 429-430)

Sugar	*7 pounds*	*3.15 kilograms*
Butter	*22 ounces*	*625 grams*
Salt	*3 ounces*	*85 grams*
Shortening, emulsified	*22 ounces*	*625 grams*
Cake flour	*6 pounds*	*2.75 kilograms*
Baking powder	*6 ounces*	*170 grams*
Milk	*2 quarts*	*2 liters*
Egg whites	*1 ½ quarts*	*1.5 liters*
Eggs	*1 pint*	*480 milliliters*
Vanilla extract	*1 fluid ounce*	*30 milliliters*

(Recipe continued on facing page)

1. Add the sugar, butter, salt, shortening, cake flour, and baking powder with 1 quart (1 liter) of milk.

2. Mix 4 minutes on medium speed, scraping bowl frequently.

3. Add egg whites and eggs, remaining milk, and vanilla to batter in three stages within 6 minutes.

4. Grease sides and paper bottom of pans.

5. Scale off batter into pans.

6. Bake at 360°F (180°C) for 20 minutes or until cake springs back when touched lightly in center.

VARIATION

Yellow High Ratio Cake: Substitute whole eggs for egg whites.

Angel Food Cake

Yield: five 8-inch (20-centimeter) cakes

Egg whites	*2 pounds*	*900 grams*
Vanilla extract	*¹/₂ fluid ounce*	*15 milliliters*
Sugar	*2 pounds*	*450 grams*
Cream of tartar	*¹/₄ ounce*	*8 grams*
Salt	*¹/₄ ounce*	*8 grams*
Cake flour	*13 ounces*	*370 grams*

1. Combine egg whites and vanilla and beat for 5 minutes.

2. Combine 1 pound (450 grams) of sugar, cream of tartar, and salt; add gradually to egg whites and beat until mixture forms a wet peak.

3. Sift rest of sugar and flour together and carefully fold into whites.

4. Scale 15 ounces (420 grams) into ungreased 8-inch (20-centimeter) tube pans.

5. Bake at 350°F (175°C) for 35 to 40 minutes or until cake bounces back on top when touched by a finger.

6. When done turn pans over on a rack; allow cakes to cool before removing from pans.

The egg whites and sugar are fully beaten.

Leaving the pan ungreased is important. The batter needs to cling to something as it bakes or it will collapse.

TECHNIQUE
Foaming method (pages 440–442)
Sifting dry ingredients (page 429)

Ladle a glaze over the cake if you you wish.

The classic frosting for this cake is a Cream Cheese Icing, found on page 749. Or, simply dust the cake with powdered sugar.

Add up to 1 pound (450 grams) of crushed pineapple in step 3 if you wish.

TECHNIQUE
*Creaming mixing method
(pages 437-439)
Preparing pans (pages 429-430)*

Carrot Cake

Yield: six, 10-inch (25-centimeter) cakes

Butter	*2 pounds*	*900 grams*
Granulated sugar	*2 pounds*	*900 grams*
Light brown sugar	*2 pounds*	*900 grams*
Eggs	*1 3/4 pounds*	*780 grams*
Carrots, grated	*4 pounds*	*1.8 kilograms*
Raisins	*1 1/4 pounds*	*720 grams*
Lemon juice	*4 fluid ounces*	*120 milliliters*
Orange juice	*4 fluid ounces*	*120 milliliters*
Lemon zest	*2 ounces*	*60 grams*
Orange zest	*2 ounces*	*60 grams*
All-purpose flour	*3 3/4 pounds*	*1.7 kilograms*
Baking powder	*1 1/4 ounces*	*40 grams*
Baking soda	*1 ounce*	*40 grams*
Salt	*1 ounce*	*30 grams*
Cinnamon	*1 ounce*	*30 grams*
Walnuts, chopped	*1 1/4 pounds*	*570 grams*

1. Cream butter with both sugars until fluffy.

2. Add eggs slowly, scraping bowl down carefully after each addition.

3. Add carrots, raisins, juices, and zests, mixing until incorporated.

4. Sift together the flour, baking powder, baking soda, salt, and cinnamon; then add the walnuts and blend in.

5. Add the dry ingredients to the batter, mixing well.

6. Portion in prepared pans and bake at 325°F (160°C) for 50 to 60 minutes or until done.

7. Remove from pan when cool.

Roman Apple Cake

Yield: 1 sheet pan or six 8-inch (20-centimeter) cakes

Butter	12 ounces	340 grams
Sugar	2 1/2 pounds	1.15 kilograms
Salt	1/2 ounces	15 grams
Mace, ground	1/2 teaspoon	1/2 teaspoon
Cinnamon	1/2 teaspoon	1/2 teaspoon
Eggs	8 ounces	225 grams
Milk	1 pint	480 milliliters
Baking soda	1 ounce	30 grams
Cake flour	42 ounces	1.9 kilograms
Baking powder	1 ounce	30 grams
Apples, peeled, cored, and chopped	3 pounds	1.3 kilograms

1. Cream together the butter, sugar, salt, and spices.

2. Add eggs slowly, scraping the bowl occasionally.

3. Alternately add remaining dry ingredients and milk in several additions.

4. Add chopped apples.

5. Spread onto a prepared sheet pan or scale at 14 ounces (400 grams) for 8-inch (20-centimeter) layers.

6. Bake at 350°F (175°C) for 30 minutes or until firm to touch and cake pulls away from sides of pan. (Timing depends on size of pan being used.)

Coring an apple.

Rome apples are a good choice for this cake. Other suitable apples include Cortland, Winesap, or York.

TECHNIQUE
*Creaming mixing method
(pages 437-439)*

Splitting a sponge cake into horizontal layers.

Slice a prepared sponge cake horizontally into 2 layers about $^1/_2$ inch (1.25 centimeters) thick. You may use a prebaked shortbread. Whatever crust you select, be sure it is fully baked before adding the cream cheese filling.

This cake can be made without cornstarch by adding 5 more eggs.

TECHNIQUE
*Creaming mixing method
(pages 437-439)
Using a water bath (pages 258-259)*

Cheesecake

Yield: two 10-inch cakes

Cornstarch	*4 ounces*	*115 grams*
Sugar	*1 $^1/_2$ pounds*	*680 grams*
Cream cheese	*5 pounds*	*2.25 kilograms*
Eggs	*1 pound*	*450 grams*
Egg yolks	*2 ounces*	*60 grams*
Vanilla extract	*1 fluid ounce*	*30 milliliters*
Lemon, zest, grated	*1 each*	*1 each*
Heavy cream	*10 fluid ounces*	*300 milliliters*
Vanilla sponge cake	*2 slices*	*2 slices*

1. Premix the cornstarch with the sugar; using a paddle, cream together the sugar mixture and the cream cheese.

2. Combine eggs, egg yolks, vanilla, and lemon zest; add gradually, one-quarter at a time, to the cream-cheese mixture, making sure to scrape sides, bottom of the bowl, and the paddle after each addition.

3. Add heavy cream and mix to incorporate.

4. Fill cake pans that have been lined with parchment paper circles and a prebaked $^1/_2$-inch-thick layer of sponge or another type of crust.

5. Using a water bath, bake at 300°F (150°C) for about 60 to 90 minutes or until the center is set.

6. Chill. Unmold the next day.

VARIATIONS

Marble Cheesecake: Add cocoa powder or melted chocolate to a small amount of batter; using a small parchment bag, pipe into cheesecake and swirl in.

For Graham Cracker Crust: Use 5 pounds (2.25 kilograms) crushed graham crackers, 1 pound (450 grams) sugar, 1 pound (450 grams) melted butter, and 4 ounces (115 grams) egg whites. Mix together, press into form and prebake at 350 to 375°F (175 to 190°C) for 5 to 7 minutes until set. Use 8 ounces (225 grams) per 10-inch pan.

Chiffon Cheesecake

Yield: two 10-inch (25-centimeter) cakes

Bakers' cheese	*2 1/2 pounds*	*1.15 kilograms*
Sugar	*1 pound*	*450 grams*
Vegetable oil, vegetable shortening, or margarine	*11 fluid ounces*	*330 milliliters*
Egg whites	*25 ounces*	*700 grams*
Water, hot, as needed	*1/2 to 1 pound*	*225 to 450 grams*
Vanilla extract	*1 fluid ounce*	*30 milliliters*
Lemon extract	*1 teaspoon*	*1 teaspoon*
Milk powder	*4 ounces*	*115 grams*
Bread flour	*4 ounces*	*115 grams*
Cornstarch	*2 1/2 ounces*	*70 grams*
Egg whites	*1 pound*	*450 grams*
Shortbread	*1 pound*	*450 grams*

Spreading the filling mixture.

1. Combine cheese, sugar, oil, and 9 ounces (255 grams) of egg whites; mix until smooth.

2. Add hot water in 3 parts, mixing until smooth (add only enough water to get cake-batter consistency).

3. Add vanilla and lemon extracts.

4. Sift together milk powder, flour, and cornstarch. Stir into the batter until smooth.

5. Beat the remaining egg whites and sugar to make a meringue, and fold into cheese mixture.

6. Line the bottom of a springform pan with shortbread dough. Pour in the batter and smooth into an even layer.

7. Bake in a water bath at (175°C) for 60 minutes or until done.

If you prefer, use a pasteurized egg product to replace the egg whites.

The water should be at or near 180°F (82°C) in step 2.

Technique
Making a hot water bath (pages 258-259)
Making meringue (page 255)

Appendices

Fruit or Vegetable	Jan.	Feb.	Mar.	Apr.	May	June	July	Aug.	Sept.	Oct.	Nov.	Dec.
Apples	☆								☆	☆	☆	☆
Apricots					○	●	●	○				
Artichokes			○	○	○	○						
Arugula	○	○	○	○	○☆	○☆	○☆	○☆	○☆	○	○	○
Asparagus			○	○★	○★	○☆						
Avocados	○	○	○	○	○	○	○	○				○
Beans, shell			○☆	○☆	○☆	○☆	○☆	○☆	○☆			
Beans, snap					○☆	○☆	○☆	○☆	○☆	○☆		
Beets, gold						○	○	○	○	○☆	○☆	○☆
Beets, red						●	●	●	○☆	○☆	○☆	
Berries						○	○	○	○	○		
Blood oranges	○	○	○									
Bok choy									☆	☆		
Boysenberries						☆	☆	☆				
Broccoli						○☆	○☆	○☆	○☆	○☆	○☆	○☆
Broccoli rabe	○	○	○	○			☆	☆	☆	☆	☆	○☆
Brussels sprouts	○	○	○						○☆	○☆	○	
Bulb fennel	○	○	○	○	○				☆		○	○
Cabbages	○	○	○	○	○	○	○	○	○	○	○	○
Cantaloupes						○	○☆	○☆	○☆	○		
Carrots	○	○	○	○	○	○	○	○	○	○	○	○
Cauliflower						○	○	○	○	○		
Celeriac	○	○	○	○	○	○	○	○	○	○	○	○
Chard	○	○	○	○	○☆	○☆	○☆	○☆	○☆	○☆	○	○
Chayote	●	●									●	●
Cherries						☆	☆					
Chinese cabbage										○	○	
Collards								○☆	○☆	○☆	○☆	
Corn						☆	★	★	★	☆		
Cucumbers	○	○	○	○	●	●★	●★	○	○	○	○	○
Eggplant, baby				○	○	○☆	○☆	○☆	○☆	○		
Eggplant, white						○☆	○☆	○☆				
Endive									○	○	○	○
Escarole	○	○	○	○	○☆	☆	☆	☆	☆	○☆	○	○
Fiddlehead ferns		☆	☆	☆	☆							
Figs							○	○	○	○		
Frisée	○	○	○	○	○	○	○	○	○	○	○☆	○☆
Gooseberries							☆					
Gourds									☆	☆	☆	☆
Grapes						○	○	○	○	○	○	○
Herbs			○	○☆	○☆	○☆	○☆	○☆	○☆	○	○	○
Jicama	○	○	○	○	○	○	○	○	○	○	○	○
Kale									☆	☆	☆	☆
Kiwi	○	○	○			○	○	○	○	○	○	○
Kohlrabi						●☆	●★	○☆				
Kumquats	○	○	○									
Leeks										○	○	○

California: ○   Local ☆
California, Peak: ●   Local, Peak ★

Standard items such as potatoes and onions are generally available year-round and are not included in this chart.

(continued on facing page)

Fruit or Vegetable	Jan.	Feb.	Mar.	Apr.	May	June	July	Aug.	Sept.	Oct.	Nov.	Dec.
Leeks, baby						○	○	○	○	○	○	○
Lettuce, baby			○	○	○	○	○	○	○	○	○	
Lettuce, bibb	○	○	○	○	○	○☆	○☆	○☆	○	○	○	
Lettuce, iceberg	○	○	○	○	○	○	○	○	○	○	○	○
Lettuce, leaf	○	○	○	○	○	○	○	○	○	○	○	○
Mache	○	○	○☆	○★	○★	○☆	○☆	○☆	○	○	○	○
Mangoes	○	○	○	○	○	○	○	○				
Mustard greens							○☆	○☆	○☆			
Nectarines						○	●	●	○			
Okra							○	○	○	○		
Papayas	○	●	●	●	○	○	○	○	○	○	○	○
Parsnips				○	○	○	○	○☆	○☆	○☆	○	○
Peaches							☆	★	☆			
Pears	○☆							★	★	★	○☆	○☆
Peas, green	○	○	○	○	○	○	○					
Peas, snow	○	○	○	○	○	○	○					
Peppers, green bell						○	○☆	○☆	○☆	○	○	○
Peppers, red bell								○☆	○☆	○☆		
Pineapples	○	○	●	●	●	●	●	○			○	○
Plums							☆	★	☆			
Potatoes, baby red					○	○☆	○☆	○☆	○☆	○		
Radicchio	○	○	○	○		☆	☆	☆	☆	○☆	○	○
Raspberries						☆	☆	☆	☆	☆		
Romaine	○	○	○	○★	○★	○☆	○☆	○☆	○	○	○	○
Rutabagas									☆	☆	☆	☆
Salsify	○	○	○	○						○	○	○
Scallions								☆	☆			
Spinach	○	○	○	○	○★	○★	○☆	○☆	○	○	○	○
Squash, acorn									☆	☆	☆	☆
Squash, baby							○☆	○☆	○☆	○☆	○☆	
Squash, butternut									☆	☆	☆	☆
Squash, cheese									☆	☆	☆	☆
Squash, crookneck							○☆	○☆	○☆	○☆		
Squash, dumpling									☆	☆	☆	☆
Squash, golden									☆	☆	☆	☆
Squash, patty pan							○☆	○☆	○☆	○☆		
Squash, spaghetti									☆	☆	☆	☆
Squash, zucchini				○	○	○	○☆	○☆	○☆	○☆	○	
Strawberries						☆	☆	☆	☆	☆		
Sunchokes	○	○	○	○	○						○	○
Tangerines	○	○	○									
Tomatoes						○☆	○☆	○☆	○☆	○☆	○☆	
Tomatoes, cherry							○☆	○☆	○☆	○☆	○☆	
Turnips	○	○	○	○	○	○	○	○	○☆	○☆	○☆	○
Watercress	○	○	●	●	○	○	○	○	○	○	○	○
Watermelons						○	○	○	○	☆		

California: ○   Local ☆
California, Peak: ●   Local, Peak ★

Standard items such as potatoes and onions are generally available year-round and are not included in this chart.

FOODBORNE ILLNESSES

Disease and (Incubation Period*)	Symptoms	Cause	Food Involved	Preventative Measures
Botulism (12–36 hours)	Sore throat, vomiting, blurred vision, cramps, diarrhea, difficulty breathing, central nervous system damaged (possible paralysis). Fatality rate up to 70%.	*Clostridium botulinum:* anaerobic bacteria that form spores with high resistance to heat. Found in animal intestines, water, and soil.	Refrigerated, low-acid foods or improperly canned foods, such as spinach, tuna, green beans, beets, fermented foods, and smoked products. Rare in commercially canned foods.	Toxin is sensitive to heat, so maintain a high temperature while canning food and boil 20 minutes before serving. Do not use food in swollen cans or home-canned food for commercial use.
Staphylococcus (2–4 hours)	Vomiting, nausea, diarrhea, cramps.	*Staphylococcus aureus:* facultative bacteria found in the nose, throat, and in skin infections of humans.	Foods that are high in protein, moist, handled much, and left in the danger zone. Milk, egg custards, turkey stuffing, chicken/tuna/potato salads, gravies, reheated food.	Store foods below 40°F (4°C) and reheat thoroughly to 165°F (74°C). People with infected cuts, burns, or respiratory illnesses should not handle food. Keep food out of the danger zone.
Ergotism (varies)	Hallucinations, convulsions, gangrene of extremities.	Ergot: a mold that grows on wheat and rye.	Wheat and rye.	Do not use moldy wheat and rye
Chemical Poisoning (minutes to hours)	Varied	Pesticides on fruits and vegetables, cyanide in silver polish, zinc inside tin cans, copper pans.		Wash fruits and vegetables before using; discard polish with cyanide; wash utensils after polishing; store pesticides away from food; avoid cooking and storing foods in cans since zinc is leached out of tin by acidic foods and is poisonous; don't allow food to touch unlined copper.
Plant and Animal Poisoning (varies—often rapid)	Varies.	Aklaloids; organic acids.		Avoid poisons: Identify wild mushrooms. Don't ingest rhubarb leaves, too much nutmeg, green-skinned potatoes, fava leaves, raw soybeans, blowfish, moray eel, or shark liver.
Salmonellosis (6–48 hours)	Headache, diarrhea, cramps, fever. Can be fatal or lead to arthritis, meningitis, and typhoid.	*Salmonella:* aerobic bacillus that lives and grows in the intestines of humans, animals, birds, and insects.	Egg, poultry, shellfish, meat, soup, sauces, gravies, milk products, warmed-over food.	Reheat leftovers to an internal temperature of 165°F (74°C). Since *Salmonella* can be killed by high temperatures, cook to proper temperatures. Eliminate rodents and flies, wash hands after using bathroom, avoid cross-contamination.

*Incubation period is the time between infection and onset of symptoms.

(continued on facing page)

FOODBORNE ILLNESSES *(continued)*

Disease and (Incubation Period*)	Symptoms	Cause	Food Involved	Preventative Measures
Shigellosis (12–48 hours)	Diarrhea, cramps, fever, dehydration.	*Shigella sonnei* and other species found in feces of infected humans, food, and water.	Beans, contaminated milk, tuna/turkey/ macaroni salads, apple cider, and mixed, moist foods.	Safe water sources, strict control of insects and rodents, good personal hygiene.
Bacillus cereus (8–16 hours)	Cramps, diarrhea, nausea, vomiting.	*Bacillus cereus:* anaerobic bacteria that produce spores and are found in soil and any food.	Cereal products, cornstarch, rice, custards, sauces, meat loaf.	Spores are able to survive heating, so reheat to 165°F (74°C) and keep foods out of the danger zone.
Streptococcus (1–4 days)	Nausea, vomiting, diarrhea	Various species of *streptococcus* bacteria which are facultative anaerobes. Some are transmitted by animals and workers contaminated with feces, others from the nose and throat of infected humans.	Milk, pudding, ice cream, eggs, meat pie, egg/potato salads, poultry.	Cook food thoroughly and chill rapidly. Strict personal hygiene. Use pasteurized dairy products.
Trichinosis (4–28 days)	Fever, diarrhea, sweating, muscle pain, vomiting, skin lesions.	*Trichinella spiralis:* a spiral worm that lives in the intestines where it matures and lays eggs and later invades muscle tissue. Transmitted by infected swine and rats.	Improperly cooked pork allows larvae to live.	Cook pork to 150°F (65°C). Avoid recontamination of raw meats. If frying, cook to 170°F (75°C).
Infectious Hepatitis (10–50 days)	Jaundice, fever, cramps, nausea, lethargy.	Hepatitis virus A: grows in feces of infected humans and human carriers. Transmitted by water and from person to person, and infects the liver.	Shellfish from polluted water, milk, whipped cream, cold cuts, potato salads.	Cook clams, and shellfish, etc., thoroughly to a temperature exceeding 150°F (65°C). Heat-treat and disinfect suspected water and milk. Enforce strict personal hygiene.
Perfringens (9–15 hours)	Diarrhea, nausea, cramps, possible fever, vomiting (rare).	*Clostridium perfringens:* spore-forming anaerobic bacteria that can withstand most cooking temperatures and are found in soil, dust, and the intestinal tract of animals.	Reheated meats, raw meat, raw vegetables, soups, gravies, stews.	Cool meat that is to be eaten later quickly and reheat to 165°F (74°C). Avoid cross-contamination of raw meat and cooked meat. The only way to kill spores is to pressure cook at 15 lb. steam pressure to reach 250°F (120°C).

*Incubation period is the time between infection and onset of symtoms.

FIRST-AID SUPPLIES

Adhesive strips in assorted sizes
Bandage compresses
Sterile gauze dressings, individually wrapped
Rolled gauze bandage
First-aid adhesive tape
Cotton swabs (for applying antiseptic or removing particles from eye)
Tourniquet
Tongue depressors (for small splints)
Scissors
Tweezers

Needle (for removing splinters)
Rubbing alcohol (for sterilizing instruments)
Mild antiseptic (for wounds)
Antibiotic cream
Syrup of ipecac (to induce vomiting)
Petroleum jelly
Aspirin or acetaminophen
Emergency numbers (post numbers for ambulance, fire, hospital, poison center, near phone)

COOKING RATIOS AND TIMES FOR SELECTED GRAINS

Type	Ratio of Grain to Liquid (Cups)	Approximate Yield (Cups)*	Cooking Time
Barley, pearled	1:2	4	35 to 45 minutes
Barley groats	1:2 $1/2$	4	50 minutes to 1 hour
Buckwheat groats (Kasha)	1:1 $1/2$ to 2	2	12 to 20 minutes
Couscous**	——	1 $1/2$ to 2	20 to 25 minutes
Hominy, whole***	1:2 $1/2$	3	2 $1/2$ to 3 hours
Hominy grits	1:4	3	25 minutes
Millet	1:2	3	30 to 35 minutes
Oat groats	1:2	2	45 minutes to 1 hour
Polenta	1:3 to 3 $1/2$	3	35 to 45 minutes
Rice, Arborio (risotta)	1:3	3	20 to 30 minutes
Rice, basmati	1:1 $1/2$	3	25 minutes
Rice, converted	1:1 $3/4$	4	25 to 30 minutes
Rice, long-grain, brown	1:3	4	40 minutes
Rice, long-grain, white	1:1 $1/2$ to 1 $3/4$	3	18 to 20 minutes
Rice, short-grain, brown	1:2 $1/2$	4	35 to 40 minutes
Rice, short-grain, white	1:1 to 1 $1/2$	3	20 to 30 minutes
Rice, wild	1:3	4	30 to 45 minutes
Rice, wild, pecan	1:1 $3/4$	4	20 minutes
Wheat berries	1:3	2	1 hour
Wheat, bulgur, soaked†	1:4	2	2 hours
Wheat, bulgur, pilaf†	1:2 $1/2$	2	15 to 20 minutes
Wheat, cracked	1:2	3	20 minutes

*From 1 cup of uncooked grain.
**Grain should be soaked briefly in tepid water and then drained before it is steamed.
***Grain should be soaked overnight in cold water and then drained before it is cooked.
†Grain may be cooked by covering it with boiling water and soaking it for 2 hours or cooking it by the pilaf method.

APPROXIMATE SOAKING AND COOKING TIMES
FOR SELECTED DRIED LEGUMES

Type	Soaking Time	Cooking Time
Adzuki beans	4 hours	1 hour
Black beans	4 hours	1 $^1/_2$ hours
Black-eyed peas*	——	1 hour
Chickpeas	4 hours	2 to 2 $^1/_2$ hours
Fava beans	12 hours	3 hours
Great Northern beans	4 hours	1 hour
Kidney beans (red or white)	4 hours	1 hour
Lentils*	——	30 to 40 minutes
Lima beans	4 hours	1 to 1 $^1/_2$ hours
Mung beans	4 hours	1 hour
Navy beans	4 hours	2 hours
Peas, split*	——	30 minutes
Peas, whole	4 hours	40 minutes
Pigeon peas*	——	30 minutes
Pink peas	4 hours	1 hour
Pinto beans	4 hours	1 to 1 $^1/_2$ hours
Soybeans	12 hours	3 to 3 $^1/_2$ hours

* Soaking is not necessary.

WEIGHT MEASURES CONVERSIONS*

U.S.	Metric (rounded)
$^1/_4$ ounce	8 grams
$^1/_2$ ounce	15 grams
1 ounce	30 grams
4 ounces	115 grams
8 ounces ($^1/_2$ pound)	225 grams
16 ounces (1 pound)	450 grams
32 ounces (2 pounds)	900 grams
40 ounces (2 $^1/_2$ pounds)	1 kilogram

*Values have been rounded.

VOLUME MEASURES CONVERSIONS*

U.S.	Metric (rounded)
1 teaspoon	5 milliliters
1 tablespoon	15 milliliters
1 fluid ounce (2 tablespoons)	30 milliliters
2 fluid ounces ($^1/_4$ cup)	60 milliliters
8 fluid ounces (1 cup)	240 milliliters
16 fluid ounces (1 pint)	480 milliliters
32 fluid ounces (1 quart)	950 milliliters (.95 liter)
128 fluid ounces (1 gallon)	3.75 liters

*Values have been rounded.

TEMPERATURE CONVERSIONS*

Degrees Fahrenheit (°F)	Degrees Celcius (C°)
32°	0°
40°	4°
140°	60°
150°	65°
160°	70°
170°	75°
212°	100°
275°	135°
300°	150°
325°	165°
350°	175°
375°	190°
400°	205°
425°	220°
450°	230°
475°	245°
500°	260°

*Values have been rounded.

INFORMATION/HINTS AND TIPS FOR CALCULATIONS

1 gallon = 4 quarts = 8 pints = 16 cups (8 fluid ounces) = 128 fluid ounces.

1 fifth bottle = approximately 1 $^1/_2$ pints or exactly 25.6 fluid ounces.

1 measuring cup holds 8 fluid ounces (A coffee cup generally holds 6 fluid ounces).

1 egg white = 2 fluid ounces (average).

1 lemon = 1 to 1 $^1/_4$ fluid ounces of juice.

1 orange = 3 to 3 $^1/_2$ fluid ounces of juice.

To convert ounces and pounds to grams: multiply ounces X 28.35; multiply pounds X 453.59.

To convert Fahrenheit to Celcius: subtract 32 from °F X 5 ÷ 9 = °C.

To round to the next closest whole number, round up if final decimal is 5 or greater; round down if less than 5.

WEIGHTS AND MEASURES EQUIVALENCIES

Dash	less than $^1/_8$ teaspoon
3 teaspoons	1 tablespoon ($^1/_2$ fluid ounce)
2 tablespoons	$^1/_8$ cup (1 fluid ounce)
4 tablespoons	$^1/_4$ cup (2 fluid ounces)
5 $^1/_3$ tablespoons	1/3 cup (2 $^2/_3$ fluid ounces)
8 tablespoons	$^1/_2$ cup (4 fluid ounces)
10 $^2/_3$ tablespoons	$^2/_3$ cup (5 $^1/_3$ fluid ounces)
12 tablespoons	$^3/_4$ cup (6 fluid ounces)
14 tablespoons	7/8 cup (7 fluid ounces)
16 tablespoons	1 cup
1 gill	$^1/_2$ cup
1 cup	8 fluid ounces (240 milliliters)
2 cups	1 pint (480 milliliters)
2 pints	1 quart (approximately 1 liter)
4 quarts	1 gallon (3.75 liters)
8 quarts	1 peck (8.8 liters)
4 pecks	1 bushel (35 liters)
1 ounce	28.35 grams (rounded to 30)
16 ounces	1 pound (453.59 grams rounded to 450)
1 kilogram	2.2 pounds

Glossary

Abalone: A mollusk with a single shell and a large, edible adductor muscle similar to that of scallops.

Aboyeur (Fr.): Expediter or announcer; a station in the brigade system. The aboyeur accepts orders from the dining room, relays them to the appropriate stations of the kitchen, and checks each plate before it leaves the kitchen.

Accelerate growth phase: The part of a pathogens life cycle in which the rate of reproduction and growth exceeds the death rate.

Acid: A substance having a sour or sharp flavor. Most foods are somewhat acidic. Foods generally referred to as "acids" include citrus juice, vinegar, and wine. A substance's degree of acidity is measured on the pH scale; acids have a pH of less than 7.

Acid/base balance: The state known as "neutral"; maintaining this state is the regulatory function of many minerals considered essential in a healthy, balanced diet.

Actual cost: A determination of an item's cost that must include cost of raw materials, labor, overhead, and any other operating expense related to that items procurement and eventual sale.

ADA (Americans with Disabilities Act): Legislation intended to assure equal access to public areas to those with disabilities. Includes building codes and other standards that must be adhered to in all new construction or remodeling.

Adulterated food: Food that has been contaminated to the point that it is considered unfit for human consumption.

Aged beef: Beef allowed to hang in a climate controlled area for a period of time in order to allow enzymes to act on meat fibers, changing texture, flavor, and color of meat.

Aerobic bacteria: Bacteria that require the presence of oxygen to function.

Aïoli (Fr.): Garlic mayonnaise. (Also, in Italian, allioli; in Spanish, aliolio.)

Albumen: The major protein in egg whites.

A la carte (Fr.): A menu in which the patron makes individual selections from various menu categories.

A l'anglaise: (1) Foods that have been breaded and fried; (2) foods that have been boiled.

A la meunière: Dishes prepare in the style of the miller's wife (dusted with flour, sautéed, served with hot butter, lemon and parsley).

Al dente (It.): To the tooth; to cook an item, such as pasta or vegetables, until it is tender but still firm, not soft.

Alkali (noun); alkaline (adj.): A substance that tests at higher than 7 on the pH scale. Alkalis are sometimes described as having a slightly soapy flavor. Olives and baking soda are some of the few alkaline foods.

Allumette: Vegetables, potatoes, or other items cut into pieces the size and shape of match sticks, inch x inch x 1 to 2 inches is the standard.

Alternivore: An individual who, while not a strict vegetarian, often prefers to order a meatless option from the menu.

Aluminum: A soft metal, frequently used to prepare cooking vessels.

American cuisine: A cooking style featuring the foods, dishes, and cooking styles indigenous to various parts of the United States.

Amino acid: The basic molecular component of proteins, one of the essential dietary components.

Anaerobic bacteria: Bacteria that do not require oxygen to function.

Animal husbandry: The practice of breeding and raising a variety of farm animals so as to maximize production of meat, dairy, and eggs.

Angel food cake: A type of sponge cake made with egg whites that are beaten until stiff.

Ante-mortem: An inspection of meats and poultry after they have been slaughtered to assure that the food is wholesome, safe, and fit for human consumption.

Antioxidants: Non-caloric nutrients (vitamins, minerals, and enzymes) capable of attaching themselves to free radicals. This has the effect of preventing free radicals from damaging healthy cells.

AP/As purchased weight: The weight of an item before trimming or other preparation (as opposed to edible portion weight or EP).

Appareil: A prepared mixture of ingredients used alone or as an ingredient in another preparation.

Appetizer: Light foods served before a meal. These may be hot or cold, plated or served as finger food.

Aquaculture: The cultivation or farm-raising of fish or shellfish.

Arkansas stone: A sharpening stone, often with a triple face, mounted in a rotating base.

Aromatics: Plant ingredients, such as herbs and spices, used to enhance the flavor and fragrance of food.

Arrowroot: A powdered starch made from a tropical root. Used primarily as a thickener. Remains clear when cooked.

Artisinal: Food produces practicing traditional methods for baking, cheese making, etc. Usually production is small and distribution is local.

Aspic gelée (Fr.): A clear jelly made from stock (or occasionally from fruit or vegetable juices) thickened with gelatin. Used to coat foods or cubed and used as a garnish.

Atherosclerosis: A condition characterized by the fatty deposits known as plague on the interior of artery walls.

Bacteria: Microscopic organisms. Some have beneficial properties, others can cause food-borne illnesses when contaminated foods are ingested.

Bain-marie: A water bath used to cook foods gently by surrounding the cooking vessel with simmering water. Also, a set of nesting pots with single, long handles used as a double boiler. Also, steam table inserts.

Bake blind; baking blind: To partially or completely bake an unfilled pastry crust.

Baking: A cooking method used to describe foods prepared in an oven; similar to roasting.

Baking powder: A chemical leavener made with an acidic ingredient and an alkaline one; most commonly these are sodium bicarbonate (baking soda) and cream of tartar. When exposed to liquid, it produces carbon dioxide gas, which leavens doughs and batters. Double-acting baking powder contains ingredients that produce two leavening reactions, one upon exposure to liquid, the second when heated.

Baking soda: Sodium bicarbonate, a leavening agent that may be used in combination with an acidic ingredient such as sour milk or as a component of baking powder.

Barbecue; barbecuing: A cooking method involving grilling food over a wood or charcoal fire. Usually some sort of marinade or sauce is brushed on the item during cooking.

Bard; barding: To cover an item with slabs or strips of fat, such as bacon or fatback, to baste it during roasting. The fat is usually tied on with butcher's twine.

Barquette: A boat-shaped tart or tartlet, which may have a sweet or savory filling.

Basic pie dough: A short dough made by combing flour, a fat, and water. Use to line pie and tart pans for sweet and savory tarts and pies.

Baste: To moisten food during cooking with pan drippings, sauce, or other liquid. Basting prevents food from drying out.

Batch cooking: The practice of preparing or reheating foods in smaller batches to maximize nutrient retention and minimize loss through waste.

Bâton/Bâtonnet (Fr.): Items cut into pieces somewhat larger than allumette or julienne; $1/4$-inch x $1/4$-inch x 2 to $2 1/2$-inches is the standard. Translated to English as "stick" or "small stick."

Batter: A mixture of flour and liquid, with sometimes the inclusion of other ingredients. Batters vary in thickness but are generally semi-liquid and thinner than doughs. Used in such preparations as cakes, quick breads, pancakes, and crêpes.

Bavarian cream/Bavaroise: A type of custard made from heavy cream and eggs; it is sweetened, flavored, and stabilized with gelatin.

Béarnaise: A classic emulsion sauce similar to hollandaise made with egg yolks; a reduction of white wine, shallots, and tarragon; and butter finished with tarragon and chervil.

Béchamel: A white sauce made of milk thickened with light roux and flavored with onion. It is one of the grand sauces.

Bench proof: In yeast dough production, the rising stage that occurs after the dough is panned and just before baking.

Beta carotene: A non-caloric nutrient found predominantly in fruits and vegetables such as carrots, squashes, leafy greens and cabbages; a Vitamin A precursor, associated with a healthful diet and possibly a decreased chance of developing various illness, such as cancer or cardio-vascular disease.

Beurre blanc (Fr.): "White butter." A classic emulsified sauce made with a reduction of white wine and shallots thickened with whole butter and possibly finished with fresh herbs or other seasonings.

Beurre manié (Fr.): "Kneaded butter." A mixture of equal parts by weight of whole butter and flour, used to thicken gravies and sauces.

Beurre noir (Fr.): "Black butter." Butter that has been cooked to a very dark brown or nearly black; a sauce made with browned butter, vinegar, chopped parsley, and capers. It is usually served with fish.

Beurre noisette (Fr.): "Hazelnut butter" or "brown butter." Whole butter that has been heated until browned.

Binder: An ingredient or appareil used to thicken a sauce or hold together another mixture of ingredients.

Biological contamination: The infection or intoxication of foods with pathogens including the following: bacteria, yeast or fungus, virus, or parasites.

Bisque: A soup based on crustaceans or a vegetable puree. It is classically thickened with rice and usually finished with cream.

Bivalve: A mollusk with two hinged shells. Examples are clams and oysters.

Blanch; blanched: To cook an item briefly in boiling water or hot fat before finishing or storing it.

Black steel: A metal used to prepare saute pans and woks; relatively thin and able to respond quickly to temperature changes.

Blade: The portion of a knife that is used for cutting, slicing, and chopping.

Blanquette: A white stew, usually of veal but sometimes of chicken or lamb. It is served after the sauce has been thickened with a liaison.

Blitz puff pastry: A dough similar to pie dough, but which contains a higher percentage of fat. It is rolled and folded in the same manner as traditional puff pastry.

Bloom: To soften gelatin in warm liquid before use.

Blue steel: A steel (sometimes referred to as rolled steel) often used for omelet, crepe, and saute pans. Typically not coated. Responds quickly to changes in cooking temperature.

Boil; boiling: A cooking method in which items are immersed in liquid at or above the boiling point ($212°F/100°C$).

Bolster: A collar or shank at the point on a knife where the blade meets the handle.

Boning knife: A thin-bladed knife used for separating raw meat from the bone; its blade is usually about 6 inches long.

Botulism: A food-borne illness caused by toxins produced by the anaerobic bacterium Clostridium botulinum.

Boucher (Fr.): Butcher.

Bouillabaisse: A hearty fish and shellfish stew flavored with saffron. A traditional specialty of Marseilles, France.

Bouillon (Fr.): Broth.

Boulanger (Fr.): Baker, specifically of breads and other nonsweetened doughs.

Bouquet garni: A small bundle of herbs tied with string. It is used to flavor stocks, braises, and other preparations. Usually contains bay leaf, parsley, thyme, and possibly other aromatics.

Boxed meat: Meat which has been slaughtered, butchered, packaged and boxed before being shipped to purveyors, retailers, and restaurants.

Braise; braising: A cooking method in which the main item, usually meat, is seared in fat, then simmered in stock or another liquid in a covered vessel.

Bran: The outer layer of a cereal grain and the part highest in fiber.

Brazier/Brasier: A pan, designed specifically for braising, that usually has two handles and a tight-fitting lid. Often is round but may be square or rectangular.

Brigade system: The kitchen organization system instituted by Auguste Escoffier. Each position has a station and well-defined responsibilities.

Brine: A salt, water, and seasonings solution used to preserve foods.

Brioche: A rich yeast dough traditionally baked in a fluted pan with a distinctive topknot of dough.

Brisket: A cut of beef from the lower forequarter, best suited for long-cooking preparations like braising. Corned beef is cured beef brisket.

Broil; broiling: A cooking method in which items are cooked by a radiant heat source placed above the food.

Broiler: The piece of equipment used to broil foods.

Broth: A flavorful, aromatic liquid made by simmering water or stock with meat, vegetables, and/or spices and herbs.

Brown stock: An amber liquid produced by simmering browned bones and meat (usually veal or beef) with vegetables and aromatics (including caramelized mirepoix).

Brown sauce: See Espagnol sauce.

Brunoise (Fr.): Small dice; $1/8$-inch square is the standard. For a brunoise cut, items are first cut in julienne, then cut crosswise. For a fine brunoise, $1/16$-inch square, cut items first in fine julienne.

Butcher: A chef or purveyor who is responsible for butchering meats, poultry, and occasionally fish. In the brigade system, the butcher may also be responsible for breading meat and fish items and other mise en place operations involving meat.

Buttercream: A mixture of butter, sugar, and eggs or custard; it is used to garnish cakes and pastries.

Butterfly: To cut an item (usually meat or seafood) and open out the edges like a book or the wings of a butterfly.

Buttermilk: A dairy beverage liquid with a slightly sour flavor similar to that of yogurt. Traditionally, the liquid by-product of butter churning, now usually made by culturing skim milk.

Calorie: A unit used to measure food energy. It is the amount of energy needed to raise the temperature of 1 gram of water by 1°C.

Canapé: An hors d'oeuvre consisting of a small piece of bread or toast, often cut in a decorative shape, garnished with a savory spread or topping.

Candy stove/stock pot range: A small, free standing single burner range with a series of rings, typically used to hold a single pot, such as a candy pot or stockpot.

Capon: A castrated male chicken, slaughtered at under 8 months of age and weighing 5 to 8 pounds (2.3 to 3.6 kilograms). Very tender, it is usually roasted or poêléed.

Caramelization: The process of browning sugar in the presence of heat. The temperature range in which sugar caramelizes is approximately 320° to 360°F (160° to 182°C).

Carbohydrate: One of the basic nutrients used by the body as a source of energy; types include simple (sugars) and complex (starches and fibers).

Carbon steel: A blend of carbon and steel, used to make knife blades; takes a good edge and resist discoloration and staining.

Carborundum stone: A sharpening stone; available in various "grits" to sharpen knives to the desired degree of fineness.

Carryover cooking: Heat retained in cooked foods that allows them to continue cooking even after removal from the cooking medium. Especially important to roasted foods.

Carte (Fr.): The general term for menu or listing.

Casing: A synthetic or natural membrane (usually pig or sheep intestines) used to enclose sausage forcemeat.

Casserole/en casserole (Fr.): A lidded cooking vessel that is used in the oven; usually round with two handles. Also, foods cooked in a casserole.

Cassoulet: A stew of beans baked with pork or other meats, duck or goose confit, and seasonings.

Cast iron: A metal that has been refined, heated, and shaped by pouring it into a mold. Typically used for frying pans, Dutch ovens, etc. Advantage is that it holds heat well and evenly; disadvantage is tendency to pit, scar, rust, and shatter.

Caul fat: A fatty membrane from a pig or sheep intestine that resembles fine netting; used to bard roasts and pâtés and to encase sausage forcemeat.

Cellulose: A complex carbohydrate; it is the main structural component of plant cells.

Center of the plate: An expression meant to focus attention on the food item that provides the primary culinary and nutritional focus. Center of the plate first came to public attention when various eating plans and pyramids suggested moving meat away from its position as "center of the plate."

Cephalopod: Marine creatures whose tentacles and arms are attached directly to their heads; includes squid and octopus.

Chafing dish: A metal dish with a heating unit (flame or electric) used to keep foods warm and to cook foods at the table side or during buffet service.

Champagne: A sparkling white wine produced in the Champagne region of France; the term is sometimes incorrectly applied to other sparkling wines.

Charcuterie (Fr.): The preparation of pork and other meat items, such as hams, terrines, sausages, pâtés, and other forcemeats.

Charcutière (Fr.): In the style of the butcher's wife. Items (usually grilled meat) are served with sauce Robert and finished with a julienne of gherkins.

Chasseur (Fr.): Hunter's style. A mushroom-tomato sauce made with a white wine reduction and demi-glace, and finished with butter and parsley.

Cheesecloth: A light, fine mesh gauze used for straining liquids and making sachets.

Chef de partie (Fr.): Station chefs. In the brigade system, these are the line-cook positions, such as saucier, grillardin, etc.

Chef de rang (Fr.): Front waiter. A demi-chef de rang is a back waiter or busboy.

Chef de salle (Fr.): Head waiter.

Chef de service (Fr.): Director of service.

Chef de vin (Fr.): Wine steward.

Chef's potato: All-purpose potato.

Chef's knife: An all-purpose knife used for chopping, slicing, and mincing; its blade is usually between 8 and 14 inches long.

Chemical contamination: The adulteration of foods with various chemicals, including chemical poisons, herbicides, insecticides, cleansers.

Chemical leavener: An ingredient or combination of ingredients (such as baking soda or baking powder) whose chemical action is used to produce carbon dioxide gas to leaven baked goods.

Chiffonade: Leafy vegetables or herbs cut into fine shreds; often used as a garnish.

Chiffon cake: A cake made by the foaming method that contains a high percentage of eggs and sugar, relatively little if any fat.

Chili/Chile: The fruit of certain types of capsicum peppers (not related to black pepper), used fresh and dry as a seasoning. Chilies come in many types (for example, jalapeño, serrano, poblano) and varying degrees of spiciness.

Chili powder: Dried, ground or crushed chilies, often with other ground spices and herbs.

Chine: Backbone. A cut of meat that includes the backbone; in butchering, to separate the backbone and ribs to facilitate carving.

Chinoise: A conical sieve used for straining and pureeing foods.

Chocolate liquor: Unsweetened chocolate.

Cholesterol: A sterol found exclusively in animal products such as meat, eggs, and cheese.

Chop: To cut into pieces of roughly the same size. Also, a small cut of meat including part of the rib.

Choron: Sauce béarnaise finished with tomato puree.

Choucroute (Fr.): Sauerkraut. Choucroute garni is sauerkraut garnished with various meats.

Chowder: A thick soup that may be made from a variety of ingredients but usually contains potatoes.

Cioppino (It.): A fish stew usually made with white wine and tomatoes, believed to have originated in Genoa.

Clarification; clarifying: The process of removing solid impurities from a liquid (such as butter or stock). Also, a mixture of ground meat, egg whites, mirepoix, tomato puree, herbs, and spices used to clarify broth for consommé.

Clarified butter: Butter from which the milk solids and water have been removed, leaving pure butterfat. Has a higher smoking point than whole butter but less butter flavor.

Cleaver: A cutting tool with a large heavy blade; available in a range of sizes. Chinese cleavers are typically sharpening on one side of the blade. Butcher's cleavers are heavy enough to cut through bones and joints.

Coagulation: The curdling or clumping of protein usually due to the application of heat or acid.

Coarse chop: To cut into pieces of roughly the same size; used for items such as mirepoix, where appearance is not important.

Cocoa powder: The pods of the cacao tree, processed to remove the cocoa butter and ground into powder. Used as a flavoring.

Cocotte (Fr.): Casserole. A cooking dish with a tight-fitting lid for braising or stewing. Also, a small ramekin used for cooking eggs. (En cocotte is often interchangeable with en casserole).

Cod, salt: Cod fish that has been salted, possibly smoked, and dried to preserve it.

Coddled eggs: Eggs cooked in simmering water, in their shells or in ramekins or coddlers, until set.

Code of conduct: A standard (may be expressed or simply understood) governing actions deemed suitable to those within a group, organization, or profession.

Colander: A perforated bowl, with or without a base or legs, used to strain foods.

Cold smoking: Preparing brined and/or cured foods in a smoker; temperatures are kept at less than 100°F (37°C).

Combination method: A cooking method that involves the application of both moist and dry heat to the main item (for example, braising or stewing).

Commis (Fr.): Apprentice. A cook who works under a chef de partie to learn the station and its responsibilities. A commis de rang is a back waiter or busboy.

Communard (Fr.): The kitchen position responsible for preparing staff meals.

Complete proteins: Foods that contain all the essential amino acids (those amino acids that cannot be produced in the body). Animal foods are considered complete proteins.

Complex carbohydrate: A large molecule made up of long chains of sugar molecules. In food, these molecules are found in starches and fiber.

Compote: A dish of fruit–fresh or dried–cooked in syrup flavored with spices or liqueur.

Compound butter: Whole butter combined with herbs or other seasonings and usually used to sauce grilled or broiled items or vegetables.

Concassé/concasser (Fr.): To pound or chop coarsely. Usually refers to tomatoes that have been peeled, seeded, and chopped.

Condiment: An aromatic mixture, such as pickles, chutney, and some sauces and relishes, that accompanies food (usually kept on the table throughout service).

Conduction: A method of heat transfer in which heat is transmitted through another substance. In cooking, when heat is transmitted to food through a pot or pan, oven walls, or racks.

Confiserie/Confiseur (Fr.): Confectionery/confectioner. A pâtissière specializing in, and responsible for, the production of candies and related items, such as petits fours.

Confit: Meat (usually goose, duck, or pork) cooked and preserved in its own fat.

Consommé: Broth that has been clarified using a mixture of ground meat, egg whites, and other ingredients that traps impurities.

Convection: A method of heat transfer in which heat is transmitted through the circulation of air or water.

Convection oven: An oven that employs convection currents by forcing hot air through fans so it circulates around food, cooking it quickly and evenly.

Convection steamer: A steamer that generates steam in a separate chamber which is then vented over the food being cooked.

Copper: A metal favored for used in pots, pans, and bowls. Typically lined with aluminum, tin, or steel for most applications, copper boils and preserving pans are often left unlined. Foods should never be allowed to remain in contact with copper for extended periods to avoid chance of toxic poisoning.

Coquilles Saint-Jacques (Fr.): Scallops. Also, a dish of broiled scallops with any of several garnishes.

Coral: Lobster roe, which is red or coral-colored when cooked.

Corned beef: Beef brisket preserved with salt and spices. The term "corned" refers to the chunks of salt spread over the brisket during the corning process.

Cornichon (Fr.): A small, sour, pickled cucumber.

Cornstarch: A fine, white powder milled from dried corn; used primarily as a thickener for sauce and occasionally as an ingredient in batters.

Cost of errors: A calculation of the total expenses involved in improperly serving or preparing an item intended for sale to the customer.

Coulibiac (Fr.): A preparation of fish (usually salmon), kasha or rice, onion, mushrooms, and herbs, baked in a pastry crust. (Also Russian, kulibyaka.)

Coulis: A thick puree, usually of vegetables but possibly of fruit. (Traditionally meat, fish, or shellfish puree; meat jus; or certain thick soups.)

Country-style: A forcemeat that is coarse in texture, usually made from pork, pork fat, liver, and various garnishes.

Court bouillon (Fr.): "Short broth." An aromatic vegetable broth that usually includes an acidic ingredient, such as wine or vinegar; most commonly used for poaching fish.

Couscous: Pellets of semolina usually cooked by steaming, traditionally in a couscoussière. Also, the stew with which this grain is traditionally served.

Couscoussière: A set of nesting pots similar to a steamer used to cook couscous.

Couverture: Fine, semi-sweet chocolate used for coating and decorating. Its high cocoa butter content gives it a glossy appearance after tempering.

CPR (cardio-pulmonary resuscitation): A means of reviving an individual whose heart has stopped beating. Individuals can be certified in CPR by authorized groups and organizations such as the American Red Cross.

Cream: The fatty component of milk; available with various fat contents. Also, a mixing method for batter cakes.

Cream soup: Traditionally a soup based on a béchamel sauce. Loosely, any soup finished with cream, a cream variant such as sour cream, or a liaison; these soups are usually based on béchamel or velouté.

Cream puff: A pastry made with pâte à choux, filled with crème pâtissière, and usually glazed. (Also in French, profiterole.)

Creaming method: A mixing method used for batters and doughs in which the fat and sugar are beaten together until light; dry and wet ingredients are added alternately to the batter.

Crème anglaise (Fr.): Custard.

Crème brulée (Fr.): Custard topped with sugar and caramelized under the broiler before service.

Crème fraîche (Fr.): Heavy cream cultured to give it a thick consistency and a slightly tangy flavor; used in hot preparations since it is less likely to curdle when heated than sour cream or yogurt.

Crème pâtissière (Fr.): "Pastry cream." Custard made with eggs, flour or other starches, milk, sugar, and flavorings, used to fill and garnish pastries or as the base for puddings, soufflés, and creams.

Crêpe: A thin pancake made with egg batter; used in sweet and savory preparations.

Critical control points (CCP): A part of HACCP standards indicating that foods must meat specific standards regarding storage, reheating, or service temperatures in order to prevent contamination.

Croissant dough: A dough consisting of a yeast dough with a butter roll-in, traditionally rolled in a crescent shape before baking.

Cross-contamination: The transference of disease-causing elements from one source to another through physical contact.

Croûte, en (Fr.): Encased in a bread or pastry crust.

Croûton (Fr.): A bread or pastry garnish, usually toasted or sautéed until crisp.

Crumb: A term used to describe the texture of baked goods; for example, an item can be said to have a fine or coarse crumb.

Crustacean: A class of hard-shelled arthropods, primarily aquatic, which includes edible species such as lobster, crab, shrimp, and crayfish.

Cryovac®: A packaging system in which foods are packed in airtight plastic after processing to minimize contamination from the pint of processing until the food reaches its final destination.

Cuisine bourgeoisie (Fr.): The cooking style of the middle class.

Cuisson (Fr.): Poaching liquid, including stock, fumet, court bouillon, or other liquid, which may be reduced and used as a base for the poached item's sauce.

Culture: A bacterial strain that induces foods to undergo a change; often used to produce such dairy items as sour cream, cheese, and buttermilk.

Curds: Milk solids that have formed into a mass; a stage in cheese production.

Cure: To preserve a food by salting, smoking, and/or drying.

Curing salt: A mixture of 94 percent table salt (sodium chloride) and 6 percent sodium nitrite used to preserve meats. (Also known as tinted curing mixture, or TCM.)

Curry: A mixture of spices used primarily in Indian cuisine; may include turmeric, coriander, cumin, cayenne or other chilies, cardamom, cinnamon, clove, fennel, fenugreek, ginger, and garlic. Also, a dish seasoned with curry.

Custard: A mixture of milk, beaten egg, and possibly other ingredients, such as

sweet or savory flavorings, which is cooked with gentle heat, often in a bain-marie or double boiler.

Cutability: A term used to indicate the overall ratio of usable meat to bones and trim.

Cutlet: A meat cut made from a boneless piece of meat; usually cut against the grain. May be pounded if necessary or desired.

Danger zone: The temperature range from 45 to 140°F (7 to 60°C), the most favorable condition for rapid growth of many pathogens.

Danish dough: A pastry dough consisting of rich yeast dough with a butter roll-in, possibly filled with nuts, fruit, or other ingredients and iced. This pastry originated in Denmark.

Date stamp: A labeling system used to indicate the last date on which an item is still fresh, wholesome, and suitable for sale in an unopened container. This assumes that the product was held and stored properly throughout processing, shipping, and all subsequent handling.

Daube: A meat stew braised in red wine, traditionally in a daubière, a specialized casserole with a tight-fitting lid and indentations to hold hot coals.

Deck oven: A variant of the conventional oven, in which the heat source is located underneath the deck or floor of the oven and the food is placed directly on the deck instead of on a rack.

Decline phase: The stage at which a pathogen's death rate exceeds the rate of growth and reproduction.

Deep-fry; deep-frying: A cooking method in which foods are cooked by immersion in hot fat; deep-fried foods are often coated with bread crumbs or batter before being cooked.

Deglaze/Déglacer: To use a liquid, such as wine, water, or stock, to dissolve food particles and/or caramelized drippings left in a pan after roasting or sautéing.

Degrease/Dégraisser: To skim the fat off the surface of a liquid, such as a stock or sauce.

Demi-glace (Fr.): "Half-glaze." A mixture of equal proportions of brown stock and brown sauce that has been reduced by half. One of the grand sauces.

Dépouillage (Fr.): To skim the surface of a cooking liquid, such as a stock or sauce. This action is simplified by placing the pot off-center on the burner and skimming impurities as they collect at one side of the pot.

Derivatives: Sauces prepared by modifying a base sauce (demi-glace, béchamel, or velouté, for instance).

Dessert soufflé: A sweet egg-based dish, served as a dessert; made by combining a sweet base such as pastry cream

or pureed fruits with beaten egg whites.

Deviled: Meat, poultry, or other food seasoned with mustard, vinegar, and possibly other seasonings; coated with bread crumbs; and grilled.

Dice: To cut ingredients into small cubes ($1/4$-inch for small, $1/2$-inch for medium, $3/4$-inch for large standard).

Dietary cholesterol: Cholesterol which is consumed in foods. (See also cholesterol.)

Diamond-impregnated steel or stone: A sharpening or honing tool that has been produced with industrial grade diamonds over the surface. Felt by many chefs to offer superior sharpening abilities.

Die: The plate in a meat grinder through which foods pass, just before a blade cuts them. The size of the die's opening determines the fineness of the grind.

Direct heat: A method of heat transfer in which heat waves radiate from a source (for example, an open burner or grill) and travel directly to the item being heated with no conductor between heat source and food. Examples are grilling, broiling, and toasting.

Dock; docked; docking: To cut the top of dough before baking to allow it to expand.

Drawn: A whole fish that has been scaled and gutted but still has its head, fins, and tail.

Dredge: To coat food with a dry ingredient such as flour or bread crumbs.

Dressed: Prepared for cooking; a dressed fish is gutted and scaled, and its head, tail, and fins are removed (same as pandressed). Dressed poultry is plucked, drawn, singed, trimmed, and trussed. Also, coated with dressing, as in a salad.

Drum sieve: A sieve consisting of a screen stretched across a shallow cylinder of wood or aluminum (see also tamis).

Dry sauté: To sauté without fat, usually using a nonstick pan.

Dry cure: A combination of salts and spices used usually before smoking to process meats and force-meats.

Dumpling: Any of a number of small soft dough or batter items, which are steamed, poached, or simmered (possibly on top of a stew); may be filled or plain.

Durum: A species of hard wheat primarily milled into semolina flour for use in dried pasta.

Dutch oven: A kettle, usually of cast iron, used for stewing and braising on the stove top or in the oven.

Dutch process: A method for treating cocoa powder with an alkali to reduce its acidity.

Duxelles: An appareil of finely chopped

mushrooms and shallots sautéed gently in butter.

Egg wash: A mixture of beaten eggs (whole eggs, yolks, or whites) and a liquid, usually milk or water, used to coat baked goods to give them a sheen.

Emincé (Fr.): To cut an item, usually meat, into very thin slices.

Empty calories: Calories derived from foods that have been refined or stripped of other nutrients.

Emulsified (emulsion) forcemeat (5/4/3): A forcemeat in which meats and fat are carefully brought into a state of emulsion, with strict adherence to temperature controls to assure a perfectly homogenous end product.

Emulsion: A mixture of two or more liquids, one of which is a fat or oil and the other of which is water-based, so that tiny globules of one are suspended in the other. This may involve the use of stabilizers, such as egg or mustard. Emulsions may be temporary, permanent, or semi-permanent.

Emulsion sauce: Sauce may by suspending two substances which normally will not mix into a permanent or temporary mixture. Hot emulsion sauces include hollandaise and beurre blanc; cold sauces include mayonnaise and vinaigrette.

Endosperm: The inside portion of a grain, usually the largest portion, composed primarily of starch and protein.

En papillote (Fr.): Foods prepared by encasing them in paper and cooking at high enough temperatures to cause steam to build up in the bag.

Entremetier (Fr.): Vegetable chef/station. The position responsible for hot appetizers and often soups, vegetables, starches, and pastas; may also be responsible for egg dishes.

EP/Edible portion: The weight of an item after trimming and preparation (as opposed to the AP weight or as purchased weight).

Escalope (Fr.): Same as scallop; a small boneless piece of meat or fish of uniform thickness.

Espagnole sauce (Fr.): "Spanish sauce." Brown sauce made with brown stock, caramelized mirepoix and tomato puree, and seasonings.

Essence: A concentrated flavoring extracted from an item, usually by infusion or distillation; includes items like vanilla and other extracts, concentrated stocks, and fumets.

Essential amino acids: Protein components that cannot be produced in the diet and which must be obtained from a dietary source.

Estouffade (Fr.): Stew. Also, a type of brown stock based on pork knuckle

and veal and beef bones that is often used in braises.

Ethylene gas: A gas emitted by various fruits and vegetables; ethylene gas speeds ripening, maturing, and eventually, rotting.

Etouffé (Fr.): "Smothered." A cooking method similar to braising in which items are cooked with little or no added liquid in a pan with a tight-fitting lid. (Also étuver, à l'étuvée.)

Extracts: Flavorings that are typically prepared by steeping a highly aromatic ingredient (vanilla or lemon zest, e.g.) in alcohol.

Extrusion/Extruding machine: A machine used to shape pasta. The dough is pushed out through perforated plates rather than being rolled.

Fabrication: The butchering, cutting, and trimming of meat, poultry, fish, and game.

Factor method: A system used to determine the menu price of various items.

Facultative bacteria: Bacteria that can survive both with and without oxygen.

Farce (Fr.): Forcemeat or stuffing; farci means stuffed.

Farina (It.): Flour or fine meal of wheat.

Fatback: Pork fat from the back of the pig, used primarily for barding.

Fat: One of the basic nutrients used by the body to provide energy. Fats also provide flavor in food and give a feeling of fullness.

Feed tray: The part of a food grinder that holds foods that are to be ground.

Fermentation: The breakdown of carbohydrates into carbon dioxide gas and alcohol, usually through the action of yeast on sugar.

Fermière/farmer style: A knife cut that results in foods cut into a tile shape.

Fiber/Dietary fiber: The structural component of plants that is necessary to the human diet. Sometimes referred to as roughage.

FIFO/First in, first out: A fundamental storage principle based on stock rotation. Products are stored and used so the oldest product is always used first.

Filé: A thickener made from ground, dried sassafras leaves; used primarily in gumbos.

Fillet/Filet: A boneless cut of meat, fish, or poultry.

Filleting knife: A flexible-bladed knife used for filleting fish; similar in size and shape to a boning knife.

Fine brunoise: See brunoise.

Fines herbes: A mixture of herbs, usually parsley, chervil, tarragon, and chives.

Fire safety: A comprehensive program put in place to assure that all individuals are free from hazards associated with

fire, including prevention and reaction strategies to cover all situations.

Fish poacher: A long, narrow pot with straight sides and possibly a perforated rack, used for poaching whole fish.

Flat fish: A fish skeletal type characterized by its flat body and both eyes on one side of its head (for example, sole, plaice, and halibut).

Flat-top range: A thick plate of cast iron or steel set over the heat source on a range; diffuses heat, making it more even than an open burner.

Foaming method: Cake batters made by first preparing a foam of eggs, egg whites, or egg yolks with sugar. Little if any fat is included in the batter.

Foie gras (Fr.): The fattened liver of a duck or goose.

Fond (Fr.): Stock.

Fondant: An icing made with sugar, water, and glucose; used primarily for pastry and confectionery.

Foodborne illness: An illness in humans caused by the consumption of an adulterated food product. In order for a food-borne illness to be considered official, it must involve two or more people who have eaten the same food and it must be confirmed by health officials.

Foodborne infection: Illness caused by consuming foods contaminated with living pathogens.

Foodborne intoxication: Illness caused by consuming foods contaminated with poisons, including those toxins produced as a by-product of the life cycle of other pathogens.

Food chopper/Buffalo chopper: A piece of cutting equipment that holds foods in a rotating bowl; blades are housed in the machine.

Food cost: Cost of all food purchased to prepare items for sale in a restaurant.

Foodgrade plastic: A material used to produce containers that are deemed suitable for holding and storing foods; typically capable of being cleaned and sanitized for re-use.

Food mill: A type of strainer with a crank-operated, curved blade. It is used to puree soft foods.

Food/meat slicer: A machine that has a rotating circular blade and a carrier, used to slice meats and other foods very thinly. May be motorized.

Food processor: A machine with interchangeable blades and disks and a removable bowl and lid separate from the motor housing. It can be used for a variety of tasks, including chopping, grinding, pureeing, emulsifying, kneading, slicing, shredding, and cutting julienne.

Forcemeat: A mixture of chopped or ground meat and other ingredients used for pâtés, sausages, and other preparations.

Fork tender: A test of doneness for foods; should be easily pierced or cut by a fork, or should slide readily from a fork when lifted.

Formula: A recipe; measurements for each ingredient may be given as percentages of the weight for the main ingredient.

Fortified wine: Wine to which a spirit, usually brandy, has been added (for example, port or sherry).

Free-range: Livestock that is raised unconfined.

French knife: See chef's knife.

Frenching: The process of scraping meat from bones before cooking.

Fricassée (Fr.): A stew of poultry or other white meat with a white sauce.

Fritter: Sweet or savory foods coated or mixed into batter and deep-fried (also in French, beignet).

Friturier (Fr.): Fry chef/station. The position responsible for all fried foods; it may be combined with the rôtisseur position.

Frozen desserts: Dishes served to conclude a meal that are churned (ice cream, sorbet, e.g.) or still frozen (soufflé, granite, parfaits).

Fructose: A simple sugar found in fruits.

Fruit curd: Similar to a hollandaise sauce, made by cooking a fruit juice with sugar, eggs, and butter.

Full tang: An extension of the blade into the handle; full tangs are associated with high quality knives.

Fully cooked: State in which foods are cooked to the exact point of doneness.

Fumet (Fr.); essence: A type of stock in which the main flavoring ingredient is allowed to smother with wine and aromatics; fish fumet is the most common type.

Galantine: Boned meat (usually poultry) that is stuffed, rolled, poached, and served cold, usually in aspic.

Game chips: Potatoes sliced into thin circles and deep-fried.

Ganache: A filling made of heavy cream, chocolate, and/or other flavorings.

Garbure (Fr.): A thick vegetable soup usually containing beans, cabbage, and/or potatoes.

Garde-manger (Fr.): Pantry chef/station. The position responsible for cold food preparations, including salads, cold appetizers, pâtés, etc.

Garni (Fr.): Garnished.

Garnish: An edible decoration or accompaniment to a dish.

Gazpacho (Sp.): A cold soup made from vegetables, typically tomatoes, cucumbers, peppers, and onions.

Gelatin: A protein-based substance found in animal bones and connective tissue.

When dissolved in hot liquid and then cooled, it can be used as a thickener and stabilizer.

Gelatinization: A phase in the process of thickening a liquid with starch in which starch molecules swell to form a network that traps water molecules.

Génoise (Fr.): A sponge cake made with whole eggs, used for petits fours, layer cakes, and other desserts.

Germ: The embryo of a cereal grain, which is usually separated from the endosperm during milling because it contains oils that accelerate the spoilage of flours and meals.

Gherkin: A small pickled cucumber.

Giblets: Organs and other trim from poultry, including the liver, heart, gizzard, and neck.

Glace (Fr.): Reduced stock; ice cream; icing.

Glacé (Fr.): Glazed or iced.

Glaze: To give an item a shiny surface by brushing it with sauce, aspic, icing, or another appareil. For meat, to coat with sauce and then brown in an oven or salamander.

Glucose: A simple sugar; the preferred source of energy for the human body.

Gluten: An elastic protein formed when hard wheat flour is moistened and agitated. Gluten gives yeast doughs their characteristic elasticity.

Goujonettes (Fr.): Fish fillet cut in strips and usually breaded or batter-coated and then deep-fried.

Government inspection: Inspection of foodstuffs to be sure that they meet all appropriate standards for purity, wholesomeness, and safety.

Graduated measuring pitchers and cups: Utensils used to measure liquid and volume of ingredients.

Grand sauce: One of several basic sauces that are used in the preparation of many other small sauces. The grand sauces are: demi-glace, velouté, béchamel, hollandaise, and tomato. (Also called mother sauce.)

Granita/granite: A still frozen mixture of a flavored, sweetened liquid that is scraped just before service to produce flakes or crystals.

GRAS (Generally Recognized as Safe): A set of standards indicating the point at which non-edible elements found in foods (often as the result of harvesting or processing) have reached levels deemed unsafe for humans to consume.

Gratin dish: A cooking vessels used to hold foods that are to be browned under the broiler or salamander.

Gratin forcemeat: A mixture of meats and fat in which the garnish meat is first seared and cooled before being incorporated.

Gratiné (Fr.): Browned in an oven or under a salamander (au gratin, gratin de). Gratin can also refer to a forcemeat in which some portion of the dominant meat is sautéed and cooled before grinding.

Griddle: A heavy metal surface, which may be either fitted with handles, built into a stove, or heated by its own gas or electric element. Cooking is done directly on the griddle.

Grill; grilling: A cooking technique in which foods are cooked by a radiant heat source placed below the food. Also, the piece of equipment on which grilling is done. Grills may be fueled by gas, electricity, charcoal, or wood.

Grill pan: A skillet with ridges that is used to simulate grilling on the stove top.

Grillardin (Fr.): Grill chef/station. The position responsible for all grilled foods; may be combined with rôtisseur.

Griswold: A pot, similar to a rondeau, made of cast iron; may have a single short handle rather than the usual loop handles.

Grit: Degree of fineness of coarseness of a sharpening stone.

Guinea hen/fowl: A bird related to the pheasant. It is slaughtered at about 6 months of age and weighs three-quarters to 1 and a half pounds (350 to 700 grams). Its tender meat is suitable to most techniques.

Gumbo: A Creole soup/stew thickened with filé or okra.

Gumbo filé powder: See filé.

HACCP (Hazard Analysis Critical Control Point): A monitoring system used to track foods from the time that they are received until they are served to consumers to assure that they are free from contamination and foodborne illness by establishing standards and controls for time and temperature, as well as safe handling practices.

Hand guard: A carrier or other protective device found on cutting and slicing equipment, intended to protect the hands from accidental injury.

Hanging meat: Meat primals or subprimals that are delivered unboxed; typically allowed to hang from hooks with air circulating around them.

Haricot (Fr.): "Bean." Haricots verts are green beans.

Hash: Chopped, cooked meat, usually with potatoes and/or other vegetables, which is seasoned, bound with a sauce, and sautéed. Also, to chop.

HDL (high-density lipoproteins): A type of fatty acid often referred to as "good cholesterol" due to its role in helping to flush the arteries of plaque that could otherwise build up on the lining of the artery wall, leading to athero-sclerosis.

Heimlich maneuver: First aid for choking; the application of sudden, upward pressure on the upper abdomen to force a foreign object from the wind-pipe.

High carbon stainless steel: A metal that contains a high percentage of carbon in relation to stainless steel. Favored for use in most knife blades.

High-ratio cake: Made by preparing a batter that includes a high percentage of sugar in relation to other ingredients. Prepared by the two-stage mixing method.

Hilum: The scar on the side of a bean where it was attached to the pod.

Hollandaise: A classic emulsion sauce made with a vinegar reduction, egg yolks, and melted butter flavored with lemon juice. It is one of the grand sauces.

Hollow-ground: A type of knife blade made by fusing two sheets of metal and beveling or fluting the edge.

Hominy: Corn that has been milled or treated with a lye solution to remove the bran and germ.

Homogenization; homogenized: A process used to prevent the milkfat from separating out of milk products. The liquid is forced through an ultra-fine mesh at high pressure, which breaks up fat globules, dispersing them evenly throughout the liquid.

Hors d'oeuvre (Fr.): "Outside the work." An appetizer.

Hotel pan: A rectangular, metal pan, in any of a number of standard sizes, with a lip that allows it to rest in a storage shelf or steam table.

Hot smoking: The process of preparing foods in a smokehouse (after they have been cured or brined) at temperatures above 145°F (63°C).

Hydrogenation: The process in which hydrogen atoms are added to an unsaturated fat molecule, making it partially or completely saturated, hence, solid at room temperature.

Hydroponics: A technique that involves growing vegetables in nutrient-enriched water, rather than in soil.

Hygiene: Conditions and practices followed to maintain health, including sanitation and personal cleanliness.

Hypertension: High blood pressure; typically cause by a constriction of the blood vessels due to a mineral imbalance (too much sodium, e.g.) tension, or stress.

Ice cream freezer: A utensil used to simultaneously churn and cool a base in order to produce frozen items such as ice cream or sherbet.

Induction burner: A type of heating unit that relies on magnetic attraction between the cook top and metals in the pot to generate the heat that cooks foods in the pan. Reaction time is significantly faster than with traditional burners.

Infection: See Foodborne infection.

Infusion: Steeping an aromatic or other item in liquid to extract its flavor. Also, the liquid resulting from this process.

Instant-reading thermometer: A thermometer used to measure the internal temperature of foods. The stem is inserted in the food, producing an instant temperature read-out.

Intoxication: See Foodborne intoxication.

Julienne: Vegetables, potatoes, or other items cut into thin strips; $1/8$-inch square x 1 to 2 inches is standard. Fine julienne is $1/16$-inch square.

Jus (Fr.): Juice. Jus de viande is meat gravy. Meat served au jus is served with its own juice or jus lié.

Jus lié (Fr.): Meat juice thickened lightly with arrowroot or cornstarch. K

Kasha (Russ.): Buckwheat groats that have been hulled and crushed; usually prepared by boiling.

Kitchen fork: A hand tool used to stabilize foods that are being sliced or carved, turn foods, or to test for doneness (fork tender).

Knead/kneading: The process of stretching dough repeatedly in order to give it a good consistency. Also helps to ensure proper quality in the finished, baked item.

Kosher meat: Butchered and prepared in accordance with Jewish dietary laws.

Kosher salt: Pure, refined rock salt used for pickling because it does not contain magnesium carbonate. It thus does not cloud brine solutions. Also used to kosher items. (Also known as coarse salt or pickling salt.)

Lacto/ovo-vegetarian: A person who consume a vegetarian diet composed of fruits, vegetables, nuts, grains, legumes, milk products and eggs

Lactose: The simple sugar found in milk.

Lag phase: The point at which a pathogen is still adjusting to its environment. Reproduction and growth is still slow..

Lard: Rendered pork fat used for pastry and frying.

Lardon (Fr.): A strip of fat used for larding; may be seasoned. (Also, lardoon.)

Lean dough: A yeast dough that includes very little or no fat.

Leavener: Any ingredient or process that produces air bubbles and causes the rising of baked goods. (See chemical and mechanical leaveners, yeast, baking soda, baking powder.)

Legume: The seeds of certain plants, including beans and peas, which are eaten for their earthy flavors and high nutritional value. Also, the French word for vegetable.

Liaison: A mixture of egg yolks and cream used to thicken and enrich sauces. (Also loosely applied to any appareil used as a thickener.)

Liqueur: A spirit flavored with fruit, spices, nuts, herbs, and/or seeds and usually sweetened.

Little neck: Small, hard-shell clams often eaten raw on the half shell.

Littleneck: A Pacific coast clam, usually steamed. (Also known as manila clam.)

LDL (low-density lipo-proteins): A substance related to cholesterol, typically associated with such conditions as atherosclerosis and cardio-vascular disease. High levels of LDL in the blood indicate an increased likelihood of fatty deposits known as plaque building up in arteries.

Low-fat milk: Milk containing less than 2 percent fat.

Lox: Salt-cured salmon.

Lozenge/diamond cut: A knife cut in which foods are cut into small diamond shapes.

Lyonnaise (Fr.): Lyons style; with onions and usually butter, white wine, vinegar, and demi-glace.

Macaroni (It.): Pasta.

Madère (Fr.): A sauce made with demi-glace flavored with Madeira.

Madeira: A Portuguese fortified wine that is treated with heat as it ages, giving it a distinctive flavor and brownish color.

Mandoline: A slicing and cutting tool, named for the stroking motion used as foods are passed over the blades.

Mahi mahi: A firm-fleshed Pacific fish with a light, delicate flavor, suitable to all cooking methods. (Also called dolphin fish.)

Maître d'hôtel (Fr.): Dining room manager or food and beverage manager, informally called maître d'. This position oversees the dining room or "front of the house" staff. Also, a compound butter flavored with chopped parsley and lemon juice.

Mandoline: A slicing device of stainless steel with carbon steel blades. The blades may be adjusted to cut items into various cuts and thicknesses.

Marbling: The intramuscular fat found in meat that makes the meat tender and juicy.

Marinade: An appareil used before cooking to flavor and moisten foods; may be liquid or dry. Liquid marinades are usually based on an acidic ingredient, such as wine or vinegar; dry marinades are usually salt-based.

Mark: To turn foods during grilling so that they are seared with a pattern of the grill rods.

Marketing: The process by which potential customers are made aware of the services, goods, or potential value of something in order to encourage them to buy or invest.

Marmite: See stock pot.

Marzipan: A paste of ground almonds, sugar, and egg whites that is used to fill and decorate pastries.

Marrow: the substance found in the interior of bones. May be used as a garnish in sauces.

Matelote (Fr.): A fish stew traditionally made with eel.

Matignon (Fr.): An edible mirepoix that is often used in poêléed dishes and is usually served with the finished dish. Typically, matignon includes two parts carrot, one part celery, one part leek, one part onion, one part mushroom (optional), and one part ham or bacon.

Mayonnaise: A cold emulsion sauce made of oil, egg yolks, vinegar, mustard, and seasonings.

Measuring spoons: A set of spoons of standard sizes, used to measure tablespoons, teaspoons, and fractions of teaspoons.

Meat grinder: A piece of equipment used to process meat by feeding meat cubes or strips through a tube, cutting the meat as it passes through a die plate.

Mechanical leavener: Air incorporated into a batter to act as a leavener. Usually, eggs or cream are whipped into a foam, then are folded into the batter.

Medallion (Fr.): A small, round scallop of meat.

Mediterranean Food Pyramid: A graphic representation of the optimal healthy diet of the Mediterranean region, developed by the World Health Organization (WHO) and Oldway's Exchange and Preservation Trust.

Meringue (Fr.): Egg whites beaten until they are stiff, then are sweetened and possibly baked until stiff. Three types are regular or common, Italian, and Swiss.

Mesophilic: A term used to describe bacteria that thrive within the middle-range temperatures between 60 to 100°F (16 to 43°C).

Metabolism: The sum of chemical processes in living cells by which energy is provided and new material is assimilated.

Meunière, à la: A cooking technique for fish.

Microwave: A method of heat transfer in which electromagnetic waves (similar to radio waves) generated by a device called a magnetron penetrate food and cause the water molecules in it to oscillate. This rapid molecular motion generates heat, which cooks the food.

Mie (Fr.): The soft part of bread (not the crust); mie de pain is fresh white bread crumbs.

Milkfat/butterfat: The fat content of fluid milk; typically expressed as a percentage.

Milled grains: Grains that have been processed by grinding or milling.

Millet: A small, round, gluten-less grain that is boiled or ground into flour.

Milling: The process by which grain is ground into flour or meal.

Mince/mincing: To chop into very small pieces.

Minestrone: A vegetable soup, typically includes dried beans and pasta.

Mirepoix: A combination of chopped aromatic vegetables–usually two parts onion, one part carrot, and one part celery–used to flavor stocks, soups, braises, and stews.

Mise en place (Fr.): "Put in place." The preparation and assembly of ingredients, pans, utensils, and plates or serving pieces needed for a particular dish or service period.

Mode, à la (Fr.): "In the style of" (usually followed by a descriptive phrase). Boeuf à la mode is braised beef; pie à la mode is served with ice cream.

Modified starch: A starch that has been purified; used to thicken products. Examples include cornstarch and arrowroot.

Molasses: The dark-brown, sweet syrup that is a by-product of sugar cane refining.

Mollusk: Any of a number of invertebrate animals with soft, unsegmented bodies usually enclosed in a hard shell; included are clams, oysters, and snails.

Monosodium glutamate (MSG): A flavor-enhancer without a distinct flavor of its own; used primarily in Chinese and processed foods. It may cause allergic reactions in some people.

Monounsaturated fat: A fat with one available bonding site not filled with a hydrogen atom. Food sources include avocado, olives, and nuts.

Monté au beurre (Fr.): "To lift with butter." A technique used to enrich sauces, thicken them slightly, and give them a glossy appearance by whisking in whole butter.

Mother sauce: See grand sauce.

Mousse (Fr.): A dish made with beaten egg whites and/or whipped cream folded into a flavored base appareil; may be sweet or savory.

Mousseline (Fr.): A mousse; a sauce made by folding whipped cream into hollandaise; or a very light forcemeat based on white meat or seafood lightened with cream and eggs.

Mouth-to-mouth resuscitation: The process by which an individual assists someone who has stopped breathing to start again, by breathing into the mouth and/or nasal passages in a rhythmic manner. Often used in conjunction with CPR.

Napoleon: A pastry made of layered puff pastry rectangles filled with pastry cream and glazed with fondant.

Napper/Nappé (Fr.): To coat with sauce; thickened.

Natural cheese: A cheese that is considered "living." The texture and flavor will continue to change as the cheese ages.

Nature (Fr.): "Ungarnished; plain." Pommes natures are boiled potatoes.

Navarin (Fr.): A stew, traditionally of lamb, with potatoes, onions, and possibly other vegetables.

New potato: A small, waxy potato that is usually prepared by boiling or steaming and is often eaten with its skin.

Nitrates/nitrates: Chemical substances used to preserve foods, found especially in cured meats and TCM (tinting curing mix, or curing salt).

Noisette (Fr.): Hazelnut. Also, a small portion of meat cut from the rib. Pommes noisette are tournéed potatoes browned in butter. Beurre noisette is browned butter.

Non-bony fish: Fish whose skeletons are made of cartilage rather than hard bone (for example, shark, skate). (Also called cartilaginous fish.)

Nonstick coating: A treatment applied to the interior of cooking and baking pans which reduces or eliminates the need for adding butter, oil or other fats to prevent foods from sticking to the pan as they cook or bake.

Nouvelle cuisine (Fr.): "New cooking." A culinary movement emphasizing freshness and lightness of ingredients, classical preparations, and innovative combinations and presentation.

Nutrients: The basic components of foods used by the body for growth, repair, restoration, and energy: carbohydrates, fats, proteins, water, vitamins, and minerals.

Nutrition: The processes by which an organism takes in and uses food.

Oblique/roll cut: A knife cut used primarily with long, cylindrical vegetables such as carrots. The item is cut on a diagonal, rolled 180 degrees, then cut on the same diagonal, producing a piece with two angled edges.

Oeuf (Fr.): Egg.

Offal: Variety meats, including organs (brains, heart, kidneys, lights or lungs, sweetbreads, tripe, tongue), head meat, tail, and feet.

Offset spatula: A hand tool with a wide,

bent blade set in a short handle, used to turn or lift foods from grills, broilers, or griddles.

Oignon brûlé (Fr.): "Burnt onion." A peeled, halved onion seared on a flat-top or in a skillet and used to enhance the color of stock and consommé.

Oignon piqué (Fr.): "Pricked onion." A whole, peeled onion to which a bay leaf is attached, using a whole clove as a tack. It is used to flavor béchamel sauce and some soups.

Oil: A substance extracted from plants sources used for cooking, baking, and in food processing.

Omelet: Beaten egg that is cooked in butter in a specialized pan or skillet and then rolled or folded into an oval. Omelets may be filled with a variety of ingredients before or after rolling.

Omelet pan: A pan used to prepare omelets.

On-site refrigeration: Refrigerated drawers, cabinets, or carts, located to avoid the necessity to leave the line during service as well as to hold foods at safe temperatures.

Open-burner range: A cook top that has one or more burners with exposed flame or heating elements (as opposed to a flat top range).

Organic leavener: A living organism operates by fermenting sugar to produce carbon dioxide gas, causing the batter to rise (see Yeast).

Organ meat: Meat from an organ, rather than the muscle tissue of an animal.

OSHA (Occupational Safety and Health Administration): An agency dedicate to assuring that workers are provided a safe, hazard free working environment.

Oven spring: The rapid initial rise of yeast doughs when placed in a hot oven. Heat accelerates the growth of the yeast, which produces more carbon dioxide gas and also causes this gas to expand.

Ovo-vegetarian: A person whose diet consists of plant based foods, with the addition of eggs.

Paella: A Spanish dish of rice cooked with onion, tomato, garlic, vegetables, and various meats, including chicken, chorizo, shellfish, and possibly other types.

Paella pan: A specialized pan for cooking paella; it is wide and shallow and usually has two loop handles.

Paillard (Fr.): A scallop of meat pounded until thin; usually grilled.

Palette knife: A flexible, round-tipped knife used to turn pancakes and grilled foods and to spread fillings and glazes; may have a serrated edge. (Also called a metal spatula.)

Panada: An appareil based on starch (such

as flour or crumbs), moistened with a liquid, that is used as a binder.

Pan-broil: A cooking method similar to dry sautéing that simulates broiling by cooking an item in a hot pan with little or no fat.

Pan-dressed: See dressed.

Pan-fry: A cooking method in which items are cooked in deep fat in a skillet; this generally involves more fat than sautéing or stir-frying but less than deep-frying.

Pan gravy: A sauce made by deglazing pan drippings from a roast and combining them with a roux or other starch and additional stock.

Pan-steaming: Cooking foods in a very small amount of liquid in a covered pan over direct heat.

Pantry: The area of the kitchen responsible for breakfast, salad, sandwich, and salad preparation.

Papillote, en (Fr.): A moist-heat cooking method similar to steaming, in which items are enclosed in parchment and cooked in the oven.

Parchment: Heat-resistant paper used in cooking for such preparations as lining baking pans, cooking items en papillote, and covering items during shallow poaching.

Parchment cones: Made from parchment paper, cut, rolled and folded to hold items that will be piped into designs.

Parcook: To partially cook an item before storing or finishing by another method; may be the same as blanching.

Paring knife: A short knife used for paring and trimming fruits and vegetables; its blade is usually 2 to 4 inches long.

Parisienne scoop: A small tool used for scooping balls out of vegetable or fruit. (Also called a melon baller.)

Parstock: The amount of stock (food and other supplies) necessary to cover operating needs between deliveries.

Partial tang: An extension of a knife's blade that extends partway into the handle.

Pasta (It.): Dough/paste; noodles made from a dough of flour (often semolina) and water or eggs. This dough is kneaded, rolled, and cut or extruded, then cooked by boiling.

Pasteurization: A process in which milk products are heated to kill microorganisms that could contaminate the milk.

Pastry bag: A bag—usually made of plastic, canvas, or nylon—that can be fitted with plain or decorative tips and used to pipe out icings and pureed foods.

Pastry cream: See creme patissiere.

Pâte (Fr.): Noodles or pasta; dough or batter.

Pâte à choux: Cream puff paste, made by boiling a mixture of water, butter, and flour, then beating in whole eggs.

Pâte brisée: Short pastry for pie crusts.

Pâte feuilletée: Puff pastry.

Pâte sucrée: Sweet short pastry.

Pâté (Fr.): A rich forcemeat of meat, game, poultry, seafood, and/or vegetables, baked in pastry or in a mold or dish.

Pâté en croûte: Pâté baked in a pastry crust.

Pâté de campagne: Country-style pâté, with a coarse texture.

Pâté dough: A lean dough used to line a pâté mold, for pâté en croûte.

Pathogen: A disease-causing microorganism.

Pâté mold: A hinged loaf pan used to prepare pâté en croûte. Pâtissière (Fr.): Pastry chef. This station is responsible for baked items, pastries, and desserts. This is often a separate area of the kitchen.

Paupiette: A fillet or scallop of fish or meat that is rolled up around a stuffing and poached or braised.

Paysanne cut: A knife cut in which ingredients are cut into flat, square pieces, $1/2$-inch by $1/2$-inch by $1/8$-inch is standard.

Peel: A paddle used to transfer shaped doughs to a hearth or deck oven.

Personal hygiene: Keeping one's person clean.

Pesco-vegetarian: A person who consumes a diet based primarily on plant-based foods with the addition of eggs, dairy and fish.

Pesto (It.): A thick, pureed mixture of an herb, traditionally basil, and oil used as a sauce for pasta and other foods and as a garnish for soup. Pesto may also contain grated cheese, nuts or seeds, and other seasonings.

pH scale: A scale with values from 0 to 14 representing degree of acidity. A measurement of 7 is neutral, 0 is most acidic and 14 is most alkaline. Chemically, pH measures the concentration/activity of the element hydrogen.

Phyllo dough: Pastry made with very thin sheets of a flour-and-water dough layered with butter and/or crumbs; similar to strudel. (Also called filo.)

Physical contamination: Adulterating foods by dropping foreign objects (hair, bandages, or non-food items) into foods during preparation or service.

Physical leavener: Name given to the action of steam when trapped in a dough.

Pickling spice: A mixture of herbs and spices used to season pickles, often includes dill weed and/or seed, coriander seed, cinnamon stick, peppercorns, bay leaves, and others.

Pilaf: A technique for cooking grains in which the grain is sautéed briefly in butter, then simmered in stock or water with various seasonings. (Also called pilau, pilaw, pullao, pilav.)

Pincé/pinçage (Fr.): To caramelize an item

by sautéing; usually refers to a tomato product.

Poach: A method in which items are cooked gently in simmering liquid.

Poêlé/poêléing: A method in which items are cooked in their own juices (usually with the addition of a matignon, other aromatics, and melted butter) in a covered pot, usually in the oven. (Also called butter roasting).

Poissonier (Fr.): Fish chef/station. The position responsible for fish items and their sauces; may be combined with the saucier position.

Polyunsaturated fat: A fat with more than one available bonding site not filled with a hydrogen atom. Food sources include corn, cottonseed, safflower, soy, and sunflower oils.

Port: A fortified dessert wine. Vintage port is high quality, unblended wine aged in the bottle for at least 12 years; ruby port may be blended and is aged in wood for a short time; white port is made with white grapes.

Portable refrigeration: Refrigerated carts that can be wheeled to the appropriate location to provide addition food storage area.

Post-mortem: Inspection of animals prior to slaughter to ensure that they are safe, wholesome, and fit for human consumption.

Pot au feu (Fr.): A classic French boiled dinner that typically includes poultry and beef, along with various root vegetables. The broth is often served as a first course, followed by the meats and vegetables.

Potentially hazardous foods: Foods that contain adequate amounts of protein, moisture and an appropriate pH, enabling them to support the growth and reproduction of pathogens at a rate conducive to establishing foodborne illness in affected foods.

Prawn: A crustacean that closely resembles shrimp; often used as a general term for large shrimp.

Prep cook: Usually the first job a novice or new-hire holds in a kitchen; typically responsible for preparing vegetables, tending stocks, and other advance preparation tasks.

Pressed steel: A term used when referring to pans made from steel that has been pressed into the desired shape. Similar in cooking abilities to black or blue steel.

Pressure steamer: A machine that cooks food using steam produced by heating water under pressure in a sealed compartment, allowing it to reach higher than boiling temperature (212°F/100°C). The food is placed in a sealed chamber that cannot be opened until the pressure has released and the

steam properly vented from the chamber.

Primal cuts: The portions produced by the initial cutting of an animal carcass. Cuts are determined standards that may vary from country to country and animal type to type. Primal cuts are further broken down into smaller, more manageable cuts.

Progressive grinding: The procedure of grinding foods through successively smaller die in order to create a good emulsion between lean and fat ingredients.

Proof: To allow yeast dough to rise. A proof box is a sealed cabinet that allows control over both temperature and humidity.

Protein: One of the basic nutrients needed by the body to maintain life, supply energy, build and repair tissues, form enzymes and hormones, and perform other essential functions. Protein can be obtained from animal and vegetable sources.

Puff pastry dough: A roll-in dough made by layering a lean, unleavened dough with butter, which is rolled and folded in the appropriate sequence.

Pulse: The edible seed of a leguminous plant, such as a bean, lentil, or pea. (Often referred to simply as legume.)

Purée: To process food (by mashing, straining, or chopping it very fine) in order to make it a smooth paste. Also, a product produced using this technique.

Puree soup: A soup may by cooking various ingredients in a broth or other liquid until tender enough to puree. Typically, the base ingredients provide all the necessary thickening.

Pusher: A tool used to help drop meat from the feed tray into a meat grinder.

Quahog: A hard-shell clam larger than 3 inches in diameter, usually used for chowder or fritters.

Quality grading: The assignment of grades to carcasses based on various standards, including ratio of meat to bone, marbling, etc. A practice paid for by meat packers and processors.

Quality service: Providing service that meets standards of quality based on the restaurant and menu type as well as the particular establishments standards and needs.

Quenelle (Fr.): A light, poached dumpling based on a forcemeat (usually chicken, veal, seafood, or game) bound with eggs that is shaped in an oval by using two spoons.

Quickbread: Bread made with chemical leaveners, which work more quickly than yeast. (Also called a batter bread.)

Radiant heat: See direct heat.

Raft: A mixture of ingredients used to clarify consommé (see clarification). The term refers to the fact that the ingredients rise to the surface and form a floating mass.

Ragout (Fr.): Stew.

Ramekin: A small, oven-proof dish, usually ceramic. (Also in French, ramequin.)

Range: A term used to describe a cooking surface. Often, an oven unit is part of a range's configuration.

Rat-tail tang: An extension of the blade into the handle that is quite narrow.

Reach-in refrigerator: A refrigeration unit, or set of units, with pass-through doors. They are often used in the pantry area for storage of salads, cold hors d'oeuvre, and other frequently used items.

Recommended Dietary Allowance (RDA): A standard recommendation of the amounts of certain nutrients that should be included in the diet in order to prevent deficiencies.

Reduce: To decrease the volume of a liquid by simmering or boiling; used to provide a thicker consistency and/or concentrated flavors.

Reduction: The product that results when a liquid is reduced.

Refined sugar: A simple carbohydrate that has been processed to remove all additional elements and separate it from its original source; table sugar, honey, corn syrup, and molasses are examples.

Refresh: To plunge an item into, or run under, cold water after blanching to prevent further cooking.

Remouillage (Fr.): "Re-wetting." A stock made from bones that have already been used for stock; it is weaker than a first-quality stock and is often reduced to make glaze.

Render: To melt fat and clarify the drippings for use in sautéing or pan-frying.

Restaurant: A business in which foods are prepared and served to a paying customer.

Resting period: See carryover cooking.

Ricer: A hand tool used to puree cooked potatoes and similar foods; the food is loaded into a hopper and a metal plate is used to press the soft food through the holds in the hopper.

Rich dough: A yeast dough that contains fats such as butter or egg yolks. May also contain sweeteners.

Ring-top range: A flat-top with removable plates that can be opened to varying degrees to expose more or less direct heat.

Risotto: Rice that is sautéed briefly in butter with onions and possibly other aromatics, then combined with stock, which is added in several additions and stirred constantly, producing a creamy texture with grains that are still al dente.

Rivets: The pieces used to attach the handle to the blade of a knife.

Roast/roasting: A cooking method in which items are cooked in an oven or on a spit over a fire.

Roasting pan: A shallow pan, with or without a cover, used to roast foods. Available in a range of sizes and materials.

Roe: Fish or shellfish eggs.

Rolled steel: See pressed steel, blue steel, black steel.

Roll-in: Butter or a butter-based mixture that is placed between layers of pastry dough, then rolled and folded repeatedly to form numerous layers. When the dough is baked, the layers remain discrete, producing a very flaky, rich pastry. (See pâte feuilletée.)

Rondeau: A shallow, wide, straight-sided pot with two loop handles.

Rondelle: A knife cut that produces flat, round or oval pieces; used on cylindrical vegetables or items trimmed into cylinders before cutting.

Rotary peeler: A vegetable peeler with a swivel blade.

Rôti (Fr.): Roasted.

Rôtisseur (Fr.): Roast chef/station. The position is responsible for all roasted foods and related sauces. Roulade (Fr.): A slice of meat or fish rolled around a stuffing; also, filled and rolled sponge cake.

Round: A cut of beef from the hind quarter that includes the top and bottom round, eye, and top sirloin. It is lean and usually braised or roasted. Also, in baking, to shape pieces of yeast dough into balls to ensure even rising and a smooth crust.

Round fish: A classification of fish based on skeletal type, characterized by a rounded body and eyes on opposite sides of its head.

Roux (Fr.): An appareil containing equal parts of flour and fat (usually butter) used to thicken liquids. Roux is cooked to varying degrees (white, pale/blond, or brown), depending on its intended use.

Royale (Fr.): A consommé garnish made of unsweetened custard cut into decorative shapes.

Sabayon (Fr.): Wine custard. Sweetened egg yolks flavored with marsala or other wine or liqueur, beaten in a double boiler until frothy. (The Italian name is zabaglione.)

Sachet d'épices (Fr.): "Bag of spices." Aromatic ingredients, encased in cheesecloth, that are used to flavor stocks and other liquids. A standard sachet contains parsley stems, cracked peppercorns, dried thyme, and a bay leaf.

Salamander: See broiler.

Salé (Fr.): Salted or pickled.

Salmonellosis: The disease associated with eating foods contaminated with the salmonella bacteria.

Saltpeter: Potassium nitrate. Used to preserve meat (a component of curing salt); it gives certain cured meats their characteristic pink color.

Sanitation: The preparation and distribution of food in a clean environment by healthy food workers.

Sanitize/sanitizing: The killing of pathogenic organisms by chemicals and/or moist heat.

Saturated fat: A fat whose available bonding sites are entirely filled with hydrogen atoms. These tend to be solid at room temperature and are primarily of animal origin. (Coconut and palm oil are vegetable sources of saturated fat.) Food sources include butter, meat, cheese, chocolate, and eggs.

Saucier (Fr.): Sauté chef/station. The chef de partie responsible for all sautéed items and their sauces.

Saucepan: A pot used for stovetop cooking; typically has a single handle and is taller than it is wide.

Saucepot: Similar to a saucepan, but often has two loop handles.

Sausage: A forcemeat mixture shaped into patties or links; typically highly seasoned.

Sauté, sautéing: A cooking method in which items are cooked quickly in a small amount of fat in a pan (see sauteuse, sautoir) on the range top.

Sauteuse: A shallow skillet with sloping sides and a single, long handle. Used for sautéing and referred to generically as a sauté pan.

Sautoir: A shallow skillet with straight sides and a single, long handle. Used for sautéing and referred to generically as a sauté pan.

Sauce vin blanc (Fr.): Literally "white wine sauce." Made by combining a reduced cooking liquid with prepared hollandaise, velouté, or diced butter.

Savory: Not sweet. Also, the name of a course (savoury) served after dessert and before port in traditional British meals. Also, a family of herbs (including summer and winter savory).

Scald: To heat a liquid, usually milk or cream, to just below the boiling point. May also refer to blanching fruits and vegetables.

Scales: Measuring tools used to determine weight.

Scale/scaling: To measure ingredients by weighing; to divide dough or batter into portions by weight.

Scallop: A bivalve whose adductor muscle (the muscle that keeps its shells closed)

and roe are eaten. Also, a thin slice of meat. (See escalope.)

Score: To cut the surface of an item at regular intervals to allow it to cook evenly.

Scrambled eggs: Eggs prepared by blending yolks and white until homogenous, then cooking in a saute pan over direct heat while stirring constantly to form soft masses, or curds.

Scrapple: A boiled mixture of pork trimmings, buckwheat, and cornmeal.

Sear: To brown the surface of food in fat over high heat before finishing by another method (for example, braising) in order to add flavor.

Sea salt: Salt produced by evaporating sea water. Available refined or unrefined, crystallized or ground. (Also sel gris, French for "gray salt.")

Seize: To stiffen the exterior of foods without browning them.

Seasoning: (1) Adding an ingredient to give foods a particular flavor; (2) the process by which a protective coating is built up on the interior of a pan.

Semi-vegetarian: An individual who consumes a diet that it predominantly plant-based, but may include dairy, eggs, fish, poultry, or even red meats on a periodic basis.

Semolina: The coarsely milled hard wheat endo-sperm used for gnocchi, some pasta, and couscous.

Serum cholesterol: A measure of the cholesterol found in an individual's blood.

Shallow-poach/shallow poaching: A method in which items are cooked gently in a shallow pan of simmering liquid. The liquid is often reduced and used as the basis of a sauce.

Sharpening stone: A stone used to restore the edge of a dull knife.

Sheet pan: A flat baking pan, often with a rolled lip, used to cook foods in the oven.

Shelf life: The amount of time in storage that a product can maintain quality.

Shellfish: Various types of marine life consumed as food including univalves, bivalves, cephalopods, and crustaceans.

Shirred egg: An egg cooked with butter (and often cream) in a ramekin.

Shorteners: Ingredients that have the effect of producing a small (or short) crumb in finished baked goods.

Shortening: An ingredient may by hydrogenating an oil. Also, the term used to describe the action of various fats on the finished texture of baked goods.

Sieve: A container made of a perforated material, such as wire mesh, used to drain, rice, or puree foods.

Sifting: Aerating flours, powders, starches, and other finely ground dry ingredients by passing them through a sieve or sifter.

Silverskin: The tough, connective tissue that surrounds certain muscles.

Simmer/simmering: To maintain the temperature of a liquid just below boiling. Also, a cooking method in which items are cooked in simmering liquid.

Simple carbohydrate: Any of a number of small carbohydrate molecules (mono- and disaccharides), including fructose, lactose, maltose, and sucrose.

Simple syrup: A mixture of water and sugar (with additional flavorings or aromatics as desired), heated until the sugar dissolves. Used to moisten cakes or to poach fruits.

Situation vegetarian: see semi-vegetarian.

Single-stage technique: A cooking technique involving only one cooking method–for example boiling or sautéing–as opposed to more than one method, as in braising.

Skim: To remove impurities from the surface of a liquid, such as stock or soup, during cooking.

Skim milk: Milk from which all but 0.5 percent of the milkfat has been removed.

Slicer: see meat slicer.

Slow cooker/combi stove: A piece of cooking equipment that prepares foods at a very low, even temperature. Some units can also steam foods and/or hold them for service.

Slurry: Starch dispersed in cold liquid to prevent it from forming lumps when added to hot liquid as a thickener.

Small sauce: A sauce that is a derivative of any of the grand sauces.

Smoker: An enclosed area in which foods are held on racks or hooks and allowed to remain in a smokebath at the appropriate temperature.

Smoke-roasting: A method for roasting foods in which items are placed on a rack in a pan containing wood chips that smolder, emitting smoke, when the pan is placed on the range top or in the oven.

Smoking: Any of several methods for preserving and flavoring foods by exposing them to smoke. Methods include cold smoking (in which smoked items are not fully cooked), hot smoking (in which the items are cooked), and smoke-roasting.

Smoking point: The temperature at which a fat begins to break when heated.

Smother: To cook in a covered pan with little liquid over low heat.

Sodium: An alkaline metal element necessary in small quantities for human nutrition; one of the components of most salts used in cooking.

Sommelier (Fr.): Wine steward or waiter.

Sorbet (Fr.): Sherbet. A frozen dessert made with fruit juice or another flavoring, a sweetener (usually sugar), and beaten egg whites, which prevent the formation of large ice crystals.

Soufflé (Fr.): "Puffed." A preparation made with a sauce base (usually béchamel for savory soufflés or pastry cream for sweet ones), whipped egg whites, and flavorings. The egg whites cause the soufflé to puff during cooking.

Soufflé dish: A ceramic, porcelain, or metal dish with straight, smooth sides used to prepare sweet or savory soufflés.

Sourdough: Yeast dough leavened with a fermented starter instead of, or in addition to, fresh yeast. Some starters are kept alive by "feeding" with additional flour and water.

Sous chef (Fr.): Under-chef. The chef who is second in command in a kitchen; usually responsible for scheduling, filling in for the chef, and assisting the chefs de partie as necessary.

Spa cooking: A cooking style that focuses on producing high-quality, well-presented dishes that are nutritionally sound, low in calories, fats, sodium, and cholesterol.

Spaetzle (Ger.): A soft noodle or small dumpling made by dropping a prepared batter into simmering liquid. Spider: A long-handled skimmer used to remove items from hot liquid or fat and to skim the surface of liquids.

Spit-roast: To roast an item on a large skewer or spit over, or in front of, an open flame or other radiant heat source.

Sponge: A thick yeast batter that is allowed to ferment and develop a light, spongy consistency and is then combined with other ingredients to form a yeast dough.

Sponge cake: A sweet-batter product that is leavened with a beaten egg foam. (Also called a genoise.)

Spring-form pan: A round, straight-sided pan whose sides are formed by a hoop that can be unclamped and detached from its base.

Squab: A domesticated pigeon that has not yet begun to fly. It is slaughtered at 3 to 4 weeks old, weighing under 1 pound (455 grams). Its light, tender meat is suitable for sautéing, roasting, and grilling.

Stabilizer: An ingredient (usually a protein or plant product) that is added to an emulsion to prevent it from separating (for example, egg yolks, cream, and mustard). Also, an ingredient, such as gelatin, that is used in various desserts to prevent them from separating (for example, Bavarian creams).

Stainless steel: A metal capable of withstanding pitting, rusting, and scarring. Typically used to line pans, as well as to make various other cooking utensils, including bain maries, spoons, ladles, and certain knife blades.

Standard breading procedure: The assembly-line procedure in which items are dredged in flour, dipped in beaten egg, then coated with crumbs before being pan-fried or deep-fried).

Standard portion (or serving) sizes: Serving sizes based on calorie and nutrient requirements.

Standardized recipes: Recipes written according to standards determined by an operation to assure consistent cooking, garnish, and service procedures.

Staphylococcus aureus: A type of facultative bacteria that can cause food-borne illness. It is particularly dangerous because it produces toxins that cannot be destroyed by heat.

Stationary phase: The point of a pathogen's life cycle in which rates of death and reproduction are equal.

Steak: A portion-size (or larger) cut of meat, poultry, or fish made by cutting across the grain of a muscle or a muscle group. May be boneless or bone-in.

Steamer: A set of stacked pots with perforations in the bottom of each pot. They fit over a larger pot that is filled with boiling or simmering water. Also, a perforated insert made of metal or bamboo that can be inserted in a pot and used to steam foods.

Steaming: A cooking method in which items are cooked in a vapor bath created by boiling water or other liquids.

Steam-jacketed kettle: A kettle with double-layered walls, between which steam circulates, providing even heat for cooking stocks, soups, and sauces. These kettles may be insulated, spigoted, and/or tilting. (The latter are also called trunnion kettles).

Steel: A tool used to hone knife blades. It is usually-ally made of steel but may be ceramic, glass, or diamond-impregnated metal.

Stew/stewing: A cooking method nearly identical to braising but generally involving smaller pieces of meat and, hence, a shorter cooking time. Stewed items also may be blanched, rather than seared, to give the finished product a pale color. Also, a dish prepared by using the stewing method.

Stir-fry/stir-frying: A cooking method similar to sautéing in which items are cooked over very high heat, using little fat. Usually this is done in a wok and the food is kept moving constantly.

Stock: A flavorful liquid prepared by simmering meat, poultry, seafood, and/or vegetables in water with aromatics until their flavor is extracted. It is used as a base for soups, sauces, and other preparations.

Stockpot: A large, straight-sided pot that is taller than it is wide. Used for making stocks and soups. Some have spigots. Also called a marmite.

Stone-ground: Meal or flour milled between grindstones; this method retains more nutrients than some other grinding methods.

Straight forcemeat: A forcemeat combining pork and pork fat with another meat in equal parts that is made by grinding the mixture together.

Straight mixing method: The dough mixing method in which all ingredients are combined at once by hand or machine.

Strengtheners: Ingredients used in baking that give structure and stability to finished items (flour and eggs are two primary examples).

Subprimals/retail cuts: Term used to describe cuts of meat produce from primal cuts.

Suprême (Fr.): The breast fillet and wing of chicken or other poultry. Sauce suprême is chicken velouté enriched with cream.

Sweat/sweating: To cook an item, usually vegetables, in a covered pan in a small amount of fat until it softens and releases moisture.

Sweetbreads: The thymus glands of young animals, usually calves, but possibly lambs or pigs. Usually sold in pairs of lobes.

Swiss: To pound meat, usually beef, with flour and seasonings; this breaks up the muscle fibers, tenderizing the meat.

Syrup: Sugar that is dissolved in liquid, usually water, with possibly the addition of flavorings such as spices or citrus zests.

Table d'hôte (Fr.): A fixed-price menu with a single price for an entire meal based on entrée selection.

Table salt: Refined, granulated rock salt. May be fortified with iodine and treated with magnesium carbonate to prevent clumping.

Tamis: See drum sieve.

Tang: The continuation of the knife blade into its handle. A full tang extends through the entire handle. A partial tang only runs through part of the knife. A rat-tail tang is thinner than the blade's spine and is encased in the handle and is not visible at the top or bottom edge.

Taper-ground: A type of knife blade forged out of a single sheet of metal, then ground so it tapers smoothly to the cutting edge. Taper-ground knives are generally the most desirable.

Tart: A pie without a top crust; may be sweet or savory.

Tartlet: A small, single-serving tart.

TCM/Tinted curing mixture: See curing salt.

Temper: To heat gently and gradually. May refer to the process of incorporating hot liquid into a liaison to gradually raise its temperature. May also refer to the proper method for melting chocolate.

Tempura (Jap.): Seafood and/or vegetables that are coated with a light batter and deep-fried.

Tenderloin: A cut of meat, usually beef or pork, from the hind quarter.

Terrine: A loaf of forcemeat, similar to a pâté, but cooked in a covered mold in a bain-marie. Also, the mold used to cook such items, usually an oval shape made of ceramic.

Terrine mold: The baking dish used to prepare terrines.

Thermometer: A tool used to measure internal or external temperatures.

Thermophilic: Heat-loving. A term used to describe bacteria that thrive within the temperature range from 110 to 171°F (43°C to 77 °C).

Thickeners: Ingredients used to give additional body to liquids; arrowroot, cornstarch, gelatin, roux, and beurre manié are examples.

Tilting kettle (Swiss kettle): A large, relatively shallow, tilting pot used for braising, stewing, and, occasionally, steaming.

Timbale:/timbale mold A small pail-shaped mold used to shape rice, custards, mousselines, and other items. Also, a preparation made in such a mold.

Tomalley: Lobster liver, which is olive green in color.

Tomato concasse: See concasse.

Tomato sauce: A sauce prepared by simmering tomatoes in a liquid (water or broth) with aromatics. One of the grand sauces.

Toque blanche (Fr.): "White hat." A chef's hat.

Total utilization: The principle advocating the use of as much of a product as possible in order to reduce waste and increase profits.

Tournant (Fr.): Roundsman or swing cook. A kitchen staff member who works as needed throughout the kitchen.

Tourner/Tourné: To cut items, usually vegetables, into barrel, olive, or football shapes.

Tourné knife: A small knife, similar to a paring knife, with a curved blade used to cut tournéed items.

Toxin: a naturally occurring poison, particularly those produced by the metabolic activity of living organisms, such as bacteria.

Toxic poisoning: A condition brought about by consuming toxins, both naturally occurring (as found in mushrooms and rhubarb leaves) or those added to foods during growing, harvesting, processing, or preparation.

Trace minerals: Nutritive, but non-caloric, elements necessary in the diet, measure in very small units. In some cases, dietary requirements may not yet have been determined.

Tranche (Fr.): A slice or cut of meat, fish, or poultry.

Trash fish: Fish that have traditionally been considered unusable. (Also called "junk fish" or underutilized fish.)

Trichinella spiralis: A spiral-shaped parasitic worm that invades the intestines and muscle tissue; transmitted primarily through infected pork that has not been cooked sufficiently.

Trichinosis: The disease associated with ingesting the Trichinella parasite.

Tripe: The edible stomach lining of a cow or other ruminant. Honeycomb trip comes from the second stomach and has a honeycomb-like texture.

Tropical oils: Oils derived from tropical plants such as coconut, palm, and palm kernel.

Truss/trussing: To tie up meat or poultry with string before cooking it in order to give it a compact shape for more even cooking and better appearance.

Tuber: The flashy root, stem, or rhizome of a plant that is able to grow into a new plant. Some, such as potatoes, are eaten as vegetables.

Tunneling: A fault in baked batter products caused by overmixing; the finished product is riddled with large holes or tunnels.

Two-stage method: A procedure for preparing a batter for high-ratio cakes.

Ultra-pasteurization: Procedure for pasteurizing dairy products at very high temperatures for short periods of time.

Univalve: A single-shelled mollusk, such as abalone and sea urchin.

Unsaturated fat: A fat with at least one available bonding site not filled with a hydrogen atom. These may be monounsaturated or polyunsaturated. They tend to be liquid at room temperature and are primarily of vegetable origin.

USDA: United State's Department of Agriculture; a large branch of the federal government charged with (among other things) overseeing the production, distribution, labeling, inspection, and sales of food items to the public.

USDA Food Guide Pyramid: A graphic representation of an optimal diet, based on several tiers. The foundation of this diet includes whole grains (breads, pasta, rice, etc.). The smaller the tier, the fewer portions should be consumed on a daily basis.

USRDA: The suggested minimum requirements for various nutrients, necessary to prevent the onset of deficiency diseases.

Utility knife: A smaller, lighter version of the chef's knife; its blade is usually between 5 and 7 inches long.

Vacuum packing: A system of packing foods in a closed environment, with as much air as possible removed.

Vanilla sauce: Custard sauce made from milk or cream, sugar, and eggs.

Variety meat: Meat from a part of an animal other than the muscle; for example, organs.

Vegan: An individual whose diet is strictly plant-based, excluding any and all animal products.

Vegetable soup: A broth- or water-based soup garnished primarily with vegetables; may include meats, legumes, and noodles as well; may be clear or thick.

Vegetarian: An individual whose diet is primarily plant-based; there are different forms of vegetarian diets including vegan, fruititarian, ovo- and lacto/ovo-vegetarian, pesco-vegetarian, and semi-vegetarian.

Vegetarian pyramid: A graphic representation of the optimal vegetarian diet.

Velouté: A sauce of white stock (chicken, veal, seafood) thickened with white roux; one of the grand sauces.

Velouté soup: A cream soup made with a velouté sauce base and flavorings (usually pureed) that is usually finished with a liaison.

Venison: Meat from large game animals; often used to refer specifically to deer meat.

Vertical chopping machine (VCM): A machine, similar to a blender, that has rotating blades used to grind, whip, emulsify, or blend foods.

Vinaigrette (Fr.): A cold sauce of oil and vinegar, usually with various flavorings; it is a temporary emulsion sauce. (The standard proportion is three parts oil to one part vinegar.)

Vinegar: An acidic liquid made by fermenting various items, including wine or cider.

Virus: A type of pathogenic microorganism that can be transmitted in food. Viruses cause such illnesses as measles, chicken pox, infectious hepatitis, and colds.

Vitamins: Any of various nutritionally essential organic substances that do not provide energy (non-caloric) but usually act as regulators in metabolic processes.

Waffle: A crisp, pancake-like batter product that is cooked in a specialized iron that gives the finished product a textured pattern, usually a grid. Also a special vegetable cut which produces a grid or basket-weave pattern.

Walk-in refrigerator: A refrigeration unit large enough to walk into. It is occasionally large enough to maintain zones of varying temperature and humidity to store a variety of foods properly. Some have reach-in doors as well. Some are large enough to accommodate rolling carts as well as may shelves of goods.

Water-soluble vitamins: Vitamin (B vitamins and C) that can dissolve in water and are therefore easily excreted from the body and are also susceptible to loss during cooking in water.

Wet cure: A curing process in which foods are completely submerged in a brine or marinade.

Whey: The liquid left after curds have formed in milk.

Whip/whisk: To beat an item, such as cream or egg whites, to incorporate air. Also, a special tool for whipping make of looped wire attached to a handle.

White chocolate: Cocoa butter flavored with sugar and milk solids. It does not contain any cocoa solids, so it does not have the characteristic brown color of regular chocolate.

White mirepoix: Mirepoix that does not include carrots and my include chipped mushrooms or mushroom trimmings. It is used for pale or white sauces and stocks.

White stock: A light-colored stock made with bones that have not been browned.

Whole grains: Unmilled or processed grains.

Whole-wheat flour: Flour milled from the whole grain, including the bran and germ. Graham flour is a whole-wheat flour named after Sylvester Graham, a 19th century American dietary reformer.

Wok (Chin.): A round-bottomed pan, usually made of rolled steel, that is used for nearly all cooking methods.

Worm: The spiral shaped piece in a meat grinder that draws food down the feed tube.

Yam: A large tuber that grows in tropical and subtropical climates; it has starchy, pale-yellow flesh and is often confused with the sweet potato.

Yeast: Microscopic fungus whose metabolic processes are responsible for fermentation. It is used for leavening bread and in cheese-, beer-, and wine-making.

Yield grade: A indication of the overall ratio of usable meat to bone on an individual carcass.

Yogurt: Milk cultured with bacteria to give it a slightly thick consistency and sour flavor.

Zabaglione: See sabayon.

Zest: The thin, brightly colored outer part of citrus rind. It contains volatile oils, making it ideal for use as a flavoring.

Zones: Specific areas that have desirable characteristics, such as hotter and cooler areas on a grill, cooler and coldest areas in a walk-in. Established to make work and food storage procedures more efficient.

Recommended Reading List

FOOD HISTORY

American Food: The Gastronomic Story. Evan Jones. Overlook Press, 1992.

August Escoffier: Memories of My Life. translated by Lawrence Escoffier, Van Nostrand Reinhold, 1996.

Consuming Passions, The Anthropology of Eating. Peter Farb and George Armelagos. Houghton Mifflin, 1980.

De Honesta Voluptate, 5 volumes. Platine (Bartolomeo de Sacehi di Padena). Mallinkrodt Chemical Works, 1967.

The Diepnosophists (Banquet of the Learned), 3 volumes. Athenaeus. Translated by C.D. Yonge. Henry G. Bohn, 1854.

Eating in America, A History. Waverley Root and Richard de Rochemont. Ecco Press, 1995.

Fabulous Feasts: Medieval Cookery and Ceremony. Madeleine Pelner Cosman. Braziller, 1976.

Food and Drink Through the Ages, 2500 B.C. to 1937 A.D. Barbara Feret. Maggs Bros. Ltd. 1937.

Food History. Reay Tannahill. Crown Publishers, Inc., 1988.

Gastronomy: The Anthropology of Food and Food Habits. Margaret Arnoh, ed. Mouton Pub. (Aldine), 1979.

History of Food. Maguelonne Toussaint-Samat. Blackwell, 1987

Kitchen and Table: A Bedside History of Eating in the Western World. Colin Clair. Abelard-Schuman, 1965.

Much Depends on Dinner. Margaret Visser. MacMillan, 1988.

Our Sustainable Table. Robert Clark, ed. North Point Press, 1990.

The Pantropheon: or, A History of Food and Its Preparation in Ancient Times. Alexis Soyer. Paddington Press, 1977.

The Rituals of Dinner. Margaret Visser. Grove Press, 1986.

The Roman Cookery of Apicius. Translated and adapted by John Edwards. Hartly & Marks, 1984.

The Travels of Marco Polo. Marta Bellonci. Translated by Teresa Waugh. Facts on File, 1984.

Why We Eat What We Eat. Raymond Sokolov. Simon & Schuster, 1993.

SANITATION AND SAFETY

Applied Foodservice Sanitation, 4th ed. Educational Foundation of the National Restaurant Association Staff. Educ. Staff, 1993.

Basic Food Sanitation. The Culinary Institute of America. Hyde Park, New York: 1986.

HACCP: Reference Book. Educational Foundation of the National Restaurant Association Staff. Educ. Staff, 1993.

NUTRITION AND NUTRITIONAL COOKING

Choices for a Healthy Heart. Joseph C. Piscatella. Workman Publishing, 1987.

Food and Culture in America: A Nutrition Handbook. Pamela Goyan Kittler and Kathryn P. Sucher. Van Nostrand Reinhold, 1989.

Handbook of the Nutritional Value of Foods: in Common Units. U.S. Department of Agriculture. Dover Publications, 1986.

Jane Brody's Good Food Book: Living the High Carbohydrate Way. Jane Brody. W. W. Norton, 1985.

Nutrition: Concepts and Controversies, 5th ed. Hamilton, Whitney, and Sizer. West Publishing Co., 1991.

Nutrition for the Foodservice Professional, 2nd ed. Karen Eich Drummond. Van Nostrand Reinhold, 1994

Techniques of Healthy Cooking. The Culinary Institute of America, Mary Donovan, ed. Van Nostrand Reinhold, 1993.

EQUIPMENT

Food Equipment Facts: A Handbook for the Foodservice Industry, 2nd ed. Carl Scriven and James Stevens. New York: Van Nostrand Reinhold, 1989.

Professional Chef's Knife Book. The Culinary Institute of America. Van Nostrand Reinhold, 1978.

The Williams-Sonoma Cookbook and Guide to Kitchenware. Chuck Williams. Random House, 1986.

GENERAL PRODUCT IDENTIFICATION

The Cook's Ingredients. Adrian Bailey, ed. Reader's Digest Association, 1990.

Tastings: The Best from Ketchup to Caviar. Jenifer Harvey Lang. Crown Publishers, Inc., 1986.

The Von Welanetz Guide to Ethnic Ingredients. Diana and Paul Von Welanetz. Warner, 1987.

MEATS, POULTRY, AND GAME

The Meat Buyers Guide. National Association of Meat Purveyors. National Assoc. of Meat Purveyors, 1992.

The Meat We Eat, 13th ed. John R. Romans, et al. Interstate Printers & Publishing, 1994.

FISH AND SHELLFISH

The Complete Cookbook of American Fish and Shellfish, 2nd ed. John F. Nicolas. Van Nostrand Reinhold, 1990.

The Encyclopedia of Fish Cookery. A. J. McClane. H. Holt, & Co., 1977.

Fish and Shell Fish: The Cook's Indispensable Companion. James Peterson. William Morrow and Company, Inc, 1996.

McClane's Fish Buyer's Guide. A. J. McClane. Henry Holt & Co., 1990.

FRUITS AND VEGETABLES

The Blue Goose Buying Guide. Blue Goose, Inc., 1990.

The Foodservice Guide to Fresh Produce. Produce Marketing Association, 1987.

Jane Grigson's Fruit Book. Jane Grigson. Atheneum, 1982.

Jane Grigson's Vegetable Book. Jane Grigson. Penguin Books, 1980.

Rodale's Illustrated Encyclopedia of Herbs. Rodale Press Staff and William H. Hylton, ed. Rodale Press, 1987.

Uncommon Fruits and Vegetables: A Commonsense Guide from Arugula to Yucca: An Encyclopedic Cookbook of America's New Produce. Elizabeth Schneider. HarperCollins, 1990.

DAIRY AND CHEESES

Cheese: A Guide to the World of Cheese and Cheese-Making. Bruno Battistotti. Facts on File, 1984.

Cheese Buyer's Handbook. Daniel O'Keefe. McGraw-Hill, 1978.

Cheeses of the World. U.S. Department of Agriculture. Dover Publications, 1972.

The World of Cheese. Evan Jones. Alfred A. Knopf, 1978.

NONPERISHABLE GOODS

The Book of Coffee and Tea. Joel, David, and Karl Schapira. St. Martin's Press, 1982.

The Complete Book of Spices: A Practical Guide to Spices & Aromatic Seeds. Jill Norman. Viking Studio Books, 1991.

Spices, Salt and Aromatics. Elizabeth David. Penguin Books, 1970.

PREPARATIONS AND RECIPES

The Art of Making Sausages, Pâtés, and other Charcuterie. (orig. title: *Charcuterie and French Pork Cookery*). Jane Grigson. Alfred A. Knopf, 1976.

Pâtés and Terrines. Frederich W. Elhart. Hearst Books, 1984.

The Professional Chef's® Art of Garde Manger, 5th ed. Frederic H. Sonnenschmidt and John Nicholas. Van Nostrand Reinhold, 1993.

Sauces. James Peterson. Van Nostrand Reinhold, 1991.

Soups for the Professional Chef. Terence Janericco. Van Nostrand Reinhold, 1993.

Art of Garnishing. Inja Nam and Arno Schmidt. Van Nostrand Reinhold, 1993.

GENERAL/CLASSIC COOKING

The Chef's Compendium of Professional Recipes, 3rd ed. John Fuller, Edward Renold, and David Faskett. Butterworth-Heinemann, 1992.

Classical Cooking the Modern Way, 2nd ed. Eugen Pauli. Van Nostrand Reinhold, 1989.

Cooking for the Professional Chef, rev. ed. Kenneth C. Wolfe. 2nd ed. Delmar Publishing, 1982.

Culinary Olympics Cookbook. American Culinary Federation and Ferdinand E. Metz. Chet Holden, ed. Cahners Publishing Company and *Restaurants & Institutions* Magazine, 1983.

Dining in France. Christian Millau. Stewart, Tabori & Chang, 1986.

Escoffier: The Complete Guide to the Art of Modern Cookery. Auguste Escoffier. Van Nostrand Reinhold, 1995.

The Grand Masters of French Cuisine. Selected and adapted by Celine Vence and Robert Courtine. G.P. Putnam & Sons, 1978.

Great Chefs of France. Anthony Blake. Harry N. Abrams, 1978.

Introductory Foods, 10th ed. Marion Bennion. Macmillan, 1994

Joy of Cooking. Irma S. Rombauer and Marion Rombauer Becker. A Plume Book (The Penguin Group), 1973.

Jacques Pepin's The Art of Cooking. Jacques Pepin. Alfred A. Knopf, 1992.

James Beard's Theory and Practice of Good Cooking. James Beard. Random House, 1990.

La Technique. Jacques Pepin. Simon & Schuster, 1989.

Le Répertoire de la Cuisine. Louis Saulnier. Barron, 1976.

Ma Gastronomie. Ferdinand Point. Lyceum, 1974.

Paul Bocuse's French Cooking. Paul Bocuse. Translated by Colette Rossant. Pantheon, 1987.

The Physiology of Taste. Jean Anthelme Brillat-Savarin. Translated by Anne Dreyton. Penguin Books, 1994.

The Saucier's Apprentice: A Modern Guide to Classic French Sauces for the Home. Raymond A. Sokolov. Alfred A. Knopf, 1976.

AMERICAN COOKING/RECIPES

An American Bounty. The Culinary Institute of America. Mary Donovan, ed. Rizzoli International Publishing, 1995.

An American Place: Celebrating the Flavors of America. Larry Forgione. William Morrow and Company, Inc. 1996.

American Cooking. James Shenton, et al. Time-Life Books, 1971.

Chez Panisse Cooking. Paul Bertolli. Random House, 1994.

City Cuisine. Susan Feniger and Mary Sue Milliken. William Morrow, 1989.

Epicurean Delight: The Life and Times of James Beard. Evan Jones. Alfred A. Knopf, 1990.

I Hear America Cooking. Betty Fussel. Viking, 1986.

Jasper White's Cooking from New England: More Than Three Hundred Traditional & Contemporary. . . . Jasper White. HarperCollins, 1993.

Jeremiah Tower's New American Classics. Jeremiah Tower. Harper & Row, 1986.

The Mansion on Turtle Creek Cookbook. Dean Fearing. Grove-Atlantic, 1987.

The New York Times Cook Book. Craig Claiborne. HarperCollins, 1990.

The Trellis Cookbook. Marcel Desaulniers. Simon & Schuster Trade, 1992.

INTERNATIONAL COOKING/RECIPES

The Art of South American Cooking. Felipe Rojas-Lombardi. HarperCollins, 1991.

The Art of Turkish Cooking. Neset Eren. Hippocrene Books, 1993.

Authentic Chinese Cuisine, 9 volumes, various authors. Shufunotomo, 1984.

The Belgian Cookbook. Enid Gordon. MacDonald, 1983.

The Book of Latin American Cooking. Elizabeth Lambert Ortiz. Ecco Press, 1994.

A Book of Mediterranean Food. Elizabeth David. Penguin Books, 1986.

A Book of Middle Eastern Food. Claudia Roden. Alfred A. Knopf, 1974.

Classical and Contemporary Italian Cooking for Professionals. Bruno Ellmer. Van Nostrand Reinhold, 1990.

Classic Indian Cooking. Julie Sahni. William Morrow, 1980.

Classic Scandinavian Cooking. Nika Hazelton. Scribner and Sons, 1987.

Essentials of Classic Italian Cooking. Marcella Hazan. Alfred A. Knopf, 1995.

The Complete Indian Cookbook. Michael Pandya. Larousse, 1980.

The Cooking of Eastern Mediterranean. Paula Wolfert. HarperCollins, 1994.

Food Associations

American Culinary Federation
P. O. Box 3466
St. Augustine, FL 32085
(904) 824–4468

American Hotel and Motel Association
1201 New York Avenue NW
Suite 600
Washington, DC 20005-3931
(202) 289-3100

American Institute of Wine and Food
1550 Bryant St.
Suite 700
San Francisco, CA 94103
(415) 255–3000

Chefs in America Foundation
3407 Toledo Street
Coral Gables, FL 33134
(305) 448–9279

**Council on Hotel/Restaurant and
Institutional Education**
1200 17th Street NW
Washington, DC 20036
(202) 331–5990

**International Association of
Women Chefs and Restaurateurs**
110 Sutter Street
Suite 305
San Francisco, CA 94104
(415) 362–7336

International Association of Culinary Professionals
304 West Liberty
Suite 201
Louisville, KY 40202
(502) 581–9786

The James Beard Foundation
167 West 12th Street
New York, NY 10011
(212) 675–4984

National Ice Carving Association
P.O. Box 3593
Oak Brook, IL 60522-3593
(708) 323–6696

National Restaurant Association
1200 17th Street, NW
Washington, DC 20036
(202) 331–5900

Oldways Preservation and Exchange Trust
45 Milk Street
Boston, MA 02109
(617) 695–9102

Roundtable for Women in Foodservice
3022 West Eastwood
Chicago, IL 60625
(800) 898–2849

Share Our Strength (SOS)
1511 K Street, NW
Suite 94
Washington, DC 20005
(202) 393–2925

Index